CONTENTS

THE NATIONWIDE
FOOTBALL ANNUAL
2012–2013

Published by SportsBooks Limited, PO Box 422, Cheltenham, GL50 2YN
First published in 1887

A CIP catalogue record for this book is available from the British Library.

Editorial compilation by Stuart Barnes

ISBN-13 9781907524202

Front cover photograph of Sergio Aguero scoring for Manchester City in added time on the last day of the season to win the Premier League title.
by PAphotos.

Printed and bound by CPI Group (UK) Ltd, Croydon, CR0 4YY

WHEN THE FEELGOOD FACTOR FADED AWAY

By Stuart Barnes

How quickly the face of football can change. A gripping Premier League title race stretching to stoppage-time on the final day of the season was followed by an engrossing, well-staged and largely trouble-free European Championship. Admittedly, England's contribution was limited, with the technical and tactical gulf between our play and that of the top teams proving as wide as ever. Few can have expected much more, particularly as Roy Hodgson had precious little time to build the squad and develop the sort of strategy that might have taken them beyond the quarter-finals. But even the most die-hard England followers must have appreciated the quality on show from the likes of Spain, Italy, Portugal and Germany, while at the same time welcoming the standard of discipline set on the pitch and the absence of serious violence off it. UEFA, in the eyes of many, have erred by increasing from 16 to 24 the countries competing at the 2016 finals in France, a move which will surely reduce the competitive element of the group stage. The European governing body were, however, justified in acclaiming this tournament in Poland and the Ukraine as a resounding success. Along with Manchester City's grandstand finish to deny Manchester United another championship, it brought about a genuine feelgood factor, one to whet the appetite for the season ahead. Then along came the John Terry court case, the collapse of Rangers, the further demise of once-proud Portsmouth and some questionable managerial sackings by new club owners to cast a cloud over the national game. 'Unedifying' was the verdict of Gordon Taylor, chief executive of the Professional Footballers' Association, after Terry was cleared of racially abusing Anton Ferdinand. The five-day trial exposed the nasty verbal exchanges which take place on the pitch and Taylor was right to point out that the 'searchlight' will be on the new season. It will also be on the FA, who have already toughened up their disciplinary machine and now face having to do more to reinforce the campaign for greater respect among players.

The absence of that quality among owners has brought about the crisis engulfing Scottish football. Rangers are now paying the ultimate price for living beyond their means and running up massive debts. It's hard to believe that the year after winning a 54th title, the old club is no more and the new one will kick-off in the third division. While many of their top players have fled, supporters have little choice but to stick with the team they have supported for a lifetime. They, as is usually the case, will be hit hardest, through no fault of their own. There could also be a financial impact on other, smaller SPL clubs reliant on the financial boost of playing Rangers, while TV rights will certainly be less attractive without the 'Old Firm' derbies for at least three seasons. Portsmouth's plight is largely confined to Fratton Park and their loyal fans, but is no less worrying for the way that successive administrations have presided over their decline. They start the League One season with another 10-point deduction – along with strict financial controls ordered by the Football League – and clearly face a struggle to prevent a third relegation in four seasons. Another salutary tale concerns Darlington, who until 2010 were playing league football in a 25,000-capacity arena built by a former owner with grandiose plans. These eventually turned to dust and the old club, formed in 1883, disappeared into a financial black hole. Its assets and goodwill were bought by a supporters' group from the administrator and Darlington 1883 emerged. The new club will begin life playing in the Northern League at a ground in Bishop Auckland, having been demoted four divisions by the FA.

Managerial sackings are now commonplace, but it's hard not to feel sympathy for Sean Dyche and Steve Cotterill, both dismissed by new owners during the summer. Dyche, in his first season in charge, led Watford to a top-half finish in the Championship and could have reasonably expected to be given a chance to build on that. Cotterill expected more than nine months in charge at Nottingham Forest and also had a case. Anyone taking over a club is perfectly entitled to bring in the manager of their choice, particularly if results have not been good. But you wonder sometimes whether they fully take account of what the present incumbent has achieved. After all, the decision-making of owners up and down the country leaves a lot to be desired.

3

EUROPEAN CHAMPIONSHIP FINALS
POLAND/UKRAINE 2012

GROUP A

POLAND 1 GREECE 1
Warsaw (55,920); Friday, June 8
Poland (4-2-3-1): Szczesny, Piszczek, Wasilewski, Perquis, Boenisch, Murawski, Polanski, Blaszczykowski, Obraniak, Rybus (Tyton 69), Lewandowski. **Scorer:** Lewandowski (17). **Sent off:** Szczesny
Greece (4-5-1): Chalkias, Torosidis, Papastathopoulos, A Papadopoulos (K Papadopoulos 36), Holebas, Ninis (Salpingidis 46), Maniatis, Katsouranis, Karagounis, Samaras, Gekas (Fortounis 68). **Scorer:** Salpingidis (51). **Booked:** Papastathopoulos, Holebas, Karagounis. **Sent off:** Papasthathopoulos
Referee: C Velasco Carballo. **Half-time:** 1-0

RUSSIA 4 CZECH REPUBLIC 1
Wroclaw (40,803); Friday, June 8
Russia (4-3-3): Malafeev, Anyukov, Berezutski, Ignashevich, Zhirkov, Shirokov, Denisov, Zyryanov, Dzagoev (Kokorin 84), Kerzhakov (Pavlyucheno 73), Arshavin. **Scorers:** Dragoev (15, 79), Shirokov (24), Pavlyuchenko (82)
Czech Republic (4-2-3-1): Cech, Selassie, Hubnik, Sivok, Kadlec, Plasil, Jiracek (Petrzela 75), Pilar, Rosicky, Rezek (Hubschman 46), Baros (Lafata 85). **Scorer:** Pilar (52)
Referee: H Webb (England). **Half-time:** 2-0

GREECE 1 CZECH REPUBLIC 2
Wroclaw (41,105); Tuesday, June 12
Greece (4-3-3): Chalkias (Sifakis 23), Torosidis, K Papadopoulos, Katsouranis, Holebas, Fotakis (Gekas 46), Maniatis, Karagounis, Salpingidis, Fortounis (Mitroglou 71), Samaras. **Scorer:** Gekas (53). **Booked:** Torosidis, Salpingidis
Czech Republic (4-2-3-1): Cech, Selassie, Sivok, Kadlec, Limbersky, Plasil, Hubschman, Jiracek, Rosicky (Kolar 46), Pilar, Baros (Pekhart 64). **Scorers:** Jiracek (3), Pilar (6). **Booked:** Rosicky, Jiracek, Kolar
Referee: S Lannoy (France). **Half-time:** 0-2

POLAND 1 RUSSIA 1
Warsaw (55,290); Tuesday, June 12
Poland (4-5-1): Tyton, Piszczek, Wasilewski, Perquis, Boenisch, Blaszczykowski, Dudka (Mierzejewski 73), Murawski, Polanski (Matuszczyk 83), Obraniak (Brozek 90), Lewandowski. **Scorer:** Blaszczykowski (57). **Booked:** Lewandowski, Polanski
Russia (4-3-3): Malafeev, Anyukov, Berezutski, Ignashevich, Zhirkov, Shirokov, Denisov, Zyryanov, Dzagoev (Izmailov 79), Kerzhakov (Pavlyuchenko 70), Arshavin. **Scorer:** Dzagoev (37). **Booked:** Denisov, Dzagoev
Referee: W Stark (Germany). **Half-time:** 0-1

CZECH REPUBLIC 1 POLAND 0
Wroclaw (41,480); Saturday, June 16
Czech Republic (4-2-3-1): Cech, Selassie, Sivok, Kadlec, Limbersky, Plasil, Hubschman, Jiracek (Rajtoral 83), Kolar, Pilar (Rezek 87), Baros (Pekhart 90). **Scorer:** Jiracek (72). **Booked:** Limbersky, Plasil, Pekhart
Poland (4-5-1): Tyton, Piszczek, Wasilewski, Perquis, Boenisch, Blaszczykowski, Dudka, Murawski (Mierzejewski 73), Polanski (Grosicki 56), Obraniak (Brozek 73), Lewandowski. **Booked:** Murawski, Polanski, Wasilewski, Blaszczykowski, Perquis
Referee: C Thomson (Scotland). **Half-time:** 0-0

GREECE 1 RUSSIA 0
Warsaw (55,614); Saturday, June 16
Greece (4-3-3): Sifakis, Torosidis, Papastathopoulos, K Papadopoulos, Tzavelas, Katsouranis, Maniatis, Salpingidis (Ninis 83), Karagounis (Makos 67), Samaras, Gekas (Holebas 65).
Scorer: Karagounis (45). Booked: Karagounis, Holebas
Russia (4-3-3): Malafeev, Anyukov (Izmailov 81), Berezutski, Ignashevich, Zhirkov, Shirokov, Denisov, Glushakov (Pogrebnyak 72), Dragoev, Kerzhakov (Pavlyuchenko 46), Arshavin.
Booked: Anyukov, Zhirkov, Dragoev, Pogrebnyak
Referee: J Eriksson (Sweden). Half-time: 1-0

FINAL TABLE

	P	W	D	L	F	A	Pts
Czech Republic Q	3	2	0	1	4	5	6
Greece Q	3	1	1	1	3	3	4
Russia	3	1	1	1	5	3	4
Poland	3	0	2	1	2	3	2

GROUP B

HOLLAND 0 DENMARK 1
Kharkiv (35,293); Saturday, June 9
Holland (4-2-3-1): Stekelenburg, Van der Wiel (Kuyt 84), Heitinga, Vlaar, Willems, Van Bommel, De Jong (Van der Vaart 71), Robben, Sneijder, Afellay (Huntelaar 71), Van Persie.
Booked: Van Bommel
Denmark (4-2-3-1): Andersen, Jacobsen, Kjaer, Agger, S Poulsen, Kvist, Zimling, Rommedahl (Mikkelsen 83), Eriksen (Schone 74), Krohn-Dehli, Bendtner. Scorer: Krohn-Dehli (24)
Referee: D Skomina (Slovenia). Half-time: 0-1

GERMANY 1 PORTUGAL 0
Lviv (32,990); Saturday, June 9
Germany (4-2-3-1): Neuer, Boateng, Hummels, Badstuber, Lahm, Khedira, Schweinsteiger, Muller (Bender 90), Ozil (Kroos 87), Podolski, Gomez (Klose 80). Scorer: Gomez (72).
Booked: Badstuber, Boateng
Portugal (4-3-3): Patricio, Pereira, Alves, Pepe, Fabio Coentrao, Meireles (Varela 80), Veloso, Moutinho, Nani, Helder Postiga (Oliveira 70), Ronaldo. Booked: Fabio Coentrao, Helder Postiga
Referee: S Lannoy (France). Half-time: 0-0

DENMARK 2 PORTUGAL 3
Lviv (31,840); Wednesday, June 13
Denmark (4-2-3-1): Andersen, Jacobsen, Kjaer, Agger, S Poulsen, Kvist, Zimling (J Poulsen 16), Rommedahl (Mikkelsen 60), Eriksen, Krohn-Dehli (Schone 90), Bendtner. Scorer: Bendtner (41, 80). Booked: J Poulsen, Jacobsen
Portugal (4-2-3-1): Patricio, Pereira, Alves, Pepe, Fabio Coentrao, Meireles (Varela 84), Veloso, Moutinho, Nani (Rolando 89), Helder Postiga (Oliveira 64), Ronaldo. Scorers: Pepe (24), Helder Postiga (36), Varela (87). Booked: Meireles, Ronaldo
Referee: C Thomson (Scotland). Half-time: 1-2

HOLLAND 1 GERMANY 2
Kharkiv (37,750); Wednesday, June 13
Holland (4-2-3-1): Stekelenburg, Van der Wiel, Heitinga, Mathijsen, Willems, Van Bommel (Van der Vaart 45), De Jong, Robben (Huntelaar 45), Sneijder, Afellay, Van Persie.
Scorer: Van Persie (73). Booked: De Jong, Willems
Germany (4-2-3-1): Neuer, Boateng, Hummels, Bastuba, Lahm, Khedira, Schweinsteiger, Muller (Bender 90), Ozil (Kroos 81), Podolski, Gomez (Klose 73). Scorer: Gomez (24, 38). Booked: Boateng
Referee: J Eriksson (Sweden). Half-time: 0-2

DENMARK 1 GERMANY 2
Lviv (32,990); Sunday, June 17
Denmark (4-1-4-1): Andersen, Kjaer, Agger, S Poulsen, Jacobsen, Kvist, Eriksen, J Poulsen (Mikkelsen 82), Zimling (C Poulsen 78), Krohn-Dehli, Bendtner. **Scorer:** Krohn-Dehli (24).
Germany (4-2-3-1): Neuer, Bender, Hummels, Badstuber, Lahm, Khedira, Schweinsteiger, Muller (Kroos 84), Ozil, Podolski (Schurrle 65), Gomez (Klose 73). **Scorers:** Podolski (19), Bender (80)
Referee: C Velasco Carballo (Spain). **Half-time:** 1-1

PORTUGAL 2 HOLLAND 1
Kharkiv (37,445); Sunday, June 17
Portugal (4-3-3): Patricio, Pereira, Alves, Pepe, Fabio Coentrao, Meireles (Custodio 72), Veloso, Moutinho, Nani (Rolando 87), Helder Postiga (Oliveira 64), Ronaldo. **Scorer:** Ronaldo (28, 74). **Booked:** Pereira
Holland (4-2-3-1): Stekelenburg, Van der Wiel, Vlaar, Mathijsen, Willems (Afellay 67), De Jong, Van der Vaart, Robben, Van Persie, Sneijder, Huntelaar. **Scorer:** Van der Vaart (11).
Booked: Willems, Van Persie
Referee: N Rizzoli (Italy). **Half-time:** 1-1

FINAL TABLE

	P	W	D	L	F	A	Pts
Germany Q	3	3	0	0	5	2	9
Portugal Q	3	2	0	1	5	4	6
Denmark	3	1	0	2	4	5	3
Holland	3	0	0	3	2	5	0

GROUP C

SPAIN 1 ITALY 1
Gdansk (38,869); Sunday, June 10
Spain (4-3-3): Casilla, Arbeloa, Pique, Sergio Ramos, Alba, Xavi, Busquets, Xabi Alonso, Silva (Navas 65), Fabregas (Torres 74), Iniesta. **Scorer:** Fabregas (64). **Booked:** Alba, Torres, Arbeloa
Italy (3-5-2): Buffon, Chiellini, De Rossi, Bonucci, Giaccherini, Marchisio, Pirlo, Motta (Nocerino 90), Maggio, Cassano (Giovinco 65), Balaotelli (Di Natale 56). **Scorer:** Di Natale (60). **Booked:** Balotelli, Bonucci, Chiellini, Maggio
Referee: V Kassai (Hungary). **Half-time:** 0-0

REPUBLIC OF IRELAND 1 CROATIA 3
Poznan (39,550); Sunday, June 10
Republic of Ireland (4-4-2): Given, O'Shea, Dunne, St Ledger, Ward, Duff, Whelan, Andrews, McGeady (Cox 54), Keane (Long 74), Doyle (Walters 53). **Scorer:** St Ledger (19). **Booked:** Andrews
Croatia (4-4-2): Pletikosa, Srna, Corluka, Schildenfeld, Strinic, Rakitic (Dumjovic 90), Vukojevic, Modric, Perisic (Eduardo 89), Mandzukic, Jelavic (Kranjcar 72). **Scorers:** Madzukic (3), Jelavic (49), Given (49 og). **Booked:** Modric, Ktanjcar
Referee: B Kuipers (Holland). **Half-time:** 1-2

ITALY 1 CROATIA 1
Poznan (37,096); Thursday, June 14
Italy (3-5-2): Buffon, Chiellini, De Rossi, Bonucci, Giaccherini, Marchiso, Pirlo, Motta (Montolivo 62), Maggio, Cassano (Giovinco 83), Balotelli (Di Natale 69). **Scorer:** Pirlo (39). **Booked:** Morra, Montolivo
Croatia (4-4-2): Pletikosa, Srna, Corluka, Schildenfeld, Strinic, Rakitic, Vukojevic, Modric, Perisic (Pranjic 68), Mandzukic (Kranjcar 90), Jelavic (Eduardo 83). **Scorer:** Mandzukic (72). **Booked:** Schildenfeld
Referee: H Webb (England). **Half-time:** 1-0

SPAIN 4 REPUBLIC OF IRELAND 0
Gdansk (39,150); Thursday, June 14
Spain (4-3-3): Casillas, Arbeloa, Pique, Sergio Ramos, Alba, Xavi, Busquets, Xabi Alonso
(Martinez 65), Iniesta (Santi Cazorla 80), Silva, Torres (Fabregas 74). **Scorers**: Torres (4, 70),
Silva (49), Fabregas (83). **Booked**: Xabi Alonso, Martinez
Republic of Ireland (4-5-1): Given, O'Shea, Dunne, St Ledger, Ward, McGeady, Whelan (Green
80), Andrews, Duff (McClean 76), Cox (Walters 46), Keane. **Booked**: Keane, Whelan, St Ledger
Referee: P Proenca (Portugal). Half-time: 1-0

ITALY 2 REPUBLIC OF IRELAND 0
Poznan (38,794); Monday, June 18
Italy (4-3-1-2): Buffon, Abate, Barzagli, Chiellini (Bonucci 56), Balzaretti, Marchisio, Pirlo, De
Rossi, Motta, Cassano (Diamenti 62), Di Natale (Balotelli 74). **Scorers**: Cassano (36), Balotelli
(90). **Booked**: Balzaretti, De Rossi, Buffon
Republic of Ireland (4-4-2): Given, O'Shea, Dunne, St Ledger, Ward, Duff, Whelan, Andrews,
McGeady (Long 64), Keane (Cox 88), Doyle (Walters 76). **Booked**: Andrews, O'Shea, St
Ledger. **Sent off**: Andrews
Referee: C Cakir (Turkey). Half-time: 1-0
(Damien Duff's 100th cap for the Republic of Ireland)

CROATIA 0 SPAIN 1
Gdansk (39,076); Monday, June 18
Croatia (4-4-1-1): Pletikosa, Vida (Jelavic 66), Corluka, Schildenfeld, Strinic, Srna, Vukojevic
(Eduardo 80), Rakitic, Pranjic (Perisic 66), Modric, Mandzukic. **Booked**: Corluka, Srna,
Strinic, Mandzukic, Jelavic, Rakitic
Spain (4-3-3): Casillas, Arbeloa, Pique, Sergio Ramos, Alba, Xavi (Negredo 89), Busquets,
Xabi Alonso, Silva (Fabregas 73), Torres (Jesus Navas 61), Iniesta. **Scorer**: Jesus Navas (88).
Referee: W Stark (Germany). Half-time: 0-0

FINAL TABLE

	P	W	D	L	F	A	Pts
Spain Q	3	2	1	0	6	1	7
Italy Q	3	1	2	0	4	2	5
Croatia	3	1	1	1	4	3	4
Republic of Ireland	3	0	0	3	1	9	0

GROUP D

FRANCE 1 ENGLAND 1
Donetsk (47,400); Monday, June 11
France (4-2-3-1): Lloris, Debuchy, Rami, Mexes, Evra, Cabaye (Ben Arfa 84), Diarra, Malouda
(Martin 84), Nasri, Ribery, Benzema. **Scorer**: Nasri (39)
England (4-4-1-1): Hart, Johnson, Terry, Lescott, Cole, Milner, Gerrard, Parker (Henderson
77), Oxlade-Chamberlain (Defoe 77), Young, Welbeck (Walcott 90). **Scorer**: Lescott (30).
Booked: Oxlade-Chamberlain, Young
Referee: N Rizzoli (Italy). Half-time: 1-1

UKRAINE 2 SWEDEN 1
Kiev (64,290); Monday, June 11
Ukraine (4-3-1-2): Pyatov, Gusev, Khacheridi, Mikhalik, Selin, Yarmolenko, Tymoschuk,
Konoplyanka (Devic 90), Nazarenko, Shevchenko (Milevskiy 81), Voronin (Rotan 85). **Scorer**:
Shevchenko (55, 62)
Sweden (4-2-3-1): Isaksson, Lustig, Mellberg, Granqvist, M Olsson, Elm, Kallstrom, Larsson
(Wilhelmsson 68), Ibrahimovic, Toivonen (Svensson 62), Rosenberg (Elmander 71). **Scorer**:
Ibrahimovic (52). **Booked**: Kallstrom, Elm
Referee: C Cakir (Turkey). Half-time: 0-0

UKRAINE 0 FRANCE 2
Donetsk (48,000); Friday, June 15
Ukraine (4-3-1-2): Pyatov, Gusev, Khacheridi, Mikhalik, Selin, Yarmolenko (Aliev 68), Tymoschuk, Konoplyanka, Nazarenko (Milevskiy 60), Shevchenko, Voronin (Devic 45). **Booked**: Selin, Tymoschuk.
France (4-1-4-1): Lloris, Debuchy, Rami, Mexes, Clichy, Diarra, Menez (Martin 73), Nasri, Cabaye (M'Vila 68), Ribery, Benzema (Giroud 75). **Scorers**: Menez (53), Cabaye (56). **Booked**: Menez, Debuchy, Mexes
Referee: B Kuipers (Holland). **Half-time**: 0-0

SWEDEN 2 ENGLAND 3
Kiev (64,640); Friday, June 15
Sweden (4-4-2): Isaksson, Granqvist (Lustig 66), Mellberg, J Olsson, M Olsson, Larsson, Svensson, Kallstrom, Elm (Wilhemsson 81), Ibrahimovic, Elmander (Rosenberg 79). **Scorers**: Mellberg (49, 59). **Booked**: Mellberg, J Olsson, Svensson
England (4-4-2): Hart, Johnson, Terry, Lescott, Cole, Milner (Walcott 59), Gerrard, Parker, Young, Carroll, Welbeck (Oxlade-Chamberlain 90). **Scorers**: Carroll (23), Walcott (64), Welbeck (78). **Booked**: Milner
Referee: D Skomina (Slovenia). **Half-time**: 0-1

ENGLAND 1 UKRAINE 0
Donetsk (48,700); Tuesday, June 19
England (4-4-1-1): Hart, Johnson, Terry, Lescott, Cole, Milner, (Walcott 70), Gerrard, Parker, Young, Rooney (Oxlade-Chamberlain 87), Welbeck (Carroll 82). **Scorer**: Rooney (48). **Booked**: Cole, Gerrard
Ukraine (4-3-1-2): Pyatov, Gusev, Khacheridi, Rakitskiy, Selin, Tymoschuk, Garmash (Nazarenko 78), Yarmolenko, Devic (Shevchenko 70), Konoplianka, Milevskiy (Butko 77). **Booked**: Tymoschuk, Shevchenko, Rakitskiy
Referee: V Kassai (Hungary). **Half-time**: 0-0

SWEDEN 2 FRANCE 0
Kiev (63.010); Tuesday, June 19
Sweden (4-2-3-1): Isaksson, Granqvist, Mellberg, J Olsson, M Olsson, Svensson (Holmen 77), Kallstrom, Larsson, Ibrahimovic, Bajrami (Wilhelmsson 45), Toivonen (Wernbloom 77).
Scorers: Ibrahimovic (54), Larsson (90). **Booked**: Svensson, Holmen
France (4-3-2-1): Lloris, Debuchy, Rami, Mexes, Clichy, Nasri (Menez 77), Diarra, M'Vila (Giroud 83), Ben Arfa (Malouda 59), Ribery, Benzema. **Booked**: Mexes
Referee: P Proenca (Portugal). **Half-time**: 0-0

FINAL TABLE

	P	W	D	L	F	A	Pts
England Q	3	2	1	0	5	3	7
France Q	3	1	1	1	3	3	4
Ukraine	3	1	0	2	2	4	3
Sweden	3	1	0	2	5	5	3

QUARTER-FINALS

CZECH REPUBLIC 0 PORTUGAL 1
Warsaw (55,590); Thursday, June 21
Czech Republic (4-2-3-1): Cech, Selassie, Sivok, Kadlec, Limbersky, Hubschman (Pekhart 86), Plasil, Jiracek, Darida (Rezek 61), Pilar, Baros. **Booked**: Limbersky
Portugal (4-3-3): Patricio, Pereira, Alves, Pepe, Fabio Coentrao, Meireles (Rolando 88), Veloso, Moutinho, Nani (Custodio 84), Helder Postiga (Almeida 39), Ronaldo. **Scorer**: Ronaldo (79). **Booked**: Nani, Veloso
Referee: H Webb (England). **Half-time**: 0-0

GERMANY 4 GREECE 2
Gdansk (38,751); Friday, June 22
Germany (4-2-3-1): Neuer, Boateng, Hummels, Badstuber, Lahm, Khedira, Schweinsteiger, Reus (Gotze 81), Ozil, Schurrie (Muller 67), Klose (Gomez 80). **Scorers:** Lahm (35), Khedira (61), Klose (68), Reus (74)
Greece (4-2-3-1): Sifakis, Torosidis, Papastathopoulos, K Papadopoulos, Tzavelas (Fotakis 46), Makos (Liberopoulos 71), Maniatis, Ninis (Gekas 46), Katsouranis, Samaras, Salpingidis. **Scorers:** Samaras (55), Salpingidis (89 pen). **Booked:** Samaras, Papastathopoulos
Referee: D Skomina (Slovenia). **Half-time:** 1-0

SPAIN 2 FRANCE 0
Donetsk (47,000); Saturday, June 23
Spain (4-3-3): Casillas, Arbeloa, Pique, Sergio Ramos, Alba, Xavi, Busquets, Xabi Alonso, Silva (Pedro 65), Fabregas (Torres 67), Iniesta (Santi Cazorla 84). **Scorer:** Xabi Alonso (19, 90 pen). **Booked:** Sergio Ramos
France (4-3-2-1): Lloris, Debuchy (Menez 64), Rami, Koscielny, Clichy, M'Vila (Giroud 79), Reveillere, Cabaye, Malouda (Nasri 64), Ribery, Benzema. **Booked:** Cabaye, Menez
Referee: N Rizzoli (Italy). **Half-time:** 1-0

ENGLAND 0 ITALY 0 (aet, Italy won 4-2 on pens)
Kiev (64,340); Sunday, June 24
England (4-4-1-1): Hart, Johnson, Terry, Lescott, Cole, Milner (Walcott 60), Gerrard, Parker (Henderson 94), Young, Rooney, Welbeck (Carroll 60)
Italy (4-3-1-2): Buffon, Abate (Maggio 90), Barzagli, Bonucci, Balzaretti, Marchisio, Pirlo, De Rossi (Nocerino 79), Montolivo, Balotelli, Cassano (Diamanti 78). **Booked:** Barzagli, Maggio
Penalty shoot-out: 0-1 (Balotelli), 1-1 (Gerrard), 1-1 (Montelivo missed), 2-1 (Rooney), 2-1 (Pirlo), 2-2 (Young hit crossbar), 2-3 (Nocerino), 2-3 (Cole saved), 2-4 (Diamanti)
Referee: P Proenca (Portugal)

SEMI-FINALS

PORTUGAL 0 SPAIN 0 (aet, Spain won 4-2 on pens)
Donetsk (48,000); Wednesday, June 27
Portugal (4-3-3): Patricio, Pereira, Pepe, Alves, Fabio Coentrao, Meireles (Varela 112), Veloso (Custodio 106), Moutinho, Nani, Almeida (Oliveira 81), Ronaldo. **Booked:** Fabio Coentrao, Pepe, Pereira, Alves, Veloso
Spain (4-3-3): Casillas, Arbeloa, Pique, Sergio Ramos, Alba, Xavi (Pedro 87), Busquets, .abi Alonso, Silva (Jesus Navas 60), Negredo (Fabregas 54), Iniesta. **Booked:** Sergio Ramos, Busquets, Arbeloa, Xabi Alonso
Penalty shoot-out: 0-0 (Xabi Alonso saved), 0-0 (Moutinho saved), 0-1 (Iniesta), 1-1 (Pepe), 1-2 (Pique), 2-2 (Nani), 2-3 (Sergio Ramos), 2-3 (Alves missed), 2-4 (Fabregas)
Referee: C Cakir (Turkey)

GERMANY 1 ITALY 2
Warsaw (58,540); Thursday, June 28
Germany (4-2-3-1): Neuer, Boateng (Muller 71), Hummels, Badstuber, Lahm, Khedira, Schweinsteiger, Kroos, Ozil, Podolski (Reus 46), Gomez (Klose 46). **Scorer:** Ozil (90 pen). **Booked:** Hummels
Italy (4-1-3-2): Buffon, Balzaretti, Barzagli, Bonucci, Chiellini, Pirlo, Marchisio, Montolivo (Motta 63), De Rossi, Balotelli (Di Natale 69), Cassano (Diamanti 58). **Scorer:** Balotelli (20, 36). **Booked:** Balotelli, Bonucci, De Rossi, Motta
Referee: S Lannoy (France). **Half-time:** 0-2

FINAL

SPAIN 4 ITALY 0
Kiev (63,170); Sunday, July 1
Spain (4-3-3): Casillas (capt), Arbeloa, Pique, Sergio Ramos, Alba, Xavi, Busquets, Xabi

Alonso, Silva (Pedro 59), Fabregas (Torres 75), Iniesta (Mata 87). **Subs not used:** Valdes, Reina, Albiol, Martinez, Juanfran, Santi Cazorla, Jesus Navas, Negredo, Llorente. **Scorers:** Silva (14), Alba (41), Torres (84), Mata (88). **Booked:** Pique. **Coach:** Vicente del Bosque
Italy (4-1-3-2): Buffon (capt), Abate, Barzagli, Bonucci, Chiellini (Balzaretti 21), Pirlo, Marchisio, Montolivo (Motta 56), De Rossi, Balotelli, Cassano (Di Natale 46). **Subs not used:** Sirigu, De Sanctis, Maggio, Ogbonna, Giaccherini, Diamanti, Nocerino, Borini, Giovinco.
Booked: Barzagli. **Coach:** Cesare Prandelli
Referee: P Proenca (Portugal). **Half-time:** 2-0

EURO 2012 FACTS AND FIGURES

- Spain, who beat Germany in the 2008 final in Vienna, became the first side to retain the European title.

- They were also the first to win three major tournaments in a row, having triumphed at the 2010 World Cup.

- Their winning margin in Kiev surpassed West Germany's 3-0 victory over the USSR in 1972. It was also bigger than in any World Cup final.

- Fernando Torres, who got the only goal in 2008, was the first player to score in two European finals.

- Torres won the Golden Boot by providing the assist for Juan Mata's goal and spending less time on the pitch than Germany's Mario Gomez. Four other players scored three times – Mario Balotelli (Italy), Alan Dzagoev (Russia), Mario Mandzukic (Croatia) and Cristiano Ronaldo (Portugal).

- Torres and Chelsea team-mate Mata joined a select group of players to feature in European Championship and Champions League/European Cup winning teams in the same season. Andres Iniesta was named the best player of the tournament.

- Iker Casillas, Spain's goalkeeper and captain, became the first player to reach 100 international wins. He has a record 79 clean sheets in 136 appearances for his country.

- With Gianluigi Buffon leading Italy, this was the first European final in which both skippers were goalkeepers.

- Spain have now kept a clean sheet in ten knock-out matches. The last time they conceded was a 3-1 defeat by France in the second round of the 2006 World Cup.

- UEFA have approved an increase from 16 to 24 teams for the 2016 finals to be held in France.

- England squad – Goalkeepers: Butland (Birmingham), Green (QPR), Hart (Manchester City). Defenders: Baines (Everton), Cole (Chelsea), Jagielka (Everton), Johnson (Liverpool), Jones (Manchester Utd), Kelly (Liverpool), Lescott (Manchester City), Terry (Chelsea). Midfielders: Downing (Liverpool), Gerrard (Liverpool), Henderson (Liverpool), Milner (Manchester City), Oxlade-Chamberlain (Arsenal), Parker (Tottenham), Walcott (Arsenal), Young (Manchester Utd). Forwards: Carroll (Liverpool), Defoe (Tottenham), Rooney (Manchester Utd), Welbeck (Manchester Utd)

- Republic of Ireland – Goalkeepers: Forde (Millwall), Given (Aston Villa), Westwood (Sunderland). Defenders: Dunne (Aston Villa), Kelly (Fulham), McShane (Hull), O'Dea (Celtic), O'Shea (Sunderland), St Ledger (Leicester), Ward (Wolves) Midfielders: Andrews (WBA), Duff (Fulham), Gibson (Everton), Green (unatt), Hunt (Wolves), McClean (Sunderland), McGeady (Spartak Moscow), Whelan (Stoke). Forwards: Cox (WBA), Doyle (Wolves), Keane (LA Galaxy), Long (WBA), Walters (Stoke)

QUOTE/UNQUOTE

'People will still be talking about Spain's performance twenty or thirty years from now. I don't think we will ever see one as good as this again' – **Alan Hansen**, BBC analyst.

'We had an extraordinary match, but don't underestimate Italy. They had no luck – one fewer player, one less day of rest and they tried throughout' – **Vicente del Bosque**, Spain's coach.

'We played against Spain in the group stage and I thought we were excellent. Here, we were so tired and as soon as we went down to ten men it was game over against a great side' – **Cesare Prandelli**, Italy's coach.

'We've watched these players taking penalties in training and they have done extremely well. But you can't reproduce the tension, the occasion and the tired legs' – **Roy Hodgson** after England's quarter-final defeat by Italy.

'You will definitely see some revolution because it is the ideal opportunity for me to look at some players who weren't with us here' – **Roy Hodgson** on the friendly with Italy which kicks off the new season.

'They will have to analyse why we aren't keeping the ball better at this level. It's the key if you want to beat the big teams' – **Steven Gerrard** on the task facing Hodgson and his coaching staff.

HOW THE FINALISTS QUALIFIED

GROUP A

	P	W	D	L	F	A	Pts
Germany Q	10	10	0	0	34	7	30
Turkey	10	5	2	3	13	11	17
Belgium	10	4	3	3	21	15	15
Austria	10	3	3	4	16	17	12
Azerbaijan	10	2	1	7	10	26	7
Kazakhstan	10	1	1	8	6	24	4

Results: Kazakhstan 0 Turkey 3, Belgium 0 Germany 1, Turkey 3 Belgium 2, Austria 2 Kazakhstan 0, Germany 6 Azerbaijan 0, Kazakhstan 0 Belgium 2, Austria 3 Azerbaijan 0, Germany 3 Turkey 0, Azerbaijan 1 Turkey 0, Kazakhstan 0 Germany 3, Belgium 4 Austria 4, Austria 0 Belgium 2, Germany 4 Kazakhstan 0, Turkey 2 Austria 0, Belgium 4 Azerbaijan 1, Austria 1 Germany 2, Belgium 1 Turkey 1, Kazakhstan 2 Azerbaijan 1, Azerbaijan 1 Germany 3, Azerbaijan 1 Belgium 1, Turkey 2 Kazakhstan 1, Germany 6 Austria 2, Azerbaijan 3 Kazakhstan 2, Austria 0 Turkey 0, Belgium 4 Kazakhstan 1, Turkey 1 Germany 3, Azerbaijan 1 Austria 4, Kazakhstan 0 Austria 0, Germany 3 Belgium 1, Turkey 1 Azerbaijan 0

GROUP B

	P	W	D	L	F	A	Pts
Russia Q	10	7	2	1	17	4	23
Rep of Ireland Q	10	6	3	1	15	7	21
Armenia	10	5	2	3	22	10	17
Slovakia	10	4	3	3	7	10	15

	P	W	D	L	F	A	Pts
Macedonia	10	2	2	6	8	14	8
Andorra	10	0	0	10	1	25	0

Results: Armenia 0 Rep of Ireland 1, Andorra 0 Russia 2, Slovakia 1 Macedonia 0, Russia 0 Slovakia 1, Macedonia 2 Armenia 2, Rep of Ireland 3 Andorra 1, Armenia 3 Slovakia 1, Andorra 0 Macedonia 2, Rep of Ireland 2 Russia 3, Armenia 4 Andorra 0, Slovakia 1 Rep of Ireland 1, Macedonia 0 Russia 1, Armenia 0 Russia 0, Andorra 0 Slovakia 1, Rep of Ireland 2 Macedonia 1, Russia 3 Armenia 1, Macedonia 0 Rep of Ireland 2, Slovakia 1 Andorra 0, Andorra 0 Armenia 3, Russia 1 Armenia 0, Rep of Ireland 0 Slovakia 0, Slovakia 0 Armenia 4, Armenia 4 Macedonia 1, Macedonia 1 Andorra 0, Russia 0 Rep of Ireland 0, Slovakia 0 Russia 1, Andorra 0 Rep of Ireland 2, Russia 6 Andorra 0, Rep of Ireland 2 Armenia 1, Macedonia 1 Slovakia 1.

GROUP C

	P	W	D	L	F	A	Pts
Italy Q	10	8	2	0	20	2	26
Estonia	10	5	1	4	15	14	16
Serbia	10	4	3	3	13	12	15
Slovenia	10	4	2	4	11	7	14
N Ireland	10	2	3	5	9	13	9
Faroe Is	10	1	1	8	6	26	4

Results: Estonia 2 Faroe Is 1, Faroe Is 0 Serbia 3, Estonia 1 Italy 2, Slovenia 0 N Ireland 1, Serbia 1 Slovenia 1, Italy 5 Faroe Is 0, Serbia 1 Estonia 3, N Ireland 0 Italy 0, Slovenia 5 Faroe Is 1, Faroe Is 1 N Ireland 1, Estonia 0 Slovenia 1, Italy 3 Serbia 0 (abandoned at 0-0 after six minutes – crowd trouble. Italy awarded 3-0 win), Serbia 2 N Ireland 1, Slovenia 0 Italy 1, Estonia 1 Serbia 1, N Ireland 0 Slovenia 0, Faroe Is 0 Slovenia 2, Italy 3 Estonia 0, Faroe Is 2 Estonia 0, N Ireland 4 Faroe Is 0, N Ireland 0 Serbia 1, Slovenia 1 Estonia 2, Faroe Is 0 Italy 1, Italy 1 Slovenia 0, Serbia 3 Faroe Is 1, Estonia 4 N Ireland 1, Serbia 1 Italy 1, N Ireland 1 Estonia 2, Slovenia 1 Serbia 0, Italy 3 N Ireland 0.

GROUP D

	P	W	D	L	F	A	Pts
France Q	10	6	3	1	15	4	21
Bosnia-Herz	10	6	2	2	17	8	20
Romania	10	3	5	2	13	9	14
Belarus	10	3	4	3	8	7	13
Albania	10	2	3	5	7	14	9
Luxembourg	10	1	1	8	3	21	4

Results: Romania 1 Albania 1, Luxembourg 0 Bosnia-Herz 3, France 0 Belarus 1, Belarus 0 Romania 0, Albania 1 Luxembourg 0, Bosnia-Herz 0 France 2, Luxembourg 0 Belarus 0, Albania 1 Bosnia-Herz 1, France 2 Romania 0, Belgium 2 Albania 0, France 2 Luxembourg 0, Luxembourg 0 France 2, Bosnia-Herz 2 Romania 1, Albania 1 Belarus 0, Romania 3 Luxembourg 1, Belarus 1 France 1, Romania 3 Bosnia-Herz 0, Belarus 2 Luxembourg 0, Bosnia-Herz 2 Albania 0, Belarus 2 Bosnia-Herz 2, Albania 1 France 2, Luxembourg 0 Romania 2, Luxembourg 2 Albania 1, Bosnia-Herz 1 Belarus 0, Romania 0 France 0, Romania 2 Belarus 2, France 3 Albania 0, Bosnia-Herz 5 Luxembourg 0, France 1 Bosnia-Herz 1, Albania 1 Romania 1.

GROUP E

	P	W	D	L	F	A	Pts
Holland Q	10	9	0	1	37	8	27
Sweden Q	10	8	0	2	31	11	24

	P	W	D	L	F	A	Pts
Hungary	10	6	1	3	22	14	19
Finland	10	3	1	6	16	16	10
Moldova	10	3	0	7	12	16	9
San Marino	10	0	0	10	0	53	0

Results: Moldova 2 Finland 0, Sweden 2 Hungary 0, San Marino 0 Holland 5, Sweden 6 San Marino 0, Holland 2 Finland 1, Hungary 2 Moldova 1, Hungary 8 San Marino 0, Moldova 0 Holland 1, Finland 1 Hungary 2, Holland 4 Sweden 1, San Marino 0 Moldova 2, Finland 8 San Marino 0, Hungary 0 Holland 4, Sweden 2 Moldova 1, Holland 5 Hungary 3, Moldova 1 Sweden 4, San Marino 0 Finland 1, Sweden 5 Finland 0, San Marino 0 Hungary 3, Hungary 2 Sweden 1, Finland 4 Moldova 1, Holland 11 San Marino 0, Finland 0 Holland 2, San Marino 0 Sweden 5, Moldova 0 Hungary 2, Finland 1 Sweden 2, Holland 1 Moldova 0, Sweden 3 Holland 2, Hungary 0 Finland 0, Moldova 4 San Marino 0

GROUP F

	P	W	D	L	F	A	Pts
Greece Q	10	7	3	0	14	5	24
Croatia Q	10	7	1	2	18	7	22
Israel	10	5	1	4	13	11	16
Latvia	10	3	2	5	9	12	11
Georgia	10	2	4	4	7	9	10
Malta	10	0	1	9	4	21	1

Results: Israel 3 Malta 1, Latvia 0 Croatia 3, Greece 1 Georgia 1, Georgia 0 Israel 0, Malta 0 Latvia 2, Croatia 0 Greece 0, Georgia 1 Malta 0, Greece 1 Latvia 0, Israel 1 Croatia 2, Latvia 1 Georgia 1, Greece 2 Israel 1, Croatia 3 Malta 0, Georgia 1 Croatia 0, Israel 2 Latvia 1, Malta 0 Greece 1, Israel 1 Georgia 0, Croatia 2 Georgia 1, Greece 3 Malta 1, Latvia 1 Israel 2, Israel 0 Greece 1, Malta 1 Croatia 3, Georgia 0 Latvia 1, Malta 1 Georgia 1, Latvia 1 Greece 1, Croatia 3 Israel 1, Greece 2 Croatia 0, Latvia 2 Malta 0, Georgia 1 Greece 2, Malta 0 Israel 2, Croatia 2 Latvia 0

GROUP G

	P	W	D	L	F	A	Pts
England Q	8	5	3	0	17	5	18
Montenegro	8	3	3	2	7	7	12
Switzerland	8	3	2	3	12	10	11
Wales	8	3	0	5	6	10	9
Bulgaria	8	1	2	5	3	13	5

Results: Montenegro 1 Wales 0, England 4 Bulgaria 0, Bulgaria 0 Montenegro 1, Switzerland 1 England 3, Wales 0 Bulgaria 1, Montenegro 1 Switzerland 0, Switzerland 4 Wales 1, England 0 Montenegro 0, Wales 0 England 2, Bulgaria 0 Switzerland 0, England 2 Switzerland 2, Montenegro 1 Bulgaria 1, Bulgaria 0 England 3, Wales 2 Montenegro 1, England 1 Wales 0, Switzerland 3 Bulgaria 1, Montenegro 2 England 2, Wales 2 Switzerland 0, Bulgaria 0 Wales 1, Switzerland 2 Montenegro 0

GROUP H

	P	W	D	L	F	A	Pts
Denmark Q	8	6	1	1	15	6	19
Portugal Q	8	5	1	2	21	12	16
Norway	8	5	1	2	10	7	16
Iceland	8	1	1	6	6	14	4
Cyprus	8	0	2	6	7	20	2

Results: Iceland 1 Norway 2, Portugal 4 Cyprus 4, Denmark 1 Iceland 0, Norway 1 Portugal 0, Cyprus 1 Norway 2, Portugal 3 Denmark 1, Denmark 2 Cyprus 0, Iceland 1 Portugal 3, Cyprus 0 Iceland 0, Norway 1 Denmark 1, Iceland 0 Denmark 2, Portugal 1 Norway 0, Norway 1 Iceland 0, Cyprus 0 Portugal 4, Iceland 1 Cyprus 0, Denmark 2 Norway 0, Cyprus 1 Denmark 4, Portugal 5 Iceland 3, Denmark 2 Portugal 1, Norway 3 Cyprus 1

GROUP I

	P	W	D	L	F	A	Pts
Spain Q	8	8	0	0	26	6	24
Czech Republic Q	8	4	1	3	12	8	13
Scotland	8	3	2	3	9	10	11
Lithuania	8	1	2	5	4	13	5
Liechtenstein	8	1	1	6	3	17	4

Results: Lithuania 0 Scotland 0, Liechtenstein 0 Spain 4, Czech Rep 0 Lithuania 1, Scotland 2 Liechtenstein 1, Czech Rep 1 Scotland 0, Spain 3 Lithuania 1, Liechtenstein 0 Czech Rep 2, Scotland 3 Spain 3, Spain 3 Czech Rep 1, Czech Rep 2 Liechtenstein 0, Lithuania 1 Spain 3, Liechtenstein 2 Lithuania 0, Lithuania 0 Liechtenstein 0, Scotland 2 Czech Rep 2, Spain 6 Liechtenstein 0, Scotland 1 Lithuania 0, Czech Rep 0 Spain 2, Liechtenstein 0 Scotland 1, Lithuania 1 Czech Rep 4, Spain 3 Scotland 1

PLAY-OFFS
First legs: Bosnia-Herz 0 Portugal 0; Czech Rep 2 Montenegro 0; Estonia 0 **Rep of Ireland** 4; Turkey 0 Croatia 3
Second legs: Croatia 0 Turkey 0 (Croatia won 3-0 on agg); Montenegro 0 Czech Republic 1 (Czech Republic won 3-0 on agg); Portugal 6 Bosnia-Herz 2 (Portugal won 6-2 on agg); **Rep of Ireland** 1 Estonia 1 (Rep of Ireland won 5-1 on agg)

PREVIOUS FINALS

1960	*USSR 2 Yugoslavia 1 (Paris)
1964	Spain 2 USSR 1 (Madrid)
1968	**Italy 2 Yugoslavia 0 (Rome)
1972	West Germany 3 USSR 0 (Brussels)
1976	***Czechoslovakia 2 West Germany 2 (Belgrade)
1980	West Germany 2 Belgium 1 (Rome)
1984	France 2 Spain 0 (Paris)
1988	Holland 2 USSR 0 (Munich)
1992	Denmark 2 Germany 0 (Gothenburg)
1996	+Germany 2 Czech Republic 1 (Wembley)
2000	+France 2 Italy 1 (Rotterdam)
2004	Greece 1 Portugal 0 (Lisbon)
2008	Spain 1 Germany 0 (Vienna)
2012	Spain 4 Italy 0 (Kiev)

* After extra-time. ** Replay after 1-1. *** Czechoslovakia won 5-3 on pens.
+ Golden goal winner

DAY BY DAY DIARY 2011–12

JULY 2011

14 Patrick Vieira retires after a successful playing career for club and country and takes up a new role as Manchester City's football development executive.

15 Stewart Downing joins Liverpool from Aston Villa for a fee of around £20m.

18 Manchester City sell Jerome Boateng to Bayern Munich for £12m, 12 months after buying him from Hamburg for £10m.

21 Football League clubs vote to reduce the number of match-day substitutes from seven to five to cut costs.

22 Mohamed Bin Hammam, former FIFA presidential candidate, is banned from football for life for attempted bribery.

23 Rangers open their defence of the title with a 1-1 draw against Hearts as the Scottish Premier League season starts three weeks early to give clubs a better chance of preparing for European qualifiers.

28 Manchester City pay a club-record £38.5m for Atletico Madrid's Argentina striker Sergio Aguero.

30 England are drawn alongside Montenegro, Poland and Ukraine in qualifying for the 2014 World Cup in Brazil. Scotland and Wales are paired in the same group, Northern Ireland have to play Portugal and Russia, while the Republic of Ireland face Germany.

31 Manchester United's Antonio Valencia signs a new four-year contract.

AUGUST 2011

1 Joey Barton, Newcastle's Player of the Year, is given a free transfer after criticising the club. Jim Jefferies is sacked as Hearts manager nine days into the new season after 11 matches without a win stretching back to March.

2 Hearts appoint former Sporting Lisbon coach Paulo Sergio to replace Jim Jefferies.

3 Rangers fall at the first Champions League hurdle, beaten 2-1 on aggregate by Malmo in the third qualifying round after having Steven Whittaker and Madjid Bougherra sent off in the second leg.

4 New-signing Tyrone Mears becomes the second Bolton player in six days to sustain a broken leg, following Chung-Yong Lee's injury in a pre-season friendly. England reach the last 16 of the World Youth Cup in Colombia after three goalless draws in their group.

5 Chelsea sell Yuri Zhirkov to the Russian club Anzhi Makhachkala for £11.7m. England goalkeeper Joe Hart agrees a new five-year contract with Manchester City. A crowd of 74,731 at Old Trafford see Manchester United play New York Cosmos in a testimonial match for Paul Scholes.

6 Conference champions Crawley are denied victory by a stoppage-time Port Vale equaliser on the opening day of the Football League season. Fellow league newcomers AFC Wimbledon lose 3-2 to Bristol Rovers.

7 Manchester United come from two goals down to retain the Community Shield by beating Manchester City 3-2 with a stoppage-time goal from Nani, his second of the game. Former Wales manager John Toshack is appointed coach to the Macedonia national team.

8 Arsenal sign 17-year-old Southampton winger Alex Oxlade-Chamberlain for £12m – a record fee for the Championship club. Chelsea pay £18m for 18-year-old Anderlecht striker Romelu Lukaku.

9 England's friendly international against Holland at Wembley is called off on safety grounds following the London riots. Also postponed are Carling Cup matches at Charlton, Crystal Palace and West Ham and ties involving Bristol City and Bristol Rovers. Five Championship sides are beaten at home by League Two teams in the first round.

10 Four players score for the first time at international level. Pat McCourt is on the mark twice and captain Aaron Hughes opens his account in his 77th appearance for Northern Ireland, who beat the Faroe Islands 4-0 in a European Championship qualifier. In friendly matches, Robert Snodgrass heads the winner against Denmark on his first start for Scotland, while Darcy Blake scores his first for club or country as Wales lose to Australia. England go out of the World Youth Cup, beaten 1-0 by Nigeria.

11 Tottenham's opening Premier League match against Everton is called off because of the riots.

13 For the first time, there are no home victories on the first weekend of the Premier League season.

14 Robbie Keane joins David Beckham at LA Galaxy in a £3.5m move from Tottenham.

15 Barcelona's pursuit of Arsenal captain Cesc Fabregas finally pays off with a £35m fee – a record for the Premier League club.

17 Arsenal's Alex Song accepts a three-match FA ban after being caught on camera stamping on Newcastle's Joey Barton. Brighton are fined £5,000 for a players' confrontation during the Carling Cup tie against Gillingham.

18 Malaysian entrepreneur Tony Fernandes, owner of the Team Lotus Formula One team and Air Asia, takes over Queens Park Rangers after buying out majority shareholder Bernie Ecclestone and Flavio Briatore.

21 Chelsea agree to pay £23.5m for Valencia's Spain midfielder player Juan Mata.

22 Manchester United sign a £40m, four-year sponsorship deal for their training kit with logistics company DHL. Arsenal manager Arsene Wenger is given a two-match touchline ban by UEFA for sending messages to his bench during the Champions League play-off first leg against Udinese while serving a previous suspension. The club are fined £8,700 for improper conduct.

23 Samir Nasri follows Cesc Fabregas out of Arsenal after another long-running transfer saga, signing for Manchester City for £25m. Newcastle and Arsenal receive £30,000 fines from the FA for a players' confrontation on the opening day of the season. Three Premier League sides suffer embarrassing defeats in round two of the Carling Cup – Norwich losing to MK Dons, Queens Park Rangers also beaten at home, by Rochdale, and Swansea going down at Shrewsbury.

24 Arsenal, helped by Wojciech Szczesny's penalty save in the second leg against Udinese, reach the group stage for the 14th successive year with a 3-1 aggregate win. The Scottish Cup gains a commercial sponsor for the first time since 2007 – bookmaker William Hill in a three-year deal worth around £3m.

25 All four English clubs, Tottenham, Fulham, Stoke and Birmingham reach the group stage of the Europa League. All three Scottish teams, Celtic, Rangers and Hearts lose play-off matches. Shamrock Rovers become the first Irish side to go that far in Europe by beating Partizan Belgrade. Sir Alex Ferguson, Manchester United manager, ends a seven-year boycott of the BBC over a documentary about his agent son Jason. Peter Jackson is the first Football League managerial casualty of the season, resigning at Bradford after a single point from four matches.

26 Football League figures show that clubs paid out £16.7m on agents' fees in 2010–11, an increase of £4m on the previous season.

27 Phil Parkinson, former Colchester, Hull and Charlton manager, takes over at Bradford.

28 Manchester United record one of the most amazing results in Premier League history, beating Arsenal 8-2. Arsenal Ladies win the inaugural FA Super League title, ahead of Birmingham. Swansea's Alan Tate sustains a broken leg in a bizarre golf buggy accident, trapping the leg between the buggy and a tree.

29 Arsenal offer around 3,000 fans who travelled to Old Trafford a free ticket for a future away fixture.

30 A bid by the Republic of Ireland to have their European Championship qualifier against Andorra played in Barcelona to accommodate supporters is rejected by UEFA.

31 Stoke pay a club-record £10m for Tottenham's Peter Crouch on transfer deadline day. Arsenal sign four players, including Everton's Mikel Arteta for £10m, after their defeat at Old Trafford. Raul Meireles leaves Liverpool for Chelsea for £12m and Fulham sign Bryan Ruiz from Twente Enschede for £10.6m. Total spending during the summer window is £518m.

SEPTEMBER 2011

1 Manchester United announce record operating profits of £110.9m for the financial year.

2 Gary Cahill chalks up his first goal for England in a 3-0 European Championship qualifying win in Bulgaria. He also becomes the first Bolton player to score for the national side since Ray Parry against Northern Ireland in 1959. Steve Morison opens his account for Wales, who collect their first points in the group by beating Montenegro 2-1. Northern Ireland lose by the only goal to Serbia, while the Republic of Ireland keep a record sixth successive clean sheet in a goalless draw with Slovakia. Celtic, beaten by FC Sion in the Europa League play-off round, are reinstated after the Swiss club are found guilty of fielding ineligible players.

3 Scotland concede a controversial stoppage-time penalty which gives the Czech Republic a 2-2 draw at Hampden Park.

5 Arsenal manager Arsene Wenger's appeal against his two-match Champions League touchline ban is rejected.

6 Fabio Capello admits England are fortunate to come away with a 1-0 win over Wales. Scotland keep their hopes flickering by beating Lithuania by the same margin and the Republic of Ireland stay on course after a goalless away draw with Russia. But Northern Ireland's chances are all but ended by a 4-1 defeat in Estonia.

7 A record 27 successive penalties are converted in a shoot-out before Leyton Orient's Ben Chorley has his spot-kick saved by Dagenham & Redbridge goalkeeper James Shea in a Johnstone's Paint Trophy first round tie.

9 Garry Cook resigns as Manchester City's chief executive after admitting sending an offensive e-mail to the mother of defender Nedum Onuoha. Port Vale and Southend are each fined £1,000 by the FA for failing to control their players, following an incident at Vale Park.

10 A year after his £13m club-record move to Sunderland, Asamoah Gyan joins the United Arab Emirates club Al-Ain on a season-long loan.

13 Ben Tomlinson scores after seven seconds for Macclesfield against Morecambe. Gabriel Tamas receives a three-match ban from the FA after being caught on camera elbowing James Vaughan in West Bromwich Albion's game at Norwich. Celtic's place in the Europa League is confirmed after Sion's appeal against expulsion from the tournament is rejected.

14 Phil Bardsley, sent off in Sunderland's match against Newcastle and banned for one match earlier in the season, is suspended for four games by the FA after being caught on camera stamping on Chelsea's Juan Mata.

15 FIFA block Swansea's deadline-day deals for Fulham's Rafik Halliche and Darnel Situ from Lens because of a delay in processing both signings.

16 Manchester City's Sergio Aguero signs a sponsorship deal with Puma worth a reported £5m.

17 Coach Hope Powell, appointed in 1998, takes charge of the England women's team for a record 140th match – a 2-2 draw against Serbia in a Euro 2013 qualifier.

18 Peter Reid is sacked as Plymouth manager with his side bottom of League Two.

19 Manchester City unveil plans for a £100m academy and training complex adjacent to the Etihad Stadium.

20 Arsene Wenger defends his coaching structure and chief executive Ivan Gazidis insists the manager's job is safe following Arsenal's troubled start to the season. Barnsley and Leicester are both fined £5,000 by the FA for a players' confrontation. Newcastle manager Alan Pardew is warned about his future conduct over comments before the local derby against Sunderland.

21 Owen Hargreaves takes a step towards rebuilding his career with a scoring debut for Manchester City, who knock holders Birmingham out of the Carling Cup.

22 Sean O'Driscoll, the Championship's longest-serving manager, is sacked after five years in charge of Doncaster, with his side bottom. He is replaced by Wrexham's Dean Saunders.

23 There is widespread condemnation of 'disgusting' chanting by rival fans at the Leeds-Manchester United Carling Cup tie.

25 Arsenal beat Birmingham 4-1 in the inaugural FA Women's Super League Continental Cup Final.

27 Carlos Tevez refuses to come off the bench and warm up during Manchester City's Champions League defeat by Bayern Munich and manager Roberto Mancini says the Argentine will never play for the club again.

28 Carlos Tevez is suspended for two weeks by the club pending an investigation. Alex Oxlade-Chamberlain, at 18 years and 44 days, becomes the youngest English scorer in the Champions League with a goal in Arsenal's win over Olympiacos.

29 Blackpool manager Ian Holloway receives a one-match touchline ban and £2,000 fine from the FA after being sent to the stands at Coventry. Bournemouth are fined £2,500 for their players surrounding referee Iain Williamson during the match against Hartlepool.

30 Brighton manager Gus Poyet signs a new five-year contract.

OCTOBER 2011

2 Steve McClaren resigns as manager of struggling Nottingham Forest after 111 days in charge, blaming financial constraints at the club.

3 Another Championship manager leaves, Bristol City's Keith Millen paying the price for his team's bottom-of-the-table position.

4 Accrington's Johnstone's Paint Trophy tie against Tranmere is abandoned after 39 minutes when their 18-year-old on-loan defender Tom Bender suffers a serious head injury.

5 Hartlepool are fined £2,500 by the FA for a players' melee during the match against Bournemouth.

6 Two players score hat-tricks in European Under-21 Championship qualifying matches – Arsenal's Alex Oxlade-Chamberlain for England in Iceland and Huddersfield's Jordan Rhodes for Scotland in Luxembourg.

7 Wayne Rooney is sent off as England make sure of a place in the European Championship Finals with a 2-2 draw in Montenegro – his second red card when playing for the national side. The Republic of Ireland move closer to the play-offs by winning 2-0 in Andorra, but Northern Ireland's elimination is confirmed by a 2-1 home defeat by Estonia. Wales beat Switzerland 2-0. Peterborough chairman Darragh MacAnthony is fined £2,000 by the FA for criticising referee Tony Bates after the defeat by West Ham.

8 Craig Mackail-Smith marks his first start for Scotland with the only goal of their group match in Liechtenstein.

9 England's failed 2018 World Cup bid cost £21m, £6m more than reported, according to FA accounts.

10 Nigel Worthington announces his intention to step down after four-and-a-half-years as Northern Ireland manager. Wayne Rooney appeals to UEFA to limit his suspension to a single match.

11 The Republic of Ireland reach the European Championship play-offs by beating Armenia 2-1 with an own goal followed by Richard Dunne's first of the qualifying campaign. Kevin Doyle is later sent off. Manchester City's David Silva scores twice to end Scotland's hopes. They lose 3-1 to Spain, David Goodwillie scoring a consolation from the penalty spot for his first international goal. Wales win 1-0 in Bulgaria for their first back-to-back successes in competitive games since 2005. Nigel Worthington's last match in charge of Northern Ireland is a 3-0 defeat by Italy. Peterborough manager Darren Ferguson and his assistant Kevin Russell both receive a one-match touchline ban and £2,000 fine from the FA for improper conduct during the match against Doncaster.

12 After a two-week investigation, Manchester City say Carlos Tevez did refuse to come on as a substitute against Bayern Munich. Manchester United's Javier Hernandez signs a new five-year contract.

13 Wayne Rooney is banned for three matches for what UEFA call his 'assault' on Montenegro's Miodrag Dzudovic.

14 Steve Cotterill leaves Portsmouth to become Nottingham Forest's new manager. Huddersfield are fined £2,500 by the FA for failing to control their players. Manager Lee Clark receives a £1,000 fine for his part in a fracas after the game with Stevenage. Bristol Rovers are fined £1,000 for a players' clash against Oxford.

16 Derby manager Nigel Clough signs a new contract through to the summer of 2015.

17 Sir Alex Ferguson leads widespread opposition to claims that a group of foreign owners want to abolish relegation from the Premier League.

18 Wayne Rooney overtakes Paul Scholes as the highest-scoring English player in the Champions League when two penalties against Otelul Galati takes his tally to 26.

19 Derek McInnes leaves St Johnstone to become Bristol City's new manager.

20 Stuart Pearce, England Under-21 manager, is named manager of Britain's Olympic team. Hope Powell, coach to England's senior women, takes charge of the women's side.

21 President Sepp Blatter promises to reform FIFA within two years following a wave of bribery and corruption allegations.

23 Manchester United manager Sir Alex Ferguson suffers the worst defeat of his career – 6-1 by Manchester City at Old Trafford.

24 Manager Sven-Goran Eriksson is sacked following Leicester's third home defeat of the season – 3-0 by Millwall. Manchester United's Nemanja Vidic retires from international football after 56 appearances for Serbia.

25 Carlos Tevez is fined four weeks' wages after a Manchester City disciplinary panel upholds a charge of misconduct relating to the incident against Bayern Munich.

26 The FA replace the 1986 FA Cup runners-up medal auctioned by Peter Reid to help pay staff wages when he was manager of Plymouth, in recognition of a 'good deed' by the former Everton player.

27 Manchester City are forced by the players' union, the PFA, to half the fine imposed on Carlos Tevez. Roman Abramovich fails to secure the freehold of Stamford Bridge at a shareholders meeting of Chelsea Pitch Owners.

30 Plymouth come out of administration following the takeover of the club by local businessman James Brent.

31 Carl Fletcher is appointed Plymouth manager after a spell as caretaker.

NOVEMBER 2011

1 Nottingham Forest's Ishmael Miller is fined £2,500 by the FA for comments on *Twitter* about Forest fans.

2 Tottenham manager Harry Redknapp has a minor heart operation and is told to take a break from the game before returning.

3 Steve Lomas, former Manchester City, West Ham and Queens Park Rangers midfielder, is named St Johnstone's new manager. It is the last appointment of the Scottish Premier League's longest-serving chairman, Geoff Brown, stepping down after 25 years in the position. Huddersfield manager Lee Clark turns down the chance to take over at Leicester.

4 FIFA refuse to allow England players to wear poppies in a friendly international against Spain, insisting there can be no changes to official kit.

5 Manchester United mark Sir Alex Ferguson's 25 years as manager by naming Old Trafford's north stand after him. Macclesfield striker Vinny Mukendi, 19, is sent off for elbowing 11 seconds after coming on as a second-half substitute against Burton.

6 Hibernian, a point away from the bottom of the Scottish Premier League, sack manager Colin Calderwood.

7 Prince William, president of the FA, and Prime Minister David Cameron add their voices to the demand for FIFA to reconsider the decision about poppies.

8 Wigan's Antolin Alcaraz is banned for three matches by the FA after being caught on camera spitting at Wolves' Richard Stearman. Manchester City fine Kolo Toure six weeks' wages for failing a drugs test earlier in the year.

9 FIFA bow to mounting pressure and allow England players to have poppies on their printed armbands. Scotland and Wales players will do the same in their games. Newcastle announce that St James' Park is to be renamed the Sports Direct Arena in a bid to pave the way for the sale of naming rights to a corporate sponsor.

10 Dario Gradi steps down after a third spell as Crewe manager and is replaced by his assistant, Steve Davis. Gradi continues as director of football. Michael Appleton leaves a coaching role at West Bromwich Albion to become Portsmouth's new manager.

11 Jonathan Walters scores his first international goal as the Republic of Ireland make virtually sure of reaching the European Championship Finals with a 4-0 away victory in the first leg of their play-off match against Estonia, who have two players sent off. Scotland defeat Cyprus 2-1 in a friendly international. England goalkeeping coach Ray Clemence is admitted to hospital after feeling unwell. Derby manager Nigel Clough is fined £2,500 by the FA for comments about referee Iain Williamson following the defeat at Peterborough. Macclesfield manager Gary Simpson and his assistant Glyn Chamberlain are also fined for improper conduct, £500 each following defeat at Burton.

12 A goal by Frank Lampard gives England a 1-0 victory over Spain, their first success against reigning world champions since beating Argentina in 1980. Substitute Sam Vokes scores twice for Wales, who defeat Norway 4-1 in another friendly, the fourth win in five games for a team rising to 45th from 117th in FIFA's world rankings under Gary Speed.

13 Six defeats in seven league and FA Cup matches cost Gary Johnson his job as Northampton manager.

14 Terry Butcher, Inverness manager and former Rangers captain, becomes the first Englishman to be inducted into the Scottish Football Hall of Fame. Chesterfield and Yeovil are fined £2,500 each by the FA for a players' scuffle.

15 The Republic of Ireland confirm a place in Euro 2012 with a 1-1 draw in the return leg with Estonia. Gareth Barry is officially credited with England's 2000th international goal, his deflected header bringing their first victory in 13 games against Sweden stretching back to 1968. Nigel Pearson leaves Hull to return to Leicester as manager.

16 Sepp Blatter, FIFA's president, comes under fire again, this time for dismissing on-pitch racism. Tony Adams, former Arsenal and England captain, resigns after 18 months as manager of FC Gabala in Azerbaijan for family reasons.

17 Adam Johnson (Manchester City) and Marouane Fellaini (Everton) sign new five-year contracts.

18 Manchester City post record annual losses of nearly £195m. Sepp Blatter apologises for his comments about racism, but says he will not resign. Pablo Zabaleta signs a new deal with Manchester City through to 2015.

19 Huddersfield make Football League history with a 43rd successive unbeaten match in League One, overtaking the 1978 record of Brian Clough's Nottingham Forest.

20 LA Galaxy's David Beckham becomes the second English player, after Trevor Steven, to win league titles in three different countries, following his success with Manchester United and Real Madrid.

21 Stoke manager Tony Pulis is fined £10,000 by the FA for critical comments about referee Lee Probert after the Carling Cup defeat by Liverpool. Manager Harry Redknapp returns to the Tottenham dug-out following heart surgery. The Scottish Premier League extend their broadcasting deal with Sky and ESPN for a further five years until 2017 for a reported fee of £16m a year, an increase of £3m per year.

22 Chelsea manager Andre Villas-Boas is fined £12,000 by the FA for his attack on referee Chris Foy after the defeat by Queens Park Rangers.

23 Arsenal reach the group stage of the Champions League for the 12th successive season. Steve Kean, manager of struggling Blackburn, signs a revision of his contract to 2013.

24 Pat Fenlon leaves the League of Ireland club Bohemians to become Hibernian's new manager.

27 Football mourns Gary Speed after the Wales manager and former captain is found dead at his home.

28 Huddersfield's record run ends with a 2-0 defeat at Charlton. Giovanni Trapattoni, the Republic of Ireland manager, signs an extension to his contract to 2014.

29 As tributes continue to be paid to Gary Speed, the Professional Footballers' Association plan to send out a guidebook to help members and former players deal with depression. Blackburn's Steven Nzonzi is banned for three games by the FA for violent conduct following video evidence of an incident with Stoke's Ryan Shawcross.

30 Sunderland sack manager Steve Bruce after two wins in 13 games. Aidy Boothroyd, former Watford, Colchester and Coventry manager, takes charge at Northampton. Premier League figures show that clubs spent £71.9m in agents' fees in the 12 months to September 30.

DECEMBER 2011

1 Stoke reach the knock-out stage of the Europa League. Liverpool's Lucas Leiva is ruled out for the rest of the season with a knee injury.

2 The Scottish Premier League game between Motherwell and Hibernian is abandoned at half-time on safety grounds following an electrical fire in one of Fir Park's floodlights.

3 Martin O'Neill returns to management with Sunderland, 16 months after resigning at Aston Villa.

4 An achilles injury rules out Newcastle's Steven Taylor for the rest of the season.

5 Hartlepool manager Mick Wadsworth is sacked after seven successive league and cup home defeats.

6 Chelsea win 3-0 in a make-or-break Champions League group game against Valencia to reach the knock-out stage.

7 Both Manchester clubs fail to reach the knock-out stage – United beaten by Basle and City losing out to Napoli for second place in their group. United also lose Nemanja Vidic for the rest of the season with a knee injury.

8 Wayne Rooney has his Euro 2012 ban cut from three to two games by UEFA on appeal. Another player faces missing the rest of the season with achilles trouble – Jermaine Jenas, on loan to Aston Villa from Tottenham.

9 Arsenal unveil statues of three of their past greats, manager Herbert Chapman and players Tony Adams and Thierry Henry, as part of the club's 125th anniversary celebrations.

10 Celtic are fined £12,700 by UEFA for pro-IRA chanting by supporters during the Europa League match against Rennes.

12 Brighton are fined £15,000 by the FA for players protesting at a penalty awarded against them at Southampton.

13 Manchester United announce that Darren Fletcher is taking an indefinite break from the game because of a debilitating bowel condition. Aberdeen's Ryan Jack scores from 50 yards in the win at St Johnstone. Notts County are fined £3,750 by the FA for failing to control their players in the match against Scunthorpe.

14 Fulham concede a stoppage-time equaliser to Odense and fail to qualify from the group stage of the Europa League. Preston sack manager Phil Brown after a single win in 16 league and cup matches.

15 Tottenham, Birmingham and Celtic are all knocked out of the Europa League, leaving Stoke as the only survivors from eight English and Scottish sides in the qualifying and group stages of the competition.

16 Coach Stuart Pearce rules out England players involved in Euro 2012 from Great Britain's squad for the Olympics.

18 Lionel Messi scores twice as Barcelona beat Santos of Brazil 4-0 in the Club World Cup Final in Yokohama.

19 Steve Eyre is sacked after six months as Rochdale manager, with his side third from bottom.

20 Liverpool's Luis Suarez is banned for eight matches and fined £40,000 by the FA for racially abusing Manchester United's Patrice Evra. World Cup Final referee Howard Webb and Scotland's Craig Thomson are included in the list of officials for Euro 2012.

21 The Crown Prosecution Service announces that Chelsea and England captain John Terry is to be prosecuted for alleged racial abuse of Queens Park Rangers defender Anton Ferdinand. Aston Villa's Marc Albrighton scores the Premier League's 20,000th goal and receives a £20,000 cheque for charity from sponsors Barclays.

22 Manchester City fine Carlos Tevez six weeks' wages – over £1m – for breaches of contract after he travelled home to Argentina without permission.

27 Michael O'Neill, winner of 33 caps and former manager of Shamrock Rovers, is named Northern Ireland's new manager.

28 Luis Suarez receives another FA ban, one match along with a £20,000 fine, for an offensive gesture towards Fulham fans. Liverpool are fined £20,000 for players remonstrating with referee Kevin Friend in the same game. Celtic, trailing by 15 points in early November, overtake Rangers as the top of the Scottish Premier League by winning the Old Firm game 1-0. Neale Cooper, who parted company with Hartlepool in May 2005, returns for a second spell as manager.

29 Former Chelsea manager Carlo Ancelotti takes charge of Paris Saint-Germain.

30 Former Aston Villa chairman Doug Ellis is awarded a knighthood in the New Year Honours list. Andy Williamson, the Football League's chief operating officer, receives an OBE.

31 A 115-page judgement, released by the FA on the Luis Suarez racial abuse case, accuses the player of unreliable and inconsistent evidence. Sir Alex Ferguson tells Manchester United TV he has three more years as manager.

JANUARY 2012

1 Wayne Rooney is dropped and fined by Manchester United – along with team-mates Jonny Evans and Darron Gibson – for not being fit to train after a night out.

2 Liverpool accept the eight-match ban imposed on Luis Suarez and decide not to appeal.

3 Paul Buckle is sacked after seven months as Bristol Rovers manager, his side having won just once in the last 11 league games. Conference club Darlington go into administration for the third time in nine years and are deducted ten points.

4 David Beckham turns down a move to Paris Saint-Germain and opts to stay with LA Galaxy.

5 Thierry Henry returns to Arsenal for six weeks on loan from New York Red Bulls. Steve McClaren takes charge of FC Twente for the second time.

6 Liverpool are at the centre of another 'racial' incident when Oldham's Tom Adeyemi breaks down in tears after being abused by a spectator during the teams' FA Cup tie at Anfield. Manchester United and Wayne Rooney issue a statement denying that the player will be sold in the January transfer window.

7 Queens Park Rangers manager Neil Warnock is sacked after his team slide to fourth from bottom.

8 Paul Scholes makes a comeback in Manchester United's FA Cup win over Manchester City. Barcelona's Lionel Messi is voted the world's best player for the third successive year.

9 Thierry Henry scores the only goal of Arsenal's FA Cup tie with Leeds. Gary Johnson returns to Yeovil as manager, six years after leaving for Bristol City, replacing Terry Skiverton, who becomes his assistant. Sir Alex Ferguson receives the FIFA President's Award for services to the game.

10 Mark Hughes returns to management with Queens Park Rangers, seven months after leaving Fulham. Nick Barmby is appointed Hull manager on a permanent basis after two months as caretaker.

11 Swindon manager Paolo Di Canio receives a one-match touchline ban and £500 fine from the FA for running across the pitch to celebrate victory at Northampton. MK Dons manager Karl Robinson is fined £1,250 for remonstrating with referee Carl Berry during the game against Colchester.

12 Steven Gerrard signs a new deal with Liverpool, taking him to the end of his playing career and then involving an ambassadorial role at the club.

13 Graham Westley leaves Stevenage after winning back-to-back promotions to become Preston's new manager.

14 Avram Grant, former Chelsea, Portsmouth and West Ham manager, takes over at Partizan Belgrade.

15 Chelsea pay the first substantial fee of the winter transfer window - £7m for Bolton's Gary Cahill.

16 Darlington's administrator sacks caretaker-manager Craig Liddle and ten players, leaving the future of the club in the balance.

17 Newcastle sign Senegal striker Papiss Cisse from Freiburg for £9m, the biggest fee of the transfer window. The FA announce a new two-year deal with ITV, worth around £90m, for England matches and FA Cup ties.

18 Liverpool sign a record kit deal, reported to be worth £150m over six years, with American firm Warrior Sports. Mark McGhee begins his eighth managerial job, most recently at Aberdeen, when he takes over Bristol Rovers.

19 Chris Coleman, winner of 32 caps and an international team-mate of Gary Speed, is named the new Wales manager.

20 Leicester's Michael Ball is fined £6,000 by the FA for posting homophobic comments on *Twitter*.

21 Supporters rally round crisis-club Darlington, with a crowd of 5,638 – nearly three times their average – watching the game against Fleetwood.

22 Sir John Madejski, Reading's owner for 22 years, agrees to sell 51 per cent of the club to a company headed by Russian tycoon Anton Zingarevich.

23 John Coleman, the Football League's longest-serving manager, leaves Accrington after nearly 13 years to take charge at Rochdale. Michael Ball has his contract with Leicester cancelled by mutual consent, say the club.

24 Cardiff beat Crystal Palace on penalties to reach the Carling Cup Final. Gary Smith, former Arsenal scout and coach of Colorado Rapids, is appointed the new Stevenage manager.

25 Mario Balotelli is banned for four matches after the FA review video evidence of the Manchester City player stamping on Tottenham's Scott Parker. City lose 3-2 on aggregate to Liverpool in the second Carling Cup semi-final.

26 In a move to clear up confusion over dangerous tackles, referees are told to punish all two-footed challenges with red cards.

28 In a move to 'defuse further tensions,' pre-match handshakes are scrapped for the Queens Park Rangers-Chelsea FA Cup tie involving Anton Ferdinand and John Terry.

30 Bournemouth pay around £800,000, nearly four times their previous record fee, for Crawley's Matt Tubbs.

31 Queens Park Rangers twice break their transfer record, first signing Djibril Cisse from Lazio for £4m, then paying £4.5m for another striker, Fulham's Bobby Zamora. The transfer window closes with total spending of £58m by Premier League clubs, compared with the record £225m in 2011. Chelsea post annual losses of £67.7m.

FEBRUARY 2012

1 Leeds manager Simon Grayson is sacked following a 4-1 home defeat by Birmingham. The FA ban Newcastle's Yohan Cabaye for three matches after studying video evidence of him kicking Brighton defender Adam El-Abd.

2 John Terry is stripped of the England captaincy for the second time following the decision to hold his trial for alleged racial abuse after the European Championship Finals.

3 Rio Ferdinand rules himself out of contention to take over as captain.

4 England manager Fabio Capello criticises the FA's decision over John Terry. Nottingham Forest owner Nigel Doughty, 54, is found dead at his home. The weather makes its first impact on the season's fixtures, with 21 Football League games and eight matches in Scotland postponed.

5 FA officials attempt to obtain an official translation of the interview Fabio Capello gave to Italian television.

7 Swansea manager Brendan Rodgers signs a new three-and-a-half-year contract.

8 Fabio Capello resigns over the John Terry affair after four years in the job. Hours earlier, Tottenham manager Harry Redknapp and his former Portsmouth chairman Milan Mandaric are cleared of tax evasion by a jury at Southwark Crown Court. Millwall's Alan Dunne is fined £2,000 by the FA for criticising referee Jon Moss on *Twitter*.

9 As the FA begin drawing up a shortlist of candidates to replace Fabio Capello, Under-21 coach Stuart Pearce is put in temporary charge for England's friendly against Holland.

10 Swindon manager Paolo Di Canio is given a second touchline ban in a month by the FA, this time for two matches after being sent off during the game against Macclesfield.

11 Sir Alex Ferguson leads the criticism after Luis Suarez refuses to shake hands with racial-abuse victim Patrice Evra before the Manchester United-Liverpool match.

12 Luis Suarez is forced by Liverpool officials to apologise. Manager Kenny Dalglish also apologises, for his reaction to post-match questions from *Sky TV* about the incident. Chelsea's Didier Drogba misses a penalty during the match and Manchester City's Kolo Toure and Arsenal's Gervinho fail with spot-kicks during a shoot-out as Ivory Coast lose to Zambia in the Africa Cup of Nations Final.

13 Wolves manager Mick McCarthy is sacked after a 5-1 home defeat by West Bromwich Albion puts his side back in the bottom three. Former Accrington midfielder Paul Cook returns to the club as manager.

14 Rangers, the club with a world record 54 domestic titles, go into administration over a multi-million-pound tax bill, are docked ten points and effectively hand the Scottish Premier League title to Celtic. Carlos Tevez returns to Manchester City after three months of self-exile over his dispute with the club.

15 Huddersfield manager Lee Clark, whose side set a Football League record of 43 unbeaten matches less than three months ago, is sacked after differences with chairman Dean Hoyle. Arsenal suffer their biggest defeat in Europe – 4-0 by AC Milan in the Champions League round of 16 first leg. Stuart Attwell loses his place on the elite list of Premier League referees following some controversial decisions.

16 Portsmouth, with debts of £4m, go into administration for the second time in two years and have ten points deducted.

17 Neil Warnock makes a rapid return to management with Leeds.

18 Martin Allen, manager of Notts County for ten months, is dismissed after a 3-0 defeat at Hartlepool.

19 Keith Curle, coach under Neil Warnock at Queens Park Rangers, takes charge at Notts County.

20 The managerial merry-go-round continues with Simon Grayson taking charge of Huddersfield.

21 Carlos Tevez backs down over his long-running rift with Manchester City and apologises for his behaviour.

22 Leading football officials attend an anti-racism summit in Downing Street, where David Cameron promises Government support to combat the problem. Ravel Morrison, West Ham's new signing from Manchester United, is fined £7,000 by the FA for a homophobic remark on *Twitter*. Manchester City reach the last 16 of the Europa League by beating Porto.

23 Manchester United follow their neighbours into the next round with victory over Ajax, but Stoke lose to Valencia.

24 Terry Connor, Mick McCarthy's assistant at Wolves, is appointed manager until the end of the season.

25 Blackburn Christopher Samba joins the wealthy Russian club Anzhi Makhachkala in a £9m transfer.

26 Liverpool beat Cardiff 3-2 on penalties in the Carling Cup Final after the teams finish 2-2 at the end of extra-time.

27 Rangers are fined £50,000 by the PLUS Stock Exchange for failing to disclose owner Craig Whyte's previous disqualification as a director when he took over the club in May 2011.

28 Tottenham's Scott Parker is voted England Player of the Year by supporters.

29 Gary Megson is sacked as Sheffield Wednesday manager three days after his side beat Sheffield United to climb to third place in League One. In Michael O'Neill's first match as Northern Ireland manager, a 3-0 defeat by Norway, David Healy makes his 92nd appearance and becomes his country's most capped outfield player. England retrieve a 2-0 deficit in their friendly against Holland, but are beaten by former Chelsea winger Arjen Robben's stoppage-time goal, his second of the game. In a memorial match for Gary Speed at Cardiff City Stadium, Wales lose 1-0 to Costa Rica, the opponents when Speed won the first of his 85 caps in 1990.

MARCH 2012

1 The FA fine Newcastle's Nile Ranger £6,000 and Walsall's Manny Smith £1,200 for homophobic comments on *Twitter*.

2 Dave Jones, former Southampton, Wolves and Cardiff manager, succeeds Gary Megson at

Hillsborough. Birmingham and Coventry have transfer embargoes imposed by the Football League for failing to file club accounts on time.

3 The rule-making International FA Board approve in principle the introduction of goal-line technology. Newcastle's Fabricio Coloccini and Tim Krul sign new four-year and five-year contracts respectively.

4 Andre Villas-Boas, Chelsea's manager for less than nine months, pays the price for a stuttering season – the sixth to be sacked since Roman Abramovich bought the club in 2003. Assistant Roberto Di Matteo takes charge until the end of the season. Also dismissed is Tranmere's Les Parry, with his side a point off the relegation zone. Former manager Ronnie Moore is appointed until the end of the season. Manchester City fine Mario Balotelli a week's wages for breaking a club curfew before the game against Bolton.

5 Another club threatened with the drop, Hereford, sack their manager Jamie Pitman and bring in Walsall coach Richard O'Kelly until the end of the season. The FA campaign to stamp out homophobia continues with a fine of £15,000 on Federico Macheda, the Manchester United striker on loan at Queens Park Rangers, for a comment on *Twitter*.

6 Arsenal go out of the Champions League, scoring three times in the first half against AC Milan but unable to add another to draw level on aggregate.

7 The Football League agree to give Portsmouth four outstanding payments totalling £800,000, enabling the club to complete the season. Wolves captain Roger Johnson is fined two weeks' wages by the club for turning up unfit for training.

8 The Scottish FA rule that Craig Whyte, owner of Rangers, is 'not a fit and proper person to run a football club', following an independent inquiry into the stricken club. Everton's Tim Howard signs an extension to his contract through to 2016. Bournemouth chairman Eddie Mitchell is fined £1,500 by the FA after swearing in a BBC radio interview and being cut off.

9 Port Vale go into administration for the second time in eight years and are deducted ten points. Players at Rangers agree a pay cut of up to 75 per cent to safeguard the club's immediate future.

10 Within minutes of Queens Park Rangers defender Clint Hill having a clear goal against Bolton missed by match officials, the FA issue a statement repeating their call for goal-line technology.

12 Tomas Rosicky wins a new two-year contract with Arsenal after a surge of form.

13 Steven Gerrard becomes the first player since Ian Rush in 1982 to score a hat-trick in the Merseyside derby as Liverpool beat Everton 3-0.

14 Chelsea reach the last eight of the Champions League with a famous victory – 4-1 over Napoli after trailing 3-1 from the first leg.

15 Rangers and owner Craig Whyte are charged by the Scottish FA with seven breaches of rules. Manchester City and Manchester United fail to reach the last eight of the Europa League, losing to Sporting and Athletic Bilbao respectively. Sir Dave Richards, chairman of the Premier League, apologises for accusing FIFA and UEFA of 'stealing' football from England.

16 Dunfermline, bottom of the Scottish Premier League, sack manager Jim McIntyre.

17 Fabrice Muamba suffers a cardiac arrest and collapses during Bolton's FA Cup tie at Tottenham. He is taken to the London Chest Hospital and the game is abandoned. Manager Paul Peschisolido is sacked after Burton lose 4-1 at home to Torquay, their sixth successive defeat.

18 Kilmarnock's 1-0 win over Celtic in the Scottish Communities League Cup Final is overshadowed when their midfield player Liam Kelly's father Jack, 59, has a heart attack while watching the game and dies in hospital. With Fabrice Muamba in a critical condition, Bolton's game at Aston Villa is postponed. Macclesfield sack manager Gary Simpson after 16 games without a win.

19 Andy Scott leaves Rotherham, after 11 months in charge, with his side eight points away from a play-off place. The sacking comes shortly after a TV interview about the heart condition which ended his playing career. Macclesfield bring in former manager Brian Horton until the end of the season.

20 Five goals are scored in eight second-half minutes as Nottingham Forest win 7-3 at Leeds. Chelsea sack reserve player Jacob Mellis for setting off a smoke grenade at the club's training ground.

21 The FA fine Newcastle £40,000 and Sunderland £20,000 for a players' melee in the Tyne-Wear derby, Newcastle's second such incident this season. Jim Jefferies, former Hearts manager, takes charge at Dunfermline.

22 James McClean, Sunderland's discovery of the season, signs a new three-year contract.

23 Bidding closes for the tenancy of the Olympic Stadium after the London 2012 Games, with West Ham among four interested parties.

25 Three players, two from Celtic and one from Rangers, are sent off in the Old Firm game, won 3-2 by Rangers to prevent their rivals clinching the title at Ibrox. Celtic manager Neil Lennon is sent from the dug-out in the second-half. Chesterfield beat Swindon 2-0 in the Johnstone's Paint Trophy Final. Bournemouth manager Lee Bradbury is sacked after six defeats in eight matches.

26 Former Chelsea manager Claudio Ranieri is dismissed by Inter Milan after one win in ten Serie A games.

27 Five players, three from Bradford and two from Crawley, are shown red cards in the dressing room by referee Ian Williamson after a mass brawl at the end of the League Two game at Valley Parade. Shrewsbury's match against Port Vale is abandoned after 65 minutes following an electrical fire in one of the stands.

28 Celtic are fined £21,000 by UEFA for the misbehaviour of supporters in the Europa League away game against Udinese.

29 Aston Villa's Stiliyan Petrov is diagnosed with acute leukaemia. Swansea's Leon Britton signs a new three-year contract.

30 Arsene Wenger receives a third touchline ban from UEFA in just over a year, this time for three matches, along with a £33,000 fine for criticising referee Damir Skomina after Arsenal's Champions League exit against AC Milan. Around £500,000 is raised for struggling Rangers by a match between legends of the Scottish club and AC Milan, watched by a crowd of more than 47,000 at Ibrox.

APRIL 2012

1 Darren Dods, making his 500th competitive appearance, scores the only goal of the SFL Ramsdens Cup Final against Hamilton to give Falkirk a record fourth win in the competition.

2 Porto are fined £16,700 by UEFA for racial abuse directed by fans at Manchester City's Yaya Toure and Mario Balotelli during the teams' Europa League game.

3 Premier League referee Peter Walton becomes general manager of the professional referee organisation for leagues in the United States and Canada.

4 Chelsea reach the Champions League semi-finals for the sixth time in nine seasons by beating Benfica 3-1 on aggregate.

5 Preston and England legend Sir Tom Finney celebrates his 90th birthday.

7 Neil Lennon, winner of five Scottish Premier League titles with Celtic as a player, gains his first as manager. Portsmouth have six players booked against Southampton, incurring a £5,000 FA fine.

8 Steve Evans leaves Crawley to become Rotherham's new manager.

10 Referees' chief Mike Riley apologises to Wigan manager Roberto Martinez following his side's defeat at Chelsea, whose two goals should have been disallowed for offside.

11 The FA fine Crawley £18,000 and Bradford £9,000 for the post-match brawl at Valley Parade. Crawley's Pablo Mills is fined £1,000 and banned for three games for violent conduct. Manchester City are fined nearly £25,000 by UEFA for delaying, by 60 seconds, the start of the second-half of their Europa League game against Sporting.

12 Branislav Ivanovic is banned for three matches by the FA after being caught on camera striking Shaun Maloney in Chelsea's game against Wigan. Liverpool's poor Premier League season results in the dismissal of director of football Damien Comolli

14 Liverpool beat Everton 2-1 in the first FA Cup semi-final. Hibernian defeat Aberdeen by the same scoreline in Scotland. Fleetwood are promoted for the first time to the Football League as Conference champions.

15 Chelsea's 5-1 victory over Tottenham in the second FA Cup semi-final is overshadowed by the decision to allow their second goal from Juan Mata to stand when the ball does not cross the line. Controversy, too, at Hampden, where Celtic dispute a stoppage-time penalty which Craig Beattie converts to give Hearts a 2-1 win.

16 Fabrice Muamba leaves hospital a month collapsing at White Hart Lane and thanks the medical staff who saved his life. Martin Allen returns for a third spell as Barnet manager, until the end of the season, following the sacking of Lawrie Sanchez.

17 Cardiff captain Mark Hudson scores from inside his own half against Derby, a goal measured at 68 yards. Phil Dowd is named as referee for the FA Cup Final.

18 A Didier Drogba goal gives Chelsea victory in their Champions League semi-final first leg against Barcelona.

19 Celtic manager Neil Lennon is given a two-match touchline ban by the Scottish FA for criticising Communities League Cup Final referee Willie Collum. Mark Clattenburg is named as the only British referee for the London Olympics.

20 Phil Gartside, FA board member and Bolton chairman, declares Harry Redknapp as the right manager for the England job. Sheffield United and Wales striker Ched Evans is jailed for five years for rape. Sunderland are fined £30,000 by the FA for the conduct of their players towards referee Phil Dowd during the game against Manchester City.

21 Reading win the Championshp title. Charlton become champions of League One. Arsenal lose 4-1 to Frankfurt in the Women's Champions League semi-finals.

22 Arsenal captain Robin van Persie is named PFA Player of the Year.

23 Rangers are given fines totalling £160,000 and a 12-month ban on signing players by the Scottish FA after going into administration. Owner Craig Whyte is banned from football for life and ordered to pay £200,000.

24 Chelsea achieve one of the Champions League's best-ever results. Playing for 54 minutes with ten men after John Terry's red card and trailing Barcelona 2-0 in the second leg, they draw level to reach the final 3-2 on aggregate. Robin van Persie completes the double when voted the Football Writers' Association Footballer of the Year. Great Britain are drawn with Senegal, United Arab Emirates and Uruguay in their group for the London Olympics. The women are paired with New Zealand, Cameroon and Brazil.

25 Bayern Munich beat Real Madrid on penalties in the second Champions League semi-final. Championship clubs vote to introduce a financial fair-play plan from the 2014-15 season to exert greater control over expenditure.

26 The Premier League scrap the pre-match handshakes ahead of the Chelsea-Queens Park Rangers game involving John Terry and Anton Ferdinand, following the lead of the FA before the teams' FA Cup tie in January.

27 Chelsea agree a deal of around £7m for Werder Bremen's Germany midfield player Marko Marin.

28 Macclesfield are relegated from the Football League. Swindon become League Two champions.

29 Roy Hodgson is revealed as the surprise choice of the FA to succeed Fabio Capello as England manager.

30 Harry Redknapp, widely expected to get the job, sends his 'best wishes' to the West Bromwich Albion manager. Arsenal agree a £10.9m fee for Lukas Podolski, Cologne's Germany striker. Hull manager Nick Barmby is suspended by the club for comments about transfer policy.

MAY 2012

1 Roy Hodgson signs a four-year contract and calls on the fans to support his appointment.

2 With Rangers ineligible after going into administration, Motherwell secure Champions League football for the first time.

3 Celtic manager Neil Lennon, just back from a two-match touchline ban, receives a six-game ban from the Scottish FA for confronting referee Euan Norris after the Scottish Cup semi-final defeat by Hearts. Half the punishment is suspended.

4 Roy Hodgson appoints Fulham coach Ray Lewington as his assistant for the European Championship Finals. Aston Villa's James Collins, Fabian Delph and Chris Herd are fined a reported total of more than £100,000 over a nightclub brawl. Darlington are bought by a supporter's group and a new club formed.

5 Chelsea beat Liverpool 2-1 in the FA Cup Final, their fourth victory in the competition in six years. Hereford are relegated from the Football League.

6 Arsenal's Bacary Sagna is ruled out of the France squad for Euro 2012 after breaking his right leg for the second time in seven months.

7 Blackburn are relegated from the Premier League. James McClean is included in the Republic of Ireland's squad for the European Championship, five months after making his Premier League debut for Sunderland. Dunfermline are relegated from the Scottish Premier League.

8 Nick Barmby is sacked after less than six months as Hull manager following comments made in a newspaper interview.

9 Norwegian Stale Solbakken, dismissed by Cologne a month ago is appointed the new manager of Wolves. Gary Rowett is confirmed as Burton's manager after a spell as caretaker.

10 Newcastle's Alan Pardew is named Premier League Manager of the Year.

11 Manchester United's Chris Smalling is ruled out of contention for a place in England's Euro 2012 squad by a groin injury. Aldershot's Danny Hylton is banned for eight matches and fined £1,000 by the FA for racist abuse during a match against Barnet. Tottenham goalkeeping coach Tony Parks is given a one-match touchline ban and £2,500 fine for using abusive language. Bournemouth appoint interim manager Paul Groves on a permanent basis.

12 York beat Newport 2-0 in the FA Trophy Final.

13 In a remarkable finish to the Premier League season, Manchester City score twice in stoppage-time to beat Queens Park Rangers 3-2 and become champions for the first time since 1968, finishing ahead of Manchester United on goal difference. Gary Hooper scores all five goals for Celtic against Hearts.

14 Manager Alex McLeish is sacked the day after Aston Villa finish fifth from bottom of the Premier League. Alan Pardew completes the double when named the League Managers' Association Manager of the Year. Gary Neville, winner of 85 caps with England, is appointed to Roy Hodgson's coaching staff. Manchester City apologise to Sir Alex Ferguson after Carlos Tevez holds up a poster with 'RIP Fergie' on it during the club's open-top bus parade.

15 Kyle Walker's toe injury ends the Tottenham player's chances of making the England squad. Doncaster chairman John Ryan is fined £3,000 by the FA for criticising referee Mick Russell.

16 Liverpool sack manager Kenny Dalgish after their poorest Premier League season for 18 years. Rio Ferdinand is left out and John Terry included in Roy Hodgson's England squad. Steven Gerrard is named captain. Rangers have their appeal against fines of £160,000 and a 12-month transfer fan turned down by a Scottish FA tribunal.

17 Sean O'Driscoll, former Bournemouth and Doncaster manager, takes charge at Crawley.

18 Fleetwood, newly promoted to the Football League, sell 31-goal striker Jamie Vardy to Leicester for a fee in the region of £1m.

19 Chelsea win a penalty shoot-out in the Champions League Final after Didier Drogba's 88th minute equaliser against Bayern Munich. West Ham beat Blackpool 2-1 with an 87th minute goal by Ricado Vaz Te in the Championship Play-off Final to make an immediate return to the Premier League. Hearts beat Hibernian 5-1 in the all-Edinburgh Scottish Cup Final.

20 York enjoy more Wembley success, defeating Luton 2-1 in the Conference Play-off Final to return to the Football League after an absence of eight years.

21 Jose Mourinho ends speculation about a return to English football by signing a new deal at Real Madrid.

22 Didier Drogba announces his decision to leave Chelsea after his biggest triumph.

23 Joey Barton, sent off in Queens Park Rangers' match against Manchester City on the final day of the Premier League season, is banned for 12 matches and fined £75,000 by the FA for elbowing Carlos Tevez, kicking Sergio Aguero and attempting to butt Vincent Kompany.

24 Nick Barmby's appeal against his sacking by Hull is turned down by club owner Assem Allam.

25 Norwich goalkeeper John Ruddy is ruled out of England's Euro 2012 squad with a broken finger and replaced by Birmingham's Jack Butland. Darlington are demoted four divisions to the Northern League by the FA after the failure to reach agreement with creditors.

26 Roy Hodgson makes a winning start as England manager – 1-0 against Norway. The Republic of Ireland defeat Bosnia and Herzegovina by the same scoreline, but lose Keith Fahey from their Euro squad with a groin injury. Huddersfield beat Sheffield United 8-7 after 22 penalties in the League One Play-off Final. Birmingham win the Women's FA Cup Final against Chelsea on penalties.

27 Chris Coleman's first match as Wales manager ends in a 2-0 defeat by Mexico. Scotland are beaten 5-1 by the USA in another friendly. Crewe defeat Cheltenham 2-0 in the League Two Play-off Final.

28 Gareth Barry, with a tear in his lower abdomen, is another England squad casualty. Phil Jagielka replaces him. Eden Hazard, Lille's Belgium midfielder, chooses Chelsea ahead of Manchester City and Manchester United for a £32m move. Petr Cech signs a new four-year contract with Chelsea.

29 A judge in the Court of Session orders the Scottish FA to reconsider the 12-month transfer ban imposed on Rangers. The takeover of Reading by Russian tycoon Anton Zingarevich is confirmed.

30 Frank Lampard, with a thigh injury, becomes England's latest withdrawal. Jordan Henderson takes his place. Credit card company Capital One take over from Carling as sponsors of the League Cup in a four year deal worth a total of £22m.

31 Swansea's Brendan Rodgers becomes Liverpool's new manager as a compensation deal is agreed between the clubs.

JUNE 2012

1 Paul Lambert resigns as Norwich manager to take over at Aston Villa.

2 Danny Welbeck's first goal for England brings a 1-0 victory over Belgium. Northern Ireland concede six for the first time for half-a-century when going down to Holland.

3 Another blow for Roy Hodgson as he loses Gary Cahill with a double fracture of the jaw, sustained in a collision with goalkeeper Joe Hart at Wembley.

4 The England manager ignores Rio Ferdinand and calls in Liverpool's Martin Kelly to replace Cahill. The Republic of Ireland draw 0-0 against Hungary in their final warm-up game for the tournament.

5 Manchester United set up the transfer of Japan midfield player Shinji Kagawa from Borussia Dortmund for £17m.

6 Birmingham's Chris Hughton succeeds Paul Lambert at Carrow Road. Steve Bruce returns to management with Hull.

7 Three weeks after winning the Scottish Cup, Hearts manager Paulo Sergio rejects the offer of a new contract and leaves the club.

8 Steve Clarke, first-team coach under Kenny Dalglish at Liverpool, succeeds Roy Hodgson at West Bromwich Albion. Arsenal goalkeeper Wojciech Szczesny is sent off after conceding a penalty in the opening match of Euro 2012 which his side, Poland, draw 1-1 with Greece.

9 Promoted Southampton pay a club record £6m for Burnley's leading scorer Jay Rodriguez.

10 The Republic of Ireland lose 3-1 to Croatia in their opening Group C fixture, the team's first defeat in 15 matches.

11 Joleon Lescott scores his first international goal as England start with a 1-1 draw against France. Peterborough coach Mark Robson is appointed Barnet manager.

12 Rangers are consigned to liquidation after a creditors' deal is turned down by Revenue and Customs. Charles Green, former chief executive of Sheffield United, heads a consortium to re-form the club. Roberto Di Matteo is rewarded for winning the Champions League and FA Cup with the Chelsea manager's job on a permanent basis. Crewe receive a club record £4m from Manchester United for 18-year-old Nick Powell.

13 The Premier League unveil a £3.018bn, three-year deal for domestic TV rights from the 2013-14 season with long-standing partners Sky and newcomers BT. It represents a 70 per cent increase on the current deal.

14 After days of speculation about his position, Tottenham manager Harry Redknapp is sacked, along with coaches Joe Jordan, Kevin Bond and Clive Allen. The Republic of Ireland become the first team to be knocked out of Euro 2012 when losing 4-0 to Spain.

15 England come from behind to beat Sweden 3-2, with substitute Theo Walcott equalising then setting up the winner for Danny Welbeck. Denmark's Michael Laudrup, who played for some of Europe's biggest clubs, is named Swansea's new manager.

16 Paul Elliott, former Chelsea, Celtic and Aston Villa defender, receives a CBE in the Queens Birthday Honours list for services to equality and diversity in football. Former England goalkeeper David James is given an MBE.

17 The FA announce that as part of their 150th anniversary celebrations England will play Scotland, for the first time since 1999, at Wembley in August 2013.

18 Keith Andrews is sent off as the Republic of Ireland complete a disappointing tournament with a 2-0 defeat by Italy in which Damien Duff wins his 100th cap. Arsenal's Nicklas Bendtner is fined £80,000 by UEFA and banned for one international for displaying sponsored underwear during Denmark's game against Portugal. 18 The Scottish Premier League announce a two-week winter break for January 2013.

19 Wayne Rooney returns from suspension to head England into the quarter-finals as group winners. But they are lucky when Marko Devic is denied a Ukraine equaliser, despite his shot crossing the line. The Croatian Football Federation are fined £65,000 by UEFA for racist chants directed by their fans at Italy's Mario Balotelli. Brentford's supporters' trust agree to sell their majority 60 per cent shareholding in the club to investor Matthew Benham.

20 The FA are fined £4,035 by UEFA for an attempted pitch invasion by England fans during the game against Sweden.

21 Coventry have their transfer embargo lifted after the Football League sign off the club's accounts.

24 England lose 4-2 on penalties after a goalless 120 minutes against Italy, their sixth defeat in seven shoot-outs in European Championship and World Cup matches.

25 Joey Barton is stripped of the Queens Park Rangers captaincy and fined six weeks' wages by the club after being sent off against Manchester City. Watford striker Troy Deeney is jailed for ten months at Birmingham Crown Court for affray.

26 Lee Clark, sacked by Huddersfield, is named Birmingham's new manager. Arsenal sign France striker Olivier Giroud from Montpellier for £12.8m. Raith manager John McGlynn takes over at Hearts.

27 Spain beat Portugal 4-2 on penalties to reach the final of Euro 2012. Gareth Bale signs a new four-year contract with Tottenham.

28 Mario Balotelli scores both goals as Italy overcome Germany 2-1 in the second semi-final. David Beckham is left out of Great Britain's squad for the Olympics. Craig Bellamy, Ryan Giggs and Micah Richards are the three over-23 players named. Laurence Bassini sells Watford to the Pozzo family, owners of Udinese in Italy and Granada in Spain.

29 Two more clubs have new owners. Lancashire businessman Keith Ryder completes a deal with Port Vale's administrators and a supporters' group takes over from Steve Hayes at Wycombe.

30 Gareth Bale is ruled out of the Olympic squad with a recurrence of a back and hip injury.

JULY 2012

1 Spain remain European champions with a 4-0 win over Italy. David Silva and Jordi Alba score in the first half, with substitutes Fernando Torres and Juan Mata adding late goals.

2 Sean Dyche, who secured a top-half finish in his first season as manager, is sacked by Watford's new owners, paving the way for Gianfranco Zola, formerly in charge of West Ham, to take over. Rafael Da Silva signs a new four-year contract with Manchester. Twin brother Fabio joins Queens Park Rangers on a season's loan.

3 Four months after being dismissed by Chelsea, Andre Villas-Boas succeeds Harry Redknapp at Tottenham and approves the club's first summer signing, midfielder Gylfi Sigurdsson from Hoffenheim for £8m. Grant Holt signs a new three-year contract with Norwich. The Football League lift Wycombe's transfer embargo.

4 The new Rangers are voted out of the Scottish Premier League. Robin van Persie tells Arsenal he will not sign a new contract. The Football League lift Birmingham's transfer embargo.

5 Goal-line technology is confirmed by the International FA Board and may be introduced in the Premier League during the 2012-13 season. Martin Allen is appointed Gillingham manager – his seventh club.

6 Ray Lewington joins England's coaching staff on a permanent basis after signing a four-year contract.

9 Manager Roberto Mancini agrees a new five-year contract with Manchester City.

10 Nottingham Forest are taken over by the Al-Hasawi family, Kuwaiti businessmen, who buy the controlling stake of the late Nigel Doughty.

11 Barclays extend their sponsorship of the Premier League until 2016 in a three-year-deal worth a total of £120m. Adel Taarabt signs a new contract through to 2016 with Queens Park Rangers.

12 Relegated Portsmouth, still in administration, receive another ten-point deduction from the start of the new season. The Football League also insist on strict financial controls. Manager Steve Cotterill is sacked by Nottingham Forest's new owners. England lose 2-1 to Greece in the semi-finals of the European Under-19 Championship.

13 After a five-day trial at Westminster Magistrates' Court, Chelsea captain John Terry is cleared of racially abusing the Queens Park Rangers defender Anton Ferdinand. Scottish Football League clubs decide to put Rangers in their Third Division.

16 Dundee, runners-up in Division One, are chosen as the replacement for Rangers in the Scottish Premier League.

17 Former England manager Fabio Capello agrees to become Russia's new head coach.

19 Tottenham captain Ledley King, whose career has been plagued by chronic knee problems, announces his retirement at the age of 31.

20 Sean O'Driscoll resigns after two months as manager of Crawley to take over at Nottingham Forest. Gareth Southgate resigns after 18 months as the FA's head of elite development and says he is no longer interested in becoming technical director.

25 Chelsea pay £25m for the Brazil midfield player Oscar from Internacional.

QUOTE/UNQUOTE

'The decision has been one of the most difficult for all concerned. But it has been taken in the best interest of sporting fairness' – **David Longmuir**, chief executive of the Scottish Football League, on the demotion of crisis-club Rangers from the Scottish Premier to Division Three.

'There will be difficult times ahead, but I know that with the support of our fans we can emerge stronger and rise to the challenge' – **Ally McCoist**, the Rangers manager.

'It has been an unedifying week for football and there is no doubt the searchlight is on our national game. We must reinforce the Respect campaign because the game has been tarnished' – **Gordon Taylor**, chief executive of the players' union, after the trial of John Terry, who was cleared of racially abusing Anton Ferdinand.

'I make decisions solely on football grounds. I don't pick on personality or on ticket sales' - **Stuart Pearce**, manager of Great Britain's Olympic team, on the omission of David Beckham from his squad.

'I'm hoping it will get invested (by clubs) in things other than playing talent. It should also be able to achieve sustainability' – **Richard Scudamore**, chief executive of the Premier League, on the new record £3bn TV rights deal with Sky and BT.

ENGLISH TABLES 2011–2012

BARCLAYS PREMIER LEAGUE

			Home				Away						
		P	W	D	L	F	A	W	D	L	F	A	GD	PTS
1	Manchester City	38	18	1	0	55	12	10	4	5	38	17	64	89
2	Manchester Utd	38	15	2	2	52	19	13	3	3	37	14	56	89
3	Arsenal	38	12	4	3	39	17	9	3	7	35	32	25	70
4	Tottenham	38	13	3	3	39	17	7	6	6	27	24	25	69
5	Newcastle	38	11	5	3	29	17	8	3	8	27	34	5	65
6	Chelsea	38	12	3	4	41	24	6	7	6	24	22	19	64
7	Everton	38	10	3	6	28	15	5	8	6	22	25	10	56
8	Liverpool	38	6	9	4	24	16	8	1	10	23	24	7	52
9	Fulham	38	10	5	4	36	26	4	5	10	12	25	-3	52
10	WBA	38	6	3	10	21	22	7	5	7	24	30	-7	47
11	Swansea	38	8	7	4	27	18	4	4	11	17	33	-7	47
12	Norwich	38	7	6	6	28	30	5	5	9	24	36	-14	47
13	Sunderland	38	7	7	5	26	17	4	5	10	19	29	-1	45
14	Stoke	38	7	8	4	25	20	4	4	11	11	33	-17	45
15	Wigan	38	5	7	7	22	27	6	3	10	20	35	-20	43
16	Aston Villa	38	4	7	8	20	25	3	10	6	17	28	-16	38
17	QPR	38	7	5	7	24	25	3	2	14	19	41	-23	37
18	Bolton	38	4	4	11	23	39	6	2	11	23	38	-31	36
19	Blackburn	38	6	1	12	26	33	2	6	11	22	45	-30	31
20	Wolves	38	3	3	13	19	43	2	7	10	21	39	-42	25

Manchester City, Manchester Utd, Arsenal and Chelsea go into Champions League group stage; Tottenham (group), Newcastle (qualifying play-off) and Liverpool (third qualifying round) into Europa League

TV/merit money: 1 £60.6m, 2 £60.3m, 3 £56.2m, 4 £57.4m, 5 £54.2m, 6 £54.4m, 7 £48.9m, 8 £54.4m, 9 £47.4m, 10 £46.6m, 11 £44.4m, 12 £45.9m, 13 £45.6m, 14 £43.6m, 15 £42.9m, 16 £42.1m, 17 £43.3m, 18 £40.6m, 19 £40.3m, 20 £39.1m
Biggest win: Manchester Utd 8 Arsenal 2, Arsenal 7 Blackburn 1, Fulham 6 QPR 0
Highest aggregate score: Manchester Utd 8 Arsenal 2
Highest attendance: 75,627 (Manchester Utd v Wolves)
Lowest attendance: 15,195 (QPR v Bolton)
Manager of Year: Alan Pardew (Newcastle)
Player of Year: Vincent Kompany (Manchester City)
Golden Boot: 30 Robin van Persie (Arsenal)
Golden Glove: 17 (clean sheets) Joe Hart (Manchester City
PFA Team of Year: Hart (Manchester City), Walker (Tottenham), Kompany (Manchester City), Colocinni (Newcastle), Baines (Everton), Silva (Manchester City), Parker (Tottenham), Y Toure (Manchester City), Bale (Tottenham), Van Persie (Arsenal), Rooney (Manchester Utd)
Leading scorers (all competitions): 37 Van Persie (Arsenal); 35 Rooney (Manchester Utd); 30 Aguero (Manchester City); 23 Dempsey (Fulham), 19 Dzeko (Manchester City); 18 Adebayor (Tottenham), Yakubu (Blackburn); 17 Balotelli (Manchester City), Defoe (Tottenham), Holt (Norwich), Suarez (Liverpool); 16 Ba (Newcastle), Lampard (Chelsea); 14 Crouch (Stoke), Graham (Swansea); 13 Cisse (Newcastle), Drogba (Chelsea), Sturridge (Chelsea), Van der Vaart (Tottenham). Also: 28 Jelavic (Everton) – 17 for Rangers

NPOWER CHAMPIONSHIP

			Home					Away						
		P	W	D	L	F	A	W	D	L	F	A	GD	PTS
1	Reading	46	14	5	4	36	18	13	3	7	33	23	28	89
2	Southampton	46	16	4	3	49	18	10	6	7	36	28	39	88
3	West Ham*	46	11	8	4	41	26	13	6	4	40	22	33	86
4	Birmingham	46	13	9	1	37	14	7	7	9	41	37	27	76
5	Blackpool	46	13	7	3	42	21	7	8	8	37	38	20	75
6	Cardiff	46	11	7	5	37	29	8	11	4	29	24	13	75
7	Middlesbrough	46	8	10	5	22	21	10	6	7	30	30	1	70
8	Hull	46	12	4	7	28	22	7	7	9	19	22	3	68
9	Leicester	46	11	6	6	36	22	7	6	10	30	33	11	66
10	Brighton	46	11	8	4	36	21	6	7	10	16	31	0	66
11	Watford	46	10	6	7	32	33	6	10	7	24	31	-8	64
12	Derby	46	11	4	8	28	23	7	6	10	22	35	-8	64
13	Burnley	46	7	9	7	33	27	10	2	11	28	31	3	62
14	Leeds	46	9	3	11	34	41	8	7	8	31	27	-3	61
15	Ipswich	46	11	3	9	39	32	6	7	10	30	45	-8	61
16	Millwall	46	7	7	9	27	30	8	5	10	28	27	-2	57
17	Crystal Palace	46	7	11	5	22	19	6	6	11	24	32	-5	56
18	Peterborough	46	10	3	10	41	38	3	8	12	26	39	-10	50
19	Nottm Forest	46	6	5	12	21	32	8	3	12	27	31	-15	50
20	Bristol City	46	7	6	10	26	32	5	7	11	18	36	-24	49
21	Barnsley	46	9	4	10	31	37	4	5	14	18	37	-25	48
22	Portsmouth	46	10	5	8	30	24	3	6	14	20	35	-9	40
23	Coventry	46	8	7	8	28	26	1	6	16	13	39	-24	40
24	Doncaster	46	4	8	11	22	35	4	4	15	21	45	-37	36

*also promoted

Biggest win: Peterborough 7 Ipswich 1, West Ham 6 Brighton 0, Millwall 0 Birmingham 6
Highest aggregate score: Leeds 3 Nottm Forest 7
Highest attendance: 35,000 (West Ham v Hull)
Lowest attendance: 6,351 (Peterborough v Cardiff)
Manager of Year: Brian McDermott (Reading)
Player of Year: Rickie Lambert (Southampton)
Top league scorer: 27 Rickie Lambert
PFA Team of Year: Davis (Southampton), Clyne (Crystal Palace), Tomkins (West Ham), Davies (Birmingham), Harte (Reading), Lallana (Southampton), Whittingham (Cardiff), Noble (West Ham), M Phillips (Blackpool), Lambert (Southampton), Rodriguez (Burnley)
Leading scorers (all competitions): 31 Lambert (Southampton); 24 Vaz Te (West Ham) – 12 for Barnsley; 21 Rodriguez (Burnley); 19 Henderson (Millwall), McCormack (Leeds), Sharp (Southampton) – 10 for Doncaster; 18 Emnes (Middlesbrough), King (Birmingham); 17 Austin (Burnley), Phillips K (Blackpool); 16 Fryatt (Hull), Nugent (Leicester); 15 Beckford (Leicester), Cole (West Ham); 14 Barnes (Brighton), Chopra (Ipswich); 13 Burke (Birmingham), Snodgrass (Leeds), Lallana (Southampton), Whittingham (Cardiff).
Also: 19 Barnett (Peterborough) – 15 for Crawley; 16 Le Fondre (Reading) – 4 for Rotherham; 14 Sinclair (Peterborough) – 4 for Macclesfield, Wood – 11 loan Birmingham, 3 loan Bristol City

NPOWER LEAGUE ONE

			Home				Away						
		P	W	D	L	F	A	W	D	L	F	A	GD	PTS
1	Charlton	46	15	6	2	46	20	15	5	3	36	16	46	101
2	Sheffield Wed	46	17	4	2	48	19	11	5	7	33	29	33	93
3	Sheffield Utd	46	16	4	3	54	27	11	5	7	38	24	41	90
4	Huddersfield*	46	14	6	3	35	19	7	12	4	44	28	32	81
5	MK Dons	46	12	6	5	45	22	10	8	5	39	25	37	80
6	Stevenage	46	10	10	3	36	23	8	9	6	33	21	25	73
7	Notts Co	46	13	5	5	42	29	8	5	10	33	34	12	73
8	Carlisle	46	12	7	4	41	30	6	8	9	24	36	-1	69
9	Brentford	46	10	6	7	36	24	8	7	8	27	28	11	67
10	Colchester	46	8	11	4	38	33	5	9	9	23	33	-5	59
11	Bournemouth	46	9	5	9	23	23	6	8	9	25	29	-4	58
12	Tranmere	46	9	11	3	27	16	5	3	15	22	37	-4	56
13	Hartlepool	46	6	6	11	21	22	8	8	7	29	33	-5	56
14	Bury	46	8	8	7	31	32	7	3	13	29	47	-19	56
15	Preston	46	7	9	7	30	35	6	6	11	24	33	-14	54
16	Oldham	46	9	5	9	26	26	5	7	11	24	40	-16	54
17	Yeovil	46	10	3	10	34	41	4	9	10	25	39	-21	54
18	Scunthorpe	46	5	10	8	28	33	5	12	6	27	26	-4	52
19	Walsall	46	7	9	7	27	27	3	11	9	24	30	-6	50
20	Leyton Orient	46	6	6	11	23	34	7	5	11	25	41	-27	50
21	Wycombe	46	7	6	10	37	38	4	4	15	28	50	-23	43
22	Chesterfield	46	7	6	10	26	33	3	6	14	30	48	-25	42
23	Exeter	46	8	8	7	31	29	2	4	17	15	46	-29	42
24	Rochdale	46	6	8	9	30	39	2	6	15	17	42	-34	38

*also promoted

Biggest win: Wycombe 0 Huddersfield 6, Yeovil 0 Stevenage 6
Highest aggregate: MK Dons 6 Chesterfield 2, Sheffield Utd 4 Exeter 4, Sheffield Wed 4 Huddersfield 4
Highest attendance: 38,082 (Sheffield Wed v Wycombe)
Lowest attendance: 2,072 (Bury v Hartlepool)
Manager of Year: Chris Powell (Charlton)
Player of Year: Jordan Rhodes (Huddersfield)
Top league scorer: 36 Jordan Rhodes
PFA Team of Year: Hamer (Charlton), Hunt (Charlton), Morrison (Charlton), Maguire (Sheffield Utd), Wiggins (Charlton), Jackson (Charlton), Quinn (Sheffield Utd), Gleeson (MK Dons), Potter (MK Dons), Rhodes (Huddersfield), Evans (Sheffield Utd)
Leading scorers (all competitions): 40 Rhodes (Huddersfield); 35 Evans (Sheffield Utd); 25 Beavon (Wycombe); 22 Wright-Phillips (Charlton); 18 Madine (Sheffield Wed); 17 Hughes J (Notts Co), Novak (Huddersfield), Williams A (Yeovil); 16 Kuqi (Oldham), Lowe (Sheffield Wed) – 7 for Bury; 15 Bowditch (MK Dons), Miller (Carlisle); 14 Zoko (Carlisle); 13 Jackson (Charlton), Williamson (Sheffield Utd), Wordsworth (Colchester); 12 Bowery (Chesterfield), Gillespie (Colchester), Kermorgant (Charlton), Lisbie (Leyton Orient). **Also**: 19 Tubbs (Bournemouth) – 18 for Crawley

NPOWER LEAGUE TWO

		P	Home					Away					GD	PTS
			W	D	L	F	A	W	D	L	F	A		
1	Swindon	46	19	3	1	49	8	10	3	10	26	24	43	93
2	Shrewsbury	46	18	5	0	37	12	8	5	10	29	29	25	88
3	Crawley	46	14	5	4	47	25	9	10	4	29	29	22	84
4	Southend	46	12	6	5	36	18	13	2	8	41	30	29	83
5	Torquay	46	12	8	3	36	23	11	4	8	27	27	13	81
6	Cheltenham	46	13	5	5	32	16	10	3	10	34	34	16	77
7	Crewe*	46	11	6	6	38	28	9	6	8	29	31	8	72
8	Gillingham	46	13	4	6	44	27	7	6	10	35	35	17	70
9	Oxford Utd	46	10	9	4	36	24	7	8	8	23	24	11	68
10	Rotherham	46	12	4	7	31	22	6	9	8	36	41	4	67
11	Aldershot	46	11	5	7	26	19	8	4	11	28	33	2	66
12	Port Vale	46	12	3	8	38	26	8	6	9	30	34	8	59
13	Bristol Rov	46	10	6	7	37	29	5	6	12	23	41	-10	57
14	Accrington	46	11	4	8	34	33	3	11	9	20	33	-12	57
15	Morecambe	46	6	6	11	31	29	8	8	7	32	28	6	56
16	AFC Wimbledon	46	9	4	10	39	40	6	5	12	23	38	-16	54
17	Burton	46	8	7	8	24	32	6	5	12	30	49	-27	54
18	Bradford	46	8	9	6	34	27	4	5	14	20	32	-5	50
19	Dag and Red	46	9	3	11	31	35	5	5	13	19	37	-22	50
20	Northampton	46	6	6	11	30	43	6	6	11	26	36	-23	48
21	Plymouth	46	6	9	8	23	26	4	7	12	24	38	-17	46
22	Barnet	46	6	6	11	29	39	6	4	13	23	40	-27	46
23	Hereford	46	5	5	13	23	41	5	9	9	27	29	-20	44
24	Macclesfield	46	5	11	7	25	26	3	2	18	14	38	-25	37

*also promoted

Biggest win: Bristol Rov 7 Burton 1, Morecambe 6 Crawley 0
Highest aggregate score: Gillingham 5 Hereford 4, Barnet 3 Burton 6, Northampton 2 Shrewsbury 7
Highest attendance: 17,014 (Bradford v Hereford)
Lowest attendance: 1,207 (Morecambe v Cheltenham)
Manager of Year: Paolo Di Canio (Swindon)
Player of Year: Matt Ritchie (Swindon)
Top league scorer: 18 Adebayo Akinfenwa (Northampton), Lewis Grabban (Rotherham), Izale McLeod (Barnet), Jack Midson (AFC Wimbledon)
PFA Team of Year: Olejnik (Torquay), Caddis (Swindon), McFadzean (Crawley), Sharps (Shrewsbury), Nicholson (Torquay), Ritchie (Swindon), Pack (Cheltenham), O'Kane (Torquay), Mansell (Torquay), McLeod (Barnet), Barnett (Crawley)
Leading scorers (all competitions): 22 McLeod (Barnet); 21 Grabban (Rotherham); 20 Midson (AFC Wimbledon); 18 Akinfenwa (Northampton), Harrold (Bristol Rov); 17 Ellison (Morecambe), Richards (Port Vale); 16 Collins (Shrewsbury), Hylton (Aldershot), Powell (Crewe); 15 Duffy (Cheltenham); 14 Hall (Southend), Hanson (Bradford), Howe (Torquay), Kedwell (Gillingham), Zola (Burton); 13 Benson (Swindon) – 1 for Charlton, Bilel (Southend), Connell (Swindon), Mansell (Torquay), Woodall (Dagenham). **Also**: 21 Alexander (Crawley) – 14 for Brentford

BARCLAYS PREMIER LEAGUE RESULTS 2011–2012

	Arsenal	Aston Villa	Blackburn	Bolton	Chelsea	Everton	Fulham	Liverpool	Manchester City	Manchester Utd	Newcastle	Norwich	QPR	Stoke	Sunderland	Swansea	Tottenham	WBA	Wigan	Wolves
Arsenal	–	3-0	7-1	3-0	0-0	1-0	1-1	0-2	1-0	1-2	2-1	3-3	1-0	3-1	2-1	1-0	5-2	3-0	1-2	1-1
Aston Villa	1-2	–	3-1	1-2	2-4	1-1	1-0	0-2	0-1	0-1	1-1	3-2	2-2	1-1	0-0	0-2	1-1	1-2	2-0	0-0
Blackburn	4-3	1-1	–	1-2	0-1	0-1	3-1	2-3	0-4	0-2	0-2	2-0	3-2	1-2	2-0	4-2	1-2	1-2	0-1	1-2
Bolton	0-0	1-2	2-1	–	1-5	0-2	0-3	3-1	2-3	0-5	0-2	1-2	2-1	5-0	0-2	1-1	1-4	2-2	1-2	1-1
Chelsea	3-5	1-3	2-1	3-0	–	3-1	1-1	1-2	2-1	3-3	0-2	3-1	6-1	0-1	1-0	4-1	0-0	1-0	2-1	3-0
Everton	0-1	2-2	1-1	1-2	2-0	–	4-0	0-2	1-0	0-1	3-1	1-1	0-1	0-1	4-0	1-0	1-0	2-0	3-1	2-1
Fulham	2-1	0-0	1-1	2-0	1-1	1-3	–	1-0	2-2	0-5	5-2	2-1	6-0	2-1	2-1	0-3	1-3	1-1	2-1	5-0
Liverpool	1-2	1-1	3-0	3-1	4-1	3-0	0-1	–	1-1	1-1	3-1	1-1	1-0	0-0	1-1	0-0	0-0	0-1	1-2	2-1
Manchester City	1-0	4-1	2-3	3-1	2-0	2-0	3-0	1-1	–	0-1	3-1	5-1	3-2	3-0	3-3	4-0	3-2	4-0	3-0	3-1
Manchester Utd	8-2	4-0	3-1	3-0	3-1	4-4	1-0	2-1	1-6	–	1-1	2-0	2-0	2-0	1-0	2-0	3-0	2-3	5-0	4-1
Newcastle	0-0	2-1	3-3	2-0	0-3	2-1	2-1	2-0	3-1	1-0	–	1-0	1-0	3-0	1-0	0-0	2-2	0-1	1-0	2-2
Norwich	1-2	2-0	1-1	0-4	0-0	2-2	2-1	0-3	1-6	1-2	4-2	–	2-1	1-1	2-1	3-1	0-2	1-1	1-1	2-1
QPR	2-1	1-1	3-1	2-2	1-0	1-1	0-1	3-2	2-3	0-2	0-0	2-3	–	1-0	2-3	3-0	0-1	1-2	3-1	1-2
Stoke	1-1	0-0	2-1	2-2	0-0	1-1	2-0	1-0	1-1	1-1	1-3	1-1	2-3	–	0-1	2-0	1-2	2-2	2-2	1-1
Sunderland	1-2	2-2	3-0	3-1	1-2	0-2	0-0	1-0	1-0	0-1	0-1	2-1	3-1	4-0	–	2-0	0-0	3-0	1-2	1-1
Swansea	2-1	0-0	3-3	3-0	1-1	2-0	2-0	0-0	1-0	0-1	0-2	3-0	1-1	2-0	2-0	–	1-1	1-0	0-0	2-2
Tottenham	2-3	2-3	0-2	2-1	1-0	0-1	0-0	0-1	1-5	1-3	5-0	1-1	3-1	1-1	0-0	3-1	–	1-1	3-1	0-2
WBA	2-3	0-0	3-0	2-0	1-0	1-1	0-2	0-1	0-0	1-2	1-3	2-3	1-0	0-1	4-0	1-2	1-3	–	1-2	1-5
Wigan	0-4	0-0	3-3	1-3	1-1	1-1	2-0	0-0	0-1	1-0	4-0	1-1	2-0	2-0	1-4	0-2	1-2	1-1	–	3-2
Wolves	0-3	2-3	0-2	2-3	1-2	0-0	2-0	0-3	0-2	0-5	2-1	2-2	1-2	1-2	2-1	2-2	0-2	1-5	3-1	–

NPOWER CHAMPIONSHIP RESULTS 2011-2012

	Barnsley	Birmingham	Blackpool	Brighton	Bristol City	Burnley	Cardiff	Coventry	Crystal Palace	Derby	Doncaster	Hull	Ipswich	Leeds	Leicester	Middlesbrough	Millwall	Nottm Forest	Peterborough	Portsmouth	Reading	Southampton	Watford	West Ham
Barnsley	–	1-3	1-1	2-0	2-0	2-0	5-3	1-0	1-0	2-0	3-1	2-1	3-5	4-1	1-2	1-3	1-3	1-1	1-0	2-0	0-4	0-1	1-1	0-4
Birmingham	1-1	–	3-0	0-0	0-2	1-3	1-0	1-1	1-0	2-1	1-1	1-1	2-1	1-4	1-1	0-6	3-0	1-2	4-1	1-0	0-2	3-0	3-0	1-1
Blackpool	2-2	2-2	–	3-1	5-0	4-0	3-1	2-1	1-0	2-1	1-3	1-0	1-0	1-0	3-3	3-0	1-0	3-7	2-1	1-1	1-0	3-0	0-0	1-4
Brighton	2-0	1-1	3-1	–	2-0	0-1	1-2	2-1	1-3	2-0	0-1	1-1	0-0	1-0	1-0	1-1	2-2	0-0	0-0	2-0	0-1	3-0	2-2	0-1
Bristol City	2-0	0-2	2-2	2-0	–	3-1	1-2	1-1	2-2	2-0	2-1	0-0	0-3	0-3	2-1	1-1	2-2	0-0	1-2	2-0	0-1	3-0	2-2	1-1
Burnley	2-0	1-3	3-1	0-1	3-1	–	1-1	1-1	2-2	1-1	0-0	1-1	4-0	0-3	1-2	0-2	1-3	1-3	3-2	1-0	2-3	1-1	2-2	0-2
Cardiff	5-3	1-0	4-0	1-2	1-2	3-1	–	2-1	2-0	2-0	3-0	0-3	4-0	3-2	0-0	2-3	0-0	2-0	1-1	3-2	3-1	0-1	1-1	0-2
Coventry	1-0	1-3	2-1	3-1	1-1	1-1	2-2	–	1-1	1-1	0-2	0-3	2-2	1-1	0-1	3-1	0-1	2-2	2-0	1-0	0-1	2-4	2-2	1-2
Crystal Palace	1-0	1-0	1-3	2-0	3-1	1-2	2-1	2-2	–	0-0	0-2	0-3	2-3	1-1	0-0	3-1	0-0	3-1	2-0	0-0	3-1	0-1	4-0	2-2
Derby	2-0	1-1	2-2	1-0	1-0	2-1	1-0	2-0	1-1	–	0-2	0-0	4-0	1-1	1-2	3-1	0-3	1-3	2-0	1-0	1-2	2-1	1-2	2-1
Doncaster	3-1	2-1	1-3	1-1	2-1	1-2	0-3	1-0	3-2	1-1	–	3-0	2-3	0-1	0-1	1-3	3-0	0-1	1-1	3-1	1-0	1-1	0-0	0-1
Hull	3-1	2-1	1-1	0-0	1-2	1-2	0-0	0-1	1-0	1-2	0-0	–	2-2	2-1	2-1	1-3	0-3	2-1	3-2	1-0	1-0	2-5	3-2	0-1
Ipswich	1-2	1-1	1-0	2-3	3-0	3-1	1-1	3-0	0-1	2-1	2-3	2-2	–	2-1	1-2	1-1	0-3	1-3	2-0	1-0	2-3	2-5	1-2	5-1
Leeds	1-2	1-4	0-5	2-1	2-1	2-1	1-1	3-0	1-2	3-1	2-0	4-1	0-1	–	1-2	2-1	2-0	3-7	4-1	1-0	0-1	0-1	0-1	1-1
Leicester	1-2	3-1	2-0	0-0	1-2	2-0	2-0	2-0	2-0	1-1	0-1	2-1	1-1	1-2	–	2-2	2-0	2-0	1-1	1-0	2-2	2-3	3-2	1-2
Middlesbrough	2-0	3-1	2-2	3-0	1-2	0-2	1-1	1-0	3-0	2-1	1-2	2-0	4-1	1-0	2-2	–	1-3	2-0	1-1	1-3	1-3	2-3	2-1	0-2
Millwall	0-0	0-6	2-0	1-0	0-1	3-0	1-3	0-0	3-0	0-0	0-1	0-3	4-1	0-2	0-0	1-1	–	2-0	2-2	3-1	0-1	0-3	2-0	0-0
Nottm Forest	0-0	1-3	3-1	1-2	0-1	0-1	2-0	3-0	0-1	0-0	3-0	3-0	1-0	2-0	1-2	1-3	0-1	–	2-3	0-1	1-0	1-3	1-0	1-4
Peterborough	3-4	3-1	3-1	0-1	0-1	2-1	3-2	2-0	2-2	1-2	2-0	1-1	7-1	2-0	2-2	2-0	3-1	0-1	–	1-0	1-0	0-3	3-2	0-2
Portsmouth	1-2	4-1	0-0	1-0	1-1	2-0	4-0	1-0	1-0	1-0	2-0	0-3	3-2	2-0	2-2	1-1	3-1	3-0	1-0	–	1-0	1-3	2-1	0-2
Reading	2-0	1-0	1-0	0-1	3-0	1-0	3-1	4-0	3-1	2-0	0-0	0-2	1-1	2-0	0-2	1-3	2-2	3-0	3-2	1-0	–	1-1	0-2	3-0
Southampton	2-1	1-0	3-0	4-1	0-1	2-2	2-0	4-1	0-2	3-1	3-1	1-2	1-1	3-1	1-1	3-0	1-0	2-0	2-1	1-3	1-0	–	4-0	1-0
Watford	2-1	2-2	3-2	1-1	0-1	2-2	2-1	0-0	3-2	1-1	1-1	2-0	1-1	1-0	3-2	0-1	2-1	2-1	3-2	0-1	1-2	0-3	–	0-4
West Ham	1-0	3-3	4-0	6-0	0-0	1-0	1-0	1-0	2-0	0-1	1-1	1-1	0-1	2-2	2-1	3-2	2-1	1-1	3-2	1-0	2-4	1-1	1-1	–

	Bournemouth	Brentford	Bury	Carlisle	Charlton	Chesterfield	Colchester	Exeter	Hartlepool	Huddersfield	Leyton Orient	MK Dons	Notts Co	Oldham	Preston	Rochdale	Scunthorpe	Sheffield Utd	Sheffield Wed	Stevenage	Tranmere	Walsall	Wycombe	Yeovil
Bournemouth	–	1-2	1-0	1-1	2-1	3-0	1-0	1-1	0-0	0-1	1-3	2-2	3-1	1-0	1-3	2-2	1-1	2-1	3-0	0-0	0-0	2-2	0-1	1-3
Brentford	1-1	–	1-1	4-0	0-1	2-2	2-3	2-1	1-2	0-4	5-0	1-3	0-0	1-3	1-2	1-2	0-0	1-3	2-1	0-1	3-0	0-1	0-1	2-0
Bury	1-0	3-0	–	0-2	1-2	1-1	4-1	3-2	0-0	3-0	1-0	1-0	2-4	0-2	1-1	1-0	1-3	4-0	4-1	3-0	2-0	2-4	0-2	1-3
Carlisle	2-1	4-1	0-2	–	0-1	1-1	1-0	2-0	0-4	2-1	3-3	3-2	2-4	3-3	2-2	2-4	1-0	0-2	1-2	2-1	2-1	1-0	4-0	1-3
Charlton	3-0	2-2	4-0	0-1	–	4-1	1-0	2-0	0-1	2-0	2-0	1-1	2-3	3-3	1-0	1-0	1-1	3-2	1-1	2-2	1-0	1-1	2-2	3-0
Chesterfield	1-0	2-0	1-0	4-0	3-1	–	3-1	2-0	2-3	0-2	2-2	2-1	2-4	1-1	2-2	3-0	2-2	3-2	0-0	0-1	3-0	1-1	2-1	3-2
Colchester	1-1	2-3	4-1	1-1	0-4	0-1	–	2-0	1-1	0-2	3-0	1-1	1-3	4-1	1-1	2-1	1-4	0-1	1-1	1-6	1-0	1-1	4-0	2-2
Exeter	1-2	2-1	3-2	0-0	0-2	2-1	0-1	–	2-0	0-4	3-0	4-2	4-2	2-0	0-2	3-1	0-1	2-2	0-1	1-1	0-2	1-0	2-2	1-1
Hartlepool	0-0	1-2	3-2	0-4	0-1	2-1	1-1	2-0	–	2-1	0-1	1-2	3-0	0-1	3-1	0-0	1-2	0-1	0-1	0-0	3-0	4-2	1-3	1-1
Huddersfield	0-1	0-0	1-1	1-1	0-4	1-0	1-1	0-4	0-1	–	2-2	3-1	2-1	1-0	2-2	1-2	1-3	1-1	0-2	1-1	1-0	1-1	3-0	2-0
Leyton Orient	1-3	3-2	1-0	1-0	1-0	1-1	3-2	1-0	2-2	1-3	–	3-1	0-3	1-3	2-1	3-1	1-3	1-0	0-1	2-0	0-1	1-1	3-0	2-2
MK Dons	1-3	2-2	1-0	1-2	3-0	6-2	0-1	3-0	2-2	2-2	4-1	–	3-0	5-0	2-5	2-1	1-0	2-4	0-0	1-0	1-0	1-1	4-3	0-1
Notts Co	3-1	1-1	2-4	2-0	0-2	1-0	4-1	2-1	1-2	2-2	3-0	1-0	–	1-0	0-0	3-2	2-5	1-0	1-1	3-2	2-1	3-3	1-1	0-1
Oldham	1-0	0-2	0-2	2-1	2-2	4-1	0-0	2-1	1-1	1-1	3-2	3-3	3-2	–	1-1	2-0	1-0	1-0	1-3	1-1	1-1	3-3	4-1	0-0
Preston	1-3	1-3	1-1	3-3	2-2	5-2	2-4	0-1	1-0	1-0	1-1	3-2	2-0	3-3	–	0-1	1-0	2-4	0-0	0-1	2-1	0-0	3-2	4-3
Rochdale	1-0	1-2	1-0	0-3	2-3	0-0	2-2	3-2	1-3	3-2	2-2	1-0	0-0	3-2	1-0	–	1-0	2-5	0-0	1-5	0-2	3-3	3-2	0-0
Scunthorpe	1-1	0-0	1-3	1-2	0-2	4-1	3-0	0-1	2-3	2-2	2-3	1-2	0-0	1-0	3-0	1-0	–	1-0	1-3	1-1	2-1	3-3	4-1	2-1
Sheffield Utd	2-1	2-1	4-0	1-0	0-2	3-1	2-2	3-1	2-1	4-4	3-1	2-3	3-1	2-0	3-2	3-0	1-0	–	2-2	2-1	2-1	3-2	3-0	4-0
Sheffield Wed	3-0	3-0	4-1	1-0	1-0	3-1	0-0	0-0	2-2	1-1	1-0	0-0	1-1	1-0	2-2	4-2	3-2	1-0	–	0-1	1-0	2-0	1-1	2-1
Stevenage	0-0	2-1	3-0	1-2	3-1	0-0	0-0	2-2	0-1	1-1	1-0	1-0	0-2	1-0	2-1	0-0	1-2	1-1	5-1	–	2-1	0-0	2-0	0-0
Tranmere	0-0	2-1	2-0	1-1	1-2	3-1	1-1	1-1	1-0	1-0	1-0	1-0	1-1	0-1	1-1	1-1	1-1	3-2	1-2	3-0	–	2-1	0-0	0-0
Walsall	2-2	0-1	2-4	1-1	1-2	3-2	3-1	1-2	1-1	1-1	1-0	1-0	3-4	0-1	3-4	0-0	1-1	2-3	1-2	1-2	2-1	–	1-1	2-3
Wycombe	0-1	0-1	0-2	1-2	1-2	3-2	0-0	5-0	0-6	4-2	4-2	2-2	3-1	2-2	3-0	0-0	2-2	1-0	1-2	0-1	2-1	1-1	–	2-3
Yeovil	1-3	2-1	1-3	0-3	2-3	3-2	2-2	0-1	0-1	2-2	1-2	3-1	1-0	3-1	0-1	3-1	2-2	0-1	2-3	0-6	2-1	2-1	1-0	–

NPOWER LEAGUE TWO RESULTS 2011–2012

	Accrington	AFC Wimbledon	Aldershot	Barnet	Bradford	Bristol Rov	Burton	Cheltenham	Crawley	Crewe	Dag & Red	Gillingham	Hereford	Macclesfield	Morecambe	Northampton	Oxford	Plymouth	Port Vale	Rotherham	Shrewsbury	Southend	Swindon	Torquay
Accrington	–	3-2	0-0	1-1	1-2	5-1	2-1	1-1	2-1	0-1	3-0	2-1	2-1	4-0	2-1	1-1	0-2	0-2	2-2	1-2	1-1	1-2	0-2	3-1
AFC Wimbledon	0-2	–	1-1	4-1	1-2	1-2	1-0	1-0	2-5	1-3	1-1	3-1	1-1	1-1	1-1	1-0	0-2	1-2	3-2	2-2	3-1	1-1	1-1	2-0
Aldershot	0-0	4-1	–	4-1	2-1	0-1	2-0	2-0	0-1	3-1	1-1	1-2	1-1	1-2	1-0	0-1	0-3	2-1	1-3	2-1	1-0	2-0	2-1	0-1
Barnet	1-1	1-1	4-1	–	1-1	1-1	3-6	1-0	0-1	2-0	1-1	2-2	1-1	3-0	0-0	0-1	0-3	0-0	1-1	1-1	2-0	0-3	2-1	0-1
Bradford	1-1	1-2	0-4	3-6	–	2-1	1-1	0-2	1-2	3-0	2-0	1-1	1-1	1-0	2-2	3-0	2-1	2-1	0-3	2-3	3-1	2-0	0-0	1-0
Bristol Rov	5-1	1-2	2-2	2-2	2-1	–	7-1	0-1	3-0	2-5	2-0	2-1	0-2	1-0	1-0	0-1	1-0	1-1	3-2	5-2	1-0	0-3	1-1	1-2
Burton	0-2	0-1	2-0	4-0	1-1	1-3	–	0-2	0-1	1-0	1-1	0-3	0-3	1-1	3-2	2-2	0-2	2-3	2-0	1-1	1-0	0-2	2-0	1-4
Cheltenham	4-1	1-0	2-0	1-0	1-1	0-2	0-2	–	3-1	1-1	3-1	1-2	0-0	1-0	1-1	0-1	3-1	2-1	3-2	1-0	0-0	0-2	0-1	2-0
Crawley	1-1	2-5	0-1	2-0	1-2	3-0	4-2	3-1	–	1-1	4-1	1-2	3-1	1-0	0-1	2-2	4-1	1-1	2-3	3-0	2-1	3-0	0-3	0-1
Crewe	2-0	1-3	3-1	2-0	3-0	2-5	1-0	1-1	1-1	–	1-0	1-2	4-1	1-0	0-1	0-0	0-1	3-2	1-1	1-2	1-1	3-0	2-0	0-3
Dag & Red	1-1	3-1	1-1	1-1	2-0	2-0	0-5	3-1	0-1	2-0	–	0-0	2-2	3-2	2-0	4-3	1-0	2-3	1-2	3-2	1-1	1-3	1-0	1-1
Gillingham	1-1	3-1	3-4	2-2	1-1	2-1	1-1	1-2	1-1	1-2	2-1	–	5-4	0-0	0-2	2-1	0-1	1-0	2-0	0-0	0-1	2-3	2-3	1-1
Hereford	1-1	1-1	1-1	1-1	1-1	0-2	1-1	0-0	1-1	1-1	1-0	1-6	–	2-0	4-3	1-2	0-0	1-1	0-0	1-1	2-7	1-2	0-1	3-2
Macclesfield	1-2	1-1	1-2	3-0	1-0	1-0	1-3	1-0	2-2	1-1	0-1	0-2	0-4	–	1-1	0-1	2-1	0-1	1-1	3-3	1-0	2-3	1-2	1-2
Morecambe	1-1	1-1	1-0	0-0	2-2	1-0	3-1	1-1	6-0	0-1	1-2	1-1	1-1	1-1	–	1-1	0-1	2-2	2-1	1-1	1-1	0-1	2-0	1-2
Northampton	0-0	1-0	0-1	0-1	3-0	0-1	2-3	0-1	1-1	1-1	2-1	1-1	0-1	1-2	0-4	–	1-2	0-1	1-1	2-1	3-1	2-5	2-1	0-0
Oxford	1-1	0-2	0-3	0-3	2-1	1-0	2-2	3-1	0-1	0-1	0-0	0-3	1-3	2-1	3-2	4-1	–	2-1	0-0	1-4	1-0	0-2	0-1	2-2
Plymouth	2-2	1-2	2-1	0-0	2-1	1-1	1-2	2-1	2-2	1-2	2-1	0-0	3-2	0-0	1-1	3-0	1-1	–	5-1	2-0	1-1	0-2	1-0	1-2
Port Vale	4-1	3-2	1-3	1-1	0-3	3-2	2-1	3-2	1-2	1-1	0-0	2-1	2-1	2-1	3-0	1-1	2-1	1-0	–	3-1	3-1	2-3	2-3	2-0
Rotherham	1-0	2-2	2-1	1-1	2-3	5-2	1-2	1-0	1-0	0-0	1-1	1-2	3-1	1-0	0-1	1-0	1-2	3-0	2-0	–	1-1	2-3	0-2	4-1
Shrewsbury	1-0	3-1	1-0	2-0	3-1	1-0	1-1	0-0	3-0	1-1	1-1	2-0	1-0	3-0	1-1	2-2	2-2	3-0	3-0	0-2	–	0-4	1-1	2-0
Southend	2-0	1-1	2-0	0-3	2-0	0-3	4-0	0-2	3-0	1-3	2-2	0-3	3-3	1-0	3-0	1-0	1-2	1-0	5-0	3-2	3-0	–	1-4	0-0
Swindon	2-0	1-1	2-1	2-1	0-0	1-1	0-1	0-1	3-0	3-0	4-0	2-5	3-0	3-0	3-0	1-2	0-0	3-1	2-1	1-4	1-1	2-0	–	1-0
Torquay	4-0	2-0	0-1	0-1	1-0	1-2	2-2	2-0	1-1	1-1	1-0	1-1	3-0	3-0	1-1	0-0	0-1	1-0	3-1	2-0	1-0	0-0	2-0	–

HIGHLIGHTS OF THE PREMIER LEAGUE
SEASON 2011–12

AUGUST 2011

13 The opening day of the season brings mixed fortunes for four players appearing for the first time for new clubs. Kieron Dyer sustains an ankle injury seven minutes into his debut for Queens Park Rangers and Danny Gabbidon later concedes an own goal. It's a bad day all round for the Championship title winners, who lose 4-0 at home to Bolton and have Clint Hill sent off. New Arsenal striker Gervinho also sees red in an incident involving Joey Barton during a goalless draw at Newcastle. Sebastian Larsson earns Sunderland a point at Anfield after Luis Suarez makes amends for missing a penalty by putting Liverpool ahead. Mauro Formica scores on his debut for Blackburn, but the home side are beaten 2-1 by Wolves, with Stephen Ward netting the winner seconds after Kevin Doyle's spot-kick is saved by Paul Robinson. Wes Hoolahan earns promoted Norwich a point at Wigan, cancelling out Ben Watson's penalty.

14 Manchester United begin their defence of the title with a 2-1 away win over West Bromwich Albion, but lose Rio Ferdinand and Nemanja Vidic to injuries, four days after another defender, Rafael, is ruled out with a dislocated shoulder sustained in training. With Stoke's match against Chelsea goalless and the Tottenham-Everton fixture postponed following the London riots, the Premier League fails to deliver a home win on the opening weekend for the first time.

15 Sergio Aguero, Manchester City's record signing, comes off the bench and scores twice in a 4-0 win over the third promoted team, Swansea.

20 More problems for Arsenal, with Emmanuel Frimpong sent off on his first senior start, Aaron Ramsey conceding an own goal and Liverpool beating them at home (2-0) for the first time since 2000. Sunderland's Phil Bardsley also sees red on his own ground against Newcastle, who take Tyne-Wear derby honours with the only goal from Ryan Taylor. Two new managers are successful for the first time. Andre Villas-Boas sees Chelsea come from behind to overcome West Bromwich Albion 2-1 with an 83rd minute winner from substitute Florent Malouda. Alex McLeish, whose move from Birmingham prompted protests from some Aston Villa fans, is off the mark with a 3-1 success against Blackburn, Gabriel Agbonlahor opening the scoring, then providing the pass for Emile Heskey's second. Delight, too, for Neil Warnock – and new owner Tony Fernandes - after Tommy Smith's strike at Everton gives Queens Park Rangers their first victory. Another newcomer, Michel Vorm, is equal to Ben Watson's penalty to earn Swansea a goalless draw against Wigan.

21 Norwich have Leon Barnett sent off for bringing down Jon Walters, but John Ruddy saves the Stoke player's spot-kick and they hold on to the lead established by loanee Ritchie de Laet's first goal for the club until the fourth minute of stoppage-time when Kenwyne Jones equalises.

27 A game of three penalties ends with Mikel Arteta's successful stoppage-time spot-kick giving Everton victory at Blackburn after the home side's Junior Hoilett and Mauro Formica fail to convert theirs. Drama, too, at Stamford Bridge, where Norwich goalkeeper John Ruddy is sent off for conceding a penalty which Frank Lampard converts. Juan Mata, on his debut, makes it 3-1 in the tenth minute of time added on, following a head injury sustained by Didier Drogba. Jordan Henderson and Charlie Adam score for the first time for Liverpool, who beat Bolton 3-1, while Franco di Santo doubles his tally for the whole of the previous season with both goals in Wigan's 3-1 victory over Queens Park Rangers.

28 Wayne Rooney's hat-trick takes him past 150 goals for the club as Manchester United punish an Arsenal side missing eight players through injury and suspension. Ashley Young opens his account with two goals in a remarkable 8-2 win – the first time Arsenal have conceded eight since 1896. Their misery is compounded by the sending-off of Carl Jenkinson and by Robin van Persie having a penalty saved by David De Gea at 1-0. Rooney, however, is upstaged by Edin Dzeko, who hits four – two of them made by former Arsenal midfielder Samir Nasri on his debut– as Manchester City overwhelm Tottenham 5-1 at White Hart Lane. Leon Best also had a good day with both goals in Newcastle's 2-1 victory over Fulham. United head City at the top on goal difference.

SEPTEMBER 2011

10 Another hat-trick for Wayne Rooney and two goals by Javier Hernandez on his first start of the season bring Manchester United a 5-0 success at Bolton – and a Premier League record of 18 in their first four matches. A hat-trick, too, for Sergio Aguero as Manchester City make light of Carlos Tevez having a penalty saved by Ali Al Habsi to defeat Wigan 3-0. Emmanuel Adebayor, who scored on his league debut for both Arsenal and Manchester City, marks his first appearance on loan for Tottenham by converting fellow-newcomer Scott Parker's pass in a 2-0 success at Wolves. South Korean Ji-Dong Won is on the mark on his first start for Sunderland, but it's not enough to prevent Chelsea's seventh successive win on Wearside, this time by 2-1.

11 The early season spate of penalty misses continues, with West Bromwich Albion's Peter Odemwingie denied by Declan Rudd at Norwich – the ninth failure out of 15 spot-kicks awarded so far. Odemwingie's earlier strike, however, is enough to win the game. Ruben Rochina's first Premier League goal earns Blackburn their first point in a 1-1 draw at Fulham.

17 Yakubu marks his debut with two goals as Blackburn twice come from behind to add to Arsenal's problems with a 4-3 victory. His side's other two are own goals. The Nigerian is one of nine players on the mark for their new clubs for the first time, including Arsenal's Mikel Arteta and Gervinho. Joey Barton and DJ Campbell help Queens Park Rangers to a 3-0 win at Wolves. Anthony Pilkington puts Norwich on the way to a 2-1 success at Bolton, achieved despite the fact that his side concede a penalty for the fifth consecutive match – a Premier League record. Bolton's Ivan Klasnic is sent off. Leroy Lita gets off the mark for Swansea in their first victory, 3-0 against West Bromwich Albion, resulting in all three promoted clubs enjoying a profitable day. Scott Sinclair's earlier penalty for Swansea is the first Premier League goal to be scored outside of England. Also opening their accounts, in the last ten minutes, are Everton substitutes Apostolos Vellios and Royston Drenthe, who secure a 3-1 victory over Wigan.

18 Chris Smalling nets his first top-flight goal as Manchester United race into a 3-0 half-time lead against Chelsea. Fernando Torres pulls one back, then perpetrates one of the worst misses in Premier League history after rounding goalkeeper David De Gea. Sergio Aguero takes his tally to eight in five games with a brace for Manchester City at Fulham, but his side drop their first points when pegged back to 2-2. Liverpool have Charlie Adam and Martin Skrtel sent off on a black day at White Hart Lane, where they suffer their biggest defeat by Tottenham – 4-0 – since 1963, Emmanuel Adebayor scoring twice. Sunderland's first win of the season is by the same scoreline against Stoke, with Craig Gardner contributing his first goal for the team.

24 Delight and despair again for Fernando Torres, who puts Chelsea on the way to a 4-1 victory over Swansea and is then sent off for a two-footed challenge on Mark Gower. For three other strikers, however, it's joy all the way. Robin van Persie chalks up his 99th and 100th goals for Arsenal at the expense of Bolton, who are beaten 3-0 and have David Wheater dismissed. Demba Ba's hat-trick, his first goals for Newcastle, account for Blackburn 3-1 in a match which produces another red card – Rovers' Martin Olsson. Peter Crouch starts to pay off his record fee with a trademark header for Stoke, who end Manchester United's 100 per cent record in a 1-1 draw. Crouch joins Les Ferdinand, Andy Cole, Marcus Bent, Nick Barmby and Craig Bellamy in scoring for six Premier League clubs. At the end of the month, United head Manchester City on goal difference after City substitutes Mario Balotelli and James Milner break Everton's resistance, with Milner's goal his first for the club in the Premier League. The day's fourth dismissal is Wigan's Steve Gohouri in the 2-1 home defeat by Tottenham.

25 Aston Villa incur a mandatory £25,000 fine for six bookings at Loftus Road, where they are denied victory by Richard Dunne's stoppage-time own goal for ten-man Queens Park Rangers, who have Armand Traore sent off.

OCTOBER 2011

1 The Merseyside derby, the fixture with the most red cards in Premier League history – 19 – produces another at Goodison Park. But this one, for Everton's Jack Rodwell, is overturned on appeal. Liverpool win 2-0, despite Dirk Kuyt having a penalty saved by Tim Howard, with goals from Andy Carroll and Luis Suarez. Manchester United defeat Norwich by the same scoreline for a club-record 19th successive home win, while substitutes Samir Nasri and Stefan Savic score for the first time for Manchester City, who win 4-0 at Blackburn. So do Nicklas Bendtner and Ahmed Elmohamady for Sunderland, who retrieve a two-goal deficit for a point against West Bromwich Albion.

2 Andy Johnson and Frank Lampard score hat-tricks as Fulham and Chelsea chalk up big wins. Johnson's treble in the 6-0 demolition of Queens Park Rangers is Fulham's first in the Premier League and comes in their first league victory of the season. He also secures the penalty converted by Danny Murphy and helps set up Clint Dempsey's goal. Lampard's strikes and two by Daniel Sturridge, who had a successful spell on loan at the Reebok the previous season, condemn Bolton to a sixth successive defeat (5-1) – their worst start since 1902-03. Kyle Walker'first goal for Tottenham earns a 2-1 success against struggling Arsenal, whose manager Arsene Wenger virtually concedes the title at this early stage of the season. Danny Graham's first for Swansea comes in a 2-0 victory over Stoke.

15 Manchester City underline their strength in depth by beating Aston Villa 4-1, despite lining up without Aguero, Silva and Dzeko and with a fourth striker, Tevez, frozen out by Roberto Mancini. Sir Alex Ferguson omits Rooney, Hernandez and Nani from his starting line-up at Anfield, but Hernandez comes off the bench to secure a point for Manchester United after Steven Gerrard scores on his first start for Liverpool since facing United in March. David Ngog is on the mark for the first time for Bolton, who end their losing run with a 3-1 victory at Wigan, despite Kevin Davies having a penalty saved by Ali Al Habsi. Anthony Pilkington gives Norwich a flying start against Swansea in the meeting of promoted teams with a goal after 50 seconds and adds a second to round off a 3-1 success.

16 Robin van Persie registers Arsenal's fastest-ever Premier League goal – after 29 seconds – and nets a second eight minutes from the end of normal time for a 2-1 win over Sunderland.

22 Maintaining their unbeaten start to the season, Newcastle defeat Wigan 1-0 thanks to Yohan Cabaye's first goal for the club. West Bromwich Albion follow up victory over Wolves by winning 2-1 at Aston Villa, who have Chris Herd sent off when conceding a penalty which Chris Brunt misses. The red card is later rescinded. Wolves put the brake on their worst top-flight run for 27 years – five successive defeats – when goals by Kevin Doyle and Jamie O'Hara in the last six minutes of normal time retrieve a 2-0 deficit against Swansea.

23 The Manchester derby at Old Trafford is billed as the biggest for years – and will be talked about for years to come. In Roberto Mancini's 100th game as manager, City win 6-1 to go five points clear at the top and set a Premier League record of 33 goals from their opening nine matches. The day after a fire at his house caused by a firework, Mario Balotelli scores the first two and there are three in the final three minutes. United, who have Jonny Evans sent off at 1-0, suffer their worst result at home since City beat them 5-0 in 1955. Drama, too, at Loftus Road, where Chelsea have Jose Bosingwa and Didier Drogba red-carded and lose to Heidar Helguson's penalty. They also have seven players booked, incurring a £25,000 fine. Robin van Persie, given a breather by Arsene Wenger, comes off the bench to score twice as Arsenal overcome Stoke 3-1. Both goals are set up by Gervinho after he scores the first himself. Also on the mark twice is Rafael van der Vaart in Tottenham's 2-1 success at Blackburn. Bryan Ruiz nets his first for Fulham and Bobby Zamora has the chance to give them victory in the 89th minute, but he misses an open goal and his side are punished as Louis Saha and Jack Rodwell then strike in quick succession to give Everton the verdict 3-1.

29 Another remarkable scoreline, this time at Stamford Bridge, where Robin van Persie's hat-trick highlights Arsenal's 5-3 defeat of Chelsea after they twice fell behind. Manchester City overcome the dismissal of captain Vincent Kompany to beat Wolves 3-1 and retain their advantage over Manchester United, 1-0 winners at Everton. Also sent off is Ricardo Gardner in Bolton's 3-1 reversal against Swansea, whose striker Danny Graham scores for both sides. Connor Wickham gets his first for Sunderland in a 2-2 draw with Aston Villa, while Grant Holt's controversial penalty in stoppage-time completes Norwich's comeback from 3-1 down for a point against Blackburn.

30 Rafael van der Vaart is on the mark for the fifth successive league game and Gareth Bale nets twice as Tottenham master Queens Park Rangers 3-1.

31 Demba Ba scores his second hat-trick of the season for Newcastle, who move up to third with a 3-1 victory at Stoke.

NOVEMBER 2011

5 Sir Alex Ferguson celebrates 25 years as Manchester United's manager with victory over Sunderland, but needs an own goal by former Old Trafford defender Wes Brown for the points. Manchester City trail for the first time in the league, but recover to win 3-2 away to Queens Park Rangers, Yaya Toure following up his two goals in midweek against Villarreal in the Champions League with the decisive strike. Newcastle extend their best start to a season for 16 years, and for a few hours go second, by beating Everton 2-1 in a lunch-time kick-off. In-form Gabriel Agbonlahor continues to press his claim for an England place by setting up two goals for Darren Bent, as well as scoring himself, in Aston Villa's 3-2 success against Norwich.

6 Chris Eagles and Ivan Klasnic both score twice as Bolton crush Stoke 5-0 – the same scoreline they suffered in the teams' FA Cup semi-final the previous season – for the club's biggest home win in the Premier League.

19 The bottom two sides deliver one of the most bizarre matches of the season. Blackburn, down to ten men after David Dunn's dismissal, make it 2-2 at the DW Stadium through Junior Hoilett after Morten Gamst Pedersen gets away with illegally playing a corner to himself, instead of to a team-mate. Then, after Albert Crusat puts Wigan ahead in the 88th minute with his first goal for the club, Rovers goalkeeper Paul Robinson is kicked in the head challenging for an equaliser and Yakubu levels at 3-3 with his second of the game, a spot-kick eight minutes into stoppage-time. In front of a record crowd for the Etihad Stadium of 47,408, penalties by Mario Balotelli and Sergio Aguero point Manchester City to a 3-1 success against previously unbeaten Newcastle, whose consolation from Dan Gosling is his first for the club. City's 11 wins and a draw in 12 fixtures is the Premier League's best-ever start. Luke Young is on the mark for the first time for Queens Park Rangers, who win 3-2 at Stoke, with Heidar Helguson netting twice. Robin van Persie's double in Arsenal's 2-1 victory at Norwich enables him to join Alan Shearer, Thierry Henry, Les Ferdinand and Ruud van Nistelrooy in scoring 30 Premier League goals in a calendar year.

20 Glen Johnson's 87th minute solo effort condemns Chelsea to a second successive home defeat for the first time since 2002 – 2-1 by Liverpool.

21 Harry Redknapp returns to the Tottenham dug-out after minor heart surgery and sees his team go third by beating Aston Villa 2-0, both goals coming from Emmanuel Adebayor.

26 Tottenham make it 28 points from ten matches, their best start since the 1960-61 Double-winning season, with a 3-1 success at West Bromwich Albion in which Emmanuel Adebayor scores twice and puts Jermain Defoe through for the other goal. They close to within two points of Manchester United, who are held 1-1 at home by Newcastle following a disputed penalty converted by Demba Ba. Thomas Vermaelen makes amends for an own goal by scoring Arsenal's equaliser against Fulham in another 1-1 scoreline. Arsene Wenger uses players with 14 different nationalities – a first for the Premier League. Wigan's lean run, eight defeats and a draw, is ended by Franco di Santo's stoppage-time goal for a 2-1 victory at Sunderland, whose manager Steve Bruce is sacked four days later. Bolton's David Wheater is sent off in the 2-0 home defeat by Everton.

27 The death of Wales manager Gary Speed casts a shadow over the two games played. Manchester City's Mario Balotelli is sent off in a 1-1 draw at Liverpool. Swansea and Aston Villa finish goalless in front of a record Liberty Stadium crowd of 20,404. City remain five points clear of Manchester United.

DECEMBER 2011

3 On the weekend when crowds across the country pay tribute to Gary Speed, Yakubu takes pride of place by scoring four goals, one a penalty, to enable Blackburn to end a troubled eight-match run with a 4-2 victory over Swansea, who have Joe Allen sent off. Arsenal also get four, without replay, at Wigan, while Manchester City transform a single-goal half-time lead against Norwich into a 5-1 success. Elsewhere, there are two controversial refereeing decisions in 'last man' situations. Mike Dean shows yellow to David Luiz after the defender hauls down Demba Ba near the penalty box and Chelsea go on to win 3-0 at Newcastle, despite Frank Lampard having a penalty saved by Tim Krul. At White Hart Lane, Stuart Attwell sends off Bolton's Gary Cahill for bringing down Scott Parker 45 yards from goal in a match Tottenham win 3-0. Cahill's red card is later overturned. Aston Villa's Emile Heskey makes his 500th Premier League appearance, but it's Manchester United's Phil Jones who takes the honours by opening his account for the club with the only goal of the game. Three players sustain non-contact injuries – United's Javier Hernandez (ankle) and Villa's Shay Given (hamstring) and Jermaine Jenas (achilles).

4 Martin O'Neill, Sunderland's new manager, watches from the stand as his team lose 2-1 at Wolves to two Steven Fletcher goals.

5 Fulham's Clint Dempsey becomes the highest-scoring American in the Premier League, overtaking Brian McBride with his 37th goal, the only one of the game against Liverpool, who have Jay Spearing sent off.

10 Clint Dempsey experiences the vagaries of football, slicing Scott Sinclair's shot into his own net and having a penalty saved by Michel Vorm in a 2-0 defeat at Swansea. Things also turn sour for Steven Reid after he puts West Bromwich Albion ahead. Reid concedes the penalty which Jordi Gomez converts to give Wigan a 2-1 success. Wayne Rooney and Nani both score twice, the pair's first Premier League goals since September, as Manchester United respond to their midweek Champions League exit by overcoming Wolves 4-1. Newcastle's ever-present defence is disrupted for the first time by injuries and the dismissal of Dan Gosling adds to their problems. Norwich take advantage with a 4-2 victory, Grant Holt scoring twice, in front of Carrow Road's biggest all-seater attendance of 26,816. The prolific Robin van Persie ends Everton's stubborn resistance with a fine volley, applauded in the stands by Thierry Henry, one of several players on parade as part of Arsenal's 125th anniversary.

11 Martin O'Neill looks to be heading for defeat in his first match in charge of Sunderland when they trail Blackburn. But two spectacular goals, David Vaughan's first for the club after 84 minutes and Sebastian Larsson's free-kick in stoppage-time, have the manager leaping for delight on the touchline. In contrast, an angry Harry Redknapp blames refereeing decisions, including the sending-off of Younes Kaboul, for the end to Tottenham's unbeaten 11-match run. His side go down 2-1 at Stoke to two Matthew Etherington goals.

12 Manchester City lead through Mario Balotelli after two minutes at Stamford Bridge. But the leaders concede an equaliser to Raul Meireles, have Gael Clichy sent off and lose their unbeaten record to Chelsea substitute Frank Lampard's 83rd minute penalty.

17 Chelsea are unable to build on that performance, conceding an 88th minute equaliser to Jordi Gomez at Wigan. Stoke come from behind to beat Wolves 2-1 away from home, making it four Premier League victories in succession for the first time. Struggling Blackburn equalise through Scott Dann's first goal for the club against West Bromwich Albion, but lose to Peter Odemwingie's 89th minute strike. Fulham, knocked out of the Europa League in midweek, add to Bolton's problems, Bryan Ruiz setting up Clint Dempsey for their first goal and Dempsey returning the compliment 65 seconds later for a 2-0 scoreline.

18 Manchester United regain the leadership with a 2-0 win at Queens Park Rangers, Wayne Rooney scoring inside a minute. But Manchester City are back in pole position after David Silva nets the only goal against Arsenal.

20 Goals in the first half-hour by Mark Davies and Nigel Reo-Coker bring Bolton a 2-1 win at Blackburn in the meeting of the two bottom teams. Substitute Simeon Jackson scores with his first touch for Norwich, but Wolves twice come from behind for a point at Molineux.

21 Premier League milestones are reached by Marc Albrighton and Ryan Giggs. Albrighton registers the league's 20,000th goal during Aston Villa's 2-1 home defeat by Arsenal in which team-mate Alan Hutton is sent off. Giggs extends his record of scoring in every league season since its formation in 1992-93 as Manchester United overwhelm Fulham 5-0 at Craven Cottage. Two goals from Sergio Aguero point Manchester City to a 3-0 success against Stoke, while Demba Ba gets two for Newcastle. But Ba's brace cannot prevent West Bromwich Albion's first league victory on Tyneside since 1977 – a 3-2 scoreline in which Gareth McAuley opens his account for the club. Wes Brown's 89th minute header is his first for Sunderland, who overcome Queens Park Rangers 3-2 at Loftus Road. The day after receiving an eight-match FA ban, and with his club considering whether to appeal, Liverpool's Luis Suarez wins a penalty at Wigan. Ali Al Habsi save Charlie Adam's spot-kick and the scoresheet remains blank.

26 Andre Villas-Boas writes off Chelsea's title chances after a third successive 1-1 draw, this time at home to Fulham, leaves his team 11 points behind Manchester City and Manchester United. City fail to score for the first time since April, held at West Bromwich Albion. United, aided by the sending-off – later rescinded on appeal – of Conor Sammon, beat Wigan 5-0. Three of their goals come from Dimitar Berbatov, a peripheral figure for much of the season. At the bottom, Bolton lose for the eighth match in nine at home, 2-0 to Newcastle, for whom Hatem Ben Arfa scores for the first time since a double break of his left leg in September 2010. Substitute Jack Colback's strike in a 1-1 draw with Everton is the first of his Sunderland career.

27 Gareth Bale keeps Tottenham in touch at the top with both goals in a 2-0 victory at Norwich. Wolves overcome the dismissal of Nenad Milijas to hold on for a 1-1 result at Arsenal.

31 Sir Alex Ferguson's 70th birthday celebrations at Old Trafford are halted as Manchester United lose 3-2 to bottom-of-the-table Blackburn. Wayne Rooney watches from a private box, after being dropped by his manager for disciplinary reasons, as United reply to two goals by Yakubu with two from Dimitar Berbatov, but go down to Grant Hanley's first of his Rovers career. Stephen Ireland's first for Aston Villa cancels out Didier Drogba's 150th for Chelsea, who concede two more in the final ten minutes on another miserable afternoon at Stamford Bridge. Orlando Sa's first for Fulham comes in a 1-1 draw at Norwich. Sam Ricketts, back after nearly 11 months out with an achilles injury, scores his first for five years as Bolton share the same scoreline with Wolves. Thierry Henry stands to applaud Robin van Persie for overtaking his Arsenal record of 34 goals in a calendar year. It's the only one of the game against Queens Park Rangers, leaving the Dutch striker one short of Alan Shearer's Premier League all-time record. Roberto Martinez sends on Ben Watson to take an 87th minute penalty at Stoke and the substitute earns a 2-2 draw for a Wigan side down to ten men after Gary Caldwell's dismissal.

JANUARY 2012

1 Manchester City miss the chance to go three points clear at the top when losing to a stoppage-time goal, the only one of the match, by Ji Dong-Won at Sunderland.

2 Joey Barton is sent off after putting Queens Park Rangers ahead at Loftus Road in what proves to be Neil Warnock's final league game as manager. The initiative is handed to Norwich, who level through Anthony Pilkington and take the points when Pilkington provides the cross for substitute Steve Morison's winner. The dismissal of Johan Djourou at Fulham proves costly for Arsenal, who lose the lead to Steve Sidwell's 85th minute header and go down to Bobby Zamora's volley in stoppage-time. Peter Crouch halts Blackburn's mini-revival with the 100th and 101st league goals of his career for a 2-1 away win by Stoke. Wayne Routledge also celebrates, his first Premier League goal and the first for his latest club completing Swansea's 2-0 success at Villa Park.

3 Manchester City make light of a red card for Gareth Barry, stretching a two-goal lead to a 3-0 victory over Liverpool. Sunderland's surge under Martin O'Neill continues with a fourth victory in six games, 4-1 at Wigan in which James McClean scores for the first time.

4 Wayne Rooney is restored to the Manchester United line-up, but his side take a 3-0 beating at Newcastle, who overcome the champions for the first time since 2001 after Demba Ba opens

the scoring with his 15th goal of the season in his final game before leaving for the Africa Cup of Nations. Goodison Park's lowest Premier League crowd in David Moyes's ten years as manager, 29,561, see Everton goalkeeper Tim Howard's wind-assisted clearance bounce over the head of his opposite number Adam Bogdan and into the net. But Bolton recover for a 2-1 win, clinched by a goal from Gary Cahill in his last match before joining Chelsea.

14 Paul Scholes makes a scoring Old Trafford comeback, putting Manchester United on the way to a 3-0 victory over Bolton after Wayne Rooney has a penalty saved by Adam Bogdan. Blackburn have leading scorer Yakubu sent off against Fulham, but a battling performance brings a 3-1 victory. Fellow-strugglers Wolves are also rewarded for a tenacious display when Steven Fletcher scores for the sixth time in seven starts to earn a 1-1 draw at Tottenham. Another consistent performer, Steve Morison, is on the mark again for Norwich, who inflict West Bromwich Albion's seventh home defeat of the season (2-1).

15 Swansea, in front of a record Liberty Stadium crowd of 20,409, join Norwich in the top half of the table, defeating Arsenal with a goal by Danny Graham 45 seconds after Theo Walcott makes it 2-2. Mark Hughes suffers a 1-0 reversal at Newcastle in his first game as manager of Queens Park Rangers.

21 The Irishman playing in the United States and the American plying his trade in London are among the goals. Much-travelled Robbie Keane, on loan from LA Galaxy, gets two against his first club, Wolves, as Aston Villa win 3-2 at Molineux. Keane becomes the seventh player to score for six Premier League clubs. Wolves have Karl Henry sent off. Clint Dempsey follows his hat-trick against Charlton in the FA Cup with another three for Fulham, who come from behind to overcome Newcastle 5-2. Nigel Reo-Coker chalks up his first official goal for Bolton in a 3-1 success against Liverpool, his strike against Wigan earlier in the season having been declared a Gary Caldwell own goal by the Dubious Goals Panel. West Bromwich Albion take maximum points at Stoke for the first time since 1982, helped by errors from the home side in a 2-1 scoreline. Jonathan Walters has a penalty saved by Ben Foster, while Thomas Sorensen, on his 400th league appearance, is beaten by two long-range shots, the second a free-kick from Graham Dorrans in stoppage-time, the midfielder's first goal for 11 months. For Everton's Tim Cahill, it's a case of mixed fortunes. Cahill is on the mark for the first time for nearly 13 months, then sees his attempted clearance from the goal-line rebound into the net off David Goodwillie to give Blackburn a point. Mark Hughes gets his first win with Queens Park Rangers, Heidar Helguson netting one penalty and having another saved by Ali Al Habsi in the 3-1 defeat of Wigan.

22 On a big day at the top, Tottenham's title challenge falters further in a dramatic second-half watched by a record crowd for the Etihad Stadium of 47,422. They retrieve a two-goal deficit against Manchester City, Jermain Defoe misses a chance to complete the recovery, then substitute Mario Balotelli makes it 3-2 for the leaders with a penalty four minutes into stoppage-time. Harry Redknapp insists Balotelli should have been sent off earlier for stamping on Scott Parker and the Italian is later banned on video evidence. Danny Welbeck's 81st minute goal gives Manchester United a 2-1 success at Arsenal.

31 Darron Gibson does former club Manchester United a favour when his first goal for Everton brings victory over Manchester City. United take advantage by beating Stoke 2-0 with penalties from Javier Hernandez and Dimitar Berbatov to draw level on points with City. Another record crowd for Swansea, 20,526, are about to celebrate victory when Chelsea, down to ten men after Ashley Cole's red card, level in stoppage-time when Jose Bosingwa's shot deflects off Neil Taylor into his own net. Andy Carroll ends three months without a league goal as Liverpool follow up Carling Cup and FA Cup success by winning 3-0 away to Wolves to complete a great week. Gareth Bale nets twice in Tottenham's 3-1 victory over Wigan, whose consolation from James McArthur is his first for the club.

FEBRUARY 2012

1 Three players celebrate notable goals at Villa Park. Djibril Cisse, a scorer on his debut for both Liverpool and Sunderland, does the same for Queens Park Rangers. His new side lead 2-0 before Darren Bent's 100th in the Premier League and Charles N'Zogbia's first for the club earn Villa a point. Gabriel Obertan is off the mark for Newcastle in their 2-0 success at Blackburn, while Fraizer Campbell crowns his return after 17 months out with knee injuries by opening the scoring for Sunderland, who see off Norwich 3-0.

4 Bobby Zamora puts Queens Park Rangers ahead in his first game for the club, but they then have Djibril Cisse sent off on his Loftus Road debut and go down 2-1 as Wolves end a run of nine games without a victory. A hat-trick by Robin van Persie and two goals from 18-year-old Alex Oxlade Chamberlain, his first in the Premier League, point Arsenal to a 7-1 rout of Blackburn, who have Gael Given dismissed at 3-1. Stoke's Robert Huth also sees red in the 1-0 home defeat by revitalised Sunderland. Chris Baird has a day to forget, conceding a penalty for a foul on Adam Johnson and later deflecting Johnson's cross into his own net as Fulham go down 3-0 at Manchester City. But on-loan Gylfi Sigurdsson is all smiles with his first goal for Swansea, 2-1 away winners against West Bromwich Albion.

5 Manchester United, seemingly out for the count when trailing Chelsea 3-0, deliver a tremendous comeback at Stamford Bridge to gain a point, with two Wayne Rooney penalties making them the first Premier League side to score four consecutive goals from the spot. Newcastle's new No 9, Papiss Cisse, hits the winner against Aston Villa (2-1) on his debut.

11 Wayne Rooney, making his 500th appearance for club and country, scores both goals as Manchester United overcome Liverpool 2-1 on an afternoon soured by the refusal of Luis Suarez to shake the hand of racial-abuse victim Patrice Evra. Manager Harry Redknapp, cleared of tax evasion three days earlier, sees Louis Saha open his account for Tottenham with a brace in the 5-0 win over Newcastle. Saha, however, has to concede match honours to Emmanuel Abebayor, who has a hand in four goals and scores one himself. Pavel Pogrebnyak marks his debut by putting Fulham on the way to a 2-1 win over Stoke and two other players on-loan have good days. Steven Pienaar nets on his return to Goodison Park as Everton see off Chelsea 2-0, while Thierry Henry strikes in stoppage-time to give Arsenal a 2-1 victory at Sunderland in his final Premier League match before rejoining New York Red Bulls. Wigan's 2-1 success at Bolton is their first in ten matches.

12 Peter Odemwingie's hat-trick and a debut goal by Keith Andrews spell the end for Wolves manager Mick McCarthy as West Bromwich Albion win 5-1 at Molineux. Joleon Lescott's volley enables Manchester City to prevail at Villa Park.

25 Frank Lampard becomes the first player to reach a double-figure goals tally in nine successive Premier League seasons when he rounds off Chelsea's 3-0 victory over Bolton. Substitute Edin Dzeko scores with his first touch as Manchester City complete a year without dropping a single point at home by beating Blackburn by the same margin. Peter Odemwingie follows up his hat-trick with a brace in West Bromwich Albion's first league success at home in three months – 4-0 against Sunderland. Terry Connor, appointed Wolves manager until the end of the season, sees his side retrieve a 2-0 deficit at Newcastle to gain a point. But fellow-strugglers Queens Park Rangers lose 1-0 at home to Fulham after Samba Diakite is sent off 33 minutes into his debut.

26 Tottenham's title chances are effectively ended by a 5-2 defeat at the Emirates, where Arsenal stage a tremendous comeback after tailing 2-0, Theo Walcott scoring twice. A stoppage-time goal by Ryan Giggs on his 900th career appearance, brings a 2-1 win at Norwich for Manchester United, who end the month two points behind Manchester City. Matthew Upson's first for the club puts Stoke on the way to a 2-0 success against Swansea.

MARCH 2012

3 Chelsea lose to West Bromwich Albion for the first time in 18 league matches between the teams – a result followed by the sacking of manager Andre Villas-Boas. Gareth McAuley scores the only goal at The Hawthorns. Arsenal move three points clear of Chelsea after two Robin van Persie goals – bringing his tally for the season in all competitions to 31 – and Wojciech Szczesny's penalty save from Dirk Kuyt earn a 2-1 success at Liverpool. Gylfi Sigurdsson also scores twice as Swansea overcome the sending-off of Nathan Dyer to win 2-0 at Wigan. Mario Balotelli completes Manchester City's 2-0 victory over Bolton before facing disciplinary action from the club for visiting a club in the early hours of Friday morning.

4 A stoppage-time goal by Shola Ameobi gives Newcastle a point in a stormy Tyne-Wear derby. Sunderland, who lead through Nicklas Bendtner's penalty, have Stephane Sessegnon and Lee Cattermole sent off, there are eight bookings, a 20-player melee and a touchline spat between managers Alan Pardew and Martin O'Neill. Referee Mike Dean, who shows Cattermole a red card after the final whistle, earns widespread praise for his handling of the game. Pavel Pogrebnyak hits a hat-trick, bringing his tally to five goals in three games, and Clint Dempsey nets twice as Fulham outplay Wolves 5-0. Two from Ashley Young set up Manchester United for a 3-1 win at Tottenham.

10 Queens Park Rangers manager Mark Hughes leads renewed calls for goal-line technology to be introduced quickly after his defender Clint Hill has a clear goal missed by match officials in the 2-1 defeat at Bolton. In another meeting of relegation-threatened teams, Junior Hoilett gives Blackburn victory with two goals at Wolves, his side keeping a clean sheet for the first time in 31 matches. Didier Drogba chalks up 100 in the Premier League for Chelsea against Stoke, who have Ricardo Fuller sent off. Two other 1-0 scorelines see players score for the first time for their clubs – Everton's Nikica Jelavic at the expense of Tottenham and substitute Andreas Weimann in time added on for Aston Villa against Fulham.

11 Joe Hart saves Scott Sinclair's penalty, but Manchester City lose the leadership after going down at Swansea to Luke Moore's 83rd minute header. Manchester United move up with two Wayne Rooney goals, the second from the penalty spot, for a 2-0 victory against West Bromwich Albion, who have Jonas Olsson sent off.

12 Thomas Vermaelen strikes in stoppage-time to give Arsenal a 2-1 win over Newcastle, to move them to within a point of Tottenham after having trailed their rivals by 12 points.

13 On his 400th Premier League appearance, Steven Gerrard becomes the first player since Ian Rush in 1982 to score a hat-trick in the Merseyside derby, giving Liverpool a 3-0 success and spoiling David Moyes's tenth anniversary as Everton manager.

17 Another two goals by Gylfi Sigurdsson set up Swansea for a 3-0 result at Fulham. Paul Scharner denies his old club Wigan a much-needed victory with an equaliser for West Bromwich Albion.

18 Jonny Evans scores his first goal for Manchester United in a 5-0 success at Wolves, who have Ronald Zubar sent off with the score 1-0. Alan Pardew's 500th league game as a manager brings a 1-0 win for Newcastle over Norwich, who record a rather less flattering statistic – the first team to concede in 29 successive Premier League away games.

20 Blackburn move six points clear of the relegation zone by beating Sunderland 2-0, with Junior Hoilett again on the mark.

21 Manchester City rebel Carlos Tevez comes off the bench to end a six-month absence and sets up an 85th minute winner for Samir Nasri against Chelsea. The 2-1 scoreline is City's 20th successive home victory – a Premier League record. Sebastian Coates scores his first goal for Liverpool, who seem to be coasting 2-0 ahead at Loftus Road. But Queens Park Rangers deliver one of the comebacks of the season to win 3-2 with goals from Shaun Derry, his first for the club, Djibril Cisse and Jamie Mackie in stoppage-time. Arsenal move above Tottenham, thanks to the only goal of the game from Thomas Vermaelen at Everton.

24 Peter Crouch describes the 30-yard angled volley which gives Stoke a 1-1 draw with Manchester City as the best of his career. On an emotional afternoon at the Reebok, Bolton return to action following the cardiac arrest suffered by Fabrice Muamba and defeat Blackburn 2-1 with two headers from David Wheater, his first league goals for the club. Grant Holt also gets two, one a penalty, and is then sent off as Norwich beat Wolves. A third 2-1 scoreline sees Wigan win at Liverpool for the first time, Shaun Maloney opening his account for the club from the spot and Gary Caldwell scoring the decider in front of the Kop. Queens Park Rangers have Djibril Cisse dismissed for the second time in five matches and go down 3-1 at Sunderland, for whom James McClean celebrates a new contract by scoring one and setting up another for Nicklas Bendtner. Taye Taiwo's consolation is his first for Rangers. Arsenal record their seventh straight win, 3-0 against Aston Villa, and have two English scorers in a Premier League game for the first time since 1997 – Kieran Gibbs, with his first in the top flight, and Theo Walcott.

26 Manchester United edge past Fulham with the only goal of the game from Wayne Rooney, but are lucky not to concede a late penalty when Michael Carrick brings down Danny Murphy.

31 Manchester City continue to falter, losing their 100 per cent home record in a 3-3 draw against Sunderland. City trail 3-1 – Sebastian Larsson netting twice – five minutes from the end of normal time before Mario Balotelli, with his second of the game, and Aleksandar Kolarov rescue a point. Earlier, the two players argue about who should take a free-kick – and tempers flare in two other games. Wolves goalkeeper Wayne Hennessey and captain Roger Johnson go head-to-head over defensive failings during the 3-2 home defeat by Bolton, for whom Marcos Alonso scores for the first time. So do West Bromwich Albion goalkeeper Ben Foster and Peter Odemwingie as their side lose 2-0 at Everton, substitute Victor Anichebe scoring his first Premier League goal at Goodison since August 2007. There is emotion of a different kind at Villa Park, where captain Stiliyan Petrov watches the game against Chelsea after being diagnosed with leukaemia. His team retrieve a 2-0 deficit, but Chelsea win 4-2 with a first league goal for six months for Fernando Torres and by full-back Branislav Ivanovic. Queens Park Rangers end Arsenal's hot streak, Samba Diakite giving them a 2-1 success with his first goal for the club. And with Wigan winning at home for the first time for seven months, 2-0 against Stoke, the pressure builds at the bottom of the table. Norwich lose 2-1 at Fulham, but it's a big day for Aaron Wilbraham, with his 100th career goal and the accompanying achievement of scoring in all four divisions.

APRIL 2012

1 Liverpool lose for the sixth time in seven games, the club's worst league run for 59 years. They go down 2-0 at Newcastle, have goalkeeper Jose Reina sent off for butting James Perch and Andy Carroll booked for diving on his return to the north-east. Papiss Cisse, Carroll's successor in the No 9 shirt, scores both goals, bringing his tally to seven in seven matches. Emmanuel Adebayor is also on the mark twice, both headers, in Tottenham's 3-1 victory over Swansea.

2 Manchester United start the month five points ahead of Manchester City after goals by Antonio Valencia and Ashley Young in the final ten minutes bring a 2-0 success at Blackburn.

6 Two more goals by Papiss Cisse give Newcastle a 2-0 victory at Swansea.

7 All four relegation-threatened teams in action are beaten. Wigan are unlucky to lose 2-1 at Stamford Bridge, with TV replays showing both Chelsea goals offside. But Bolton have no complaints after a 3-0 defeat at home to Fulham, for whom Clint Dempsey takes his Premier League tally for the season to a club-record 15 and Mahamadou Diarra scores his first. Neither do Blackburn, beaten by the same scoreline at West Bromwich Albion, with Liam Ridgewell heading his first for the team. Rovers have substitute Anthony Modeste sent off. Wolves suffer their sixth successive defeat, 2-1 at Stoke, and look doomed. Two other players score for the first time for their clubs – Aston Villa's Chris Herd in a 1-1 draw at Liverpool and Jonny Howson for Norwich in a 2-2 scoreline against Everton, who are twice pegged back after goals from Nikica Jelavic.

8 Manchester United continue on their winning ways with Wayne Rooney's penalty and a Paul Scholes special against Queens Park Rangers. Rangers are aggrieved after Ashley Young is shown to be a yard offside when falling under the challenge of Shaun Derry, who is sent off. Just as angry is Manchester City manager Roberto Mancini, who sees Mario Balotelli dismissed and his side beaten at Arsenal by the only goal of the game from Mikel Arteta.

9 Frank Lampard and Hatem Ben Arfa score notable goals as Chelsea and Newcastle continue to pursue a Champions League place. Lampard becomes the first midfield player to score 150 in the Premier League, but Fulham earn a point with Clint Dempsey's 22nd of the season in all competitions. A stunning solo effort by Ben Arfa, starting inside his own half, paves the way for Newcastle's fifth successive win, 2-0 against Bolton. Elliott Bennett opens his account for Norwich, who score an excellent 2-1 win at Tottenham with a starting line of players all born in England. Magaye Gueye gets his first for Everton in the 4-0 defeat of Sunderland.

10 Andy Carroll's stoppage-time header gives Liverpool a 3-2 victory on an eventful night at Ewood Park. Leading Blackburn by two Maxi Rodriguez goals, they have second-choice goalkeeper Alexander Doni sent off for bringing down Junior Hoilett and conceding a penalty which his replacement, Brad Jones, saves. Yakubu makes amends for that miss by making it 2-1, then converts the game's second spot-kick after Jones pushes him to the ground.

11 Wigan, beaten in all 13 previous games with Manchester United, put the brake on their championship charge with the only goal from Shaun Maloney. Carlos Tevez makes his first start since September and scores for the first time this season as Manchester City cut the deficit by beating West Bromwich Albion 4-0. Joey Barton, left out of the Queens Park Rangers team at Old Trafford with the threat of a ban hanging over him, returns against Swansea and opens the scoring in a 3-0 victory. Luckless Wolves have Sebastien Bassong sent off after nine minutes and lose 3-0 at home to Arsenal.

14 Carlos Tevez scores a hat-trick as Manchester City overwhelm Norwich 6-1 at Carrow Road with four goals in the final 20 minutes. Blackburn suffer a fifth successive defeat, 3-0 at Swansea, while Queens Park Rangers are beaten by the only goal at West Bromwich Albion.

15 Manchester United restore a five-point advantage by beating Aston Villa 4-0, but controversy surrounds another Wayne Rooney penalty after another fall by Ashley Young.

16 Wigan's bid to beat the drop gathers pace when goals by Franco di Santo and Jordi Gomez in the first eight minutes bring a 2-1 victory at the Emirates, the first time they have taken anything from an away game against Arsenal.

21 Newcastle climb into a Champions League place as Yohan Cabaye scores twice and sets up Papiss Cisse for one in the 3-0 victory over Stoke. With relegation pressure building, Adel Taarabt gives Queens Park Rangers a lifeline when scoring the only goal against Tottenham, but is then sent off. Tottenham goalkeeper Brad Friedel makes his 300th successive Premier League appearance. Blackburn end their losing run by beating Norwich 2-0, but Wigan go down 2-1 to an 89th minute header by Philippe Senderos at Fulham, his first for the club, and Bolton are held 1-1 by Swansea. Sunderland's Craig Gardner receives a last-minute red card in a goalless draw at Aston Villa.

22 The title race takes another twist. Manchester United lead Everton 3-1 and 4-2, but concede twice in the final 10 minutes and have to share an eight-goal thriller. Wayne Rooney overtakes George Best and Dennis Viollet with his 179th and 180th goals for the club, while Nikica Jelavic gets two for Everton. Manchester City close the gap by winning 2-0 at Molineux, a result which confirms relegation for Wolves. Roy Hodgson returns to Anfield for the first time since being sacked by Liverpool and sees his West Bromwich Albion side win there for the first time since 1967, Peter Odemwingie netting the only goal.

24 Aston Villa lead through Stephen Warnock, but are drawn into the relegation struggle when goals by Martin Petrov (pen) and David Ngog within three minutes give Bolton victory.

28 Luis Suarez completes a hat-trick in Liverpool's 3-0 win at Norwich with a stunning 50-yard shot over the head of goalkeeper John Ruddy. Victor Moses is on the mark twice in the first 15 minutes as Wigan overwhelm Newcastle 4-0 and a brace by Kevin Davies earns Bolton a 2-2 draw at Sunderland. Andrea Orlandi, after 24 seconds, scores the Premier League's fastest goal of the season and Swansea lead 3-0 with a quarter-of-an-hour gone against Wolves, who then show great spirit to earn a 4-4 scoreline, with Matt Jarvis netting twice. Another two-goal marksman is Nikica Jelkavic as Everton defeat Fulham 4-0.

29 Fernando Torres hits a hat-trick in Chelsea's 6-1 win over Queens Park Rangers. Like Rangers, Blackburn have a bad day, losing 2-0 at Tottenham to slip closer to going down.

29 What is billed as the biggest-ever Manchester derby goes the way of City. Captain Vincent Kompany heads the only goal of the game to put his side ahead of United on goal difference with two matches to play.

MAY 2012

1 Kenny Dalglish starts without eight of his side for the FA Cup Final against Chelsea and Liverpool lose to Fulham at Anfield for the first time, Martin Skrtel putting the ball into his own net for the only goal.

2 Roberto Di Matteo starts with six of his team for Wembley, but Chelsea lose 2-0 at home to Newcastle. Papiss Cisse scores both goals to equal the Premier League record of 13 in his first

12 appearances. Fabrice Muamba, making an emotional return to the Reebok, sees Bolton beaten 4-1 by Tottenham, for whom Emmanuel Adebayor scores twice.

5 Robin van Persie's brace for Arsenal in Arsene Wenger's 900th game in charge looks to be decisive until Steve Morison's 85th minute goal for Norwich makes it 3-3 at the Emirates.

6 Manchester City move to within reach of the title when two goals by Yaya Toure bring a 2-0 victory at Newcastle. Manchester United beat Swansea 2-0 at a subdued Old Trafford. Goals in the 89th minute by two substitutes have a significant bearing on the battle to avoid relegation. Djibril Cisse scores the only one of the game for Queens Park Rangers against Stoke at Loftus Road to boost their chances of survival. At the Reebok, James Morrison completes West Bromwich Albion's recovery from 2-0 down to deny Bolton a badly-needed win. Aston Villa secure the point they need to make sure of staying up in a 1-1 draw with Tottenham, who have Danny Rose sent off.

7 Blackburn are relegated after a seventh defeat in eight matchers – 1-0 at home to Wigan, whose winner from Antolin Alcaraz completes his side's impressive climb to safety.

8 Chelsea make eight changes from the side that beat Liverpool in the FA Cup Final three days earlier and lose 4-1 in the rearranged league match at Anfield.

13 In front of a 48,000 full house, Manchester City become champions for the first time since 1968 on a day of unrivalled drama. They lead through Pablo Zabaleta at the Etihad Stadium, but Djibril Cisse equalises and despite having Joey Barton sent off, Queens Park Rangers go ahead through Jamie Mackie. Then, in stoppage time Edin Dzeko and Sergio Aguero make it 3-2 for City, who finish ahead of Manchester United on goal difference. United hear the news after beating Sunderland with Wayne Rooney's 27th goal of the season. Despite losing, Rangers stay up and Bolton are relegated after drawing 2-2 at the Britannia Stadium, where they argue that Jon Walters unfairly bundled goalkeeper Adam Bogdan and the ball into the net for Stoke's first goal. Arsenal keep hold of third position, thanks to Laurent Koscielny's winner for 3-2 in Roy Hodgson's last game as West Bromwich Albion manager before concentrating on the England job. Fourth-place Tottenham, 2-0 winners over Fulham, are left to sweat on Chelsea's Champions League Final against Bayern Munich before knowing which European tournament they will be playing in. Newcastle have to be satisfied with the Europa League after going down 3-1 at Everton, who make sure of finishing above Liverpool for the first time since 2005. Everton's Tim Cahill is shown a red card after the final whistle. Liverpool lose to Danny Graham's 100th career goal for Swansea in what proves to be Kenny Dalglish's final game as manager watched by another Liberty Stadium record crowd of 20,605.

● A total of 32 goals on the final day takes the season's total to 1,066, a record for a 38-match programme

HOW MANCHESTER CITY BECAME CHAMPIONS

AUGUST 2011

15	Manchester City 4 (Dzeko 57, Aguero 68, 90, Silva 71) Swansea 0. Att: 46,802
21	Bolton 2 (Klasnic 39, K Davies 63) Manchester City 3 (Silva 26, Barry 37, Dzeko 47). Att: 24,273
28	Tottenham 1 (Kaboul 68) Manchester City 5 (Dzeko 34, 41, 55, 90, Aguero 60). Att: 36,150

SEPTEMBER 2011

10	Manchester City 3 (Aguero 13, 63, 69) Wigan 0. Att: 46,509
18	Fulham 2 (Zamora 55, Murphy 75) Manchester City 2 (Aguero 18, 46). Att: 24,750
24	Manchester City 2 (Balotelli 68, Milner 89) Everton 0. Att: 47,293

OCTOBER 2011

1 Blackburn 0 Manchester City 4 (Johnson 56, Balotelli 59, Nasri 73, Savic 87).
Att: 24,760
15 Manchester City 4 (Balotelli 28, Johnson 47, Kompany 52, Milner 71)
Aston Villa 1 (Warnock 65). Att: 47,019
23 Manchester Utd 1 (Fletcher 81) Manchester City 6 (Balotelli 22, 60, Aguero 69,
Dzeko 90, 90, Silva 90). Att: 75,487
29 Manchester City 3 (Dzeko 52, Kolarov 67, Johnson 90) Wolves 1 (Hunt 75 pen).
Att: 47,142

NOVEMBER 2011

5 QPR 2 (Bothroyd 28, Helguson 69) Manchester City 3 (Dzeko 43, Silva 52,
Y Toure 74). Att: 18,076
19 Manchester City 3 (Balotelli 41 pen, Richards 44, Aguero 72 pen) Newcastle 1
(Gosling 89). Att: 47,408
27 Liverpool 1 (Lescott 33 og) Manchester City 1 (Kompany 31). Att: 45,071

DECEMBER 2011

3 Manchester City 5 (Aguero 32, Nasri 51, Y Toure 68, Balotelli 88, Johnson 90)
Norwich 1 (Morison 81). Att: 47,201
12 Chelsea 2 (Meireles 34, Lampard 83 pen) Manchester City 1 (Balotelli 2).
Att: 41,730
18 Manchester City 1 (Silva 53) Arsenal 0. Att: 47,303
21 Manchester City 3 (Aguero 29, 54, Johnson 36) Stoke 0. Att: 46,321
26 WBA 0 Manchester City 0. Att: 25,938

JANUARY 2012

1 Sunderland 1 (Ji 90) Manchester City 0. Att: 40,625
3 Manchester City 3 (Aguero 10, Y Toure 33, Milner 75 pen) Liverpool 0. Att: 47,131
16 Wigan 0 Manchester City 1 (Dzeko 22). Att: 16,026
22 Manchester City 3 (Nasri 56, Lescott 59, Balotelli 90 pen) Tottenham 2
(Defoe 60, Bale 65). Att: 47,422
31 Everton 1 (Gibson 60) Manchester City 0. Att: 29,856

FEBRUARY 2012

4 Manchester City 3 (Aguero 10 pen, Baird 30 og, Dzeko 72) Fulham 0. Att: 46,963
12 Aston Villa 0 Manchester City 1 (Lescott 63). Att: 35,132
25 Manchester City 3 (Balotelli 30, Aguero 52, Dzeko 81) Blackburn 0. Att: 46,782

MARCH 2012

3 Manchester City 2 (Steinsson 23 og, Balotelli 69) Bolton 0. Att: 47,219
11 Swansea 1 (Moore 83) Manchester City 0. Att: 20,510
21 Manchester City 2 (Aguero 78 pen, Nasri 85) Chelsea 1 (Cahill 60). Att: 46,324
24 Stoke 1 (Crouch 59) Manchester City 1 (Y Toure 76). Att: 27,535
31 Manchester City 3 (Balotelli 43 pen, 85, Kolarov 86) Sunderland 3
(Larsson 31, 55, Bendtner 45). Att: 47,007

APRIL 2012

1 Arsenal 1 (Arteta 87) Manchester City 0. Att: 60,096
11 Manchester City 4 (Aguero 6, 54, Tevez 61, Silva 64) WBA 0. Att: 46,746

14	Norwich 1 (Surman 51) Manchester City 6 (Tevez 18, 73, 80, Aguero 27, 75, Johnson 90). Att: 26,812
22	Wolves 0 Manchester City 2 (Aguero 27, Nasri 74). Att: 24,576
30	Manchester City 1 (Kompany 45) Manchester Utd 0. Att: 47,259

MAY 2012

| 6 | Newcastle 0 Manchester City 2 (Y Toure 70, 89). Att: 52,389 |
| 13 | Manchester City 3 (Zabaleta 39, Dzeko 90, Aguero 90) QPR 2 (Cisse 48, Mackie 66). Att: 48,000 (clinched title) |

QUOTE UNQUOTE

'A crazy finish for a crazy season' – **Roberto Mancini** after his Manchester City side scored twice in stoppage-time against Queens Park Rangers to win the Premier League.

'It wasn't our turn today' – **Sir Alex Ferguson** on Manchester United losing out on goal difference.

'If you had asked me three months ago if we would win this competition, I would have laughed' – **Frank Lampard**, Chelsea's captain-for-the-night on their Champions League triumph.

'The caretaker has taken care of everything' – **Clive Tyldesley**, ITV commentator, on Roberto Di Matteo's success as Chelsea's interim manager.

'Who knows, I could come back as manager one day – I'd cut the grass if they asked me to' – **Didier Drogba**, man of the match in Munich, after announcing his decision to leave the club.

'What happened to me is more than a miracle' – **Fabrice Muamba**, Bolton midfielder, on his recovery from a cardiac arrest suffered during the FA Cup tie with Tottenham atWhite Hart Lane.

'Their dedication, professionalism and expertise are amazing and I will forever be in their debt' – **Fabrice Muamba** on the medical staff who saved his life.

'I realise what I'm getting into. I'm not naïve. I have been in football a long while and know we're dealing with enormous expectations' – **Roy Hodgson** on being appointed England manager

'I wish him all the best. He's a great guy. I don't hold grudges' – **Harry Redknapp**, Tottenham manager, offers his congratulations to Hodgson.

'He's a good man and a good manager. It's important he's given a chance and I'm looking forward to working with him again' – **Steven Gerrard**, Liverpoool captain.

'I can't accept this. For me, he's finished' – **Roberto Mancini**, Manchester City manager, after Carlos Tevez refused to come off the bench and warm up against Bayern Munich.

'I didn't feel right to play. I have always done my best for the club. If he doesn't want me to play again, that's up to him' – **Carlos Tevez**.

'What happened with Carlos finished when he came back. Carlos is one of us' – **Roberto Mancini** after the Argentinian exile made his comeback against Chelsea.

END OF SEASON PLAY-OFFS

West Ham were third in the Championship and second best in the Play-off Final. But they passed the post first at Wembley, thanks to an 87th minute goal by Ricardo Vaz Te which secured an immediate return to the Premier League. Manager Sam Allardyce signed the Portuguese striker as a 17-year-old at Bolton in 2003 and brought him to Upton Park from Barnsley for £500,000 in the January transfer window – a fee dwarfed by the millions his goal was worth to the club. It was the 12th in 18 appearances and Allardyce rated him one of his best-ever acquisitions. The goal left Ian Holloway and his Blackpool players crestfallen at not making it back themselves at the first attempt. Holloway had set his heart on another tilt at the top flight. When Thomas Ince cancelled out Carlton Cole's strike, Blackpool looked to have seized the initiative. But they paid for several missed chances, notably one before Vaz Te struck, by Stephen Dobbie, a winner in the two previous years with Blackpool and then Swansea.

Goalkeepers took centre stage in the League One Final, with **Huddersfield** and Sheffield United goalless after 120 minutes and still locked in a marathon shoot-out. Alex Smithies put the 21st penalty past his opposite number Steve Simonsen, who then drove over the crossbar to hand Huddersfield victory by 8-7. They had lost the previous year to Peterborough and looked set for more disappointment when missing their first three spot-kicks. Nick Powell, 18, lit up the League Two Final with a spectacular volley to put youthful **Crewe** on the way to a 2-0 victory over Cheltenham, clinched by Byron Moore late on. Eight days after winning the FA Trophy, **York** returned to Wembley to defeat Luton in the Conference decider. They conceded a second minute goal to Andre Gray, but responded through Ashley Chambers and Matty Blair to regain a Football League place after an absence of eight years.

SEMI-FINALS, FIRST LEG

NPOWER CHAMPIONSHIP
Cardiff 0 **West Ham** 2 (Collison 9, 41). Att: 23,029. **Blackpool** 1 (Davies 45 og) **Birmingham** 0. Att: 13,832

LEAGUE ONE
Stevenage 0 **Sheffield Utd** 0. Att: 5,802. **MK Dons** 0 **Huddersfield** 2 (Rhodes 32, Hunt 73). Att: 11,893

LEAGUE TWO
Cheltenham 2 (McGlashan 27, Burgess 50) **Torquay** 0. Att: 5,273. **Crewe** 1 (Dugdale 49) **Southend** 0. Att: 7,221

BLUE SQUARE PREMIER LEAGUE
Luton 2 (Gray 22, Fleetwood 30) **Wrexham** 0. Att: 9,012. **York** 1 (Geohaghon 42 og) **Mansfield** 1 (Dyer 26). Att: 6,057

SEMI-FINALS, SECOND LEG

NPOWER CHAMPIONSHIP
Birmingham 2 (Zigic 64, Davies 73) **Blackpool** 2 (Dobbie 45, M Phillips 48). Att: 28,483 (Blackpool won 3-2 on agg). **West Ham** 3 (Nolan 15, Vaz Te 40, Maynard 90) **Cardiff** 0. Att: 34,682 (West Ham won 5-0 on agg)

LEAGUE ONE
Huddersfield 1 (Rhodes 18) **MK Dons** 2 (Powell 39, Smith 90). Att: 15,085 (Huddersfield won 3-2 on agg). **Sheffield Utd 1** (Porter 85) **Stevenage** 0. Att: 21,182 (Sheffield Utd won 1-0 on agg)

LEAGUE TWO
Southend 2 (Harris 64, Barker 88) **Crewe** 2 (Leitch-Smith 24, Clayton 86). Att: 8,190 (Crewe won 3-2 on agg). **Torquay** 1 (Atieno 85) **Cheltenham** 2 (McGlashan 75, Pack 87). Att: 3,606 (Cheltenham won 4-1 on agg)

BLUE SQUARE PREMIER LEAGUE
Mansfield 0 **York** 1 (Blair 111). Att: 7,295 (aet, York won 2-1 on agg). **Wrexham** 2 (Cieslewicz 63, Morrell 77) **Luton** 1 (Pilkington 25 pen). Att: 9,087 (Luton won 3-2 on agg)

FINALS

NPOWER CHAMPIONSHIP – MAY 19 2012
Blackpool 1 (Ince 48) **West Ham United** 2 (Cole 35, Vaz Te 87). Att: 78,523 (Wembley)
Blackpool (4-2-3-1): Gilks, Eardley, Baptiste, Evatt, Crainey, Angel (Dicko 90), Ferguson (capt), M Phillips, Dobbie (Bednar 90), Ince, K Phillips (Sylvestre 71). **Subs not used:** Cathcart, Southern. **Manager:** Ian Holloway
West Ham (4-4-2): Green, Demel (Faubert 57), Tomkins, Reid, Taylor, O'Neil (McCartney 53), Noble, Nolan (capt), Collison, Cole, Vaz Te. **Subs not used:** Henderson, Lansbury, Maynard. **Booked:** Vaz Te. **Manager:** Sam Allardyce
Referee: H Webb (Yorks). **Half-time:** 0-1

LEAGUE ONE – MAY 26 2012
Huddersfield Town 0 **Sheffield United** 0 (aet, Huddersfield won 8-7 on pens). Att: 52,100 (Wembley)
Huddersfield (4-4-2): Smithies, Woods, P Clarke (capt), Morrison, Hunt, Ward (Lee 98), Miller, Johnson, Higginbotham (Roberts 79) Novak (Arfield 110), Rhodes. **Subs not used:** Colgan, T Clarke. **Booked:** Higginbotham, Johnson. **Manager:** Simon Grayson
Sheffield United (4-4-2): Simonsen, Lowton, Maguire, Collins, Hill, Williamson, Montgomery (Taylor 119), Doyle (capt), Flynn (O'Halloran 108), Quinn, Cresswell (Porter 85). **Subs not used:** Howard, McAllister. **Booked:** Maguire. **Manager:** Danny Wilson
Referee: R East (Wilts)

LEAGUE TWO – MAY 27 2012
Cheltenham Town 0 **Crewe Alexandra** 2 (Powell 15, Moore 82). Att: 24,029 (Wembley)
Cheltenham (4-4-2): Brown, Jombati, Elliott, Bennett (capt), Garbutt, McGlashan, Summerfield, Pack (Penn 84), Mohamed, Burgess (Spencer 83), Goulding (Duffy 75). **Subs not used:** Lowe, Smikle. **Manager:** Mark Yates
Crewe (4-4-2): Phillips; Davis, Artell (capt), Dugdale, Mellor; Moore (Bell 89), Westwood, Murphy, Tootle; Leitch-Smith (Martin 85), Powell (Clayton 80). **Subs not used:** Bodin, Martin. **Manager:** Steve Davis
Referee: C Pawson (Yorks). **Half-time** 0-1

BLUE SQUARE PREMIER LEAGUE – MAY 20 2012
Luton Town 1 (Gray 71) **York City** 2 (Chambers 26, Blair 47). Att: 39,265 (Wembley)
Luton (4-3-3): Tyler, Osano, Pilkington (capt), Kovacs, Howells, Lawless, Watkins (Kissock 60), Keane, Willmott, Fleetwood (McAllister 60) (O'Connor 72), Gray. **Subs not used:** Gleeson, Blackett. **Booked:** Lawless. **Manager:** Paul Buckle
York (4-4-2): Ingham, Challinor (Brown 37), Smith (capt), Doig, Gibson, Meredith, Parslow, Oyebanjo, Chambers (Reed 77), Blair, Walker (McLaughlin 85). **Subs not used:** Musselwhite, Moke. **Booked:** Gibson. **Manager:** Gary Mills
Referee: J Simpson (Lancs). **Half-time:** 1-1

PLAY-OFF FINALS – HOME & AWAY

1987: Divs 1/2: Charlton beat Leeds 2-1 in replay (Birmingham) after 1-1 agg (1-0h, 0-1a). Charlton remained in Div 1 Losing semi-finalists: Ipswich and Oldham. **Divs 2/3: Swindon** beat Gillingham 2-0 in replay (Crystal Palace) after 2-2 agg (0-1a, 2-1h). Swindon promoted to Div 2. Losing semi-finalists: Sunderland and Wigan; Sunderland relegated to Div 3. **Divs 3/4: Aldershot** beat Wolves 3-0 on agg (2-0h, 1-0a) and promoted to Div 3. Losing semi-finalists: Bolton and Colchester; Bolton relegated to Div 4

1988: Divs 1/2: Middlesbrough beat Chelsea 2-1 on agg (2-0h, 0-1a) and promoted to Div 1; Chelsea relegated to Div 2. Losing semi-finalists: Blackburn and Bradford City. **Divs 2/3: Walsall** beat Bristol City 4-0 in replay (h) after 3-3 agg (3-1a, 0-2h) and promoted to Div 2. Losing semi-finalists: Sheffield Utd and Notts County; Sheffield Utd relegated to Div 3. **Divs 3/4: Swansea** beat Torquay 5-4 on agg (2-1h, 3-3a) and promoted to Div 3. Losing semi-finalists: Rotherham and Scunthorpe.; Rotherham relegated to Div 4

1989: Div 2: Crystal Palace beat Blackburn 4-3 on agg (1-3a, 3-0h). Losing semi-finalists: Watford and Swindon. **Div 3: Port Vale** beat Bristol Rovers 2-1 on agg (1-1a, 1-0h). Losing semi-finalists: Fulham and Preston **Div.4: Leyton Orient** beat Wrexham 2-1 on agg (0-0a, 2-1h). Losing semi-finalists: Scarborough and Scunthorpe

PLAY-OFF FINALS AT WEMBLEY

1990: Div 2: Swindon 1 Sunderland 0 (att: 72,873). Swindon promoted, then demoted for financial irregularities; Sunderland promoted. Losing semi-finalists: Blackburn and Newcastle Utd **Div 3: Notts County** 2 Tranmere 0 (att: 29,252). Losing semi-finalists: Bolton and Bury. **Div 4: Cambridge Utd** 1 Chesterfield 0 (att: 26,404). Losing semi-finalists: Maidstone and Stockport County

1991: Div 2: Notts County 3 Brighton 1 (att: 59,940). Losing semi-finalists: Middlesbrough and Millwall. **Div 3: Tranmere** 1 Bolton 0 (att: 30,217). Losing semi-finalists: Brentford and Bury. **Div 4: Torquay** 2 Blackpool 2 – Torquay won 5-4 on pens (att: 21,615). Losing semi-finalists: Burnley and Scunthorpe

1992: Div 2: Blackburn 1 Leicester 0 (att: 68,147). Losing semi-finalists: Derby and Cambridge Utd. **Div 3: Peterborough** 2 Stockport 1 (att: 35,087). Losing semi-finalists: Huddersfield and Stoke. **Div 4: Blackpool** 1 Scunthorpe 1 aet, Blackpool won 4-3 on pens (att: 22,741). Losing semi-finalists: Barnet and Crewe

1993: Div 1: Swindon 4 Leicester 3 (att: 73,802). Losing semi-finalists: Portsmouth and Tranmere. **Div 2: WBA** 3 Port Vale 0 (att: 53,471). Losing semi-finalists: Stockport and Swansea. **Div 3: York** 1 Crewe 1 aet, York won 5-3 on pens (att: 22,416). Losing semi-finalists: Bury and Walsall

1994: Div 1: Leicester 2 Derby 1 (att: 73,671). Losing semi-finalists: Millwall and Tranmere. **Div 2: Burnley** 2 Stockport 1 (att: 44,806). Losing semi-finalists: Plymouth Argyle and York. **Div 3: Wycombe** 4 Preston 2 (att: 40,109). Losing semi-finalists: Carlisle and Torquay

1995: Div 1: Bolton 4 Reading 3 (att: 64,107). Losing semi-finalists: Tranmere and Wolves. **Div 2: Huddersfield** 2 Bristol Rov 1 (att: 59,175). Losing semi-finalists: Brentford and Crewe. **Div 3: Chesterfield** 2 Bury 0 (att: 22,814). Losing semi-finalists: Mansfield and Preston

1996: Div 1: Leicester 2 Crystal Palace 1 aet (att: 73,573). Losing semi-finalists: Charlton and Stoke. **Div 2: Bradford City** 2 Notts Co 0 (att: 39,972). Losing semi-finalists: Blackpool and Crewe. **Div 3: Plymouth Argyle** 1 Darlington 0 (att: 43,431). Losing semi-finalists: Colchester and Hereford

1997: Div 1: Crystal Palace 1 Sheffield Utd 0 (att: 64,383). Losing semi-finalists: Ipswich and Wolves. **Div 2: Crewe** 1 Brentford 0 (att: 34,149). Losing semi-finalists: Bristol City and Luton. **Div 3: Northampton** 1 Swansea 0 (att: 46,804). Losing semi-finalists: Cardiff and Chester

1998: Div 1: Charlton 4 Sunderland 4 aet, Charlton won 7-6 on pens (att: 77, 739). Losing semi-finalists: Ipswich and Sheffield Utd. **Div 2: Grimsby** 1 Northampton 0 (att: 62,988). Losing semi-finalists: Bristol Rov and Fulham. **Div 3: Colchester** 1 Torquay 0 (att: 19,486). Losing semi-finalists: Barnet and Scarborough

1999: Div 1: Watford 2 Bolton 0 (att: 70,343). Losing semi-finalists: Ipswich and Birmingham. **Div 2: Manchester City** 2 Gillingham 2 aet, Manchester City won 3-1 on pens (att: 76,935). Losing semi-finalists: Preston and Wigan. **Div 3: Scunthorpe** 1 Leyton Orient 0 (att: 36,985). Losing semi-finalists: Rotherham and Swansea

2000: Div 1: Ipswich 4 Barnsley 2 (att: 73,427). Losing semi-finalists: Birmingham and Bolton. **Div 2: Gillingham** 3 Wigan 2 aet (att: 53,764). Losing semi-finalists: Millwall and Stoke. **Div 3: Peterborough** 1 Darlington 0 (att: 33,383). Losing semi-finalists: Barnet and Hartlepool

PLAY-OFF FINALS AT MILLENNIUM STADIUM

2001: Div 1: Bolton 3 Preston 0 (att: 54,328). Losing semi-finalists: Birmingham and WBA. **Div 2: Walsall** 3 Reading 2 aet (att: 50,496). Losing semi-finalists: Stoke and Wigan. **Div 3: Blackpool** 4 Leyton Orient 2 (att: 23,600). Losing semi-finalists: Hartlepool and Hull.

2002: Div 1: Birmingham 1 Norwich 1 aet, Birmingham won 4-2 on pens, (att: 71,597). Losing semi-finalists: Millwall and Wolves. **Div 2: Stoke** 2 Brentford 0 (att: 42,523). Losing semi-finalists: Cardiff and Huddersfield. **Div 3: Cheltenham** 3 Rushden & Diamonds 1 (att: 24,368). Losing semi-finalists: Hartlepool and Rochdale

2003: Div 1: Wolves 3 Sheffield Utd 0 (att: 69,473). Losing semi-finalists: Nott'm Forest and Reading. **Div 2: Cardiff** 1 QPR. 0 aet (att: 66,096). Losing semi-finalists: Bristol City and Oldham. **Div 3: Bournemouth** 5 Lincoln 2 (att: 32,148). Losing semi-finalists: Bury and Scunthorpe

2004: Div 1: Crystal Palace 1 West Ham 0 (att: 72,523). Losing semi-finalists: Ipswich and Sunderland. **Div 2: Brighton** 1 Bristol City 0 (att: 65,167). Losing semi-finalists: Hartlepool and Swindon. **Div 3: Huddersfield** 0 Mansfield 0 aet, Huddersfield won 4-1 on pens (att: 37,298). Losing semi-finalists: Lincoln and Northampton

2005: Championship: West Ham 1 Preston 0 (att: 70,275). Losing semifinalists: Derby Co and Ipswich. **League 1: Sheffield Wed** 4 Hartlepool 2 aet (att: 59,808). Losing semi-finalists: Brentford and Tranmere **League 2: Southend** 2 Lincoln 0 aet (att: 19532). Losing semi-finalists: Macclesfield and Northampton

2006: Championship: Watford 3 Leeds 0 (att: 64,736). Losing semi-finalists: Crystal Palace and Preston. **League 1: Barnsley** 2 Swansea 2 aet (att: 55,419), Barnsley won 4-3 on pens. Losing semi-finalists: Huddersfield and Brentford. **League 2: Cheltenham** 1 Grimsby 0 (att: 29,196). Losing semi-finalists: Wycombe and Lincoln

PLAY-OFF FINALS AT WEMBLEY

2007: Championship: Derby 1 WBA 0 (att: 74,993). Losing semi-finalists: Southampton and Wolves. **League 1: Blackpool** 2 Yeovil 0 (att: 59,313). Losing semi-finalists: Nottm Forest and Oldham. **League 2: Bristol Rov** 3 Shrewsbury 1 (att: 61,589). Losing semi-finalists: Lincoln and MK Dons

2008: Championship: Hull 1 Bristol City 0 (att: 86,703). Losing semi-finalists: Crystal Palace and Watford. **League 1: Doncaster** 1 Leeds 0 (att: 75,132). Losing semi-finalists: Carlisle and Southend. **League 2: Stockport** 3 Rochdale 2 (att: 35,715). Losing semi-finalists: Darlington and Wycombe

2009: Championship: Burnley 1 Sheffield Utd 0 (att: 80,518). Losing semi-finalists: Preston and Reading. **League 1: Scunthorpe** 3 Millwall 2 (att: 59,661). Losing semi-finalists: Leeds and MK Dons. **League 2: Gillingham** 1 Shrewsbury 0 (att: 53,706). Losing semi-finalists: Bury and Rochdale

2010: Championship: Blackpool 3 Cardiff 2 (att: 82,244). Losing semi-finalists: Leicester and Nottm Forest. **League 1: Millwall** 1 Swindon 0 (att:73,108). Losing semi-finalists: Charlton and Huddersfield. **League 2: Dagenham & Redbridge** 3 Rotherham 2 (att: 32,054). Losing semi-finalists: Aldershot and Morecambe
2011: Championship: Swansea 4 Reading 2 (att: 86,581). Losing semi-finalists: Cardiff and Nottm Forest. **League 1: Peterborough** 3 Huddersfield 0 (Old Trafford, att:48,410). Losing semi-finalists: Bournemouth and MK Dons. **League 2: Stevenage** 1 Torquay 0 (Old Trafford, att: 11,484. Losing semi-finalists: Accrington and Shrewsbury

HISTORY OF THE PLAY-OFFS

Play-off matches were introduced by the Football League to decide final promotion and relegation issues at the end of season 1986-87. A similar series styled 'Test Matches' had operated between Divisions One and Two for six seasons from 1893-98, and was abolished when both divisions were increased from 16 to 18 clubs.

Eighty-eight years later, the play-offs were back in vogue. In the first three seasons (1987-88-89), the Finals were played home-and-away, and since they were made one-off matches in 1990, they have featured regularly in Wembley's spring calendar, until the old stadium closed its doors and the action switched to the Millennium Stadium in Cardiff in 2001.

Through the years, these have been the ups and downs of the play-offs:

1987: Initially, the 12 clubs involved comprised the one that finished directly above those relegated in Divisions One, Two and Three and the three who followed the sides automatically promoted in each section. Two of the home-and-away Finals went to neutral-ground replays, in which **Charlton** clung to First Division status by denying Leeds promotion while **Swindon** beat Gillingham to complete their climb from Fourth Division to Second in successive seasons, via the play-offs, Sunderland fell into the Third and Bolton into Division Four, both for the first time. **Aldershot** went up after finishing only sixth in Division Four; in their Final, they beat Wolves, who had finished nine points higher and missed automatic promotion by one point.

1988: Chelsea were relegated from the First Division after losing on aggregate to **Middlesbrough**, who had finished third in Division Two. So Middlesbrough, managed by Bruce Rioch, completed the rise from Third Division to First in successive seasons, only two years after their very existence had been threatened by the bailiffs. Also promoted via the play-offs: **Walsall** from Division Three and **Swansea** from the Fourth. Relegated, besides Chelsea: Sheffield Utd (to Division Three) and Rotherham (to Division Four).

1989: After two seasons of promotion-relegation play-offs, the system was changed to involve the four clubs who had just missed automatic promotion. That format has remained. Steve Coppell's **Crystal Palace**, third in Division Two, returned to the top flight after eight years, beating Blackburn 4-3 on aggregate after extra time. Similarly, **Port Vale** confirmed third place in Division Three with promotion via the play-offs. For **Leyton Orient**, promotion seemed out of the question in Division Four when they stood 15th on March 1. But eight wins and a draw in the last nine home games swept them to sixth in the final table, and two more home victories in the play-offs completed their season in triumph.

1990: The play-off Finals now moved to Wembley over three days of the Spring Holiday weekend. On successive afternoons, **Cambridge Utd** won promotion from Division Four and **Notts Co** from the Third. Then, on Bank Holiday Monday, the biggest crowd for years at a Football League fixture (72,873) saw Ossie Ardiles' **Swindon** beat Sunderland 1-0 to reach the First Division for the first time. A few weeks later, however, Wembley losers **Sunderland** were promoted instead, by default; Swindon were found guilty of "financial irregularities" and stayed in Division Two.

1991: Again, the season's biggest League crowd (59,940) gathered at Wembley for the First Division Final in which **Notts Co** (having missed promotion by one point) still fulfilled their ambition, beating Brighton 3-1. In successive years, County had climbed from Third Division to First via the play-offs – the first club to achieve double promotion by this route. Bolton were denied automatic promotion in Division Three on goal difference, and lost at Wembley to an extra-time goal by **Tranmere**. The Fourth Division Final made history, with Blackpool beaten 5-4 on penalties by **Torquay** – first instance of promotion being decided by a shoot-out. In the table, Blackpool had finished seven points ahead of Torquay.

1992: Wembley on that Spring Bank Holiday was the turning point in the history of **Blackburn**. Bolstered by Kenny Dalglish's return to management and owner Jack Walker's millions, they beat Leicester 1-0 by Mike Newell's 45th-minute penalty to achieve their objective – a place in the new Premier League. Newell, who also missed a second-half penalty, had recovered from a broken leg just in time for the play-offs. In the Fourth Division Final **Blackpool** (denied by penalties the previous year) this time won a shoot-out 4-3 against Scunthorpe., who were unlucky in the play-offs for the fourth time in five years. **Peterborough** climbed out of the Third Division for the first time, beating Stockport County 2-1 at Wembley.

1993: The crowd of 73,802 at Wembley to see **Swindon** beat Leicester 4-3 in the First Division Final was 11,000 bigger than that for the FA Cup Final replay between Arsenal and Sheffield Wed Leicester rallied from three down to 3-3 before Paul Bodin's late penalty wiped away **Swindon**'s bitter memories of three years earlier, when they were denied promotion after winning at Wembley. In the Third Division Final, **York** beat Crewe 5-3 in a shoot-out after a 1-1 draw, and in the Second Division decider, **WBA** beat Port Vale 3-0. That was tough on Vale, who had finished third in the table with 89 points – the highest total never to earn promotion in any division. They had beaten Albion twice in the League, too.

1994: Wembley's record turn-out of 158,586 spectators at the three Finals started with a crowd of 40,109 to see Martin O'Neill's **Wycombe** beat Preston 4-2. They thus climbed from Conference to Second Division with successive promotions. **Burnley's** 2-1 victory in the Second Division Final was marred by the sending-off of two Stockport players, and in the First Division decider **Leicester** came from behind to beat Derby Co and and the worst Wembley record of any club. They had lost on all six previous appearances there – four times in the FA Cup Final and in the play-offs of 1992 and 1993.

1995: Two months after losing the Coca-Cola Cup Final to Liverpool, Bruce Rioch's **Bolton** were back at Wembley for the First Division play-off Final. From two goals down to Reading in front of a crowd of 64,107, they returned to the top company after 15 years, winning 4-3 with two extra-time goals. **Huddersfield** ended the first season at their new £15m. ground with promotion to the First Division via a 2-1 victory against Bristol Rov – manager Neil Warnock's third play-off success (after two with Notts Co). Of the three clubs who missed automatic promotion by one place, only **Chesterfield** achieved it in the play-offs, comfortably beating Bury 2-0.

1996: Under new manager Martin O'Neill (a Wembley play-off winner with Wycombe in 1994), **Leicester** returned to the Premiership a year after leaving it. They had finished fifth in the table, but in the Final came from behind to beat third-placed Crystal Palace by Steve Claridge's shot in the last seconds of extra time. In the Second Division **Bradford City** came sixth, nine points behind Blackpool (3rd), but beat them (from two down in the semi-final first leg) and then clinched promotion by 2-0 v Notts County at Wembley. It was City's greatest day since they won the Cup in 1911. **Plymouth Argyle** beat Darlington in the Third Division Final to earn promotion a year after being relegated. It was manager Neil Warnock's fourth play-off triumph in seven seasons after two with Notts County (1990 and 1991) and a third with Huddersfield in 1995.

1997: High drama at Wembley as **Crystal Palace** left it late against Sheffield Utd in the First Division play-off final. The match was scoreless until the last 10 seconds when David Hopkin lobbed Blades' keeper Simon Tracey from 25 yards to send the Eagles back to the Premiership after two seasons of Nationwide action. In the Second Division play-off final, **Crewe** beat

Brentford 1-0 courtesy of a Shaun Smith goal. **Northampton** celebrated their first Wembley appearance with a 1-0 victory over Swansea thanks to John Frain's injury-time free-kick in the Third Division play-off final.

1998: In one of the finest games ever seen at Wembley, **Charlton** eventually triumphed 7-6 on penalties over Sunderland. For Charlton, Wearside-born Clive Mendonca scored a hat-trick and Richard Rufus his first career goal in a match that lurched between joy and despair for both sides as it ended 4-4. Sunderland defender Michael Gray's superb performance ill-deserved to end with his weakly struck spot kick being saved by Sasa Ilic. In the Third Division, the penalty spot also had a role to play, as **Colchester**'s David Gregory scored the only goal to defeat Torquay, while in the Second Division a Kevin Donovan goal gave **Grimsby** victory over Northampton.

1999: Elton John, watching via a personal satellite link in Seattle, saw his **Watford** side overcome Bolton 2-0 to reach the Premiership. Against technically superior opponents, Watford prevailed with application and teamwork. They also gave Bolton a lesson in finishing through match-winners by Nick Wright and Allan Smart. **Manchester City** staged a remarkable comeback to win the Second Division Final after trailing to goals by Carl Asaba and Robert Taylor for Gillingham. Kevin Horlock and Paul Dickov scored in stoppage time and City went on to win on penalties. A goal by Spaniard Alex Calvo-Garcia earned **Scunthorpe** a 1-0 success against Leyton Orient in the Third Division Final.

2000: After three successive play-off failures, **Ipswich** finally secured a place in the Premiership. They overcame the injury loss of leading scorer David Johnson to beat Barnsley 4-2 with goals by 36-year-old Tony Mowbray, Marcus Stewart and substitutes Richard Naylor and Martijn Reuser. With six minutes left of extra-time in the Second Division Final, **Gillingham** trailed Wigan 2-1. But headers by 38-year-old player-coach Steve Butler and fellow substitute Andy Thomson gave them a 3-2 victory. Andy Clarke, approaching his 33rd birthday, scored the only goal of the Third Division decider for **Peterborough** against Darlington.

2001: Bolton, unsuccessful play-off contenders in the two previous seasons, made no mistake at the third attempt. They flourished in the new surroundings of the Millennium Stadium to beat Preston 3-0 with goals by Gareth Farrelly, Michael Ricketts - his 24th of the season - and Ricardo Gardner to reach the Premiership. **Walsall**, relegated 12 months earlier, scored twice in a three-minute spell of extra time to win 3-2 against Reading in the Second Division Final, while **Blackpool** capped a marked improvement in the second half of the season by overcoming Leyton Orient 4-2 in the Third Division Final.

2002: Holding their nerve to win a penalty shoot-out 4-2, **Birmingham** wiped away the memory of three successive defeats in the semi-finals of the play-offs to return to the top division after an absence of 16 years. Substitute Darren Carter completed a fairy-tale first season as a professional by scoring the fourth spot-kick against Norwich. **Stoke** became the first successful team to come from the south dressing room in 12 finals since football was adopted by the home of Welsh rugby, beating Brentford 2-0 in the Second Division Final with Deon Burton's strike and a Ben Burgess own goal. Julian Alsop's 26th goal of the season helped **Cheltenham** defeat League newcomers Rushden & Diamonds 3-1 in the Third Division decider.

2003: Wolves benefactor Sir Jack Hayward finally saw his £60m investment pay dividends when the club he first supported as a boy returned to the top flight after an absence of 19 years by beating Sheffield Utd 3-0. It was also a moment to savour for manager Dave Jones, who was forced to leave his previous club Southampton because of child abuse allegations, which were later found to be groundless. **Cardiff**, away from the game's second tier for 18 years, returned with an extra-time winner from substitute Andy Campbell against QPR after a goalless 90 minutes in the Division Two Final. **Bournemouth**, relegated 12 months earlier, became the first team to score five in the end-of-season deciders, beating Lincoln 5-2 in the Division Three Final.

2004: Three tight, tense Finals produced only two goals, the lowest number since the Play-offs were introduced. One of them, scored by Neil Shipperley, gave **Crystal Palace** victory over West Ham, the much-travelled striker tapping in a rebound after Stephen Bywater parried Andy Johnson's shot. It completed a remarkable transformation for Crystal Palace, who were 19th in the table when Iain Dowie left Oldham to become their manager. **Brighton** made an immediate return to Division One in a poor game against Bristol City which looked set for extra-time until Leon Knight netted his 27th goal of the campaign from the penalty spot after 84 minutes. **Huddersfield** also went back up at the first attempt, winning the Division Three Final in a penalty shoot-out after a goalless 120 minutes against Mansfield.

2005: Goals were few and far between for Bobby Zamora during **West Ham**'s Championship season – but what a difference in the Play-offs. The former Brighton and Tottenham striker scored three times in the 4-2 aggregate win over Ipswich in the semi-finals and was on the mark again with the only goal against Preston at the Millennium Stadium. **Sheffield Wed** were eight minute away from defeat against Hartlepool in the League One decider when Steven MacLean made it 2-2 from the penalty spot and they went on to win 4-2 in extra-time. **Southend**, edged out of an automatic promotion place, won the League Two Final 2-0 against Lincoln, Freddy Eastwood scoring their first in extra-time and making the second for Duncan Jupp. **Carlisle** beat Stevenage 1-0 with a goal by Peter Murphy in the Conference Final to regain their League place 12 months after being relegated.

2006: From the moment Marlon King scored his 22nd goal of the season to set up a 3-0 win over Crystal Palace in the semi-final first leg, **Watford** had the conviction of a team going places. Sure enough, they went on to beat Leeds just as comfortably in the final. Jay DeMerit, who was playing non-league football 18 months earlier, headed his side in front. James Chambers fired in a shot that hit a post and went in off goalkeeper Neil Sullivan. Then Darius Henderson put away a penalty after King was brought down by Shaun Derry, the man whose tackle had ended Boothroyd's playing career at the age of 26. **Barnsley** beat Swansea on penalties in the League One Final, Nick Colgan making the vital save from Alan Tate, while Steve Guinan's goal earned **Cheltenham** a 1-0 win over Grimsby in the League Two Final. **Hereford** returned to the Football League after a nine-year absence with Ryan Green's extra-time winner against Halifax in the Conference Final.

2007: Record crowds, plenty of goals and a return to Wembley for the finals made for some eventful and entertaining matches. Stephen Pearson, signed from Celtic for £650,000 in the January transfer window, took **Derby** back to the Premier League after an absence of five seasons with a 61st minute winner, his first goal for the club, against accounted for West Bromwich Albion. It was third time lucky for manager Billy Davies, who had led Preston into the play-offs, without success, in the two previous seasons. **Blackpool** claimed a place in the game's second tier for the first time for 30 years by beating Yeovil 2-0 – their tenth successive victory in a remarkable end-of-season run. Richard Walker took his tally for the season to 23 with two goals for **Bristol Rov**, who beat Shrewsbury 3-1 in the League Two Final. Sammy McIlroy, who led Macclesfield into the league in 1997, saw his Morecambe side fall behind in the Conference Final against Exeter, but they recovered to win 2-1.

2008: Wembley has produced some unlikely heroes down the years, but rarely one to match 39-year-old Dean Windass. The **Hull** striker took his home-town club into the top-flight for the first time with the only goal of the Championship Final against Bristol City – and it was a goal fit to grace any game. In front of a record crowd for the final of 86,703, Fraizer Campbell, his 20-year-old partner up front, picked out Windass on the edge of the penalty box and a sweetly-struck volley flew into the net. **Doncaster**, who like Hull faced an uncertain future a few years earlier, beat Leeds 1-0 in the League One Final with a header by James Hayer from Brian Stock's corner. Jim Gannon had lost four Wembley finals with **Stockport** as a player, but his first as manager brought a 3-2 win against Rochdale in the League Two Final by goals by Anthony Pilkington and Liam Dickinson and a Nathan Stanton own goal. Exeter's 1-0 win over Cambridge United in the Conference Final took them back into the Football League after an absence of five years.

2009: Delight for Burnley, back in the big time after 33 years thanks to a fine goal from 20 yards by Wade Elliott, and for their town which became the smallest to host Premier League football. Despair for Sheffield Utd, whose bid to regain a top-flight place ended with two players, Jamie Ward and Lee Hendrie, sent off by referee Mike Dean. Martyn Woolford capped a man-of-the-match performance with an 85th minute winner for Scunthorpe, who beat Millwall 3-2 to make an immediate return to the Championship, Matt Sparrow having scored their first two goals. Gillingham also went back up at the first attempt, beating Shrewsbury with Simeon Jackson's header seconds from the end of normal time in the League Two Final. Torquay returned to the Football League after a two-year absence by beating Cambridge United 2-0 in the Conference Final.

2010: Blackpool, under the eccentric yet shrewd Ian Holloway, claimed the big prize two years almost to the day after the manager was sacked from his previous job at Leicester. On a scorching afternoon, with temperatures reaching 106 degrees, they twice came back from a goal down to draw level against Cardiff through Charlie Adam and Gary Taylor-Fletcher, then scored what proved to be the winner through Brett Ormerod at the end of a pulsating first half. **Millwall,** beaten in five previous play-offs, reached the Championship with the only goal of the game against Swindon from captain Paul Robinson. **Dagenham & Redbridge** defeated Rotherham 3-2 in the League Two Final, Jon Nurse scoring the winner 20 minutes from the end. **Oxford** returned to the Football League after an absence of four years with a 3-1 over York in the Conference Final.

2011: Scott Sinclair scored a hat-trick as **Swansea** reached the top flight, just eight years after almost going out of the Football League. Two of his goals came from the penalty spot as Reading were beaten 4-2 in the Championship Final, with Stephen Dobbie netting their other goal. The day after his father's side lost to Barcelona in the Champions League Final, Darren Ferguson led **Peterborough** back to the Championship at the first attempt with goals by Tommy Rowe, Craig Mackail-Smith and Grant McCann in the final 12 minutes against Huddersfield. John Mousinho scored the only one of the League Two Final for **Stevenage,** who won a second successive promotion by beating Torquay. **AFC Wimbledon,** formed by supporters in 2002 after the former FA Cup-winning club relocated to Milton Keynes, completed their rise from the Combined Counties to the Football League by winning a penalty shoot-out against Luton after a goalless draw in the Conference Final.

LEAGUE PLAY-OFF CROWDS YEAR BY YEAR

Year	Matches	Agg. Att	Year	Matches	Agg. Att
1987	20	310,000	2000	15	333,999
1988	19	305,817	2001	15	317,745
1989	18	234,393	2002	15	327,894
1990	15	291,428	2003	15	374,461
1991	15	266,442	2004	15	388,675
1992	15	277,684	2005	15	353,330
1993	15	319,907	2006	15	340,804
1994	15	314,817	2007	15	405,278 (record)
1995	15	295,317	2008	15	382,032
1996	15	308,515	2009	15	380,329
1997	15	309,085	2010	15	370,055
1998	15	320,795	2011	15	310,998
1999	15	372,969	2012	15	332,930

NATIONAL REFEREES

Adcock, James (Derbys)
Atkinson, Martin (Yorks)
Attwell, Stuart (Warwicks)
Bates, Tony (Staffs)
Berry, Carl (Surrey)
Booth, Russell (Notts)
Boyeson, Carl (Yorks)
Brown, Mark (Yorks)
Clattenburg, Mark (Co Durham)
Collins, Lee (Surrey)
Coote, David (Notts)
Deadman, Darren (Cambs)
Dean, Mike (Wirral)
Dowd, Phil (Staffs)
Drysdale, Darren (Lincs)
D'Urso, Andy (Essex)
East, Roger (Wilts)
Eltringham, Geoff (Tyne & Wear)
Evans, Karl (Lancs)
Foster, David (Tyne & Wear)
Foy, Chris (Merseyside)
Friend, Kevin (Leics)
Gibbs, Phil (West Mids)
Graham, Fred (Essex)
Haines, Andy (Tyne & Wear)
Hall, Andy (West Mids)
Halsey, Mark (Lancs)
Haywood, Mark (Cheshire)
Hegley, Grant (Herts)
Hill, Keith (Herts)
Hooper, Simon (Wilts)
Horwood, Graham (Beds)
Ilderton, Eddie (Tyne & Wear)
Jones, Mike (Cheshire)
Kettle, Trevor (Rutland)
Langford, Oliver (West Mids)
Lewis, Rob (Shrops)
Linington, James (IOW)
Madley, Andrew (Yorks)
Madley, Bobby (Yorks)
Malone, Brendan (Wilts)

Marriner, Andre (West Mids)
Mason, Lee (Lancs)
Mathieson, Scott (Cheshire)
McDermid, Danny (Hants)
Miller, Nigel (Co Durham)
Miller, Pat (Beds)
Mohareb, Dean (Cheshire)
Moss, Jon (Yorks)
Naylor, Michael (Yorks)
Oliver, Michael (Northumberland)
Pawson, Craig (Yorks)
Penn, Andy (West Mids)
Phillips, David (Sussex)
Probert, Lee (Wilts)
Quinn, Peter (Cleveland)
Rushton, Steve (Staffs)
Russell, Mick (Herts)
Salisbury, Graham (Lancs)
Sarginson, Chris (Staffs)
Scott, Graham (Oxon)
Sheldrake, Darren (Surrey)
Shoebridge, Rob (Derbys)
Stroud, Keith (Hants)
Sutton, Gary (Lincs)
Swarbrick, Neil (Lancs)
Tanner, Steve (Somerset))
Taylor, Anthony (Cheshire)
Tierney, Paul (Lancs)
Walton, Peter (Northants)
Ward, Gavin (Surrey)
Waugh, Jock (Yorks)
Webb, David (Co Durham)
Webb, Howard (Yorks)
Webster, Colin (Tyne & Wear)
Whitestone, Dean (Northants)
Williamson, Iain (Berks)
Woolmer, Andy (Northants)
Wright, Kevin (Cambs)

ENGLISH HONOURS LIST

FA PREMIER LEAGUE

	First	Pts	Second	Pts	Third	Pts
1992–3a	Manchester Utd	84	Aston Villa	74	Norwich	72
1993–4a	Manchester Utd	92	Blackburn	84	Newcastle	77
1994–5a	Blackburn	89	Manchester Utd	88	Nottm Forest	77
1995–6b	Manchester Utd	82	Newcastle	78	Liverpool	71
1996–7b	Manchester Utd	75	Newcastle	68	Arsenal	68
1997–8b	Arsenal	78	Manchester Utd	77	Liverpool	65
1998–9b	Manchester Utd	79	Arsenal	78	Chelsea	75
1999–00b	Manchester Utd	91	Arsenal	73	Leeds	69
2000–01b	Manchester Utd	80	Arsenal	70	Liverpool	69
2001–02b	Arsenal	87	Liverpool	80	Manchester Utd	77
2002–03b	Manchester Utd	83	Arsenal	78	Newcastle	69
2003–04b	Arsenal	90	Chelsea	79	Manchester Utd	75
2004–05b	Chelsea	95	Arsenal	83	Manchester Utd	77
2005–06b	Chelsea	91	Manchester Utd	83	Liverpool	82
2006–07b	Manchester Utd	89	Chelsea	83	Liverpool	68
2007–08b	Manchester Utd	87	Chelsea	85	Arsenal	83
2008–09b	Manchester Utd	90	Liverpool	86	Chelsea	83
2009–10b	Chelsea	86	Manchester Utd	85	Arsenal	75
2010–11b	Manchester Utd	80	Chelsea	71	Manchester City	71
2011–12b	*Manchester City	89	Manchester Ud	89	Arsenal	70

* won on goal difference. Maximum points: a, 126; b, 114

FOOTBALL LEAGUE

FIRST DIVISION

1992–3	Newcastle	96	West Ham	88	††Portsmouth	88
1993–4	Crystal Palace	90	Nottm Forest	83	††Millwall	74
1994–5	Middlesbrough	82	††Reading	79	Bolton	77
1995–6	Sunderland	83	Derby	79	††Crystal Palace	75
1996–7	Bolton	98	Barnsley	80	††Wolves	76
1997–8	Nottm Forest	94	Middlesbrough	91	††Sunderland	90
1998–9	Sunderland	105	Bradford City	87	††Ipswich	86
1999–00	Charlton	91	Manchester City	89	Ipswich	87
2000–01	Fulham	101	Blackburn	91	Bolton	87
2001–02	Manchester City	99	WBA	89	††Wolves	86
2002–03	Portsmouth	98	Leicester	92	††Sheffield Utd	80
2003–04	Norwich	94	WBA	86	††Sunderland	79

CHAMPIONSHIP

2004–05	Sunderland	94	Wigan	87	††Ipswich	85
2005–06	Reading	106	Sheffield Utd	90	Watford	81
2006–07	Sunderland	88	Birmingham	86	Derby	84
2007–08	WBA	81	Stoke	79	Hull	75
2008–09	Wolves	90	Birmingham	83	††Sheffield Utd	80
2009–10	Newcastle	102	WBA	91	††Nottm Forest	79
2010–11	QPR	88	Norwich	84	Swansea	80
2011–12	Reading	89	Southampton	88	West Ham	86

Maximum points: 138 ††Not promoted after play–offs

SECOND DIVISION

1992–3	Stoke	93	Bolton	90	††Port Vale	89

1993–4	Reading	89	Port Vale	88	††Plymouth Argyle	85
1994–5	Birmingham	89	††Brentford	85	††Crewe	83
1995–6	Swindon	92	Oxford Utd	83	††Blackpool	82
1996–7	Bury	84	Stockport	82	††Luton	78
1997–8	Watford	88	Bristol City	85	Grimsby	72
1998–9	Fulham	101	Walsall	87	Manchester City	82
1999–00	Preston	95	Burnley	88	Gillingham	85
2000–01	Millwall	93	Rotherham	91	††Reading	86
2001–02	Brighton	90	Reading	84	††Brentford	83
2002–03	Wigan	100	Crewe	86	††Bristol City	83
2003–04	Plymouth Argyle	90	QPR	83	††Bristol City	82

LEAGUE ONE

2004–05	Luton	98	Hull	86	††Tranmere	79
2005–06	Southend	82	Colchester	79	††Brentford	76
2006–07	Scunthorpe	91	Bristol City	85	Blackpool	83
2007–08	Swansea	92	Nottm Forest	82	Doncaster	80
2008-09	Leicester	96	Peterborough	89	††MK Dons	87
2009–10	Norwich	95	Leeds	86	Millwall	85
2010–11	Brighton	95	Southampton	92	††Huddersfield	87
2011–12	Charlton	101	Sheffield Wed	93	††Sheffield Utd	90

Maximum points: 138 †† Not promoted after play–offs

THIRD DIVISION

1992–3a	Cardiff	83	Wrexham	80	Barnet	79
1993–4a	Shrewsbury	79	Chester	74	Crewe	73
1994–5a	Carlisle	91	Walsall	83	Chesterfield	81
1995–6b	Preston	86	Gillingham	83	Bury	79
1996–7b	Wigan	87	Fulham	87	Carlisle	84
1997–8b	Notts Co	99	Macclesfield	82	Lincoln	75
1998–9b	Brentford	85	Cambridge Utd	81	Cardiff	80
1999–00b	Swansea	85	Rotherham	84	Northampton	82
2000–01b	Brighton	92	Cardiff	82	*Chesterfield	80
2001–02b	Plymouth Argyle	102	Luton	97	Mansfield	79
2002–03b	Rushden & D	87	Hartlepool Utd	85	Wrexham	84
2003–04b	Doncaster	92	Hull	88	Torquay	81

* Deducted 9 points for financial irregularities

LEAGUE TWO

2004–05b	Yeovil	83	Scunthorpe	80	Swansea	80
2005–06b	Carlisle	86	Northampton	83	Leyton Orient	81
2006–07b	Walsall	89	Hartlepool	88	Swindon	85
2007-08b	MK Dons	97	Peterborough	92	Hereford	88
2008-09b	Brentford	85	Exeter	79	Wycombe	78
2009–10b	Notts Co	93	Bournemouth	83	Rochdale	82
2010–11b	Chesterfield	86	Bury	81	Wycombe	80
2011–12b	Swindon	93	Shrewsbury	88	Crawley	84

Maximum points: a, 126; b, 138;

FOOTBALL LEAGUE 1888–1992

1888–89a	Preston	40	Aston Villa	29	Wolves	28
1889–90a	Preston	33	Everton	31	Blackburn	27
1890–1a	Everton	29	Preston	27	Notts Co	26
1891–2b	Sunderland	42	Preston	37	Bolton	36

OLD FIRST DIVISION

Season	Champions	Pts	Runners-up	Pts	Third	Pts
1892–3c	Sunderland	48	Preston	37	Everton	36
1893–4c	Aston Villa	44	Sunderland	38	Derby	36
1894–5c	Sunderland	47	Everton	42	Aston Villa	39
1895–6c	Aston Villa	45	Derby	41	Everton	39
1896–7c	Aston Villa	47	Sheffield Utd	36	Derby	36
1897–8c	Sheffield Utd	42	Sunderland	39	Wolves	35
1898–9d	Aston Villa	45	Liverpool	43	Burnley	39
1899–1900d	Aston Villa	50	Sheffield Utd	48	Sunderland	41
1900–1d	Liverpool	45	Sunderland	43	Notts Co	40
1901–2d	Sunderland	44	Everton	41	Newcastle	37
1902–3d	The Wednesday	42	Aston Villa	41	Sunderland	41
1903–4d	The Wednesday	47	Manchester City	44	Everton	43
1904–5d	Newcastle	48	Everton	47	Manchester City	46
1905–6e	Liverpool	51	Preston	47	The Wednesday	44
1906–7e	Newcastle	51	Bristol City	48	Everton	45
1907–8e	Manchester Utd	52	Aston Villa	43	Manchester City	43
1908–9e	Newcastle	53	Everton	46	Sunderland	44
1909–10e	Aston Villa	53	Liverpool	48	Blackburn	45
1910–11e	Manchester Utd	52	Aston Villa	51	Sunderland	45
1911–12e	Blackburn	49	Everton	46	Newcastle	44
1912–13e	Sunderland	54	Aston Villa	50	Sheffield Wed	49
1913–14e	Blackburn	51	Aston Villa	44	Middlesbrough	43
1914–15e	Everton	46	Oldham	45	Blackburn	43
1919–20f	WBA	60	Burnley	51	Chelsea	49
1920–1f	Burnley	59	Manchester City	54	Bolton	52
1921–2f	Liverpool	57	Tottenham	51	Burnley	49
1922–3f	Liverpool	60	Sunderland	54	Huddersfield	53
1923–4f	*Huddersfield	57	Cardiff	57	Sunderland	53
1924–5f	Huddersfield	58	WBA	56	Bolton	55
1925–6f	Huddersfield	57	Arsenal	52	Sunderland	48
1926–7f	Newcastle	56	Huddersfield	51	Sunderland	49
1927–8f	Everton	53	Huddersfield	51	Leicester	48
1928–9f	Sheffield Wed	52	Leicester	51	Aston Villa	50
1929–30f	Sheffield Wed	60	Derby	50	Manchester City	47
1930–1f	Arsenal	66	Aston Villa	59	Sheffield Wed	52
1931–2f	Everton	56	Arsenal	54	Sheffield Wed	50
1932–3f	Arsenal	58	Aston Villa	54	Sheffield Wed	51
1933–4f	Arsenal	59	Huddersfield	56	Tottenham	49
1934–5f	Arsenal	58	Sunderland	54	Sheffield Wed	49
1935–6f	Sunderland	56	Derby	48	Huddersfield	48
1936–7f	Manchester City	57	Charlton	54	Arsenal	52
1937–8f	Arsenal	52	Wolves	51	Preston	49
1938–9f	Everton	59	Wolves	55	Charlton	50
1946–7f	Liverpool	57	Manchester Utd	56	Wolves	56
1947–8f	Arsenal	59	Manchester Utd	52	Burnley	52
1948–9f	Portsmouth	58	Manchester Utd	53	Derby	53
1949–50f	*Portsmouth	53	Wolves	53	Sunderland	52
1950–1f	Tottenham	60	Manchester Utd	56	Blackpool	50
1951–2f	Manchester Utd	57	Tottenham	53	Arsenal	53
1952–3f	*Arsenal	54	Preston	54	Wolves	51
1953–4f	Wolves	57	WBA	53	Huddersfield	51
1954–5f	Chelsea	52	Wolves	48	Portsmouth	48

1955–6f	Manchester Utd	60	Blackpool	49	Wolves	49
1956–7f	Manchester Utd	64	Tottenham	56	Preston	56
1957–8f	Wolves	64	Preston	59	Tottenham	51
1958–9f	Wolves	61	Manchester Utd	55	Arsenal	50
1959–60f	Burnley	55	Wolves	54	Tottenham	53
1960–1f	Tottenham	66	Sheffield Wed	58	Wolves	57
1961–2f	Ipswich	56	Burnley	53	Tottenham	52
1962–3f	Everton	61	Tottenham	55	Burnley	54
1963–4f	Liverpool	57	Manchester Utd	53	Everton	52
1964–5f	*Manchester Utd	61	Leeds	61	Chelsea	56
1965–6f	Liverpool	61	Leeds	55	Burnley	55
1966–7f	Manchester Utd	60	Nottm Forest	56	Tottenham	56
1967–8f	Manchester City	58	Manchester Utd	56	Liverpool	55
1968–9f	Leeds	67	Liverpool	61	Everton	57
1969–70f	Everton	66	Leeds	57	Chelsea	55
1970–1f	Arsenal	65	Leeds	64	Tottenham	52
1971–2f	Derby	58	Leeds	57	Liverpool	57
1972–3f	Liverpool	60	Arsenal	57	Leeds	53
1973–4f	Leeds	62	Liverpool	57	Derby	48
1974–5f	Derby	53	Liverpool	51	Ipswich	51
1975–6f	Liverpool	60	QPR	59	Manchester Utd	56
1976–7f	Liverpool	57	Manchester City	56	Ipswich	52
1977–8f	Nottm Forest	64	Liverpool	57	Everton	55
1978–9f	Liverpool	68	Nottm Forest	60	WBA	59
1979–80f	Liverpool	60	Manchester Utd	58	Ipswich	53
1980–1f	Aston Villa	60	Ipswich	56	Arsenal	53
1981–2g	Liverpool	87	Ipswich	83	Manchester Utd	78
1982–3g	Liverpool	82	Watford	71	Manchester Utd	70
1983–4g	Liverpool	80	Southampton	77	Nottm Forest	74
1984–5g	Everton	90	Liverpool	77	Tottenham	77
1985–6g	Liverpool	88	Everton	86	West Ham	84
1986–7g	Everton	86	Liverpool	77	Tottenham	71
1987–8h	Liverpool	90	Manchester Utd	81	Nottm Forest	73
1988–9j	††Arsenal	76	Liverpool	76	Nottm Forest	64
1989–90j	Liverpool	79	Aston Villa	70	Tottenham	63
1990–1j	Arsenal	83	Liverpool	76	Crystal Palace	69
1991–2g	Leeds	82	Manchester Utd	78	Sheffield Wed	75

Maximum points: *a*, 44; *b*, 52; *c*, 60; *d*, 68; *e*, 76; *f*, 84; *g*, 126; *h*, 120; *j*, 114
*Won on goal average †Won on goal diff ††Won on goals scored No comp 1915–19 –1939–46

OLD SECOND DIVISION 1892–1992

1892–3a	Small Heath	36	Sheffield Utd	35	Darwen	30
1893–4b	Liverpool	50	Small Heath	42	Notts Co	39
1894–5c	Bury	48	Notts Co	39	Newton Heath	38
1895–6c	*Liverpool	46	Manchester City	46	Grimsby	42
1896–7c	Notts Co	42	Newton Heath	39	Grimsby	38
1897–8c	Burnley	48	Newcastle	45	Manchester City	39
1898–9d	Manchester City	52	Glossop	46	Leicester Fosse	45
1899–1900d	The Wednesday	54	Bolton	52	Small Heath	46
1900–1d	Grimsby	49	Small Heath	48	Burnley	44
1901–2d	WBA	55	Middlesbrough	51	Preston	42
1902–3d	Manchester City	54	Small Heath	51	Woolwich Arsenal	48
1903–4d	Preston	50	Woolwich Arsenal	49	Manchester Utd	48
1904–5d	Liverpool	58	Bolton	56	Manchester Utd	53

Season	1st	Pts	2nd	Pts	3rd	Pts
1905–6e	Bristol City	66	Manchester Utd	62	Chelsea	53
1906–7e	Nottm Forest	60	Chelsea	57	Leicester Fosse	48
1907–8e	Bradford City	54	Leicester Fosse	52	Oldham	50
1908–9e	Bolton	52	Tottenham	51	WBA	51
1909–10e	Manchester City	54	Oldham	53	Hull	53
1910–11e	WBA	53	Bolton	51	Chelsea	49
1911–12e	*Derby	54	Chelsea	54	Burnley	52
1912–13e	Preston	53	Burnley	50	Birmingham	46
1913–14e	Notts Co	53	Bradford PA	49	Woolwich Arsenal	49
1914–15e	Derby	53	Preston	50	Barnsley	47
1919–20f	Tottenham	70	Huddersfield	64	Birmingham	56
1920–1f	*Birmingham	58	Cardiff	58	Bristol City	51
1921–2f	Nottm Forest	56	Stoke	52	Barnsley	52
1922–3f	Notts Co	53	West Ham	51	Leicester	51
1923–4f	Leeds	54	Bury	51	Derby	51
1924–5f	Leicester	59	Manchester Utd	57	Derby	55
1925–6f	Sheffield Wed	60	Derby	57	Chelsea	52
1926–7f	Middlesbrough	62	Portsmouth	54	Manchester City	54
1927–8f	Manchester City	59	Leeds	57	Chelsea	54
1928–9f	Middlesbrough	55	Grimsby	53	Bradford City	48
1929–30f	Blackpool	58	Chelsea	55	Oldham	53
1930–1f	Everton	61	WBA	54	Tottenham	51
1931–2f	Wolves	56	Leeds	54	Stoke	52
1932–3f	Stoke	56	Tottenham	55	Fulham	50
1933–4f	Grimsby	59	Preston	52	Bolton	51
1934–5f	Brentford	61	Bolton	56	West Ham	56
1935–6f	Manchester Utd	56	Charlton	55	Sheffield Utd	52
1936–7f	Leicester	56	Blackpool	55	Bury	52
1937–8f	Aston Villa	57	Manchester Utd	53	Sheffield Utd	53
1938–9f	Blackburn	55	Sheffield Utd	54	Sheffield Wed	53
1946–7f	Manchester City	62	Burnley	58	Birmingham	55
1947–8f	Birmingham	59	Newcastle	56	Southampton	52
1948–9f	Fulham	57	WBA	56	Southampton	52
1949–50f	Tottenham	61	Sheffield Wed	52	Sheffield Utd	52
1950–1f	Preston	57	Manchester City	52	Cardiff	50
1951–2f	Sheffield Wed	53	Cardiff	51	Birmingham	51
1952–3f	Sheffield Utd	60	Huddersfield	58	Luton	52
1953–4f	*Leicester	56	Everton	56	Blackburn	55
1954–5f	*Birmingham	54	Luton	54	Rotherham	54
1955–6f	Sheffield Wed	55	Leeds	52	Liverpool	48
1956–7f	Leicester	61	Nottm Forest	54	Liverpool	53
1957–8f	West Ham	57	Blackburn	56	Charlton	55
1958–9f	Sheffield Wed	62	Fulham	60	Sheffield Utd	53
1959–60f	Aston Villa	59	Cardiff	58	Liverpool	50
1960–1f	Ipswich	59	Sheffield Utd	58	Liverpool	52
1961–2f	Liverpool	62	Leyton Orient	54	Sunderland	53
1962–3f	Stoke	53	Chelsea	52	Sunderland	52
1963–4f	Leeds	63	Sunderland	61	Preston	56
1964–5f	Newcastle	57	Northampton	56	Bolton	50
1965–6f	Manchester City	59	Southampton	54	Coventry	53
1966–7f	Coventry	59	Wolves	58	Carlisle	52
1967–8f	Ipswich	59	QPR	58	Blackpool	58
1968–9f	Derby	63	Crystal Palace	56	Charlton	50
1969–70f	Huddersfield	60	Blackpool	53	Leicester	51

1970–1 f	Leicester	59	Sheffield Utd	56	Cardiff	53
1971–2 f	Norwich	57	Birmingham	56	Millwall	55
1972–3 f	Burnley	62	QPR	61	Aston Villa	50
1973–4 f	Middlesbrough	65	Luton	50	Carlisle	49
1974–5 f	Manchester Utd	61	Aston Villa	58	Norwich	53
1975–6 f	Sunderland	56	Bristol City	53	WBA	53
1976–7 f	Wolves	57	Chelsea	55	Nottm Forest	52
1977–8 f	Bolton	58	Southampton	57	Tottenham	56
1978–9 f	Crystal Palace	57	Brighton	56	Stoke	56
1979–80 f	Leicester	55	Sunderland	54	Birmingham	53
1980–1 f	West Ham	66	Notts Co	53	Swansea	50
1981–2 g	Luton	88	Watford	80	Norwich	71
1982–3 g	QPR	85	Wolves	75	Leicester	70
1983–4 g	†Chelsea	88	Sheffield Wed	88	Newcastle	80
1984–5 g	Oxford Utd	84	Birmingham	82	Manchester City	74
1985–6 g	Norwich	84	Charlton	77	Wimbledon	76
1986–7 g	Derby	84	Portsmouth	78	††Oldham	75
1987–8 h	Millwall	82	Aston Villa	78	Middlesbrough	78
1988–9 j	Chelsea	99	Manchester City	82	Crystal Palace	81
1989–90 j	†Leeds	85	Sheffield Utd	85	†† Newcastle	80
1990–1 j	Oldham	88	West Ham	87	Sheffield Wed	82
1991–2 j	Ipswich	84	Middlesbrough	80	†† Derby	78

Maximum points: *a*, 44; *b*, 56; *c*, 60; *d*, 68; *e*, 76; *f*, 84; *g*, 126; *h*, 132; *j*, 138 * Won on goal average † Won on goal difference †† Not promoted after play–offs

THIRD DIVISION 1958–92

1958–9	Plymouth Argyle	62	Hull	61	Brentford	57
1959–60	Southampton	61	Norwich	59	Shrewsbury	52
1960–1	Bury	68	Walsall	62	QPR	60
1961–2	Portsmouth	65	Grimsby	62	Bournemouth	59
1962–3	Northampton	62	Swindon	58	Port Vale	54
1963–4	*Coventry	60	Crystal Palace	60	Watford	58
1964–5	Carlisle	60	Bristol City	59	Mansfield	59
1965–6	Hull	69	Millwall	65	QPR	57
1966–7	QPR	67	Middlesbrough	55	Watford	54
1967–8	Oxford Utd	57	Bury	56	Shrewsbury	55
1968–9	*Watford	64	Swindon	64	Luton	61
1969–70	Orient	62	Luton	60	Bristol Rov	56
1970–1	Preston	61	Fulham	60	Halifax	56
1971–2	Aston Villa	70	Brighton	65	Bournemouth	62
1972–3	Bolton	61	Notts Co	57	Blackburn	55
1973–4	Oldham	62	Bristol Rov	61	York	61
1974–5	Blackburn	60	Plymouth Argyle	59	Charlton	55
1975–6	Hereford	63	Cardiff	57	Millwall	56
1976–7	Mansfield	64	Brighton	61	Crystal Palace	59
1977–8	Wrexham	61	Cambridge Utd	58	Preston	56
1978–9	Shrewsbury	61	Watford	60	Swansea	60
1979–80	Grimsby	62	Blackburn	59	Sheffield Wed	58
1980–1	Rotherham	61	Barnsley	59	Charlton	59
†1981–2	**Burnley	80	Carlisle	80	Fulham	78
†1982–3	Portsmouth	91	Cardiff	86	Huddersfield	82
†1983–4	Oxford Utd	95	Wimbledon	83	Sheffield Utd	83
†1984–5	Bradford City	94	Millwall	90	Hull	87
†1985–6	Reading	94	Plymouth Argyle	87	Derby	84
†1986–7	Bournemouth	97	Middlesbrough	94	Swindon	87
†1987–8	Sunderland	93	Brighton	84	Walsall	82

* Won on goal average ** Won on goal difference † Maximum points 138 (previously 92) †† Not promoted after play–offs

FOURTH DIVISION 1958–92

1958–9	Port Vale	64	Coventry	60	York	60	Shrewsbury	58
1959–60	Walsall	65	Notts Co	60	Torquay	60	Watford	57
1960–1	Peterborough	66	Crystal Palace	64	Northampton	60	Bradford PA	60
1961–2	Millwall	56	Colchester	55	Wrexham	53	Carlisle	52
1962–3	Brentford	62	Oldham	59	Crewe	59	Mansfield	57
1963–4	*Gillingham	60	Carlisle	60	Workington	59	Exeter	58
1964–5	Brighton	63	Millwall	62	York	62	Oxford Utd	61
1965–6	*Doncaster	59	Darlington	59	Torquay	58	Colchester	56
1966–7	Stockport	64	Southport	59	Barrow	59	Tranmere	58
1967–8	Luton	66	Barnsley	61	Hartlepool Utd	60	Crewe	58
1968–9	Doncaster	59	Halifax	57	Rochdale	56	Bradford City	56
1969–70	Chesterfield	64	Wrexham	61	Swansea	60	Port Vale	59
1970–1	Notts Co	69	Bournemouth	60	Oldham	59	York	56
1971–2	Grimsby	63	Southend	60	Brentford	59	Scunthorpe	57
1972–3	Southport	62	Hereford	58	Cambridge Utd	57	Aldershot	56
1973–4	Peterborough	65	Gillingham	62	Colchester	60	Bury	59
1974–5	Mansfield	68	Shrewsbury	62	Rotherham	58	Chester	57
1975–6	Lincoln	74	Northampton	68	Reading	60	Tranmere	58
1976–7	Cambridge Utd	65	Exeter	62	Colchester	59	Bradford City	59
1977–8	Watford	71	Southend	60	Swansea	56	Brentford	59
1978–9	Reading	65	Grimsby	61	Wimbledon	61	Barnsley	61
1979–80	Huddersfield	66	Walsall	64	Newport	61	Portsmouth	60
1980–1	Southend	67	Lincoln	65	Doncaster	56	Wimbledon	55
†1981–2	Sheffield Utd	96	Bradford City	91	Wigan	91	Bournemouth	88
†1982–3	Wimbledon	98	Hull	90	Port Vale	88	Scunthorpe	83
†1983–4	York	101	Doncaster	85	Reading	82	Bristol City	82
†1984–5	Chesterfield	91	Blackpool	86	Darlington	85	Bury	84
†1985–6	Swindon	102	Chester	84	Mansfield	81	Port Vale	79
†1986–7	Northampton	99	Preston	90	Southend	80	††Wolves	79
†1987–8	Wolves	90	Cardiff	85	Bolton	78	††Scunthorpe	77
†1988–9	Rotherham	82	Tranmere	80	Crewe	78	††Scunthorpe	77
†1989–90	Exeter	89	Grimsby	79	Southend	75	††Stockport	74
†1990–1	Darlington	83	Stockport	82	Hartlepool Utd	82	Peterborough	80
1991–2a	Burnley	83	Rotherham	77	Mansfield	77	Blackpool	76

* Won on goal average Maximum points: †, 138; *a*, 126; previously 92 †† Not promoted after play–offs

THIRD DIVISION – SOUTH 1920–58

1920–1a	Crystal Palace	59	Southampton	54	QPR	53
1921–2a	*Southampton	61	Plymouth Argyle	61	Portsmouth	53
1922–3a	Bristol City	59	Plymouth Argyle	53	Swansea	53
1923–4a	Portsmouth	59	Plymouth Argyle	55	Millwall	54
1924–5a	Swansea	57	Plymouth Argyle	56	Bristol City	53
1925–6a	Reading	57	Plymouth Argyle	56	Millwall	53
1926–7a	Bristol City	62	Plymouth Argyle	60	Millwall	56
1927–8a	Millwall	65	Northampton	55	Plymouth Argyle	53
1928–9a	*Charlton	54	Crystal Palace	54	Northampton	52
1929–30a	Plymouth Argyle	68	Brentford	61	QPR	51
1930–31a	Notts Co	59	Crystal Palace	51	Brentford	50
1931–2a	Fulham	57	Reading	55	Southend	53

1932–3a	Brentford	62	Exeter	58	Norwich	57
1933–4a	Norwich	61	Coventry	54	Reading	54
1934–5a	Charlton	61	Reading	53	Coventry	51
1935–6a	Coventry	57	Luton	56	Reading	54
1936–7a	Luton	58	Notts Co	56	Brighton	53
1937–8a	Millwall	56	Bristol City	55	QPR	53
1938–9a	Newport	55	Crystal Palace	52	Brighton	49
1946–7a	Cardiff	66	QPR	57	Bristol City	51
1947–8a	QPR	61	Bournemouth	57	Walsall	51
1948–9a	Swansea	62	Reading	55	Bournemouth	52
1949–50a	Notts Co	58	Northampton	51	Southend	51
1950–1d	Nottm Forest	70	Norwich	64	Reading	57
1951–2d	Plymouth Argyle	66	Reading	61	Norwich	61
1952–3d	Bristol Rov	64	Millwall	62	Northampton	62
1953–4d	Ipswich	64	Brighton	61	Bristol City	56
1954–5d	Bristol City	70	Leyton Orient	61	Southampton	59
1955–6d	Leyton Orient	66	Brighton	65	Ipswich	64
1956–7d	*Ipswich	59	Torquay	59	Colchester	58
1957–8d	Brighton	60	Brentford	58	Plymouth Argyle	58

THIRD DIVISION – NORTH 1921–58

1921–2b	Stockport	56	Darlington	50	Grimsby	50
1922–3b	Nelson	51	Bradford PA	47	Walsall	46
1923–4a	Wolves	63	Rochdale	62	Chesterfield	54
1924–5a	Darlington	58	Nelson	53	New Brighton	53
1925–6a	Grimsby	61	Bradford PA	60	Rochdale	59
1926–7a	Stoke	63	Rochdale	58	Bradford PA	57
1927–8a	Bradford PA	63	Lincoln	55	Stockport	54
1928–9a	Bradford City	63	Stockport	62	Wrexham	52
1929–30a	Port Vale	67	Stockport	63	Darlington	50
1930–1a	Chesterfield	58	Lincoln	57	Wrexham	54
1931–2c	*Lincoln	57	Gateshead	57	Chester	50
1932–3a	Hull	59	Wrexham	57	Stockport	54
1933–4a	Barnsley	62	Chesterfield	61	Stockport	59
1934–5a	Doncaster	57	Halifax	55	Chester	54
1935–6a	Chesterfield	60	Chester	55	Tranmere	54
1936–7a	Stockport	60	Lincoln	57	Chester	53
1937–8a	Tranmere	56	Doncaster	54	Hull	53
1938–9a	Barnsley	67	Doncaster	56	Bradford City	52
1946–7a	Doncaster	72	Rotherham	64	Chester	56
1947–8a	Lincoln	60	Rotherham	59	Wrexham	50
1948–9a	Hull	65	Rotherham	62	Doncaster	50
1949–50a	Doncaster	55	Gateshead	53	Rochdale	51
1950–1d	Rotherham	71	Mansfield	64	Carlisle	62
1951–2d	Lincoln	69	Grimsby	66	Stockport	59
1952–3d	Oldham	59	Port Vale	58	Wrexham	56
1953–4d	Port Vale	69	Barnsley	58	Scunthorpe	57
1954–5d	Barnsley	65	Accrington	61	Scunthorpe	58
1955–6d	Grimsby	68	Derby	63	Accrington	59
1956–7d	Derby	63	Hartlepool Utd	59	Accrington	58
1957–8d	Scunthorpe	66	Accrington	59	Bradford City	57

Maximum points: a, 84; b, 76; c, 80; d, 92 * Won on goal average

TITLE WINNERS
FA PREMIER LEAGUE
Manchester Utd	12
Arsenal	3
Chelsea	3
Blackburn	1
Manchester City	1

FOOTBALL LEAGUE CHAMPIONSHIP
Reading	2
Sunderland	2
Newcastle	1
QPR	1
WBA	1
Wolves	1

DIV 1 (NEW)
Sunderland	2
Bolton	1
Brighton	1
Charlton	1
Crystal Palace	1
Fulham	1
Manchester City	1
Middlesbrough	1
Newcastle	1
Norwich	1
Nottm Forest	1
Portsmouth	1

DIV 1 (ORIGINAL)
Liverpool	18
Arsenal	10
Everton	9
Aston Villa	7
Manchester Utd	7
Sunderland	6
Newcastle	4
Sheffield Wed	4
Huddersfield	3
Leeds	3
Wolves	3
Blackburn	2

Burnley	2
Derby	2
Manchester City	2
Portsmouth	2
Preston	2
Tottenham	2
Chelsea	1
Ipswich	1
Nottm Forest	1
Sheffield Utd	1
WBA	1

LEAGUE ONE
Brighton	1
Charlton	1
Leicester	1
Luton	1
Norwich	1
Scunthorpe	1
Southend	1
Swansea	1

DIV 2 (NEW)
Birmingham	1
Brighton	1
Bury	1
Chesterfield	1
Fulham	1
Millwall	1
Plymouth Argyle	1
Preston	1
Reading	1
Stoke	1
Swindon	1
Watford	1
Wigan	1
Notts Co	1

DIV 2 (ORIGINAL)
Leicester	6
Manchester City	6
Sheffield Wed	5
Birmingham	4
Derby	4
Liverpool	4
Ipswich	3

Leeds	3
Middlesbrough	3
Notts County	3
Preston	3
Aston Villa	2
Bolton	2
Burnley	2
Chelsea	2
Grimsby	2
Manchester Utd	2
Norwich	2
Nottm Forest	2
Stoke	2
Tottenham	2
WBA	2
West Ham	2
Wolves	2
Blackburn	1
Blackpool	1
Bradford City	1
Brentford	1
Bristol City	1
Bury	1
Coventry	1
Crystal Palace	1
Everton	1
Fulham	1
Huddersfield	1
Luton	1
Millwall	1
Newcastle	1
Oldham	1
Oxford Utd	1
QPR	1
Sheffield Utd	1
Sunderland	1

LEAGUE TWO
Brentford	1
Carlisle	1
Chesterfield	1
MK Dons	1
Notts County	1
Swindon	1
Walsall	1
Yeovil	1

APPLICATIONS FOR RE-ELECTION (System discontinued 1987)

14	Hartlepool	7	Walsall	4	Norwich
12	Halifax	7	Workington	3	Aldershot
11	Barrow	7	York	3	Bradford City
11	Southport	6	Stockport	3	Crystal Palace
10	Crewe	5	Accrington	3	Doncaster
10	Newport	5	Gillingham	3	Hereford
10	Rochdale	5	Lincoln	3	Merthyr
8	Darlington	5	New Brighton	3	Swindon
8	Exeter	4	Bradford PA	3	Torquay
7	Chester	4	Northampton	3	Tranmere

2	Aberdare	2	Oldham	1	Cardiff
2	Ashington	2	QPR	1	Carlisle
2	Bournemouth	2	Rotherham	1	Charlton
2	Brentford	2	Scunthorpe	1	Mansfield
2	Colchester	2	Southend	1	Port Vale
2	Durham	2	Watford	1	Preston
2	Gateshead	1	Blackpool	1	Shrewsbury
2	Grimsby	1	Brighton	1	Swansea
2	Millwall	1	Bristol Rov	1	Thames
2	Nelson	1	Cambridge Utd	1	Wrexham

RELEGATED CLUBS (TO 1992)

1892–3	In Test matches, Darwen and Sheffield Utd won promotion in place of Accrington and Notts Co
1893–4	Tests, Liverpool and Small Heath won promotion Darwen and Newton Heath relegated
1894–5	After Tests, Bury promoted, Liverpool relegated
1895–6	After Tests, Liverpool promoted, Small Heath relegated
1896–7	After Tests, Notts Co promoted, Burnley relegated
1897–8	Test system abolished after success of Burnley and Stoke, League extended Blackburn and Newcastle elected to First Division

Automatic promotion and relegation introduced

FIRST DIVISION TO SECOND DIVISION

1898–9	Bolton, Sheffield Wed
1899–00	Burnley, Glossop
1900–1	Preston, WBA
1901–2	Small Heath, Manchester City
1902–3	Grimsby, Bolton
1903–4	Liverpool, WBA
1904–5	League extended Bury and Notts Co, two bottom clubs in First Division, re–elected
1905–6	Nottm Forest, Wolves
1906–7	Derby, Stoke
1907–8	Bolton, Birmingham
1908–9	Manchester City, Leicester Fosse
1909–10	Bolton, Chelsea
1910–11	Bristol City, Nottm Forest
1911–12	Preston, Bury
1912–13	Notts Co, Woolwich Arsenal
1913–14	Preston, Derby
1914–15	Tottenham, *Chelsea
1919–20	Notts Co, Sheffield Wed
1920–1	Derby, Bradford PA
1921–2	Bradford City, Manchester Utd
1922–3	Stoke, Oldham
1923–4	Chelsea, Middlesbrough
1924–5	Preston, Nottm Forest
1925–6	Manchester City, Notts Co
1926–7	Leeds, WBA
1927–8	Tottenham, Middlesbrough
1928–9	Bury, Cardiff
1929–30	Burnley, Everton
1930–1	Leeds, Manchester Utd
1931–2	Grimsby, West Ham
1932–3	Bolton, Blackpool
1933–4	Newcastle, Sheffield Utd
1934–5	Leicester, Tottenham
1935–6	Aston Villa, Blackburn
1936–7	Manchester Utd, Sheffield Wed
1937–8	Manchester City, WBA

1938–9	Birmingham, Leicester
1946–7	Brentford, Leeds
1947–8	Blackburn, Grimsby
1948–9	Preston, Sheffield Utd
1949–50	Manchester City, Birmingham
1950–1	Sheffield Wed, Everton
1951–2	Huddersfield, Fulham
1952–3	Stoke, Derby
1953–4	Middlesbrough, Liverpool
1954–5	Leicester, Sheffield Wed
1955–6	Huddersfield, Sheffield Utd
1956–7	Charlton, Cardiff
1957–8	Sheffield Wed, Sunderland
1958–9	Portsmouth, Aston Villa
1959–60	Luton, Leeds
1960–61	Preston, Newcastle
1961–2	Chelsea, Cardiff
1962–3	Manchester City, Leyton Orient
1963–4	Bolton, Ipswich
1964–5	Wolves, Birmingham
1965–6	Northampton, Blackburn
1966–7	Aston Villa, Blackpool
1967–8	Fulham, Sheffield Utd
1968–9	Leicester, QPR
1969–70	Sheffield Wed, Sunderland
1970–1	Burnley, Blackpool
1971–2	Nottm Forest, Huddersfield
1972–3	WBA, Crystal Palace
1973–4	Norwich, Manchester Utd, Southampton
1974–5	Chelsea, Luton, Carlisle
1975–6	Sheffield Utd, Burnley, Wolves
1976–7	Tottenham, Stoke, Sunderland
1977–8	Leicester, West Ham, Newcastle
1978–9	QPR, Birmingham, Chelsea
1979–80	Bristol City, Derby, Bolton
1980–1	Norwich, Leicester, Crystal Palace
1981–2	Leeds, Wolves, Middlesbrough
1982–3	Manchester City, Swansea, Brighton
1983–4	Birmingham, Notts Co, Wolves
1984–5	Norwich, Sunderland, Stoke
1985–6	Ipswich, Birmingham, WBA
1986–7	Leicester, Manchester City, Aston Villa
1987–8	Chelsea**, Portsmouth, Watford, Oxford Utd
1988–9	Middlesbrough, West Ham, Newcastle
1989–90	Sheffield Wed, Charlton, Millwall
1990–1	Sunderland, Derby
1991–2	Luton, Notts Co, West Ham

* Subsequently re-elected to First Division when League extended after the war
** Relegated after play–offs

SECOND DIVISION TO THIRD DIVISION

1920–1	Stockport
1921–2	Bradford City, Bristol City
1922–3	Rotherham, Wolves
1923–4	Nelson, Bristol City
1924–5	Crystal Palace, Coventry
1925–6	Stoke, Stockport
1926–7	Darlington, Bradford City
1927–8	Fulham, South Shields

1928–9	Port Vale, Clapton Orient
1929–30	Hull, Notts County
1930–1	Reading, Cardiff
1931–2	Barnsley, Bristol City
1932–3	Chesterfield, Charlton
1933–4	Millwall, Lincoln
1934–5	Oldham, Notts Co
1935–6	Port Vale, Hull
1936–7	Doncaster, Bradford City
1937–8	Barnsley, Stockport
1938–9	Norwich, Tranmere
1946–7	Swansea, Newport
1947–8	Doncaster, Millwall
1948–9	Nottm Forest, Lincoln
1949–50	Plymouth Argyle, Bradford PA
1950–1	Grimsby, Chesterfield
1951–2	Coventry, QPR
1952–3	Southampton, Barnsley
1953–4	Brentford, Oldham
1954–5	Ipswich, Derby
1955–6	Plymouth Argyle, Hull
1956–7	Port Vale, Bury
1957–8	Doncaster, Notts Co
1958–9	Barnsley, Grimsby
1959–60	Bristol City, Hull
1960–1	Lincoln, Portsmouth
1961–2	Brighton, Bristol Rov
1962–3	Walsall, Luton
1963–4	Grimsby, Scunthorpe
1964–5	Swindon, Swansea
1965–6	Middlesbrough, Leyton Orient
1966–7	Northampton, Bury
1967–8	Plymouth Argyle, Rotherham
1968–9	Fulham, Bury
1969–70	Preston, Aston Villa
1970–1	Blackburn, Bolton
1971–2	Charlton, Watford
1972–3	Huddersfield, Brighton
1973–4	Crystal Palace, Preston, Swindon
1974–5	Millwall, Cardiff, Sheffield Wed
1975–6	Portsmouth, Oxford Utd, York
1976–7	Carlisle, Plymouth Argyle, Hereford
1977–8	Hull, Mansfield, Blackpool
1978–9	Sheffield Utd, Millwall, Blackburn
1979–80	Fulham, Burnley, Charlton
1980–1	Preston, Bristol City, Bristol Rov
1981–2	Cardiff, Wrexham, Orient
1982–3	Rotherham, Burnley, Bolton
1983–4	Derby, Swansea, Cambridge Utd
1984–5	Notts Co, Cardiff, Wolves
1985–6	Carlisle, Middlesbrough, Fulham
1986–7	Sunderland**, Grimsby, Brighton
1987–8	Sheffield Utd**, Reading, Huddersfield
1988–9	Shrewsbury, Birmingham, Walsall
1989–90	Bournemouth, Bradford City, Stoke
1990–1	WBA, Hull
1991–2	Plymouth Argyle, Brighton, Port Vale

** Relegated after play-offs

THIRD DIVISION TO FOURTH DIVISION

1958–9   Rochdale, Notts Co, Doncaster, Stockport
1959–60   Accrington, Wrexham, Mansfield, York
1960–1   Chesterfield, Colchester, Bradford City, Tranmere
1961–2   Newport, Brentford, Lincoln, Torquay
1962–3   Bradford PA, Brighton, Carlisle, Halifax
1963–4   Millwall, Crewe, Wrexham, Notts Co
1964–5   Luton, Port Vale, Colchester, Barnsley
1965–6   Southend, Exeter, Brentford, York
1966–7   Doncaster, Workington, Darlington, Swansea
1967–8   Scunthorpe, Colchester, Grimsby, Peterborough (demoted)
1968–9   Oldham, Crewe, Hartlepool Utd, Northampton
1969–70   Bournemouth, Southport, Barrow, Stockport
1970–1   Gillingham, Doncaster, Bury, Reading
1971–2   Mansfield, Barnsley, Torquay, Bradford City
1972–3   Scunthorpe, Swansea, Brentford, Rotherham
1973–4   Cambridge Utd, Shrewsbury, Rochdale, Southport
1974–5   Bournemouth, Watford, Tranmere, Huddersfield
1975–6   Aldershot, Colchester, Southend, Halifax
1976–7   Reading, Northampton, Grimsby, York
1977–8   Port Vale, Bradford City, Hereford, Portsmouth
1978–9   Peterborough, Walsall, Tranmere, Lincoln
1979–80   Bury, Southend, Mansfield, Wimbledon
1980–1   Sheffield Utd, Colchester, Blackpool, Hull
1981–2   Wimbledon, Swindon, Bristol City, Chester
1982–3   Reading, Wrexham, Doncaster, Chesterfield
1983–4   Scunthorpe, Southend, Port Vale, Exeter
1984–5   Burnley, Orient, Preston, Cambridge Utd
1985–6   Lincoln, Cardiff, Wolves, Swansea
1986–7   Bolton**, Carlisle, Darlington, Newport
1987–8   Doncaster, York, Grimsby, Rotherham**
1988–9   Southend, Chesterfield, Gillingham, Aldershot
1989–90   Cardiff, Northampton, Blackpool, Walsall
1990–1   Crewe, Rotherham, Mansfield
1991–2   Bury, Shrewsbury, Torquay, Darlington
** Relegated after plays-offs

DEMOTED FROM FOURTH DIVISION TO CONFERENCE

1987   Lincoln
1988   Newport
1989   Darlington
1990   Colchester
1991   No demotion
1992   No demotion

DEMOTED FROM THIRD DIVISION TO CONFERENCE

1993   Halifax
1994–6 No demotion
1997   Hereford
1998   Doncaster
1999   Scarborough
2000   Chester
2001   Barnet
2002   Halifax
2003   Exeter, Shrewsbury
2004   Carlisle, York

DEMOTED FROM LEAGUE TWO TO BLUE SQUARE PREMIER LEAGUE

2005	Kidderminster, Cambridge Utd
2006	Oxford Utd, Rushden & Diamonds
2007	Boston, Torquay
2008	Mansfield, Wrexham
2009	Chester Luton
2010	Grimsby, Darlington
2011	Lincoln, Stockport
2012	Hereford, Macclesfield

RELEGATED CLUBS (SINCE 1993)

1993
Premier League to Div 1: Crystal Palace, Middlesbrough, Nottm Forest
Div 1 to Div 2: Brentford, Cambridge Utd, Bristol Rov
Div 2 to Div 3: Preston, Mansfield, Wigan, Chester

1994
Premier League to Div 1: Sheffield Utd, Oldham, Swindon
Div 1 to Div 2: Birmingham, Oxford Utd, Peterborough
Div 2 to Div 3: Fulham, Exeter, Hartlepool Utd, Barnet

1995
Premier League to Div 1: Crystal Palace, Norwich, Leicester, Ipswich
Div 1 to Div 2: Swindon, Burnley, Bristol City, Notts Co
Div 2 to Div 3: Cambridge Utd, Plymouth Argyle, Cardiff, Chester, Leyton Orient

1996
Premier League to Div 1: Manchester City, QPR, Bolton
Div 1 to Div 2: Millwall, Watford, Luton
Div 2 to Div 3: Carlisle, Swansea, Brighton, Hull

1997
Premier League to Div 1: Sunderland, Middlesbrough, Nottm Forest
Div 1 to Div 2: Grimsby, Oldham, Southend
Div 2 to Div 3: Peterborough, Shrewsbury, Rotherham, Notts Co

1998
Premier League to Div 1: Bolton, Barnsley, Crystal Palace
Div 1 to Div 2: Manchester City, Stoke, Reading
Div 2 to Div 3: Brentford, Plymouth Argyle, Carlisle, Southend

1999
Premier League to Div 1: Charlton, Blackburn, Nottm Forest
Div 1 to Div 2: Bury, Oxford Utd, Bristol City
Div 2 to Div 3: York, Northampton, Lincoln, Macclesfield

2000
Premier League to Div 1: Wimbledon, Sheffield Wed, Watford
Div 1 to Div 2: Walsall, Port Vale, Swindon
Div 2 to Div 3: Cardiff, Blackpool, Scunthorpe, Chesterfield

2001
Premier League to Div 1: Manchester City, Coventry, Bradford City
Div 1 to Div 2: Huddersfield, QPR, Tranmere
Div 2 to Div 3: Bristol Rov, Luton, Swansea, Oxford Utd

2002
Premier League to Div 1: Ipswich, Derby, Leicester
Div 1 to Div 2: Crewe, Barnsley, Stockport
Div 2 to Div 3: Bournemouth, Bury, Wrexham, Cambridge Utd

2003
Premier League to Div 1: West Ham, WBA, Sunderland
Div 1 to Div 2: Sheffield Wed, Brighton, Grimsby
Div 2 to Div 3: Cheltenham, Huddersfield, Mansfield, Northampton

2004
Premier League to Div 1: Leicester, Leeds, Wolves
Div 1 to Div 2: Walsall, Bradford City, Wimbledon
Div 2 to Div 3: Grimsby, Rushden & Diamonds, Notts Co, Wycombe

2005
Premier League to Championship: Crystal Palace, Norwich, Southampton
Championship to League 1: Gillingham, Nottm Forest, Rotherham
League 1 to League 2: Torquay, Wrexham, Peterborough, Stockport

2006
Premier League to Championship: Birmingham, WBA, Sunderland
Championship to League 1: Crewe, Millwall, Brighton
League 1 to League 2: Hartlepool Utd, MK Dons, Swindon, Walsall

2007
Premier League to Championship: Sheffield Utd, Charlton, Watford
Championship to League 1: Southend, Luton, Leeds
League 1 to League 2: Chesterfield, Bradford City, Rotherham, Brentford

2008
Premier League to Championship: Reading, Birmingham, Derby
Championship to League 1: Leicester, Scunthorpe, Colchester
League 1 to League 2: Bournemouth, Gillingham, Port Vale, Luton

2009
Premier League to Championship: Newcastle, Middlesbrough, WBA
Championship to League 1: Norwich, Southampton, Charlton
League 1 to League 2: Northampton, Crewe, Cheltenham, Hereford

2010
Premier League to Championship: Burnley, Hull, Portsmouth
Championship to League 1: Sheffield Wed, Plymouth, Peterborough
League 1 to League 2: Gillingham, Wycombe, Southend, Stockport

2011
Premier League to Championship: Birmingham, Blackpool, West Ham
Championship to League 1: Preston, Sheffield Utd, Scunthorpe
League 1 to League 2: Dagenham & Redbridge, Bristol Rov, Plymouth, Swindon

2012
Premier League to Championship: Bolton, Blackburn, Wolves
Championship to League 1: Portsmouth, Coventry, Doncaster
League 1 to League 2: Wycombe, Chesterfield, Exeter, Rochdale

ANNUAL AWARDS

FOOTBALL WRITERS' ASSOCIATION

Footballer of the Year: 1948 Stanley Matthews (Blackpool); **1949** Johnny Carey (Manchester Utd); **1950** Joe Mercer (Arsenal); **1951** Harry Johnston (Blackpool); **1952** Billy Wright (Wolves); **1953** Nat Lofthouse (Bolton); **1954** Tom Finney (Preston); **1955** Don Revie (Manchester City); **1956** Bert Trautmann (Manchester City); **1957** Tom Finney (Preston); **1958** Danny Blanchflower (Tottenham); **1959** Syd Owen (Luton); **1960** Bill Slater (Wolves); **1961** Danny Blanchflower (Tottenham); **1962** Jimmy Adamson (Burnley); **1963** Stanley Matthews (Stoke); **1964** Bobby Moore (West Ham); **1965** Bobby Collins (Leeds); **1966** Bobby Charlton (Manchester Utd); **1967** Jack Charlton (Leeds); **1968** George Best (Manchester Utd); **1969** Tony Book (Manchester City) & Dave Mackay (Derby) – shared; **1970** Billy Bremner (Leeds); **1971** Frank McLintock (Arsenal); **1972** Gordon Banks (Stoke); **1973** Pat Jennings (Tottenham); **1974** Ian Callaghan (Liverpool); **1975** Alan Mullery (Fulham); **1976** Kevin Keegan (Liverpool); **1977** Emlyn Hughes (Liverpool); **1978** Kenny Burns (Nott'm Forest); **1979** Kenny Dalglish (Liverpool); **1980** Terry McDermott (Liverpool); **1981** Frans Thijssen (Ipswich); **1982** Steve Perryman (Tottenham); **1983** Kenny Dalglish (Liverpool); **1984** Ian Rush (Liverpool); **1985** Neville Southall (Everton); **1986** Gary Lineker (Everton); **1987** Clive Allen (Tottenham); **1988** John Barnes (Liverpool); **1989** Steve Nicol (Liverpool); Special award to the Liverpool players for the compassion shown to bereaved families after the Hillsborough Disaster; **1990** John Barnes (Liverpool); **1991** Gordon Strachan (Leeds); **1992** Gary Lineker (Tottenham); **1993** Chris Waddle (Sheffield Wed); **1994** Alan Shearer (Blackburn); **1995** Jurgen Klinsmann (Tottenham); **1996** Eric Cantona (Manchester Utd); **1997** Gianfranco Zola (Chelsea); **1998** Dennis Bergkamp (Arsenal); **1999** David Ginola (Tottenham); **2000** Roy Keane (Manchester Utd); **2001** Teddy Sheringham (Manchester Utd); **2002** Robert Pires (Arsenal); **2003** Thierry Henry (Arsenal); **2004** Thierry Henry (Arsenal); **2005** Frank Lampard (Chelsea); **2006** Thierry Henry (Arsenal); **2007** Cristiano Ronaldo (Manchester Utd); **2008** Cristiano Ronaldo (Manchester Utd); **2009** Steven Gerrard (Liverpool), **2010** Wayne Rooney (Manchester Utd), **2011** Scott Parker (West Ham), **2012** Robin van Persie (Arsenal)

PROFESSIONAL FOOTBALLERS' ASSOCIATION

Player of the Year: 1974 Norman Hunter (Leeds); **1975** Colin Todd (Derby); **1976** Pat Jennings (Tottenham); **1977** Andy Gray (Aston Villa); **1978** Peter Shilton (Nott'm Forest); **1979** Liam Brady (Arsenal); **1980** Terry McDermott (Liverpool); **1981** John Wark (Ipswich); **1982** Kevin Keegan (Southampton); **1983** Kenny Dalglish (Liverpool); **1984** Ian Rush (Liverpool); **1985** Peter Reid (Everton); **1986** Gary Lineker (Everton); **1987** Clive Allen (Tottenham); **1988** John Barnes (Liverpool); **1989** Mark Hughes (Manchester Utd); **1990** David Platt (Aston Villa); **1991** Mark Hughes (Manchester Utd); **1992** Gary Pallister (Manchester Utd); **1993** Paul McGrath (Aston Villa); **1994** Eric Cantona (Manchester Utd); **1995** Alan Shearer (Blackburn); **1996** Les Ferdinand (Newcastle); **1997** Alan Shearer (Newcastle); **1998** Dennis Bergkamp (Arsenal); **1999** David Ginola (Tottenham); **2000** Roy Keane (Manchester Utd); **2001** Teddy Sheringham (Manchester Utd); **2002** Ruud van Nistelrooy (Manchester Utd); **2003** Thierry Henry (Arsenal); **2004** Thierry Henry (Arsenal); **2005** John Terry (Chelsea); **2006** Steven Gerrard (Liverpool); **2007** Cristiano Ronaldo (Manchester Utd); **2008** Cristiano Ronaldo (Manchester Utd); **2009** Ryan Giggs (Manchester Utd); **2010** Wayne Rooney (Manchester Utd); **2011** Gareth Bale (Tottenham), **2012** Robin van Persie (Arsenal)

Young Player of the Year: 1974 Kevin Beattie (Ipswich); **1975** Mervyn Day (West Ham); **1976** Peter Barnes (Manchester City); **1977** Andy Gray (Aston Villa); **1978** Tony Woodcock (Nott'm Forest); **1979** Cyrille Regis (WBA); **1980** Glenn Hoddle (Tottenham); **1981** Gary

Shaw (Aston Villa); **1982** Steve Moran (Southampton); **1983** Ian Rush (Liverpool); **1984** Paul Walsh (Luton); **1985** Mark Hughes (Manchester Utd); **1986** Tony Cottee (West Ham); **1987** Tony Adams (Arsenal); **1988** Paul Gascoigne (Newcastle); **1989** Paul Merson (Arsenal); **1990** Matthew Le Tissier (Southampton); **1991** Lee Sharpe (Manchester Utd); **1992** Ryan Giggs (Manchester Utd); **1993** Ryan Giggs (Manchester Utd); **1994** Andy Cole (Newcastle); **1995** Robbie Fowler (Liverpool); **1996** Robbie Fowler (Liverpool); **1997** David Beckham (Manchester Utd); **1998** Michael Owen (Liverpool); **1999** Nicolas Anelka (Arsenal); **2000** Harry Kewell (Leeds); **2001** Steven Gerrard (Liverpool); **2002** Craig Bellamy (Newcastle); **2003** Jermaine Jenas (Newcastle); **2004** Scott Parker (Chelsea); **2005** Wayne Rooney (Manchester Utd); **2006** Wayne Rooney (Manchester Utd); **2007** Cristiano Ronaldo (Manchester Utd); **2008** Cesc Fabregas (Arsenal); **2009** Ashley Young (Aston Villa); **2010** James Milner (Aston Villa); **2011** Jack Wilshere (Arsenal), **2012** Kyle Walker (Tottenham)

Merit Awards: 1974 Bobby Charlton & Cliff Lloyd; **1975** Denis Law; **1976** George Eastham; **1977** Jack Taylor; **1978** Bill Shankly; **1979** Tom Finney; **1980** Sir Matt Busby; **1981** John Trollope; **1982** Joe Mercer; **1983** Bob Paisley; **1984** Bill Nicholson; **1985** Ron Greenwood; **1986** England 1966 World Cup-winning team; **1987** Sir Stanley Matthews; **1988** Billy Bonds; **1989** Nat Lofthouse; **1990** Peter Shilton; **1991** Tommy Hutchison; **1992** Brian Clough; **1993** Manchester Utd, 1968 European Champions; Eusebio; **1994** Billy Bingham; **1995** Gordon Strachan; **1996** Pele; **1997** Peter Beardsley; **1998** Steve Ogrizovic; **1999** Tony Ford; **2000** Gary Mabbutt; **2001** Jimmy Hill; **2002** Niall Quinn; **2003** Sir Bobby Robson; **2004** Dario Gradi; **2005** Shaka Hislop; **2006** George Best; **2007** Sir Alex Ferguson; **2008** Jimmy Armfield; **2009** John McDermott, **2010** Lucas Radebe, **2011** Howard Webb, **2012** Graham Alexander

MANAGER OF THE YEAR (1)

(Chosen by a panel from the governing bodies, media and fans)
1966 Jock Stein (Celtic); **1967** Jock Stein (Celtic); **1968** Matt Busby (Manchester Utd); **1969** Don Revie (Leeds); **1970** Don Revie (Leeds); **1971** Bertie Mee (Arsenal); **1972** Don Revie (Leeds); **1973** Bill Shankly (Liverpool); **1974** Jack Charlton (Middlesbrough); **1975** Ron Saunders (Aston Villa); **1976** Bob Paisley (Liverpool); **1977** Bob Paisley (Liverpool); **1978** Brian Clough (Nott'm Forest); **1979** Bob Paisley (Liverpool); **1980** Bob Paisley (Liverpool); **1981** Ron Saunders (Aston Villa); **1982** Bob Paisley (Liverpool); **1983** Bob Paisley (Liverpool); **1984** Joe Fagan (Liverpool); **1985** Howard Kendall (Everton); **1986** Kenny Dalglish (Liverpool); **1987** Howard Kendall (Everton); **1988** Kenny Dalglish (Liverpool); **1989** George Graham (Arsenal); **1990** Kenny Dalglish (Liverpool); **1991** George Graham (Arsenal); **1992** Howard Wilkinson (Leeds); **1993** Alex Ferguson (Manchester Utd); **1994** Alex Ferguson (Manchester Utd); **1995** Kenny Dalglish (Blackburn); **1996** Alex Ferguson (Manchester Utd); **1997** Alex Ferguson (Manchester Utd); **1998** Arsene Wenger (Arsenal); **1999** Alex Ferguson (Manchester Utd); **2000** Sir Alex Ferguson (Manchester Utd); **2001** George Burley (Ipswich); **2002** Arsene Wenger (Arsenal); **2003** Sir Alex Ferguson (Manchester Utd); **2004** Arsene Wenger (Arsenal); **2005** Jose Mourinho (Chelsea); **2006** Jose Mourinho (Chelsea); **2007** Sir Alex Ferguson (Manchester Utd); **2008** Sir Alex Ferguson (Manchester Utd); **2009** Sir Alex Ferguson (Manchester Utd); **2010** Harry Redknapp (Tottenham), **2011** Sir Alex Ferguson (Manchester Utd), **2012**: Alan Pardew (Newcastle)

MANAGER OF THE YEAR (2)

(Chosen by the League Managers' Association)
1993 Dave Bassett (Sheffield Utd); **1994** Joe Kinnear (Wimbledon); **1995** Frank Clark (Nott'm Forest); **1996** Peter Reid (Sunderland); **1997** Danny Wilson (Barnsley); **1998** David Jones (Southampton); **1999** Alex Ferguson (Manchester Utd); **2000** Alan Curbishley (Charlton Athletic); **2001** George Burley (Ipswich); **2002** Arsene Wenger (Arsenal); **2003** David Moyes (Everton); **2004** Arsene Wenger (Arsenal); **2005** David Moyes (Everton); **2006** Steve Coppell (Reading); **2007** Steve Coppell (Reading); **2008** Sir Alex Ferguson (Manchester Utd); **2009** David Moyes (Everton); **2010** Roy Hodgson (Fulham), **2011** Sir Alex Ferguson (Manchester Utd), **2012**: Alan Pardew (Newcastle)

SCOTTISH FOOTBALL WRITERS' ASSOCIATION

Player of the Year: 1965 Billy McNeill (Celtic); 1966 John Greig (Rangers); 1967 Ronnie Simpson (Celtic); 1968 Gordon Wallace (Raith); 1969 Bobby Murdoch (Celtic); 1970 Pat Stanton (Hibernian); 1971 Martin Buchan (Aberdeen); 1972 David Smith (Rangers); 1973 George Connelly (Celtic); 1974 World Cup Squad; 1975 Sandy Jardine (Rangers); 1976 John Greig (Rangers); 1977 Danny McGrain (Celtic); 1978 Derek Johnstone (Rangers); 1979 Andy Ritchie (Morton); 1980 Gordon Strachan (Aberdeen); 1981 Alan Rough (Partick Thistle); 1982 Paul Sturrock (Dundee Utd); 1983 Charlie Nicholas (Celtic); 1984 Willie Miller (Aberdeen); 1985 Hamish McAlpine (Dundee Utd); 1986 Sandy Jardine (Hearts); 1987 Brian McClair (Celtic); 1988 Paul McStay (Celtic); 1989 Richard Gough (Rangers); 1990 Alex McLeish (Aberdeen); 1991 Maurice Malpas (Dundee Utd); 1992 Ally McCoist (Rangers); 1993 Andy Goram (Rangers); 1994 Mark Hateley (Rangers); 1995 Brian Laudrup (Rangers); 1996 Paul Gascoigne (Rangers); 1997 Brian Laudrup (Rangers); 1998 Craig Burley (Celtic); 1999 Henrik Larsson (Celtic); 2000 Barry Ferguson (Rangers); 2001 Henrik Larsson (Celtic); 2002 Paul Lambert (Celtic); 2003 Barry Ferguson (Rangers); 2004 Jackie McNamara (Celtic); 2005 John Hartson (Celtic); 2006 Craig Gordon (Hearts); 2007 Shunsuke Nakamura (Celtic); 2008 Carlos Cuellar (Rangers); 2009 Gary Caldwell (Celtic), 2010 David Weir (Rangers), 2011 Emilio Izaguirre (Celtic), 2012 Charlie Mulgrew (Celtic)

PROFESSIONAL FOOTBALLERS' ASSOCIATION SCOTLAND

Player of the Year: 1978 Derek Johnstone (Rangers); 1979 Paul Hegarty (Dundee Utd); 1980 Davie Provan (Celtic); 1981 Mark McGhee (Aberdeen); 1982 Sandy Clarke (Airdrieonians); 1983 Charlie Nicholas (Celtic); 1984 Willie Miller (Aberdeen); 1985 Jim Duffy (Morton); 1986 Richard Gough (Dundee Utd); 1987 Brian McClair (Celtic); 1988 Paul McStay (Celtic); 1989 Theo Snelders (Aberdeen); 1990 Jim Bett (Aberdeen); 1991 Paul Elliott (Celtic); 1992 Ally McCoist (Rangers); 1993 Andy Goram (Rangers); 1994 Mark Hateley (Rangers); 1995 Brian Laudrup (Rangers); 1996 Paul Gascoigne (Rangers); 1997 Paolo Di Canio (Celtic) 1998 Jackie McNamara (Celtic); 1999 Henrik Larsson (Celtic); 2000 Mark Viduka (Celtic); 2001 Henrik Larsson (Celtic); 2002 Lorenzo Amoruso (Rangers); 2003 Barry Ferguson (Rangers); 2004 Chris Sutton (Celtic); 2005 John Hartson (Celtic) and Fernando Ricksen (Rangers); 2006 Shaun Maloney (Celtic); 2007 Shunsuke Nakamura (Celtic); 2008 Aiden McGeady (Celtic); 2009 Scott Brown (Celtic), 2010 Steven Davis (Rangers), 2011 Emilio Izaguirre (Celtic), 2012 Charlie Mulgrew (Celtic)

Young Player of the Year: 1978 Graeme Payne (Dundee Utd); 1979 Ray Stewart (Dundee Utd); 1980 John McDonald (Rangers); 1981 Charlie Nicholas (Celtic); 1982 Frank McAvennie (St Mirren); 1983 Paul McStay (Celtic); 1984 John Robertson (Hearts); 1985 Craig Levein (Hearts); 1986 Craig Levein (Hearts); 1987 Robert Fleck (Rangers); 1988 John Collins (Hibernian); 1989 Billy McKinlay (Dundee Utd); 1990 Scott Crabbe (Hearts); 1991 Eoin Jess (Aberdeen); 1992 Phil O'Donnell (Motherwell); 1993 Eoin Jess (Aberdeen); 1994 Phil O'Donnell (Motherwell); 1995 Charlie Miller (Rangers); 1996 Jackie McNamara (Celtic); 1997 Robbie Winters (Dundee Utd); 1998 Gary Naysmith (Hearts); 1999 Barry Ferguson (Rangers) ; 2000 Kenny Miller (Hibernian); 2001 Stilian Petrov (Celtic); 2002 Kevin McNaughton (Aberdeen); 2003 James McFadden (Motherwell); 2004 Stephen Pearson (Celtic); 2005 Derek Riordan (Hibernian); 2006 Shaun Maloney (Celtic); 2007 Steven Naismith (Kilmarnock); 2008 Aiden McGeady (Celtic); 2009 James McCarthy (Hamilton), 2010 Danny Wilson (Rangers), 2011: David Goodwillie (Dundee Utd), 2012 James Forrest (Celtic)

SCOTTISH MANAGER OF THE YEAR

1987 Jim McLean (Dundee Utd); 1988 Billy McNeill (Celtic); 1989 Graeme Souness (Rangers); 1990 Andy Roxburgh (Scotland); 1991 Alex Totten (St Johnstone); 1992 Walter Smith (Rangers); 1993 Walter Smith (Rangers); 1994 Walter Smith (Rangers); 1995 Jimmy Nicholl (Raith); 1996 Walter Smith (Rangers); 1997 Walter Smith (Rangers); 1998 Wim Jansen (Celtic); 1999 Dick Advocaat (Rangers); 2000 Dick Advocaat (Rangers); 2001 Martin

O'Neill (Celtic); **2002** John Lambie (Partick Thistle); **2003** Alex McLeish (Rangers); **2004** Martin O'Neill (Celtic); **2005** Alex McLeish (Rangers); **2006** Gordon Strachan (Celtic); **2007** Gordon Strachan (Celtic); **2008** Billy Reid (Hamilton); **2009** Csaba Laszlo (Hearts), **2010** Walter Smith (Rangers), **2011:** Mixu Paatelainen (Kilmarnock), **2012** Neil Lennon (Celtic)

EUROPEAN FOOTBALLER OF THE YEAR

1956 Stanley Matthews (Blackpool); **1957** Alfredo di Stefano (Real Madrid); **1958** Raymond Kopa (Real Madrid); **1959** Alfredo di Stefano (Real Madrid); **1960** Luis Suarez (Barcelona); **1961** Omar Sivori (Juventus); **1962** Josef Masopust (Dukla Prague); **1963** Lev Yashin (Moscow Dynamo); **1964** Denis Law (Manchester Utd); **1965** Eusebio (Benfica); **1966** Bobby Charlton (Manchester Utd); **1967** Florian Albert (Ferencvaros); **1968** George Best (Manchester Utd); **1969** Gianni Rivera (AC Milan); **1970** Gerd Muller (Bayern Munich); **1971** Johan Cruyff (Ajax); **1972** Franz Beckenbauer (Bayern Munich); **1973** Johan Cruyff (Barcelona); **1974** Johan Cruyff (Barcelona); **1975** Oleg Blokhin (Dynamo Kiev); **1976** Franz Beckenbauer (Bayern Munich); **1977** Allan Simonsen (Borussia Moenchengladbach); **1978** Kevin Keegan (SV Hamburg); **1979** Kevin Keegan (SV Hamburg); **1980** Karl-Heinz Rummenigge (Bayern Munich); **1981** Karl-Heinz Rummenigge (Bayern Munich); **1982** Paolo Rossi (Juventus); **1983** Michel Platini (Juventus); **1984** Michel Platini (Juventus); **1985** Michel Platini (Juventus); **1986** Igor Belanov (Dynamo Kiev); **1987** Ruud Gullit (AC Milan); **1988** Marco van Basten (AC Milan); **1989** Marco van Basten (AC Milan); **1990** Lothar Matthaus (Inter Milan); **1991** Jean-Pierre Papin (Marseille); **1992** Marco van Basten (AC Milan); **1993** Roberto Baggio (Juventus); **1994** Hristo Stoichkov (Barcelona); **1995** George Weah (AC Milan); **1996** Matthias Sammer (Borussia Dortmund); **1997** Ronaldo (Inter Milan); **1998** Zinedine Zidane (Juventus); **1999** Rivaldo (Barcelona); **2000** Luis Figo (Real Madrid); **2001** Michael Owen (Liverpool); **2002** Ronaldo (Real Madrid); **2003** Pavel Nedved (Juventus); **2004** Andriy Shevchenko (AC Milan); **2005** Ronaldinho (Barcelona); **2006** Fabio Cannavaro (Real Madrid); **2007** Kaka (AC Milan); **2008** Cristiano Ronaldo (Manchester United), **2009** Lionel Messi (Barcelona)

WORLD FOOTBALLER OF YEAR

1991 Lothar Matthaus (Inter Milan and Germany); **1992** Marco van Basten (AC Milan and Holland); **1993** Roberto Baggio (Juventus and Italy); **1994** Romario (Barcelona and Brazil); **1995** George Weah (AC Milan and Liberia); **1996** Ronaldo (Barcelona and Brazil); **1997** Ronaldo (Inter Milan and Brazil); **1998** Zinedine Zidane (Juventus and France); **1999** Rivaldo (Barcelona and Brazil); **2000** Zinedine Zidane (Juventus and France); **2001** Luis Figo (Real Madrid and Portugal); **2002** Ronaldo (Real Madrid and Brazil); **2003** Zinedine Zidane (Real Madrid and France); **2004** Ronaldinho (Barcelona and Brazil); **2005** Ronaldinho (Barcelona and Brazil); **2006** Fabio Cannavaro (Real Madrid and Italy); **2007** Kaka (AC Milan and Brazil); **2008** Cristiano Ronaldo (Manchester United and Portugal), **2009** Lionel Messi (Barcelona and Argentina)

FIFA BALLON D'OR

(replaces European and World Footballer of the Year)
2010: Lionel Messi (Barcelona). **2011** Lionel Messi (Barcelona)

FIFA WORLD COACH OF THE YEAR

2010: Jose Mourinho (Inter Milan). **2011** Pep Guardiola (Barcelona)

BARCLAYS PREMIER LEAGUE

REVIEWS, APPEARANCES, SCORERS 2011–12

(Figures in brackets denote appearances as substitute)

ARSENAL

Robin van Persie rescued his side from a nightmare start, continued to lead from the front and played the major role in securing a 15th successive season of Champions League football. Four defeats in the first seven matches had manager Arsene Wenger virtually writing off their championship chances. They were already 12 points behind Manchester United and Manchester City and had been mauled 8-2 at Old Trafford. It was the club's worst opening in top flight football since 1953-54. To their credit, Arsenal began picking up the pieces, boosted by Van Persie's hat-trick in a 5-3 victory over Chelsea at Stamford Bridge. A second came in the 7-1 win over Blackburn which, after another lean spell, had helped make inroads into the 12-point advantage Tottenham were holding in third place. The pursuit continued when a two-goal deficit against Spurs at the Emirates was transformed into a 5-2 success and they eventually finished a point ahead of their north London rivals. Van Persie took the Premier League's Golden Boot award and was named top player by the players' union and football writers. He finished with 37 in all competitions, one of them coming as Arsenal went close to pulling back a 4-0 Champions League deficit in a last 16 tie against AC Milan by winning the second leg 3-0. The end of the season marked Pat Rice's retirement after a 44-year association with the club and Steve Bould's promotion as Wenger's No 2.

Arshavin A 8 (11)	Henry T .... - (4)	Sagna B.................. 20 (1)
Arteta M 29	Jenkinson C 5 (4)	Santos A.................. 10 (5)
Benayoun Y.............. 10 (9)	Koscielny L..................33	Song A 34
Bendtner N .... - (1)	Lansbury H .... - (2)	Squillaci S .... - (1)
Chamakh M............. 1 (10)	Mertesacker P 21	Szczesny W...................38
Coquelin F 6 (4)	Miquel I.................... 1 (3)	Traore A 1
Diaby A...................... - (4)	Nasri S............................1	Van Persie R 37 (1)
Djourou J 14 (4)	Oxlade-Chamberlain A. 6 (10)	Vermaelen T 28 (1)
Frimpong E 3 (3)	Park Chu-Young........... - (7)	Walcott T 32 (3)
Gervinho 19 (9)	Ramsey A 27 (7)	Yennaris N .... - (1)
Gibbs K 15 (1)	Rosicky T................ 19 (9)	

League goals (74): Van Persie 30, Walcott 8, Arteta 6, Vermaelen 6, Benayoun 4, Gervinho 4, Koscielny 2, Oxlade-Chamberlain 2, Ramsey 2, Santos 2, Gibbs 1, Arshavin 1, Chamakh 1, Rosicky 1, Sagna 1, Song 1, Henry 1, Opponents 1
FA Cup goals (4): Van Persie 2, Henry 1, Walcott 1. **Carling Cup goals** (5): Arshavin 1, Benayoun 1, Gibbs 1, Oxlade-Chamberlain 1, Park Chu-Young 1. **Champions League goals** (13): Van Persie 5, Walcott 2, Benayoun 1, Koscielny 1, Oxlade-Chamberlain 1, Ramsey 1, Rosicky 1, Santos 1
Average home league attendance: 60,000. **Player of Year:** Robin van Persie

ASTON VILLA

From the start, Alex McLeish faced a huge job winning over supporters unhappy at the appointment of a manager straight from rivals Birmingham City. It was a task he struggled with and one that grew increasingly fraught as Villa slid towards the relegation zone. They made sure of staying up with a point gained against Tottenham in the final home fixture. But it was not enough to save the Scot, who was sacked by owner Randy Lerner the day after the season ended, with Villa having failed to win any of their last ten matches and finishing two places above the bottom three. A youthful squad found it hard going after the loss of leading scorer Darren Bent, with ruptured ankle ligaments, and midfielder Stiliyan Petrov, who was diagnosed with acute leukaemia. The team had also conceded, over the course of the season, too many goals from dead-ball situations to make any real impression. The cause was not helped late on when three players were disciplined by the club over a nightclub brawl. On a brighter note, Marc Albrighton scored the Premier League's 20,000th goal during the home game against Arsenal, receiving a £20,000 cheque for charity from sponsors Barclays. Norwich's Paul Lambert was charged with reviving Villa's fortunes.

Agbonlahor G 32 (1)	Delfouneso N 1 (5)	Ireland S.................. 19 (5)
Albrighton M 15 (11)	Delph F 10 (1)	Jenas J 1 (2)
Baker N 6 (2)	Dunne R 28	Keane R 5 (1)
Bannan B 10 (18)	Gardner G 5 (9)	Lichaj E................... 9 (1)
Bent D..................... 21 (1)	Given S........................32	N'Zogbia C 24 (6)
Carruthers S............. - (3)	Guzan B 6 (1)	Petrov S................. 26 (1)
Clark C 13 (2)	Herd C........................19	Warnock S 34 (1)
Collins J 31 (1)	Heskey E 18 (10)	Weimann A 5 (9)
Cuellar C................. 17 (1)	Hutton A................. 29 (2)	Young L 2

League goals (37): Bent 9, Agbonlahor 5, Petrov 4, Keane 3, N'Zogbia 2, Albrighton 2, Warnock 2, Weimann 2, Bannan 1, Clark 1, Collins 1, Dunne 1, Herd 1, Heskey 1, Ireland 1, Lichaj 1
FA Cup goals (5): Agbonlahor 1, Albrighton 1, Bent 1, Clark 1, Dunne 1. **Carling Cup goals** (2): Delfouneso 1, Lichaj 1
Average home league attendance: 33,873. **Player of Year**: Stephen Ireland

BLACKBURN ROVERS

Steve Kean was a manager under pressure from the word go. Rovers made the club's worst start to a league season for 60 years, with three defeats, and supporters were soon calling for him to go. They were still voicing disapproval when relegation was confirmed, after 11 years in the top flight, by a defeat by revitalised Wigan in the final home game. Their team were bottom at Christmas and lost Christopher Samba in the New Year, the defensive strongman demanding a move and eventually joining the wealthy Russian club Anzhi Makhachkala for £9m. Brief respite for Kean came not long after one of the season's many low points – a 7-1 beating at Arsenal. Junior Hoilett gave them victory with two goals over Wolves at Molineux, where Rovers kept a clean sheet for the first time in 31 matches. Then a 2-0 victory over Sunderland moved them five points clear of the relegation zone, with Hoilett and Yakubu on the mark. But it proved a false dawn. They lost the next five and eight of the season's last nine. Yakubu netted 17 goals in the league, including all four against Swansea and a brace in the 3-2 victory away to Manchester United.

Blackman N .... - (1)	Hoilett J 34	Petrovic R 10 (9)
Bunn M 3	Kean J...........................1	Roberts J 5 (5)
Dann S.......................27	Lowe J 30 (2)	Robinson P 34
Dunn D..................... 21 (5)	Modeste A.................. 3 (6)	Rochina R................. 9 (9)
Emerton B 2	Morris J .... - (2)	Salgado M.....................9
Formica M 25 (9)	Nelsen R.......................1	Samba C....................16
Givet G 21 (1)	Nzonzi S 31 (1)	Slew J .... - (1)
Goodwillie D........... 4 (16)	Olsson Marcus.......... 10 (2)	Vukcevic S 4 (3)
Grella V .... - (1)	Olsson Martin 23 (4)	Yakubu 29 (1)
Hanley G.................. 19 (4)	Orr B 10 (2)	
Henley A................. 4 (3)	Pedersen M G................33	

League goals (48): Yakubu 17, Hoilett 7, Formica 4, Pedersen 3, Dunn 2, Goodwillie 2, Nzonzi 2, Rochina 2, Samba 2, Dann 1, Hanley 1, Vukcevic 1, Opponents 4
FA Cup goals (1): Goodwillie 1. **Carling Cup goals** (10): Rochina 4, Givet 1, Goodwillie 1, Pedersen 1, Roberts 1, Vukcevic 1, Yakubu 1
Average home league attendance: 22,551. **Player of Year**: Yakubu

BOLTON WANDERERS

The feelgood factor generated around the Reebok by Fabrice Muamba's 'miracle' recovery from a cardiac arrest was not enough to save his side from relegation after 11 years in the Premier League. When Bolton resumed their bid to beat the drop after the fixture against Aston Villa was postponed because of the midfielder's illness, they overcame two other struggling sides to climb out of the bottom three. Two headers from David Wheater, his first in the league for the club, accounted for Blackburn, while Marcos Alonso was also on the mark for the first time in victory at Wolves. But they did not win another home game and needed three points at Stoke on the final afternoon to survive. Here, they had grounds for complaint when Adam Bogdan was barged into the net by Jon Walters while holding the ball. The goalkeeper then brought down Peter Crouch for the penalty which Walters converted for 2-2. Bolton's troubles had started pre-season, with Chung-Yong Lee and new signing Tyrone Mears sustaining broken legs. Player of the Year Stuart Holden never kicked a ball because of knee trouble. They had also lost leading scorers Johan Elmander and on-loan Daniel Sturridge. If that wasn't enough, Bolton faced both Manchester clubs, Liverpool, Arsenal and Chelsea in their opening seven games.

Alonso, M 4 (1)	Jaaskelainen J...............18	Ream T...........................13
Blake R .... - (1)	Kakuta G .... - (4)	Reo-Coker N..................37
Bogdan A....................20	Klasnic I 16 (13)	Ricketts S......................20
Boyata D.............. 13 (1)	Knight Z 21 (4)	Riley J 2 (1)
Cahill G 19	Mears T 1	Robinson P 15 (2)
Chung-Yong Lee...........- (2)	Miyaichi R 8 (4)	Sordell M .... - (3)
Davies K 21 (10)	Muamba F 18 (2)	Steinsson G.............. 20 (3)
Davies M.............. 29 (6)	Ngog D 24 (9)	Tuncay....................... 3 (13)
Eagles C 26 (8)	Petrov M 30 (1)	Vela J .... - (3)
Gardner R 2 (2)	Pratley D.............. 14 (11)	Wheater D....................24

League goals (46): Klasnic 8, Davies K 6, Davies M 4, Eagles 4, Petrov 4, Ngog 3, Reo-Coker 3, Cahill 2, Wheater 2, Alonso 1, Boyata 1, Muamba 1, Pratley 1, Ricketts 1, Steinsson 1, Opponents 4
FA Cup goals (9): Davies K 2, Eagles 1, Klasnic 1, Miyaichi 1, Ngog 1, Petrov 1, Pratley 1, Wheater 1. **Carling Cup goals** (5): Eagles 1, Kakuta 1, Muamba 1, Petrov 1, Tuncay 1
Average home league attendance: 23,670. **Player of Year**: Adam Bogdan

CHELSEA

Roberto Di Matteo secured a place in Chelsea's hall of fame as a player with goals in two FA Finals, a League Cup victory and more success in the Cup Winners' Cup. Now, he is guaranteed one as a manager after bringing the Champions League trophy to Stamford Bridge for the first time. Didier Drogba's 88th minute equaliser and subsequent decisive penalty in a shoot-out against Bayern Munich in the final came at the end of a remarkable season for the club and their caretaker boss. He also won the FA Cup against Liverpool, having transformed their fortunes when Andre Villas-Boas was sacked after less than nine months in charge. Mood, morale and results deteriorated under the young Portuguese, appointed to succeed Carlo Ancelotti after achieving domestic and European success with Porto. He had a difficult working relationship with senior players, there were disagreements over tactics and he paid the price for a lean run of 12 Premier League matches, culminating in a defeat by West Bromwich Albion. Di Matteo, dismissed by Albion the previous season, had none of those problems, having worked well with the team during his time as No 2 to Villas-Boas. Chelsea's championship chances had disappeared before the midway point of the campaign. But they showed tremendous character to beat both Napoli and Barcelona against all the odds, while returning to Wembley with a 5-1 victory over Tottenham in the semi-finals. Di Matteo was rewarded with the job on a permanent basis.

Alex..................................3	Cahill G 9 (1)	Hilario 2
Anelka N.................. 3 (6)	Cech P 34	Hutchinson S 1 (1)
Benayoun Y.................. - (1)	Cole A 31 (1)	Ivanovic B.............. 26 (3)
Bertrand R 6 (1)	Drogba D 16 (8)	Kalou S 7 (5)
Bosingwa J.............. 24 (3)	Essien M.................. 10 (4)	Lampard F 26 (4)

Luiz D 18 (2)	Mikel J O 15 (7)	Sturridge D 28 (2)
Lukaku R 1 (7)	Meireles R 23 (5)	Terry J 31
Malouda F............. 11 (15)	Paulo Ferreira............ 3 (3)	Torres F 20 (12)
Mata J 29 (5)	Ramires 28 (2)	Turnbull R.......................2
McEachran J .... - (2)	Romeu O 11 (5)	

League goals (65): Lampard 11, Sturridge 11, Mata 6, Terry 6, Torres 6, Drogba 5, Ramires 5, Ivanovic 3, Luiz 2, Malouda 2, Meireles 2, Anelka 1, Bosingwa 1, Cahill 1, Kalou 1, Opponents 2 **FA Cup goals** (20): Mata 4, Ramires 4, Drogba 2, Lampard 2, Ramires 2, Meireles 2, Torres 2, Cahill 1, Kalou 1, Malouda 1, Sturridge 1. **Carling Cup goals** (2): Kalou 1, Sturridge 1. **Champions League goals** (25): Drogba 6, Lampard 3, Ramires 3, Torres 3, Ivanovic 2, Kalou 2, Mata 2, Meireles 2, Luiz 1, Terry 1
Average home league attendance: 41,478. **Player of Year**: Juan Mata

EVERTON

David Moyes would have loved an FA Cup Final to mark ten years as manager at Goodison. Instead, he had to settle for a major 'consolation' prize – finishing above Liverpool for the first time since 2005. Everton were denied by their neighbours in the semi-finals, having led through Nikica Jelavic, and lost to them home and away in the league. But they showed great character to respond to that cup defeat by scoring twice in the final ten minutes and pegging back Manchester United to 4-4 at Old Trafford. Fulham were seen off 4-0 and Newcastle beaten 3-1 on the final afternoon of the season, extending an unbeaten run to nine games from which 19 points were accumulated. That confirmed seventh place, one higher than Liverpool, with the improvement in results in the second half of the season attributed to three signings Moyes made in the January transfer window. Jelavic, a £5m buy from Rangers, scored 11 goals in 13 starts; Steven Pienaar, back at the club on loan from Tottenham where he failed to make an impression, was a major provider; Gibson, from Manchester United, gave the midfield a more solid look.

Anichebe V 5 (7)	Donovan L.......................7	Jelavic N.................. 10 (3)
Arteta M 1 (1)	Drenthe R 10 (11)	McAleny C .... - (2)
Baines L 33	Duffy S 2 (2)	McFadden J 2 (5)
Barkley R 2 (4)	Fellaini M 31 (3)	Neville P 24 (3)
Baxter J .... - (1)	Gibson D.....................11	Osman L 28 (2)
Beckford J 1 (1)	Gueye M 3 (14)	Pienaar S.......................14
Bilyaletdinov D 7 (3)	Heitinga J 29 (1)	Rodwell J 11 (3)
Cahill T 27 (8)	Hibbert T 31 (1)	Saha L 15 (3)
Coleman S 14 (4)	Howard T......................38	Stracqualursi D 7 (14)
Distin S 24 (3)	Jagielka P 29 (1)	Vellios A 2 (1)

League goals (50): Jelavic 9, Osman 5, Anichebe 4, Baines 4, Pienaar 4, Drenthe 3, Fellaini 3, Vellios 3, Cahill 2, Jagielka 2, Rodwell 2, Arteta 1, Gibson 1, Gueye 1, Heitinga 1, Howard 1, Saha 1, Stracqualursi 1, Opponents 2
FA Cup goals (10): Jelavic 2, Stacqualursi 2, Baines 1, Cahill 1, Drenthe 1, Fellaini 1, Heitinga 1, Opponents 1. **Carling Cup goals** (6): Anichebe 1, Arteta 1, Fellaini 1, Neville 1, Saha 1, Opponents 1
Average home league attendance: 33,228. **Player of Year**: John Heitinga

FULHAM

Clint Dempsey collected a clutch of personal honours as Fulham capably negotiated a gruelling season which started in June with a Europa League qualifier. They secured a third top-ten place in four years and finished level on points with Liverpool, having won at Anfield for the first time in their penultimate away match. Dempsey's winner in the home game against Liverpool made him the highest scoring American in the Premier League with 37 goals. He became the first United States player to score a hat-trick in the league – in a 5-2 win over Newcastle – and went on to take his tally for the season to a club record 17. Dempsey, who netted another three against

Charlton in the FA Cup, was also US male Player of the Year for the second time. Fulham failed to win any of their opening six matches, but a hat-trick by Andrew Johnson put them on the right track with a 6-0 win over Queens Park Rangers and there was another big victory to come against Wolves (5-0). Their luck was out in Europe, a stoppage-time equaliser conceded to Odense resulting in a failure to qualify from their group.

Baird C 13 (6)	Grygera Z 5	Ruiz B 17 (10)
Briggs M 1 (1)	Hangeland B 38	Sa O 3 (4)
Davies S 3 (3)	Hughes A 18 (1)	Schwarzer M 30
Dembele M 33 (3)	Johnson A 13 (7)	Senderos P 21
Dempsey C 37	Kacaniklic A 2 (2)	Sidwell S 12 (2)
Diarra M 8 (3)	Kasami P 3 (4)	Stockdale D 8
Duff D 23 (5)	Kelly S 21 (3)	Trotta R .... - (1)
Etuhu D 9 (13)	Murphy D 33 (3)	Zamora R 14 (1)
Frei K 6 (10)	Pogrebnyak P 12	
Gecov M .... - (2)	Riise J A 35 (1)	

League goals (48): Dempsey 17, Pogrebnyak 6, Zamora 5, Johnson 3, Dembele 2, Duff 2, Murphy 2, Ruiz 2, Diarra 1, Sa 1, Senderos 1, Sidwell 1, Opponents 5
FA Cup goals (5): Dempsey 3, Duff 1, Murphy 1. **Carling Cup goals**: None. **Europa League goals** (24): Johnson 3, Dempsey 3, Duff 3, Murphy 3, Sidwell 2, Zamora 2, Briggs 1, Frei 1, Hughes 1
Average home league attendance. 25,293. **Player of Year**: Clint Dempsey

LIVERPOOL

Carling Cup success counted for little; neither did reaching the FA Cup Final. All that mattered was eighth place in the Premier League, the lowest for 18 years and a long way short of Champions League football the club's American owners demanded. They sacked Kenny Dalglish after 15 months of his second spell in charge, dissatisfied with the return on £100m spent on new players. He was replaced by Swansea's highly-rated Brendan Rodgers. Anfield supporters are among the most loyal in the country, but even they were concerned about a season which brought just six home wins and never much sign of an improvement. Dalglish, who followed director of football Damien Comolli out of the door, did himself no favours by his handling the Luis Suarez affair in which the Uruguayan was found to have abused Manchester United's Patrice Evra and banned for eight matches. The manager subsequently apologised, but the damage had been done. Despite his actions, Suarez was one of the few success stories on the pitch, with 17 goals in all competitions and a quite brilliant hat-trick against Norwich, completed with a shot from 50 yards. The contrast between Liverpool's league and cup form was marked. They overcame Stoke, Chelsea and Manchester City on the way to winning the Carling Cup against Cardiff and beat Manchester United in the FA Cup before finishing the better side against Chelsea at Wembley.

Adam C 27 (1)	Flanagan J 5	Maxi Rodriguez 10 (2)
Agger D 24 (3)	Gerrard S 12 (6)	Meireles R .... - (2)
Aurelio F 1 (1)	Henderson J 31 (6)	Reina J 34
Bellamy C 12 (15)	Johnson G 22 (1)	Shelvey J 8 (5)
Carragher J 19 (2)	Jones B .... - (1)	Skrtel M 33 (1)
Carroll A 21 (14)	Jose Enrique 33 (2)	Spearing J 15 (1)
Coates S 4 (3)	Kelly M 12	Sterling R .... - (3)
Doni A 4	Kuyt D 22 (12)	Suarez L 29 (2)
Downing S 28 (8)	Lucas Leiva 12	

League goals (47): Suarez 11, Bellamy 6, Gerrard 5, Carroll 4, Maxi Rodriguez 4, Adam 2, Henderson 2, Kuyt 2, Skrtel 2, Agger 1, Coates 1, Johnson 1, Shelvey 1, Opponents 5
FA Cup goals (18): Carroll 4, Suarez 3, Downing 2, Agger 1, Bellamy 1, Gerrard 1, Kuyt 1, Shelvey 1, Skrtel 1, Opponents 3. **Carling Cup goals** (14): Suarez 3, Bellamy 2, Gerrard 2, Kuyt 2, Maxi Rodriguez 2. Carroll 1, Kelly 1, Skrtel 1
Average home league attendance: 44,253. **Player of Year**: Martin Skrtel

MANCHESTER CITY

They were written off when falling eight points behind Manchester United with six matches remaining and again when trailing ten-man Queens Park Rangers going into stoppage-time of a must-win game. Yet City had the final say in one last twist to the tightest and most dramatic Premier League finish in its 20-year history. Edin Dzeko headed an equaliser and, remarkably, Sergio Aguero scored his 23rd goal of the campaign to make them champions for the first time for 44 years on goal difference. Roberto Mancini called it 'a crazy finish to a crazy season.' The manager was also correct to insist his team deserved it. Their persistence had been rewarded with important late goals in previous matches, overall they scored more and conceded fewer than United and beat their neighbours home and away. The 6-1 victory at Old Trafford, in his 100th game in charge, formed part of a record-breaking start of 11 in 12 games. City stayed on top for the next four-and-a-half months, until defeats at Swansea and Arsenal, along with draws against Stoke and Sunderland. That seemed to take the pressure off and ten goals flowed in the next two against West Bromwich Albion and at Norwich, where the rehabilitated Carlos Tevez went some way to justifying his previous indiscretions with a hat-trick. Then came captain Vincent Kompany's decisive header in the return fixture with United. And on the gound where City won the title in 1968, Mancini pushed Yaya Toure forward from his normal holding midfied role for the Ivorian to score both goals in a crucial win over Newcastle.

Aguero S	31 (3)	Johnson A	10 (16)	Razak A	- (1)
Balotelli M	14 (9)	Kolarov A	9 (3)	Richards M	23 (6)
Barry G	31 (3)	Kompany V	31	Savic S	5 (6)
Clichy G	28	Lescott J	30 (1)	Silva D	33 (3)
De Jong N	11 (10)	Milner J	17 (9)	Tevez C	7 (6)
Dzeko E	16 (14)	Nasri S	26 (4)	Toure K	8 (6)
Hargreaves O	- (1)	Onuoha N	- (1)	Toure Y	31 (1)
Hart J	38	Pizarro D	1 (4)	Zabaleta P	18 (3)

League goals (93): Aguero 23, Dzeko 14, Balotelli 13, Johnson 6, Silva 6, Toure Y 6, Nasri 5, Tevez 4, Kompany 3, Milner 3, Kolarov 2, Lescott 2, Barry 1, Richards 1, Savic 1, Zabaleta 1, Opponents 2
FA Cup goals (2): Aguero 1, Kolarov 1. **Carling Cup goals** (10): Dzeko 3, Aguero 1, Balotelli 1, Hargreaves 1, Johnson 1, Nasri 1, De Jong 1, Opponents 1. **Champions League goals** (9): Toure Y 3, Balotelli 2, Aguero 1, Kolarov 1, Silva 1, Opponents 1. **Europa League goals** (9): Aguero 4, Balotelli 1, Dzeko 1, Pizarro 1, Silva 1, Opponents 1. **Community Shield goals** (2): Dzeko 1, Lescott 1
Average home league attendance: 47,045. **Player of Year**: Sergio Aguero

MANCHESTER UNITED

Sir Alex Ferguson reached 25 years as manager at Old Trafford, but it was a landmark overshadowed by the way his side lost the title to Manchester City. United looked to have it all sewn up when going eight points clear with six fixtures left after winning 11 out of 12 matches. Instead, they faltered, losing to Wigan for the first time in the initial ten minutes against Everton and giving a pallid performance in a second defeat by City, who had previously routed them 6-1 at Old Trafford. Wayne Rooney's 27th goal, a campaign best, on the final day at Sunderland looked to have earned them a reprieve. Then word came through that City had scored twice in stoppage-time against Queens Park Rangers to stay on top on goal difference. Sir Alex complimented Roberto Mancinci on his achievement, while acknowledging it had not been a vintage season for his own players, even allowing for the fact that United had encountered injury problems, notably the one that restricted Nemanja Vidic to just six matches. There were some high spots, including a Premier League record of 18 goals in the opening four matches which embraced the 8-2 win over Arsenal. But they conceded three or more seven times, two in European games where standards also fell. United failed to qualify from a non-too-difficult Champions League group and were outplayed by Athletic Bilbao in the Europa League.

Amos B.................................1	Fletcher D................... 7 (1)	Owen M........................ - (1)
Anderson 8 (2)	Fryers E...................... - (2)	Pogba P....................... - (3)
Berbatov D................. 5 (7)	Gibson D.........................1	Rooney W 32 (2)
Carrick M 27 (3)	Giggs R 14 (11)	Scholes P 14 (3)
Cleverley T................ 5 (5)	Hernandez J.......... 18 (10)	Smalling C 14 (5)
Evans J................... 28 (1)	Ji-Sung Park 10 (7)	Valencia A.............. 22 (5)
Evra P.............................37	Jones P............... 25 (4)	Vidic N..............................6
Da Silva F................. 2 (3)	Keane W...................... - (1)	Welbeck D 23 (7)
Da Silva R............. 10 (2)	Lindegaard A.....................8	Young A 19 (6)
De Gea D.......................29	Macheda F.................. - (3)	
Ferdinand R 29 (1)	Nani.......................... 24 (5)	

League goals (89): Rooney 27, Hernandez 10, Welbeck 9, Nani 8, Berbatov 7, Young 6, Scholes 4, Valencia 4, Anderson 2, Carrick 2, Giggs 2, Ji-Sung Park 2, Evans 1, Fletcher 1, Jones 1, Smalling 1, Opponents 2
FA Cup goals (4): Rooney 2, Ji-Sung Park 1, Welbeck 1. **Carling Cup goals (7):** Owen 3, Berbatov 1, Giggs 1, Macheda 1, Valencia 1. **Champions League goals (11):** Rooney 3, Welbeck 2, Berbatov 1, Fletcher 1, Giggs 1, Jones 1, Valencia 1, Young 1. **Europa League goals (6):** Rooney 3, Hernandez 2, Young 1. **Community Shield goals (3):** Nani 2, Smalling 1
Average home league attendance: 75,387. **Player of Year:** Antonio Valencia

NEWCASTLE UNITED

Alan Pardew collected both Manager of the Year awards and his players qualified for Europe as Newcastle silenced the sceptics. They were written off in some quarters as relegation candidates after Kevin Nolan and Joey Barton followed Andy Carroll out of the club. Instead, there were 11 unbeaten matches to start the season, with Yohan Cabaye an immediate success in midfield and Demba Ba scoring hat-tricks against Blackburn and Stoke. Some momentum was lost when injuries forced defensive changes for the first time, but Newcastle came through a lean spell and another signing, this time in the winter transfer window, proved an even bigger hit. Ba's fellow Sengalese, Papiss Cisse, a £9m buy from the German club Freiburg, scored on his debut and went on to deliver 13 goals in 14 appearances, some of them right out of the top drawer. Six successive wins lifted his side into Champions League contention and they remained in there until defeat at Everton, along with results elsewhere on the final day, left them heading for the Europa League from fifth place. Pardew was voted top man by the Premier League and League Managers' Association, while goalkeeper Tim Krul earned plaudits for outstanding form.

Ameobi Sammy 1 (9)	Ferguson S.................. - (7)	Santon D 19 (5)
Ameobi Shola........... 8 (19)	Gosling D................. 1 (11)	Simpson D 35
Barton J............................2	Guthrie D................. 13 (3)	Smith A...................... - (2)
Ben Arfa H............. 16 (10)	Gutierrez J.......................37	Taylor R 23 (8)
Best L 16 (2)	Krul T...........................38	Taylor S...........................14
Cabaye Y.......................34	Lovenkrands P.......... 2 (7)	Tiote C...........................24
Cisse P 13 (1)	Marveaux S 1 (6)	Vuckic H................. 2 (2)
Coloccini F.....................35	Obertan G 18 (5)	Williamson M 21 (1)
Demba Ba................ 32 (2)	Perch J.................. 13 (12)	

League goals (56): Ba 16, Cisse 13, Ben Arfa 5, Best 4, Cabaye 4, Ameobi Shola 2, Gutierrez 2, Taylor R 2, Gosling 1, Guthrie 1, Obertan 1, Opponents 5
FA Cup goals (2): Ben Arfa 1, Gutierrez 1. **Carling Cup goals (9):** Lovenkrands 3, Ameobi Sammy 1, Cabaye 1, Coloccini 1, Guthrie 1, Simpson 1, Taíyor R 1
Average home league attendance: 49,936. **Player of Year:** Fabricio Coloccini

NORWICH CITY

Never overawed, and never in danger of being drawn into a relegation struggle, Norwich negotiated their return to the Premier League with considerable aplomb. Paul Lambert used the rotation system shrewdly and his players responded with great organisation and no little skill to spend most of the season in the middle reaches of the table. If there was a single match which embraced this approach, it came at Old Trafford, where they attacked Manchester United head on and with sharper finishing might have come away with a victory against Tottenham instead of losing 2-0. They also won plenty admirers at White Hart Lane for a winning performance earned with a starting line-up of all English players and rated by Lambert the best of his time in charge. Only Manchester City really turned them over, a 5-1 defeat at the Etihad followed by a 6-1 reversal at Carrow Road, where they conceded four goals in the final 20 minutes. A strong finish, 3-3 at Arsenal and 2-0 against Aston Villa meant 12th place, with Grant Holt scoring in each to take his tally to 15. The manager's success brought a move to Aston Villa, with Birmingham's Chris Hughton taking over.

Ayala D..................... 6 (1)	Hoolahan W 25 (8)	Pilkington A 23 (7)
Barnett L 13 (4)	Howson J 11	Rudd D.......................... 1 (1)
Bennett E 22 (10)	Jackson S 10 (12)	Ruddy J...........................37
Bennett R 8	Johnson B................ 25 (3)	Surman A 21 (4)
Crofts A 13 (11)	Lappin S..........................4	Tierney M.......................17
De Laet R 6	Martin R 30 (3)	Vaughan J.................. 1 (4)
Drury A........................12	Martin C 3 (1)	Ward E 12
Fox D 23 (5)	Morison S 22 (12)	Whitbread Z 18
Holt G 24 (12)	Naughton K............ 29 (3)	Wilbraham 2 (9)

League goals (52): Holt 15, Morison 9, Pilkington 8, Hoolahan 4, Surman 4, Jackson 3, Johnson 2, Martin R 2, Barnett 1, Bennett E 1, Howson 1, Wilbraham 1, De Laet 1
FA Cup goals (7): Holt 2, Jackson 2, Hoolahan 1, Morison 1, Surman 1. **Carling Cup goals**: None
Average home league attendance: 26,548. **Player of Year**: Grant Holt

QUEENS PARK RANGERS

Rangers escaped an immediate return to the Championship on the final day of the season, while at the same time playing an eye-catching role in events at the top of the table. They overcame Joey Barton's sending-off – the club's ninth red card – to lead Manchester City 2-1 through goals by Djibril Cisse and Jamie Mackie. A stirring performance looked as if it had made them safe, as well as delivering the title to Manchester United. Instead, Rangers caved in twice in stoppage-time and were relieved to hear that Bolton had fallen short of the win at Stoke which would have sent them down. Key to survival under Mark Hughes was victory in the final five home matches against Liverpool, Arsenal, Swansea, Tottenham and Stoke. It was in sharp contrast to early results at Loftus Road which prompted Neil Warnock to bring in five players with wide-ranging Premier League experience. His new-look side climbed into top half of table after 12 matches, but failed to win any of next eight, slipped fourth from bottom and Warnock was sacked. Hughes became the club's ninth 'permanent' manager in six years.

Agyemang P......................2	Dyer K...............................1	Mackie J.................. 24 (7)
Andrade B................. - (1)	Ephraim H .... - (2)	Onuoha N 16
Barton J.........................31	Faurlin A........................20	Orr B 2 (4)
Bothroyd J .... `12 (9)	Ferdinand A 31	Puncheon J................ - (2)
Perone B...........................1	Gabbidon D............ 15 (2)	Smith T 4 (13)
Buzsaky A 10 (8)	Hall F................... 11 (3)	Taarabt A 24 (3)
Campbell D J 2 (9)	Harriman M.............. - (1)	Taiwo T 13 (2)
Cerny R 5	Helguson H 13 (3)	Traore A 18 (5)
Cisse D 7 (1)	Hill C 19 (3)	Wright-Phillips S 24 (8)
Connolly M 5 (1)	Hulse R 1 (1)	Young L 23
Derry S 28 (1)	Kenny P..........................33	Zamora A 14
Diakite S.........................9	Macheda F .... - (3)	

League goals (43): Helguson 8, Mackie 7, Cisse 6, Barton 3, Bothroyd 2, Buzsaky 2, Smith 2, Taarabt 2, Young 2, Zamora 2, Campbell 1, Derry 1, Diakite 1, Faurlin 1, Taiwo 1, Opponents 2
FA Cup goals (2): Helguson 1, Gabbidon 1. **Carling Cup goals**: None
Average home league attendance: 17,295. **Player of Year**: Clint Hill

STOKE CITY

Stoke were on course for their highest Premier League finish until a long season began to catch up with them. They won only one of the final 11 matches and dropped back to 14th in a congested middle section of the table. Nevertheless, they could look back with some satisfaction at reaching the 40-point 'safety' mark with six games still to play and achieving a measure of success in the FA Cup and Europa League. With Peter Crouch proving a good signing, Tony Pulis led them to the cup quarter-finals for the third successive year before a 2-1 defeat at Liverpool in their fourth away tie. In Europe for the first time since the mid-1970s, Stoke were the only one of eight English and Scottish teams to come through qualifying and group matches to the knock-out stage of the tournament. The run ended with defeat by Valencia, with Pulis having to defend his decision to leave nine first-teamers behind for the second leg. Stoke also lost that one 1-0, with Kenwyne Jones missing two chances to keep them in contention.

Begovic A 22 (1)	Jerome C 7 (16)	Upson M 10 (4)
Crouch P 31 (1)	Jones K 10 (11)	Walters J 38
Delap R 18 (8)	Palacios W 9 (9)	Whelan G 27 (3)
Diao S 2 (4)	Pennant J 18 (9)	Whitehead D 24 (9)
Etherington M 30	Pugh D .... - (3)	Wilkinson A 20 (5)
Fuller R 3 (10)	Shawcross R 36	Wilson M 35
Higginbotham D 1 (1)	Shotton R 14 (9)	Woodgate J 16 (1)
Huth R 31 (3)	Sorensen T 16	

League goals (36): Crouch 10, Walters 7, Jerome 4, Etherington 3, Huth 3, Delap 2, Shawcross 2, Jones 1, Shotton 1, Upson 1, Whelan 1, Opponents 1
FA Cup goals (8): Crouch 2, Huth 2, Jerome 2, Walters 2. **Carling Cup goals** (1): Jones 1. **Europa League goals** (17): Jones 4, Crouch 2, Jerome 2, Shotton 2, Walters 2, Fuller 1, Pugh 1, Upson 1, Whelan 1, Whitehead 1
Average home league attendance: 27,226. **Player of Year:** Peter Crouch

SUNDERLAND

Martin O'Neill returned to management 16 months after resigning his job at Aston Villa and immediately made a mark at the Stadium of Light. In his first game in charge after Steve Bruce was sacked for two wins in 13 matches, O'Neill looked to be heading for defeat until spectacular goals by David Vaughan in the 84th minute and Sebastian Larsson in stoppage-time earned victory over Blackburn. He gave James McClean his debut in that match and the midfielder seized the chance to become an influential figure in Sunderland's climb from fourth from bottom. With Frenchman Stephane Sessegnon scoring freely, they won seven of the first ten Premier League games under the new manager and rose as high as eighth in the table. Manchester City were among their victims and a notable double was on the cards when they led 3-1 at the Etihad Stadium with 85 minutes gone before City rescued a point. After that, Sunderland lost momentum, failing to score in the next four matches and winning only one of the final eight.

Bardsley P 29 (2)	Gardner C 22 (8)	Noble R .... - (1)
Bendtner N 25 (3)	Gordon C 1	O'Shea J 29
Bramble T 8	Gyan A 3	Richardson K 26 (3)
Bridge W 3 (5)	Kilgallon M 9 (1)	Sessegnon S 36
Brown W 20	Ji Dong-Won 2 (17)	Turner M 23 (1)
Campbell F 6 (6)	Kyrgiakos S 2 (1)	Vaughan D 17 (5)
Cattermole L 23	Larsson S 32	Westwood K 8 (1)
Colback J 29 (6)	McClean J 20 (3)	Wickham C 5 (11)
Elmohamady A 7 (11)	Meyler D 1 (6)	
Ferdinand A 3	Mignolet S 29	

League goals (45): Bendtner 8, Larsson 7, Sessegnon 7, McClean 5, Gardner 3, Ji Dong-Won 2, Richardson 2, Vaughan 2, Bardsley 1, Bramble 1, Brown 1, Campbell 1, Colback

1, Elmohamady 1, Wickham 1, Opponents 2
FA Cup goals (8): Bardsley 1, Campbell 1, Colback 1, Larsson 1, McClean 1, Richardson 1, Sessegnon 1, Opponents 1. **Carling Cup goals:** None
Average home league attendance: 39,095. **Player of Year**: Stephane Sessegnon

SWANSEA CITY

Humour in the stands blended with style on the pitch as victory over Liverpool rounded off a commendable first Premier League season. Hundreds of fans in a record crowd of 20,605 turned up as Elvis Presley impersonators to remind the bookmaker how wrong he had been to insist there was more chance of Elvis being spotted in south Wales than of Swansea avoiding relegation. Brendan Rodgers and his promoted team had emerged from a harsh introduction to the top flight to earn widespread acclaim for the standard of their football. The manager's insistence on playing a passing game paid dividend once the opening four matches without a goal to show from them were out of the way. Manchester City and Arsenal were also defeated at the Liberty Stadium and Tottenham and Chelsea held to draws. Rodgers, however, rated the 3-0 win at Fulham as their best performances, with the Fulham goalkeeper Mark Schwarzer adding his praise to the quality on display that day. Two of the goals were scored by Gylfi Sigurdsson, who made a big impression after joining on loan from the German club Hoffenheim in the January transfer window and who finished with seven to his credit. Rodgers was lost to Liverpool and replaced by Michael Laudrup.

Agustien K 7 (6)	Lita L 4 (12)	Sigurdsson G............ 17 (1)
Allen J 31 (5)	McEachran J 1 (3)	Sinclair S................. 35 (3)
Bessone F .... - (1)	Monk G 14 (2)	Tate A 1 (4)
Britton L 35 (1)	Moore L 3 (17)	Taylor N 35 (1)
Caulker A 26	Moras V .... - (1)	Tremmel G 1
Dobbie S 2 (6)	Orlandi A 2 (1)	Vorm M 37
Dyer N 29 (5)	Rangel A 32 (2)	Williams A 37
Gower M 14 (6)	Richards A 6 (2)	
Graham D 32 (4)	Routledge W 17 (11)	

League goals (44): Graham 12, Sinclair 8, Sigurdsson 7, Dyer 5, Allen 4, Lita 2, Moore 2, Orlandi 1, Routledge 1, Williams 1, Opponents 1.
FA Cup goals (5): Graham 2, Dyer 1, Moore 1, Rangel 1. **Carling Cup goals** (1): Opponents 1
Average home league attendance: 19,946. **Player of Year**: Nathan Dyer

TOTTENHAM HOTSPUR

Opinion was divided on whether speculation about Harry Redknapp becoming England manager had a detrimental effect on Tottenham's season. Redknapp himself maintained that his squad was not big enough to compensate for injuries and a drop in performance level. Even so, there was no argument that a costly run of nine games producing a single victory came in the aftermath of Fabio Capello resigning and Redknapp being installed as favourite for the job. The run ended any chance of his side having a say in the title race and offered Arsenal the incentive to make further inroads into what was once a 12-point gap between the teams. Tottenham lost the north London derby 5-2 after leading 2-0, eventually conceded third place and were in danger of surrendering fourth spot before three wins in the final four matches saw off Newcastle's challenge. But it proved not enough for a Champions League place, which went to Chelsea after their victory over Bayern Munich in the final. After that, speculation mounted about Redknapp's position and he was eventually sacked by chairman Daniel Levy, who replaced him with the former Chelsea manager Andre Villas-Boas.

Adebayor E 32 (1)	Crouch P.........................1	Gallas W 15
Assou-Ekotto B...............34	Dawson M.................. 6 (1)	Huddlestone T............. - (2)
Bale G 36	Defoe J 11 (14)	Kaboul Y........................33
Bassong S 1 (4)	Dos Santos G .... - (7)	King L 21
Corluka V 1 (2)	Friedel B.......................38	Kranjcar N 9 (3)

Lancaster C	- (1)	Parker S	28 (1)	Sando	17 (6)
Lennon A	19 (4	Pavlyuchenko R	- (5)	Smith A	- (1)
Livermore J	7 (17)	Pienaar S	- (2)	Walker K	37
Modric L	36	Rose D	3 (8)	Van der Vaart R	28 (5)
Nelsen R	- (5)	Saha L	5 (5)		

League goals (66): Adebayor 17, Defoe 11, Van der Vaart 11, Bale 9, Modric 4, Lennon 3, Saha 3, Assou-Ekotto 2, Walker 2, Kaboul 1, Kranjcar 1, Pavlyuchenko 1, Opponents 1
FA Cup goals (11): Defoe 3, Bale 2, Adebayor 1, Dos Santos 1, Nelsen 1, Pavlyuchenko 1, Saha 1, Van der Vaart 1. **Carling Cup goals:** None. **Europa League goals (14):** Defoe 3, Pavlyuchenko 2, Bale 1, Dos Santos 1, Kane H 1, Lennon 1, Livermore 1, Modric 1, Pienaar 1, Townsend 1, Van der Vaart 1
Average home league attendance: 36,026. **Player of Year:** Scott Parker

WEST BROMWICH ALBION

Roy Hodgson and his players were entitled to feel pleased with their work over the course of the season. It started with three successive defeats. But come May, they had achieved the club's highest Premier League finish of tenth and were top dogs in the West Midlands for the first time since third place in 1979. Ten points out of 12 gained against Aston Villa and Wolves added to the satisfaction, with the 5-1 success at Molineux featuring a hat-trick from Peter Odemwingie. Sunderland and Chelsea were then defeated, giving Albion a healthy 11-point cushion from the relegation places. This spell also marked an improvement in results at The Hawthorns, where they had already lost eight times. Another victory to savour was achieved by Odemwingie's winner at Anfield on Hodgson's first return to the club that sacked him the previous season. Albion were unable to give Hodgson a winning send-off to the England job, losing at home to Arsenal. But he left with the knowledge that considerable progress had been made at the club during his 14 months in charge. Steve Clarke replaced him after leaving a coaching job at Liverpool.

Andrews K	8 (6)	Jara G	1 (3)	Ridgewell L	13
Brunt C	25 (4)	Jones B	17 (1)	Scharner P	18 (11)
Cox S	7 (11)	Long S	24 (8)	Shorey N	22 (3)
Dawson C	6 (2)	McAuley G	32	Tamas G	7 (1)
Dorrans G	16 (15)	Morrison J	23 (7)	Tchoyi S	6 (12)
Fortune M-A	12 (5)	Mulumbu Y	34 (1)	Thomas J	26 (3)
Foster B	37	Odemwingie P	25 (5)	Thorne G	1 (2)
Fulop M	1	Olsson J	33		
Gera Z	3	Reid S	21 (1)		

League goals (45): Odemwingie 10, Long 8, Morrison 5, Dorrans 3, Scharner 3, Andrews 2, Brunt 2, Fortune 2, McAuley 2, Olsson 2, Mulumbu 1, Reid 1, Ridgewell 1, Tchoyi 1, Thomas 1, Opponents 1
FA Cup goals (5): Cox 3, Fortune 1, Odemwingie 1. **Carling Cup goals (5):** Fortune 2, Brunt 1, Cox 1, Thomas 1
Average home league attendance: 24,798. **Player of Year:** Jonas Olsson

WIGAN ATHLETIC

Even during the best part of six months in the bottom three and even though a daunting run of fixtures lay ahead, Roberto Martinez remained adamant that his players were capable of beating the drop. Few outside the DW Stadium would have agreed with him. Yet the manager was true to his word. Not only did they pull off a great escape, they did it in some style and despite some cruel luck. A first win at Anfield was followed by victory over Stoke. Then came defeat at Stamford Bridge, where both Chelsea goals were shown to be offside. Far from feeling sorry for themselves, Wigan regrouped to beat Manchester United for the first time, with the increasingly influential Shaun Maloney scoring the only goal. Five days later, Franco di Santo and Jordi Gomez stunned the Emirates with goals in the opening eight minutes which brought the club's first win in an away game against Arsenal. It put them five points clear of trouble and although there was still work to do, there was now no stopping them. Newcastle, Blackburn and Wolves were seen off, making it seven victories in the last nine matches, stretching the safety margin to seven points and prompting some observers to suggest Martinez should have been rewarded with a Manager of the Year award.

Al Habsi A 38	Figueroa M............... 37 (1)	Moses V.................. 36 (2)
Alcaraz A 25	Gohouri S 8 (2)	Piscu.............................5
Beausejour J 16	Gomez J 24 (4)	Rodallega H 11 (12)
Boyce E..........................26	Jones D 13 (3)	Sammon C 8 (17)
Caldwell G 36	Maloney S 8 (5)	Stam R 13 (7)
Crusat A 4 (11)	McArthur J......... 18 (13)	Watson B 14 (7)
Di Santo F 24 (8)	McCarthy J....................33	Van Aanholt P 3
Diame M 18 (8)	McManaman C .... - (2)	

League goals (42): Di Santo 7, Moses 6, Gomez 5, Boyce 3, Maloney 3, McArthur 3, Watson 3, Caldwell 3, Diame 3, Alcaraz 2, Rodallega 2, Crusat 1, Opponents 1
FA Cup goals (1): McManaman 1. **Carling Cup goals (1):** Watson 1
Average home league attendance: 18,634. **Player of Year:** Gary Caldwell

WOLVERHAMPTON WANDERERS

Hindsight can be a wonderful thing, but there was every justification for asking whether the sacking of Mick McCarthy was a mistake and accelerated his team's demise. Admittedly, unrest among supporters had reached a peak with a 5-1 home defeat by West Bromwich Albion. And with 13 games remaining, there was plenty of time for a new manager to spark a revival. But the club were unable to deliver a replacement with the necessary experience and expertise. A number of candidates, among them Steve Bruce, were interviewed, before the decision was made to install McCarthy's assistant, Terry Connor, until the end of the season. Connor started encouragingly, Wolves retrieving a 2-0 deficit for a point at Newcastle. But 5-0 beatings by Fulham and Manchester United cast them adrift at the bottom. Steve Fletcher's goals, which had previously offered a lifeline, dried up and seven successive defeats effectively confirmed a return to the Championship with five games still remaining. By the end, Connor was without a win in his 13 games in charge and in came Norwegian Stale Solbakken to pick up the pieces.

Bassong S.......................9	Foley K 11 (1)	Johnson R................... 26 (1)
Berra C 29 (1)	Forde A.................... 3 (3)	Jonsson E 2 (1)
Craddock J.....................1	Frimpong E 5	Kightly M................. 14 (4)
Davis D.................... 6 (1)	Gorman J .... - (1)	Maierhofer S .... - (1)
De Vries D......................4	Guedioura A 2 (8)	Milijas N............. 6 (14)
Doherty M .... - (1)	Hammill A 3 (6)	O'Hara J 19
Doyle K..................... 26 (7)	Hennessey W.................34	Stearman R............ 28 (2)
Ebanks-Blake S 8 (15)	Henry K 30 (1)	Vokes S .... - (4)
Edwards D 24 (2)	Hunt S 16 (8)	Ward S 38
Elokobi G............. 3 (6)	Ikeme C..................... - (1)	Zubar R 14 (1)
Fletcher S................ 26 (6)	Jarvis M................. 31 (6)	

League goals (40): Fletcher 12, Jarvis 8, Doyle 4, Edwards 3, Hunt 3, Kightly 3, Ward 3, O'Hara 2, Ebanks-Blake 1, Zubar 1
FA Cup goals: None. **Carling Cup goals (11):** Ebanks-Blake 2, Milijas 2, Edwards 1, Elokobi 1, Guedioura 1, Hammill 1, O'Hara 1, Spray J 1, Vokes 1
Average home league attendance: 25,672. **Player of Year:** Wayne Hennessey

NPOWER CHAMPIONSHIP

BARNSLEY

The loss of Jacob Butterfield and Ricardo Vaz Te had a pronounced effect on fortunes at Oakwell. Butterfield, at 21 the club's youngest-ever captain, sustained cruciate ligament damage against Leeds on New Year's Eve and was ruled out for the rest of the season. A month later, leading scorer Vaz Te joined West Ham after turning down the offer of a new contract. He had scored 12 league and FA Cup goals in 14 starts, including a hat-trick in the 4-1 win over Leeds. The pair had been key to Barnsley maintaining a mid-table position. Without them, goals and points were increasingly hard to come by. From the beginning of February to the end of the campaign, they won just two of 18 matches. There was no danger of being drawn into a relegation struggle because of the number of points previously accumulated. But the slide meant they dropped to fourth from bottom, the club's lowest finish since returning to the game's second tier in 2006.

Addison M 9 (2)	Edwards, R 17	Perkins D................. 31 (2)
Butterfield J 24	Foster S..........................41	Preece D...........................1
Button D.........................9	Golbourne S 10 (2)	Ranger N 3 (2)
Clark J....................... 1 (1)	Gray A 25 (7)	Rose D 2 (2)
Collins L 4 (3)	Hassell B 17 (2)	Smith K..................... 10 (2)
Cotterill D 6 (5)	Haynes D 4 (8)	Steele L...........................36
Dagnall C 4 (5)	Higginbotham K 2 (3)	Stones J .... - (2)
Davies C 33 (7)	McEveley J............... 25 (4)	Taylor A .... - (1)
Dawson S................. 9 (3)	McNulty J 43 (1)	Tonge M................. 7 (3)
Digby P.................... 2 (2)	Noble-Lazarus R 2 (6)	Vaz Te R 12 (10)
Done M.................... 22 (9)	Nouble F.................... 5 (1)	Wiseman S.............. 34 (9)
Doyle N 16 (5)	O'Brien J 23 (8)	
Drinkwater D 16 (1)	Park, C 1 (2)	

League goals (49): Vaz Te 10, Davies 11, Gray 9, Butterfield 5, Done 4, McNulty 2, O'Brien 2, Cotterill 1, Foster 1, Perkins 1, Wiseman 1, Drinkwater 1, Opponents 1
FA Cup goals (2): Vaz Te 2. **Carling Cup goals**: None.
Average home league attendance: 10,331. **Player of Year**: Luke Steele

BIRMINGHAM CITY

A marathon season ended with Chris Hughton's side beaten but not bowed in the play-offs. In their 62nd match, they trailed Blackpool 3-0 on aggregate in the second leg at St Andrew's and looked a spent force. But the resilience which had been a hallmark of the whole campaign again shone through as Nikola Zigic and Curtis Davies pulled two goals back to ensure a tight finish. Helped by 20 goals scored in the final ten minutes of matches, Birmingham had held their league form together to finish fourth, despite the added demands of the Europa League, in which they went close to qualifying from the group stage, and the FA Cup, which brought victory over Wolves and a replay against Chelsea in the fifth round. All this against a backdrop of the club's severe financial problems which restricted Hughton's rebuilding programme following relegation from the Premier League and eventually led to a transfer embargo imposed by the Football League for the failure to file accounts on time. Norwich gave the former Newcastle manager the chance of a return to the Premier League and he was succeeded at St Andrew's by Lee Clark, formerly in charge of Huddersfield.

Beausejour J 22	Fahey K 34 (1)	Mutch J 18 (3)
Burke C 45 (1)	Gomis M 13 (3)	Myhill B..........................42
Caldwell S......................43	Huseklepp E 4 (7)	N'Daw, G 17 (2)
Carr S..........................20	Ibanez P 7 (6)	Ramage P 14
Davies C 42	Jerome C .... - (1)	Redmond N............. 5 (19)
Doyle C........................ 4 (1)	King M 37 (3)	Ridgewell L 13 (1)
Elliott W 15 (14)	Murphy D................ 30 (3)	Rooney A 6 (12)

Spector J 31   Wood C................. 13 (10)
Townsend A............. 11 (4)   Zigic N.................. 20 (15)

Play-offs – appearances: Burke 2, Davies 2, Doyle 2, Ibanez 2, King 2, Murphy 2, Mutch 2, Ramage 2, N'Daw 1 (1), Redmond 1 (1), Spector 1 (1), Elliott 1, Townsend 1, Zigic 1
League goals (78): King 16, Burke 12, Zigic 11, Wood 9, Davies 5, Redmond 5, Fahey 4, Murphy 4, Rooney 4, Elliott 2, Huseklepp 2, Mutch 2, Beausejour 1, Opponents 1. **Play-offs – goals** (2): Davies 1, Zigic 1
FA Cup goals (6): Elliott 2, Rooney 2, Murphy 1, Redmond 1. **Carling Cup goals**: None
Europa League goals (11): King 2, Murphy 2, Wood 2, Beausejour 1, Burke 1, Elliott 1, Redmond 1, Rooney 1
Average home league attendance: 19,126. **Player of Year**: Chris Burke

BLACKPOOL

They went close to defying the odds and preserving Premier League status on the final day of the season 12 months earlier. This time, they were within three minutes of keeping alive the dream of a return to the big-time. But again there was heartbreak for Ian Holloway's side, who conceded a goal to Ricardo Vaz Te and lost the Play-off Final 2-1 to West Ham. The manager was left to rue costly missed chances, along with the ankle injury sustained in training by striker Gary Taylor-Fletcher, who might have made a difference. Holloway rebuilt his squad shrewdly after losing some key players, with the experience of Barry Ferguson and Kevin Phillips blending well with young midfielder Tom Ince, son of the former England player Paul Ince. Blackpool were in contention for a top-six place throughout, made sure by beating Burnley 4-0 in the final home fixture and overcame Birmingham 3-2 in the semi-finals, resisting a late comeback in the second leg at St Andrew's after Stephen Dobbie and Matt Phillips had stretched their aggregate lead to 3-0.

Angel C 10 (5)	Eardley N................. 22 (4)	LuaLua L 18 (11)
Baptiste A......................43	Evatt I 37 (2)	McManaman C 9 (5)
Basham C 8 (9)	Ferguson B 40 (2)	Ormerod B 10 (7)
Bednar R 3 (6)	Fleck J 4 (3)	Phillips M 25 (8)
Bogdanovic D............. 1 (7)	Gilks M..........................42	Phillips K............... 20 (18)
Bruna G...................... - (1)	Grandin E 4 (3)	Shelvey J 10
Cathcart C....................27	Harris R 4 (1)	Southern K 24 (1)
Clarke B 4 (5)	Hill M..............................4	Sutherland C............. 2 (5)
Crainey S 40 (2)	Howard M 4	Sylvestre L 20 (8)
Dicko N 4 (6)	Hurst J .... - (2)	Taylor-Fletcher G 34 (3)
Dobbie S................... 5 (2)	Ince T.................... 22 (11)	Wilson D...........................6

Play-offs – appearances: Angel 3, Baptiste 3, Crainey 3, Dobbie 3, Eardley 3, Evatt 3, Ferguson 3, Gilks 3, Ince 3, Phillips M 3, Taylor-Fletcher 2, Phillips K 1 (2), Dicko – (3), Bednar – (1), Southern – (1), Sylvestre – (1)
League goals (79): Phillips K 16, Taylor-Fletcher 8, Phillips M 7, Ince 6, Shelvey 6, Dobbie 5, Dicko 4, LuaLua 4, Crainey 3, Evatt 3, Basham 2, Bogdanovic 2, Grandin 2, McManaman 2, Angel 1, Baptiste 1, Bednar 1, Eardley 1, Ferguson 1, Ormerod 1, Southern 1, Sylvestre 1, Opponents 1. **Play – offs goals** (4): Ince 1, Phillips M 1, Taylor-Fletcher 1, Opponents 1
FA Cup goals (9): Phillips M 4, LuaLua 2, Ince 1, Phillips K 1, Sylvestre 1. **Carling Cup goals**: None
Average home league attendance: 12,764. **Player of Year**: Matt Gilks

BRIGHTON AND HOVE ALBION

Even when his side climbed to fourth in the table with little more than a month of the season remaining, manager Gus Poyet doubted whether they were ready for a crack at Premier League football. That frank assessment proved correct as Brighton faltered in the face of a demanding run-in and were particularly exposed in a 6-0 defeat at West Ham. They failed to win any of their last eight matches, slipped out of contention and finished nine points adrift of the play-off positions. Nevertheless, the League One champions won plenty of admirers during the club's first season in the American Express Stadium after the best part of 16 years as footballing nomads without a home to call their own. They were top after taking 16 points from the opening six games, but slipped into the bottom half after losing the last four matches of 2011 without a goal to show from any of them. A 3-0 win over Southampton provided the perfect start to the New Year, launching a run of 12 without defeat, plus an FA Cup victory over Newcastle.

Agdestein T................ - (4)	Dunk L...........................31	Mattock J.............. 14 (1)
Ankergren C 19	El-Abd A................. 21 (2)	Navarro A................. 24 (9)
Assulin G.................. 2 (5)	Gonzalez D.....................2	Noone C 18 (15)
Barnes A.................. 36 (7)	Greer G.........................42	Painter M....................20
Brezovan, P...................20	Hall G......................... - (1)	Paynter B.............. 6 (4)
Bridcutt L.....................43	Harley R............... 13 (3)	Razak A 4 (2)
Buckley W 16 (13)	Harper S.........................5	Sparrow M 15 (3)
Calderon I.............. 30 (2)	Hoskins W................. 2 (5)	Taricco M.................. 9 (2)
Caskey J 3 (1)	Jara G............................14	Vicente 11 (6)
Cook S........................1	LuaLua K 11 (16)	Vincelot R 10 (5)
Dicker G 17 (1)	Mackail-Smith C....... 40 (5)	Vokes S 7 (7)

League goals (52): Barnes 11, Mackail-Smith 9, Buckley 8 Calderon 4, Vicente 3, Vokes 3, Harley 2, Noone 2, Sparrow 2, Caskey 1, Greer 1, Hoskins 1, LuaLua 1, Mattock 1, Navarro 1, Vincelot 1, Opponents 1
FA Cup goals (4): Barnes 1, Caskey 1, LuaLua 1, Opponents 1. **Carling Cup goals (3):** Barnes 2, Mackail-Smith 1
Average home league attendance: 20,029. **Player of Year:** Liam Bridcutt

BRISTOL CITY

Easter opened up an escape route for a side who had struggled against the threat of relegation for much of the time. A 1-0 away win over Nottingham Forest, earned by a Chris Wood penalty, lifted them out of the bottom three. Two days later, they overcame the dismissal of Brett Pitman to see off fellow-strugglers Coventry 3-1, with Wood again on the mark. Then, a point each against promotion-chasing Birmingham and West Ham reflected this new-found confidence. By the end of the season, City had extended their unbeaten run to eight games – a run which coincided with the replacement of former England goalkeeper David James by Dean Gerken. Manager Derek McInnes felt the reserve player deserved his chance after James conceded an own goal against Watford. McInnes had left St Johnstone to replace Keith Millen, sacked with City bottom after ten matches. A gradual improvement in results looked as if it might be taking them clear, but a single point gained from seven matches, in which 18 goals were conceded, knocked them back.

Adomah A 39 (6)	Ephraim H 3 (2)	Nyatanga L 28 (1)
Amougou A 7	Fontaine L 26	Pearson S 28
Bolasie Y 7 (16)	Foster R........................20	Pitman B 12 (23)
Bryan J.........................1	Gerken D 10	Skuse C 36
Campbell-Ryce J....... 12 (5)	James D 36	Spence J.................. 9 (1)
Carey L 18 (2)	Keinan D .... - (1)	Stead J................ 16 (8)
Cisse K 26 (6)	Kilkenny N 32 (9)	Stewart D..........................3
Clarkson D .... - (4)	Maynard N 26 (1)	Taylor R .... - (7)
Davis S 2 (1)	McAllister J............. 11 (1)	Wilson A 14 (7)
Edwards L 1 (1)	McGivern R 26 (5)	Wood C 12 (7)
Elliott M 28	McManus S....................6	Woolford M 11 (14)

League goals (44): Maynard 8, Pitman 7, Stead 6, Adomah 5, Pearson 3, Wood 3, Cisse 2, Elliott 2, Skuse 2, Bolasie 1, Ephraim 1, Kilkenny 1, Taylor 1, Woolford 1, Opponents 1
FA Cup goals: None. **Carling Cup goals:** None
Average home league attendance: 13,907. **Player of Year:** Jon Stead

BURNLEY

Burnley went into the New Year with high hopes of developing a promotion challenge. They were on a run of six victories in seven matches, taking maximum points at West Ham, Brighton and Hull and, for once, showing a measure of consistency at Turf Moor. It was not maintained and overall was nowhere near good enough for success, with only seven victories in front of their own supporters. In contrast, they won ten times away from home and were unlucky not to have equalled the club record of 11 at Leicester, where Charlie Austin could not have gone closer to breaking the stalemate. He had one header strike both posts and another cleared off the line before the game ended goalless. There was one more chance to reach the target, but this brought a 4-0 defeat at Blackpool and eventually a finish in the bottom half of the table. Austin's tally of 16 goals, all in the Championship, included two in stoppage-time for a hat-trick at Portsmouth after he came off the bench.

Amougou A 9 (5)	Hines Z..................... - (13)	Mee B 29 (2)
Austin C 30 (11)	Ings D 9 (6)	Paterson M 9 (5)
Bartley M............... 25 (14)	Jackson J .... - (1)	Rodriguez J 36 (1)
Duff M 30 (1)	Jensen B.........................4	Stanislas J 25 (6)
Easton B 17 (4)	Lafferty D 5	Treacy K 16 (8)
Edgar D 44	MacDonald A............... - (5)	Trippier K......................46
Elliott W 2 (2)	Marney D 29 (8)	Vokes S 3 (6)
Fox D 1	McCann C 45 (1)	Wallace R 41 (3)
Grant L 42 (1)	McCartan S.................. - (1)	
Hewitt S .... - (1)	McQuoid J 9 (8)	

League goals (61): Austin 16, Rodriguez 15, Wallace 5, McCann 4, Bartley 3, Ings 3, Paterson 3, Trippier 3, Edgar 2, Treacy 2, Vokes 2, McQuoid 1, Opponents 2
FA Cup goals (1): Rodriguez 1. **Carling Cup goals (11):** Rodriguez 5, Amougou 1, Austin 1, Elliott 1, McCann 1, Tripper 1, Wallace 1
Average home league attendance:14,048. **Player of Year:** Kieran Trippier

CARDIFF CITY

Heartbreak at Wembley was followed by defeat in the play-offs for the third successive season. Cardiff, however, were able to look back on it with considerable satisfaction after going so close with a squad that had to be rebuilt by Malky Mackay following the departure of a dozen players. Resilience was a key factor in negotiating a tough passage in the Carling Cup and that quality was again on display in the final as odds-on favourites Liverpool were stretched all the way to a somewhat fortuitous victory by way of a penalty shoot-out. After that there was a spell out of the Championship's top six, with the effects of a demanding campaign evident in a 3-0 home defeat by Hull. The team regrouped, won impressively at Middlesbrough and clinched a play-off place by beating Derby, helped by captain Mark Hudson's spectacular goal measured at 68 yards. But they found West Ham too strong, losing the first leg 2-0, unable to capitalise on their opponents' indifferent form at Upton Park and going down 5-0 on aggregate.

Blake D 9 (11)	Hudson M................. 38 (1)	Miller K 41 (2)
Conway C 24 (7)	Keinan D .... - (1)	Naylor L...........................2
Cowie D......................43	Kiss F.................. 13 (13)	Quinn P .... - (1)
Earnshaw R............. 8 (11)	Lawrence L 12 (1)	Ralls J 5 (5)
Gerrard A 18 (2)	Marshall D 45	Taylor A 42
Gestede R............... 5 (20)	McNaughton K 41 (1)	Turner B 36 (1)
Gunnarsson A.......... 41 (1)	McPhail S 11 (8)	Vuckic H 2 (3)
Heaton T.................. 1 (1)	Mason J 23 (16)	Whittingham P 46

Play-offs – appearances: Gunnarsson 2, Hudson 2, Lawrence 2, Marshall 2, Miller 2, Mason 2, Taylor 2, Turner 2, Whittingham 2, Blake 1, Cowie 1 (1), McPhail 1 (1), McNaughton 1, Blake – (1), Earnshaw – (1), Kiss – (1)
League goals (66): Whittingham 12, Miller 10, Mason 9, Gunnarsson 5, Hudson 5, Cowie 4,

Conway 3, Earnshaw 3, Gestede 2, Turner 2, Gerrard 1, Kiss 1, Lawrence 1, Ralls 1, Taylor 1, Vuckic 1, Opponents 5. **Play-offs – goals**: None
FA Cup goals (2): Earnshaw 1, Mason 1. **Carling Cup goals** (16): Cowie 3, Conway 3, Mason 2, Gerrard 1, Gestede 1, Gyepes G 1, Jarvis N 1, Miller 1, Parkin J 1, Turner 1, Whittingham 1, Opponents 1
Average home league attendance: 22,100. **Player of Year**: Peter Whittingham

COVENTRY CITY

Coventry were condemned to the game's third tier for the first time since 1964 after months of turmoil on and off the pitch. It ended with manager Andy Thorn criticising the club's ever-changing hierarchy which, he insisted, failed to provide him with anything like the resources needed to be competitive. Thorn saw key players depart in the close season, lost leading scorer Lukas Jutkiewicz in the January transfer window and was told there was no money for replacements. Not surprisingly, the team spent virtually the whole campaign in the bottom three and never really looked like finding safe ground. There was a glimmer of hope during the run-in with successive 2-0 victories over Portsmouth and Hull. But a 3-1 defeat by Bristol City, the team immediately above them, was a hammer blow. Then, Gary McSheffrey had a penalty saved in the home defeat by Millwall which could have offered another lifeline. Another reversal, by Doncaster, confirmed relegation, although Thorn was later asked to stay in charge.

Baker C 20 (6)	Gardner G 4	Nimely A.................. 16 (1)
Bell D..................... 19 (9)	Henderson J .... - (1)	Norwood, O.............. 17 (1)
Bigirimana G........... 16 (10)	Hreidarsson H 2	O'Donovan R 6 (5)
Cameron N............. 11 (3)	Hussey C 28 (1)	Platt C 23 (10)
Christie C............... 27 (10)	Jeffers S .... - (2)	Roberts W................. - (1)
Clarke J 17 (2)	Jutkiewicz L................25	Ruffles J .... - (1)
Clingan S 34 (2)	Keogh R 45	Thomas C 24 (3)
Cranie M.......................38	McDonald C 16 (7)	Willis J 1 (2)
Deegan G 19 (5)	McPake J 3 (2)	Wood R.................. 12 (5)
Dunn C .... - (2)	McSheffrey G 37 (2)	
Eastwood F .... - (4)	Murphy J....................46	

League goals (41): Jutkiewicz 9, McSheffrey 8, McDonald 4, Platt 4, Deegan 3, Clingan 2, Norwood 2, Baker 1, Clarke 1, Gardner 1, Nimely 1, Thomas 1, Wood 1, Opponents 3
FA Cup goals (1): McSheffrey 1. **Carling Cup goals** (1): O'Donovan 1
Average home league attendance: 15,118. **Player of Year**: Richard Keogh

CRYSTAL PALACE

The club's best start for a decade leading to a successful first half of the season gave way to double disappointment at Selhurst Park. Palace had been on the fringes of the play-off positions and reached the semi-finals of the Carling Cup with notable wins over Wigan, Middlesbrough, Southampton and then Manchester United at Old Trafford, where Darren Ambrose scored from 30 yards and Glenn Murray headed in an Ambrose free-kick for a 2-1 success. There was also a club record of 619 minutes of league and cup football without conceding a goal. But hopes of reaching Wembley were dashed in a penalty shoot-out against Cardiff which followed a 1-1 deadlock over the two legs. After that, Palace's promotion bid stalled, with manager Dougie Freedman admitting that the demands of competing on two fronts had been too much for his players. Their season went into reverse, with the final nine matches bringing just three points and resulting in a third successive finish in the lower reaches of the table.

Ambrose D 26 (10)	Davies A 1	Easter J 18 (15)
Andrew C 2 (4)	De Silva K................. 2 (4)	Egan J............................1
Appiah K .... - (4)	Dikgacoi K 24 (3)	Gardner A 25 (3)
Cadogan K 1	Dorman A .... - (1)	Garvan O................. 13 (9)
Clyne N 28	Dumbuya M 2	Iversen S .... - (3)

Jedinak M 29 (2)	Murray G 25 (12)	Sekajja I 1
Keinan D 3	O'Keefe S 13	Speroni J 42
Marrow A .... - (1)	Parr J 35 (4)	Tunchev A 9
Martin C 20 (6)	Parsons M 3 (1)	Wright D 22
McCarthy P 42 (1)	Pedroza A 1 (3)	Williams J 5 (9)
McGivern R 5	Price L 4 (1)	Zaha W 34 (7)
McShane P 9 (2)	Ramage P 14 (3)	
Moxey D 20 (4)	Scannell S 27 (10)	

League goals (46):Ambrose 7, Martin 7, Murray 6, Zaha 6, Easter 5, Scannell 4, Garvan 3, Dikgacoi 2, McCarthy 2, Parr 2, Jedinak 1, Opponents 1
FA Cup goals: None. **Carling Cup goals (11):** Ambrose 3, Zaha 3, Andrew 1, Easter 1, Gardner 1, Murray 1, Williams 1
Average home league attendance: 15,219. **Player of Year:** Jonathan Parr

DERBY COUNTY

Four straight wins, the club's best start for 106 years, offered hope of a successful season. But that level of consistency was never repeated, with the lack of a cutting edge a constant problem for manager Nigel Clough, who believed that with more clinical finishing his side could have reached the play-offs. As it was, Derby lost eight times at Pride Park, too many for a serious promotion challenge. At one stage, well into the second half of the campaign, they were 12 points away from a top-six place after acquiring just three from a run of seven matches. They closed the gap, helped by the first league double over Nottingham Forest since the First Division title-winning season under Brian Clough in 1971-72. But there were more disappointing performances at home, a goalless draw against Ipswich and a 1-0 defeat by Middlesbrough and an eventual mid-table finish. One bright spot was the emergence of 17-year-old midfielder Will Hughes, who was given his chance towards the end and looked a genuine prospect.

Anderson R 5 (2)	Cwyka T 3 (5)	Maguire C 2 (5)
Bailey J 17 (5)	Davies B 30 (5)	Naylor T 8
Ball C 11 (12)	Davies S 20 (6)	Noble R 1 (1)
Barker S 19 (1)	Doyle C 1 (5)	O'Brien M 15 (5)
Bennett M 2 (7)	Fielding F 44	Priskin T 4 (1)
Brayford J 22 (1)	Green P 26 (1)	Roberts G 39 (2)
Bryson C 44	Hendrick J 38 (4)	Robinson T 27 (12)
Buxton J 12 (9)	Hughes W 1 (2)	Shackell J 46
Carroll T 8 (4)	Kilbane K 7 (2)	Tyson N 13 (10)
Croft L 4 (5)	Legzdins A 2 (2)	Ward J 35 (2)

League goals (50): Davies S 12, Robinson 10, Bryson 6, Ward 4, Ball 3, Hendrick 3, Buxton 2, Carroll 1, Cwyka 1, Davies B 1, Green 1, Kilbane 1, McGuire 1, Priskin 1, Roberts 1, Shackell 1, Opponents 1
FA Cup goals (1): Robinson 1. **Carling Cup goals (2):** Maguire 1, Robinson 1.
Average home league attendance: 26,020. **Player of Year:** Craig Bryson

DONCASTER ROVERS

A controversial transfer policy, dubbed 'the experiment,' failed to save Rovers from relegation after four years of Championship football. Dean Saunders insisted the club's FA-approved policy, involving agent-turned-consultant Willie McKay, had injected life into the season. At the same time, he admitted that the influx of high-profile players, some on loan or short-term contracts, had been difficult to manage. Saunders left Wrexham to replace Sean O'Driscoll when the division's longest-serving manager was sacked after five years in charge, with his side having taken a single point from the first seven games. The former Wales striker's first three matches netted seven points against Crystal Palace, Hull and Peterborough. But Rovers soon slipped back into the bottom three and stayed there, despite the introduction of players like El-Hadji Diouf, Pascal Chimbonda and Frederic Piquionne. The sale of leading scorer Billy Sharp to Southampton for £1.8m in the January transfer window was followed by a run of just one win in 15 games, ending with defeats by Leicester and Burnley over Easter which sealed their fate.

Bagayoko M 2 (3)	Friend G 24 (3)	Naylor R 13
Bamogo H.........................4	Gillett S 43 (3)	O'Connor J 24 (4)
Barnes G 24 (9)	Goulon H 5 (1)	Oster J.................... 23 (7)
Baxendale J .... - (2)	Hayter J 18 (13)	Parkin J 4 (1)
Bennett K 15 (21)	Hird S 23 (8)	Piquionne F 8
Beye H 22	Husband J 2 (1)	Robert F 7 (6)
Brown C........................ 7 (4)	Ikeme C......................15	Sharp B................. 18 (2)
Brown R 1 (1)	Ilunga H.....................19	Spurr T..........................19
Button D..........................7	Keegan P 1 (1)	Stock B 24 (2)
Chimbonda P 16	Kirkland C......................1	Sullivan N..........................9
Diouf, E-H 22	Lalkovic 1 .... (5)	Wilson M .... - (3)
Coppinger, J............. 31 (7)	Lockwood A.......... 11 (3)	Woods G 14
Dumbuya M 6 (4)	Martis S............ 14 (1)	Woods M............... 2 (2)
Fortune M-A.....................5	Mason R 2 (2)	

League goals (43): Sharp 10, Diouf 6, Bennett 4, Hayter 4, Gillett 3, Bagayoko 2, Beye 2, Brown C 2, Coppinger 2, Piquionne 2, Robert 2, Barnes 1, Fortune 1, Oster 1, Stock 1
FA Cup goals: None. **Carling Cup goals (4):** Bennett 1, Brown C 1, Hayter 1, Mason 1
Average home league attendance: 9,341. **Player of Year:** George Friend

HULL CITY

Nick Barmby's affinity with his home-town club ended in bitter controversy. After less than six months as manager, he was suspended then sacked by the owners, who claimed he had questioned their ambition. Barmby, who described the dismissal as unjustified, was appointed caretaker, after seven years as a Hull player, when Nigel Pearson returned to Leicester. Two months later, he was given the job on a permanent basis and saw his side break into the play-off positions with a 3-0 away win over Cardiff. Barmby expected them to go on and develop a strong challenge for promotion. Instead, the stay-was shortlived, with a single goal scored in the next six matches, five of which resulted in defeats. He felt the team were in a rut and by the time things improved – victory over Middlesbrough and a hat-trick from leading scorer Matty Fryatt against Barnsley – too much ground had been lost, Hull finishing seven points adrift. The club went for experience this time, with Steve Bruce appointed.

Adebola D................ 2 (8)	Dudgeon J................ 17 (7)	McKenna P 37 (4)
Barmby N .... - (8)	Evans C 38 (5)	Mclean A 28 (11)
Basso A 12 (1)	Fryatt M 39 (7)	McShane P 1
Bradley S................. 1 (1)	Garcia R 6 (4)	Olofinjana S 1 (2)
Brady R 24 (15)	Gulacsi P 13 (2)	Pusic M.........................2
Cairney T 18 (9)	Harper J .... - (1)	Rosenior L 44
Chester J.........................44	Hobbs J......................40	Simpson J.................. - (3)
Cooper L..........................7	King J............. 8 (10)	Stewart C........... 26 (5)
Cullen M.................... - (4)	Koren R......................41	Waghorn M......................5
Dawson A............... 31 (1)	Mannone V...................21	

League goals (47): Fryatt 16, Koren 10, Mclean 5, Brady 3, Chester 2, Evans 2, Barmby 1, Hobbs 1, King 1, Stewart 1, Waghorn 1, Opponents 4
FA Cup goals (3): Cairney 1, Mclean 1, Stewart 1 **Carling Cup goals:** None
Average home league attendance: 18,790. **Player of Year:** James Chester

IPSWICH TOWN

Twelve goals conceded in successive games against Southampton and Peterborough provided an early indication of another patchy season at Portman Road. The signs were later confirmed by a run of seven straight defeats and another 20 goals conceded – the club's worst run since 1994-95. That pushed them down to fourth from bottom approaching the mid-way point. The sequence was ended by a 5-3 victory at Barnsley, achieved after trailing 2-0 at half-time. And a handsome 5-1 success against promotion-minded West Ham offered some New Year cheer. But although there was a marginal improvement in results in the second half of the campaign, another lean run towards the end meant a third successive finish in the bottom half of the table. They had conceded 77 goals – only relegated Doncaster's record was worse – and manager Paul Jewell expressed the need for four or five new players to strengthen the squad.

Ainsley J.....................1	Ellington N 1 (14)	Murphy D................. 31 (2)
Andrews K 19 (1)	Emmanuel-Thomas J28 (13)	Priskin T................... 1 (1)
Bowyer L............. 24 (5)	Healy C.............................1	Scotland J.............. 20 (16)
Bullard J............... 12 (9)	Hyam L 7 (1)	Smith T 24 (2)
Carson J............. 5 (11)	Ingimarsson I 6 (2)	Sonko I................... 20 (2)
Chopra M............. 39 (6)	Kennedy M 6 (1)	Stevenson R.............. 3 (8)
Collins D.....................16	Lawrence B.............. - (1)	Stockdale D 18
Cresswell A 44	Leadbitter G 32 (2)	Wabara R 1 (5)
Delaney D 26 (3)	Lee-Barrett A........... 17 (1)	Wright R 1
Drury A 20 (1)	Martin L 28 (6)	
Edwards C.....................45	McCarthy A 10	

League goals (69): Chopra 14, Andrews 9, Scotland 8, Emmanuel-Thomas 6, Leadbitter 5, Martin 5, Murphy 4, Collins 3, Smith 3, Bowyer 2, Carson 2, Drury 2, Bullard 1, Cresswell 1, Sonko 1, Stevenson 1, Opponents 2
FA Cup goals (1): Scotland 1. **Carling Cup goals** (1): Emmanuel-Thomas 1
Average home league attendance: 18,266. **Player of Year**: Carlos Edwards

LEEDS UNITED

Neil Warnock promised a major rebuilding programme after admitting his side had not been good enough to sustain a promotion challenge. Ken Bates brought in the manager with the knack of gaining promotion after sacking Simon Grayson in the wake of a 4-1 home defeat by Birmingham in late January. Warnock, himself dismissed by Queens Park Rangers three weeks earlier, kept Leeds on the fringe of the play-off places until an embarrassing 7-3 beating by Nottingham Forest at Elland Road underlined their shortcomings. A single goal win at Millwall followed. Then three successive 2-0 reversals against Watford, Reading and Derby, accompanied by three sendings-off, sent them sliding into the bottom half of the table. There was another red card picked up at Blackpool, suggesting that Warnock also has a disciplinary problem to address. Leeds finished 14th after a last-day defeat by Leicester, a club record 11th on their own ground.

Becchio L 25 (16)	Kisnorbo P 18 (1)	Rogers R................... 1 (3)
Bromby L.................. 7 (3)	Lees T 41 (1)	Sam L 3 (14)
Brown M............... 21 (3)	Lonergan A 35	Smith A 3
Bruce A.........................8	McCarthy A 6	Snodgrass R 42 (1)
Cairns A................... - (1)	McCormack R........... 42 (3)	Taylor C 2
Clayton A............. 42 (1)	Nunez R 6 (12)	Thompson Z 7 (1)
Connolly P 23 (5)	O'Brien A 2 (2)	Townsend A.............. 5 (1)
Delph F 5	O'Dea D........................35	Vayrynen M 2 (8)
Forssell M 1 (14)	Paynter B................. 2 (3)	Webber D............... 2 (11)
Gradel M........................4	Pugh D 31 (3)	White A 35 (1)
Howson J.....................19	Rachubka P 5 (1)	
Keogh A............... 17 (5)	Robinson P 9 (1)	

League goals (65): McCormack 18, Snodgrass 13, Beccho 11, Clayton 6, Keogh 2, Lees 2, O'Dea 2, Paynter 2, Pugh 2, Brown 1, Gradel 1, Howson 1, Nunez 1, Townsend 1, Webber 1, Opponents 1
FA Cup goals: None. **Carling Cup goals (5):** Nunez 4, McCormack 1
Average home league attendance: 23,379. **Player of Year:** Robert Snodgrass

LEICESTER CITY

Sven-Goran Eriksson spent £10m on new players in an attempt to bring Premier League football to the King Power Stadium and satisfy the club's wealthy owners. The spending spree did not pay off and the former England manager paid the price after a third home defeat, 3-0 by Millwall, before the end of October. Nigel Pearson returned to the club he left to manage Hull in June 2010 and experienced the same degree of inconsistency which brought about Eriksson's dismissal. Even so, Leicester never completely lost touch with the leading group and Easter victories over Doncaster and Ipswich left them three points away from a play-off place. But defeat at Millwall, followed by a goalless draw with Burnley, underlined the problems which Pearson promised to address during the summer. At least there was a successful finish, with 17-year-old Harry Panayiotou coming off the bench for his debut and scoring a stoppage-time winner at Leeds.

Bamba S.	32 (4)	Kennedy T	4 (1)	Peltier L	39 (1)
Beckford J	33 (6)	King A	24 (6)	Schlupp J	3 (18)
Danns N	22 (7)	Konchesky P	42	Schmeichel K	46
Delfouneso N	- (4)	Marshall B	12 (4)	St Ledger S	23 (3)
Drinkwater D	13 (6)	Mills M	25	Tunchev A	2
Dyer L	27 (9)	Moore L	2	Vassell N	10 (3)
Gallagher P	18 (10)	Morgan W	15 (2)	Waghorn M	1 (3)
Gelson Fernandes	10 (5)	Nugent D	41 (1)	Weale C	- (1)
Howard S	3 (17)	Paintsil J	4 (2)	Wellens R	39 (2)
Johnson M	3 (4)	Panayiotou H	- (1)	Yuke Abe	13 (3)

League goals (66): Nugent 15, Beckford 9, Gallagher 8, Danns 5, Dyer 4, King 4, Marshall 3, Drinkwater 2, Konchesky 2, Peltier 2, Schlupp 2, Vassell 2, Bamba 1, Gelson Fernandes 1, Mills 1, Panayiotou 1, Waghorn 1, Wellens 1, Yuke Abe 1, Opponents 1
FA Cup goals (10): Beckford 6, Marshall 1, Nugent 1, St Ledger 1, Opponents 1. **Carling Cup goals (10):** Schlupp 4, Dyer 2, Gallagher 2, Danns 1, Howard 1
Average home league attendance: 23,036. **Player of Year:** Kasper Schmeichel

MIDDLESBROUGH

A record-breaking start; a disappointing finish. That, in a nutshell, was the story of Middlesbrough's season in which indifferent form in front of their own supporters proved the overriding factor. When Tony Mowbray's team were held to a goalless draw by bottom-of-the-table Doncaster in the penultimate game at the Riverside, it meant 35 points had been dropped there during the course of the campaign. That result was particularly damaging because previously impressive away form had also stalled through a lack of goals, forcing them out of the play-off positions. There was still a chance after the final home game brought a 2-1 victory over Southampton – the first time in 11 that more than a one goal had been scored. It meant a difference of two points between sixth-placed Cardiff. But Middlesbrough lost at Watford on the last day of the regular campaign and finished five adrift. They had opened with 11 unbeaten matches, five wins and six draws, to overtake the 101-year-old club record.

Arca J	22 (8)	Emnes M	37 (5)	Hoyte J	39
Bailey N	37	Halliday A	- (1)	Ikeme C	10
Bates M	37	Hammill A	8 (2)	Jutkiewicz L	17 (2)
Bennett J	40 (1)	Haroun F	23 (9)	Kink T	- (1)
Coyne D	1	Hines S	20 (3)	Main C	- (12)

Martin M.................... - (15)	Ogbeche B 5 (12)	Steele J 34
McDonald S 31 (2)	Reach A...................... - (1)	Thomson K 10 (12)
McMahon T............... 28 (6)	Ripley C............................1	Williams R 34 (1)
McManus S............. 21 (3)	Robson S 37	Zemmama M.............. 7 (8)
Nimely A.................... - (9)	Smallwood R 7 (6)	

League goals (52): Emnes 14, McDonald 9, Robson 7, Martin 3, Ogbeche 3, Bailey 2, Bates 2, Haroun 2, Jutkiewicz 2, Main 2, Williams 2, Bennett 1, Hines 1, McMahon 1, Zemmama 1
FA Cup goals (3): Emnes 1, Jutkiewicz 1, Robson 1. **Carling Cup goals** (6): Emnes 3, Hines 1, Robson 1, Zemmama 1
Average home league attendance: 17,557. **Player of Year**: Barry Robson

MILLWALL

Four successive wins at a crucial time took the pressure off Kenny Jackett's team. They beat Hull, Portsmouth and Leicester, with Tottenham loanee Harry Kane scoring in each match. Then, Shane Lowry netted his first goal for the club and Maik Taylor saved a penalty to secure victory over Coventry and move their team well clear of trouble. In all, Millwall's unbeaten run to the end of the season spanned seven games, during which Andy Keogh brought his tally to ten since moving from Wolves in the January transfer window. Keogh formed a productive partnership with Kane to compensate for the absence of leading marksman Darius Henderson. Millwall had won only one of their opening 12 league matches, then scored ten in the next three, with Henderson netting a hat-trick against Leicester. Another lean run yielded a single goal in seven, before he scored three against Barnsley and for good measure delivered another hat-trick in the FA Cup tie against Dagenham and Redbridge.

Abdou N 35 (5)	Henderson D 25 (6)	Montgomery N............. - (2)
Agyemang P 1 (1)	Henry J 24 (15)	N'Guessan D 6 (9)
Baker N 6	Howard B................. 11 (1)	Robinson P 41
Barron S 18 (2)	Kane H 19 (3)	Simpson J.............. 13 (3)
Batt S............................ - (4)	Keogh A 17 (1)	Smith J................... 30 (3)
Bouazza H 19 (7)	Lowry S.......................22	Stewart J 3 (1)
Craig T 21 (2)	Marquis J 7 (10)	Taylor M.........................10
Dunne A 25 (5)	Mason R 3 (2)	Trotter L 33 (2)
Feeney L.................. 27 (7)	McQuoid J 1 (4)	Ward D 27 (3)
Forde D 27	Mildenhall S 9 (1)	Wright J 16 (2)
Hackett C .... - (3)	Mkandawire T............. 10 (3)	

League goals (55): Henderson 15, Keogh 10, Kane 7, Trotter 7, Feeney 4, Simpson 4, Bouazza 2, Lowry 1, Marquis 1, N'Guessan 1, Robinson 1, Wright 1, Opponents 1
FA Cup goals (9): Henderson 4, Kane 2, Feeney 1, N'Guessan 1, Trotter 1. **Carling Cup goals** (3): Bouazza 1, Mkandawire 1, N'Guessan 1
Average home league attendance: 11,484. **Player of Year**: Nadjim Abdou

NOTTINGHAM FOREST

After reaching the play-offs in the two previous seasons, Forest experienced a difficult one, with the sudden death of owner Nigel Doughty, the departure of manager Steve McClaren and an uncomfortable time spent in the relegation zone. McClaren resigned, citing financial restraints at the club, after a 3-1 home defeat by Birmingham, only his tenth Championship game in charge. Portsmouth's Steve Cotterill came in to win four of his first six games, but a club record seven in succession without a goal sent them sliding into the bottom three. Forest spent two months there and remained on the fringes until a remarkable 7-3 win over Leeds at Elland Road, in which Garath McCleary scored four goals, eased the pressure. That was followed by a hat-trick from Radoslaw Majewski in a 3-0 success against Crystal Palace which put his side comfortably clear of trouble. Dexter Blackstock was also among the goals, with eight in 16 starts after returning from a career-threatening knee injury. Doughty's controlling stake was bought by Kuwaiti businessmen the Al-Hasawi family, who sacked Cotterill after completing their summer takeover.

Anderson P 10 (6)	Garner J..................... 1 (1)	McGoldrick D 3 (6)
Bamford P .... - (2)	Greening J 24 (7)	McGugan L 27 (8)
Blackstock D........... 16 (6)	Guedioura A.................19	Miller I 13 (8)
Boateng G........................5	Gunter C 44 (2)	Moloney B................. 3 (5)
Camp L.........................46	Harewood M.....................4	Morgan W 22
Chambers L..................43	Higginbotham D 5 (1)	Moussi G 33 (1)
Cohen C...........................7	Hill C 5	Reid A 22 (17)
Cunningham G 25 (2)	Lascelles J 1	Tudgay M 24 (10)
Derbyshire M........... 7 (8)	Lynch J................... 28 (7)	Wootton S 7 (6)
Elokobi G 8 (4)	Majewski R 23 (5)	
Findley R 10 (13)	McCleary G 21 (1)	

League goals (48): McCleary 9, Blackstock 8, Majewski 6, Tudgay 5, Findley 3, Lynch 3, McGugan 3, Miller 3, Reid 2, Boateng 1, Derbyshire 1, Guedioura 1, Gunter 1, Higginbotham 1, Morgan 1
FA Cup goals: None. **Carling Cup goals** (10): Findley 3, McGugan 2, Derbyshire 1, Majewski 1, Miller 1, Morgan 1, Tudgay 1
Average home league attendance: 21,969. **Player of Year**: Garath McCleary

PETERBOROUGH UNITED

In terms of value for money, Peterborough are hard to beat. They traded a stack of goals for the second successive season, this time while managing to stay clear of any relegation worries on their return to the Championship. It wasn't quite on a par with the promotion-winning campaign, but an aggregate of 144 goals in their 46 matches kept the entertainment level high. Top performance was the 7-1 drubbing of Ipswich, with Lee Tomlin scoring a hat-trick. For last-minute drama, Paul Taylor's winner against Cardiff took some beating. Another 4-3 thriller at London Road had Darren Ferguson's side retrieving a 3-0 deficit against Barnsley, then conceding the deciding goal. Leading marksman Taylor helped set up victory over champions-to-be Reading and signed off in style with a thumping shot against Watford. The final nine games yielded a single victory, but sufficient points had been accumulated for Peterborough to finish ten points clear of trouble.

Ajose N..................... 1 (1)	Coulson C .... - (1)	Newell J 8 (6)
Alcock C 40 (1)	Frecklington L 35 (2)	Ntlhe K........................ - (2)
Ball D..................... 6 (16)	Gordon B .... - (1)	Rowe T 40 (3)
Barnett T 12 (1)	Jones P...........................35	Sinclair E 21 (14)
Basey G 2 (1)	Kearns D.................. 5 (15)	Taylor P 36 (8)
Bennett R 32	Kennedy T 8 (2)	Tomlin L 31 (6)
Boyd G..........................45	Lewis J.........................11	Tunnicliffe R 10 (17)
Briggs M........................5	Little M 26 (9)	Wootton S 7 (4)
Brisley S.......................11	McCann G 38 (3)	Zakuani G 41

League goals (67): Taylor 12, Sinclair 10, McCann 8, Tomlin 8, Boyd 7, Frecklington 5, Ball 4, Barnett 4, Rowe 4, Bennett 1, Little 1, Newell 1, Zakuani 1, Opponents 1
FA Cup goals: None. **Carling Cup goals** (4): Ball 2, Boyd 1, Tomlin 1
Average home league attendance: 9,110. **Player of Year**: Gabriel Zakuani

PORTSMOUTH

Premier League football and FA Cup glory seemed a distant memory as this troubled club lurched from crisis to crisis and will now play in the game's third tier for the first time since 1983. Continuing financial problems resulted in administration for the second time in two years, another ten-point deduction and a drop into the relegation zone. There were even doubts about surviving the season until the Football League handed over four outstanding payments totalling £800,000 to enable the club to see it through. Michael Appleton, who had left a coaching role at West Bromwich Albion three months earlier to become manager when Steve Cotterill resigned to take over at Nottingham Forest, had a thankless task motivating an already depleted squad. A 4-1 win over promotion-chasing Birmingham followed closely by victory over Hull raised hopes of staying up. There was also a spirited performance to earn a point away to leaders Southampton. But successive home defeats by Burnley and Millwall took a heavy toll and Portsmouth finished eight points adrift.

Allan S 15	Huseklepp E 21 (6)	Rekik K 8
Ashdown J 21	Kanu N......................3 (3)	Riise B H...........................2
Ben-Haim T 33	Kitson D 22 (11)	Rocha R 31 (2)
Benjani...................6 (11)	Lawrence L 23	Scapuzzi L .... - (2)
Dailly C....................... - (1)	Maguire C 10 (1)	Thorne G.........................14
Etuhu K 9 (4)	Mattock J.........................7	Varney L 28 (2)
Futacs M 12 (17)	Mokoena A.............. 15 (2)	Ward J.................... 38 (6)
Halford G.......................42	Mullins H.......................34	Webster A .... - (3)
Harris A 2 (3)	Norris D 39 (1)	Williams R .... - (4)
Henderson S 25	Pearce J 43	
Hreidarsson H 2	Razak A 1 (2)	

League goals (50): Norris 8, Halford 7, Huseklepp 6, Varney 6, Futacs 5, Kitson 4, Maguire 3, Ward 3, Pearce 2, Allan 1, Benjani 1, Etuhu 1, Kanu 1, Mullins 1, Opponents 1
FA Cup goals: None. **Carling Cup goals:** None
Average home league attendance: 15,044. **Player of Year:** Jason Pearce

READING

Reading fell at the final hurdle in 2011, but this time there was no barrier to a return to the Premier League under Brian McDermott. They overcame a poor start, which left them second from bottom after six matches, worked their way up the table, then surged ahead in the second half of the season – helped by the shrewd signing of Blackburn's Jason Roberts in the January transfer window – to wipe away the disappointment of losing to Swansea in the Play-off Final. No-one could dispute their supremacy, particularly after five successive wins against promotion-chasing opposition, capped by two late goals from Adam Le Fondre which saw off long-time leaders Southampton 3-1 at St Mary's. Reading clinched promotion next time out by beating Nottingham Forest and were confirmed champions by Southampton's defeat at Middlesbrough. By then, they had won 15 and drawn two of 18 matches, a tribute to the management skills of the long-serving McDermott, who joined the club as chief scout in 2000, served as reserve team manager, then succeeded Brendan Rodgers in January 2010 after a spell as caretaker.

Afobe B 1 (2)	Gunnarsson B............ 1 (4)	Long S.............................1
Antonio M 2 (4)	Harte I.....................30 (2)	Manset M 4 (11)
Church S 19 (12)	Howard B...................... - (1)	McAnuff J.......................40
Connolly M.....................6	Hunt N 33 (8)	Mills J 13 (2)
Cummings S 32 (2)	Karacan J 36 (1)	Mullins H................... 6 (1)
Cywka T....................1 (3)	Kebe J 30 (3)	Pearce A.......................46
Federici A.....................46	Khumalo B......................4	Roberts J.......................17
Gorkss K.......................42	Le Fondre A 17 (15)	Robson-Kanu H....... 19 (16)
Griffin A.........................9	Leigertwood M...............41	Tabb J 10 (9)

League goals (69): Le Fondre 12, Hunt 8, Church 7, Roberts 6, Leigertwood 5, McAnuff 5, Pearce 5, Harte 4, Robson-Kanu 4, Gorkss 3, Karacan 3, Kebe 3, Manset 3, Opponents 1
FA Cup goals: None. **Carling Cup goals (1):** Morrison S 1
Average home league attendance: 19,219. **Player of Year:** Alex Pearce

SOUTHAMPTON

Nigel Adkins delivered another master class in management and Rickie Lambert's goals echoed the days of Mick Channon as Saints marched back to the Premier League. It was their second successive promotion and for Adkins a fourth in six seasons after twice taking Scunthorpe into the Championship. His target was to establish a launch pad in the top ten by Christmas. In the event, they were three points clear at the top, having made the club's best start for 103 years and reaching a record 19 straight home wins in the league. There was a wobble around the turn of the year, with only one win in six. But Lambert, the division's Player of the Year, scored his third and fourth hat-tricks of the season to put them back on track, aided by winter transfer window signing Billy Sharp. A home defeat by Reading left their rivals in pole position for the title and West Ham applying pressure for the runners-up spot. But an all-time record crowd of 32,363, saw their team overcome Coventry 4-0 on the final day to finish two points clear. Lambert's tally of 27 made him the club's first player to top 20 league goals in three successive seasons since Channon in the mid 1970s.

Barnard L .... - (6)	Falque I 1	Lambert R....................42
Bialkowski B 1	Fonte J 42	Martin A 7 (3)
Butterfield D 9 (1)	Forte J .... - (1)	Lee T.................... 4 (3)
Chaplow R 17 (8)	Fox D 37 (4)	Puncheon J................ 4 (4)
Connolly D 17 (9)	Hammond D.......... 31 (12)	Reeves B .... - (2)
Cork J 39 (7)	Harding D 12 (8)	Richardson F............. 33 (1)
Davis K..........................45	Holmes L .... - (6)	Schnerderlin M....... 29 (13)
De Ridder S 5 (27)	Hooiveld J...................39	Seaborne D 4
Do Prado G 36 (6)	Lallana A 41	Sharp B 11 (4)

League goals (85): Lambert 27, Lallana 11, Do Prado 10, Sharp 9, Hooiveld 7, Connolly 6, Chaplow 3, De Ridder 3, Schneiderlin 2, Fonte 1, Hammond 1, Harding 1, Holmes 1, Lee 1, Martin 1, Opponents 1
FA Cup goals (5): Lambert 2, Lallana 1, Martin 1, Ward-Prowse J 1. **Carling Cup goals (9):** Forte 2, Lambert 2, Chaplow 1, De Ridder 1, Do Prado 1, Hooiveld 1, Lallana 1
Average home league attendance: 26,419. **Player of Year:** Rickie Lambert

WATFORD

Sean Dyche was entitled to look back on his first taste of management with considerable satisfaction. Watford were among the favourites to go down after selling the prolific Danny Graham to Swansea for £3.5m and certainly gave little indication of upsetting the odds in the early part of the season. The first 13 matches yielded just two victories, 10 points and resulted in a place in the bottom three. But Dyche, a former defender at Vicarage Road who stepped up when Malky Mackay took over at Cardiff, saw his side develop into a force in the second part of the campaign, despite losing another leading marksman, Marvin Sordell, to Bolton in the January transfer window. Sean Murray, an 18-year-old midfielder with the scoring touch, and Troy Deeney provided a steady stream of goals which set up a productive, 13-match run with a single defeat. Deeney was on the mark in all the final four matches, bringing Watford an 11th place finish. But it was not enough for the club's new owners, the Pozzo family, who sacked Dyche and brought in former West Ham manager Gianfranco Zola days after taking over.

Assombalonga B 2 (2)	Hodson L 20	Murray S.................. 17 (1)
Beattie C 1 (3)	Hogg J............................40	Nosworthy N 32
Bond J........................ - (1)	Iwelumo C............. 21 (17)	Prince Buaben.......... 21 (9)
Bennett D 1 (1)	Jenkins R................ 4 (5)	Sordell M................. 25 (1)
Deeney T 28 (15)	Kacaniklic A............. 11 (1)	Taylor M................. 20 (2)
Dickinson C 38 (1)	Kightly M.............. 11 (1)	Trotta M...........................1
Doyley L.......................33	Kuszczak T..................13	Walker J....................... - (1)
Eustace J 34 (5)	Loach S 31	Weimann A 3
Forsyth C 15 (5)	Mariappa A 37 (2)	Whichelow M............... - (2)
Garner C 14 (8)	Massey G .... - (3)	Yeates M.................. 28 (5)
Gilmartin R 2	Mirfin D 3 (1)	

League goals (56): Deeney 11, Sordell 8, Murray 7, Eustace 4, Iwelumo 4, Forsyth 3, Kightly 3,

Yeates 3, Dickinson 2, Nosworthy 2, Beattie 1, Buaben 1, Garner 1, Kacaniklic 1, Mariappa 1, Taylor 1, Opponents 3
FA Cup goals (4): Forsyth 2, Sordell 1, Deeney 1. **Carling Cup goals** (1): Sordell 1
Average home league attendance: 12,710. **Player of Year**: Adrian Mariappa

WEST HAM UNITED

Sam Allardyce overcame some rocky patches to lead West Ham back to the Premier League at the first time of asking and in his first season as manager. Ricardo Vaz Te, a £500,000 January signing from Barnsley scored an 87th minute goal worth millions for a 2-1 win over Blackpool in the Play-off Final. The Portuguese striker had also been on the mark in the 5-0 aggregate victory over Cardiff in the semi-finals, while ten league goals underlined the significance of that signing. Eight of them, including a hat-trick against Brighton, came in a five-match run when his side were attempting to close the gap on the top two, Reading and Southampton. They fell two points short, largely through previous indifferent form at Upton Park, where unrest among supporters came to a head when seven successive games failed to produce a win and included a particularly damaging 4-2 defeat by Reading. In contrast, West Ham scored 13 wins on their travels, a club record, the last of which, 2-1 at Leicester, kept alive slim hopes of overtaking Southampton on the final day of the regular season. But two goals by Carlton Cole against Hull were not enough, with their rivals making no mistake against relegated Coventry.

Almunia M 4	Faye A 25 (4)	O'Brien J 27 (5)
Baldock S 10 (13)	Green R 42	O'Neil G 9 (7)
Barrera P .... - (1)	Hall R.................... - (3)	Parker S 4
Bentley D 2 (3)	Ilunga N 4	Piquionne F 8 (12)
Bouba Diop P 14 (2)	Lansbury H 13 (9)	Potts D 3
Carew J.................. 7 (12)	Maynard N 9 (5)	Reid W 27 (1)
Cole C 28 (12)	McCartney G 36 (2)	Sears F 2 (7)
Collins D.................. 4 (7)	Morrison R .... - (1)	Stanislas J .... - (1)
Collison J................ 26 (5)	Noble M 43 (2)	Taylor M.................. 26 (2)
Demel G 7	Nolan K......................42	Tomkins J 42 (2)
Faubert J 28 (6)	Nouble F 1 (2)	Vaz Te R 13 (2)

Play-offs – appearances: Cole 3, Collison 3, Demel 3, Green 3, Noble 3, Nolan 3, O'Neil 3, Reid 3, Taylor 3, Tomkins 3, Vaz Te 3, McCartney – (3), Faubert – (2), Maynard – (2), Lansbury – (1)
League goals (81): Cole 14, Nolan 12, Vaz Te 10, Noble 8, Baldock 5, Collison 4, Tomkins 4, Reid 3, Carew 2, Maynard 2, O'Neil 2, Piquionne 2, Collins 1, Diop 1, Faubert 1, Lansbury 1, McCartney 1, Nouble 1, O'Brien 1, Faye 1, Parker 1, Taylor 1, Opponents 3. **Play-offs goals (7)**: Collison 2, Vaz Te 2, Cole 1, Maynard 1, Nolan 1
FA Cup goals: None. **Carling Cup goals** (1): Stanislas 1
Average home league attendance: 30,923. **Player of Year**: Mark Noble

NPOWER LEAGUE ONE

BOURNEMOUTH

A record signing and a change of manager were not enough keep Bournemouth's season alive. The club spent around £800,000 – nearly four times their previous highest fee – in the January transfer window bringing in Crawley's Matt Tubbs to reinforce the drive for a second successive place in the play-offs. Tubbs made an immediate impact with a goal, and an assist for Scot Malone, in a 2-0 win over Exeter which took their side to within two points of the top six. But it was to be his only one in seven appearances before a groin injury, followed by an operation, ended his season. A fortnight later, Lee Bradbury was sacked after a single win in nine matches led to the gap widening to ten points. Youth team coach Paul Groves, appointed caretaker, had little chance of closing it, managing two victories in his eight games in charge. Groves, a former Grimsby manager, was later given the job on a permanent basis.

Addison M 14	Francis S 29	Partington J 1 (4)
Arter H 28 (6)	Gregory S 23 (5)	Peters J 8
Barrett A 21	Hines Z 7 (1)	Pugh M 42
Baudry M 5 (2)	Feeney L 5	Purches S 20 (4)
Byrne N 9	Fletcher S 2 (18)	Sheringham C 2 (4)
Carmichael J ...... - (1)	Ings D 1	Stockley J 1 (9)
Cook S 26	Jalal S 2 (1)	Strugnell D ...... - (1)
Cooper S 25 (1)	Lovell S 1 (1)	Symes M 7 (8)
Cummings W 10 (4)	MacDonald S 22 (3)	Taylor L 7 (11)
Daniels C 20 (1)	Malone S 28 (4)	Thomas W 36
Doble R 4 (3)	McDermott D 10 (4)	Tubbs M 5 (2)
Flahavan D 44	Molesley M 4 (7)	Wakefield J ...... - (2)
Fogden W 20 (7)	Parsons A ...... - (1)	Zubar S 17 (5)

League goals (48): Thomas 11, Pugh 8, Arter 5, Malone 5, Fogden 3, Symes 3, Daniels 2, Gregory 2, Addison 1, Barrett 1, Fletcher 1, Hines 1, MacDonald 1, McDermott 1, Sheringham 1, Tubbs 1, Opponents 1
FA Cup goals (5): Arter 1, Malone 1, Purches 1, Zubar 1, Opponents 1. **Carling Cup goals (6):** Taylor 2, Cooper 1, Feeney 1, Lovell 1, Pugh 1. **Johnstone's Paint Trophy goals (7):** Pugh 3. Stockley 2, MacDonald 1, Opponents 1
Average home league attendance: 5,881. **Player of Year:** Marc Pugh

BRENTFORD

Just when it seemed as if they had timed to perfection a run towards the play-offs, Brentford's bid ran out of steam and petered out in the final month of the season. Five successive wins and 12 goals scored enabled Uwe Rosler's side to close the gap on a top-six place from ten points to three. But successive goalless draws against Hartlepool and Notts County put the brake on their charge. Then, they paid the price for two missed penalties in a crucial game at Stevenage. Clayton Donaldson struck the crossbar with his spot-kick and Sam Saunders hit a post, enabling their rivals for a place to move right into contention with a 2-1 victory. Brentford were left with too much to do in the final two matches, with former Manchester City striker Rosler, in his first season as manager, blaming previous inconsistency for having to play catch-up after starting the New Year on the fringes.

Adams B 6 (1)	Eger M 13 (3)	Moore S 9 (1)
Alexander G 20 (4)	Forrester H 7 (12)	Morrison C 4 (4)
Balkestein P 2 (3)	Forshaw A 6 (1)	O'Connor K 9 (5)
Bean M 22 (10)	German A ...... - (2)	Osborne K 22 (3)
Bennett D 5	Grella M 1 (10)	Oyeleke E 1
Berahino S 5 (3)	Hacker L ...... - (1)	Reeves J 7 (1)
Bidwell J 24	Lee R 37	Saunders S 29 (8)
Clarkson D 4	Legge L 23 (5)	Spillane M ...... - (1)
Dean H 23 (3)	Llera M 10 (1)	Thompson A 16 (4)
Diagouraga T 30 (5)	Logan S 26 (1)	Weston M 11 (15)
Donaldson C 40 (6)	MacDonald C ...... - (3)	Wood S 3 (2)
Douglas J 46	McGinn N 27 (10)	Woodman C 18

League goals (63): Alexander 12, Donaldson 11, Saunders 10, McGinn 5, Berahino 4, Diagouraga 4, Legge 4, Logan 3, Bean 2, Douglas 2, Bennett 1, Clarkson 1, Dean 1, O'Connor 1, Weston 1, Opponents 1
FA Cup goals (1): Saunders 1. **Carling Cup goals:** None. **Johnstone's Paint Trophy goals (12):** Grella 4, Alexander 2, Adams 1, Diagouraga 1, Logan 1, O'Connor 1, Saunders 1, Thompson 1
Average home league attendance: 5,643. **Player of Year:** Jonathan Douglas

BURY

Mike Grella played a key role as Bury recorded three successive victories at a vital time of the season to overcome the threat of an immediate return to League Two. The American striker scored against Colchester and Bournemouth, then struck twice in a 4-2 success away from home against promotion-minded Notts County. Manager Richie Barker reckoned that finishing just below mid-table was an even better achievement than winning promotion, because of the need to rebuild after losing players during the summer. His side had run into trouble after moving to within four points of a play-off place early in the New Year. Little went right during a two-month spell, apart from a spirited comeback from 3-0 down within half an hour to Huddersfield, rounded off by Ashley Eastham's stoppage-time equaliser. That performance suggested the corner might have been turned. But it was followed by successive 4-1 defeats by Sheffield Wednesday, Carlisle and Wycombe and their run without a win eventually stretched to 13 matches.

Amoo D 19 (8)	Doble R 3 (2)	Lowe R 5
Belford C 23	Eastham A 22 (3)	Mozika D 3 (1)
Bishop A 33 (7)	Elford-Alliyu L............ 4 (9)	Oyenuga K .... - (1)
Bond J.........................6	Grella M 8 (2)	Picken P 36 (1)
Byrne S 10 (4)	Harrad S 14 (12)	Schumacher S.......... 29 (3)
Carrington M 12 (9)	Harrop M .... - (5)	Skarz J 45
Carson T 17	Haworth A.................. - (6)	Sodje E 40 (1)
Clarke N 11	Hughes M 21 (4)	Sweeney P 41
Coke G 28 (2)	John-Lewis L........... 8 (20)	Worrall D 29 (12)
Cregg P.................... 5 (2)	Jones A 9 (2)	
Cullen M 1 (3)	Jones M........................24	

League goals (60): Bishop 8, Coke 6, Schumacher 6, John-Lewis 5, Amoo 4, Grella 4, Lowe 4, Sweeney 4, Jones M 3, Worrall 3, Eastham 2, Elford-Alliyu 2, Harrad 2, Sodje 2, Carrington 1, Mozika 1, Skarz 1, Opponents 2
FA Cup goals: None. **Carling Cup goals** (5): Lowe 3, Bishop 1, Jones M 1. **Johnstone's Paint Trophy goals**: None
Average home league attendance: 3,552. **Player of Year**: David Worrall

CARLISLE UNITED

Manager Greg Abbott was always conscious of the difficulty of competing for promotion against bigger clubs with considerably more resources. So, although disappointed that his side eventually missed out, he drew satisfaction from leading their bid for a play-off place into the final round of fixtures. Had leading scorer Lee Miller been able to complete the season, it might have been a different story. But Miller was ruled out with a groin injury sustained in a goalless draw with Scunthorpe and Abbott struggled to find a way to compensate for his height and strength. Carlisle lost the next three matches against leaders Charlton, eventual runners-up Sheffield Wednesday and another leading side, Stevenage. A 4-1 victory over Exeter put them back in contention, but defeat at Oldham, along with results elsewhere, meant they finished four points off the top six.

Beck M....................... - (2)	Loy R 18 (2)	Ribeiro C 5
Berrett J 42	Madden P 6 (12)	Robson M 25 (2)
Chantler C............... 10 (2)	McGovern J-P.......... 40 (5)	Simek F........................25
Collin A 46	Michalik L............... 33 (3)	Taiwo T 32 (5)
Cook J 6 (8)	Miller L........................33	Tavernier J 16
Curran C 2 (10)	Murphy P 38 (2)	Thirlwell P 25 (1)
Helan J .... - (2)	Noble L 32 (8)	Welsh A 4 (17)
Lakeland S.....................1	O'Halloran S 3	Zoko F 33 (11)
Livesey D 26 (2)	Parker B 5	

League goals (65): Miller 14, Zoko 13, Berrett 9, Noble 6, Cook 4, Loy 3, McGovern 3, Taiwo 3, Robson 2, Livesey 1, Madden 1, Murphy 1, Parker 1, Thirlwell 1, Opponents 3

FA Cup goals (4): Berrett 1, Loy 1, Miller 1, Noble 1. **Carling Cup goals** (1): McGovern 1.
Johnstone's Paint Trophy goals (2): McGovern 1, Zoko 1
Average home league attendance: 5,284. **Player of Year:** Lee Miller

CHARLTON ATHLETIC

In his first full season as manager, Chris Powell brought success back to The Valley after some
lean years. His team made a flying start by equalling the club record of 12 matches without
defeat stretching back to the 1927-28 season. Later, there was a run of eight successive victories
in the league and FA Cup, with Bradley Wright-Phillips continuing to be a regular source of goals.
Powell, who had three spells as a player with Charlton, saw them wobble a little when losing two
home matches in the space of five days to Colchester and Notts County. But having established a
13-point lead at the top, they were able to absorb those setbacks and retain a healthy advantage.
They made sure of going up by beating Carlisle, thanks to a 22nd goal from Wright-Phillips, and
clinched the title a week later with the winner from Dale Stephens against Wycombe. That
enabled Powell to become the first man to win a league title as Charlton player and manager.
And there was a perfect finish, with victory over Hartlepool enabling them to reach 100 points.

Benson P .... - (1)	Hamer B 41	Russell D 8 (3)
Clarke L 1 (6)	Hayes P 12 (7)	Solly C............................44
Cook L...................... 3 (1)	Haynes D 3 (11)	Stephens D 28 (2)
Cort L...................... 10 (5)	Hollands D....................43	Sullivan J.................... 1 (2)
Doherty G .... - (3)	Hughes A................. 5 (10)	Taylor M..................... 38 (3)
Elliot R..........................4	Jackson J................. 35 (1)	Wagstaff S 19 (15)
Ephraim H 4 (1)	Kermorgant Y 33 (3)	Wiggins R 45
Euell J..................... - (11)	Morrison M 45	Wright-Phillips B 41 (1)
Evina C...................... 2 (1)	N'Guessan D 6 (1)	
Green D.................. 25 (7)	Pritchard B 10 (10)	

League goals (82): Wright-Phillips 22, Jackson 12, Kermorgant 12, Hollands 7, Stephens 5,
Morrison 4, N'Guessan 4, Wagstaff 4, Green 3, Hayes 3, Haynes 2, Russell 2, Ephraim 1,
Wiggins 1
FA Cup goals (6): Euell 1, Hollands 1, Jackson 1, Morrison 1, Pritchard 1, Taylor 1. **Carling Cup
goals** (2): Benson 1, Euell 1. **Johnstone's Paint Trophy goals:** None
Average home league attendance: 17,485. **Player of Year:** Chris Solly

CHESTERFIELD

Celebrations turned to commiserations in the space of a week for Chesterfield. They overcame
Swindon 2-0 in the Johnstone's Paint Trophy Final through an own goal by Oliver Risser and a
stoppage-time strike from Craig Westcarr. But hopes that it would provide a lift in their bid to
avoid an immediate return to League Two were shortlived. A 4-1 beating at Sheffield United
followed by a home defeat by the same scoreline against Scunthorpe cast them adrift. Then, they
fell 13 points away from safety when losing to Walsall. There was some improvement as three
wins lifted John Sheridan's team off the bottom and sparked a glimmer of hope. But another
defeat, by Yeovil, confirmed the drop. The previous season's champions had made the club's
worst start since 1901 – two points from six games. Soon after came the start of a costly run of
17 matches without a win. It was a different story in the knock-out competition, with victories
over Notts County, Tranmere, Preston on penalties and Oldham on the way to Wembley.

Ajose N...................... 5 (7)	Davis D...........................9	Hurst J 10
Allott M 36	Downes A........... 8 (1)	Johnson L 11
Boden S 7 (19)	Fleming G................. 9 (1)	Juan J 6 (1)
Bowery J............... 23 (17)	Ford S......................18	Lee T............................35
Clarke L........................14	Griffiths S 3	Lester J 16 (5)
Clay C......................... - (5)	Grounds J 13	Lowry J....................... 2 (4)
Darikwa T 2	Holden D 9 (1)	Mattis D 6 (1)

Mendy A	31 (3)	Randall M	10 (6)	Talbot D	43
Morgan D	10 (7)	Ridehalgh L	20	Thompson J	20
Moussa F	10	Robertson G	11 (1)	Trotman N	23
Niven D	4 (3)	Smith N	22 (3)	Westcarr C	32 (6)
Obadeyi T	3 (2)	Soderberg O	2	Whitaker D	23 (7)

League goals (56): Clarke 9, Bowery 8, Westcarr 8, Whitaker 5, Boden 4, Moussa 4, Lester 3, Morgan 3, Mendy 2, Talbot 2, Ajose 1, Allott 1, Holden 1, Juan 1, Randall 1, Ridehalgh 1, Thompson 1, Trotman 1
FA Cup goals (1): Bowery 1. **Carling Cup goals** (2): Whitaker 2. **Johnstone's Paint Trophy goals** (13): Bowery 3, Westcarr 3, Boden 1, Lester 1, Mendy 1, Morgan 1, Randall 1, Whitaker 1, Opponents 1
Average home league attendance: 6,530. **Player of Year**: Tommy Lee

COLCHESTER UNITED

Colchester negotiated a fourth successive middle-of-the-road season, not close enough to threaten the leading group and never in danger of being dragged into trouble. This time it contained a club record 20 draws, 11 of them at home. When they were not sharing the points, there were some sparkling performances at the Community Stadium, with four goals scored against Oldham, Notts County, Bury and in the final game there against Tranmere. Colchester also got four against Crewe in the FA Cup. That victory over Tranmere was the first in 12, although they still managed to hold their opponents to tenth through the nine drawn matches. Low point of the campaign was a 6-1 home defeat by Stevenage. Manager John Ward was also disappointed to finish off with a 4-1 loss at Notts County. End of season brought a testimonial match for midfielder Kemal Izzet for ten years at the club embracing more than 400 league appearances.

Antonio M	14 (1)	Heath M	22 (4)	Rowlands M	7 (2)
Baldwin P	4 (1)	Henderson I	45 (1)	Sears F	5 (6)
Bond A	28 (12)	Izzet K	29 (5)	Thomas C	- (2)
Coker B	15 (5)	James L	17 (6)	Vincent A	5 (4)
Cousins M	10	Massey G	4 (4)	White J	21 (5)
Duguid K	16 (9)	O'Toole J	8 (7)	Williams B	36
Eastman T	24 (1)	Odejayi K	33 (10)	Wilson B	46
Gillespie S	19 (14)	Okuonghae M	42	Wordsworth A	44
Hamilton B	- (1)	Rose M	12 (2)		

League goals (61): Wordsworth 13, Gillespie 11, Henderson 9, Antonio 4, Odejayi 4, Bond 3, Duguid 3, Eastman 3, Heath 2, Rowlands 2, Sears 2, James 1, Vincent 1, Opponents 3
FA Cup goals (4): James 2, Bond 1, Coker 1. **Carling Cup goals** (3): Gillespie 1, Henderson 1, Odejayi 1. **Johnstone's Paint Trophy goals** (1): Baldwin 1
Average home league attendance: 3,865. **Player of Year**: Kayode Odejayi

EXETER CITY

A singe goal from their opening four matches was a taste of things to come for Exeter. Manager Paul Tisdale had been forced to rebuild after losing the 'spine' of the team that finished a single point away from the play-offs. Leading scorer Jamie Cureton was among the players who left and it was perhaps no coincidence that his old team finished as the division's lowest scorers, drawing a blank in 22 of the 46 matches. They just managed to keep their head above water until a damaging run of two points from nine matches left them deep in trouble with a month of the season remaining. Ironically, the goals then started to flow – nine in home matches against Leyton Orient, Walsall and Sheffield United. But it was too late, with a 3-2 defeat away to fellow-strugglers Rochdale, in which a two-goal lead was surrendered in the final 11 minutes, having effectively ruled out any chance of escaping the drop.

Archibald-Henville T 45	Frear E 5 (5)	O'Brien L 2 (1)
Baldwin P 9	Golbourne S 26	O'Flynn J 8 (16)
Bauza G................ 12 (15)	Gow A........................ 6 (1)	Oakley M 7
Bennett S 13 (2)	Hackett C 5	Pidgeley L................ 8 (2)
Bignall N 3	Jones B 16 (3)	Ricketts R............... - (1)
Coles D................... 28 (3)	Keohane J.................. - (4)	Sercombe L............. 27 (6)
Cureton J................. 5 (2)	Krysiak A 38	Shephard C............... 7 (4)
Dalla Valle L......... 4 (1)	Logan R 11 (17)	Taylor J................ 26 (4)
Dawson A......................2	McNish C.................. 2 (3)	Tully S 42 (2)
Duffy R................. 22 (6)	Nardiello D 28 (8)	Vine R 4 (1)
Dunne J................. 44 (1)	Nicholls T 2 (5)	Whichelow M...................2
Fortune J 5	Noble D 42	

League goals (46): Nardiello 9, Sercombe 7, Logan 5, Bennett 3, Gow 3, Taylor 3, Archibald-Henville 2, Bauza 2, Coles 2, Dunne 2, Noble 2, O'Flynn 2, Cureton 1, Jones 1, Nicholls 1, Opponents 1
FA Cup goals (3): Frear 1, Logan 1, Noble 1. **Carling Cup goals** (3): Bauza 1, Nardiello 1, Shephard 1. **Johnstone's Paint Trophy goals** (2): Dunne 1, Nardiello 1
Average home attendance: 4,474. **Player of Year**: Troy Archibald-Henville

HARTLEPOOL UNITED

A successful start gave way to a nightmare run at Victoria Park as Hartlepool experienced a rollercoaster season. They were up to third after five wins and four draws under Mick Wadsworth. Two months later, Wadsworth was gone, sacked after another club record – this time seven successive home defeats, including one by Stevenage in the FA Cup. There were two more before Neale Cooper, back in charge at the club he left in 2005, stabilised things and stopped the rot with a 2-0 victory over Rochdale. Seven goals against Carlisle and Notts County gave the supporters more to cheer about. But after that they were hard to come by – seven in 13 games home and away. Nevertheless, Hartlepool finished 13th, their highest league position since 2005. Adam Boyd, whose 22 goals provided a major contribution to that year's achievement of reaching the play-offs, was released at the end of this season after a 12-year association with the club.

Adjei S .... - (1)	Holden D 2 (1)	Poole J 15 (12)
Austin N 46	Horwood E 38 (3)	Rafferty A 1
Baldwin J................ 14 (3)	Humphreys R 19 (10)	Richards J................. 1 (1)
Boyd A 13 (20)	James L................ 12 (7)	Rowbotham J 1
Brown J 10 (14)	Larkin C.....................2	Rutherford G............... - (1)
Collins S................ 35 (1)	Liddle G 37 (2)	Solano N.................. 11 (3)
Flinders S 45	Luscombe N............. 3 (10)	Sweeney A 39
Hartley P 44	Monkhouse A 39 (6)	Wright S 10
Haslam S.................. 3 (7)	Murray P................ 44 (1)	
Hassan C .... - (1)	Nish C................ 12 (7)	
Hawkins L......................1	Noble R 9	

League goals (50): Sweeney 8, Poole 7, Boyd 6, Hartley 4, Liddle 4, Nish 4, James 3, Monkhouse 3, Noble 2, Solano 2, Austin 1, Brown 1, Collins 1, Horwood 1, Humphreys 1, Luscombe 1, Murray 1
FA Cup goals: None. **Carling Cup goals** (1): Sweeney 1. **Johnstone's Paint Trophy goals**: None
Average home league attendance: 4,960. **Player of Year**: Paul Murray

HUDDERSFIELD TOWN

The country's top goalscorer led Huddersfield into the Championship – but it was a goalkeeper they finally had to thank for going up. Sheffield United's Steve Simonsen fired over the crossbar with the 22nd penalty of a marathon Play-off Final shoot-out to hand their Yorkshire rivals victory by 8-7 after a goalless 120 minutes. It was a dramatic end to a remarkable season for Huddersfield and 40-goal Jordan Rhodes. Two of them against Notts County enabled his side to overtake Nottingham Forest's Football League record of 42 unbeaten league matches, a run which ended against Charlton in their next game. League One's Player of the Year netted five times in a 6-0 win over Wycombe and got all four in the 4-4 draw with Sheffield Wednesday. There were also hat-tricks in successive games against Exeter and Preston. Despite all this, manager Lee Clark was sacked in mid-February by chairman Dean Hoyle after a breakdown in their relationship and replaced by Simon Grayson, himself dismissed by Leeds earlier in the month. The goals dried up in the final month of the campaign, when three successive defeats ruled out any chance of automatic promotion, but Rhodes was back on song with two as MK Dons were beaten in the semi-finals.

Arfield S 24 (11)	Gudjonsson J.............. 6 (2)	Naysmith G 20 (2)
Arismendi D............... 7 (2)	Higginbotham K 3 (1)	Novak L 29 (12)
Atkinson C .... - (1)	Hunt J..........................43	Parkin J 2 (1)
Bennett I 33	Johnson D.............⁒... 16 (2)	Rhodes J................... 36 (4)
Bruce A 3	Kay A 25 (3)	Roberts G 28 (11)
Cadamarteri D 6 (9)	Lee A 18 (13)	Robinson A 12 (3)
Clarke P.........................31	McCombe J 20	Smithies A 13
Clarke T...................... 7 (7)	McDermott D.............. 6 (3)	Ward D 31 (8)
Cooper L 2 (2)	Miller T 24 (2)	Woods C 23 (3)
Gobern O 19 (2)	Morrison S 19	

Play-offs – appearances: Clarke P 3, Hunt 3, Johnson 3, Miller 3, Morrison 3, Novak 3, Rhodes 3, Ward 3, Woods 3, Higginbotham 2 (1), Bennett 2, Arfield 1 (1), Smithies 1 (1), Clarke T – (2), Lee – (2), Roberts – (1), Robinson – (1)
League goals (79): Rhodes 36, Novak 13, Lee 7, Roberts 6, Ward 4, McCombe 3, Arfield 2, Gobern 2, Hunt 1, Kay 1, Miller 1, Morrison 1, Robinson 1, Opponents 1. **Play-offs – goals** (3): Rhodes 2, Hunt 1
FA Cup goals (1): Novak 1. **Carling Cup goals** (7): Novak 2, Rhodes 2, Hunt 1, Roberts 1, Ward 1. **Johnstone's Paint Trophy goals** (4): Clarke P 1, McDermott 1, Miller 1, Novak 1
Average home league attendance: 14,131. **Player of Year**: Jordan Rhodes

LEYTON ORIENT

A season which manager Russell Slade rated the toughest of his career ended with Orient spared from a relegation cliffhanger. His side were dragged into trouble when losing seven out of eight games, then being held at home by Yeovil after surrendering a two-goal lead in the last ten minutes. But although there was another defeat, at Hartlepool, they were relieved at not having to go in the final fixture still under threat when Wycombe and Chesterfield were both beaten and a four-point safety net preserved. Orient had opened with five successive defeats and took just three points from the first ten games. Ben Chorley's stoppage-time equaliser at Huddersfield, followed by the first victory, 2-1 against Preston, provided badly-needed confidence. So much so that the next 13 matches yielded 25 points and Orient went into the New Year looking to consolidate a mid-table position. Instead, they faltered again and starting slipping back towards trouble.

Alnwick B 6	Clarke T..........................10	Forbes T 38 (1)
Andrew C................... 2 (8)	Cook L 9	Jones J 6
Ben Youssef S 6 (3)	Cox D 35 (3)	Laird M................... 11 (11)
Butcher L 23	Craig T 4	Leacock D.....................15
Button D.........................1	Cureton J 9 (10)	Lisbie K 34 (3)
Campbell-Ryce J........ 7 (1)	Cuthbert S 33	Lobjoit B.................... - (1)
Cestor M 1	Daniels C 13	McSweeney L 28 (1)
Chicksen A......................3	Dawson S.....................20	Mooney D 28 (9)
Chorley B................ 30 (2)	Dickson R 9	Obafemi A.................. - (1)

114

Odubajo M	1 (2)	Reed A	10 (1)	Spring M	41
Omozusi E	8 (2)	Revell A	4 (1)	Stech M	2
Porter G	9 (25)	Richardson M	1 (2)	Taiwo S	2 (3)
Rachubka P	8	Smith J	35 (3)	Tehoue J	4 (10

League goals (48): Lisbie 12, Cox 8, Smith 6, Mooney 5, Spring 4, Tehoue 3, Laird 2, Campbell-Ryce 1, Cook 1, Cureton 1, Cuthbert 1, Dawson 1, Odubajo 1, Porter 1, Opponents 1
FA Cup goals (3): Porter 1, Smith 1, Spring 1. **Carling Cup goals** (6): Mooney 2, Chorley 1, Cox 1, Dawson 1, Richardson 1. **Johnstone's Paint Trophy goals** (1): Mooney 1
Average home league attendance: 4,298. **Player of Year**: Scott Cuthbert

MILTON KEYNES DONS

More disappointment in the play-offs for Dons, this time at the hands of the country's leading marksman. They lost 2-0 at home to Huddersfield, with Jordan Rhodes scoring for the 39th time. And it was Rhodes who stretched the advantage in the second leg, before a comeback brought goals from Daniel Powell and, in stoppage-time, gave Alan Smith to give their side some consolation with a victory. Manager Karl Robinson felt they were superior overall, but that Rhodes was the deciding factor. It was the club's fourth semi-final defeat in six years. Dons had signalled their intentions with 16 points from the opening six matches. They were top for a fortnight and always in or around the leading group. With six weeks remaining, the chance came to close to within four points of Sheffield Wednesday when Shaun Williams converted a penalty against Carlisle, only they conceded twice in the final ten minutes. Smith, on loan from Newcastle, scored his first goal in five years to make sure of going through with victory over Sheffield United.

Balanta A	10 (10)	Guy L	- (1)	O'Shea J	12 (15)
Baldock S	4	Hall R	- (2)	Potter D	40
Beevers M	14	Ibehre J	23 (16)	Powell D	22 (21)
Bowditch D	33 (8)	Lewington D	46	Slane P	- (5)
Chadwick L	34 (8)	MacDonald C	29 (6)	Smith Adam	17
Chicksen A	14 (6)	MacKenzie G	26	Smith Alan	14 (2)
Doumbe M	19 (1)	Martin D	46	Tavernier J	7
Flanagan T	18 (3)	McLoughlin I	- (1)	Williams S	32 (6)
Galloway B	1	McNamee A	- (7)	Williams G	- (2)
Gleeson S	39	Morrison C	5 (1)		

Play-offs – appearances: Bowditch 2, Chicksen 2, Gleeson 2, Lewington 2, MacDonald 2, MacKenzie 2, Martin 2, Potter 2, Powell 2, Williams 2, O'Shea 1 (1), Smith Alan 1 (1), Ibehre – (2), Chadwick – (1)
League goals (84): Bowditch 12, MacDonald 9, Ibehre 8, Williams 8, Powell 6, Gleeson 5, O'Shea 5, Baldock 4, Balanta 4, Doumbe 4, Flanagan 3, Lewington 3, Morrison 3, Chadwick 2, Potter 2, Smith Adam 2, Beevers 1, MacKenzie 1, Smith Alan 1, Opponents 1. **Play-offs – goals** (2): Powell 1, Smith 1
FA Cup goals (10): Bowditch 3, Powell 2, Doumbe 1, MacDonald 1, O'Shea 1, Potter 1, Williams 1. **Carling Cup goals** (9): Baldock 2, Chadwick 2, Powell 2, Balanta 1, Ibehre 1, Lewington 1.
Johnstone's Paint Trophy goals (3): Chadwick 1, MacDonald 1, Opponents 1
Average home league attendance: 8,659. **Player of Year**: Darren Potter

NOTTS COUNTY

County were left counting the cost of a 4-2 home defeat by Bury after Keith Curle had revived their promotion bid. It knocked them out of a play-off position and wins in the final two matches against Wycombe – after trailing with 88 minutes gone – and Colchester were not enough to compensate. County lost out for the fourth slot on goal difference to fast-finishing Stevenage, who had also prevailed when the teams met in the FA Cup. Curle, coaching under Neil Warnock at Queens Park Rangers until both were sacked, replaced Martin Allen, dismissed after ten months as manager with his side eight points adrift. The impact was immediate, five wins and a draw in six games, including a 4-2 success away to leaders Charlton in which Jonathan Forte scored a hat-trick. Home defeats by the two Sheffield clubs in the space of four days ended that sequence, but they were back on track with the help of another hat-trick from a player brought in on loan, Lloyd Sam, against Yeovil.

Adebola D 3 (3)	Harris L 1 (1)	Ravenhill R 5
Allen C 4 (5)	Hawley K 15 (11)	Sam L 8 (2)
Bencherif H 14 (6)	Hollis H 1	Sheehan A 39
Bishop N 41	Hughes J 44 (1)	Sodje S 7 (9)
Bogdanovic D 8	Hughes L 28 (12)	Speiss F .... - (1)
Burgess B 20 (8)	Judge A 40 (3)	Spicer J .... - (1)
Chilvers L 16 (1)	Kelly J 29 (3)	Stewart D 16 (1)
Demontagnac I 2 (15)	Mahon G 23 (8)	Stirling J .... - (8)
Edwards M 27 (3)	Montano C 5 (10)	Westcarr C 2 (2)
Forte J 6 (4)	Nelson S 46	Yennaris N 2
Freeman K 18 (1)	Orenuga F .... - (2)	
Harley L 11 (3)	Pearce K 25 (2)	

League goals (75): Hughes J 13, Hughes L 10, Judge 7, Forte 5, Sam 5, Burgess 4, Montano 4, Kelly 3, Pearce 3, Bencherif 2, Bishop 2, Bogdanovic 2, Hawley 2, Sheehan 2, Sodje 2, Stewart 2, Adebola 1, Edwards 1, Freeman 1, Opponents 4
FA Cup goals (8): Hughes J 4, Hawley 1, Judge 1, Sheehan 1. **Carling Cup goals (3)** Edwards 1, Hughes L 1, Westcarr. **Johnstone's Paint Trophy goals (1):** Hawley 1
Average home league attendance: 6,807. **Player of Year:** Alan Judge

OLDHAM ATHLETIC

Going into the final part of the season, manager Paul Dickov felt his side were good enough to emerge from a tightly-packed bunch in the middle reaches of the table and climb into the top half. Instead, they gained just three points from eight matches, failed to score in six of them and finished a third successive indifferent campaign in 16th place. At least there was a victory over Carlisle to end on for a young line-up put together with an eye on the future – 19 year-old local boy James Tarkowski scoring his first goal for the club and Oumane Tounkara netting his first of a second spell on loan from Sunderland. Goals had been increasingly hard to come by once a regular flow from much-travelled Shefki Kuqi began to dry up. Kuqi, playing for his tenth club, rounded off Oldham's best result of the season, 3-2 away to promotion-minded Sheffield United, with a stoppage-time penalty.

Adeyemi T 33 (3)	Gerrard P .... - (1)	Parker J 7 (6)
Belezika G .... - (1)	Hughes C .... - (4)	Reid R 17 (3)
Black P 13	Kuqi S 39 (1)	Scapuzzi L 8 (2)
Bouzanis D 8 (1)	Lee K 43	Simpson R 26 (3)
Brown R 15	Lund M 2 (1)	Smith M 3 (25)
Bunn H 8 (3)	M'Changama Y 8 (2)	Tarkowski J 13 (3)
Cisak A 38	Marsh-Brown K 5 (6)	Taylor C 38
Clarke N 16	Mellor D 19 (2)	Tounkara O 3 (5)
Diallo B 12 (3)	Millar K 2 (2)	Wesolowski J 21
Diamond Z 21 (2)	Morais F 23 (13)	Winchester C 9 (3)
Furman D 21 (2)	Mvoto J-Y 35 (1)	

League goals (50): Kuqi 11, Simpson 6, Morais 5, Reid 5, Smith 3, Wesolowski 3, Adeyemi 2, Diamond 2, Lee 2, Taylor 2, Clarke 1, Furman 1, Marsh-Brown 1, Mellor 1, Mvoto 1, Scapuzzi 1, Tarkowski 1, Tounkara 1, Opponents 1
FA Cup goals (6): Simpson 2, Furman 1, Kuqi 1, Taylor 1, Wesolowski 1. **Carling Cup goals (1):** Reid 1. **Johnstone's Paint Trophy goals (7):** Kuqi 4, Adeyemi 1, Scapuzzi 1, Simpson 1
Average home league attendance: 4,432. **Player of Year:** Kieran Lee

PRESTON NORTH END

Early season optimism gave way to troubled times at Deepdale. Seven successive victories and 18 goals scored suggested a strong challenge for a quick return to the Championship. Instead, leading scorer Neil Mellor sustained an ankle injury and his side fell away alarmingly, winning only one of the next 16 league and cup matches. Manager Phil Brown was sacked soon after Peter Ridsdale took over as chairman. Then, Mellor was ruled out again, this time with knee trouble which eventually forced him to retire. Graham Westley succeeded Brown after winning back-to-back promotions with Stevenage, but was unable to stop the slide. If anything, the mood deteriorated, with dressing room opposition to some of his methods and four players accused of leaking tactics to Sheffield Wednesday ahead of the teams' match. The outcome was Preston finishing in the bottom half of the table and Westley planning a new-look squad.

Alexander G	17 (1)	Ehmer M	7 (2)	Miller G	2 (4)
Aneke C	3 (4)	Forte J	2 (1)	Morgan C	18 (1)
Arestidou A	7	Gray D	18 (5)	Murphy R	1 (4)
Ashbee I	3 (4)	Hayhurst W	1 (1)	Nicholson B	22 (8)
Barton A	12 (4)	Holroyd C	14 (6)	Parry P	39 (1)
Brown A	4	Hume I	21 (7)	Proctor A	19
Bunn H	1	Hunt N	15 (2)	Proctor J	24 (7)
Carlisle C	20	Jervis J	3 (2)	Robertson C	17 (1)
Clark L	2	Marrow A	3 (1)	Russell D	2
Clucas S	- (1)	Mayor D	22 (14)	Smith S	9 (4)
Coutts P	41	McAllister J	4	Stuckmann T	28
Cummins G	13 (2)	McCombe J	6	Tsoumou J	5 (11)
Daley K	- (8)	McLaughlin C	10 (7)	Turner I	11
Devine D	13	McLean B	15 (1)	Wright B	11 (2)
Douglas J	- (4)	Mellor N	15 (2)		
Doyle N	5	Middleton D	1		

League goals (54): Hume 9, Mellor 8, Parry 4, Carlisle 3, Proctor 3, Tsoumou 3, Coutts 2, Cummins 2, Alexander 2, Jervis 2, Mayor 2, Nicholson 2, Aneke 1, Bunn1, Daley 1, Devine 1, Douglas 1, Holroyd 1, Hunt 1, McLean 1, Morgan 1, Robertson 1, Turner 1, Wright 1
FA Cup goals: None. **Carling Cup goals (6):** Barton 1, Hume 1, Mayor 1, Mellor 1, Russell 1, Opponents 1. **Johnstone's Paint Trophy goals (4):** Barton 1, McCombe 1, McLean 1, Tsoumou 1
Average home league attendance: 11,820. **Player of Year:** Thorsten Stuckmann

ROCHDALE

Two points from the first six matches suggested a tough season ahead for Rochdale – and so it proved. They spent most of the time in the relegation zone and finished bottom, 12 points from safety. Steve Eyre was sacked a week before Christmas, six months after taking over from Keith Hill as manager. In came Accrington's John Coleman, whose first game in charge brought a 3-0 win over Bury, ending a run of nine games without success. Victory over Bournemouth and a point gained away from home against leaders Charlton closed the gap on teams above them. But Rochdale were unable to achieve that final push and Coleman was 'sickened' when his team conceded a stoppage-time equaliser to Walsall after coming from two goals down to lead 3-2. A 5-2 home defeat by Sheffield United then effectively killed off any hope of staying up, despite a spirited recovery next time out when they retrieved a two-goal deficit to beat fellow-strugglers Exeter 3-2 with three goals in last 11 minutes.

Ababaka G	- (2)	Barnes-Homee M	1 (4)	Byrne N	2 (1)
Adams N	30 (11)	Barry-Murphy B	17 (5)	Darby S	34 (1)
Akpa Akpro J-L	30 (11)	Benali A	- (2)	Eccleston N	3 (2)
Amankwaah K	15 (1)	Bergkamp R	2 (1)	Edwards M	6 (2)
Balkestein P	12 (1)	Bogdanovic D	5	Gray R	1 (3)
Ball D	12 (2)	Bunn H	5 (1)	Grimes A	27 (9)

Hackney S 1 (1)	Long K 16	Symes M.................. 14 (1)
Holden D 20 (1)	Lucas D 16	Thompson J 8 (9)
Holness M 23 (1)	Marshall P .... - (1)	Trotman N...................12
Jones G 45	McConville S 2 (2)	Tutte A 28 (12)
Jordan S 17 (2)	Miniham S 1	Twaddle M 1 (1)
Kean J............................14	Grady C .... - (1)	Widdowson J 30 (2)
Kennedy J 38 (6)	Obadeyi T 3 (3)	
Kurucz P...........................11	Ormerod B 4 (1)	

League goals (47): Grimes 8, Akpa Akpro 7, Jones 5, Adams 4, Kennedy 4, Symes 4, Ball 3, Holness 3, Barry-Murphy 1, Bogdanovic 1, Eccleston 1, Gray 1, Obadeyi 1, Ormerod 1, Thompson 1, Tutte 1, Opponents 1
FA Cup goals: None. **Carling Cup goals (6):** Grimes 3, Akpa Apkro 1, Jones 1, Opponents 1.
Johnstone's Paint Trophy goals (2): Ball 1, Bunn 1
Average home league attendance: 3,108. **Player of Year:** Jason Kennedy

SCUNTHORPE UNITED

Nine matches without a win represented the club's worst start for 37 years. At the half-way point of the season, only a superior goal difference kept Scunthorpe out of the bottom four, raising the spectre of a second successive relegation. A poor disciplinary record added to their problems and that continued, with nine players in all receiving red cards. But there was a marked improvement in performances, with Alan Knill's loan signings a key factor. Defender David Mirfin returned to Glanford Park, and together with another Watford player, midfielder Josh Walker, and Cardiff striker Jon Parkin, gave the team much-needed impetus. The result was a run of ten matches without defeat and the 'safety' mark of 50 points reached after a goalless draw at Carlisle with four fixture remaining. That was the 20th time they had shared the points and there were another two to come for a club record total.

Ajose N..................... 2 (5)	Jennings C .... -(4)	Parkin J 13 (1)
Barcham A............... 37 (4)	Johnstone S...................12	Reckord J....................17
Byrne C 13 (1)	Lillis J 6	Reid P 36
Canavan N 11 (1)	McAleny C 2 (1)	Ribeiro C 10
Collins M .... - (1)	Mirfin D.......................19	Robertson J............. 12 (7)
Dagnall C 19 (4)	Mozika D 17 (1)	Ryan J 20 (4)
Duffy M 27 (10)	Nelson M 8 (2)	Slocombe S...................28
Duffy S..........................18	Nolan E 29 (1)	Thompson G 19 (20)
Gibbons R 3 (1)	Norwood O 14 (1)	Togwell S 35 (4)
Godden M .... - (1)	O'Connor M............... 29 (4)	Walker J................... 17 (1)
Grant R 19 (10)	Palmer A..................... - (1)	Wright A 14 (4)

League goals (55): Barcham 9, Grant 7, Thompson 7, Parkin 6, Dagnall 4, Robertson 3, Walker 3, Duffy M 2, Mozika 2, O'Connor 2, Ryan 2, Canavan 1, Duffy S 1, Mirfin 1, Nelson 1, Nolan 1, Norwood 1, Reid 1, Togwell 1
FA Cup goals: None. **Carling Cup goals (3):** Dagnall 2, Barcham 1. **Johnstone's Paint Trophy goals (2):** Grant 2
Average home league attendance: 4,331. **Player of Year:** Paul Reid

SHEFFIELD UNITED

Losing their top scorer at a criticial time of the season was a blow; losing out on automatic promotion to Sheffield Wednesday was hard to take; losing on penalties in the Play-off Final was the worst of all. That was the fate of Danny Wilson's side, beaten 8-7 by Huddersfield when goalkeeper Steve Simonsen fired over the crossbar with the 22nd spot-kick of a marathon shoot-out which followed a goalless 120 minutes. It all went wrong for United in second place, four points clear of their neighbours and just three matches remaining. The day after 35-goal Ched

Evans was sent to prison, there was a defeat by MK Dons. They had to retrieve a two-goal deficit for a point against Stevenage at Bramall Lane. Then, another 2-2 draw, against relegated Exeter, meant Wednesday claimed the runners-up spot, thanks to three successive wins. A red card for James Beattie at St James Park ruled him out of the play-offs, while doubts about the fitness of Richard Cresswell and Kevin McDonald compounded United's problems. Chris Porter's 85th minute winner in the second leg of the semi-finals against Stevenage took them to Wembley, but not in the shape they wanted.

Beattie J 2 (16)	Hill M 11 (1)	O'Halloran M 1 (6)
Bogdanovic D .... - (2)	Hoskins W 4 (8)	Phillips M 5 (1)
Clarke B 5	Lescinal J-F 22 (3)	Porter C 18 (16)
Collins N 42	Long G 2	Quinn S 43 (2)
Cresswell R 32 (10)	Lowton M 44	Simonsen S 44
Doyle M 39 (4)	Maguire H 44	Slew J 3 (1)
Egan J 1	McAllister D 3 (1)	Taylor A 4
Ertl J 2 (5)	McDonald K 30 (1)	Tonne E .... - (2)
Evans C 30 (6)	Mendez-Laing N 4 (4)	Williams M 14 (5)
Flynn R 12 (14)	Montgomery N 14 (6)	Williamson L 31 (9)

Play-offs – appearances: Collins 3, Doyle 3, Flynn 3, Hill 3, Lowton 3, Maguire 3, Quinn 3, Simonsen 3, Williamson 3, Porter 2 (1), McDonald 2, Montgomery 1 (1), Cresswell 1 (1), Ertl – (1), O'Halloran – (1), Taylor – (1)

League goals (92): Evans 29, Williamson 13, Cresswell 9, Lowton 6, Phillips 5, Porter 5, Quinn 4, Doyle 3, McDonald 3, Collins 2, Flynn 2, Hoskins 2, Clarke 1, Maguire 1, Mendez-Laing 1, Montgomery 1, Slew 1, Tonne 1, Opponents 3. **Play-offs – goals** (1): Porter 1

FA Cup goals (9): Evans 5, Flynn 1, Porter 1, Opponents 2. **Carling Cup goals** (2): Cresswell 1, Quinn 1. **Johnstone's Paint Trophy goals** (5): Evans 1, McAllister 1, Phillips 1, Porter 1, Tonne 1

Average home league attendance: 18,701. **Player of Year**: Harry Maguire

SHEFFIELD WEDNESDAY

Gary Megson developed Wednesday's return to the Championship and Dave Jones completed the job when chairman Milan Mandaric decided on a controversial change of manager with two months of the season remaining. Three days after victory over Sheffield United lifted them to within two points of their second-placed neighbours, Mandaric decided that Jones, sacked by Cardiff at the end of the previous season was the better bet to achieve promotion. The two sides remained neck and neck until the penultimate game when Wednesday forged ahead by winning at Brentford. They then clinched the runners-up spot behind Charlton with a 2-0 victory over relegated Wycombe, earned by goals from two loan players, Reading's Michail Antonio and Newcastle's Nile Ranger, in front of a 38,000 Hillsborough crowd. It was Jones's tenth win in 12 games in charge, with the other two drawn. Wednesday had also started with a flourish, seven straight home wins representing their best since the early 1960s.

Antonio M 14	Lines C 37 (4)	Prutton D 19 (6)
Batth D 44	Llera M 15 (5)	Ranger N 7 (1)
Beevers M 4 (3)	Lowe R 11 (15)	Reynolds M 3
Bennett J 16 (5)	Madine G 36 (2)	Sedgwick C 5 (5)
Bostock J 2 (2)	Marshall B 22	Semedo J 46
Buxton L 36 (1)	McGoldrick D 3 (1)	Tavernier J 6
Bywater S 32	Morrison C 7 (12)	Treacy K 2 (5)
Johnson J 12 (12)	O'Connor J 11 (7)	Uchechi D .... - (1)
Johnson R 22 (2)	O'Donnell R 6	Watt S 2 (2)
Jones D 1 (2)	O'Grady C 25 (7)	Weaver N 8
Jones M 6 (4)	Otsemobor J 8 (3)	
Jones R 32 (1)	Palmer L 6 (8)	

League goals (81): Madine 18, Lowe 8, Johnson R 7, Antonio 5, Marshall 5, O'Grady 5, Johnson J 4, Jones R 4, Llera 4, Lines 3, Batth 2, Bennett 2, Prutton 2, Ranger 2, Buxton 1, McGoldrick 1, Morrison 1, O'Connor 1, Palmer 1, Sedgwick 1, Semedo 1, Treacy 1, Opponents 2
FA Cup goals (5): O'Grady 2, Lines 1, Lowe 1, Morrison 1. **Carling Cup goals** (1): Morrison 1.
Johnstone's Paint Trophy goals:None
Average home league attendance: 21,336. **Player of Year**: Jose Semedo

STEVENAGE

Even though the dream of a third successive promotion eventually died, this was another season to remember. The club lost manager Graham Westley to Preston half-way through it and a place in the top six after managing a single win in 13 games. When he returned to the Lamex Stadium with his new team and secured a 1-1 draw, his old one were six points adrift of the play-offs. Westley's successor, Gary Smith, then engineered a big recovery, beginning with a 6-0 win at Yeovil and netting 13 points from the last five games. Stevenage had finished 19 points behind Sheffield United, but the teams' semi-final was settled by a single goal, headed by Chris Porter with five minutes of normal time left in the second leg at Bramall Lane. Westley's last game was an FA Cup third round win at Reading. Under Smith, late of Colorado Rapids, they overcame Notts County to reach the last 16 for the first time, held Tottenham to a goalless draw and led through Joel Byrom's penalty before losing the replay 3-1.

Agyemang P 10 (3)	Freeman L 22 (4)	Myrie-Williams J 3 (14)
Aneke C 2 (4)	Harrison B 10 (8)	Reid C 24 (5)
Ashton J 42 (1)	Henry R 32	Roberts M 46
Beardsley C 15 (16)	Julian A 2 (1)	Shroot R 11 (14)
Bostwick M 43	Laird S 46	Slew J 6 (3)
Byrom J 29 (3)	Lascelles J 5 (2)	Thalassitis M .... - (3)
Charles D 23 (5)	Long S 18 (12)	Walker J .... - (5)
Cowan D 2 (6)	Madjo G .... - (1)	Wilson L 44 (2)
Day C 44	May B 2 (5)	
Edwards P 11 (11)	Mousinho J 14 (5)	

Play-offs – appearances: Agyemang 2, Ashton 2, Bostwick 2, Byrom 2, Day 2, Freeman 2, Laird 2, Lascelles 2,Roberts 2, Wilson 2, Reid 1 (1), Shroot 1 (1), Mousinho – (2), Beardsley – (1), Myrie-Williams – (1)
League goals (69): Laird 8, Beardsley 7, Bostwick 7, Freeman 7, Reid 6, Roberts 6, Wilson 5, Byrom 4, Charles 4, Mousinho 3, Shroot 3, Harrison 2, Agyemang 1, Ashton 1, Lascelles 1, Long 1, Walker 1, Opponents 2. **Play-offs – goals**: None
FA Cup goals (7): Beardsley 2, Byrom 1, Charles 1, Laird 1, Shroot 1, Opponents 1. **Carling Cup goals** (3): Beardsley 1, Bostwick 1, Long 1. **Johnstone's Paint Trophy goals** (2): Roberts, Wilson.
Average home league attendance: 3,558. **Player of Year**: Mark Roberts

TRANMERE ROVERS

Ronnie Moore returned to Prenton Park for a second spell as manager and steered Tranmere away from the threat of relegation towards respectability. Moore was appointed until the end of the season when Les Parry paid the price for a single win in 18 matches, along with an FA Cup home defeat by Cheltenham. That resulted in a slide from sixth to within a point of the bottom four, with Parry blaming the 'fear factor' among his players. Moore, himself dismissed by the club after failing to reach the play-offs in 2009, put that right, beginning with a point against Notts County, thanks to a stoppage-time equaliser by John Welsh. His side went on to accumulate 14 points from six matches and when Jake Cassidy, on loan from Wolves, scored twice in a 3-0 win over Stevenage to bring his tally to four in four matches, Rovers moved into the top half of the table. Moore later signed a one year contract.

Akins L 36 (8)	Baxter J 14	Buchanan D....................41
Bakayogo Z 8 (18)	Brunt R 11 (4)	Cassidy J 7 (3)

Coughlin A	1 (1)	Kirby J	- (1)	Showunmi E	21 (6)
Devaney M	16 (4)	Labadie J	9 (18)	Stockton C	- (1)
Donaldson R	1	McChrystal M	17 (1)	Taylor A	36 (1)
Elford-Alliyu L	2 (2)	McGurk A	25 (6)	Tiryaki M	16 (14)
Fon Williams O	35	Power M	2 (2)	Wallace J	18
Goodison I	41 (2)	Rachubka P	10	Weir R	29 (10)
Holmes D	25 (1)	Raven D	17	Welsh J	43 (1)
Kay M	4 (2)	Robinson A	21 (4)		

League goals (49): Akins 5, Cassidy 5, Labadie 5, McGurk 4, Robinson 4, Baxter 3, Showunmi 3, Tiryaki 3, Weir 3, Welsh 3, Devaney 2, Taylor 2, Wallace 2, Brunt 1, Buchanan 1, Goodison 1, McChrystal 1, Opponents 1

FA Cup goals: None. **Carling Cup goals**: None. **Johnstone's Paint Trophy goals** (5): Taylor 2, McGurk 1, Showunmi 1, Tiryaki 1

Average home league attendance: 5,130. **Player of Year**: David Buchanan

WALSALL

Walsall overcame a disputed goal-line decision and a controversial sending-off to survive a relegation threat for the second successive season. It wasn't as tight as 2011 when everything hinged on results on the final day. But nerves still became frayed when a position of relative comfort was transformed by three successive defeats. The third was a 4-2 setback at Exeter in which they claimed Florent Cuvelier's shot, which hit both posts, was over the line and Manny Smith's red card a harsh one. But a hard-earned point in the penultimate game against Huddersfield, gained by Cuvelier's goal, and results elsewhere ensured safety. Walsall had previously been in the bottom four when winning only once in 16 matches, before a 2-0 victory over Wycombe sparked a run of 12 points from six. During that lean spell, goalkeeper Jimmy Walker broke Colin Harrison's all-time club record with his 530th appearance – and kept a clean sheet against Brentford.

Beevers L	28 (7)	Hurst K	30 (4)	Peterlin A	20 (6)
Bowerman G	3 (19)	Jarvis R	9 (10)	Sadler M	46
Butler A	42	Lancashire O	17 (3)	Smith E	31 (2)
Chambers A	26 (3)	Ledesma E	9 (1)	Taundry R	31 (4)
Cuvelier F	17 (1)	Macken J	33 (4)	Walker J	24
Gnakpa C	8 (12)	Mantom S	13	Westlake M	14 (3)
Grigg W	17 (12)	Martin D	4	Wilson M	4
Grof D	22 (1)	Nicholls A	32 (13)		
Halliday A	2 (5)	Paterson J	24 (10)		

League goals (51): Macken 7, Nicholls 7, Butler 5, Cuvelier 4, Grigg 4, Ledesma 4, Bowerman 3, Mantom 3, Paterson 3, Chambers 2, Hurst 2, Jarvis 2, Gnakpa 1, Lancashire 1, Sadler 1, Smith 1, Opponents 1

FA Cup goals (5): Bowerman 1, Gnakpa 1, Macken 1, Nicholls 1, Wilson 1. **Carling Cup goals**: None. **Johnstone's Paint Trophy goals** (3): Hurst 1, Jarvis 1, Taundry 1

Average home league attendance: 4,274. **Player of Year**: Andy Butler

WYCOMBE WANDERERS

Just when it seemed as if Wycombe would take their bid for survival to the last game of the season, it all went wrong. They conceded an equaliser in the 89th minute to Notts County, who then scored again three minutes into stoppage-time to win 4-3 at Adams Park. It left them four points adrift of Leyton Orient and Walsall and having to make an immediate return to League Two. The leakiest defence in the four divisions was the root of the problem. Wycombe conceded 88 goals in 46 matches and never really looked like sorting things out at the back. They had briefly climbed out of the bottom four by scoring 16 of their own to beat Hartlepool, Leyton Orient, Bury and Exeter as Stuart Beavon forged a prolific strike partnership with on-loan Paul

Hayes. But after Hayes was recalled by Charlton, they did not win another match. Beavon was the division's second overall top scorer behind Huddersfield's Jordan Rhodes with 25 goals, including hat-tricks against Bury and in the Johnstone's Paint Trophy tie against Bristol Rovers.

Ainsworth G 16 (16)	Grant J 22 (8)	McCoy M 24 (4)
Basey G 29 (3)	Hackett C 6 (2)	McNamee A 11 (4)
Beavon S 40 (3)	Halls J 5 (2)	Rendell S................... 2 (4)
Benyon E 2 (7)	Harding B 3 (4)	Rowlands M 8 (2)
Betsy K..................... 1 (2)	Harper J 5	Sandell A....................11
Bignall N .... - (1)	Harris K 10 (7)	Stewart A......................4
Bloomfield M........... 24 (7)	Hayes P.......................6	Strevens B 29 (7)
Bull N.........................46	Ibe J 2 (5)	Trotta M 8
Doherty G 13	Johnson L 24 (3)	Tunnicliffe J............. 16 (1)
Donnelly S 16 (2)	Kewley-Graham J....... - (1)	Whichelow M...............4
Dunne C .... - (3)	Laing L 10 (1)	Winfield D....................25
Eastmond C 14	Lewis S................... 38 (3)	
Foster D......................29	McClure M 3 (9)	

League goals (65): Beavon 21, Trotta 8, Hayes 6, Donnelly 4, Grant 4, Strevens 4, Ainsworth 2, Basey 2, Bloomfield 2, McNamee 2, Winfield 2, Doherty 1, Ibe 1, Lewis 1, McClure 1, Rendell 1, Tunnicliffe 1, Whichelow 1, Opponents 1
FA Cup goals: None. **Carling Cup goals** (4): Beavon 1, Benyon 1, Donnelly 1, Grant 1. **Johnstone's Paint Trophy goals** (4): Beavon 3, Betsy 1
Average home league attendance: 4,843. **Player of Year:** Stuart Beavon

YEOVIL TOWN

Six years after leaving the club for Bristol City, Gary Johnson returned to Huish Park to lead a revival in fortunes. Johnson, who parted company with Northampton two months earlier, replaced Terry Skiverton as manager with Yeovil in the bottom four and out of the FA Cup after losing to non-league Fleetwood. His second spell in charge started with a 4-0 defeat by promotion-chasing Sheffield United. Then came a run of eight wins in the next 12 games, in which Andy Williams scored 11 goals, and a rise into the top half of the table. There was a loss of momentum after that, accompanied by a 6-0 home defeat by Stevenage, the club's biggest at home since 1958 and their worst anywhere since 1982. In the tightly-packed middle reaches of the division, they slipped back to 17th, although Williams took his tally to 16 with a 25-yard winner against Chesterfield.

Agard K 13 (16)	Gilbert K 3 (5)	Obika J 24 (3)
Ayling L.......................44	Gilmartin R 8	Parrett D................... 9 (1)
Belson F 1	Grounds J 13 (1)	Purse D 5
Blizzard D 24 (6)	Haynes-Brown C 1 (9)	Stech M...........................5
Clifford C 6 (1)	Hinds R 15 (1)	Steer J..........................12
D'Ath L 12 (2)	Huntington P.................37	Stewart G.......................1
Dickson R......................5	Johnson O 5 (1)	Upson E 40 (1)
Edgar A 5 (5)	Jones N 21 (1)	Walker S......................20
Edwards J....................4	MacLean S 14 (6)	Williams G 23 (5)
Ehmer M.......................24	Massey G 8 (8)	Williams A 31 (4)
Fallon R..................... - (5)	Morris J 3 (2)	Woods M 2 (3)
Franks J................. 13 (1)	N'Gala B 24 (7)	Wotton P......................22
Gibson B 1 (4)	O'Brien A 8 (5)	Youga K .... - (1)

League goals (59): Williams A 16, Agard 6, Obika 4, Williams G 4, Blizzard 3, Franks 3, MacLean 3, Massey 3, Upson 3, Huntington 2, N'Gala 2, Wotton 2, D'Ath 1, Dickson 1, Edgar 1, Edwards 1, Hinds 1, Parrett 1, Woods 1, Opponents 1
FA Cup goals (5): Upson 2, Blizzard 1, Clifford 1, Williams A 1. **Carling Cup goals**: None.
Johnstone's Paint Trophy goals (2): Ehmer 1, MacLean 1
Average home league attendance: 3,984. **Player of Year:** Andy Williams

NPOWER LEAGUE TWO

AFC WIMBLEDON

Jack Midson's goals helped Wimbledon's return to the Football League to be a satisfactory as well as a nostalgic one. The club founded in 2002 by fans after the former FA Cup winners relocated to Milton Keynes, settled in quickly and there was talk of a promotion challenge when the reward for 23 points from the first 12 games was a place behind joint leaders Southend and Crawley. It was premature because the next 12 failed to deliver a single win. Manager Terry Brown made a number of signings in the January transfer window and successive victories over Port Vale, Gillingham and Macclesfield followed. The one at Priestfield was notable for the way AFC came from 3-1 down with less than 20 minutes remaining to finish 4-3 ahead. After that, they were up and down before finishing their home programme on a high by beating promotion-chasing Torquay and Shrewsbury. Midson scored 18 times in the league and two more in cup ties.

Ademano C 5 (10)	Jackson R 3 (4)	Moore L 29 (8)
Balkestein P.....................6	Johnson B 14 (4)	Moore S 40 (1)
Brown S..........................44	Jolley C 23 (14)	Mulley J..................... 3 (7)
Bush C 16 (6)	Jones R 1	Porter M 11 (4)
Djilali K 4 (8)	Kiernan R 1 (8)	Prior J 2 (1)
Euell J 8 (1)	Knott B................. 14 (6)	Stuart J 33 (1)
Franks F 3 (1)	McNaughton C 18	Turner J 2
Gwillim G......................27	Midson J 43 (3)	Wellard R 16 (6)
Harrison B 11 (8)	Minshull L 13 (5)	Yussuff R 29 (11)
Hatton S 41 (3)	Mitchell-King M............24	
Hoyte G 2 (1)	Moncur G......................20	

League goals (62): Midson 18, Moore L 9, Jolley 7, Moore S 6, Yussuff 4, Knott 3, Harrison 2, Moncur 2, Ademano 1, Djilali 1, Gwillim 1, Hatton 1, Porter 1, Stuart 1,Wellard 1, Opponents 4
FA Cup goals (2): Midson 1, Moore L 1. **Carling Cup goals (2):** Midson 1, Moore L 1. **Johnstone's Paint Trophy goals (3):** Yussuff 2, Hatton 1
Average home league attendance: 4,294. **Player of Year:** Sammy Moore

ACCRINGTON STANLEY

Former midfield player Paul Cook had a difficult introduction to Football League management when returning to the club to succeed John Coleman, who joined Rochdale after nearly 13 years in charge. Cook, appointed on the back of success at the Irish club Sligo, took over a side challenging to make the play-offs for the second successive year. He started with a 4-0 defeat by Plymouth, lost the next two as well and had to wait for his seventh game for a first win – 2-1 against Northampton. Two more, by the same scoreline, came against AFC Wimbledon and Hereford, but they were only ones in 17 matches through to the end of the season. Accrington slipped out of the running for a top-seven repeat and finished in the lower half of the table. One of the high spots was Michael Smith's hat-trick in the 4-3 victory over Gillingham, ironically immediately after Coleman's departure and before Cook came in. A cause for concern was a total of nine red cards.

Amond P...................37 (5)	Dunbavin I 25	Joyce L...........................43
Barnett C 27 (15)	Evans M 14 (9)	Kiernan R 3
Bender T..................... - (2)	Fletcher W 10	Liddle M........................12
Burton A .... - (1)	Grant R...........................8	Lindfield C 29 (10)
Carver M ....-1(1)	Guthrie K 6 (7)	Long K.........................24
Coid D 16 (5)	Hatfield W 4 (13)	McIntyre K 44 (1)
Craney I 7 (15)	Hessey S........................17	Miller K 2
Devitt J 15 (1)	Hopper R 1 (3)	Moult L 1 (3)
Dobie L...................... - (4)	Hughes B................ 15 (6)	Murdoch S 12 (1)

Murphy P 36 (2)	Richardson L .... - (1)	Taylor N 1 (1)
Nicholls L 9	Smith M 4 (2)	Willis L 1 (1)
Nsiala A 19	Spray J 3	Winnard D.....................30
Procter A 25	Stockley J 5 (4)	

League goals (54): Amond 7, Lindfield 4, Long 4, Murphy 4, Evans 3, Grant 3, Hatfield 3, Hughes 3, Smith 3, Stockley 3, Devitt 2, Fletcher 2, Hessey 2, Joyce 2, McIntyre 2, Proctor 2, Barnett 1, Coid 1, Craney 1, Winnard 1, Opponents 1
FA Cup goals (1): Joyce 1. **Carling Cup goals:** None. **Johnstone's Paint Trophy goals (3):** Amond 1, Lindfield 1, Proctor 1
Average home league attendance: 1,784.

ALDERSHOT TOWN

Aldershot continued to make progress under Dean Holdsworth, up three places to 11th with a squad featuring some promising young players. Particularly pleasing was the response to a worrying run of six successive matches without a goal around the turn of the year which sent his side sliding to sixth from bottom. The slump was arrested by a club record six successive victories, including Guy Madjo, signed from Stevenage, justifying the manager's faith that he would make a difference to their attack. Madjo was also prominent in five unbeaten matches at the end of the season, which included a 2-1 victory over champions-elect Swindon and their biggest win – 4-0 away at Burton. Aldershot also made progress in the Carling Cup, beating West Ham, Carlisle and Rochdale, then giving a creditable account against Manchester United when losing 3-0 in front of a sell-out crowd of 7,000.

Andrade B .... - (1)	Henry C 3 (3)	Pulis A 1 (4)
Bergqvist D .... - (2)	Herd B 45	Rankine M 21 (1)
Bradley S 13 (1)	Hylton D 43 (1)	Risser W 9 (7)
Brown A.................... 6 (5)	Jones D 42	Roberts J 1 (3)
Brown J 2 (1)	Madjo G 15 (5)	Rodman A 15 (3)
Brown T 14 (3)	McGlashan J 18 (5)	Sinclair R 1 (3)
Bubb B 1 (8)	Mekki A 16 (9)	Smith A..................... 7 (5)
Collins C .... - (1)	Molesley M 2 (6)	Smith B 3 (5)
Collins J 21 (4)	Morris A 36 (3)	Straker A 44
Connolly R .... -1(6)	Murphy D................... 2 (1)	Taylor J .... - (3)
Davies S 3 (5)	Panther E .... - (1)	Vincenti P 33 (9)
Doig C 2	Payne J 14 (3)	Worner R 22
Doughty M 2 (3)	Payne S .... -(1)	Young J................... 24 (1)
Guttridge L 24 (1)	Pearson G 1 (4)	

League goals (54): Hylton 13, Madjo 8, Vincenti 6, Guttridge 4, McGlashan 4, Risser 3, Brown T 2, Morris 2, Payne J 2, Rankine 2, Straker 2, Davies 1, Mekki 1, Molesley 1, Rodman 1, Opponents 2
FA Cup goals (3): Guttridge 1, Rankine 1, Rodman 1. **Carling Cup goals (6):** Hylton 2, Rankine 2, Guttridge 1, Opponents 1. **Johnstone's Paint Trophy goals (1):** Hylton 1
Average home league attendance: 2,864. **Player of Year:** Darren Jones

BARNET

No wonder Barnet are known as the 'Houdini' club. For the third successive season, their bid to beat the drop went to the final fixture – and for the third time they were successful. A 2-1 victory at Burton maintained a two-point cushion over second-from-bottom Hereford, who won their last match. Although 22-goal leading marksman Izale McLeod was not fit enough to start the game, Mark Byrne put his side ahead. Then, after it was cancelled out and Calvin Zola had missed a penalty for Burton, skipper Mark Hughes came up with the decider. Back in charge to supervise the escape was Martin Allen, brought in for the final three games after the sacking of Lawrie Sanchez. It was Allen's third spell as manager and after a 3-0 defeat at Southend, Barnet kept their noses in front by beating AFC Wimbledon 4-0, with Hughes again on the mark.

Previously, they had gone ten points clear of the relegation zone with four successive wins in January. But just one victory in the next 17 outings spelled trouble. Job done, Allen was on his way again, with Peterborough coach Mark Robson coming in.

Baseya C...................... - (2)	Holmes R................. 33 (8)	Obita J 3 (2)
Borrowdale G...............11	Hughes M................. 44 (1)	O'Brien L....................10
Brill D 36	Kabba S 5 (4)	Owusu L .... - (5)
Byrne M.................. 38 (5	Kamdjo C....................41	Parkes J.....................11
Deering S............... 39 (5)	Leach D....................9(1)	Price J..........................5
Dennehy D.............. 18 (1)	Marshall M............. 24 (1)	Saville J.................. 14 (3)
Downing P 25 (1)	May B.................... 9 (2)	Senda D 19
Fraser T.................... 2 (3)	McCallum G .... - (2)	Taylor C 2 (16)
Gambin L.................. - (1)	McGleish S 5 (4)	Uddin A........................9
Geohaghon E............. - (2)	McLeod I 43 (1)	Vilhete N .... - (3)
Hajrovic S................ 7 (3)	Mustoe J................. 15 (3)	Yiadom A................. 1 (6)
Hector M .... 26(1)	N'Diaye A 2 (4)	

League goals (52): McLeod 18, Holmes 8, Byrne 5, May 4, Deering 3, Hughes 3, Kamdjo 3, Hector 2, Kabba 1, Leach 1, Marshall 1, Price 1, Taylor 1, Yiadom 1
FA Cup goals (3): Kamdjo 1, McLeod 1, Taylor 1. **Carling Cup goals (3):** Holmes 1, Hughes 1, Kabba 1. **Johnstone's Paint Trophy goals (9):** McLeod 3, Marshall 2, Holmes 1, Hughes 1, Kabba 1,Taylor 1
Average home league attendance: 2,288.

BRADFORD CITY

Peter Jackson was the Football League's first managerial casualty of the season, resigning after the opening four matches netted a single point. It was a taste of things to come for his successor Phil Parkinson, formerly in charge of Colchester, Hull and Charlton, as Bradford flirted with the relegation zone for much of the campaign. Successive wins over promotion-minded Southend, Crewe and Shrewsbury put them in better heart going into the New Year. But they failed to maintain that momentum and were not helped by a poor disciplinary record. Three red cards in a mass brawl after the home defeat by Crawley, took the total for the season to nine. Eventually, Bradford opened up daylight between the bottom two by completing the double over Southend. Then a hat-trick by Nahki Wells provided a 3-1 victory at Northampton to put them comfortably clear. Despite all the inconsistency, a special ticket offer attracted a crowd of over 17,000 for the game against Hereford.

Atkinson W 6 (6)	Hannah R 4 (14)	Ravenhill R 25 (1)
Baker A .... - (1)	Hansen M 4	Reed A 4
Branston G.............. 15 (1)	Hanson J 36 (3)	Reid K 32 (5)
Bryan M.................... 5 (3)	Haworth A 2 (1)	Rodney N.................... - (5)
Bullock L 14 (5)	Hunt L........................ - (1)	Seip M 23
Compton J 9 (5)	Jansson O 1	Smalley D 7 (6)
Dagnall C................ 5 (2)	Jones R 31 (1)	Stewart M 5 (7)
Davies A......................26	Kozluk R....................17	Syers D.................. 8 (10)
Dean L .... - (1)	McLaughlan J...............23	Taylor C 1 (2)
Devitt J .... 5(2)	Mitchell C 10 (1)	Threlfall R................ 16 (1)
Duke M........................18	Moore L 16 (1)	Wells N................. 18 (15)
Fagan C 29 (2)	O'Brien L 3 (6)	Williams S 1
Flynn M 27 (3)	Oliver L........................39	
Fry M .... 5(1)	Ramsden S 16 (1)	

League goals (54): Hanson 13, Wells 10, Fagan 7, Flynn 4, Reid 4, Davies 2, Hannah 2, Syers 2, Atkinson 1, Branston 1, Dagnall 1, Devitt 1, Jones 1, Mitchell 1, Oliver 1, Ravenhill 1, Seip 1, Opponents 1
FA Cup goals (6): Wells 2, Fagan 1, Hannah 1, Hanson 1, Opponents 1. **Carling Cup goals (2):**

Compton 1, Flynn 1. **Johnstone's Paint Trophy goals** (3): Flynn 1, Oliver 1, Opponents 1
Average home league attendance: 10,171. **Player of Year**: Luke Oliver

BRISTOL ROVERS

Much-travelled Mark McGhee steered Rovers away from the threat of a relegation struggle amid more managerial upheaval at the Memorial Ground. McGhee took over his eighth club, the last one Aberdeen, when Paul Buckle, the fourth man in charge from the previous relegation season, was sacked after seven months in charge. His side had a single win to show from a run of 11 matches and were sixth from bottom as a consequence. McGhee effected an immediate improvement — victories over Cheltenham, Bradford and Morecambe taking Rovers well clear of trouble. But their form after that was patchy, without proving damaging. The inconsistency was reflected by a 7-1 drubbing of Burton in which Eliot Richards scored a hat-trick, a 5-1 success against Accrington, then disappointingly, a subdued performance at Dagenham, where a 4-0 defeat cost them the chance of finishing in the top half of the table.

Anthony B.............. 14 (2)	Gill M...................... 32 (1)	Paterson J..................17
Anyinsah J 23 (8)	Gough C 1	Poke M..........................8
Bevan S..........................37	Harding M.................. - (1)	Rendell S................. 4 (1)
Bolger C 38 (1)	Harrold M 35 (5)	Richards E 18 (14)
Brown L.................. 35 (7)	Kuffour J 3 (2)	Sawyer G 23 (1)
Brown W 4 (8)	Lines C...................... - (1)	Smith M 8 (12)
Campbell S 10 (1)	Lund M 9 (4)	Stanley C 30 (4)
Carayol M 24 (6)	McGleish S 14 (13)	Virgo A..........................9
Cronin L .... - (1)	McLaggon K.............. - (1)	Woodards D..................39
Dorman A 20 (5)	Norburn O.............. 1 (4)	Zebroski C............ 28 (11)
Downes A..........................8	Parkes T 14	

League goals (60): Harrold 16, Brown L 7, McGleish 7, Richards 7, Anyinsah 4, Carayol 4, Zebroski 3, Bolger 2, Dorman 2, Lund 2, Anthony 1, Kuffour 1, Paterson 1, Stanley 1, Virgo 1, Woodwards 1
FA Cup goals (10): Carayol 2, McGleish 2, Richards 2, Anthony 1, Anyinsah 1, Woodards 1, Zebroski 1. **Carling Cup goals** (3): Harrold 1, Richards 1, Zebroski 1. **Johnstone's Paint Trophy goals** (1): Harrold 1
Average home league attendance: 6,035. **Player of Year**: Danny Woodards

BURTON ALBION

Burton seemed capable of mounting a challenge for the play-offs when climbing to fifth with a 3-2 Boxing Day win at Northampton. Instead, the season turned sour, they failed to win any of the next 14 games and dropped ten places in the table. A 4-1 defeat by Torquay, the sixth in succession was followed by the sacking of manager Paul Peschisolido, and there were two more under caretaker Gary Rowett. Victory over Gillingham, courtesy of an own goal, stopped the rot. Then, Ross Atkins saved an injury-time penalty from Morecambe's Kevin Ellison to preserve a 3-2 advantage and ensure his team were safe. Long-serving manager Aaron Webster was among the scorers with his 100th goal for the club. Burton slumped again, conceding six second-half goals to lose 7-1 at Bristol Rovers and three after the break for a 4-0 home defeat by Aldershot. Rowett, however, had done enough to win a permanent appointment at the end of the campaign.

Ada P..........................5 (4)	Clucas S.................. 1 (1)	Legzdins A 1
Ainsworth L.............. 4 (3)	Corbett A 31 (2)	Lucas L 1
Amankwaah K 8	Driver C..........................8	Maghoma J 32 (4)
Atkins R 45	Dyer J 16 (1)	McGrath J 28 (3)
Austin R 34 (4)	Gurrieri A.............. 6 (7)	Moore D.................. 1 (3)
Banton J.................. - (1)	Harriott M 3 (1)	Palmer C.............. 16 (18)
Blanchett D.............. 9 (5)	James T.................. 29 (1)	Parkes T 4
Bolder A 41 (3)	Kee B.................. 14 (6)	Pearson G 6 (6)

126

Phillips J 21 (12)	Taylor C 23 (8)	Zola C...................... 34 (2)
Richards J................ 28 (7)	Webster A 33 (2)	
Stanton N 22	Yussuf A 2 (15)	

League goals (54): Kee 12, Zola 12, Richards 11, Maghoma 4, Bolder 3, Palmer 3, Webster 3, Taylor 2, Driver 1, Dyer 1, Yussuf 1, Opponents 1
FA Cup goals (1): Zola 1. **Carling Cup goals (3):** Maghoma 1, Taylor 1, Zola 1. **Johnstone's Paint Trophy goals (1):** Richards 1
Average home league attendance: 2,809. **Player of Year:** Nathan Stanton

CHELTENHAM TOWN

Mark Yates found consolation in defeat at Wembley when assessing the performance of his players there and the way they had exceeded expectations to reach the Play-off Final. There was no argument about a stunning finish from Crewe's £4m rated 18-year-old Nick Powell. But luck was against them when Jeff Goulding struck the crossbar from 25 yards and Steve Elliott's header was cleared off the line, before a second goal late on ended their chances. Cheltenham's promotion bid had been launched with a run of nine wins in ten matches which lifted them into the top three. They enjoyed a brief spell as leaders and remainedl well placed to go up automatically until a barren run of six matches produced a single goal and a single point. Momentum was restored with victories over Barnet and Accrington. Then they beat Bradford and Plymouth in the final two games to seal sixth place. It brought a semi-final against Torquay and a 4-1 aggregate success, with Jermaine McGlashan scoring in each leg.

Andrew D........................10	Graham B 1 (6)	Mohamed K 39 (6)
Bennett A 44	Hooman H 1 (1)	Pack M...........................43
Brown S........................22	Jackson M................. - (1)	Penn R 39 (4)
Burgess B 6 (1)	Jombati S 33 (3)	Reid B .... - (1)
Butland J.....................24	Lewis T............................1	Smikle B.................. 3 (32)
Duffy D................ 25 (16)	Low J 25 (13)	Spencer J 27 (14)
Elliott S 38	Lowe K 25 (6)	Summerfield L.......... 37 (4)
Garbutt L 34	MacLean S.......................3	
Goulding J 16 (19)	McGlashan J 10 (6)	

Play-offs – appearances: Bennett 3, Brown 3, Burgess 3, Elliott 3, Jombati 3, McGlashan 3, Mohamed 3, Pack 3, Summerfield 3, Spencer 2 (1), Lowe 2, Goulding 1 (2), Garbutt 1, Duffy – (2), Penn – (2), Hooman – (1), Smikle – (1),
League goals (66): Duffy 11, Mohamed 11, Spencer 10, Goulding 5, Pack 5, Summerfield 4, Jombati 3, Low 3, Bennett 2, Burgess 2, Elliott 2, Garbutt 2, Lowe 1, MacLean 1, McGlashan 1, Penn 1, Smikle 1, Opponents 1. **Play-offs – goals (4):** McGlashan 2, Burgess 1, Pack 1
FA Cup goals (5): Duffy 2, Pack 1, Penn 1, Summerfield 1. **Carling Cup goals (1):** Summerfield 1. **Johnstone's Paint Trophy goals (5):** Duffy 2, Goulding 1, Smikle 1, Spencer 1
Average home league attendance: 3,424. **Player of Year:** Sido Jombati

CRAWLEY TOWN

League football held no worries for the new boys. Neither did the loss of manager Steve Evans, who walked out to join Rotherham with six games of the season remaining, disturb their challenge for back-to-back promotions. With coach Craig Brewster taking over as caretaker and former Reading manager Steve Coppell appointed director of football, Crawley extended an unbeaten run to 13 matches. A surprise home defeat by relegation-threatened Hereford threatened to knock them off course. But Scott Neilson scored the only goal of the final game at Accrington to preserve the third automatic place, a point ahead of Southend. It was a notable achievement by a side who had also lost leading marksman Matt Tubbs to Bournemouth in the January transfer window and his strike partner Tyrone Barnett to Peterborough soon after. There was also a second successive run to the fifth round of the FA Cup, with Hull and Bristol City among their victims before Stoke proved too strong. Sean O'Driscoll, sacked by Doncaster, was appointment permanent replacement for Evans.

Akinde J	7 (18)	Doughty M	2 (14)	Neilson S	11 (19)
Akpan H	17 (9)	Drury A	13	Pittman J-P	- (4)
Alexander G	14	Eastman T	6	Shearer S	25
Barnett T	25 (1)	Gilmartin R	6	Simpson J	31 (9)
Batt S	2 (3)	Griffiths S	6	Smith B	3 (2)
Bulman D	41	Hawley K	1 (3)	Thomas W	2 (4)
Clarke L	4	Howell D	36 (1)	Torres S	37 (1)
Clarke B	16 (1)	Hunt D	26 (1)	Tubbs M	23 (1)
Cummings W	6 (3)	James L	6	Wassmer C	12 (1)
Davies S	17 (3)	Kuipers M	15	Watt S	6 (8)
Davis C	27 (2)	McFadzean K	36 (1)	Wilson G	2 (2)
Dempster J	6 (1)	Mills P	19 (2)		

League goals (76): Barnett 14, Tubbs 14, Alexander 7, Bulman 3, Clarke B 3, Davis 3, Drury 3, Howell 3, Neilson 3, Torres 3, Davies 2, McFadzean 2, Mills 2, Simpson 2, Wassmer 2, Watt 2, Akinde 1, Akpan 1, Clarke L 1, Dempster 1, Pittman 1, Smith 1, Thomas 1, Opponents 3
FA Cup goals (9): Tubbs 5, Barnett 1, Doughty 1, Drury 1, McFadzean 1. **Carling Cup goals (3):** Akpan 1, Torres 1, Tubbs 1.
Johnstone's Paint Trophy goals: None.
Average home league attendance: 3,212. **Player of Year:** Kyle McFadzean

CREWE ALEXANDRA

When Steve Davis stepped up from assistant manager to take over from Dario Gradi in mid-November, he was given a single brief: make sure of preserving Football League status. Crewe had started the season with four successive defeats and despite showing some improvement, were still finding it hard going down in 18th place. Six months later, on a sun-drenched afternoon at Wembley, a youthful team – nine of the starting line-up had progressed through the club's renowned academy – were celebrating a 2-0 victory over Cheltenham in the Play-off Final. Highly-rated Nick Powell, 18, put them ahead with a spectacular dipping left-foot shot and Byron Moore made sure late on, a performance which extended their record unbeaten run to 19 matches. Former central defender Davis, who made his debut for the club at 18 and later helped Barnsley to promotion to the Premier League, saw confidence increase with improved results and his youngsters playing closer to their potential. They moved into the play-off positions by beating Cheltenham 1-0 in the penultimate home game and saw off Southend, the last team to defeat them, 3-2 on aggregate in the semi-finals.

Artell D	31 (1)	Leitch-Smith A J	31 (7)	Powell N	34 (4)
Bell L	22 (8)	Lowry J	9 (1)	Sarcevic A	1 (5)
Bodin B	8	Martin C	26 (3)	Shelley D	12 (14)
Brown J	2 (5)	Mellor K	6 (6)	Tootle M	36 (1)
Clayton M	1 (23)	Miller S	26 (7)	Tunnicliffe J	2
Davis H	39 (2)	Moore B	42	Turton O	- (2)
Dugdale A	43	Murphy L	39 (3)	Westwood A	39 (2)
Fletcher W	3 (3)	Pearson G	8 (1)		
Hughes C	- (4)	Phillips S	46		

Play-offs –appearances: Davis 3, Dugdale 3, Leitch-Smith 3, Mellor 3, Moore 3, Phillips 3, Powell 3, Tootle 3, Westwood 3, Artell 2, Murphy 2, Bell 1 (2), Martin 1 (1), Clayton – (3), Bodin – (1)
League goals (67): Powell 14, Leitch-Smith 8, Moore 8, Murphy 8, Davis 5, Miller 5, Clayton 3, Dugdale 3, Pearson 3, Westwood 3, Artell 2, Fletcher 1, Mellor 1, Shelley 1, Opponents 2.
Play-offs – goals (5): Clayton 1, Dugdale 1, Leitch-Smith 1, Moore 1, Powell 1
FA Cup goals (1): Moore 1. **Carling Cup goals (2):** Artell 1, Miller 1. **Johnstone's Paint Trophy goals (2):** Clayton 1, Powell 1
Average home league attendance: 4,124. **Player of Year:** Nick Powell

DAGENHAM AND REDBRIDGE

John Still, the longest-serving manager in League Two, has done an admirable job with limited resources at Victoria Road and here was another job completed against the odds. Still, who has been in charge since 2004, led his team to safety when a return to Conference football was beginning to look a distinct possibility. With ten games remaining Dagenham were rock bottom and leaking too many goals. But a surge of form and a run of 14 points from the next six was unmatched by their relegation rivals. And when Dominic Green scored the winner at Gillingham, his first goal of the season, safety was assured, with Still rating it one of his most satisfying moments. There was also a spakling finish as Brian Woodall scored his first league hat-trick in a 4-0 victory over Bristol Rovers. Dagenham had also started the campaign strongly, winning three games out of four before nine successive defeats spelled trouble.

Abdullah A 4 (1)	Hewitt T 3 (3)	Rose R 9 (1)
Akinde J 4 (1)	Hogan D .... - (1)	Saunders M..................5
Arber M 32 (1)	Howell L.....................10	Scannell D................ 7 (7)
Baudry M.......................11	Ilesanmi F.......................17	Scott J 12 (8)
Bingham B 17 (10)	Lee O 15 (1)	Shea J .... - (1)
Bond J............................5	Lewington C 41	Spillane M 29
Cunnington A 2 (7)	Maher K 8	Tomlin G................. 15 (2)
Doe S............................41	McCrory D............... 32 (1)	Walsh P 4 (4)
Edmans R................. - (3)	Montano C 10	Wassmer C.................. - (1)
Elito M 20 (4)	Nurse J 36 (3)	Wearen E .... - (2)
Gain P 16 (4)	Ogogo A......................40	Williams S 10
Geohaghon E............. 1 (1)	Parker J 6 (2)	Woodall B 26 (13)
Green Danny 4 (4)	Reed J 1 (6)	
Green Dominic 8 (8)	Reeves B 5	

League goals (50): Woodall 11, Doe 6, Nurse 5, Elito 4, Spillane 4, Lee 3, Montano 3, Arber 2, Bingham 2, Williams 2, Green Danny 1, Green Dominic 1 McCrory 1, Ogogo 1, Rose 1, Saunders 1, Scott 1, Opponents 1
FA Cup goals (5): Nurse 3, Woodall 2. **Carling Cup goals:** None. **Johnstone's Paint Trophy goals (2):** McCrory 1, Williams 1
Average home league attendance: 2,090. **Player of Year:** Mickey Spillane

GILLINGHAM

Andy Hessenthaler's side were among the favourites for promotion after missing the 2011 play-offs on goal difference. So expectancy was high at Priestfield. But there was more disappointment to come, another eighth-place finish, and Hessenthaler paid the price. He was replaced by much-travelled Martin Allen, fresh from keeping Barnet in the league. No team chalked up more goals in the division, with three or more scored in 13 matches. But too many were conceded and a poor start to the New Year in which six games delivered a single point meant Gillingham were always playing catch-up. That run included 4-3 defeats by AFC Wimbledon and Accrington, demonstrating how vulnerable they could be. Even a tremendous comeback against Hereford, when a 4-2 deficit was transformed into a 5-4 win in the final ten minutes, had its down side, with defensive deficiencies again exposed. Victory over leaders Swindon in the penultimate home match was not enough and they finished two points adrift.

Brown A..................... - (1)	Gazzaniga P 19 (1)	Martin J 32 (3)
Davies C .... - (2)	Jackman D 36 (4)	Miller A 2 (3)
Essam C 17 (1)	Kedwell D 37 (3)	Montrose L............. 28 (9)
Evans J..................... 4 (3)	King S 8 (1)	Nouble F................... 12 (1)
Fish M 19 (4)	Kuffour J 26 (4)	Obita J 5 (1)
Flitney R........................27	Lawrence M 24 (2)	Oli D 4 (19)
Frampton A.............. 27 (1)	Lee C 28 (6)	Payne S .... - (12)
Fuller B 9	Lee O 5 (2)	Payne J 29 (1)

Richards	G24	Tomlin G	9 (1)	Whelpdale C	34 (5)
Rooney L	11 (6)	Vine R	3 (6)		
Spiller D	6 (9)	Weston C	21 (9)		

League goals (79): Kedwell 12, Whelpdale 12, Kuffour 9, Lee 6, Tomlin 6, Nouble 5, Jackman 4, Montrose 4, Obita 3, Rooney 3, Oli 2, Payne J 2, Spiller 2, Fish 1, King 1, Martin 1, Miller 1, Payne S 1, Richards 1, Vine 1, Opponents 2
FA Cup goals (8): Kedwell 2, Weston 2, Jackman 1, Payne J 1, Payne S 1, Richards 1. **Carling Cup goals**: None. **Johnstone's Paint Trophy goals** (1): Richards 1
Average home league attendance: 5,146. **Player of Year**: Danny Jackman

HEREFORD UNITED

Hereford did just enough to preserve Football League status under Jamie Pitman in 2011. But there was no escape this time, despite a change of manager and a fighting finish which brought a 3-0 away win over promotion-chasing Crawley and a 3-2 victory over Torquay in front of a sell-out Edgar Street crowd. It was not enough because Barnet maintained a two-point advantage by beating Burton in their last fixture. Three defeats and eight goals conceded in the opening three games had suggested another difficult season. The first 12 brought a single success and although spirits improved when Bradford, Barnet and Northampton were beaten in consecutive matches, they were always up against it. Pitman was sacked soon after a 4-2 lead with ten minutes left at Gillingham turned into a 5-4 defeat and Walsall coach Richard O'Kelly given two months for a rescue act. He made an encouraging start, lifting the side three points clear of the relegation zone, but was unable to prevent a lean run of eight matches which dragged them back into it. O'Kelly later declined the offer to stay in charge.

Anthony B	13 (2)	Dalibard B	9 (1)	McQuilkin J	3 (4)
Arquin Y	16 (18)	Elder N	13 (13)	Pell H	22 (8)
Barkhuizen T	32 (6)	Evans W	21 (4)	Peniket R	4 (3)
Bartlett A	18	Facey D	32 (8)	Purkiss B	15
Baxendale J	- (1)	Featherstone N	36 (2)	Purdie R	34
Chambers J	7	Fleetwood S	4 (1)	Stam S	21 (3)
Clist S	27 (1)	Green R	26 (2)	Taylor L	6 (2)
Clucas S	3 (14)	Heath J	15 (2)	Todd A	4
Colbeck J	19 (9)	Hoult R	2	Townsend M	36 (3)
Connor D	1	Leslie S	10	Williams D	3 (2)
Cornell D	25	Lunt K	24 (1)	Winnall S	5 (3)

League goals (50): Barkhuizen 11, Arquin 8, Facey 6, Evans 5, Purdie 4, Elder 3, Pell 3, Leslie 2, Taylor 2, Winnall 2, Anthony 1, Colbeck 1, Opponents 2
FA Cup goals: None. **Carling Cup goals** (1): Arquin 1. **Johnstone's Paint Trophy goals** (1): Barkhuizen 1
Average home league attendance: 2,553. **Player of Year**: Rob Purdie

MACCLESFIELD TOWN

Fifteen years of league football at Moss Rose came to an end after the second-half of the season failed to bring a single victory. Low crowds, a lack of resources and having to sell players finally caught up with a club who had done well to beat the odds for so long. Brian Horton saw off the threat of relegation during his first spell as manager. This time he had only nine games to turn the tide when brought in to replace Gary Simpson, sacked in the wake of a defeat by fellow-strugglers Dagenham and Redbridge. It was no time at all, considering the way Macclesfield had gone into freefall after reaching the midway-point 12 points clear of trouble. Sixteen matches were lost, seven drawn. They fell into the bottom two when losing at Gillingham and the drop was confirmed, along with bottom place, by a 2-0 home defeat by Burton in the penultimate match. Afterwards, the club issued a dignified statement saying that had been 'proud to represent the community in the Football League' and would make every effort to regain a place.

Aley Z.............1	Fairhurst W 4 (14)	Morgan P 2 (1)
Bakare M............ - (9)	Fisher T .... - (1)	Mukendi V 4 (12)
Bateson J............17 (4)	Futcher B 10	O'Donnell R 11
Boden S 6 (1)	Grant J .... - (4)	Roberts A..................1 (1)
Brisley S.............29	Gray D 2	Sinclair E 4 (1)
Brown N.............37	Hamshaw M 30 (8)	Smith M 6 (2)
Chalmers L 17 (6)	Hewitt E 17 (4)	Thomas M...........2 (4)
Connolly M.............7	Kay S 10 (5)	Tomlinson B 15 (10)
Daniel C 30 (6)	Marshall M 13 (1)	Tramarco C...........35
Diagne T 40 (1)	Mattis D 1	Veiga J M...........35
Donnelly G.............28	Mendy A 23 (5)	Wedgbury S.............37 (2)
Draper R 27 (1)	Mills B 5 (7)	

League goals (39): Donnelly 6, Tomlinson 6, Draper 4, Brisley 3, Chalmers 3, Diagne 3, Daniel 2, Hamshaw 2, Mendy 2, Marshall 1, Mattis 1, Mukendi 1, Sinclair 1, Smith 1, Wedgbury 1, Opponents 2
FA Cup goals (6): Tremarco 2, Daniel 1, Diagne 1, Donnelly 1, Hamshaw 1: **Carling Cup goals (3):** Sinclair 3. **Johnstone's Paint Trophy goals:** None
Average home league attendance: 2,227. **Player of Year:** Jose Veiga

MORECAMBE

Jim Bentley, in his first season as manager, put Morecambe back on a sounder footing after they slipped to fifth from bottom in 2011. His side were up five places and with a better finish would have gone higher. The last six fixtures yielded only two points, with patchy home form continuing to prove a problem. Overall, they won only six times and suffered 11 defeats at Globe Arena after some early results suggested it might prove to be a stronghold. Notably, there was the 6-0 drubbing of fancied Crawley in which Danny Carlton scored a hat-trick and Kevin Ellison netted one of his 15 league goals. That put them on top of the table, a position held for three weeks. Morecambe remained in the leading group until hitting a bad patch approaching the midway point which stretched to a single victory in 11 games. After that, they defeated promotion-contenders Southend, Cheltenham and Oxford, without showing the consistency required to get back among them.

Alessandra L 24 (18)	Fleming A 11 (6)	Mwasilie J.................... - (6)
Burrow J 14 (5)	Haining W................36 (4)	Parkinson D .... - (3)
Carlton D 34 (10)	Hunter G................30 (7)	Parrish A.................29 (9)
Charnock K .... - (4)	Jevons P 14 (13)	Price J.....................12 (6)
Cowperthwaite N 1 (2)	Kettings C........................2	Redshaw J 7 (4)
Curran C 6 (1)	McCready C.......................46	Reid I................26 (10
Drummond S............36 (2)	McDonald G 39 (3)	Roche B 44
Ellison K.................26 (8)	McGee J ..... - (1)	Wilson L.....................30
Fenton N........................35	McGinty S........................4	

League goals (63): Ellison 15, Carlton 9, Drummond 5, Wilson 5, Alessandra 4, Burrow 4, Jevons 4, Fenton 3, McDonald 3, Fleming 2, Price 2, Redshaw 2, Reid 2, Curran 1, Hunter 1, Opponents 1
FA Cup goals (1): Wilson 1. **Carling Cup goals (2):** Carlton 1, Ellison 1. **Johnstone Paint Trophy goals (2):** Ellison 1, Jevons 1
Average home league attendance: 2,144. **Player of Year:** Chris McCready

NORTHAMPTON TOWN

Aidy Boothroyd turned around a season that was threatening to bring Conference football to Sixfields. Results had gone from bad to worse with the departure, after eight months as manager, of Gary Johnson in the wake of an FA Cup loss to Luton. It was followed by a 7-2 home drubbing by Shrewsbury and a 4-1 reversal at Plymouth before Boothroyd, formerly in charge of Watford,

Colchester and Coventry, came in to address a run of eight defeats in nine matches. There was no instant cure, with his team hitting rock bottom at the midway point of the season. But gradually results began to improve, with the much-travelled Adebayo Akinfenwa playing an important role. He scored seven goals in seven matches, of which Northampton won five to move clear of trouble. Akinfenwa, in his second spell with the club, took his tally to 18, all in the league, although overall there was a disappointing end to the campaign, with six games failing to deliver a win.

Adams B. 21 (1)	Hall M 1	Savage B 3 (5)
Akinfenwa A............. 33 (6)	Harding B 19	Silva T 12 (3)
Arthur C..................... 5 (2)	Higgs S.........................3	Thornton K.................. - (2)
Asante A. 3 (1)	Holt A 5 (4)	Tozer B 42 (3)
Baldock G. 4 (1)	Jackson M.................. 5 (1)	Turnbull P.................. 9 (5)
Berahino S...................14	Jacobs M 45 (1)	Walker S.....................21
Carlisle C....................18	Johnson J 43 (2)	Weale C............................3
Charles A.................... 5 (4)	Kaziboni G................. - (3)	Webster B 8 (5)
Corker A..................... 9 (7)	Kitson N............................8	Wedderburn N..................1
Crowe J.......................11	Langmead K 39 (2)	Westwood A 14 (3)
Davies A 15	McKoy N................... 5 (4)	Williams B 8 (10)
Duke M.........................9	Niven D.........................4	Wilson L 2 (1)
Gilligan R .... - (2)	Ofori-Twumasi N......... 4 (1)	Young L 20 (10)
Guttridge L 19	Robinson J............. 15 (17)	
Hall F 1 (1)	Salihu L........................ - (1)	

League goals (56): Akinfenwa 18, Berahino 6, Jacobs 6, Davies 4, Langmead 4, Guttridge 3, Tozer 3, Williams 3, Johnson 2, Asante 1, Carlisle 1, Jackson 1, Silva 1, Westwood 1, Wilson 1, Opponents 1
FA Cup goals: None. **Carling Cup goals** (2): Tozer 1, Turnbull 1. **Johnstone's Paint Trophy goals** (1): Jacobs 1
Average home league attendance: 4,867. **Player of Year**: Michael Jacobs

OXFORD UNITED

Chris Wilder admitted his side had only themselves blame for missing out on the play-offs. The manager pointed to too many draws – 17 – and too many late goals conceded as significant failings. They looked a good bet holding a four-point advantage in sixth place after a 2-0 victory at Accrington with six weeks of the season remaining. But the final seven matches, four of them at home, yielded just three points from three draws. One of them came against ten-man Torquay, who levelled at 2-2 in the last minute. There was still a slim chance of making it going into the final fixture at Port Vale. But Oxford lost 3-0 and finished four points adrift of Crewe, the team who came through with a strong finish. It was particularly disappointing in view of the way they had beaten champions Swindon home and away and taken four points off runners-up Shrewsbury. James Constable scored both goals in the away success against local rivals Swindon, their first in 38 years. At home, they overcame the dismissal of the leading scorer after ten minutes to complete the double.

Batt D. 34 (6)	Hall R.................... 11 (2)	Payne J..................... 2 (4)
Brown W.........................2	Haworth A................. 2 (2)	Philliskirk D 2 (2)
Capaldi T........................1	Heslop S................ 26 (3)	Pittman J-P............... 6 (9)
Chapman A 10 (4)	Holmes L 5 (2)	Potter A 21 (4)
Clarke R.....................42	Johnson O................ 8 (9)	Rendell S............... 15 (3)
Constable J 32 (8)	Kerrouche M 1 (3)	Ripley C...........................1
Craddock T 6 (3)	Kinninburgh S........... - (1)	Smalley D............... 7 (15)
Davis L 41 (3)	Leven P 36 (3)	Tonkin A 6 (8)
Duberry M....................36	Martinez D....................1	Whing A................. 36 (5)
Franks J..................... - (1)	McLaren P 16 (2)	Wilson M 3 (3)
Guy L 2	Montano C 6 (3)	Worley H.................. 6 (4)
Hall A.................. 24 (10)	Morgan D...................10	Wright J.....................43

League goals (59): Constable 11, Hall A 7, Leven 6, Hall R 5, Duberry 3, Heslop 3, Johnson 3, Pittman 3, Rendell 3, Davis 2, Holmes 2, Montano 2, Potter 2, Batt 1, Chapman 1, Craddock 1, Guy 1, McLaren 1, Morgan 1, Smalley 1
FA Cup goals: None. **Carling Cup goals** (1): Clist S 1. **Johnstone's Paint Trophy goals** (2): Hall R 1, Smalley 1
Average home league attendance: 7,451. **Player of Year**: Andy Whing

PLYMOUTH ARGYLE

For much of the season, Argyle were staring at a third successive relegation and the prospect of Conference football. Their first nine games yielded only one point and brought the sacking of manager Peter Reid, who had battled against ever-mounting odds at this troubled club. Five months later, they were still in the bottom two. Discipline was also a major problem, with seven red cards in the league and three more in FA Cup ties. But eventually the tide turned under the guidance of former captain Carl Fletcher, who replaced Reid as caretaker and was given the job on a permanent basis when the club came out of administration following a takeover by local businessman James Brent. A 4-0 victory at Accrington pointed the way clear, confidence grew and narrow wins over AFC Wimbledon, Shrewsbury and Bradford followed. When Aldershot were beaten 1-0 over Easter, Fletcher's side had virtually ensured survival, having gathered enough points to offset a run of four games without a win to finish with.

Atkinson W 20 (2)	Gibson B.................. 12 (1)	Sims J 3
Berry D................... 33 (2)	Griffiths J............... 4 (5)	Soukouna L 15 (5)
Bhasera O................ 24 (3)	Hemmings A 18 (5)	Sutherland C 5 (4)
Bignot P 14	Hitchcock T 3 (5)	Tsoumou J 4 (7)
Blanchard M 28	Hourihane C............. 32 (6)	Vassell I .... - (6)
Chadwick N........... 19 (3)	King S.........................6	Walton S 36 (5)
Chenoweth O................1	Larrieu R 8 (2)	Williams R 26
Cole J 37	Lecointe M............. 8 (11)	Wotton P.......................19
Daley L 14 (4)	Lennox J 2 (6)	Young L 21 (7)
Feeney W............... 25 (3)	MacDonald A........... 15 (3)	Zubar S 4
Fletcher C............ 8 (1)	Nelson C................ 16 (1)	
Fletcher S................. 2 (4)	Purse D 24	

League goals (47): Walton 8, Chadwick 5, Atkinson 4, MacDonald 4, Blanchard 2, Feeney 2, Hemmings 2, Hourihane 2, Lecointe 2, Purse 2, Tsoumou 2, Williams 2, Young 2, Bhasera 1, Daley 1, Fletcher C 1, Soukouna 1, Sutherland 1, Wotton 1, Opponents 2
FA Cup goals (3): Bhasera 1, Feeney 1, Fletcher C 1. **Carling Cup goals**: None. **Johnstone's Paint Trophy goals** (1): Daley 1
Average home league attendance: 6,915. **Player of Year**: Maxime Blanchard

PORT VALE

Vale worked hard to restore some impetus to their season after four successive defeats around the turn of the year. The reward was a haul of 18 points from eight matches and a climb to within two points of a play-off place. But all their efforts counted for nothing when the club went into administration for the second time in eight years and had the mandatory ten points deducted. That meant a fall into the bottom half of the table and left little to play for apart from pride. Not surprisingly, the level of performance dipped, with manager Micky Adams struggling to lift himself and his players. There were five defeats in the next six matches before a measure of order was restored. A place in the top half was regained and although beaten 5-0 by champions Swindon, Vale finished on a positive note, defeating Oxford 3-0 and Marc Richards taking his tally for the season to 17, all in the league.

Collins L 15 (1)	Dodds L 21 (14)	Haldane L .... - (3)
Chilvers L 12	Green M 4	James K .... - (5)
Davis J 7 (1)	Griffith A.....................43	Kozluk R 4 (2)

Little A 2 (5)	McDonald C 23 (7)	Roberts G 9 (2)
Lloyd R....................... - (2)	Morsy S 11 (15)	Roe P .... - (2)
Loft D...................... 42 (2)	Myrie-Williams J................6	Shuker C................... 12 (4)
Madjo G..................... 5 (1)	Owen G................... 21 (3)	Taylor R 28 (3)
Marshall P 10 (5)	Pope T..................... 34 (7)	Tomlinson S 38
Martin C 8	Richards M 31 (5)	Williamson B.......... 12 (23)
McCombe J.....................40	Rigg S 33 (9)	Yates A 35 (3)

League goals (68): Richards 17, Rigg 10, Dodds 8, Pope 5, Loft 4, Madjo 4, McCombe 4, Roberts 4, Williamson 3, Taylor 2, Yates 2, Griffith 1, Morsy 1, Myrie-Williams 1, Shuker 1, Opponents 1
FA Cup goals: None. **Carling Cup goals** (2): Loft 1, Roberts 1. **Johnstone's Paint Trophy goals** (1): Taylor 1
Average home league attendance: 4,819. **Player of Year**: Doug Loft

ROTHERHAM UNITED

Steve Evans took over as manager with four matches remaining and immediately saw his new side's slim chance of bringing League One football to their new stadium effectively ended. They were beaten 3-1 by eventual runners-up Shrewsbury and remained too far away from the play-offs. Evans gained his first win, 3-2 over Morecambe in which Lewis Grabban scored his 17th and 18th league goals of the season. Then came draws against Aldershot and Northampton and a finishing position five points adrift. Evans left Crawley, who clinched automatic promotion on the final day of the season, to succeed Andy Scott, sacked three weeks earlier after 11 months in the job. Rotherham were up to second after a solid start which netted 16 points from seven matches. Nine games without a win followed and this inconsistency continued. Grabban also scored three times in the FA Cup and was second to Barnet's Izale McLeod in the division's overall scoring list.

Bradley M 18 (3)	Harrad S 6 (2)	Raynes M.................. 31 (2)
Branston G.......................2	Harrison D 35 (6)	Revell A...........................40
Brown T 4 (2)	Holroyd C 5 (10)	Schofield D 35 (2)
Cadogan K 7 (6)	Hoskins S 2 (6)	Taylor J 38 (1)
Cresswell R 13 (3)	Le Fondre A 4	Taylor R..................20
Denton A .... - (1)	Logan C.....................19	Tonge D 28 (4)
Evans G 29 (3)	Marshall M 8 (7)	Warne P................. - (3)
Foster L................ 1 (4)	Mullins J............. 34 (1)	Warrington A.................7
Grabban L 39 (4)	Naylor R.....................5	Williams B 4 (7)
Griffiths S.....................8	Newey T 15 (5)	Wood S 24 (2)
Harley J 11 (1)	Pringle B 14 (7)	

League goals (67): Grabban 18, Revell 10, Evans 7, Cresswell 4, Le Fondre 4, Pringle 4, Harrad 3, Harrison 2, Hoskins 2, Mullins 2, Taylor J 2, Williams 2, Bradley 1, Brown 1, Cadogan 1, Holroyd 1, Marshall 1, Schofield 1, Wood 1
FA Cup goals (3): Grabban 3. **Carling Cup goals** (1): Opponents 1. **Johnstone's Paint Trophy goals** (1): Revell 1
Average home league attendance: 3,498. **Player of Year**: John Mullins

SHREWSBURY TOWN

Graham Turner bridged a gap of three decades to lead Shrewsbury to promotion. A record crowd for the Greenhous Meadow Stadium of 9,441 saw leading marksman James Collins score the only goal against Dagenham and Redbridge in the final home game to confirm the runners-up spot behind Swindon. It came 33 years after Turner took the club to the old Third Division title as a young player-manager. He returned there in June 2010 after a 15-year association with Hereford and went close in his first season back, losing to Torquay in the semi-finals of the play-offs. The teams were again rivals and this time Shrewsbury gained the upper hand. Making the most of a run-in against sides from the middle and lower reaches of the division, they knocked

Torquay off second place and held off a challenge from Crawley during a run of ten unbeaten matches which netted 26 points. Collins finished with 16 goals, including one in the 7-2 away win over Northampton.

Ainsworth L............... 19 (2)	Jacobson J............... 37 (2)	Sharps I.........................43
Bradshaw T............... 5 (3)	McAllister D 15	Smith B.........................11
Cansdell-Sherriff S.... 35 (2)	McAllister S 14 (3)	Taylor J.................. 15 (18)
Collins J 32 (10)	McLaughlin C...................4	Wallace J 1 (2)
Goldson C 2 (2)	Morgan M 26 (16)	Wildig A 10 (2)
Gornell T............... 28 (13)	Neal C 35	Wright M.................. 45 (1)
Grandison J............... 36 (2)	Regan C 12 (1)	Wroe N 32 (6)
Hazell R 5 (2)	Richards M 35 (7)	
Hurst J 7	Sawyers R 2 (5)	

League goals (66): Collins 14, Wright 10, Gornell 9, Morgan 8, Richards 5, Cansdell-Sherriff 4, Wroe 4, Ainsworth 2, Grandison 2, Wildig 2, Bradshaw 1, Jacobson 1, McAllister S 1, Sharps 1, Opponents 2
FA Cup goals (3): Gornell 1, Sharps 1, Wroe 1. **Carling Cup goals (7):** Morgan 3, Collins 2, Wright 1, Wroe 1. **Johnstone's Paint Trophy goals (1):** Opponents 1
Average home league attendance: 5,769. **Player of Year:** Matt Richards

SOUTHEND UNITED

Southend equalled a club record of 17 league and cup matches without defeat in the first half of the season and looked a solid bet for automatic promotion. They spent nearly six months in the top three, with a good few weeks in pole position before Swindon assumed the leadership. Then, three defeats in four games leading up to Easter proved costly and not even a storming finish could retrieve the situation. Despite collecting 13 points from the last five matches, with Bilel Mohsni scoring a hat-trick against Barnet and not a goal conceded in any of them, they were still a point adrift of third-place Crawley. That run of form augured well for the play-offs against Crewe, but Paul Sturrock's side were below par for the first hour of both legs. They lost the first 1-0 and were held 2-2 in the home game when twice coming from behind through Chris Barker in his 100th game for club and substitute Neil Harris.

Baldwin P 2	Dickinson L............... 28 (2)	Kalala J-P 23 (1)
Barker C 42 (1)	Eastwood F 6 (1)	Leonard R 13 (4)
Belford C 13	Ferdinand K 28 (8)	Martin D 11 (6)
Bentley D.................... - (1)	Flood A........................ - (1)	Morris G 24
Benyon E 8 (8)	Gilbert P 29 (2)	N'Diaye A .... - (1)
Bilel M 23 (8)	Grant A..................... 25 (8)	Phillips M 38 (1)
Clohessy S 45	Hall R....................... 35 (8)	Prosser L 18 (3)
Coughlan G 2 (2)	Harris N 21 (12)	Sampson J 5 (4)
Crawford H.................. - (3)	Hills L 5 (2)	Sawyer L 5 (5)
Dailly C............................3	James-Lewis M .... - (1)	Sturrock B 5 (4)
Daniels L........................9	Johnson J 1 (4)	Timlin M 39

Play-offs – appearances: Barker 2, Belford 2, Bilel 2, Clohessy 2, Gilbert 2, Grant 2, Hall 2, Timlin 2, Eastwood 1 (1), Harris 1 (1), Prosser 1 (1), Benyon 1, Ferdinand 1, Phillips 1, Hills – (1), Leonard – (1)
League goals (77): Bilel 13, Dickinson 10, Hall 10, Harris 8, Ferdinand 7, Phillips 7, Timlin 4, Gilbert 3, Martin 3, Benyon 2, Eastwood 2, Grant 1, Kalala 1, Leonard 1, Prosser 1, Opponents 4. **Play-offs – goals (2):** Barker 1, Harris 1
FA Cup goals (2): Dickinson 1, Hall 1. **Carling Cup goals (1):** Phillips 1. **Johnstone's Paint Trophy goals (6):** Hall 3 Dickinson 1, Harris 1, Sturrock 1
Average home league attendance: 5,969. **Player of Year:** Mark Phillips

SWINDON TOWN

Paolo Di Canio left a big impression on English football as a player and his first taste of management here was also a memorable one. His appointment by a club just relegated was intriguing. Many thought it a gamble. When his new side lost four of the opening five matches, they seemed to have a case. But when the Italian finally assembled the squad he wanted, with a sprinkling of Continental players, Swindon flourished. He made another influential signing in the January transfer window – Charlton's Paul Benson, whose goals helped them go top in late February and reach a club record of ten successive league wins. They effectively secured promotion by beating Plymouth on an emotional afternoon at the County Ground – the day after the manager's mother died – and became champions with a 5-0 victory over Port Vale. Further honours came with the League Two Manager of the Year award and the Player of the Year for midfielder Matt Ritchie. The one disappointment was defeat by Chesterfield in the Johnstone's Paint Trophy Final.

Abdullah A 1 (5)	Esajas E 2 (4)	Montano C 3 (1)
Benson P 20 (2)	Ferry S 36 (8)	Murray R 9 (11)
Boateng D 2	Flint A 28 (4)	Ridehalgh L 9 (2)
Bodin B 9 (2)	Foderingham W 33	Risser O 23 (9)
Bostock J 3	Gabilondo L 4 (6)	Ritchie M 40
Caddis P 39	Holmes L 7 (3)	Rooney L 13 (7)
Cibbochi A 11 (7)	Jervis J 10 (2)	Smith C .... - (1)
Clarke L 2	Kennedy C 18	Smith J 28 (10)
Comazzi A 4	Kerrouche M 9 (4)	Smith P 8
Connell A 13 (19)	Lanzano M 5 (1)	Storey M .... - (4)
Cox L 2 (5)	Magera L 7 (5)	Tehoue J 1 (2)
De Vita R 30 (8)	McCormack A 38 (2)	Thompson N 2 (3)
Devera J 28	McEveley J 8	Timlin M 1

League goals (75): Benson 11, Connell 11, Ritchie 10, Kerrouche 6, Caddis 4, De Vita 4, Bodin 3, Jervis 3, Murray 3, Risser 3, Smith J 3, Devera 2, Flint 2, McCormack 2, Rooney 2, Ferry 1, Holmes 1, Kennedy 1, Magera 1, Montano 1, Opponents 1
FA Cup goals (7): Benson 1, Connell 1, De Vita 1, Ferry 1, Flint 1, Kerrouche 1, Richie 1. **Carling Cup goals** (2): De Vita 1, Kerrouche 1. **Johnstone's Paint Trophy goals** (7): Jervis 2, Caddis 1, Connell 1, Flint 1, Murray 1, Risser 1
Average home league attendance: 8,410. **Player of Year**: Alan McCormack

TORQUAY UNITED

There were mixed feelings at Plainmoor following defeat by Cheltenham in the semi-finals of the play-offs. Martin Ling did not expect to deliver promotion during a squad-building first season as manager, so the disappointment was offset by the satisfaction of getting that far. Even so, Torquay knew that a golden chance of going up automatically had not been taken. They built on a run of seven successive victories, launched in the New Year and all by a single-goal margin, to eventually establish a five-point cushion in the runners-up spot. But late goals contributed to their failure to win any of the final five games. Two conceded in the last 11 minutes brought defeat against AFC Wimbledon, while Crewe scored in stoppage-time for a point. Torquay were defeated in the final fixture by struggling Hereford to miss out by three points after being overtaken first by Shrewsbury, then by Crawley. Ling's side lost the first leg 2-0 at Cheltenham and the return 2-1 after hitting the woodwork three times.

Atieno T 17 (26)	Kee B 1 (3)	McPhee C 6 (20)
Bodin B 15 (2)	Lathrope D 35 (5)	Morris I 33 (4)
Ellis M 34 (1)	Leadbitter D .... - (2)	Nicholson K 46
Halpin S .... - (1)	MacDonald A 1 (1)	Oastler J 45
Howe R 36 (3)	Macklin L 1 (3)	O'Kane E 45
Jarvis R 3 (11)	Mansell L 45	Olejnik R 46

Play-offs – appearances: Ellis 2, Jarvis 2, Lathrope 2, Mansell 2, Morris 2, Nicholson 2, Oastler 2, O'Kane 2, Olejnik 2, Saah 2, Howe 1, Stevens 1, Atieno – (2), Rowe-Turner – (1), MacDonald – (1)

League goals (63): Howe 12, Mansell 12. Stevens 8, Atieno 6, Bodin 5, O'Kane 5, Nicholson 4, Ellis 3, Jarvis 2, McPhee 2, Morris 2, Robertson 1, Saah 1. **Play-offs – goals** (1): Atieno 1 **FA Cup goals** (5): Howe 2, Stevens 2, Nicholson 1. **Carling Cup goals** (1): Mansell 1. **Johnstone's Paint Trophy goals** (1): Macklin 1.

Average home league attendance: 2,869. **Player of Year:** Lee Mansell

QUOTE/UNQUOTE

'The conduct of Mr Suarez has damaged the image of English football around the world. Mr Suarez's evidence was unreliable in relation to matters of critical importance' – **FA Commission** verdict after imposing an eight-match ban and £40,000 fine on Liverpool's Luis Suarez for racially abusing Manchester United's Patrice Evra.

'He's a disgrace to a club with their history, I'd get rid of him. It could have caused a riot' – **Sir Alex Ferguson**, Manchester United manager, after Suarez refused to shake hands with Evra before the game at Old Trafford.

'I've not only let him (the manager) down, but also the club and what it stands for. I made a mistake and I'm sorry' –**Suarez** apologises the following day.

'I did not conduct myself in a way befitting of a Liverpool manager and I'd like to apologise for that' – **Kenny Dalglish** also says sorry for the boorish way he handled a *Sky TV* interview.

'An hour later, when I went into his office to carry on the conversations, he came up with the desire to come out of this post' – **David Bernstein**, FA chairman, on Fabio Capello's resignation as England manager following the decision to strip John Terry of the captaincy.

'I'm a fantastic manager, not a hard-headed businessman. I've got no business acumen whatsoever' – **Harry Redknapp** giving evidence and denying tax evasion charges during his crown court trial.

'This was the most difficult week I've ever had, but it's turned out good' – **Redknapp**, whose acquittal was followed by Tottenham's 5-0 win over Newcastle.

'Absolutely ridiculous' – **Sir Alex Ferguson**, Manchester United manager, on the FA decision to switch kick-off for the FA Cup Final from 3pm to 5.15pm

'Looking for an eighth manager in nine years is a serious embarrassment to the owner, the club, the fans and the league' – **Richard Bevan**, chief executive of the League Managers' Association after the sacking of Chelsea manager Andre Villas-Boas by Roman Abramovich.

'If any of our fans are worried about me and Chelsea, they need not panic. I am trying to build my career, not wreck it' – **Brendan Rodgers**, Swansea manager, making it clear he had no interest in the Stamford Bridge job.

LEAGUE CLUB MANAGERS

Figure in brackets = number of managerial changes at club since the War

BARCLAYS PREMIER LEAGUE

Arsenal (11)	Arsene Wenger	October 1996
Aston Villa (22)	Paul Lambert	June 2012
Chelsea (25)	Roberto Di Matteo	June 2012
Everton (16)	David Moyes	March 2002
Fulham (28)	Martin Jol	June 2011
Liverpool (13)	Brendan Rodgers	May 2012
Manchester City (28)	Roberto Mancini	December 2009
Manchester Utd (8)	Sir Alex Ferguson	November 1986
Newcastle (25)	Alan Pardew	December 2010
Norwich (26)	Chris Hughton	June 2012
QPR (30)	Mark Hughes	January 2012
Reading (18)	Brian McDermott	January 2010
Southampton (23)	Nigel Adkins	September 2010
Stoke (22)	Tony Pulis†	June 2006
Sunderland (24)	Martin O'Neill	December 2011
Swansea (31)	Michael Laudrup	June 2012
Tottenham (21)	Andre Villas-Boas	July 2012
WBA (29)	Steve Clarke	June 2012
West Ham (13)	Sam Allardyce	June 2011
Wigan (18)	Roberto Martinez	June 2009

†Second spell at club. Number of changes since elected to Football League: Wigan 1978

NPOWER CHAMPIONSHIP

Barnsley (21)	Keith Hill	June 2011
Birmingham (24)	Lee Clark	June 2012
Blackburn (25)	Steve Kean	December 2010
Blackpool (25)	Ian Holloway	May 2009
Bolton (20)	Owen Coyle	January 2010
Brighton (30)	Gus Poyet	November 2009
Bristol City (23)	Derek McInnes	October 2011
Burnley (23)	Eddie Howe	January 2011
Cardiff (27)	Malky Mackay	June 2011
Charlton (17)	Chris Powell	January 2011
Crystal Palace (36)	Dougie Freedman	January 2011
Derby (21)	Nigel Clough	December 2008
Huddersfield (25)	Simon Grayson	February 2012
Hull (26)	Steve Bruce	June 2012
Ipswich (12)	Paul Jewell	January 2011
Leeds (23)	Neil Warnock	February 2012
Leicester (27)	Nigel Pearson†	November 2011
Middlesbrough (19)	Tony Mowbray	October 2010
Millwall (28)	Kenny Jackett	November 2007
Nottm Forest (18)	Sean O'Driscoll	July 2012
Peterborough (27)	Darren Ferguson†	January 2011
Sheffield Wed (27)	Dave Jones	March 2012
Watford (28)	Gianfranco Zola	July 2012
Wolves (21)	Stale Solbakken	May 2012

† Second spell at club. Number of changes since elected to Football League: Peterborough 1960

NPOWER LEAGUE ONE

Bournemouth (23)	Paul Groves	May 2012
Brentford (30)	Uwe Rosler	June 2011
Bury (23)	Richie Barker	March 2011
Carlisle (3)	Greg Abbott	November 2008
Colchester (24)	John Ward	May 2010

Coventry (30)	Andy Thorn	March 2011
Crawley (1)		
Crewe (21)	Steve Davis	November 2011
Doncaster (2)	Dean Saunders	September 2011
Hartlepool (32)	Neale Cooper†	December 2011
Leyton Orient (22)	Russell Slade	April 2010
MK Dons (15)	Karl Robinson	April 2010
Notts Co (36)	Keith Curle	February 2012
Oldham (25)	Paul Dickov	June 2010
Portsmouth (29)	Michael Appleton	November 2011
Preston (27)	Graham Westley	January 2012
Scunthorpe (24)	Alan Knill	March 2011
Sheffield Utd (34)	Danny Wilson	May 2011
Shrewsbury (3)	Graham Turner†	June 2010
Stevenage (1)	Gary Smith	January 2012
Swindon (26)	Paolo Di Canio	May 2011
Tranmere (20)	Ronnie Moore†	March 2012
Walsall (33)	Dean Smith	January 2011
Yeovil (4)	Gary Johnson†	January 2012

†Second spell at club. Number of changes since elected to Football League: Yeovil 2003, Stevenage 2010. Since returning: Shrewsbury 2004, Carlisle 2005

NPOWER LEAGUE TWO

AFC Wimbledon (-)	Terry Brown	May 2007
Accrington (1)	Paul Cook	February 2012
Aldershot (2)	Dean Holdsworth	January 2011
Barnet (5)	Mark Robson	June 2012
Bradford (33)	Phil Parkinson	August 2011
Bristol Rov (25)	Mark McGhee	January 2012
Burton (1)	Gary Rowett	May 2012
Cheltenham (6)	Mark Yates	December 2009
Chesterfield (18)	John Sheridan	June 2009
Dagenham (-)	John Still	April 2004
Exeter (-)	Paul Tisdale	June 2006
Fleetwood (-)	Micky Mellon	September 2008
Gillingham (22)	Martin Allen	July 2012
Morecambe (1)	Jim Bentley	May 2011
Northampton (30)	Aidy Boothroyd	November 2011
Oxford Utd (-)	Chris Wilder	December 2008
Plymouth (32)	Carl Fletcher	October 2011
Port Vale (23)	Micky Adams†	May 2011
Rochdale (31)	John Coleman	January 2012
Rotherham (24)	Steve Evans	April 2012
Southend (27)	Paul Sturrock	July 2010
Torquay (1)	Martin Ling	June 2011
Wycombe (9)	Gary Waddock	October 2009
York (-)	Gary Mills	October 2010

† Second spell at club. Number of changes since elected to Football League: Wycombe 1993, Cheltenham 1999, Dagenham 2007, Morecambe 2007, Burton 2009, AFC Wimbledon 2011, Fleetwood 2012. Since returning: Barnet 2005, Accrington 2006, Aldershot 2008, Exeter 2008, Torquay 2009, Oxford Utd 2010, York 2012

MANAGERIAL INS AND OUTS 2011–12

PREMIER LEAGUE

Aston Villa: Out – Alex McLeish (May 2012); In – Paul Lambert
Chelsea: Out – Andre Villas-Boas (March 2012); In – Roberto Di Matteo
Liverpool: Out – Kenny Dalglish (May 2012); In – Brendan Rodgers
Norwich: Out – Paul Lambert (June 2012); In – Chris Hughton
QPR: Out – Neil Warnock (January 2012); In –Mark Hughes
Sunderland: Out – Steve Bruce (November 2011); In – Martin O'Neill
Swansea: Out – Brendan Rodgers (May 2012); In – Michael Laudrup
Tottenham Out – Harry Redknapp (June 2012); In – Andre Villas-Boas
WBA: Out – Roy Hodgson (May 2012); In – Steve Clarke
Wolves: Out – Mick McCarthy (February 2012); In – Stale Solbakken

CHAMPIONSHIP

Birmingham: Out – Chris Hughton (June 2012); In – Lee Clark
Bristol City: Out – Keith Millen (October 2011); In – Derek McInnes
Doncaster: Out – Sean O'Driscoll (September 2011); In – Dean Saunders
Hull: Out – Nigel Pearson (November 2011); In – Nick Barmby – Out – (April 2012); In – Steve Bruce
Leeds: Out – Simon Grayson (February 2012); In – Neil Warnock
Leicester: Out – Sven-Goran Eriksson (October 2011); In – Nigel Pearson
Nottm Forest: Out – Steve McClaren (October 2011); In – Steve Cotterill – Out – (July 2012); In – Sean O'Driscoll
Portsmouth: Out – Steve Cotterill (October 2011); In – Michael Appleton
Watford Out – Sean Dyche (July 2012); In – Gianfranco Zola

LEAGUE ONE

Bournemouth: Out – Lee Bradbury (March 2012); In – Paul Groves
Hartlepool: Out – Mick Wadsworth (December 2011); In – Neale Cooper
Huddersfield: Out – Lee Clark (February 2012); In – Simon Grayson
Notts Co: Out – Martin Allen (February 2012); In – Keith Curle
Preston: Out – Phil Brown (December 2011); In – Graham Westley
Rochdale: Out – Steve Eyre (December 2011); In – John Coleman
Sheffield Wednesday: Out – Gary Megson (February 2012); In – Dave Jones
Stevenage: Out – Graham Westley (January 2012); In – Gary Smith
Tranmere: Out – Les Parry (March 2012); In – Ronnie Moore
Yeovil: Out – Terry Skiverton (January 2012); In – Gary Johnson

LEAGUE TWO

Accrington: Out – John Coleman (January 2012); In –Paul Cook
Barnet: Out – Lawrie Sanchez (April 2012); In – Mark Robson
Bradford: Out – Peter Jackson (August 2011); In – Phil Parkinson
Bristol Rov: Out – Paul Buckle (January 2012); In – Mark McGhee
Burton: Out – Paul Peschisolido (March 2012); In – Gary Rowett
Crawley: Out – Steve Evans (April 2012); In – Sean O'Driscoll; Out – (July 2012)
Crewe: Out – Dario Gradi (November 2011); In – Steve Davis
Gillingham: Out – Andy Hessenthaler (May 2012); In – Martin Allen
Hereford: Out – Jamie Pitman (March 2012); In – Martin Foyle
Macclesfield: Out – Gary Simpson (March 2012); In - Steve King
Northampton: Out – Gary Johnson (November 2011); In – Aidy Boothroyd
Plymouth: Out – Peter Reid (September 2011); In – Carl Fletcher
Rotherham: Out – Andy Scott (March 2012); In – Steve Evans

FA CUP 2011–12
(sponsored by Budweiser)

FIRST ROUND

AFC Wimbledon 0 Scunthorpe 0
Alfreton 0 Carlisle 4
Barrow 1 Rotherham 2
Blyth 0 Gateshead 2
Bournemouth 3 Gillingham 3
Bradford 1 Rochdale 1
Brentford 1 Basingstoke 0
Bristol Rov 3 Corby 1
Bury 0 Crawley 2
Cambridge Utd 2 Wrexham 2
Chelmsford 4 Telford 0
Chesterfield 1 Torquay 3
Crewe 1 Colchester 4
Dagenham 1 Bath 1
East Thurrock 0 Macclesfield 3
Exeter 1 Walsall 1
Fleetwood 2 Wycombe 0
Halifax 0 Charlton 4
Hartlepool 0 Stevenage 1
Hereford 0 Yeovil 3
Hinckley 2 Tamworth 2
Leyton Orient 3 Bromley 0
Luton 1 Northampton 0
Maidenhead 1 Aldershot 1
MK Dons 6 Nantwich 0
Morecambe 1 Sheffield Wed 2
Newport 0 Shrewsbury 1
Notts Co 4 Accrington 1
Oldham 3 Burton 1
Plymouth 3 Stourbridge 3
Port Vale 0 Grimsby 0
Preston 0 Southend 0
Redbridge 0 Oxford City 0
Salisbury 3 Arlesey 1
Sheffield Utd 3 Oxford Utd 0
Southport 1 Barnet 2
Sutton 1 Kettering 0
Swindon 4 Huddersfield 1
Totton 8 Bradford PA 1
Tranmere 0 Cheltenham 1

REPLAYS

Aldershot 2 Maidenhead 0
Bath 1 Dagenham 3 (aet)
Gillingham 3 Bournemouth 2
Grimsby 1 Port Vale 0
Oxford City 1 Redbridge 2 (aet)

Scunthorpe 0 AFC Wimbledon 1
Southend 1 Preston 0
Stourbridge 2 Plymouth 0
Tamworth 1 Hinckley 0
Walsall 3 Exeter 2 (aet)
Wrexham 2 Cambridge Utd 1

SECOND ROUND

Barnet 1 MK Dons 3
Bradford 3 AFC Wimbledon 1
Brentford 0 Wrexham 1
Charlton 2 Carlisle 0
Chelmsford 1 Macclesfield 1
Colchester 0 Swindon 1
Crawley 5 Redbridge 0
Dagenham 1 Walsall 1
Fleetwood 2 Yeovil 2
Gateshead 1 Tamworth 2
Leyton Orient 0 Gillingham 1
Luton 2 Cheltenham 4
Salisbury 0 Grimsby 0
Sheffield Utd 3 Torquay 2
Sheffield Wed 1 Aldershot 0
Shrewsbury 2 Rotherham 1
Southend 1 Oldham 1
Stourbridge 0 Stevenage 3
Sutton 0 Notts Co 2
Totton 1 Bristol Rov 6

REPLAYS

Grimsby 2 Salisbury 3 (aet)
Macclesfield 1 Chelmsford 0
Oldham 1 Southend 0
Walsall 0 Dagenham 0
(aet, Dagenham won 3-2 on pens)
Yeovil 0 Fleetwood 2

CHELSEA SURVIVE LIVERPOOL FIGHT BACK

THIRD ROUND	FOURTH ROUND	FIFTH ROUND	SIXTH ROUND	SEMI-FINALS	FINAL
*Chelsea....4					Chelsea....2
Portsmouth....0	Chelsea....1				
*MK Dons....1:0		*Chelsea....1:2			
QPR....1:1	*QPR....0		*Chelsea....5		
*Sheffield Utd....3					
Salisbury....1	*Sheffield Utd....0				
*Birmingham....0:1		Birmingham....1:0			
Wolves....0:0	Birmingham....4			Chelsea....5	
*WBA....4					
Cardiff....2	*WBA....1				
*Norwich....4		*Norwich....1			
Burnley....1	Norwich....2		Leicester....2		
*Nottm Forest....0:0					
Leicester....0:4	*Leicester....2	*Leicester....2			
*Swindon....2					
Wigan....1	Swindon....0				
*Reading....0					
Stevenage....1	*Stevenage....1	*Stevenage....0:1			
*Doncaster....1					
Notts Co....2	Notts Co....0		*Tottenham....B3		
*Watford....4					
Bradford....2	*Watford....0				
*Tottenham....3		Tottenham....0:3		Tottenham....1	
Cheltenham....0	Tottenham....1				
*Dagenham....0:0					
Millwall....0:5	*Millwall....1:3	*Millwall....0			
*Coventry....1					
Southampton....2	Southampton....1:2		Bolton....1		
*Macclesfield....2:0					
Bolton....2:2	*Bolton....2	Bolton....2			
*Barnsley....2					
Swansea....4	Swansea....1				

Round 1

*Everton	2
Tamworth	0
*Fulham	4
Charlton	0
*Fleetwood	1
Blackpool	5
*Sheffield Wed	1
West Ham	0
*Peterborough	0
Sunderland	2
*Middlesbrough	1
Shrewsbury	0
*Arsenal	1
Leeds	0
*Bristol Rov	3
Aston Villa	3
*Hull	3
Ipswich	1
*Crawley	1
Bristol City	0
*Derby	1
Crystal Palace	0
*Gillingham	1
Stoke	3
*Brighton	1 +A1
Wrexham	1:1
*Newcastle	2
Blackburn	0
*Manchester City	2
Manchester Utd	3
Oldham	1
*Liverpool	5

Round 2

*Everton	2
Fulham	1
*Blackpool	1:3
Sheffield Wed	1:0
*Sunderland	1+2
Middlesbrough	1:1
*Arsenal	3
Aston Villa	2
*Hull	0
Crawley	1
*Derby	0
Stoke	2
*Brighton	1
Newcastle	0
Manchester Utd	1
*Liverpool	6

Round 3

*Everton	1:2
Blackpool	0
*Sunderland	2
Arsenal	0
*Crawley	0
Stoke	1
Brighton	1
*Liverpool	2

Round 4

Everton	1
Sunderland	1:0
Stoke	1
Liverpool	2

Semi-finals

Everton	1
Liverpool	2

Final

Liverpool 1

*Drawn at home. +After extra-time. A – Brighton won 4-1 on pens. B – Restaged tie. First match abandoned, 41 minutes, after Fabrice Muamba collapsed. Both semi-finals at Wembley

ROUND BY ROUND HIGHLIGHTS

FIRST ROUND

Stourbridge reach the second round for the first time in their history, at the expense of crisis-club Plymouth. They concede an 88th minute equaliser and have to be satisfied with a 3-3 draw at Home Park, but make no mistake in the replay, winning 2-0 with second-half goals by Paul McCone and Sean Evans. Three other non-league teams spring surprises. Fleetwood put out Wycombe 2-0, despite having Richard Brodie sent off. Jamie Vardy's 12th goal in as many games and one from Andy Mangan do the trick. Adam Watkins comes off the bench to score the only goal for Luton against Northampton, while Grimsby overcome Port Vale by the same scoreline, thanks to Serge Makofo's strike in a replay. Barrow also look to be heading for a notable success until the final ten minutes when Rotherham come from behind to score twice through Lewis Grabban. George Williams,16, becomes the youngest-ever scorer for MK Dons in his side's 6-0 victory over Nantwich. Biggest winners of the round are Totton, with Stefan Brown scoring a hat-trick in their 8-1 beating of Bradford Park Avenue, who have two players sent off. A total of 14 red cards are handed out during the course of the round, including one to Hartlepool goalkeeper Scott Flinders, dismissed after eight minutes when conceding the penalty which puts Stevenage through.

SECOND ROUND

Two teams go through to the third round for the first time in replays away from home. Fleetwood earn a second chance against Yeovil by retrieving a 2-0 deficit in the final eight minutes through Kieran Charnock's header and Jamie Milligan's penalty. They make the most of it when goals by Jamie McGuire and Jamie Vardy set up a local derby against Blackpool. After a goalless draw at home, Salisbury win 3-2 at Grimsby, Stuart Anderson's extra-time penalty settling the tie after goals by Dan Fitchett and Brian Dutton keep their hopes alive. Wrexham, Fleetwood's rivals for promotion from the Conference, are also impressive on their travels, beating Brentford with the only goal of the tie from Jamie Tolley. Matt Tubbs converts two penalties in a hat-trick for Crawley, who beat Redbridge 5.0.

THIRD ROUND

Paul Scholes and Thierry Henry turn back the clock as the competition's two most successful clubs progress. Scholes, 37, comes out of retirement for Manchester United and plays the final half-hour against holders Manchester City. United threaten to fully avenge the 6-1 Premier League home defeat by their neighbours when leading 3-0 after two goals by Wayne Rooney and the dismissal of City's Vincent Kompany. But they are hanging on at the end after the home side pull two back. Henry, 34, back at Arsenal on loan from New York Red Bulls, delivers a trademark finish ten minutes after leaving the bench for the only goal of the tie against Leeds. Paolo Di Canio chalks up his first FA Cup upset as a manager when Swindon come from behind with goals from Alan Connell and substitute Paul Benson to master a Wigan side showing nine changes from their previous Premier League game. Newcastle manager Alan Pardew hails Hatem Ben Arfa's solo effort in the 2-1 success against Blackburn as 'technically the greatest I have ever seen.' Graham Westley, of Stevenage, is another proud manager after Darius Charles scores the only goal at Reading. It proves to be the last game in charge for Westley, who takes over at Preston a week later. MK Dons are denied victory over Queens Park Rangers by Heidar Helguson's 89th minute equaliser, but have the consolation of a record crowd of 19,506. Matt Phillips is on the mark three times in the second half as Blackpool break Fleetwood's resistance for a 5-1 victory. There are four other hat-tricks: Clint Dempsey in Fulham's 4-0 win over Charlton; Simon Cox for West Bromwich Albion, who go through 4-2 against Cardiff; Jermaine Beckford as Leicester see off Nottingham Forest 4-0 in a replay; Darius Henderson as Millwall beat Dagenham and Redbridge 5-0 at the second attempt.

FOURTH ROUND

Dirk Kuyt's 88th minute goal gives Liverpool a 2-1 win over Manchester United in the 'heavyweight' tie of the round. The other high-profile game, bringing together John Terry and Anton Ferdinand for the first time since their conflict earlier in the season, is settled by Juan Mata's controversial penalty for Chelsea at Queens Park Rangers. Two penalties by Robin van Persie and a Theo Walcott goal, all in the space of eight minutes, enable Arsenal to overhaul a 2-0 half-time deficit for victory against Aston Villa. Fraizer Campbell, out of 17 months with knee injuries, makes a scoring comeback for Sunderland, who draw 1-1 with Middlesbrough and win the replay 2-1 at the Riverside. Newcastle go down to a single goal set up by a lifelong fan – Brighton's Will Buckley, whose shot is deflected into his own net by Mike Williamson. Matt Tubbs scores the only one at Hull to put Crawley into round five for the second successive season, then two days later joins Bournemouth in an £800,000 deal. Another own goal, from Notts County's Damion Stewart, is enough to put Stevenage into the last 16 for the first time and give Gary Smith a successful start as manager.

FIFTH ROUND

Leicester keep the Football League flag flying with a 2-1 success at Norwich, earned by goals from Sean St Ledger, his first for the club, and David Nugent, a cup winner with Portsmouth in 2008. Brighton give Liverpool a big helping hand towards a 6-1 victory with three own goals, two from Liam Bridcutt and one by Lewis Dunk. But Stevenage do themselves proud by holding Tottenham 0-0, then taking the lead in the replay at White Hart Lane through Joel Byrom's penalty, before Jermain Defoe's brace paves the way for a 3-1 victory by the Premier League side. Birmingham lead at Stamford Bridge through David Murphy, but Daniel Sturridge levels and Chelsea are 2-0 winners in the replay. Crawley go down by the same scoreline, against Stoke. So do Millwall after Japanese winger Ryo Miyaichi marks his first start on loan from Arsenal with Bolton's opener. Arsenal's week goes from bad to worse, with a 4-0 Champions League beating by AC Milan followed by defeat at the Stadium of Light, where Kieran Richardson and an own goal by Alex Oxlade-Chamberlain give Sunderland the verdict. Everton are quickest out of the blocks – Dutchman Royston Drenthe scoring after 49 seconds against Blackpool, then setting up a second after six minutes for Argentinian Denis Stracqualursi.

SIXTH ROUND

White Hart Lane is silent after Bolton's Fabrice Muamba suffers a cardiac arrest and collapses during the tie against Tottenham. Referee Howard Webb abandons it after 41 minutes with the score 1-1. Nine days later, with Muamba out of danger, Tottenham win the restaged game 3-1, thanks to goals from Ryan Nelsen, his first for the club, Gareth Bale and Louis Saha. Fernando Torres ends a five-month drought by scoring twice in Chelsea's 5-2 victory over Leicester. Carling Cup winners Liverpool book a return to Wembley for the semi-finals by beating Stoke 2-1 with goals from Luis Suarez and Stewart Downing. Sunderland's Simon Mignolet evokes memories of Jim Montgomery's double save in the 1973 final against Leeds by denying Everton's John Heitinga and Nikica Jelavic. The match ends 1-1, but Mignolet is beaten by Jelavic and David Vaughan's own goal as Everton prevail 2-0 in the replay at the Stadium of Light.

SEMI-FINALS

The thorny issue of goal-line technology overshadows Chelsea's 5-1 win against Tottenham. Referee Martin Atkinson rules that Juan Mata has put them 2-0 ahead, but replays show the ball does not cross the line. Tottenham pull one back through Gareth Bale, but Ramires, Frank Lampard and substitute Florent Malouda score in the final 13 minutes of normal time, adding to Didier Drogba's opener. Liverpool beat Everton 2-1 in an error-strewn tie. They trail when Jamie Carragher's attempted clearance strikes Tim Cahill and falls kindly for Nikica Jelavic. Luis Suarez punishes Sylvain Distin's underhit back pass to equalise. Then, after 87 minutes, Andy Carroll makes amend for one headed miss by glancing in Craig Bellamy's free-kick.

FINAL

Somehow, it didn't seem like FA Cup Final day. For one thing, the kick-off had been moved from 3pm to 5.15pm to accommodate television, upsetting the traditionalists and the travel plans of Liverpool supporters. For another, an occasion which normally commanded all the attended had to share the media spotlight with the all-Manchester struggle for the Premier League title. And for almost an hour at Wembley there was little in the way of a competitive element to the match as Chelsea eased into a two-goal lead through Ramires and Didier Drogba, the latter with his customary goal at the stadium. Then it took off, largely as a result of the way Andy Carroll came on to disrupt their defensive calm, cut the deficit and give his side much needed purpose. From then on it was Liverpool calling the tune and providing the game's major talking point, with Carroll's header further strengthening the case – if more evidence was ever needed – for the introduction of goal-line technology. He was convinced it was in. Television replays were inconclusive. The man who mattered, referee Phil Dowd, had no option but to credit Petr Cech with a stunning save. Dowd's decision meant Chelsea held on and the fact that they finished on the back foot came as no surprise. It was their 18th game in 61 days since Roberto Di Matteo took charge for a fifth round replay at Birmingham – a punishing schedule for any team and particularly so because so many of those were high-profile fixtures.

CHELSEA 2 LIVERPOOL 1
Wembley (89,102); Saturday, May 5 2012

Chelsea (4-2-3-1): Cech, Bosingwa, Ivanovic, Terry (capt), Cole, Mikel, Lampard, Ramires (Meireles 76), Mata (Malouda 90), Kalou, Drogba. **Subs not used**: Turnbull, Paulo Ferreira, Essien, Torres, Sturridge. **Scorers**: Ramires (11), Drogba (52). **Booked**: Mikel. **Manager**: Roberto Di Matteo
Liverpool (4-1-4-1): Reina, Johnson, Skrtel, Agger, Luis Enrique, Spearing (Carroll 55), Bellamy (Kuyt 78), Henderson, Gerrard (capt), Downing, Suarez. **Subs not used**: Doni, Carragher, Kelly, Shelvey, Rodriguez. **Scorer**: Carroll (64). **Booked**: Agger, Suarez. **Manager**: Kenny Dalglish
Referee: P Dowd (Staffs). **Half-time**: 1-0

HOW THEY REACHED THE FINAL

CHELSEA
Round 3: 4-0 home to Portsmouth (Ramires 2, Mata, Lampard)
Round 4: 1-0 away to QPR (Mata pen)
Round 5: 1-1 home to Birmingham (Sturridge); 2-0 away to Birmingham (Mata, Meireles)
Round 6: 5-2 home to Leicester (Torres 2, Cahill, Kalou, Meireles)
Semi-final: 5-1 v Tottenham (Drogba, Mata, Ramires, Lampard, Malouda)

LIVERPOOL
Round 3: 5-1 home to Oldham (Bellamy, Gerrard pen, Shelvey, Carroll, Downing)
Round 4: 2-1 home to Manchester Utd (Agger, Kuyt)
Round 5: 6-1 home to Brighton (Skrtel, Carroll, Suarez, Bridcutt 2 ogs, Dunk og)
Round 6: 2-1 home to Stoke (Suarez, Downing)
Semi-final: 2-1 v Everton (Suarez, Carroll)

LEADING SCORERS (from first round)
6 Beckford (Leicester); 5 Evans (Sheffield Utd), Tubbs (Crawley); 4 Carroll (Liverpool), Henderson (Millwall), Hughes J (Notts Co), Mata (Chelsea), Phillips M (Blackpool), Ramires (Chelsea)

FACTS AND FIGURES

● John Terry made history by lifting the trophy for the fourth time as Chelsea captain, following his teams' victories over Manchester Utd (2007), Everton (2009) and Portsmouth (2010).

- Didier Drogba was on the mark in those games and with his goal this time became the first player to score in four FA Cup finals. He has also netted at Wembley in three semi-finals and in the 2008 Carling Cup Final against Tottenham.

- Ashley Cole extended his record of winning medals to seven, four with Chelsea and three with Arsenal.

- Roberto Di Matteo has now won the trophy as a Chelsea manager and player. He scored the fastest goal at the old Wembley in 43 seconds against Middlesbrough in the 1997 final and was on the mark again against Aston Villa three years later.

- This win meant Di Matteo became the third former Italy player in successive years to triumph at Wembley as a manager, following Chelsea's Carlo Ancelotti and Manchester City's Roberto Mancini.

- Only two British managers have been successful in the competition since 1995 – Manchester United's Sir Alex Ferguson and Harry Redknapp with Portsmouth.

- Chelsea drew level with Liverpool on seven FA Cup wins. They had never previously met in the final.

- The FA defended their controversial decision to move the kick-off time from 3pm, claiming research showed 5.15 pm to be more popular.

QUOTE/UNQOUTE

'We think, sometimes, of football being important, but it's not really' – **Gary Neville**, former Manchester United and England stalwart, on the death of Gary Speed,

'The whole nation is still in mourning. We're a passionate nation and it needed to be one of us' – **Chris Coleman**, Swansea-born, on his appointment as Speed's successor as Wales manager.

'I take full responsibility for where we are. We are in the Premier League' – **Neil Warnock** responding to his sacking by Queens Park Rangers for a slide down the table.

'Who needs Mourinho, we've got Di Canio' – **Swindon** supporters saluting manager Paolo after the FA Cup victory over Wigan.

'I told David Platt he was now on the bench!' – **Roberto Mancini**, Manchester City manager, asked about his reaction to seeing Paul Scholes back in Manchester United's squad for the teams' FA Cup tie.

"If (Thierry) Henry is still in the Arsenal team when we play them next month we'll have to bring back Graham Roberts or Paul Miller out of retirement to kick him!" – **Harry Redknapp**, Tottenham manager.

'I will always remember tonight. I don't know why, but when it comes to Arsenal something happens with me' – **Thierry Henry**, after scoring the FA Cup winner against Leeds in his first match back on loan.

'The way it was pounced on by some people, you'd have thought I was the bloke at RBS getting a £1m bonus' – **Ian Holloway**, Blackpool manager, on receiving a slice of Charlie Adam's £7m transfer to Liverpool.

147

FA CUP FINAL SCORES & TEAMS

1872 **Wanderers 1** (Betts) Bowen, Alcock, Bonsor, Welch; Betts, Crake, Hooman, Lubbock, Thompson, Vidal, Wollaston. Note: Betts played under the pseudonym 'AH Chequer' on the day of the match **Royal Engineers 0** Capt Merriman; Capt Marindin, Lieut Addison, Lieut Cresswell, Lieut Mitchell, Lieut Renny-Tailyour, Lieut Rich, Lieut George Goodwyn, Lieut Muirhead, Lieut Cotter, Lieut Bogle

1873 **Wanderers 2** (Wollaston, Kinnaird) Bowen; Thompson, Welch, Kinnaird, Howell, Wollaston, Sturgis, Rev Stewart, Kenyon-Slaney, Kingsford, Bonsor **Oxford University 0** Kirke-Smith; Leach, Mackarness, Birley, Longman, Chappell-Maddison, Dixon, Paton, Vidal, Sumner, Ottaway. March 29; 3,000; A Stair

1874 **Oxford University 2** (Mackarness, Patton) Neapean; Mackarness, Birley, Green, Vidal, Ottaway, Benson, Patton, Rawson, Chappell-Maddison, Rev Johnson **Royal Engineers 0** Capt Merriman; Major Marindin, Lieut W Addison, Gerald Onslow, Lieut Oliver, Lieut Digby, Lieut Renny-Tailyour, Lieut Rawson, Lieut Blackman Lieut Wood, Lieut von Donop. March 14; 2,000; A Stair

1875 **Royal Engineers 1** (Renny-Tailyour) Capt Merriman; Lieut Sim, Lieut Onslow, Lieut (later Sir) Ruck, Lieut Von Donop, Lieut Wood, Lieut Rawson, Lieut Stafford, Capt Renny-Tailyour, Lieut Mein, Lieut Wingfield-Stratford **Old Etonians 1** (Bonsor) Thompson; Benson, Lubbock, Wilson, Kinnaird, (Sir) Stronge, Patton, Farmer, Bonsor, Ottaway, Kenyon-Slaney. March 13; 2,000; CW Alcock. aet **Replay – Royal Engineers 2** (Renny-Tailyour, Stafford) Capt Merriman; Lieut Sim, Lieut Onslow, Lieut (later Sir) Ruck, Lieut Von Donop, Lieut Wood, Lieut Rawson, Lieut Stafford, Capt Renny-Tailyour, Lieut Mein, Lieut Wingfield-Stratford **Old Etonians 0** Capt Drummond-Moray; Kinnaird, (Sir) Stronge, Hammond, Lubbock, Patton, Farrer, Bonsor, Lubbock, Wilson, Farmer. March 16; 3,000; CW Alcock

1876 **Wanderers 1** (Edwards) Greig; Stratford, Lindsay, Chappell-Maddison, Birley, Wollaston, C Heron, G Heron, Edwards, Kenrick, Hughes **Old Etonians 1** (Bonsor) Hogg; Rev Welldon, Lyttleton, Thompson, Kinnaird, Meysey, Kenyon-Slaney, Lyttleton, Sturgis, Bonsor, Allene. March 11; 3,500; WS Rawson aet **Replay – Wanderers 3** (Wollaston, Hughes 2) Greig; Stratford, Lindsay, Chappel-Maddison, Birley, Wollaston, C Heron, G Heron, Edwards, Kenrick, Hughes **Old Etonians 0** Hogg, Lubbock, Lyttleton, Farrer, Kinnaird, (Sir) Stronge, Kenyon-Slaney, Lyttleton, Sturgis, Bonsor, Allene. March 18; 1,500; WS Rawson

1877 **Wanderers 2** (Kenrick, Lindsay) Kinnaird; Birley, Denton, Green, Heron, Hughes, Kenrick, Lindsay, Stratford, Wace, Wollaston **Oxford University 1** (Kinnaird og) Allington; Bain, Dunnell, Rev Savory, Todd, Waddington, Rev Fernandez, Otter, Parry, Rawson. March 24; 3,000; SH Wright, aet

1878 **Wanderers 3** (Kinnaird, Kenrick 2) (Sir) Kirkpatrick; Stratford, Lindsay, Kinnaird, Green, Wollaston, Heron, Wylie, Wace, Denton, Kenrick **Royal Engineers 1** (Morris) Friend; Cowan, (Sir) Morris, Mayne, Heath, Haynes, Lindsay, Hedley, (Sir) Bond, Barnet, Ruck. March 23; 4,500; SR Bastard

1879 **Old Etonians 1** (Clerke) Hawtrey; Edward, Bury, Kinnaird, Lubbock, Clerke, Pares, Goodhart, Whitfield, Chevalier, Beaufoy **Clapham Rovers 0** Birkett; Ogilvie, Field, Bailey, Prinsep, Rawson, Stanley, Scott, Bevington, Growse, Keith-Falconer. March 29; 5,000; CW Alcock

1880 **Clapham Rovers 1** (Lloyd-Jones) Birkett; Ogilvie, Field, Weston, Bailey, Stanley, Brougham, Sparkes, Barry, Ram, Lloyd-Jones **Oxford University 0** Parr; Wilson, King, Phillips, Rogers, Heygate, Rev Childs, Eyre, (Dr) Crowdy, Hill, Lubbock. April 10; 6,000; Major Marindin

1881 **Old Carthusians 3** (Page, Wynyard, Parry) Gillett; Norris, (Sir) Colvin, Prinsep, (Sir) Vintcent, Hansell, Richards, Page, Wynyard, Parry, Todd **Old Etonians 0** Rawlinson; Foley, French, Kinnaird, Farrer, Macauley, Goodhart, Whitfield, Novelli, Anderson, Chevallier. April 9; 4,000; W Pierce-Dix

1882 **Old Etonians 1** (Macauley) Rawlinson; French, de Paravicini, Kinnaird, Foley, Novelli, Dunn, Macauley, Goodhart, Chevallier, Anderson **Blackburn Rov 0** Howarth; McIntyre, Suter, Hargreaves, Sharples, Hargreaves, Avery, Brown, Strachan, Douglas, Duckworth. March 25; 6,500; JC Clegg

1883 **Blackburn Olympic 2** (Matthews, Costley) Hacking; Ward, Warburton, Gibson, Astley, Hunter, Dewhurst, Matthews, Wilson, Costley, Yates **Old Etonians 1** (Goodhart) Rawlinson; French, de Paravicini, Kinnaird, Foley, Dunn, Bainbridge, Chevallier, Anderson, Goodhart, Macauley. March 31; 8,000; Major Marindin, aet

1884   **Blackburn Rov 2** (Sowerbutts, Forrest) Arthur; Suter, Beverley, McIntyre, Forrest, Hargreaves, Brown, Inglis Sowerbutts, Douglas, Lofthouse **Queen's Park 1** (Christie) Gillespie; MacDonald, Arnott, Gow, Campbell, Allan, Harrower, (Dr) Smith, Anderson, Watt, Christie. March 29; 4,000; Major Marindin

1885   **Blackburn Rov 2** (Forrest, Brown) Arthur; Turner, Suter, Haworth, McIntyre, Forrest, Sowerbutts, Lofthouse, Douglas, Brown, Fecitt **Queen's Park 0** Gillespie; Arnott, MacLeod, MacDonald, Campbell, Sellar, Anderson, McWhammel, Hamilton, Allan, Gray. April 4; 12,500; Major Marindin

1886   **Blackburn Rov 0** Arthur; Turner, Suter, Heyes, Forrest, McIntyre, Douglas, Strachan, Sowerbutts, Fecitt, Brown **WBA 0** Roberts; Green, Bell, Horton, Perry, Timmins, Woodhall, Green, Bayliss, Loach, Bell. April 3; 15,000; Major Marindin **Replay – Blackburn Rov 2** (Sowerbutts, Brown) Arthur; Turner, Suter, Walton, Forrest, McIntyre, Douglas, Strachan, Sowerbutts, Fecitt, Brown **WBA 0** Roberts; Green, Bell, Horton, Perry, Timmins, Woodhall, Green, Bayliss, Loach, Bell. April 10; 12,000; Major Marindin

1887   **Aston Villa 2** (Hodgetts, Hunter) Warner; Coulton, Simmonds, Yates, Dawson, Burton, Davis, Albert Brown, Hunter, Vaughton, Hodgetts **WBA 0** Roberts; Green, Aldridge, Horton, Perry, Timmins, Woodhall, Green, Bayliss, Paddock, Pearson. April 2; 15,500; Major Marindin

1888   **WBA 2** (Bayliss), Woodhall) Roberts; Aldridge, Green, Horton, Perry, Timmins, Woodhall, Bassett, Bayliss, Wilson, Pearson **Preston 1** (Dewhurst) Mills-Roberts; Howarth, Holmes, Ross, Russell, Gordon, Ross, Goodall, Dewhurst, Drummond, Graham. March 24; 19,000; Major Marindin

1889   **Preston 3** (Dewhurst, Ross, Thomson) Mills-Roberts; Howarth, Holmes, Drummond, Russell, Graham, Gordon, Goodall, Dewhurst, Thompson, Ross **Wolves 0** Baynton; Baugh, Mason, Fletcher, Allen, Lowder, Hunter, Wykes, Brodie, Wood, Knight. March 30; 22,000; Major Marindin

1890   **Blackburn Rov 6** (Lofthouse, Jack Southworth, Walton, Townley 3) Horne; James Southworth, Forbes, Barton, Dewar, Forrest, Lofthouse, Campbell, Jack Southworth, Walton, Townley **Sheffield Wed 1** (Bennett) Smith; Morley, Brayshaw, Dungworth, Betts, Waller, Ingram, Woolhouse, Bennett, Mumford, Cawley. March 29; 20,000; Major Marindin

1891   **Blackburn Rov 3** (Dewar, Jack Southworth, Townley) Pennington; Brandon, Forbes, Barton, Dewar, Forrest, Lofthouse, Walton, Southworth, Hall, Townley **Notts Co 1** (Oswald) Thraves; Ferguson, Hendry, Osborne, Calderhead, Shelton, McGregor, McInnes Oswald, Locker, Daft. March 21; 23,000; CJ Hughes

1892   **WBA 3** (Geddes, Nicholls, Reynolds) Reader; Nicholson, McCulloch, Reynolds, Perry, Groves, Bassett, McLeod, Nicholls, Pearson, Geddes **Aston Villa 0** Warner; Evans, Cox, Devey, Cowan, Baird, Athersmith, Devey, Dickson, Hodgetts, Campbell. March 19; 32,810; JC Clegg

1893   **Wolves 1** (Allen) Rose; Baugh, Swift, Malpass, Allen, Kinsey, Topham, Wykes, Butcher, Griffin, Wood **Everton 0** Williams; Kelso, Howarth, Boyle, Holt, Stewart, Latta, Gordon, Maxwell, Chadwick, Milward. March 25; 45,000; CJ Hughes

1894   **Notts Co 4** (Watson, Logan 3) Toone; Harper, Hendry, Bramley, Calderhead, Shelton, Watson, Donnelly, Logan Bruce, Daft **Bolton 1** (Cassidy) Sutcliffe; Somerville, Jones , Gardiner, Paton, Hughes, Tannahill, Wilson, Cassidy, Bentley, Dickenson. March 31; 37,000; CJ Hughes

1895   **Aston Villa 1** (Chatt) Wilkes; Spencer, Welford, Reynolds, Cowan, Russell, Athersmith Chatt, Devey, Hodgetts, Smith **WBA 0** Reader; Williams, Horton, Perry, Higgins, Taggart, Bassett, McLeod, Richards, Hutchinson, Banks. April 20; 42,560; J Lewis

1896   **Sheffield Wed 2** (Spikesley 2) Massey; Earp, Langley, Brandon, Crawshaw, Petrie, Brash, Brady, Bell, Davis, Spikesley **Wolves 1** (Black) Tennant; Baugh, Dunn, Owen, Malpass, Griffiths, Tonks, Henderson, Beats, Wood, Black. April 18; 48,836; Lieut Simpson

1897   **Aston Villa 3** (Campbell, Wheldon, Crabtree) Whitehouse; Spencer, Reynolds, Evans, Cowan, Crabtree, Athersmith, Devey, Campbell, Wheldon, Cowan **Everton 2** (Bell, Boyle) Menham; Meechan, Storrier, Boyle, Holt, Stewart, Taylor, Bell, Hartley, Chadwick, Milward. April 10; 65,891; J Lewis

1898   **Nottm Forest 3** (Capes 2, McPherson) Allsop; Ritchie, Scott, Forman, McPherson, Wragg, McInnes, Richards, Benbow, Capes, Spouncer **Derby 1** (Bloomer) Fryer; Methven, Leiper, Cox, Goodall, Bloomer, Boag, Stevenson, McQueen. April 16; 62,017; J Lewis

1899   **Sheffield Utd 4** (Bennett, Beers, Almond, Priest) Foulke; Thickett, Boyle, Johnson, Morren, Needham, Bennett, Beers, Hedley, Almond, Priest **Derby 1** (Boag) Fryer; Methven, Staley, Cox,

149

Paterson, May, Arkesden, Bloomer, Boag, McDonald, Allen. April 15; 73,833; A Scragg

1900 **Bury 4** (McLuckie 2, Wood, Plant) Thompson; Darroch, Davidson, Pray, Leeming, Ross, Richards, Wood, McLuckie, Sagar, Plant **Southampton 0** Robinson; Meechan, Durber, Meston, Chadwick, Petrie, Turner, Yates, Farrell, Wood, Milward. April 21; 68,945; A Kingscott

1901 **Tottenham 2** (Brown 2) Clawley; Erentz, Tait, Morris, Hughes, Jones, Smith, Cameron, Brown, Copeland, Kirwan **Sheffield Utd 2** (Priest, Bennett) Foulke; Thickett, Boyle, Johnson, Morren, Needham, Bennett, Field, Hedley, Priest, Lipsham. April 20; 110,820; A Kingscott **Replay – Tottenham 3** (Cameron, Smith, Brown) Clawley; Erentz, Tait, Morris, Hughes, Jones, Smith, Cameron, Brown, Copeland, Kirwan. **Sheffield Utd 1** (Priest) Foulke; Thickett, Boyle, Johnson, Morren, Needham, Bennett, Field, Hedley, Priest, Lipsham. April 27; 20,470; A Kingscott

1902 **Sheffield Utd 1** (Common) Foulke; Thickett, Boyle, Needham, Wilkinson, Johnson, Bennett, Common, Hedley, Priest, Lipsham **Southampton 1** (Wood) Robinson; Fry, Molyneux, Meston, Bowman, Lee, Turner, Wood Brown, Chadwick, Turner. April 19; 76,914; T Kirkham. **Replay – Sheffield Utd 2** (Hedley, Barnes) Foulke; Thickett, Boyle, Needham, Wilkinson, Johnson, Barnes, Common, Hedley, Priest, Lipsham **Southampton 1** (Brown) Robinson; Fry, Molyneux, Meston, Bowman, Lee, Turner, Wood, Brown, Chadwick, Turner. April 26; 33,068; T Kirkham

1903 **Bury 6** (Leeming 2, Ross, Sagar, Wood, Plant) Monteith; Lindsey, McEwen, Johnston, Thorpe, Ross, Richards, Wood, Sagar Leeming, Plant **Derby 0** Fryer; Methven, Morris, Warren, Goodall, May, Warrington, York, Boag, Richards, Davis. April 18; 63,102; J Adams

1904 **Manchester City 1** (Meredith) Hillman; McMahon, Burgess, Frost, Hynds, Ashworth, Meredith, Livingstone, Gillespie, Turnbull, Booth **Bolton 0** Davies; Brown, Struthers, Clifford, Greenhalgh, Freebairn, Stokes, Marsh, Yenson, White, Taylor. April 23; 61,374; AJ Barker

1905 **Aston Villa 2** (Hampton 2) George; Spencer, Miles, Pearson, Leake, Windmill, Brawn, Garratty, Hampton, Bache, Hall **Newcastle 0** Lawrence; McCombie, Carr, Gardner, Aitken, McWilliam, Rutherford, Howie, Appleyard, Veitch, Gosnell. April 15; 101,117; PR Harrower

1906 **Everton 1** (Young) Scott; Crelley, W Balmer, Makepeace, Taylor, Abbott, Sharp, Bolton, Young, Settle, Hardman **Newcastle 0** Lawrence; McCombie, Carr, Gardner, Aitken, McWilliam, Rutherford, Howie, Orr, Veitch, Gosnell. April 21; 75,609; F Kirkham

1907 **Sheffield Wed 2** (Stewart, Simpson) Lyall; Layton, Burton, Brittleton, Crawshaw, Bartlett, Chapman, Bradshaw, Wilson, Stewart, Simpson **Everton 1** (Sharp) Scott; W Balmer, B Balmer, Makepeace, Taylor, Abbott, Sharp, Bolton, Young, Settle, Hardman. April 20; 84,594; N Whittaker

1908 **Wolves 3** (Hunt, Hedley, Harrison) Lunn; Jones, Collins, Rev Hunt, Wooldridge, Bishop, Harrison, Shelton, Hedley, Radford, Pedley **Newcastle 1** (Howie) Lawrence; McCracken, Pudan, Gardner, Veitch, McWilliam, Rutherford, Howie, Appleyard, Speedie, Wilson. April 25; 74,697; TP Campbell

1909 **Manchester Utd 1** (Sandy Turnbull) Moger; Stacey, Hayes, Duckworth, Roberts, Bell, Meredith, Halse, J Turnbull, S Turnbull, Wall **Bristol City 0** Clay; Annan, Cottle, Hanlin, Wedlock, Spear, Staniforth, Hardy, Gilligan, Burton, Hilton. April 24; 71,401; J Mason

1910 **Newcastle 1** (Rutherford) Lawrence; McCracken, Whitson, Veitch, Low, McWilliam, Rutherford, Howie, Higgins, Shepherd, Wilson **Barnsley 1** (Tufnell) Mearns; Downs, Ness, Glendinning, Boyle, Utley, Tufnell, Lillycrop, Gadsby, Forman, Bartrop. April 23; 77,747; JT Ibbotson **Replay – Newcastle 2** (Shepherd 2, 1pen) Lawrence; McCracken, Carr, Veitch, Low, McWilliam, Rutherford, Howie, Higgins, Shepherd, Wilson **Barnsley 0** Mearns; Downs, Ness, Glendinning, Boyle, Utley, Tufnell, Lillycrop, Gadsby, Forman, Bartrop. April 28; 69,000; JT Ibbotson

1911 **Bradford City 0** Mellors; Campbell, Taylor, Robinson, Gildea, McDonald, Logan, Speirs, O'Rourke, Devine, Thompson **Newcastle 0** Lawrence; McCracken, Whitson, Veitch, Low, Willis, Rutherford, Jobey, Stewart, Higgins, Wilson. April 22; 69,068; JH Pearson **Replay – Bradford City 1** (Speirs) Mellors; Campbell, Taylor, Robinson, Torrance, McDonald, Logan, Speirs, O'Rourke, Devine, Thompson **Newcastle 0** Lawrence; McCracken, Whitson, Veitch, Low, Willis, Rutherford, Jobey, Stewart, Higgins, Wilson. April 26; 58,000; JH Pearson

1912 **Barnsley 0** Cooper; Downs, Taylor, Glendinning, Bratley, Utley, Bartrop, Tufnell, Lillycrop, Travers, Moore **WBA 0** Pearson; Cook, Pennington, Baddeley, Buck, McNeal, Jephcott, Wright, Pailor, Bowser, Shearman. April 20; 54,556; JR Shumacher **Replay – Barnsley 1** (Tufnell) Cooper; Downs, Taylor, Glendinning, Bratley, Utley, Bartrop, Harry, Lillycrop, Travers, Jimmy Moore **WBA 0** Pearson; Cook,

Pennington, Baddeley, Buck, McNeal, Jephcott, Wright, Pailor, Bowser, Shearman. April 24; 38,555; JR Schumacher. aet

1913 **Aston Villa 1** (Barber) Hardy; Lyons, Weston, Barber, Harrop, Leach, Wallace, Halse, Hampton, Stephenson, Bache **Sunderland 0** Butler; Gladwin, Ness, Cuggy, Thomson, Low, Mordue, Buchan, Richardson, Holley, Martin. April 19; 120,081; A Adams

1914 **Burnley 1** (Freeman) Sewell; Bamford, Taylor, Halley, Boyle, Watson, Nesbit, Lindley, Freeman, Hodgson, Mosscrop **Liverpool 0** Campbell; Longworth, Pursell, Fairfoul, Ferguson, McKinley, Sheldon, Metcalfe, Miller, Lacey, Nicholl. April 25; 72,778; HS Bamlett

1915 **Sheffield Utd 3** (Simmons, Fazackerly, Kitchen) Gough; Cook, English, Sturgess, Brelsford, Utley, Simmons, Fazackerly, Kitchen, Masterman, Evans **Chelsea 0** Molyneux; Bettridge, Harrow, Taylor, Logan, Walker, Ford, Halse, Thomson, Croal, McNeil. April 24; 49,557; HH Taylor

1920 **Aston Villa 1** (Kirton) Hardy; Smart, Weston, Ducat, Barson, Moss, Wallace, Kirton, Walker, Stephenson, Dorrell **Huddersfield 0** Mutch; Wood, Bullock, Slade, Wilson, Watson, Richardson, Mann, Taylor, Swann, Islip. April 24; 50,018; JT Howcroft. aet

1921 **Tottenham 1** (Dimmock) Hunter; Clay, McDonald, Smith, Walters, Grimsdell, Banks, Seed, Cantrell, Bliss, Dimmock **Wolves 0** George; Woodward, Marshall, Gregory, Hodnett, Riley, Lea, Burrill, Edmonds, Potts, Brooks. April 23; 72,805; S Davies

1922 **Huddersfield 1** (Smith pen) Mutch; Wood, Wadsworth, Slade, Wilson, Watson, Richardson, Mann, Islip, Stephenson, Billy Smith **Preston 0** Mitchell; Hamilton, Doolan, Duxbury, McCall, Williamson, Rawlings, Jefferis, Roberts, Woodhouse, Quinn. April 29; 53,000; JWP Fowler

1923 **Bolton 2** (Jack, JR Smith) Pym; Haworth, Finney, Nuttall, Seddon, Jennings, Butler, Jack, JR Smith, Joe Smith, Vizard **West Ham 0** Hufton; Henderson, Young, Bishop, Kay, Tresadern, Richards, Brown, Watson, Moore, Ruffell. April 28; 126,047; DH Asson

1924 **Newcastle 2** (Harris, Seymour) Bradley; Hampson, Hudspeth, Mooney, Spencer, Gibson, Low, Cowan, Harris, McDonald, Seymour **Aston Villa 0** Jackson; Smart, Mort, Moss, Milne, Blackburn, York, Kirton, Capewell, Walker, Dorrell. April 26; 91,695; WE Russell

1925 **Sheffield Utd 1** (Tunstall) Sutcliffe; Cook, Milton, Pantling, King, Green, Mercer, Boyle, Johnson, Gillespie, Tunstall **Cardiff 0** Farquharson; Nelson, Blair, Wake, Keenor, Hardy, Davies, Gill, Nicholson, Beadles, Evans. April 25; 91,763; GN Watson

1926 **Bolton 1** (Jack) Pym; Haworth, Greenhalgh, Nuttall, Seddon, Jennings, Butler, JR Smith, Jack, Joe Smith, Vizard **Manchester City 0** Goodchild; Cookson, McCloy, Pringle, Cowan, McMullan, Austin, Browell, Roberts, Johnson, Hicks. April 24; 91,447; I Baker

1927 **Cardiff 1** (Ferguson) Farquharson; Nelson, Watson, Keenor, Sloan, Hardy, Curtis, Irving, Ferguson, Davies, McLachlan **Arsenal 0** Lewis; Parker, Kennedy, Baker, Butler, John, Hulme, Buchan, Brain, Blythe, Hoar. April 23; 91,206; WF Bunnell

1928 **Blackburn 3** (Roscamp 2, McLean) Crawford; Hutton, Jones, Healless, Rankin, Campbell, Thornewell, Puddefoot, Roscamp, McLean, Rigby **Huddersfield 1** (Jackson) Mercer; Goodall, Barkas, Redfern, Wilson, Steele, Jackson, Kelly, Brown, Stephenson, Smith. April 21; 92,041; TG Bryan

1929 **Bolton 2** (Butler, Blackmore) Pym; Haworth, Finney, Kean, Seddon, Nuttall, Butler, McClelland, Blackmore, Gibson, Cook **Portsmouth 0** Gilfillan; Mackie, Bell, Nichol, McIlwaine, Thackeray, Forward, Smith, Weddle, Watson, Cook. April 27; 92,576; A Josephs

1930 **Arsenal 2** (James, Lambert) Preedy; Parker, Hapgood, Baker, Seddon, John, Hulme, Jack, Lambert, James, Bastin **Huddersfield 0** Turner; Goodall, Spence, Naylor, Wilson, Campbell, Jackson, Kelly, Davies, Raw, Smith. April 26; 92,488; T Crew

1931 **WBA 2** (WG Richardson 2) Pearson; Shaw, Trentham, Magee, Bill Richardson, Edwards, Glidden, Carter, WG Richardson, Sandford, Wood **Birmingham 1** (Bradford) Hibbs; Liddell, Barkas, Cringan, Morrall, Leslie, Briggs, Crosbie, Bradford, Gregg, Curtis. April 25; 92,406; AH Kingscott

1932 **Newcastle 2** (Allen 2) McInroy; Nelson, Fairhurst, McKenzie, Davidson, Weaver, Boyd, Richardson, Allen, McMenemy, Lang **Arsenal 1** (John) Moss; Parker, Hapgood, Jones, Roberts, Male, Hulme, Jack, Lambert, Bastin, John. April 23; 92,298; WP Harper

1933 **Everton** 3 (Stein, Dean, Dunn) Sagar; Cook, Cresswell, Britton, White, Thomson, Geldard, Dunn, Dean, Johnson, Stein **Manchester City** 0 Langford; Cann, Dale, Busby, Cowan, Bray, Toseland, Marshall, Herd, McMullan, Eric Brook. April 29; 92,950; E Wood

1934 **Manchester City** 2 (Tilson 2) Swift; Barnett, Dale, Busby, Cowan, Bray, Toseland, Marshall, Tilson, Herd, Brook **Portsmouth** 1 (Rutherford) Gilfillan; Mackie, Smith, Nichol, Allen, Thackeray, Worrall, Smith, Weddle, Easson, Rutherford. April 28; 93,258; Stanley Rous

1935 **Sheffield Wed** 4 (Rimmer 2, Palethorpe, Hooper) Brown; Nibloe, Catlin, Sharp, Millership, Burrows, Hooper, Surtees, Palethorpe, Starling, Rimmer **WBA** 2 (Boyes, Sandford) Pearson; Shaw, Trentham, Murphy, Bill Richardson, Edwards, Glidden, Carter, WG Richardson, Sandford, Wally. April 27; 93,204; AE Fogg

1936 **Arsenal** 1 (Drake) Wilson; Male, Hapgood, Crayston, Roberts, Copping, Hulme, Bowden, Drake, James, Bastin **Sheffield Utd** 0 Smith; Hooper, Wilkinson, Jackson, Johnson, McPherson, Barton, Barclay, Dodds, Pickering, Williams. April 25; 93,384; H Nattrass

1937 **Sunderland** 3 (Gurney, Carter, Burbanks) Mapson; Gorman, Hall, Thomson, Johnston, McNab, Duns, Carter, Gurney, Gallacher, Burbanks **Preston** 1 (Frank O'Donnell) Burns; Gallimore, Beattie, Shankly, Tremelling, Milne, Dougal, Beresford, O'Donnell, Fagan, O'Donnell. May 1; 93,495; RG Rudd

1938 **Preston** 1 (Mutch pen) Holdcroft; Gallimore, Beattie, Shankly, Smith, Batey, Watmough, Mutch, Maxwell, Beattie, O'Donnell **Huddersfield** 0 Hesford; Craig, Mountford, Willingham, Young, Boot, Hulme, Issac, MacFadyen, Barclay, Beasley. April 30; 93,497; AJ Jewell. aet

1939 **Portsmouth** 4 (Parker 2, Barlow, Anderson) Walker; Morgan, Rochford, Guthrie, Rowe, Wharton, Worrall, McAlinden, Anderson, Barlow, Parker **Wolves** 1 (Dorsett) Scott; Morris, Taylor, Galley, Cullis, Gardiner, Burton, McIntosh, Westcott, Dorsett, Maguire. April 29; 99,370; T Thompson

1946 **Derby** 4 (Stamps 2. Doherty, B Turner og) Woodley; Nicholas, Howe, Bullions, Leuty, Musson, Harrison, Carter, Stamps, Doherty, Duncan **Charlton Athletic** 1 (B Turner) Bartram; Phipps, Shreeve, Turner, Oakes, Johnson, Fell, Brown, Turner, Welsh, Duffy. April 27; 98,000; ED Smith. aet

1947 **Charlton Athletic** 1 (Duffy) Bartram; Croker, Shreeve, Johnson, Phipps, Whittaker, Hurst, Dawson, Robinson, Welsh, Duffy **Burnley** 0 Strong; Woodruff, Mather, Attwell, Brown, Bray, Chew, Morris, Harrison, Potts, Kippax. April 26; 99,000; JM Wiltshire. aet

1948 **Manchester Utd** 4 (Rowley 2, Pearson, Anderson) Crompton; Carey, Aston, Anderson, Chilton, Cockburn, Delaney, Morris, Rowley, Pearson, Mitten **Blackpool** 2 (Shimwell pen, Mortensen) Robinson; Shimwell, Crosland, Johnston, Hayward, Kelly, Matthews, Munro, Mortensen, Dick, Rickett. April 24; 99,000; CJ Barrick

1949 **Wolves** 3 (Pye 2, Smyth) Williams; Pritchard, Springthorpe Crook, Shorthouse, Wright, Hancocks, Smyth, Pye, Dunn, Mullen **Leicester** 1 (Griffiths) Bradley; Jelly, Scott, Harrison, Plummer, King, Griffiths, Lee, Harrison, Chisholm, Adam. April 30; 99,500; RA Mortimer

1950 **Arsenal** 2 (Lewis 2) Swindin; Scott, Barnes, Forbes, Compton, Mercer, Cox, Logie, Goring, Lewis, Compton **Liverpool** 0 Sidlow; Lambert, Spicer, Taylor, Hughes, Jones, Payne, Baron, Stubbins, Fagan, Liddell. April 29; 100,000; H Pearce

1951 **Newcastle** 2 (Milburn 2) Fairbrother; Cowell, Corbett, Harvey, Brennan, Crowe, Walker, Taylor, Milburn, Jorge Robledo, Mitchell **Blackpool** 0 Farm; Shimwell, Garrett, Johnston, Hayward, Kelly, Matthews, Mudie, Mortensen, Slater, Perry. April 28; 100,000; W Ling

1952 **Newcastle** 1 (G Robledo) Simpson; Cowell, McMichael, Harvey, Brennan, Eduardo Robledo, Walker, Foulkes, Milburn, Jorge Robledo, Mitchell **Arsenal** 0 Swindin; Barnes, Smith, Forbes, Daniel Mercer, Cox, Logie, Holton, Lishman, Roper. May 3; 100,000; A Ellis

1953 **Blackpool** 4 (Mortensen 3, Perry) Farm; Shimwell, Garrett, Fenton, Johnston, Robinson, Matthews, Taylor, Mortensen, Mudie, Perry **Bolton** 3 (Lofthouse, Moir, Bell) Hanson; Ball, Banks, Wheeler, Barass, Bell, Holden, Moir, Lofthouse, Hassall, Langton. May 2; 100,000; M Griffiths

1954 **WBA** 3 (Allen 2 [1pen], Griffin) Sanders; Kennedy, Millard, Dudley, Dugdale, Barlow, Griffin, Ryan, Allen, Nicholls, Lee **Preston** 2 (Morrison, Wayman) Thompson; Cunningham, Walton, Docherty, Marston, Forbes, Finney, Foster, Wayman, Baxter, Morrison. May 1; 100,000; A Luty

1955 **Newcastle** 3 (Milburn, Mitchell, Hannah) Simpson; Cowell, Batty, Scoular, Stokoe, Casey, White,

Milburn, Keeble, Hannah, Mitchell **Manchester City 1** (Johnstone) Trautmann; Meadows, Little, Barnes, Ewing, Paul, Spurdle, Hayes, Revie, Johnstone, Fagan. May 7; 100,000; R Leafe

1956 Manchester City 3 (Hayes, Dyson, Johnstone) Trautmann; Leivers, Little, Barnes, Ewing, Paul, Johnstone, Hayes, Revie, Dyson, Clarke **Birmingham 1** (Kinsey) Merrick; Hall, Green, Newman, Smith, Boyd, Astall, Kinsey, Brown, Murphy, Govan. May 5; 100,000; A Bond

1957 Aston Villa 2 (McParland 2) Sims; Lynn, Aldis, Crowther, Dugdale, Saward, Smith, Sewell, Myerscough, Dixon, McParland **Manchester Utd 1** (Taylor) Wood; Foulkes, Byrne, Colman, Blanchflower, Edwards, Berry, Whelan, Taylor, Charlton, Pegg. May 4; 100,000; F Coultas

1958 Bolton 2 (Lofthouse 2) Hopkinson; Hartle, Banks, Hennin, Higgins, Edwards, Birch, Stevens, Lofthouse, Parry, Holden **Manchester Utd 0** Gregg; Foulkes, Greaves, Goodwin, Cope, Crowther, Dawson, Taylor, Charlton, Viollet, Webster. May 3; 100,000; J Sherlock

1959 Nottingham Forest 2 (Dwight, Wilson) Thomson; Whare, McDonald, Whitefoot, McKinlay, Burkitt, Dwight, Quigley, Wilson, Gray, Imlach **Luton Town 1** (Pacey) Baynham; McNally, Hawkes, Groves, Owen, Pacey, Bingham, Brown, Morton, Cummins, Gregory. May 2; 100,000; J Clough

1960 Wolves 3 (McGrath og, Deeley 2) Finlayson; Showell, Harris, Clamp, Slater, Flowers, Deeley, Stobart, Murray, Broadbent, Horne **Blackburn 0** Leyland; Bray, Whelan, Clayton, Woods, McGrath, Bimpson, Dobing, Dougan, Douglas, McLeod. May 7; 100,000; K Howley

1961 Tottenham 2 (Smith, Dyson) Brown; Baker, Henry, Blanchflower, Norman, Mackay, Jones, White, Smith, Allen, Dyson **Leicester 0** Banks; Chalmers, Norman, McLintock, King, Appleton, Riley, Walsh, McIlmoyle, Keyworth, Cheesebrough. May 6; 100,000; J Kelly

1962 Tottenham 3 (Greaves, Smith, Blanchflower pen) Brown; Baker, Henry, Blanchflower, Norman, Mackay, Medwin, White, Smith, Greaves, Jones **Burnley 1** (Robson) Blacklaw; Angus, Elder, Adamson, Cummings, Miller, Connelly, McIlroy, Pointer, Robson, Harris. May 5; 100,000; J Finney

1963 Manchester Utd 3 (Law, Herd 2) Gaskell; Dunne, Cantwell, Crerand, Foulkes, Setters, Giles, Quixall, Herd, Law, Charlton **Leicester 1** (Keyworth) Banks; Sjoberg, Norman, McLintock, King, Appleton, Riley, Cross, Keyworth, Gibson, Stringfellow. May 25; 100,000; K Aston

1964 West Ham 3 (Sissons, Hurst, Boyce) Standen; Bond, Burkett, Bovington, Brown, Moore, Brabrook, Boyce, Byrne, Hurst, Sissons **Preston 2** (Holden, Dawson) Kelly; Ross, Lawton, Smith, Singleton, Kendall, Wilson, Ashworth, Dawson, Spavin, Holden. May 2; 100,000; A Holland

1965 Liverpool 2 (Hunt, St John) Lawrence; Lawler, Byrne, Strong, Yeats, Stevenson, Callaghan, Hunt, St John, Smith, Thompson **Leeds 1** (Bremner) Sprake; Reaney, Bell, Bremner, Charlton, Hunter, Giles, Storrie, Peacock, Collins, Johanneson. May 1; 100,000; W Clements. aet

1966 Everton 3 (Trebilcock 2, Temple) West; Wright, Wilson, Gabriel, Labone, Harris, Scott, Trebilcock, Young, Harvey, Temple **Sheffield Wed 2** (McCalliog, Ford) Springett; Smith, Megson, Eustace, Ellis, Young, Pugh, Fantham, McCalliog, Ford, Quinn. May 14; 100,000; JK Taylor

1967 Tottenham 2 (Robertson, Saul) Jennings; Kinnear, Knowles, Mullery, England, Mackay, Robertson, Greaves, Gilzean, Venables, Saul. Unused sub: Jones **Chelsea 1** (Tambling) Bonetti; Allan Harris, McCreadie, Hollins, Hinton, Ron Harris, Cooke, Baldwin, Hateley, Tambling, Boyle. Unused sub: Kirkup. May 20; 100,000; K Dagnall

1968 WBA 1 (Astle) John Osborne; Fraser, Williams, Brown, Talbot, Kaye, Lovett, Collard, Astle Hope, Clark Sub: Clarke rep Kaye 91 **Everton 0** West; Wright, Wilson, Kendall, Labone, Harvey, Husband, Ball, Royle, Hurst, Morrissey. Unused sub: Kenyon. May 18; 100,000; L Callaghan. aet

1969 Manchester City 1 (Young) Dowd; Book, Pardoe, Doyle, Booth, Oakes, Summerbee, Bell, Lee, Young, Coleman. Unused sub: Connor **Leicester 0** Shilton; Rodrigues, Nish, Roberts, Woollett, Cross, Fern, Gibson, Lochhead, Clarke, Glover. Sub: Manley rep Glover 70. April 26; 100,000; G McCabe

1970 Chelsea 2 (Houseman, Hutchinson) Bonetti; Webb, McCreadie, Hollins, Dempsey, Ron Harris, Baldwin, Houseman, Osgood, Hutchinson, Cooke. Sub: Hinton rep Harris 91 **Leeds 2** (Charlton, Jones) Sprake; Madeley, Cooper, Bremner, Charlton, Hunter, Lorimer, Clarke, Jones, Giles, Gray Unused sub: Bates. April 11; 100,000; E Jennings. aet **Replay – Chelsea 2** (Osgood, Webb) Bonetti, Webb, McCreadie, Hollins, Dempsey, Ron Harris, Baldwin, Houseman, Osgood, Hutchinson, Cooke. Sub: Hinton rep Osgood 105 **Leeds 1** (Jones) Harvey; Madeley, Cooper, Bremner, Charlton, Hunter, Lorimer, Clarke, Jones, Giles, Gray Unused sub: Bates. April 29; 62,078; E Jennings. aet

153

1971 **Arsenal 2** (Kelly, George) Wilson; Rice, McNab, Storey, McLintock Simpson, Armstrong, Graham, Radford, Kennedy, George. Sub: Kelly rep Storey 70 **Liverpool 1** (Heighway) Clemence; Lawler, Lindsay, Smith, Lloyd, Hughes, Callaghan, Evans, Heighway, Toshack, Hall. Sub: Thompson rep Evans 70. May 8; 100,000; N Burtenshaw. aet

1972 **Leeds 1** (Clarke) Harvey; Reaney, Madeley, Bremner, Charlton, Hunter, Lorimer, Clarke, Jones, Giles, Gray. Unused sub: Bates **Arsenal 0** Barnett; Rice, McNab, Storey, McLintock, Simpson, Armstrong, Ball, George, Radford, Graham. Sub: Kennedy rep Radford 80. May 6; 100,000; DW Smith

1973 **Sunderland 1** (Porterfield) Montgomery; Malone, Guthrie, Horswill, Watson, Pitt, Kerr, Hughes, Halom, Porterfield, Tueart. Unused sub: Young **Leeds 0** Harvey; Reaney, Cherry, Bremner, Madeley, Hunter, Lorimer, Clarke, Jones, Giles, Gray. Sub: Yorath rep Gray 75. May 5; 100,000; K Burns

1974 **Liverpool 3** (Keegan 2, Heighway) Clemence; Smith, Lindsay, Thompson, Cormack, Hughes, Keegan, Hall, Heighway, Toshack, Callaghan. Unused sub: Lawler **Newcastle 0** McFaul; Clark, Kennedy, McDermott, Howard, Moncur, Smith, Cassidy, Macdonald, Tudor, Hibbitt. Sub: Gibb rep Smith 70. May 4; 100,000; GC Kew

1975 **West Ham 2** (Taylor 2) Day; McDowell, Taylor, Lock, Lampard, Bonds, Paddon, Brooking, Jennings, Taylor, Holland. Unused sub: Gould **Fulham 0** Mellor; Cutbush, Lacy, Moore, Fraser, Mullery, Conway, Slough, Mitchell, Busby, Barrett. Unused sub: Lloyd. May 3; 100,000; P Partridge

1976 **Southampton 1** (Stokes) Turner; Rodrigues, Peach, Holmes, Blyth, Steele, Gilchrist, Channon, Osgood, McCalliog, Stokes. Unused sub: Fisher **Manchester Utd 0** Stepney; Forsyth, Houston, Daly, Greenhoff, Buchan, Coppell, McIlroy, Pearson, Macari, Hill. Sub: McCreery rep Hill 66. May 1; 100,000; C Thomas

1977 **Manchester Utd 2** (Pearson, J Greenhoff) Stepney; Nicholl, Albiston, McIlroy, B Greenhoff, Buchan, Coppell, J Greenhoff, Pearson, Macari, Hill. Sub: McCreery rep Hill 81 **Liverpool 1** (Case) Clemence; Neal, Jones, Smith, Kennedy, Hughes, Keegan, Case, Heighway, Johnson, McDermott. Sub: Callaghan rep Johnson 64. May 21; 100,000; R Matthewson

1978 **Ipswich Town 1** (Osborne) Cooper; Burley, Mills, Talbot, Hunter, Beattie, Osborne, Wark, Mariner, Geddis, Woods. Sub: Lambert rep Osborne 79 **Arsenal 0** Jennings; Rice, Nelson, Price, Young, O'Leary, Brady, Hudson, Macdonald, Stapleton, Sunderland. Sub: Rix rep Brady 65. May 6; 100,000; D Nippard

1979 **Arsenal 3** (Talbot, Stapleton, Sunderland) Jennings; Rice, Nelson, Talbot, O'Leary, Young, Brady, Sunderland, Stapleton, Price, Rix. Sub: Walford rep Rix 83 **Manchester Utd 2** (McQueen, McIlroy) Bailey; Nicholl, Albiston, McIlroy, McQueen, Buchan, Coppell, J Greenhoff, Jordan, Macari, Thomas. Unused sub: Greenhoff. May 12; 100,000; R Challis

1980 **West Ham 1** (Brooking) Parkes; Stewart, Lampard, Bonds, Martin, Devonshire, Allen, Pearson, Cross, Brooking, Pike. Unused sub: Brush **Arsenal 0** Jennings; Rice, Devine, Talbot, O'Leary, Young, Brady, Sunderland, Stapleton, Price, Rix. Sub: Nelson rep Devine 61. May 10; 100,000; G Courtney

1981 **Tottenham 1** (Hutchinson og) Aleksic; Hughton, Miller, Roberts, Perryman, Villa, Ardiles, Archibald, Galvin, Hoddle, Crooks. Sub: Brooke rep Villa 68. **Manchester City 1** (Hutchinson) Corrigan; Ranson, McDonald, Reid, Power, Caton, Bennett, Gow, Mackenzie, Hutchison Reeves. Sub: Henry rep Hutchison 82. May 9; 100,000; K Hackett. aet **Replay – Tottenham 3** (Villa 2, Crooks) Aleksic; Hughton, Miller, Roberts, Perryman, Villa, Ardiles, Archibald, Galvin, Hoddle, Crooks. Unused sub: Brooke **Manchester City 2** (Mackenzie, Reeves pen) Corrigan; Ranson, McDonald, Reid, Power, Caton, Bennett, Gow, Mackenzie, Hutchison Reeves. Sub: Tueart rep McDonald 79. May 14; 92,000; K Hackett

1982 **Tottenham 1** (Hoddle) Clemence; Hughton, Miller, Price, Hazard, Perryman, Roberts, Archibald, Galvin, Hoddle, Crooks. Sub: Brooke rep Hazard 104 **Queens Park Rangers 1** (Fenwick) Hucker; Fenwick, Gillard, Waddock, Hazell, Roeder, Currie, Flanagan, Allen, Stainrod, Gregory. Sub: Micklewhite rep Allen 50. May 22; 100,000; C White. aet **Replay – Tottenham 1** (Hoddle pen) Clemence; Hughton, Miller, Price, Hazard, Perryman, Roberts, Archibald, Galvin, Hoddle, Crooks. Sub: Brooke rep Hazard 67 **Queens Park Rangers 0** Hucker; Fenwick, Gillard, Waddock, Hazell, Neill, Currie, Flanagan, Micklewhite, Stainrod, Gregory. Sub: Burke rep Micklewhite 84. May 27; 90,000; C White

1983 **Manchester Utd 2** (Stapleton, Wilkins) Bailey; Duxbury, Moran, McQueen, Albiston, Davies, Wilkins, Robson, Muhren, Stapleton, Whiteside. Unused sub: Grimes **Brighton 2** (Smith, Stevens) Moseley; Ramsey, Gary A Stevens, Pearce, Gatting, Smillie, Case, Grealish, Howlett, Robinson, Smith. Sub: Ryan rep Ramsey 56. May 21; 100,000; AW Grey, aet **Replay – Manchester Utd 4** (Robson 2, Whiteside, Muhren pen) Bailey; Duxbury, Moran, McQueen, Albiston, Davies, Wilkins, Robson, Muhren, Stapleton, Whiteside. Unused sub: Grimes **Brighton 0** Moseley; Gary A Stevens, Pearce, Foster, Gatting, Smillie, Case, Grealish, Howlett, Robinson, Smith. Sub: Ryan rep Howlett 74. May 26; 100,000; AW Grey

1984 **Everton 2** (Sharp, Gray) Southall; Gary M Stevens, Bailey, Ratcliffe, Mountfield, Reid, Steven, Heath, Sharp, Gray, Richardson. Unused sub: Harper **Watford 0** Sherwood; Bardsley, Price, Taylor, Terry, Sinnott, Callaghan, Johnston, Reilly, Jackett, Barnes. Sub: Atkinson rep Price 58. May 19; 100,000; J Hunting

1985 **Manchester Utd 1** (Whiteside) Bailey; Gidman, Albiston, Whiteside, McGrath, Moran, Robson, Strachan, Hughes, Stapleton, Olsen. Sub: Duxbury rep Albiston 91 Moran sent off 77. **Everton 0** Southall; Gary M Stevens, Van den Hauwe, Ratcliffe, Mountfield, Reid, Steven, Sharp, Gray, Bracewell, Sheedy. Unused sub: Harper. May 18; 100,000; P Willis. aet

1986 **Liverpool 3** (Rush 2, Johnston) Grobbelaar; Lawrenson, Beglin, Nicol, Whelan, Hansen, Dalglish, Johnston, Rush, Molby, MacDonald. Unused sub: McMahon **Everton 1** (Lineker) Mimms; Gary M Stevens, Van den Hauwe, Ratcliffe, Mountfield, Reid, Steven, Lineker, Sharp, Bracewell, Sheedy. Sub: Heath rep Stevens 65. May 10; 98,000; A Robinson

1987 **Coventry City 3** (Bennett, Houchen, Mabbutt og) Ogrizovic; Phillips, Downs, McGrath, Kilcline, Peake, Bennett, Gynn, Regis, Houchen, Pickering. Sub: Rodger rep Kilcline 88. Unused sub: Sedgley **Tottenham 2** (Allen, Mabbutt) Clemence; Hughton Thomas, Hodge, Gough, Mabbutt, C Allen, P Allen, Waddle, Hoddle, Ardiles. Subs: Gary A Stevens rep Ardiles 91; Claesen rep Hughton 97. May 16; 98,000; N Midgley. aet

1988 **Wimbledon 1** (Sanchez) Beasant; Goodyear, Phelan, Jones, Young, Thorn, Gibson Cork, Fashanu, Sanchez, Wise. Subs: Cunningham rep Cork 56; Scales rep Gibson 63 **Liverpool 0** Grobbelaar; Gillespie, Ablett, Nicol, Spackman, Hansen, Beardsley, Aldridge, Houghton, Barnes, McMahon. Subs: Johnston rep Aldridge 63; Molby rep Spackman 72. May 14; 98,203; B Hill

1989 **Liverpool 3** (Aldridge, Rush 2) Grobbelaar; Ablett, Staunton, Nichol, Whelan, Hansen, Beardsley, Aldridge Houghton, Barnes, McMahon. Subs: Rush rep Aldridge 72; Venison rep Staunton 91 **Everton 2** (McCall 2) Southall; McDonald, Van den Hauwe, Ratcliffe, Watson, Bracewell, Nevin, Trevor Steven, Cottee, Sharp, Sheedy. Subs: McCall rep Bracewell 58; Wilson rep Sheedy 77. May 20; 82,500; J Worrall. aet

1990 **Manchester Utd 3** (Robson, Hughes 2) Leighton; Ince, Martin, Bruce, Phelan, Pallister, Robson, Webb, McClair, Hughes, Wallace. Subs: Blackmore rep Martin 88; Robins rep Pallister 93. **Crystal Palace 3** (O'Reilly, Wright 2) Martyn; Pemberton, Shaw, Gray, O'Reilly, Thorn, Barber, Thomas, Bright, Salako, Pardew. Subs: Wright rep Barber 69; Madden rep Gray 117. May 12; 80,000; A Gunn. aet **Replay – Manchester Utd 1** (Martin) Sealey; Ince, Martin, Bruce, Phelan, Pallister, Robson, Webb, McClair, Hughes, Wallace. Unused subs: Robins, Blackmore **Crystal Palace 0** Martyn; Pemberton, Shaw, Gray, O'Reilly, Thorn, Barber, Thomas, Bright, Salako, Pardew. Subs: Wright rep Barber 64; Madden rep Salako 79. May 17; 80,000; A Gunn

1991 **Tottenham 2** (Stewart, Walker og) Thorstvedt; Edinburgh, Van den Hauwe, Sedgley, Howells, Mabbutt, Stewart, Gascoigne, Samways, Lineker, Allen. Subs: Nayim rep Gascoigne 18; Walsh rep Samways 82. **Nottingham Forest 1** (Pearce) Crossley; Charles, Pearce, Walker, Chettle, Keane, Crosby, Parker, Clough, Glover, Woan. Subs: Hodge rep Woan 62; Laws rep Glover 108. May 18; 80,000; R Milford. aet

1992 **Liverpool 2** (Thomas, Rush) Grobbelaar; Jones, Burrows, Nicol, Molby, Wright, Saunders, Houghton, Rush, McManaman, Thomas. Unused subs: Marsh, Walters **Sunderland 0** Norman; Owers, Ball, Bennett, Rogan, Rush, Bracewell, Davenport, Armstrong, Byrne, Atkinson. Subs: Hardyman rep Rush 69; Hawke rep Armstrong 77. May 9; 80,000; P Don

1993 **Arsenal 1** (Wright) Seaman; Dixon, Winterburn, Linighan, Adams, Jensen, Davis, Parlour, Merson, Campbell, Wright. Subs: Smith rep Parlour 66; O'Leary rep Wright 90. **Sheffield Wed 1** (Hirst) Woods; Nilsson Worthington, Palmer, Hirst, Anderson, Waddle, Warhurst, Bright, Sheridan, Harkes. Subs: Hyde rep Anderson 85; Bart-Williams rep Waddle 112. May 15; 79,347; K Barratt. aet **Replay – Arsenal 2** (Wright, Linighan) Seaman; Dixon, Winterburn, Linighan, Adams, Jensen, Davis, Smith, Merson, Campbell, Wright. Sub: O'Leary rep Wright 81. Unused sub: Selley **Sheffield Wed 1** (Waddle) Woods; Nilsson, Worthington, Palmer, Hirst, Wilson, Waddle, Warhurst, Bright, Sheridan, Harkes. Subs: Hyde rep Wilson 62; Bart-Williams rep Nilsson 118. May 20; 62,267; K Barratt. aet

1994 Manchester Utd 4 (Cantona 2 [2pens], Hughes, McClair) Schmeichel; Parker, Bruce, Pallister, Irwin, Kanchelskis, Keane, Ince, Giggs, Cantona, Hughes. Subs: Sharpe rep Irwin 84; McClair rep Kanchelskis 84. Unused sub: Walsh (gk) **Chelsea 0** Kharine; Clarke, Sinclair, Kjeldberg, Johnsen, Burley, Spencer, Newton, Stein, Peacock, Wise Substitutions Hoddle rep Burley 65; Cascarino rep Stein 78. Unused sub: Kevin Hitchcock (gk) May 14; 79,634; D Elleray

1995 Everton 1 (Rideout) Southall; Jackson, Hinchcliffe, Ablett, Watson, Parkinson, Unsworth, Horne, Stuart, Rideout, Limpar. Subs: Ferguson rep Rideout 51; Amokachi rep Limpar 69. Unused sub: Kearton (gk) **Manchester Utd 0** Schmeichel; Neville, Irwin, Bruce, Sharpe, Pallister, Keane, Ince, Brian McClair, Hughes, Butt. Subs: Giggs rep Bruce 46; Scholes rep Sharpe 72. Unused sub: Gary Walsh (gk) May 20; 79,592; G Ashby

1996 Manchester Utd 1 (Cantona) Schmeichel; Irwin, P Neville, May, Keane, Pallister, Cantona, Beckham, Cole, Butt, Giggs. Subs: Scholes rep Cole 65; G Neville rep Beckham 89. Unused sub: Sharpe **Liverpool 0** McAteer, Scales, Wright, Babb, Jones, McManaman, Barnes, Redknapp, Collymore, Fowler. Subs: Rush rep Collymore 74; Thomas rep Jones 85. Unused sub: Warner (gk) May 11; 79,007; D Gallagher

1997 Chelsea 2 (Di Matteo, Newton) Grodas; Petrescu, Minto, Sinclair, Lebouef, Clarke, Zola, Di Matteo, Newton, Hughes, Wise. Sub: Vialli rep Zola 89. Unused subs: Hitchcock (gk), Myers **Middlesbrough 0** Roberts; Blackmore, Fleming, Stamp, Pearson, Festa, Emerson, Mustoe, Ravanelli, Juninho, Hignett. Subs: Beck rep Ravanelli 24; Vickers rep Mustoe 29; Kinder, rep Hignett 74. May 17; 79,160; S Lodge

1998 Arsenal 2 (Overmars, Anelka) Seaman; Dixon, Winterburn, Vieira, Keown, Adams, Parlour, Anelka, Petit, Wreh, Overmars. Sub: Platt rep Wreh 63. Unused subs: Manninger (gk); Bould, Wright, Grimandi **Newcastle 0** Given; Pistone, Pearce, Batty, Dabizas, Howey, Lee, Barton, Shearer, Ketsbaia, Speed. Subs: Andersson rep Pearce 72; Watson rep Barton 77; Barnes rep Ketsbaia 85. Unused subs: Hislop (gk); Albert. May 16; 79,183; P Durkin

1999 Manchester Utd 2 (Sheringham, Scholes) Schmeichel; G Neville, Johnsen, May, P Neville, Beckham, Scholes, Keane, Giggs, Cole, Solskjaer. Subs: Sheringham rep Keane 9; Yorke rep Cole 61; Stam rep Scholes 77. Unused subs: Blomqvist, Van Der Gouw **Newcastle 0** Harper; Griffin, Charvet, Dabizas, Domi, Lee, Hamann, Speed, Solano, Ketsbaia, Shearer. Subs: Ferguson rep Hamann 46; Maric rep Solano 68; Glass rep Ketsbaia 79. Unused subs: Given (gk); Barton. May 22; 79,101; P Jones

2000 Chelsea 1 (Di Matteo) de Goey; Melchiot Desailly, Lebouef, Babayaro, Di Matteo, Wise, Deschamps, Poyet, Weah, Zola. Subs: Flo rep Weah 87; Morris rep Zola 90. Unused subs: Cudicini (gk), Terry , Harley **Aston Villa 0** James; Ehiogu, Southgate, Barry, Delaney, Taylor, Boateng, Merson, Wright, Dublin, Carbone. Subs: Stone rep Taylor 79; Joachim rep Carbone 79; Hendrie rep Wright 88. Unused subs: Enckelman (gk); Samuel May 20; 78,217; G Poll

2001 Liverpool 2 (Owen 2) Westerveld; Babbel, Henchoz, Hyypia, Carragher, Murphy, Hamann, Gerrard, Smicer, Heskey, Owen. Subs: McAllister rep Hamann 60; Fowler rep Smicer 77; Berger rep Murphy 77. Unused subs: Arphexad (gk); Vignal **Arsenal 1** (Ljungberg) Seaman; Dixon, Keown, Adams, Cole, Ljungberg, Grimandi, Vieira, Pires, Henry, Wiltord Subs: Parlour rep Wiltord 76; Kanu rep Ljungberg 85; Bergkamp rep Dixon 90. Unused subs: Manninger (gk); Lauren. May 12; 72,500; S Dunn

2002 Arsenal 2 (Parlour, Ljungberg) Seaman; Lauren, Campbell, Adams, Cole, Parlour, Wiltord, Vieira, Ljungberg, Bergkamp, Henry Subs: Edu rep Bergkamp 72; Kanu rep Henry 81; Keown rep Wiltord 90. Unused subs: Wright (gk); Dixon **Chelsea 0** Cudicini; Melchiot, Desailly, Gallas, Babayaro, Gronkjaer, Lampard, Petit, Le Saux, Floyd Hasselbaink, Gudjohnsen. Subs: Terry rep Babayaro 46; Zola rep Hasselbaink 68; Zenden rep Melchiot 77. Unused subs: de Goey (gk); Jokanovic. May 4; 73,963; M Riley

2003 Arsenal 1 (Pires) Seaman; Lauren, Luzhny, Keown, Cole, Ljungberg, Parlour, Gilberto, Pires, Bergkamp, Henry. Sub: Wiltord rep Bergkamp 77. Unused sub: Taylor (gk); Kanu, Toure, van Bronckhorst **Southampton 0** Niemi; Baird, Svensson, Lundekvam, Bridge, Telfer, Svensson, Oakley, Marsden, Beattie, Ormerod. Subs: Jones rep Niemi 66; Fernandes rep Baird 87; Tessem rep Svensson 75. Unused subs: Williams, Higginbotham. May 17; 73,726; G Barber

2004   **Manchester Utd 3** (Van Nistelrooy [2, 1 pen], Ronaldo) Howard; G Neville, Brown, Silvestre, O'Shea, Fletcher, Keane, Ronaldo, Scholes, Giggs, Van Nistelrooy. Subs: Carroll rep Howard, Butt rep Fletcher, Solskjaer rep Ronaldo 84. Unused subs: P Neville, Djemba-Djemba **Millwall 0** Marshall; Elliott, Lawrence, Ward, Ryan, Wise, Ifill, Cahill, Livermore, Sweeney, Harris. Subs: Cogan rep Ryan, McCammon rep Harris 74 Weston rep Wise 88. Unused subs: Gueret (gk); Dunne. May 22; 71,350; J Winter

2005   **Arsenal 0** Lehmann; Lauren, Toure, Senderos, Cole, Fabregas, Gilberto, Vieira, Pires, Reyes, Bergkamp Subs: Ljungberg rep Bergkamp 65, Van Persie rep Fabregas 86, Edu rep Pires 105. Unused subs: Almunia (gk); Campbell **Manchester Utd 0** Carroll; Brown, Ferdinand, Silvestre, O'Shea, Fletcher, Keane, Scholes, Rooney, Van Nistelrooy, Ronaldo. Subs: Fortune rep O'Shea 77, Giggs rep Fletcher 91. Unused subs: Howard; G Neville, Smith. **Arsenal** (Lauren, Ljungberg, van Persie, Cole, Vieira) beat Manchester Utd (van Nistelrooy, Scholes [missed], Ronaldo, Rooney, Keane) 5-4 on penalties

2006   **Liverpool 3** (Gerrard 2, Cisse) Reina; Finnan, Carragher, Hyypiä, Riise, Gerrard, Xabi, Sissoko, Kewell, Cisse, Crouch. Subs: Morientes rep Kewell 48, Kromkamp rep Alonso 67, Hamman rep Crouch 71. Unused subs: Dudek (gk); Traoré **West Ham 3** (Ashton, Konchesky, Carragher (og)) Hislop; Scaloni, Ferdinand, Gabbidon, Konchesky, Benayoun, Fletcher, Reo-Coker, Etherington, Ashton, Harewood. Subs: Zamora rep Ashton 71, Dailly rep Fletcher, Sheringham rep Etherington 85. Unused subs: Walker (gk); Collins. **Liverpool** (Hamann, Hyypiä [missed], Gerrard, Riise) beat **West Ham** (Zamora [missed], Sheringham, Konchesky [missed], Ferdinand [missed]) 3-1 on penalties. May 13; 71,140; A Wiley

2007   **Chelsea 1** (Drogba) Cech; Ferreira, Essien, Terry, Bridge, Mikel, Makelele, Lampard, Wright-Phillips, Drogba, J Cole Subs: Robben rep J Cole 45, Kalou rep Wright-Phillips 93, A Cole rep Robben 108. Unused subs: Cudicini (gk); Diarra. **Manchester Utd 0** Van der Sar, Brown, Ferdinand, Vidic, Heinze, Fletcher, Scholes, Carrick, Ronaldo, Rooney, Giggs Subs: Smith rep Fletcher 92, O'Shea rep Carrick, Solskjaer rep Giggs 112. Unused subs: Kuszczak (gk); Evra. May 19; 89,826; S Bennett

2008   **Portsmouth 1** (Kanu) James; Johnson, Campbell, Distin, Hreidarsson, Utaka, Muntari, Mendes, Diarra, Kranjcar, Kanu. Subs: Nugent rep Utaka 69, Diop rep Mendes 78, Baros rep Kanu 87. Unused subs: Ashdown (gk); Pamarot. **Cardiff 0** Enckelman; McNaughton, Johnson, Loovens, Capaldi, Whittingham, Rae, McPhail, Ledley, Hasselbaink, Parry. Subs: Ramsey rep Whittingham 62, Thompson rep Hasselbaink 70, Sinclair rep Rae 87. Unused subs: Oakes (gk); Purse. May 17; 89,874; M Dean

2009 **Chelsea 2** (Drogba, Lampard), Cech; Bosingwa, Alex, Terry, A Cole, Essien, Mikel, Lampard, Drogba, Anelka, Malouda. Subs: Ballack rep Essien 61. Unused subs: Hilario (gk), Ivanovic, Di Santo, Kalou, Belletti, Mancienne. **Everton** 1 (Saha) Howard; Hibbert, Yobo, Lescott, Baines, Osman, Neville, Cahill, Pienaar, Fellaini, Saha. Subs: Jacobsen rep Hibbert 46, Vaughan rep Saha 77, Gosling rep Osman 83. Unused subs: Nash, Castillo, Rodwell, Baxter. May 30; 89,391; H Webb

2010 **Chelsea 1** (Drogba) Cech; Ivanovic, Alex, Terry, A Cole, Lampard, Ballack, Malouda, Kalou, Drogba, Anelka. Subs: Belletti rep Ballack 44, J Cole rep Kalou 71, Sturridge rep Anelka 90. Unused subs: Hilario (gk), Zhirkov, Paulo Ferreira, Matic. **Portsmouth 0** James; Finnan, Mokoena, Rocha, Mullins, Dindane, Brown, Diop, Boateng, O'Hara, Piquionne. Subs: Utaka rep Boateng 73, Belhadj rep Mullins 81, Kanu rep Diop 81. Unused subs: Ashdown (gk), Vanden Borre, Hughes, Ben Haim. May 15; 88,335; C Foy

2011 **Manchester City 1** (Y Toure) Hart; Richards, Kompany, Lescott, Kolarov, De Jong, Barry, Silva, Y Toure, Balotelli, Tevez. Subs: Johnson rep Barry73, Zabaleta rep Tevez 87, Vieira rep Silva 90. Unused subs: Given (gk), Boyata, Milner, Dzeko. **Stoke 0** Sorensen; Wilkinson, Shawcross, Huth, Wilson, Pennant, Whelan, Delap, Etherington, Walters, Jones. Subs: Whitehead rep Etherington 62, Carew rep Delap 80, Pugh rep Whelan 84. Unused subs: Nash (gk), Collins, Faye, Diao. May 14; 88,643; M Atkinson

VENUES

Kennington Oval 1872; **Lillie Bridge** 1873; **Kennington Oval** 1874 – 1892 (1886 replay at the **Racecourse Ground, Derby**); **Fallowfield**, Manchester, 1893; **Goodison Park** 1894; **Crystal Palace** 1895 – 1915 (1901 replay at **Burnden Park**; 1910 replay at **Goodison Park**; 1912 replay at **Bramall Lane**); **Old Trafford** 1915; **Stamford Bridge** 1920 – 1922; **Wembley** 1923 – 2000 (1970 replay at **Old Trafford**; all replays after 1981 at **Wembley**); **Millennium Stadium** 2001 – 2006; **Wembley** 2007 – 2012

SUMMARY OF FA CUP WINS

Manchester Utd	11	Wolves	4	Cardiff	1
Arsenal	10	Sheffield Wed	3	Charlton	1
Tottenham	8	West Ham	3	Clapham Rov	1
Aston Villa	7	Bury	2	Coventry	1
Liverpool	7	Nottm Forest	2	Derby	1
Chelsea	7	Old Etonians	2	Huddersfield	1
Blackburn Rov	6	Portsmouth	2	Ipswich	1
Newcastle	6	Preston	2	Leeds	1
Everton	5	Sunderland	2	Notts Co	1
Manchester City	5	Barnsley	1	Old Carthusians	1
The Wanderers	5	Blackburn Olympic	1	Oxford University	1
WBA	5	Blackpool	1	Royal Engineers	1
Bolton	4	Bradford City	1	Southampton	1
Sheffield Utd	4	Burnley	1	Wimbledon	1

APPEARANCES IN FINALS

(Figures do not include replays)

Manchester Utd	18	The Wanderers*	5	Queen's Park (Glas)	2
Arsenal	17	West Ham	5	Blackburn Olympic*	1
Liverpool	14	Derby	4	Bradford City*	1
Everton	13	Leeds	4	Brighton	1
Newcastle	13	Leicester	4	Bristol City	1
Chelsea	11	Oxford University	4	Coventry*	1
Aston Villa	10	Royal Engineers	4	Crystal Palace	1
West Brom	10	Southampton	4	Fulham	1
Manchester City	9	Sunderland	4	Ipswich*	1
Tottenham	9	Blackpool	3	Luton	1
Blackburn Rov	8	Burnley	3	Middlesbrough	1
Wolves	8	Cardiff	3	Millwall	1
Bolton	7	Nottm Forest	3	Old Carthusians*	1
Preston	7	Barnsley	2	QPR	1
Old Etonians	6	Birmingham	2	Stoke	1
Sheffield Utd	6	Bury*	2	Watford	1
Sheffield Wed	6	Charlton	2	Wimbledon*	1
Huddersfield	5	Clapham Rov	2		
Portsmouth	5	Notts Co	2		

(* Denotes undefeated)

APPEARANCES IN SEMI-FINALS

(Figures do not include replays)

Manchester Utd 27, Arsenal 26, Everton 25, Liverpool 23, Aston Villa 20, Chelsea 20, WBA 20, Tottenham 19, Blackburn 18, Newcastle 19, Sheffield Wed 16, Bolton 14, Wolves 14, Derby 13, Sheffield Utd 13, Nottm Forest 12, Sunderland 12, Manchester City 11, Southampton 11, Preston 10, Birmingham 9, Burnley 8, Leeds 8, Huddersfield 7, Leicester 7, Portsmouth 7, West Ham 7, Fulham 6, Old Etonians 6, Oxford University 6, Notts Co 5, The Wanderers 5, Watford 5, Cardiff 4, Luton 4, Millwall 4, Queen's Park (Glasgow) 4, Royal Engineers 4, Stoke 4, Barnsley 3, Blackpool 3, Clapham Rov 3, *Crystal Palace 3, Ipswich Town 3, Middlesbrough 3, Norwich 3, Old Carthusians 3, Oldham 3, The Swifts 3, Blackburn Olympic 2, Bristol City 2, Bury 2, Charlton 2, Grimsby Town 2, Swansea 2, Swindon 2, Wimbledon 2, Bradford City 1, Brighton 1, Cambridge University 1, Chesterfield 1, Coventry 1, Crewe 1, Darwen 1, Derby Junction 1, Hull 1, Marlow 1, Old Harrovians 1, Orient 1, Plymouth Argyle 1, Port Vale 1, QPR 1, Rangers (Glasgow) 1, Reading 1, Shropshire Wand 1, Wycombe 1, York 1 (*A previous and different Crystal Palace club also reached the semi-final in season 1871–72)

QUOTE/UNQOUTE

'Wayne hasn't trained well this week. He's missed a few days. It's little strains here and there' – **Sir Alex Ferguson**, Manchester United manager, before it emerged that Rooney had been dropped after a Boxing Day night out.

'I don't know what that stuff is. For all I know, he could have been blowing bubbles' – **Alex McLeish** after his Aston Villa midfielder Stephen Ireland was pictured with a shisha pipe in his hand.

'I've been a manager for 30 years and made 50,000 substitutions. I do not have to justify every decision I make to you' – **Arsene Wenger**, Arsenal manager, gets his maths wrong when responding to criticism for bringing off Alex Oxlade-Chamberlain against Manchester United.

'I think they should have made the chin just a little bit longer' – **Jimmy Hill**, former manager and chairman of Coventry, at the unveiling of a bronze statue at the club's Ricoh Arena.

'I can't understand, personally, what the hell they get out of it. I think it's a bit of an ego thing to see who can have the most followers' – **Steve Bruce**, former Sunderland manager, struggling to understand the fascination of *Twitter* for modern-day players.

'This is as important as any game I have ever played. I felt straight away the butterflies in my stomach' – **Paolo Di Canio**, Swindon manager, putting the match against Oxford on a par with Old Firm and Rome derbies.

'I was hoping it wouldn't go down to the managers taking one' – **John Still**, Dagenham and Redbridge manager, after his side's record 14-13 penalty shoot-out win over Leyton Orient in a Johnstone's Paint Trophy tie.

'I'm devasted. I know I should have scored and my team-mates know I should have scored. There's absolutely no chance of me watching it again' – **Robert Earnshaw**, Wales striker, on missing an open goal against England.

'I told the players that St Patrick was looking down on us' – **Giovanni Trapattoni**, Republic of Ireland manager, after a fortunate goalless draw against Russia.

I'm sure some of you are going bald, so you know it's a bit stressful. I made a decision to get it done' – **Wayne Rooney**, Manchester United striker, questioned about his hair replacement treatment.

'I want to show the people who think I needed a tablet to be a better footballer that it's not the case. It was an accident' – **Kolo Toure**, Manchester City defender, returning after a six-month ban for failing a drugs test.

'As a manager, I've played four and lost four in the Carlsberg Cup, or whatever it is called' – **Roy Hodgson**, former West Bromwich Albion manager, showing that the Carling Cup was not high on the list of his priorities.

'We are Liverpool Football Club and we want to win every game we play' – **Kenny Dalglish** offering a different slant on the competition.

LIVERPOOL THWART BRAVE CARDIFF ON PENALTIES

THIRD ROUND	FOURTH ROUND	FIFTH ROUND	SEMI-FINALS	FINAL
*Cardiff.........+A2				
Leicester.........2	*Cardiff.........1			
*Burnley.........2	Burnley.........0	*Cardiff.........2		
MK Dons.........1				
*Blackburn.........3	*Blackburn.........+4		Cardiff.........0;+D1	
Leyton Orient.........2	Newcastle.........3	Blackburn.........0		
*Nottm Forest.........3				Cardiff.........2
Newcastle.........+4				
*Aldershot.........2	*Aldershot.........0			
Rochdale.........1	Manchester Utd.........3	*Manchester Utd.........1		
*Leeds.........0			*Crystal Palace.........1:0	
Manchester Utd.........3				
*Crystal Palace.........2	*Crystal Palace.........2	Crystal Palace.........+2		
Middlesbrough.........1	Southampton.........0			
*Southampton.........2				
Preston.........1				
*Arsenal.........3	*Arsenal.........2			
Shrewsbury.........1	Bolton.........1	*Arsenal.........0		
*Aston Villa.........0			*Manchester City0:2	
Bolton.........2				
*Wolves.........5	*Wolves.........2	Manchester City.........1		
Millwall.........0				

Manchester City....5

Liverpool.........+E2

*Manchester City..2
Birmingham 0

*Everton ....+2
WBA..............1

*Everton 1

*Chelsea 0

*Chelsea ....+BO
Fulham 0

Chelsea ....+2

Liverpool.........1:2

*Stoke.........+CO
Tottenham........0

*Stoke.........1

Liverpool.........2

*Brighton.........1
Liverpool.........2

*Drawn at home; in semi-finals, first leg; + After extra-time; A – Cardiff won 7-6 on pens; B Chelsea won 4-3 on pens; C Stoke won 7-6 on pens; D Cardiff won 3-1 on pens; E – Liverpool won 3-2 on pens

PRELIMINARY ROUND: Crawley 3 AFC Wimbledon 2

FIRST ROUND: Accrington 0 Scunthorpe 2; Barnsley 0 Morecambe 2; Bournemouth 5 Dagenham 0; Brighton 1 Gillingham 0; Bristol City 0 Swindon 1; Bristol Rov 1 Watford 1 (aet, Bristol Rov won 4-2 on pens); Burnley 6 Burton 3 (aet); Bury 3 Coventry 1; Charlton 2 Reading 1; Cheltenham 1 MK Dons 4; Crystal Palace 2 Crawley 0; Derby 2 Shrewsbury 3; Doncaster 3 Tranmere 0; Exeter 2 Yeovil 0; Hartlepool 1 Sheffield Utd 1 (aet, Sheffield Utd won 4-3 on pens); Hereford 1 Brentford 0; Hull 0 Macclesfield 2; Ipswich 1 Northampton 2; Leeds 3 Bradford 2; Nottm Forest 3 Notts Co 3 (aet, Nottm Forest won 4-3 on pens); Oldham 1 Carlisle 1 (aet, Carlisle won 4-2 on pens); Oxford 1 Cardiff 3 (aet); Plymouth 0 Millwall 1; Portsmouth 0 Barnet 1; Port Vale 2 Huddersfield 4; Preston 3 Crewe 2; Rochdale 3 Chesterfield 2 (aet); Rotherham 1 Leicester 4; Sheffield Wed 0 Blackpool 0 (aet, Sheffield Wed won 4-2 on pens); Southampton 4 Torquay 1; Southend 1 Leyton Orient 1 (aet, Leyton Orient won 4-3 on pens); Stevenage 3 Peterborough 4 (aet); Walsall 0 Middlesbrough 3; West Ham 1 Aldershot 2; Wycombe 3 Colchester 3 (aet, Wycombe won 5-4 on pens)

SECOND ROUND: Aldershot 2 Carlisle 0; Aston Villa 2 Hereford 0; Blackburn 3 Sheffield Wed 1; Bolton 2 Macclesfield 1; Bournemouth 1 WBA 4; Brighton 1 Sunderland 0 (aet); Burnley 3 Barnet 2 (aet); Bury 2 Leicester 4; Charlton 0 Preston 2; Crystal Palace 2 Wigan 1; Doncaster 1 Leeds 2; Everton 3 Sheffield Utd 1; Exeter 1 Liverpool 3; Leyton Orient 3 Bristol Rov 2; Millwall 2 Morecambe 0; Northampton 0 Wolves 4; Norwich 0 MK Dons 4; Peterborough 0 Middlesbrough 2; QPR 0 Rochdale 2; Scunthorpe 1 Newcastle 2 (aet); Shrewsbury 3 Swansea 1; Swindon 1 Southampton 3; Wycombe 3 Nottm Forest 4

CARLING CUP FINAL

CARDIFF 2 LIVERPOOL 2
(aet, Liverpool won 3-2 on pens)
Wembley (89,044); Sunday, February 26 2012

Cardiff (4-4-1-1): Heaton, McNaughton (Blake 106), Hudson (capt) (A Gerrard 99), Turner, Taylor, Mason (Kiss 91), Whittingham, Gunnarsson, Cowie, Miller, Gestede. **Subs not used:** Marshall, Naylor, Conway, Earnshaw. **Scorers:** Mason (19), Turner (118). **Booked:** Kiss, Turner. **Manager:** Malky Mackay

Liverpool (4-4-1-1): Reina, Johnson, Skrtel, Agger (Carragher 87), Jose Enrique, Henderson (Bellamy 58), S Gerrard (capt), Adam, Downing, Suarez, Carroll (Kuyt 103). **Subs not used:** Doni, Kelly, Maxi Rodriguez, Spearing. **Scorers:** Skrtel (60), Kuyt (108). **Booked:** Henderson. **Manager:** Kenny Dalglish

Penalty shoot-out (Liverpool first): S Gerrard saved, Miller missed, Adam missed, Cowie 0-1 Kuyt 1-1, Gestede missed, Downing 2-1, Whittingham 2-2, Johnson 3-2, A Gerrard missed **Referee:** M Clattenburg. **Half-time:** 1-0

For Liverpool a first trophy since 2006, along with a reputation restored; for manager Kenny Dalglish a place in the record books; for Cardiff a widely-acclaimed performance which took them so close to a shock win; for Wembley a final to rank among the finest of recent years. There were so many strands to this enthralling afternoon, although it was the way the underdogs set about their task, and almost carried it through, that will be remembered most. Cardiff were finally broken in a penalty shoot-out which left one family member celebrating and another in despair. After his opening spot-kick had been brilliantly saved by Tom Heaton, Steven Gerrard was a relieved captain when lifting the trophy. Before that, Gerrard sought out and offered commiserations to cousin Anthony, the Cardiff substitute whose miss decided the outcome. His team had beaten Leicester and Crystal Palace on penalties on the way to the final. Two other ties went to extra-time, so perhaps the resilience they displayed when equalising through Ben Turner in the 118th minute when the match looked lost was not such a surprise. Cardiff had earlier been rewarded for their enterprise with the opening goal from Joe Mason, then offered great organisation to prevent their opponents from taking any sort of grip. Liverpool also successfully negotiated a demanding route to Wembley, winning at Stoke and Chelsea, then overcoming Manchester City in the semi-finals. The trophy was badly needed after their much-criticised handling of the eight-match ban imposed on Luis Suarez for racially abusing Manchester United's Patrice Evra and of his subsequent refusal to shake Evra's hand. Dalglish did not distinguish himself, either, in this affair, so becoming the first man to achieve a clean sweep of domestic honours as player and manager couldn't have been better timed.

HOW THEY REACHED THE FINAL

CARDIFF
Round 1: 3-1 away to Oxford (Conway, Whittingham, Jarvis) – aet
Round 2: 5-3 home to Huddersfield (Cowie 2, Gyepes, Parkin, Conway) – aet
Round 3: 2-2 home to Leicester (Cowie, Gestede) – aet, won 7-6 on pens
Round 4: 1-0 home to Burnley (Mason)
Round 5: 2-0 home to Blackburn (Miller, A Gerrard)
Semi-finals: v Crystal Palace – first leg, 0-1 away; second leg, 1-0 home (Gardner og) – aet, won 3-1 on pens

LIVERPOOL
Round 2: 3-1 away to Exeter (Suarez, Maxi Rodriguez, Carroll)
Round 3: 2-1 away to Brighton (Bellamy, Kuyt)
Round 4: 2-1 away to Stoke (Suarez 2)
Round 5: 2-0 away to Chelsea (Maxi Rodriguez, Kelly)
Semi-finals: v Manchester City – first leg, 1-0 away (S Gerrard pen); second leg, 2-2 home (S Gerrard pen, Bellamy)

LEAGUE CUP – COMPLETE RESULTS

LEAGUE CUP FINALS

1961*   Aston Villa beat Rotherham 3-2 on agg (0-2a, 3-0h)
1962   Norwich beat Rochdale 4-0 on agg (3-0a, 1-0h)
1963   Birmingham beat Aston Villa 3-1 on agg (3-1h, 0-0a)
1964   Leicester beat Stoke 4-3 on agg (1-1a, 3-2h)
1965   Chelsea beat Leicester 3-2 on agg (3-2h, 0-0a)
1966   WBA beat West Ham 5-3 on agg (1-2a, 4-1h)

AT WEMBLEY

1967   QPR beat WBA (3-2)
1968   Leeds beat Arsenal (1-0)
1969*   Swindon beat Arsenal (3-1)
1970*   Manchester City beat WBA (2-1)
1971   Tottenham beat Aston Villa (2-0)
1972   Stoke beat Chelsea (2-1)
1973   Tottenham beat Norwich (1-0)
1974   Wolves beat Manchester City (2-1)
1975   Aston Villa beat Norwich (1-0)
1976   Manchester City beat Newcastle (2-1)
1977†*   Aston Villa beat Everton (3-2 after 0-0 and 1-1 draws)
1978††   Nottm Forest beat Liverpool (1-0 after 0-0 draw)
1979   Nottm Forest beat Southampton (3-2)
1980   Wolves beat Nottm Forest (1-0)
1981††† Liverpool beat West Ham (2-1 after 1-1 draw)

MILK CUP

1982*   Liverpool beat Tottenham (3-1)
1983*   Liverpool beat Manchester Utd (2-1)
1984**   Liverpool beat Everton (1-0 after *0-0 draw)
1985   Norwich beat Sunderland (1-0)
1986   Oxford Utd beat QPR (3-0)

LITTLEWOODS CUP

1987   Arsenal beat Liverpool (2-1)
1988   Luton beat Arsenal (3-2)
1989   Nottm Forest beat Luton (3-1)
1990   Nottm Forest beat Oldham (1-0)

RUMBELOWS CUP

1991   Sheffield Wed beat Manchester Utd (1-0)
1992   Manchester Utd beat Nottm Forest (1-0)

COCA-COLA CUP

1993   Arsenal beat Sheffield Wed (2-1)
1994   Aston Villa beat Manchester Utd (3-1)
1995   Liverpool beat Bolton (2-1)
1996   Aston Villa beat Leeds (3-0)
1997*** Leicester beat Middlesbrough (*1-0 after *1-1 draw)
1998   Chelsea beat Middlesbrough (2-0)

WORTHINGTON CUP (at Millennium Stadium from 2001)

1999	Tottenham beat Leicester (1-0)
2000	Leicester beat Tranmere (2-1)
2001	Liverpool beat Birmingham (5-4 on pens after *1-1 draw)
2002	Blackburn beat Tottenham (2-1)
2003	Liverpool beat Manchester Utd (2-0)

CARLING CUP (at Wembley from 2008)

2004	Middlesbrough beat Bolton (2-1)
2005*	Chelsea beat Liverpool (3-2)
2006	Manchester Utd beat Wigan (4-0)
2007	Chelsea beat Arsenal (2-1)
2008*	Tottenham beat Chelsea (2-1)
2009	Manchester Utd beat Tottenham (4-1 on pens after *0-0 draw)
2010	Manchester Utd beat Aston Villa (2-1)
2011	Birmingham beat Arsenal (2-1)
2012	Liverpool beat Cardiff (3-2 on pens after *2-2 draw)

* After extra time. † First replay at Hillsborough, second replay at Old Trafford. †† Replayed at Old Trafford. ††† Replayed at Villa Park. ** Replayed at Maine Road. *** Replayed at Hillsborough

SUMMARY OF LEAGUE CUP WINNERS

Liverpool	8	Birmingham	2	Middlesbrough	1
Aston Villa	5	Manchester City	2	Oxford Utd	1
Chelsea	4	Norwich	2	QPR	1
Nottm Forest	4	Wolves	2	Sheffield Wed	1
Tottenham	4	Blackburn	1	Stoke	1
Manchester Utd	4	Leeds	1	Swindon	1
Leicester	3	Luton	1	WBA	1
Arsenal	2				

LEAGUE CUP FINAL APPEARANCES

11 Liverpool; **8** Aston Villa, Manchester Utd; **7** Arsenal, Tottenham; **6** Chelsea, Nottm Forest; **5** Leicester; **4** Norwich; **3** Birmingham, Manchester City, Middlesbrough, WBA; **2** Bolton, Everton, Leeds, Luton , QPR, Sheffield Wed, Stoke, West Ham, Wolves; **1** Blackburn, Cardiff, Newcastle, Oldham, Oxford Utd, Rochdale, Rotherham, Southampton, Sunderland, Swindon, Tranmere, Wigan (Figures do not include replays).

LEAGUE CUP SEMI-FINAL APPEARANCES

14 Arsenal, Liverpool, **13** Aston Villa, Tottenham; **12** Manchester Utd **10** Chelsea; **8** West Ham; **7** Manchester City; **6** Blackburn, Nottm Forest, **5** Birmingham, Leeds, Leicester, Middlesbrough, Norwich; **4** Bolton, Burnley, Crystal Palace, Everton, Ipswich, Sheffield Wed, WBA; **3**, QPR, Sunderland, Swindon , Wolves; **2** Bristol City, Cardiff, Coventry, Derby, Luton, Oxford Utd, Plymouth, Southampton, Stoke City, Tranmere, Watford, Wimbledon; **1** Blackpool, Bury, Carlisle, Chester, Huddersfield, Newcastle, Oldham, Peterborough, Rochdale, Rotherham, Sheffield Utd, Shrewsbury, Stockport, Walsall, Wigan, Wycombe
(Figures do not include replays).

OTHER COMPETITIONS 2011–12

JOHNSTONE'S PAINT TROPHY

FIRST ROUND
Northern: Accrington 3 Carlisle 2; Bradford 0 Sheffield Wed 0 (Bradford won 3-1 on pens); Burton 1 Sheffield Utd 2; Bury 0 Crewe 0 (Crewe won 4-2 on pens); Northampton 1 Huddersfield 2; Scunthorpe 2 Hartlepool 0; Tranmere 1 Port Vale 1 (Tranmere won 4-2 on pens); Walsall 2 Shrewsbury 1
Southern: Bournemouth 4 Hereford 1; Cheltenham 2 Torquay 1; Colchester 1 Barnet 3; Exeter 1 Plymouth 1 (Exeter won 3-0 on pens); Leyton Orient 1 Dagenham 1 (Dagenham won 14-13 on pens); MK Dons 3 Brentford 3 (Brentford won 4-3 on pens); Southend 1 Crawley 0; Wycombe 3 Bristol Rov 1

SECOND ROUND
Northern: Accrington 0 Tranmere 1 (after Accrington 1 Tranmere 2, abandoned after 39 mins; serious injury); Crewe 1 Macclesfield 0; Huddersfield 2 Bradford 2 (Bradford won 4-3 on pens); Morecambe 2 Preston 2 (Preston won 7-6 on pens); Notts Co 1 Chesterfield 3; Rochdale 1 Walsall 1 (Rochdale won 3-1 on pens); Rotherham 1 Sheffield Utd 2; Scunthorpe 0 Oldham 1
Southern: AFC Wimbledon 2 Stevenage 2 (AFC Wimbledon won 4-3 on pens); Aldershot 1 Oxford 2; Bournemouth 3 Yeovil 2; Charlton 0 Brentford 3; Dagenham 1 Southend 2; Exeter 1 Swindon 2; Gillingham 1 Barnet 3; Wycombe 1 Cheltenham 3

THIRD ROUND
Northern: Chesterfield 4 Tranmere 3; Oldham 3 Crewe 1; Rochdale 1 Preston 1 (Preston won 4-2 on pens); Sheffield Utd 1 Bradford 1 (Bradford won 6-5 on pens)
Southern: Brentford 6 Bournemouth 0; Cheltenham 0 Barnet 2; Oxford 0 Southend 1; Swindon 1 AFC Wimbledon 1 (Swindon won 3-1 on pens)

SEMI-FINALS
Northern: Oldham 2 Bradford 0; Preston 1 Chesterfield 1 (Chesterfield won 4-2 on pens)
Southern: Barnet 0 Brentford 0 (Barnet won 5-3 on pens); Southend 1 Swindon 2

AREA FINALS
Northern first leg: Chesterfield 2 (Boden 49, Whitaker 67 pen) Oldham 1 (Simpson 58). Att: 5,724. **Second leg**: Oldham 0 Chesterfield 1 (Lester 88). Att: 5,622 (Chesterfield won 3-1 on agg)
Southern first leg: Barnet 1 (Hughes 72) Swindon 1 (Flint 44). Att: 3,915. **Second leg**: Swindon 1 (Connell 17) Barnet 0. Att: 10,408 (Swindon won 2-1 on agg)

FINAL

CHESTERFIELD 2 SWINDON TOWN 0
Wembley (49,602); Sunday, March 25 2012
Chesterfield (4-4-2): Lee; Hurst, Ford, Thompson, N Smith, Mendy, Allott, Moussa (Randall 81), Talbot, Bowery (Boden 87), Lester (capt) (Westcarr 37). **Subs not used**: Fleming, Whitaker. **Scorers**: Risser (47 og), Westcarr (90). **Booked**: Westcarr. **Manager**: John Sheridan
Swindon (4-4-2): Foderingham; Devera, McCormack (capt), Risser (Murray 62), McEveley (Cibocchi 77), Ritchie, Ferry, J Smith (Bostock 72), Holmes, Benson, Connell. **Subs not used**: P Smith, De Vita. **Booked**: Connell. **Manager**: Paolo Di Canio
Referee: T Bates (Staffs). **Half-time**: 0-0

FA CARLSBERG TROPHY

FIRST ROUND

Alfreton 4 Southport 0; Barrow 3 Harrogate 2; Boreham Wood 0 Cambridge Utd 1; Boston 2 Hyde 1; Brackley 0 Dartford 3; Carshalton 5 Bishop's Stortford 0; Chelmsford 2 Bath 3; Colwyn Bay 1 Lincoln 3; Didcot 0 Basingstoke 1; Droylsden 2 Mansfield 1; East Thurrock 2 Welling 1; Gateshead 3 Kettering 0; Gosport 0 Braintree 1; Grimsby 3 Darlington 0; Guiseley 2 FC United Manchester 0; Hampton 2 Hayes 0; Hornchurch 0 Farnborough 0; Luton 2 Swindon Super 0; Newport 0 Forest Green 0; North Ferriby 1 Chester 5; Northwich 3 Fleetwood 1; Nuneaton 0 Telford 2; Salisbury 4 Lowestoft 1; Staines 0 Maidenhead 1; Stockport 2 Stalybridge 2; Truro 0 Ebbsfleet 5; Vauxhall 4 Kidderminster 4; Wealdstone 5 Uxbridge 0; Weymouth 2 Chippenham 1; Worksop 1 Tamworth 0; Wrexham 1 Hinckley 2; York 2 Solihull 2. **Replays:** Farnborough 2 Hornchurch 3; Forest Green 0 Newport 2; Kidderminster 2 Vauxhall 0; Maidenhead 1 Staines 2; Stalybridge 2 Stockport 1; Solihull 0 York 3

SECOND ROUND

Bath 1 Basingstoke 0; Cambridge Utd 4 Telford 1; Dartford 4 Boston 2; East Thurrock 1 Hampton 1; Ebbsfleet 3 Chester 2; Gateshead 2 Braintree 2; Grimsby 4 Hornchurch 0; Guiseley 2 Stalybridge 0; Hinckley 0 Luton 1; Kidderminster 5 Droylsden 1; Lincoln 0 Carshalton 0; Northwich 1 Staines 0; Salisbury 2 York 6; Wealdstone 2 Barrow 1; Weymouth 0 Alfreton 6; Worksop 1 Newport 3. **Replays:** Braintree 1 Gateshead 1 (aet, Gateshead won 4-3 on pens); Carshalton 2 Lincoln 1; Hampton 4 East Thurrock 1; Luton 3 Hinckley 0

THIRD ROUND

Bath 1 Grimsby 2; Cambridge Utd 1 Guiseley 0; Dartford 2 Wealdstone 2; Gateshead 2 Alfreton 1; Kidderminster 1 Luton 2; Newport 4 Carshalton 0; Northwich 4 Hampton 1; York 1 Ebbsfleet 0. **Replay:** Wealdstone 1 Dartford 0

FOURTH ROUND

Grimsby 0 York 1; Luton 2 Gateshead 0; Northwich 2 Newport 3; Cambridge Utd 1 Wealdstone 2

SEMI-FINALS, FIRST LEG

Newport 3 (Buchanan 7, Jarvis 22, Knights 78) Wealdstone 1 (Jolly 49). Att: 2,206. York 1 (Reed 18) Luton 0. Att: 3,365

SEMI-FINALS, SECOND LEG

Luton 1 (Willmott 43) York 1 (Blair 90). Att: 5,796 (York won 2-1 on agg). Wealdstone 0 Newport 0. Att: 2,092 (Newport won 3-1 on agg)

FINAL

NEWPORT COUNTY 0 YORK CITY 2
Wembley (19,884); Saturday, May 12 2012

Newport (4-1-4-1): Thompson, Pipe, Warren (capt), Yakubu, Hughes, Jarvis (Harris 69), Porter (Knights 80), Evans, Rose (Buchanan 69), Foley, Minshull. **Subs not used:** Swan, Rodgers. •
Manager: Justin Edinburgh
York (4-4-2): Ingham, Challinor, Smith (capt), Parslow, Gibson, Meredith, Oyebanjo, McLaughlin (Fyfield 83), Blair, Chambers (Moke 89), Walker (Reed 90). **Subs not used:** Musselwhite, Potts. **Scorers:** Blair (65), Oyebanjo (72). **Manager:** Gary Mills
Referee: A. Taylor (Cheshire). **Half-time:** 0-0

FINALS – RESULTS
Associated Members' Cup
1984 (Hull) Bournemouth 2 Hull 1

Freight Rover Trophy
1985   (Wembley) Wigan 3 Brentford 1
1986   (Wembley) Bristol City 3 Bolton 0
1987   (Wembley) Mansfield 1 Bristol City 1 (aet; Mansfield won 5-4 on pens)

Sherpa Van Trophy
1988   (Wembley) Wolves 2 Burnley 0
1989   (Wembley) Bolton 4 Torquay 1

Leyland Daf Cup
1990   (Wembley) Tranmere 2 Bristol Rov 1
1991   (Wembley) Birmingham 3 Tranmere 2

Autoglass Trophy
1992   (Wembley) Stoke 1 Stockport 0
1993   (Wembley) Port Vale 2 Stockport 1
1994   (Wembley) Huddersfield 1 Swansea 1 (aet; Swansea won 3-1 on pens)

Auto Windscreens Shield
1995   (Wembley) Birmingham 1 Carlisle 0 (Birmingham won in sudden-death overtime)
1996   (Wembley) Rotherham 2 Shrewsbury 1
1997   (Wembley) Carlisle 0 Colchester 0 (aet; Carlisle won 4-3 on pens)
1998   (Wembley) Grimsby 2 Bournemouth 1 (Grimsby won with golden goal in extra-time)
1999   (Wembley) Wigan 1 Millwall 0
2000   (Wembley) Stoke 2 Bristol City 1

LDV Vans Trophy
2001   (Millennium Stadium) Port Vale 2 Brentford 1
2002   (Millennium Stadium) Blackpool 4 Cambridge Utd 1
2003   (Millennium Stadium) Bristol City 2 Carlisle 0
2004   (Millennium Stadium) Blackpool 2 Southend 0
2005   (Millennium Stadium) Wrexham 2 Southend 0

Football League Trophy
2006   (Millennium Stadium) Swansea 2 Carlisle 1

Johnstone's Paint Trophy
2007   (Millennium Stadium) Doncaster 3 Bristol Rov 2 (aet)
2008   (Wembley) MK Dons 2 Grimsby 0
2009   (Wembley) Luton 3 Scunthorpe 2 (aet)
2010   (Wembley) Southampton 4 Carlisle 1
2011   (Wembley) Carlisle 1 Brentford 0
2012   (Wembley) Chesterfield 2 Swindon 0

FERGUSON AND GIGGS TOP POLL

Sir Alex Ferguson was voted top manager and Ryan Giggs finest player in a poll to mark 20 years of Premier League football. The poll, among fans, journalists and leading figures in the game, had Manchester United's 4-3 win over Manchester City in 2009 as the best match and Wayne Rooney's acrobatic volley against City in 2011 as top goal. Arsenal's 'invincibles' of the 2003–04 season were the leading team, while Craig Gordon's reflex save from Zat Knight in the 2010 Sunderland-Bolton match received most votes. Fans' fantasy team was: Schmeichel, Gary Neville, Adams, Vidic, Cole, Ronaldo, Scholes, Gerrard, Giggs, Henry, Shearer. The panel's choice had Ferdinand instead of Vidic and Keane in place of Gerrard.

OTHER LEAGUE CLUBS' CUP COMPETITIONS

FINALS – AT WEMBLEY

Full Members' Cup (Discontinued after 1992)

1985–86	Chelsea 5 Manchester City 4
1986–87	Blackburn 1 Charlton 0

Simod Cup

1987–88	Reading 4 Luton 1
1988–89	Nottm Forest 4 Everton 3

Zenith Data Systems Cup

1989–90	Chelsea 1 Middlesbrough 0
1990–91	Crystal Palace 4 Everton 1
1991–92	Nottm Forest 3 Southampton 2

ANGLO-ITALIAN CUP (Discontinued after 1996: * Home club)

1970	*Napoli 0 Swindon 3
1971	*Bologna 1 Blackpool 2 (aet)
1972	*AS Roma 3 Blackpool 1
1973	*Fiorentina 1 Newcastle 2
1993	Derby 1 Cremonese 3 (at Wembley)
1994	Notts Co 0 Brescia 1 (at Wembley)
1995	Ascoli 1 Notts Co 2 (at Wembley)
1996	Port Vale 2 Genoa 5 (at Wembley)

FA VASE FINALS

At Wembley (until 2000 and from 2007)

1975	Hoddesdon 2 Epsom & Ewell 1
1976	Billericay 1 Stamford 0*
1977	Billericay 2 Sheffield 1 (replay Nottingham after a 1-1 draw at Wembley)
1978	Blue Star 2 Barton Rov 1
1979	Billericay 4 Almondsbury Greenway 1
1980	Stamford 2 Guisborough Town 0
1981	Whickham 3 Willenhall 2*
1982	Forest Green 3 Rainworth Miners' Welfare 0
1983	VS Rugby 1 Halesowen 0
1984	Stansted 3 Stamford 2
1985	Halesowen 3 Fleetwood 1
1986	Halesowen 3 Southall 0
1987	St Helens 3 Warrington 2
1988	Colne Dynamoes 1 Emley 0*
1989	Tamworth 3 Sudbury 0 (replay Peterborough after a 1-1 draw at Wembley)
1990	Yeading 1 Bridlington 0 (replay Leeds after 0-0 draw at Wembley)
1991	Guiseley 3 Gresley Rov 1 (replay Bramall Lane Sheffield after a 4-4 draw at Wembley)
1992	Wimborne 5 Guiseley 3
1993	Bridlington 1 Tiverton 0
1994	Diss 2 Taunton 1*
1995	Arlesey 2 Oxford City 1
1996	Brigg Town 3 Clitheroe 0
1997	Whitby Town 3 North Ferriby 0
1998	Tiverton 1 Tow Law 0
1999	Tiverton 1 Bedlington 0
2000	Deal 1 Chippenham 0

2001	Taunton 2 Berkhamsted 1 (Villa Park)
2002	Whitley Bay 1 Tiptree 0* (Villa Park)
2003	Brigg 2 AFC Sudbury 1 (Upton Park)
2004	Winchester 2 AFC Sudbury 0 (St Andrews)
2005	Didcot 3 AFC Sudbury 2 (White Hart Lane)
2006	Nantwich 3 Hillingdon 1 (St Andrews)
2007	Truro 3 AFC Totton 1
2008	Kirkham & Wesham (Fylde) 2 Lowestoft 1
2009	Whitley Bay 2 Glossop 0
2010	Whitley Bay 6 Wroxham1
2011	Whitley Bay 3 Coalville 2
2012	Dunston 2 West Auckland 0

* After extra-time

FA TROPHY FINALS

At Wembley

1970	Macclesfield 2 Telford 0
1971	Telford 3 Hillingdon 2
1972	Stafford 3 Barnet 0
1973	Scarborough 2 Wigan 1*
1974	Morecambe 2 Dartford 1
1975	Matlock 4 Scarborough 0
1976	Scarborough 3 Stafford 2*
1977	Scarborough 2 Dagenham 1
1978	Altrincham 3 Leatherhead 1
1979	Stafford 2 Kettering 0
1980	Dagenham 2 Mossley 1
1981	Bishop's Stortford 1 Sutton 0
1982	Enfield 1 Altrincham 0*
1983	Telford 2 Northwich 1
1984	Northwich 2 Bangor 1 (replay Stoke after a 1-1 draw at Wembley)
1985	Wealdstone 2 Boston 1
1986	Altrincham 1 Runcorn 0
1987	Kidderminster 2 Burton 1 (replay WBA after a 0-0 draw at Wembley)
1988	Enfield 3 Telford 2 (replay WBA after a 0-0 draw at Wembley)
1989	Telford 1 Macclesfield 0*
1990	Barrow 3 Leek 0
1991	Wycombe 2 Kidderminster 1
1992	Colchester 3 Witton 1
1993	Wycombe 4 Runcorn 1
1994	Woking 2 Runcorn 1
1995	Woking 2 Kidderminster 1
1996	Macclesfield 3 Northwich 1
1997	Woking 1 Dagenham & Redbridge 0*
1998	Cheltenham 1 Southport 0
1999	Kingstonian 1 Forest Green 0
2000	Kingstonian 3 Kettering 2

At Villa Park

2001	Canvey 1 Forest Green 0
2002	Yeovil 2 Stevenage 0
2003	Burscough 2 Tamworth 1
2004	Hednesford Town 3 Canvey 2
2005	Grays 1 Hucknall 1* (Grays won 6-5 on pens)

At Upton Park
2006   Grays 2 Woking 0

At Wembley
2007   Stevenage 3 Kidderminster 2
2008   Ebbsfleet 1 Torquay 0
2009   Stevenage 2 York 0
2010   Barrow 2 Stevenage 1*
2011   Darlington 1 Mansfield 0 *
2012   York 2 Newport 0
(*After extra-time)

FA YOUTH CUP WINNERS

Year	Winners	Runners-up	Aggregate
1953	Manchester Utd	Wolves	9-3
1954	Manchester Utd	Wolves	5-4
1955	Manchester Utd	WBA	7-1
1956	Manchester Utd	Chesterfield	4-3
1957	Manchester Utd	West Ham	8-2
1958	Wolves	Chelsea	7-6
1959	Blackburn	West Ham	2-1
1960	Chelsea	Preston	5-2
1961	Chelsea	Everton	5-3
1962	Newcastle	Wolves	2-1
1963	West Ham	Liverpool	6-5
1964	Manchester Utd	Swindon	5-2
1965	Everton	Arsenal	3-2
1966	Arsenal	Sunderland	5-3
1967	Sunderland	Birmingham	2-0
1968	Burnley	Coventry	3-2
1969	Sunderland	WBA	6-3
1970	Tottenham	Coventry	4-3
1971	Arsenal	Cardiff	2-0
1972	Aston Villa	Liverpool	5-2
1973	Ipswich	Bristol City	4-1
1974	Tottenham	Huddersfield	2-1
1975	Ipswich	West Ham	5-1
1976	WBA	Wolves	5-0
1977	Crystal Palace	Everton	1-0
1978	Crystal Palace	Aston Villa	*1-0
1979	Millwall	Manchester City	2-0
1980	Aston Villa	Manchester City	3-2
1981	West Ham	Tottenham	2-1
1982	Watford	Manchester Utd	7-6
1983	Norwich	Everton	6-5
1984	Everton	Stoke	4-2
1985	Newcastle	Watford	4-1
1986	Manchester City	Manchester Utd	3-1
1987	Coventry	Charlton	2-1
1988	Arsenal	Doncaster	6-1
1989	Watford	Manchester City	2-1
1990	Tottenham	Middlesbrough	3-2
1991	Millwall	Sheffield Wed	3-0
1992	Manchester Utd	Crystal Palace	6-3
1993	Leeds	Manchester Utd	4-1
1994	Arsenal	Millwall	5-3

1995	Manchester Utd	Tottenham	†2-2
1996	Liverpool	West Ham	4-1
1997	Leeds	Crystal Palace	3-1
1998	Everton	Blackburn	5-3
1999	West Ham	Coventry	9-0
2000	Arsenal	Coventry	5-1
2001	Arsenal	Blackburn	6-3
2002	Aston Villa	Everton	4-2
2003	Manchester Utd	Middlesbrough	3-1
2004	Middlesbrough	Aston Villa	4-0
2005	Ipswich	Southampton	3-2
2006	Liverpool	Manchester City	3-2
2007	Liverpool	Manchester Utd	††2-2
2008	Manchester City	Chelsea	4-2
2009	Arsenal	Liverpool	6-2
2010	Chelsea	Aston Villa	3-2
2011	Manchester Utd	Sheffield Utd	6-3
2012	Chelsea	Blackburn	4-1

(*One match only; † Manchester Utd won 4-3 on pens, †† Liverpool won 4-3 on pens)

WELSH CUP FINAL

Cefn Druids 0 New Saints 2 (Draper 14, Darlington 15) – Bangor. Att: 731

FA VASE FINAL

West Auckland 0 Dunston 2 (Bulford 32, 79) – Wembley. Att: 5,126

FA WOMEN'S CUP FINAL

Birmingham 2 (Williams 90, Carney 112) Chelsea 2 (Lander 69, Longhurst 101) – aet, Birmingham won 3-2 on pens. Ashton Gate, Bristol. Att: 8,723

FA SUNDAY CUP FINAL

Hetton Lyons 5 (Byrne 4, 19, Moore 52, Capper 60, Craggs 90) Canada FC (Liverpool) 1 (Fargan 70) – Stadium of Light, Sunderland

FA COMMUNITY SHIELD

CHARITY/COMMUNITY SHIELD RESULTS (POST WAR)

[CHARITY SHIELD]

Year	Winners	Runners-up	Score
1948	Arsenal	Manchester Utd	4-3
1949	Portsmouth	Wolves	*1-1
1950	England World Cup XI	FA Canadian Tour Team	4-2
1951	Tottenham	Newcastle	2-1
1952	Manchester Utd	Newcastle	4-2
1953	Arsenal	Blackpool	3-1
1954	Wolves	WBA	*4-4
1955	Chelsea	Newcastle	3-0
1956	Manchester Utd	Manchester City	1-0
1957	Manchester Utd	Aston Villa	4-0

1958	Bolton	Wolves	4-1
1959	Wolves	Nottm Forest	3-1
1960	Burnley	Wolves	*2-2
1961	Tottenham	FA XI	3-2
1962	Tottenham	Ipswich Town	5-1
1963	Everton	Manchester Utd	4-0
1964	Liverpool	West Ham	*2-2
1965	Manchester Utd	Liverpool	*2-2
1966	Liverpool	Everton	1-0
1967	Manchester Utd	Tottenham	*3-3
1968	Manchester City	WBA	6-1
1969	Leeds	Manchester City	2-1
1970	Everton	Chelsea	2-1
1971	Leicester	Liverpool	1-0
1972	Manchester City	Aston Villa	1-0
1973	Burnley	Manchester City	1-0
1974	Liverpool	Leeds	1-1
	(Liverpool won 6-5 on penalties)		
1975	Derby Co	West Ham	2-0
1976	Liverpool	Southampton	1-0
1977	Liverpool	Manchester Utd	*0-0
1978	Nottm Forest	Ipswich	5-0
1979	Liverpool	Arsenal	3-1
1980	Liverpool	West Ham	1-0
1981	Aston Villa	Tottenham	*2-2
1982	Liverpool	Tottenham	1-0
1983	Manchester Utd	Liverpool	2-0
1984	Everton	Liverpool	1-0
1985	Everton	Manchester Utd	2-0
1986	Everton	Liverpool	*1-1
1987	Everton	Coventry	1-0
1988	Liverpool	Wimbledon	2-1
1989	Liverpool	Arsenal	1-0
1990	Liverpool	Manchester Utd	*1-1
1991	Arsenal	Tottenham	*0-0
1992	Leeds	Liverpool	4-3
1993	Manchester Utd	Arsenal	1-1
	(Manchester Utd won 5-4 on penalties)		
1994	Manchester Utd	Blackburn	2-0
1995	Everton	Blackburn	1-0
1996	Manchester Utd	Newcastle	4-0
1997	Manchester Utd	Chelsea	1-1
	(Manchester Utd won 4-2 on penalties)		
1998	Arsenal	Manchester Utd	3-0
1999	Arsenal	Manchester Utd	2-1
2000	Chelsea	Manchester Utd	2-0
2001	Liverpool	Manchester Utd	2-1

COMMUNITY SHIELD

Year	Winners	Runners-up	Score
2002	Arsenal	Liverpool	1-0
2003	Manchester Utd	Arsenal	1-1
	(Manchester Utd won 4-3 on penalties)		
2004	Arsenal	Manchester Utd	3-1
2005	Chelsea	Arsenal	2-1

2006	Liverpool	Chelsea	2-1
2007	Manchester Utd	Chelsea	1-1
	(Manchester Utd won 3-0 on penalties)		
2008	Manchester Utd	Portsmouth	0-0
	(Manchester Utd won 3-1 on pens)		
2009	Chelsea	Manchester Utd	2-2
	(Chelsea won 4-1 on pens)		
2010	Manchester Utd	Chelsea	3-1
2011	Manchester Utd	Manchester City	3-2

(Fixture played at Wembley 1974–2000 and from 2007). Millennium Stadium 2001–2006)
*Trophy shared

QUOTE/UNQOUTE

'The defeat is painful. I feel humiliated. But quitting has never entered my mind. How much of the blame is mine? As much as you want it to be. The time for working that out is at the end of the season' – **Arsene Wenger**, Arsenal manager, after the 8-2 defeat by Manchester United.

'I play football for money. You musn't undersell yourself because you like the club. True relationships don't exist. It's not about friendship or camaraderie' – **Benoit Assou-Ekotto**, Tottenham defender, in a frank assessment of why he plays the game.

'I told him I preferred him as a player rather than a writer' – **Fabio Capello**, former England manager, on criticism from Arsenal winger Theo Walcott in his book.

'You would not believe the chasm that's left when the Premier League goes away. The excitement, the tension, even looking forward to the games. That's not there any more' – **Ian Holloway**, Blackpool manager, on relegation.

'No disrespect to Abu Dhabi, or wherever he's gone, but I find it baffling that he can leave the biggest stage in the world' – **Steve Bruce**, former Sunderland manager, blaming 'parasites' for turning the head of record-signing Asamoah Gyan.

'Loads of footballers are taking it. They've got lots of money and it brings the girls in, so they do it' – **Leon Knight**, former Chelsea, Brighton and Swansea striker, interviewed on a Channel Four programme about players' cocaine use.

'He told us we played in the Premier League against Manchester City and we should remember that. Then he told us we'd lost to Shrewsbury in the Carling Cup and we should make sure we told our grandchildren about that too' – **Leon Britton**, Swansea midfielder, on the psychology of manager Brendan Rodgers.

SCOTTISH TABLES 2011–2012

CLYDESDALE BANK PREMIER LEAGUE

			Home				Away						
		P	W	D	L	F	A	W	D	L	F	A	GD	PTS
1	Celtic	38	17	1	1	41	6	13	2	4	43	15	63	93
2	Rangers*	38	12	5	2	38	14	14	0	5	39	14	49	73
3	Motherwell	38	9	3	7	27	24	9	5	5	22	20	5	62
4	Dundee Utd	38	8	6	5	27	16	8	5	6	35	34	12	59
5	Hearts	38	11	0	8	30	19	4	7	8	15	24	2	52
6	St Johnstone	38	6	2	10	20	30	8	6	6	23	20	-7	50
7	Kilmarnock	38	7	6	6	29	35	4	7	7	15	26	-17	47
8	St Mirren	38	6	4	7	23	25	3	10	6	16	26	-12	43
9	Aberdeen	38	6	8	5	22	16	3	6	10	14	28	-8	41
10	Inverness	38	5	5	9	19	27	5	4	10	23	33	-18	39
11	Hibernian	38	2	7	10	17	30	6	2	11	23	37	-27	33
12	Dunfermline	38	1	7	11	22	44	4	3	12	18	38	-42	25

League split after 33 matches with teams staying in top six and bottom six regardless of points won

*Rangers deducted ten points for going into administration

League split after 33 matches with teams staying in top six and bottom six regardless of points won. Celtic and Motherwell go into Champions League third qualifying round; Hearts (qualifying play-off), Dundee Utd (third qualifying round) and St Johnstone (second qualifying round) into Europa League

Leading scorers (all competitions): 29 Hooper (Celtic); 22 Daly (Dundee Utd); 21 Stokes (Celtic); 18 Skacel (Hearts); 17 Jelavic (Rangers), Sandaza (St Johnstone); 16 Higdon (Motherwell), O'Connor (Hibernian), Thompson (St Mirren); 15 Heffernan (Kilmarnock), Russell (Dundee Utd), Shiels (Kilmarnock); 13 Murphy (Motherwell), Vernon (Aberdeen)

Manager of Year: Neil Lennon (Celtic). **Player of Year**: Charlie Mulgrew (Celtic)

IRN-BRU FIRST DIVISION

			Home				Away						
		P	W	D	L	F	A	W	D	L	F	A	GD	PTS
1	Ross	36	11	7	0	40	14	11	6	1	32	18	40	79
2	Dundee	36	7	5	6	25	20	8	5	5	28	23	10	55
3	Falkirk	36	9	6	3	29	21	4	7	7	24	27	5	52
4	Hamilton	36	8	3	7	33	30	6	4	8	22	26	-1	49
5	Livingston	36	5	6	7	26	29	8	3	7	30	25	2	48
6	Partick	36	7	6	5	27	16	5	5	8	23	23	11	47
7	Raith	36	7	4	7	24	21	4	7	7	22	28	-3	44
8	Morton*	36	5	5	8	24	29	5	7	6	16	26	-15	42
9	Ayr*	36	5	7	6	22	25	4	4	10	22	42	-23	38
10	Queen of South	36	6	5	7	21	31	1	6	11	17	33	-26	32

*Also relegated

Play-offs (on agg) – Semi-finals: Airdrie 3 Ayr 1; Dumbarton 2 Arbroath 1. Final: Dumbarton 6 Airdrie 2

Leading scorers (all competitions): 27 El Alagui (Falkirk); 20 McMenamin (Ross); 18 Gardyne (Ross); 16 McNulty (Livingston); 15 Cairney (Partick), MacDonald (Morton), Milne (Dundee);13 Baird (Raith), Boulding (Livingston), Doohlan (Partick)

Manager of Year: Derek Adams (Ross). **Player of Year**: Colin McMenamin (Ross)

IRN-BRU SECOND DIVISION

			Home					Away						
		P	W	D	L	F	A	W	D	L	F	A	GD	PTS
1	Cowdenbeath	36	13	4	1	37	10	7	7	4	31	19	39	71
2	Arbroath	36	10	5	3	44	23	7	7	4	32	28	25	63
3	Dumbarton*	36	10	2	6	30	30	7	5	6	31	31	0	58
4	Airdrie	36	9	4	5	43	30	5	6	7	25	30	8	52
5	Stenhousemuir	36	9	2	7	32	23	6	4	8	22	26	5	51
6	East Fife	36	7	4	7	27	29	7	2	9	28	28	-2	48
7	Forfar	36	6	5	7	33	34	5	4	9	26	38	-13	42
8	Brechin	36	5	6	7	24	30	5	5	8	23	32	-15	41
9	Albion	36	6	6	6	25	22	4	1	13	18	44	-23	37
10	Stirling	36	4	5	9	22	29	5	2	11	24	41	-24	34

*Also promoted
Play-offs (on agg) – **Semi-finals**: Albion 2 Elgin 1; Stranraer 5 Queen's Park 1. **Final**: Albion 3 Stranraer 3 (aet, Albion won 5-3 on pens)
Leading scorers (all competitions): 27 Donnelly (Airdrie); 26 Wallace (East Fife); 21 Doris (Arbroath); 19 Templeman (Forfar); 18 McKenzie (Cowdenbeath); 17 McManus (Brechin), Prunty (Dumbarton), Rodgers (Stenhousemuir); 15 Coult (Cowdenbeath); 13 Agnew (Dumbarton)
Manager of Year: Colin Cameron (Cowdenbeath). **Player of Year**: Ryan Donnelly (Airdrie)

IRN-BRU THIRD DIVISION

			Home					Away						
		P	W	D	L	F	A	W	D	L	F	A	GD	PTS
1	Alloa	36	13	4	1	43	13	10	4	4	27	26	31	77
2	Queen's Park	36	10	4	4	41	17	9	2	7	29	31	22	63
3	Stranraer	36	10	2	6	43	33	7	5	6	34	24	20	58
4	Elgin	36	11	3	4	43	17	5	6	7	25	43	8	57
5	Peterhead	36	7	5	6	25	23	8	1	9	26	30	-2	51
6	Annan	36	7	5	6	28	26	6	5	7	25	27	0	49
7	Berwick	36	6	5	7	30	28	6	7	5	31	30	3	48
8	Montrose	36	7	3	8	34	33	4	2	12	24	42	-17	38
9	Clyde	36	5	5	8	24	23	3	6	9	11	27	-15	35
10	East Stirling	36	5	4	9	24	33	1	2	15	14	55	-50	24

Leading scorers (all competitions): 23 McAllister (Peterhead); 22 Boyle (Montrose); 21 Gunn (Elgin), Longworth (Queen's Park); 19 May (Alloa); 18 Malcolm (Stranraer); 13 Moore (Stranraer)
Manager of Year: Paul Hartley (Alloa). **Player of Year**: Stevie May (Alloa)

SCOTTISH LEAGUE RESULTS 2011–2012

CLYDESDALE BANK PREMIER LEAGUE

	Aberdeen	Celtic	Dundee Utd	Dunfermline	Hearts	Hibernian	Inverness	Kilmarnock	Motherwell	Rangers	St Johnstone	St Mirren
Aberdeen	–	0-1	3-1	4-0	0-0	1-0	2-1	2-2	1-2	1-2	0-0	2-2
	–	1-1	3-1	1-0	–	1-2	0-1	0-0	–		0-0	0-0
Celtic	2-1	–	5-1	2-1	1-0	0-0	2-0	2-1	4-0	1-0	0-1	5-0
		–	2-1	2-0	5-0	–	1-0	–	1-0	3-0	2-0	
										1-0	1-0	
Dundee Utd	1-2	0-1	–	0-1	1-0	3-1	3-1	1-1	1-3	0-1	0-0	1-1
		1-0	–	3-0	2-2	–	3-0	4-0	1-1	2-1		0-0
Dunfermline	3-3	0-3	1-4	–	0-2	2-2	3-3	1-1	2-4	0-4	0-3	0-0
	3-0			–	1-2	2-3	1-1	1-2	0-2	1-4		1-1
Hearts	3-0	2-0	0-1	4-0	–	2-0	2-1	0-1	2-0	0-2	1-2	2-0
	3-0	0-4	0-2		–	2-0			0-1	0-3	2-0	5-2
Hibernian	0-0	0-2	3-3	0-1	1-3	–	1-1	1-1	0-1	0-2	3-2	1-2
	0-0	0-5	0-2	4-0	–		0-1	1-1	–	2-3		0-0
Inverness	2-1	0-2	2-3	1-1	1-1	0-1	–	2-1	2-3	0-2	0-1	2-1
	0-2			0-0	1-0	2-3	–	1-1		1-4		0-0
	–				2-0							
Kilmarnock	2-0	3-3	1-1	3-2	0-0	4-1	3-6	–	0-0	1-0	1-2	2-1
	1-1	0-6		0-3	1-1	1-3	4-3	–	2-0		0-0	0-2
Motherwell	1-0	1-2	0-0	3-1	1-0	4-3	0-0		–	0-3	0-3	1-1
	1-0	0-3	0-2	3-0			0-1		–	1-2	3-2	
									–		5-1	
Rangers	2-0	4-2	3-1	2-1	1-1	1-0	2-1	2-0	3-0	–	0-0	1-1
	1-1	3-2	5-0		1-2	4-0		0-1	0-0	–		3-1
St Johnstone	1-2	0-2	3-3	0-1	2-0	3-1	2-0	2-0	0-3	0-2	–	0-1
			1-5	3-1	2-1		0-0			1-2	–	
			0-2							0-4	–	
St Mirren	1-0	0-2	2-2	2-1	0-0	2-3	1-2	3-0	0-1	2-1	0-0	–
	1-1	0-2		4-4		1-0	0-1	4-2	0-0		0-3	–

IRN-BRU FIRST DIVISION

	Ayr	Dundee	Falkirk	Hamilton	Livingston	Morton	Partick	Queen of Sth	Raith	Ross
Ayr	–	1-3	2-2	1-2	0-0	0-1	0-0	1-0	2-1	2-3
	–	3-2	1-0	2-2	3-1	0-0	1-3	1-1	1-1	1-3
Dundee	1-1	–	4-2	0-1	3-0	0-1	0-1	2-1	1-0	1-2
	4-1	–	3-1	2-2	1-0	0-1	0-3	1-1	1-1	1-1
Falkirk	0-0	2-1	–	0-0	4-3	1-0	2-1	1-0	2-0	1-1
	3-2	1-1	–	3-0	2-5	0-2	1-1	3-0	2-3	1-1
Hamilton	2-3	1-6	0-1	–	1-1	1-2	1-0	3-1	2-2	5-1
	3-2	3-1	0-1	–	0-1	4-3	2-2	3-0	2-1	0-2
Livingston	1-2	4-2	1-1	1-0	–	1-1	2-1	2-2	1-1	0-3
	0-1	2-3	1-2	0-4	–	0-0	3-1	2-2	4-0	1-3
Morton	4-1	1-2	3-2	0-2	2-1	–	1-2	2-2	1-1	0-2
	3-1	0-2	0-0	1-2	1-3	–	1-0	2-2	1-3	1-1
Partick	4-0	0-1	2-2	1-1	2-1	5-0	–	2-1	0-1	0-1
	4-2	0-0	1-1	2-0	2-3	0-0	–	1-0	1-1	0-1
Queen of Sth	4-1	0-0	1-5	1-0	0-2	4-1	0-0	–	1-3	0-0
	2-1	1-1	0-0	1-2	0-4	2-1	0-5	–	1-0	3-5
Raith	0-1	0-1	1-0	3-2	0-1	1-1	2-0	0-2	–	0-1
	2-2	0-1	2-2	2-1	0-3	5-0	2-1	3-1	–	1-1
Ross	4-0	1-1	3-1	1-0	1-1	0-0	2-2	2-0	4-2	–
	1-1	3-0	2-1	5-1	3-0	2-2	3-0	2-1	1-1	–

IRN-BRU SECOND DIVISION

	Airdree	Albion	Arbroath	Brechin	Cowdenbeath	Dumbarton	East Fife	Forfar	Stenhousemuir	Stirling
Airdree	–	4-0	3-3	2-3	1-5	3-0	1-3	4-4	5-2	1-1
	–	1-0	2-0	4-1	1-1	2-3	2-0	3-0	0-3	4-1
Albion	7-2	–	1-0	1-2	3-3	3-1	0-3	1-0	1-1	0-1
	0-1	–	1-1	0-1	1-0	1-1	1-1	2-2	1-0	1-2
Arbroath	3-1	6-2	–	1-1	1-1	4-3	3-0	4-1	1-0	4-2
	2-2	6-1	–	2-3	1-1	2-0	2-2	0-1	0-2	2-0
Brechin	1-1	1-4	2-3	–	1-0	3-3	0-2	0-1	2-0	1-3
	1-1	2-1	1-1	–	2-2	2-2	1-3	2-1	1-0	1-2
Cowdenbeath	2-0	2-1	0-0	3-1	–	0-0	3-2	3-1	2-0	2-0
	0-0	3-0	2-3	1-0	–	4-1	4-0	2-0	0-0	4-1
Dumbarton	1-1	2-1	3-4	1-0	0-4	–	3-0	1-1	3-0	1-5
	2-1	1-0	3-2	4-2	0-2	–	0-4	1-0	0-2	4-1
East Fife	2-0	2-0	2-2	1-1	1-3	0-6	–	4-3	1-3	1-0
	2-0	1-2	1-3	2-2	0-1	1-2	–	4-0	1-1	1-0
Forfar	3-2	0-2	1-1	0-0	2-2	0-2	3-2	–	2-3	2-2
	2-3	4-0	2-4	4-1	1-0	1-1	1-4	–	1-2	4-3
Stenhousemuir	1-1	3-0	2-0	1-1	3-1	3-1	2-1	2-3	–	4-0
	0-3	1-2	1-3	2-1	0-2	1-2	1-0	1-2	–	4-0
Stirling	1-4	2-2	0-1	1-0	1-1	0-1	1-0	2-4	2-2	–
	0-2	3-0	1-1	2-3	0-2	1-2	0-1	2-2	3-1	–

IRN-BRU THIRD DIVISION

	Alloa	Annan	Berwick	Clyde	East Stirling	Elgin	Montrose	Peterhead	Queen's Park	Stranraer
Alloa	–	1-0	1-1	2-2	1-1	3-0	4-2	2-1	1-0	1-0
	–	1-1	0-1	1-0	5-1	8-1	2-0	3-1	4-0	3-1
Annan	2-0	–	2-2	1-0	3-0	1-1	2-1	2-0	5-2	0-3
	1-2	–	1-1	1-0	2-2	1-1	1-2	0-3	2-3	1-3
Berwick	2-2	0-1	–	0-2	4-2	1-1	1-2	2-1	2-0	2-2
	5-0	1-3	–	3-0	0-2	3-3	2-2	0-1	1-4	1-0
Clyde	0-1	0-0	1-4	–	7-1	1-2	1-0	2-0	0-2	1-1
	1-1	1-1	2-2	–	3-0	0-2	1-2	0-1	1-2	2-1
East Stirling	0-1	1-0	1-3	1-1	–	1-1	1-0	0-2	1-3	1-3
	1-3	0-4	2-1	0-1	–	2-2	3-1	6-3	1-2	2-2
Elgin	5-0	3-0	4-1	0-3	2-0	–	3-1	6-1	2-0	1-1
	3-0	1-2	4-0	1-1	3-1	–	2-1	1-2	1-1	1-2
Montrose	1-1	2-3	3-5	4-0	2-1	3-0	–	2-1	0-1	0-6
	0-2	1-1	1-1	5-0	3-1	2-3	–	1-3	3-1	1-3
Peterhead	1-1	2-3	1-0	0-0	1-0	1-3	2-3	–	1-1	1-3
	0-1	3-2	1-2	1-1	2-0	3-0	2-1	–	2-1	1-1
Queen's Park	1-3	0-0	1-1	3-0	2-0	6-0	3-1	1-1	–	2-0
	1-2	2-0	2-2	3-0	5-1	1-3	5-0	0-1	–	3-2
Stranraer	2-3	4-2	2-1	0-0	6-0	1-0	4-4	2-1	2-3	–
	0-4	4-2	1-3	1-0	4-1	5-2	3-1	0-3	2-3	–

HOW CELTIC REGAINED THE TITLE

JULY 2011

24   Hibernian 0 Celtic 2 (Stokes 14, Ki 63). Att: 12,523

AUGUST 2011

7   Aberdeen 0 Celtic 1 (Stokes 74). Att: 12,497
13   Celtic 5 (Stokes 4, Hooper 33, Ki 58, Ledley 71, Forrest 90) Dundee Utd 1 (Russell 31). Att: 50,589
21   Celtic 0 St Johnstone 1 (MacKay 60). Att: 52,067
28   St Mirren 0 Celtic 2 (Hooper 6, 12). Att: 6,223

SEPTEMBER 2011

10   Celtic 4 (Forrest 9, 74, Ledley 33, Ki 67) Motherwell 0. Att: 48,793
18   Rangers 4 (Naismith 23, 90, Jelavic 55, Lafferty 67) Celtic 2 (Hooper 34, El Kaddouri 41)). Att: 50,221
24   Celtic 2 (Ledley 28, Forest 33) Inverness 0. Att: 47,382

OCTOBER 2011

2   Hearts 2 (Skacel 58, Stevenson 81) Celtic 0. Att: 14,749
15   Kilmarnock 3 (Shiels 26, Heffernan 40, Fowler 45) Celtic 3 (Stokes 73, 76, Mulgrew 80). Att: 8,011
23   Celtic 2 (Ki 17, Mulgrew 72) Aberdeen 1 (Jack 59). Att: 49,037
29   Celtic 0 Hibernian 0. Att: 48,670

NOVEMBER 2011

6   Motherwell 1 (Higdon 11) Celtic 2 (Stokes 14, Hooper 80). Att: 10,440
19   Inverness 0 Celtic 2 (Stokes 61, 72). Att: 6,435
23   Celtic 2 (Hooper 6, Forrest 13) Dunfermline 1 (Barrowman 86). Att: 41,000
26   Celtic 5 (Samaras 4, Hooper 8, 53, 57, McGeouch 72) St Mirren 0. Att: 48,406

DECEMBER 2011

4   Dundee Utd 0 Celtic 1 (Hooper 12). Att: 10,980
10   Celtic 1 (Wanyama 72) Hearts 0. Att: 49,023
18   St Johnstone 0 Celtic 2 (Hooper 60, Ki 64). Att: 6,759
24   Celtic 2 (Samaras 45, 53) Kilmarnock 1 (Racchi 87). Att: 49,352
28   Celtic 1 (Ledley 52) Rangers 0. Att: 58,658

JANUARY 2012

2   Dunfermline 0 Celtic 3 (Stokes 18, Wanyama 40, Mulgrew 69). Att: 10,140
14   Celtic 2 (Hooper 12, Wanyama 17) Dundee Utd 1 (Rankin 50). Att: 50,139
21   St Mirren 0 Celtic 2 (Forrest 71, Brown 88). Att: 6,129

FEBRUARY 2012

8   Hearts 0 Celtic 4 (Brown 3, Wanyama 20, Ledley 31, Hooper 60). Att: 14,787
11   Celtic 1 (Ledley 16) Inverness 0. Att: 50,014
19   Hibernian 0 Celtic 5 (Stokes 14, Hooper 20, 52, Mulgrew 47, Ki 77). Att: 12,161
22   Celtic 2 (Mulgrew 32, Forrest 75) Dunfermline 0. Att: 45,000
25   Celtic 1 (Hooper 59) Motherwell 0. Att: 53,486

MARCH 2012

3	Aberdeen 1 (Blackman 44 og) Celtic 1 (Stokes 28). Att: 13,127
25	Rangers 3 (Aluko 11, Little 72, Wallace 77) Celtic 2 (Brown 89 pen, Rogne 90). Att: 50,191

APRIL 2012

1	Celtic 2 (Samaras 66, Millar 70 og) St Johnstone 0. Att: 57,848
7	Kilmarnock 0 Celtic 6 (Mulgrew 8, 35, Loovens 17, Hooper 45, 90, Ledley 88). Att: 15,926 (clinched title)
22	Motherwell 0 Celtic 3 (Watt 63, 66, Cha 83). Att: 8,760
29	Celtic 3 (Mulgrew 17, Commons 31, Hooper 54) Rangers 0. Att: 58,546

MAY 2012

3	Celtic 1 (Stokes 28) St Johnstone 0. Att: 50,297
6	Dundee Utd 1 (Robertson 21) Celtic 0. Att: 9,144
13	Celtic 5 (Hooper 5, 8, 39 pen, 66, 87) Hearts 0. Att: 58,875

QUOTE/UNQOUTE

'Football is a short-lived thing and it can change, literally, from day to day' – **John Ryan**, Doncaster chairman, on sacking manager Sean O'Driscoll three days after giving him a vote of confidence.

'I've said a thousand times before, I'm not here to pick my nose' – **Anders Lindegaard**, Manchester United goalkeeper, refusing to settle for the No 2 spot at Old Trafford

'We lose a game where we score five times and that's quite disappointing' – **Arsene Wenger**, Arsenal manager, on a 4-3 defeat at Blackburn, where his side concede two own goals.

'The only gambling I do is on a Saturday afternoon when I might put on two wingers or two strikers' – **Alan Pardew**, Newcastle manager, denying he spends to much time in casinos.

It's football pressure – not the pressure of a dad with five kids who has to work to feed his family' – **Owen Coyle**, Bolton manager, on coping with the threat of relegation.

'He has had to put up with more in a short period of time than most managers have to put up with in a whole career. But ultimately, whatever the challenges, football is a results business' – **Peter Ridsdale**, acting chairman of crisis-club Plymouth, on the sacking of manager Peter Reid with his side bottom of League Two.

'It's the worst result in my history. I can't believe the scoreline' – **Sir Alex Ferguson**, Manchester United manager, after the 6-1 home defeat by Manchester City.

SCOTTISH HONOURS LIST

PREMIER DIVISION

	First	Pts	Second	Pts	Third	Pts
1975–6	Rangers	54	Celtic	48	Hibernian	43
1976–7	Celtic	55	Rangers	46	Aberdeen	43
1977–8	Rangers	55	Aberdeen	53	Dundee Utd	40
1978–9	Celtic	48	Rangers	45	Dundee Utd	44
1979–80	Aberdeen	48	Celtic	47	St Mirren	42
1980–81	Celtic	56	Aberdeen	49	Rangers	44
1981–2	Celtic	55	Aberdeen	53	Rangers	43
1982–3	Dundee Utd	56	Celtic	55	Aberdeen	55
1983–4	Aberdeen	57	Celtic	50	Dundee Utd	47
1984–5	Aberdeen	59	Celtic	52	Dundee Utd	47
1985–6	*Celtic	50	Hearts	50	Dundee Utd	47
1986–7	Rangers	69	Celtic	63	Dundee Utd	60
1987–8	Celtic	72	Hearts	62	Rangers	60
1988–9	Rangers	56	Aberdeen	50	Celtic	46
1989–90	Rangers	51	Aberdeen	44	Hearts	44
1990–1	Rangers	55	Aberdeen	53	Celtic	41
1991–2	Rangers	72	Hearts	63	Celtic	62
1992–3	Rangers	73	Aberdeen	64	Celtic	60
1993–4	Rangers	58	Aberdeen	55	Motherwell	54
1994–5	Rangers	69	Motherwell	54	Hibernian	53
1995–6	Rangers	87	Celtic	83	Aberdeen	55
1996–7	Rangers	80	Celtic	75	Dundee Utd	60
1997–8	Celtic	74	Rangers	72	Hearts	67

PREMIER LEAGUE

	First	Pts	Second	Pts	Third	Pts
1998–99	Rangers	77	Celtic	71	St Johnstone	57
1999–2000	Rangers	90	Celtic	69	Hearts	54
2000–01	Celtic	97	Rangers	82	Hibernian	66
2001–02	Celtic	103	Rangers	85	Livingston	58
2002–03	*Rangers	97	Celtic	97	Hearts	63
2003–04	Celtic	98	Rangers	81	Hearts	68
2004–05	Rangers	93	Celtic	92	Hibernian	61
2005–06	Celtic	91	Hearts	74	Rangers	73
2006–07	Celtic	84	Rangers	72	Aberdeen	65
2007-08	Celtic	89	Rangers	86	Motherwell	60
2008-09	Rangers	86	Celtic	82	Hearts	59
2009–10	Rangers	87	Celtic	81	Dundee Utd	63
2010–11	Rangers	93	Celtic	92	Hearts	63
2011–12	Celtic	93	**Rangers	73	Motherwell	62

Maximum points: 72 except 1986–8, 1991–4 (88), 1994–2000 (108), 2001–10 (114)
* Won on goal difference. **Deducted 10 pts for administration

FIRST DIVISION (Scottish Championship until 1975–76)

	First	Pts	Second	Pts	Third	Pts
1890–1a	††Dumbarton	29	Rangers	29	Celtic	24
1891–2b	Dumbarton	37	Celtic	35	Hearts	30
1892–3a	Celtic	29	Rangers	28	St Mirren	23
1893–4a	Celtic	29	Hearts	26	St Bernard's	22
1894–5a	Hearts	31	Celtic	26	Rangers	21
1895–6a	Celtic	30	Rangers	26	Hibernian	24
1896–7a	Hearts	28	Hibernian	26	Rangers	25
1897–8a	Celtic	33	Rangers	29	Hibernian	22
1898–9a	Rangers	36	Hearts	26	Celtic	24

Season	Team	Pts	Team	Pts	Team	Pts
1899–1900a	Rangers	32	Celtic	25	Hibernian	24
1900–1c	Rangers	35	Celtic	29	Hibernian	25
1901–2a	Rangers	28	Celtic	26	Hearts	22
1902–3b	Hibernian	37	Dundee	31	Rangers	29
1903–4d	Third Lanark	43	Hearts	39	Rangers	38
1904–5a	†Celtic	41	Rangers	41	Third Lanark	35
1905–6a	Celtic	46	Hearts	39	Rangers	38
1906–7f	Celtic	55	Dundee	48	Rangers	45
1907–8f	Celtic	55	Falkirk	51	Rangers	50
1908–9f	Celtic	51	Dundee	50	Clyde	48
1909–10f	Celtic	54	Falkirk	52	Rangers	49
1910–11f	Rangers	52	Aberdeen	48	Falkirk	44
1911–12f	Rangers	51	Celtic	45	Clyde	42
1912–13f	Rangers	53	Celtic	49	Hearts	41
1913–14g	Celtic	65	Rangers	59	Hearts	54
1914–15g	Celtic	65	Hearts	61	Rangers	50
1915–16g	Celtic	67	Rangers	56	Morton	51
1916–17g	Celtic	64	Morton	54	Rangers	53
1917–18f	Rangers	56	Celtic	55	Kilmarnock	43
1918–19f	Celtic	58	Rangers	57	Morton	47
1919–20h	Rangers	71	Celtic	68	Motherwell	57
1920–1h	Rangers	76	Celtic	66	Hearts	56
1921–2h	Celtic	67	Rangers	66	Raith	56
1922–3g	Rangers	55	Airdrieonians	50	Celtic	40
1923–4g	Rangers	59	Airdrieonians	50	Celtic	41
1924–5g	Rangers	60	Airdrieonians	57	Hibernian	52
1925–6g	Celtic	58	Airdrieonians	50	Hearts	50
1926–7g	Rangers	56	Motherwell	51	Celtic	49
1927–8g	Rangers	60	Celtic	55	Motherwell	55
1928–9g	Rangers	67	Celtic	51	Motherwell	50
1929–30g	Rangers	60	Motherwell	55	Aberdeen	53
1930–1g	Rangers	60	Celtic	58	Motherwell	56
1931–2g	Motherwell	66	Rangers	61	Celtic	48
1932–3g	Rangers	62	Motherwell	59	Hearts	50
1933–4g	Rangers	66	Motherwell	62	Celtic	47
1934–5g	Rangers	55	Celtic	52	Hearts	50
1935–6g	Celtic	68	Rangers	61	Aberdeen	61
1936–7g	Rangers	61	Aberdeen	54	Celtic	52
1937–8g	Celtic	61	Hearts	58	Rangers	49
1938–9f	Rangers	59	Celtic	48	Aberdeen	46
1946–7f	Rangers	46	Hibernian	44	Aberdeen	39
1947–8g	Hibernian	48	Rangers	46	Partick	46
1948–9i	Rangers	46	Dundee	45	Hibernian	39
1949–50i	Rangers	50	Hibernian	49	Hearts	43
1950–1i	Hibernian	48	Rangers	38	Dundee	38
1951–2i	Hibernian	45	Rangers	41	East Fife	37
1952–3i	*Rangers	43	Hibernian	43	East Fife	39
1953–4i	Celtic	43	Hearts	38	Partick	35
1954–5f	Aberdeen	49	Celtic	46	Rangers	41
1955–6f	Rangers	52	Aberdeen	46	Hearts	45
1956–7f	Rangers	55	Hearts	53	Kilmarnock	42
1957–8f	Hearts	62	Rangers	49	Celtic	46
1958–9f	Rangers	50	Hearts	48	Motherwell	44
1959–60f	Hearts	54	Kilmarnock	50	Rangers	42
1960–1f	Rangers	51	Kilmarnock	50	Third Lanark	42
1961–2f	Dundee	54	Rangers	51	Celtic	46
1962–3f	Rangers	57	Kilmarnock	48	Partick	46
1963–4f	Rangers	55	Kilmarnock	49	Celtic	47
1964–5f	*Kilmarnock	50	Hearts	50	Dunfermline	49

183

1965–6f	Celtic	57	Rangers	55	Kilmarnock	45
1966–7f	Celtic	58	Rangers	55	Clyde	46
1967–8f	Celtic	63	Rangers	61	Hibernian	45
1968–9f	Celtic	54	Rangers	49	Dunfermline	45
1969–70f	Celtic	57	Rangers	45	Hibernian	44
1970–1f	Celtic	56	Aberdeen	54	St Johnstone	44
1971–2f	Celtic	60	Aberdeen	50	Rangers	44
1972–3f	Celtic	57	Rangers	56	Hibernian	45
1973–4f	Celtic	53	Hibernian	49	Rangers	48
1974–5f	Rangers	56	Hibernian	49	Celtic	45

*Won on goal average †Won .... on deciding match ††Title shared. Competition suspended 1940–46 (Second World War)

SCOTTISH CHAMPIONSHIP WINS

Rangers	*54	Hibernian	4	Kilmarnock	1
Celtic	43	Dumbarton	*2	Motherwell	1
Aberdeen	4	Dundee	1	Third Lanark	1
Hearts	4	Dundee Utd	1	(* Incl 1 shared)

FIRST DIVISION (Since formation of Premier Division)

	First	Pts	Second	Pts	Third	Pts
1975–6d	Partick	41	Kilmarnock	35	Montrose	30
1976–7j	St Mirren	62	Clydebank	58	Dundee	51
1977–8j	*Morton	58	Hearts	58	Dundee	57
1978–9j	Dundee	55	Kilmarnock	54	Clydebank	54
1979–80j	Hearts	53	Airdrieonians	51	Ayr	44
1980–1j	Hibernian	57	Dundee	52	St Johnstone	51
1981–2j	Motherwell	61	Kilmarnock	51	Hearts	50
1982–3j	St Johnstone	55	Hearts	54	Clydebank	50
1983–4j	Morton	54	Dumbarton	51	Partick	46
1984–5j	Motherwell	50	Clydebank	48	Falkirk	45
1985–6j	Hamilton	56	Falkirk	45	Kilmarnock	44
1986–7k	Morton	57	Dunfermline	56	Dumbarton	53
1987–8k	Hamilton	56	Meadowbank	52	Clydebank	49
1988–9j	Dunfermline	54	Falkirk	52	Clydebank	48
1989–90j	St Johnstone	58	Airdrieonians	54	Clydebank	44
1990–1j	Falkirk	54	Airdrieonians	53	Dundee	52
1991–2k	Dundee	58	Partick	57	Hamilton	57
1992–3k	Raith	65	Kilmarnock	54	Dunfermline	52
1993–4k	Falkirk	66	Dunfermline	65	Airdrieonians	54
1994–5l	Raith	69	Dunfermline	68	Dundee	68
1995–6l	Dunfermline	71	Dundee Utd	67	Morton	67
1996–7l	St Johnstone	80	Airdrieonians	60	Dundee	58
1997–8l	Dundee	70	Falkirk	65	Raith	60
1998–9l	Hibernian	89	Falkirk	66	Ayr	62
1999–2000l	St Mirren	76	Dunfermline	71	Falkirk	68
2000–01l	Livingston	76	Ayr	69	Falkirk	56
2001–02l	Partick	66	Airdie	56	Ayr	52
2002–03l	Falkirk	81	Clyde	72	St Johnstone	67
2003–04l	Inverness	70	Clyde	69	St Johnstone	57
2004–05l	Falkirk	75	St Mirren	60	Clyde	60
2005–06l	St Mirren	76	St Johnstone	66	Hamilton	59
2006–07l	Gretna	66	St Johnstone	65	Dundee	53
2007–08l	Hamilton	76	Dundee	69	St Johnstone	58
2008–09l	St Johnstone	65	Partick	55	Dunfermline	51
2009–10l	Inverness	73	Dundee	61	Dunfermline	58
2010–11l	Dunfermline	70	Raith	60	Falkirk	58
2011–12l	Ross	79	Dundee	55	Falkirk	52

Maximum points: a, 36; b, 44; c, 40; d, 52; e, 60; f, 68; g, 76; h, 84; i, 60; j, 78; k, 88; l, 108 *Won on goal difference

SECOND DIVISION

	First	Pts	Second	Pts	Third	Pts
1921–2a	Alloa	60	Cowdenbeath	47	Armadale	45
1922–3a	Queen's Park	57	Clydebank	52	St Johnstone	50
1923–4a	St Johnstone	56	Cowdenbeath	55	Bathgate	44
1924–5a	Dundee Utd	50	Clydebank	48	Clyde	47
1925–6a	Dunfermline	59	Clyde	53	Ayr	52
1926–7a	Bo'ness	56	Raith	49	Clydebank	45
1927–8a	Ayr	54	Third Lanark	45	King's Park	44
1928–9b	Dundee Utd	51	Morton	50	Arbroath	47
1929–30a	*Leith Athletic	57	East Fife	57	Albion	54
1930–1a	Third Lanark	61	Dundee Utd	50	Dunfermline	47
1931–2a	*E Stirling	55	St Johnstone	55	Stenhousemuir	46
1932–3c	Hibernian	55	Queen of South	49	Dunfermline	47
1933–4c	Albion	45	Dunfermline	44	Arbroath	44
1934–5c	Third Lanark	52	Arbroath	50	St Bernard's	47
1935–6c	Falkirk	59	St Mirren	52	Morton	48
1936–7c	Ayr	54	Morton	51	St Bernard's	48
1937–8c	Raith	59	Albion	48	Airdrieonians	47
1938–9c	Cowdenbeath	60	Alloa	48	East Fife	48
1946–7d	Dundee Utd	45	Airdrieonians	42	East Fife	31
1947–8e	East Fife	53	Albion	42	Hamilton	40
1948–9e	*Raith	42	Stirling	42	Airdrieonians	41
1949–50e	Morton	47	Airdrieonians	44	St Johnstone	36
1950–1e	*Queen of South	45	Stirling	45	Ayr	36
1951–2e	Clyde	44	Falkirk	43	Ayr	39
1952–3	E Stirling	44	Hamilton	43	Queen's Park	37
1953–4e	Motherwell	45	Kilmarnock	42	Third Lanark	36
1954–5e	Airdrieonians	46	Dunfermline	42	Hamilton	39
1955–6b	Queen's Park	54	Ayr	51	St Johnstone	49
1956–7b	Clyde	64	Third Lanark	51	Cowdenbeath	45
1957–8b	Stirling	55	Dunfermline	53	Arbroath	47
1958–9b	Ayr	60	Arbroath	51	Stenhousemuir	46
1959–60b	St Johnstone	53	Dundee Utd	50	Queen of South	49
1960–1b	Stirling	55	Falkirk	54	Stenhousemuir	50
1961–2b	Clyde	54	Queen of South	53	Morton	44
1962–3b	St Johnstone	55	E Stirling	49	Morton	48
1963–4b	Morton	67	Clyde	53	Arbroath	46
1964–5b	Stirling	59	Hamilton	50	Queen of South	45
1965–6b	Ayr	53	Airdrieonians	50	Queen of South	47
1966–7b	Morton	69	Raith	58	Arbroath	57
1967–8b	St Mirren	62	Arbroath	53	East Fife	49
1968–9b	Motherwell	64	Ayr	53	East Fife	48
1969–70b	Falkirk	56	Cowdenbeath	55	Queen of South	50
1970–1b	Partick	56	East Fife	51	Arbroath	46
1971–2b	*Dumbarton	52	Arbroath	52	Stirling	50
1972–3b	Clyde	56	Dunfermline	52	Raith	47
1973–4b	Airdrieonians	60	Kilmarnock	58	Hamilton	55
1974–5b	Falkirk	54	Queen of South	53	Montrose	53

SECOND DIVISION (MODERN)

	First	Pts	Second	Pts	Third	Pts
1975–6d	*Clydebank	40	Raith	40	Alloa	35
1976–7f	Stirling	55	Alloa	51	Dunfermline	50
1977–8f	*Clyde	53	Raith	53	Dunfermline	48
1978–9f	Berwick	54	Dunfermline	52	Falkirk	50
1979–80f	Falkirk	50	E Stirling	49	Forfar	46
1980–1f	Queen's Park	50	Queen of South	46	Cowdenbeath	45

1981–2f	Clyde 59	Alloa.................50	Arbroath 50
1982–3f	Brechin 55	Meadowbank 54	Arbroath 49
1983–4f	Forfar 63	East Fife 47	Berwick 43
1984–5f	Montrose 53	Alloa.................50	Dunfermline 49
1985–6f	Dunfermline............. 57	Queen of South..........55	Meadowbank 49
1986–7f	Meadowbank 55	Raith 52	Stirling 52
1987–8f	Ayr 61	St Johnstone 59	Queen's Park 51
1988–9f	Albion 50	Alloa.................45	Brechin............... 43
1989–90f	Brechin 49	Kilmarnock...........48	Stirling 47
1990–1f	Stirling............... 54	Montrose.............46	Cowdenbeath 45
1991–2f	Dumbarton 52	Cowdenbeath.........51	Alloa............... 50
1992–3f	Clyde 54	Brechin.............53	Stranraer............... 53
1993–4f	Stranraer 56	Berwick 48	Stenhousemuir 47
1994–5g	Morton 64	Dumbarton 60	Stirling 58
1995–6g	Stirling 81	East Fife 67	Berwick 60
1996–7g	Ayr 77	Hamilton.............74	Livingston 64
1997–8g	Stranraer 61	Clydebank.............60	Livingston 59
1998–9g	Livingston 77	Inverness.............72	Clyde............... 53
1999–2000g	Clyde 65	Alloa.................64	Ross Co 62
2000–01g	Partick 76	Arbroath.............58	Berwick 54
2001–02g	Queen of South 67	Alloa.................59	Forfar Athletic 53
2002–03g	Raith 59	Brechin.............55	Airdrie 54
2003–04g	Airdrie 70	Hamilton.............62	Dumbarton 60
2004–05g	Brechin 72	Stranraer.............63	Morton............... 62
2005–06g	Gretna 88	Morton.............70	Peterhead 57
2006–07g	Morton 77	Stirling 69	Raith 62
2007–08g	Ross 73	Airdrie 66	Raith 60
2008–09g	Raith 76	Ayr 74	Brechin............... 62
2009–10g	*Stirling 65	Alloa.................65	Cowdenbeath............... 59
2010–11g	Livingston 82	*Ayr.................59	Forfar 59
2011–12g	Cowdenbeath 71	Arbroath.............63	Dumbarton 58

Maximum points: a, 76; b, 72; c, 68; d, 52; e, 60; f, 78; g, 108 *Won on goal average/goal difference

THIRD DIVISION (MODERN)

1994–5	Forfar............... 80	Montrose.................67	Ross Co 60
1995–6	Livingston 72	Brechin.................63	Caledonian Th 57
1996–7	Inverness 76	Forfar.................67	Ross Co 77
1997–8	Alloa 76	Arbroath.................68	Ross Co 67
1998–9	Ross Co 77	Stenhousemuir.................64	Brechin............... 59
1999–2000	Queen's Park 69	Berwick.................66	Forfar............... 61
2000–01	*Hamilton............... 76	Cowdenbeath.................76	Brechin............... 72
2001–02	Brechin 73	Dumbarton.................61	Albion............... 59
2002–03	Morton 72	East Fife 71	Albion............... 70
2003–04	Stranraer 79	Stirling 77	Gretna............... 68
2004–05	Gretna 98	Peterhead 78	Cowdenbeath 51
2005–06	*Cowdenbeath........... 76	Berwick 76	Stenhousemuir 73
2006–07	Berwick 75	Arbroath.................70	Queen's Park 68
2007–08	East Fife 88	Stranraer.................65	Montrose............... 59
2008–09	Dumbarton 67	Cowdenbeath.................63	East Stirling 61
2009–10	Livingston 78	Forfar 63	East Stirling 61
2010–11	Arbroath 66	Albion.................61	Queen's Park 59
2011–12	Alloa 77	Queen's Park 63	Stranraer............... 58

Maximum points: 108 * Won on goal difference

RELEGATED FROM PREMIER DIVISION/PREMIER LEAGUE

1975–6	Dundee, St Johnstone	1979–80	Dundee, Hibernian
1976–7	Kilmarnock, Hearts	1980–1	Kilmarnock, Hearts
1977–8	Ayr, Clydebank	1981–2	Partick, Airdrieonians
1978–9	Hearts, Motherwell	1982–3	Morton, Kilmarnock

1983–4	St Johnstone, Motherwell	1999–2000	No relegation
1984–5	Dumbarton, Morton	2000–01	St Mirren
1985–6	No relegation	2001–02	St Johnstone
1986–7	Clydebank, Hamilton	2002–03	No relegation
1987–8	Falkirk, Dunfermline, Morton	2003–04	Partick
1988–9	Hamilton	2004–05	Dundee
1989–90	Dundee	2005–06	Livingston
1990–1	No relegation	2006–07	Dunfermline
1991–2	St Mirren, Dunfermline	2007–08	Gretna
1992–3	Falkirk, Airdrieonians	2008–09	Inverness
1993–4	St J'stone, Raith, Dundee	2009–10	Falkirk
1994–5	Dundee Utd	2010–11	Hamilton
1995–6	Falkirk, Partick	2011–12	Dunfermline *Rangers
1996–7	Raith	*Following administration, liquidation and	
1997–8	Hibernian	new club formed	
1998–9	Dunfermline		

RELEGATED FROM FIRST DIVISION

1975–6	Dunfermline, Clyde	1994–5	Ayr, Stranraer
1976–7	Raith, Falkirk	1995–6	Hamilton, Dumbarton
1977–8	Alloa, East Fife	1996–7	Clydebank, East Fife
1978–9	Montrose, Queen of South	1997–8	Partick, Stirling
1979–80	Arbroath, Clyde	1998–9	Hamilton, Stranraer
1980–1	Stirling, Berwick	1999–2000	Clydebank
1981–2	E Stirling, Queen of South	2000–01	Morton, Alloa
1982–3	Dunfermline, Queen's Park	2001–02	Raith
1983–4	Raith, Alloa	2002–03	Alloa Athletic, Arbroath
1984–5	Meadowbank, St Johnstone	2003–05	Ayr, Brechin
1985–6	Ayr, Alloa	2004–05	Partick, Raith
1986–7	Brechin, Montrose	2005–06	Brechin, Stranraer
1987–8	East Fife, Dumbarton	2006–07	Airdrie Utd, Ross Co
1988–9	Kilmarnock, Queen of South	2007–08	Stirling
1989–90	Albion, Alloa	2008–09	*Livingston, Clyde
1990–1	Clyde, Brechin	2009–10	Airdrie, Ayr
1991–2	Montrose, Forfar	2010–11	Cowdenbeath, Stirling
1992–3	Meadowbank, Cowdenbeath	2011–12	Ayr, Queen of South
1993–4	Dumbarton, Stirling, Clyde, Morton, Brechin	*relegated to Division Three for breaching insolvency rules	

RELEGATED FROM SECOND DIVISION

1993–4	Alloa, Forfar, E Stirling, Montrose, Queen's Park, Arbroath, Albion, Cowdenbeath	2001–02	Morton
		2002–03	Stranraer, Cowdenbeath
		2003–04	East Fife, Stenhousemuir
		2004–05	Arbroath, Berwick
1994–5	Meadowbank, Brechin	2005–06	Dumbarton
1995–6	Forfar, Montrose	2006–07	Stranraer, Forfar
1996–7	Dumbarton, Berwick	2007–08	Cowdenbeath , Berwick
1997–8	Stenhousemuir, Brechin	2008–09	Queen's Park, Stranraer
1998–9	East Fife, Forfar	2009–10	Arbroath, Clyde
1999–2000	Hamilton	2010–11	Alloa, Peterhead
2000–01	Queen's Park, Stirling	2011–12	Stirling

CLYDESDALE BANK PREMIER LEAGUE 2011–2012

ABERDEEN

Anderson R 4 (2)	Hughes S 3 (2)	Milsom R 22
Arnason K 31 (2)	Jack R 30 (1)	Osbourne I 22 (1)
Brown J 20	Langfield J 4	Paton M .... - (2)
Chalali M 4 (12)	Low N .... - (2)	Pawlett P 5 (16)
Clark C 16 (8)	Mackie D 8 (11)	Rae G 12
Considine A 36	Magennis J 13 (10)	Reynolds M 16
Fallon R 18 (4)	Masson J 3 (1)	Robertson C 9
Foster R 22	Mawene Y 19 (3)	Smith C .... - (2)
Fraser R .... - (3)	McArdle R 20 (5)	Uchechi D .... - (1)
Fyvie F 26 (1)	McManus D .... - (2)	Vernon S 34 (1)
Gonzalez D 14	Megginson M 7 (9)	

League goals (36): Vernon 11, Arnason 3, Considine 3, Jack 3, Fallon 2, Mawene 2, Chalali 1, Clark 1, Foster 1, Fyvie 1, Mackie 1, Magennis 1, Masson 1, Milsom 1, Opponents 4
Scottish Cup goals (10): Fallon 4, Vernon 2, Chalali 1, Considine 1, Fyvie 1, Megginson 1.
Communities League Cup goals (4): Mackie 2, Fallon 1, McArdle 1
Average home league attendance: 9,296

CELTIC

Bangura M 2 (8)	Izaguirre E 9 (3)	Mulgrew C 29 (1)
Blackman A 1 (2)	Kayal B 18 (1)	Rogne T 15 (2)
Brown S 20 (2)	Ki Sung-Yeung 21 (9)	Samaras G 20 (6)
Brozek P 1 (2)	Ledley J 31 (1)	Stokes A 25 (9)
Cha Du-Ri 11 (4)	Loovens G 11	Twardzik F .... - (1)
Commons K 16 (7)	Lustig M 3 (1)	Wanyama V 24 (5)
El Kaddouri B 5 (1)	Majstorovic D 15 (2)	Watt T .... - (3)
Forrest J 23 (6)	Maloney S 1 (2)	Wilson K 14 (1)
Forster F 33	Matthews A 25 (2)	Wilson M 5 (2)
Hooper G 34 (3)	McCourt P .... - (13)	Zaluska L 5
Ibrahim R .... - (1)	McGeouch D 1 (5)	

League goals (84): Hooper 24, Stokes 12, Mulgrew 8, Forrest 7, Ledley 7, Ki Sung-Yeung 6, Samaras 4, Wanyama 4, Brown 3, Watt 2, Cha Du-Ri 1, Commons 1, El Kaddouri 1, Loovens 1, McGeouch 1, Rogne 1, Opponents 1
Scottish Cup goals (10): Stokes 4, Brown 2, Samaras 2, Hooper 1, Ledley 1. **Communities League Cup goals (9):** Stokes 3, Forrest 2, Hooper 2, Brown 1, Opponents 1. **Europa League goals (7):** Hooper 2, Stokes 2, Ki Sung-Yeung 1, Ledley 1, Mulgrew 1
Average home league attendance: 50,904

DUNDEE UNITED

Allan S 4 (4)	Gauld R .... - (1)	Rankin J 38
Armstrong S 11 (12)	Goodwillie D 1	Robertson S 34 (3)
Dalla Valle L 5 (7)	Gunning G 29 (2)	Russell J 33 (4)
Daly J 35 (1)	Kennedy G 20 (5)	Ryan R 2 (12)
Dillon S 26 (2)	Lacny M .... - (4)	Severin S 2
Dixon P 37	Mackay-Steven G ... 24 (7)	Swanson D 6 (8)
Douglas B 5 (4)	Marsh-Brown K .... - (1)	Watson K 14 (3)
Dow R 3 (7)	Neilson R 21	
Flood W 30 (2)	Pernis D 38	

League goals (62): Daly 19, Russell 9, Robertson 6, Mackay-Steven 4, Rankin 4, Dalla Valle 3, Dixon 3, Swanson 3, Gunning 2, Armstrong 1, Douglas 1, Flood 1, Lacny 1, Watson 1, Opponents 4

Scottish Cup goals (8): Russell 4, Gunning 1, Mackay-Steven 1, Rankin 1, Robertson 1.
Communities League Cup goals (4): Daly 2, Dow 1, Russell 1. Europa League goals (3): Daly 1, Goodwillie 1, Russell 1
Average home league attendance: 7,481

DUNFERMLINE ATHLETIC

Barrowman A 13 (9)	Graham D 33 (5)	Phinn N .... - (1)
Bernado 1	Hardie M 18 (10)	Potter J-P 15 (1)
Boyle P.................... 20 (1)	Hutton K 8 (1)	Rutkiewicz K 8
Buchanan L 14 (13)	Keddie A 36	Smith C.....................15
Burns P................. 21 (4)	Kerr M............................13	Thomson R 11 (14)
Cardle J 24 (12)	Kirk A 23 (13)	Thomson J....................12
Clarke P.................... - (3)	Mason G.....................32	Turner I 4
Dowie A..................... 30	McCann A.................22 (1)	Willis P 11 (10)
Easton C....................3	McDougall S 2 (10)	
Gallacher P.................18	McMillan J.................11	

League goals (40): Kirk 11, Cardle 8, Buchanan 5, Barrowman 3, Burns 2, Graham 2, Thomson R 2, Hardie 1, McCann 1, McMillan 1, Thomson J 1, Willis 1, Opponents 2
Scottish Cup goals (2): Barrowman 2. Communities League Cup goals (3): Barrowman 1, Buchanan 1, Kirk 1
Average home league attendance: 4,799

HEARTS

Barr D 13 (2)	Kello M 20	Santana S................ 3 (10)
Beattie C....................4 (1)	MacDonald J............17 (1)	Skacel R.................19 (10)
Black I 28 (1)	McGowan R 23 (5)	Smith G........................ - (6)
Driver A.................. 15 (6)	McHattie K .... - (1)	Stevenson R............. 15 (4)
Elliott S 19 (7)	Mrowiec A............... 27 (2)	Sutton J 9 (5)
Glen G..................... 4 (4)	Novikovas A..............4 (11)	Taouil M 15 (9)
Grainger D 27	Obua D 11 (8)	Templeton D 20 (7)
Hamill J...................28 (1)	Prychynenko D............ - (3)	Webster A.....................31
Holt J...........................1 (1)	Ridgers M 1 (1)	Zaliukas M..................... 36
Jonsson E................ 14 (2)	Robinson S 14 (6)	

League goals (45): Skacel 12, Webster 4, Elliott 3, Sutton 3, Black 2, Hamill 2, McGowan 2, Novikovas 2, Santana 2, Stevenson 2, Taouil 2, Barr 1, Beattie 1, Glen 1, Holt 1, Jonsson 1, Obua 1, Templeton 1, Zaliukas 1, Opponents 1
Scottish Cup goals (15): Skacel 5, Beattie 2, Hamill 2, Barr 1, Grainger 1, McGowan 1, Smith 1, Templeton 1, Zalikiukas 1. Communities League Cup goals (1): Robinson 1. Europa League goals (5): Stevenson 2, Driver 1, Hamill 1, Skacel 1
Average home league attendance: 13,381

HIBERNIAN

Agogo J 9 (3)	Grant P............................1`	Scott M 8 (7)
Airey P .... - (1)	Griffiths L................ 24 (6)	Soares T....................9 (1)
Booth C................... 10 (2)	Hanlon P.....................35	Sodje A .... - (13)
Brown M....................7	Hart M..........................6	Sproule I 26 (8)
Caldwell R .... - (1)	Saikou Kujabi P.........12 (1)	Stack G 30
Claros C...................10	McPake J.................11	Stanton S .... - (2)
Crawford D .... - (2)	Murray I 13 (2)	Stephens D 14 (2)
De Graaf E................ - (1)	O'Connor G 27 (6)	Stevenson L 27 (2)
Doherty M 11 (2)	O'Donovan R 5 (9)	Thornhill M.................5 (1)
Doyle E...................... 6 (7)	O'Hanlon S 22	Towell R 11 (3)
Francomb G 11 (3)	Osbourne I................ 29 (1)	Wotherspoon D....... 20 (10)
Galbraith D 7 (9)	Palsson V................. 12 (3)	

League goals (40): O'Connor 12, Griffiths 8, Sproule 3, Doherty 2, Hanlon 2, O'Hanlon 2, Soares 2, Agogo 1, Booth 1, Doyle 1, O'Donovan 1, Osbourne 1, Towell 1, Opponents 3
Scottish Cup goals (9): Griffiths 3, Doyle 2, McPake 1, O'Connor 1, O'Donovan 1, Wotherspoon 1. **Communities League Cup goals (9):** O'Connor 3, Scott 2, Sodje 1, Sproule 1, Opponents 1
Average home league attendance: 9,909

INVERNESS CALEDONIAN THISTLE

Aldred T	2 (2)	Hayes J	25 (1)	Sutherland S	9 (18)
Chippendale A	1 (4)	Hogg C	9	Tade G	30 (6)
Cox L	4 (3)	McKay B	17 (5)	Tansey A	33 (3)
Davis D	14	Meekings J	18 (1)	Tokely R	28 (1)
Doran A	7 (3)	Morrison G	3 (1)	Tudur Jones O	8 (7)
Esson R	33	Piermayr T	16 (4)	Tuffey J	5
Foran R	37	Proctor D	9 (8)	Williams S	6 (3)
Gillet K	25	Ross N	18 (11)	Winnall S	1 (1)
Gnakpa C	2 (5)	Shinnie A	15 (4)		
Golobart R	18 (4)	Shinnie G	25 (1)		

League goals (42): Tade 9, Hayes 7, Shinnie A 7, Tansey 4, McKay 3, Foran 2, Golobart 2, Ross 2, Williams 2, Davis 1, Shinnie G 1, Sutherland 1, Tokely 1
Scottish Cup goals (4): Hayes 2, Shinnie A 1, Tansey 1. **Communities League Cup goals:** None
Average home league attendance: 4,023

KILMARNOCK

Ada P	3	Harkins G	29 (1)	Mendes Silva D	3 (13)
Barbour R	1 (1)	Hay G	20 (4)	Nelson M	15
Bell C	32	Heffernan P	26 (3)	O'Leary R	7 (1)
Buijs D	12 (2)	Hutchinson B	3 (1)	Panikvar L	2
Clancy T	1	Jaakkola A	5	Pascali M	24
Davidson R	- (1)	Johnson L	7 (2)	Pursehouse A	8
Dayton J	13 (15)	Johnston C	- (2)	Racchi D	9 (10)
Fisher G	3 (3)	Kelly L	33 (1)	Shiels D	33 (2)
Fowler J	34 (3)	Kennedy M	2 (9)	Sissoko M	24 (3)
Galan J	- (4)	Kroca Z	13 (1)	Toshney L	12
Gordon B	17	Letheren K	1 (1)	Van Tornhout D	6 (5)
Gros W	2 (6)	McKeown R	18	Winchester J	- (2)

League goals (44): Shiels 13, Heffernan 11, Dayton 3, Fowler 3, Pascali 3, Racchi 2, Harkins 1, Kelly 1, Kroca 1, McKeown 1, Nelson 1, Van Tornhout 1, Winchester 1, Opponents 2
Scottish Cup goals (3): Heffernan 1, Pascali 1, Shiels 1. **Communities League Cup goals (9):** Heffernan 3, Harkins 2, Hutchinson 1, Shiels 1, Sissoko 1, Van Tornhout 1
Average home league attendance: 5,537

MOTHERWELL

Carswell S	4 (10)	Higdon M	35	Murphy J	32 (4)
Clancy T	24 (2)	Hughes S	2 (2)	Ojamaa H	12 (6)
Craigan S	24 (2)	Humphrey C	23 (12)	Page J	2 (2)
Cummins A	1	Hutchinson S	29 (1)	Randolph D	38
Daley O	11 (14)	Jennings S	33 (1)	Saunders S	1 (1)
Forbes R	1 (3)	Lasley K	32	Smith G	- (1)
Hammell S	37	Law N	38		
Hateley T	38	McHugh R	1 (8)		

League goals (49): Higdon 14, Murphy 9, Ojamaa 7, Lasley 4, Law 4, Daley 2, Hammell 2, Hateley 2, Humphrey 2, Hutchinson 1, McHugh 1, Opponents 1
Scottish Cup goals (11): Murphy 4, Law 2, Ojamaa 2, Daley 1, Hateley 1, Hutchinson 1
Communities League Cup goals (6): Higdon 2, Hateley 1, Lasley 1, Law 1, Lawless S 1

RANGERS

Alexander N 1	Healy D 6 (5)	McMillan J...................1 (1)
Aluko S................... 19 (2)	Hemmings K .... - (4)	Mitchell A...................1 (1)
Bartley K 18 (1)	Jelavic N 21 (1)	Naismith S...................11
Bedoya A 5 (7)	Kerkar S 5 (10)	Ness J 3 (2)
Bocanegra C 29	Bendiksen T............... 1 (2)	Ortiz J 5 (5)
Bougherra M...................2	Lafferty K 14 (6)	Papac S...................21
Broadfoot K 11 (5)	Little A 6 (4)	Perry R 8 (4)
Celik M................... - (5)	McCabe R...................8 (1)	Wallace L 26 (2)
Davis S 33	McCulloch L 20 (6)	Whittaker S...............24 (1)
Edu M 34 (2)	McGregor A...................37	Wylde G 13 (8)
Fleck J .... - (4)	McKay B................... - (1)	
Goian D 33	McKay M...................2 (1)	

League goals (77): Jelavic 14, Aluko 12, Naismith 9, Lafferty 7, Davis 5, Little 5, McCulloch 5, Edu 3, Healy 3, Bocanegra 2, Wallace 2, Whittaker 2, Wylde 2, Bedoya 1, Kerkar 1, Ness 1, Opponents 3
Scottish Cup goals (4): Healy 1, Jelavic 1, Kerkar 1, Opponents 1. **Communities League Cup goals** (2): Goian 1, Jelavic 1. **Champions League goals** (1): Jelavic 1. **Europa League goals** (2): Bocanegra 1, Ortiz 1
Average home league attendance: 46,324

ST JOHNSTONE

Adams J 6 (1)	Haber M 14 (17)	Morris J 28
Anderson S 26 (3)	Higgins S................... - (3)	Oyenuga K................... - (1)
Compton J .... - (3)	Keatings J................... - (4)	Parkin S...................1 (1)
Craig L 36	MacKay D 36	Riordan D 2 (2)
Croft L 10 (1)	Mannus A 13	Robertson D............ 10 (6)
Davidson C 26	May S................... - (1)	Sandaza F 28 (1)
Davidson M 24 (2)	Maybury A 15 (7)	Sheridan C 25 (3)
Enckelman P...................25	McCracken D 27 (1)	Wright F 23
Finnigan C 3 (8)	Millar C 26 (4)	
Gibson W 1 (10)	Moon K 13 (6)	

League goals (43): Sandaza 14, Craig 7, MacKay 4, Sheridan 4, Croft 3, Davidson M 2, Haber 2, Anderson 1, Davidson C 1, McCracken 1, Morris 1, Opponents 3
Scottish Cup goals (4): Davidson M 2, Sandaza 1, Sheridan 1. **Communities League Cup goals** (3): Sandaza 3
Average home league attendance: 4,169

ST MIRREN

Barron D................ 12 (5)	McGowan P 37	Naismith J................... - (2)
Carey G 20 (9)	McGregor D 6 (3)	Reilly T...................- (4)
Goodwin J...................31	McKee J .... - (2)	Samson C...................38
Haddad I...................4 (6)	McLean K 24 (4)	Teale G...................21 (13)
Hasselbaink N........ 22 (12)	McQuade P............... - (1)	Tesselaar J...................33
Imrie D 12 (2)	McShane J 1 (8)	Thompson S 35 (1)
Mair L 34	Mooy A 3 (5)	Thomson S 18 (5)
McAusland M...........31 (1)	Murray H 1 (6)	Van Zanten D...............35

League goals (39): Thompson 13, McGowan 8, Hasselbaink 6, McLean 4, Carey 2, Thomson 2, Goodwin 1, Mair 1, McAusland 1, Mooy 1
Scottish Cup goals (6): Carey 2, Hasselbaink 1, Teale 1, Thompson 1, Opponents 1. **Communities League Cup goals** (6): Thompson 2, Goodwin 1, Hasselbaink 1, Teale 1, Opponents 1.
Average home league attendance: 4,492

FIRST LEAGUE CUP SUCCESS FOR KILMARNOCK

SECOND ROUND	THIRD ROUND	FOURTH ROUND	SEMI-FINALS	FINAL
Bye	Celtic 2	Celtic 4	Celtic 3	Celtic 0
*Hamilton......1 / Ross......2	*Ross......0			
*Clyde......0 / Motherwell......4	*Motherwell......2	*Hibernian......1		
*Hibernian......5 / Berwick......0	Hibernian......†A2			
*Airdrie......2 / Raith......0	*Airdrie......0	*Dundee Utd......2	Falkirk......1	
Bye	Dundee Utd......2			
*Falkirk......3 / Stenhousemuir......1	*Falkirk......3	Falkirk......†D2		
Bye	Rangers......2			Kilmarnock......1
*St Johnstone......3 / Livingston......0	*St Johnstone......0	*St Mirren......0	Ayr......0	
*Morton......3 / St Mirren......4	St Mirren......2			
*Ayr......1 / Inverness......0 †B1	*Ayr......†B1	Ayr......1		
Bye	Hearts......1			

192

*Aberdee 1
Dundee 0

*East Fife 2
Dunfermline 1

*Queen of South 3
Forfar 0

Bye

*Aberdeen 3

East Fife .... †3

Queen of South 0

*Kilmarnock 5

*Aberdeen 0

*Kilmarnock 2

East Fife 0

Kilmarnock 1

† Drawn at home; after extra-time; A – Hibernian won 7-6 on pens; B – Ayr won 4-1 on pens; C – East Fife won 4-3 on pens; D – Falkirk won 5-4 on pens; both semi-finals at Hampden Park

FIRST ROUND

Airdrie 5 Stirling 0; Albion 2 Falkirk 4; Alloa 0 Morton 3; Annan 1 Dunfermline 2; Brechin 2 Clyde 4; Cowdenbeath 2 Stenhousemuir 2 (aet, Stenhousemuir won 4-3 on pens); Dumbarton 0 Dundee 4; East Fife 2 Elgin 1; East Stirling 0 Ayr 3; Forfar 2 Peterhead 0; Livingston 6 Arbroath 0; Montrose 1 Raith 4; Partick 1 Berwick 3; Queen of South 2 Stranraer 1; Ross 2 Queen's Park 1

SCOTTISH COMMUNITIES LEAGUE CUP FINAL

CELTIC 0 KILMARNOCK 1

Hampden Park (49,572); Sunday, March 18 2012

Celtic (4-4-2): Forster, Matthews, Rogne (Ki Sung-Yueng 56), Wilson, Mulgrew, Forrest, Brown (capt), Wanyama, Ledley (Commons 86), Hooper (Samaras 80), Stokes. **Subs not used:** Zaluska, Ch Du-Ri. **Booked:** Stokes. **Manager:** Neil Lennon
Kilmarnock (4-5-1): Bell, Fowler (capt), Nelson, Sissoko (Kroca 86), Gordon, Buijs (Johnson 20), Dean Shiels, Kelly, Hay, Harkins (Van Tornhout 73), Heffernan. **Subs not used:** Letheren, Dayton. **Scorer:** Van Tornhout (83). **Booked:** Kelly, Johnson. **Manager:** Kenny Shiels
Referee: W Collum. **Half-time:** 0-0

SCOTTISH LEAGUE CUP FINALS

1946	Aberdeen beat Rangers (3-2)
1947	Rangers beat Aberdeen (4-0)
1948	East Fife beat Falkirk (4-1 after 0-0 draw)
1949	Rangers beat Raith Rov (2-0)
1950	East Fife beat Dunfermline Athletic (3-0)
1951	Motherwell beat Hibernian (3-0)
1952	Dundee beat Rangers (3-2)
1953	Dundee beat Kilmarnock (2-0)
1954	East Fife beat Partick (3-2)
1955	Hearts beat Motherwell (4-2)
1956	Aberdeen beat St Mirren (2-1)
1957	Celtic beat Partick (3-0 after 0-0 draw)
1958	Celtic beat Rangers (7-1)
1959	Hearts beat Partick (5-1)
1960	Hearts beat Third Lanark (2-1)
1961	Rangers beat Kilmarnock (2-0)
1962	Rangers beat Hearts (3-1 after 1-1 draw)
1963	Hearts beat Kilmarnock (1-0)
1964	Rangers beat Morton (5-0)
1965	Rangers beat Celtic (2-1)
1966	Celtic beat Rangers (2-1)
1967	Celtic beat Rangers (1-0)
1968	Celtic beat Dundee (5-3)
1969	Celtic beat Hibernian (6-2)
1970	Celtic beat St Johnstone (1-0)
1971	Rangers beat Celtic (1-0)
1972	Partick beat Celtic (4-1)
1973	Hibernian beat Celtic (2-1)
1974	Dundee beat Celtic (1-0)
1975	Celtic beat Hibernian (6-3)
1976	Rangers beat Celtic (1-0)
1977†	Aberdeen beat Celtic (2-1)
1978†	Rangers beat Celtic (2-1)
1979	Rangers beat Aberdeen (2-1)
1980	Dundee Utd beat Aberdeen (3-0 after 0-0 draw)
1981	Dundee Utd beat Dundee (3-0)
1982	Rangers beat Dundee Utd (2-1)
1983	Celtic beat Rangers (2-1)
1984†	Rangers beat Celtic (3-2)
1985	Rangers beat Dundee Utd (1-0)
1986	Aberdeen beat Hibernian (3-0)
1987	Rangers beat Celtic (2-1)
1988†	Rangers beat Aberdeen (5-3 on pens after 3-3 draw)
1989	Rangers beat Aberdeen (3-2)
1990†	Aberdeen beat Rangers (2-1)
1991†	Rangers beat Celtic (2-1)
1992	Hibernian beat Dunfermline Athletic (2-0)
1993†	Rangers beat Aberdeen (2-1)
1994	Rangers beat Hibernian (2-1)
1995	Raith Rov beat Celtic (6-5 on pens after 2-2 draw)
1996	Aberdeen beat Dundee (2-0)
1997	Rangers beat Hearts (4-3)

1998	Celtic beat Dundee Utd (3-0)
1999	Rangers beat St Johnstone (2-1)
2000	Celtic beat Aberdeen (2-0)
2001	Celtic beat Kilmarnock (3-0)
2002	Rangers beat Ayr (4-0)
2003	Rangers beat Celtic (2-1)
2004	Livingston beat Hibernian (2-0)
2005	Rangers beat Motherwell (5-1)
2006	Celtic beat Dunfermline Athletic (3-0)
2007	Hibernian beat Kilmarnock (5-1)
2008	Rangers beat Dundee Utd (3-2 on pens after 2-2 draw)
2009†	Celtic beat Rangers (2-0)
2010	Rangers beat St Mirren (1-0)
2011+	Rangers beat Celtic (2-1)
2012	Kilmarnock beat Celtic (1-0)

(† After extra time; Skol Cup 1985-93, Coca-Cola Cup 1995-97, Co-operative Insurance Cup 1999 onwards)

SUMMARY OF SCOTTISH LEAGUE CUP WINNERS

Rangers	27	Dundee	3	Kilmarnock	1
Celtic	14	East Fife	3	Livingston	1
Aberdeen	6	Hibernian	3	Motherwell	1
Hearts	4	Dundee Utd	2	Partick	1
				Raith Rov	1

RAMSDENS CUP 2011–12

First round (north-east): Arbroath 1 Dundee 2 (aet); Brechin 1 Falkirk 2; Deveronvale 1 Stirling 3; Forfar 1 Buckie 1 (aet, Forfar won 5-4 on pens); Montrose 1 East Fife 6; Peterhead 2 Alloa 2 (aet, Peterhead won 5-4 on pens); Raith 2 Cowdenbeath 1; Ross 1 Elgin 2

First round (south-west): Airdrie 0 Livingston 5; Albion 0 Annan 2; Ayr 2 Queen of South 0; Clyde 2 Berwick 2 (aet, Berwick won 4-3 on pens); Dumbarton 3 East Stirling 2; Partick 2 Stenhousemuir 1; Queen's Park 0 Hamilton 2; Stranraer 0 Morton 8

Second round: Annan 4 Peterhead 2; Ayr 3 Raith 0; Dumbarton 0 Berwick 2; East Fife 2 Elgin 0; Falkirk 1 Dundee 0; Forfar 0 Morton 5; Hamilton 1 Partick 0; Livingston 5 Stirling 0

Third round: Ayr 0 Annan 1; Berwick 1 Livingston 2; East Fife 1 Falkirk 4; Hamilton 2 Morton 1

Semi-finals: Annan 0 Falkirk 3; Hamilton 1 Livingston 0

FINAL
FALKIRK 1 HAMILTON ACADEMICAL 0
Braidwood Stadium, Livingston (5,210); Sunday, April 1 2012

Falkirk: McGovern, Duffie, Scobbie, Dods (capt), Wallace, Fulton, Sibbald (Alston 86), Millar, El Alagui, Gibson, Weatherston. **Subs not used:** Bowman, Kingsley, White, Bennett. **Scorer:** Dods (2). **Booked:** Fulton. **Manager:** Steven Pressley

Hamilton Academical: Hutton , McAlister, Kilday, Kirkpatrick (Hendrie 46), Mensing, McLaughlin (Ryan 71), Routledge, Redmond, McShane, Neil, Stewart (Spence 46). **Subs not used:** Currie, Gillespie. **Booked:** Neil. **Manager:** Billy Reid

Referee: B Winter. **Half-time:** 1-0

EASY FOR HEARTS IN ALL-EDINBURGH FINAL

FOURTH ROUND	FIFTH ROUND	SIXTH ROUND	SEMI-FINALS	FINAL
*Hearts ....1 / Auchinleck 0	Hearts 1:f2	*Hearts 2:2	Hearts 2	Hearts 5
*St Johnstone ....2 / Brechin 1	*St Johnstone 1:1			
*St Mirren ....0:1 / Hamilton 0:0	*St Mirren 1:2	St Mirren 2:0		
*Ross ....7 / Stenhousemuir 0	Ross 1:1			
*Arbroath ....0 / Rangers 4	*Rangers 0	*Dundee Utd 0	Celtic 1	
*Airdrie ....2 / Dundee Utd 6	Dundee Utd 2			
*Inverness ....1:f3 / Dunfermline 1:1	*Inverness 0	Celtic 4		
*Peterhead ....0 / Celtic 3	Celtic 2			
*Motherwell ....4 / Queen's Park 0	*Motherwell 6	*Motherwell 1	Aberdeen 1	
*Raith ....1 / Morton 2	Morton 0			
*Forfar ....0 / Aberdeen 4	*Aberdeen 1:2	Aberdeen 2		
*Partick ....0 / Queen of South 1	Queen of South 1:1			Hibernian 1

*Livingston 1			
Ayr 2	*Ayr 2		
		*Ayr 0	
*Falkirk 1			
East Fife 0	Falkirk 1		
			Hibernian 2
*Dundee 1:1			
Kilmarnock 1:2	Kilmarnock 0		
		Hibernian 1	
*Cowdenbeath 2			
Hibernian 3	Hibernian 1		

*Drawn at home. †After extra-time. Both semi-finals played at Hampden Park

FIRST ROUND: Culter 1 Burntisland 0; Dalbeattie 1 Inverurie 6; Edinburgh City 3 Brora 0; Edinburgh Univ 0 Whitehill 3; Forres 2 Irvine 2; Fort William 0 Bo'Ness 4; Fraserburgh 4 Civil Service 3; Gala 8 Hawick 1; Glasgow Univ 0 Cove 4; Huntly 6 Newton Stewart 1; Lossiemouth 1 Auchinleck 2, Nairn 2 Selkirk 1; Rothes 0 Clachnacuddin 3; St Cuthbert 0 Keith 2; Vale of Leithen 1 Girvan 0; Wick 9 Coldstream 1; Wigtown 2 Preston 0. **Replay:** Irvine 6 Forres 3

SECOND ROUND: Alloa 2 Annan 2; Auchinleck 8 Threave 1; Bo'Ness 2 Whitehill 1; Clachnacuddin 1 Inverurie 1; Culter 0 Spartans 2 (Spartans expelled for ineligible player); Deveronvale 4 Berwick 0; East Stirling 1 Buckie 1; Edinburgh City 0 Irvine 1; Fraserburgh 0 Elgin 0; Gala 5 Golspie 2; Huntly 0 Queen's Park 3; Montrose 2 Clyde 1; Peterhead 2 Nairn 0; Vale of Leithen 3 Cove 2; Wick 0 Keith 1; Wigtown 0 Stranraer 9. **Replays:** Annan 2 Alloa 0; Buckie 2 East Stirling 4 (aet); Elgin 5 Fraserburgh 2; Inverurie 3 Clachnacuddin 2

THIRD ROUND: Airdrie 11 Gala 0; Auchinleck 3 Vale of Leithen 1; Ayr 2 Montrose 2; Bo'Ness 0 Cowdenbeath 3; Brechin 3 Dumbarton 0; Culter 1 Partick 1; East Fife 5 East Stirling 0; Elgin 1 Queen's Park 1; Inverurie 2 Peterhead 4; Irvine 0 Livingston 6; Keith 0 Arbroath 1; Morton 5 Deveronvale 1; Ross 4 Albion 0; Stenhousemuir 4 Annan 0; Stirling 1 Dundee 2; Stranraer 1 Forfar 1. **Replays:** Forfar 3 Stranraer 0; Montrose 1 Ayr 2; Partick 4 Culter 0; Queen's Park 3 Elgin 1

WILLIAM HILL SCOTTISH CUP FINAL

HEARTS 5 HIBERNIAN 1

Hampden Park (51,041); Saturday, May 19 2012

Hearts (4-4-2): MacDonald, McGowan, Webster, Zaliukas (capt), Grainger, Black (Robinson 36), Barr, Santana (Beattie 76), Skacel, Driver (Taouil 84), Elliott. **Subs not used:** Ridgers, Prychynenko. **Scorers:** Barr (15), Skacel (27, 75), Grainger (48 pen), McGowan (50). **Manager:** Paulo Sergio
Hibernian (4-4-2): Brown, Doherty, McPake (capt), Hanlon, Kujabi, Soares (Francomb 76), Osbourne, Claros (Sproule 42), Stevenson, O'Connor (Doyle 54), Griffiths. **Subs not used:** Grant, O'Hanlon. **Scorer:** McPake (41). **Booked:** Doherty. **Sent off:** Kujabi. **Manager:** Pat Fenlon
Referee: C Thomson. **Half-time:** 2-1

SCOTTISH FA CUP FINALS

1874	Queen's Park beat Clydesdale (2-0)
1875	Queen's Park beat Renton (3-0)
1876	Queen's Park beat Third Lanark (2-0 after 1-1 draw)
1877	Vale of Leven beat Rangers (3-2 after 0-0, 1-1 draws)
1878	Vale of Leven beat Third Lanark (1-0)
1879	Vale of Leven awarded Cup (Rangers withdrew after 1-1 draw)
1880	Queen's Park beat Thornlibank (3-0)
1881	Queen's Park beat Dumbarton (3-1)
1882	Queen's Park beat Dumbarton (4-1 after 2-2 draw)
1883	Dumbarton beat Vale of Leven (2-1 after 2-2 draw)
1884	Queen's Park awarded Cup (Vale of Leven withdrew from Final)
1885	Renton beat Vale of Leven (3-1 after 0-0 draw)
1886	Queen's Park beat Renton (3-1)
1887	Hibernian beat Dumbarton (2-1)
1888	Renton beat Cambuslang (6-1)
1889	Third Lanark beat Celtic (2-1)
1890	Queen's Park beat Vale of Leven (2-1 after 1-1 draw)
1891	Hearts beat Dumbarton (1-0)
1892	Celtic beat Queen's Park (5-1)
1893	Queen's Park beat Celtic (2-1)
1894	Rangers beat Celtic (3-1)
1895	St Bernard's beat Renton (2-1)
1896	Hearts beat Hibernian (3-1)
1897	Rangers beat Dumbarton (5-1)
1898	Rangers beat Kilmarnock (2-0)
1899	Celtic beat Rangers (2-0)
1900	Celtic beat Queen's Park (4-3)
1901	Hearts beat Celtic (4-3)
1902	Hibernian beat Celtic (1-0)
1903	Rangers beat Hearts (2-0 after 0-0, 1-1 draws)
1904	Celtic beat Rangers (3-2)
1905	Third Lanark beat Rangers (3-1 after 0-0 draw)
1906	Hearts beat Third Lanark (1-0)
1907	Celtic beat Hearts (3-0)
1908	Celtic beat St Mirren (5-1)
1909	Cup withheld because of riot after two drawn games in final between Celtic and Rangers (2-2, 1-1)
1910	Dundee beat Clyde (2-1 after 2-2, 0-0 draws)
1911	Celtic beat Hamilton (2-0 after 0-0 draw)
1912	Celtic beat Clyde (2-0)
1913	Falkirk beat Raith (2-0)
1914	Celtic beat Hibernian (4-1 after 0-0 draw)
1915–19	No competition (World War 1)
1920	Kilmarnock beat Albion (3-2)
1921	Partick beat Rangers (1-0)
1922	Morton beat Rangers (1-0)
1923	Celtic beat Hibernian (1-0)
1924	Airdrieonians beat Hibernian (2-0)
1925	Celtic beat Dundee (2-1)
1926	St Mirren beat Celtic (2-0)
1927	Celtic beat East Fife (3-1)

1928	Rangers beat Celtic (4-0)
1929	Kilmarnock beat Rangers (2-0)
1930	Rangers beat Partick (2-1 after 0-0 draw)
1931	Celtic beat Motherwell (4-2 after 2-2 draw)
1932	Rangers beat Kilmarnock (3-0 after 1-1 draw)
1933	Celtic beat Motherwell (1-0)
1934	Rangers beat St Mirren (5-0)
1935	Rangers beat Hamilton (2-1)
1936	Rangers beat Third Lanark (1-0)
1937	Celtic beat Aberdeen (2-1)
1938	East Fife beat Kilmarnock (4-2 after 1-1 draw)
1939	Clyde beat Motherwell (4-0)
1940–6	No competition (World War 2)
1947	Aberdeen beat Hibernian (2-1)
1948†	Rangers beat Morton (1-0 after 1-1 draw)
1949	Rangers beat Clyde (4-1)
1950	Rangers beat East Fife (3-0)
1951	Celtic beat Motherwell (1-0)
1952	Motherwell beat Dundee (4-0)
1953	Rangers beat Aberdeen (1-0 after 1-1 draw)
1954	Celtic beat Aberdeen (2-1)
1955	Clyde beat Celtic (1-0 after 1-1 draw)
1956	Hearts beat Celtic (3-1)
1957†	Falkirk beat Kilmarnock (2-1 after 1-1 draw)
1958	Clyde beat Hibernian (1-0)
1959	St Mirren beat Aberdeen (3-1)
1960	Rangers beat Kilmarnock (2-0)
1961	Dunfermline beat Celtic (2-0 after 0-0 draw)
1962	Rangers beat St Mirren (2-0)
1963	Rangers beat Celtic (3-0 after 1-1 draw)
1964	Rangers beat Dundee (3-1)
1965	Celtic beat Dunfermline (3-2)
1966	Rangers beat Celtic (1-0 after 0-0 draw)
1967	Celtic beat Aberdeen (2-0)
1968	Dunfermline beat Hearts (3-1)
1969	Celtic beat Rangers (4-0)
1970	Aberdeen beat Celtic (3-1)
1971	Celtic beat Rangers (2-1 after 1-1 draw)
1972	Celtic beat Hibernian (6-1)
1973	Rangers beat Celtic (3-2)
1974	Celtic beat Dundee Utd (3-0)
1975	Celtic beat Airdrieonians (3-1)
1976	Rangers beat Hearts (3-1)
1977	Celtic beat Rangers (1-0)
1978	Rangers beat Aberdeen (2-1)
1979†	Rangers beat Hibernian (3-2 after two 0-0 draws)
1980†	Celtic beat Rangers (1-0)
1981	Rangers beat Dundee Utd (4-1 after 0-0 draw)
1982†	Aberdeen beat Rangers (4-1)
1983†	Aberdeen beat Rangers (1-0)
1984†	Aberdeen beat Celtic (2-1)
1985	Celtic beat Dundee Utd (2-1)
1986	Aberdeen beat Hearts (3-0)
1987†	St Mirren beat Dundee Utd (1-0)

1988	Celtic beat Dundee Utd (2-1)
1989	Celtic beat Rangers (1-0)
1990†	Aberdeen beat Celtic (9-8 on pens after 0-0 draw)
1991†	Motherwell beat Dundee Utd (4-3)
1992	Rangers beat Airdrieonians (2-1)
1993	Rangers beat Aberdeen (2-1)
1994	Dundee Utd beat Rangers (1-0)
1995	Celtic beat Airdrieonians (1-0)
1996	Rangers beat Hearts (5-1)
1997	Kilmarnock beat Falkirk (1-0)
1998	Hearts beat Rangers (2-1)
1999	Rangers beat Celtic (1-0)
2000	Rangers beat Aberdeen (4-0)
2001	Celtic beat Hibernian (3-0)
2002	Rangers beat Celtic (3-2)
2003	Rangers beat Dundee (1-0)
2004	Celtic beat Dunfermline (3-1)
2005	Celtic beat Dundee Utd (1-0)
2006†	Hearts beat Gretna (4-2 on pens after 1-1 draw)
2007	Celtic beat Dunfermline (1-0)
2008	Rangers beat Queen of the South (3-2)
2009	Rangers beat Falkirk (1-0)
2010	Dundee Utd bt Ross Co (3-0)
2011	Celtic bt Motherwell (3-0)
2012	Hearts bt Hibernian (5-1)

† After extra time

SUMMARY OF SCOTTISH CUP WINNERS

Celtic 35, Rangers 33, Queen's Park 10, Hearts 8, Aberdeen 7, Clyde 3, Kilmarnock 3, St Mirren 3, Vale of Leven 3, Dundee Utd 2, Dunfermline 2, Falkirk 2, Hibernian 2, Motherwell 2, Renton 2, Third Lanark 2, Airdrieonians 1, Dumbarton 1, Dundee 1, East Fife 1, Morton 1, Partick 1, St Bernard's 1

FA WOMEN'S PREMIER LEAGUE

	P	W	D	L	F	A	GD	Pts
Sunderland	18	13	3	2	49	18	31	42
Leeds	18	13	2	3	36	10	26	41
Aston Villa	18	7	6	5	24	21	3	27
Barnet	18	7	5	6	30	21	9	26
Charlton	18	7	5	6	24	23	1	26
Coventry	18	7	5	6	19	19	0	26
Watford	18	5	2	11	16	39	-23	17
Cardiff	18	4	4	10	11	19	-8	16
Reading	18	5	1	12	25	43	-18	16
Nottm Forest	18	4	3	11	21	42	-21	15

BLUE SQUARE PREMIER LEAGUE 2011–2012

		P	W	D	L	F	A	W	D	L	F	A	GD	PTS
					Home			Away						
1	Fleetwood	46	13	8	2	50	25	18	2	3	52	23	54	103
2	Wrexham	46	16	3	4	48	17	14	5	4	37	16	52	98
3	Mansfield	46	14	6	3	50	25	11	8	4	37	23	39	89
4	York*	46	11	6	6	43	24	12	8	3	38	21	36	83
5	Luton	46	15	4	4	48	15	7	11	5	30	27	36	81
6	Kidderminster	46	10	7	6	44	32	12	3	8	38	31	19	76
7	Southport	46	8	8	7	36	39	13	5	5	36	30	3	76
8	Gateshead	46	11	8	4	39	26	10	3	10	30	36	7	74
9	Cambridge	46	11	6	6	31	16	8	8	7	26	25	16	71
10	Forest Green	46	11	5	7	37	25	8	8	7	29	20	21	70
11	Grimsby	46	12	4	7	51	28	7	9	7	28	32	19	70
12	Braintree	46	11	5	7	39	34	6	6	11	37	46	-4	62
13	Barrow	46	12	6	5	39	25	5	3	15	23	51	-14	60
14	Ebbsfleet	46	7	6	10	34	39	7	6	10	35	45	-15	54
15	Alfreton	46	8	6	9	39	48	7	3	13	23	38	-24	54
16	Stockport	46	8	7	8	35	28	4	8	11	23	46	-16	51
17	Lincoln	46	8	6	9	32	24	5	4	14	24	42	-10	49
18	Tamworth	46	7	9	7	30	30	4	6	13	17	40	-23	48
19	Newport	46	8	6	9	22	22	3	8	12	31	43	-12	47
20	Telford	46	6	8	9	24	26	1	10	12	21	39	-20	46
21	Hayes	46	5	5	13	26	41	6	3	14	32	49	-32	41
22	Darlington**	46	8	7	8	24	24	3	6	14	23	49	-26	36
23	Bath	46	5	4	14	27	41	2	6	15	16	48	-46	31
24	Kettering***	46	5	5	13	25	47	3	4	16	15	53	-60	30

* Also promoted; ** 10pts deducted; *** 3pts deducted

Manager of Year: Micky Mellon (Fleetwood). **Fair Play award**: Stockport
Leading league scorers: 31 Vardy (Fleetwood); 29 Green (Mansfield); 28 Shaw (Gateshead); 27 Hearn (Grimsby); 24 Gray (Southport); 21 Speight (Wrexham); 19 Mangan (Fleetwood), Willock (Ebbsfleet)
Team of Year: Tyler (Luton), Beeley (Fleetwood), Creighton (Wrexham), Kovacs (Luton), Knight-Percival (Wrexham), Blair (York), Fowler (Fleetwood), Meredith (York), Vardy (Fleetwood), Shaw (Gateshead), Hearn (Grimsby)

CHAMPIONS

1979–80	Altrincham	1997–98*	Halifax
1980–81	Altrincham	1998–99*	Cheltenham
1981–82	Runcorn	1999–2000*	Kidderminster
1982–83	Enfield	2000–01*	Rushden
1983–84	Maidstone	2001–02*	Boston
1984–85	Wealdstone	2002–03*	Yeovil
1985–86	Enfield	2003–04*	Chester
1986–87*	Scarborough	2004–05*	Barnet
1987–88*	Lincoln	2005–06*	Accrington
1988–89*	Maidstone	2006–07*	Dagenham
1989–90*	Darlington	2007–08*	Aldershot
1990–91*	Barnet	2008–09*	Burton
1991–92*	Colchester	2009–10*	Stevenage
1992–93*	Wycombe	2010–11*	Crawley
1993–94	Kidderminster	2011–2012*	Fleetwood
1994–95	Macclesfield	(*Promoted to Football League
1995–96	Stevenage	*Conference – Record Attendance*: 11,065
1996–97*	Macclesfield	*Oxford v Woking, December 26, 2006*

BLUE SQUARE PREMIER LEAGUE RESULTS 2011–2012

	AFC Telford	Alfreton	Barrow	Bath	Braintree	Cambridge	Darlington	Ebbsfleet	Fleetwood	Forest Green	Gateshead	Grimsby	Hayes	Kettering	Kidderminster	Lincoln	Luton	Mansfield	Newport	Southport	Stockport	Tamworth	Wrexham	York
AFC Telford	—	1-0	1-0	2-1	2-1	1-2	3-3	0-2	2-4	2-0	2-0	0-0	1-1	3-1	2-1	1-2	0-2	0-0	2-1	0-1	0-0	1-0	0-2	0-0
Alfreton	0-0	—	2-1	0-3	0-1	3-0	1-1	1-1	4-0	4-1	2-0	5-2	3-1	0-2	3-1	1-0	1-0	1-0	1-0	2-1	0-0	0-5	2-0	0-1
Barrow	2-1	1-0	—	0-1	1-1	1-0	0-1	0-1	4-1	3-0	2-0	5-2	1-1	2-1	1-2	1-0	2-0	7-0	2-2	2-1	3-2	2-0	2-0	3-1
Bath	3-1	0-3	0-1	—	3-3	3-3	2-2	2-2	4-1	0-2	1-0	6-0	1-1	4-1	4-1	2-0	3-1	0-0	3-0	2-1	4-0	0-1	6-2	1-0
Braintree	2-1	0-1	0-4	1-1	—	3-2	1-0	0-0	0-2	2-1	2-2	0-0	1-2	5-4	0-0	3-3	4-1	3-4	1-0	1-0	1-0	1-0	5-1	1-1
Cambridge	1-0	3-0	1-3	3-4	3-2	—	2-0	2-0	0-0	2-1	1-1	0-0	1-1	0-0	0-1	0-1	1-2	5-2	1-0	4-1	4-1	2-2	1-1	1-1
Darlington	1-0	3-1	3-0	2-0	3-1	2-0	—	1-3	1-3	0-0	3-1	1-2	0-0	3-1	3-1	5-0	5-2	2-0	3-3	0-3	3-4	1-0	2-1	1-0
Ebbsfleet	3-2	2-3	1-1	2-3	2-3	2-0	2-0	—	6-2	1-3	3-1	0-2	3-2	1-2	2-1	3-0	3-0	0-0	0-6	3-3	1-1	1-2	1-0	3-2
Fleetwood	2-2	1-4	2-0	1-4	1-4	2-0	0-1	0-1	—	1-2	2-1	1-3	2-3	2-3	2-3	1-2	1-1	0-6	1-1	0-6	2-4	0-3	0-1	1-0
Forest Green	2-1	1-6	0-0	0-2	1-5	1-1	0-0	0-1	1-2	—	2-1	2-0	2-0	2-1	4-1	1-1	1-1	1-1	1-3	1-1	1-1	1-1	2-1	1-0
Gateshead	3-0	1-1	1-1	2-1	4-2	3-1	0-1	0-1	3-1	1-0	—	3-0	0-1	0-1	3-1	1-0	5-1	4-0	2-0	1-1	0-1	0-1	0-0	1-0
Grimsby	2-0	2-5	2-2	6-0	5-0	0-1	0-0	3-1	1-0	2-1	1-1	—	3-0	1-0	2-2	0-1	1-0	3-2	0-0	1-2	1-1	4-1	2-0	2-0
Hayes	0-0	3-2	3-1	0-1	0-3	0-3	2-1	3-1	1-0	1-0	3-0	3-0	—	3-0	6-1	0-1	4-2	3-2	4-0	1-2	3-3	2-0	2-0	7-0
Kettering	2-1	1-1	3-0	0-1	0-1	2-1	3-1	1-0	2-0	1-1	3-3	1-0	3-0	—	3-1	1-0	5-0	4-0	3-1	1-2	1-0	2-2	7-0	2-3
Kidderminster	2-2	0-2	3-1	1-2	1-4	1-2	1-2	3-3	5-2	1-1	1-1	3-1	1-2	0-1	—	1-0	1-3	3-1	1-3	2-2	2-0	0-0	2-3	2-0
Lincoln	1-2	1-3	2-0	2-1	1-0	2-0	2-0	2-3	2-2	0-2	0-2	3-1	1-2	2-1	1-0	—	2-1	1-3	1-0	4-0	1-1	3-0	3-2	3-0
Luton	0-2	1-0	1-0	1-1	3-1	1-1	1-1	2-2	2-2	3-0	2-2	0-0	2-2	0-5	0-0	1-0	—	0-0	2-0	3-3	1-0	3-0	1-2	1-1
Mansfield	0-0	3-6	2-3	2-3	1-1	1-1	1-2	0-3	1-1	1-1	0-3	1-3	1-3	1-2	0-0	0-0	0-0	—	5-0	5-1	2-1	4-0	2-2	1-0
Newport	2-1	3-1	3-1	1-2	3-0	1-0	3-0	1-2	1-4	1-1	1-1	0-4	1-0	2-0	0-3	2-0	2-0	1-0	—	0-3	1-0	1-1	2-0	1-1
Southport	0-1	1-1	2-2	1-2	1-2	3-0	0-3	0-1	2-3	2-3	1-1	2-3	2-3	0-1	1-1	1-0	0-0	5-1	0-3	—	5-0	1-1	2-1	2-0
Stockport	0-0	6-1	1-0	0-2	0-2	2-2	2-2	2-1	2-2	1-1	1-1	7-0	1-3	1-1	1-3	1-1	1-0	2-1	1-0	5-0	—	4-0	2-1	2-1
Tamworth	1-0	5-2	6-1	0-2	3-1	3-1	3-0	3-0	3-0	3-1	1-1	1-0	1-0	0-1	4-0	3-0	3-0	4-0	1-1	1-1	4-0	—	1-2	3-0
Wrexham	0-2	1-4	3-1	3-1	0-0	0-0	2-4	0-5	2-4	1-0	1-0	1-3	1-4	0-1	0-1	1-2	1-2	2-0	2-0	0-5	1-0	1-2	—	0-3
York	0-0	0-2	0-0	0-1	0-1	0-1	2-2	1-2	2-2	1-1	1-1	2-3	2-4	1-5	1-5	1-1	1-1	1-0	1-1	0-2	2-1	3-0	0-3	—

BLUE SQUARE NORTH

		P	Home W	D	L	F	A	Away W	D	L	F	A	GD	PTS
1	Hyde	42	15	5	1	55	17	12	4	5	35	19	54	90
2	Guiseley	42	15	3	3	52	24	10	7	4	35	26	37	85
3	Halifax	42	10	5	6	41	33	11	6	4	39	26	21	74
4	Gainsborough	42	14	2	5	38	23	9	3	9	36	38	13	74
5	Nuneaton*	42	13	4	4	36	19	9	8	4	38	22	33	72
6	Stalybridge	42	13	2	6	48	33	7	9	5	35	31	19	71
7	Worcester	42	10	7	4	31	20	8	4	9	32	38	5	65
8	Altrincham	42	10	6	5	49	31	7	4	10	41	40	19	61
9	Droylsden	42	10	6	5	46	35	6	5	10	37	51	-3	59
10	B Stortford	42	8	4	9	35	30	9	3	9	35	45	-5	58
11	Boston United	42	6	8	7	28	29	9	1	11	32	38	-7	54
12	Colwyn Bay	42	9	3	9	31	39	6	5	10	24	31	-15	53
13	Workington	42	8	6	7	31	28	6	4	11	25	33	-5	52
14	Gloucester	42	8	3	10	25	27	7	4	10	28	33	-7	52
15	Harrogate	42	7	7	7	25	26	7	3	11	34	43	-10	52
16	Histon	42	5	9	7	41	41	7	6	8	26	31	-5	51
17	Corby	42	6	1	14	33	43	8	7	6	32	28	-6	50
18	Vauxhall	42	8	4	9	27	33	6	4	11	36	45	-15	50
19	Solihull	42	9	4	8	29	25	4	6	11	15	29	-10	49
20	Hinckley	42	5	5	11	36	43	8	4	9	39	47	-15	48
21	Blyth	42	5	5	11	30	38	2	8	11	21	43	-30	34
22	Eastwood	42	1	7	13	22	53	3	1	17	15	52	-68	20

* Also promoted and deducted 6pts; **Play-off final:** Nuneaton 1 Gainsborough 0

BLUE SQUARE SOUTH

		P	Home W	D	L	F	A	Away W	D	L	F	A	GD	PTS
1	Woking	42	15	4	2	43	18	15	3	3	49	23	51	97
2	Dartford*	42	15	4	2	52	19	11	6	4	37	21	49	88
3	Welling	42	14	6	1	42	18	10	3	8	37	29	32	81
4	Sutton	42	12	6	3	39	24	8	8	5	29	29	15	74
5	Basingstoke	42	10	6	5	35	29	10	5	6	30	21	15	71
6	Chelmsford	42	8	5	8	33	25	10	8	3	34	19	23	67
7	Dover	42	7	8	6	26	24	10	7	4	36	25	13	66
8	Boreham Wood	42	11	5	5	43	26	6	5	10	23	32	8	61
9	Tonbridge	42	10	4	7	41	34	5	8	8	29	33	3	57
10	Salisbury	42	9	4	8	27	21	6	8	7	28	33	1	57
11	Dorchester	42	7	4	10	30	37	9	4	8	28	28	-7	56
12	Eastleigh	42	10	5	6	36	25	5	4	12	21	38	-6	54
13	Weston-s-Mare	42	8	6	7	34	35	6	3	12	24	36	-13	51
14	Truro	42	7	3	11	33	37	6	6	9	32	43	-15	48
15	Staines	42	4	6	11	25	39	8	4	9	28	24	-10	46
16	Farnborough **	42	9	0	12	21	32	6	6	9	31	47	-27	46
17	Bromley	42	4	10	7	23	24	6	5	10	29	42	-14	45
18	Eastbourne	42	7	4	10	29	33	5	5	11	25	36	-15	45
19	Havant	42	7	6	8	39	34	4	5	12	25	41	-11	44
20	Maidenhead	42	4	6	11	25	41	7	4	10	24	33	-25	43
21	Hampton	42	3	7	11	22	39	7	5	9	31	30	-16	42
22	Thurrock	42	2	7	12	13	36	3	4	14	20	48	-51	26

* Also promoted; ** deducted 5pts; **Play-off final:** Dartford 1 Welling 0

OTHER LEAGUES 2011–12

CORBETT SPORTS WELSH PREMIER LEAGUE

	P	W	D	L	F	A	GD	Pts
New Saints	32	23	5	4	75	31	44	74
Bangor	32	22	3	7	72	46	26	69
Neath	32	18	8	6	60	36	24	62
Llanelli	32	18	5	9	63	36	27	59
Bala	32	14	7	11	48	41	7	49
Prestatyn	32	8	4	20	41	63	-22	28
Airbus	32	10	9	13	48	50	-2	39
Aberystwyth**	32	8	10	14	44	50	-6	33
Port Talbot	32	8	9	15	39	51	-12	33
Afan Lido	32	7	11	14	40	55	-15	32
Carmarthen	32	10	2	20	33	67	-34	32
Newtown*	32	7	5	20	44	82	-38	23

League split after 22 games, with teams staying in top six and bottom six regardless of points won. * 3 pts deducted, ** 1 pt deducted. **Cup Final**: Afan Lido 1 Newtown 1 (aet, Afan Lido won 3-2 on pens)

RYMAN PREMIER LEAGUE

	P	W	D	L	F	A	GD	Pts
Billericay	42	24	13	5	82	38	44	85
Hornchurch*	42	26	4	12	68	35	33	82
Lowestoft	42	25	7	10	80	53	27	82
Wealdstone	42	20	15	7	76	39	37	75
Bury	42	22	9	11	85	55	30	75
Lewes	42	21	10	11	55	47	8	73
Hendon	42	21	9	12	69	44	25	72
Canvey	42	22	5	15	66	55	11	71
Cray	42	20	8	14	74	55	19	68
East Thurrock	42	18	8	16	70	65	5	62
Kingstonian	42	18	7	17	58	64	-6	61
Met Police	42	18	6	18	63	46	17	60
Wingate	42	16	11	15	63	79	-16	59
Concord	42	16	9	17	72	66	6	57
Margate	42	15	9	18	66	65	1	54
Carshalton	42	14	10	18	48	55	-7	52
Harrow	42	13	8	21	53	70	-17	47
Hastings	42	13	8	21	43	61	-18	47
Leatherhead	42	11	8	23	46	62	-16	41
Aveley	42	5	12	25	41	88	-47	27
Tooting	42	7	6	29	47	116	-69	27
Horsham **	42	3	6	33	38	105	-67	14

*Also promoted, **1 pt deducted. **Play-off Final**: Hornchurch 2 Lowestoft 1 (aet)

EVOSTICK NORTH PREMIER LEAGUE

	P	W	D	L	F	A	GD	Pts
Chester	42	31	7	4	102	29	73	100
Northwich+	42	26	8	8	73	43	30	83
Chorley	42	24	7	11	76	48	28	79
Bradford PA*	42	24	6	12	77	49	28	78
Hednesford	42	21	10	11	67	49	18	73
FC United	42	21	9	12	83	51	32	72
Marine	42	19	9	14	56	50	6	66
Rushall	42	17	10	15	52	51	1	61
North Ferriby	42	16	10	16	56	70	-14	58
Nantwich***	42	15	13	14	65	61	4	57
Kendal	42	15	8	19	78	83	-5	53
Ashton	42	15	8	19	61	67	-6	53
Buxton	42	15	8	19	64	77	-13	53
Matlock	42	12	14	16	52	54	-2	50
Worksop	42	13	10	19	56	76	-20	49
Stafford	42	12	12	18	60	65	-5	48
Whitby	42	12	11	19	57	80	-23	47
Stocksbridge	42	10	12	20	57	75	-18	42
Frickley	42	10	12	20	48	69	-21	42
Chasetown	42	10	11	21	50	75	-25	41
Mickleover**	42	11	10	21	67	85	-18	40
Burscough	42	5	11	26	54	104	-50	26

+Expelled for breach of financial rules, *also promoted, **3 pts deducted; *** 1 pt deducted.
Play-off Final: Bradford PA 1 FC United 0 (aet)

EVOSTICK SOUTH PREMIER LEAGUE

	P	W	D	L	F	A	GD	Pts
Brackley	42	25	10	7	92	48	44	85
Oxford City*	42	22	11	9	68	41	27	77
Totton	42	21	11	10	81	43	38	74
Chesham	42	21	10	11	76	53	23	73
Cambridge City	42	21	9	12	78	52	26	72
Stourbridge	42	20	12	10	67	45	22	72
Leamington	42	18	15	9	60	47	13	69
St Albans	42	17	11	14	72	77	-5	62
Barwell	42	17	10	15	70	61	9	61
Bedford	42	15	10	17	60	69	-9	55
Chippenham	42	14	11	17	55	53	2	53
Frome	42	12	16	14	44	49	-5	52
Bashley	42	13	13	16	58	74	-16	52
Hitchin	42	13	12	17	54	57	-3	51
Redditch	42	14	9	19	45	50	-5	51
Banbury	42	13	10	19	54	61	-7	49
Weymouth	42	13	9	20	54	75	-21	48
Arlesey	42	12	11	19	43	60	-17	47
Hemel Hempstead	42	10	14	18	46	66	-20	44
Evesham	42	12	8	22	49	71	-22	44
Swindon Super	42	11	11	20	50	86	-36	44
Cirencester	42	7	9	26	40	78	-38	30

*Also promoted. **Play-off Final**: Oxford City 4 Totton 2

PRESS AND JOURNAL HIGHLAND LEAGUE

	P	W	D	L	F	A	GD	Pts
Forres	34	24	5	5	85	35	50	77
Cove	34	23	7	4	93	33	60	76
Nairn	34	19	9	6	92	44	48	66
Inverurie	34	20	5	9	71	35	36	65
Buckie	34	18	7	9	79	45	34	61
Fraserburgh	34	17	8	9	79	63	16	59
Deveronvale	34	17	4	13	75	50	25	55
Wick	34	16	7	11	77	55	22	55
Keith	34	16	6	12	85	57	28	54
Clachnacuddin	34	14	8	12	79	65	14	50
Formartine	34	14	7	13	62	60	2	49
Lossiemouth	34	15	4	15	51	52	-1	49
Huntly	34	14	4	16	50	67	-17	46
Turriff	34	13	4	17	61	64	-3	43
Rothes	34	7	5	22	31	80	-49	26
Brora	34	6	2	26	33	115	-82	20
Strathspey	34	3	2	29	27	102	-75	11
Fort William	34	1	4	29	14	122	-108	7

Cup Final: Buckie 2 Cove 0

BARCLAYS PREMIER RESERVE LEAGUE

NORTH

	P	W	D	L	F	A	GD	Pts
Manchester Utd	22	15	4	3	58	23	35	49
Liverpool	22	9	8	5	44	30	14	35
Everton	22	9	8	5	38	29	9	35
Sunderland	22	9	5	8	38	36	2	32
Newcastle	22	7	4	11	38	58	-20	25
Wigan	22	5	9	8	27	37	-10	24
Blackburn	22	4	10	8	18	22	-4	22
Bolton	22	3	8	11	23	40	-17	17

SOUTH

	P	W	D	L	F	A	GD	Pts
Aston Villa	22	13	4	5	45	22	23	43
Fulham	22	12	4	6	46	25	21	40
Arsenal	22	11	5	6	36	25	11	38
WBA	22	11	2	9	36	31	5	35
Chelsea	22	7	7	8	42	43	-1	28
Wolves	22	6	5	11	26	41	-15	23
Swansea	22	4	8	10	21	38	-17	20
Norwich	22	2	7	13	26	62	-36	13

Play-off Final: Manchester Utd 0 Aston Villa 0 – Old Trafford (Manchester Utd won 3-1 on pens)

IRISH FOOTBALL 2011–12

AIRTRICITY LEAGUE OF IRELAND

PREMIER DIVISION

	P	W	D	L	F	A	Pts
Shamrock Rov	36	23	8	5	69	24	77
Sligo Rov	36	22	7	7	73	19	73
Derry City	36	18	14	4	63	23	68
St Patrick's Ath	36	17	12	7	62	35	63
Bohemians	36	17	9	10	39	27	60
Bray Wdrs	36	15	6	15	53	50	51
Dundalk	36	11	11	14	50	53	44
UCD	36	10	4	22	42	80	34
Drogheda Utd	36	7	4	25	32	77	25
Galway Utd	36	1	3	32	20	115	6

Leading scorer: 22 Eamon Zayed (Derry City). **Player of Year:** Eamon Zayed. **Young Player of Year:** Enda Stevens (Shamrock Rov). **Goalkeeper of Year:** Gerard Doherty (Derry City). **Personality of Year:** Michael O'Neill (Shamrock Rov)

FIRST DIVISION

	P	W	D	L	F	A	Pts
Cork City	30	20	9	1	73	26	69
Shelbourne	30	22	2	6	61	24	68
Monaghan Utd	30	21	4	5	60	27	67
Limerick	30	20	6	4	49	22	66
Waterford Utd	30	13	3	14	37	31	42
Longford Town	30	12	4	14	38	41	40
Mervue Utd	30	10	4	16	37	45	34
Athlone Town	30	9	5	16	25	53	32
Finn Harps	30	8	4	18	29	45	28
Wexford Youths	30	4	2	24	29	68	14
Salthill Devons	30	2	5	23	18	74	11

Leading scorer: 23 Graham Cummins (Cork City). **Player of Year:** Graham Cummins

FAI FORD CUP FINAL

Sligo Rov 1 (Davoran) **Shelbourne** 1 (Hughes) – aet, Sligo won 4-1 on pens. Aviva Stadium, Dublin, November 6, 2011
Sligo: Clarke (Kelly), Keane, Davoran, Peers, Ventre, Ryan, Dillon (Blinkhorn), Russell (Cretaro), McGuinness, Greene, Doyle
Shelbourne: Delany, Ryan, S Byrne, Boyle, Paisley, Sullivan (C Byrne), Clancy, Cassidy (James), Hughes, Dawson, McGill (Bermingham). Sent off: Clancy
Referee: R Winter (Wicklow)

EA SPORTS LEAGUE CUP FINAL

Derry City 1 (Zayed) **Cork City** 0. Turner's Cross, Cork, September 24, 2011

SETANTA SPORTS CUP FINAL

Crusaders 2 (Coates 2) **Derry City** 2 (Patterson 2) – aet, Crusaders won 5-4 on pens. Oval, Belfast, May 12 2012

CARLING IRISH PREMIER LEAGUE

	P	W	D	L	F	A	Pts
Linfield	38	27	4	7	79	29	85
Portadown	38	22	5	11	72	47	71
Cliftonville	38	21	6	11	83	62	69
Coleraine	38	18	12	8	61	38	66
Crusaders	38	18	10	10	63	47	64
Glentoran	38	16	9	13	67	52	57
Ballymena Utd	38	14	8	16	66	71	50
Donegal Celtic	38	12	5	21	44	80	41
Dungannon Swifts	38	8	11	19	42	71	35
Glenavon	38	8	10	20	60	71	34
Lisburn Distillery	38	8	8	22	56	84	32
Carrick Rgrs	38	7	10	21	50	91	31

Leading scorer: 27 Gary McCutcheon (Ballymena Utd). **Player of Year:** Chris Morrow (Crusaders).
Young Player of Year: Rory Donnelly (Cliftonville). **Manager of Year:** David Jeffrey (Linfield)

BELFAST TELEGRAPH CHAMPIONSHIP – DIVISION 1

	P	W	D	L	F	A	Pts
Ballinamallard Utd	26	20	3	3	62	24	63
Newry City	26	15	6	5	51	22	51
Institute	26	13	4	9	37	34	43
Bangor	26	12	6	8	45	34	42
Ards	26	11	6	9	39	31	39
Limavady Utd	26	12	2	12	48	43	38
Loughhall	26	11	5	10	45	41	38
Dergview	26	8	10	8	38	37	34
HW Welders	26	10	4	12	30	35	34
Larne	26	9	5	12	37	47	32
Tobermore Utd	26	8	7	11	34	44	31
Warrenpoint Town	26	7	7	12	34	37	28
Banbridge Town	26	5	4	17	30	70	19
Glebe Rgrs	26	3	7	16	25	56	16

Leading scorer: 16 Andy Crawford (Ballinamallard Utd). **Player of Year:** Chris Curran (Ballinamallard Utd)

JJB IRISH CUP FINAL

Linfield 4 (McAllister 2, Carvill, Mulgrew) **Crusaders** 1 (Coates) – Windsor Park, May 5 2012
Linfield: Blayney, Curran, Murphy, Watson Ervin, Carvill, Garrett (Casement) Mulgrew (Burns), Lowry, McAllister (Fordyce) Thompson
Crusaders: O'Neill, McKeown (Leeman), McBride (Watson), Magowan, Coates, Dallas, Morrow, Adamson, Rainey, Caddell, McMaster (Owens)
Referee: R Crangle (Belfast)

IRN-BRU LEAGUE CUP FINAL

Crusaders 1 (Morrow) **Coleraine** 0 – Ballymena Showgrounds, January 28, 2012

PADDY POWER COUNTY ANTRIM SHIELD FINAL

Cliftonville 2 (M Donnelly, Gormley) **Glentoran** 1 (Taylor) – Oval, Belfast, November 29 2011

WORLD CUP 2014 – QUALIFYING

The 2014 World Cup draw which brought together Scotland and Wales evoked poignant memories of when the teams last shared a qualifying group. In September 1985, a penalty by Rangers winger Davie Cooper in the 81st minute at Ninian Park, Cardiff gave Scotland a 1-1 draw and a play-off with Australia. Minutes after the goal, their 62-year-old manager Jock Stein collapsed in the dug-out and died of a heart attack in the stadium's medical room. Stein's assistant Alex Ferguson, then manager of Aberdeen, supervised a 2-0 victory in the two-leg play-off and took the side to the finals in Mexico, where they were eliminated after losing to Denmark and West Germany and drawing with Uruguay. Since then, three Home Internationals brought three wins for Wales, while the most recent meeting, in the Carling Nations Cup in May 2011, resulted in a 3-1 victory for Scotland under Craig Levein thanks to goals from James Morrison, Kenny Miller and Christophe Berra. Now they resume rivalry in Cardiff on October 12, with Chris Coleman having succeeded the late Gary Speed and looking to maintain the improvement Wales showed before Speed's death with four wins in five games. The return fixture is in Glasgow on March 22, 2013.

Michael O'Neill makes his competitive debut after replacing Nigel Worthington as Northern Ireland manager. It's a tough one, away to Russia on September 7, in a group which also includes Portugal and in which the Irish will need to show an improvement on their European Championship qualifying results in order to stand any chance of going through. Unlike Euro 2012, Roy Hodgson will have plenty of time to prepare for England's bid, which starts with an away match against Moldova. It becomes more demanding, with fixtures against Ukraine, the team they overcame in Donetsk to finish group winners, Poland and Montenegro, who held them twice in qualifying games. The Republic of Ireland kick off against Kazakhstan, a team they have never met, before the serious business gets under way against Germany. Winners of the nine European groups qualify for the finals in Brazil. The best eight runners-up are paired in two-leg play-offs for four further places.

South American qualifying is already well under way, with Luis Suarez leading Uruguay's bid for a place. The Liverpool striker scored all their goals in a 4-0 win over Chile, one in the 4-2 success against Peru and another as they beat Bolivia by the score scoreline. Sergio Aguero, whose stoppage-time winner against Queens Park Rangers gave Manchester City the Premier League title, was also on the mark in Argentina's wins over Equador (4-0) and Colombia (2-1).

EUROPE QUALIFYING

Group A: Croatia, Serbia, Belgium, **Scotland**, Macedonia, **Wales**
Group B: Italy, Denmark, Czech Republic, Bulgaria, Armenia, Malta
Group C: Germany, Sweden, **Republic of Ireland**, Austria, Faroe Islands, Kazakhstan
Group D: Holland, Turkey, Hungary, Romania, Estonia, Andorra
Group E: Norway, Slovenia, Switzerland, Albania, Cyprus, Iceland
Group F: Portugal, Russia, Israel, **Northern Ireland**, Azerbaijan, Luxembourg
Group G: Greece, Slovakia, Bosnia-Herzegovina, Lithuania, Latvia, Liechtenstein
Group H: **England**, Montenegro, Ukraine, Poland, Moldova, San Marino
Group I: Spain, France, Belarus, Georgia, Finland

SOUTH AMERICA QUALIFYING

	P	W	D	L	F	A	Pts
Chile	6	4	0	2	11	10	12
Uruguay	5	3	2	0	14	6	11
Argentina	5	3	1	1	11	4	10
Ecuador	5	3	0	2	6	6	9
Venezuela	6	2	2	2	4	6	8
Colombia	5	2	1	2	5	5	7

Bolivia	6	1	1	4	7	11	4
Paraguay	5	1	1	3	4	9	4
Peru	5	1	0	4	6	11	3

(Brazil qualify as hosts. Top four also go through – fifth team plays off against Asian side)

WORLD CUP SUMMARIES 1930–2010

1930 – URUGUAY

WINNERS: Uruguay RUNNERS-UP: Argentina THIRD: USA FOURTH: Yugoslavia
Other countries taking part: Belgium, Bolivia, Brazil, Chile, France, Mexico, Paraguay, Peru, Romania. **Total entries:** 13
Venue: All matches played in Montevideo
Top scorer: Stabile (Argentina) 8 goals
Final (30/7/30): **Uruguay 4** (Dorado 12, Cea 55, Iriarte 64, Castro 89) **Argentina 2** (Peucelle 29, Stabile 35). **Att:** 90,000
Uruguay: Ballesteros; Nasazzi (capt), Mascheroni, Andrade, Fernandez, Gestido, Dorado, Scarone, Castro, Cea, Iriarte
Argentina: Botasso; Della Torre, Paternoster, J Evaristo, Monti, Suarez, Peucelle, Varallo, Stabile, Ferreira (capt), M Evaristo
Referee: Langenus (Belgium). **Half-time:** 1-2

1934 – ITALY

WINNERS: Italy RUNNERS-UP: Czechoslovakia THIRD: Germany FOURTH: Austria
Other countries in finals: Argentina, Belgium, Brazil, Egypt, France, Holland, Hungary, Romania, Spain, Sweden, Switzerland, USA. **Total entries:** 29 (16 qualifiers)
Venues: Bologna, Florence, Genoa, Milan, Naples, Rome, Trieste, Turin
Top scorers: Conen (Germany), Nejedly (Czechoslovakia), Schiavio (Italy), each 4 goals. **Final** (Rome, 10/6/34): **Italy 2** (Orsi 82, Schiavio 97) **Czechoslovakia 1** (Puc 70) after extra-time. **Att:** 50,000
Italy: Combi (capt); Monzeglio, Allemandi, Ferraris, Monti, Bertolini, Guaita, Meazza, Schiavio, Ferrari, Orsi
Czechoslovakia: Planicka (capt); Zenisek, Ctyroky, Kostalek, Cambal, Krcil, Junek, Svoboda, Sobotka, Nejedly, Puc
Referee: Eklind (Sweden). **Half-time:** 0-0 (90 mins: 1-1)

1938 – FRANCE

WINNERS: Italy RUNNERS-UP: Hungary THIRD: Brazil FOURTH: Sweden
Other countries in finals: Belgium, Cuba, Czechoslovakia, Dutch East Indies, France, Germany, Holland, Norway, Poland, Romania, Switzerland. **Total entries:** 25 (15 qualifiers)
Venues: Antibes, Bordeaux, Le Havre, Lille, Marseilles, Paris, Reims, Strasbourg, Toulouse
Top scorer: Leonidas (Brazil) 8 goals
Final (Paris, 19/6/38): **Italy 4** (Colaussi 6, 36, Piola 15, 81) **Hungary 2** (Titkos 7, Sarosi 65). **Att:** 45,000
Italy: Olivieri; Foni, Rava, Serantoni, Andreolo, Locatelli, Biavati, Meazza (capt), Piola, Ferrari, Colaussi
Hungary: Szabo; Polgar, Biro, Szalay, Szucs, Lazar, Sas, Vincze, Sarosi (capt), Szengeller, Titkos
Referee: Capdeville (France). **Half-time:** 3-1

1950 – BRAZIL

WINNERS: Uruguay RUNNERS-UP: Brazil THIRD: Sweden FOURTH: Spain
Other countries in finals: Bolivia, Chile, England, Italy, Mexico, Paraguay, Switzerland, USA, Yugoslavia. **Total entries:** 29 (13 qualifiers)
Venues: Belo Horizonte, Curitiba, Porto Alegre, Recife, Rio de Janeiro, Sao Paulo

Top scorer: Ademir (Brazil) 9 goals
Deciding Match (Rio de Janeiro, 16/7/50): **Uruguay 2** (Schiaffino 64, Ghiggia 79) **Brazil 1** (Friaca 47). **Att:** 199,850
(For the only time, the World Cup was decided on a final pool system, in which the winners of the four qualifying groups met in a six-match series So, unlike previous and subsequent tournaments, there was no official final as such, but Uruguay v Brazil was the deciding match in the final pool)
Uruguay: Maspoli; Gonzales, Tejera, Gambetta, Varela (capt), Andrade, Ghiggia, Perez, Miguez, Schiaffino, Moran
Brazil: Barbosa; Augusto (capt), Juvenal, Bauer, Danilo, Bigode, Friaca, Zizinho, Ademir, Jair, Chico
Referee: Reader (England). **Half-time:** 0-0

1954 – SWITZERLAND
WINNERS: West Germany RUNNERS-UP: Hungary THIRD: Austria FOURTH: Uruguay
Other countries in finals: Belgium, Brazil, Czechoslovakia, England, France, Italy, Korea, Mexico, Scotland, Switzerland, Turkey, Yugoslavia. **Total entries:** 35 (16 qualifiers)
Venues: Basle, Berne, Geneva, Lausanne, Lugano, Zurich
Top scorer: Kocsis (Hungary) 11 goals
Final (Berne, 4/7/54): **West Germany 3** (Morlock 12, Rahn 17, 84) **Hungary 2** (Puskas 4, Czibor 9). **Att:** 60,000
West Germany: Turek; Posipal, Kohlmeyer, Eckel, Liebrich, Mai, Rahn, Morlock, O Walter, F Walter (capt), Schaefer
Hungary: Grosics; Buzansky, Lantos, Bozsik, Lorant, Zakarias, Czibor, Kocsis, Hidegkuti, Puskas (capt), J Toth
Referee: Ling (England). **Half-time:** 2-2

1958 – SWEDEN
WINNERS: Brazil RUNNERS-UP: Sweden THIRD: France FOURTH: West Germany
Other countries in finals: Argentina, Austria, Czechoslovakia, England, Hungary, Mexico, Northern Ireland, Paraguay, Scotland, Soviet Union, Wales, Yugoslavia. **Total entries:** 47 (16 qualifiers)
Venues: Boras, Eskilstuna, Gothenburg, Halmstad, Helsingborgs, Malmo, Norrkoping, Orebro, Sandviken, Stockholm, Vasteras
Top scorer: Fontaine (France) 13 goals
Final (Stockholm, 29/6/58): **Brazil 5** (Vava 10, 32, Pele 55, 88, Zagalo 76) **Sweden 2** (Liedholm 4, Simonsson 83). **Att:** 49,737
Brazil: Gilmar; D Santos, N Santos, Zito, Bellini (capt), Orlando, Garrincha, Didi, Vava, Pele, Zagalo
Sweden: Svensson; Bergmark, Axbom, Boerjesson, Gustavsson, Parling, Hamrin, Gren, Simonsson, Liedholm (capt), Skoglund
Referee: Guigue (France). **Half-time:** 2-1

1962 – CHILE
WINNERS: Brazil RUNNERS-UP: Czechoslovakia THIRD: Chile FOURTH: Yugoslavia
Other countries in finals: Argentina, Bulgaria, Colombia, England, Hungary, Italy, Mexico, Soviet Union, Spain, Switzerland, Uruguay, West Germany. **Total entries:** 53 (16 qualifiers)
Venues: Arica, Rancagua, Santiago, Vina del Mar
Top scorer: Jerkovic (Yugoslavia) 5 goals
Final (Santiago, 17/6/62): **Brazil 3** (Amarildo 17, Zito 69, Vava 77) **Czechoslovakia 1** (Masopust 16). **Att:** 68,679
Brazil: Gilmar; D Santos, Mauro (capt), Zozimo, N Santos, Zito, Didi, Garrincha, Vava, Amarildo, Zagalo
Czechoslovakia: Schroiff; Tichy, Novak, Pluskal, Popluhar, Masopust (capt), Pospichal, Scherer,

Kvasnak, Kadraba, Jelinek
Referee: Latychev (Soviet Union). **Half-time:** 1-1

1966 – ENGLAND

WINNERS: England RUNNERS-UP: West Germany THIRD: Portugal FOURTH: USSR
Other countries in finals: Argentina, Brazil, Bulgaria, Chile, France, Hungary, Italy, Mexico,
North Korea, Spain, Switzerland, Uruguay. **Total entries:** 53 (16 qualifiers)
Venues: Birmingham (Villa Park), Liverpool (Goodison Park), London (Wembley and White City),
Manchester (Old Trafford), Middlesbrough, Sheffield (Hillsborough), Sunderland
Top scorer: Eusebio (Portugal) 9 goals
Final (Wembley, 30/7/66): **England 4** (Hurst 19, 100, 120, Peters 78) **West Germany 2**
(Haller 13, Weber 89) after extra-time. **Att:** 93,802
England: Banks; Cohen, Wilson, Stiles, J Charlton, Moore (capt), Ball, Hurst, Hunt, R Charlton, Peters
West Germany: Tilkowski; Hottges, Schnellinger, Beckenbauer, Schulz, Weber, Haller, Held,
Seeler (capt), Overath, Emmerich
Referee: Dienst (Switzerland). **Half-time:** 1-1 (90 mins: 2-2)

1970 – MEXICO

WINNERS: Brazil RUNNERS-UP: Italy THIRD: West Germany FOURTH: Uruguay
Other countries in finals: Belgium, Bulgaria, Czechoslovakia, El Salvador, England, Israel,
Mexico, Morocco, Peru, Romania, Soviet Union, Sweden. **Total entries:** 68 (16 qualifiers)
Venues: Guadalajara, Leon, Mexico City, Puebla, Toluca
Top scorer: Muller (West Germany) 10 goals
Final (Mexico City, 21/6/70): **Brazil 4** (Pele 18, Gerson 66, Jairzinho 71, Carlos Alberto 87)
Italy 1 (Boninsegna 38). **Att:** 107,412
Brazil: Felix; Carlos Alberto (capt), Brito, Piazza, Everaldo, Clodoaldo, Gerson, Jairzinho,
Tostao, Pele, Rivelino
Italy: Albertosi; Burgnich, Facchetti (capt), Cera, Rosato, Bertini (Juliano 72), Domenghini, De
Sisti, Mazzola, Boninsegna (Rivera 84), Riva
Referee: Glockner (East Germany). **Half-time:** 1-1

1974 – WEST GERMANY

WINNERS: West Germany RUNNERS-UP: Holland THIRD: Poland FOURTH: Brazil
Other countries in finals: Argentina, Australia, Bulgaria, Chile, East Germany, Haiti, Italy,
Scotland, Sweden, Uruguay, Yugoslavia, Zaire. **Total entries:** 98 (16 qualifiers)
Venues: Berlin, Dortmund, Dusseldorf, Frankfurt, Gelsenkirchen, Hamburg, Hanover, Munich,
Stuttgart
Top scorer: Lato (Poland) 7 goals
Final (Munich, 7/7/74): **West Germany 2** (Breitner 25 pen, Muller 43) **Holland 1** (Neeskens 2
pen). **Att:** 77,833
West Germany: Maier; Vogts, Schwarzenbeck, Beckenbauer (capt), Breitner, Bonhof, Hoeness,
Overath, Grabowski, Muller, Holzenbein
Holland: Jongbloed; Suurbier, Rijsbergen (De Jong 69), Haan, Krol, Jansen, Van Hanegem,
Neeskens, Rep, Cruyff (capt), Rensenbrink (R Van der Kerkhof 46)
Referee: Taylor (England). **Half-time:** 2-1

1978 – ARGENTINA

WINNERS: Argentina RUNNERS-UP: Holland THIRD: Brazil FOURTH: Italy
Other countries in finals: Austria, France, Hungary, Iran, Mexico, Peru, Poland, Scotland,
Spain, Sweden, Tunisia, West Germany. **Total entries:** 102 (16 qualifiers)
Venues: Buenos Aires, Cordoba, Mar del Plata, Mendoza, Rosario
Top scorer: Kempes (Argentina) 6 goals
Final (Buenos Aires, 25678): **Argentina 3** (Kempes 38, 104, Bertoni 115) **Holland 1**
(Nanninga 82) after extra-time. **Att:** 77,000

Argentina: Fillol; Passarella (capt), Olguin, Galvan, Tarantini, Ardiles (Larrosa 66), Gallego, Ortiz (Houseman 74), Bertoni, Luque, Kempes
Holland: Jongbloed; Krol (capt), Poortvliet, Brandts, Jansen (Suurbier 73), Haan, Neeskens, W Van der Kerkhof, Rep (Nanninga 58), R Van der Kerkhof, Rensenbrink
Referee: Gonella (Italy). **Half-time**: 1-0 (90 mins: 1-1)

1982 – SPAIN

WINNERS: Italy RUNNERS-UP: West Germany THIRD: Poland FOURTH: France
Other countries in finals: Algeria, Argentina, Austria, Belgium, Brazil, Cameroon, Chile, Czechoslovakia, El Salvador, England, Honduras, Hungary, Kuwait, New Zealand, Northern Ireland, Peru, Scotland, Soviet Union, Spain, Yugoslavia. **Total entries**: 109 (24 qualifiers)
Venues: Alicante, Barcelona, Bilbao, Coruna, Elche, Gijon, Madrid, Malaga, Oviedo, Seville, Valencia, Valladolid, Vigo, Zaragoza
Top scorer: Rossi (Italy) 6 goals
Final (Madrid, 11/7/82): **Italy** 3 (Rossi 57, Tardelli 69, Altobelli 81) **West Germany** 1 (Breitner 84). **Att**: 90,089
Italy: Zoff (capt); Bergomi, Scirea, Collovati, Cabrini, Oriali, Gentile, Tardelli, Conti, Rossi, Graziani (Altobelli 18 – Causio 88)
West Germany: Schumacher; Kaltz, Stielike, K-H Forster, B Forster, Dremmler (Hrubesch 63), Breitner, Briegel, Rummenigge (capt) (Muller 70), Fischer, Littbarski
Referee: Coelho (Brazil). **Half-time**: 0-0

1986 – MEXICO

WINNERS: Argentina RUNNERS-UP: West Germany THIRD: France FOURTH: Belgium
Other countries in finals: Algeria, Brazil, Bulgaria, Canada, Denmark, England, Hungary, Iraq, Italy, Mexico, Morocco, Northern Ireland, Paraguay, Poland, Portugal, Scotland, South Korea, Soviet Union, Spain, Uruguay. **Total entries**: 118 (24 qualifiers)
Venues: Guadalajara, Irapuato, Leon, Mexico City, Monterrey, Nezahualcoyotl, Puebla, Queretaro, Toluca
Top scorer: Lineker (England) 6 goals
Final (Mexico City, 29/6/86): **Argentina** 3 (Brown 23, Valdano 56, Burruchaga 85) **West Germany** 2 (Rummenigge 74, Voller 82). **Att**: 115,026
Argentina: Pumpido; Cuciuffo, Brown, Ruggeri, Olarticoechea, Batista, Giusti, Maradona (capt), Burruchaga (Trobbiani 89), Enrique, Valdano
West Germany: Schumacher; Berthold, K-H Forster, Jakobs, Brehme, Briegel, Eder, Matthaus, Magath (Hoeness 62), Allofs (Voller 45), Rummenigge (capt)
Referee: Filho (Brazil). **Half-time**: 1-0

1990 – ITALY

WINNERS: West Germany RUNNERS-UP: Argentina THIRD: Italy FOURTH: England
Other countries in finals: Austria, Belgium, Brazil, Cameroon, Colombia, Costa Rica, Czechoslovakia, Egypt, Holland, Republic of Ireland, Romania, Scotland, Spain, South Korea, Soviet Union, Sweden, United Arab Emirates, USA, Uruguay, Yugoslavia. **Total entries**: 103 (24 qualifiers)
Venues: Bari, Bologna, Cagliari, Florence, Genoa, Milan, Naples, Palermo, Rome, Turin, Udine, Verona
Top scorer: Schillaci (Italy) 6 goals
Final (Rome, 8/7/90): **Argentina 0 West Germany 1** (Brehme 85 pen). **Att**: 73,603
Argentina: Goycochea; Ruggeri (Monzon 45), Simon, Serrizuela, Lorenzo, Basualdo, Troglio, Burruchaga (Calderon 53), Sensini, Maradona (capt), Dezotti **Sent-off**: Monzon (65), Dezotti (86) – first players ever to be sent off in World Cup Final
West Germany: Illgner; Berthold (Reuter 75), Buchwald, Augenthaler, Kohler, Brehme, Matthaus (capt), Littbarski, Hassler, Klinsmann, Voller
Referee: Codesal (Mexico). **Half-time**: 0-0

1994 – USA

WINNERS: Brazil RUNNERS-UP: Italy THIRD: Sweden FOURTH: Bulgaria
Other countries in finals: Argentina, Belgium, Bolivia, Cameroon, Colombia, Germany, Greece, Holland, Mexico, Morocco, Nigeria, Norway, Republic of Ireland, Romania, Russia, Saudi Arabia, South Korea, Spain, Switzerland, USA. **Total entries:** 144 (24 qualifiers)
Venues: Boston, Chicago, Dallas, Detroit, Los Angeles, New York City, Orlando, San Francisco, Washington
Top scorers: Salenko (Russia), Stoichkov (Bulgaria), each 6 goals
Final (Los Angeles, 17/7/94): **Brazil 0 Italy 0** after extra-time; Brazil won 3-2 on pens
Att: 94,194
Brazil: Taffarel; Jorginho (Cafu 21), Aldair, Marcio Santos, Branco, Mazinho, Mauro Silva, Dunga (capt), Zinho (Viola 105), Romario, Bebeto
Italy: Pagliuca; Mussi (Apolloni 35), Baresi (capt), Maldini, Benarrivo, Berti, Albertini, D Baggio (Evani 95), Donadoni, R Baggio, Massaro
Referee: Puhl (Hungary)
Shoot-out: Baresi missed, Marco Santos saved, Albertini 1-0, Romario 1-1, Evani 2-1, Branco 2-2, Massaro saved, Dunga 2-3, R Baggio over

1998 – FRANCE

WINNERS: France RUNNERS-UP: Brazil THIRD: Croatia FOURTH: Holland
Other countries in finals: Argentina, Austria, Belgium, Bulgaria, Cameroon, Chile, Colombia, Denmark, England, Germany, Iran, Italy, Jamaica, Japan, Mexico, Morocco, Nigeria, Norway, Paraguay, Romania, Saudi Arabia, Scotland, South Africa, South Korea, Spain, Tunisia, USA, Yugoslavia. **Total entries:** 172 (32 qualifiers)
Venues: Bordeaux, Lens, Lyon, Marseille, Montpellier, Nantes, Paris (St Denis, Parc des Princes), Saint-Etienne, Toulouse
Top scorer: Davor Suker (Croatia) 6 goals
Final (Paris St Denis, 12/7/98): **Brazil 0 France 3** (Zidane 27, 45, Petit 90). **Att:** 75,000
Brazil: Taffarel; Cafu, Junior Baiano, Aldair, Roberto Carlos; Dunga (capt), Leonardo (Denilson 46), Cesar Sampaio (Edmundo 74), Rivaldo; Bebeto, Ronaldo
France: Barthez; Thuram, Leboeuf, Desailly, Lizarazu; Karembeu (Boghossian 56), Deschamps (capt), Petit, Zidane, Djorkaeff (Viera 75); Guivarc'h (Dugarry 66) **Sent-off:** Desailly (68)
Referee: Belqola (Morocco). **Half-time:** 0-2

2002 – JAPAN/SOUTH KOREA

WINNERS: Brazil RUNNERS-UP: Germany THIRD: Turkey FOURTH: South Korea
Other countries in finals: Argentina, Belgium, Cameroon, China, Costa Rica, Croatia, Denmark, Ecuador, England, France, Italy, Japan, Mexico, Nigeria, Paraguay, Poland, Portugal, Republic of Ireland, Russia, Saudi Arabia, Senegal, Slovenia, South Africa, Spain, Sweden, Tunisia, USA, Uruguay. **Total entries:** 195 (32 qualifiers)
Venues: Japan – Ibaraki, Kobe, Miyagi, Niigata, Oita, Osaka, Saitama, Sapporo, Shizuoka, Yokohama. **South Korea** – Daegu, Daejeon, Gwangju, Incheon, Jeonju, Busan, Seogwipo, Seoul, Suwon Ulsan
Top scorer: Ronaldo (Brazil) 8 goals
Final (Yokohama, 30/6/02): **Germany 0, Brazil 2** (Ronaldo 67, 79). **Att:** 69,029
Germany: Kahn (capt), Linke, Ramelow, Metzelder, Frings, Jeremies (Asamoah 77), Hamann, Schneider, Bode (Zeige 84), Klose (Bierhoff 74), Neuville
Brazil: Marcos, Lucio, Edmilson, Roque Junior, Cafu (capt) Kleberson, Gilberto Silva, Roberto Carlos, Ronaldinho (Juninho 85), Rivaldo, Ronaldo (Denilson 90)
Referee: Collina (Italy). **Half-time:** 0-0

2006 – GERMANY

WINNERS: Italy RUNNERS-UP: France THIRD: Germany FOURTH: Portugal
Other countries in finals: Angola, Argentina, Australia, Brazil, Costa Rica, Croatia, Czech

Republic, Ecuador, England, Ghana, Holland, Iran, Ivory Coast, Japan, Mexico, Paraguay, Poland, Saudi Arabia, Serbia & Montenegro, South Korea, Spain, Sweden, Switzerland, Trinidad & Tobago, Togo, Tunisia, Ukraine, USA. **Total entries:** 198 (32 qualifiers)
Venues: Berlin, Cologne, Dortmund, Frankfurt, Gelsenkirchen, Hamburg, Hanover, Kaiserslautern, Leipzig, Munich, Nuremberg, Stuttgart
Top scorer: Klose (Germany) 5 goals
Final (Berlin, 9/7/06): **Italy** 1 (Materazzi 19) **France** 1 (Zidane 7 pen) after extra-time: Italy won 5-3 on pens. **Att:** 69,000
Italy: Buffon; Zambrotta, Cannavaro (capt), Materazzi, Grosso, Perrotta (De Rossi 61), Pirlo, Gattuso, Camoranesi (Del Piero 86), Totti (Iaquinta 61), Toni
France: Barthez; Sagnol, Thuram, Gallas, Abidal, Makelele, Vieira (Diarra 56), Ribery (Trezeguet 100), Malouda, Zidane (capt), Henry (Wiltord 107) **Sent-off:** Zidane (110)
Referee: Elizondo (Argentina). **Half-time:** 1-1 90 mins: 1-1
Shoot-out: Pirlo 1-0, Wiltord 1-1, Materazzi 2-1, Trezeguet missed, De Rossi 3-1, Abidal 3-2, Del Piero 4-2, Sagnol 4-3, Grosso 5-3

2010 – SOUTH AFRICA

WINNERS: Spain RUNNERS-UP: Holland THIRD: Germany FOURTH: Uruguay
Other countries in finals: Algeria, Argentina, Australia, Brazil, Cameroon, Chile, Denmark, England, France, Ghana, Greece, Honduras, Italy, Ivory Coast, Japan, Mexico, New Zealand, Nigeria, North Korea, Paraguay, Portugal, Serbia, Slovakia, Slovenia, South Africa, South Korea, Switzerland, USA. **Total entries:** 204 (32 qualifiers)
Venues: Bloemfontein, Cape Town, Durban, Johannesburg (Ellis Park), Johannesburg (Soccer City), Nelspruit, Polokwane, Port Elizabeth, Pretoria, Rustenburg
Top scorers: Forlan (Uruguay), Muller (Germany), Sneijder (Holland), Villa (Spain) 5 goals
Final (Johannesburg, Soccer City, 11/7/10): **Holland** 0 **Spain** 1 (Iniesta 116) after extra-time; **Att:** 84,490
Holland: Stekelenburg, Van der Wiel, Heitinga, Mathijsen, Van Bronckhorst (capt) (Braafheid 105), Van Bommel, De Jong (Van der Vaart 99), Robben, Sneijder, Kuyt (Elia 71), Van Persie.
Sent off: Heitinga (109)
Spain: Casillas (capt), Sergio Ramos, Puyol, Piquet, Capdevila, Busquets, Xabi Alonso (Fabregas 87), Iniesta, Xavi, Pedro (Jesus Navas 60), Villa (Torres 106)
Referee: H Webb (England). **Half-time:** 0-0

---

300 UP FOR FRIEDEL

Brad Friedel stretched his Premier League record of continuous appearances to 304 by completing an eighth successive season without missing a match. This time it was with Tottenham after four for Blackburn and three at Aston Villa. The 41-year-old goalkeeper, who won 82 caps during his international career with the United States, last missed a game in May 2004

FAIRYTALE FINISH FOR ALEXANDER

Graham Alexander ended a 22-year career by scoring a stoppage-time equaliser for Preston with a free-kick against League One champions Charlton. The 40-year-old-midfielder-cum-defender, making his 1023rd appearances, was then booked for over-celebrating. Alexander, who also served Scunthorpe, Luton and Burnley and won 40 caps with Scotland, described it as a 'fairytale finish'. A week earlier, he had received the PFA's Merit Award for 2012 for services to the game.

UEFA CHAMPIONS LEAGUE 2011–12

FIRST QUALIFYING ROUND, ON AGGREGATE

Dudelange 4 Santa Coloma 0; Valletta 5 Tre Fiori 1

SECOND QUALIFYING ROUND, FIRST LEG

Bangor 0 HJK Helsinki 3 (Sadik 14, 55, Sorsa 89). Att: 1,189. **Linfield** 1 (Fordyce 5) Bate Borisov 1 (Bressan 38 pen). Att: 1,212. **Shamrock** 1 (Turner 33) Flora Tallinn 0. Att: 5,026

SECOND QUALIFYING ROUND, SECOND LEG

Bate Borisov 2 (Nekhaychik 58, Pavlov 61) **Linfield** 0. Att: 5,225 (Bate Borisov won 3-1 on agg). HJK Helsinki 10 (Ring 37, Sadik 44, Zeneli 47, 54, Rafinha 52, Pukki 64, 67, Kastrati 66, 88, Parikka 71) **Bangor** 0. Att: 5,944 (HJK Helsinki won 13-0 on agg). Flora Tallinn 0 **Shamrock** 0. Att: 2,850 (**Shamrock** won 1-0 on agg)

SECOND QUALIFYING ROUND, ON AGGREGATE

Apoel Nicosia 6 Skenderbeu 0; Dinamo Zagreb 3 Neftchi 0; Ekranas 4 Valletta 2; Litex Lovech 5 Mogren 1; Maccabi Haifa 7 Borac 4; Malmo 3 Torshavn 1; Maribor 5 Dudelange 1; Partizan Belgrade 1 Shkendija Tetovo 0; Pizen 9 Pyunik 1; Rosenborg 5 Breidablik 2; Slovan Bratislava 3 Tobol 1; Sturm Graz 4 Videoton 3; Wislaw Krakow 2 Skonto 0; Zestafoni 3 Dacia 2

THIRD QUALIFYING ROUND, FIRST LEG

Copenhagen 1 (Ottesen 4) **Shamrock** 0. Att: 11,751; **Rangers** 0 Malmo 1 (Larsson 18). Att: 28,828

THIRD QUALIFYING ROUND, SECOND LEG

Malmo 1 (Hamad 80) **Rangers** 1 (Jelavic 23). Att: 19,084 (Malmo won 2-1 on agg); **Shamrock** 0 Copenhagen 2 (Ndoye 42, Bolanos 73). Att: 5,901 (Copenhagen won 3-0 on agg)

THIRD QUALIFYING ROUND, ON AGGREGATE

Apoel Nicosia 2 Slovan Bratislava 0; Bate Borisov 3 Ekranas 1; Benfica 3 Trabzonspor 1 (Trabzonspor reinstated by UEFA to group stage, replacing Fenerbahce following match-fixing probe); Dinamo Zagreb 3 HJK Helsinki 1; Genk 3 Partizan Belgrade 2; Maccabi Haifa 3 Maribor 2; Odense 5 Panathinaikos 4; Pizen 4 Rosenborg 2; Rubin Kazan 4 Dynamo Kiev 1; Sturm Graz 2 Zestafoni 1; Twente 2 Vaslui 0; Wisla Krakow 5 Litex Lovech 2; Zurich 2 Standard Liege 1

PLAY-OFFS, FIRST LEG

Arsenal 1 (Walcott 4) Udinese 0. Att: 58,159.

PLAY-OFFS, SECOND LEG

Udinese 1 (Di Natale 39) **Arsenal** 2 (Van Persie 55, Walcott 69). Att: 25,687 (**Arsenal** won 3-1 on agg)

PLAY OFFS, ON AGGREGATE

Apoel Nicosia 3 Wisla Krakow 2; Bate Borisov 3 Sturm Graz 1; Bayern Munich 3 Zurich 0;

Benfica 5 Twente 3; Dinamo Zagreb 4 Malmo 3; Genk 3 Maccabi Haifa 3 (aet, Genk won 4-1 on pens); Lyon 4 Rubin Kazan 2; Viktor Plzen 5 Copenhagen 2; Villarreal 3 Odense 0

GROUP A

September 14, 2011
Manchester City 1 (Kolarov 75) **Napoli** 1 (Cavani 69). Att: 44,026
Manchester City (4-2-3-1): Hart, Zabaleta, Kompany, Lescott, Kolarov (Clichy 75), Y Toure, Barry, Silva, Aguero, Nasri (Johnson 75), Dzeko (Tevez 80). Booked: Zabaleta
Villarreal 0 **Bayern Munich** 2 (Kroos 7, Rafinha 76). Att: 19,168

September 27, 2011
Bayern Munich 2 (Gomez 38, 45) **Manchester City** 0. Att: 65,000
Manchester City (4-4-2): Hart, Richards, K Toure, Kompany, Clichy, Nasri (Milner 69), Y Toure, Barry (Kolarov 73), Silva, Aguero, Dzeko (De Jong 55). Booked: Aguero, Clichy, Y Toure, K Toure
Napoli 2 (Hamsik 14, Cavani 17 pen) **Villarreal** 0. Att: 46,747

October 18, 2011
Manchester City 2 (Marchena 43 og, Aguero 90) **Villarreal** 1 (Cani 4). Att: 42,236
Manchester City (4-2-3-1): Hart, Zabaleta, Kompany, Lescott, Kolarov, De Jong (Aguero 62), Y Toure, Johnson (Barry 40), Silva, Nasri (Milner 81), Dzeko
Napoli 1 (Badstuber 39 og), **Bayern Munich** 1 (Kroos 2). Att: 60,074

November 2, 2011
Bayern Munich 3 (Gomez 17, 23, 42) **Napoli** 2 (Fernandez 45, 79). Att: 61,523
Villarreal 0 **Manchester City** 3 (Y Toure 30, 71, Balotelli 45 pen). Att: 24,235
Manchester City (4-2-3-1): Hart, Zabaleta, Kompany, Savic, Clichy, De Jong, Y Toure (Aguero 74), Milner, Silva (Johnson 65), Nasri, Balotelli (Kolarov 82). Booked: Balotelli

November 22, 2011
Bayern Munich 3 (Ribery 3, 69, Gomez 23) **Villarreal** 1 (De Guzman 50). Att: 66,000
Napoli 2 (Cavano 17, 49) **Manchester City** 1 (Balotelli 33). Att: 57,575
Manchester City (4-3-2-1): Hart, Zabaleta (Johnson 86), Kompany, Lescott, Kolarov, Milner, Y Toure, De Jong (Nasri 70), Silva, Balotelli, Dzeko (Aguero 81). Booked: Balotelli, Silva, Kompany, Kolarov

December 7, 2011
Manchester City 2 (Silva 37, Y Toure 52) **Bayern Munich** 0. Att: 46,002
Manchester City (4-2-3-1): Hart, Savic, Kompany, Lescott, Clichy, Y Toure (Balotelli 81), Barry, Nasri, Aguero, Silva (Johnson 83), Dzeko (De Jong 77)
Villarreal 0 **Napoli** 2 (Inler 65, Hamsik 77). Att: 15,350

FINAL TABLE

	P	W	D	L	F	A	Pts
Bayern Munich Q	6	4	1	1	11	6	13
Napoli Q	6	3	2	1	10	6	11
Manchester City	6	3	1	2	9	6	10
Villarreal	6	0	0	6	2	14	0

GROUP B

September 14, 2011
Inter Milan 0 **Trabzonspor** 1 (Celustka 76). Att: 24,444
Lille 2 (Sow 45, Pedretti 57) **CSKA Moscow** 2 (Doumbia 72, 90). Att: 15,274

September 27, 2011
CSKA Moscow 2 (Dzagoev 45, Vagner Love 77) **Inter Milan** 3 (Lucio 6, Pazzini 23, Zarate 78). Att: 35,000
Trabzonspor 1 (Colman 75 pen) **Lille** 1 (Sow 30). Att: 17,349

October 18, 2011
CSKA Moscow 3 (Doumbia 29, 86, Cauna 76) **Trabzonspor** 0. Att: 18,000
Lille 0 **Inter Milan** 1 (Pazzini 21). Att: 16,996

November 2, 2011
Inter Milan 2 (Samuel 18, Milito 65) **Lille** 1 (De Melo 83). Att: 24,299
Trabzonspor 0 **CSKA Moscow** 0. Att: 22,486

November 22, 2011
CSKA Moscow 0 **Lille** 2 (Berezutsky 49 og, Sow 64). Att: 19,100
Trabzonspor 1 (Altintop 23) **Inter Milan** 1 (Alvarez 18). Att: 17,349

December 7, 2011
Inter Milan 1 (Cambiasso 51) **CSKA Moscow** 2 (Doumbia 50, Berezutsky 87). Att: 65,412
Lille 0 **Trabzonspor** 0. Att: 16,551

FINAL TABLE

	P	W	D	L	F	A	Pts
Inter Milan Q	6	3	1	2	8	7	10
CSKA Moscow Q	6	2	2	2	9	8	8
Trabzonspor	6	1	4	1	3	5	7
Lille	6	1	3	2	6	6	6

GROUP C

September 14, 2011
Basle 2 (F Frei 39, A Frei 84 pen) **Otelul Galati** 1 (Pena 58). Att: 30,126
Benfica 1 (Cardozo 24) **Manchester Utd** 1 (Giggs 42). Att: 63,822
Manchester Utd (4-3-2-1): Lindegaard, Fabio (Jones 77), Evans, Smalling, Evra, Fletcher (Hernandez 68), Carrick, Giggs, Valencia (Nani 69), Park, Rooney. Booked: Rooney, Carrick

September 27, 2011
Manchester Utd 3 (Welbeck 16, 17, Young 90) **Basle** 3 (F Frei 58, A Frei 60, 76 pen). Att: 73,115
Manchester Utd (4-3-3): De Gea, Fabio (Nani 69), Ferdinand, Jones, Evra, Anderson (Berbatov 82), Carrick, Giggs (Park 61), Valencia, Welbeck, Young
Otelul Galati 0 **Benfica** 1 (Bruno Cesar 40). Att: 6,824

October 18, 2011
Basle 0 **Benfica** 2 (Bruno Cesar 20, Cardozo 75). Att: 35,831
Otelul Galati 0 **Manchester Utd** 2 (Rooney 64 pen, 90 pen). Att: 28,047
Manchester Utd (4-4-2): Lindegaard, Fabio (Jones 76), Smalling, Vidic, Evra, Valencia (Evans 71), Carrick, Anderson, Nani, Rooney, Hernandez. Booked: Carrick. Sent off: Vidic

November 2, 2011
Benfica 1 (Machado 4) **Basle** 1 (Huggel 64). Att: 39,270
Manchester Utd 2 (Valencia 8, Rooney 87) **Otelul Galati** 0. Att: 74,847
Manchester Utd (4-4-2): De Gea, Jones, Ferdinand, Evans (Fryers 89), Fabio, Valencia, Rooney, Anderson (Park 80), Nani, Owen (Hernandez 11), Berbatov. Booked: Evans

November 22, 2011
Manchester Utd 2 (Berbatov 30, Fletcher 59) **Benfica** 2 (Jones 4 og, Aimar 60). Att: 74,853
Manchester Utd (4-4-2): De Gea, Fabio (Smalling 82), Jones, Ferdinand, Evra, Valencia (Hernandez 80), Fletcher, Carrick, Nani, Young, Berbatov. Booked: Fletcher, Carrick
Otelul Galati 2 (Giurgui 75, Antal 81) **Basle** 3 (F Frei 10, A Frei 14, Streller 37). Att: 5,787

December 7, 2011
Basle 2 (Streller 9, A Frei 84) **Manchester Utd** 1 (Jones 89). Att: 36,894
Manchester Utd (4-5-1): De Gea, Smalling, Ferdinand, Vidic (Evans 44), Evra, Nani, Jones, Giggs, Park (Macheda 82), Young (Welbeck 64), Rooney. Booked: Young, Evra
Benfica 1 (Cardozo 7) **Otelul Galati** 0. Att: 37,116

FINAL TABLE

	P	W	D	L	F	A	Pts
Benfica Q	6	3	3	0	8	4	12
Basle Q	6	3	2	1	11	10	11
Manchester Utd	6	2	3	1	11	8	9
Otelul Galati	6	0	0	6	3	11	0

GROUP D

September 14, 2011
Ajax 0 **Lyon** 0. Att: 49,504
Dinamo Zagreb 0 **Real Madrid** 1 (Di Maria 53). Att: 27,055

September 27, 2011
Lyon 2 (Gomis 23, Kone 42) **Dinamo Zagreb** 0. Att: 34,432
Real Madrid 3 (Ronaldo 25, Kaka 41, Benzema 49) **Ajax** 0. Att: 70,320

October 18, 2011
Dinamo Zagreb 0 **Ajax** 2 (Boerrigter 49, Eriksen 90). Att: 25,714
Real Madrid 4 (Benzema 18, Khedira 47, Lloris 55 og, Sergio Ramos 81) **Lyon** 0. Att: 76,102

November 2, 2011
Ajax 4 (Van Der Wiel 20, Sulejmani 25, De Jong 65, Lodeiro 90) **Dinamo Zagreb** 0. Att: 49,707
Lyon 0 **Real Madrid** 2 (Ronaldo 24, 70 pen). Att: 40,099

November 22, 2011
Lyon 0 **Ajax** 0. Att: 35,070
Real Madrid 6 (Benzema 2, 66, Callejon 6, 49, Higuain 9, Ozil 20). **Dinamo Zagreb** 2. (Beqiraj 81, Tomecak 90). Att: 65,415

December 7, 2011
Ajax 0 **Real Madrid** 3 (Callejon 13, 90, Higuain 41). Att: 51,557
Dinamo Zagreb 1 (Kovacic 41) **Lyon** 7 (Gomis 45, 49, 52, 70, Gonalons 47, Lopez 64, Briand 75). Att: 25,657

FINAL TABLE

	P	W	D	L	F	A	Pts
Real Madrid Q	6	6	0	0	19	2	18
Lyon Q	6	2	2	2	9	7	8
Ajax	6	2	2	2	6	6	8
Dinamo Zagreb	6	0	0	6	3	22	0

GROUP E

September 13, 2011
Chelsea 2 (Luiz 67, Mata 90) **Bayer Leverkusen** 0. Att: 33,820
Chelsea (4-3-3): Cech, Bosingwa, Ivanovic, Luiz (Alex 76), Cole, Meireles (Lampard 65),
Mikel, Malouda, Sturridge (Anelka 65), Torres, Mata. Booked; Torres, Luiz
Genk 0 **Valencia** 0. Att: 20,248

September 28, 2011
Bayer Leverkusen 2 (Bender 29, Ballack 90) **Genk** 0. Att: 25,138
Valencia 1 (Soldado 87 pen) **Chelsea** 1 (Lampard 56). Att: 33,791
Chelsea (4-3-3): Cech, Bosingwa, Luiz, Terry, Cole, Ramirez (Meireles 66), Mikel, Lampard
(Kalou 83), Mata, Torres (Anelka 72), Malouda. Booked: Kalou, Malouda, Cole, Mata

October 19, 2011
Bayer Leverkusen 2 (Schurrie 52, Sam 56) **Valencia** 1 (Jonas 24). Att: 26,384
Chelsea 5 (Meireles 8, Torres 11, 27, Ivanovic 42, Kalou 73) **Genk** 0. Att: 38,518
Chelsea (4-3-3): Cech, Bosingwa (Alex 78), Ivanovic, Luiz, Cole (Paulo Ferreira 46), Meireles,
Romeu, Lampard (Kalou 68), Anelka, Torres, Malouda. Booked: Luiz

November 1, 2011
Genk 1 (Vossen 61) **Chelsea** 1 (Ramires 25). Att: 22,584
Chelsea (4-3-3): Cech, Bosingwa, Ivanovic, Luiz, Cole, Ramires (Lampard 66), Romeu (Mata
77), Meireles, Anelka (Sturridge 66), Torres, Malouda
Valencia 3 (Jonas 1, Soldado 65, Rami 75) **Bayer Leverkusen** 1 (Kiessling 31). Att: 37,047

November 23, 2011
Bayer Leverkusen 2 (Derdiyok 73, Friedrich 90) **Chelsea** 1 (Drogba 48). Att: 28,551
Chelsea (4-3-3): Cech, Ivanovic, Terry, Luiz (Alex 68), Bosingwa, Ramires, Meireles (Mikel
80), Lampard, Sturridge, Drogba, Mata (Malouda 65). Booked: Ivanovic, Meireles
Valencia 7 (Jonas 10, Soldado 13, 36, 39, Pablo 68, Aduriz 70, Tino Costa 81) **Genk** 0. Att:
49,026

December 6, 2011
Chelsea 3 (Drogba 3, 76, Ramires 22) **Valencia** 0. Att: 41,109
Chelsea (4-1-2-3): Cech, Ivanovic, Luiz, Terry, Cole, Romeu, Ramires (Mikel 65), Meireles,
Sturridge, Drogba (Torres 77), Mata (Malouda 83). Booked: Romeu
Genk 1 (Vossen 30) **Bayer Leverkusen** 1 (Derdiyok 79). Att: 21,187

FINAL TABLE

	P	W	D	L	F	A	Pts
Chelsea Q	6	3	2	1	13	4	11
Bayer Leverkusen Q	6	3	1	2	8	8	10
Valencia	6	2	2	2	12	7	8
Genk	6	0	3	3	2	16	3

GROUP F

September 13, 2011
Borussia Dortmund 1 (Perisic 88) **Arsenal** 1 (Van Persie 42). Att: 65,590
Arsenal (4-2-3-1): Szczesny, Sagna, Mertesacker, Koscielny, Gibbs, Song, Arteta, Walcott
(Frimpong 86), Benayoun, Gervinho (Santos 86), Van Persie (Chamakh 86). Booked: Sagna
Olympiacos 0 **Marseille** 1 (Gonzalez 51). Att: 30,040

September 28, 2011
Arsenal 2 (Oxlade-Chamberlain 8, Santos 20) **Olympiacos** 1 (Fuster 27). Att: 59,676
Arsenal (4-1-4-1): Szczesny, Sagna, Mertesacker, Song, Santos, Frimpong, Oxlade-

Chamberlain (Ramsey 67), Arteta, Rosicky, Arshavin (Gibbs 82), Chamakh (Van Persie 70).
Booked: Rosicky, Arteta
Marseille 3 (Ayew 20, 69 pen, Remy 62) **Borussia Dortmund** 0. Att: 26,142

October 19, 2011
Marseille 0 **Arsenal** 1 (Ramsey 90). Att: 33,258
Arsenal (4-3-2-1): Szczesny, Jenkinson (Djourou 62),Mertesacker, Koscielny, Santos, Song,
Arteta, Rosicky, Walcott (Gervinho 67), Arshavin (Ramsey 78), Van Persie. Booked: Song,
Santos, Djourou
Olympiacos 3 (Holebas 8, Djebbour 40, Modesto 79) **Borussia Dortmund** 1 (Lewandowski 26).
Att: 29,638

November 1, 2011
Arsenal 0 **Marseille** 0. Att: 59,961
Arsenal (4-3-2-1): Szczesny, Jenkinson, Mertesacker, Vermaelen, Santos, Song, Ramsey
(Rosicky 66), Arteta, Gervinho (Arshavin 76), Walcott, Park (Van Persie 62). Booked: Rosicky
Borussia Dortmund 1 (Grosskreutz 7) **Olympiacos** 0. Att: 65,590

November 23, 2011
Arsenal 2 (Van Persie 49, 86) **Borussia Dortmund** 1 (Kagawa 90). Att: 59,531
Arsenal (4-2-3-1): Szczesny, Koscielny (Djourou 83), Mertesacker, Vermaelen, Santos, Arteta,
Song, Walcott (Diaby 85), Ramsey, Gervinho (Benayoun 74), Van Persie. Booked: Walcott,
Ramsey, Benayoun
Marseille 0 **Olympiacos** 1 (Fetfatzidis 82). Att: 25,392

December 6, 2011
Borussia Dortmund 2 (Blaszczykowski 23, Hummels 32 pen) **Marseille** 3 (Remy 45, Ayew 85,
Valbuena 87). Att: 65,590
Olympiacos 3 (Djebbour 16, Fuster 36, Modesto 89) **Arsenal** 1 (Benayoun 57). Att: 30,816
Arsenal (4-3-2-1): Fabianski (Mannone 25), Djourou, Vermaelen, Squillaci, Santos (Miquel
51), Frimpong, Coquelin (Rosicky 67), Oxlade-Chamberlain, Benayoun, Arshavin, Chamakh.
Booked: Frimpong, Oxlade-Chamberlain

FINAL TABLE

	P	W	D	L	F	A	Pts
Arsenal Q	6	3	2	1	7	6	11
Marseille Q	6	3	1	2	7	4	10
Olympiacos	6	3	0	3	8	6	9
Borussia Dortmund	6	1	1	4	6	12	4

GROUP G

September 13, 2011
Apoel Nicosia 2 (Manduca 73, Almeida 75) **Zenit St Petersburg** 1 (Zyryanov 63). Att: 21,269
Porto 2 (Hulk 28, Kleber 51) **Shakhtar Donetsk** 1 (Luiz Adriano 13). Att: 36,612

September 28, 2011
Shakhtar Donetsk 1 (Jadson 64) **Apoel Nicosia** 1 (Trickovski 61). Att: 40,736
Zenit St Petersburg 3 (Shirokov 20, 63, Danny 72) **Porto** 1 (Rodriguez 10). Att: 21,405

October 19, 2011
Porto 1 (Hulk 13) **Apoel Nicosia** 1 (Almeida 19). Att: 32,512
Shakhtar Donetsk 2 (Willian 15, Luiz Adriano 45) **Zenit St Petersburg** 2 (Shirokov 33,
Faitzulin 60). Att: 50,578

November 1, 2011
Apoel Nicosia 2 (Almeida 42 pen, Manduca 90) **Porto** 1 (Hulk 89 pen). Att: 22,301
Zenit St Petersburg 1 (Lombaerts 45) **Shakhtar Donetsk** 0. Att: 21,405

November 23 2011
Shakhtar Donetsk 0 **Porto** 2 (Hulk 79, Rat 90 og). Att: 33,451
Zenit St Petersburg 0 **Apoel Nicosia** 0. Att: 21,500

December 6, 2011
Apoel Nicosia 0 **Shakhtar Donetsk** 2 (Luiz Adriano 62, Seleznev 78). Att: 22,537
Porto 0 **Zenit St Petersburg** 0. Att: 46,512

FINAL TABLE

	P	W	D	L	F	A	Pts
Apoel Nicosia Q	6	2	3	1	6	6	9
Zenit St Petersburg Q	6	2	3	1	7	5	9
Porto	6	2	2	2	7	7	8
Shakhtar Donetsk	6	1	2	3	6	8	5

GROUP H

September 13, 2011
Barcelona 2 (Pedro 36, Villa 50) **AC Milan** 2 (Pato 1, Thiago Silva 90). Att: 89,861
Viktor Plzen 1 (Bakos 45) **Bate Borisov** 1 (Bressan 90). Att: 19,541

September 28, 2011
AC Milan 2 (Ibrahimovic 53 pen, Cassano 66) **Viktor Plzen** 0. Att: 66,859
Bate Borisov 0 **Barcelona** 5 (Volodko 20 og, Pedro 22, Messi 38, 55, Villa 90). Att: 29,555

October 19, 2011
AC Milan 2 (Ibrahimovic 33, Boateng 70) **Bate Borisov** 0. Att: 66,040
Barcelona 2 (Iniesta 10, Villa 82) **Viktor Plzen** 0. Att: 74,376

November 1, 2011
Bate Borisov 1 (Bressan 55 pen) **AC Milan** 1 (Ibrahimovic 22). Att: 29,100
Viktor Plzen 0 **Barcelona** 4 (Messi 24 pen, 45, 90, Fabregas 72). Att: 20,145

November 23, 2011
AC Milan 2 (Ibrahimovic 20, Boateng 54) **Barcelona** 3 (Van Bommel 14 og, Messi 31 pen, Xavi 63). Att: 77,394
Bate Borisov 0 **Viktor Plzen** 1 (Bakos 42). Att: 16,598

December 6, 2011
Barcelona 4 (Roberto 35, Montoya 60, Pedro 63, 89 pen) **Bate Borisov** 0. Att: 36,452
Viktor Plzen 2 (Bystron 89, Duris 90) **AC Milan** 2 (Pato 47, Robinho 48). Att: 19,854

FINAL TABLE

	P	W	D	L	F	A	Pts
Barcelona Q	6	5	1	0	20	4	16
AC Milan Q	6	2	3	1	11	8	9
Viktor Plzen	6	1	2	3	4	11	5
Bate Borisov	6	0	2	4	2	14	2

ROUND OF 16, FIRST LEG

February 14, 2012
Bayer Leverkusen 1 (Kadlec 52) **Barcelona** 3 (Sanchez 41, 55, Messi 88). Att: 29,412
Lyon 1 (Lacazette 58) **Apoel Nicosia** 0. Att: 32,010

February 15, 2012
AC Milan 4 (Boateng 15, Robinho 38, 49, Ibrahimovic 79 pen) **Arsenal** 0. Att: 64,462
Arsenal (4-2-3-1): Szczesny, Sagna, Kosielny (Djourou 44), Vermaelen, Gibbs (Oxlade-Chamberlain 66), Song, Arteta, Walcott (Henry 46), Ramsey, Rosicky, Van Persie. Booked: Song, Djourou
Zenit St Petersburg 3 (Shirokov 27, 89, Semak 71) **Benfica** 2 (Maxi Pereira 21, Cardozo 87). Att: 18,200

February 21, 2012
CSKA Moscow 1 (Wernbloom 90) **Real Madrid** 1 (Ronaldo 28). Att: 70,000
Napoli 3 (Lavezzi 38, 65, Cavani 45) **Chelsea** 1 (Mata 27). Att: 52,495
Chelsea (4-3-3): Cech, Ivanovic, Cahill, Luiz, Bosingwa (Cole 12), Ramires, Meireles (Essien 70) Malouda (Lampard 70), Sturridge, Drogba, Mata. Booked: Meireles, Cahill

February 22, 2012
Basle 1 (Stocker 86) **Bayern Munich** 0. Att: 38,512
Marseille 1 (Ayew 90) **Inter Milan** 0. Att: 37,646

ROUND OF 16, SECOND LEG

March 6, 2012
Arsenal 3 (Koscielny 7, Rosicky 26, Van Persie 42 pen) **AC Milan** 0. Att: 59,973 (AC Milan won 4-3 on agg)
Arsenal (4-3-2-1):Szczesny, Sagna, Koscielny, Vermaelen, Gibbs, Song, Oxlade-Chamberlain (Chamakh 75), Rosicky, Walcott (Park 84) Gervinho, Van Persie. Booked: Sagna, Gibbs, Song
Benfica 2 (Maxi Pereira 45, Nelson Oliveira 90) **Zenit St Petersburg** 0. Att: 48,909 (Benfica won 4-3 on agg)

March 7, 2012
Apoel Nicosia 1 (Manduca 9) **Lyon** 0. Att: 18,500 (aet, agg 1-1, Apoel Nicosia won 4-3 on pens)
Barcelona 7 (Messi 25, 42, 49, 58, 85, Tello 55, 62) **Bayer Leverkusen** 1 (Bellarabi 90). Att: 75,632 (Barcelona won 10-2 on agg)

March 13, 2012
Bayern Munich 7 (Robben 11, 81, Muller 42, Gomez 44, 50, 61, 67) **Basle** 0. Att: 66,000 (Bayern Munich won 7-1 on agg)
Inter Milan 2 (Milito 75, Pazzini 90 pen) **Marseille** 1 (Brandao 90). Att: 62,632 (agg 2-2, Marseille won on away goal)

March 14, 2012
Chelsea 4 (Drogba 29, Terry 48, Lampard 75 pen, Ivanovic 105) **Napoli** 1 (Inler 55). Att: 37,784 (aet, Chelsea won 5-4 on agg)
Chelsea (4-2-3-1): Cech, Ivanovic, Luiz, Terry (Bosingwa 98), Cole, Essien, Lampard, Ramires, Mata (Malouda 95), Sturridge (Torres 63), Drogba. Booked: Lampard, Cole
Real Madrid 4 (Higuain 26, Ronaldo 55, 90, Benzema 70) **CSKA Moscow** 1 (Tosic 77). Att: 83,493 (Real Madrid won 5-2 on agg)

QUARTER-FINALS, FIRST LEG

March 27, 2012
Apoel Nicosia 0 **Real Madrid** 3 (Benzema 74, 90, Kaka 82). Att: 22,500

Benfica 0 **Chelsea** 1 (Kalou 75). Att: 60,000
Chelsea (4-2-3-1): Cech, Paulo Ferreira (Bosingwa 80), Luiz, Terry, Cole, Mikel, Meireles (Lampard 68), Ramires, Mata, Kalou (Sturridge 84), Torres. Booked: Meireles

March 28, 2012
AC Milan 0 **Barcelona** 0. Att: 70,628
Marseille 0 **Bayern Munich** 2 (Gomez 44, Robben 69). Att: 31,683

QUARTER-FINALS SECOND LEG

April 3, 2012
Barcelona 3 (Messi 11 pen, 41 pen, Iniesta 53) **AC Milan** 1 (Nocerino 32). Att: 94,629 (Barcelona won 3-1 on agg)
Bayern Munich 2 (Olic 13, 37) **Marseille** 0. Att: 66,000 (Bayern Munich won 4-0 on agg)

April 4, 2012
Chelsea 2 (Lampard 21 pen, Meireles 90) **Benfica** 1 (Garcia 85). Att: 37,264 (Chelsea won 3-1 on agg)
Chelsea (4-2-3-1): Cech, Ivanovic, Luiz, Terry (Cahill 59), Cole, Mikel, Lampard, Ramires, Mata (Meireles 79), Kalou, Torres (Drogba 88). Booked: Ivanovic, Ramires, Mikel
Real Madrid 5 (Ronaldo 26, 75, Kaka 36, Callejon 80, Di Maria 84) **Apoel Nicosia** 2 (Manduca 67, Solari 82 pen). Att: 50,865 (Real Madrid won 8-2 on agg)

SEMI-FINALS, FIRST LEG

April 17, 2012
Bayern Munich 2 (Ribery 17, Gomez 90) **Real Madrid** 1 (Ozil 53). Att: 69,000

April 18, 2012
Chelsea 1 (Drogba 45) **Barcelona** 0. Att: 38,039
Chelsea (4-2-3-1): Cech, Ivanovic, Cahill, Terry, Cole, Lampard, Mikel, Meireles, Mata (Kalou 74), Ramires (Bosingwa 88), Drogba. Booked: Drogba, Ramires

SEMI-FINALS, SECOND LEG

April 24, 2012
Barcelona 2 (Busquets 35, Iniesta 43) **Chelsea** 2 (Ramires 45, Torres 90). Att: 95,845 (Chelsea won 3-2 on agg)
Chelsea (4-2-3-1): Cech, Ivanovic, Cahill (Bosingwa 12), Terry, Cole, Ramires, Lampard, Mikel, Meireles, Mata (Kalou 598), Drogba (Torres 80). Booked: Mikel, Ramires, Ivanovic, Cech, Lampard, Meireles. Sent off: Terry
Real Madrid 2 (Ronaldo 6 pen, 14) **Bayern Munich** 1 (Robben 27 pen). Att: 82,619 (aet, agg 3-3, Bayern Munich won 3-1 on pens)

FINAL

BAYERN MUNICH 1 CHELSEA 1 (aet, Chelsea won 4-3 on pens)
Allianz Arena, Munich (69,901); Saturday, May 19 2012
Bayern Munich (4-2-3-1): Neuer, Lahm (capt), Tymoshchuk, Boateng, Contento, Kroos, Schweinsteiger, Robben, Muller (Van Buyten 86), Ribery (Olic 96), Gomez. **Subs not used**: Butt, Petersen, Rafinha, Usami, Pranjic. **Scorer**: Muller (83). **Booked**: Schweinsteiger. **Coach**: Jupp Heynckes
Chelsea (4-2-3-1): Cech, Bosingwa, Cahill, Luiz, Cole, Mikel, Lampard (capt), Kalou (Torres 84), Mata, Bertrand (Malouda 73), Drogba. **Subs not used**: Turnbull, Paulo Ferreira, Essien, Romeu, Sturridge. **Scorer**: Drogba (88). **Booked**: Cole, Luiz, Drogba, Torres. **Manager**: Roberto Di Matteo
Penalty shoot-out: 1-0 (Lahm), 1-0 (Mata saved), 2-0 (Gomez), 2-1 (Luiz), 3-1 (Neuer), 3-2

(Lampard), 3-2 (Olic saved), 3-3 (Cole), 3-3 (Schweinsteiger hit post), 3-4 (Drogba)
Referee: P Proenca (Portugal). **Half-time**: 0-0

In the 57-year history of Europe's premier club competition, many teams have upset the odds to win this coveted trophy. Yet few can have matched the way Chelsea overcame adversity, not just in the final but through the knock-out rounds. Who would have expected a 3-1 deficit against Napoli to be overturned by a 4-1 victory in the second leg? Who would have thought they were capable of playing for 53 minutes with ten men after John Terry's red card and overcoming Barcelona when trailing 2-0 in the Nou Camp? That performance convinced some observers it might just be their year. But the task was still a formidable one – facing Bayern Munich on their own ground without three other suspended players, Branislav Ivanovic, Ramires and Raul Meireles. It grew even more daunting as events unfolded in the Allianz Arena. Each time, though, damaging situations were rescued – Didier Drogba cancelling out Thomas Muller's 83rd minute goal; Petr Cech saving Arjen Robben's extra-time spot-kick after Drogba tripped Franck Ribery; the Germans leading 2-0 in the penalty shoot-out before Cech denied Ivica Olic and Bastian Schweinsteiger struck a post. After all that, Drogba, off a run of three paces and cool as a cucumber, stroked his penalty into the corner to underline his status as the man for the big occasion. Little more than three months earlier, Chelsea were in turmoil, with senior players in open revolt under manager Andre Villas-Boas. Frank Lampard, after lifting the cup, admitted he would have laughed at any suggestion then that they would win it for the first time. It was a tribute to every Chelsea player and Roberto Di Matteo, who picked up all the pieces and put them back together after Villas-Boas was sacked, that no-one was laughing any more.

FINAL FACTS AND FIGURES

● Chelsea's triumph was the 12th for England in the tournament, one short of Spain's record.

● English sides have now won five of the six finals contested with German teams.

● Ryan Bertrand became the first player of the modern era to make his Champions League debut in the final. The 22-year-old had started for the first time for Chelsea against Wigan six weeks earlier after loan spells with Bournemouth, Oldham, Norwich, Reading and Nottingham Forest.

● Frank Lampard was playing in his 100th European match – 96 for Chelsea after four for his previous club, West Ham.

● Lampard scored three times and Didier Drogba twice in the teams' only other Champions League tie, a quarter-final which Chelsea won 6-5 on aggregate in 2005. Their other goal was an own goal by Bayern's Lucio.

● Chelsea's victory meant they qualified for the next Champions League and denied a place to Tottenham who finished fourth in the Premier League.

● Bayern had also lost the German Cup Final 5-2 to Borussia Dortmund and finished eight points behind their rivals in the Bundesliga.

● Bayern were the first team to benefit from a home stadium since the Champions League was inaugurated in 1992. The last time a side played at home, when it was the European Cup, was 1984 when Roma lost to Liverpool on penalties in Rome.

● Petr Cech and David Luiz were included in the Champions League's team of the season. Team: Cech (Chelsea), Dani Alves (Barcelona), Luiz (Chelsea), Paulo Jorge (Apoel Nicosia), Alaba (Bayern Munich), Ronaldo (Real Madrid), Manduca (Apoel Nicosia), Boateng (AC Milan), Ribery (Bayern Munich), Messi (Barcelona), Gomez (Bayer Munich).

Leading scorers (from group stage): 14 Messi (Barcelona); 12 Gomez (Bayern Munich); 10 Ronaldo (Real Madrid); 7 Benzema (Real Madrid); 6 (Drogba (Chelsea); 5 Callejon (Real Madrid), Cavani (Napoli), Doumbia (CSKA Moscow), Frei A (Basle), Ibrahimovic (AC Milan), Shirokov (Zenit St Petersburg), Soldado (Valencia).

EUROPEAN CUP FINALS

1956	Real Madrid 4, Reims 3 (Paris)
1957	Real Madrid 2, Fiorentina 0 (Madrid)
1958†	Real Madrid 3, AC Milan 2 (Brussels)
1959	Real Madrid 2, Reims 0 (Stuttgart)
1960	Real Madrid 7, Eintracht Frankfurt 3 (Glasgow)
1961	Benfica 3, Barcelona 2 (Berne)
1962	Benfica 5, Real Madrid 3 (Amsterdam)
1963	AC Milan 2, Benfica 1 (Wembley)
1964	Inter Milan 3, Real Madrid 1 (Vienna)
1965	Inter Milan 1, Benfica 0 (Milan)
1966	Real Madrid 2, Partizan Belgrade 1 (Brussels)
1967	Celtic 2, Inter Milan 1 (Lisbon)
1968†	Manchester Utd 4, Benfica 1 (Wembley)
1969	AC Milan 4, Ajax 1 (Madrid)
1970†	Feyenoord 2, Celtic 1 (Milan)
1971	Ajax 2, Panathinaikos 0 (Wembley)
1972	Ajax 2, Inter Milan 0 (Rotterdam)
1973	Ajax 1, Juventus 0 (Belgrade)
1974	Bayern Munich 4, Atletico Madrid 0 (replay Brussels, after a 1-1 draw, Brussels)
1975	Bayern Munich 2, Leeds Utd 0 (Paris)
1976	Bayern Munich 1, St. Etienne 0 (Glasgow)
1977	Liverpool 3, Borussia Moenchengladbach 1 (Rome)
1978	Liverpool 1, Brugge 0 (Wembley)
1979	Nott'm. Forest 1, Malmo 0 (Munich)
1980	Nott'm. Forest 1, Hamburg 0 (Madrid)
1981	Liverpool 1, Real Madrid 0 (Paris)
1982	Aston Villa 1, Bayern Munich 0 (Rotterdam)
1983	SV Hamburg 1, Juventus 0 (Athens)
1984†	Liverpool 1, AS Roma 1 (Liverpool won 4-2 on penalties) (Rome)
1985	Juventus 1, Liverpool 0 (Brussels)
1986†	Steaua Bucharest 0, Barcelona 0 (Steaua won 2-0 on penalties) (Seville)
1987	Porto 2, Bayern Munich 1 (Vienna)
1988†	PSV Eindhoven 0, Benfica 0 (PSV won 6-5 on penalties) (Stuttgart)
1989	AC Milan 4, Steaua Bucharest 0 (Barcelona)
1990	AC Milan 1, Benfica 0 (Vienna)
1991†	Red Star Belgrade 0, Marseille 0 (Red Star won 5-3 on penalties) (Bari)
1992	Barcelona 1, Sampdoria 0 (Wembley)
1993	Marseille 1, AC Milan 0 (Munich)
1994	AC Milan 4, Barcelona 0 (Athens)
1995	Ajax 1, AC Milan 0 (Vienna)
1996†	Juventus 1, Ajax 1 (Juventus won 4-2 on penalties) (Rome)
1997	Borussia Dortmund 3, Juventus 1 (Munich)
1998	Real Madrid 1, Juventus 0 (Amsterdam)
1999	Manchester Utd 2, Bayern Munich 1 (Barcelona)
2000	Real Madrid 3, Valencia 0 (Paris)
2001	Bayern Munich 1, Valencia 1 (Bayern Munich won 5-4 on penalties) (Milan)
2002	Real Madrid 2, Bayer Leverkusen 1 (Glasgow)
2003†	AC Milan 0, Juventus 0 (AC Milan won 3-2 on penalties) (Manchester)
2004	FC Porto 3, Monaco 0 (Gelsenkirchen)
2005†	Liverpool 3, AC Milan 3 (Liverpool won 3-2 on penalties) (Istanbul)
2006	Barcelona 2, Arsenal 1 (Paris)
2007	AC Milan 2, Liverpool 1 (Athens)
2008†	Manchester Utd 1, Chelsea 1 (Manchester Utd won 6-5 on penalties) (Moscow)
2009	Barcelona 2 Manchester Utd 0 (Rome)
2010	Inter Milan 2 Bayern Munich 0 (Madrid)
2011	Barcelona 3 Manchester Utd 1 (Wembley)
2012†	Chelsea 1 Bayern Munich 1 (Chelsea won 4-3 on pens) (Munich)

(† After extra time)
● Champions League since 1993

UEFA EUROPA LEAGUE 2011–12

FIRST QUALIFYING ROUND, FIRST LEG

Aalesund 4 (Fuhre 35, Olsen 37, Ulvestad 48 pen, Sellin 77) **Neath** 1 (Trundle 23). Att: 2,847. **Fulham** 3 (Duff 33, Murphy 61 pen, Johnson 70) Runavik 0. Att: 14,910. **New Saints** 1 (Darlington 28) **Cliftonville** 1 (Johnston 40). Att: 927. Renova 2 (Jancevski 14 pen, Bajrami 87) **Glentoran** 1 (Nixon 45). Att: 2,000. Vestmannaeyjar 1 (Olafsson 50 pen) **St Patrick's** 0. Att: 608

FIRST QUALIFYING ROUND, SECOND LEG

Cliftonville 0 New Saints 1 (Baker 4). Att: 1,221 (**New Saints** won 2-1 on agg). Glentoran 2 (Clarke 31, Murray 74) Renova 1 (Ismaili 59). Att: 1,424 (aet, agg 3-3, Glentoran won 3-2 on pens). **Neath** 0 Aalesund 2 (Barrantes 53, Olsen 79). Att: 600 (Aalesund won 6-1 on agg). Runavik 0 **Fulham** 0. Att: 1,245 (Fulham won 3-0 on agg). **St Patrick's** 2 (Daly 24, Doyle 36) Vestmannaeyjar 0. Att: 2,100 (St Patrick's won 2-1 on agg)

FIRST QUALIFYING ROUND, ON AGGREGATE

Dinamo Tbilisi 5 Milsami 1; Elfsborg 5 Fola Esch 1; Ferencvaros 5 Uliss Yerevan 0; Flamurtari 4 Buducnost Podgorica 3; Hacken 6 Kaerjeng 2; Honka 2 Nomme Kalju 0; Irtysh 2 Jagiellonia Bialystock 1; Karabakh Azersun 7 Banga 0; Minsk 3 AZAL 2; Olimpi Rustavi 2 Banants Yerevan 1; Olimpija Ljubljana 3 Siroki Brijeg 0; Paks 5 Santa Coloma 0; Rabotnicki 4 Trans Narva 1; Rad Belgrade 9 Tre Penne 1; Reykjavik 8 Fuglafjordur 2; Shakhtyor Karaganda 3 Koper 2; Spartak Trnava 4 Zeta 2; Tromso 7 Daugava 1; Varazdin 6 Lusitanos 1; Vllaznia Shkoder 2 Birkirkara 1

SECOND QUALIFYING ROUND, FIRST LEG

Crusaders 1 (Adamson 54) **Fulham** 3 (Briggs 39, Zamora 74, Murphy 77 pen). Att: 3,011. **Glentoran** 0 Vorskla Poltava 2 (Bezus 29, Januzi 38). Att: 1,527. **Llanelli** 2 (Follows 8, 51) Dinamo Tbilisi 1 (Odikadze 81 pen). Att: 643. **New Saints** 1 (Evans 59) Midtjylland 3 (Hassan 65, Olsen 86 pen, Albaek 90). Att: 914; Olimpija Ljubljana 2 (Vrsic 45 pen, 76) **Bohemians** 0. Att: 7,000. Shakhtyor Karaganda 2 (Vasiljevic 52, 86) **St Patrick's** 1 (McMillan 76). Att: 12,000. Slask Wroclaw 1 (Voskamp 76) **Dundee Utd** 0. Att: 8,300

SECOND QUALIFYING ROUND, SECOND LEG

Bohemians 1 (Fagan 34) Olimpija Ljubljana 1 (O'Brien 81 og). Att: 1,802 (Olimpija Ljubljana won 3-1 on agg); Dinamo Tbilisi 5 (Ixisco 5, 50, Yague 10, Robertinho 27, Coto 55) **Llanelli** 0. Att: 18,027 (Dinamo Tbilisi won 6-2 on agg); **Dundee Utd** 3 (Watson 2, Goodwillie 5, Daly 44 pen) Slask Wroclaw 2 (Elsner 14, Dudek 74). Att: 11,306 (agg 3-3, Slask Wroclaw won on away goals); **Fulham** 4 (Johnson 19, Duff 56, Zamora 66, Sidwell 70) **Crusaders** 0. Att: 15,676 (Fulham won 7-1 on agg); Midtjylland 5 (Emeka 23, Nworuh 24, 51, Olsen 31 pen, Hvilsom 90) **New Saints** 2 (Darlington 55, 90). Att: 2,650 (Midtjylland won 8-3 on agg); **St Patrick's** 2 (McMillan 14, Doyle 70) Shakhtyor Karaganda 0. Att: 2,250 (St Patrick's won 3-2 on agg); Vorskla Poltava 3 (Januzi 33, 73, Kurilov 36) **Glentoran** 0. Att: 5,500 (Vorskla Poltava won 5-0 on agg)

SECOND QUALIFYING ROUND, ON AGGREGATE

Aalesund 4 Ferencvaros 3; AEK Larnarca 9 Floriana 0; Aktobe 1 Kecskemeti 1 (Aktobe won on away goal); Anorthosis Famagusta 3 Gagra 2; Austria Vienna 5 Rudar Pljevlja 0; Bnei Yehuda 4 Sant Julia 0; Den Haag 5 Tauras 2; Differdange 1 Levadia Tallinn 0; Elfsborg 4 Suduva 0; Gaziantepspor 5 Minsk 2; Gaz Metan 2 Kuopio 1; Hacken 3 Honka 0; Jablonec 7

Flamurtai 1; Lokomotiv Sofia 3 Metalurg 2; Maccabi Tel-Aviv 3 Khazar Lenkoran 1; Nacional
3 Hafnarfjordur 1; Olimpi Rustavi 3 Irtysh 0; Olympiacos Volou 2 Rad Belgrade 1; Qarabag
1 Streymur 1 (Qarabag won on away goal); Paks 4 Tromso 1; Rabotnicki 4, Juvenes 0; Red
Bull Salzburg 4 Liepajas 1; Reykjavik 3 Zilina 2; RNK Split 5 Domzale 1; Sarajevo 2 Orebro
0; Spartak Trnava 3 Tirana 1; Thun 2 Vilaznia Shkoder 1; Vaduz 3 Vojvodina 3 (Vaduz won on
away goals); Valerenga 2 Mika Ashtarak 0; Varazdin 4 Iskra-Stal 2; Ventspils 4 Shakhter 2;
Westerlo 1 TPS 0; Zeljeznicar 1 Sheriff 0

THIRD QUALIFYING ROUND, FIRST LEG

Karpaty Lviv 2 (Fedetskiy 34, Voronkov 90) **St Patrick's** 0. Att: 13,000. Paks 1 (Sipeki 32)
Hearts 1 (Hamill 45 pen). Att: 3,500. RNK Split 0 **Fulham** 0. Att: 9,987. **Stoke** 1 (Walters 3)
Hajduk Split 0. Att: 26,322. Vorksla 0 **Sligo** 0. Att: 8,500

THIRD QUALIFYING ROUND, SECOND LEG

Fulham 2 (Johnson 19, Murphy 57 pen) RNK Split 0. Att: 17,087 (Fulham won 2-0 on
agg). Hajduk Split 0 **Stoke** 1 (Shotton 90). Att: 29,548 (Stoke won 2-0 on agg). **Hearts** 4
(Stevenson 34, 45, Driver 50, Skacel 76) Paks 1 (Bode 89). Att: 12,611 (Hearts won 5-2
on agg). **Sligo** 0 Vorskla 2 (Zakarliuka 16, Rebenok 17). Att: 3,800 (Vorskla won 2-0 on agg).
St Patrick's 1 (McMillan 57) Karpaty Lviv 3 (Zenjov 22, Khudobyak 64, Oschypko 83). Att:
2,109 (Karpaty Lviv won 5-1 on agg)

THIRD QUALIFYING ROUND, ON AGGREGATE

Aalesund 2 Elfsborg 1; AEK Larnaca 5 Mlada Boleslav 2; Alania 2 Aktobe 2 (aet, Alania
won 4-2 on pens); Atletico Madrid 4 Stromsgodset 1; Austria Vienna 4 Olimpija Ljubljana 3;
AZ 3 Jablonec 1; Bursaspor 5 Gomel 2; Club Bruges 4 Karabakh Azersun 2; Crvena Zvezda
9 Ventspils 1; Dinamo Bucharest 4 Varazdin 3; Dinamo Tbilisi 6 Reykjavik 1; Gaz Metan 2
Mainz 2 (aet, Gaz Metan won 4-3 on pens); Guimaraes 2 Midtjylland 1; Hapoel Tel-Aviv 5
Vaduz 2; Helsingborgs 3 Bnei Yehuda 0; Legia Warsaw 1 Gaziantepspor 0; Lokomotiv Sofia
0 Slask Wroclaw 0 (aet, Slask Wroclaw won 4-3 on pens); Maccabi Tel-Aviv 8 Zeljeznicar
0; Nacional 4 Hacken 2; Olympiacos Volou 6 Differdange 0 (Olympiacos Volou expelled for
domestic points deduction, Differdange reinstated); Omonia Nicosia 3 Den Haag 1; PAOK
Salonika 5 Valerenga 0; Rabotkicki 3 Anorthosis Famagusta 2; Red Bull Salzburg 4 Senica 0;
Rennes 7 Rustavi 2; Ried 4 Brondby 4 (Ried won on away goals); Sparta Prague 7 Sarajevo
0; Spartak Trnava 3 Levski Sofia 3 (aet, Spartak Trnava won 5-4 on pens); Thun 3 Palermo 3
(Thun won on away goals); Young Boys 5 Westerlo 1

PLAY-OFFS, FIRST LEG

Celtic 0 Sion 0. Att: 51,525; **Fulham** 3 (Hughes 39, Dempsey 43, 49) Dnipro 0. Att: 14,823;
Hearts 0 **Tottenham** 5 (Van der Vaart 5, Defoe 13, Livermore 28, Bale 63, Lennon 78). Att:
16,279. Maribor 2 (Ibraimi 52, Velikonja 90) **Rangers** 1 (Ortiz 31). Att: 10,900. Nacional 0
Birmingham 0. Att: 4,323. **Shamrock** 1 (McCabe 81) Partizan Belgrade 1 (Tomic 14). Att:
4,650. Thun 0 **Stoke** 1 (Pugh 19). Att: 7,850

PLAY-OFFS, SECOND LEG

Birmingham 3 (Redmond 15, Murphy 24, Wood 86) Nacional 0. Att: 27,698 (Birmingham
won 3-0 on agg). Dnipro 1 (Shakov 23) **Fulham** 0. Att: 12,100 (Fulham won 3-1 on agg);
Partizan Belgrade 1 (Volkov 35) **Shamrock** 2 (Sullivan 58, Rice 113 pen). Att: 13,706. (aet,
Shamrock won 3-2 on agg); **Rangers** 1 (Bocanagra 75) Maribor 1 (Volas 55). Att: 32,223
(Maribor won 3-2 on agg). Sion 3 (Feindouno 3 pen, 63, Sio 82) **Celtic** 1 (Mulgrew 78). Att:
10,145 (Sion won 3-1 on agg. Sion expelled for fielding ineligible players, Celtic reinstated).
Stoke 4 (Upson 25, Jones 31, 72, Whelan 38) Thun 1 (Wittwer 77). Att: 24,148 (Stoke won
5-1 on agg). **Tottenham** 0 **Hearts** 0. Att: 32,590 (Tottenham won 5-0 on agg)

PLAY-OFFS, ON AGGREGATE

AEK Athens 2 Dinamo Tbilisi 1 (aet); AEK Larnaca 2 Rosenborg 1; Athletic Bilbao v
Trabzonspor (Athletic Bilbao through to group stage after Trabzonspor elevated to Champions
League); Atletico Madrid 6 Guimaraes 0; Austria Vienna 3 Gaz Metan 2; AZ 7 Aalesund 2;
Anderlecht 4 Bursaspor 3; Besiktas 3 Alania 2; Braga 2 Young Boys 2 (Braga won on away
goals); Club Bruges 5 Zestafoni 3; Dynamo Kiev 3 Litex Lovech 1; Hannover 3 Sevilla 2;
Hapoel Tel-Aviv 4 Ekranas 1; Lazio 9 Rabotnicki 1; Legia Warsaw 5 Spartak Moscow 4;
Lokomotiv Moscow 3 Spartak Trnava 1; Maccabi Tel-Aviv 4 Panathinaikos 2; Metalist Kharkiv
4 Sochaux 0; PAOK Salonika 3 Karpaty Lviv 1; Paris SG 6 Differdange 0; PSV 5 Ried
0; Rapid Bucharest 4 Slask Wroclaw 2; Red Bull Salzburg 2 Omonia Nicosia 2 (Red Bull
Salzburg won on away goals); Rennes 6 Crvena Zvezda 1; Schalke 6 HJK Helsinki 3; Slovan
Bratislava 2 Roma 1; Sporting 2 Nordsjaelland 1; Standard Liege 4 Helsingborgs 1; Steaua
Bucharest 3 CSKA Sofia 1; Vaslui 2 Sparta Prague 1; Vorskla 5 Dinamo Bucharest 3

GROUP A

Match-day 1: PAOK Salonika 0 Tottenham 0. Att: 24,645. **Shamrock** 0 Rubin Kazan 3
(Martins 3, Noboa 52, Karadeniz 62). Att: 6,920
Match-day 2: Rubin Kazan 2 (Valdez 52, Dyadyun 67) PAOK Salonika 2 (Athanasiadis
22, Fotakis 80). Att: 14,350. Tottenham 3 (Pavlyuchenko 60, Defoe 61, Dos Santos 65)
Shamrock 1 (Rice 50). Att: 24,782
Match-day 3: PAOK Salonika 2 (Lazar 12, Vieirinha 63) **Shamrock** 1 (Sheppard 48). Att:
12,776. **Tottenham** 1 (Pavlyuchenko 33) Rubin Kazan 0. Att: 24,058
Match-day 4: Rubin Kazan 1 (Natcho 55) Tottenham 0. Att: 21,250. **Shamrock** 1 (Dennehy
51) PAOK Salonika 3 (Salpingidis 7, 38, Fotakis 35). Att: 6,100
Match-day 5: Rubin Kazan 4 (Valdez 10, 51, Natcho 36, Martins 62) **Shamrock** 1 (Oman 12).
Att: 15,740. Tottenham 1 (Modric 39 pen) PAOK Salonika 2 (Salpingidis 6, Athanasiadis 13).
Att: 26,229
Match-day 6: PAOK Salonika 1 (Vieirinha 16 pen) Rubin Kazan 1 (Valdez 48). Att: 15,500.
Shamrock 0 Tottenham 4 (Pienaar 29, Townsend 38, Defoe 45, Kane 90). Att: 7,500

FINAL TABLE

	P	W	D	L	F	A	Pts
PAOK Salinoka Q	6	3	3	0	10	6	12
Rubin Kazan Q	6	3	2	1	11	5	11
Tottenham	6	3	1	2	9	4	10
Shamrock	6	0	0	6	4	19	0

GROUP B

Match-day 1: Copenhagen 1 (Nordstrand 54 pen) Vorskla 0. Att: 10,420. Hannover 0
Standard Liege 0. Att: 42,540
Match-day 2: Standard Liege 3 (Seijas 27, Felipe 72, Kanu 79) Copenhagen 0. Att: 13,368.
Vorskla 1 (Kurilov 50) Hannover 2 (Abdellaoui 32, Pander 44). Att: 11,000
Match-day 3: Hannover 2 (Pander 29, Pinto 82) Copenhagen 2 (N'doye 68, Santin 89). Att:
43,100. Standard Liege 0 Vorskla 0. Att: 13,496
Match-day 4: Copenhagen 1 (N'doye 66) Hannover 2 (Schlaudraff 71, Stindl 74). Att:
27,853. Vorskla 1 (Kurilov 5) Standard Liege 3 (Seijas 16, Kanu 45, Tchite 74). Att: 5,000
Match-day 5: Standard Liege 2 (Tchite 25, Cyriac 59) Hannover 0. Att: 18,104. Vorskla 1
(N'doye 31 og) Copenhagen 1 (N'doye 37). Att: 3,000
Match-day 6: Copenhagen 0 Standard Liege 1 (Batshuayi 31). Att: 9,722. Hannover 3
(Rausch 24, Konan 33, Sobiech 78) Vorskla 1 (Bezues 45 pen). Att: 40,000

FINAL TABLE

	P	W	D	L	F	A	Pts
Standard Liege Q	6	4	2	0	9	1	14
Hannover Q	6	3	2	1	9	7	11
Copenhagen	6	1	2	3	5	9	5
Vorskla	6	0	2	4	4	10	2

GROUP C

Match-day 1: Hapoel Tel-Aviv 0 Rapid Bucharest 1 (Herea 55). Att: 7,700. PSV 1 (Mertens 21) Legia Warsaw 0. Att: 13,000

Match-day 2: Legia Warsaw 3 (Ljuboja 67, Komorowski 72 pen, Radovic 89) Hapoel Tel-Aviv 2 (Tamuz 34, Lala 79). Att: 20,150. Rapid Bucharest 1 (Alexa 28) PSV 3 (Bouma 42, Toivonen 88, Matavz 90). Att: 21,320.

Match-day 3: Hapoel Tel-Aviv 0 PSV 1 (Wijnaldum 70 pen). Att: 9,468. Rapid Bucharest 0 Legia Warsaw 1 (Radovic 73). Att: 13,726.

Match-day 4: Legia Warsaw 3 (Radovic 53, 68, Kucharczyk 90) Rapid Bucharest 1 (Teixeira 64). Att: 30,786. PSV 3 (Wijnaldum 12, Toivonen 59, Strootman 87) Hapoel Tel-Aviv 3 (Damari 10, Tamuz 33, 47). Att: 23,500.

Match-day 5: Legia Warsaw 0 PSV 3 (Zewlakow 32 og, Mertens 60 pen, Labyad 68). Att: 28,786. Rapid Bucharest 1 (Deac 43 pen) Hapoel Tel-Aviv 3 (Igiebor 12, Tamuz 40 pen, Toama 45). Att: 4,529

Match-day 6: Hapoel Tel-Aviv 2 (Toama 33, Yadin 76) Legia Warsaw 0. Att: 5,500. PSV 2 (Manolev 75, Matavz 79) Rapid Bucharest 1 (Pancu 90). Att: 27,000.

FINAL TABLE

	P	W	D	L	F	A	Pts
PSV Q	6	5	1	0	13	5	16
Legia Warsaw Q	6	3	0	3	7	9	9
Hapoel Tel-Aviv	6	2	1	3	10	9	7
Rapid Bucharest	6	1	0	5	5	12	3

GROUP D

Match-day 1: Lazio 2 (Cisse 35 pen, Sculli 71) Vaslui 2 (Wesley 59 63 pen). Att:13,913. Zurich 0 Sporting 2 (Insua 4, Van Wolfswinkel 20). Att: 10,400

Match-day 2: Sporting 2 (Van Wolfswinkel 21, Insua 45) Lazio 1 (Klose 40). Att: 33,725. Vaslui 2 (Wesley 62 pen, Tamwanyera 76) Zurich 2 (Alphonse 32, Mehmedi 79) Att: 4,000

Match-day 3: Sporting 2 (Evaldo 43, Fernandez 70) Vaslui 0. Att: 28,106. Zurich 1 (Nikci 23) Lazio 1 (Sculli 22). Att: 10,800

Match-day 4: Lazio 1 (Brocchi 62) Zurich 0. Att: 13,414. Vaslui 1 (Zmeu 30) Sporting 0. Att: 5,000

Match-day 5: Sporting 2 (Van Wolfswinkel 15, Bojinov 58) Zurich 0. Att: 25,309. Vaslui 0 Lazio 0. Att: 7,000

Match-day 6: Lazio 2 (Kozak 43, Sculli 15) Sporting 0. Att: 8,295. Zurich 2 (Margairaz 69, Buff 90) Vaslui 0. Att: 6,200

FINAL TABLE

	P	W	D	L	F	A	Pts
Sporting Q	6	4	0	2	8	4	12
Lazio Q	6	2	3	1	7	5	9
Vaslui	6	1	3	2	5	8	6
Zurich	6	1	2	3	5	8	5

GROUP E

Match-day 1: Besiktas 5 (Almeida 3, 28, Aurelio 51, Korkmaz 53, De Oliveira 88) Maccabi Tel-

Aviv 1 (Kahat 49). Att: 17,936. Dynamo Kiev 1 (Vukojevic 90) **Stoke** 1 (Jerome 55). Att: 14,500
Match-day 2: Maccabi Tel-Aviv 1 (Micha 44) Dynamo Kiev 1 (Ideye 9). Att: 13,835. **Stoke** 2
(Crouch 15, Walters 78 pen) Besiktas 1 (Hilbert 14). Att: 23,551
Match-day 3: Dynamo Kiev 1 (Garmash 90) Besiktas 0. Att: 13,500. **Stoke** 3 (Jones 12,
Jerome 24, Shotton 32) Maccabi Tel-Aviv 0. Att: 22,756
Match-day 4: Besiktas 1 (Korkmaz 68) Dynamo Kiev 0. Att: 24,183. Maccabi Tel-Aviv 1
(Colautti 90) **Stoke** 2 (Whitehead 51, Crouch 64). Att: 10,368
Match-day 5: Maccabi Tel-Aviv 2 (Yeyni 60, Lugasi 72) Besiktas 3 (Quaresma 45, 90,
Toraman 49). Att: 9,420. **Stoke** 1 (Jones 81) Dynamo Kiev 1 (Upson 28 og). Att: 23,774
Match-day 6: Besiktas 3 (Fernandes 59 pen, Pektemek 74, De Oliveria 82) **Stoke** 1 (Fuller
29). Att: 26,118. Dynamo Kiev 3 (Yeyni 12 og, Gusev 17, 80) Maccabi Tel-Aviv 3 (Vered 50,
Atar 62, Dabbur 75). Att: 3,850

FINAL TABLE

	P	W	D	L	F	A	Pts
Besiktas Q	6	4	0	2	13	7	12
Stoke Q	6	3	2	1	10	7	11
Dynamo Kiev	6	1	4	1	7	7	7
Maccabi Tel-Aviv	6	0	2	4	8	17	2

GROUP F

Match-day 1: Paris SG 3 (Nene 35 pen, Bodmer 44, Menez 67) Red Bull Salzburg 1 (Sekagya
87). Att: 23,039. Slovan Bratislava 1 (Guede 34) Athletic Bilbao 2 (Susaeta 13, Muniain 40).
Att: 6,328
Match day 2: Athletic Bilbao 2 (Gabilondo 20, Susaeta 45) Paris SG 0. Att: 23,487. Red Bull
Salzburg 3 (Leonardo 60, Zarate 76, Svento 90) Slovan Bratislava 0. Att: 7,500
Match-day 3: Athletic Bilbao 2 (Llorente 69 pen, 75 pen) Red Bull Salzburg 2 (Wallner 30,
Leonardo 36). Att: 22,566. Slovan Bratislava 0 Paris SG 0. Att: 7,238
Match-day 4: Paris SG 1 (Pastore 63) Slovan Bratislava 0. Att: 32,046. Red Bull Salzburg 0
Athletic Bilbao 1 (Herrera 37). Att: 10,350
Match-day 5: Athletic Bilbao 2 (De Marcos 15, Susaeta 75) Slovan Bratislava 1 (Sebo 39).
Att: 28,314. Red Bull Salzburg 2 (Jantscher 20, Svento 90) Paris SG 0. Att: 8,304
Match-day 6: Paris SG 4 (Pastore 21, Bodmer 41, Perez 85 og, Hoarau 90 pen) Athletic
Bilbao 2 (Aurtenetxe 3, Lopez 55). Att: 37,114. Slovan Bratislava 2 (Lacny 3, 6) Red Bull
Salzburg 3 (Jantscher 19 pen, Leonardo 23, Had 52 og). Att: 4,586

FINAL TABLE

	P	W	D	L	F	A	Pts
Athletic Bilbao Q	6	4	1	1	11	8	13
Red Bull Salzburg Q	6	3	1	2	11	8	10
Paris SG	6	3	1	2	8	7	10
Slovan Bratislava	6	0	1	5	4	11	1

GROUP G

Match-day 1: Austria Vienna 1 (Jun 7) Metalist Kharkiv 2 (Gueye 56, Cleiton Xavier 79 pen).
Att: 9,120. AZ 4 (Altidore 21, Elm 33 pen, Maher 39, Holman 49) Malmo 1 (Larsson 72
pen). Att: 11,095
Match-day 2: Malmo 1 (Mehmeti 82) Austria Vienna 2 (Barazite 17, Grunwald 37). Att:
10,802. Metalist Kharkiv 1 (Taison 77) AZ 1 (Altidore 26). Att: 37,122
Match-day 3: AZ 2 (Hlinka 80 og, Wernbloom 83) Austria Vienna 2 (Marcellis 19 og, Gorgon
29). Att: 15,321. Malmo 1 (Hamad 22) Metalist Kharkiv 4 (Cristaldo 32, Fininho 45, Edmar
57, Devic 73). Att: 8,466
Match-day 4: Austria Vienna 2 (Ortlechner 58, Barazite 61) AZ 2 (Elm 19 pen, Wernbloom 44).
Att: 10,450. Metalist Kharkiv 3 (Taison 46, 56, Finiho 90) Malmo 1 (Ranegie 66). Att: 25,883

Match-day 5: Malmo 0 AZ 0. Att: 7,632. Metalist Kharkiv 4 (Devic 17, Edmar 40, Gueye 60, Sosa 89) Austria Vienna 1 (Mader 19). Att: 25,810.
Match-day 6: Austria Vienna 2 (Liendl 63, Barazite 80) Malmo 0. Att: 10,000. AZ 1 (Maher 37) Metalist Kharkiv 1 (Devic 37). Att: 13,268

FINAL TABLE

	P	W	D	L	F	A	Pts
Metalist Kharkiv Q	6	4	2	0	15	6	14
AZ Q	6	1	5	0	10	7	8
Austria Vienna	6	2	2	2	10	11	8
Malmo	6	0	1	5	4	15	1

GROUP H

Match-day 1: Birmingham 1 (King 71) Braga 3 (Helder Barbosa 6, 88, Lima 59). Att: 21,747. Club Bruges 2 (Odjija Ofoe 7, Dirar 24) Maribor 0. Att: 16,668
Match-day 2: Braga 1 (Helder Barbosa 63) Club Bruges 2 (Akpala 71, Donk 90). Att: 9,145. Maribor 1 (Volas 29) Birmingham 2 (Burke 64, Elliott 79). Att: 11,000
Match-day 3: Club Bruges 1 (Akpala 3) Birmingham 2 (Murphy 26, Wood 90). Att: 23,396. Maribor 1 (Ibraimi 14) Braga 1 (Echiejile 44). Att: 8,500
Match-day 4: Birmingham 2 (Beausejour 55, King 74 pen) Club Bruges 2 (Meunier 39, Akpala 44). Att: 26,849. Braga 5 (Lima 4, Alan 7, Echiejile 38, Paulo Vinicius 85, Merida 90) Maribor 1 (Volas 62). Att: 7,185
Match-day 5: Braga 1 (Hugo Viana 51) Birmingham 0. Att: 9,957. Maribor 3 (Volas 11, 68, Hoefkens 51 og) Club Bruges 4 (Dirar 74, 77, Akpala 81, Donk 90). Att: 9,500
Match-day 6: Birmingham 1 (Rooney 24) Maribor 0. Att: 21,436. Club Bruges 1 (Vleminckx 50) Braga 1 (Ewerton 64). Att: 21,000

FINAL TABLE

	P	W	D	L	F	A	Pts
Club Bruges Q	6	3	2	1	12	9	11
Braga Q	6	3	2	1	12	6	11
Birmingham	6	3	1	2	8	8	10
Maribor	6	0	1	5	6	15	1

GROUP I

Match-day 1: Atletico Madrid 2 (Falcao 3, Diego 68) Celtic 0. Att: 24,868. Udinese 2 (Di Natale 39, Armero 83) Rennes 1 (Hadji 19). Att: 8,383
Match-day 2: Celtic 1 (Ki Sung-Yueng 3 pen), Udinese 1 (Abdi 88 pen). Att: 28,476. Rennes 1 (Montano 56) Atletico Madrid 1 (Juanfran 87). Att: 24,298
Match-day 3: Rennes 1 (Cha Du-Ri 30 og) Celtic 1 (Ledley 70). Att: 21,825. Udinese 2 (Benatia 88, Floro Flores 90) Atletico Madrid 0. Att: 10,026
Match-day 4: Atletico Madrid 4 (Adrian 6, 12, Diego 36, Falcao 67) Udinese 0. Att: 18,300. Celtic 3 (Stokes 30, 43, Hooper 82) Rennes 1 (Mangane 2). Att: 28,578
Match-day 5: Celtic 0 Atletico Madrid 1 (Turan 30). Att: 33,257. Rennes 0 Udinese 0. Att: 17,428
Match-day 6: Atletico Madrid 3 (Falcao 38 pen, Dominguez 42, Turan 79) Rennes 1 (Mandjeck 86). Att: 8,000. Udinese 1 (Di Natale 45) Celtic 1 (Hooper 29). Att: 15,000

FINAL TABLE

	P	W	D	L	F	A	Prs
Atletico Madrid Q	6	4	1	1	11	4	13
Udinese Q	6	2	3	1	6	7	9
Celtic	6	1	3	2	6	7	6
Rennes	6	0	3	3	5	10	3

GROUP J

Match-day 1: Maccabi Haifa 1 (Gadir 54) AEK Larnaca 0. Att: 9,250. Steaua Bucharest 0 Schalke 0. Att: 12,390
Match-day 2: AEK Larnaca 1 (Mrdakovic 59) Steaua Bucharest 1 (Costea 65). Att: 4,058. Schalke 3 (Fuchs 7, 65, Manuel Jurado 82) Maccabi Haifa 1 (Vered 34). Att: 49,070
Match-day 3: AEK Larnaca 0 Schalke 5 (Holtby 23, Huntelaar 35, 88, Howedes 41, Draxler 87). Att: 5,344. Maccabi Haifa 5 (Amasha 10, 20, Katan 38 pen, Tawatcha 72, Vered 79) Steaua Bucharest 0. Att: 14,000
Match-day 4: Schalke 0 AEK 0. Att: 52,077. Steaua Bucharest 4 (Tatu 13, Costea 28, Tanase 64, 84) Maccabi Haifa 2 (Meshumar 36, Katan 40). Att: 31,233
Match-day 5: AEK Larnaca 2 (Garcia 14, Pintado 51) Maccabi Haifa 1 (Buljat 75). Att: 3,132. Schalke 2 (Papadopoulos 26, Raul 57) Steaua Bucharest 1 (Rusescu 33). Att: 53,123
Match-day 6: Maccabi Haifa 0 Schalke 3 (Buljat 8 og, Marica 84, Wiegel 90). Att: 11,234. Steaua Bucharest 3 (Rusescu 55 pen, Nikolic 70, 85) AEK Larnaca 1 (Pintado 61). Att: 50,051

FINAL TABLE

	P	W	D	L	F	A	Pts
Schalke Q	6	4	2	0	13	2	14
Steaua Bucharest Q	6	2	2	2	9	11	8
Maccabi Haifa	6	2	0	4	10	12	6
AEK Larnaca	6	1	2	3	4	11	5

GROUP K

Match-day 1: Fulham 1 (Johnson 19) Twente 1 (Schwarzer 41 og). Att: 14,110. Wisla Krakow 1 (Kirm 54) Odense 3 (Johansson 35, Utaka 80, Jensen 90). Att: 12,920
Match-day 2: Odense 0 Fulham 2 (Johnson 36, 88). Att: 9,969. Twente 4 (De Jong 32, Janko 45, 57, Janssen 80). Att: 20,000.
Match-day 3: Odense 1 (Djiby Fall 71) Twente 4 (Brama 13, Bajrami 31, Chadli 65, De Jong 82). Att: 6,834. Wisla Krakow 1 (Biton 60) Fulham 0. Att: 16,577
Match-day 4: Fulham 4 (Duff 5, Johnson 30, 57, Sidwell 79) Wisla Krakow 1 (Kirm 9). Att: 20,319. Twente 3 (Landzaat 35, 37, Fer 82) Odense 2 (Djiby Fall 11, 62). Att: 21,000
Match-day 5: Odense 1 (Jensen 51) Wisla Krakow 2 (Biton 19, Malecki 30). Att: 5,824. Twente 1 (Janko 89) Fulham 0. Att: 25,250
Match-day 6: Fulham 2 (Dempsey 27, Frei 31) Odense 2 (Andreasen 64, Djiby Fall 90). Att: 15,757. Wisla Krakow 2 (Gargula 12, Genkov 46) Twente 1 (De Jong 39). Att: 15,500

FINAL TABLE

	P	W	D	L	F	A	Pts
Twente Q	6	4	1	1	14	7	13
Wisla Krakow Q	6	3	0	3	8	13	9
Fulham	6	2	2	2	9	6	8
Odense	6	1	1	4	9	14	4

GROUP L

Match-day 1: Anderlecht 4 (Suarez 16, 41, 84, Jovanovic 34) AEK Athens 1 (Leonardo 36). Att: 11,480. Sturm Graz 1 (Szabics 14) Lokomotiv Moscow 2 (Obinna 28, Sychev 29). Att: 13,356
Match-day 2: AEK Athens 1 (Standfest 51 og) Sturm Graz 2 (Burgstaller 87, Haas 90). Att: 10,074. Lokomotiv Moscow 0 Anderlecht 2 (Suarez 10, Mbokani 70). Att: 11,495
Match-day 3: Lokomotiv Moscow 3 (Sychev 47, 72 pen, Caicedo 90) AEK Athens 1 (Sialmas 88). Att: 8,279. Sturm Graz 0 Anderlecht 2 (Gillet 66, Suarez 75). Att: 14,297

Match-day 4: AEK Athens 1 (Leonardo 61 pen) Lokomotiv Moscow 3 (Glushakov 50, Maicon 72, Ignatiev 80). Att: 4,042. Anderlecht 3 (Gillet 23, Suarez 74, De Sutter 81) Sturm Graz 0. Att: 15,460
Match-day 5: AEK Athens 1 (Sialmas 19) Anderlecht 2 (Gillet 4, 36). Att: 3,703. Lokomotiv Moscow 3 (Maicon 62, Sychev 72 pen, Glushakov 89). Sturm Graz 1 (Kainz 63). Att: 13,423
Match-day 6: Anderlecht 5 (Kljestan 13, Canesin 39, Wasilewski 58, Suarez 61, Gillet 78) Lokomotiv Moscow 3 (Ignatiev 21, Sychev 69 pen, 89). Att: 14,609. Sturm Graz 1 (Kainz 59) AEK Athens 3 (Manolas 10, Burns 43, Victor 77). Att: 13,681

FINAL TABLE

	P	W	D	L	F	A	Pts
Anderlecht Q	6	6	0	0	18	5	18
Lokomotiv Moscow Q	6	4	0	2	14	11	12
AEK Athens	6	1	0	5	8	15	3
Sturm Graz	6	1	0	5	5	14	3

ROUND OF 32, FIRST LEG

Ajax 0 **Manchester Utd** 2 (Young 59, Hernandez 85). Att: 48,966. AZ 1 (Maher 35) Anderlecht 0. Att: 13,744
Braga 0 Besiktas 2 (Sivok 37, Sabrosa 58). Att: 9,088. Hannover 2 (Sobiech 73, Schlaudraff 81 pen) Club Bruges 1 (Lestienne 51). Att: 42,000
Lazio 1 (Klose 19) Atletico Madrid 3 (Adrian 25, Falcao 37, 63). Att: 30,604. Legia Warsaw 2 (Wawrzyniak 37, Gol 79) Sporting 2 (Carrico 60, Santos 88). Att: 27,234
Lokomotiv Moscow 2 (Glushakov 61 pen, Caicedo 71) Athletic Bilbao 1 (Muniain 35). Att: 13,160. Porto 1 (Varela 27) **Manchester City** 2 (Pereira 55 og, Aguero 84). Att: 47,417
Red Bull Salzburg 0 Metalist Kharkiv 4 (Taison 1, Cristaldo 38, 41, Marlos 90). Att: 8,100. Rubin Kazan 0 Olympicos 1 (Fuster 72). Att: 1,741
Steaua Bucharest 0 Twente 1 (John 53). Att: 49,588. **Stoke** 0 Valencia 1 (Topal 36). Att: 24,185
Trabzonspor 1 (Adin 33) PSV 2 (Matavz 6, Toivonen 12). Att: 18,866. Udinese 0 PAOK Salonika 0. Att: 11,641
Viktor Plzen 1 (Darida 22) Schalke 1 (Huntelaar 75). Att: 11,437. Wisla Krakow 1 (Genkov 88) Standard Liege 1 (Cyriac 27 pen). Att: 19,266

ROUND OF 32, SECOND LEG

Anderlecht 0 AZ 0. Att: 25,000 (AZ won 2-0 on agg). Athletic Bilbao 1 (Muniain 62) Lokomotiv Moscow 0. Att: 35,000 (agg 2-2, Athletic Bilbao won on away goal)
Atletico Madrid 1 (Godin 48) Lazio 0. Att: 30,000 (Atletico Madrid won 4-1 on agg). Besiktas 0 Braga 1 (Lima 25). Att: 25,000 (Besiktas won 2-1 on agg)
Club Bruges 0 Hannover 1 (Diouf 21). Att: 22,000 (Hannover won 3-1 on agg). **Manchester City** 4 (Aguero 1, Dzeko 76, Silva 84, Pizarro 86) Porto 0. Att: 39,638 (Manchester City won 6-1 on agg)
Manchester Utd 1 (Hernandez 6) Ajax 2 (Ozbiliz 37, Alderweireld 87). Att: 67,328 (Manchester Utd won 3-2 on agg). Metalist Kharkiv 4 (Hinteregger 29 og, Cristaldo 62, Blanco 64, Marlos 87) Red Bull Salzburg 1 (Jantscher 56). Att: 30,826 (Metalist Kharkiv won 8-1 on agg)
Olympiacos 1 (Djebbour 14) Rubin Kazan 0. Att: 30,000 (Olympiacos won 2-0 on agg). PAOK Salonika 0 Udinese 3 (Danilo 6, Flores 14, Domizzi 51 pen). Att: 20,000 (Udinese won 3-0 on agg)
PSV 4 (Mertens 15 pen, Matavz 31, 53, Strootman 38) Trabzonspor 1 (Yilmaz 43). Att: 18,300 (PSV won 6-2 on agg)
Schalke 3 (Huntelaar 7, 106, 120) Viktor Plzen 1 (Rajtoral 88). Att: 54,142 (aet, Schalke won 4-2 on agg). Sporting 1 (Fernandez 84) Legia Warsaw 0. Att: 20,144 (Sporting won 3-2 on agg)

Standard Liege 0 Wisla Krakow 0. Att: 23,000 (agg 1-1, Standard Liege won on away goal).
Valencia 1 (Jonas 24) Stoke 0. Att: 35,000 (Valencia won 2-0 on agg)

ROUND OF 16, FIRST LEG

Atletico Madrid 3 (Salvio 24, 27, Adrian 37) Besiktas 1 (Sabrosa 53). Att: 40,000. AZ 2
(Martens 63, Falkenburg 84) Udinese 0. Att: 12,579
Manchester Utd 2 (Rooney 22, 90 pen) Athletic Bilbao 3 (Llorente 44, De Marcos 72,
Muniain 90). Att: 59,265. Metalist Kharkiv 0 Olympiacos 1 (Fuster 50). Att: 11,000
Sporting 1 (Xandao 51) Manchester City 0. Att: 34,371. Standard Liege 2 (Buyens 27, Tchite
30) Hannover 2 (Stindl 22 pen, Diouf 56). Att: 21,000
Twente 1 (De Jong 61 pen) Schalke 0. Att: 30,000. Valencia 4 (Ruiz 11, Soldado 13, 43
pen, Piatti 56) PSV 2 (Toivonen 83, Wijnaldum 90). Att: 30,000

ROUND OF 16, SECOND LEG

Athletic Bilbao 2 (Llorente 23, De Marcos 65) Manchester Utd 1 (Rooney 80). Att: 40,000
(Athletic Bilbao won 5-3 on agg). Besiktas 0 Atletico Madrid 3 (Adrian 26, Falcao 84, Salvio
90). Att: 23,000 (Atletico Madrid won 6-1 on agg)
Hannover 4 (Abdellaoui 4, Kanu 21 og, 73 og, Pinto 90) Standard Liege 0. Att: 43,000
(Hannover won 6-2 on agg). Manchester City 3 (Aguero 60, 82, Balotelli 75 pen) Sporting 2
(Fernandez 33, Van Wolfswinkel 40). Att: 38,021 (agg 3-3, Sporting won on away goals)
Olympiacos 1 (Marcano 15) Metalist Kharkiv 2 (Villagra 81, Devic 87). Att: 30,000 (agg 2-2,
Metalist Kharkiv won on away goals). PSV 1 (Toivonen 64) Valencia 1 (Rami 47). Att: 22,000
(Valencia won 5-3 on agg)
Schalke 4 (Huntelaar 29, 57 pen, 81, Jones 70) Twente 1 (Janssen 14). Att: 54,142
(Schalke won
4-2 on agg). Udinese 2 (Di Natale 3 pen, 15) AZ 1 (Falkenburg 31). Att: 9,500 (AZ won 3-2
on agg)

QUARTER-FINALS, FIRST LEG

Atletico Madrid 2 (Falcao 9, Salvio 89) Hannover 1 (Diouf 38). Att: 29,223. AZ 2 (Holman
45, Martens 79) Valencia 1 (Topal 51). Att: 16,100. Schalke 2 (Raul 22, 59) Athletic Bilbao
4 (Llorente 20, 73, De Marcos 81, Muniain 90). Att: 53,883. Sporting 2 (Izmailov 51, Insua
64) Metalist Kharkiv 1 (Xavier 90 pen). Att: 40,512

QUARTER-FINALS, SECOND LEG

Athletic Bilbao 2 (Ibai 41, Susaeta 55) Schalke 2 (Huntelaar 28, Raul 52). Att: 39,750
(Athletic Bilbao won 6-4 on agg). Hannover 1 (Diouf 81) Atletico Madrid 2 (Adrian 63, Falcao
87). Att: 44,000 (Atletico Madrid won 4-2 on agg). Metalist Kharkiv 1 (Cristaldo 57) Sporting
1 (Van Wolfswinkel 45). Att: 38,683 (Sporting won 3-2 on agg). Valencia 4 (Rami 15, 17,
Jordi Alba 56, Pablo 80) AZ 0. Att: 35,000 (Valencia won 5-2 on agg)

SEMI-FINALS, FIRST LEG

Atletico Madrid 4 (Falcao 18, 78, Miranda 49, Adrian 54) Valencia 2 (Jonas 45, Ricardo
Costa 90). Att: 49,400. Sporting 2 (Insua 75, Diego Capel 80) Athletic Bilbao 1 (Aurtenetxe
54). Att: 37,213

SEMI-FINALS, SECOND LEG

Athletic Bilbao 3 (Susaeta 17, Ibai 45, Llorente 88) Sporting 1 (Van Wolfswinkel 44). Att:
37,000 (Athletic Bilbao won 4-3 on agg). Valencia 0 Atletico Madrid 1 (Adrian 60). Att:
45,000 (Atletico Madrid won 5-2 on agg)

FINAL

ATLETICO MADRID 3 ATHLETIC BILBAO 0
National Arena, Bucharest (52,347); Wednesday, May 9 2012

Atletico Madrid (4-2-3-1): Courtois, Juanfran, Godin, Miranda, Luis Filipe, Mario Suarez, Gabi (capt), Diego (Koke 90), Adrian (Salvio 88), Turan (Dominguez 90), Falcao. **Subs not used:** Sergio Asenjo, Antonio Lopez, Paulo Assuncao, Martin. **Scorers:** Falcao (7, 34), Diego (85). **Booked:** Falcao. **Coach:** Diego Simeone.
Athletic Bilbao (4-2-3-1): Iraizoz, Iraolo (capt), Javi Martinez, Amorebieta, Aurtenetxe (Ibai 46), De Marcos, Iturraspe (Inigo Perez 46), Borges (Kardec 78), Muniain, Ander Herrera (Toquero 63), Susaeta, Llorente. **Subs not used:** Raul, San Jose, Gabilondo, Ekiza. **Booked:** Ander Herrera, Amorebieta, Inigo Perez, Susaeta. **Coach:** Marcelo Bielsa
Referee: W Stark (Germany). **Half-time:** 2-0

Leading scorers (from group stage): 12 Falcao (Atletico Madrid); 10 Huntelaar (Schalke); 8 Adrian (Atletico Madrid); 7 Suarez (Anderlecht), Llorente (Athletic Bilbao); 6 Sychev (Lokomotiv Moscow), Van Wolfswinkel (Sporting)

CLUB WORLD CUP FINAL

SANTOS 0 BARCELONA 4
Yokohama (68,166); Sunday, December 18 2011

Santos (4-4-2): Rafael, Edu Dracena (capt), Leo, Danilo (Elano 31), Durval, Bruno Rodrigo, Arouca, Henrique, Ganso (Ibson 83), Borges (Kardec 78), Neymar. **Subs not used:** Aranha, Vladimir, Bruno Aguiar, Carvalho, Vinicius, Anderson, Renteria, Para, Diogo. **Booked:** Edu Dracena, Ganso. **Coach:** Muricy Ramalho
Barcelona (4-2-3-1): Valdes, Dani Alves, Pique (Mascherano 56), Puyol (capt) (Fontas 85), Abidal, Fabregas, Xavi, Iniesta, Thiago (Pedro 78), Busquets, Messi. **Subs not used:** Olazabal, Pinto, Sanchez, Keita, Dos Santos, Maxwell, Adriano, Cuenca. **Scorers:** Messi (17, 82), Xavi (24), Fabregas (45). **Booked:** Pique, Mascherano. **Coach:** Pep Guardiola
Referee: R Irmatov (Uzbekistan). **Half-time:** 0-3

EUROPEAN SUPER CUP

BARCELONA 2 PORTO 0
Monaco (18,048); Friday, August 26 2011

Barcelona (4-3-3): Valdes, Dani Alves, Adriano (Busquets 63), Mascherano, Abidal, Keita, Xavi (capt), Iniesta, Villa (Sanchez 60), Messi, Pedro (Fabregas 80). **Subs not used:** Olazabal, Alcantara, Fontas, Dos Santos. **Scorers:** Messi (39), Fabregas (87). **Booked:** Iniesta. **Coach:** Pep Guardiola
Porto (4-5-1): Helton (capt), Otamendi, Fucile, Sapunaru, Rolando, Souza (Fernando 77), Guarin, Joao Moutinho, Rodriguez (Varela 68), Kleber (Belluschi 77), Hulk. **Subs not used:** Bracalli, Maicon, Djalma, Defour. **Booked:** Rodriguez, Rolando, Guarin. **Sent off:** Rolando, Guarin. **Coach:** Vitor Pereira
Referee: B Kuipers (Holland). **Half-time:** 1-0

UEFA CUP FINALS

1972	Tottenham beat Wolves 3-2 on agg (2-1a, 1-1h)
1973	Liverpool beat Borussia Moenchengladbach 3-2 on agg (3-0h, 0-2a)
1974	Feyenoord beat Tottenham 4-2 on agg (2-2a, 2-0h)
1975	Borussia Moenchengladbach beat Twente Enschede 5-1 on agg (0-0h, 5-1a)
1976	Liverpool beat Brugge 4-3 on agg (3-2h, 1-1a)
1977	Juventus beat Atletico Bilbao on away goals after 2-2 agg (1-0h, 1-2a)
1978	PSV Eindhoven beat Bastia 3-0 on agg (0-0a, 3-0h)
1979	Borussia Moenchengladbach beat Red Star Belgrade 2-1 on agg (1-1a, 1-0h)

1980	Eintracht Frankfurt beat Borussia Moenchengladbach on away goals after 3-3 agg (2-3a, 1-0h)
1981	Ipswich Town beat AZ 67 Alkmaar 5-4 on agg (3-0h, 2-4a)
1982	IFK Gothenburg beat SV Hamburg 4-0 on agg (1-0h, 3-0a)
1983	Anderlecht beat Benfica 2-1 on agg (1-0h, 1-1a)
1984	Tottenham beat Anderlecht 4-3 on penalties after 2-2 agg (1-1a, 1-1h)
1985	Real Madrid beat Videoton 3-1 on agg (3-0a, 0-1h)
1986	Real Madrid beat Cologne 5-3 on agg (5-1h, 0-2a)
1987	IFK Gothenburg beat Dundee Utd 2-1 on agg (1-0h, 1-1a)
1988	Bayer Leverkusen beat Espanol 3-2 on penalties after 3-3 agg (0-3a, 3-0h)
1989	Napoli beat VfB Stuttgart 5-4 on agg (2-1h, 3-3a)
1990	Juventus beat Fiorentina 3-1 on agg (3-1h, 0-0a)
1991	Inter Milan beat AS Roma 2-1 on agg (2-0h, 0-1a)
1992	Ajax beat Torino on away goals after 2-2 agg (2-2a, 0-0h)
1993	Juventus beat Borussia Dortmund 6-1 on agg (3-1a, 3-0h)
1994	Inter Milan beat Salzburg 2-0 on agg (1-0a, 1-0h)
1995	Parma beat Juventus 2-1 on agg (1-0h, 1-1a)
1996	Bayern Munich beat Bordeaux 5-1 on agg (2-0h, 3-1a)
1997	FC Schalke beat Inter Milan 4-1 on penalties after 1-1 agg (1-0h, 0-1a)
1998	Inter Milan beat Lazio 3-0 (one match) – Paris
1999	Parma beat Marseille 3-0 (one match) – Moscow
2000	Galatasaray beat Arsenal 4-1 on penalties after 0-0 (one match) – Copenhagen
2001	Liverpool beat Alaves 5-4 on golden goal (one match) – Dortmund
2002	Feyenoord beat Borussia Dortmund 3-2 (one match) – Rotterdam
2003	FC Porto beat Celtic 3-2 on silver goal (one match) – Seville
2004	Valencia beat Marseille 2-0 (one match) – Gothenburg
2005	CSKA Moscow beat Sporting Lisbon 3-1 (one match) – Lisbon
2006	Sevilla beat Middlesbrough 4-0 (one match) – Eindhoven
2007	Sevilla beat Espanyol 3-1 on penalties after 2-2 (one match) – Hampden Park
2008	Zenit St Petersburg beat Rangers 2-0 (one match) – City of Manchester Stadium
2009†	Shakhtar Donetsk beat Werder Bremen 2-1 (one match) – Istanbul

EUROPA LEAGUE FINALS

2010†	Atletico Madrid beat Fulham 2-1 (one match) – Hamburg
2011	Porto beat Braga 1-0 (one match) – Dublin
2012	Atletico Madrid beat Athletic Bilbao 3-0 (one match) – Bucharest

(† After extra-time)

FAIRS CUP FINALS

(As UEFA Cup previously known)

1958	Barcelona beat London 8-2 on agg (2-2a, 6-0h)
1960	Barcelona beat Birmingham 4-1 on agg (0-0a, 4-1h)
1961	AS Roma beat Birmingham City 4-2 on agg (2-2a, 2-0h)
1962	Valencia beat Barcelona 7-3 on agg (6-2h, 1-1a)
1963	Valencia beat Dynamo Zagreb 4-1 on agg (2-1a, 2-0h)
1964	Real Zaragoza beat Valencia 2-1 (Barcelona)
1965	Ferencvaros beat Juventus 1-0 (Turin)
1966	Barcelona beat Real Zaragoza 4-3 on agg (0-1h, 4-2a)
1967	Dinamo Zagreb beat Leeds Utd 2-0 on agg (2-0h, 0-0a)
1968	Leeds Utd beat Ferencvaros 1-0 on agg (1-0h, 0-0a)
1969	Newcastle Utd beat Ujpest Dozsa 6-2 on agg (3-0h, 3-2a)
1970	Arsenal beat Anderlecht 4-3 on agg (1-3a, 3-0h)
1971	Leeds Utd beat Juventus on away goals after 3-3 agg (2-2a, 1-1h)

CUP-WINNERS' CUP FINALS

1961	Fiorentina beat Rangers 4-1 on agg (2-0 Glasgow first leg, 2-1 Florence second leg)
1962	Atletico Madrid beat Fiorentina 3-0 (replay Stuttgart, after a 1-1 draw, Glasgow)
1963	Tottenham beat Atletico Madrid 5-1 (Rotterdam)
1964	Sporting Lisbon beat MTK Budapest 1-0 (replay Antwerp, after a 3-3 draw, Brussels)
1965	West Ham Utd beat Munich 1860 2-0 (Wembley)
1966†	Borussia Dortmund beat Liverpool 2-1 (Glasgow)
1967†	Bayern Munich beat Rangers 1-0 (Nuremberg)
1968	AC Milan beat SV Hamburg 2-0 (Rotterdam)
1969	Slovan Bratislava beat Barcelona 3-2 (Basle)
1970	Manchester City beat Gornik Zabrze 2-1 (Vienna)
1971†	Chelsea beat Real Madrid 2-1 (replay Athens, after a 1-1 draw, Athens)
1972	Rangers beat Moscow Dynamo 3-2 (Barcelona)
1973	AC Milan beat Leeds Utd 1-0 (Salonika)
1974	Magdeburg beat AC Milan 2-0 (Rotterdam)
1975	Dynamo Kiev beat Ferencvaros 3-0 (Basle)
1976	Anderlecht beat West Ham Utd 4-2 (Brussels)
1977	SV Hamburg beat Anderlecht 2-0 (Amsterdam)
1978	Anderlecht beat Austria WAC 4-0 (Paris)
1979†	Barcelona beat Fortuna Dusseldorf 4-3 (Basle)
1980†	Valencia beat Arsenal 5-4 on penalties after a 0-0 draw (Brussels)
1981	Dynamo Tbilisi beat Carl Zeiss Jena 2-1 (Dusseldorf)
1982	Barcelona beat Standard Liege 2-1 (Barcelona)
1983†	Aberdeen beat Real Madrid 2-1 (Gothenburg)
1984	Juventus beat Porto 2-1 (Basle)
1985	Everton beat Rapid Vienna 3-1 (Rotterdam)
1986	Dynamo Kiev beat Atletico Madrid 3-0 (Lyon)
1987	Ajax beat Lokomotiv Leipzig 1-0 (Athens)
1988	Mechelen beat Ajax 1-0 (Strasbourg)
1989	Barcelona beat Sampdoria 2-0 (Berne)
1990	Sampdoria beat Anderlecht 2-0 (Gothenburg)
1991	Manchester Utd beat Barcelona 2-1 (Rotterdam)
1992	Werder Bremen beat Monaco 2-0 (Lisbon)
1993	Parma beat Royal Antwerp 3-1 (Wembley)
1994	Arsenal beat Parma 1-0 (Copenhagen)
1995†	Real Zaragoza beat Arsenal 2-1 (Paris)
1996	Paris St Germain beat Rapid Vienna 1-0 (Brussels)
1997	Barcelona beat Paris St Germain 1-0 (Rotterdam)
1998	Chelsea beat VfB Stuttgart 1-0 (Stockholm)
1999	Lazio beat Real Mallorca 2-1 (Villa Park, Birmingham)

(† After extra time)

INTER-CONTINENTAL CUP

Year	Winners	Runners-up	Score
1960	Real Madrid (Spa)	Penarol (Uru)	0-0 5-1
1961	Penarol (Uru)	Benfica (Por)	0-1 2-1 5-0
1962	Santos (Bra)	Benfica (Por)	3-2 5-2
1963	Santos (Bra)	AC Milan (Ita)	2-4 4-2 1-0
1964	Inter Milan (Ita)	Independiente (Arg)	0-1 2-0 1-0
1965	Inter Milan (Ita)	Independiente (Arg)	3-0 0-0
1966	Penarol (Uru)	Real Madrid (Spa)	2-0 2-0
1967	Racing (Arg)	**Celtic** (Sco)	0-1 2-1 1-0
1968	Estudiantes (Arg)	Manchester Utd (Eng)	1-0 1-1

1969	AC Milan (Ita)	Estudiantes (Arg)	3-0 1-2
1970	Feyenoord (Hol)	Estudiantes (Arg)	2-2 1-0
1971	Nacional (Uru)	Panathanaikos (Gre)	* 1-1 2-1
1972	Ajax (Hol)	Independiente (Arg)	1-1 3-0
1973	Independiente (Arg)	Juventus* (Ita)	1-0 #
1974	Atletico Madrid (Spa)*	Independiente (Arg)	0-1 2-0
1975	Not played		
1976	Bayern Munich (WGer)	Cruzeiro (Bra)	2-0 0-0
1977	Boca Juniors (Arg)	Borussia Mönchengladbach* (WGer)	2-2 3-0
1978	Not played		
1979	Olimpia Asuncion (Par)	Malmö* (Swe)	1-0 2-1
1980	Nacional (Arg)	Nott'm Forest (Eng)	1-0
1981	Flamengo (Bra)	Liverpool (Eng)	3-0
1982	Penarol (Uru)	Aston Villa (Eng)	2-0
1983	Porto Alegre (Bra)	SV Hamburg (WGer)	2-1
1984	Independiente (Arg)	Liverpool (Eng)	1-0
1985	Juventus (Ita)	Argentinos Juniors (Arg)	2-2 (aet)
	(Juventus won 4-2 on penalties)		
1986	River Plate (Arg)	Steaua Bucharest (Rom)	1-0
1987	Porto (Por)	Penarol (Uru)	2-1 (aet)
1988	Nacional (Uru)	PSV Eindhoven (Hol)	1-1 (aet)
	(Nacional won 7-6 on penalties)		
1989	AC Milan (Ita)	Nacional (Col)	1-0 (aet)
1990	AC Milan (Ita)	Olimpia Asuncion (Par)	3-0
1991	Red Star (Yug)	Colo Colo (Chi)	3-0
1992	Sao Paulo (Bra)	Barcelona (Spa)	2-1
1993	Sao Paulo (Bra)	AC Milan (Ita)	3-2
1994	Velez Sarsfield (Arg)	AC Milan (Ita)	2-0
1995	Ajax (Hol)	Gremio (Bra)	0-0 (aet)
	(Ajax won 4-3 on penalties)		
1996	Juventus (Ita)	River Plate (Arg)	1-0
1997	Borussia Dortmund (Ger)	Cruzeiro (Arg)	2-0
1998	Real Madrid (Spa)	Vasco da Gama (Bra)	2-1
1999	Manchester Utd (Eng)	Palmeiras (Bra)	1-0
2000	Boca Juniors (Arg)	Real Madrid (Spa)	2-1
2001	Bayern Munich (Ger)	Boca Juniors (Arg)	1-0
2002	Real Madrid (Spa)	Olimpia Ascuncion (Par)	2-0
2003	Boca Juniors (Arg)	AC Milan (Ita)	1-1
	(Boca Juniors won 3-1 on penalties)		
2004	FC Porto (Por)	Caldas (Col)	0-0
	(FC Porto won 8-7 on penalties)		

Played as a single match in Japan since 1980
* European Cup runners-up # One match only
Summary: 43 contests; South America 22 wins, Europe 23 wins

CLUB WORLD CHAMPIONSHIP

2005	Sao Paulo beat Liverpool	1-0
2006	Internacional (Bra) beat Barcelona	1-0
2007	AC Milan beat Boca Juniors (Arg)	4-2

CLUB WORLD CUP

2008	Manchester Utd beat Liga de Quito	1-0
2009	Barcelona beat Estudiantes	2-1 (aet)
2010	Inter Milan beat TP Mazembe	3-0
2011	Barcelona beat Santos	4-0

QUOTE/UNQOUTE

'I don't know how I stayed on the pitch' – **Wojciech Szczesny**, Arsenal goalkeeper, admits to escaping with a yellow card after bringing down Chelsea's Ashley Cole

'I don't pick them, they're a bit dodgy. But we have to wear them' – **Gabriel Agbonlahor**, Aston Villa striker, on his luminous green boots.

'It's a bit of a fairy-tale to last so long. When I look back, I say to myself how fortunate I am to have had these players' – **Sir Alex Ferguson** on 25 years as manager of Manchester United.

This was a really good moment for me, with my son getting married and England winning' – **Fabio Capello** after his team's victory over Spain.

'I totally respect the tradition and history of the club, but we need to move with the times and this is progression' – **Derek Llambias,** Newcastle managing director, on the controversial decision to re-name St James's Park.

'He has scored 27 goals in 26 Premier League games and still people tell me he is not a centre-forward. How many goals does a centre-forward need to score? – **Arsene Wenger**, Arsenal manager, on the prolific Robin van Persie, who finished with 37 for the season.

'Airdrie United 11, Gala Fairydean 0' – **Tim Gudgin**, 81, during the reading of his final set of classified l results after six decades on *BBC Grandstand* and *Final Score.*

'To me, David Luiz looks like he's being controlled by a ten-year-old in the crowd on a playstation' – **Gary Neville**, Sky Sports pundit, on the Chelsea defender.

'That's ridiculous. He's one of the best central defenders in the world. So be careful what you're saying' – **Andre Villas-Boas**, then Chelsea manager, giving his response.

'We owned the game. We wrote the rules, designed the pitches and everything else. Then, 50 years later, some guy came along and said "You're liars" and they actually stole it. It was called Fifa. Fifty years later, another gang came along called UEFA and stole a bit more' – **Sir Dave Richards**, chairman of the Premier League, with comments at a conference in Qatar for which he later apologised.

EUROPEAN TABLES 2011–2012

FRANCE

	P	W	D	L	F	A	Pts
Montpellier	38	25	7	6	68	34	82
Paris SG	38	23	10	5	75	41	79
Lille	38	21	11	6	72	39	74
Lyon	38	19	7	12	64	51	64
Bordeaux	38	16	13	9	53	41	61
Rennes	38	17	9	12	53	44	60
St Etienne	38	16	9	13	49	45	57
Toulouse	38	15	11	12	37	34	56
Evian	38	13	11	14	54	55	50
Marseille	38	12	12	14	45	41	48
Nancy	38	11	12	15	38	48	45
Valenciennes	38	12	7	19	40	50	43
Nice	38	10	12	16	39	46	42
Sochaux	38	11	9	18	40	60	42
Brest	38	8	17	13w	31	38	41
Ajaccio	38	9	14	15	40	61	41
Lorient	38	9	12	17	35	49	39
Caen	38	9	11	18	39	59	38
Dijon	38	9	9	20	38	63	36
Auxerre	38	7	13	18	46	57	34

Leading league scorers: 21 Giroud (Montpellier), Nene (Paris SG); 20 Hazard (Lille); 16 Aubameyang (St Etienne), Lopez (Lyon); 14 Gomis (Lyon), Gouffran (Bordeaux); 13 Pastore (Paris SG); 12 Belhanda (Montpellier), Remy (Marseille). **Cup Final:** Lyon 1 (Lopez 28) Quevilly 0

HOLLAND

	P	W	D	L	F	A	Pts
Ajax	34	23	7	4	93	36	76
Feyenoord	34	21	7	6	70	37	70
PSV	34	21	6	7	87	47	69
AZ	34	19	8	7	64	35	65
Heerenveen	34	18	10	6	79	59	64
Twente	34	17	9	8	82	46	60
Vitesse	34	15	8	11	48	43	53
NEC	34	13	6	15	42	45	45
RKC	34	13	6	15	40	49	45
Roda	34	14	2	18	55	70	44
Utrecht	34	11	10	13	55	58	43
Heracles	34	11	7	16	52	62	40
Breda	34	10	8	16	45	54	38
Groningen	34	10	7	17	41	61	37
Den Haag	34	8	8	18	38	67	32
Venlo	34	9	4	21	42	78	31
De Graafschap	34	6	6	22	36	74	24
Excelsior	34	4	7	23	28	76	19

Leading league scorers: 32 Bas Dost (Heerenveen); 25 De Jong (Twente); 23 Malki (Roda); 20 Mertens (PSV); 18 Toivonen (PSV), Guidetti (Feyenoord); 15 Altidore (AZ); 14 Matavz (PSV), Wilfried (Vitesse). **Cup Final**: PSV 3 (Toivonen 31, Mertens 56, Lens 63) Heracles 0

GERMANY

	P	W	D	L	F	A	Pts
Borussia Dortmund	34	25	6	3	80	25	81
Bayern Munich	34	23	4	7	77	22	73
Schalke	34	20	4	10	74	44	64
Borussia M'gladbach	34	17	9	8	49	24	60
Bayer Leverkusen	34	15	9	10	52	44	54
Stuttgart	34	15	8	11	63	46	53
Hannover	34	12	12	10	41	45	48
Wolfsburg	34	13	5	16	47	60	44
Werder Bremen	34	11	9	14	49	58	42
Nuremberg	34	12	6	16	38	49	42
Hoffenheim	34	10	11	13	41	47	41
Freiburg	34	10	10	14	45	61	40
Mainz	34	9	12	13	47	51	39
Augsburg	34	8	14	12	36	49	38
Hamburg	34	8	12	14	35	57	36
Hertha Berlin	34	7	10	17	38	64	31
Cologne	34	8	6	20	39	75	30
Kaiserslautern	34	4	11	19	24	54	23

Leading league scorers: 29 Huntelaar (Schalke); 26 Gomez (Bayern Munich); 22 Lewandowski (Borussia Dortmund); 18 Pizarro (Werder Bremen), Podolski (Cologne), Reus (Borussia M'gladbach); 17 Harnik (Stuttgart); 16 Kiessling (Bayer Leverkusen); 15 Raul (Schalke). **Cup Final**: Borussia Dortmund 5 (Kagawa 3, Hummels 41 pen, Lewandowski 45, 58, 81) Bayern Munich 2 (Robben 25 pen, Ribery 75)

ITALY

	P	W	D	L	F	A	Pts
Juventus	38	23	15	0	68	20	84
AC Milan	38	24	8	6	74	33	80
Udinese	38	18	10	10	52	35	64
Lazio	38	18	8	12	56	47	62
Napoli	38	16	13	9	66	46	61
Inter Milan	38	17	7	14	58	55	58
Roma	38	16	8	14	60	54	56
Parma	38	15	11	12	54	53	56
Bologna	38	13	12	13	41	43	51
Chievo	38	12	13	13	35	45	49
Catania	38	11	15	12	47	52	48
Atalanta *	38	13	13	12	41	43	46
Fiorentina	38	11	13	14	37	43	46
Siena	38	11	11	16	45	45	44
Cagliari	38	10	13	15	37	46	43
Palermo	38	11	10	17	52	62	43
Genoa	38	11	9	18	50	69	42
Lecce	38	8	12	18	40	56	36
Novara	38	7	11	20	35	65	32
Cesena	38	4	10	24	24	60	22

*6 pts deducted, match fixing

Leading league scorers: 28 Ibrahimovic (AC Milan); 24 Milito (Inter Milan); 23 Cavani (Napoli), Di Natale (Udinese); 19 Palacio (Genoa); 16 Denis (Atalanta), Miccoli (Palermo); 15 Giovinco (Parma); 14 Jovetic (Fiorentina). **Cup Final**: Napoli 2 (Cavani 60 pen, Hamsik 83) Juventus 0

PORTUGAL

	P	W	D	L	F	A	Pts
Porto	30	23	6	1	69	19	75
Benfica	30	21	6	3	66	27	69
Braga	30	19	5	6	59	29	62
Sporting	30	18	5	7	47	26	59
Maritimo	30	14	8	8	41	38	50
Guimaraes	30	14	3	13	40	40	45
Nacional	30	12	5	13	47	51	41
Olhanense	30	9	12	9	36	38	39
Gil Vicente	30	8	10	12	31	42	34
Pacos Ferreira	30	8	7	15	35	53	31
Vitoria Setubal	30	8	6	16	24	49	30
Academica	30	7	8	15	27	38	29
Beira Mar	30	8	5	17	26	38	29
Rio Ave	30	7	7	16	33	42	28
Feirense	30	5	9	16	27	49	24
Uniao Leiria	30	6	4	20	26	55	22

Leading league scorers: 20 Cardozo (Benfica), Lima (Braga); 16 Hulk (Porto); 14 Van Wolfswinkel (Sporting); 13 Rodriguez (Porto); 11 Edgar (Guimaraes), Nolito (Benfica). **Cup Final**: Academica 1 (Marinho 3) Sporting 0

SPAIN

	P	W	D	L	F	A	Pts
Real Madrid	38	32	4	2	121	32	100
Barcelona	38	28	7	3	114	29	91
Valencia	38	17	10	11	59	44	61
Malaga	38	17	7	14	54	53	58
Atletico Madrid	38	15	11	12	53	46	56
Levante	38	16	7	15	54	50	55
Osasuna	38	13	15	10	44	61	54
Mallorca	38	14	10	14	42	46	52
Sevilla	38	13	11	14	48	47	50
Athletic Bilbao	38	12	13	13	49	52	49
Sociedad	38	12	11	15	46	52	47
Betis	38	13	8	17	47	56	47
Getafe	38	12	11	15	40	51	47
Espanyol	38	12	10	16	46	56	46
Vallecano	38	13	4	21	53	73	43
Zaragoza	38	12	7	19	36	61	43
Granada	38	12	6	20	35	56	42
Villarreal	38	9	14	15	39	53	41
Gijon	38	10	7	21	42	69	37
Santander	38	4	15	19	28	63	27

Leading league scorers: 50 Messi (Barcelona); 46 Ronaldo (Real Madrid); 25 Falcao (Atletico Madrid); 22 Higuain (Real Madrid); 21 Benzema (Real Madrid); 17 Llorente (Athletic Bilbao), Soldado (Valencia); 16 Castro (Betis); 15 Kone (Levante), Michu (Vallecano). **Cup Final**: Barcelona 3 (Pedro 3, 25, Messi 20) Athletic Bilbao 0

FOOTBALL'S CHANGING HOMES

In the summer of 2011, Brighton and Hove Albion moved into the American Express Stadium after 16 years as footballing nomads. Now, **Rotherham United** have a new home to call their own and it too has a strong United States connection. The 12,000-capacity ground, costing £17m, is situated in an area of the town that used to be known as New York and is on the site of an old foundry which used to export fire hydrants across the Atlantic. So, after growing support from fans, the club decided to name it The New York Stadium. 'It is strongly rooted in more than 150 years of Rotherham's proud history of industry and enterprise,' said chairman Tony Stewart, announcing the decision alongside World Cup referee Howard Webb, the club's honorary ambassador. The ground is less than a mile from Millmoor, their home for 101 years until negotiations with the landlords to continue playing there broke down, resulting in a move four years ago to Sheffield's Don Valley Stadium. Brighton, meanwhile, have been given planning permission for a two-phase increase in capacity from 22,500 to 30,750. The average attendance for the first season was over 20,000.

Tottenham moved a step nearer to building a new stadium adjacent to White Hart Lane after reaching a new funding agreement with London Mayor Boris Johnson and Haringey Council. The club scrapped plans to challenge West Ham for the right to become tenants of the Olympic Stadium in Stratford in favour of a 56,000-seater arena as part of regeneration plans for the area in north London.

Queens Park Rangers are looking for a new home in the west of the capital to replace Loftus Road, the smallest in the Premier League with a capacity of just 18,500. Owner Tony Fernandes acknowledges the benefits of an 'intimidating' atmosphere there, but stresses the need for somewhere bigger and has been evaluating three potential sites. After owner Roman Abramovich failed with a bid to purchase the freehold of Stamford Bridge, **Chelsea** proposed a new stadium at Battersea Power Station. But that has been unsuccessful, with a Malaysian consortium paying £400m for the 39-acre site. Neighbours **Fulham** confirmed they are staying at Craven Cottage, with plans to increase the capacity from 25,700 to 30,000 by developing the Riverside Stand. **Swansea City**, whose attendance record at the Liberty Stadium was broken six times during their first season in the Premier League, want to increase capacity from 25,500 to 30,000.

Four clubs have been given the thumbs-up to move. **Bristol Rovers** will build a £40m, 21,700-seater stadium on the northern fringes of the city, providing Sainsbury's receive permission for a supermarket at the club's Memorial Ground site in order to fund much of the cost. Rovers are in partnership with the University of the West of England. **Barnet** aim to leave Underhill and be in a new ground seven miles away at their training ground in Edgware from 2013–14. **York City** received council approval for a 6,000-capacity community stadium, on the outskirts of the city at Monks Cross, to be shared with York Knights rugby league side. It rounded off a momentous ten days in their history in which they secured promotion back to the Football League via the play-offs after an absence of eight years and won the FA Trophy. **Southend United** were granted an extension of planning permission for a 14,000-seater ground at Fossetts Farm to be funded largely by the sale of Roots Hall ground to supermarket chain Sainsbury's.

Carlisle United held an exhibition of plans for a 12,000-seater stadium at Kingmoor Park in the north of the city and received almost 100 per cent support from fans visiting it. **Cheltenham Town** shelved a proposal to move to the town's racecourse because of the cost and have been looking at improving facilities at Whaddon Road. In Scotland, **Aberdeen** put back their planned move to a 21,000-seater stadium at Loirston Loch by 12 months to the summer of 2014 because of issues with land at the new site. Newly-promoted **Ross County** have been spending £1.4m to bring Victoria Park in Dingwall up to Scottish Premier League standard, including a new stand for away supporters and under-soil heating.

BRITISH AND IRISH INTERNATIONALS 2011–12

* Denotes new cap

EUROPEAN CHAMPIONSHIP 2012 – QUALIFYING

NORTHERN IRELAND 4 FAROE ISLANDS 0
Group C: Windsor Park (13,183); Wednesday, August 10 2011

Northern Ireland (4-4-2): Camp (Nottm Forest), Baird (Fulham), McAuley (WBA) (Cathcart, Blackpool 46), Hughes (Fulham), J Evans (Manchester Utd), Davis (Rangers), Clingan (Coventry), McCann (Peterborough), C Evans (Hull) (McGinn, Celtic 60), Healy (Rangers) (*Ward, Derby 83), McCourt (Celtic). **Scorers:** Hughes (5), Davis (66), McCourt (71, 88).
Booked: McCourt
Faroe Islands (4-4-2): Mikkelsen, Davidsen, Baldvinsson, Gregersen, Naes, Elttor (Mouritsen 75), Benjaminsen, Olsen (Danielsen 75), Udsen, Holst (Hansen 67), Edmundsson
Referee: E Aleckovic (Bosnia-Herzegovina). **Half-time:** 1-0

BULGARIA 0 ENGLAND 3
Group G: Sofia (36,521); Friday, September 2 2011

Bulgaria (4-2-3-1): Mihaylov, Bandalovski (Sarmov 45), Bodurov, Ivanov, Zanev, Georgiev, S Petrov, Milanov, Popov (Marquinhos 80), M Petrov, Genkov (Bozhilov 61). **Booked:** Sarmov, Milanov
England (4-2-3-1): Hart (Manchester City), *Smalling (Manchester Utd), Cahill (Bolton), Terry (Chelsea), Cole (Chelsea), Parker (Tottenham), Barry (Manchester City) (Lampard, Chelsea 79), Walcott (Arsenal) (Johnson, Manchester City), Young (Manchester Utd) (Milner, Manchester City 61), Downing (Liverpool), Rooney (Manchester Utd). **Scorers:** Cahill (13), Rooney (21, 45). **Booked:** Parker
Referee: F de Bleeckere (Belgium). **Half-time:** 0-3

WALES 2 MONTENEGRO 1
Group G: Cardiff City Stadium (8,194); Friday, September 2 2011

Wales (4-3-3): Hennessey (Wolves), Gunter (Nottm Forest), Blake (Cardiff), Williams (Swansea), Taylor (Swansea), Ledley (Celtic), Ramsey (Arsenal) (Crofts, Norwich 64), Vaughan (Sunderland), Bellamy (Liverpool), Morison (Norwich) (Robson-Kanu, Reading 83), Bale (Tottenham) (Earnshaw, Cardiff 90). **Scorers:** Morison (9), Ramsey (50). **Booked:** Williams, Vaughan, Bellamy
Montenegro (4-2-3-1): Bozovic, Zverotic, Batak, Savic, Balic (Jovanovic 83), Pekovic, Drincic, Vukcevic, Jovetic, Dalovic (Damjanovic 57), Vucinic (Delibasic 79). **Scorer:** Jovetic (71). **Booked:** Balic, Drincic, Vukcevic
Referee: L Banti (Italy). **Half-time:** 1-0

NORTHERN IRELAND 0 SERBIA 1
Group C: Windsor Park (13,026); Friday, September 2 2011

Northern Ireland (4-4-1-1): Camp (Nottm Forest), Cathcart (Blackpool), McAuley (WBA), Hughes (Fulham), J Evans (Manchester Utd), C Evans (Hull) (McGinn, Celtic 59), Baird (Fulham), Davis (Rangers), McCann (Peterborough) (Feeney, Plymouth 70), Brunt (WBA), Healy (Rangers) (McQuoid, Millwall 83). **Booked:** McCann, C Evans, J Evans
Serbia (4-4-2): Jorgacevic, Ivanovic, Subotic, Rajkovic, Kolarov, Stankovic, Kuzmanovic (Fejsa 89), Ninkovic (Petrovic 73), Tosic (Ljajic 77), Jovanovic, Pantelic. **Scorer:** Pantelic (67). **Booked:** Ninkovic, Rajkovic, Petrovic
Referee: T Einwaller (Austria). **Half-time:** 0-0

REPUBLIC OF IRELAND 0 SLOVAKIA 0
Group B: Aviva Stadium (44,761); Friday, September 2 2011

Republic of Ireland (4-4-2): Given (Aston Villa), O'Shea (Sunderland), Dunne (Aston Villa), St Ledger (Leicester), Ward (Wolves), Duff (Fulham), Whelan (Stoke), Andrews (Blackburn), McGeady (Spartak Moscow) (Hunt, Wolves 85), Keane (LA Galaxy), Doyle (Wolves) (Cox, WBA

64). **Booked:** Dunne, St Ledger
Slovakia (4-5-1): Mucha, Pekarik, Skrtel, Durica, Cech, Weiss (Jendrisek 86), Karhan, Stoch, Hamsik, Kucka (Guede 77), Holosko (Vittek 88). **Booked:** Kucka, Mucha
Referee: P Garcia (Portugal)

SCOTLAND 2 CZECH REPUBLIC 2
Group I: Hampden Park (51,457); Saturday, September 3 2011
Scotland (4-5-1): McGregor (Rangers), Hutton (Aston Villa), G Caldwell (Wigan), Berra (Wolves), Bardsley (Sunderland) (Wilson, Liverpool 75), Naismith (Rangers) (Robson, Middlesbrough 86), Fletcher (Manchester Utd), Adam (Liverpool) (Cowie, Cardiff 79), Brown (Celtic), Morrison (WBA), Miller (Cardiff). **Scorers:** Miller (44), Fletcher (83). **Booked:** Brown, Miller, Berra, Wilson
Czech Republic (4-5-1): Lastuvka, Hubnik, Rajnoch, Sivok, Kadlec, Petrezela (Rezek 56), Rosicky, Hubschman, Jiracek (Pekhart 77), Plasil, Baros (Vacek 90). **Scorers:** Plasil (78), Kadlec (90 pen). **Booked:** Jiracek, Plasil, Rezek, Baros, Pekhart
Referee: K Blom (Holland). **Half-time:** 1-0

ENGLAND 1 WALES 0
Group G: Wembley (77,128); Tuesday, September 6 2011
England (4-3-3): Hart (Manchester City), Smalling (Manchester Utd), Cahill (Bolton), Terry (Chelsea), Cole (Chelsea), Lampard (Chelsea) (Parker, Tottenham 72), Barry (Manchester City), Milner (Manchester City), Downing (Liverpool) (Johnson, Manchester City 79), Rooney (Manchester Utd) (Carroll, Liverpool 89), Young (Manchester Utd). **Scorer:** Young (35).
Booked: Milner
Wales (4-1-4-1): Hennessey (Wolves), Gunter (Nottm Forest), Blake (Cardiff), Williams (Swansea), Taylor (Swansea), Crofts (Norwich), Bale (Tottenham), Collison (West Ham) (King, Leicester 85), Ramsey (Arsenal), Ledley (Celtic), Morison (Norwich) (Earnshaw, Cardiff 68)
Referee: R Schorgenhofer (Austria). **Half-time:** 1-0

SCOTLAND 1 LITHUANIA 0
Group I: Hampden Park (34,071); Tuesday, September 6 2011
Scotland (4-1-4-1): McGregor (Rangers), Whittaker (Rangers), G Caldwell (Wigan), Berra (Wolves), Bardsley (Sunderland) (Crainey, Blackpool 70), Fletcher (Manchester Utd), Bannan (Aston Villa) (Snodgrass, Leeds 84), Cowie (Cardiff), Morrison (WBA) (Dorrans, WBA 79), Naismith (Rangers), Goodwillie (Blackburn). **Scorer:** Naismith (50). **Booked:** Dorrans
Lithuania (4-5-1): Karcemarskas, Cesnauskis, Kijanskas (Danilevicius 60), Zaliukas, Klimavicius, Radavicius, Labukas (Novikovas 46), Semberas, Pilibaitis, Mikoliunas (Beniusis 77), Sernas. **Booked:** Labukas, Semberas
Referee: K Jacobsson (Iceland). **Half-time:** 0-0

ESTONIA 4 NORTHERN IRELAND 1
Group C: Tallinn (8,660); Tuesday, September 6 2011
Estonia (4-2-3-1): Pareiko, Jaager, Rahn, Piiroja, Klavan, Puri (Purje 63), Vunk, Vassiljev, Kink (Saag 88), Kruglov, Ahjupera (Zenjov 53). **Scorers:** Vunk (29), Kink (32), Zenjov (59), Saag (90). **Booked:** Rahn
Northern Ireland (4-5-1): Camp (Nottm Forest), Baird (Fulham), McAuley (WBA), Hughes (Fulham), Cathcart (Blackpool), McGinn (Celtic) (Feeney, Plymouth 65), Clingan (Coventry), Davis (Rangers), McCann (Peterborough), Brunt (WBA), Healy (Rangers) (McQuoid, Millwall 65). **Scorer:** Piroja (39 og)
Referee: D Stalhammar (Sweden). **Half-time:** 2-1

RUSSIA 0 REPUBLIC OF IRELAND 0
Group B: Moscow (48,717); Tuesday, September 6 2011
Russia (4-3-2-1): Malafeev, Anyukov, V Berezutski, Ignashevich, A Berezutski, Semshov, Shirokov, Zyryanov, Arshavin, Zhirkov (Bilyaletdinov 76), Kerzhakov (Pavlyuchenko 54).
Booked: Anyukov
Republic of Ireland (4-4-2): Given (Aston Villa), Kelly (Fulham), Dunne (Aston Villa),

O'Dea (Celtic), Ward (Wolves), Duff (Fulham) (Hunt, Wolves 67), Whelan (Stoke), Andrews (Blackburn), McGeady (Spartak Moscow), Keane (LA Galaxy), Doyle (Wolves) (Cox, WBA 58).
Booked: Dunne, Ward
Referee: F Brych (Germany)

MONTENEGRO 2 ENGLAND 2
Group G: Podgorica (11,340); Friday, October 7 2011
Montenegro (4-4-2): M Bozovic, Zverotic, Dzudovic, Savic, Kascelan (Jovanovic 46), Vukcevic, Pekovic, V Bozovic (Delibasic 80), Beciraj (Darnjanovic 64), Jovetic, Vucinic. **Scorers**: Zverotic (45), Delibasic (90). **Booked**: Jovanovic, Pekovic, Delibasic, Vucinic
England (4-4-1-1): Hart (Manchester City) *Jones (Manchester Utd), Cahill (Bolton), Terry (Chelsea), Cole (Chelsea), Walcott (Arsenal) (Welbeck, Manchester Utd 76), Barry (Manchester City), Parker (Tottenham), Young (Manchester Utd) (Downing, Liverpool 60), Rooney (Manchester Utd), Bent (Aston Villa) (Lampard, Chelsea 64). **Scorers**: Young (11), Bent (31).
Sent off: Rooney (73)
Referee: W Stark (Germany). **Half-time**: 1-2

WALES 2 SWITZERLAND 0
Group G: Liberty Stadium (12,317); Friday, October 7 2011
Wales (4-3-3): Hennessey (Wolves), Gunter (Nottm Forest), Blake (Cardiff), Williams (Swansea), Taylor (Swansea), Crofts (Norwich) (Vaughan, Sunderland 81), Allen (Swansea), Ramsey (Arsenal), Bellamy (Liverpool), Morison (Norwich) (Church, Reading 81), Bale (Tottenham). **Scorers**: Ramsey (60 pen), Bale (71). **Booked**: Blake
Switzerland (4-2-3-1): Benaglio, Lichtsteiner, Von Bergen, Klose, Ziegler, Behrami, Inler, Shaqiri (Rodriguez 62), Xhaka (Mehmedi 80), Frei (Emeghara 71) Derdiyok. **Booked**: Klose.
Sent off: Ziegler (55)
Referee: B Kuipers (Holland). **Half-time**: 0-0

NORTHERN IRELAND 1 ESTONIA 2
Group C: Windsor Park (12,768); Friday, October 7 2011
Northern Ireland (4-4-1-1): Camp (Nottm Forest), Hodson (Watford), Cathcart (Blackpool), McAuley (WBA), Baird (Fulham), McCourt (Celtic), Clingan (Coventry) (C Evans, Hull 32)), Davis (Rangers), McCann (Peterborough) (Healy, Rangers 83), Brunt (WBA), Lafferty (Rangers) (Feeney, Plymouth 69). **Scorer**: Davis (22). **Booked**: Lafferty, Camp, Cathcart, McAuley
Estonia (4-2-3-1): Pareiko, Piirola, Klavan, Jaager, Stepanov, Kruglov, Dmitrijev, Puri (Purje 57), Vunk, Kink (Vassiljev 65), Ahjupera (Zenjov 46). **Scorer**: Vassiljev (77 pen, 84). **Booked**: Zenjov
Referee: M Grafe (Germany). **Half-time**: 1-0

ANDORRA 0 REPUBLIC OF IRELAND 2
Group B: Andorra La Vella (860); Friday, October 7 2011
Andorra (4-5-1):Gomes, A Martinez (Lorenzo 77), Garcia, Lima (Sonegee 81), Bernaus, C Martinez, Vieira, Ayala, Moreno, Pujol (Peppe 60), Silva. **Booked**: C Martinez, Ayala
Republic of Ireland (4-4-2): Given (Aston Villa), O'Shea (Sunderland), St Ledger (Leicester), O'Dea (Celtic), Ward (Wolves), Duff (Fulham) (Hunt, Wolves 76), Whelan (Stoke), Fahey, Birmingham 65), Andrews (Blackburn), McGeady (Spartak Moscow), Keane (LA Galaxy), Doyle (Wolves) (Long, WBA 71). **Scorers**: Doyle (7), McGeady (20). **Booked**: Ward
Referee: L Kovarik (Czech Republic). **Half-time**: 0-2

LIECHTENSTEIN 0 SCOTLAND 1
Group I: Vaduz (5,636); Saturday, October 8 2011
Liechtenstein (4-4-2): Jehle, Ritzberger, Stocklasa, Kaufmann, Rechsteiner, Buchel (Kieber 71), Hanselmann (Eberle 75), Hasler, Poverino, Beck, Frick. **Booked**: Polverino, Stocklasa, Beck
Scotland (4-1-4-1): McGregor (Rangers), Hutton (Aston Villa), G Caldwell (Wigan), Berra (Wolves), Bardsley (Sunderland), Fletcher (Manchester Utd), Bannan (Aston Villa) (Forrest, Celtic 73), Adam (Liverpool) (Cowie, Cardiff 76), Morrison (WBA), Naismith (Rangers),

Mackail-Smith (Brighton). **Scorer**: Mackail-Smith(32). **Booked**: Mackail-Smith
Referee: T Hagen (Norway). **Half-time**: 0-1

SPAIN 3 SCOTLAND 1
Group I: Alicante (24,896); Tuesday, October 11 2011
Spain (4-3-3): Valdes, Sergio Ramos, Pique, Puyol (Arbeloa 46), Alba, Xavi (Llorente 64), Busquets, Santi Cazorla, Pedro, Silva (Thiago 55), Villa. **Booked**: Sergio Ramos. **Scorers**: Silva (6, 44), Villa (54). **Booked**: Sergio Ramos
Scotland (4-1-4-1): McGregor (Rangers), Hutton (Aston Villa), G Caldwell (Wigan), Berra (Wolves), Bardsley (Sunderland), Fletcher (Manchester Utd) (Cowie, Cardiff 85), Bannan (Aston Villa) (Goodwillie, Blackburn 63), Adam (Liverpool) (Forrest, Celtic 64), Morrison (WBA), Naismith (Rangers), Mackail-Smith (Brighton). **Scorer**: Goodwillie (66 pen). **Booked**: Fletcher, Goodwillie, Morrison
Referee: S Johannesson (Sweden). **Half-time**: 2-0

BULGARIA 0 WALES 1
Group G: Sofia (1,672); Tuesday, October 11 2011
Bulgaria (4-4-2): Mihailov, Manolev (Delev 52), Zanev, Miliev, Terziev, Gadzhev, Tonev, S Petrov, Popov (Rangelov 70), Domovchiyski (Bojinov 62), Ivanov. **Booked**: Gadzhev, Ivanov, S Petrov
Wales (4-3-3): Hennessey (Wolves), Gunter (Nottm Forest), Blake (Cardiff) (Mathews, Celtic 41),Williams (Swansea), Taylor (Swansea), Crofts (Norwich), Allen (Swansea), Ramsey (Arsenal), Bellamy (Liverpool), Morison (Norwich) (Church, Reading 70), Bale (Tottenham).
Scorer: Bale (45). **Booked**: Allen
Referee: P Gil (Poland). **Half-time**: 0-1

ITALY 3 NORTHERN IRELAND 0
Group C: Pescara (15,875); Tuesday, October 11 2011
Italy (4-2-3-1): Buffon (De Sanctis 76), Cassani, Barzagli, Chiellini, Balzaretti, Montolivo, De Rossi, Pirlo, Aquilani (Nocerino 69), Giovinco, Cassano (Osvaldo 56). **Scorers**: Cassano (21, 53), McAuley (75 og)
Northern Ireland (4-1-4-1): Taylor (unatt), Hodson (Watford), McGivern (Manchester City), McAuley (WBA), Baird (Fulham), Evans (Hull), Little (Rangers), Norwood (Manchester Utd) (*McLaughlin, Preston 73), Davis (Rangers), Gorman (Wolves) (McGinn, Celtic 78). Healy (Rangers) (Feeney, Plymouth 65)
Referee: A Lohoz (Spain). **Half-time**: 1-0
(Nigel Worthington's last match as Northern Ireland manager)

REPUBLIC OF IRELAND 2 ARMENIA 1
Group B: Aviva Stadium (40,283); Tuesday, October 11 2011
Republic of Ireland (4-4-2): Given (Aston Villa), O'Shea (Sunderland), Dunne (Aston Villa), St Ledger (Leicester), Kelly (Fulham), Duff (Fulham), Whelan (Stoke) (Fahey, Birmingham 76), Andrews (Blackburn), McGeady (Spartak Moscow) (Hunt, Wolves 68), Doyle (Wolves), Cox (WBA) (Walters, Stoke 80). **Scorers**: Aleksanyan (43 og), Dunne (59). **Booked**: Kelly, St Ledger, Andrews, Doyle. **Sent off**: Doyle
Armenia (4-5-1): Berezovsky, Hovsepyan, Mkoyan, Aleksanyan, Hayrapetyan, Mkrtchyan, Mkhitaryan, Pizelli (Manucharyan 53), Malakyan (Petrosyan 27), Ghazaryan (Sarkisov 66), Movsisyan. **Scorer**: Mkhitaryan (62). **Booked**: Petrosyan, Aleksanyan, Mkoyan. **Sent off**: Berezovsky (26)
Referee: E Gonzalez (Spain). **Half-time**: 1-0

ESTONIA 0 REPUBLIC OF IRELAND 4
Play-off, first leg: Tallinn (9,692); Friday, November 11 2011
Estonia (4-5-1): Pareiko, Jaager, Stepanov, Piiroja, Klavan, Kink (Purje 68), Dmitrijev, Vunk (Lindpere 61), Vassiljev, Kruglov, Ahjupera (Voskoboinikov 60). **Booked**: Stepanov, Ahjupera, Piiroja, Pareiko. **Sent off**: Stepanov, Piiroja
Republic of Ireland (4-4-2): Given (Aston Villa), Kelly (Fulham), Dunne (Aston Villa), St Ledger (Leicester), Ward (Wolves), Duff (Fulham) (Hunt, Wolves 73), Whelan (Stoke) (Fahey, Birmingham 78), Andrews (Blackburn), McGeady (Spartak Moscow), Keane (LA Galaxy),

Walters (Stoke) (Cox, WBA 83). **Scorers**: Andrews (13), Walters (67), Keane (71, 88 pen)
Referee: V Kassai (Hungary). **Half-time**: 0-1

REPUBLIC OF IRELAND 1 ESTONIA 1
Play-off, second leg: Aviva Stadium (51,151); Tuesday, November 15 2011
Republic of Ireland (4-4-2): Given (Aston Villa), O'Shea (Sunderland), Dunne (Aston Villa), St Ledger (Leicester), Ward (Wolves), Hunt (Wolves) (McGeady, Spartak Moscow 59), Whelan (Stoke), Andrews (Blackburn), Duff (Fulham) (Fahey, Birmingham 79), Keane (LA Galaxy) (Cox, WBA 67), Doyle (Wolves). **Scorer**: Ward (32)
Estonia (4-4-2): Londak, Jaager, Rahn, Klavan, Kruglov (Puri 18), Teniste, Vassiljev, Vunk, Lindpere (Kink 54), Saag, Voskoboinikov (Purje 72). **Scorer**: Vassiljev (57). **Booked**: Rahn, Vunk
Referee: B Kuipers (Holland). **Half-time**: 1-0

INTERNATIONAL FRIENDLIES

SCOTLAND 2 DENMARK 1
Hampden Park (17,582); Wednesday, August 10 2011
Scotland (4-1-4-1): McGregor (Rangers), Bardsley (Wigan), G Caldwell (Wigan), Wilson (Liverpool), Crainey (Blackpool), Adam (Liverpool), (Dorrans, WBA 57), Snodgrass (Leeds), (Hanley, Blackburn 87), Brown (Celtic) (Cowie, Cardiff 20), Morrison (WBA) (Bannan, Aston Villa 67), Naismith (Rangers) (Forrest, Celtic 73), Miller (Cardiff) (Mackail-Smith, Brighton 57). **Scorers**: Kvist (23 og), Snodgrass (44). **Booked**: Snodgrass
Denmark (4-2-3-1): Sorensen, Jacobsen (Silberbauer 72), Agger (Jorgensen 57), Kjaer, Boilesen, S Poulsen, Kvist, Rommedahl (Pederson 46), Eriksen, Krone-Dehli (Zimling 46), Bendtner (Schone 46). **Scorer**: Eriksen (31)
Referee: M Borg (Malta). **Half-time**: 2-1

WALES 1 AUSTRALIA 2
Cardiff City Stadium (6,378); Wednesday, August 10 2011
Wales (4-4-2): Hennessey (Wolves), Gunter (Nottm Forest) (Matthews, Celtic 62), Gabbidon (QPR) (Blake, Cardiff 46), A Williams (Swansea), Taylor (Swansea), Vaughan (Sunderland) (Allen, Swansea 70), Ramsey (Arsenal) (Collison, West Ham 47), Ledley (Celtic), Bale (Tottenham), Earnshaw (Cardiff) (Morison, Norwich 62), Bellamy (Manchester City). **Scorer**: Blake (82)
Australia (4-4-2): Schwarzer, Wilkshire (Kruse 46), Neill, Spiranovic, Zullo (Sarota 83), Emerton (R Williams 48), Kilkenny, Valeri, McKay, Cahill (Troisi 70), McDonald (Jedinak 90). **Scorers**: Cahill (44), Kruse (60). **Booked**: Zullo
Referee: K Tohver (Estonia). **Half-time**: 0-1

REPUBLIC OF IRELAND 0 CROATIA 0
Aviva Stadium (20,000); Wednesday, August 10 2011
Republic of Ireland (4-4-2): Given (Aston Villa) (Westwood, Sunderland 64), Kelly (Fulham), Dunne (Aston Villa), St Ledger (Leicester), Ward (Wolves), Duff (Fulham) (Treacy, Burnley 83), Whelen (Stoke) (O'Dea, Celtic 74), Gibson (Manchester Utd), Hunt (Wolves) (Keogh, Wolves 64), Keane (Tottenham), Long (WBA) (Cox, WBA 83). **Booked**: Gibson
Croatia (4-5-1): Pletikosa, Corluka (Vrsaljko 74), Lovren, Simunic, Strinic, Srna, Vukojevic (Dujmovic 87), Modric, Kranjcar (Ilicevic 65), Mandzukic (Kalinic 74), Eduardo (Olic 46).
Booked: Vukojevic
Referee: T Hagen (Norway)

CYPRUS 1 SCOTLAND 2
Larnarca (2,000); Friday, November 11 2011
Cyprus (4-5-1): Georgallides (Kissas 46), Merkis, Alexandrou (Katsis 69), Demetriou (Sielis 46), Parpas (Nicolaou 58), Satsias, Dobrasinovic (Vasilou 74), Solomou, Avraam (Mitidis 46), Christofi, Efrem. **Scorer**: Christofi (59). **Booked**: Demetriou, Dobrasinovic

Scotland (4-1-4-1): McGregor (Rangers), Whittaker (Rangers), G Caldwell (Wigan), Berra (Wolves), Bardsley (Sunderland) (Crainey, Blackpool 73), Robson (Middlesbrough) (Conway, Cardiff 79), Fletcher (Manchester Utd) (McArthur, Wigan 62), Cowie (Cardiff), Morrison (WBA), Mackie (QPR) (*Rhodes, Huddersfield 86), Miller (Cardiff) (Mackail-Smith, Brighton 62). **Scorers:** Miller (23), Mackie (56) **Booked:** Whittaker
Referee: M Levi (Israel). **Half-time:** 0-1

ENGLAND 1 SPAIN 0
Wembley (87,189); Saturday, November 12 2011
England (4-1-4-1): Hart (Manchester City), G Johnson (Liverpool), Jagielka (Everton), Lescott (Manchester City), Cole (Chelsea); Parker (Tottenham) (*Walker, Tottenham 85), Walcott (Arsenal) (Downing, Liverpool 46), Jones (Manchester Utd) (*Rodwell, Everton 56), Lampard (Chelsea) (Barry, Manchester City 56), Milner (Manchester City) (Johnson, Manchester City 76), Bent (Aston Villa) (Welbeck, Manchester Utd 63).
Scorer: Lampard (49). **Booked:** Milner
Spain (4-3-3): Casillas (Reina 46), Arbeloa, Pique, Sergio Ramos (Puyol 74), Alba, Xavi (Fabregas 46), Xabi Alonso, Busquets (Torres 64), Iniesta (Santi Cazorla 85), Silva (Mata 46), Villa. **Booked:** Fabregas, Sergio Ramos
Referee: F De Bleeckere (Belgium). **Half-time:** 0-0

WALES 4 NORWAY 1
Cardiff City Stadium (12,637); Saturday, November 12 2011
Wales (4-4-2): Hennessey (Wolves), Gunter (Nottm Forest), Matthews (Celtic), Williams (Swansea), Blake (Cardiff), Allen (Swansea) (Robson-Kanu, Reading 76), Crofts (Norwich), Ramsey (Arsenal) (King, Leicester 90), Bale (Tottenham) Bellamy (Liverpool)) (Edwards, Wolves 90), Morison (Norwich) (Vokes, Wolves 70). **Scorers:** Bale (11), Bellamy (16), Vokes (88, 89)
Norway (4-4-2): Jarstein (Pettersen 46), Ruud, Waehler (Demidov 46), Hangeland, Riise, Pedersen, Tettey, Grindheim (Brenne 54). Jenssen (Parr 85), Abdellaoui (Braaten 77), Huseklepp. **Scorer:** Huseklepp (61). **Booked:** Ruud
Referee: G Grobelnik (Austria). **Half-time:** 2-0
(Gary Speed's last match as Wales manager)

ENGLAND 1 SWEDEN 0
Wembley (48,876); Tuesday, November 15 2011
England (4-3-3): Hart (Manchester City) (Carson, Bursaspor 46), Walker (Tottenham), Cahill (Bolton), Terry (Chelsea), Baines (Everton), Rodwell (Everton) (Milner, Manchester City 58), Jones (Manchester Utd), Barry (Manchester City), Walcott (Arsenal) (*Sturridge, Chelsea 58), Zamora (Fulham) (Bent, Aston Villa 70), Downing (Liverpool). **Scorer:** Barry (22)
Sweden (4-4-2): Isaksson, Lustig (Wilhelmsson 54), Mellberg (J Olsson 46), Majstorovic, M Olsson, Elm (Bajrami 87), Wernbloom, Kallstrom (Svensson 70), Larsson, Ibrahimovic (Toivonen 46), Elmander. **Booked:** Elmander
Referee: P Kravolec (Czech Republic). **Half-time:** 1-0
(Fabio Capello's last match as England manager)

ENGLAND 2 HOLLAND 3
Wembley (76,283); Wednesday, February 29 2012
England (4-3-3): Hart (Manchester City), Richards (Manchester City), Smalling (Manchester Utd) (Jones, Manchester Utd 62), Cahill (Chelsea), Baines (Everton), Gerrard (Liverpool) (Sturridge, Chelsea 33) (Walcott, Arsenal 88), Parker (Tottenham), Barry (Manchester City) (Milner, Manchester City 46), Johnson (Manchester City) (Downing, Liverpool 62), Welbeck (Manchester Utd) (*Campbell, Sunderland 79), Young (Manchester United). **Scorers:** Cahill (85), Young (90). **Booked:** Richards
Holland (4-2-3-1): Stekelenburg, Boulahrouz (Vlaar 82), Heitinga, Mathijsen, Pieters (Schaars 46), Van Bommel, N De Jong, Robben, Sneijder (Emanuelson 76), Kuyt, Van Persie (Huntelaar 46) (L De Jong 63). **Scorers:** Robben (57, 90), Huntelaar (59). **Booked:** Mathijsen
Referee: F Brych (Germany). **Half-time:** 0-0

SLOVENIA 1 SCOTLAND 1
Koper (4,200); Wednesday, February 29 2012

Slovenia (4-4-2): Handanovic, Brecko, Suler, Cesar, Jokic, Birsa (Vuckic 61), Kirm (Pecnik 88), Radosavljevic, Krhin (Matic 84), Dedic (Ljubijankic 82), Ilic. **Scorer:** Kirm (33)
Scotland (4-1-4-1): McGregor (Rangers), Martin (Norwich), G Caldwell (Wigan), Berra (Wolves), *Mulgrew (Celtic), Adam (Liverpool) (Bannan, Aston Villa 46), Forrest (Celtic) (Robson, Middlesbrough 87), McArthur (Wigan), Morrison (WBA) (Dorrans, WBA 72), Mackie (QPR) (Miller, Cardiff 80) Mackail-Smith (Brighton) (Snodgrass, Leeds 60). **Scorer:** Berra (39)
Referee: A Sravrev (Macedonia). **Half-time:** 1-1

WALES 0 COSTA RICA 1 (Gary Speed memorial match)
Cardiff City Stadium (23,193); Wednesday, February 29 2012

Wales (4-4-1-1): Price (Crystal Palace), Gunter (Nottm Forest), Blake (Cardiff), Williams (Swansea) (Gabbidon, QPR 70), Matthews (Celtic) (Ricketts, Bolton 74), Robson-Kanu (Reading), Allen (Swansea) (Collison, West Ham 63), Crofts (Norwich), Vaughan (Sunderland) (Ledley, Celtic 70), Bellamy (Liverpool) (Earnshaw, Cardiff 74), Morison (Norwich) (Vokes, Wolves 68)
Costa Rica (4-5-1): Navas, Umana, Salvatierra, Miller, Cunningham (Diaz 88), Barrantes, Azofeifa, Wallace (Gabas 68), Oviedo, Ruiz, Campbell (McDonald 78). **Scorer:** Campbell (7)
Referee: H Webb (England). **Half-time:** 0-1

NORTHERN IRELAND 0 NORWAY 3
Windsor Park (10,500); Wednesday, February 29 2012

Northern Ireland (4-4-2): Camp (Nottm Forest), McAuley (WBA) (Hodson, Watford 57), Hughes (Fulham) (Duff, Burnley 46), J Evans (Manchester Utd), McGivern (Manchester City), Davis (Rangers), C Evans (Hull) (McCann, Peterborough 46), Clingan (Coventry), Ferguson (Newcastle) (McCourt, Celtic 69), Shiels (Kilmarnock), Paterson (Burnley) (Healy, Rangers 73)
Norway (4-4-2): Jarstein, Hogli (Ruud 89), Rogne, Demidov (Elyounoussi 60), Riise, Henriksen (Jenssen 78), Nordtveit, Grindheim (Reginiussen 60), Pedersen, Abdellaoui (Braaten 46), Huseklepp (Berisha 66). **Scorers:** Nordtveid (44), Elyounoussi (87), Ruud (90)
Referee: H Jones (Wales). **Half-time:** 0-1
(Michael O'Neill's first match as Northern Ireland manager)

REPUBLIC OF IRELAND 1 CZECH REPUBLIC 1
Aviva Stadium (37,741); Wednesday, February 29 2012

Republic of Ireland (4-4-2): Given (Aston Villa), O'Shea (Sunderland), St Ledger (Leicester), O'Dea (Celtic), Ward (Wolves), Duff (Fulham), (Hunt, Wolves 63), Andrews (WBA), Whelan (Stoke) (Green, Derby 63), McGeady (Spartak Moscow) (*McClean, Sunderland 79), Keane (LA Galaxy) (Cox, WBA 71), Long (WBA) (Walters, Stoke 71). **Scorer:** Cox (86)
Czech Republic (4-4-2): Cech, Selassie (Rajtoral 66), Limbersky, Sivok, Kadlec, Petrzela (Pilar 66), Rezek (Pekhart 87), Stajner (Lafata 59), Plasil, Baros (Kolar 59), Jiracek (Hubschman 46). **Scorer:** Baros (50)
Referee: M de Sousa (Portugal). **Half-time:** 0-0

NORWAY 0 ENGLAND 1
Oslo (21,496); Saturday, May 26 2012

Norway (4-4-2): Jarstein, Hogli (Ruud 40), Demidov, Hangeland, Riise, Tettey (Jenssen 90), Elyounoussi, Henriksen (Berisha 84), Pedersen (Grindheim 63), Braaten (Huseklepp 74), Abdellaoui
England (4-4-2): Green (West Ham), Jones (Manchester Utd) (*Kelly, Liverpool 88), Jagielka (Everton), Lescott (Manchester City), Baines (Everton), Milner (Manchester City), Gerrard (Liverpool) (Barry, Manchester City 46), Henderson, Liverpool 73), Parker (Tottenham) (Walcott, Arsenal 56), Downing (Liverpool) (Johnson, Manchester City 85), Young (Manchester Utd) (*Oxlade-Chamberlain, Arsenal 73), Carroll (Liverpool). **Scorer:** Young (9)
Referee: M Weiner (Germany). **Half-time:** 0-1

REPUBLIC OF IRELAND 1 BOSNIA-HERZEGOVINA 0
Aviva Stadium (37,100); Saturday, May 26 2012
Republic of Ireland (4-4-2): Westwood (Sunderland), McShane (Hull) (Kelly, Fulham 78), Dunne (Aston Villa) (St Ledger, Leicester 70), O'Dea (Celtic), Ward (Wolves), Duff (Fulham) (McGeady, Spartak Moscow 46), Gibson (Everton), Whelan (Stoke) (Andrews, WBA 46), McClean (Sunderland), Keane (LA Galaxy) (Long, WBA 62), Doyle (Wolves) (Walters, Stoke 62). **Scorer**: Long (78)
Bosnia-Herzegovina (4-4-2): Begovic, Mujdza (Zahirovic 56), Pandza, Jahic, Lulic, Pjanic, Medunjanin (Stevanovic 46), Rahimic (Vrancic 46), Misimovic (Alispahic 81), Ibisevic (Vranjes 70), Dzeko. **Booked**: Vrancic
Referee: N Haenni (Switzerland). **Half-time**: 0-0

USA 5 SCOTLAND 1
Jacksonville (44,438); Sunday, May 27 2012
USA (4-4-2): Howard (Guzan 71), Cherundolo, Cameron, Bocanegra (Onyewu 63), Johnson (Castillo 73), Edu (Beckerman 63), Bradley, Jones, Donovan, Boyd (Gomez 63), Torres (Corona 68). **Scorers**: Donovan (4, 60, 65), Bradley (11), Jones (70). **Booked**: Bocanegra
Scotland (4-4-1-1): McGregor (Rangers), Bardsley (Sunderland) (Martin, Norwich 59), Caldwell (Wigan), Webster (Hearts) (Berra, Wolves 82), Mulgrew (Celtic), Brown (Celtic), McArthur (Wigan) (Whittaker, Rangers 59), Bannan (Aston Villa) (Cowie, Cardiff 51), *Phillips (Blackpool), Maloney (Wigan) (Mackail-Smith, Brighton 82), Miller (Cardiff). **Scorer**: Cameron (15 og)
Referee: E Bonilla (El Salvador). **Half-time**: 2-1

MEXICO 2 WALES 0
New York (35,518); Sunday, May 27 2012
Mexico (4-4-2): Corona, Moreno, Meza, Salcido, Rodriguez, , Barrera (Marquez 76), Zavala (Granados 64), Perez (Torres 71), Andrade, Giovani (Reyna 71), De Nigris. **Scorer**: Di Nigris (43, 89)
Wales (4-4-1-1): Brown (Aberdeen), Matthews (Celtic) (Ricketts, Bolton 60), Williams (Swansea), Gunter (Nottm Forest), Taylor (Swansea) (*Richards, Swansea 80), Allen (Swansea), Edwards (Wolves) (King, Leicester 71), Robson-Kanu (Reading), Church, Reading 60), Ramsey (Arsenal), Bellamy (Liverpool), Morison (Norwich) (Vokes, Wolves 60). **Booked**: Ramsey
Referee: R Salazar (USA). **Half-time**: 1-0
(Chris Coleman's first match as Wales manager)

ENGLAND 1 BELGIUM 0
Wembley (85,091); Saturday, June 2 2012
England (4-4-1-1): Hart (Manchester City), Johnson (Liverpool), Cahill (Chelsea) (Lescott, Manchester City 19), Terry (Chelsea) (Jagielka, Everton 70), Cole (Chelsea), Milner (Manchester City), Gerrard (Liverpool) (Henderson, Liverpool 83), Parker (Tottenham), Oxlade-Chamberlain (Arsenal) (Walcott, Arsenal 66), Young (Manchester Utd) (Defoe, Tottenham 66), Welbeck (Manchester Utd) (Rooney (Manchester Utd 53). **Scorer**: Welbeck (36). **Booked**: Parker
Belgium (4-4-1-1): Mignolet, Gillet, Simons, Vermaelen, Vertonghen, Mertens (Lukaku 72), Witsel, Dembele, Mirallas (Chadli 59), Fellaini, Hazard. **Booked**: Mertens
Referee: P Rasmussen (Denmark). **Half-time**: 1-0

HOLLAND 6 NORTHERN IRELAND 0
Amsterdam (45,000); Saturday, June 2 2012
Holland (4-2-3-1): Stekelenburg, Van der Wiel, Heitinga, Vlaar, Willems (Schaars 78), De Jong, Van Bommel (Van der Vaart 57), Robben (Narsingh 82), Sneijder (Kuyt 70), Afellay, Van Persie (Huntelaar 57). **Scorers**: Van Persie (11, 29 pen), Sneijder (15), Afellay (37, 51), Vlaar (78)
Northern Ireland (4-5-1): Camp (Nottm Forest) (Carroll, Olympiacos 46), Hodson (Watford), Duff (Burnley), (McArdle, Aberdeen 61), *McPake (Coventry), *Lafferty (Burnley) (McGivern,

Manchester City 46), Little (Rangers) (McGinn Celtic 56), Clingan (Coventry), McCann (Peterborough) (Carson, Ipswich 46), Norwood (Manchester Utd), Ferguson (Newcastle) (Healy, Rangers 81) *Grigg (Walsall). **Booked:** Duff, Hodson
Referee: R Schorgenhofer (Austria). **Half-time:** 4-0

HUNGARY 0 REPUBLIC OF IRELAND 0
Budapest (17,000); Monday, June 4 2012

Hungary (4-2-3-1): Bogdan, Varga, Meszaros, Gyurcso (Koltai 80), Korcsmar, Halmosi (Kadar 69), Pinter (Vanczak 46), Koman, Dzsudzsak, Szakaly (Szabics 66), Szalai (Nemeth 79). **Booked:** Korcsmar
Republic of Ireland (4-4-2): Given (Aston Villa) (Westwood, Sunderland 46), O'Shea (Sunderland), St Ledger (Leicester), Dunne (Aston Villa), Ward (Wolves), Duff (Fulham) (Hunt, Wolves 63), Andrews (WBA) (Gibson, Everton 66), Whelan (Stoke) (Green, Derby 85), McGeady (Spartak Moscow), Keane (LA Galaxy) (Cox, WBA 60), Doyle (Wolves) (Walters, Stoke 46). **Booked:** Ward
Referee: K Hansen (Denmark)

LEAGUE OF NATIONS

Arsenal set a Premier League record by using players of 14 different nationalities during the 1-1 Premier League draw against Fulham at the Emirates. Their line-up was: Szeczesny (Poland), Djourou (Switzerland), Mertesacker (Germany), Vermaelen (Belgium), Santos (Brazil), Song (Cameroon), Arteta (Spain), Ramsey (Wales), Walcott (England), Arshavin (Russia), Van Persie (Holland). The substitutes were Diaby (France), Gervinho (Ivory Coast) and Chamakh (Morocco)

ALL-ENGLISH FOR NORWICH

Norwich had a starting line-up of all English-born players for the Premier League game at Tottenham which they won 2-1. The team was: Ruddy, Martin, Drury, Ward, Ryan Bennett, Johnson, Pilkington, Elliott Bennett, Howson, Holt, Wilbraham.

JAPANESE REFEREE FOR FA CUP TIE

Masaaki Toma became the first non-British official to take charge of an FA Cup tie. The Japanese, who was spending time in the UK as part of a referee exchange programme, showed yellow cards to three players during the Brentford-Basingstoke first round match.

RULEBOOK FETCHES A FORTUNE

The world's oldest football rulebook, belonging to the world's oldest club, went for £881,250 to an anonymous bidder at a Sotherby's auction. The handwritten pamphlet, dating from 1857, was sold by Sheffield FC to raise money to improve their ground.

QUICK-FIRE CENTURY FOR RONALDO

Former Manchester United star Cristiano Ronaldo reached 100 goals in his first 105 appearances for Real Madrid with two in the Champions League game against Lyon. The £80m player scored 46 in La Liga last season, but still finished four behind Barcelona's Lionel Messi.

OTHER BRITISH & IRISH INTERNATIONAL RESULTS

ENGLAND

v ALBANIA

		E	A
1989	Tirana (WC)	2	0
1989	Wembley (WC)	5	0
2001	Tirana (WC)	3	1
2001	Newcastle (WC)	2	0

v ALGERIA

		E	A
2010	Cape Town (WC)	0	0

v ANDORRA

		E	A
2006	Old Trafford (EC)	5	0
2007	Barcelona (EC)	3	0
2008	Barcelona (WC)	2	0
2009	Wembley (WC)	6	0

v ARGENTINA

		E	A
1951	Wembley	2	1
1953*	Buenos Aires	0	0
1962	Rancagua (WC)	3	1
1964	Rio de Janeiro	0	1
1966	Wembley (WC)	1	0
1974	Wembley	2	2
1977	Buenos Aires	1	1
1980	Wembley	3	1
1986	Mexico City (WC)	1	2
1991	Wembley	2	2
1998†	St Etienne (WC)	2	2
2000	Wembley	0	0
2002	Sapporo (WC)	1	0
2005	Geneva	3	2

(*Abandoned after 21 mins – rain)
(† England lost 3-4 on pens)

v AUSTRALIA

		E	A
1980	Sydney	2	1
1983	Sydney	0	0
1983	Brisbane	1	0
1983	Melbourne	1	1
1991	Sydney	1	0
2003	West Ham	1	3

v AUSTRIA

		E	A
1908	Vienna	6	1
1908	Vienna	11	1
1909	Vienna	8	1
1930	Vienna	0	0
1932	Stamford Bridge	4	3
1936	Vienna	1	2
1951	Wembley	2	2
1952	Vienna	3	2
1958	Boras (WC)	2	2
1961	Vienna	1	3
1962	Wembley	3	1

1965	Wembley	2	3
1967	Vienna	1	0
1973	Wembley	7	0
1979	Vienna	3	4
2004	Vienna (WC)	2	2
2005	Old Trafford (WC)	1	0
2007	Vienna	1	0

v AZERBAIJAN

		E	A
2004	Baku (WC)	1	0
2005	Newcastle (WC)	2	0

v BELARUS

		E	B
2008	Minsk (WC)	3	1
2009	Wembley (WC)	3	0

v BELGIUM

		E	B
1921	Brussels	2	0
1923	Highbury	6	1
1923	Antwerp	2	2
1924	West Bromwich	4	0
1926	Antwerp	5	3
1927	Brussels	9	1
1928	Antwerp	3	1
1929	Brussels	5	1
1931	Brussels	4	1
1936	Brussels	2	3
1947	Brussels	5	2
1950	Brussels	4	1
1952	Wembley	5	0
1954	Basle (WC)	4	4
1964	Wembley	2	2
1970	Brussels	3	1
1980	Turin (EC)	1	1
1990	Bologna (WC)	1	0
1998*	Casablanca	0	0
1999	Sunderland	2	1
2012	Wembley	1	0

(*England lost 3-4 on pens)

v BOHEMIA

		E	B
1908	Prague	4	0

v BRAZIL

		E	B
1956	Wembley	4	2
1958	Gothenburg (WC)	0	0
1959	Rio de Janeiro	0	2
1962	Vina del Mar (WC)	1	3
1963	Wembley	1	1
1964	Rio de Janeiro	1	5
1969	Rio de Janeiro	1	2
1970	Guadalajara (WC)	0	1
1976	Los Angeles	0	1
1977	Rio de Janeiro	0	0
1978	Wembley	1	1
1981	Wembley	0	1
1984	Rio de Janeiro	2	0
1987	Wembley	1	1

1990	Wembley	1	0
1992	Wembley	1	1
1993	Washington	1	1
1995	Wembley	1	3
1997	Paris (TF)	0	1
2000	Wembley	1	1
2002	Shizuoka (WC)	1	2
2007	Wembley	1	1
2009	Doha	0	1

v BULGARIA

		E	B
1962	Rancagua (WC)	0	0
1968	Wembley	1	1
1974	Sofia	1	0
1979	Sofia (EC)	3	0
1979	Wembley (EC)	2	0
1996	Wembley	1	0
1998	Wembley (EC)	0	0
1999	Sofia (EC)	1	1
2010	Wembley (EC)	4	0
2011	Sofia (EC)	3	0

v CAMEROON

		E	C
1990	Naples (WC)	3	2
1991	Wembley	2	0
1997	Wembley	2	0
2002	Kobe (Japan)	2	2

v CANADA

		E	C
1986	Vancouver	1	0

v CHILE

		E	C
1950	Rio de Janeiro (WC)	2	0
1953	Santiago	2	1
1984	Santiago	0	0
1989	Wembley	0	0
1998	Wembley	0	2

v CHINA

		E	C
1996	Beijing	3	0

v CIS

(formerly Soviet Union)

		E	CIS
1992	Moscow	2	2

v COLOMBIA

		E	C
1970	Bogota	4	0
1988	Wembley	1	1
1995	Wembley	0	0
1998	Lens (WC)	2	0
2005	New York	3	2

v CROATIA

		E	C
1995	Wembley	0	0
2003	Ipswich	3	1
2004	Lisbon (EC)	4	2
2006	Zagreb (EC)	0	2
2007	Wembley (EC)	2	3
2008	Zagreb (WC)	4	1
2009	Wembley (WC)	5	1

v CYPRUS

		E	C
1975	Wembley (EC)	5	0
1975	Limassol (EC)	1	0

v CZECH REPUBLIC

		E	C
1998	Wembley	2	0
2008	Wembley	2	2

v CZECHOSLOVAKIA

		E	C
1934	Prague	1	2
1937	White Hart Lane	5	4
1963	Bratislava	4	2
1966	Wembley	0	0
1970	Guadalajara (WC)	1	0
1973	Prague	1	1
1974	Wembley (EC)	3	0
1975*	Bratislava (EC)	1	2
1978	Wembley (EC)	1	0
1982	Bilbao (WC)	2	0
1990	Wembley	4	2
1992	Prague	2	2

(* Aband 0-0, 17 mins prev day – fog)

v DENMARK

		E	D
1948	Copenhagen	0	0
1955	Copenhagen	5	1
1956	W'hampton (WC)	5	2
1957	Copenhagen (WC)	4	1
1966	Copenhagen	2	0
1978	Copenhagen (EC)	4	3
1979	Wembley (EC)	1	0
1982	Copenhagen (EC)	2	2
1983	Wembley (EC)	0	1
1988	Wembley	1	0
1989	Copenhagen	1	1
1990	Wembley	1	0
1992	Malmo (EC)	0	0
1994	Wembley	1	0
2002	Niigata (WC)	3	0
2003	Old Trafford	2	3
2005	Copenhagen	1	4
2011	Copenhagen	2	1

v EAST GERMANY

		E	EG
1963	Leipzig	2	1
1970	Wembley	3	1
1974	Leipzig	1	1
1984	Wembley	1	0

v ECUADOR

		E	Ec
1970	Quito	2	0
2006	Stuttgart (WC)	1	0

v EGYPT

		E	Eg
1986	Cairo	4	0
1990	Cagliari (WC)	1	0
2010	Wembley	3	1

v ESTONIA

		E	Est
2007	Tallinn (EC)	3	0
2007	Wembley (EC)	3	0

v FIFA

		E	F
1938	Highbury	3	0
1953	Wembley	4	4
1963	Wembley	2	1

v FINLAND

		E	F
1937	Helsinki	8	0
1956	Helsinki	5	1
1966	Helsinki	3	0
1976	Helsinki (WC)	4	1
1976	Wembley (WC)	2	1
1982	Helsinki	4	1
1984	Wembley (WC)	5	0
1985	Helsinki (WC)	1	1
1992	Helsinki	2	1
2000	Helsinki (WC)	0	0
2001	Liverpool (WC)	2	1

v FRANCE

		E	F
1923	Paris	4	1
1924	Paris	3	1
1925	Paris	3	2
1927	Paris	6	0
1928	Paris	5	1
1929	Paris	4	1
1931	Paris	2	5
1933	White Hart Lane	4	1
1938	Paris	4	2
1947	Highbury	3	0
1949	Paris	3	1
1951	Highbury	2	2
1955	Paris	0	1
1957	Wembley	4	0
1962	Hillsborough (EC)	1	1
1963	Paris (EC)	2	5
1966	Wembley (WC)	2	0
1969	Wembley	5	0
1982	Bilbao (WC)	3	1
1984	Paris	0	2
1992	Wembley	2	0
1992	Malmo (EC)	0	0
1997	Montpellier (TF)	1	0
1999	Wembley	0	2
2000	Paris	1	1
2004	Lisbon (EC)	1	2
2008	Paris	0	1
2010	Wembley	1	2
2012	Donetsk (EC)	1	1

v GEORGIA

		E	G
1996	Tbilisi (WC)	2	0
1997	Wembley (WC)	2	0

v GERMANY/WEST GERMANY

		E	G
1930	Berlin	3	3
1935	White Hart Lane	3	0
1938	Berlin	6	3
1954	Wembley	3	1
1956	Berlin	3	1
1965	Nuremberg	1	0
1966	Wembley	1	0
1966	Wembley (WCF)	4	2
1968	Hanover	0	1
1970	Leon (WC)	2	3
1972	Wembley (EC)	1	3
1972	Berlin (EC)	0	0
1975	Wembley	2	0
1978	Munich	1	2
1982	Madrid (WC)	0	0
1982	Wembley	1	2
1985	Mexico City	3	0
1987	Dusseldorf	1	3
1990*	Turin (WC)	1	1
1991	Wembley	0	1
1993	Detroit	1	2
1996†	Wembley (EC)	1	1
2000	Charleroi (EC)	1	0
2000	Wembley (WC)	0	1
2001	Munich (WC)	5	1
2007	Wembley	1	2
2008	Berlin	2	1
2010	Bloemfontein (WC)	1	4
2012	Donetsk (EC)	1	1

(*England lost 3-4 on pens)
(† England lost 5-6 on pens)

v GHANA

		E	G
2011	Wembley	1	1

v GREECE

		E	G
1971	Wembley (EC)	3	0
1971	Athens (EC)	2	0
1982	Salonika (EC)	3	0
1983	Wembley (EC)	0	0
1989	Athens	2	1
1994	Wembley	5	0
2001	Athens (WC)	2	0
2001	Old Trafford (WC)	2	2
2006	Old Trafford	4	0

v HOLLAND

		E	H
1935	Amsterdam	1	0
1946	Huddersfield	8	2
1964	Amsterdam	1	1
1969	Amsterdam	1	0
1970	Wembley	0	0
1977	Wembley	0	2
1982	Wembley	2	0
1988	Wembley	2	2
1988	Dusseldorf (EC)	1	3
1990	Cagliari (WC)	0	0
1993	Wembley (WC)	2	2
1993	Rotterdam (WC)	0	2
1996	Wembley (EC)	4	1
2001	White Hart Lane	0	2

2002	Amsterdam	1	1
2005	Villa Park	0	0
2006	Amsterdam	1	1
2009	Amsterdam	2	2
2012	Wembley	2	3

v HUNGARY

		E	H
1908	Budapest	7	0
1909	Budapest	4	2
1909	Budapest	8	2
1934	Budapest	1	2
1936	Highbury	6	2
1953	Wembley	3	6
1954	Budapest	1	7
1960	Budapest	0	2
1962	Rancagua (WC)	1	2
1965	Wembley	1	0
1978	Wembley	4	1
1981	Budapest (WC)	3	1
1981	Wembley (WC)	1	0
1983	Wembley (EC)	2	0
1983	Budapest (EC)	3	0
1988	Budapest	0	0
1990	Wembley	1	0
1992	Budapest	1	0
1996	Wembley	3	0
1999	Budapest	1	1
2006	Old Trafford	3	1
2010	Wembley	2	1

v ICELAND

		E	I
1982	Reykjavik	1	1
2004	City of Manchester	6	1

v ISRAEL

		E	I
1986	Tel Aviv	2	1
1988	Tel Aviv	0	0
2006	Tel Aviv (EC)	0	0
2007	Wembley (EC)	3	0

v ITALY

		E	I
1933	Rome	1	1
1934	Highbury	3	2
1939	Milan	2	2
1948	Turin	4	0
1949	White Hart Lane	2	0
1952	Florence	1	1
1959	Wembley	2	2
1961	Rome	3	2
1973	Turin	0	2
1973	Wembley	0	1
1976	New York	3	2
1976	Rome (WC)	0	2
1977	Wembley (WC)	2	0
1980	Turin (EC)	0	1
1985	Mexico City	1	2
1989	Wembley	0	0
1990	Bari (WC)	1	2
1996	Wembley (WC)	0	1

1997	Nantes (TF)	2	0
1997	Rome (WC)	0	0
2000	Turin	0	1
2002	Leeds	1	2
2012*	Kiev (EC)	0	0
(*England lost 2-4 on pens)			

v JAMAICA

		E	J
2006	Old Trafford	6	0

v JAPAN

		E	J
1995	Wembley	2	1
2004	City of Manchester	1	1
2010	Graz	2	1

v KAZAKHSTAN

		E	K
2008	Wembley (WC)	5	1
2009	Almaty (WC)	4	0

v KUWAIT

		E	K
1982	Bilbao (WC)	1	0

v LIECHTENSTEIN

		E	L
2003	Vaduz (EC)	2	0
2003	Old Trafford (EC)	2	0

v LUXEMBOURG

		E	L
1927	Luxembourg	5	2
1960	Luxembourg (WC)	9	0
1961	Highbury (WC)	4	1
1977	Wembley (WC)	5	0
1977	Luxembourg (WC)	2	0
1982	Wembley (EC)	9	0
1983	Luxembourg (EC)	4	0
1998	Luxembourg (EC)	3	0
1999	Wembley (EC)	6	0

v MACEDONIA

		E	M
2002	Southampton (EC)	2	2
2003	Skopje (EC)	2	1
2006	Skopje (EC)	1	0
2006	Old Trafford (EC)	0	0

v MALAYSIA

		E	M
1991	Kuala Lumpur	4	2

v MALTA

		E	M
1971	Valletta (EC)	1	0
1971	Wembley (EC)	5	0
2000	Valletta	2	1

v MEXICO

		E	M
1959	Mexico City	1	2
1961	Wembley	8	0
1966	Wembley (WC)	2	0
1969	Mexico City	0	0
1985	Mexico City	0	1
1986	Los Angeles	3	0

1997	Wembley	2	0
2001	Derby	4	0
2010	Wembley	3	1

v MOLDOVA

		E	M
1996	Kishinev	3	0
1997	Wembley (WC)	4	0

v MONTENEGRO

		E	M
2010	Wembley (EC)	0	0
2011	Podgorica (EC)	2	2

v MOROCCO

		E	M
1986	Monterrey (WC)	0	0
1998	Casablanca	1	0

v NEW ZEALAND

		E	NZ
1991	Auckland	1	0
1991	Wellington	2	0

v NIGERIA

		E	NZ
1994	Wembley	1	0
2002	Osaka (WC)	0	0

v NORWAY

		E	NZ
1937	Oslo	6	0
1938	Newcastle	4	0
1949	Oslo	4	1
1966	Oslo	6	1
1980	Wembley (WC)	4	0
1981	Oslo (WC)	1	2
1992	Wembley (WC)	1	1
1993	Oslo (WC)	0	2
1994	Wembley	0	0
1995	Oslo	0	0
2012	Oslo	1	0

v PARAGUAY

		E	P
1986	Mexico City (WC)	3	0
2002	Anfield	4	0
2006	Frankfurt (WC)	1	0

v PERU

		E	P
1959	Lima	1	4
1961	Lima	4	0

v POLAND

		E	P
1966	Goodison Park	1	1
1966	Chorzow	1	0
1973	Chorzow (WC)	0	2
1973	Wembley (WC)	1	1
1986	Monterrey (WC)	3	0
1989	Wembley (WC)	3	0
1989	Katowice (WC)	0	0
1990	Wembley (EC)	2	0
1991	Poznan (EC)	1	1
1993	Chorzow (WC)	1	1
1993	Wembley (WC)	3	0
1996	Wembley (WC)	2	1
1997	Katowice (WC)	2	0

1999	Wembley (EC)	3	1
1999	Warsaw (EC)	0	0
2004	Katowice (WC)	2	1
2005	Old Trafford (WC)	2	1

v PORTUGAL

		E	P
1947	Lisbon	10	0
1950	Lisbon	5	3
1951	Goodison Park	5	2
1955	Oporto	1	3
1958	Wembley	2	1
1961	Lisbon (WC)	1	1
1961	Wembley (WC)	2	0
1964	Lisbon	4	3
1964	Sao Paulo	1	1
1966	Wembley (WC)	2	1
1969	Wembley	1	0
1974	Lisbon	0	0
1974	Wembley (EC)	0	0
1975	Lisbon (EC)	1	1
1986	Monterrey (WC)	0	1
1995	Wembley	1	1
1998	Wembley	3	0
2000	Eindhoven (EC)	2	3
2002	Villa Park	1	1
2004	Faro	1	1
2004*	Lisbon (EC)	2	2
2006†	Gelsenkirchen (WC)	0	0

(† England lost 1–3 on pens)
(*England lost 5–6 on pens)

v REPUBLIC OF IRELAND

		E	RoI
1946	Dublin	1	0
1950	Goodison Park	0	2
1957	Wembley (WC)	5	1
1957	Dublin (WC)	1	1
1964	Dublin	3	1
1977	Wembley	1	1
1978	Dublin (EC)	1	1
1980	Wembley (EC)	2	0
1985	Wembley	2	1
1988	Stuttgart (EC)	0	1
1990	Cagliari (WC)	1	1
1990	Dublin (EC)	1	1
1991	Wembley (EC)	1	1
1995*	Dublin	0	1

(*Abandoned 27 mins – crowd riot)

v ROMANIA

		E	R
1939	Bucharest	2	0
1968	Bucharest	0	0
1969	Wembley	1	1
1970	Guadalajara (WC)	1	0
1980	Bucharest (WC)	1	2
1981	Wembley (WC)	0	0
1985	Bucharest (WC)	0	0
1985	Wembley (WC)	1	1
1994	Wembley	1	1
1998	Toulouse (WC)	1	2
2000	Charleroi (EC)	2	3

v RUSSIA

		E	R
2007	Wembley (EC)	3	0
2007	Moscow (EC)	1	2

v SAN MARINO

		E	SM
1992	Wembley (WC)	6	0
1993	Bologna (WC)	7	1

v SAUDI ARABIA

		E	SA
1988	Riyadh	1	1
1998	Wembley	0	0

v SERBIA-MONTENEGRO

		E	S-M
2003	Leicester	2	1

v SLOVAKIA

		E	S
2002	Bratislava (EC)	2	1
2003	Middlesbrough (EC)	2	1
2009	Wembley	4	0

v SLOVENIA

		E	S
2009	Wembley	2	1
2010	Port Elizabeth (WC)	1	0

v SOUTH AFRICA

		E	SA
1997	Old Trafford	2	1
2003	Durban	2	1

v SOUTH KOREA

		E	SK
2002	Seoguipo	1	1

v SOVIET UNION (see also CIS)

		E	SU
1958	Moscow	1	1
1958	Gothenburg (WC)	2	2
1958	Gothenburg (WC)	0	1
1958	Wembley	5	0
1967	Wembley	2	2
1968	Rome (EC)	2	0
1973	Moscow	2	1
1984	Wembley	0	2
1986	Tbilisi	1	0
1988	Frankfurt (EC)	1	3
1991	Wembley	3	1

v SPAIN

		E	S
1929	Madrid	3	4
1931	Highbury	7	1
1950	Rio de Janeiro (WC)	0	1
1955	Madrid	1	1
1955	Wembley	4	1
1960	Madrid	0	3
1960	Wembley	4	2
1965	Madrid	2	0
1967	Wembley	2	0
1968	Wembley (EC)	1	0
1968	Madrid (EC)	2	1
1980	Barcelona	2	0
1980	Naples (EC)	2	1

1981	Wembley	1	2
1982	Madrid (WC)	0	0
1987	Madrid	4	2
1992	Santander	0	1
1996*	Wembley (EC)	0	0
2001	Villa Park	3	0
2004	Madrid	0	1
2007	Old Trafford	0	1
2009	Seville	0	2
2011	Wembley	1	0

(*England won 4-2 on pens)

v SWEDEN

		E	S
1923	Stockholm	4	2
1923	Stockholm	3	1
1937	Stockholm	4	0
1948	Highbury	4	2
1949	Stockholm	1	3
1956	Stockholm	0	0
1959	Wembley	2	3
1965	Gothenburg	2	1
1968	Wembley	3	1
1979	Stockholm	0	0
1986	Stockholm	0	1
1988	Wembley (WC)	0	0
1989	Stockholm (WC)	0	0
1992	Stockholm (EC)	1	2
1995	Leeds	3	3
1998	Stockholm (EC)	1	2
1999	Wembley (EC)	0	0
2001	Old Trafford	1	1
2002	Saitama (WC)	1	1
2004	Gothenburg	0	1
2006	Cologne (WC)	2	2
2011	Wembley	1	0
2012	Kiev (EC)	3	2

v SWITZERLAND

		E	S
1933	Berne	4	0
1938	Zurich	1	2
1947	Zurich	0	1
1949	Highbury	6	0
1952	Zurich	3	0
1954	Berne (WC)	2	0
1962	Wembley	3	1
1963	Basle	8	1
1971	Basle (EC)	3	2
1971	Wembley (EC)	1	1
1975	Basle	2	1
1977	Wembley	0	0
1980	Wembley (WC)	2	1
1981	Basle (WC)	1	2
1988	Lausanne	1	0
1995	Wembley	3	1
1996	Wembley (EC)	1	1
1998	Berne	1	1
2004	Coimbra (EC)	3	0
2008	Wembley	2	1
2010	Basle (EC)	3	1
2011	Wembley (EC)	2	2

259

v TRINIDAD & TOBAGO

		E	T
2006	Nuremberg (WC)	2	0
2008	Port of Spain	3	0

v TUNISIA

		E	T
1990	Tunis	1	1
1998	Marseille (WC)	2	0

v TURKEY

		E	T
1984	Istanbul (WC)	8	0
1985	Wembley (WC)	5	0
1987	Izmir (EC)	0	0
1987	Wembley (EC)	8	0
1991	Izmir (EC)	1	0
1991	Wembley (EC)	1	0
1992	Wembley (WC)	4	0
1993	Izmir (WC)	2	0
2003	Sunderland (EC)	2	0
2003	Istanbul (EC)	0	0

v UKRAINE

		E	U
2000	Wembley	2	0
2004	Newcastle	3	0
2009	Wembley (WC)	2	1
2009	Dnipropetrovski (WC)	0	1
2012	Donetsk (EC)	1	0

v URUGUAY

		E	U
1953	Montevideo	1	2
1954	Basle (WC)	2	4
1964	Wembley	2	1
1966	Wembley (WC)	0	0
1969	Montevideo	2	1
1977	Montevideo	0	0
1984	Montevideo	0	2
1990	Wembley	1	2
1995	Wembley	0	0
2006	Anfield	2	1

v USA

		E	USA
1950	Belo Horizonte (WC)	0	1
1953	New York	6	3
1959	Los Angeles	8	1
1964	New York	10	0
1985	Los Angeles	5	0
1993	Boston	0	2
1994	Wembley	2	0
2005	Chicago	2	1
2008	Wembley	2	0
2010	Rustenburg (WC)	1	1

v YUGOSLAVIA

		E	Y
1939	Belgrade	1	2
1950	Highbury	2	2
1954	Belgrade	0	1
1956	Wembley	3	0
1958	Belgrade	0	5
1960	Wembley	3	3
1965	Belgrade	1	1
1966	Wembley	2	0
1968	Florence (EC)	0	1
1972	Wembley	1	1
1974	Belgrade	2	2
1986	Wembley (EC)	2	0
1987	Belgrade (EC)	4	1
1989	Wembley	2	1

ENGLAND'S RECORD

England's first international was a 0-0 draw against Scotland in Glasgow, on the West of Scotland cricket ground, Partick, on November 30, 1872 Their complete record at the start of 2012–13 is:

P	W	D	L	F	A
909	516	219	174	2009	909

ENGLAND'S 'B' TEAM RESULTS

England scores first

1937	Stockholm	4	0
1948	Highbury	4	2
1949	Stockholm	1	3
1956	Stockholm	0	0
1959	Wembley	2	3
1965	Gothenburg	2	1
1968	Wembley	3	1
1979	Stockholm	0	0
1986	Stockholm	0	1
1988	Wembley (WC)	0	0
1989	Stockholm (WC)	0	0
1992	Stockholm (EC)	1	2
1995	Leeds	3	3
1998	Stockholm (EC)	1	2
1999	Wembley (EC)	0	0
2001	Old Trafford	1	1
2002	Saitama (WC)	1	1
2004	Gothenburg	0	1
2006	Cologne (WC)	2	
1949	Finland (A)	4	0
1949	Holland (A)	4	0
1950	Italy (A)	0	5
1950	Holland (H)	1	0
1950	Holland (A)	0	3
1950	Luxembourg (A)	2	1
1950	Switzerland (H)	5	0
1952	Holland (H)	1	0
1952	France (A)	1	7
1953	Scotland (A)	2	2
1954	Scotland (H)	1	1
1954	Germany (A)	4	0
1954	Yugoslavia (A)	1	2
1954	Switzerland (A)	0	2
1955	Germany (H)	1	1
1955	Yugoslavia (H)	5	1
1956	Switzerland (H)	4	1

1956	Scotland (A)	2	2
1957	Scotland (H)	4	1
1978	W Germany (A)	2	1
1978	Czechoslovakia (A)	1	0
1978	Singapore (A)	8	0
1978	Malaysia (A)	1	1
1978	N Zealand (A)	4	0
1978	N Zealand (A)	3	1
1978	N Zealand (A)	4	0
1979	Austria (A)	1	0
1979	N Zealand (H)	4	1
1980	USA (H)	1	0
1980	Spain (H)	1	0
1980	Australia (H)	1	0
1981	Spain (A)	2	3
1984	N Zealand (A)	2	0
1987	Malta (A)	2	0
1989	Switzerland (A)	2	0
1989	Iceland (A) .	2	0
1989	Norway (A)	1	0
1989	Italy (H)	1	1
1989	Yugoslavia (H)	2	1
1990	Rep of Ireland (A)	1	4
1990	Czechoslovakia (H)	2	0
1990	Algeria (A)	0	0
1991	Wales (A)	1	0
1991	Iceland (H)	1	0
1991	Switzerland (H)	2	1
1991	Spanish XI (A)	1	0
1992	France (H)	3	0
1992	Czechoslovakia (A)	1	0
1992	CIS (A)	1	1
1994	N Ireland (H)	4	2
1995	Rep of Ireland (H)	2	0
1998	Chile (H)	1	2
1998	Russia (H)	4	1
2006	Belarus (H)	1	2
2007	Albania	3	1

GREAT BRITAIN v REST OF EUROPE (FIFA)

		GB	RofE
1947	Glasgow	6	1

SCOTLAND

v ARGENTINA

		S	A
1977	Buenos Aires	1	1
1979	Glasgow	1	3
1990	Glasgow	1	0
2008	Glasgow	0	1

v AUSTRALIA

		S	A
1985*	Glasgow (WC)	2	0
1985*	Melbourne (WC)	0	0
1996	Glasgow	1	0
2000	Glasgow	0	2

(* World Cup play-off)

v AUSTRIA

		S	A
1931	Vienna	0	5
1933	Glasgow	2	2
1937	Vienna	1	1
1950	Glasgow	0	1
1951	Vienna	0	4
1954	Zurich (WC)	0	1
1955	Vienna	4	1
1956	Glasgow	1	1
1960	Vienna	1	4
1963*	Glasgow	4	1
1968	Glasgow (WC)	2	1
1969	Vienna (WC)	0	2
1978	Vienna (EC)	2	3
1979	Glasgow (EC)	1	1
1994	Vienna	2	1
1996	Vienna (WC)	0	0
1997	Glasgow (WC)	2	0

(* Abandoned after 79 minutes)

2003	Glasgow	0	2
2005	Graz	2	2
2007	Vienna	1	0

v BELARUS

		S	B
1997	Minsk (WC)	1	0
1997	Aberdeen (WC)	4	1
2005	Minsk (WC)	0	0
2005	Glasgow (WC)	0	1

v BELGIUM

		S	B
1947	Brussels	1	2
1948	Glasgow	2	0
1951	Brussels	5	0
1971	Liege (EC)	0	3
1971	Aberdeen (EC)	1	0
1974	Brugge	1	2
1979	Brussels (EC)	0	2
1979	Glasgow (EC)	1	3
1982	Brussels (EC)	2	3
1983	Glasgow (EC)	1	1
1987	Brussels (EC)	1	4
1987	Glasgow (EC)	2	0
2001	Glasgow (WC)	2	2
2001	Brussels (WC)	0	2

v BOSNIA

		S	B
1999	Sarajevo (EC)	2	1
1999	Glasgow (EC)	1	0

v BRAZIL

		S	B
1966	Glasgow	1	1

261

1972	Rio de Janeiro	0	1
1973	Glasgow	0	1
1974	Frankfurt (WC)	0	0
1977	Rio de Janeiro	0	2
1982	Seville (WC)	1	4
1987	Glasgow	0	2
1990	Turin (WC)	0	1
1998	St Denis (WC)	1	2
2011	Arsenal	0	2

v BULGARIA

		S	B
1978	Glasgow	2	1
1986	Glasgow (EC)	0	0
1987	Sofia (EC)	1	0
1990	Sofia (EC)	1	1
1991	Glasgow (EC)	1	1
2006	Kobe	5	1

v CANADA

		S	C
1983	Vancouver	2	0
1983	Edmonton	3	0
1983	Toronto	2	0
1992	Toronto	3	1
2002	Edinburgh	3	1

v CHILE

		S	C
1977	Santiago	4	2
1989	Glasgow	2	0

v CIS (formerly Soviet Union)

		S	C
1992	Norrkoping (EC)	3	0

v COLOMBIA

		S	C
1988	Glasgow	0	0
1996	Miami	0	1
1998	New York	2	2

v COSTA RICA

		S	C
1990	Genoa (WC)	0	1

v CROATIA

		S	C
2000	Zagreb (WC)	1	1
2001	Glasgow (WC)	0	0
2008	Glasgow	1	1

v CYPRUS

		S	C
1968	Nicosia (WC)	5	0
1969	Glasgow (WC)	8	0
1989	Limassol (WC)	3	2
1989	Glasgow (WC)	2	1
2011	Larnaca	2	1

v CZECH REPUBLIC

		S	C
1999	Glasgow (EC)	1	2
1999	Prague (EC)	2	3
2008	Prague	1	3
2010	Glasgow	1	0
2010	Prague (EC)	0	1
2011	Glasgow (EC)	2	2

v CZECHOSLOVAKIA

		S	C
1937	Prague	3	1
1937	Glasgow	5	0
1961	Bratislava (WC)	0	4
1961	Glasgow (WC)	3	2
1961*	Brussels (WC)	2	4
1972	Porto Alegre	0	0
1973	Glasgow (WC)	2	1
1973	Bratislava (WC)	0	1
1976	Prague (WC)	0	2
1977	Glasgow (WC)	3	1
(*World Cup play-off)			

v DENMARK

		S	D
1951	Glasgow	3	1
1952	Copenhagen	2	1
1968	Copenhagen	1	0
1970	Glasgow (EC)	1	0
1971	Copenhagen (EC)	0	1
1972	Copenhagen (WC)	4	1
1972	Glasgow (WC)	2	0
1975	Copenhagen (EC)	1	0
1975	Glasgow (EC)	3	1
1986	Neza (WC)	0	1
1996	Copenhagen	0	2
1998	Glasgow	0	1
2002	Glasgow	0	1
2004	Copenhagen	0	1
2011	Glasgow	2	1

v EAST GERMANY

		S	EG
1974	Glasgow	3	0
1977	East Berlin	0	1
1982	Glasgow (EC)	2	0
1983	Halle (EC)	1	2
1986	Glasgow	0	0
1990	Glasgow	0	1

v ECUADOR

		S	E
1995	Toyama, Japan	2	1

v EGYPT

		S	E
1990	Aberdeen	1	3

v ESTONIA

		S	E
1993	Tallinn (WC)	3	0
1993	Aberdeen	3	1
1996	Tallinn (WC)	*No result	
1997	Monaco (WC)	0	0
1997	Kilmarnock (WC)	2	0
1998	Edinburgh (EC)	3	2
1999	Tallinn (EC)	0	0
(* Estonia absent)			
2004	Tallinn	1	0

v FAROE ISLANDS

		S	F
1994	Glasgow (EC)	5	1
1995	Toftir (EC)	2	0

1998	Aberdeen (EC)	2	1
1999	Toftir (EC)	1	1
2002	Toftir (EC)	2	2
2003	Glasgow (EC)	3	1
2006	Glasgow (EC)	6	0
2007	Toftir (EC)	2	0
2010	Aberdeen	3	0

v FINLAND

		S	F
1954	Helsinki	2	1
1964	Glasgow (WC)	3	1
1965	Helsinki (WC)	2	1
1976	Glasgow	6	0
1992	Glasgow	1	1
1994	Helsinki (EC)	2	0
1995	Glasgow (EC)	1	0
1998	Edinburgh	1	1

v FRANCE

		S	F
1930	Paris	2	0
1932	Paris	3	1
1948	Paris	0	3
1949	Glasgow	2	0
1950	Paris	1	0
1951	Glasgow	1	0
1958	Orebro (WC)	1	2
1984	Marseilles	0	2
1989	Glasgow (WC)	2	0
1990	Paris (WC)	0	3
1997	St Etienne	1	2
2000	Glasgow	0	2
2002	Paris	0	5
2006	Glasgow (EC)	1	0
2007	Paris (EC)	1	0

v GEORGIA

		S	G
2007	Glasgow (EC)	2	1
2007	Tbilisi (EC)	0	2

v GERMANY/WEST GERMANY

		S	G
1929	Berlin	1	1
1936	Glasgow	2	0
1957	Stuttgart	3	1
1959	Glasgow	3	2
1964	Hanover	2	2
1969	Glasgow (WC)	1	1
1969	Hamburg (WC)	2	3
1973	Glasgow	1	1
1974	Frankfurt	1	2
1986	Queretaro (WC)	1	2
1992	Norrkoping (EC)	0	2
1993	Glasgow	0	1
1999	Bremen	1	0
2003	Glasgow (EC)	1	1
2003	Dortmund (EC)	1	2

v GREECE

		S	G
1994	Athens (EC)	0	1
1995	Glasgow	1	0

v HOLLAND

		S	H
1929	Amsterdam	2	0
1938	Amsterdam	3	1
1959	Amsterdam	2	1
1966	Glasgow	0	3
1968	Amsterdam	0	0
1971	Amsterdam	1	2
1978	Mendoza (WC)	3	2
1982	Glasgow	2	1
1986	Eindhoven	0	0
1992	Gothenburg (EC)	0	1
1994	Glasgow	0	1
1994	Utrecht	1	3
1996	Birmingham (EC)	0	0
2000	Arnhem	0	0
2003*	Glasgow (EC)	1	0
2003*	Amsterdam (EC)	0	6
2009	Amsterdam (WC)	0	3
2009	Glasgow (WC)	0	1
(*Qual Round play-off)			

v HUNGARY

		S	H
1938	Glasgow	3	1
1955	Glasgow	2	4
1955	Budapest	1	3
1958	Glasgow	1	1
1960	Budapest	3	3
1980	Budapest	1	3
1987	Glasgow	2	0
2004	Glasgow	0	3

v ICELAND

		S	I
1984	Glasgow (WC)	3	0
1985	Reykjavik (WC)	1	0
2002	Reykjavik (EC)	2	0
2003	Glasgow (EC)	2	1
2008	Reykjavik (WC)	2	1
2009	Glasgow (WC)	2	1

v IRAN

		S	I
1978	Cordoba (WC)	1	1

v ISRAEL

		S	I
1981	Tel Aviv (WC)	1	0
1981	Glasgow (WC)	3	1
1986	Tel Aviv	1	0

v ITALY

		S	I
1931	Rome	0	3
1965	Glasgow (WC)	1	0
1965	Naples (WC)	0	3
1988	Perugia	0	2
1992	Glasgow (WC)	0	0
1993	Rome (WC)	1	3
2005	Milan (WC)	0	2
2005	Glasgow (WC)	1	1
2007	Bari (EC)	0	2
2007	Glasgow (EC)	1	2

v JAPAN

		S	J
1995	Hiroshima	0	0
2006	Saitama	0	0
2009	Yokohama	0	2

v LATVIA

		S	L
1996	Riga (WC)	2	0
1997	Glasgow (WC)	2	0
2000	Riga (WC)	1	0
2001	Glasgow (WC)	2	1

v LIECHTENSTEIN

		S	L
2010	Glasgow (EC)	2	1
2011	Vaduz (EC)	1	0

v LITHUANIA

		S	L
1998	Vilnius (EC)	0	0
1999	Glasgow (EC)	3	0
2003	Kaunus (EC)	0	1
2003	Glasgow (EC)	1	0
2006	Kaunas (EC)	2	1
2007	Glasgow (EC)	3	1
2010	Kaunas (EC)	0	0
2011	Glasgow (EC)	1	0

v LUXEMBOURG

		S	L
1947	Luxembourg	6	0
1986	Glasgow (EC)	3	0
1987	Esch (EC)	0	0

v MACEDONIA

		S	M
2008	Skopje (WC)	0	1
2009	Glasgow (WC)	2	0

v MALTA

		S	M
1988	Valletta	1	1
1990	Valletta	2	1
1993	Glasgow (WC)	3	0
1993	Valletta (WC)	2	0
1997	Valletta	3	2

v MOLDOVA

		S	M
2004	Chisinau (WC)	1	1
2005	Glasgow (WC)	2	0

v MOROCCO

		S	M
1998	St Etienne (WC)	0	3

v NEW ZEALAND

		S	NZ
1982	Malaga (WC)	5	2
2003	Edinburgh	1	1

v NIGERIA

		S	N
2002	Aberdeen	1	2

v NORWAY

		S	N
1929	Bergen	7	3
1954	Glasgow	1	0
1954	Oslo	1	1
1963	Bergen	3	4
1963	Glasgow	6	1
1974	Oslo	2	1
1978	Glasgow (EC)	3	2
1979	Oslo (EC)	4	0
1988	Oslo (WC)	2	1
1989	Glasgow (WC)	1	1
1992	Oslo	0	0
1998	Bordeaux (WC)	1	1
2003	Oslo	0	0
2004	Glasgow (WC)	0	1
2005	Oslo (WC)	2	1
2008	Glasgow (WC)	0	0
2009	Oslo (WC)	0	4

v PARAGUAY

		S	P
1958	Norrkoping (WC)	2	3

v PERU

		S	P
1972	Glasgow	2	0
1978	Cordoba (WC)	1	3
1979	Glasgow	1	1

v POLAND

		S	P
1958	Warsaw	2	1
1960	Glasgow	2	3
1965	Chorzow (WC)	1	1
1965	Glasgow (WC)	1	2
1980	Poznan	0	1
1990	Glasgow	1	1
2001	Bydgoszcz	1	1

v PORTUGAL

		S	P
1950	Lisbon	2	2
1955	Glasgow	3	0
1959	Lisbon	0	1
1966	Glasgow	0	1
1971	Lisbon (EC)	0	2
1971	Glasgow (EC)	2	1
1975	Glasgow	1	0
1978	Lisbon (EC)	0	1
1980	Glasgow (EC)	4	1
1980	Glasgow (WC)	0	0
1981	Lisbon (WC)	1	2
1992	Glasgow (WC)	0	0
1993	Lisbon (WC)	0	5
2002	Braga	0	2

v REPUBLIC OF IRELAND

		S	RoI
1961	Glasgow (WC)	4	1
1961	Dublin (WC)	3	0
1963	Dublin	0	1
1969	Dublin	1	1
1986	Dublin (EC)	0	0
1987	Glasgow (EC)	0	1
2000	Dublin	2	1
2003	Glasgow (EC)	0	2
2011	Dublin (CC)	0	1

v ROMANIA

		S	R
1975	Bucharest (EC)	1	1
1975	Glasgow (EC)	1	1

1986	Glasgow	3	0
1990	Glasgow (EC)	2	1
1991	Bucharest (EC)	0	1
2004	Glasgow	1	2

v RUSSIA

		S	R
1994	Glasgow (EC)	1	1
1995	Moscow (EC)	0	0

v SAN MARINO

		S	SM
1991	Serravalle (EC)	2	0
1991	Glasgow (EC)	4	0
1995	Serravalle (EC)	2	0
1995	Glasgow (EC)	5	0
2000	Serravalle (WC)	2	0
2001	Glasgow (WC)	4	0

v SAUDI ARABIA

		S	SA
1988	Riyadh	2	2

v SLOVENIA

		S	SL
2004	Glasgow (WC)	0	0
2005	Celje (WC)	3	0
2012	Koper	1	1

v SOUTH AFRICA

		S	SA
2002	Hong Kong	0	2
2007	Aberdeen	1	0

v SOUTH KOREA

		S	SK
2002	Busan	1	4

v SOVIET UNION (see also CIS and RUSSIA)

		S	SU
1967	Glasgow	0	2
1971	Moscow	0	1
1982	Malaga (WC)	2	2
1991	Glasgow	0	1

v SPAIN

		S	Sp
1957	Glasgow (WC)	4	2
1957	Madrid (WC)	1	4
1963	Madrid	6	2
1965	Glasgow	0	0
1975	Glasgow (EC)	1	2
1975	Valencia (EC)	1	1
1982	Valencia	0	3
1985	Glasgow (WC)	3	1
1985	Seville (WC)	0	1
1988	Madrid	0	0
2004*	Valencia	1	1
(*Abandoned after 59 mins – floodlight failure)			
2010	Glasgow (EC)	2	3
2011	Alicante (EC)	1	3

v SWEDEN

		S	Swe
1952	Stockholm	1	3
1953	Glasgow	1	2
1975	Gothenburg	1	1
1977	Glasgow	3	1
1980	Stockholm (WC)	1	0

1981	Glasgow (WC)	2	0
1990	Genoa (WC)	2	1
1995	Solna	0	2
1996	Glasgow (WC)	1	0
1997	Gothenburg (WC)	1	2
2004	Edinburgh	1	4
2010	Stockholm	0	3

v SWITZERLAND

		S	Sw
1931	Geneva	3	2
1948	Berne	1	2
1950	Glasgow	3	1
1957	Basle (WC)	2	1
1957	Glasgow (WC)	3	2
1973	Berne	0	1
1976	Glasgow	1	0
1982	Berne (EC)	0	2
1983	Glasgow (EC)	2	2
1990	Glasgow (EC)	2	1
1991	Berne (EC)	2	2
1992	Berne (WC)	1	3
1993	Aberdeen (WC)	1	1
1996	Birmingham (EC)	1	0
2006	Glasgow	1	3

v TRINIDAD & TOBAGO

		S	T
2004	Hibernian	4	1

v TURKEY

		S	T
1960	Ankara	2	4

v UKRAINE

		S	U
2006	Kiev (EC)	0	2
2007	Glasgow (EC)	3	1

v USA

		S	USA
1952	Glasgow	6	0
1992	Denver	1	0
1996	New Britain, Conn	1	2
1998	Washington	0	0
2005	Glasgow	1	1
2012	Jacksonville	1-5	

v URUGUAY

		S	U
1954	Basle (WC)	0	7
1962	Glasgow	2	3
1983	Glasgow	2	0
1986	Neza (WC)	0	0

v YUGOSLAVIA

		S	Y
1955	Belgrade	2	2
1956	Glasgow	2	0
1958	Vaasteras (WC)	1	1
1972	Belo Horizonte	2	2
1974	Frankfurt (WC)	1	1
1984	Glasgow	6	1
1988	Glasgow (WC)	1	1
1989	Zagreb (WC)	1	3

v ZAIRE

		S	Z
1974	Dortmund (WC)	2	0

WALES

v ALBANIA

		W	A
1994	Cardiff (EC)	2	0
1995	Tirana (EC)	1	1

v ARGENTINA

		W	A
1992	Gifu (Japan)	0	1
2002	Cardiff	1	1

v ARMENIA

		W	A
2001	Yerevan (WC)	2	2
2001	Cardiff (WC)	0	0

v AUSTRALIA

		W	A
2011	Cardiff	1	2

v AUSTRIA

		W	A
1954	Vienna	0	2
1955	Wrexham	1	2
1975	Vienna (EC)	1	2
1975	Wrexham (EC)	1	0
1992	Vienna	1	1
2005	Cardiff	0	2
2005	Vienna	0	1

v AZERBAIJAN

		W	A
2002	Baku (EC)	2	0
2003	Cardiff (EC)	4	0
2004	Baku (WC)	1	1
2005	Cardiff (WC)	2	0
2008	Cardiff (WC)	1	0
2009	Baku (WC)	1	0

v BELARUS

		W	B
1998	Cardiff (EC)	3	2
1999	Minsk (EC)	2	1
2000	Minsk (WC)	1	2
2001	Cardiff (WC)	1	0

v BELGIUM

		W	B
1949	Liege	1	3
1949	Cardiff	5	1
1990	Cardiff (EC)	3	1
1991	Brussels (EC)	1	1
1992	Brussels (WC)	0	2
1993	Cardiff (WC)	2	0
1997	Cardiff (WC)	1	2
1997	Brussels (WC)	2	3

v BOSNIA-HERZEGOVINA

		W	B-H
2003	Cardiff	2	2

v BRAZIL

		W	B
1958	Gothenburg (WC)	0	1
1962	Rio de Janeiro	1	3
1962	Sao Paulo	1	3
1966	Rio de Janeiro	1	3
1966	Belo Horizonte	0	1
1983	Cardiff	1	1
1991	Cardiff	1	0
1997	Brasilia	0	3
2000	Cardiff	0	3
2006	White Hart Lane	0	2

v BULGARIA

		W	B
1983	Wrexham (EC)	1	0
1983	Sofia (EC)	0	1
1994	Cardiff (EC)	0	3
1995	Sofia (EC)	1	3
2006	Swansea	0	0
2007	Bourgas	1	0
2010	Cardiff (EC)	0	1
2011	Sofia (EC)	1	0

v CANADA

		W	C
1986	Toronto	0	2
1986	Vancouver	3	0
2004	Wrexham	1	0

v CHILE

		W	C
1966	Santiago	0	2

v COSTA RICA

		W	C
1990	Cardiff	1	0
2012	Cardiff	0	1

v CROATIA

		W	C
2002	Varazdin	1	1
2010	Osijek	0	2

v CYPRUS

		W	C
1992	Limassol (WC)	1	0
1993	Cardiff (WC)	2	0
2005	Limassol	0	1
2006	Cardiff (EC)	3	1
2007	Nicosia (EC)	1	3

v CZECHOSLOVAKIA (see also RCS)

		W	C
1957	Cardiff (WC)	1	0
1957	Prague (WC)	0	2
1971	Swansea (EC)	1	3
1971	Prague (EC)	0	1
1977	Wrexham (WC)	3	0
1977	Prague (WC)	0	1
1980	Cardiff (WC)	1	0
1981	Prague (WC)	0	2
1987	Wrexham (EC)	1	1
1987	Prague (EC)	0	2

v CZECH REPUBLIC

		W	CR
2002	Cardiff	0	0
2006	Teplice (EC)	1	2
2007	Cardiff (EC)	0	0

v DENMARK

Year	Venue	W	D
1964	Copenhagen (WC)	0	1
1965	Wrexham (WC)	4	2
1987	Cardiff (EC)	1	0
1987	Copenhagen (EC)	0	1
1990	Copenhagen	0	1
1998	Copenhagen (EC)	2	1
1999	Anfield (EC)	0	2
2008	Copenhagen	1	0

v EAST GERMANY

Year	Venue	W	EG
1957	Leipzig (WC)	1	2
1957	Cardiff (WC)	4	1
1969	Dresden (WC)	1	2
1969	Cardiff (WC)	1	3

v ESTONIA

Year	Venue	W	E
1994	Tallinn	2	1
2009	Llanelli	1	0

v FAROE ISLANDS

Year	Venue	W	FI
1992	Cardiff (WC)	6	0
1993	Toftir (WC)	3	0

v FINLAND

Year	Venue	W	F
1971	Helsinki (EC)	1	0
1971	Swansea (EC)	3	0
1986	Helsinki (EC)	1	1
1987	Wrexham (EC)	4	0
1988	Swansea (WC)	2	2
1989	Helsinki (WC)	0	1
2000	Cardiff	1	2
2002	Helsinki (EC)	2	0
2003	Cardiff (EC)	1	1
2009	Cardiff (WC)	0	2
2009	Helsinki (WC)	1	2

v FRANCE

Year	Venue	W	F
1933	Paris	1	1
1939	Paris	1	2
1953	Paris	1	6
1982	Toulouse	1	0

v GEORGIA

Year	Venue	W	G
1994	Tbilisi (EC)	0	5
1995	Cardiff (EC)	0	1
2008	Swansea	1	2

v GERMANY/WEST GERMANY

Year	Venue	W	G
1968	Cardiff	1	1
1969	Frankfurt	1	1
1977	Cardiff	0	2
1977	Dortmund	1	1
1979	Wrexham (EC)	0	2
1979	Cologne (EC)	1	5
1989	Cardiff (WC)	0	0
1989	Cologne (WC)	1	2
1991	Cardiff (EC)	1	0

v GREECE (continued)

Year	Venue	W	D/...
1991	Nuremberg (EC)	1	4
1995	Dusseldorf (EC)	1	1
1995	Cardiff (EC)	1	2
2002	Cardiff	1	0
2007	Cardiff (EC)	0	2
2007	Frankfurt (EC)	0	0
2008	Moenchengladbach (WC)	0	1
2009	Cardiff (WC)	0	2

v GREECE

Year	Venue	W	G
1964	Athens (WC)	0	2
1965	Cardiff (WC)	4	1

v HOLLAND

Year	Venue	W	H
1988	Amsterdam (WC)	0	1
1989	Wrexham (WC)	1	2
1992	Utrecht	0	4
1996	Cardiff (WC)	1	3
1996	Eindhoven (WC)	1	7
2008	Rotterdam	0	2

v HUNGARY

Year	Venue	W	H
1958	Sanviken (WC)	1	1
1958	Stockholm (WC)	2	1
1961	Budapest	2	3
1963	Budapest (EC)	1	3
1963	Cardiff (EC)	1	1
1974	Cardiff (EC)	2	0
1975	Budapest (EC)	2	1
1986	Cardiff	0	3
2004	Budapest	2	1
2005	Cardiff	2	0

v ICELAND

Year	Venue	W	I
1980	Reykjavik (WC)	4	0
1981	Swansea (WC)	2	2
1984	Reykjavik (WC)	0	1
1984	Cardiff (WC)	2	1
1991	Cardiff	1	0
2008	Reykjavik	1	0

v IRAN

Year	Venue	W	I
1978	Tehran	1	0

v ISRAEL

Year	Venue	W	I
1958	Tel Aviv (WC)	2	0
1958	Cardiff (WC)	2	0
1984	Tel Aviv	0	0
1989	Tel Aviv	3	3

v ITALY

Year	Venue	W	I
1965	Florence	1	4
1968	Cardiff (WC)	0	1
1969	Rome (WC)	1	4
1988	Brescia	1	0
1996	Terni	0	3
1998	Anfield (EC)	0	2
1999	Bologna (EC)	0	4
2002	Cardiff (EC)	2	1
2003	Milan (EC)	0	4

v JAMAICA

		W	J
1998	Cardiff	0	0

v JAPAN

		W	J
1992	Matsuyama	1	0

v KUWAIT

		W	K
1977	Wrexham	0	0
1977	Kuwait City	0	0

v LATVIA

		W	L
2004	Riga	2	0

v LIECHTENSTEIN

		W	L
2006	Wrexham	4	0
2008	Cardiff (WC)	2	0
2009	Vaduz (WC)	2	0

v LUXEMBOURG

		W	L
1974	Swansea (EC)	5	0
1975	Luxembourg (EC)	3	1
1990	Luxembourg (EC)	1	0
1991	Luxembourg (EC)	1	0
2008	Luxembourg	2	0
2010	Llanelli	5	1

v MALTA

		W	M
1978	Wrexham (EC)	7	0
1979	Valletta (EC)	2	0
1988	Valletta	3	2
1998	Valletta	3	0

v MEXICO

		W	M
1958	Stockholm (WC)	1	1
1962	Mexico City	1	2
2012	New York	0	2

v MOLDOVA

		W	M
1994	Kishinev (EC)	2	3
1995	Cardiff (EC)	1	0

v MONTENEGRO

		W	M
2009	Podgorica	1	2
2010	Podgorica (EC)	0	1
2011	Cardiff (EC)	2	1

v NEW ZEALAND

		W	NZ
2007	Wrexham	2	2

v NORWAY

		W	N
1982	Swansea (EC)	1	0
1983	Oslo (EC)	0	0
1984	Trondheim	0	1
1985	Wrexham	1	1
1985	Bergen	2	4
1994	Cardiff	1	3
2000	Cardiff (WC)	1	1
2001	Oslo (WC)	2	3

v PARAGUAY

		W	P
2004	Oslo	0	0
2008	Wrexham	3	0
2011	Cardiff	4	1
2006	Cardiff	0	0

v POLAND

		W	P
1973	Cardiff (WC)	2	0
1973	Katowice (WC)	0	3
1991	Radom	0	0
2000	Warsaw (WC)	0	0
2001	Cardiff (WC)	1	2
2004	Cardiff (WC)	2	3
2005	Warsaw (WC)	0	1
2009	Vila-Real (Por)	0	1

v PORTUGAL

		W	P
1949	Lisbon	2	3
1951	Cardiff	2	1
2000	Chaves	0	3

v QATAR

		W	Q
2000	Doha	1	0

v RCS (formerly Czechoslovakia)

		W	RCS
1993	Ostrava (WC)	1	1
1993	Cardiff (WC)	2	2

v REPUBLIC OF IRELAND

		W	RI
1960	Dublin	3	2
1979	Swansea	2	1
1981	Dublin	3	1
1986	Dublin	1	0
1990	Dublin	0	1
1991	Wrexham	0	3
1992	Dublin	1	0
1993	Dublin	1	2
1997	Cardiff	0	0
2007	Dublin (EC)	0	1
2007	Cardiff (EC)	2	2
2011	Dublin (CC)	0	3

v REST OF UNITED KINGDOM

		W	UK
1951	Cardiff	3	2
1969	Cardiff	0	1

v ROMANIA

		W	R
1970	Cardiff (EC)	0	0
1971	Bucharest (EC)	0	2
1983	Wrexham	5	0
1992	Bucharest (WC)	1	5
1993	Cardiff (WC)	1	2

v RUSSIA (See also Soviet Union)

		W	R
2003*	Moscow (EC)	0	0
2003*	Cardiff (EC)	0	1
2008	Moscow (WC)	1	2
2009	Cardiff (WC)	1	3

(*Qual Round play-offs)

v SAN MARINO

		W	SM
1996	Serravalle (WC)	5	0
1996	Cardiff (WC)	6	0
2007	Cardiff (EC)	3	0
2007	Serravalle (EC)	2	1

v SAUDI ARABIA

		W	SA
1986	Dahran	2	1

v SERBIA & MONTENEGRO

		W	S
2003	Belgrade (EC)	0	1
2003	Cardiff (EC)	2	3

v SLOVAKIA

		W	S
2006	Cardiff (EC)	1	5
2007	Trnava (EC)	5	2

v SLOVENIA

		W	S
2005	Swansea	0	0

v SOVIET UNION (See also Russia)

		W	SU
1965	Moscow (WC)	1	2
1965	Cardiff (WC)	2	1
1981	Wrexham (WC)	0	0
1981	Tbilisi (WC)	0	3
1987	Swansea	0	0

v SPAIN

		W	S
1961	Cardiff (WC)	1	2
1961	Madrid (WC)	1	1
1982	Valencia	1	1
1984	Seville (WC)	0	3
1985	Wrexham (WC)	3	0

v SWEDEN

		W	S
1958	Stockholm (WC)	0	0
1988	Stockholm	1	4
1989	Wrexham	0	2
1990	Stockholm	2	4
1994	Wrexham	0	2
2010	Swansea	0	1

v SWITZERLAND

		W	S
1949	Berne	0	4
1951	Wrexham	3	2
1996	Lugano	0	2
1999	Zurich (EC)	0	2
1999	Wrexham (EC)	0	2
2010	Basle (EC)	1	4
2011	Swansea (EC)	2	0

v TRINIDAD & TOBAGO

		W	T
2006	Graz	2	1

v TUNISIA

		W	T
1998	Tunis	0	4

v TURKEY

		W	T
1978	Wrexham (EC)	1	0
1979	Izmir (EC)	0	1
1980	Cardiff (WC)	4	0
1981	Ankara (WC)	1	0
1996	Cardiff (WC)	0	0
1997	Istanbul (WC)	4	6

v UKRAINE

		W	U
2001	Cardiff (WC)	1	1
2001	Kiev (WC)	1	1

v URUGUAY

		W	U
1986	Wrexham	0	0

v USA

		W	USA
2003	San Jose	0	2

v YUGOSLAVIA

		W	Y
1953	Belgrade	2	5
1954	Cardiff	1	3
1976	Zagreb (EC)	0	2
1976	Cardiff (EC)	1	1
1982	Titograd (EC)	4	4
1983	Cardiff (EC)	1	1
1988	Swansea	1	2

NORTHERN IRELAND

v ALBANIA

		NI	A
1965	Belfast (WC)	4	1
1965	Tirana (WC)	1	1
1983	Tirana (EC)	0	0
1983	Belfast (EC)	1	0
1992	Belfast (WC)	3	0
1993	Tirana (WC)	2	1
1996	Belfast (WC)	2	0
1997	Zurich (WC)	0	1
2010	Tirana	0	1

v ALGERIA

		NI	A
1986	Guadalajara (WC)	1	1

v ARGENTINA

		NI	A
1958	Halmstad (WC)	1	3

v ARMENIA

		NI	A
1996	Belfast (WC)	1	1
1997	Yerevan (WC)	0	0
2003	Yerevan (EC)	0	1
2003	Belfast (EC)	0	1

v AUSTRALIA

		NI	A
1980	Sydney	2	1
1980	Melbourne	1	1
1980	Adelaide	2	1

v AUSTRIA

		NI	A
1982	Madrid (WC)	2	2
1982	Vienna (EC)	0	2
1983	Belfast (EC)	3	1
1990	Vienna (EC)	0	0
1991	Belfast (EC)	2	1
1994	Vienna (EC)	2	1
1995	Belfast (EC)	5	3
2004	Belfast (WC)	3	3
2005	Vienna (EC)	0	2

v AZERBAIJAN

		NI	A
2004	Baku (WC)	0	0
2005	Belfast (WC)	2	0

v BARBADOS

		NI	B
2004	Bridgetown	1	1

v BELGIUM

		NI	B
1976	Liege (WC)	0	2
1977	Belfast (WC)	3	0
1997	Belfast	3	0

v BRAZIL

		NI	B
1986	Guadalajara (WC)	0	3

v BULGARIA

		NI	B
1972	Sofia (WC)	0	3
1973	Sheffield (WC)	0	0
1978	Sofia (EC)	2	0
1979	Belfast (EC)	2	0
2001	Sofia (WC)	3	4
2001	Belfast (WC)	0	1
2008	Belfast	0	1

v CANADA

		NI	C
1995	Edmonton	0	2
1999	Belfast	1	1
2005	Belfast	0	1

v CHILE

		NI	C
1989	Belfast	0	1
1995	Edmonton, Canada	0	2
2010	Chillan	0	1

v COLOMBIA

		NI	C
1994	Boston, USA	0	2

v CYPRUS

		NI	C
1971	Nicosia (EC)	3	0
1971	Belfast (EC)	5	0
1973	Nicosia (WC)	0	1
1973	Fulham (WC)	3	0
2002	Belfast	0	0

v CZECHOSLOVAKIA/CZECH REP

		NI	C
1958	Halmstad (WC)	1	0
1958	Malmo (WC)	2	1

v DENMARK

		NI	D
1978	Belfast (EC)	2	1
1979	Copenhagen (EC)	0	4
1986	Belfast	1	1
1990	Belfast (EC)	1	1
1991	Odense (EC)	1	2
1992	Belfast (WC)	0	1
1993	Copenhagen (WC)	0	1
2000	Belfast (WC)	1	1
2001	Copenhagen (WC)	1	1
2006	Copenhagen (EC)	0	0
2007	Belfast (EC)	2	1

v ESTONIA

		NI	E
2004	Tallinn	1	0
2006	Belfast	1	0
2011	Tallinn (EC)	1	4
2011	Belfast (EC)	1	2

v FAROE ISLANDS

		NI	FI
1991	Belfast (EC)	1	1
1991	Landskrona, Sw (EC)	5	0
2010	Toftir (EC)	1	1
2011	Belfast (EC)	4	0

v FINLAND

		NI	F
1984	Pori (WC)	0	1
1984	Belfast (WC)	2	1
1998	Belfast (EC)	1	0
1999	Helsinki (EC)	1	4
2003	Belfast	0	1
2006	Helsinki	2	1

v FRANCE

		NI	F
1951	Belfast	2	2
1952	Paris	1	3
1958	Norrkoping (WC)	0	4
1982	Paris	0	4
1982	Madrid (WC)	1	4
1986	Paris	0	0
1988	Belfast	0	0
1999	Belfast	0	1

v GEORGIA

		NI	G
2008	Belfast	4	1

v GERMANY/WEST GERMANY

		NI	G
1958	Malmo (WC)	2	2
1960	Belfast (WC)	3	4
1961	Berlin (WC)	1	2
1966	Belfast	0	2
1977	Cologne	0	5
1982	Belfast (EC)	1	0
1983	Hamburg (EC)	1	0
1992	Bremen	1	1
1996	Belfast	1	1

1997	Nuremberg (WC)	1	1
1997	Belfast (WC)	1	3
1999	Belfast (EC)	0	3
1999	Dortmund (EC)	0	4
2005	Belfast	1	4

v GREECE

		NI	G
1961	Athens (WC)	1	2
1961	Belfast (WC)	2	0
1988	Athens	2	3
2003	Belfast (EC)	0	2
2003	Athens (EC)	0	1

v HOLLAND

		NI	H
1962	Rotterdam	0	4
1965	Belfast (WC)	2	1
1965	Rotterdam (WC)	0	0
1976	Rotterdam (WC)	2	2
1977	Belfast (WC)	0	1
2012	Amsterdam	0	6

v HONDURAS

		NI	H
1982	Zaragoza (WC)	1	1

v HUNGARY

		NI	H
1988	Budapest (WC)	0	1
1989	Belfast (WC)	1	2
2000	Belfast	0	1
2008	Belfast	0	2

v ICELAND

		NI	I
1977	Reykjavik (WC)	0	1
1977	Belfast (WC)	2	0
2000	Reykjavik (WC)	0	1
2001	Belfast (WC)	3	0
2006	Belfast (EC)	0	3
2007	Reykjavik (EC)	1	2

v ISRAEL

		NI	I
1968	Jaffa	3	2
1976	Tel Aviv	1	1
1980	Tel Aviv (WC)	0	0
1981	Belfast (WC)	1	0
1984	Belfast	3	0
1987	Tel Aviv	1	1
2009	Belfast	1	1

v ITALY

		NI	I
1957	Rome (WC)	0	1
1957	Belfast	2	2
1958	Belfast (WC)	2	1
1961	Bologna	2	3
1997	Palermo	0	2
2003	Campobasso	0	2
2009	Pisa	0	3
2010	Belfast (EC)	0	0
2011	Pescara (EC)	0	3

v LATVIA

		NI	L
1993	Riga (WC)	2	1
1993	Belfast (WC)	2	0

1995	Riga (EC)	1	0
1995	Belfast (EC)	1	2
2006	Belfast (EC)	1	0
2007	Riga (EC)	0	1

v LIECHTENSTEIN

		NI	L
1994	Belfast (EC)	4	1
1995	Eschen (EC)	4	0
2002	Vaduz	0	0
2007	Vaduz (EC)	4	1
2007	Belfast (EC)	3	1

v LITHUANIA

		NI	L
1992	Belfast (WC)	2	2

v LUXEMBOURG

		NI	L
2000	Luxembourg	3	1

v MALTA

		NI	M
1988	Belfast (WC)	3	0
1989	Valletta (WC)	2	0
2000	Ta'Qali	3	0
2000	Belfast (WC)	1	0
2001	Valletta (WC)	1	0
2005	Valletta	1	1

v MEXICO

		NI	M
1966	Belfast	4	1
1994	Miami	0	3

v MOLDOVA

		NI	M
1998	Belfast (EC)	2	2
1999	Kishinev (EC)	0	0

v MONTENEGRO

		W	M
2010	Podgorica	0	2

v MOROCCO

		NI	M
1986	Belfast	2	1
2010	Belfast	1	1

v NORWAY

		NI	N
1974	Oslo (EC)	1	2
1975	Belfast (EC)	3	0
1990	Belfast	2	3
1996	Belfast	0	2
2001	Belfast	0	4
2004	Belfast	1	4
2012	Belfast	0	3

v POLAND

		NI	P
1962	Katowice (EC)	2	0
1962	Belfast (EC)	2	0
1988	Belfast	1	1
1991	Belfast	3	1
2002	Limassol (Cyprus)	1	4
2004	Belfast (WC)	0	3
2005	Warsaw (WC)	0	1
2009	Belfast (WC)	3	2
2009	Chorzow (WC)	1	1

v PORTUGAL

		NI	P
1957	Lisbon (WC)	1	1
1957	Belfast (WC)	3	0
1973	Coventry (WC)	1	1
1973	Lisbon (WC)	1	1
1980	Lisbon (WC)	0	1
1981	Belfast (WC)	1	0
1994	Belfast (EC)	1	2
1995	Oporto (EC)	1	1
1997	Belfast (WC)	0	0
1997	Lisbon (WC)	0	1
2005	Belfast	1	1

v REPUBLIC OF IRELAND

		NI	RI
1978	Dublin (EC)	0	0
1979	Belfast (EC)	1	0
1988	Belfast (WC)	0	0
1989	Dublin (WC)	0	3
1993	Dublin (WC)	0	3
1993	Belfast (WC)	1	1
1994	Belfast (EC)	0	4
1995	Dublin (EC)	1	1
1999	Dublin	1	0
2011	Dublin (CC)	0	5

v ROMANIA

		NI	R
1984	Belfast (WC)	3	2
1985	Bucharest (WC)	1	0
1994	Belfast	2	0
2006	Chicago	0	2

v SAN MARINO

		NI	SM
2008	Belfast (WC)	4	0
2009	Serravalle (WC)	3	0

v SERBIA & MONTENEGRO

		NI	S
2004	Belfast	1	1

v SERBIA

		NI	S
2009	Belfast	0	1
2011	Belgrade (EC)	1	2
2011	Belfast (EC)	0	1

v SLOVAKIA

		NI	S
1998	Belfast	1	0
2008	Bratislava (WC)	1	2
2009	Belfast (WC)	0	2

v SLOVENIA

		NI	S
2008	Maribor (WC)	0	2
2009	Belfast (WC)	1	0
2010	Maribor (EC)	1	0
2011	Belfast (EC)	0	0

v SOVIET UNION

		NI	SU
1969	Belfast (WC)	0	0
1969	Moscow (WC)	0	2
1971	Moscow (EC)	0	1
1971	Belfast (EC)	1	1

v SPAIN

		NI	S
1958	Madrid	2	6
1963	Bilbao	1	1
1963	Belfast	0	1
1970	Seville (EC)	0	3
1972	Hull (EC)	1	1
1982	Valencia (WC)	1	0
1985	Palma, Majorca	0	0
1986	Guadalajara (WC)	1	2
1988	Seville (WC)	0	4
1989	Belfast (WC)	0	2
1992	Belfast (WC)	0	0
1993	Seville (WC)	1	3
1998	Santander	1	4
2002	Belfast	0	5
2002	Albacete (EC)	0	3
2003	Belfast (EC)	0	0
2006	Belfast (EC)	3	2
2007	Las Palmas (EC)	0	1

v ST KITTS & NEVIS

		NI	SK
2004	Basseterre	2	0

v SWEDEN

		NI	S
1974	Solna (EC)	2	0
1975	Belfast (EC)	1	2
1980	Belfast (WC)	3	0
1981	Stockholm (WC)	0	1
1996	Belfast	1	2
2007	Belfast (EC)	2	1
2007	Stockholm (EC)	1	1

v SWITZERLAND

		NI	S
1964	Belfast (WC)	1	0
1964	Lausanne (WC)	1	2
1998	Belfast	1	0
2004	Zurich	0	0
2010	Basle (EC)	1	4

v THAILAND

		NI	T
1997	Bangkok	0	0

v TRINIDAD & TOBAGO

		NI	T
2004	Port of Spain	3	0

v TURKEY

		NI	T
1968	Belfast (WC)	4	1
1968	Istanbul (WC)	3	0
1983	Belfast (EC)	2	1
1983	Ankara (EC)	0	1
1985	Belfast (WC)	2	0
1985	Izmir (WC)	0	0
1986	Izmir (EC)	0	0
1987	Belfast (EC)	1	0
1998	Istanbul (EC)	0	3
1999	Belfast (EC)	0	3
2010	Connecticut	0	2

v UKRAINE

		NI	U
1996	Belfast (WC)	0	1

1997	Kiev (WC)	1	2
2002	Belfast (EC)	0	0
2003	Donetsk (EC)	0	0

v URUGUAY

		NI	U
1964	Belfast	3	0
1990	Belfast	1	0
2006	New Jersey	0	1

v YUGOSLAVIA

		NI	Y
1975	Belfast (EC)	1	0
1975	Belgrade (EC)	0	1
1982	Zaragoza (WC)	0	0
1987	Belfast (EC)	1	2
1987	Sarajevo (EC)	0	3
1990	Belfast (EC)	0	2
1991	Belgrade (EC)	1	4
2000	Belfast	1	2

REPUBLIC OF IRELAND

v ALBANIA

		RI	A
1992	Dublin (WC)	2	0
1993	Tirana (WC)	2	1
2003	Tirana (EC)	0	0
2003	Dublin (EC)	2	1

v ALGERIA

		RI	A
1982	Algiers	0	2
2010	Dublin	3	0

v ANDORRA

		RI	A
2001	Barcelona (WC)	3	0
2001	Dublin (WC)	3	1
2010	Dublin (EC)	3	1
2011	La Vella (EC)	2	0

v ARGENTINA

		RI	A
1951	Dublin	0	1
1979*	Dublin	0	0
1980	Dublin	0	1
1998	Dublin	0	2
2010	Dublin	0	1

(*Not regarded as full Int)

v ARMENIA

		RI	A
2010	Yerevan (EC)	1	0
2011	Dublin (EC)	2	1

v AUSTRALIA

		RI	A
2003	Dublin	2	1
2009	Limerick	0	3

v AUSTRIA

		RI	A
1952	Vienna	0	6
1953	Dublin	4	0
1958	Vienna	1	3
1962	Dublin	2	3
1963	Vienna (EC)	0	0
1963	Dublin (EC)	3	2
1966	Vienna	0	1
1968	Dublin	2	2
1971	Dublin (EC)	1	4
1971	Linz (EC)	0	6
1995	Dublin (EC)	1	3
1995	Vienna (EC)	1	3
2009	Limerick	0	3
2009	Limerick	0	3

v BELGIUM

		RI	B
1928	Liege	4	2
1929	Dublin	4	0
1930	Brussels	3	1
1934	Dublin (WC)	4	4
1949	Dublin	0	2
1950	Brussels	1	5
1965	Dublin	0	2
1966	Liege	3	2
1980	Dublin (WC)	1	1
1981	Brussels (WC)	0	1
1986	Brussels (EC)	2	2
1987	Dublin (EC)	0	0
1997*	Dublin (WC)	1	1
1997*	Brussels (WC)	1	2

(*World Cup play-off)

v BOLIVIA

		RI	B
1994	Dublin	1	0
1996	East Rutherford, NJ	3	0
2007	Boston	1	1

v BOSNIA HERZEGOVINA

		RI	B-H
2012	Dublin	1	0

v BRAZIL

		RI	B
1974	Rio de Janeiro	1	2
1982	Uberlandia	0	7
1987	Dublin	1	0
2004	Dublin	0	0
2008	Dublin	0	1
2010	Arsenal	0	2

v BULGARIA

		RI	B
1977	Sofia (WC)	1	2
1977	Dublin (WC)	0	0
1979	Sofia (EC)	0	1
1979	Dublin (EC)	3	0
1987	Sofia (EC)	1	2
1987	Dublin (EC)	2	0
2004	Dublin	1	1
2009	Dublin (WC)	1	1
2009	Sofia (WC)	1	1

v CAMEROON

		RI	C
2002	Niigata (WC)	1	1

v CANADA

		RI	C
2003	Dublin	3	0

v CHILE

		RI	C
1960	Dublin	2	0
1972	Recife	1	2
1974	Santiago	2	1
1982	Santiago	0	1
1991	Dublin	1	1
2006	Dublin	0	1

v CHINA

		RI	C
1984	Sapporo	1	0
2005	Dublin	1	0

v COLOMBIA

		RI	C
2008	Fulham	1	0

v CROATIA

		RI	C
1996	Dublin	2	2
1998	Dublin (EC)	2	0
1999	Zagreb (EC)	0	1
2001	Dublin	2	2
2004	Dublin	1	0
2011	Dublin	0	0
2012	Poznan (EC)	1	3

v CYPRUS

		RI	C
1980	Nicosia (WC)	3	2
1980	Dublin (WC)	6	0
2001	Nicosia (WC)	4	0
2001	Dublin (WC)	4	0
2004	Dublin (WC)	3	0
2005	Nicosia (WC)	1	0
2006	Nicosia (EC)	2	5
2007	Dublin (EC)	1	1
2008	Dublin (WC)	1	0
2009	Nicosia (WC)	2	1

v CZECHOSLOVAKIA/CZECH REP

		RI	C
1938	Prague	2	2
1959	Dublin (EC)	2	0
1959	Bratislava (EC)	0	4
1961	Dublin (WC)	1	3
1961	Prague (WC)	1	7
1967	Dublin (EC)	0	2
1967	Prague (EC)	2	1
1969	Dublin (WC)	1	2
1969	Prague (WC)	0	3
1979	Prague	1	4
1981	Dublin	3	1
1986	Reykjavik	1	0
1994	Dublin	1	3
1996	Prague	0	2
1998	Olomouc	1	2
2000	Dublin	3	2
2004	Dublin	2	1
2006	Dublin (EC)	1	1
2007	Prague (EC)	0	1
2012	Dublin	1	1

v DENMARK

		RI	D
1956	Dublin (WC)	2	1
1957	Copenhagen (WC)	2	0
1968*	Dublin (WC)	1	1
1969	Copenhagen (WC)	0	2
1969	Dublin (WC)	1	1
1978	Copenhagen (EC)	3	3
1979	Dublin (EC)	2	0
1984	Copenhagen (WC)	0	3
1985	Dublin (WC)	1	4
1992	Copenhagen (WC)	0	0
1993	Dublin (WC)	1	1
2002	Dublin	3	0

(*Abandoned after 51 mins – fog)

2007	Aarhus	4	0

v ECUADOR

		RI	E
1972	Natal	3	2
2007	New York	1	1

v EGYPT

		RI	E
1990	Palermo (WC)	0	0

v ESTONIA

		RI	E
2000	Dublin (WC)	2	0
2001	Tallinn (WC)	2	0
2011	Tallinn (EC)	4	0
2011	Dublin (EC)	1	1

v FAROE ISLANDS

		RI	F
2004	Dublin (WC)	2	0
2005	Torshavn (WC)	2	0

v FINLAND

		RI	F
1949	Dublin (WC)	3	0
1949	Helsinki (WC)	1	1
1990	Dublin	1	1
2000	Dublin	3	0
2002	Helsinki	3	0

v FRANCE

		RI	F
1937	Paris	2	0
1952	Dublin	1	1
1953	Dublin (WC)	3	5
1953	Paris (WC)	0	1
1972	Dublin (WC)	2	1
1973	Paris (WC)	1	1
1976	Paris (WC)	0	2
1977	Dublin (WC)	1	0
1980	Paris (WC)	0	2
1981	Dublin (WC)	3	2
1989	Dublin	0	0
2004	Paris (WC)	0	0
2005	Dublin (WC)	0	1
2009	Dublin (WC)	0	1
2009	Paris (WC)	1	1

v GEORGIA

		RI	G
2002	Tbilisi (EC)	2	1

2003	Dublin (EC)	2	0
2008	Mainz (WC)	2	1
2009	Dublin (WC)	2	1

v GERMANY/WEST GERMANY

		RI	G
1935	Dortmund	1	3
1936	Dublin	5	2
1939	Bremen	1	1
1951	Dublin	3	2
1952	Cologne	0	3
1955	Hamburg	1	2
1956	Dublin	3	0
1960	Dusseldorf	1	0
1966	Dublin	0	4
1970	Berlin	1	2
1975*	Dublin	1	0
1979	Dublin	1	3
1981	Bremen	0	3
1989	Dublin	1	1
1994	Hanover	2	0
2002	Ibaraki (WC)	1	1
2006	Stuttgart (EC)	0	1
2007	Dublin (EC)	0	0

(*v W Germany 'B')

v GREECE

		RI	G
2000	Dublin	0	1
2002	Athens	0	0

v HOLLAND

		RI	H
1932	Amsterdam	2	0
1934	Amsterdam	2	5
1935	Dublin	3	5
1955	Dublin	1	0
1956	Rotterdam	4	1
1980	Dublin (WC)	2	1
1981	Rotterdam (WC)	2	2
1982	Rotterdam (EC)	1	2
1983	Dublin (EC)	2	3
1988	Gelsenkirchen (EC)	0	1
1990	Palermo (WC)	1	1
1994	Tilburg	1	0
1994	Orlando (WC)	0	2
1995*	Liverpool (EC)	0	2
1996	Rotterdam	1	3

(*Qual Round play-off)

2000	Amsterdam (WC)	2	2
2001	Dublin (WC)	1	0
2004	Amsterdam	1	0
2006	Dublin	0	4

v HUNGARY

		RI	H
1934	Dublin	2	4
1936	Budapest	3	3
1936	Dublin	2	3
1939	Cork	2	2
1939	Budapest	2	2
1969	Dublin (WC)	1	2
1969	Budapest (WC)	0	4
1989	Budapest (WC)	0	0
1989	Dublin (WC)	2	0

1992	Gyor	2	1
2012	Budapest	0	0

v ICELAND

		RI	I
1962	Dublin (EC)	4	2
1962	Reykjavik (EC)	1	1
1982	Dublin (EC)	2	0
1983	Reykjavik (EC)	3	0
1986	Reykjavik	2	1
1996	Dublin (WC)	0	0
1997	Reykjavik (WC)	4	2

v IRAN

		RI	I
1972	Recife	2	1
2001*	Dublin (WC)	2	0
2001*	Tehran (WC)	0	1

(*Qual Round play-off)

v ISRAEL

		RI	I
1984	Tel Aviv	0	3
1985	Tel Aviv	0	0
1987	Dublin	5	0
2005	Tel Aviv (WC)	1	1
2005	Dublin (WC)	2	2

v ITALY

		RI	I
1926	Turin	0	3
1927	Dublin	1	2
1970	Florence (EC)	0	3
1971	Dublin (EC)	1	2
1985	Dublin	1	2
1990	Rome (WC)	0	1
1992	Boston, USA	0	2
1994	New York (WC)	1	0
2005	Dublin	1	2
2009	Bari (WC)	1	1
2009	Dublin (WC)	2	2
2012	Poznan (EC)	0	2

v JAMAICA

		RI	J
2004	Charlton	1	0

v LATVIA

		RI	L
1992	Dublin (WC)	4	0
1993	Riga (WC)	2	0
1994	Riga (EC)	3	0
1995	Dublin (EC)	2	1

v LIECHTENSTEIN

		RI	L
1994	Dublin (WC)	4	0
1995	Eschen (EC)	0	0
1996	Eschen (WC)	5	0
1997	Dublin (WC)	5	0

v LITHUANIA

		RI	L
1993	Vilnius (WC)	1	0
1993	Dublin (WC)	2	0
1997	Dublin (WC)	0	0
1997	Zalgiris (WC)	2	1

v LUXEMBOURG

		RI	L
1936	Luxembourg	5	1
1953	Dublin (WC)	4	0
1954	Luxembourg (WC)	1	0
1987	Luxembourg (EC)	2	0
1987	Luxembourg (EC)	2	1

v MACEDONIA

		RI	M
1996	Dublin (WC)	3	0
1997	Skopje (WC)	2	3
1999	Dublin (EC)	1	0
1999	Skopje (EC)	1	1
2011	Dublin (EC)	2	1
2011	Skopje (EC)	2	0

v MALTA

		RI	M
1983	Valletta (EC)	1	0
1983	Dublin (EC)	8	0
1989	Dublin (WC)	2	0
1989	Valletta (WC)	2	0
1990	Valletta	3	0
1998	Dublin (EC)	1	0
1999	Valletta (EC)	3	2

v MEXICO

		RI	M
1984	Dublin	0	0
1994	Orlando (WC)	1	2
1996	New Jersey	2	2
1998	Dublin	0	0
2000	Chicago	2	2

v MONTENEGRO

		RI	M
2008	Podgorica (WC)	0	0
2009	Dublin (WC)	0	0

v MOROCCO

		RI	M
1990	Dublin	1	0

v NIGERIA

		RI	N
2002	Dublin	1	2
2004	Charlton	0	3
2009	Fulham	1	1

v NORWAY

		RI	N
1937	Oslo (WC)	2	3
1937	Dublin (WC)	3	3
1950	Dublin	2	2
1951	Oslo	3	2
1954	Dublin	2	1
1955	Oslo	3	1
1960	Dublin	3	1
1964	Oslo	4	1
1973	Oslo	1	1
1976	Dublin	3	0
1978	Oslo	0	0
1984	Oslo (WC)	0	1
1985	Dublin (WC)	0	0
1988	Oslo	0	0
1994	New York (WC)	0	0
2003	Dublin	1	0
2008	Oslo	1	1
2010	Dublin	1	2

v PARAGUAY

		RI	P
1999	Dublin	2	0
2010	Dublin	2	1

v POLAND

		RI	P
1938	Warsaw	0	6
1938	Dublin	3	2
1958	Katowice	2	2
1958	Dublin	2	2
1964	Cracow	1	3
1964	Dublin	3	2
1968	Dublin	2	2
1968	Katowice	0	1
1970	Dublin	1	2
1970	Poznan	0	2
1973	Wroclaw	0	2
1973	Dublin	1	0
1976	Poznan	2	0
1977	Dublin	0	0
1978	Lodz	0	3
1981	Bydgoszcz	0	3
1984	Dublin	0	0
1986	Warsaw	0	1
1988	Dublin	3	1
1991	Dublin (EC)	0	0
1991	Poznan (EC)	3	3
2004	Bydgoszcz	0	0
2008	Dublin	2	3

v PORTUGAL

		RI	P
1946	Lisbon	1	3
1947	Dublin	0	2
1948	Lisbon	0	2
1949	Dublin	1	0
1972	Recife	1	2
1992	Boston, USA	2	0
1995	Dublin (EC)	1	0
1995	Lisbon (EC)	0	3
1996	Dublin	0	1
2000	Lisbon (WC)	1	1
2001	Dublin (WC)	1	1
2005	Dublin	1	0

v ROMANIA

		RI	R
1988	Dublin	2	0
1990*	Genoa	0	0
1997	Bucharest (WC)	0	1
1997	Dublin (WC)	1	1

(*Rep won 5-4 on pens)

v RUSSIA (See also Soviet Union)

		RI	R
1994	Dublin	0	0
1996	Dublin	0	2
2002	Dublin	2	0
2002	Moscow (EC)	2	4
2003	Dublin (EC)	1	1
2010	Dublin (EC)	2	3
2011	Moscow (EC)	0	0

v SAN MARINO

		RI	SM
2006	Dublin (EC)	5	0

| 2007 | Rimini (EC) | 2 | 1 |

v SAUDI ARABIA

		RI	SA
2002	Yokohama (WC)	3	0

v SERBIA

		RI	S
2008	Dublin	1	1

v SLOVAKIA

		RI	S
2007	Dublin (EC)	1	0
2007	Bratislava (EC)	2	2
2010	Zilina (EC)	1	1
2011	Dublin (EC)	0	0

v SOUTH AFRICA

		RI	SA
2000	New Jersey	2	1
2009	Limerick	1	0

v SOVIET UNION (See also Russia)

		RI	SU
1972	Dublin (WC)	1	2
1973	Moscow (WC)	0	1
1974	Dublin (EC)	3	0
1975	Kiev (EC)	1	2
1984	Dublin (WC)	1	0
1985	Moscow (WC)	0	2
1988	Hanover (EC)	1	1
1990	Dublin	1	0

v SPAIN

		RI	S
1931	Barcelona	1	1
1931	Dublin	0	5
1946	Madrid	1	0
1947	Dublin	3	2
1948	Barcelona	1	2
1949	Dublin	1	4
1952	Madrid	0	6
1955	Dublin	2	2
1964	Seville (EC)	1	5
1964	Dublin (EC)	0	2
1965	Dublin (WC)	1	0
1965	Seville (WC)	1	4
1965	Paris (WC)	0	1
1966	Dublin (EC)	0	0
1966	Valencia (EC)	0	2
1977	Dublin	0	1
1982	Dublin (EC)	3	3
1983	Zaragoza (EC)	0	2
1985	Cork	0	0
1988	Seville (WC)	0	2
1989	Dublin (WC)	1	0
1992	Seville (WC)	0	0
1993	Dublin (WC)	1	3
2002*	Suwon (WC)	1	1
(*Rep lost 3-2 on pens)			
2012	Gdansk (EC)	0	4

v SWEDEN

		RI	S
1949	Stockholm (WC)	1	3
1949	Dublin (WC)	1	3
1959	Dublin	3	2

1960	Malmo	1	4
1970	Dublin (EC)	1	1
1970	Malmo (EC)	0	1
1999	Dublin	2	0
2006	Dublin	3	0

v SWITZERLAND

		RI	S
1935	Basle	0	1
1936	Dublin	1	0
1937	Berne	1	0
1938	Dublin	4	0
1948	Dublin	0	1
1975	Dublin (EC)	2	1
1975	Berne (EC)	0	1
1980	Dublin	2	0
1985	Dublin (WC)	3	0
1985	Berne (WC)	0	0
1992	Dublin	2	1
2002	Dublin (EC)	1	2
2003	Basle (EC)	0	2
2004	Basle (WC)	1	1
2005	Dublin (WC)	0	0

v TRINIDAD & TOBAGO

		RI	T&T
1982	Port of Spain	1	2

v TUNISIA

		RI	T
1988	Dublin	4	0

v TURKEY

		RI	T
1966	Dublin (EC)	2	1
1967	Ankara (EC)	1	2
1974	Izmir (EC)	1	1
1975	Dublin (EC)	4	0
1976	Ankara	3	3
1978	Dublin	4	2
1990	Izmir	0	0
1990	Dublin (EC)	5	0
1991	Istanbul (EC)	3	1
1999	Dublin (EC)	1	1
1999	Bursa (EC)	0	0
2003	Dublin	2	2

v URUGUAY

		RI	U
1974	Montevideo	0	2
1986	Dublin	1	1
2011	Dublin	2	3

v USA

		RI	USA
1979	Dublin	3	2
1991	Boston	1	1
1992	Dublin	4	1
1992	Washington	1	3
1996	Boston	1	2
2000	Foxboro	1	1
2002	Dublin	2	1

v YUGOSLAVIA

		RI	Y
1955	Dublin	1	4
1988	Dublin	2	0
1998	Belgrade (EC)	0	1
1999	Dublin (EC)	2	1

BRITISH AND IRISH INTERNATIONAL APPEARANCES SINCE THE WAR (1946–2012)

(As at start of season 2012–13 In year shown 2012 = season 2011–12)
*Also a pre-war International player. Totals include appearances as substitute)

ENGLAND

Agbonlahor G (Aston Villa, 2009–10)	3
A'Court A (Liverpool, 1958–59)	5
Adams T (Arsenal, 1987–2001)	66
Allen A (Stoke, 1960)	3
Allen C (QPR, Tottenham, 1984–88)	5
Allen R (WBA, 1952–55)	5
Anderson S (Sunderland, 1962)	2
Anderson V (Nottm Forest, Arsenal, Manchester Utd, 1979–88)	30
Anderton D (Tottenham, 1994–2002)	30
Angus J (Burnley, 1961)	1
Armfield J (Blackpool, 1959–66)	43
Armstrong D (Middlesbrough, Southampton, 1980–4)	3
Armstrong K (Chelsea, 1955)	1
Ashton D (West Ham, 2008)	1
Astall G (Birmingham, 1956)	2
Astle J (WBA, 1969–70)	5
Aston J (Manchester Utd, 1949–51)	17
Atyeo J (Bristol City, 1956–57)	6
Bailey G (Manchester Utd, 1985)	2
Bailey M (Charlton, 1964–5)	2
Baily E (Tottenham, 1950–3)	9
Baines L (Everton, 2010–12)	8
Baker J (Hibs, Arsenal, 1960–6)	8
Ball A (Blackpool, Everton, Arsenal, 1965–75)	72
Ball M (Everton, 2001)	1
Banks G (Leicester, Stoke, 1963–72)	73
Banks T (Bolton, 1958–59)	6
Bardsley D (QPR, 1993)	2
Barham M (Norwich, 1983)	2
Barlow R (WBA, 1955)	1
Barmby N (Tottenham, Middlesbrough, Everton, Liverpool, 1995–2002)	23
Barnes J (Watford, Liverpool, 1983–96)	79
Barnes P (Manchester City, WBA, Leeds, 1978–82)	22
Barrass M (Bolton, 1952–53)	3
Barrett E (Oldham, Aston Villa, 1991–93)	3
Barry G (Aston Villa, Manchester City, 2000–12)	53
Barton J (Manchester City, 2007)	1
Barton W (Wimbledon, Newcastle, 1995)	3
Batty D (Leeds, Blackburn, Newcastle, Leeds, 1991–2000)	42
Baynham R (Luton, 1956)	3
Beardsley P (Newcastle, Liverpool, Newcastle, 1986–96)	59
Beasant D (Chelsea, 1990)	2
Beattie J (Southampton, 2003–04)	5
Beattie K (Ipswich, 1975–58)	9
Beckham D (Manchester Utd, Real Madrid, LA Galaxy, AC Milan 1997–2010)	115
Bell C (Manchester City, 1968–76)	48
Bent D (Charlton, Tottenham Sunderland, Aston Villa, 2006–12)	13
Bentley D (Blackburn, 2008–09)	7
Bentley R (Chelsea, 1949–55)	12
Berry J (Manchester Utd, 1953–56)	4
Birtles G (Nottm Forest, 1980–81)	3
Blissett L (Watford, AC Milan, 1983–84)	14
Blockley J (Arsenal, 1973)	1
Blunstone F (Chelsea, 1955–57)	5
Bonetti P (Chelsea, 1966–70)	7
Bothroyd J (Cardiff, 2011)	1
Bould S (Arsenal, 1994)	2
Bowles S (QPR, 1974–77)	5
Bowyer L (Leeds, 2003)	1
Boyer P (Norwich, 1976)	1
Brabrook P (Chelsea, 1958–60)	3
Bracewell P (Everton, 1985–86)	3
Bradford G (Bristol Rov, 1956)	1
Bradley W (Manchester Utd, 1959)	3
Bridge W (Southampton, Chelsea, Manchester City 2002–10)	36
Bridges B (Chelsea, 1965–66)	4
Broadbent P (Wolves, 1958–60)	7
Broadis I (Manchester City, Newcastle, 1952–54)	14
Brooking T (West Ham, 1974–82)	47
Brooks J (Tottenham, 1957)	3
Brown A (WBA, 1971)	1
Brown K (West Ham, 1960)	1
Brown W (Manchester Utd, 1999–2010)	23
Bull S (Wolves, 1989–91)	13
Butcher T (Ipswich, Rangers, 1980–90)	77
Butt N (Manchester Utd, Newcastle, 1997–2005)	39
Byrne G (Liverpool, 1963–66)	2
Byrne J (Crystal Palace, West Ham, 1962–65)	11
Byrne R (Manchester Utd, 1954–58)	33
Cahill G (Bolton, Chelsea 2011–12)	13
Callaghan I (Liverpool, 1966–78)	4
Campbell F (Sunderland, 2012)	1
Campbell S (Tottenham, Arsenal, Portsmouth, 1996–2008)	73
Carragher J (Liverpool, 1999–2010)	38
Carrick M (West Ham, Tottenham, Manchester Utd, 2001–10)	22
Carroll A (Newcastle, Liverpool 2011– 12)	7
Carson S (Liverpool, Aston Villa WBA, Bursaspor 2008–12)	4

Green R (Norwich, West Ham 2005–12) 12
Greenhoff B (Manchester Utd, Leeds, 1976–80) 18
Gregory J (QPR, 1983–84) 6
Guppy S (Leicester, 2000) 1

Hagan J (Sheffield Utd, 1949) 1
Haines A (WBA, 1949) 1
Hall J (Birmingham, 1956–57) 17
Hancocks J (Wolves, 1949–50) 3
Hardwick G (Middlesbrough, 1947–48) 13
Harford M (Luton, 1988–89) 2
Hargreaves O (Bayern Munich, Manchester Utd, 2002–08) 42
Harris G (Burnley, 1966) 1
Harris P (Portsmouth, 1950–54) 2
Hart J (Manchester City, 2010–12) 22
Harvey C (Everton, 1971) 1
Hassall H (Huddersfield, Bolton, 1951–54) 5
Hateley M (Portsmouth, AC Milan, Monaco, Rangers, 1984–92) 32
Haynes J (Fulham, 1955–62) 56
Hector K (Derby, 1974) 2
Hellawell M (Birmingham, 1963) 2
Henderson J (Sunderland, Liverpool 2011–12) 5
Hendrie L (Aston Villa, 1999) 1
Henry R (Tottenham, 1963) 1
Heskey E (Leicester, Liverpool, Birmingham, Wigan, Aston Villa 1999–2010) 62
Hill F (Bolton, 1963) 2
Hill G (Manchester Utd, 1976–78) 6
Hill R (Luton, 1983–86) 3
Hinchcliffe A (Everton, Sheffield Wed, 1997–99) 7
Hinton A (Wolves, Nottm Forest, 1963–65) 3
Hirst D (Sheffield Wed, 1991–92) 3
Hitchens G (Aston Villa, Inter Milan, 1961–62) 7
Hoddle G (Tottenham, Monaco, 1980–88) 53
Hodge S (Aston Villa, Tottenham, Nottm Forest, 1986–91) 24
Hodgkinson A (Sheffield Utd, 1957–61) 5
Holden D (Bolton, 1959) 5
Holliday E (Middlesbrough, 1960) 3
Hollins J (Chelsea, 1967) 1
Hopkinson E (Bolton, 1958–60) 14
Howe D (WBA, 1958–60) 23
Howe J (Derby, 1948–49) 3
Howey S (Newcastle, 1995–96) 4
Huddlestone T (Tottenham, 2010) 3
Hudson A (Stoke, 1975) 2
Hughes E (Liverpool, Wolves, 1970–80) 62
Hughes L (Liverpool, 1950) 3
Hunt R (Liverpool, 1962–69) 34
Hunt S (WBA, 1984) 2
Hunter N (Leeds, 1966–75) 28
Hurst G (West Ham, 1966–72) 49

Ince P (Manchester Utd, Inter Milan, Liverpool, Middlesbrough, 1993–2000) 53

Jagielka P (Everton, 2008–12) 12
James D (Liverpool, Aston Villa, West Ham, Manchester City, Portsmouth, 1997–2010) 53
Jarvis M (Wolves, 2011) 1
Jeffers F (Arsenal, 2003) 1
Jenas J (Newcastle, Tottenham, 2003–10) 21
Jezzard B (Fulham, 1954–56) 2
Johnson A (Crystal Palace, Everton, 2005–08) 8
Johnson A (Manchester City, 2010–12) 11
Johnson D (Ipswich, Liverpool, 1975–80) 8
Johnson G (Chelsea, Portsmouth, Liverpool, 2004–12) 40
Johnson S (Derby, 2001) 1
Johnston H (Blackpool, 1947–54) 10
Jones M (Leeds, Sheffield Utd, 1965–70) 3
Jones P (Manchester Utd, 2012) 5
Jones R (Liverpool, 1992–95) 8
Jones W H (Liverpool, 1950) 2

Kay A (Everton, 1963) 1
Keegan K (Liverpool, Hamburg, Southampton, 1973–82) 63
Kelly, M (Liverpool, 2012) 1
Kennedy A (Liverpool, 1984) 2
Kennedy R (Liverpool, 1976–80) 17
Keown M (Everton, Arsenal, 1992–2002) 43
Kevan D (WBA, 1957–61) 14
Kidd B (Manchester Utd, 1970) 2
King L (Tottenham, 2002–10) 21
Kirkland C (Liverpool, 2007) 1
Knight Z (Fulham, 2005) 2
Knowles C (Tottenham, 1968) 4
Konchesky P (Charlton, 2003–06) 2

Labone B (Everton, 1963–70) 26
Lampard F Snr (West Ham, 1973–80) 2
Lampard F Jnr (West Ham, Chelsea, 2000–12) 90
Langley J (Fulham, 1958) 3
Langton R (Blackburn, Preston, Bolton, 1947–51) 11
Latchford R (Everton, 1978–9) 12
Lawler C (Liverpool, 1971–72) 4
*Lawton T (Chelsea, Notts Co, 1947–49) 15
Lee F (Manchester City, 1969–72) 27
Lee J (Derby, 1951) 1
Lee R (Newcastle, 1995–99) 21
Lee S (Liverpool, 1983–84) 14
Lennon A (Tottenham, 2006–10) 19
Le Saux G (Blackburn, Chelsea, 1994–2001) 36
Lescott J (Everton, Manchester City, 2008–12) 20
Le Tissier M (Southampton, 1994–97) 8
Lindsay A (Liverpool, 1974) 4
Lineker G (Leicester, Everton, Barcelona, Tottenham, 1985–92) 80
Little B (Aston Villa, 1975) 1
Lloyd L (Liverpool, Nottm Forest, 1971–80) 4
Lofthouse N (Bolton, 1951–59) 33
Lowe E (Aston Villa, 1947) 3

Mabbutt G (Tottenham, 1983–92)	16
Macdonald M (Newcastle, 1972–76)	14
Madeley P (Leeds, 1971–77)	24
Mannion W (Middlesbrough, 1947–52)	26
Mariner P (Ipswich, Arsenal, 1977–85)	35
Marsh R (QPR, Manchester City, 1972–73)	9
Martin A (West Ham, 1981–87)	17
Martyn N (Crystal Palace, Leeds, 1992–2002)	23
Marwood B (Arsenal, 1989)	1
Matthews R (Coventry, 1956–57)	5
*Matthews S (Stoke, Blackpool, 1947–57)	37
McCann G (Sunderland, 2001)	1
McDermott T (Liverpool, 1978–82)	25
McDonald C (Burnley, 1958–59)	8
McFarland R (Derby, 1971–77)	28
McGarry W (Huddersfield, 1954–56)	4
McGuinness W (Manchester Utd, 1959)	2
McMahon S (Liverpool, 1988–91)	17
McManaman S (Liverpool, Real Madrid, 1995–2002)	37
McNab R (Arsenal, 1969)	4
McNeil M (Middlesbrough, 1961–62)	9
Meadows J (Manchester City, 1955)	1
Medley L (Tottenham, 1951–52)	6
Melia J (Liverpool, 1963)	2
Merrick G (Birmingham, 1952–54)	23
Merson P (Arsenal, Middlesbrough, Aston Villa, 1992–99)	21
Metcalfe V (Huddersfield, 1951)	2
Milburn J (Newcastle, 1949–56)	13
Miller B (Burnley, 1961)	1
Mills D (Leeds, 2001–04)	19
Mills M (Ipswich, 1973–82)	42
Milne G (Liverpool, 1963–65)	14
Milner J (Aston Villa, Manchester City, 2010–12)	30
Milton A (Arsenal, 1952)	1
Moore R (West Ham, 1962–74)	108
Morley A (Aston Villa, 1982–83)	6
Morris J (Derby, 1949–50)	3
Mortensen S (Blackpool, 1947–54)	25
Mozley B (Derby, 1950)	3
Mullen J (Wolves, 1947–54)	12
Mullery A (Tottenham, 1965–72)	35
Murphy D (Liverpool, 2002–04)	9
Neal P (Liverpool, 1976–84)	50
Neville G (Manchester Utd, 1995–2009)	85
Neville P (Manchester Utd, Everton, 1996–2008)	59
Newton K (Blackburn, Everton, 1966–70)	27
Nicholls J (WBA, 1954)	2
Nicholson W (Tottenham, 1951)	1
Nish D (Derby, 1973–74)	5
Norman M (Tottenham, 1962–5)	23
Nugent D (Preston, 2007)	1
O'Grady M (Huddersfield, Leeds, 1963–9)	2
Osgood P (Chelsea, 1970–74)	4
Osman R (Ipswich, 1980–84)	11

Owen M (Liverpool, Real Madrid, Newcastle, 1998–2008)	89
Owen S (Luton, 1954)	3
Oxlade-Chamberlain A (Arsenal, 2012)	5
Paine T (Southampton, 1963–66)	19
Pallister G (Middlesbrough, Manchester Utd 1988–97)	22
Palmer C (Sheffield Wed, 1992–94)	18
Parker P (QPR, Manchester Utd, 1989–94)	19
Parker S (Charlton, Chelsea, Newcastle, West Ham, Tottenham 2004–12)	17
Parkes P (QPR, 1974)	1
Parlour R (Arsenal, 1999–2001)	10
Parry R (Bolton, 1960)	2
Peacock A (Middlesbrough, Leeds, 1962–66)	6
Pearce S (Nottm Forest, West Ham, 1987–2000)	78
Pearson Stan (Manchester Utd, 1948–52)	8
Pearson Stuart (Manchester Utd, 1976–78)	15
Pegg D (Manchester Utd, 1957)	1
Pejic M (Stoke, 1974)	4
Perry W (Blackpool, 1956)	3
Perryman S (Tottenham, 1982)	1
Peters M (West Ham, Tottenham, 1966–74)	67
Phelan M (Manchester Utd, 1990)	1
Phillips K (Sunderland, 1999–2002)	8
Phillips L (Portsmouth, 1952–55)	3
Pickering F (Everton, 1964–65)	3
Pickering N (Sunderland, 1983)	1
Pilkington B (Burnley, 1955)	1
Platt D (Aston Villa, Bari, Juventus, Sampdoria, Arsenal, 1990–96)	62
Pointer R (Burnley, 1962)	3
Powell C (Charlton, 2001–02)	5
Pye J (Wolves, 1950)	1
Quixall A (Sheffield Wed, 1954–55)	5
Radford J (Arsenal, 1969–72)	2
Ramsey A (Southampton, Tottenham, 1949–54)	32
Reaney P (Leeds, 1969–71)	3
Redknapp J (Liverpool, 1996–2000)	17
Reeves K (Norwich, Manchester City, 1980)	2
Regis C (WBA, Coventry, 1982–88)	5
Reid P (Everton, 1985–88)	13
Revie D (Manchester City, 1955–57)	6
Richards J (Wolves, 1973)	1
Richards M (Manchester City, 2007–12)	13
Richardson K (Aston Villa, 1994)	1
Richardson K (Manchester Utd, 2005–07)	8
Rickaby S (WBA, 1954)	1
Ricketts M (Bolton, 2002)	1
Rimmer J (Arsenal, 1976)	1
Ripley S (Blackburn, 1994–97)	2
Rix G (Arsenal, 1981–84)	17
Robb G (Tottenham, 1954)	1

Roberts G (Tottenham, 1983–84) 6
Robinson P (Leeds, Tottenham, 2003–08) 41
Robson B (WBA, Manchester Utd, 1980–92) 90
Robson R (WBA, 1958–62) 20
Rocastle D (Arsenal, 1989–92) 14
Rodwell, J (Everton, 2012) 2
Rooney W (Everton, Manchester Utd, 2003–12) 76
Rowley J (Manchester Utd, 1949–52) 6
Royle J (Everton, Manchester City, 1971–77) 6
Ruddock N (Liverpool, 1995) 1

Sadler D (Manchester Utd, 1968–71) 4
Salako J (Crystal Palace, 1991–92) 5
Sansom K (Crystal Palace, Arsenal, 1979–88) 86
Scales J (Liverpool, 1995) 3
Scholes P (Manchester Utd, 1997–2004) 66
Scott L (Arsenal, 1947–49) 17
Seaman D (QPR, Arsenal, 1989–2003) 75
Sewell J (Sheffield Wed, 1952–54) 6
Shackleton L (Sunderland, 1949–55) 5
Sharpe L (Manchester Utd, 1991–94) 8
Shaw G (Sheffield Utd, 1959–63) 5
Shearer A (Southampton, Blackburn, Newcastle, 1992–2000) 63
Shellito K (Chelsea, 1963) 1
Sheringham E (Tottenham, Manchester Utd, Tottenham, 1993–2002) 51
Sherwood T (Tottenham, 1999) 3
Shilton P (Leicester, Stoke, Nottm Forest, Southampton, Derby, 1971–90) 125
Shimwell E (Blackpool, 1949) 1
Shorey N (Reading, 2007) 2
Sillett P (Chelsea, 1955) 3
Sinclair T (West Ham, Manchester City, 2002–04) 12
Sinton A (QPR, Sheffield Wed, 1992–94) 12
Slater W (Wolves, 1955–60) 12
Smalling C (Manchester Utd, 2012) 3
Smith A (Arsenal, 1989–92) 13
Smith A (Leeds, Manchester Utd, Newcastle, 2001–08) 19
Smith L (Arsenal, 1951–53) 6
Smith R (Tottenham, 1961–64) 15
Smith T (Birmingham, 1960) 2
Smith T (Liverpool, 1971) 1
Southgate G (Aston Villa, Middlesbrough, 1996–2004) 57
Spink N (Aston Villa, 1983) 1
Springett R (Sheffield Wed, 1960–66) 33
Staniforth R (Huddersfield, 1954–55) 8
Statham D (WBA, 1983) 3
Stein B (Luton, 1984) 1
Stepney A (Manchester Utd, 1968) 1
Sterland M (Sheffield Wed, 1989) 1
Steven T (Everton, Rangers, Marseille, 1985–92) 36

Stevens G (Everton, Rangers, 1985–92) 46
Stevens G (Tottenham, 1985–86) 7
Stewart P (Tottenham, 1992) 3
Stiles N (Manchester Utd, 1965–70) 28
Stone S (Nottm Forest, 1996) 9
Storey P (Arsenal, 1971–73) 19
Storey–Moore I (Nottm Forest, 1970) 1
Streten B (Luton, 1950) 1
Sturridge D (Chelsea, 2012) 2
Summerbee M (Manchester City, 1968–73) 8
Sunderland, A (Arsenal, 1980) 1
Sutton C (Blackburn, 1997) 1
Swan P (Sheffield Wed, 1960–62) 19
Swift F (Manchester City, 1947–79) 19

Talbot B (Ipswich, Arsenal, 1977–80) 6
Tambling R (Chelsea, 1963–66) 3
Taylor E (Blackpool, 1954) 1
Taylor J (Fulham, 1951) 2
Taylor P (Liverpool, 1948) 3
Taylor P (Crystal Palace, 1976) 4
Taylor T (Manchester Utd, 1953–58) 19
Temple D (Everton, 1965) 1
Terry J (Chelsea, 2003–12) 77
Thomas D (QPR, 1975–76) 8
Thomas D (Coventry, 1983) 2
Thomas G (Crystal Palace, 1991–92) 9
Thomas M (Arsenal, 1989–90) 2
Thompson A (Celtic, 2004) 1
Thompson Peter (Liverpool, 1964–70) 16
Thompson Phil (Liverpool, 1976–83) 42
Thompson T (Aston Villa, Preston, 1952–57) 2
Thomson R (Wolves, 1964–65) 8
Todd C (Derby, 1972–77) 27
Towers A (Sunderland, 1978) 3
Tueart D (Manchester City, 1975–77) 6

Ufton D (Charlton, 1954) 1
Unsworth D (Everton, 1995) 1
Upson M (Birmingham, West Ham, 2003–10) 21

Vassell D (Aston Villa, 2002–04) 22
Venables T (Chelsea, 1965) 2
Venison B (Newcastle, 1995) 2
Viljoen C (Ipswich, 1975) 2
Viollet D (Manchester Utd, 1960) 2

Waddle C (Newcastle, Tottenham, Marseille, 1985–92) 62
Waiters A (Blackpool, 1964–65) 5
Walcott T (Arsenal, 2006–12) 28
Walker D (Nottm Forest, Sampdoria, Sheffield Wed, 1989–94) 59
Walker I (Tottenham, Leicester, 1996–2004) 4
Walker, K (Tottenham, 2012) 2
Wallace D (Southampton, 1986) 1
Walsh P (Luton, 1983–4) 5
Walters M (Rangers, 1991) 1

Ward P (Brighton, 1980) 1
Ward T (Derby, 1948) 2
Warnock S (Blackburn, Aston Villa, 2008–11) 2
Watson D (Sunderland, Manchester City,
Werder Bremen, Southampton,
Stoke, 1974–82) 65
Watson D (Norwich, Everton, 1984–8) 12
Watson W (Sunderland, 1950–1) 4
Webb N (Nottm Forest, Manchester
Utd, 1988–92) 26
Welbeck D (Manchester Utd, 2011) 9
Weller K (Leicester, 1974) 4
West G (Everton, 1969) 3
Wheeler J (Bolton, 1955) 1
White D (Manchester City, 1993) 1
Whitworth S (Leicester, 1975–76) 7
Whymark T (Ipswich, 1978) 1
Wignall F (Nottm Forest, 1965) 2
Wilcox J (Blackburn, Leeds, 1996–2000) 3
Wilkins R (Chelsea, Manchester Utd,
AC Milan, 1976–87) 84
Williams B (Wolves, 1949–56) 24
Williams S (Southampton, 1983–85) 6
Willis A (Tottenham, 1952) 1
Wilshaw D (Wolves, 1954–57) 12
Wilshere J (Arsenal, 2011) 5
Wilson R (Huddersfield, Everton,
1960–8) 63

Winterburn N (Arsenal, 1990–93) 2
Wise D (Chelsea, 1991–2001) 21
Withe P (Aston Villa, 1981–85) 11
Wood R (Manchester Utd, 1955–56) 3
Woodcock A (Nottm Forest, Cologne,
Arsenal, 1977–86) 42
Woodgate J (Leeds, Newcastle, Middlesbrough,
Tottenham, 1999–2008) 8
Woods C (Norwich, Rangers,
Sheffield Wed, 1984–93) 43
Worthington F (Leicester, 1974–75) 8
Wright I (Crystal Palace, Arsenal, West Ham,
1991–99) 33
Wright M (Southampton, Derby,
Liverpool, 1984–96) 45
Wright R (Ipswich, Arsenal, 2000–02) 2
Wright T (Everton, 1968–70) 11
Wright W (Wolves, 1947–59) 105
Wright-Phillips S (Manchester City,
Chelsea, Manchester City, 2005–11) 36

Young A (Aston Villa, Manchester Utd,
2008–12) 25
Young G (Sheffield Wed, 1965) 1
Young L (Charlton, 2005) 7

Zamora R (Fulham, 2011–12) 2

SCOTLAND

Adam C (Rangers, Blackpool, Liverpool
2007–12) 16
Aird J (Burnley, 1954) 4
Aitken G (East Fife, 1949–54) 8
Aitken R (Celtic, Newcastle, St Mirren,
1980–92) 57
Albiston A (Manchester Utd, 1982–6) 14
Alexander G (Preston, Burnley, 2002–10) 40
Alexander N (Cardiff, 2006) 3
Allan T (Dundee, 1974) 2
Anderson J (Leicester, 1954) 1
Anderson R (Aberdeen, Sunderland,
2003–08) 11
Archibald S (Aberdeen, Tottenham,
Barcelona, 1980–86) 27
Auld B (Celtic, 1959–60) 3

Baird H (Airdrie, 1956) 1
Baird S (Rangers, 1957–58) 7
Bannan B (Aston Villa, 2011–12) 11
Bannon E (Dundee Utd, 1980–86) 11
Bardsley P (Sunderland, 2011–12) 12
Barr D (Falkirk, 2009) 1
Bauld W (Hearts, 1950) 3
Baxter J (Rangers, Sunderland, 1961–68) 34
Beattie C (Celtic, WBA, 2006–08) 7
Bell C (Kilmarnock, 2011) 1
Bell W (Leeds, 1966) 2
Bernard P (Oldham, 1995) 2
Berra C (Hearts, Wolves, 2008–12) 20
Bett J (Rangers, Lokeren, Aberdeen, 1982–90) 26

Black E (Metz, 1988) 2
Black I (Southampton, 1948) 1
Blacklaw A (Burnley, 1963–66) 3
Blackley J (Hibs, 1974–77) 7
Blair J (Blackpool, 1947) 1
Blyth J (Coventry, 1978) 2
Bone J (Norwich, 1972–73) 2
Booth S (Aberdeen, Borussia Dortmund,
Twente Enschede 1993–2002) 22
Bowman D (Dundee Utd, 1992–94) 6
Boyd K (Rangers, Middlesbrough, 2006–11) 18
Boyd T (Motherwell, Chelsea, Celtic,
1991–2002) 72
Brand R (Rangers, 1961–62) 8
Brazil A (Ipswich, Tottenham, 1980–83) 13
Bremner D (Hibs, 1976) 1
Bremner W (Leeds, 1965–76) 54
Brennan F (Newcastle, 1947–54) 7
Broadfoot K (Rangers, 2009–11) 4
Brogan J (Celtic, 1971) 4
Brown A (East Fife, Blackpool, 1950–54) 13
Brown H (Partick, 1947) 3
Brown J (Sheffield Utd, 1975) 1
Brown R (Rangers, 1947–52) 3
Brown S (Hibs, Celtic, 2007–12) 28
Brown W (Dundee, Tottenham, 1958–66) 28
Brownlie J (Hibs, 1971–76) 7
Bryson C (Kilmarnock, 2011) 1
Buchan M (Aberdeen, Manchester Utd,
1972–8) 34
Buckley P (Aberdeen, 1954–55) 3

Burchill M (Celtic, 2000) 6
Burke C (Rangers, 2006) 2
Burley C (Chelsea, Celtic, Derby, 1995–2003) 46
Burley G (Ipswich, 1979–82) 11
Burns F (Manchester Utd, 1970) 1
Burns K (Birmingham, Nottm Forest, 1974–81) 20
Burns T (Celtic, 1981–88) 8

Calderwood C (Tottenham, Aston Villa, 1995–2000) 36
Caldow E (Rangers, 1957–63) 40
Caldwell G (Newcastle, Sunderland, Hibs, Wigan, 2002–12) 48
Caldwell S (Newcastle, Sunderland, Celtic, Wigan, 2001–11) 12
Callaghan T (Dunfermline, 1970) 2
Cameron C (Hearts, Wolves, 1999–2005) 28
Campbell R (Falkirk, Chelsea, 1947–50) 5
Campbell W (Morton, 1947–48) 5
Canero P (Leicester, 2004) 1
Carr W (Coventry, 1970–73) 6
Chalmers S (Celtic, 1965–67) 5
Clark J (Celtic, 1966–67) 4
Clark R (Aberdeen, 1968–73) 17
Clarke S (Chelsea, 1988–94) 6
Clarkson D (Motherwell, 2008–09) 2
Collins J (Hibs, Celtic, Monaco, Everton, 1988–2000) 58
Collins R (Celtic, Everton, Leeds, 1951–65) 31
Colquhoun E (Sheffield Utd, 1972–73) 9
Colquhoun J (Hearts, 1988) 2
Combe J (Hibs, 1948) 3
Commons K (Derby, Celtic, 2009–11) 9
Conn A (Hearts, 1956) 1
Conn A (Tottenham, 1975) 2
Connachan E (Dunfermline, 1962) 2
Connelly G (Celtic, 1974) 2
Connolly J (Everton, 1973) 1
Connor R (Dundee, Aberdeen, 1986–91) 4
Conway C (Dundee Utd, 2010–12) 3
Cooke C (Dundee, Chelsea, 1966–75) 16
Cooper D (Rangers, Motherwell, 1980–90) 22
Cormack P (Hibs, 1966–72) 9
Cowan J (Morton, 1948–52) 25
Cowie D (Dundee, 1953–58) 20
Cowie D (Watford, 2010–12) 10
Cox C (Hearts, 1948) 1
Cox S (Rangers, 1948–54) 25
Craig JP (Celtic, 1968) 1
Craig J (Celtic, 1977) 1
Craig T (Newcastle, 1976) 1
Crainey S (Celtic, Southampton, Blackpool, 2002–12) 12
Crawford S (Raith, Dunfermline, Plymouth Argyle, 1995–2005) 25

Crerand P (Celtic, Manchester Utd, 1961–66) 16
Cropley A (Hibs, 1972) 2
Cruickshank J (Hearts, 1964–76) 6
Cullen M (Luton, 1956) 1
Cumming J (Hearts, 1955–60) 9
Cummings W (Chelsea, 2002) 1
Cunningham W (Preston, 1954–55) 8
Curran H (Wolves, 1970–71) 5

Dailly C (Derby, Blackburn, West Ham, 1997–2008) 67
Dalglish K (Celtic, Liverpool, 1972–87) 102
Davidson C (Blackburn, Leicester, Preston, 1999–2010) 19
Davidson J (Partick, 1954–55) 8
Dawson A (Rangers, 1980–83) 5
Deans J (Celtic, 1975) 2
*Delaney J (Manchester Utd, 1947–48) 4
Devlin P (Birmingham, 2003–04) 10
Dick J (West Ham, 1959) 1
Dickov P (Manchester City, Leicester, Blackburn, 2001–05) 10
Dickson W (Kilmarnock, 1970–71) 5
Dobie S (WBA, 2002–03) 6
Docherty T (Preston, Arsenal, 1952–59) 25
Dodds D (Dundee Utd, 1984) 2
Dodds W (Aberdeen, Dundee Utd, Rangers, 1997–2002) 26
Donachie W (Manchester City, 1972–79) 35
Donnelly S (Celtic, 1997–99) 10
Dorrans G (WBA, 2010–12) 8
Dougall C (Birmingham, 1947) 1
Dougan R (Hearts, 1950) 1
Douglas R (Celtic, Leicester, 2002–06) 19
Doyle J (Ayr, 1976) 1
Duncan A (Hibs, 1975–76) 6
Duncan D (East Fife, 1948) 3
Duncanson J (Rangers, 1947) 1
Durie G (Chelsea, Tottenham, Rangers, 1988–98) 43
Durrant I (Rangers, Kilmarnock, 1988–2000) 20

Elliott M (Leicester, 1997–2002) 18
Evans A (Aston Villa, 1982) 4
Evans R (Celtic, Chelsea, 1949–60) 48
Ewing T (Partick, 1958) 2
Farm G (Blackpool, 1953–59) 10
Ferguson B (Rangers, Blackburn, Rangers, 1999–2009) 45
Ferguson D (Dundee Utd, Everton, 1992–97) 7
Ferguson D (Rangers, 1988) 2
Ferguson I (Rangers, 1989–97) 9
Ferguson R (Kilmarnock, 1966–67) 7
Fernie W (Celtic, 1954–58) 12
Flavell R (Airdrie, 1947) 2
Fleck R (Norwich, 1990–91) 4
Fleming C (East Fife, 1954) 1
Fletcher D (Manchester Utd, 2004–12) 58

Fletcher S (Hibs, Burnley, Wolves, 2008–11) 8
Forbes A (Sheffield Utd, Arsenal, 1947–52) 14
Ford D (Hearts, 1974) 2
Forrest J (Motherwell, 1958) 1
Forrest J (Rangers, Aberdeen, 1966–71) 5
Forrest J (Celtic, 2011–12) 5
Forsyth A (Partick, Manchester Utd, 1972–76) 10
Forsyth C (Kilmarnock, 1964) 4
Forsyth T (Motherwell, Rangers, 1971–78) 22
Fox, D (Burnley, 2010) 1
Fraser D (WBA, 1968–69) 2
Fraser W (Sunderland, 1955) 2
Freedman D (Crystal Palace, 2002) 2

Gabriel J (Everton, 1961–64) 2
Gallacher K (Dundee Utd, Coventry, Blackburn, Newcastle, 1988–2001) 53
Gallacher P (Dundee Utd, 2003–04) 8
Gallagher P (Blackburn, 2004) 1
Galloway M (Celtic, 1992) 1
Gardiner I (Motherwell, 1958) 1
Gemmell T (St Mirren, 1955) 2
Gemmell T (Celtic, 1966–71) 18
Gemmill A (Derby, Nottm Forest, Birmingham, 1971–81) 43
Gemmill S (Nottm Forest, Everton, 1995–2003) 26
Gibson D (Leicester, 1963–65) 7
Gillespie G (Liverpool, 1988–91) 13
Gilzean A (Dundee, Tottenham, 1964–71) 22
Glass S (Newcastle Utd 1999) 1
Glavin R (Celtic, 1977) 1
Glen A (Aberdeen, 1956) 2
Goodwillie D (Dundee Utd, Blackburn, 2011–12) 3
Goram A (Oldham, Hibs, Rangers, 1986–98) 43
Gordon C (Hearts, Sunderland, 2004–11) 40
Gough R (Dundee Utd, Tottenham, Rangers, 1983–93) 61
Gould J (Celtic, 2000–01) 2
Govan J (Hibs, 1948–49) 6
Graham A (Leeds, 1978–81) 10
Graham J (Arsenal, Manchester Utd, 1972–73) 12
Gray A (Aston Villa, Wolves, Everton, 1976–85) 20
Gray A (Bradford City, 2003) 2
Gray E (Leeds, 1969–77) 12
Gray F (Leeds, Nottm Forest, 1976–83) 32
Grant J (Hibs, 1958) 2
Grant P (Celtic, 1989) 2
Green A (Blackpool, Newcastle, 1971–72) 6
Greig J (Rangers, 1964–76) 44
Gunn B (Norwich, 1990–94) 6

Haddock H (Clyde, 1955–58) 6
Haffey F (Celtic, 1960–61) 2
Hamilton A (Dundee, 1962–66) 24
Hamilton G (Aberdeen, 1947–54) 5
Hamilton W (Hibs, 1965) 1
Hammell S (Motherwell, 2005) 1
Hanley G (Blackburn, 2011–12) 3
Hansen A (Liverpool, 1979–87) 26
Hansen J (Partick, 1972) 2
Harper J (Aberdeen, Hibs, 1973–78) 4
Hartford A (WBA, Manchester City, Everton, 1972–82) 50
Hartley P (Hearts, Celtic, Bristol City, 2005–10) 25
Harvey D (Leeds, 1973–77) 16
Haughney M (Celtic, 1954) 1
Hay D (Celtic, 1970–74) 27
Hegarty P (Dundee Utd, 1979–83) 8
Henderson J (Portsmouth, Arsenal, 1953–59) 7
Henderson W (Rangers, 1963–71) 29
Hendry C (Blackburn, Rangers, Coventry, Bolton, 1994–2001) 51
Herd D (Arsenal, 1959–61) 5
Herd G (Clyde, 1958–61) 5
Herriot J (Birmingham, 1969–70) 8
Hewie J (Charlton, 1956–60) 19
Holt D (Hearts, 1963–64) 5
Holt G (Kilmarnock, Norwich, 2001–05) 10
Holton J (Manchester Utd, 1973–75) 15
Hope R (WBA, 1968–69) 2
Hopkin D (Crystal Palace, Leeds, 1997–2000) 7
Houliston W (Queen of the South, 1949) 3
Houston S (Manchester Utd, 1976) 1
Howie H (Hibs, 1949) 1
Hughes J (Celtic, 1965–70) 8
Hughes R (Portsmouth, 2004–06) 5
Hughes S (Norwich, 2010) 1
Hughes W (Sunderland, 1975) 1
Humphries W (Motherwell, 1952) 1
Hunter A (Kilmarnock, Celtic, 1972–74) 4
Hunter W (Motherwell, 1960–61) 3
Husband J (Partick, 1947) 1
Hutchison D (Everton, Sunderland, West Ham, 1999–2004) 26
Hutchison T (Coventry, 1974–76) 17
Hutton A (Rangers, Tottenham, Aston Villa, 2007–12) 23

Imlach S (Nottm Forest, 1958) 4
Irvine B (Aberdeen, 1991–94) 9
Iwelumo C (Wolves, Burnley, 2009–11) 4

Jackson C (Rangers, 1975–77) 21
Jackson D (Hibs, Celtic, 1995–99) 29
Jardine A (Rangers, 1971–80) 38
Jarvie A (Airdrie, 1971) 3
Jess E (Aberdeen, Coventry, Aberdeen, 1993–99) 17
Johnston A (Sunderland, Rangers, Middlesbrough, 1999–2003) 18

Johnston M (Watford, Celtic, Nantes, Rangers, 1984–92) 38
Johnston W (Rangers, WBA, 1966–78) 21
Johnstone D (Rangers, 1973–80) 14
Johnstone J (Celtic, 1965–75) 23
Johnstone L (Clyde, 1948) 2
Johnstone R (Hibs, Manchester City, 1951–56) 17
Jordan J (Leeds, Manchester Utd, AC Milan, 1973–82) 52

Kelly H (Blackpool, 1952) 1
Kelly J (Barnsley, 1949) 2
Kennedy J (Celtic, 1964–65) 6
Kennedy J (Celtic, 2004) 1
Kennedy S (Rangers, 1975) 5
Kennedy S (Aberdeen, 1978–82) 8
Kenneth G (Dundee Utd, 2011) 2
Kerr A (Partick, 1955) 2
Kerr B (Newcastle, 2003–04) 3
Kyle K (Sunderland, Kilmarnock, 2002–10) 10

Lambert P (Motherwell, Borussia Dortmund, Celtic, 1995–2003) 40
Law D (Huddersfield, Manchester City, Torino, Manchester Utd, 1959–74) 55
Lawrence T (Liverpool, 1963–69) 3
Leggat G (Aberdeen, Fulham, 1956–60) 18
Leighton J (Aberdeen, Manchester Utd, Hibs, Aberdeen, 1983–99) 91
Lennox R (Celtic, 1967–70) 10
Leslie L (Airdrie, 1961) 5
Levein C (Hearts, 1990–95) 16
Liddell W (Liverpool, 1947–55) 28
Linwood A (Clyde, 1950) 1
Little R (Rangers, 1953) 1
Logie J (Arsenal, 1953) 1
Long H (Clyde, 1947) 1
Lorimer P (Leeds, 1970–76) 21

Macari L (Celtic, Manchester Utd, 1972–78) 24
Macaulay A (Brentford, Arsenal, 1947–48) 7
MacDonald A (Rangers, 1976) 1
MacDougall E (Norwich, 1975–76) 7
Mackail–Smith C (Peterborough, Brighton 2011–12) 7
Mackay D (Hearts, Tottenham, 1957–66) 22
Mackay G (Hearts, 1988) 4
Mackay M (Norwich, 2004–05) 5
Mackie J (QPR, 2011–12) 5
MacLeod J (Hibs, 1961) 4
MacLeod M (Celtic, Borussia Dortmund, Hibs, 1985–91) 20
Maguire C (Aberdeen, 2011) 2
Maloney S (Celtic, Aston Villa, Celtic, Wigan, 2006–12) 20
Malpas M (Dundee Utd, 1984–93) 55
Marshall D (Celtic, Cardiff, 2005–10) 5
Marshall G (Celtic, 1992) 1

Martin B (Motherwell, 1995) 2
Martin F (Aberdeen, 1954–55) 6
Martin N (Hibs, Sunderland, 1965–66) 3
Martin R (Norwich, 2011–12) 3
Martis J (Motherwell, 1961) 1
Mason J (Third Lanark 1949–51) 7
Masson D (QPR, Derby, 1976–78) 17
Mathers D (Partick, 1954) 1
Matteo D (Leeds, 2001–02) 6
McAllister B (Wimbledon, 1997) 3
McAllister G (Leicester, Leeds, Coventry, 1990–99) 57
McAllister J (Livingston, 2004) 1
McArthur J (Wigan, 2011–12) 7
McAvennie F (West Ham, Celtic, 1986–88) 5
McBride J (Celtic, 1967) 2
McCall S (Everton, Rangers, 1990–98) 40
McCalliog J (Sheffield Wed, Wolves, 1967–71) 5
McCann N (Hearts, Rangers, Southampton, 1999–2006) 26
McCann R (Motherwell, 1959–61) 5
McClair B (Celtic, Manchester Utd, 1987–93) 30
McCloy P (Rangers, 1973) 4
McCoist A (Rangers, Kilmarnock, 1986–99) 61
McColl I (Rangers, 1950–58) 14
McCormack R (Motherwell, Cardiff, Leeds, 2008–11) 7
McCreadie E (Chelsea, 1965–9) 23
McCulloch L (Wigan, Rangers, 2005–11) 18
McDonald J (Sunderland, 1956) 2
McEveley, J (Derby, 2008) 3
McFadden J (Motherwell, Everton, Birmingham, 2002–11) 48
McFarlane W (Hearts, 1947) 1
McGarr E (Aberdeen, 1970) 2
McGarvey F (Liverpool, Celtic, 1979–84) 7
McGhee M (Aberdeen, 1983–84) 4
McGinlay J (Bolton, 1995–97) 14
McGrain D (Celtic, 1973–82) 62
McGregor A (Rangers, 2007–12) 21
McGrory J (Kilmarnock, 1965–66) 3
McInally A (Aston Villa, Bayern Munich, 1989–90) 8
McInally J (Dundee Utd, 1987–93) 10
McInnes D (WBA, 2003) 2
McKay D (Celtic, 1959–62) 14
McKean R (Rangers, 1976) 1
McKenzie J (Partick, 1954–56) 9
McKimmie S (Aberdeen, 1989–96) 40
McKinlay T (Celtic, 1996–98) 22
McKinlay W (Dundee Utd, Blackburn, 1994–99) 29
McKinnon R (Rangers, 1966–71) 28
McKinnon R (Motherwell, 1994–95) 3
McLaren A (Preston, 1947–48) 4
McLaren A (Hearts, Rangers, 1992–96) 24
McLaren A (Kilmarnock, 2001) 1
McLean G (Dundee, 1968) 1

McLean T (Kilmarnock, Rangers, 1969–71) 6
McLeish A (Aberdeen, 1980–93) 77
McLintock F (Leicester, Arsenal, 1963–71) 9
McManus S (Celtic, Middlesbrough, 2007–11) 26
McMillan I (Airdrie, 1952–61) 6
McNamara J (Celtic, Wolves, 1997–2006) 33
McNamee D (Livingston, 2004–06) 4
McNaught W (Raith, 1951–55) 5
McNaughton K (Aberdeen, Cardiff, 2002–08) 4
McNeill W (Celtic, 1961–72) 29
McPhail J (Celtic, 1950–54) 5
McPherson D (Hearts, Rangers, 1989–93) 27
McQueen G (Leeds, Manchester Utd, 1974–81) 30
McStay P (Celtic, 1984–97) 76
McSwegan G (Hearts, 2000) 2
Millar J (Rangers, 1963) 2
Miller C (Dundee Utd, 2001) 1
Miller K (Rangers, Wolves, Celtic, Derby, Rangers, Bursaspor, Cardiff, 2001–12) 60
Miller L (Dundee Utd, Aberdeen 2006–10) 3
Miller W (Celtic, 1946–47) 6
Miller W (Aberdeen, 1975–90) 65
Mitchell R (Newcastle, 1951) 2
Mochan N (Celtic, 1954) 3
Moir W (Bolton, 1950) 1
Moncur R (Newcastle, 1968–72) 16
Morgan W (Burnley, Manchester Utd, 1968–74) 21
Morris H (East Fife, 1950) 1
Morrison J (WBA, 2008–12) 20
Mudie J (Blackpool, 1957–58) 17
Mulgrew C (Celtic, 2012) 2
Mulhall G (Aberdeen, Sunderland, 1960–64) 3
Munro F (Wolves, 1971–75) 9
Munro I (St Mirren, 1979–80) 7
Murdoch R (Celtic, 1966–70) 12
Murray I (Hibs, Rangers, 2003–06) 6
Murray J (Hearts, 1958) 5
Murray S (Aberdeen, 1972) 1
Murty G (Reading, 2004–08) 4

Naismith S (Kilmarnock, Rangers, 2007–12) 15
Narey D (Dundee Utd, 1977–89) 35
Naysmith G (Hearts, Everton, Sheffield Utd, 2000–09) 46
Neilson R (Hearts, 2007) 1
Nevin P (Chelsea, Everton, Tranmere, 1987–96) 28
Nicholas C (Celtic, Arsenal, Aberdeen, 1983–89) 20
Nicholson B (Dunfermline, 2001–05) 3
Nicol S (Liverpool, 1985–92) 27

O'Connor G (Hibs, Lokomotiv Moscow, Birmingham, 2002–10) 16
O'Donnell P (Motherwell, 1994) 1
O'Hare J (Derby, 1970–72) 13
O'Neil B (Celtic, VfL Wolfsburg, Derby, Preston, 1996–2006) 7
O'Neil J (Hibs, 2001) 1
Ormond W (Hibs, 1954–59) 6
Orr T (Morton, 1952) 2

Parker A (Falkirk, Everton, 1955–56) 15
Parlane D (Rangers, 1973–77) 12
Paton A (Motherwell, 1952) 2
Pearson S (Motherwell, Celtic, Derby, 2004–07) 10
Pearson T (Newcastle, 1947) 2
Penman A (Dundee, 1966) 1
Pettigrew W (Motherwell, 1976–77) 5
Phillips M (Blackpool, 2012) 1
Plenderleith J (Manchester City, 1961) 1
Pressley S (Hearts, 2000–07) 32
Provan D (Rangers, 1964–66) 5
Provan D (Celtic, 1980–82) 10
Quashie N (Portsmouth, Southampton, WBA, 2004–07) 14
Quinn P (Motherwell, 1961–62) 9

Rae G (Dundee, Rangers, Cardiff, 2001–09) 14
Redpath W (Motherwell, 1949–52) 9
Reilly L (Hibs, 1949–57) 38
Rhodes, J (Huddersfield, 2012) 1
Ring T (Clyde, 1953–58) 12
Rioch B (Derby, Everton, 1975–78) 24
Riordan D (Hibs, 2006–10) 3
Ritchie P (Hearts, Bolton, 1999–2000) 6
Ritchie W (Rangers, 1962) 1
Robb D (Aberdeen, 1971) 5
Robertson A (Clyde, 1955) 5
Robertson D (Rangers, 1992–94) 3
Robertson H (Dundee, 1962) 1
Robertson J (Tottenham, 1964) 1
Robertson J (Nottm Forest, Derby, 1978–84) 28
Robertson J (Hearts, 1991–96) 16
Robertson S (Dundee Utd, 2009–11) 1
Robinson R (Dundee, 1974–75) 4
Robson B (Celtic, Middlesbrough, 2008–12) 17
Ross M (Rangers, 2002–04) 12
Rough A (Partick, Hibs, 1976–86) 53
Rougvie D (Aberdeen, 1984) 1
Rutherford E (Rangers, 1948) 1

Saunders S (Motherwell, 2011) 1
Schaedler E (Hibs, 1974) 1
Scott A (Rangers, Everton, 1957–66) 16
Scott J (Hibs, 1966) 1
Scott J (Dundee, 1971) 2
Scoular J (Portsmouth, 1951–53) 9
Severin S (Hearts, Aberdeen, 2002–07) 15
Sharp G (Everton, 1985–88) 12

Shaw D (Hibs, 1947–49) 8
Shaw J (Rangers, 1947) 4
Shearer D (Aberdeen, 1994–96) 7
Shearer R (Rangers, 1961) 4
Simpson N (Aberdeen, 1983–88) 4
Simpson R (Celtic, 1967–69) 5
Sinclair J (Leicester, 1966) 1
Smith D (Aberdeen, Rangers, 1966–68) 2
Smith G (Hibs, 1947–57) 18
Smith H (Hearts, 1988–92) 3
Smith JE (Celtic, 1959) 2
Smith J (Aberdeen, Newcastle, 1968–74) 4
Smith J (Celtic, 2003) 2
Snodgrass R (Leeds, 2011–12) 5
Souness G (Middlesbrough, Liverpool, Sampdoria, Rangers, 1975–86) 54
Speedie D (Chelsea, Coventry, 1985–89) 10
Spencer J (Chelsea, QPR, 1995–97) 14
Stanton P (Hibs, 1966–74) 16
Steel W (Morton, Derby, Dundee, 1947–53) 30
Stein C (Rangers, Coventry, 1969–73) 21
Stephen J (Bradford City, 1947–48) 2
Stewart D (Leeds, 1978) 1
Stewart J (Kilmarnock, Middlesbrough, 1977–79) 2
Stewart M (Manchester Utd, Hearts 2002–09) 4
Stewart R (West Ham, 1981–7) 10
St John I (Motherwell, Liverpool, 1959–65) 21
Stockdale R (Middlesbrough, 2002–03) 5
Strachan G (Aberdeen, Manchester Utd, Leeds, 1980–92) 50
Sturrock P (Dundee Utd, 1981–87) 20
Sullivan N (Wimbledon, Tottenham, 1997–2003) 28

Teale G (Wigan, Derby, 2006–09) 13
Telfer P (Coventry, 2000) 1
Telfer W (St Mirren, 1954) 1
Thomson K (Rangers, Middlesbrough, 2009–11) 3
Thompson S (Dundee Utd, Rangers, 2002–05) 16
Thomson W (St Mirren, 1980–84) 7
Thornton W (Rangers, 1947–52) 7

Toner W (Kilmarnock, 1959) 2
Turnbull E (Hibs, 1948–58) 8

Ure I (Dundee, Arsenal, 1962–68) 11

Waddell W (Rangers, 1947–55) 17
Walker A (Celtic, 1988–95) 3
Walker N (Hearts, 1993–96) 2
Wallace I (Coventry, 1978–79) 3
Wallace L (Hearts, 2010–11) 5
Wallace R (Preston, 2010) 1
Wallace W (Hearts, Celtic, 1965–69) 7
Wardhaugh J (Hearts, 1955–57) 2
Wark J (Ipswich, Liverpool, 1979–85) 29
Watson J (Motherwell, Huddersfield, 1948–54) 2
Watson R (Motherwell, 1971) 1
Webster A (Hearts, Rangers, Hearts, 2003–12) 24
Weir A (Motherwell, 1959–60) 6
Weir D (Hearts, Everton, Rangers, 1997–2011) 69
Weir P (St Mirren, Aberdeen, 1980–84) 6
White J (Falkirk, Tottenham, 1959–64) 22
Whittaker S (Rangers, 2010–12) 15
Whyte D (Celtic, Middlesbrough, Aberdeen, 1988–99) 12
Wilkie L (Dundee, 2002–03) 11
Williams G (Nottm Forest, 2002–03) 5
Wilson A (Portsmouth, 1954) 1
Wilson D (Liverpool, 2011–12) 5
Wilson D (Rangers, 1961–65) 22
Wilson I (Leicester, Everton, 1987–8) 5
Wilson M (Celtic, 2011) 1
Wilson P (Celtic, 1975) 1
Wilson R (Arsenal, 1972) 2
Wood G (Everton, Arsenal, 1978–82) 4
Woodburn W (Rangers, 1947–52) 24
Wright K (Hibs, 1992) 1
Wright S (Aberdeen, 1993) 2
Wright T (Sunderland, 1953) 3

Yeats R (Liverpool, 1965–66) 2
Yorston H (Aberdeen, 1955) 1
Young A (Hearts, Everton, 19606–6) 8
Young G (Rangers, 1947–57) 53
Younger T (Hibs, Liverpool, 1955–58) 24

WALES

Aizlewood M (Charlton, Leeds, Bradford City, Bristol City, Cardiff, 1986–95) 39
Allchurch I (Swansea City, Newcastle, Cardiff, 1951–66) 68
Allchurch L (Swansea City, Sheffield Utd, 1955–64) 11
Allen B (Coventry, 1951) 2
Allen J (Swansesa, 2009–12) 8

Allen M (Watford, Norwich, Millwall, Newcastle, 1986–94) 14

Baker C (Cardiff, 1958–62) 7
Baker W (Cardiff, 1948) 1
Bale G (Southampton, Tottenham, 2006–12) 33
Barnard D (Barnsley, Bradford City, Barnsley, Grimsby, 1998–2004) 22
Barnes W (Arsenal, 1948–55) 22

Bellamy C (Norwich, Coventry, Newcastle, Blackburn, Liverpool, West Ham, Manchester City, Liverpool 1998–2012) 69

Berry G (Wolves, Stoke, 1979–83) 5

Blackmore C (Manchester Utd, Middlesbrough, 1985–97) 39

Blake D (Cardiff, 2011–12) 9

Blake N (Sheffield Utd, Bolton, Blackburn, Wolves, 1994–2004) 29

Bodin P (Swindon, Crystal Palace, Swindon, 1990–95) 23

Bowen D (Arsenal, 1955–59) 19

Bowen J (Swansea City, Birmingham, 1994–97) 2

Bowen M (Tottenham, Norwich, West Ham, 1986–97) 41

Boyle T (Crystal Palace, 1981) 2

Bradley M (Walsall, 2010) 1

Brown J (Gillingham, Blackburn, Aberdeen, 2006–12) 3

Browning M (Bristol Rov, Huddersfield, 1996–97) 5

Burgess R (Tottenham, 1947–54) 32

Burton A (Norwich, Newcastle, 1963–72) 9

Cartwright L (Coventry, Wrexham, 1974–79) 7

Charles Jeremy (Swansea City, QPR, Oxford Utd, 1981–87) 19

Charles John (Leeds, Juventus, Cardiff, 1950–65) 38

Charles M (Swansea City, Arsenal, Cardiff, 1955–63) 31

Church S (Reading, 2009–12) 15

Clarke R (Manchester City, 1949–56) 22

Coleman C (Crystal Palace, Blackburn, Fulham, 1992–2002) 32

Collins D (Sunderland, Stoke, 2005–11) 12

Collins J (Cardiff, West Ham, Aston Villa, 2004–11) 39

Collison J (West Ham, 2008–12) 11

Cornforth J (Swansea City, 1995) 2

Cotterill D (Bristol City, Wigan, Sheffield Utd, Swansea, 2006–11) 19

Coyne D (Tranmere, Grimsby, Leicester, Burnley, Tranmere, 1996–2008) 16

Crofts A (Gillingham, Brighton, Norwich, 2006–12) 23

Crossley M (Nottm Forest, Middlesbrough, Fulham, 1997–2005) 8

Crowe V (Aston Villa, 1959–63) 16

Curtis A (Swansea City, Leeds, Southampton, Cardiff, 1976–87) 35

Daniel R (Arsenal, Sunderland, 1951–57) 21

Davies A (Manchester Utd, Newcastle, Swansea City, Bradford City, 1983–90) 13

Davies A (Yeovil 2006) 1

Davies C (Charlton, 1972) 1

Davies C (Oxford Utd, Verona, Oldham, 2006–08) 5

Davies D (Everton, Wrexham, Swansea City 1975–83) 52

Davies ER (Newcastle, 1953–58) 6

Davies G (Fulham, Chelsea, Manchester City, 1980–86) 16

Davies RT (Norwich, Southampton, Portsmouth, 1964–74) 29

Davies RW (Bolton, Newcastle, Manr Utd, Man City, Blackpool, 1964–74) 34

Davies S (Manchester Utd, 1996) 1

Davies S (Tottenham, Everton, Fulham, 2001–10) 58

Davis G (Wrexham, 1978) 3

Deacy N (PSV Eindhoven, Beringen, 1977–79) 12

Delaney M (Aston Villa, 2000–07) 36

Derrett S (Cardiff, 1969–71) 4

Dibble A (Luton, Manchester City, 1986–89) 3

Dorman A (St Mirren, Crystal Palace, 2010–11) 3

Duffy R (Portsmouth, 2006–08) 13

Durban A (Derby, 1966–72) 27

Dwyer P (Cardiff, 1978–80) 10

Eardley N (Oldham, Blackpool, 2008–11) 16

Earnshaw R (Cardiff, WBA, Norwich, Derby, Nottm Forest, Cardiff 2002–12) 58

Easter J (Wycombe, Crystal Palace, 2007–11) 9

Eastwood F (Wolves, Coventry, 2008–11) 11

Edwards C (Swansea City, 1996) 1

Edwards D (Luton, Wolves, 2008–12) 24

Edwards, G (Birmingham, Cardiff, 1947–50) 12

Edwards, I (Chester, Wrexham, 1978–80) 4

Edwards, L (Charlton, 1957) 2

Edwards, R (Bristol City, 1997–98) 4

Edwards, R (Aston Villa, Wolves, 2003–07) 15

Emmanuel W (Bristol City, 1973) 2

England M (Blackburn, Tottenham, 1962–75) 44

Evans B (Swansea City, Hereford, 1972–74) 7

Evans C (Manchester City, Sheffield Utd, 2008–11) 13

Evans I (Crystal Palace, 1976–78) 13

Evans P (Brentford, Bradford City, 2002–03) 2

Evans R (Swansea City, 1964) 1

Evans S (Wrexham, 2007–09) 7

Felgate D (Lincoln, 1984) 1

Fletcher C (Bournemouth, West Ham, Crystal Palace, 2004–09) 36

Flynn B (Burnley, Leeds, 1975–84) 66

Ford T (Swansea City, Sunderland, Aston Villa, Cardiff, 1947–57) 38

Foulkes W (Newcastle, 1952–54) 11

Freestone R (Swansea City, 2000–03) 1

Gabbidon D (Cardiff, West Ham, QPR, 2002–12) 46

Garner G (Leyton Orient, 2006) 1
Giggs R (Manchester Utd, 1992–2007) 64
Giles D (Swansea City, Crystal Palace,
 1980–83) 12
Godfrey B (Preston, 1964–65) 3
Goss J (Norwich, 1991–96) 9
Green C (Birmingham, 1965–69) 15
Green R (Wolves, 1998) 2
Griffiths A (Wrexham, 1971–77) 17
Griffiths H (Swansea City, 1953) 1
Griffiths M (Leicester, 1947–54) 11
Gunter C (Cardiff, Tottenham, Nottm Forest,
 2007–12) 37

Hall G (Chelsea, 1988–92) 9
Harrington A (Cardiff, 1956–62) 11
Harris C (Leeds, 1976–82) 23
Harris W (Middlesbrough, 1954–58) 6
Hartson J (Arsenal, West Ham, Wimbledon,
 Coventry, Celtic, 1995–2006) 51
Haworth S (Cardiff, Coventry, 1997–8) 5
Hennessey T (Birmingham, Nottm Forest,
 Derby, 1962–73) 39
Hennessey W (Wolves, 2007–12) 38
Hewitt R (Cardiff, 1958) 5
Hill M (Ipswich, 1972) 2
Hockey T (Sheffield Utd, Norwich,
 Aston Villa, 1972–74) 9
Hodges G (Wimbledon, Newcastle,
 Watford, Sheffield Utd, 1984–96) 18
Holden A (Chester, 1984) 1
Hole B (Cardiff, Blackburn, Aston Villa,
 Swansea City, 1963–71) 30
Hollins D (Newcastle, 1962–66) 11
Hopkins J (Fulham, Crystal Palace,
 1983–90) 16
Hopkins M (Tottenham, 1956–63) 34
Horne B (Portsmouth, Southampton,
 Everton, Birmingham, 1988–97) 59
Howells R (Cardiff, 1954) 2
Hughes C (Luton, Wimbledon, 1992–97) 8
Hughes I (Luton, 1951) 4
Hughes M (Manchester Utd, Barcelona,
 Bayern Munich, Manchester Utd, Chelsea,
 Southampton, 1984–99) 72
*Hughes W (Birmingham, 1947) 3
Hughes WA (Blackburn, 1949) 5
Humphreys J (Everton, 1947) 1

Jackett K (Watford, 1983–88) 31
James EG (Blackpool, 1966–71) 9
James L (Burnley, Derby, QPR, Swansea City,
 Sunderland, 1972–83) 54
James R (Swansea, Stoke, QPR,
 Leicester, Swansea, 1979–88) 47
Jarvis A (Hull, 1967) 3
Jenkins S (Swansea, Huddersfield,
 1996–2002) 16
Johnson A (Nottm Forest, WBA,
 1999–2005) 15
Johnson M (Swansea, 1964) 1

Jones A (Port Vale, Charlton, 1987–90) 6
Jones Barrie (Swansea, Plymouth Argyle,
 Cardiff, 1963–9) 15
*Jones Bryn (Arsenal, 1947–9) 4
Jones C (Swansea, Tottenham,
 Fulham, 1954–69) 59
Jones D (Norwich, 1976–80) 8
Jones E (Swansea, Tottenham, 1947–9) 4
Jones J (Liverpool, Wrexham, Chelsea,
 Huddersfield, 1976–86) 72
Jones K (Aston Villa, 1950) 1
Jones L (Liverpool, Tranmere, 1997) 2
Jones M (Leeds, Leicester, 2000–03) 13
Jones M (Wrexham, 2007–08) 2
Jones P (Stockport, Southampton, Wolves,
 Millwall, QPR, 1997–2007) 50
Jones R (Sheffield Wed, 1994) 1
*Jones TG (Everton, 1946–49) 13
Jones V (Wimbledon, 1995–97) 9
Jones W (Bristol Rov, 1971) 1

Kelsey J (Arsenal, 1954–62) 41
King A (Leicester, 2009–12) 12
King J (Swansea, 1955) 1
Kinsey N (Norwich, Birmingham,
 1951–56) 7
Knill A (Swansea, 1989) 1
Koumas J (Tranmere, WBA, Wigan,
 2001–09) 34
Krzywicki R (WBA, Huddersfield,
 1970–72) 8

Lambert R (Liverpool, 1947–9) 5
Law B (QPR, 1990) 1
Ledley J (Cardiff, Celtic, 2006–12) 41
Lee C (Ipswich, 1965) 2
Leek K (Leicester, Newcastle, Birmingham,
 Northampton, 1961–65) 13
Legg A (Birmingham, Cardiff,
 1996–2001) 6
Lever A (Leicester, 1953) 1
Lewis D (Swansea, 1983) 1
Llewellyn C (Norwich, Wrexham,
 1998–2007) 6
Lloyd B (Wrexham, 1976) 3
Lovell S (Crystal Palace, Millwall,
 1982–86) 6
Lowndes S (Newport, Millwall, Brighton,
 Barnsley, 1983–88) 10
Lowrie G (Coventry, Newcastle, 1948–49) 4
Lucas M (Leyton Orient, 1962–63) 4
Lucas W (Swansea, 1949–51) 7

MacDonald, S (Swansea, 2011) 1
Maguire G (Portsmouth, 1990–92) 7
Mahoney J (Stoke, Middlesbrough,
 Swansea, 1968–83) 51
Mardon P (WBA, 1996) 1
Margetson M (Cardiff, 2004) 1
Marriott A (Wrexham, 1996–98) 5
Marustik C (Swansea, 1982–83) 6

Matthews A (Cardiff, Celtic, 2011–12) 7
Medwin T (Swansea, Tottenham, 1953–63) 29
Melville A (Swansea, Oxford Utd, Sunderland, Fulham, West Ham, 1990–2005) 65
Mielczarek R (Rotherham, 1971) 1
Millington A (WBA, Peterborough, Swansea, 1963–72) 21
Moore G (Cardiff, Chelsea, Manchester Utd, Northampton, Charlton, 1960–71) 21
Morgan C (MK Dons, Peterborough, Preston, 2007–11) 23
Morison S (Millwall, Norwich, 2011–12) 15
Morris W (Burnley, 1947–52) 5
Myhill B (Hull, WBA, 2008–11) 10

Nardiello D (Coventry, 1978) 2
Nardiello D (Barnsley, QPR, 2007–08) 3
Neilson A (Newcastle, Southampton, 1992–97) 5
Nicholas P (Crystal Palace, Arsenal, Crystal Palace, Luton, Aberdeen, Chelsea, Watford, 1979–92) 73
Niedzwiecki E (Chelsea, 1985–88) 2
Nogan L (Watford, Reading, 1991–96) 2
Norman T (Hull, 1986–88) 5
Nurse M (Swansea, Middlesbrough, 1960–63) 12
Nyatanga L (Derby, Bristol City, 2006–11) 34

O'Sullivan P (Brighton, 1973–78) 3
Oster J (Everton, Sunderland, 1997–2005) 13

Page M (Birmingham, 1971–79) 28
Page R (Watford, Sheffield Utd, Cardiff, Coventry, 1997–2006) 41
Palmer D (Swansea, 1957) 3
Parry J (Swansea, 1951) 1
Parry P (Cardiff, 2004–07) 11
Partridge D (Motherwell, Bristol City, 2005–06) 7
Pascoe C (Swansea, Sunderland, 1984–92) 10
Paul R (Swansea, Manchester City, 1949–56) 33
Pembridge M (Luton, Derby, Sheffield Wed, Benfica, Everton, Fulham, 1992–2005) 54
Perry J (Cardiff, 1994) 1
Phillips D (Plymouth Argyle, Manchester City, Coventry, Norwich, Nottm Forest, 1984–96) 62
Phillips J (Chelsea, 1973–78) 4
Phillips L (Cardiff, Aston Villa, Swansea, Charlton, 1971–82) 58
Pipe D (Coventry, 2003) 1
Pontin K (Cardiff, 1980) 2
Powell A (Leeds, Everton, Birmingham, 1947–51) 8

Powell D (Wrexham, Sheffield Utd, 1968–71) 11
Powell I (QPR, Aston Villa, 1947–51) 8
Price L (Ipswich, Derby, Crystal Palace, 2006–12) 9
Price P (Luton, Tottenham, 1980–84) 25
Pring K (Rotherham, 1966–67) 3
Pritchard H (Bristol City, 1985) 1

Ramsey A (Arsenal, 2009–12) 21
Rankmore F (Peterborough, 1966) 1
Ratcliffe K (Everton, Cardiff, 1981–93) 59
Ready K (QPR, 1997–98) 5
Reece G (Sheffield Utd, Cardiff, 1966–75) 29
Reed W (Ipswich, 1955) 2
Rees A (Birmingham, 1984) 1
Rees J (Luton, 1992) 1
Rees R (Coventry, WBA, Nottm Forest, 1965–72) 39
Rees W (Cardiff, Tottenham, 1949–50) 4
Ribeiro C (Bristol City, 2010–11) 2
Richards J (Swansea, 2012) 1
Richards, S (Cardiff, 1947) 1
Ricketts S (Swansea, Hull, Bolton, 2005–12) 44
Roberts A (QPR, 1993) 1
Roberts D (Oxford Utd, Hull, 1973–78) 17
Roberts G (Tranmere, 2000–06) 8
Roberts I (Watford, Huddersfield, Leicester, Norwich, 1990–2002) 15
Roberts J (Arsenal, Birmingham, 1971–76) 21
Roberts J (Bolton, 1949) 1
Roberts M (QPR, 1997) 1
Roberts N (Wrexham, Wigan, 2000–04) 4
Roberts P (Portsmouth, 1974) 4
Roberts S (Wrexham, 2005) 1
Robinson C (Wolves, Portsmouth, Sunderland, Norwich, Toronto 2000–08) 46
Robinson J (Charlton, 1996–2002) 30
Robson-Kanu H (Reading, 2010–12) 7
Rodrigues P (Cardiff, Leicester, City Sheffield Wed, 1965–74) 40
Rouse V (Crystal Palace, 1959) 1
Rowley T (Tranmere, 1959) 1
Rush I (Liverpool, Juventus, Liverpool, 1980–96) 73

Saunders D (Brighton, Oxford Utd, Derby, Liverpool, Aston Villa, Galatasaray, Nottm Forest, Sheffield Utd, Benfica, Bradford City, 1986–2001) 75
Savage R (Crewe, Leicester, Birmingham, 1996–2005) 39
Sayer P (Cardiff, 1977–8) 7
Scrine F (Swansea, 1950) 2
Sear C (Manchester City, 1963) 1
Sherwood A (Cardiff, Newport, 1947–57) 41
Shortt W (Plymouth Argyle, 1947–53) 12
Showers D (Cardiff, 1975) 2

Sidlow C (Liverpool, 1947–50) 7
Slatter N (Bristol Rov, Oxford Utd, 1983–89) 22
Smallman D (Wrexham, Everton, 1974–6) 7
Southall N (Everton, 1982–97) 92
Speed G (Leeds, Everton, Newcastle, 1990–2004) 85
Sprake G (Leeds, Birmingham, 1964–75) 37
Stansfield F (Cardiff, 1949) 1
Stevenson B (Leeds, Birmingham, 1978–82) 15
Stevenson N (Swansea, 1982–83) 4
Stitfall R (Cardiff, 1953–57) 2
Stock B (Doncaster, 2010–11) 3
Sullivan D (Cardiff, 1953–60) 17
Symons K (Portsmouth, Manchester City, Fulham, Crystal Palace, 1992–2004) 37

Tapscott D (Arsenal, Cardiff, 1954–59) 14
Taylor G (Crystal Palace, Sheffield Utd, Burnley, Nottm Forest, 1996–2005) 15
Taylor N (Wrexham, Swansea, 2010–12) 9
Thatcher B (Leicester, Manchester City, 2004–05) 7
Thomas D (Swansea, 1957–58) 2
Thomas M (Wrexham, Manchester Utd, Everton, Brighton, Stoke, Chelsea, WBA, 1977–86) 51
Thomas M (Newcastle, 1987) 1
Thomas R (Swindon, Derby, Cardiff, 1967–78) 50
Thomas S (Fulham, 1948–49) 4
Toshack J (Cardiff, Liverpool, Swansea, 1969–80) 40
Trollope P (Derby, Fulham, Northampton, 1997–2003) 9
Tudur Jones O (Swansea, Norwich, 2008–11) 6

Van den Hauwe P (Everton, 1985–89) 13
Vaughan D (Crewe, Real Sociedad, Blackpool, Sunderland, 2003–12) 29
Vaughan N (Newport, Cardiff, 1983–85) 10
Vearncombe G (Cardiff, 1958–61) 2
Vernon R (Blackburn, Everton, Stoke, 1957–68) 32
Villars A (Cardiff, 1974) 3
Vokes S (Wolves, 2008–12) 21

Walley T (Watford, 1971) 1
Walsh I (Crystal Palace, 1980–82) 18
Ward D (Bristol Rov, Cardiff, 1959–62) 2
Ward D (Notts Co, Nottm Forest, 2000–04) 5
Webster C (Manchester Utd, 1957–58) 4
Weston R (Arsenal, Cardiff, 2000–05) 7
Williams A (Stockport, Swansea, 2008–12) 33
Williams A (Reading, Wolves, Reading, 1994–2003) 13
Williams A (Southampton, 1997–98) 2
Williams D (Norwich, 1986–87) 5
Williams G (Cardiff, 1951) 1
Williams G (Derby, Ipswich, 1988–96) 13
Williams G (West Ham, 2006) 2
Williams GE (WBA, 1960–69) 26
Williams GG (Swansea, 1961–62) 5
Williams HJ (Swansea, 1965–72) 3
Williams HT (Newport, Leeds, 1949–50) 4
Williams S (WBA, Southampton, 1954–66) 43
Witcomb D (WBA, Sheffield Wed, 1947) 3
Woosnam P (Leyton Orient, West Ham, Aston Villa, 1959–63) 17
Yorath T (Leeds, Coventry, Tottenham, Vancouver Whitecaps 1970–81) 59
Young E (Wimbledon, Crystal Palace, Wolves, 1990–96) 21

NORTHERN IRELAND

Aherne T (Belfast Celtic, Luton, 1947–50) 4
Anderson T (Manchester Utd, Swindon, Peterborough, 1973–79) 22
Armstrong G (Tottenham, Watford, Real Mallorca, WBA, 1977–86) 63

Baird C (Southampton, Fulham, 2003–12) 56
Barr H (Linfield, Coventry, 1962–63) 3
Barton A (Preston, 2011) 1
Best G (Manchester Utd, Fulham, 1964–77) 37
Bingham W (Sunderland, Luton, Everton, Port Vale, 1951–64) 56
Black K (Luton, Nottm Forest, 1988–94) 30
Blair R (Oldham, 1975–76) 5
Blanchflower RD (Barnsley, Aston Villa, Tottenham, 1950–63) 56
Blanchflower J (Manchester Utd, 1954–58) 12

Blayney A (Doncaster, Linfield, 2006–11) 5
Bowler G (Hull, 1950) 3
Boyce L (Werder Bremen, 2011) 4
Braithwaite R (Linfield, Middlesbrough, 1962–65) 10
Braniff K (Portadown, 2010) 2
Brennan R (Luton, Birmingham, Fulham, 1949–51) 5
Briggs W (Manchester Utd, Swansea, 1962–65) 2
Brotherston N (Blackburn, 1980–85) 27
Bruce W (Glentoran, 1961–67) 2
Brunt C (Sheffield Wed, WBA, 2005–12) 36
Bryan, M (Watford, 2010) 2
Camp L (Nottm Forest, 2011–12) 8
Campbell D (Nottm Forest, Charlton, 1987–88) 10
Campbell J (Fulham, 1951) 2
Campbell R (Crusaders, 1963–65) 2

293

Hamilton W (QPR, Burnley, Oxford Utd, 1978–86) 41

Harkin J (Southport, Shrewsbury, 1968–70) 5

Harvey M (Sunderland, 1961–71) 34

Hatton S (Linfield, 1963) 2

Healy D (Manchester Utd, Preston, Leeds, Fulham, Sunderland, Rangers, 2000–12) 93

Healy F (Coleraine, Glentoran, 1982–83) 4

Hegan D (WBA, Wolves, 1970–73) 7

Hill C (Sheffield Utd, Leicester, Trelleborg, Northampton, 1990–99) 27

Hill J (Norwich, Everton, 1959–64) 7

Hinton E (Fulham, Millwall, 1947–51) 7

Hodson L (Watford, 2011–12) 8

Holmes S (Wrexham, 2002) 1

Horlock K (Swindon, Manchester City, 1995–2003) 32

Hughes A (Newcastle, Aston Villa, Fulham, 1997–2012) 80

Hughes J (Lincoln, 2006) 2

Hughes M (Oldham, 2006) 1

Hughes M (Manchester City, Strasbourg, West Ham, Wimbledon, Crystal Palace, 1992–2005) 71

Hughes P (Bury, 1987) 3

Hughes W (Bolton, 1951) 1

Humphries W (Ards, Coventry, Swansea, 1962–65) 14

Hunter A (Blackburn, Ipswich, 1970–80) 53

Hunter B (Wrexham, Reading, 1995–2000) 15

Hunter V (Coleraine, 1962) 2

Ingham M (Sunderland, Wrexham, 2005–07) 3

Irvine R (Linfield, Stoke, 1962–5) 8

Irvine J (Burnley, Preston, Brighton, 1963–72) 23

Jackson T (Everton, Nottm Forest, Manchester Utd, 1969–77) 35

Jamison J (Glentoran, 1976) 1

Jenkins I (Chester, Dundee Utd, 1997–2000) 6

Jennings P (Watford, Tottenham, Arsenal, Tottenham, 1964–86) 119

Johnson D (Blackburn, Birmingham, 1999–2010) 56

Johnston W (Glenavon, Oldham, 1962–66) 2

Jones J (Glenavon, 1956–57) 3

Jones S (Crewe, Burnley, 2003–08) 29

Keane T (Swansea, 1949) 1

Kee P (Oxford Utd, Ards, 1990–95) 9

Keith R (Newcastle, 1958–62) 23

Kelly H (Fulham, Southampton, 1950–51) 4

Kelly P (Barnsley, 1950) 1

Kennedy P (Watford, Wigan, 1999–2004) 20

Kirk A (Hearts, Boston, Northampton, Dunfermline, 2000–10) 11

Lafferty D (Burnley, 2012) 1

Lafferty K (Burnley, Rangers, 2006–12) 30

Lawrie J (Port Vale, 2009–10) 3

Lawther W (Sunderland, Blackburn, 1960–62) 4

Lennon N (Crewe, Leicester, Celtic, 1994–2002) 40

Little A (Rangers, 2009–12) 8

Lockhart N (Linfield, Coventry, Aston Villa, 1947–56) 8

Lomas S (Manchester City, West Ham, 1994–2003) 45

Lutton B (Wolves, West Ham, 1970–4) 6

Magennis J (Cardiff, Aberden, 2010–11) 3

Magill E (Arsenal, Brighton, 1962–66) 26

Magilton J (Oxford Utd, Southampton, Sheffield Wed, Ipswich, 1991–2002) 52

Mannus A (Linfield, 2004–09) 4

Martin C (Glentoran, Leeds, Aston Villa, 1947–50) 6

McAdams W (Manchester City, Bolton, Leeds, 1954–62) 15

*McAlinden J (Portsmouth, Southend, 1947–49) 2

McArdle R (Rochdale, Aberdeen, 2010–12) 5

McAuley G (Lincoln, Leicester, Ipswich, WBA, 2005–12) 36

McBride S (Glenavon, 1991–92) 4

McCabe J (Leeds, 1949–54) 6

McCann G (West Ham, Cheltenham, Barnsley, Scunthorpe, Peterborough, 2002–12) 39

McCarthy J (Port Vale, Birmingham, 1996–2001) 18

McCartney G (Sunderland, West Ham, Sunderland 2002–10) 34

McCavana T (Coleraine, 1954–55) 3

McCleary J (Cliftonville, 1955) 1

McClelland J (Arsenal, Fulham, 1961–67) 6

McClelland J (Mansfield, Rangers, Watford, Leeds, 1980–90) 53

McCourt F (Manchester City, 1952–53) 6

McCourt P (Rochdale, Celtic, 2002–12) 10

McCoy R (Coleraine, 1987) 1

McCreery D (Manchester Utd, QPR, Tulsa, Newcastle, 1976–90) 67

McCrory S (Southend, 1958) 1

McCullough W (Arsenal, Millwall, 1961–67) 10

McCurdy C (Linfield, 1980) 1

McDonald A (QPR, 1986–96) 52

McElhinney G (Bolton, 1984–85) 6

McEvilly L (Rochdale, 2002) 1

McFaul W (Linfield, Newcastle, 1967–74) 6

McGarry J (Cliftonville, 1951) 3

McGaughey M (Linfield, 1985) 1

McGibbon P (Manchester Utd, Wigan, 1995–2000) 7

McGinn N (Derry, Celtic, 2009–12) 18

McGivern R (Manchester City, 2009–12) 16

McGovern, M (Ross Co, 2010) 1
McGrath C (Tottenham, Manchester 1974–79) 21
McIlroy J (Burnley, Stoke, 1952–66) 55
McIlroy S (Manchester Utd, Stoke, Manchester City, 1972–87) 88
McKeag W (Glentoran, 1968) 2
McKenna J (Huddersfield, 1950–52) 7
McKenzie R (Airdrie, 1967) 1
McKinney W (Falkirk, 1966) 1
McKnight A (Celtic, West Ham, 1988–89) 10
McLaughlin C (Preston, 2012) 1
McLaughlin J (Shrewsbury, Swansea, 1962–66) 12
McLean B (Motherwell, 2006) 1
McMahon G (Tottenham, Stoke, 1995–98) 17
McMichael A (Newcastle, 1950–60) 40
McMillan S (Manchester Utd, 1963) 2
McMordie A (Middlesbrough, 1969–73) 21
McMorran E (Belfast Celtic, Barnsley, Doncaster, 1947–57) 15
McNally B (Shrewsbury, 1987–88) 5
McPake J (Coventry, 2012) 1
McParland P (Aston Villa, Wolves, 1954–62) 34
McQuoid J (Millwall, 2011–12) 5
McVeigh P (Tottenham, Norwich, 1999–2005) 20
Montgomery F (Coleraine, 1955) 1
Moore C (Glentoran, 1949) 1
Moreland V (Derby, 1979–80) 6
Morgan S (Port Vale, Aston Villa, Brighton, Sparta Rotterdam, 1972–99) 18
Morrow S (Arsenal, QPR, 1990–2000) 39
Mulgrew J (Linfield, 2010) 2
Mullan G (Glentoran, 1983) 5
Mulryne P (Manchester Utd, Norwich, 1997–2005) 26
Murdock C (Preston, Hibs, Crewe, Rotherham, 2000–06) 34

Napier R (Bolton, 1966) 1
Neill T (Arsenal, Hull, 1961–73) 59
Nelson S (Arsenal, Brighton, 1970–82) 51
Nicholl C (Aston Villa, Southampton, Grimsby, 1975–83) 51
Nicholl J (Manchester Utd, Toronto, Sunderland, Rangers, WBA, 1976–86) 73
Nicholson J (Manchester Utd, Huddersfield, 1961–72) 41
Nolan I (Sheffield Wed, Bradford City, Wigan, 1997–2002) 18
Norwood O (Manchester Utd, 2011–12) 6

O'Boyle G (Dunfermline, St Johnstone, 1994–99) 13
O'Connor M (Crewe, Scunthorpe, 2008–11) 10
O'Doherty A (Coleraine, 1970) 2
O'Driscoll J (Swansea, 1949) 3
O'Kane W (Nottm Forest, 1970–75) 20
O'Neill C (Motherwell, 1989–91) 3

O'Neill J (Sunderland, 1962) 1
O'Neill J (Leicester, 1980–86) 39
O'Neill M (Distillery, Nottm Forest, Norwich, Manchester City, Notts Co, 1972–85) 64
O'Neill M (Newcastle, Dundee Utd, Hibs, Coventry, 1989–97) 31
Owens J (Crusaders, 2011) 1

Parke J (Linfield, Hibs, Sunderland, 1964–68) 14
Paterson M (Scunthorpe, Burnley, 2008–12) 13
Patterson D (Crystal Palace, Luton, Dundee Utd, 1994–99) 17
Patterson R (Coleraine, Plymouth, 2010–11) 5
Peacock R (Celtic, Coleraine, 1952–62) 31
Penney S (Brighton, 1985–89) 17
Platt J (Middlesbrough, Ballymena, Coleraine, 1976–86) 23

Quinn J (Blackburn, Swindon, Leicester, Bradford City, West Ham, Bournemouth, Reading, 1985–96) 46
Quinn SJ (Blackpool, WBA, Willem 11, Sheffield Wed, Peterborough, Northampton, 1996–2007) 50

Rafferty W (Wolves, 1980) 1
Ramsey P (Leicester, 1984–89) 14
Rice P (Arsenal, 1969–80) 49
Robinson S (Bournemouth, Luton, 1997–2008) 7
Rogan A (Celtic, Sunderland, Millwall, 1988–97) 17
Ross W (Newcastle, 1969) 1
Rowland K (West Ham, QPR, 1994–99) 19
Russell A (Linfield, 1947) 1
Ryan R (WBA, 1950) 1

Sanchez L (Wimbledon, 1987–89) 3
Scott J (Grimsby, 1958) 2
Scott P (Everton, York, Aldershot, 1976–79) 10
Sharkey P (Ipswich, 1976) 1
Shields J (Southampton, 1957) 1
Shiels D (Hibs, Doncaster, Kilmarnock, 2006–12) 10
Simpson W (Rangers, 1951–59) 12
Sloan D (Oxford Utd, 1969–71) 2
Sloan J (Arsenal, 1947) 1
Sloan T (Manchester Utd, 1979) 3
Smith A (Glentoran, Preston, 2003–05) 18
Smyth S (Wolves, Stoke, 1948–52) 9
Smyth W (Distillery, 1949–54) 4
Sonner D (Ipswich, Sheffield Wed, Birmingham, Nottm Forest, Peterborough, 1997–2005) 13
Spence D (Bury, Blackpool, Southend, 1975–82) 27

Sproule I (Hibs, 2006–08) 11
*Stevenson A (Everton, 1947–48) 3
Stewart A (Glentoran, Derby, 1967–69) 7
Stewart D (Hull, 1978) 1
Stewart I (QPR, Newcastle, 1982–87) 31
Stewart T (Linfield, 1961) 1

Taggart G (Barnsley, Bolton,
  Leicester, 1990–2003) 51
Taylor M (Fulham, Birmingham, 1999–2012) 88
Thompson A (Watford, 2011) 2
Thompson P (Linfield, 2006–08) 7
Todd S (Burnley, Sheffield Wed,
  1966–71) 11
Toner C (Leyton Orient, 2003) 2
Trainor D (Crusaders, 1967) 1
Tuffey J (Partick, Inverness, 2009–11) 8
Tully C (Celtic, 1949–59) 10

Uprichard W (Swindon, Portsmouth,
  1952–59) 18

Vernon J (Belfast Celtic, WBA,
  1947–52) 17
Walker J (Doncaster, 1955) 1
Walsh D (WBA, 1947–50) 9
Walsh M (Manchester City, 1948–49) 5

Ward J (Derby, 2012) 1
Watson P (Distillery, 1971) 1
Webb S (Ross Co, 2006–07) 4
Welsh E (Carlisle, 1966–67) 4
Whiteside N (Manchester Utd, Everton,
  1982–90) 38
Whitley Jeff (Manchester City, Sunderland,
  Cardiff, 1997–2006) 20
Whitley Jim (Manchester City,
  1998–2000) 3
  Williams M (Chesterfield, Watford,
  Wimbledon, Stoke, Wimbledon,
  MK Dons, 1999–2005) 36
Williams P (WBA, 1991) 1
Wilson D (Brighton, Luton,
  Sheffield Wed, 1987–92) 24
Wilson K (Ipswich, Chelsea, Notts Co,
  Walsall, 1987–95) 42
Wilson S (Glenavon, Falkirk, Dundee,
  1962–68) 12
Winchester C (Oldham, 2011) 1
Wood T (Walsall, 1996) 1
Worthington N (Sheffield Wed, Leeds,
  Stoke, 1984–97) 66
Wright T (Newcastle, Nottm Forest, Reading,
  Manchester City, 1989–2000) 31

REPUBLIC OF IRELAND

Aherne T (Belfast Celtic, Luton,
  1946–54) 16
Aldridge J (Oxford Utd, Liverpool, Real
  Sociedad, Tranmere, 1986–97) 69
Ambrose P (Shamrock R, 1955–64) 5
Anderson J (Preston, Newcastle,
  1980–89) 16
Andrews K (Blackburn, WBA, 2009–12) 32

Babb P (Coventry, Liverpool, Sunderland,
  1994–2003) 35
Bailham E (Shamrock R, 1964) 1
Barber E (Bohemians, Birmingham, 1966) 2
Barrett G (Arsenal, Coventry, 2003–05) 6
Beglin J (Liverpool, 1984–87) 15
Bennett A (Reading, 2007) 2
Best L (Coventry, 2009–10) 7
Braddish S (Dundalk, 1978) 2
Branagan K (Bolton, 1997) 1
Bonner P (Celtic, 1981–96) 80
Brady L (Arsenal, Juventus, Sampdoria,
  Inter–Milan, Ascoli, West Ham,
  1975–90) 72
Brady R (QPR, 1964) 6
Breen G (Birmingham, Coventry, West Ham,
  Sunderland, 1996–2006) 63
*Breen T (Shamrock R, 1947) 3
Brennan F (Drumcondra, 1965) 1
Brennan S (Manchester Utd, Waterford,
  1965–71) 19
Browne W (Bohemians, 1964) 3

Bruce A (Ipswich, 2007–09) 2
Buckley L (Shamrock R, Waregem,
  1984–85) 2
Burke F (Cork Ath, 1952) 1
Butler P (Sunderland, 2000) 1
Butler T (Sunderland, 2003) 2
Byrne A (Southampton, 1970–74) 14
Byrne J (Shelbourne, 2004–06) 2
Byrne J (QPR, Le Havre, Brighton,
  Sunderland, Millwall, 1985–93) 23
Byrne P (Shamrock R, 1984–86) 8

Campbell A (Santander, 1985) 3
Campbell N (St Patrick's Ath,
  Fortuna Cologne, 1971–77) 11
Cantwell N (West Ham, Manchester Utd,
  1954–67) 36
Carey B (Manchester Utd, Leicester,
  1992–94) 3
*Carey J (Manchester Utd, 1946–53) 21
Carolan J (Manchester Utd, 1960) 2
Carr S (Tottenham, Newcastle,
  1999–2008) 44
Carroll B (Shelbourne, 1949–50) 2
Carroll T (Ipswich, 1968–73) 17
Carsley L (Derby, Blackburn, Coventry,
  Everton, 1997–2008) 39
Cascarino A (Gillingham, Millwall,
  Aston Villa, Chelsea, Marseille, Nancy,
  1986–2000) 88
Chandler J (Leeds, 1980) 2

296

Clark C (Aston Villa, 2011) — 2
Clarke C (Stoke, 2004) — 2
Clarke J (Drogheda, 1978) — 1
Clarke K (Drumcondra, 1948) — 2
Clarke M (Shamrock R, 1950) — 1
Clinton T (Everton, 1951–54) — 3
Coad P (Shamrock R, 1947–52) — 11
Coffey T (Drumcondra, 1950) — 1
Colfer M (Shelbourne, 1950–51) — 2
Coleman S (Everton, 2011) — 4
Colgan N (Hibs, 2002–07) — 9
Conmy O (Peterborough, 1965–70) — 5
Connolly D (Watford, Feyenoord, Excelsior Feyenoord, Wimbledon, West Ham, Wigan, 1996–2006) — 41
Conroy G (Stoke, 1970–77) — 27
Conway J (Fulham, Manchester City, 1967–77) — 20
Corr P (Everton, 1949–50) — 4
Courtney E (Cork Utd, 1946) — 1
Cox S (WBA, 2011–12) — 15
Coyle O (Bolton, 1994) — 1
Coyne T (Celtic, Tranmere, Motherwell, 1992–98) — 22
Crowe G (Bohemians, 2003) — 2
Cummins G (Luton, 1954–61) — 19
Cuneen T (Limerick, 1951) — 1
Cunningham G (Manchester City, 2010–11) — 3
Cunningham K (Wimbledon, Birmingham, 1996–2006) — 72
Curtis D (Shelbourne, Bristol City, Ipswich, Exeter, 1956–63) — 17
Cusack S (Limerick, 1953) — 1

Daish L (Cambridge Utd, Coventry, 1992–96) — 5
Daly G (Manchester Utd, Derby, Coventry, Birmingham, Shrewsbury, 1973–87) — 48
Daly M (Wolves, 1978) — 2
Daly P (Shamrock R, 1950) — 1
Deacy E (Aston Villa, 1982) — 4
Delaney D (QPR, Ipswich 2008–11) — 5
Delap R (Derby, Southampton, 1998–2004) — 11
De Mange K (Liverpool, Hull, 1987–89) — 2
Dempsey J (Fulham, Chelsea, 1967–72) — 19
Dennehy J (Cork Hibs, Nottm Forest, Walsall, 1972–77) — 11
Desmond P (Middlesbrough, 1950) — 4
Devine J (Arsenal, 1980–85) — 13
Doherty G (Tottenham, Norwich, 2000–06) — 34
Donovan D (Everton, 1955–57) — 5
Donovan T (Aston Villa, 1980) — 2
Douglas J (Blackburn, Leeds, 2004–08) — 8
Doyle C (Shelbourne, 1959) — 1
Doyle C (Birmingham, 2007) — 1
Doyle K (Reading, Wolves, 2006–12) — 50
Doyle M (Coventry, 2004) — 1
Duff D (Blackburn, Chelsea, Newcastle, Fulham, 1998–2012) — 100

Duffy B (Shamrock R, 1950) — 1
Dunne A (Manchester Utd, Bolton, 1962–76) — 33
Dunne J (Fulham, 1971) — 1
Dunne P (Manchester Utd, 1965–67) — 5
Dunne R (Everton, Manchester City, Aston Villa, 2000–12) — 76
Dunne S (Luton, 1953–60) — 15
Dunne T (Bolton, 1975) — 1
Dunning P (Shelbourne, 1971) — 2
Dunphy E (York, Millwall, 1966–71) — 23
Dwyer N (West Ham, Swansea, 1960–65) — 14

Eccles P (Shamrock R, 1986) — 1
Eglington T (Shamrock R, Everton, 1946–56) — 24
Elliott S (Sunderland, 2005–07) — 9
Evans M (Southampton, 1997) — 1

Fagan E (Shamrock R, 1973) — 1
Fagan F (Manchester City, Derby, 1955–61) — 8
Fahey K (Birmingham, 2010–12) — 15
Fairclough M (Dundalk, 1982) — 2
Fallon S (Celtic, 1951–55) — 8
Farrell P (Shamrock R, Everton, 1946–57) — 28
Farrelly G (Aston Villa, Everton, Bolton, 1996–2000) — 6
Finnan S (Fulham, Liverpool, Espanyol 2000–09) — 53
Finucane A (Limerick, 1967–72) — 11
Fitzgerald F (Waterford, 1955–6) — 2
Fitzgerald P (Leeds, 1961–2) — 5
Fitzpatrick K (Limerick, 1970) — 1
Fitzsimons A (Middlesbrough, Lincoln, 1950–59) — 26
Fleming C (Middlesbrough, 1996–8) — 10
Fogarty A (Sunderland, Hartlepool Utd, 1960–64) — 11
Folan C (Hull, 2009–10) — 7
Foley D (Watford, 2000–01) — 6
Foley K (Wolves, 2009–11) — 8
Foley T (Northampton, 1964–67) — 9
Fullam J (Preston, Shamrock R, 1961–70) — 11
Forde D (Millwall, 2011) — 2

Gallagher C (Celtic, 1967) — 2
Gallagher M (Hibs, 1954) — 1
Galvin A (Tottenham, Sheffield Wed, Swindon, 1983–90) — 29
Gamble J (Cork City, 2007) — 2
Gannon E (Notts Co, Sheffield Wed, Shelbourne, 1949–55) — 14
Gannon M (Shelbourne, 1972) — 1
Gavin J (Norwich, Tottenham, Norwich, 1950–57) — 7
Gibbons A (St Patrick's Ath, 1952–56) — 4
Gibson D (Manchester Utd, Everton 2008–12) — 19
Gilbert R (Shamrock R, 1966) — 1

Giles C (Doncaster, 1951) 1

Giles J (Manchester Utd, Leeds, WBA, Shamrock R, 1960–79) 59

Given S (Blackburn, Newcastle, Manchester City, Aston Villa 2006–12) 125

Givens D (Manchester Utd, Luton, QPR, Birmingham, Neuchatel, 1969–82) 56

Gleeson S (Wolves, 2007) 2

Glynn D (Drumcondra, 1952–55) 2

Godwin T (Shamrock R, Leicester, Bournemouth, 1949–58) 13

Goodman J (Wimbledon, 1997) 4

Goodwin J (Stockport, 2003) 1

*Gorman W (Brentford, 1947) 2

Grealish A (Orient Luton, Brighton, WBA, 1976–86) 45

Green P (Derby, 2010–12) 12

Gregg E (Bohemians, 1978–80) 8

Grimes A (Manchester Utd, Coventry, Luton, 1978–88) 18

Hale A (Aston Villa, Doncaster, Waterford, 1962–72) 14

Hamilton T (Shamrock R, 1959) 2

Hand E (Portsmouth, 1969–76) 20

Harte I (Leeds, Levante, 1996–2007) 64

Hartnett J (Middlesbrough, 1949–54) 2

Haverty J (Arsenal, Blackburn, Millwall, Celtic, Bristol Rov, Shelbourne, 1956–67) 32

Hayes A (Southampton, 1979) 1

*Hayes W (Huddersfield, 1947) 2

Hayes W (Limerick, 1949) 1

Healey R (Cardiff, 1977–80) 2

Healy C (Celtic, Sunderland, 2002–04) 13

Heighway S (Liverpool, Minnesota, 1971–82) 34

Henderson B (Drumcondra, 1948) 2

Henderson W (Brighton, Preston, 2006–08) 6

Hennessy J (Shelbourne, St Patrick's Ath, 1956–69) 5

Herrick J (Cork Hibs, Shamrock R, 1972–73) 3

Higgins J (Birmingham, 1951) 1

Holland M (Ipswich, Charlton, 2000–06) 49

Holmes J (Coventry, Tottenham, Vancouver W'caps, 1971–81) 30

Hoolahan W (Blackpool, 2008) 1

Houghton R (Oxford Utd, Liverpool, Aston Villa, Crystal Palace, Reading, 1986–97) 73

Howlett G (Brighton, 1984) 1

Hughton C (Tottenham, West Ham, 1980–92) 53

Hunt N (Reading, 2009) 2

Hunt S (Reading, Hull, Wolves, 2007–12) 39

Hurley C (Millwall, Sunderland, Bolton, 1957–69) 40

Ireland S (Manchester City, 2006–08) 6

Irwin D (Manchester Utd, 1991–2000) 56

Kavanagh G (Stoke, Cardiff, Wigan, 1998–2007) 16

Keane Robbie (Wolves, Coventry, Inter Milan, Leeds, Tottenham, Liverpool, Tottenham, LA Galaxy, 1998–2012) 119

Keane Roy (Nottm Forest, Manchester Utd, 1991–2006) 67

Keane T (Swansea, 1949) 4

Kearin M (Shamrock R, 1972) 1

Kearns F (West Ham, 1954) 1

Kearns M (Oxford Utd, Walsall, Wolves, 1970–80) 18

Kelly A (Sheffield Utd, Blackburn, 1993–2002) 34

Kelly D (Walsall, West Ham, Leicester, Newcastle, Wolves, Sunderland, Tranmere, 1988–98) 26

Kelly G (Leeds, 1994–2003) 52

Kelly JA (Drumcondra, Preston, 1957–73) 47

Kelly J (Wolves, 1961–62) 5

Kelly M (Portsmouth, 1988–91) 4

Kelly N (Nottm Forest, 1954) 1

Kelly S (Tottenham, Birmingham Fulham, 2006–12) 30

Kenna J (Blackburn, 1995–2000) 27

Kennedy M (Portsmouth, 1986) 2

Kennedy M (Liverpool, Wimbledon, Manchester City, Wolves, 1996–2004) 34

Kenny P (Sheffield Utd, 2004–07) 7

Keogh A (Wolves, 2007–12) 22

Keogh J (Shamrock R, 1966) 1

Keogh S (Shamrock R, 1959) 1

Kernaghan A (Middlesbrough, Manchester City, 1993–96) 22

Kiely D (Charlton, WBA, 2000–09) 11

Kiernan F (Shamrock R, Southampton, 1951–2) 5

Kilbane K (WBA, Sunderland, Everton, Wigan, Hull, 1997–2011) 110

Kinnear J (Tottenham, Brighton, 1967–76) 26

Kinsella M (Charlton, Aston Villa, WBA, 1998–2004) 48

Langan D (Derby, Birmingham, Oxford Utd, 1978–88) 26

Lapira J (Notre Dame, 2007) 1

Lawler R (Fulham, 1953–56) 8

Lawlor J (Drumcondra, Doncaster, 1949–51) 3

Lawlor M (Shamrock R, 1971–73) 5

Lawrence L (Stoke, Portsmouth, 2009–11) 15

Lawrenson M (Preston, Brighton, Liverpool, 1977–88) 39

Lee A (Rotherham, Cardiff, Ipswich, 2003–07) 9

Leech M (Shamrock R, 1969–73) 8

Long (Reading, WBA, 2007–12) 27

Lowry D (St Patrick's Ath, 1962) 1

298

McAlinden J (Portsmouth, 1946) 2
McCarthy J (Wigan, 2011) 3
McAteer J (Bolton, Liverpool, Blackburn, Sunderland, 1994–2004) 52
McCann J (Shamrock R, 1957) 1
McCarthy M (Manchester City, Celtic, Lyon, Millwall, 1984–92) 57
McClean J (Sunderland, 2012) 3
McConville T (Dundalk, Waterford, 1972–73) 6
McDonagh J (Everton, Bolton, Sunderland, Notts Co, 1981–86) 25
McDonagh J (Shamrock R, 1984–85) 3
McEvoy A (Blackburn, 1961–67) 17
McGeady A (Celtic, Spartak Moscow, 2004–12) 52
McGee P (QPR, Preston, 1978–81) 15
McGoldrick E (Crystal Palace, Arsenal, 1992–95) 15
McGowan D (West Ham, 1949) 3
McGowan J (Cork Utd, 1947) 1
McGrath M (Blackburn, Bradford City, 1958–66) 22
McGrath P (Manchester Utd, Aston Villa, Derby, 1985–97) 83
Macken J (Manchester City, 2005) 1
Mackey G (Shamrock R, 1957) 3
McLoughlin A (Swindon, Southampton, Portsmouth, 1990–2000) 42
McMillan W (Belfast Celtic, 1946) 2
McNally B (Luton, 1959–63) 3
McPhail S (Leeds, 2000–04) 10
McShane P (WBA, Sunderland, Hull, 2008–12) 27
Macken A (Derby, 1977) 1
Mahon A (Tranmere, 2000) 3
Malone G (Shelbourne, 1949) 1
Mancini T (QPR, Arsenal, 1974–75) 5
Martin C (Glentoran, Leeds, Aston Villa, 1946–56) 30
Martin M (Bohemians, Manchester Utd, 1972–83) 52
Maybury, A (Leeds, Hearts, Leicester, 1998–2005) 10
Meagan M (Everton, Huddersfield, Drogheda, 1961–70) 17
Miller L (Celtic, Manchester Utd, Sunderland, QPR 2004–10) 21
Milligan M (Oldham, 1992) 1
Mooney J (Shamrock R, 1965) 2
Moore A (Middlesbrough, 1996–97) 8
Moran K (Manchester Utd, Sporting Gijon, Blackburn, 1980–94) 71
Moroney T (West Ham, 1948–54) 12
Morris C (Celtic, Middlesbrough, 1988–93) 35
Morrison C (Crystal Palace, Birmingham, Crystal Palace, 2002–07) 36
Moulson G (Lincoln, 1948–49) 3
Mucklan C (Drogheda, 1978) 1
Mulligan P (Shamrock R, Chelsea,

Crystal Palace, WBA, Shamrock R, 1969–80) 50
Munroe L (Shamrock R, 1954) 1
Murphy A (Clyde, 1956) 1
Murphy B (Bohemians, 1986) 1
Murphy D (Sunderland, 2007–09) 9
Murphy J (Crystal Palace, 1980) 3
Murphy J (Scunthorpe, 2009–10) 2
Murphy J (WBA, 2004) 1
Murphy P (Carlisle, 2007) 1
Murray T (Dundalk, 1950) 1

Newman W (Shelbourne, 1969) 1
Nolan E (Preston, 2009–10) 3
Nolan R (Shamrock R, 1957–63) 10

O'Brien Alan (Newcastle, 2007) 5
O'Brien Andy (Newcastle, Portsmouth, 2001–07) 26
O'Brien F (Philadelphia Forest, 1980) 3
O'Brien J (Bolton, 2006–08) 3
O'Brien L (Shamrock R, Manchester Utd, Newcastle, Tranmere, 1986–97) 16
O'Brien R (Notts Co, 1976–77) 5
O'Byrne L (Shamrock R, 1949) 1
O'Callaghan B (Stoke, 1979–82) 6
O'Callaghan K (Ipswich, Portsmouth, 1981–87) 21
O'Cearuill J (Arsenal, 2007) 2
O'Connell A (Dundalk, Bohemians, 1967–71) 2
O'Connor T (Shamrock R, 1950) 4
O'Connor T (Fulham, Dundalk, Bohemians, 1968–73) 8
O'Dea D (Celtic, 2010–12) 14
O'Driscoll J (Swansea, 1949) 3
O'Driscoll S (Fulham, 1982) 3
O'Farrell F (West Ham, Preston, 1952–59) 9
*O'Flanagan Dr K (Arsenal, 1947) 3
O'Flanagan M (Bohemians, 1947) 1
O'Halloran S (Aston Villa, 2007) 2
O'Hanlon K (Rotherham, 1988) 1
O'Keefe E (Everton, Port Vale, 1981–85) 5
O'Leary D (Arsenal, 1977–93) 68
O'Leary P (Shamrock R, 1980–1) 7
O'Neill F (Shamrock R, 1962–72) 20
O'Neill J (Everton, 1952–59) 17
O'Neill J (Preston, 1961) 1
O'Neill K (Norwich, Middlesbrough, 1996–2000) 13
O'Regan K (Brighton, 1984–85) 4
O'Reilly J (Cork Utd, 1946) 3
O'Shea J (Manchester Utd, Sunderland 2002–12) 79

Peyton G (Fulham, Bournemouth, Everton, 1977–92) 33
Peyton N (Shamrock R, Leeds, 1957–61) 6
Phelan T (Wimbledon, Manchester City, Chelsea, Everton, Fulham,

1992–2000)	42	Staunton S (Liverpool, Aston Villa, Liverpool, Crystal Palace, Aston Villa, 1989–2002)	102
Potter D (Wolves, 2007–08)	5		
		*Stevenson A (Everton, 1947–49)	6
Quinn A (Sheffield Wed, Sheffield Utd, 2003–07)	7	Stokes A (Sunderland, Celtic 2007–11)	4
		Strahan F (Shelbourne, 1964–65)	5
Quinn B (Coventry, 2000)	4	Swan M (Drumcondra, 1960)	1
Quinn N (Arsenal, Manchester City, Sunderland, 1986–2002)	91	Synnott N (Shamrock R, 1978–79)	3
		Thomas P (Waterford, 1974)	2
Reid A (Nottm Forest, Tottenham, Charlton, Sunderland, 2004–08)	27	Thompson J (Nottm Forest, 2004)	1
		Townsend A (Norwich, Chelsea, Aston Villa, Middlesbrough, 1989–97)	70
Reid S (Millwall, Blackburn, 2002–09)	23		
Richardson D (Shamrock R, Gillingham, 1972–80)	3	Traynor T (Southampton, 1954–64)	8
		Treacy K (Preston, Burnley 2011–12)	6
Ringstead A (Sheffield Utd, 1951–59)	20	Treacy P (WBA, Charlton, Swindon, Preston, Shamrock R, 1966–80)	42
Robinson M (Brighton, Liverpool, QPR, 1981–86)	24		
		Tuohy L (Shamrock R, Newcastle, Shamrock R, 1956–65)	8
Roche P (Shelbourne, Manchester Utd, 1972–76)	8		
		Turner A (Celtic, 1963)	2
Rogers E (Blackburn, Charlton, 1968–73)	19		
		Vernon J (Belfast Celtic, 1946)	2
Rowlands M (QPR, 2004–10)	5		
Ryan G (Derby, Brighton, 1978–85)	18	Waddock G (QPR, Millwall, 1980–90)	21
Ryan R (WBA, Derby, 1950–56)	16	Walsh D (WBA, Aston Villa, 1946–54)	20
		Walsh J (Limerick, 1982)	1
Sadlier R (Millwall, 2002)	1	Walsh M (Blackpool, Everton, QPR, Porto, 1976–85)	21
Savage D (Millwall, 1996)	5		
Saward P (Millwall, Aston Villa, Huddersfield, 1954–63)	18	Walsh M (Everton, Norwich, 1982–83)	4
		Walsh W (Manchester City, 1947–50)	9
Scannell T (Southend, 1954)	1	Walters J (Stoke, 2011–2012)	10
Scully P (Arsenal, 1989)	1	Ward S (Wolves, 2011–12)	15
Sheedy K (Everton, Newcastle, 1984–93)	46	Waters J (Grimsby, 1977–80)	2
		Westwood K (Coventry, Sunderland 2009–12)	10
Sheridan C (Celtic, CSKA Sofia, 2010–11)	3		
Sheridan J (Leeds, Sheffield Wed, 1988–96)	34	Whelan G (Stoke, 2009–12)	42
		Whelan R (St Patrick's Ath, 1964)	2
Slaven B (Middlesbrough, 1990–93)	7	Whelan R (Liverpool, Southend, 1981–95)	53
Sloan P (Arsenal, 1946)	2		
Smyth M (Shamrock R, 1969)	1	Whelan L (Manchester Utd, 1956–57)	4
St Ledger S (Preston, Leicester, 2009–12)	30	Whittaker R (Chelsea, 1959)	1
		Wilson M (Stoke, 2011)	1
Stapleton F (Arsenal, Manchester Utd, Ajax Derby, Le Havre, Blackburn, 1977–90)	71		

INTERNATIONAL GOALSCORERS 1946–2012

(start of season 2012–13)

ENGLAND

Charlton R	49	Kevan	8	McDermott	3
Lineker	48	Anderton	7	McManaman	3
Greaves	44	Connelly	7	Matthews S	3
Owen	40	Coppell	7	Merson	3
Finney	30	Fowler	7	Morris	3
Lofthouse	30	Heskey	7	O'Grady	3
Shearer	30	Paine	7	Peacock	3
Rooney	29	Charlton J	6	Ramsey	3
Platt	27	Johnson D	6	Sewell	3
Robson B	26	Macdonald	6	Walcott	3
Hurst	24	Mullen	6	Wilkins	3
Mortensen	23	Rowley	6	Wright W	3
Lampard Frank jnr	23	Terry	6	Allen R	2
Crouch	22	Vassell	6	Anderson	2
Channon	21	Waddle	6	Bradley	2
Keegan	21	Wright-Phillips S	6	Broadbent	2
Peters	20	Young A	6	Brooks	2
Gerrard	19	Adams	5	Cahill	2
Haynes	18	Atyeo	5	Carroll	2
Hunt R	18	Baily	5	Cowans	2
Beckham	17	Brooking	5	Eastham	2
Lawton	16	Carter	5	Froggatt J	2
Taylor T	16	Edwards	5	Froggatt R	2
Woodcock	16	Ferdinand L	5	Haines	2
Defoe	15	Hitchens	5	Hancocks	2
Scholes	14	Latchford	5	Hunter	2
Chivers	13	Neal	5	Ince	2
Mariner	13	Pearce	5	Johnson A	2
Smith R	13	Pearson Stan	5	Keown	2
Francis T	12	Pearson Stuart	5	King	2
Barnes J	11	Pickering F	5	Lee R	2
Douglas	11	Barmby	4	Lee S	2
Mannion	11	Barnes P	4	Moore	2
Sheringham	11	Bent	4	Perry	2
Clarke A	10	Bull	4	Pointer	2
Cole J	10	Dixon K	4	Richardson	2
Flowers R	10	Hassall	4	Royle	2
Gascoigne	10	Revie	4	Smith A (1989–92)	2
Lee F	10	Robson R	4	Southgate	2
Milburn	10	Steven	4	Stone	2
Wilshaw	10	Watson Dave (Sunderland)	4	Taylor P	2
Beardsley	9	Webb	4	Tueart	2
Bell	9	Baker	3	Upson	2
Bentley	9	Barry	3	Welbeck	2
Hateley	9	Blissett	3	Wignall	2
Wright I	9	Butcher	3	Worthington	2
Ball	8	Currie	3	A'Court	1
Broadis	8	Elliott	3	Astall	1
Byrne J	8	Ferdinand R	3	Beattie K	1
Hoddle	8	Francis G	3	Bowles	1
		Grainger	3	Bradford	1
		Kennedy R	3	Bridge	1

Robertson A	2	
Shearer D	2	
Aitken R	1	
Bannon	1	
Beattie	1	
Bett	1	
Bone	1	
Boyd T	1	
Brazil	1	
Broadfoot	1	
Buckley	1	
Burns	1	
Calderwood	1	
Campbell R	1	
Clarkson	1	
Combe	1	
Conn	1	
Craig	1	
Curran	1	
Davidson	1	
Dickov	1	
Dobie	1	
Docherty	1	
Duncan M	1	
Elliott	1	
Fernie	1	
Fletcher S	1	
Freedman	1	
Goodwillie	1	
Gray F	1	
Gemmell T	1	
Hartley	1	
Henderson J	1	
Holt	1	
Howie	1	
Hughes J	1	
Hunter W	1	
Hutchison T	1	
Goodwillie	1	
Jackson C	1	
Jardine	1	
Johnstone L	1	
Kyle	1	
Lambert	1	
Linwood	1	
Mackail-Smith	1	
Mackay G	1	
MacLeod	1	
Maloney	1	
McAvennie	1	
McCall	1	
McCalliog	1	
McArthur	1	
McCormack	1	
McCulloch	1	

McKenzie	1
McKimmie	1
McKinnon	1
McLean	1
McLintock	1
McSwegan	1
Miller W	1
Mitchell	1
Morgan	1
Morrison	1
Mulhall	1
Murray J	1
Narey	1
Naysmith	1
Ormond	1
Orr	1
Parlane	1
Provan D	1
Quashie	1
Quinn	1
Ritchie P	1
Sharp	1
Snodgrass	1
Stewart R	1
Thornton	1
Wallace I	1
Webster	1
Weir A	1
Weir D	1
Wilkie	1
Wilson Danny	1

WALES

Rush	28
Allchurch I	23
Ford	23
Saunders	22
Bellamy	19
Earnshaw	16
Hughes M	16
Charles John	15
Jones C	15
Hartson	14
Toshack	13
Giggs	12
James L	10
Koumas	10
Davies RT	8
James R	8
Vernon	8
Davies RW	7
Flynn	7
Speed	7
Walsh I	7
Bale	6

Charles M	6
Curtis A	6
Davies S	6
Griffiths A	6
Medwin	6
Pembridge	6
Clarke R	5
Leek	5
Ramsey	5
Blake	4
Coleman	4
Deacy	4
Eastwood	4
Edwards I	4
Tapscott	4
Thomas M	4
Vokes	4
Woosnam	4
Allen M	3
Bodin	3
Bowen M	3
Edwards D	3
England	3
Ledley	3
Melville	3
Palmer D	3
Rees R	3
Robinson J	3
Collins J	2
Davies G	2
Durban A	2
Dwyer	2
Edwards G	2
Evans C	2
Giles D	2
Godfrey	2
Griffiths M	2
Hodges	2
Horne	2
Jones Barrie	2
Jones Bryn	2
Lowrie	2
Nicholas	2
Phillips D	2
Reece G	2
Savage	2
Slatter	2
Symons	2
Yorath	2
Barnes	1
Blackmore	1
Blake	1
Bowen D	1
Boyle T	1
Burgess R	1

Charles Jeremy	1	
Church	1	
Cotterill	1	
Evans I	1	
Fletcher	1	
Foulkes	1	
Harris C	1	
Hewitt R	1	
Hockey	1	
Jones A	1	
Jones D	1	
Jones J	1	
King	1	
Krzywicki	1	
Llewellyn	1	
Lovell	1	
Mahoney	1	
Moore G	1	
Morison	1	
O'Sullivan	1	
Parry	1	
Paul	1	
Powell A	1	
Powell D	1	
Price P	1	
Roberts P	1	
Robinson C	1	
Smallman	1	
Taylor	1	
Vaughan	1	
Williams Adrian	1	
Williams Ashley	1	
Williams GE	1	
Williams GG	1	
Young	1	

N IRELAND

Healy	35
Clarke	13
Armstrong	12
Quinn JM	12
Dowie	11
Bingham	10
Crossan J	10
McIlroy J	10
McParland	10
Best	9
Whiteside	9
Dougan	8
Irvine W	8
Lafferty	8
O'Neill M (1972–85)	8
McAdams	7
Taggart G	7
Wilson S	7
Gray	6
McLaughlin	6
Nicholson J	6
Wilson K	6
Cush	5
Feeney ((2002–9))	5
Hamilton W	5
Hughes M	5
Magilton	5
McIlroy S	5
Simpson	5
Smyth S	5
Walsh D	5
Anderson T	4
Davis	4
Elliott	4
Hamilton B	4
McCann	4
McGrath	4
McMorran	4
O'Neill M (1989–96)	4
Quinn SJ	4
Brotherston	3
Harvey M	3
Lockhart	3
Lomas	3
McDonald	3
McMordie	3
Morgan S	3
Mulryne	3
Nicholl C	3
Spence D	3
Tully	3
Blanchflower D	3
Casey	2
Clements	2
Doherty P	2
Finney	2
Gillespie	2
Harkin	2
Lennon	2
McAuley	2
McCourt	2
McMahon	2
Neill W	2
O'Neill J	2
Peacock	2
Penney	2
Stewart I	2
Whitley	2
Barr	1
Black	1
Blanchflower J	1
Brennan	1
Brunt	1
Campbell W	1
Caskey	1
Cassidy	1
Cochrane T	1
Crossan E	1
D'Arcy	1
Doherty L	1
Elder	1
Evans C	1
Evans J	1
Ferguson	1
Ferris	1
Griffin	1
Hill C	1
Hughes	1
Humphries	1
Hunter A	1
Hunter B	1
Johnston	1
Jones J	1
Jones, S	1
McCartney	1
McClelland (1961)	1
McCrory	1
McCurdy	1
McGarry	1
McVeigh	1
Moreland	1
Morrow	1
Murdock	1
Nelson	1
Nicholl J	1
O'Boyle	1
O'Kane	1
Patterson D	1
Patterson R	1
Rowland	1
Sproule	1
Stevenson	1
Thompson	1
Walker	1
Welsh	1
Williams	1
Wilson D	1

REP OF IRELAND

Keane Robbie	53
Quinn N	21
Stapleton	20
Aldridge	19
Cascarino	19
Givens	19
Cantwell	14
Daly	13
Harte	11
Doyle	10

Brady	9	Tuohy	4	Ward	2
Connolly	9	Andrews	3	Ambrose	1
Duff	9	Carey J	3	Anderson	1
Keane Roy	9	Coad	3	Carroll	1
Kelly D	9	Conway	3	Dempsey	1
Morrison	9	Cox	3	Duffy	1
Sheedy	9	Fahey	3	Elliott	1
Curtis	8	Farrell	3	Fitzgerald J	1
Dunne R	8	Fogarty	3	Fullam J	1
Grealish	8	Haverty	3	Galvin	1
Kilbane	8	Kennedy Mark	3	Gibson	1
McGrath P	8	Kinsella	3	Glynn	1
Staunton	8	McAteer	3	Green	1
Breen G	7	Ryan R	3	Grimes	1
Fitzsimons	7	St Ledger S	3	Healy	1
Long	7	Waddock	3	Holmes	1
Ringstead	7	Walsh M	3	Hughton	1
Townsend	7	Whelan R	3	Hunt	1
Coyne	6	Barrett	2	Gibson	1
Houghton	6	Conroy	2	Kavanagh	1
McEvoy	6	Dennehy	2	Keogh	1
Martin C	6	Eglington	2	Kernaghan	1
Moran	6	Fallon	2	Mancini	1
Cummins	5	Finnan	2	McCann	1
Fagan F	5	Fitzgerald P	2	McPhail	1
Giles	5	Foley	2	Miller	1
Holland	5	Gavin	2	Mooney	1
Lawrenson	5	Hale	2	Moroney	1
Rogers	5	Hand	2	Mulligan	1
Sheridan	5	Hurley	2	O'Brien A	1
Treacy	5	Kelly G	2	O'Callaghan K	1
Walsh D	5	Lawrence	2	O'Keefe	1
Byrne J	4	Leech	2	O'Leary	1
Doherty	4	McCarthy	2	O'Neill F	1
Ireland	4	McGeady	2	O'Shea	1
Irwin	4	McLoughlin	2	Ryan G	1
McGee	4	O'Connor	2	Slaven	1
Martin M	4	O'Farrell	2	Sloan	1
O'Neill K	4	O'Reilly J	2	Strahan	1
Reid A	4	Whelan G	2	Walters	1
Robinson	4	Reid S	2	Waters	1

HOME INTERNATIONAL RESULTS

Note: In the results that follow, WC = World Cup, EC = European Championship, CC = Carling Cup
TF = Tournoi de France For Northern Ireland read Ireland before 1921

ENGLAND V SCOTLAND
Played 110; England 45; Scotland 41; drawn 24 Goals: England 192, Scotland 169

		E	S					
1872	Glasgow	0	0	1879	The Oval		5	4
1873	The Oval	4	2	1880	Glasgow		4	5
1874	Glasgow	1	2	1881	The Oval		1	6
1875	The Oval	2	2	1882	Glasgow		1	5
1876	Glasgow	0	3	1883	Sheffield		2	3
1877	The Oval	1	3	1884	Glasgow		0	1
1878	Glasgow	2	7	1885	The Oval		1	1
				1886	Glasgow		1	1

Year	Venue	E/Scot		Year	Venue		
1887	Blackburn	2	3	1947	Wembley	1	1
1888	Glasgow	5	0	1948	Glasgow	2	0
1889	The Oval	2	3	1949	Wembley	1	3
1890	Glasgow	1	1	1950	Glasgow (WC)	1	0
1891	Blackburn	2	1	1951	Wembley	2	3
1892	Glasgow	4	1	1952	Glasgow	2	1
1893	Richmond	5	2	1953	Wembley	2	2
1894	Glasgow	2	2	1954	Glasgow (WC)	4	2
1895	Goodison Park	3	0	1955	Wembley	7	2
1896	Glasgow	1	2	1956	Glasgow	1	1
1897	Crystal Palace	1	2	1957	Wembley	2	1
1898	Glasgow	3	1	1958	Glasgow	4	0
1899	Birmingham	2	1	1959	Wembley	1	0
1900	Glasgow	1	4	1960	Glasgow	1	1
1901	Crystal Palace	2	2	1961	Wembley	9	3
1902	Birmingham	2	2	1962	Glasgow	0	2
1903	Sheffield	1	2	1963	Wembley	1	2
1904	Glasgow	1	0	1964	Glasgow	0	1
1905	Crystal Palace	1	0	1965	Wembley	2	2
1906	Glasgow	1	2	1966	Glasgow	4	3
1907	Newcastle	1	1	1967	Wembley (EC)	2	3
1908	Glasgow	1	1	1968	Glasgow (EC)	1	1
1909	Crystal Palace	2	0	1969	Wembley	4	1
1910	Glasgow	0	2	1970	Glasgow	0	0
1911	Goodison Park	1	1	1971	Wembley	3	1
1912	Glasgow	1	1	1972	Glasgow	1	0
1913	Stamford Bridge	1	0	1973	Glasgow	5	0
1914	Glasgow	1	3	1973	Wembley	1	0
1920	Sheffield	5	4	1974	Glasgow	0	2
1921	Glasgow	0	3	1975	Wembley	5	1
1922	Birmingham	0	1	1976	Glasgow	1	2
1923	Glasgow	2	2	1977	Wembley	1	2
1924	Wembley	1	1	1978	Glasgow	1	0
1925	Glasgow	0	2	1979	Wembley	3	1
1926	Manchester	0	1	1980	Glasgow	2	0
1927	Glasgow	2	1	1981	Wembley	0	1
1928	Wembley	1	5	1982	Glasgow	1	0
1929	Glasgow	0	1	1983	Wembley	2	0
1930	Wembley	5	2	1984	Glasgow	1	1
1931	Glasgow	0	2	1985	Glasgow	0	1
1932	Wembley	3	0	1986	Wembley	2	1
1933	Glasgow	1	2	1987	Glasgow	0	0
1934	Wembley	3	0	1988	Wembley	1	0
1935	Glasgow	0	2	1989	Glasgow	2	0
1936	Wembley	1	1	1996	Wembley (EC)	2	0
1937	Glasgow	1	3	1999	Glasgow (EC)	2	0
1938	Wembley	0	1	1999	Wembley (EC)	0	1
1939	Glasgow	2	1				

ENGLAND v WALES

Played 101; England won 66; Wales 14; drawn 21; Goals: England 245 Wales 90

Year	Venue	E	W	Year	Venue	E	W
1879	The Oval	2	1	1889	Stoke	4	1
1880	Wrexham	3	2	1890	Wrexham	3	1
1881	Blackburn	0	1	1891	Sunderland	4	1
1882	Wrexham	3	5	1892	Wrexham	2	0
1883	The Oval	5	0	1893	Stoke	6	0
1884	Wrexham	4	0	1894	Wrexham	5	1
1885	Blackburn	1	1	1895	Queens Club, London	1	1
1886	Wrexham	3	1	1896	Cardiff	9	1
1887	The Oval	4	0	1897	Bramall Lane	4	0
1888	Crewe	5	1	1898	Wrexham	3	0
				1899	Bristol	4	0

Year	Venue	E	W		Year	Venue	E	W
1900	Cardiff	1	1		1951	Cardiff	1	1
1901	Newcastle	6	0		1952	Wembley	5	2
1902	Wrexham	0	0		1953	Cardiff (WC)	4	1
1903	Portsmouth	2	1		1954	Wembley	3	2
1904	Wrexham	2	2		1955	Cardiff	1	2
1905	Anfield	3	1		1956	Wembley	3	1
1906	Cardiff	1	0		1957	Cardiff	4	0
1907	Fulham	1	1		1958	Villa Park	2	2
1908	Wrexham	7	1		1959	Cardiff	1	1
1909	Nottingham	2	0		1960	Wembley	5	1
1910	Cardiff	1	0		1961	Cardiff	1	1
1911	Millwall	3	0		1962	Wembley	4	0
1912	Wrexham	2	0		1963	Cardiff	4	0
1913	Bristol	4	3		1964	Wembley	2	1
1914	Cardiff	2	0		1965	Wembley	0	0
1920	Highbury	1	2		1966	Wembley (EC)	5	1
1921	Cardiff	0	0		1967	Cardiff (EC)	3	0
1922	Anfield	1	0		1969	Wembley	2	1
1923	Cardiff	2	2		1970	Cardiff	1	1
1924	Blackburn	1	2		1971	Wembley	0	0
1925	Swansea	2	1		1972	Cardiff	3	0
1926	Selhurst Park	1	3		1972	Cardiff (WC)	1	0
1927	Wrexham	3	3		1973	Wembley (WC)	1	1
1927	Burnley	1	2		1973	Wembley	3	0
1928	Swansea	3	2		1974	Cardiff	2	0
1929	Stamford Bridge	6	0		1975	Wembley	2	2
1930	Wrexham	4	0		1976	Wrexham	2	1
1931	Anfield	3	1		1976	Cardiff	1	0
1932	Wrexham	0	0		1977	Wembley	0	1
1933	Newcastle	1	2		1978	Cardiff	3	1
1934	Cardiff	4	0		1979	Wembley	0	0
1935	Wolverhampton	1	2		1980	Wrexham	1	4
1936	Cardiff	1	2		1981	Wembley	0	0
1937	Middlesbrough	2	1		1982	Cardiff	1	0
1938	Cardiff	2	4		1983	Wembley	2	1
1946	Maine Road	3	0		1984	Wrexham	0	1
1947	Cardiff	3	0		2004	Old Trafford (WC)	2	0
1948	Villa Park	1	0		2005	Cardiff (WC)	1	0
1949	Cardiff (WC)	4	1		2011	Cardiff (EC)	2	0
1950	Sunderland	4	2		2011	Wembley (EC)	1	0

ENGLAND v N IRELAND

Played 98; England won 75; Ireland 7; drawn 16 Goals: England 323, Ireland 81

Year	Venue	E	I		Year	Venue	E	I
1882	Belfast	13	0		1901	Southampton	3	0
1883	Aigburth, Liverpool	7	0		1902	Belfast	1	0
1884	Belfast	8	1		1903	Wolverhampton	4	0
1885	Whalley Range	4	0		1904	Belfast	3	1
1886	Belfast	6	1		1905	Middlesbrough	1	1
1887	Bramall Lane	7	0		1906	Belfast	5	0
1888	Belfast	5	1		1907	Goodison Park	1	0
1889	Goodison Park	6	1		1908	Belfast	3	1
1890	Belfast	9	1		1909	Bradford PA	4	0
1891	Wolverhampton	6	1		1910	Belfast	1	1
1892	Belfast	2	0		1911	Derby	2	1
1893	Perry Barr	6	1		1912	Dublin	6	1
1894	Belfast	2	2		1913	Belfast	1	2
1895	Derby	9	0		1914	Middlesbrough	0	3
1896	Belfast	2	0		1919	Belfast	1	1
1897	Nottingham	6	0		1920	Sunderland	2	0
1898	Belfast	3	2		1921	Belfast	1	1
1899	Sunderland	13	2		1922	West Bromwich	2	0
1900	Dublin	2	0		1923	Belfast	1	2
					1924	Goodison Park	3	1

Year	Venue			Year	Venue		
1925	Belfast	0	0	1962	Belfast	3	1
1926	Anfield	3	3	1963	Wembley	8	3
1927	Belfast	0	2	1964	Belfast	4	3
1928	Goodison Park	2	1	1965	Wembley	2	1
1929	Belfast	3	0	1966	Belfast (EC)	2	0
1930	Bramall Lane	5	1	1967	Wembley (EC)	2	0
1931	Belfast	6	2	1969	Belfast	3	1
1932	Blackpool	1	0	1970	Wembley	3	1
1933	Belfast	3	0	1971	Belfast	1	0
1935	Goodison Park	2	1	1972	Wembley	0	1
1935	Belfast	3	1	1973	*Goodison Park	2	1
1936	Stoke	3	1	1974	Wembley	1	0
1937	Belfast	5	1	1975	Belfast	0	0
1938	Old Trafford	7	0	1976	Wembley	4	0
1946	Belfast	7	2	1977	Belfast	2	1
1947	Goodison Park	2	2	1978	Wembley	1	0
1948	Belfast	6	2	1979	Wembley (EC)	4	0
1949	Maine Road (WC)	9	2	1979	Belfast	2	0
1950	Belfast	4	1	1979	Belfast (EC)	5	1
1951	Villa Park	2	0	1980	Wembley	1	1
1952	Belfast	2	2	1982	Wembley	4	0
1953	Goodison Park (WC)	3	1	1983	Belfast	0	0
1954	Belfast	2	0	1984	Wembley	1	0
1955	Wembley	3	0	1985	Belfast (WC)	1	0
1956	Belfast	1	1	1985	Wembley (WC)	0	0
1957	Wembley	2	3	1986	Wembley (EC)	3	0
1958	Belfast	3	3	1987	Belfast (EC)	2	0
1959	Wembley	2	1	2005	Old Trafford (WC)	4	0
1960	Belfast	5	2	2005	Belfast (WC)	0	1
1961	Wembley	1	1				

(*Switched from Belfast because of political situation)

SCOTLAND v WALES
Played 105; Scotland won 61; Wales 21; drawn 23 Goals: Scotland 241, Wales 120

Year	Venue	S	W	Year	Venue	S	W
1876	Glasgow	4	0	1905	Wrexham	1	3
1877	Wrexham	2	0	1906	Edinburgh	0	2
1878	Glasgow	9	0	1907	Wrexham	0	1
1879	Wrexham	3	0	1908	Dundee	2	1
1880	Glasgow	5	1	1909	Wrexham	2	3
1881	Wrexham	5	1	1910	Kilmarnock	1	0
1882	Glasgow	5	0	1911	Cardiff	2	2
1883	Wrexham	3	0	1912	Tynecastle	1	0
1884	Glasgow	4	1	1913	Wrexham	0	0
1885	Wrexham	8	1	1914	Glasgow	0	0
1886	Glasgow	4	1	1920	Cardiff	1	1
1887	Wrexham	2	0	1921	Aberdeen	2	1
1888	Edinburgh	5	1	1922	Wrexham	1	2
1889	Wrexham	0	0	1923	Paisley	2	0
1890	Paisley	5	0	1924	Cardiff	0	2
1891	Wrexham	4	3	1925	Tynecastle	3	1
1892	Edinburgh	6	1	1926	Cardiff	3	0
1893	Wrexham	8	0	1927	Glasgow	3	0
1894	Kilmarnock	5	2	1928	Wrexham	2	2
1895	Wrexham	2	2	1929	Glasgow	4	2
1896	Dundee	4	0	1930	Cardiff	4	2
1897	Wrexham	2	2	1931	Glasgow	1	1
1898	Motherwell	5	2	1932	Wrexham	3	2
1899	Wrexham	6	0	1933	Edinburgh	2	5
1900	Aberdeen	5	2	1934	Cardiff	2	3
1901	Wrexham	1	1	1935	Aberdeen	3	2
1902	Greenock	5	1	1936	Cardiff	1	1
1903	Cardiff	1	0	1937	Dundee	1	2
1904	Dundee	1	1	1938	Cardiff	1	2
				1939	Edinburgh	3	2

Year	Venue	Score		Year	Venue	Score	
1946	Wrexham	1	3	1971	Cardiff	0	0
1947	Glasgow	1	2	1972	Glasgow	1	0
1948	Cardiff (WC)	3	1	1973	Wrexham	2	0
1949	Glasgow	2	0	1974	Glasgow	2	0
1950	Cardiff	3	1	1975	Cardiff	2	2
1951	Glasgow	0	1	1976	Glasgow	3	1
1952	Cardiff (WC)	2	1	1977	Glasgow (WC)	1	0
1953	Glasgow	3	3	1977	Wrexham	0	0
1954	Cardiff	1	0	1977	Anfield (WC)	2	0
1955	Glasgow	2	0	1978	Glasgow	1	1
1956	Cardiff	2	2	1979	Cardiff	0	3
1957	Glasgow	1	1	1980	Glasgow	1	0
1958	Cardiff	3	0	1981	Swansea	0	2
1959	Glasgow	1	1	1982	Glasgow	1	0
1960	Cardiff	0	2	1983	Cardiff	2	0
1961	Glasgow	2	0	1984	Glasgow	2	1
1962	Cardiff	3	2	1985	Glasgow (WC)	0	1
1963	Glasgow	2	1	1985	Cardiff (WC)	1	1
1964	Cardiff	2	3	1997	Kilmarnock	0	1
1965	Glasgow (EC)	4	1	2004	Cardiff	0	4
1966	Cardiff (EC)	1	1	2009	Cardiff	0	3
1967	Glasgow	3	2	2011	Dublin (CC)	3	1
1969	Wrexham	5	3				
1970	Glasgow	0	0				

SCOTLAND v NORTHERN IRELAND

Played 95; Scotland won 63; Northern Ireland 15; drawn 17; Goals: Scotland 257, Northern Ireland 80

Year	Venue	S	I	Year	Venue	S	I
1884	Belfast	5	0	1922	Glasgow	2	1
1885	Glasgow	8	2	1923	Belfast	1	0
1886	Belfast	7	2	1924	Glasgow	2	0
1887	Belfast	4	1	1925	Belfast	3	0
1888	Belfast	10	2	1926	Glasgow	4	0
1889	Glasgow	7	0	1927	Belfast	2	0
1890	Belfast	4	1	1928	Glasgow	0	1
1891	Glasgow	2	1	1929	Belfast	7	3
1892	Belfast	3	2	1930	Glasgow	3	1
1893	Glasgow	6	1	1931	Belfast	0	0
1894	Belfast	2	1	1932	Glasgow	3	1
1895	Glasgow	3	1	1933	Belfast	4	0
1896	Belfast	3	3	1934	Glasgow	1	2
1897	Glasgow	5	1	1935	Belfast	1	2
1898	Belfast	3	0	1936	Edinburgh	2	1
1899	Glasgow	9	1	1937	Belfast	3	1
1900	Belfast	3	0	1938	Aberdeen	1	1
1901	Glasgow	11	0	1939	Belfast	2	0
1902	Belfast	5	1	1946	Glasgow	0	0
1902	Belfast	3	0	1947	Belfast	0	2
1903	Glasgow	0	2	1948	Glasgow	3	2
1904	Dublin	1	1	1949	Belfast	8	2
1905	Glasgow	4	0	1950	Glasgow	6	1
1906	Dublin	1	0	1951	Belfast	3	0
1907	Glasgow	3	0	1952	Glasgow	1	1
1908	Dublin	5	0	1953	Belfast	3	1
1909	Glasgow	5	0	1954	Glasgow	2	2
1910	Belfast	0	1	1955	Belfast	1	2
1911	Glasgow	2	0	1956	Glasgow	1	0
1912	Belfast	4	1	1957	Belfast	1	1
1913	Dublin	2	1	1958	Glasgow	2	2
1914	Belfast	1	1	1959	Belfast	4	0
1920	Glasgow	3	0	1960	Glasgow	5	1
1921	Belfast	2	0	1961	Belfast	6	1
				1962	Glasgow	5	1

1963	Belfast	1	2	1977	Glasgow	3	0
1964	Glasgow	3	2	1978	Glasgow	1	1
1965	Belfast	2	3	1979	Glasgow	1	0
1966	Glasgow	2	1	1980	Belfast	0	1
1967	Belfast	0	1	1981	Glasgow (WC)	1	1
1969	Glasgow	1	1	1981	Glasgow	2	0
1970	Belfast	1	0	1981	Belfast (WC)	0	0
1971	Glasgow	0	1	1982	Belfast	1	1
1972	Glasgow	2	0	1983	Glasgow	0	0
1973	Glasgow	1	2	1984	Belfast	0	2
1974	Glasgow	0	1	1992	Glasgow	1	0
1975	Glasgow	3	0	2008	Glasgow	0	0
1976	Glasgow	3	0	2011	Dublin (CC)	3	0

WALES v NORTHERN IRELAND

Played 95; Wales won 44; Northern Ireland won 27; drawn 24; Goals: Wales 189, Northern Ireland 131

		W	I				
1882	Wrexham	7	1	1935	Wrexham	3	1
1883	Belfast	1	1	1936	Belfast	2	3
1884	Wrexham	6	0	1937	Wrexham	4	1
1885	Belfast	8	2	1938	Belfast	0	1
1886	Wrexham	5	0	1939	Wrexham	3	1
1887	Belfast	1	4	1947	Belfast	1	2
1888	Wrexham	11	0	1948	Wrexham	2	0
1889	Belfast	3	1	1949	Belfast	2	0
1890	Shrewsbury	5	2	1950	Wrexham (WC)	0	0
1891	Belfast	2	7	1951	Belfast	2	1
1892	Bangor	1	1	1952	Swansea	3	0
1893	Belfast	3	4	1953	Belfast	3	2
1894	Swansea	4	1	1954	Wrexham (WC)	1	2
1895	Belfast	2	2	1955	Belfast	3	2
1896	Wrexham	6	1	1956	Cardiff	1	1
1897	Belfast	3	4	1957	Belfast	0	0
1898	Llandudno	0	1	1958	Cardiff	1	1
1899	Belfast	0	1	1959	Belfast	1	4
1900	Llandudno	2	0	1960	Wrexham	3	2
1901	Belfast	1	0	1961	Belfast	5	1
1902	Cardiff	0	3	1962	Cardiff	4	0
1903	Belfast	0	2	1963	Belfast	4	1
1904	Bangor	0	1	1964	Swansea	2	3
1905	Belfast	2	2	1965	Belfast	5	0
1906	Wrexham	4	4	1966	Cardiff	1	4
1907	Belfast	3	2	1967	Belfast (EC)	0	0
1908	Aberdare	0	1	1968	Wrexham (EC)	2	0
1909	Belfast	3	2	1969	Belfast	0	0
1910	Wrexham	4	1	1970	Swansea	1	0
1911	Belfast	2	1	1971	Belfast	0	1
1912	Cardiff	2	3	1972	Wrexham	0	0
1913	Belfast	1	0	1973	*Goodison Park	0	1
1914	Wrexham	1	2	1974	Wrexham	1	0
1920	Belfast	2	2	1975	Belfast	0	1
1921	Swansea	2	1	1976	Swansea	1	0
1922	Belfast	1	1	1977	Belfast	1	1
1923	Wrexham	0	3	1978	Wrexham	1	0
1924	Belfast	1	0	1979	Belfast	1	1
1925	Wrexham	0	0	1980	Cardiff	0	1
1926	Belfast	0	3	1982	Wrexham	3	0
1927	Cardiff	2	2	1983	Belfast	1	0
1928	Belfast	2	1	1984	Swansea	1	1
1929	Wrexham	2	2	2004	Cardiff (WC)	2	2
1930	Belfast	0	7	2005	Belfast (WC)	3	2
1931	Wrexham	3	2	2007	Belfast	0	0
1932	Belfast	0	4	2008	Glasgow	0	0
1933	Wrexham	4	1	2011	Dublin (CC)	2	0
1934	Belfast	1	1				

(*Switched from Belfast because of political situation in N Ireland)

BRITISH AND IRISH UNDER-21 INTERNATIONALS 2011–12

EUROPEAN CHAMPIONSHIP 2013 – QUALIFYING

NORTHERN IRELAND 4 FAROE ISLANDS 0
Group 4: Oval, Belfast (1,500); Wednesday, August 10 2011

Northern Ireland: Devlin (unatt), Knowles (Blackburn), Dudgeon (Hull), McLaughlin (York), Hegarty (Rangers), McKeown (Kilmarnock), Lund (Stoke) (Breeze, Wigan 60), Norwood (Manchester Utd), Kee (Torquay), Magennis (Aberdeen) (Boyce, Werder Bremen 65), Carson (Ipswich) (Grigg, Walsall 73). **Booked:** McLaughlin, Hegarty, Knowles. **Sent off:** Knowles
Scorers – Northern Ireland: Kee (25, 29, 75), Magennis (32). **Half-time:** 3-0

ENGLAND 6 AZERBAIJAN 0
Group 8: Vicarage Road, Watford (7,738); Thursday, September 1 2011

England: Butland (Birmingham), Flanagan (Liverpool), Caulker (Tottenham), Dawson (WBA), Briggs (Fulham), Rodwell (Everton), Henderson (Liverpool), Oxlade-Chamberlain (Arsenal) (Shelvey, Liverpool 79), Lansbury (Arsenal), Delfouneso (Aston Villa) (Sordell, Watford 69), Wickham (Sunderland) (Waghorn, Leicester 69)
Scorers – England: Dawson (5, 89), Lansbury (21, 73), Henderson (45), Waghorn (79). **Half-time:** 3-0

REPUBLIC OF IRELAND 2 HUNGARY 1
Group 7: Showgrounds, Sligo (2,500); Thursday, September 1 2011

Republic of Ireland: McLoughlin (MK Dons), Connolly (Bolton), Canavan (Scunthorpe), Kiernan (Wigan) , Gunning (Dundee Utd), Towell (Celtic), Barton (Preston), McCarthy (Wigan), Brady (Manchester Utd), Murphy (Arsenal), White (Leeds). **Booked:** Towell
Scorers – Republic of Ireland: Brady (15), Murphy (69). **Hungary:** Futacs (38). **Half-time:** 1-1

SERBIA 1 NORTHERN IRELAND 0
Group 4: Novi Sad (2,250); Friday, September 2 2011

Northern Ireland: Devlin (unatt), C McLaughlin (Preston), McKeown (Kilmarnock), P McLaughlin (York), McCashin (Glenn Hoddle Acad) (Clucas, Preston 64), Ramsey (Portadown), Grigg (Walsall) (Magennis, Aberdeen 64), Norwood (Manchester Utd), Kee (Burton), Carson (Ipswich), Ferguson (Newcastle) (Breeze, Wigan 77). **Booked:** Carson, Norwood, Kee
Scorer – Serbia: Milivojevic (17). **Half-time:** 1-0

SCOTLAND 0 BULGARIA 0
Group 10: St Mirren Park (2,769); Monday, September 5 2011

Scotland: Adam (Rangers), Wotherspoon (Hibernian), Perry (Rangers), Hanlon (Hibernian), Booth (Hibernian), Cairney (Hull), Kelly (Kilmarnock), Armstrong (Dundee Utd), Allan (Dundee Utd) (Pawlett, Aberdeen 75), Russell (Dundee Utd), Rhodes (Huddersfield) (Griffiths, Wolves 61). **Booked:** Perry

MONTENEGRO 3 WALES 1
Group 3: Podgorica (2,650); Tuesday, September 6 2011

Wales: Maxwell (Wrexham), Freeman (Nottm Forest), Richards (Swansea), Lucas (Swansea), Alfei (Swansea), Brown (Rotherham), Williams (Crystal Palace) (Taylor, Reading 62), Hewitt (Macclesfield) (Meades, Cardiff 74), Bradshaw (Shrewsbury), Doble (Southampton), Bodin (Swindon) (Chamberlain, Leicester 71)
Scorers – Montenegro: Golubovic (65), Mugosa (77), Nikolic (88). **Wales :** Bradshaw (55)
Half-time: 0-0

NORTHERN IRELAND 0 DENMARK 3
Group 4: Oval, Belfast (172); Tuesday, September 6 2011

Northern Ireland: Devlin (unatt), Winchester (Oldham), McKeown (Kilmarnock), Breeze (Wigan) (Ball, Norwich 65), Hegarty (Rangers), Ramsey (Portadown), Dallas (Crusaders) (Grigg, Walsall 65), Norwood (Manchester Utd), Boyce (Werder Bremen) (McLellan, Preston 80), Magennis

(Aberdeen), Ferguson (Newcastle). **Booked**: Magennis, Ramsey, Hegarty, Breeze, Norwood
Scorers – Denmark: Helenius (6), Laudrup (81), Larsen (88). **Half-time**: 0-1

TURKEY 1 REPUBLIC OF IRELAND 0
Group 7: Manisa (2,712): Tuesday, September 6 2011
Republic of Ireland: McLoughlin (MK Dons), Oyebanjo (York) (Duffy, Everton 75), Canavan
(Scunthorpe), Kiernan (Wigan), Gunning (Dundee Utd), Towell (Celtic) (Hourihane, Plymouth
80), Connolly (Bolton), Clifford (Chelsea), White (Leeds), Hendrick (Derby) (Collins,
Shrewsbury 66), Brady (Manchester Utd). **Booked**: Hendrick, Gunning
Scorer – Turkey: Sahin (10). **Half-time**: 1-0

ICELAND 0 ENGLAND 3
Group 8: Reykjavik (2,599); Thursday, October 6 2011
England: Butland (Birmingham), Flanagan (Liverpool), Kelly (Liverpool), Dawson (WBA), Briggs
(Fulham), Oxlade-Chamberlain (Arsenal) (Barkley, Everton 83), Henderson (Liverpool), Rodwell
(Everton), Lansbury (Arsenal), Sordell (Watford), Delfouneso (Aston Villa) (Waghorn, Leicester
24) (McEachran (Chelsea 63). **Booked**: Kelly
Scorer – England: Oxlade-Chamberlain (12, 15, 50). **Half-time**: 0-2

LUXEMBOURG 1 SCOTLAND 5
Group 10: Josy Barthel (320); Thursday, October 6 2011
Scotland: Adam (Rangers), Jack (Aberdeen), Hanlon (Hibernian), Wilson (Liverpool), Perry
(Rangers), Palmer (Sheffield Wed), MacDonald (Burnley), Wotherspoon (Hibernian), Rhodes
(Huddersfield), (Griffiths,Wolves 73), Allan (Dundee Utd), (Russell, Dundee Utd 78), Wylde
(Rangers), (Pawlett, Aberdeen 64)
Scorers – Luxembourg: Almeida (82). **Scotland**: MacDonald (29), Rhodes (33, 43, 63),
Hanlon (87). **Half-time**: 0-3

WALES 1 MONTENEGRO 0
Group 3: Racecourse Ground, Wrexham (525); Saturday, October 8 2011
Wales: Maxwell (Wrexham), Freeman (Nottm Forest), Richards (Swansea), Lucas (Swansea),
Brown (Rotherham), Alfei (Swansea), Taylor (Reading) (Bodin, Swindon 79), Hewitt
(Macclesfield), Bradshaw (Shrewsbury), Doble (Southampton), Howells (Luton). **Booked**: Maxwell
Scorer – Wales: Alfei (58 pen). **Half-time**: 0-0

NORWAY 1 ENGLAND 2
Group 8: Drammen (2,323): Monday, October 10 2011
England: Butland (Birmingham), Smith (Tottenham), Baker (Aston Villa) (Flanagan, Liverpool
72), Dawson (WBA), Bennett (Peterborough), Oxlade-Chamberlain (Arsenal), Henderson
(Liverpool), Lansbury (Arsenal), Barkley (Everton) (Gardner, Aston Villa 55), Lowe (Blackburn),
Sordell (Watford) (Shelvey, Liverpool 81)
Scorers – Norway: Berisha (21). **England**: Dawson (4), Henderson (6). **Half-time**: 1-2

SCOTLAND 2 AUSTRIA 2
Group 10: St Mirren Park (3,058); Monday, October 10 2011
Scotland: Adam (Rangers), Jack (Aberdeen), Hanlon (Hibernian), Wilson (Liverpool), Perry
(Rangers), Palmer (Sheffield Wed), Wotherspoon (Hibernian), Russell (Dundee Utd) (Pawlett,
Aberdeen 61), Allan (Dundee Utd) (MacDonald, Burnley 45), Wylde (Rangers) (Griffiths,Wolves
75), Rhodes (Huddersfield). **Booked**: Allan
Scorers – Scotland: Rhodes (37, 64). **Austria**: Weimann (14), Alar (42). **Half-time**: 1-2

WALES 0 CZECH REPUBLIC 1
Group 3: Racecourse Ground, Wrexham (595): Tuesday, October 11 2011
Wales: Maxwell (Wrexham), Freeman (Nottm Forest), Richards (Swansea), Lucas
(Swansea), Brown (Rotherham), Alfei (Swansea), Taylor (Reading) (Bodin, Swindon 46),
Hewitt (Macclesfield), Bradshaw (Shrewsbury) (Ogleby, Hearts 74), Doble (Southampton)
(Chamberlain, Leicester 66), Howells (Luton). **Booked**: Richards, Alfei
Scorer – Czech Republic: Kadlec (5). **Half-time**: 0-1

LIECHTENSTEIN 1 REPUBLIC OF IRELAND 4
Group 7: Eschen (293); Tuesday, October 11 2011
Republic of Ireland: McLoughlin (MK Dons), Connolly (Bolton), Duffy (Everton), Kiernan (Wigan), Cunningham (Manchester City) (Stevens, Shamrock 69), Brady (Manchester Utd) (Greene, Sligo 79), Towell (Celtic), Clifford (Chelsea) (Hourihane, Plymouth 66), White (Leeds), Barton (Preston), Collins (Shrewsbury)
Scorers – Liechtenstein: Pirker (14). **Republic of Ireland**: Collins (26, 30, 33), Duffy (39). **Half-time**: 1-4

ENGLAND 5 ICELAND 0
Group 8: Community Stadium, Colchester (10,051); Thursday, November 10 2011
England: Butland (Birmingham), Smith (Tottenham), Kelly (Liverpool), Dawson (WBA), Clyne (Crystal Palace), Henderson (Liverpool), Lowe (Blackburn) (Gardner, Aston Villa 62), Oxlade-Chamberlain (Arsenal), McEachran (Chelsea) (Keane, Manchester Utd 78), Delfouneso (Aston Villa) (Sammy Ameobi, Newcastle 11), Sordell (Watford)
Scorers – England: Sordell (39), Kelly (58), Dawson (86), Gardner (90, 90). **Half-time**: 1-0

BELGIUM 2 ENGLAND 1
Group 8: Mons (3,519); Monday, November 14 2011
England: Butland (Birmingham), Smith (Tottenham), Kelly (Liverpool), Dawson (WBA), Clyne (Crystal Palace), Henderson (Liverpool), Lowe (Blackburn) (Barkley, Everton 90), Oxlade-Chamberlain (Arsenal), McEachran (Chelsea), Sammy Ameobi (Newcastle) (Gardner, Aston Villa 62), Sordell (Watford) (Keane, Manchester Utd 78). **Booked**: Smith
Scorers – Belgium: Naessens (72), El Kaddouri (90). **England**: Kelly (14). **Half-time**: 0-1

REPUBLIC OF IRELAND 2 LIECHTENSTEIN 0
Group 7: Showgrounds, Sligo (2,108); Monday, November 14 2011
Republic of Ireland: McLoughlin (MK Dons), Connolly (Bolton), Duffy (Everton), Kiernan (Wigan), Cunningham (Manchester City), Towell (Hibernian), Clifford (Chelsea) (Greene, Sligo 86), Barton (Preston) (Hendrick, Derby 81), Brady (Manchester Utd), Collins (Shrewsbury) (Sheppard, Shamrock 72), White (Leeds). **Booked**: Clifford, Collins
Scorers – Republic of Ireland: Brady (13 pen), White (37). **Half-time**: 2-0

ARMENIA 0 WALES 0
Group 3: Yerevan (750); Tuesday, November 15 2011
Wales: Maxwell (Wrexham), Freeman (Nottm Forest) (Ogleby, Hearts 83), Richards (Swansea), Lucas (Swansea), Alfei (Swansea) (Brown, Rotherham 59), Stephens (Hibernian), Taylor (Reading), Hewitt (Macclesfield), Bradshaw (Shrewsbury), Bodin (Swindon), Williams (Crystal Palace) (Chamberlain, Leicester 72). **Booked**: Alfei, Taylor

NORTHERN IRELAND 0 SERBIA 2
Group 4: Showground, Coleraine (300); Tuesday, November 15 2011
Northern Ireland: Devlin (unatt); Hodson (Watford), Dudgeon (Hull), Clucas (Preston), Thompson (Watford), McLaughlin (Preston), Ferguson (Newcastle) (Lavery, unatt 79), Carson (Ipswich), Magennis (Aberdeen), Grigg (Walsall) (Knowles, Blackburn 46), Gorman (Wolves (Winchester, Oldham 79). **Booked**: Carson, Dudgeon, Ferguson, Knowles, Magennis
Scorers – Serbia: Marlkovic (80), Gudelj (83 pen). **Half-time**: 0-0

ENGLAND 4 BELGIUM 0
Group 8: Riverside Stadium, Middlesbrough (22,647); Wednesday, February 29 2012
England: Butland (Birmingham), Kelly (Liverpoool), Caulker (Tottenham), Dawson (WBA), Rose (Tottenham), Oxlade-Chamberlain (Arsenal), Henderson (Liverpool), McEachran (Chelsea), Zaha (Crystal Palace) (Shelvey, Liverpool 67), Lansbury (Arsenal) (Gardner, Aston Villa 73), Sordell (Bolton) (Keane, Manchester Utd 82). **Booked**: Dawson
Scorers – England: Lansbury (9, 53), Caulker (36), Oxlade-Chamberlain (90 pen). **Half-time**: 2-0

SCOTLAND 0 HOLLAND 0
Group 10: St Mirren Park (6,607); Wednesday, February 29 2012
Scotland: Ridgers (Hearts), Jack (Aberdeen), Hanlon (Hibernian), Wilson (Liverpool), Perry (Rangers), Kelly (Kilmarnock), Russell (Dundee Utd), Cairney (Hull) (Allan, WBA 68), Rhodes (Huddersfield) (O'Halloran, Bolton 86), Wotherspoon (Hibernian), Mackay-Steven (Dundee Utd)

WALES 4 ANDORRA 0
Group 3: Racecourse Ground, Wrexham (2,013); Wednesday, February 29 2012
Wales: Maxwell (Wrexham), Henley (Blackburn), Freeman (Nottm Forest) (Dummett, Newcastle 61), Richards (Swansea), Stephens (Hibernian), Brown (Rotherham) (A Taylor, Tranmere 57), Bodin (Swindon), Howells (Luton), Cassidy (Wolves) (Bradshaw, Shrewsbury 69), J Taylor (Reading), Doble (Southampton). **Booked:** Cassidy
Scorers – Wales: Bodin (22, 33), Vieira (44 og), Doble (59). **Half-time:** 3-0

MACEDONIA 1 NORTHERN IRELAND 0
Group 4: Kumanovo (1,100); Thursday, May 10 2012
Northern Ireland: Devlin (unatt), Hodson (Watford), McGivern (Manchester City), Thompson (Watford), C McLaughlin (Preston), Clucas (Preston), R McLaughlin (Liverpool) (Lavery, unatt 77), Norwood (Manchester Utd), Grigg (Walsall), Lund (Stoke) (McClure, Wycombe 86), Ferguson (Newcastle). **Booked:** McGivern, Clucas, Norwood, Devlin. **Sent off:** Ferguson
Scorer – Macedonia: Urdinov (83 pen). **Half-time:** 0-0

BULGARIA 2 SCOTLAND 2
Group 10: Lovech (1,500); Thursday, May 31 2012
Scotland: Ridgers (Hearts), Jack (Aberdeen) (Toshney, Celtic 81), Hanlon (Hibernian), Wilson (Liverpool), Perry (Rangers), Kelly (Kilmarnock), Russell (Dundee Utd) (Palmer, Sheffield Wed 83), Wotherspoon (Hibernian) (Armstrong, Dunde Utd 67), Rhodes (Huddersfield), Allan (WBA), Mackay-Steven (Dundee Utd). **Booked:** Wotherspoon
Scorers – Bulgaria: Milanov (33), Kostadinov (90). **Scotland:** Rhodes (69, 90). **Half-time:** 1-0

REPUBLIC OF IRELAND 2 ITALY 2
Group 7: Showgrounds, Sligo (2,600); Monday, June 4 2012
Republic of Ireland: McLoughlin (MK Dons) (McCarey, Wolves 59), Egan (Sunderland), Duffy (Everton), Canavan (Scunthorpe), Cunningham (Manchester City), Hendrick (Derby), Towell (Celtic), O'Kane (Torquay), White (Leeds), Murphy (unatt) (Collins, Shrewsbury 89), Brady (Manchester Utd). **Booked:** Duffy, Murphy
Scorers – Republic of Ireland: Brady (67 pen), Cunningham (71). **Italy:** Duffy (3 og), Immobile (55). **Half-time:** 0-1

CURRENT STANDINGS

GROUP 1

	P	W	D	L	F	A	Pts
Germany	8	8	0	0	32	5	24
Bosnia-Herzegovina	8	5	1	2	17	8	16
Greece	8	3	1	4	13	11	10
Belarus	7	3	1	3	10	11	10
Cyprus	8	3	0	5	13	19	9
San Marino	9	0	1	8	2	33	1

GROUP 2

	P	W	D	L	F	A	Pts
Slovenia	8	5	2	1	13	5	17
Sweden	7	5	1	1	12	7	16
Ukraine	7	3	2	2	13	7	11
Finland	7	2	3	2	6	6	9
Lithuania	8	2	0	6	4	12	6
Malta	9	1	2	6	7	18	5

GROUP 3

	P	W	D	L	F	A	Pts
Czech Republic	6	5	1	0	19	3	16
Armenia	6	3	2	1	10	5	11
Wales	6	3	1	2	7	4	10

	P	W	D	L	F	A	Pts
Montenegro	6	3	0	3	14	8	9
Andorra	8	0	0	8	2	32	0

GROUP 4

	P	W	D	L	F	A	Pts
Serbia	6	4	2	0	11	2	14
Denmark	5	3	2	0	14	6	11
Macedonia	6	2	3	1	10	9	9
Northern Ireland	6	1	1	4	4	7	4
Faroe Islands	7	0	2	5	2	17	2

GROUP 5

	P	W	D	L	F	A	Pts
Spain	6	6	0	0	21	2	18
Switzerland	6	4	1	1	12	4	13
Georgia	6	2	0	4	5	16	6
Croatia	6	2	0	4	6	9	6
Estonia	6	0	1	5	1	14	1

GROUP 6

	P	W	D	L	F	A	Pts
Portugal	7	4	2	1	15	6	14
Russia	6	4	1	1	11	2	13
Poland	6	3	1	2	12	9	10
Albania	7	1	2	4	10	16	5
Moldova	6	1	0	5	6	21	3

GROUP 7

	P	W	D	L	F	A	Pts
Italy	6	5	1	0	18	4	16
Turkey	7	4	0	3	12	7	12
Republic of Ireland	5	3	1	1	10	5	10
Hungary	6	2	0	4	7	9	6
Liechtenstein	6	0	0	6	4	26	0

GROUP 8

	P	W	D	L	F	A	Pts
England	6	5	0	1	21	3	15
Norway	6	4	1	1	10	5	13
Belgium	6	2	2	2	11	12	8
Azerbaijan	7	2	1	4	6	16	7
Iceland	7	1	0	6	4	16	3

GROUP 9

	P	W	D	L	F	A	Pts
France	7	7	0	0	18	0	21
Romania	7	3	2	2	7	6	11
Slovakia	6	3	0	3	9	6	9
Kazakhstan	6	0	3	3	1	7	3
Latvia	6	0	1	5	0	16	1

GROUP 10

	P	W	D	L	F	A	Pts
Holland	7	5	1	1	17	2	16
Scotland	6	2	4	0	11	6	10
Bulgaria	7	2	3	2	8	11	9
Austria	6	2	2	2	11	8	8
Luxembourg	6	0	0	6	5	25	0

INTERNATIONAL FRIENDLIES

REPUBLIC OF IRELAND 2 AUSTRIA 1
Showgrounds, Sligo (1,810); Tuesday, August 9 2011
Republic of Ireland: McLoughlin (MK Dons) (McCarey, Wolves 46), Connolly (Bolton), Kiernan (Wigan), Canavan (Scunthorpe) (Oyebanjo, York 46), Gunning (Blackburn) (Stevens, Shamrock 46), Clifford (Chelsea) (Mason, Cardiff 46), Towell (Celtic), Hendrick (Derby) (Duffy, Everton 46), Brady (Manchester Utd), Doran (Inverness) (Kearns, Dundalk 80), White (Leeds) (Greene, Sligo 73)
Scorers – Republic of Ireland: Brady (72, 90 pen). **Austria:** Holzhauser (68). **Half-time:** 0-0

SCOTLAND 3 NORWAY 0
St Mirren Park (1,654); Wednesday, August 10 2011
Scotland: Adam (Rangers), Jack (Aberdeen), Saunders (Motherwell) (Perry, Rangers 4), Hanlon (Hibernian), Booth (Hibernian), Cairney (Hull) (Armstrong, Dundee Utd 46), Kelly (Kilmarnock), Allan (Dundee Utd) (Cole, Rangers 68), Wylde (Rangers) (Ross, Inverness 58), Russell (Dundee Utd) (MacDonald (Burnley 58), Rhodes (Huddersfield) (Griffiths, Wolves 46).
Booked: Rhodes, Russell, Perry
Scorers – Scotland: Cairney (20), Jack (72), Armstrong (75). **Half-time:** 1-0

WALES 1 HUNGARY 2
Meadow Stadium, Haverfordwest (400); Wednesday, August 10, 2011
Wales: Maxwell (Wrexham) (Taylor, Chelsea 46), Alfei (Swansea), Freeman (Nottm Forest) (Bender, Colchester 74), Lucas (Swansea), Stephens (Hibernian) (Hewitt, Macclesfield 46), Brown (Rotherham) (Walsh, Swansea 61), Taylor (Reading), Howells (Luton), Peniket (Fulham) (Ogleby, Hearts 46), Bodin (Swindon) (Thomas, Swansea 78), Williams (Crystal Palace)
Scorers – Wales: Lucas (37). **Hungary:** Balazs (6), Haraszti (90). **Half-time:** 1-1

ENGLAND 4 ISRAEL 1
Oakwell, Barnsley (9,152); Monday, September 5 2011
England: Amos (Manchester Utd), Wisdom (Liverpool) (Smith, Tottenham 46), Bennett (Middlesbrough), Dawson (WBA), Baker (Aston Villa) (Caulker, Tottenham 45), Gosling (Newcastle) (Gardner, Aston Villa 62), Rodwell (Everton) (Lansbury, Arsenal 46), Barkley (Everton) (Wickham, Sunderland 73), Shelvey (Liverpool) (Oxlade-Chamberlain, Arsenal 46), Waghorn (Leicester) (Delfouneso, Aston Villa 62), Sordell (Watford)
Scorers – England: Waghorn (58), Sordell (61), Delfouneso (83 pen), Lansbury (90). **Israel:** Klivat (25). **Half-time:** 0-1

SCOTLAND 1 ITALY 4
Easter Road, Edinburgh (4,665); Wednesday, April 25 2012
Scotland: Ridgers (Hearts), (Adam, Rangers 46), Edwards, Rochdale 52), Jack (Aberdeen) (Toshney,Celtic 80), Wilson (Liverpool), Perry (Rangers), Hanlon (Hibernian) (G Shinnie, Inverness 80), Kelly (Kilmarnock) (McGeouch, Celtic46), Wotherspoon (Hibernian) (Palmer, Sheffield Wed 74), Allan (WBA), (Feruz, Chelsea 62), Russell (Dundee Utd) (McGeouch, Celtic 46), MacDonald (Burnley) (McLean,St Mirren 62), Mackay-Steven (Dundee Utd) (Armstrong, Dundee Utd 74)
Scorers – Scotland: Mackay-Steven (33). **Italy:** Florenzi (8), Immobile (55), Insigne (75), Longo (89). **Half-time:** 1-1

REPUBLIC OF IRELAND 1 DENMARK 2
Tallaght Stadium, Dublin (500); Monday, May 28 2012
Republic of Ireland: McLoughlin (MK Dons) (McCarey, Wolves 77), Egan (Sunderland), Duffy (Everton), Canavan (Scunthorpe), Cunningham (Manchester City), Hendrick (Derby) (Clifford, Chelsea 55), Towell (unatt), O'Kane (Torquay) (Houihane, Plymouth 55), White (Leeds), Murphy (unatt) (Collins, Shrewsbury 55), Brady (Manchester Utd) (Murray, Ipswich 77)
Scorers – Republic of Ireland: Brady (54). **Denmark:** Albaek (57, 74 pen). **Half-time:** 0-0

TRANSFER TRAIL

I	=	World record fee	D	=	Record fee paid by Scottish club
A	=	Record all-British deal	F	=	Record for teenager
B	=	British record for goalkeeper	G	=	Most expensive foreign import
C	=	Record deal between English and Scottish clubs			

	Player	From	To	Date	£
I	Cristiano Ronaldo	Manchester Utd	Real Madrid	7/09	80,000,000
A	Fernando Torres	Liverpool	Chelsea	1/11	50,000,000
G	Sergio Aguero	Atletico Madrid	Manchester City	7/11	38,500,000
	Andy Carroll	Newcastle	Liverpool	1/11	35,000,000
	Cesc Fabregas	Arsenal	Barcelona	8/11	35,000,000
	Robinho	Real Madrid	Manchester City	9/08	32,500,000
	Eden Hazard	Lille	Chelsea	6/12	32,000,000
	DimitarBerbatov	Tottenham	Manchester Utd	9/08	30,750,000
	Andriy Shevchenko	AC Milan	Chelsea	5/06	30,800,000
	Xabi Alonso	Liverpool	Real Madrid	8/09	30,000,000
	Rio Ferdinand	Leeds	Manchester Utd	7/02	29,100,000
	Juan Sebastian Veron	Lazio	Manchester Utd	7/01	28,100,000
	YayaToure	Barcelona	Manchester City	7/10	28,000,000
F	Wayne Rooney	Everton	Manchester Utd	8/04	27,000,000
	Edin Dzeko	Wolfsburg	Manchester City	1/11	27,000,000
	Marc Overmars	Arsenal	Barcelona	7/00	25,000,000
	Carlos Tevez	Manchester Utd	Manchester City	7/09	25,000,000
	Emmanuel Adebayor	Arsenal	Manchester City	7/09	25,000,000
	Samir Nasri	Arsenal	Manchester City	8/11	25,000,000
	Oscar	Internacional	Chelsea	7/12	25,000,000
	ArjenRobben	Chelsea	Real Madrid	8/07	24,500,000
	Michael Essien	Lyon	Chelsea	8/05	24,400,000
	David Silva	Valencia	Manchester City	7/10	24,000,000
	James Milner	Aston Villa	Manchester City	8/10	24,000,000
	Mario Balotelli	Inter Milan	Manchester City	8/10	24,000,000
	Darren Bent	Sunderland	Aston Villa	1/11	24,000,000
	Juan Mata	Valencia	Chelsea	8/11	23,500,000
	David Beckham	Manchester Utd	Real Madrid	7/03	23,300,000
	Didier Drogba	Marseille	Chelsea	7/04	23,200,000
	Luis Suarez	Ajax	Liverpool	1/11	22,700,000
	Nicolas Anelka	Arsenal	Real Madrid	8/99	22,300,000
	Fernando Torres	Atletico Madrid	Liverpool	7/07	22,000,000
	JoloenLescott	Everton	Manchester City	8/09	22,000,000
	David Luiz	Benfica	Chelsea	1/11	21,300,000
	Shaun Wright-Phillips	Manchester City	Chelsea	7/05	21,000,000
	LassanaDiarra	Portsmouth	Real Madrid	12/08	20,000,000
	Alberto Aquilani	Roma	Liverpool	8/09	20,000,000
	Stewart Downing	Aston Villa	Liverpool	7/11	20,000,000
	Ricardo Carvalho	Porto	Chelsea	7/04	19,850,000
	Ruud van Nistelrooy	PSV Eindhoven	Manchester Utd	4/01	19,000,000
	Robbie Keane	Tottenham	Liverpool	7/08	19,000,000
	Michael Carrick	Tottenham	Manchester Utd	8/06	18,600,000
	Javier Mascherano	Media Sports	Liverpool	2/08	18,600,000
	Rio Ferdinand	West Ham	Leeds	11/00	18,000,000
	Anderson	Porto	Manchester Utd	7/07	18,000,000

	Jo	CSKA Moscow	Manchester City	6/08	18,000,000
	Yuri Zhirkov	CSKA Moscow	Chelsea	7/09	18,000,000
	Ramires	Benfica	Chelsea	8/10	18,000,000
	Romelu Lukaku	Anderlecht	Chelsea	8/11	18,000,000
B	David De Gea	Atletico Madrid	Manchester Utd	6/11	17,800,000
	Roque Santa Cruz	Blackburn	Manchester City	6/09	17,500,000
	Jose Reyes	Sevilla	Arsenal	1/04	17,400,000
	Javier Mascherano	Liverpool	Barcelona	8/10	17,250,000
	Damien Duff	Blackburn	Chelsea	7/03	17,000,000
	Owen Hargreaves	Bayern Munich	Manchester Utd	6/07	17,000,000
	Glen Johnson	Portsmouth	Liverpool	6/09	17,000,000
	Shinji Kagawa	Borussia Dortmund	Manchester Utd	6/12	17,000,000
	AndreyArshavin	Zenit St Petersburg	Arsenal	2/09	16,900,000
	HernanCrespo	Inter Milan	Chelsea	8/03	16,800,000
	Claude Makelele	Real Madrid	Chelsea	9/03	16,600,000
	Luka Modric	Dinamo Zagreb	Tottenham	6/08	16,600,000
	Darren Bent	Charlton	Tottenham	6/07	16,500,000
	Phil Jones	Blackburn	Manchester Utd	6/11	16,500,000
	Jose Bosingwa	Porto	Chelsea	6/08	16,200,000
	Michael Owen	Real Madrid	Newcastle	8/05	16,000,000
	Thierry Henry	Arsenal	Barcelona	6/07	16,000,000
	Aleksandar Kolarov	Lazio	Manchester City	7/10	16,000,000
	Robinho	Manchester City	AC Milan	8/10	16,000,000
	Jordan Henderson	Sunderland	Liverpool	6/11	16,000,000
	Ashley Young	Aston Villa	Manchester Utd	6/11	16,000,000
	Adrian Mutu	Parma	Chelsea	8/03	15,800,000
	Samir Nasri	Marseille	Arsenal	7/08	15,800,000
	Jermain Defoe	Portsmouth	Tottenham	1/09	15,750,000
	Antonio Valencia	Wigan	Manchester Utd	6/09	15,250,000
	Alan Shearer	Blackburn	Newcastle	7/96	15,000,000
	Jimmy F Hasselbaink	Atletico Madrid	Chelsea	6/00	15,000,000
	Juan Sebastian Veron	Manchester Utd	Chelsea	8/03	15,000,000
	Nicolas Anelka	Bolton	Chelsea	1/08	15,000,000
	David Bentley	Blackburn	Tottenham	7/08	15,000,000
	MarouaneFellaini	Standard Liege	Everton	9/08	15,000,000
	Nigel de Jong	Hamburg	Manchester City	1/09	15,000,000
	KoloToure	Arsenal	Manchester City	7/09	15,000,000
	DjibrilCisse	Auxerre	Liverpool	7/04	14,000,000
	Wilson Palacios	Wigan	Tottenham	1/09	14,000,000
	Roman Pavlyuchenko	Spartak Moscow	Tottenham	8/08	14,000,000
	Patrick Vieira	Arsenal	Juventus	7/05	13,700,000
	Paulo Ferreira	Porto	Chelsea	7/04	13,500,000
	FlorentMalouda	Lyon	Chelsea	7/07	13,500,000
	Jonathan Woodgate	Newcastle	Real Madrid	8/04	13,400,000
	JaapStam	Manchester Utd	Lazio	8/01	13,300,000
	Robbie Keane	Coventry	Inter Milan	7/00	13,000,000
	Sylvain Wiltord	Bordeaux	Arsenal	8/00	13,000,000
	AsamoahGyan	Rennes	Sunderland	8/10	13,000,000
	Olivier Giroud	Montpellier	Arsenal	6/12	13,000,000
	Louis Saha	Fulham	Manchester Utd	1/04	12,825,000
	Olivier Giroud	Montpellier	Arsenal	6/12	12,800,000
	SulleyMuntari	Portsmouth	Inter Milan	7/08	12,700,000
	Dwight Yorke	Aston Villa	Manchester Utd	8/98	12,600,000
	AfonsoAlves	Heerenveen	Middlesbrough	1/08	12,500,000

	Cristiano Ronaldo	Sporting Lisbon	Manchester Utd	8/03	12,240,000
	Juninho	Middlesbrough	Atletico Madrid	7/97	12,000,000
	Jimmy F Hasselbaink	Leeds	Atletico Madrid	8/99	12,000,000
CD	Tore Andre Flo	Chelsea	Rangers	11/00	12,000,000
	Robbie Keane	Inter Milan	Leeds	12/00	12,000,000
	Gareth Barry	Aston Villa	Manchester City	6/09	12,000,000
	Nicolas Anelka	Paris St Germain	Manchester City	5/02	12,000,000
	ArjenRobben	PSV Eindhoven	Chelsea	4/04	12,000,000
	Theo Walcott	Southampton	Arsenal	1/06	12,000,000
	John Obi Mikel	Manchester Utd	Chelsea	6/06	12,000,000
	Nani	Sporting Lisbon	Manchestèr Utd	7/07	12,000,000
	Johan Elmander	Toulouse	Bolton	6/08	12,000,000
	James Milner	Newcastle	Aston Villa	8/08	12,000,000
	Craig Bellamy	West Ham	Manchester City	1/09	12,000,000
	Wayne Bridge	Chelsea	Manchester City	1/09	12,000,000
	Robbie Keane	Liverpool	Tottenham	2/09	12,000,000
	Stewart Downing	Middlesbrough	Aston Villa	7/09	12,000,000
	Jerome Boateng	Manchester City	Bayern Munich	7/11	12,000,000
	Alex Oxlade-Chamberlain	Southampton	Arsenal	8/11	12,000,000
	Raul Meireles	Liverpool	Chelsea	8/11	12,000,000
	Alexander Hleb	Arsenal	Barcelona	7/08	11,800,000
	Yuri Zhirkov	Chelsea	Makhachkala	8/11	11,700,000
	Steve Marlet	Lyon	Fulham	8/01	11,500,000
	Raul Meireles	Porto	Liverpool	8/10	11,500,000
	AiyegbeniYakubu	Middlesbrough	Everton	8/07	11,250,000
	Sergei Rebrov	Dynamo Kiev	Tottenham .	5/00	11,000,000
	Frank Lampard	West Ham	Chelsea	6/01	11,000,000
	Robbie Fowler	Liverpool	Leeds	11/01	11,000,000
	Ryan Babbel	Ajax	Liverpool	7/07	11,000,000
	Gervinho	Lille	Arsenal	7/11	11,000,000
	DimitarBerbatov	Bayer Leverkusen	Tottenham	5/06	10,900,000
	Lukas Podolski	Cologne	Arsenal	6/12	10,900,000
	JaapStam	PSV Eindhoven	Manchester Utd	5/98	10,750,000
	Xabi Alonso	Real Sociedad	Liverpool	8/04	10,700,000
	Bryan Ruiz	Twente Enschede	Fulham	8/11	10,600,000
	Thierry Henry	Juventus	Arsenal	8/99	10,500,000
	Laurent Robert	Paris St Germain	Newcastle	8/01	10,500,000
	Andrew Johnson	Everton	Fulham	8/08	10,500,000
	Ruud van Nistelrooy	Manchester Utd	Real Madrid	7/06	10,200,000
	Dirk Kuyt	Feyenoord	Liverpool	8/06	10,200,000
	Chris Sutton	Blackburn	Chelsea	7/99	10,000,000
	Emile Heskey	Leicester	Liverpool	2/00	10,000,000
	El HadjiDiouf	Lens	Liverpool	6/02	10,000,000
	Scott Parker	Charlton	Chelsea	1/04	10,000,000
	Alexander Hleb	Stuttgart	Arsenal	6/05	10,000,000
	Obafemi Martins	Inter Milan	Newcastle ·	8/06	10,000,000
	Shaun Wright-Phillips	Chelsea	Manchester City	8/08	10,000,000
	FabricioColoccini	Dep La Coruna	Newcastle	8/08	10,000,000
	Thomas Vermaelen	Ajax	Arsenal	6/09	10,000,000
	Darren Bent	Tottenham	Sunderland	8/09	10,000,000
	DiniyarBilyaletdinov	Lokomotiv Moscow	Tottenham	7/09	10,000,000
	Jerome Boateng	Hamburg	Manchester City	7/10	10,000,000
	Peter Crouch	Tottenham	Stoke	8/11	10,000,000
	Mikel Arteta	Everton	Arsenal	8/11	10,000,000

BRITISH RECORD TRANSFERS FROM FIRST £1,000 DEAL

Player	From	To	Date	£
Alf Common	Sunderland	Middlesbrough	2/1905	1,000
SydPuddefoot	West Ham	Falkirk	2/22	5,000
WarneyCresswell	South Shields	Sunderland	3/22	5,500
Bob Kelly	Burnley	Sunderland	12/25	6,500
David Jack	Bolton	Arsenal	10/28	10,890
Bryn Jones	Wolves	Arsenal	8/38	14,500
Billy Steel	Morton	Derby	9/47	15,000
Tommy Lawton	Chelsea	Notts Co	11/47	20,000
Len Shackleton	Newcastle	Sunderland	2/48	20,500
Johnny Morris	Manchester Utd	Derby	2/49	24,000
Eddie Quigley	Sheffield Wed	Preston	12/49	26,500
Trevor Ford	Aston Villa	Sunderland	10/50	30,000
Jackie Sewell	Notts Co	Sheffield Wed	3/51	34,500
Eddie Firmani	Charlton	Sampdoria	7/55	35,000
John Charles	Leeds	Juventus	4/57	65,000
Denis Law	Manchester City	Torino	6/61	100,000
Denis Law	Torino	Manchester Utd	7/62	115,000
Allan Clarke	Fulham	Leicester	6/68	150,000
Allan Clarke	Leicester	Leeds	6/69	165,000
Martin Peters	West Ham	Tottenham	3/70	200,000
Alan Ball	Everton	Arsenal	12/71	220,000
David Nish	Leicester	Derby	8/72	250,000
Bob Latchford	Birmingham	Everton	2/74	350,000
Graeme Souness	Middlesbrough	Liverpool	1/78	352,000
Kevin Keegan	Liverpool	Hamburg	6/77	500,000
David Mills	Middlesbrough	WBA	1/79	516,000
Trevor Francis	Birmingham	Nottm Forest	2/79	1,180,000
Steve Daley	Wolves	Manchester City	9/79	1,450,000
Andy Gray	Aston Villa	Wolves	9/79	1,469,000
Bryan Robson	WBA	Manchester Utd	10/81	1,500,000
Ray Wilkins	Manchester Utd	AC Milan	5/84	1,500,000
Mark Hughes	Manchester Utd	Barcelona	5/86	2,300,000
Ian Rush	Liverpool	Juventus	6/87	3,200,000
Chris Waddle	Tottenham	Marseille	7/89	4,250,000
David Platt	Aston Villa	Bari	7/91	5,500,000
Paul Gascoigne	Tottenham	Lazio	6/92	5,500,000
Andy Cole	Newcastle	Manchester Utd	1/95	7,000,000
Dennis Bergkamp	Inter Milan	Arsenal	6/95	7,500,000
Stan Collymore	Nottm Forest	Liverpool	6/95	8,500,000
Alan Shearer	Blackburn	Newcastle	7/96	15,000,000
Nicolas Anelka	Arsenal	Real Madrid	8/99	22,500,000
Juan Sebastian Veron	Lazio	Manchester Utd	7/01	28,100,000
Rio Ferdinand	Leeds	Manchester Utd	7/02	29,100,000
Andriy Shevchenko	AC Milan	Chelsea	5/06	30,800,000
Robinho	Real Madrid	Manchester City	9/08	32,500,000
Cristiano Ronaldo	Manchester Utd	Real Madrid	7/09	80,000,000

• World's first £1m transfer: GuiseppeSavoldi, Bologna to Napoli, July 1975

TOP FOREIGN SIGNINGS

Player	From	To	Date	£
Zlatan Ibrahimovic	Inter Milan	Barcelona	7/09	60.300,000
Kaka	AC Milan	Real Madrid	6/08	56,000,000

ZinedineZidane	Juventus	Real Madrid	7/01	47,200,000
Luis Figo	Barcelona	Real Madrid	7/00	37,200,000
Javier Pastore	Palermo	Paris SG	8/11	36,600,000
KarimBenzema	Lyon	Real Madrid	7/09	35,800,000
HernanCrespo	Parma	Lazio	7/00	35,000,000
Radamel Falcao	Porto	Atletico Madrid	8/11	34,700,000
David Villa	Valencia	Barcelona	5/10	34,000,000
Ronaldo	Inter Milan	Real Madrid	8/02	33,000,000
Gianluigi Buffon	Parma	Juventus	7/01	32,600,000
Christian Vieri	Lazio	Inter Milan	6/99	31,000,000
Alessandro Nesta	Lazio	AC Milan	8/02	30,200,000
KarimBenzema	Lyon	Real Madrid	7/08	30,000,000
HernanCrespo	Lazio	Inter Milan	8/02	29,000,000
GaizkaMendieta	Valencia	Lazio	7/01	28,500,000
Mario Gomez	Stuttgart	Bayern Munich	5/09	27,000,000
PavelNedved	Lazio	Juventus	7/01	25,000,000
Danny	Dynamo Moscow	Zenit St Petersburg	8/08	25,000,000

WORLD RECORD FOR 16-YEAR-OLD
£12m for Theo Walcott, Southampton to Arsenal, Jan 2006

RECORD FEE BETWEEN SCOTTISH CLUBS
£4.4m for Scott Brown, Hibernian to Celtic, May 2007

RECORD CONFERENCE FEE
£260,000: George Boyd, Stevenage to Peterborough, Jan 2007

RECORD FEE BETWEEN NON-LEAGUE CLUBS
£275,000: Richard Brodie, York to Crawley, Aug 2010

MILESTONES OF SOCCER

1848: First code of rules compiled at Cambridge University.
1857: Sheffield FC, world's oldest football club, formed.
1862: Notts Co (oldest League club) formed.
1863: Football Association founded – their first rules of game agreed.
1871: FA Cup introduced.
1872: First official International: Scotland 0 England 0. Corner-kick introduced.
1873: Scottish FA formed; Scottish Cup introduced.
1874: Shinguards introduced.
1875: Crossbar introduced (replacing tape).
1876: FA of Wales formed.
1877: Welsh Cup introduced.
1878: Referee's whistle first used.
1880: Irish FA founded; Irish Cup introduced.
1883: Two-handed throw-in introduced.
1885: Record first-class score (Arbroath 36 Bon Accord 0 – Scottish Cup). Professionalism legalised.
1886: International Board formed.
1887: Record FA Cup score (Preston 26 Hyde 0).
1888: Football League founded by William McGregor. First matches on Sept 8.
1889 Preston win Cup and League (first club to complete Double).

1890: Scottish League and Irish League formed.

1891: Goal-nets introduced. Penalty-kick introduced.

1892: Inter-League games began. Football League Second Division formed.

1893: FA Amateur Cup launched.

1894: Southern League formed.

1895: FA Cup stolen from Birmingham shop window – never recovered.

1897: First Players' Union formed. Aston Villa win Cup and League.

1898: Promotion and relegation introduced.

1901: Maximum wage rule in force (£4 a week). Tottenham first professional club to take FA Cup south. First six-figure attendance (110,802) at FA Cup Final.

1902: Ibrox Park disaster (25 killed). Welsh League formed.

1904: FIFA founded (7 member countries).

1905: First £1,000 transfer (Alf Common, Sunderland to Middlesbrough).

1907: Players' Union revived.

1908: Transfer fee limit (£350) fixed in January and withdrawn in April.

1911: New FA Cup trophy – in use to 1991. Transfer deadline introduced.

1914: King George V first reigning monarch to attend FA Cup Final.

1916: Entertainment Tax introduced.

1919: League extended to 44 clubs.

1920: Third Division (South) formed.

1921: Third Division (North) formed.

1922: Scottish League (Div II) introduced.

1923: Beginning of football pools. First Wembley Cup Final.

1924: First International at Wembley (England 1 Scotland 1). Rule change allows goals to be scored direct from corner-kicks.

1925: New offside law.

1926: Huddersfield complete first League Championship hat-trick.

1927: First League match broadcast (radio): Arsenal v Sheffield United. First radio broadcast of Cup Final (winners Cardiff City). Charles Clegg, president of FA, becomes first knight of football.

1928: First £10,000 transfer – David Jack (Bolton to Arsenal). WR ('Dixie') Dean (Everton) creates League record – 60 goals in season. Britain withdraws from FIFA

1930: Uruguay first winners of World Cup.

1931: WBA win Cup and promotion.

1933: Players numbered for first time in Cup Final (1-22).

1934: Sir Frederick Wall retires as FA secretary; successor Stanley Rous. Death of Herbert Chapman (Arsenal manager).

1935: Arsenal equal Huddersfield's Championship hat-trick record. Official two-referee trials.

1936: Joe Payne's 10-goal League record (Luton 12 Bristol Rov 0).

1937: British record attendance: 149,547 at Scotland v England match.

1938: First live TV transmission of FA Cup Final. Football League 50th Jubilee. New pitch marking – arc on edge of penalty-area. Laws of Game re-drafted by Stanley Rous. Arsenal pay record £14,500 fee for Bryn Jones (Wolves).

1939: Compulsory numbering of players in Football League. First six-figure attendance for League match (Rangers v Celtic 118,567). All normal competitions suspended for duration of Second World War.

1945: Scottish League Cup introduced.

1946: British associations rejoin FIFA. Bolton disaster (33 killed) during FA Cup tie with Stoke. Walter Winterbottom appointed England's first director of coaching.

1947: Great Britain beat Rest of Europe 6-1 at Hampden Park, Glasgow. First £20,000 transfer – Tommy Lawton, Chelsea to Notts Co

1949: Stanley Rous, secretary FA, knighted. England's first home defeat outside British Champ. (0-2 v Eire).

1950: Football League extended from 88 to 92 clubs. World record crowd (203,500) at World

Cup Final, Brazil v Uruguay, in Rio. Scotland's first home defeat by foreign team (0-1 v Austria).

1951: White ball comes into official use.

1952: Newcastle first club to win FA Cup at Wembley in successive seasons.

1953: England's first Wembley defeat by foreign opponents (3-6 v Hungary).

1954: Hungary beat England 7-1 in Budapest.

1955: First FA Cup match under floodlights (prelim round replay): Kidderminster v Brierley Hill Alliance.

1956: First FA Cup ties under floodlights in competition proper. First League match by floodlight (Portsmouth v Newcastle). Real Madrid win first European Cup.

1957: Last full Football League programme on Christmas Day. Entertainment Tax withdrawn.

1958: Manchester United air crash at Munich. League re-structured into four divisions.

1960: Record transfer fee: £55,000 for Denis Law (Huddersfield to Manchester City). Wolves win Cup, miss Double and Championship hat-trick by one goal. For fifth time in ten years FA Cup Final team reduced to ten men by injury. FA recognise Sunday football. Football League Cup launched.

1961: Tottenham complete the first Championship–FA Cup double this century. Maximum wage (£20 a week) abolished in High Court challenge by George Eastham. First British £100-a-week wage paid (by Fulham to Johnny Haynes). First £100,000 British transfer – Denis Law, Manchester City to Torino. Sir Stanley Rous elected president of FIFA

1962: Manchester United raise record British transfer fee to £115,000 for Denis Law.

1963: FA Centenary. Season extended to end of May due to severe winter. First pools panel. English "retain and transfer" system ruled illegal in High Court test case.

1964: Rangers' second great hat-trick – Scottish Cup, League Cup and League. Football League and Scottish League guaranteed £500,000 a year in new fixtures copyright agreement with Pools. First televised 'Match of the Day' (BBC2): Liverpool 3 Arsenal 2.

1965: Bribes scandal – ten players jailed (and banned for life by FA) for match-fixing 1960–63. Stanley Matthews knighted in farewell season. Arthur Rowley (Shrewsbury) retires with record of 434 League goals. Substitutes allowed for injured players in Football League matches (one per team).

1966: England win World Cup (Wembley).

1967: Alf Ramsey, England manager, knighted; OBE for captain Bobby Moore. Celtic become first British team to win European Cup. First substitutes allowed in FA Cup Final (Tottenham v Chelsea) but not used. Football League permit loan transfers (two per club).

1968: First FA Cup Final televised live in colour (BBC2 – WBA v Everton). Manchester United first English club to win European Cup.

1970: FIFA/UEFA approve penalty shoot-out in deadlocked ties.

1971: Arsenal win League Championship and FA Cup.

1973: Football League introduce 3-up, 3-down promotion/relegation between Divisions 1, 2 and 3 and 4-up, 4-down between Divisions 3 and 4.

1974: First FA Cup ties played on Sunday. League football played on Sunday for first time. Last FA Amateur Cup Final. Joao Havelange (Brazil) succeeds Sir Stanley Rous as FIFA president.

1975: Scottish Premier Division introduced.

1976: Football League introduce goal difference (replacing goal average) and red/yellow cards.

1977: Liverpool achieve the double of League Championship and European Cup. Don Revie defects to United Arab Emirates when England manager – successor Ron Greenwood.

1978: Freedom of contract for players accepted by Football League. PFA lifts ban on foreign players in English football. Football League introduce Transfer Tribunal. Viv Anderson (Nottm Forest) first black player to win a full England cap. Willie Johnston (Scotland) sent home from World Cup Finals in Argentina after failing dope test.

1979: First all-British £500,000 transfer – David Mills, Middlesbrough to WBA. First British million pound transfer (Trevor Francis – Birmingham to Nottm Forest). Andy Gray moves from Aston Villa to Wolves for a record £1,469,000 fee.

1981: Tottenham win 100th FA Cup Final. Liverpool first British side to win European Cup three times. Three points for a win introduced by Football League. QPR install Football League's first artificial pitch. Death of Bill Shankly, manager–legend of Liverpool 1959–74. Record British transfer – Bryan Robson (WBA to Manchester United), £1,500,000.

1982: Aston Villa become sixth consecutive English winners of European Cup. Tottenham retain FA Cup – first club to do so since Tottenham 1961 and 1962. Football League Cup becomes the (sponsored) Milk Cup.

1983: Liverpool complete League Championship–Milk Cup double for second year running. Manager Bob Paisley retires. Aberdeen first club to do Cup-Winners' Cup and domestic Cup double. Football League clubs vote to keep own match receipts. Football League sponsored by Canon, Japanese camera and business equipment manufacturers – 3-year agreement starting 1983–4. Football League agree two-year contract for live TV coverage of ten matches per season (5 Friday night, BBC, 5 Sunday afternoon, ITV).

1984: One FA Cup tie in rounds 3, 4, 5 and 6 shown live on TV (Friday or Sunday). Aberdeen take Scottish Cup for third successive season, win Scottish Championship, too. Tottenham win UEFA Cup on penalty shoot-out. Liverpool win European Cup on penalty shoot-out to complete unique treble with Milk Cup and League title (as well as Championship hat-trick). N Ireland win the final British Championship. France win European Championship – their first honour. FA National Soccer School opens at Lilleshall. Britain's biggest score this century: Stirling Alb 20 Selkirk 0 (Scottish Cup).

1985: Bradford City fire disaster – 56 killed. First £1m receipts from match in Britain (FA Cup Final). Kevin Moran (Manchester United) first player to be sent off in FA Cup Final. Celtic win 100th Scottish FA Cup Final. European Cup Final horror (Liverpool v Juventus, riot in Brussels) 39 die. UEFA ban all English clubs indefinitely from European competitions. No TV coverage at start of League season – first time since 1963 (resumption delayed until January 1986). Sept: first ground-sharing in League history – Charlton Athletic move from The Valley to Selhurst Park (Crystal Palace).

1986: Liverpool complete League and Cup double in player-manager Kenny Dalglish's first season in charge. Swindon (4th Div Champions) set League points record (102). League approve reduction of First Division to 20 clubs by 1988. Everton chairman Philip Carter elected president of Football League. Death of Sir Stanley Rous (91). 100th edition of News of the World Football Annual. League Cup sponsored for next three years by Littlewoods (£2m). Football League voting majority (for rule changes) reduced from three-quarters to two-thirds. Wales move HQ from Wrexham to Cardiff after 110 years. Two substitutes in FA Cup and League (Littlewoods) Cup. Two-season League/TV deal (£6.2m):- BBC and ITV each show seven live League matches per season, League Cup semi-finals and Final. Football League sponsored by Today newspaper. Luton first club to ban all visiting supporters; as sequel are themselves banned from League Cup. Oldham and Preston install artificial pitches, making four in Football League (following QPR and Luton).

1987: League introduce play-off matches to decide first promotion/relegation places in all divisions. Re-election abolished – bottom club in Div 4 replaced by winners of GM Vauxhall Conference. Two substitutes approved for Football League 1987–8. Red and yellow disciplinary cards (scrapped 1981) re-introduced by League and FA Football League sponsored by Barclays. First Div reduced to 21 clubs.

1988: Football League Centenary. First Division reduced to 20 clubs.

1989: Soccer gets £74m TV deal: £44m over 4 years, ITV; £30m over 5 years, BBC/BSB. But it costs Philip Carter the League Presidency. Ted Croker retires as FA chief executive; successor Graham Kelly, from Football League. Hillsborough disaster: 95 die at FA Cup semi-final (Liverpool v Nottm Forest). Arsenal win closest-ever Championship with last kick. Peter Shilton sets England record with 109 caps.

1990: Nottm Forest win last Littlewoods Cup Final. Both FA Cup semi-finals played on Sunday and televised live. Play-off finals move to Wembley; Swindon win place in Div 1, then relegated back to Div 2 (breach of financial regulations) – Sunderland promoted instead.

England reach World Cup semi-final in Italy and win FIFA Fair Play Award. Peter Shilton retires as England goalkeeper with 125 caps (world record). Graham Taylor (Aston Villa) succeeds Bobby Robson as England manager. International Board amend offside law (player 'level' no longer offside). FIFA make "professional foul" a sending-off offence. English clubs back in Europe (Manchester United and Aston Villa) after 5-year exile.

1991: First FA Cup semi-final at Wembley (Tottenham 3 Arsenal 1). Bert Millichip (FA chairman) and Philip Carter (Everton chairman) knighted. End of artificial pitches in Div 1 (Luton, Oldham). Scottish League reverts to 12-12-14 format (as in 1987–8). Penalty shoot-out introduced to decide FA Cup ties level after one replay.

1992: Introduction of fourth FA Cup (previous trophy withdrawn). FA launch Premier League (22 clubs). Football League reduced to three divisions (71 clubs). Record TV-sport deal: BSkyB/BBC to pay £304m for 5-year coverage of Premier League. ITV do £40m, 4-year deal with Football League. Channel 4 show Italian football live (Sundays). FIFA approve new back-pass rule (goalkeeper must not handle ball kicked to him by team-mate). New League of Wales formed. Record all-British transfer, £3.3m: Alan Shearer (Southampton to Blackburn). Charlton return to The Valley after 7-year absence.

1993: Barclays end 6-year sponsorship of Football League. For first time both FA Cup semi-finals at Wembley (Sat, Sun). Arsenal first club to complete League Cup/FA Cup double. Rangers pull off Scotland's domestic treble for fifth time. FA in record British sports sponsorship deal (£12m over 4 years) with brewers Bass for FA Carling Premiership, from Aug. Brian Clough retires after 18 years as Nottm Forest manager; as does Jim McLean (21 years manager of Dundee Utd). Football League agree 3-year, £3m sponsorship with Endsleigh Insurance. Premier League introduce squad numbers with players' names on shirts. Record British transfer: Duncan Ferguson, Dundee Utd to Rangers (£4m). Record English-club signing: Roy Keane, Nottm Forest to Manchester United (£3.75m). Graham Taylor resigns as England manager after World Cup exit (Nov). Death of Bobby Moore (51), England World Cup winning captain 1966.

1994: Death of Sir Matt Busby. Terry Venables appointed England coach. Manchester United complete the Double. Last artificial pitch in English football goes – Preston revert to grass, summer 1994. Bobby Charlton knighted. Scottish League format changes to four divisions of ten clubs. Record British transfer: Chris Sutton, Norwich to Blackburn (£5m). FA announce first sponsorship of FA Cup – Littlewoods Pools (4-year, £14m deal, plus £6m for Charity Shield). Death of Billy Wright.

1995: New record British transfer: Andy Cole, Newcastle to Manchester United (£7m). First England match abandoned through crowd trouble (v Republic of Ireland, Dublin). Blackburn Champions for first time since 1914. Premiership reduced to 20 clubs. British transfer record broken again: Stan Collymore, Nottm Forest to Liverpool (£8.5m). Starting season 1995–6, teams allowed to use 3 substitutes per match, not necessarily including a goalkeeper. European Court of Justice upholds Bosman ruling, barring transfer fees for players out of contract and removing limit on number of foreign players clubs can field.

1996: Death of Bob Paisley (77), ex-Liverpool, most successful manager in English Football. FA appoint Chelsea manager Glenn Hoddle to succeed Terry Venables as England coach after Euro 96. Manchester United first English club to achieve Double twice (and in 3 seasons). Football League completes £125m, 5-year TV deal with BSkyB starting 1996–7. England stage European Championship, reach semi-finals, lose on pens to tournament winners Germany. Keith Wiseman succeeds Sir Bert Millichip as FA Chairman. Linesmen become known as "referees' assistants". Coca-Cola Cup experiment with own disciplinary system (red, yellow cards). Alan Shearer football's first £15m player (Blackburn to Newcastle). Nigeria first African country to win Olympic soccer. Nationwide Building Society sponsor Football League in initial 3-year deal worth £5.25m Peter Shilton first player to make 1000 League appearances.

1997: Howard Wilkinson appointed English football's first technical director. England's first home defeat in World Cup (0-1 v Italy). Ruud Gullit (Chelsea) first foreign coach to win FA Cup. Rangers equal Celtic's record of 9 successive League titles. Manchester United win Premier League for fourth time in 5 seasons. New record World Cup score: Iran 17, Maldives 0 (qualifying round). Season 1997–8 starts Premiership's record £36m, 4-year sponsorship extension with brewers Bass (Carling).

1998: In French manager Arsene Wenger's second season at Highbury, Arsenal become second English club to complete the Double twice. Chelsea also win two trophies under new player-manager Gianluca Vialli (Coca-Cola Cup, Cup Winners' Cup). France win 16th World Cup competition. In breakaway from Scottish League, top ten clubs form new Premiership under SFA, starting season 1998–9. Football League celebrates its 100th season, 1998–9. New FA Cup sponsors – French insurance giants AXA (25m, 4-year deal). League Cup becomes Worthington Cup in £23m, 5-year contract with brewers Bass. Nationwide Building Society's sponsorship of Football League extended to season 2000–1.

1999: FA buy Wembley Stadium (£103m) for £320m, plan rebuilding (Aug 2000–March 2003) as new national stadium (Lottery Sports fund contributes £110m) Scotland's new Premier League takes 3-week mid-season break in January. Sky screen Oxford Utd v Sunderland (Div 1) as first pay-per-view match on TV. FA sack England coach Glenn Hoddle; Fulham's Kevin Keegan replaces him at £1m a year until 2003. Sir Alf Ramsey, England's World Cup-winning manager, dies aged 79. With effect 1999, FA Cup Final to be decided on day (via penalties, if necessary). Hampden Park re-opens for Scottish Cup Final after £63m refit. Alex Ferguson knighted after Manchester United complete Premiership, FA Cup, European League treble. Starting season 1999–2000, UEFA increase Champions League from 24 to 32 clubs. End of Cup-Winners' Cup (merged into 121-club UEFA Cup). FA allow holders Manchester United to withdraw from FA Cup to participate in FIFA's inaugural World Club Championship in Brazil in January. Chelsea first British club to field an all-foreign line-up at Southampton (Prem). FA vote in favour of streamlined 14-man board of directors to replace its 92-member council.

2000: Scot Adam Crozier takes over as FA chief executive. Wales move to Cardiff's £125m Millennium Stadium (v Finland). Brent Council approve plans for new £475m Wembley Stadium (completion target spring 2003); demolition of old stadium to begin after England v Germany (World Cup qual.). Fulham Ladies become Britain's first female professional team. FA Premiership and Nationwide League to introduce (season 2000–01) rule whereby referees advance free-kick by 10 yards and caution player who shows dissent, delays kick or fails to retreat 10 yards. Scottish football increased to 42 League clubs in 2000–01 (12 in Premier League and 3 divisions of ten; Peterhead and Elgin elected from Highland League). France win European Championship – first time a major international tournament has been jointly hosted (Holland/ Belgium). England's £10m bid to stage 2006 World Cup fails; vote goes to Germany. England manager Kevin Keegan resigns after 1-0 World Cup defeat by Germany in Wembley's last International. Lazio's Swedish coach Sven-Goran Eriksson agrees to become England head coach.

2001: Scottish Premier League experiment with split into two 5-game mini leagues (6 clubs in each) after 33 matches completed. New transfer system agreed by FIFA/UEFA is ratified. Barclaycard begin £48m, 3-year sponsorship of the Premiership, and Nationwide's contract with the Football League is extended by a further 3 years (£12m). ITV, after winning auction against BBC's Match of the Day, begin £183m, 3-season contract for highlights of Premiership matches; BSkyB's live coverage (66 matches per season) for next 3 years will cost £1.1bn. BBC and BSkyB pay £400m (3-year contract) for live coverage of FA Cup and England home matches. ITV and Ondigital pay £315m to screen Nationwide League and Worthington Cup matches. In new charter for referees, top men can earn up to £60,000 a season in Premiership. Real Madrid break world transfer record, buying Zinedine Zidane from Juventus for £47.2m. FA introduce prize money, round by round, in FA Cup.

2002: Scotland appoint their first foreign manager, Germany's former national coach Bertie

Vogts replacing Craig Brown. Collapse of ITV Digital deal, with Football League owed £178m, threatens lower-division clubs. Arsenal complete Premiership/FA Cup Double for second time in 5 seasons, third time in all. Newcastle manager Bobby Robson knighted in Queen's Jubilee Honours. Brazil win World Cup for fifth time. New record British transfer and world record for defender, £29.1m Rio Ferdinand (Leeds to Manchester United). Transfer window introduced to British football. FA Charity Shield renamed FA Community Shield. After 2-year delay, demolition of Wembley Stadium begins. October: Adam Crozier, FA chief executive, resigns.

2003: FA Cup draw (from 4th Round) reverts to Monday lunchtime. Scottish Premier League decide to end mid-winter shut-down. Mark Palios appointed FA chief executive. For first time, two Football League clubs demoted (replaced by two from Conference). Ban lifted on loan transfers between Premiership clubs. July: David Beckham becomes record British export (Manchester United to Real Madrid, £23.3m). Biggest takeover in British football history – Russian oil magnate Roman Abramovich buys control of Chelsea for £150m Wimbledon leave rented home at Selhurst Park, become England's first franchised club in 68-mile move to Milton Keynes.

2004: Arsenal first club to win Premiership with unbeaten record and only the third in English football history to stay undefeated through League season. Trevor Brooking knighted in Queen's Birthday Honours. Wimbledon change name to Milton Keynes Dons. Greece beat hosts Portugal to win European Championship as biggest outsiders (80-1 at start) ever to succeed in major international tournament. New contracts – Premiership in £57m deal with Barclays, seasons 2004–07. Coca-Cola replace Nationwide as Football League sponsors (£15m over 3 years), rebranding Div 1 as Football League Championship, with 2nd and 3rd Divisions, becoming Leagues 1 and 2. After 3 years, BBC Match of the Day wins back Premiership highlights from ITV with 3-year, £105m contract (2004–07). All-time League record of 49 unbeaten Premiership matches set by Arsenal. Under new League rule, Wrexham forfeit 10 points for going into administration.

2005: Brian Barwick, controller of ITV Sport, becomes FA chief executive. Foreign managers take all major trophies for English clubs: Chelsea, in Centenary year, win Premiership (record 95 points) and League Cup in Jose Mourinho's first season; Arsene Wenger's Arsenal win FA Cup in Final's first penalty shoot-out; under new manager Rafael Benitez, Liverpool lift European Cup on penalties after trailing 0-3 in Champions League Final. Wigan, a League club only since 1978, promoted to Premiership. In new record British-club take-over, American tycoon Malcolm Glazer buys Manchester United for £790m Bury become the first club to score 1,000 goals in each of the four divisions. Tributes are paid world-wide to George Best, who dies aged 59.

2006: Steve Staunton succeeds Brian Kerr as Republic of Ireland manager. Chelsea post record losses of £140m Sven-Goran Eriksson agrees a settlement to step down as England coach. Steve McClaren replaces him. The Premier League announce a new 3-year TV deal worth £1.7 billion under which Sky lose their monopoly of coverage. Chelsea smash the British transfer record, paying £30.8m for Andriy Shevchenko. Italy win the World Cup on penalties. Aston Villa are taken over by American billionaire Randy Lerner. Clydesdale Bank replace Bank of Scotland as sponsor of the SPL. An Icelandic consortium buy West Ham.

2007: Michel Platini becomes the new president of UEFA. Walter Smith resigns as Scotland manager to return to Rangers and is replaced by Alex McLeish. American tycoons George Gillett and Tom Hicks finalise a £450m takeover of Liverpool. The new £800m Wembley Stadium is finally completed. The BBC and Sky lose TV rights for England's home matches and FA Cup ties to ITV and Setanta. World Cup-winner Alan Ball dies aged 61. Lawrie Sanchez resigns as Northern Ireland manager to take over at Fulham. Nigel Worthington succeeds him. Lord Stevens names five clubs in his final report into alleged transfer irregularities. Former Thai Prime Minister Thaksin Shinawatra becomes Manchester City's new owner. Steve McClaren is sacked after England fail to qualify for the European Championship Finals and is replaced by Fabio Capello. The Republic of Ireland's

Steve Staunton also goes. Scotland's Alex McLeish resigns to become Birmingham manager.

2008: The Republic of Ireland follow England's lead in appointing an Italian coach – Giovanni Trapattoni. George Burley leaves Southampton to become Scotland manager. Derby are taken over by an American sports and entertainment group in a deal worth around £50m. David Beckham wins his 100th England cap. Manchester United beat Chelsea in the first all-English Champions League Final. Spain beat Germany 1-0 in the European Championship Final. Thaksin Shinawatra, who bought Manchester City for £81m in July 2007, agrees to sell the club to the Abu Dhabi United Group for a reported £200m. With their new-found wealth, City smash the British transfer record when signing Robinho from Real Madrid for £32.5m. Cristiano Ronaldo is named European Footballer of the Year.

2009: Sky secure the rights to five of the six Premier League packages from 2010–13 with a bid of £1.6bn. Setanta keep the Saturday evening slot. Cristiano Ronaldo wins the World Footballer of the Year accolade. Reading's Steve Coppell reaches 1,000 games as a manager. David Beckham breaks Bobby Moore's record number of caps for an England outfield player with his 109th appearance. A British league record for not conceding a goal ends on 1,311 minutes for Manchester United's Edwin van der Sar. AC Milan's Kaka moves to Real Madrid for a world record fee of £56m. Nine days later, Manchester United agree to sell Cristiano Ronaldo to Real for £80m. Setanta goes into administration and ESPN takes over its live games. Sir Bobby Robson dies aged 76 after a long battle with cancer. Shay Given and Kevin Kilbane win their 100th caps for the Republic of Ireland. The Premier League vote for clubs to have eight home-grown players in their squads. George Burley is sacked as Scotland manager and replaced by Craig Levein.

2010: Former Birmingham owners David Gold and David Sullivan take control of West Ham. nPower succeed Coca-Cola as sponsors of the Football League. Portsmouth become the first Premier League club to go into administration. Chelsea achieve the club's first League and FA Cup double. Lord Triesman resigns as chairman of the FA and of England's 2018 World Cup bid after making embarrassing remarks about bribes. Fabio Capello agrees to stay on as England manager for another two years. Robbie Keane wins his 100th Republic of Ireland cap. John Toshack resigns as Wales manager and is replaced by former captain Gary Speed. Liverpool are taken over by New England Sports Ventures. England are humiliated in the vote for the 2018 World Cup which goes to Russia, with the 2022 tournament awarded to Qatar. Sir Alex Ferguson, appointed in 1986, becomes Manchester United's longest-serving manager.

2011: Seven club managers are sacked in a week. The transfer record between British clubs is broken twice in a day, with Liverpool buying Newcastle's Andy Carroll for £35m and selling Fernando Torres to Chelsea for £50m. Vauxhall replace Nationwide as sponsors of England and the other home nations. Businessman Craig Whyte takes over Rangers from Sir David Murray. John Terry is restored as England captain. Burnley's Graham Alexander makes his 1,000th career appearance. FIFA are rocked by bribery and corruption allegations. Football League clubs vote to reduce the number of substitutes from seven to five. Malaysian entrepreneur Tony Fernandes takes over Queens Park Rangers. Nigel Worthington steps down as Northern Ireland manager and is succeeded by Michael O'Neill. Sir Alex Ferguson completes 25 years as Manchester United manager. Manchester City post record annual losses of nearly £195m. Huddersfield set a Football League record of 43 successive unbeaten league games. Football mourns Gary Speed after the Wales manager is found dead at his home.

2012: Chris Coleman is appointed the new Wales manager. Fabio Capello resigns as manager after John Terry is stripped of the England captaincy for the second time. Roy Hodgson takes over. Rangers are forced into liquidation by crippling debts and a newly-formed club are demoted from the Scottish Premier League to Division Three. Manchester City become champions for the first time since 1968 after the tightest finish to a Premier League season. Chelsea win a penalty shoot-out against Bayern Munich in the Champions League Final. Capital One replace Carling as League Cup sponsors.

FINAL WHISTLE – OBITUARIES 2011–12

AUGUST 2011

STAN WILLEMSE, 86, was part of Chelsea's first League Championship-winning team, playing in 36 of the 42 matches of the 1954–55 season when his side finished four points ahead of Wolves and Portsmouth. Most of them were at left-back, although he scored a vital winner from the left-wing position against Sunderland during the run-in when Frank Blunstone was away on England duty. The former Royal Marine commando, described by the legendary Tom Finney as the league's hardest defender, signed from Brighton in 1949 for £6,500 – then a record fee for his home-town club. Throughout his time at Stamford Bridge he commuted by train from Brighton, along with team-mates Eric Parsons and John McNichol. He made 221 appearances, played one match for England B and later served Leyton Orient.

FRANK MUNRO, 63, won league, cup and international honours in a nine-year career with Wolves which embraced 371 appearances. He played in the first UEFA Cup Final, a 3-2 aggregate defeat by Tottenham in 1972, after scoring in both legs of the semi-final against Ferencvaros. Two years later, his side beat Manchester City 2-1 in the League Cup Final and in 1977 the central defender led Wolves to the Second Division title. Munro, capped nine times by Scotland, was a £55,000 signing in 1968 from Aberdeen. He scored the club's first European goal on the way to a hat-trick against Reykjavik in the Cup Winners' Cup, having started out at Dundee United. Leaving Molineux, he became the last player Jock Stein signed as manager of Celtic, later moved to Australia to join South Melbourne club Hellas and had a brief spell as player-coach at Albion.

ROGER BROWN, 58, led Bournemouth to one of the FA Cup's biggest upsets – a 2-0 third round win over Manchester United in 1984. Fledgling manager Harry Redknapp turned to the big centre-half after captain John Beck went down with flu. In the same year, Brown also skippered the team to victory over Hull in the Football League Trophy. It was his second spell at the club, following an £85,000 move to Norwich in 1979 and a £100,000 transfer to Fulham eight months later. At Craven Cottage, he scored 12 goals in the 1981–82 Third Division promotion-winning season. Brown later had a brief spell as manager of Colchester.

MARK OVENDALE, 37, was a much-travelled goalkeeper who commanded a £425,000 fee when joining Luton from Bournemouth in 2000. He helped the club win promotion from Division Three in the 2001–02 season, but was unable to make the position his own and moved on in 2003 after 55 appearances. Ovendale, who died of cancer, also played for Northampton and York, as well as non-league sides Wisbech, Barry, Tiverton, Carmarthen and Newport. He was forced to retire with a hip injury in 2007 and later had a coaching role with Wimborne.

BERNIE GALLACHER, 44, played in every match but one of the 1987–88 season when Aston Villa returned to top-flight football under Graham Taylor by finishing runners-up to Millwall in Division Two. The full-back, who joined Villa from school and rose through the youth and reserve ranks, had limited opportunities after that. A spell on loan with Blackburn was followed by moves to Doncaster, Brighton and Northampton, before his career was cut short by injury at the age of 27.

PETER HOOPER, (78), joined Bristol Rovers in 1953 and shared in the club's most successful years in the Second Division. He had one of the hardest shots in the game, scoring 101 goals in 297 league appearances. One of them came in front of the Kop at Liverpool and he said afterwards: 'What more does a man want in life?' Hooper, an outside-left, moved to Cardiff in 1962 and also played for Bristol City.

GEORGE KNIGHT, 90, was Burnley's oldest surviving former player. The inside-right made his debut in 1939, but his career was interrupted by the War and curtailed in 1948 by a knee injury when he had played only nine games. He later scouted for the club and for Manchester United.

GORDON HAIGH, 90, was Burnley's second oldest surviving former player and also an inside-right. He scored on his league debut with a spectacular overhead kick against Newport in 1946 and had four years at the club. He went on to join Bournemouth and Watford, before returning to Lancashire to play for Rossendale and Nelson.

JOHN PARKE, 74, was a Northern Ireland international who made his name with Linfield, where he was a member of the team that won seven trophies during the 1961–62 season. He spent a year with Hibernian, then had four seasons at Sunderland. The full-back began his career as an amateur with Cliftonville and ended it playing for the Belgian side Mechelen.

ALLAN WATKINS, 89, the England and Glamorgan cricket all-rounder, also played professional football for Plymouth and Cardiff. His maiden century for Glamorgan against Surrey at the Arms Park in 1946 came after the Plymouth manager agreed to release the winger from training.

BOB PATERSON, 80, helped Aberdeen win their first Scottish League title when they finished three points ahead of Celtic in 1955. The right-back joined the club from Queen's Park in 1948 and later played for Dumbarton at the end of a career cut short by illness.

FRANK SMITH, 78, scored Wycombe's goal in their 3-1 defeat by Bishop Auckland in the 1957 FA Amateur Cup Final, watched by a 90,000 crowd at Wembley. Smith, who once turned down professional terms at Newcastle to continue his studies, joined the club from Loughborough College and played for four seasons.

SEPTEMBER 2011

LAURIE HUGHES, 87 was the first Liverpool player to appear in the World Cup Finals, winning all his three England caps in Brazil in 1950, including the 1-0 defeat by the United States. The centre-half signed professional forms for the club in 1943 after starting his career with Tranmere. He made 326 appearances and was a League Championship winner in 1947 when Liverpool finished a point ahead of Manchester United. Hughes also played in the 1950 FA Cup Final defeat by Arsenal. His last game was in 1957.

RALPH GUBBINS, 79, played an important role in Bolton's FA Cup success in 1958. The inside-forward replaced the injured Nat Lofthouse for the semi-final against Blackburn at Maine Road and scored both goals in a 2-1 victory. Lofthouse returned for the final and netted both goals in the 2-0 victory over Manchester United. Gubbins spent seven years at the club before joining Hull, then finishing his career with Tranmere.

NORMAN LAWSON, 75, joined Swansea from Bury in 1958 and played alongside club legends Ivor Allchurch and Mel Charles during three seasons at the club. The left-back or left-winger moved on to Watford when the management wanted a team of all-Welsh players, but returned to the area as player-manager of Merthyr and Ton Pentre. Then he went back to the Vetch Field to help coach the youth team alongside 'Gentle Giant' John Charles.

DEREK GRIERSON, 79, joined Rangers from Queen's Park in 1952 and in his first season played a key role in their 'Double' triumph. The inside-right scored 23 goals in 30 matches as his side won the title on goal average from Hibernian. He netted five more on the way to the Scottish Cup Final, which Rangers won 1-0 in a replay against Aberdeen, and his tally in five years at Ibrox was 69 in 128 matches. Grierson then joined Falkirk and was in the side that defeated Kilmarnock 2-1 in a replay of the 1957 Final. He later played for Arbroath, Stirling, Coleraine and Cowdenbeath.

BRIAN RICHARDSON, 72, turned professional with West Bromwich Albion in 1957. After a handful of reserve team games, he joined Walsall, where his career was interrupted by national service before he could make a first-team appearance, and he later moved into non-league football. He was the son of WG Richardson, who scored 228 times for Albion, in 354 appearances, including both goals in their FA Cup Final win over Birmingham in 1931.

OCTOBER 2011

FLORIAN ALBERT, 70, gave one of the finest performances of the 1966 World Cup in England when he masterminded Hungary's 3-1 victory over Brazil in a group match at Goodison Park.

The following year he succeeded Bobby Charlton as European Footballer of the Year. Albert, a deep-lying centre-forward, played 75 times and scored 31 goals for his country. He spent all his club career with Ferencvaros.

REG WILLIAMS, 89, was Chelsea's oldest surviving former player and their last link to a famous friendly against Moscow Dynamo at the end of the Second World War. The wing-half scored in that 3-3 draw, watched by a crowd officially given as 74,496 but believed to be more than 100,000. Williams spent six seasons at Stamford Bridge, having his best one in 1949–50 when playing 25 matches in a side that reached the semi-finals of the FA Cup before losing to Arsenal in a replay.

ROY WILLIAMS, 79, scored 154 goals in 357 appearances in two spells with Hereford during their non-league days – the club's second highest tally. One of them came in their biggest FA Cup win over Football League opposition, 6-1 against Queens Park Rangers in a second round tie in 1957. The inside-forward also featured in the third round 3-0 defeat by Sheffield Wednesday which drew Edgar Street's record crowd of 18,114. Williams spent two seasons with Southampton after a £4,000 transfer in 1952.

PETER RHODES, 90, was a leading Football League referee in the 1950s and 60s. A colourful and often controversial figure, he resigned after 22 years on the league list and sold his memoirs to a Sunday newspaper, saying: 'It is the only way I can speak up for the most abused person in football – the referee.' Rhodes, from York, once sent off, for abusive language, Manchester United's Denis Law, who argued unsuccessfully at an appeal that it was directed not at the official but towards his team-mate Paddy Crerand.

HOWARD MADLEY, 72, was a centre-half with Exeter, Bristol Rovers, Cardiff and Newport. He then made more than 400 appearances for Worcester between 1963–70, before returning to Wales to captain Merthyr.

IAN RUNDLE, 67, made 357 appearances for Wycombe in their non-league days. The defender came from Oxford City and returned there as a scout following the departure of manager Bobby Moore, England's World Cup-winning captain, and his assistant Harry Redknapp. He later became manager.

DERRICK WARD, 76, was a Potteries-born winger who joined Stoke in 1950 and spent a decade at the club, much of the time in the reserves. He then had two years with Stockport. Younger brother Terry, a full-back, also played for Stoke.

NOVEMBER 2011

GARY SPEED, 42, had an outstanding career as a player for club and country and was beginning to make a mark as an international manager when his death shocked and saddened the world of football. It came hours after an appearance on the BBC's *Football Focus* programme with Gary McAllister, one of his midfield partners along with Gordon Strachan and David Batty in Leeds' League Championship success of the 1991–92 season. Speed made 312 appearances and scored 57 goals for the club he joined as a schoolboy, before a £3.5m move to Everton, the team he supported as a boy. There, he scored his first hat-trick, against Southampton, in one of 65 appearances which brought 18 goals. Newcastle paid £5.5m for his services and were rewarded by FA Cup Finals against Arsenal in 1998 (0-2) and Manchester United (0-2) a year later, followed by Champions League football. After 285 matches and 40 goals, the Welshman was given the chance to extend his career in the top flight by Bolton and became the first man to play 500 Premier League games. After 139 matches and 14 goals for Wanderers, Speed played another 37 for Sheffield United, scoring six times, before retiring at 41. He took over as manager when Kevin Blackwell was sacked, but had been in the job for only four months when agreeing to succeed John Toshack as Wales manager in December 2010. The holder of 85 Wales caps, and a proud possessor of an MBE, Speed began the task of restoring his country's fortunes. He installed Arsenal's 20-year-old midfielder Aaron Ramsey as captain and after a difficult start had led his team to four victories in five matches, bringing a rise in the FIFA world rankings to 45th from 117th. His first cap came in 1990 against Costa Rica and that country were the opposition for a memorial match staged by the FA of Wales, watched by a crowd of 23,193 at Cardiff City Stadium.

JIMMY ADAMSON, 82, captained Burnley to the League Championship in 1960 when they finished one point ahead of Wolves, title winners for the two previous seasons. He also won the Footballer Writers' Association Footballer of the Year award in 1962, despite defeat in the FA Cup Final by Tottenham (1–3). One of the finest wing-halves of his day was a one-club man, who made 486 appearances in a 17-year career at Turf Moor. At 33, he was included in England's squad for the 1962 World Cup in Chile, but never won an international cap. Later, Adamson turned down the chance to succeed Walter Winterbottom as manager, believing he lacked experience, and opened the way for Alf Ramsey to take charge of the national side. He became manager of Burnley in 1970, experienced relegation in his first season and promotion back to the top flight two years later. He had a spell in charge of Sparta Rotterdam, before taking charge of Sunderland, then succeeding Jock Stein at Leeds.

JIM LEWIS, 84, achieved major honours in amateur and professional football during a remarkable career. Throughout, he kept his amateur status, even when winning a League Championship medal with Chelsea in 1955. In those days, the maximum wage was less than his earnings as a salesman, so he did not receive a new suit from Chelsea to mark their first title. Instead, the club presented him with an illuminated address. Manager Ted Drake brought Lewis to Stamford Bridge after the prolific centre-forward equalised for Walthamstow Avenue – one of the most famous amateur sides – in a fourth round FA Cup tie against Manchester United at Old Trafford in 1953 and netted twice in the replay, which United won 5–2 at Highbury. He was on the mark 40 times in 95 appearances for Chelsea, before returning to Walthamstow, for whom his father had also played. He scored 423 goals in 522 games for the club, forerunners of Dagenham and Redbridge, and 39 in 49 appearances for the England amateur side. Lewis was twice a winner of the FA Amateur Cup and played for Great Britain in the 1952, 1956 and 1960 Olympics.

ALF FIELDS, 92, was believed to have been Arsenal's oldest former player. He turned professional in 1937 and during the course of 47 years at the club also served as a coach, trainer and physiotherapist. The centre-half also turned actor in 1939, playing himself in the film *The Arsenal Stadium Mystery*. He was restricted to 19 league appearances because of the War, the form of Leslie Compton and a knee injury sustained in a collision with his own goalkeeper George Swindin.

JOHNNY WILLIAMS, 76, made his debut for Plymouth in 1955, scored for the first time against Liverpool at Anfield and made 477 appearances in 11 years at Home Park. A ferocious shot brought many of his 58 goals from outside the penalty area, attracting the interest of several First Division clubs, including Wolves who had a substantial offer rejected. The wing-half helped Plymouth win the Third Division title in 1959, and reach the League Cup semi-finals in 1965. He left for Bristol Rovers the following season, briefly returning as a coach under Billy Bingham, before spells with Bodmin and Falmouth.

FRANK BEAUMONT, 71, helped Barnsley to a successful FA Cup run in the 1960–61 season when they reached the sixth round before losing 2–1 to Leicester. He also featured in Bury's progress to the semi-finals of the 1962–63 League Cup before a 4–3 aggregate defeat by Birmingham. The inside-forward later played for Stockport, then led Macclesfield to victory in the first FA Trophy Final against Telford (2–0) in 1970.

CHARLIE DORE, 80, made his debut for Portsmouth against Bolton in March 1952 and played for the remainder of that season when they finished fourth behind champions Manchester United, Tottenham and Arsenal. He faced keen competition for the goalkeeping spot and moved on in the summer of 1954, having spells with Worcester and Guildford.

ALUN EVANS, 69, succeeded Trevor Morris as secretary of the Football Association of Wales in 1982. He held the position until 1995 and sat on several FIFA and UEFA regulatory bodies. He was also instrumental in the formation of the Welsh Premier League.

DAVID CARGILL, 75, was an outside-left who made 56 league appearances for Derby between

1958-60. He also played for Burnley, Sheffield Wednesday and Lincoln, before spending four years with home-town club Arbroath.

DECEMBER 2011

SOCRATES, 57, was the 6ft 4in footballing doctor regarded as one of the most gifted midfield players of his era. He made 60 appearances for Brazil, scoring 22 goals, captained the 1982 World Cup team in Spain and featured in the 1986 tournament in Mexico. His club career spanned Corinthians, Botafogo, Flamengo and Santos, along with a spell in Italy with Fiorentina, and in 1983 he was named South American Player of the Year. In 2004, the owner of Northern Counties League club Garforth, Simon Clifford, used contacts in Brazil to bring Socrates to England on a one-month deal as player-coach. More than a decade after retiring, he played in one match, coming on as a substitute against Tadcaster for 12 minutes, before returning home to his medical practice.

LEN PHILLIPS, 89, was Portsmouth's last link to the team that won back-to-back League Championships. The inside-forward played 40 games and scored 11 goals in 1948–49 when they finished five points clear of Manchester United. The following season, he made 34 appearances and netted five times as Portsmouth edged out Wolves on goal average. Phillips spent the whole of his eight-year career at the club, playing 261 matches and scoring 62 goals, and was inducted into their Hall of Fame in 2010. He won three England caps and later played non-league football well into his 40s.

GEORGE ROBB, 85, died on Christmas Day, exactly 60 years after scoring on his Football League debut for Tottenham against Charlton. He was one of the last of the 'gentleman players,' combining a football career with a job in teaching. The left-winger netted 58 goals in 200 appearances for the club, before an injury sustained in a five-a-side tournament ended his playing days in 1958. His one international cap came in the 6-3 Wembley defeat by Hungary in 1953 – the first time England had lost at home to overseas opposition. Previously, Robb made 18 appearances for the England amateur side and was in Great Britain's team for the 1952 Olympics in Helsinki.

PETER CROKER, 89, was the last surviving member of Charlton's FA Cup-winning team of 1947 when they beat Burnley 1-0 in the final after extra-time. The previous season, he played in every round of the competition, but missed that final against Derby (1-4) with a fractured leg sustained ten days earlier. The injury also cost him the chance of an England call-up. Croker joined Watford after six years at the club, then returned to The Valley to serve as chief scout and assistant manager to Bob Stokoe. He also scouted for Blackpool and Sunderland.

NEIL DAVIDS, 56, made his debut for Wigan in their first match as a Football League club, a goalless draw at Hereford on the opening day of the 1978–79 Fourth Division season. The central defender made 68 league appearances, before a broken leg ended his career. Davids, an England youth international, started out with Leeds in 1973 and also appeared for Norwich, Northampton, Stockport and Swansea.

RON HOWELLS, 84, made his league debut for Cardiff in a 3-0 victory over former club Swansea on Boxing Day 1951 in front of a 46,000 crowd at Ninian Park. The goalkeeper helped them reach the old First Division that season as runners-up to Sheffield Wednesday and won two Wales caps in World Cup qualifiers against England and Scotland. He moved to Worcester in 1957, but returned to league football at Chester towards the end of his career.

KEN JOHNSON, 80, spent the whole of his career from 1949–64 at Hartlepool and remains their all-time leading Football League scorer with 98 goals. The inside-right is part of another Victoria Park record – the 17,426 attendance for an FA Cup third round tie against Manchester United in 1957. He scored in that match, which United manager Matt Busby described as one of the most exciting he had ever seen after a 4-3 win. Johnson made a total of 413 appearances and was voted by supporters the club's Player of the 50s.

PETER BROWN, 77, was restricted to 16 league appearances during six years with Southampton by strong competition for places. The outside-right doubled that total after moving to Wrexham in

1958 and later turned out for Poole, Dorchester and Andover. Son Kevan left Southampton after failing to break into the first team to join Brighton, then Aldershot and Yeovil.

LAWRIE TIERNEY, 52, played for both Edinburgh clubs, helping Hearts gain promotion back to the Premier Division in the 1977–78 season and having a spell with Hibernian in 1980. The midfielder moved on to Wigan, then played in the American indoor league with Phoenix and Tacoma.

ALF SETCHELL, 87, was one of Coventry's oldest surviving former players. The left-winger made his debut for the club in War-time football, appeared 18 times during that period and played a handful of matches afterwards. He then moved on to Kidderminster, then Hereford.

JANUARY 2012

GARY ABLETT, 46, the only player to win the FA Cup with both Liverpool and Everton, died after a 16-month battle against cancer. He first became ill at the Ipswich training ground, having taken up a coaching role under Roy Keane in July 2010. Ablett joined Liverpool as an apprentice in 1982. In Kenny Dalglish's first spell as manager, he helped them win the League title in 1988 and 1990, along with the FA Cup in 1989 when they beat Everton 3-2. After loan spells with Derby and Hull, he moved to Goodison Park for £750,000 and featured in the 1995 final – a 1-0 victory over Manchester United. Ablett, who played at full-back or in central defence, also served Birmingham and Blackpool, along with Sheffield United and Wycombe on loan, finishing his career with Long Island in America after a total of 468 appearances. He then coached Everton's youngsters and became Liverpool's reserve team manager, followed by a season as manager of Stockport, a club crippled by financial problems and relegated to League Two in 2010. He left when new owners took over.

ERNIE GREGORY, 90, had a 51-year association with West Ham as player and coach. The goalkeeper made 481 appearances, 50 of them in war-time before his Football League debut in 1946. He was a key figure in the side that won the Division Two title in 1958 and played one match for England B before hanging up his gloves in 1959. Gregory stayed with the club to coach the reserves, then the first team. Although retiring in 1987, he remained a regular visitor to the Chadwell Heath training ground, passing on knowledge and experience to the club's young players and coaching staff.

CLIFF PORTWOOD, 74, scored twice for Portsmouth when they first featured on BBC's *Match of the Day* against Wolves in 1967. The inside-forward spent five years at Fratton Park after helping Grimsby win promotion from Division Three in the 1961–62 season. He started his career at Preston, then netted 38 goals in two seasons with Port Vale. After retiring, Portwood had a successful singing career, appearing at the London Palladium and in Las Vegas and releasing several albums.

GRAHAM RATHBONE, 69, made 255 appearances for Grimsby after a £10,000 move from home-town club Newport in 1966. The centre-half was part of Lawrie McMenemy's team that won the Division Four title in the 1971–72 season and later helped Cambridge United gain promotion from the same division.

SID OTTEWELL, 92, was a much-travelled inside-forward who between 1946–1953 played for Chesterfield, Birmingham, Luton, Nottingham Forest, Mansfield and Scunthorpe. His most successful spell was at Mansfield, where he scored 21 goals in 68 league matches and helped the club to the runners-up spot in the Third Division North in 1951. He also guested for six other clubs during the War.

BILL DICKIE, 82, was for many years one of the most influential officials in Scottish football. He served on all the major SFA committees, was president from 1993–97 and frequently acted as a FIFA and UEFA match observer. He spent nearly 40 years as a director of Motherwell, having three separate spells as chairman.

SIR TOM COWIE, 89, spent six years as chairman of Sunderland from 1980. He was one of the north-east's best-known entrepreneurs, but his tenure at Roker Park was a troubled one.

It involved a long-running power struggle and he eventually grew tired with the politics and in-fighting and sold out in, while remaining a devoted fan.

PAUL FEASEY, 78, spent his entire 17-year professional career with Hull, joining the club in 1949 after training as a bricklayer. At 5ft 8in he was small for a centre-half, but gave little away in the air. Feasey captained the promotion-winning side of 1958–59, missing only one of the 46 matches that brought the runners-up spot behind Plymouth in Division Three. He made a total of 271 appearances and after retiring from league football became player-manager of Goole.

SYD THOMAS, 92, won four caps for Wales in the 1940s, one of them a 3-0 defeat by England in front of a crowd of 55,000 at Ninian Park, Cardiff. The right-winger was in Fulham's Second Division Championship-winning side of the 1948–49 season and later played for Bristol City following a £9,000 transfer. His career was cut short by tuberculosis.

FEBRUARY 2012

NIGEL DOUGHTY, 54, bought Nottingham Forest for £11m in 1999, saved the club from administration and over the years invested £75m of his personal fortune. The life-long Forest fan stepped down as chairman in October, 2011 after the sacking of manager Steve McClaren. He was replaced by former City Ground player and manager Frank Clark.

EAMONN 'CHICK' DEACY, 53, was part of Aston Villa's First Division Championship-winning squad of 1980–81 when they finished four points ahead of Ipswich. The left-back spent a lot of the time on the bench – starting five matches – and was reluctant to collect his title medal because he felt he had not done enough. But manager Ron Saunders, who remarkably used only 14 players in that season, told him he had contributed to the team's success when coming off the bench. Deacy, who made four international appearances for the Republic of Ireland, spent five years at Villa Park, before returning home to Galway, with whom he won the FA of Ireland Cup in 1991.

TOM MCANEARNEY, 79, made nearly 400 appearances during 13 years with Sheffield Wednesday from 1952. In his time, they twice won promotion back to the First Division as champions after being relegated and in 1961 were runners-up to Tottenham in the top flight. The wing-half, whose brother Jim was also at the club, had a brief spell at Peterborough, then began a long association with Aldershot both as player and manager. It began in 1966, was interrupted by a return to Hillsborough as coach and a spell as manager of Bury, and resumed at the start of the 1972–73 season. He immediately led the club to their first promotion – using just 16 players in that Fourth Division campaign – and to their highest league placing of eighth a year later. McAnearney was manager for more than 500 matches, a club record, before his departure in 1981.

MALCOLM DEVITT, 75, made 110 appearances in five years for home-town club Bradford City. The inside-forward left in 1963 after a contract dispute and joined Wisbech, where he made a record 246 appearances for the club during their days in the Southern League.

PETER KING, 47, was a youth player at Liverpool signed by Crewe in 1983 on the recommendation of Anfield secretary Peter Robinson. The midfielder spent two years in the senior team at Gresty Road, then had spells with non-league Southport and Morecambe.

CHARLES AMER, 100, became chairman of Middlesbrough in 1973 and the following year celebrated winning the Second Division title by a then record margin of 15 points under manager Jack Charlton. But his time was shrouded in controversy. Star players left the club, there were mounting financial problems and Amer, a property developer, resigned in 1982.

GEORGE DUNCAN, 75, was a Scotland schoolboy international who went on to play for Rangers between 1957–60. His chances were limited because Alex Scott occupied that position and after a spell on loan with Raith, he joined Southend, then Chesterfield.

MARCH 2012

RAY BARLOW, 85, was one of West Bromwich Albion's best-ever players and an inspiration for England's World Cup-winning captain Bobby Moore. In his autobiography, Moore said he modelled his game on the wing-half, who made 482 appearances in a 16-year career at The Hawthorns, starting in 1944. Barlow was the last surviving member of the team that beat Preston 3-2 in the 1954 FA Cup Final. In the same season, Albion finished runners-up to Wolves in the First Division. He won one England cap, against Northern Ireland, and finished his career with Birmingham.

BARRY KITCHENER, 64, made 602 appearances for Millwall, a club record, between 1967–82. He signed at 16 and played at left-back in the youth and reserve teams before making the centre-half position his own in the senior side. Apart from a brief loan spell with Tampa Bay in the United States in 1979, Kitchener was a one-club man, who won the Player of the Year award three times. After retiring, he coached the youths and reserves and was in charge of the Football League squad for six games before the arrival as manager of George Graham.

GERRY BRIDGWOOD, 67, played his first game for home-town club Stoke in 1961 at the age of 16. He spent nine seasons there, much of the time as a back-up winger because of the return to the Potteries of Stanley Matthews. Bridgwood played a part in Stoke's successful League Cup campaign of 1963–64, although not featuring in the losing two-leg final against Leicester. He was sold to Shrewsbury for £12,000 in 1969, but had his career cut short by injuries at 29.

BRIAN BROMLEY, 65, made his senior debut as a 16-year-old. He was an England youth international who played for Bolton between 1963–68, then for Portsmouth after a £25,000 transfer. The inside-forward also had spells with Brighton, Reading and Darlington, followed by non-league football with Wigan and Waterlooville.

BRIAN PHILLIPS, 80, was one of ten players jailed in 1965 in the match-fixing scandal which rocked English football. The Mansfield centre-half received 15 months. Phillips had previously been with Middlesbrough, where he was a team-mate of Brian Clough.

APRIL 2012

EDDIE MAY, 68, was one of the most respected figures in Welsh football, both as a player and manager. The centre-half made 334 appearances for Wrexham between 1968–76 and also played for Swansea and Southend. He twice managed Cardiff, winning the Division Three title and Welsh Cup in 1993, and had spells in charge of Newport, Torquay and Brentford. He also coached extensively in Africa, the Middle-East and Europe.

GIORGIO CHINAGLIA, 65, was born in Italy, grew up in Wales and once set up a goal at Wembley for the future England manager Fabio Capello. Spotted scoring a hat-trick in a schools match, he joined Swansea as an apprentice in 1962 and spent four years at Vetch Field. The centre-forward went on to play for Napoli, Lazio and alongside Pele at New York Cosmos. He won 14 caps for his country, one of them in 1973 when he eluded Bobby Moore and provided Capello with a tap-in which gave Italy a 1-0 victory, their first in England.

ALFIE BIGGS, 76, scored 199 goals in two spells with Bristol Rovers and was second in the list of the club's all-time leading marksmen behind Geoff Bradford. Two of them came in a 4-0 FA Cup third round win over Manchester United, watched by a 35,000 crowd at the old Eastville Stadium in 1956. After a season with Preston, the centre-forward returned to the club and netted a record 37 goals in all competitions during the 1963–64 campaign. Biggs, nicknamed 'Baron' for his sharp dress sense, made more than 400 appearances for Rovers. He later played for Walsall and Swansea.

JOSE MARIA ZARRAGA, 81, captained Real Madrid in their renowned 7-3 victory over Eintracht Frankfurt in the 1960 European Cup Final at Hampden Park. It was one of five successive triumphs for the legendary team of Puskas, Di Stefano, Gento and Del Sol. Zarraga, a defensive midfield player, also won six Spanish titles with the club.

LARRY CANNING, 86, became known as Mr Football of the Midlands for his time with Aston Villa and as a broadcaster. The wing-half was at Villa Park from 1947–54 and later played for

Kettering and Northampton. He moved into broadcasting with the help of BBC presenter David Coleman.

ARTHUR BOTTOM, 82, scored a hat-trick on his debut for York and equalled the club record of 31 league goals in his first season. The centre-forward was part of the side that reached the semi-finals of the FA Cup in 1955 before losing 2-0 to Newcastle in a replay. He joined the club from Sheffield United and later played for Newcastle and Chesterfield.

JIMMY LAWLOR, 78, joined Bradford City from Coleraine in 1957 and spent five years at Valley Parade, initially as a centre-half and then at wing-half. He made 155 league appearances before a fractured leg, sustained in a reserve match at Sunderland, forced him to retire at 29. Lawlor started his career with another Irish club, Drumcondra, and later had a spell at Doncaster, alongside brother John.

JACK EVANS, 86, was on Coventry's books between 1942–52, making eight first-team appearances and playing mainly for the reserves. The centre-forward moved into local non-league football, where he had a long and successful career.

MAY 2012

BARRY LOWES, 73, was part of Workington's Fourth Division promotion-winning side of 1963–64. The right-winger made 141 appearances and scored 38 goals for the club after spells with Barrow and Blackpool. He went on to play for Bury, then under Jimmy Hill at Coventry, where he struggled with a knee injury sustained in his first game.

RASHIDI YEKINI, 48, was the first Nigerian to become Africa's Footballer of the Year. The 6ft 3in striker scored his country's first-ever World Cup goal, against Bulgaria in the 1994 finals in the United States and was a key figure in their Africa Cup of Nations victory in the same year. He remained Nigeria's top international scorer with 37 goals from 58 games.

DAVE HAINING, 68, began a 47-year association with Crawley as a player in 1965. He made more than 500 appearances for the club, scoring 80 goals, then had five separate spells as manager or caretaker-manager.

JUNE 2012

GORDON WEST, 69, spent 11 years with Everton following a £27,000 move from Blackpool, then a British record fee for a goalkeeper. He made 402 appearances, won League Championships in 1963 and 1970 and the FA Cup in 1966 when his side beat Sheffield Wednesday 3-2. West played three times for England and was part of the squad for the 1968 European Championship. Two years later, he turned down the chance to go to the World Cup in Mexico for family reasons. He later had a spell with Tranmere.

CHRIS THOMPSON, 52, scored 26 goals in 100 appearances for Blackburn after joining the club from Bolton. The former England youth international played up front alongside Simon Garner and was leading league scorer in the 1984–85 Second Division season. He went on to play for Wigan, Blackpool and Cardiff, before ending his career with Walsall.

BOBBY BLACK, 85, won the Scottish League Cup with East Fife in the 1949–50 season when they beat Dunfermline 3-0. His team also reached the Scottish Cup Final, losing to Rangers by the same score, and finished fourth in the First Division. Two years later, they were up to third. The winger went on to score 120 goals in 346 appearances for Queen of the South, the club's second highest all-time tally.

STEVE BUTTLE, 59, was among the first wave of English players to move to the United States. After starting his career at Ipswich, then serving Bournemouth, he began a succesful five years with Seattle in the North American Soccer League in 1977. The midfielder then played for Pittsburg and coached Tacoma.

DENNIS SIGNY, 85, spent a lifetime involved in different aspects of football. He was a respected journalist and chairman of the Football Writers' Association. On the administrative side of the game, he was chief executive of Queens Park Rangers, general manager of Brentford and, latterly,

PR consultant to Barnet and the Football League.

ALAN MCDONALD, 48, made nearly 500 appearances in a 17-year career with Queens Park Rangers beginning in 1981. He also captained Northern Ireland, winning 52 caps and playing in the 1986 Mexico World Cup against Algeria (1-1), Spain (1-2) and Brazil (0-3). The centre-half, who collapsed while playing golf, led Rangers to the League Cup Final that year when they were beaten 3-0 by Oxford United. He also played on loan for Swindon and Charlton and had a spell as assistant manager under Gary Waddock at Loftus Road. McDonald went on to manage Glentoran, winning the Irish League title in 2009.

JACKIE NEILSON, 83, won the Scottish Cup with St Mirren in 1959 when they beat Aberdeen 3-1 in front of a crowd of 109,000 at Hampden Park, their first success in the competition for 33 years. Four years earlier, the wing-half and his team lost 2-1 to the same opponents in the League Cup Final. Neilson made nearly 400 appearances in 12 seasons with the Paisley club before a knee injury forced him to retire at 31.

TEDDY SCOTT, 83, made a single appearance for Aberdeen's senior side, but became a Pittodrie legend during a 49-year association with the club. He served under 15 managers as trainer, coach and kit man and was a key member of Alex Ferguson's backroom team in the club's glory years in the early 1980s. Sir Alex took a full-strength Manchester United team to play Aberdeen for Scott's testimonial in 1999, during their treble-winning season.

JULY 2012

JOE MCBRIDE, 74, scored 86 goals in 94 games for Celtic between 1965-68, winning two Scottish titles and two League Cups. But injury forced him to miss their biggest triumph – the 2-1 win over Inter Milan in the 1967 European Cup Final when the 'Lisbon Lions' became the first British side to win the trophy. McBride started his senior career with Kilmarnock, had spells with Wolves, Luton, Partick and then Motherwell, where three successive seasons as leading marksman persuaded Jock Stein to bring him to Parkhead for a £22,000 fee at the age of 27. After the injury he was unable to regain his place and joined Hibernian, where his tally was 58 goals in 91 matches. He also played for Dunfermline and Clyde and won two Scotland caps.

EDDY BROWN, 86, gave up training to be a catholic priest to pursue a career in football and became one of the biggest characters of his era. A prolific scorer, he was credited with inventing the goal celebration, often hugging on-duty policemen or shaking hands with the corner flag. The centre-forward also used to quote Shakespeare to his team-mates, opponents and referees. He helped Birmingham win the Second Division title on goal average from Luton in 1955 and finish sixth the following year, the club's highest placing in the top flight. In the 1956 FA Cup Final, which his side lost 3-1 to Manchester City, his header led to the collision between Peter Murphy and Bert Trautmann which left City goalkeeper Trautmann with a broken neck. Ten days after that, Birmingham became the first English club to compete in a European competition, the new Inter-Cities Fairs Cup in which they lost 2-1 to Barcelona in a play-off game in Berne, Switzerland, after the two-leg semi-final ended 4-4 on aggregate. Brown also played for Preston, Southampton, Coventry and Leyton Orient, scoring 232 goals in 488 league games.

JIMMY TANSEY, 83, was a left-back who came through the youth ranks to make 142 appearances for Everton between 1952-59. After spending time on the fringes of the senior team, he made the breakthrough during the club's second season back in the First Division, playing 39 times in the league. He eventually lost his place to John Bramwell and moved on to Crewe, his only other club.

ERNIE MACHIN, 68, was a key figure in the transformation of Coventry's fortunes under manager Jimmy Hill. The inside-forward spent a decade at the club from 1962, making nearly 300 appearances and gaining two promotions. His side won the Third Division title on goal average from Crystal Palace in 1964. Three years later, they became Second Division champions, finishing a point clear of Wolves, who they beat 3-1 in front of Highfield Road's biggest-ever attendance – 51,455. Machin, who scored in that game, captained the team in Division One before joining Plymouth for £35,000, then Brighton for £30,000.

RECORDS SECTION

INDEX

GOALSCORING

(†Football League pre-1992–93)

Highest: Arbroath 36 Bon Accord (Aberdeen) 0 in Scottish Cup 1, Sep 12, 1885. On same day, also in Scottish Cup 1, Dundee Harp beat Aberdeen Rov 35-0.

Internationals: France 0 England 15 in Paris, 1906 (Amateur); Ireland 0 England 13 in Belfast Feb 18, 1882 (record in UK); England 9 Scotland 3 at Wembley, Apr 15, 1961; Biggest England win at Wembley, 9-0 v Luxembourg (Euro Champ), Dec 15, 1982.

Other record wins: Scotland: 11-0 v Ireland (Glasgow, Feb 23, 1901); **Northern Ireland:** 7-0 v Wales (Belfast, Feb 1, 1930); **Wales:** 11-0 v Ireland (Wrexham, Mar 3, 1888); **Rep of Ireland:** 8-0 v Malta (Euro Champ, Dublin, Nov 16, 1983).

Record international defeats: England: 1-7 v Hungary (Budapest, May 23, 1954); **Scotland:** 3-9 v England (Wembley, Apr 15, 1961); **Ireland:** 0-13 v England (Belfast, Feb 18, 1882); **Wales:** 0-9 v Scotland (Glasgow, Mar 23, 1878); **Rep of Ireland:** 0-7 v Brazil (Uberlandia, May 27, 1982).

World Cup: Qualifying round – Australia 31 American Samoa 0, world record international score (Apr 11, 2001); Australia 22 Tonga 0 (Apr 9, 2001); Iran 19 Guam 0 (Nov 25, 2000); Maldives 0 Iran 17 (Jun 2, 1997). **Finals – highest scores:** Hungary 10 El Salvador 1 (Spain, Jun 15, 1982); Hungary 9 S Korea 0 (Switzerland, Jun 17, 1954); Yugoslavia 9 Zaire 0 (W Germany, Jun 18, 1974).

European Championship: Qualifying round – highest scorers: San Marino 0 Germany 13 (Serravalle, Sep 6, 2006). **Finals – highest score:** Holland 6 Yugoslavia 1 (quarter-final, Rotterdam, Jun 25, 2000).

FA Cup: Preston 26 Hyde 0 1st round, Oct 15, 1887.

League Cup: West Ham 10 Bury 0 (2nd round, 2nd leg, Oct 25, 1983); Liverpool 10 Fulham 0 (2nd round, 1st leg, Sep 23, 1986). **Record aggregates:** Liverpool 13 Fulham 2 (10-0h, 3-2a), Sep 23, Oct 7, 1986; West Ham 12 Bury 1 (2-1a, 10-0h), Oct 4, 25, 1983; Liverpool 11 Exeter 0 (5-0h, 6-0a), Oct 7, 28, 1981.

Premier League (beginning 1992–93): Manchester Utd 9 Ipswich 0, Mar 4, 1995. Tottenham 9 Wigan 1, Nov 22, 2009. **Record away win:** Nottm Forest 1 Manchester Utd 8 Feb 6, 1999.

Highest aggregate scores in Premier League –11: Portsmouth 7 Reading 4, Sep 29, 2007; **10:** Tottenham 6 Reading 4, Dec 29, 2007; Tottenham 9 Wigan 1, Nov 22, 2009; Manchester Utd 8 Arsenal 2, Aug 28, 2011; **9:** Norwich 4 Southampton 5, Apr 9, 1994; Manchester Utd 9 Ipswich 0, Mar 4, 1995; Southampton 6 Manchester Utd 3, Oct 26, 1996; Blackburn 7 Sheffield Wed 2, Aug 25, 1997; Nottm Forest 1 Manchester Utd 8 Feb 6, 1999; Tottenham 7 Southampton 2, Mar 11, 2000; Tottenham 4 Arsenal 5, Nov 13, 2004; Middlesbrough 8 Manchester City 1, May 11, 2008; Chelsea 7 Sunderland 2, Jan 16, 2010

†Football League (First Division): Aston Villa 12 Accrington 2, Mar 12, 1892; Tottenham 10 Everton 4, Oct 11, 1958 (highest Div 1 aggregate that century); WBA 12 Darwen 0, Apr 4, 1892; Nottm Forest 12 Leicester Fosse 0, Apr 21, 1909. **Record away win:** Newcastle 1 Sunderland 9, Dec 5, 1908; Cardiff 1 Wolves 9, Sep 3, 1955; Wolves 0 WBA 8, Dec 27, 1893.

New First Division (beginning 1992–93): Bolton 7 Swindon 0, Mar 8, 1997; Sunderland 7 Oxford Utd 0, Sep 19, 1998. **Record away win:** Stoke 0 Birmingham 7, Jan 10, 1998; Oxford Utd 0 Birmingham 7, Dec 12, 1998. **Record aggregate:** Grimsby 6 Burnley 5, Oct 29, 2002; Burnley 4 Watford 7, Apr 5, 2003.

Championship (beginning 2004–05): WBA 7 Barnsley 0, May 6, 2007. Record away win: Wolves 0 Southampton 6, Mar 31, 2007; Bristol City 0 Cardiff 6, Jan 26, 2010; Doncaster 0 Ipswich 6, Feb 15, 2011; Millwall 0 Birmingham 6, Jan 14, 2012. Record agregate: Leeds 4 Preston 6, Sep 29, 2010; Leeds 3 Nottm Forest 7, Mar 20, 2012.

†**Second Division**: Newcastle 13 Newport Co 0, Oct 5, 1946; Small Heath 12 Walsall Town Swifts 0, Dec 17, 1892; Darwen 12 Walsall 0, Dec 26, 1896; Woolwich Arsenal 12 Loughborough 0, Mar 12, 1900; Small Heath 12 Doncaster 0, Apr 11, 1903. **Record away win:** *Burslem Port Vale 0 Sheffield Utd 10, Dec 10, 1892. **Record aggregate:** Manchester City 11 Lincoln 3, Mar 23, 1895.

New Second Division (beginning 1992–93): Hartlepool 1 Plymouth Argyle 8, May 7, 1994; Hartlepool 8 Grimsby 1, Sep 12, 2003.

New League 1 (beginning 2004–05): Swansea 7 Bristol City 1, Sep 10, 2005; Nottm Forest 7 Swindon 1, Feb 25, 2006; Bristol City 6 Gillingham 0, Mar 18, 2006; Swindon 6 Port Vale 0, Apr 19, 2008; Norwich 1 Colchester 7, Aug 8, 2009; Huddersfield 7 Brighton 1, Aug 18, 2009; Huddersfield 6 Wycombe 0, Nov 14, 2009; Stockport 0 Huddersfield 6, Apr 24, 2010; Oldham 0 Southampton 6, Jan 11, 2011; Wycombe 0 Huddersfield 6, Jan 6, 2012; Yeovil 0 Stevenage 6, Apr 14, 2012. Record aggregate: Hartlepool 4 Wrexham 6, Mar 5, 2005.

†**Third Division**: Gillingham 10 Chesterfield 0, Sep 5, 1987; Tranmere 9 Accrington 0, Apr 18, 1959; Brentford 9 Wrexham 0, Oct 15, 1963. **Record away win:** Halifax 0 Fulham 8, Sep 16, 1969. Record aggregate: Doncaster 7 Reading 5, Sep 25, 1982.

New Third Division (beginning 1992–93): Barnet 1 Peterborough 9, Sep 5, 1998. Record aggregate: Hull 7 Swansea 4, Aug 30, 1997.

†**New League 2 (beginning 2004–05):** Peterborough 7 Brentford 0, Nov 24, 2007 Shrewsbury 7 Gillingham 0, Sep 13, 2008; Crewe 7 Barnet 0, Aug 21, 2010; Crewe 8 Cheltenham 1, Apr 2, 2011.

Record away win: Boston 0 Grimsby 6, Feb 3, 2007; Macclesfield 0 Darlington 6, Aug 30, 2008; Lincoln 0 Rotherham 6, Mar 25, 2011. **Record aggregate:** Burton 5 Cheltenham 6, Mar 13, 2010; Accrington 7 Gillingham 4, Oct 2, 2010.

†**Third Division (North)**: Stockport 13 Halifax 0 (still joint biggest win in Football League – see Div 2) Jan 6, 1934; Tranmere 13 Oldham 4, Dec 26, 1935. (17 is highest Football League aggregate score). **Record away win:** Accrington 0 Barnsley 9, Feb 3, 1934.

†**Third Division (South)**: Luton 12 Bristol Rov 0, Apr 13, 1936; Bristol City 9 Gillingham 4, Jan 15, 1927; Gillingham 9 Exeter 4, Jan 7, 1951. **Record away win:** Northampton 0 Walsall 8, Apr 8, 1947.

†**Fourth Division**: Oldham 11 Southport 0, Dec 26, 1962. Record away win: Crewe 1 Rotherham 8, Sep 8, 1973. Record aggregate: Hartlepool 10 Barrow 1, Apr 4, 1959; Crystal Palace 9 Accrington 2, Aug 20, 1960; Wrexham 10 Hartlepool 1, Mar 3, 1962; Oldham 11 Southport 0, Dec 26, 1962; Torquay 8 Newport 3, Oct 19, 1963; Shrewsbury 7 Doncaster 4, Feb 1, 1975; Barnet 4 Crewe 7, Aug 17, 1991. **Record away win:** Crewe 1 Rotherham 8 Sep 8, 1973.

Scottish Premier – Highest aggregate: 12: Motherwell 6 Hibernian 6, May 5, 2010; **11:** Celtic 8 Hamilton 3, Jan 3, 1987; Motherwell 5 Aberdeen 6, Oct 20, 1999. **Other highest team scores:** Aberdeen 8 Motherwell 0 (Mar 26, 1979); Hamilton 0 Celtic 8 (Nov 5, 1988); Celtic 9 Aberdeen 0 (Nov 6, 2010).

Scottish League Div 1: Celtic 11 Dundee 0, Oct 26, 1895. **Record away win:** Hibs 11 *Airdrie 1, Oct 24, 1959.

Scottish League Div 2: Airdrieonians 15 Dundee Wanderers 1, Dec 1, 1894 (biggest win in history of League football in Britain).

Record modern Scottish League aggregate: 12 – Brechin 5 Cowdenbeath 7, Div 2, Jan 18, 2003.

Record British score since 1900: Stirling 20 Selkirk 0 (Scottish Cup 1, Dec 8, 1984). Winger Davie Thompson (7 goals) was one of 9 Stirling players to score.

LEAGUE GOALS – BEST IN SEASON (Before restructure in 1992)

Div		Goals	Games
1	WR (Dixie) Dean, Everton, 1927–28	60	39
2	George Camsell, Middlesbrough, 1926–27	59	37
3(S)	Joe Payne, Luton, 1936–37	55	39
3(N)	Ted Harston, Mansfield, 1936–37	55	41
3	Derek Reeves, Southampton, 1959–60	39	46
4	Terry Bly, Peterborough, 1960–61	52	46

(Since restructure in 1992)

Div		Goals	Games
1	Guy Whittingham, Portsmouth, 1992–93	42	46
2	Jimmy Quinn, Reading, 1993–94	35	46
3	Andy Morrell, Wrexham, 2002–03	34	45

Premier League – BEST IN SEASON
Andy Cole **34 goals** (Newcastle – 40 games, 1993–94); Alan Shearer **34 goals** (Blackburn – 42 games, 1994–95).

FOOTBALL LEAGUE – BEST MATCH HAULS

(Before restructure in 1992)

Div	Goals	
1	Ted Drake (Arsenal), away to Aston Villa, Dec 14, 1935	7
	James Ross (Preston) v Stoke, Oct 6, 1888	7
2	*Neville (Tim) Coleman (Stoke) v Lincoln, Feb 23, 1957	7
	Tommy Briggs (Blackburn) v Bristol Rov, Feb 5, 1955	7
3(S)	Joe Payne (Luton) v Bristol Rov, Apr 13, 1936	10
3(N)	Robert ('Bunny') Bell (Tranmere) v Oldham, Dec 26, 1935 he also missed a penalty	9
3	Barrie Thomas (Scunthorpe) v Luton, Apr 24, 1965	5
	Keith East (Swindon) v Mansfield, Nov 20, 1965	5
	Steve Earle (Fulham) v Halifax, Sep 16, 1969	5
	Alf Wood (Shrewsbury) v Blackburn, Oct 2, 1971	5
	Tony Caldwell (Bolton) v Walsall, Sep 10, 1983	5
	Andy Jones (Port Vale) v Newport Co., May 4, 1987	5
4	Bert Lister (Oldham) v Southport, Dec 26, 1962	6

*Scored from the wing

(Since restructure in 1992)

Div Goals -

1 **4** in match – John Durnin (Oxford Utd v Luton, 1992–93); Guy Whittingham (Portsmouth v Bristol Rov 1992–3); Craig Russell (Sunderland v Millwall, 1995–6); David Connolly (Wolves at Bristol City 1998–99); Darren Byfield (Rotherham at Millwall, 2002–03); David Connolly (Wimbledon at Bradford City, 2002–03); Marlon Harewood (Nottm Forest v Stoke, 2002–03); Michael Chopra (Watford at Burnley, 2002–03); Robert Earnshaw (Cardiff v Gillingham, 2003–04).

2 **5** in match – Paul Barnes (Burnley v Stockport, 1996–97); Robert Taylor (all 5, Gillingham at Burnley, 1998–99); Lee Jones (all 5, Wrexham v Cambridge Utd, 2001–02).

3 **5** in match – Tony Naylor (Crewe v Colchester, 1992–93); Steve Butler (Cambridge Utd v Exeter, 1993–4); Guiliano Grazioli (Peterborough at Barnet, 1998–99).

Champ 4 in match – Gareth McCleary (Nottm Forest at Leeds 2011–12); Nikola Zigic (Birmingham at Leeds 2011–12

Lge 1 4 in match – Jordan Rhodes (all 4, Huddersfield at Sheffield Wed, 2011–12)

5 in match – Juan Ugarte (Wrexham at Hartlepool, 2004–05); Jordan Rhodes (Huddersfield at Wycombe, 2011–12)

PREMIER LEAGUE – BEST MATCH HAULS

5 goals in match: Andy Cole (Manchester Utd v Ipswich, Mar 4, 1995); Alan Shearer (Newcastle v Sheffield Wed, Sep 19, 1999); Jermain Defoe (Tottenham v Wigan, Nov 22, 2009); Dimitar Berbatov (Manchester Utd v Blackburn, Nov 27, 2010).

SCOTTISH LEAGUE

Div		Goals
Prem	Gary Hooper (Celtic) v Hearts, May 13, 2012	5
	Kris Boyd (Rangers) v Dundee Utd, Dec 30, 2009	5
	Kris Boyd (Kilmarnock) v Dundee Utd, Sep 25, 2004	5
	Kenny Miller (Rangers) v St Mirren, Nov 4, 2000	5
	Marco Negri (Rangers) v Dundee Utd, Aug. 23, 1997	5
	Paul Sturrock (Dundee Utd) v Morton, Nov 17, 1984	5
1	Jimmy McGrory (Celtic) v Dunfermline, Jan 14, 1928	8
1	Owen McNally (Arthurlie) v Armadale, Oct 1, 1927	8
2	Jim Dyet (King's Park) v Forfar, Jan 2, 1930 on his debut for the club	8
2	John Calder (Morton) v Raith, Apr 18, 1936	8
2	Norman Haywood (Raith) v Brechin, Aug. 20, 1937	8

SCOTTISH LEAGUE – BEST IN SEASON

Prem	Brian McClair (Celtic, 1986–87)	35
	Henrik Larsson (Celtic, 2000–01)	35
1	William McFadyen (Motherwell, 1931–32)	53
2	*Jimmy Smith (Ayr, 1927–28 – 38 appearances)	66
	(*British record)	

SCOTTISH CUP FOOTBALL

Scottish Cup: John Petrie (Arbroath) v Bon Accord, at Arbroath, 1st round, Sep 12, 1885 — 13
FA Cup: Ted MacDougall (Bournemouth) v Margate, 1st round, Nov 20,1971 — 9
FA Cup Final: Billy Townley (Blackburn) v Sheffield Wed, at Kennington Oval, 1890; Jimmy Logan (Notts Co) v Bolton, at Everton, 1894; Stan Mortensen (Blackpool) v Bolton, at Wembley, 1953 — 3
League Cup: Frank Bunn (Oldham) v Scarborough (3rd round), Oct 25, 1989 — 6
Scottish League Cup: Jim Fraser (Ayr) v Dumbarton, Aug. 13, 1952; Jim Forrest (Rangers) v Stirling Albion, Aug. 17, 1966 — 5

Scottish Cup: Most goals in match since war: 10 by **Gerry Baker** (St Mirren) in 15-0 win (1st round) v Glasgow Univ, Jan 30, 1960; 9 by his brother **Joe Baker** (Hibernian) in 15-1 win (2nd round) v Peebles, Feb 11, 1961.

AGGREGATE LEAGUE SCORING RECORDS

	Goals
*Arthur Rowley (1947–65, WBA, Fulham, Leicester, Shrewsbury)	434
†Jimmy McGrory (1922–38, Celtic, Clydebank)	410
Hughie Gallacher (1921–39, Airdrieonians, Newcastle, Chelsea, Derby, Notts Co, Grimsby, Gateshead)	387
William ('Dixie') Dean (1923–37, Tranmere, Everton, Notts Co)	379
Hugh Ferguson (1916–30, Motherwell, Cardiff, Dundee)	362
● Jimmy Greaves (1957–71, Chelsea, Tottenham, West Ham)	357
Steve Bloomer (1892–1914, Derby, Middlesbrough, Derby)	352

George Camsell (1923–39, Durham City, Middlesbrough) **348**
Dave Halliday (1920–35, St Mirren, Dundee, Sunderland, Arsenal,
Manchester City, Clapton Orient) **338**
John Aldridge (1979–98, Newport, Oxford Utd, Liverpool, Tranmere) **329**
Harry Bedford (1919–34, Nottm Forest, Blackpool, Derby, Newcastle,
Sunderland, Bradford PA, Chesterfield..326
John Atyeo (1951–66, Bristol City) **315**
Joe Smith (1908–29, Bolton, Stockport) **315**
Victor Watson (1920–36, West Ham, Southampton) **312**
Harry Johnson (1919–36, Sheffield Utd, Mansfield) **309**
Bob McPhail (1923–1939, Airdrie, Rangers) **306**

(***Rowley** scored 4 for WBA, 27 for Fulham, 251 for Leicester, 152 for Shrewsbury.
●**Greaves**'s 357 is record top-division total (he also scored 9 League goals for AC Milan).
Aldridge also scored 33 League goals for Real Sociedad. †**McGrory** scored 397 for Celtic, 13
for Clydebank.)

Most League goals for one club: 349 – Dixie Dean (Everton 1925–37); **326**–George Camsell
    (Middlesbrough 1925–39); **315** –John Atyeo (Bristol City 1951–66); **306** – Vic Watson
    (West Ham 1920–35); **291** – Steve Bloomer (Derby 1892–1906, 1910–14); **259** – Arthur
    Chandler (Leicester 1923–35); **255** – Nat Lofthouse (Bolton 1946–61); **251** – Arthur
    Rowley (Leicester 1950–58).
More than 500 Goals: Jimmy McGrory (Celtic, Clydebank and Scotland) scored a total of **550**
    goals in his first-class career (1922–38).
More than 1,000 goals: Brazil's **Pele** is reputedly the game's all-time highest scorer with **1,283**
    goals in 1,365 matches (1956–77), but many of them were scored in friendlies for his club,
    Santos. He scored his 1,000th goal, a penalty, against Vasco da Gama in the Maracana
    Stadium, Rio, on Nov 19, 1969. ● Pele (born Oct 23, 1940) played regularly for Santos from
    the age of 16. During his career, he was sent off only once. He played 95 'A' internationals
    for Brazil and in their World Cup-winning teams in 1958 and 1970. † Pele (Edson Arantes
    do Nascimento) was subsequently Brazil's Minister for Sport. He never played at Wembley,
    apart from being filmed there scoring a goal for a commercial. Aged 57, Pele received
    an 'honorary knighthood' (Knight Commander of the British Empire) from the Queen at
    Buckingham Palace on Dec 3, 1997.
Romario (retired Apr, 2008, aged 42) scored more than 1,000 goals for Vasco da Gama,
    Barcelona, PSV Eindhoven, Valencia and Brazil (56 in 73 internationals).

MOST LEAGUE GOALS IN SEASON: DEAN'S 60

WR ('Dixie') Dean, Everton centre-forward, created a League scoring record in 1927–28 with 60
    in 39 First Division matches. He also scored three in FA Cup ties, and 19 in representative
    games, totalling 82 for the season.
George Camsell, of Middlesbrough, previously held the record with 59 goals in 37 Second
    Division matches in 1926–27, his total for the season being 75.

SHEARER'S RECORD 'FIRST'

Alan Shearer (Blackburn) is the only player to score more than 30 top-division goals in 3
    successive seasons since the War: 31 in 1993–94, 34 in 1994–95, 31 in 1995–96.
Thierry Henry (Arsenal) is the first player to score more than 20 Premiership goals in five
    consecutive seasons (2002–06). **David Halliday** (Sunderland) topped 30 First Division
    goals in 4 consecutive seasons with totals of 38, 36, 36 and 49 from 1925–26 to 1928–29.

MOST GOALS IN A MATCH

Sep 12, 1885: John Petrie set the all-time British individual record for a first-class match
    when, in Arbroath's 36-0 win against Bon Accord (Scottish Cup 1), he scored **13**
Apr 13, 1936: Joe Payne set the still-existing individual record on his debut as a
    centre-forward, for Luton v Bristol Rov (Div 3 South). In a 12-0 win he scored **10**

ROWLEY'S ALL-TIME RECORD

Arthur Rowley is English football's top club scorer with a total of 464 goals for WBA, Fulham, Leicester and Shrewsbury (1947–65). There were 434 in the League, 26 FA Cup, 4 League Cup.

Jimmy Greaves is second with a total of 420 goals for Chelsea, AC Milan, Tottenham and West Ham, made up of 366 League, 35 FA Cup, 10 League Cup and 9 in Europe. He also scored nine goals for AC Milan.

John Aldridge retired as a player at the end of season 1997–98 with a career total of 329 League goals for Newport, Oxford Utd, Liverpool and Tranmere (1979–98). In all competitions for those clubs he scored 410 in 737 appearances. He also scored 45 in 63 games for Real Sociedad.

MOST GOALS IN INTERNATIONAL MATCHES

13 by **Archie Thompson** for Australia v American Samoa in World Cup (Oceania Group qualifier) at Coff's Harbour, New South Wales, Apr 11, 2001. Result: 31-0.

7 by **Stanley Harris** for England v France in Amateur International in Paris, Nov 1, 1906. Result: 15-0.

6 by **Nat Lofthouse** for Football League v Irish League, at Wolverhampton, Sep 24, 1952. Result: 7-1.

Joe Bambrick for Ireland against Wales, in Belfast, Feb 1, 1930. Result: 7-0.

WC Jordan in Amateur International for England v France, at Park Royal, Mar 23, 1908. Result: 12-0.

Vivian Woodward for England v Holland in Amateur International, at Chelsea, Dec 11,1909. Result: 9-1.

5 by **Howard Vaughton** for England v Ireland (Belfast) Feb 18, 1882. Result: 13-0.

Steve Bloomer for England v Wales (Cardiff) Mar 16, 1896. Result: 9-1.

Hughie Gallacher for Scotland against Ireland (Belfast), Feb 23, 1929. Result: 7-3.

Willie Hall for England v Northern Ireland, at Old Trafford, Nov 16, 1938. Five in succession (first three in 3·5 mins – fastest international hat-trick). Result: 7-0.

Malcolm Macdonald for England v Cyprus (Wembley) Apr 16, 1975. Result: 5-0.

Hughie Gallacher for Scottish League against Irish League (Belfast) Nov 11, 1925. Result: 7-3.

Barney Battles for Scottish League against Irish League (Firhill Park, Glasgow) Oct 31, 1928. Result: 8-2.

Bobby Flavell for Scottish League against Irish League (Belfast) Apr 30, 1947. Result: 7-4.

Joe Bradford for Football League v Irish League (Everton) Sep 25, 1929. Result: 7-2.

Albert Stubbins for Football League v Irish League (Blackpool) Oct 18, 1950. Result: 6-3.

Brian Clough for Football League v Irish League (Belfast) Sep 23, 1959. Result: 5-0.

LAST ENGLAND PLAYER TO SCORE ...

3 goals: Jermain Defoe v Bulgaria (4-0), Euro Champ qual, Wembley, Sep 3, 2010

4 goals: Ian Wright v San Marino (7-1), World Cup qual, Bologna, Nov 17, 1993.

5 goals: Malcolm Macdonald v Cyprus (5-0), Euro Champ qual, Wembley, Apr 16, 1975.

INTERNATIONAL TOP SHOTS

		Goals	Games
England	Bobby Charlton (1958–70)	49	106
N Ireland	David Healy (2000–12)	35	92
Scotland	Denis Law (1958–74)	30	55
	Kenny Dalglish (1971–86)	30	102
Wales	Ian Rush (1980–96)	28	73
Rep of Ire	Robbie Keane (1998–2012)	53	119

ENGLAND'S TOP MARKSMEN
(As at start of season 2012–13)

	Goals	Games
Bobby Charlton (1958–70)	49	106
Gary Lineker (1984–92)	48	80
Jimmy Greaves (1959–67)	44	57
Michael Owen (1998–2008)	40	89
Tom Finney (1946–58)	30	76
Nat Lofthouse (1950–58)	30	33
Alan Shearer (1992–2000)	30	63
Vivian Woodward (1903–11)	29	23
Steve Bloomer (1895–1907)	28	23
Wayne Rooney (2003–12)	29	76
David Platt (1989–96)	27	62
Bryan Robson (1979–91)	26	90
Geoff Hurst (1966–72)	24	49
Stan Mortensen (1947–53)	23	25
Frank Lampard (2003–12)	23	90
Tommy Lawton (1938–48)	22	23
Peter Crouch (2005–11)	22	42
Mike Channon (1972–77)	21	46
Kevin Keegan (1972–82)	21	63

CONSECUTIVE GOALS FOR ENGLAND

Steve Bloomer scored in **TEN** consecutive appearances (19 goals) for **England** between Mar 1895 and Mar 1899.

Jimmy Greaves scored 11 goals in five consecutive England matches from the start of season 1960–61.

Paul Mariner scored in five consecutive England appearances (7 goals) between Nov 1981 and Jun 1982.

ENGLAND'S TOP FINAL SERIES MARKSMAN

Gary Lineker with 6 goals at 1986 World Cup in Mexico.

ENGLAND TOP SCORERS IN COMPETITIVE INTERNATIONALS

Michael Owen 26 goals in 53 matches; **Gary Lineker** 22 in 39; **Alan Shearer** 20 in 31.

MOST ENGLAND GOALS IN SEASON

13 – **Jimmy Greaves** (1960–61 in 9 matches); 12 – **Dixie Dean** (1926–27 in 6 matches); 10 – **Gary Lineker** (1990–91 in 10 matches); 10 – **Wayne Rooney** – (2008–09 in 9 matches).

MOST ENGLAND HAT-TRICKS

Jimmy Greaves 6; **Gary Lineker** 5, **Bobby Charlton** 4, **Vivian Woodward** 4, **Stan Mortensen** 3.

MOST GOALS FOR ENGLAND U-21s

13 – Alan Shearer (11 apps) Francis Jeffers (13 apps)

GOLDEN GOAL DECIDERS

The Football League, in an experiment to avoid penalty shoot-outs, introduced a new golden goal system in the 1994–95 **Auto Windscreens Shield** to decide matches in the knock-out stages of the competition in which scores were level after 90 minutes. The first goal scored in overtime ended play.

Iain Dunn (Huddersfield) became the first player in British football to settle a match by this sudden-death method. His 107th-minute goal beat Lincoln 3-2 on Nov 30, 1994, and to mark his 'moment in history' he was presented with a golden football trophy.

The AWS Final of 1995 was decided when Paul Tait headed the only goal for Birmingham against Carlisle 13 minutes into overtime – the first time a match at Wembley had been decided by the 'golden goal' formula.

First major international tournament match to be decided by sudden death was the Final of the **1996 European Championship** at Wembley in which Germany beat Czech Rep 2-1 by **Oliver Bierhoff**'s goal in the 95th minute.

In the **1998 World Cup Finals** (2nd round), host country France beat Paraguay 1-0 with **Laurent Blanc**'s goal (114).

France won the **2000 European Championship** with golden goals in the semi-final, 2-1 v Portugal (Zinedine Zidane pen, 117), and in the Final, 2-1 v Italy (David Trezeguet, 103).

Galatasaray (Turkey) won the **European Super Cup** 2-1 against Real Madrid (Monaco, Aug 25, 2000) with a 103rd minute golden goal, a penalty.

Liverpool won the **UEFACup** 5-4 against Alaves with a 117th min golden goal, an own goal, in the Final in Dortmund (May 19, 2001).

In the **2002 World Cup Finals**, 3 matches were decided by Golden Goals: in the 2nd round Senegal beat Sweden 2-1 (Henri Camara, 104) and South Korea beat Italy 2-1 (Ahn Jung – hwan, 117); in the quarter-final, Turkey beat Senegal 1-0 (Ilhan Mansiz, 94).

France won the 2003 **FIFA Confederations Cup** Final against Cameroon (Paris, Jun 29) with a 97th-minute golden goal by Thierry Henry.

Doncaster won promotion to Football League with a 110th-minute golden goal winner (3-2) in the Conference Play-off Final against Dagenham at Stoke (May 10, 2003).

Germany won the **Women's World Cup Final** 2-1 v Sweden (Los Angeles, Oct 12, 2003) with a 98th-minute golden goal.

GOLD TURNS TO SILVER

Starting with the 2003 Finals of the UEFA Cup and Champions League/European Cup, UEFA introduced a new rule by which a silver goal could decide the winners if the scores were level after 90 minutes.

Team leading after 15 minutes' extra time win match. If sides level, a second period of 15 minutes to be played. If still no winner, result to be decided by penalty shoot-out.

UEFA said the change was made because the golden goal put too much pressure on referees and prompted teams to play negative football.

Although both 2003 European Finals went to extra-time, neither was decided by a silver goal. The new rule applied in the 2004 European Championship Finals, and Greece won their semi-final against the Czech Republic in the 105th minute.

The **International Board** decided (Feb 28 2004) that the golden/silver goal rule was 'unfair' and that from July 1 competitive international matches level after extra-time would, when necessary, be settled on penalties.

PREMIER LEAGUE TOP SHOTS (1992–2012)

Alan Shearer	260	Nicolas Anelka	123
Andy Cole	187	Dwight Yorke	123
Thierry Henry	175	Ian Wright	113
Robbie Fowler	163	Jermain Defoe	112
Frank Lampard	150	Dion Dublin	111
Les Ferdinand	149	Emile Heskey	111
Michael Owen	149	Ryan Giggs	107
Teddy Sheringham	147	Paul Scholes	106
Wayne Rooney	144	Matthew Le Tissier	102
Jimmy Floyd Hasselbaink	127	Darren Bent	100
Robbie Keane	126	Didier Drogba	100

LEAGUE GOAL RECORDS

The highest goal-scoring aggregates in the Football League, Premier and Scottish League are as follows:

For

	Goals	Games	Club	Season
Prem	103	38	Chelsea	2009–10
Div 1	128	42	Aston Villa	1930–31
New Div 1	108	46	Manchester City	2001–02
New Champ	99	46	Reading	2005–06
Div 2	122	42	Middlesbrough	1926–27
New Div 2	89	46	Millwall	2000–01
New Lge 1	106	46	Peterborough	2010–11
Div 3(S)	127	42	Millwall	1927–28
Div 3(N)	128	42	Bradford City	1928–29
Div 3	111	46	QPR	1961–62
New Div 3	96	46	Luton	2001–02
New Lge 2	96	46	Notts Co	2009–10
Div 4	134	46	Peterborough	1960–61
Scot Prem	105	38	Celtic	2003–04
Scot L 1	132	34	Hearts	1957–58
Scot L 2	142	34	Raith Rov	1937–38
Scot L 3 (Modern)	130	36	Gretna	2004–05

Against

	Goals	Games	Club	Season
Prem	100	42	Swindon	1993–94
Div 1	125	42	Blackpool	1930–31
New Div 1	102	46	Stockport	2001–02
New Champ	86	46	Crewe	2004–05
Div 2	141	34	Darwen	1898–99
New Div 2	102	46	Chester	1992–93
New Lge 1	98	46	Stockport	2004–05
Div 3(S)	135	42	Merthyr T	1929–30
Div 3(N)	136	42	Nelson	1927–28
Div 3	123	46	Accrington Stanley	1959–60
New Div 3	113	46	Doncaster	1997–98
New Lge 2	96	46	Stockport	2010–11
Div 4	109	46	Hartlepool Utd	1959–60
Scot Prem	100	36	Morton	1984–85
Scot Prem	100	44	Morton	1987–88
Scot L 1	137	38	Leith A	1931–32
Scot L 2	146	38	Edinburgh City	1931–32
Scot L 3 (Modern)	118	36	East Stirling	2003–04

BEST DEFENSIVE RECORDS

*Denotes under old offside law

Div	Goals Agst	Games	Club	Season
Prem	15	38	Chelsea	2004–05
1	16	42	Liverpool	1978–79
1	*15	22	Preston	1888–89
New Div 1	28	46	Sunderland	1998–99
New Champ	30	46	Preston	2005–06
2	18	28	Liverpool	1893–94

2	*22	34	Sheffield Wed	1899–1900	
2	24	42	Birmingham	1947–48	
2	24	42	Crystal Palace	1978–79	
New Div 2	25	46	Wigan	2002–03	
New Lge 1	32	46	Nottm Forest	2007–08	
3(S)	*21	42	Southampton	1921–22	
3(S)	30	42	Cardiff	1946–47	
3(N)	*21	38	Stockport	1921–22	
3(N)	21	46	Port Vale	1953–54	
3	30	46	Middlesbrough	1986–87	
New Div 3	20	46	Gillingham	1995–96	
New Lge 2	31	46	Notts Co	2009–10	
4	25	46	Lincoln	1980–81	

SCOTTISH LEAGUE

Div	Goals Agst	Games	Club	Season	
Prem	18	38	Celtic	2001–02	
1	*12	22	Dundee	1902–03	
1	*14	38	Celtic	1913–14	
2	20	38	Morton	1966–67	
2	*29	38	Clydebank	1922–23	
2	29	36	East Fife	1995–96	
New Div 3	21	36	Brechin	1995–96	

TOP SCORERS (LEAGUE ONLY)

		Goals	Div
2011–12	Jordan Rhodes (Huddersfield)	36	Lge 1
2010–11	Clayton Donaldson (Crewe)	28	Lge 2
2009–10	Rickie Lambert (Southampton)	31	Lge 1
2008– 09	Simon Cox (Swindon)		
	Rickie Lambert (Bristol Rov)	29	Lge 1
2007–08	Cristiano Ronaldo (Manchester Utd)	31	Prem
2006–07	Billy Sharp (Scunthorpe)	30	Lge 1
2005–06	Thierry Henry (Arsenal)	27	Prem
2004–05	Stuart Elliott (Hull)	27	1
	Phil Jevons (Yeovil)	27	2
	Dean Windass (Bradford City)	27	1
2003–04	Thierry Henry (Arsenal)	30	Prem
2002–03	Andy Morrell (Wrexham)	34	3
2001–02	Shaun Goater (Manchester City)	28	1
	Bobby Zamora (Brighton)	28	2
2000–01	Bobby Zamora (Brighton)	28	3
1999–00	Kevin Phillips (Sunderland)	30	Prem
1998–99	Lee Hughes (WBA)	31	1
1997–98	Pierre van Hooijdonk (Nottm Forest)	29	1
	Kevin Phillips (Sunderland)	29	1
1996–97	Graeme Jones (Wigan)	31	3
1995–96	Alan Shearer (Blackburn)	31	Prem
1994–95	Alan Shearer (Blackburn)	34	Prem
1993–94	Jimmy Quinn (Reading)	35	2
1992–93	Guy Whittingham (Portsmouth)	42	1
1991–92	Ian Wright (Crystal Palace 5, Arsenal 24)	29	1
1990–91	Teddy Sheringham (Millwall)	33	2
1989–90	Mick Quinn (Newcastle)	32	2

1988–89	Steve Bull (Wolves)	37	3
1987–88	Steve Bull (Wolves)	34	4
1986–87	Clive Allen (Tottenham)	33	1
1985–86	Gary Lineker (Everton)	30	1
1984–85	Tommy Tynan (Plymouth Argyle)	31	3
	John Clayton (Tranmere)	31	4
1983–84	Trevor Senior (Reading)	36	4
1982–83	Luther Blissett (Watford)	27	1
1981–82	Keith Edwards (Hull 1, Sheffield Utd 35)	36	4
1980–81	Tony Kellow (Exeter)	25	3
1979–80	Clive Allen (Queens Park Rangers)	28	2
1978–79	Ross Jenkins (Watford)	29	3
1977–78	Steve Phillips (Brentford)	32	4
	Alan Curtis (Swansea City)	32	4
1976–77	Peter Ward (Brighton)	32	3
1975–76	Dixie McNeil (Hereford)	35	3
1974–75	Dixie McNeil (Hereford)	31	3
1973–74	Brian Yeo (Gillingham)	31	4
1972–73	Bryan (Pop) Robson (West Ham)	28	1
1971–72	Ted MacDougall (Bournemouth)	35	3
1970–71	Ted MacDougall (Bournemouth)	42	4
1969–70	Albert Kinsey (Wrexham)	27	4
1968–69	Jimmy Greaves (Tottenham)	27	1
1967–68	George Best (Manchester Utd)	28	1
	Ron Davies (Southampton)	28	1
1966–67	Ron Davies (Southampton)	37	1
1965–66	Kevin Hector (Bradford PA)	44	4
1964–65	Alick Jeffrey (Doncaster)	36	4
1963–64	Hugh McIlmoyle (Carlisle)	39	4
1962–63	Jimmy Greaves (Tottenham)	37	1
1961–62	Roger Hunt (Liverpool)	41	2
1960–61	Terry Bly (Peterborough)	52	4

100 LEAGUE GOALS IN SEASON

Manchester City, First Div Champions in 2001–02, scored 108 goals.

Bolton, First Div Champions in 1996–97, reached 100 goals, the first side to complete a century in League football since 103 by **Northampton** (Div 4 Champions) in 1986–87.

Last League Champions to reach 100 League goals: Chelsea (103 in 2009–10). Last century of goals in the top division: 111 by runners-up **Tottenham** in 1962–63.

Only club to score a century of Premier League goals in season: **Chelsea** (103 in 2009–10, including home scores of 7, 7, 8)

Wolves topped 100 goals in four successive First Division seasons (1957–58, 1958–59, 1959–60, 1960–61).

In **1930–31**, the top three all scored a century of League goals: 1 Arsenal (127), 2 Aston Villa (128), 3 Sheffield Wed (102).

Latest team to score a century of League goals: Peterborough with 106 in 2010–11 (Lge 1).

100 GOALS AGAINST

Swindon, relegated with 100 goals against in 1993–94, were the first top-division club to concede a century of League goals since **Ipswich** (121) went down in 1964. Most goals conceded in the top division: 125 by **Blackpool** in 1930–31, but they avoided relegation.

MOST LEAGUE GOALS ON ONE DAY

A record of 209 goals in the four divisions of the Football League (43 matches) was set on **Jan**

2, 1932: 56 in Div 1, 53 in Div 2, 57 in Div 3 South and 43 in Div 3 North.
There were two 10-goal aggregates: Bradford City 9, Barnsley 1 in Div 2 and Coventry City 5, Fulham 5 in Div 3 South.
That total of 209 League goals on one day was equalled on **Feb 1, 1936** (44 matches): 46 in Div 1, 46 in Div 2, 49 in Div 3 South and 69 in Div 3 North. Two matches in the Northern Section produced 23 of the goals: Chester 12, York 0 and Crewe 5, Chesterfield 6.

MOST GOALS IN TOP DIV ON ONE DAY

This record has stood since **Dec 26, 1963**, when 66 goals were scored in the ten First Division matches played.

MOST PREMIER LEAGUE GOALS ON ONE DAY

47, in nine matches on **May 8, 1993** (last day of season). For the first time, all 20 clubs scored in the Premier League programme over the weekend of Nov 27-28, 2010

FEWEST PREMIER LEAGUE GOALS IN ONE WEEK-END

10, in 10 matches on **Nov 24/25, 2001**

FEWEST FIRST DIV GOALS ON ONE DAY

For full/near full programme: **Ten goals**, all by home clubs, in ten matches on Apr 28, 1923 (day of Wembley's first FA Cup Final).

SCORERS IN CONSECUTIVE TOP-DIVISION MATCHES

Stan Mortensen scored in 11 consecutive Division One games for Blackpool in season 1950–51. **Ruud van Nistelrooy** (Manchester Utd) scored 13 goals in last 8 games of season 2002–03 and in first 2 of 2003–04. Since the last war, 3 other players scored in 10 successive matches in the old First Division: **Billy McAdams** (Man City, 1957–58), **Ron Davies** (Southampton, 1966–67) and **John Aldridge** (Liverpool, May–Oct 1987).

SCORERS FOR 6 PREMIER LEAGUE CLUBS

Les Ferdinand (QPR, Newcastle, Tottenham, West Ham, Leicester, Bolton); **Andy Cole** (Newcastle, Manchester Utd, Blackburn, Fulham, Manchester City, Portsmouth); **Marcus Bent** (Crystal Palace, Ipswich, Leicester, Everton, Charlton, Wigan); **Nick Barmby** (Tottenham, Middlesbrough, Everton, Liverpool, Leeds, Hull); **Craig Bellamy** (Coventry, Newcastle, Blackburn, Liverpool, West Ham, Manchester City); **Peter Crouch** (Tottenham, Aston Villa, Southampton, Liverpool, Portsmouth, Stoke); **Robbie Keane** (Coventry, Leeds, Tottenham, Liverpool, West Ham, Aston Villa)

SCORERS FOR 5 PREMIER LEAGUE CLUBS

Stan Collymore (Nottm Forest, Liverpool, Aston Villa, Leicester, Bradford); **Mark Hughes** (Manchester Utd, Chelsea, Southampton, Everton, Blackburn); **Benito Carbone** (Sheffield Wed, Aston Villa, Bradford, Derby, Middlesbrough); **Ashley Ward** (Norwich, Derby, Barnsley, Blackburn Bradford); **Teddy Sheringham** (Nottm Forest, Tottenham, Manchester Utd, Portsmouth, West Ham); **Chris Sutton** (Norwich, Blackburn, Chelsea, Birmingham, Aston Villa); **Nicolas Anelka** (Arsenal, Liverpool, Manchester City, Bolton, Chelsea).

SCORERS IN MOST CONSECUTIVE LEAGUE MATCHES

Arsenal broke the record by scoring in 55 successive Premiership fixtures: the last match in season 2000–01, then all 38 games in winning the title in 2001–02, and the first 16 in season 2002–03. The sequence ended with a 2–0 defeat away to Manchester Utd on December 7, 2002.
Chesterfield previously held the record, having scored in 46 consecutive matches in Div 3 (North), starting on Christmas Day, 1929 and ending on December 27, 1930.

SIX-OUT-OF-SIX HEADERS

When **Oxford Utd** beat Shrewsbury 6-0 (Div 2) on Apr 23, 1996, all six goals were headers.

ALL–ROUND MARKSMEN

Alan Cork scored in four divisions of the Football League and in the Premier League in his 18-season career with Wimbledon, Sheffield Utd and Fulham (1977–95).

Brett Ormerod scored in all four divisions (2, 1, Champ and Prem Lge) for Blackpool in two spells (1997–2002, 2008–11). **Grant Holt** (Sheffield Wed, Rochdale, Nottm Forest, Shrewsbury, Norwich) has scored in all four divisions (2003–12).

MOST CUP GOALS

FA Cup – most goals in one season: 20 by **Jimmy Ross** (Preston, runners-up 1887–88); 15 by **Alex (Sandy) Brown** (Tottenham, winners 1900–01).

Most FA Cup goals in individual careers: 49 by **Harry Cursham** (Notts Co 1877–89); this century: **44** by **Ian Rush** (39 for Liverpool, 4 for Chester, 1 for Newcastle 1979–98). **Denis Law** was the previous highest FA Cup scorer in the 20th century with 41 goals for Huddersfield Town, Manchester City and Manchester Utd (1957–74).

Most FA Cup Final goals by individual: 5 by **Ian Rush** for Liverpool (2 in 1986, 2 in 1989, 1 in 1992).

HOTTEST CUP HOT-SHOT

Geoff Hurst scored 21 cup goals in season 1965–66: 11 League Cup, 4 FA Cup and 2 Cup-Winners' Cup for West Ham, and 4 in the World Cup for England.

SCORERS IN EVERY ROUND

Twelve players have scored in every round of the FA Cup in one season, from opening to Final inclusive: **Archie Hunter** (Aston Villa, winners 1887); **Sandy Brown** (Tottenham, winners 1901); **Harry Hampton** (Aston Villa, winners 1905); **Harold Blackmore** (Bolton, winners 1929); **Ellis Rimmer** (Sheffield Wed, winners 1935); **Frank O'Donnell** (Preston, beaten 1937); **Stan Mortensen** (Blackpool, beaten 1948); **Jackie Milburn** (Newcastle, winners 1951); **Nat Lofthouse** (Bolton, beaten 1953); **Charlie Wayman** (Preston, beaten 1954); **Jeff Astle** (WBA, winners 1968); **Peter Osgood** (Chelsea, winners 1970).

Blackmore and the next seven completed their 'set' in the Final at Wembley; Osgood did so in the Final replay at Old Trafford.

Only player to score in every **Football League Cup** round possible in one season: **Tony Brown** for WBA, winners 1965–66, with 9 goals in 10 games (after bye in Round 1).

TEN IN A ROW

Dixie McNeill scored for Wrexham in ten successive FA Cup rounds (18 goals): 11 in Rounds 1-6, 1977–78; 3 in Rounds 3-4, 1978–79; 4 in Rounds 3-4, 1979–80.

Stan Mortensen (Blackpool) scored 25 goals in 16 FA Cup rounds out of 17 (1946–51).

TOP MATCH HAULS IN FA CUP

Ted MacDougall scored nine goals, a record for the competition proper, in the FA Cup first round on Nov 20, 1971, when Bournemouth beat Margate 11-0. On Nov 23, 1970 he had scored six in an 8-1 first round replay against Oxford City.

Other six-goal FA Cup scorers include **George Hilsdon** (Chelsea v Worksop, 9-1, 1907– 08), **Ronnie Rooke** (Fulham v Bury, 6-0, 1938–39), **Harold Atkinson** (Tranmere v Ashington, 8-1, 1952–53), **George Best** (Manchester Utd v Northampton 1969–70, 8-2 away), **Duane Darby** (Hull v Whitby, 8-4, 1996–97).

Denis Law scored all six for Manchester City at Luton (6-2) in an FA Cup 4th round tie on Jan 28, 1961, but none of them counted – the match was abandoned (69 mins) because of a waterlogged pitch. He also scored City's goal when the match was played again, but they lost 3-1.

Tony Philliskirk scored **five** when Peterborough beat Kingstonian 9-1 in an FA Cup 1st round replay on Nov 25, 1992, but had them wiped from the records.

With the score at 3-0, the Kingstonian goalkeeper was concussed by a coin thrown from the crowd and unable to play on. The FA ordered the match to be replayed at Peterborough behind closed doors, and Kingstonian lost 1-0.

I Two players have scored **ten goals** in FA Cup preliminary round matches: **Chris Marron** for South Shields against Radcliffe in Sep 1947; **Paul Jackson** when Sheffield-based club Stocksbridge Park Steels beat Oldham Town 17-1 on Aug 31, 2002. He scored 5 in each half and all ten with his feet – goal times 6, 10, 22, 30, 34, 68, 73, 75, 79, 84 mins

QUICKEST GOALS AND RAPID SCORING

A goal in **4 sec** was claimed by **Jim Fryatt**, for Bradford PA v Tranmere (Div 4, Apr 25, 1965), and by **Gerry Allen** for Whitstable v Danson (Kent League, Mar 3,1989). **Damian Mori** scored in **4 sec** for Adelaide v Sydney (Australian National League, December 6, 1995).

Goals after **6 sec** – **Albert Mundy** for Aldershot v Hartlepool, Oct 25, 1958; **Barrie Jones** for Notts Co v Torquay, Mar 31, 1962; **Keith Smith** for Crystal Palace v Derby, Dec 12, 1964.

9.6 sec by **John Hewitt** for Aberdeen at Motherwell, 3rd round, Jan 23, 1982 (fastest goal in Scottish Cup history).

Colin Cowperthwaite reputedly scored in **3.5 sec** for Barrow v Kettering (Alliance Premier League) on Dec 8, 1979, but the timing was unofficial.

Phil Starbuck for Huddersfield **3 sec** after entering the field as 54th min substitute at home to Wigan (Div 2) on Easter Monday, Apr 12, 1993. Corner was delayed, awaiting his arrival and he scored with a header.

Malcolm Macdonald after **5 sec** (officially timed) in Newcastle's 7-3 win in a pre-season friendly at St Johnstone on Jul 29, 1972.

World's fastest goal: 2.8 sec, direct from kick-off, Argentinian **Ricardo Olivera** for Rio Negro v Soriano (Uruguayan League), December 26, 1998.

Fastest international goal: 8.3 sec, Davide Gualtieri for San Marino v England (World Cup qual, Bologna, Nov 17, 1993).

Fastest England goals: 17 sec, Tommy Lawton v Portugal in Lisbon, May 25, 1947. **27 sec, Bryan Robson** v France in World Cup qual at Bilbao, Spain on Jun 16, 1982; **37 sec, Gareth Southgate** v South Africa in Durban, May 22, 2003; **30 sec, Jack Cock** v Ireland, Belfast, Oct 25, 1919; **30 sec, Bill Nicholson** v Portugal at Goodison Park, May 19, 1951. **38 sec, Bryan Robson** v Yugoslavia at Wembley, Dec 13, 1989; **42 sec, Gary Lineker** v Malaysia in Kuala Lumpur, Jun 12, 1991.

Fastest international goal by substitute: 5 sec, John Jensen for Denmark v Belgium (Euro Champ), Oct 12, 1994.

Fastest by England substitute: 10 sec, Teddy Sheringham v Greece (World Cup qualifier) at Old Trafford, Oct 6, 2001.

Fastest FA Cup goal: 4 sec, Gareth Morris (Ashton Utd) v Skelmersdale, 1st qual round, Sept 15, 2001.

Fastest FA Cup goal (comp proper): 9.7 sec, Jimmy Kebe for Reading v WBA, 5th Round, Feb 13, 2010.

Fastest FA Cup Final goal: 25 sec, Louis Saha for Everton v Chelsea at Wembley, May 30, 2009.

Fastest goal by substitute in FA Cup Final: 96 sec, Teddy Sheringham for Manchester Utd v Newcastle at Wembley, May 22, 1999.

Fastest League Cup Final goal: 45 sec, John Arne Riise for Liverpool v Chelsea, 2005.

Fastest goal on full League debut: 7.7 sec, Freddy Eastwood for Southend v Swansea (Lge 2), Oct 16, 2004. He went on to score hat-trick in 4-2 win.

Fastest goal in cup final: 4.07 sec, 14-year-old Owen Price for Ernest Bevin College, Tooting, beaten 3-1 by Barking Abbey in Heinz Ketchup Cup Final at Arsenal on May 18, 2000. Owen, on Tottenham's books, scored from inside his own half when the ball was played back to him from kick-off.

Fastest Premier League goals: 10 sec, Ledley King for Tottenham away to Bradford, Dec 9, 2000; **10.4 sec, Alan Shearer** for Newcastle v Manchester City, Jan 18, 2003: **11 sec, Mark Viduka** for Leeds v Charlton, Mar 17, 2001; **12.5 sec. James Beattie** for Southampton at Chelsea, Aug 28, 2004; **13 sec, Chris Sutton** for Blackburn at Everton, Apr 1, 1995; **13 sec, Dwight Yorke** for Aston Villa at Coventry, Sep 30, 1995.

Fastest top-division goal: 7 sec, Bobby Langton for Preston v Manchester City (Div 1), Aug 25, 1948.

Fastest goal in Champions League: 10 sec, Roy Makaay for Bayern Munich v Real Madrid (1st ko rd), Mar 7, 2007.

Fastest Premier League goal by substitute: 9 sec, Shaun Goater, Manchester City's equaliser away to Manchester Utd (1-1), Feb 9, 2003.

Fastest goal in women's football: 7 sec, Angie Harriott for Launton v Thame (Southern League, Prem Div), season 1998–99.

Fastest hat-trick in League history: 2 min 20 sec, Bournemouth's 84th-minute substitute **James Hayter** in 6-0 home win v Wrexham (Div 2) on Feb 24, 2004 (goal times 86, 87, 88 mins).

Fastest First Division hat-tricks since war: Graham Leggat, 3 goals in 3 minutes (first half) when Fulham beat Ipswich 10-1 on Boxing Day, 1963; **Nigel Clough**, 3 goals in 4 minutes (81, 82, 85 pen) when Nottm Forest beat QPR 4-0 on Dec 13, 1987.

Premier League – fastest hat-trick: 4 min30 sec (26, 29, 31) by **Robbie Fowler** in Liverpool 3, Arsenal 0 on Aug 28, 1994.

Fastest international hat-trick: 3 min 15 sec, Masashi Nakayami for Japan in 9-0 win v Brunei in Macao (Asian Cup), Feb 16, 2000.

Fastest international hat-trick in British matches: 3.5 min, Willie Hall for England v N Ireland at Old Trafford, Manchester, Nov 16, 1938. (Hall scored 5 in 7-0 win); **4.5 min, Arif Erdem** for Turkey v N Ireland, European Championship, at Windsor Park, Belfast, on Sep 4, 1999.

Fastest FA Cup hat-trick: In 3 min, Billy Best for Southend v Brentford (2nd round, Dec 7, 1968); **2 min 20 sec, Andy Locke** for Nantwich v Droylsden (1st Qual round, Sep 9, 1995).

Fastest Scottish hat-trick: 2 min 30 sec, Ian St John for Motherwell away to Hibernian (Scottish League Cup), Aug 15, 1959.

Fastest hat-trick of headers: Dixie Dean's 5 goals in Everton's 7-2 win at home to Chelsea (Div 1) on Nov 14, 1931 included 3 headers between 5th and 15th-min.

Fastest all-time hat-trick: Reported at 1 min 50 sec, Eduardo Maglioni for Independiente against Gimnasia de la Plata in Argentina Div , Mar 18, 1973.

Scored first kick: Billy Foulkes (Newcastle) for Wales v England at Cardiff, Oct 20, 1951, in his first international match.

Preston scored six goals in **7 min** in record 26-0 FA Cup 1st round win v Hyde, Oct 15, 1887.

Notts Co scored six second-half goals in **12 min** (Tommy Lawton 3, Jackie Sewell 3) when beating Exeter 9-0 (Div 3 South) at Meadow Lane on Oct 16, 1948.

Arsenal scored six in **18 min** (71-89 mins) in 7-1 home win (Div 1) v Sheffield Wed, Feb 15, 1992.

Tranmere scored sixin first **19 min** when beating Oldham 13-4 (Div 3 North), December 26, 1935.

Sunderland scored eight in **28 min** at Newcastle (9-1 Div 1), December 5, 1908. Newcastle went on to win the title.

Southend scored all seven goals in **29 min** in 7-0 win at home to Torquay (Leyland Daf Cup, Southern quarter-final), Feb 26, 1991. Score was 0-0 until 55th minute.

Plymouth Argyle scored five in first **18 min** in 7-0 home win v Chesterfield (Div 2), Jan 3, 2004.

Five in 20 min: Frank Keetley in Lincoln's 9-1 win over Halifax in Div 3 (North), Jan 16, 1932; **Brian Dear** for West Ham v WBA (6-1, Div 1) Apr 16, 1965. **Kevin Hector** for Bradford PA v Barnsley (7-2, Div 4), Nov 20, 1965.

Four in 5 min: John McIntyre for Blackburn v Everton (Div 1), Sep 16, 1922; **WG (Billy) Richardson** for WBA v West Ham (Div 1), Nov 7, 1931.

Three in 2'5 min: Jimmy Scarth for Gillingham v Leyton Orient (Div 3S), Nov 1, 1952.

Three in three minutes: Billy Lane for Watford v Clapton Orient (Div 3S), December 20, 1933;

Johnny Hartburn for Leyton Orient v Shrewsbury (Div 3S), Jan 22, 1955; **Gary Roberts** for Brentford v Newport, (Freight Rover Trophy, South Final), May 17, 1985; **Gary Shaw** for Shrewsbury v Bradford City (Div 3), December 22, 1990.

Two in 9 sec: Jamie Bates with last kick of first half, **Jermaine McSporran** 9 sec into second half when Wycombe beat Peterborough 2-0 at home (Div 2) on Sep 23, 2000.

Premier League – fastest scoring: Four goals in 4 min 44 sec, Tottenham home to Southampton on Sunday, Feb 7, 1993.

Premiership – fast scoring away: When **Aston Villa** won 5-0 at Leicester (Jan 31, 2004), all goals scored in **18 second-half min** (50-68).

Four in 13 min by Premier League sub: Ole Gunnar Solskjaer for Manchester Utd away to Nottm Forest, Feb 6, 1999.

FASTEST GOALS IN WORLD CUP FINAL SERIES

10.8 sec, Hakan Sukur for Turkey against South Korea in 3rd/4th-place match at Taegu, Jun 29, 2002; **15 sec, Vaclav Masek** for Czechoslovakia v Mexico (in Vina, Chile, 1962); **27 sec, Bryan Robson** for England v France (in Bilbao, Spain, 1982).

TOP MATCH SCORES SINCE WAR

By English clubs: 13-0 by Newcastle v Newport (Div 2, Oct 1946); 13-2 by Tottenham v Crewe (FA Cup 4th. Rd. replay, Feb 1960); 13-0 by Chelsea v Jeunesse Hautcharage, Lux. (Cup-Winners' Cup 1st round, 2nd leg, Sep 1971).

By Scottish club: 20-0 by Stirling v Selkirk (E. of Scotland League) in Scottish Cup 1st round. (Dec 1984). That is the highest score in British first-class football since Preston beat Hyde 26-0 in FA Cup, Oct 1887.

GOALS BY GOALKEEPERS

(Long clearances unless stated)

Pat Jennings for Tottenham v Manchester Utd (goalkeeper Alex Stepney), Aug 12, 1967 (FA Charity Shield).

Peter Shilton for Leicester v Southampton (Campbell Forsyth), Oct 14, 1967 (Div 1).

Ray Cashley for Bristol City v Hull (Jeff Wealands), Sep 18, 1973 (Div 2).

Steve Sherwood for Watford v Coventry (Raddy Avramovic), Jan 14, 1984 (Div 1).

Steve Ogrizovic for Coventry v Sheffield Wed (Martin Hodge), Oct 25, 1986 (Div 1).

Andy Goram for Hibernian v Morton (David Wylie), May 7, 1988 (Scot Prem Div).

Andy McLean, on Irish League debut, for Cliftonville v Linfield (George Dunlop), Aug 20, 1988.

Alan Paterson for Glentoran v Linfield (George Dunlop), Nov 30, 1988 (Irish League Cup Final – only instance of goalkeeper scoring winner in a senior cup final in UK).

Ray Charles for East Fife v Stranraer (Bernard Duffy), Feb 28, 1990 (Scot Div 2).

Iain Hesford for Maidstone v Hereford (Tony Elliott), Nov 2, 1991 (Div 4).

Chris Mackenzie for Hereford v Barnet (Mark Taylor), Aug 12, 1995 (Div 3).

Peter Schmeichel for Manchester Utd v Rotor Volgograd, Sep 26, 1995 (header, UEFA Cup 1).

Mark Bosnich (Aston Villa) for Australia v Solomon Islands, Jun 11, 1997 (penalty in World Cup qual – 13-0)).

Peter Keen for Carlisle away to Blackpool (goalkeeper John Kennedy), Oct 24, 2000 (Div 3).

Steve Mildenhall for Notts Co v Mansfield (Kevin Pilkington), Aug 21, 2001 (free-kick inside own half, League Cup 1).

Peter Schmeichel for Aston Villa v Everton (Paul Gerrard), Oct 20, 2001 (volley, first goalkeeper to score in Premiership)

Mart Poom for Sunderland v Derby (Andy Oakes), Sep 20, 2003 (header, Div 1).

Brad Friedel for Blackburn v Charlton (Dean Kiely), Feb 21, 2004 (shot, Prem).

Paul Robinson for Leeds v Swindon (Rhys Evans), Sep 24, 2003 (header, League Cup 2).

Andy Lonergan for Preston v Leicester (Kevin Pressman), Oct 2, 2004 (Champ).

Gavin Ward for Tranmere v Leyton Orient (Glenn Morris), Sept 2, 2006 (free-kick Lge 1).

Mark Crossley for Sheffield Wed v Southampton (Kelvin Davis), Dec 23, 2006 (header, Champ

Paul Robinson for Tottenham v Watford (Ben Foster), Mar 17, 2007 (Prem).
Adam Federici for Reading v Cardiff (Peter Enckelman), Dec 28, 2008 (shot, Champ)
Chris Weale for Yeovil v Hereford (Peter Gulacsi), Apr 21, 2009 (header, Lge 1)
Scot Flinders for Hartlepool v Bournemouth (Shwan Jalal), Apr 30, 2011 (header, Lge 1)
Iain Turner for Preston v Notts Co (Stuart Nelson), Aug 27 2011 (shot, Lge 1)
Tim Howard for Everton v Bolton (Adam Bogdan), Jan 4, 2012 (clearance, Prem)

MORE GOALKEEPING HEADLINES

Arthur Wilkie, sustained a hand injury in Reading's Div 3 match against Halifax on Aug 31, 1962, then played as a forward and scored twice in a 4-2 win.

Alex Stepney was Manchester Utd's joint top scorer for two months in season 1973-74 with two penalties.

Alan Fettis scored twice for Hull in 1994-95 Div 2 season, as a substitute in 3-1 home win over Oxford Utd (Dec 17) and, when selected outfield, with last-minute winner (2-1) against Blackpool on May 6.

Roger Freestone scored for Swansea with a penalty at Oxford Utd (Div 2, Apr 30, 1995) and twice from the spot the following season against Shrewsbury (Aug 12) and Chesterfield (Aug 26).

Jimmy Glass, on loan from Swindon, kept Carlisle in the Football League on May 8, 1999. With ten seconds of stoppage-time left, he went upfield for a corner and scored the winner against Plymouth that sent Scarborough down to the Conference instead.

Paul Smith, Nottm Forest goalkeeper, was allowed to run through Leicester's defence unchallenged and score direct from the kick-off of a Carling Cup second round second match on Sept 18, 2007. It replicated the 1-0 score by which Forest had led at half-time when the original match was abandoned after Leicester defender Clive Clarke suffered a heart attack. Leicester won the tie 3-2.

Tony Roberts (Dagenham), is the only known goalkeeper to score from open play in the FA Cup, his last-minute goal at Basingstoke in the fourth qualifying round on Oct 27, 2001 earning a 2-2 draw. Dagenham won the replay 3-0 and went on to reach the third round proper.

The only known instance in first-class football in Britain of a goalkeeper scoring direct from a goal-kick was in a First Division match at Roker Park on Apr 14, 1900. The kick by Manchester City's **Charlie Williams** was caught in a strong wind and Sunderland keeper J. E Doig fumbled the ball over his line.

Jose Luis Chilavert, Paraguay's international goalkeeper, scored a hat-trick of penalties when his club Velez Sarsfield beat Ferro Carril Oeste 6-1 in the Argentine League on Nov 28, 1999. In all, he scored 8 goals in 72 internationals. He also scored with a free-kick from just inside his own half for Velez Sarsfield against River Plate on Sep 20, 2000.

Most goals by a goalkeeper in a League season: 5 (all penalties) by **Arthur Birch** for Chesterfield (Div 3 North), 1923-24.

When Brazilian goalkeeper Rogerio Ceni (37) converted a free-kick for Sao Paulo's winner (2-1) v Corinthians in a championship match on Mar 27, 2011, it was his 100th goal (56 free-kicks, 44 ;pens) in a 20-season career.

OWN GOALS

Most by player in one season: 5 by **Robert Stuart** (Middlesbrough) in 1934-35.

Three in match by one team: Sheffield Wed's **Vince Kenny, Norman Curtis** and **Eddie Gannon** in 5-4 defeat at home to WBA (Div 1) on Dec 26, 1952; Rochdale's **George Underwood, Kenny Boyle** and **Danny Murphy** in 7-2 defeat at Carlisle (Div 3 North), Dec 25, 1954; Sunderland's **Stephen Wright** and **Michael Proctor** (2) in 24, 29, 32 minutes at home to Charlton (1-3, Prem), Feb 1, 2003; Brighton's **Liam Bridcutt** (2) and **Lewis Dunk** in 6-1 FA Cup 5th rd defeat at Liverpool, Feb 19, 2012.

Two in match by one player: Chris Nicholl (Aston Villa) scored all 4 goals in 2-2 draw away to Leicester (Div 1), Mar 20, 1976; **Jamie Carragher** (Liverpool) in first half at home to Manchester Utd (2-3) in Premiership, Sep 11, 1999; **Jim Goodwin** (Stockport) in 1-4 defeat away to Plymouth (Div 2), Sep 23, 2002; **Michael Proctor** (Sunderland) in 1-3 defeat at home to Charlton (Premiership), Feb 1, 2003.

Fastest own goals: 8 sec by **Pat Kruse** of Torquay, for Cambridge Utd (Div 4), Jan 3, 1977; in First Division, 16 sec by **Steve Bould** (Arsenal) away to Sheffield Wed, Feb 17, 1990.

Late own-goal man: Frank Sinclair (Leicester) put through his own goal in the 90th minute of Premiership matches away to Arsenal (L1-2) and at home to Chelsea (2-2) in Aug 1999.

Half an own goal each: Chelsea's second goal in a 3-1 home win against Leicester on December 18, 1954 was uniquely recorded as 'shared own goal'. Leicester defenders **Stan Milburn** and **Jack Froggatt**, both lunging at the ball in an attempt to clear, connected simultaneously and sent it rocketing into the net.

Match of 149 own goals: When Adama, Champions of Malagasy (formerly Madagascar) won a League match 149-0 on Oct 31, 2002, all 149 were own goals scored by opponents Stade Olympique De L'Emryne. They repeatedly put the ball in their own net in protest at a refereeing decision.

MOST SCORERS IN MATCH

Liverpool set a Football League record with **eight** scorers when beating Crystal Palace 9-0 (Div 1) on Sep 12, 1989. Marksmen were: Steve Nicol (7 and 88 mins), Steve McMahon (16), Ian Rush (45), Gary Gillespie (56), Peter Beardsley (61), John Aldridge (67 pen), John Barnes (79), Glenn Hysen (82).

Fifteen years earlier, **Liverpool** had gone one better with **nine** different scorers when they achieved their record win, 11-0 at home to Stromsgodset (Norway) in the Cup-Winners' Cup 1st round, 1st leg on Sep 17, 1974.

Eight players scored for **Swansea** when they beat Sliema, Malta, 12-0 in the Cup-Winners' Cup 1st round, 1st leg on Sep 15, 1982.

Nine Stirling players scored in the 20-0 win against Selkirk in the Scottish Cup 1st Round on December 8, 1984.

LONG SCORING RUNS

Tom Phillipson scored in 13 consecutive matches for Wolves (Div 2) in season 1926–27, which is still an English League record. **Bill Prendergast** scored in 13 successive League and Cup appearances for Chester (Div 3 North) in season 1938–39.

Dixie Dean scored in 12 consecutive games (23 goals) for Everton in Div 2 in 1930–31.

Danish striker **Finn Dossing** scored in 15 consecutive matches (Scottish record) for Dundee Utd (Div 1) in 1964–65.

50-GOAL PLAYERS

With **52** goals for **Wolves** in 1987–78 (34 League, 12 Sherpa Van Trophy, 3 Littlewoods Cup, 3 FA Cup), **Steve Bull** became the first player to score 50 in a season for a League club since **Terry Bly** for Div 4 newcomers Peterborough in 1960–61. Bly's 54 comprised 52 League goals and 2 in the FA Cup, and included 7 hat-tricks, still a post-war League record. Bull was again the country's top scorer with 50 goals in season 1988–89: 37 League, 2 Littlewoods Cup and 11 Sherpa Van Trophy. Between Bly and Bull, the highest individual scoring total for a season was 49 by two players: **Ted MacDougall** (Bournemouth 1970–71, 42 League, 7 FA Cup) and **Clive Allen** (Tottenham 1986–87, 33 League, 12 Littlewoods Cup, 4 FA Cup).

HOT SHOTS

Jimmy Greaves was top Div 1 scorer (League goals) six times in 11 seasons: 32 for Chelsea (1958–59), 41 for Chelsea (1960–61) and, for Tottenham, 37 in 1962–63, 35 in 1963–64, 29 in 1964–65 (joint top) and 27 in 1968–69.

Brian Clough (Middlesbrough) was leading scorer in Div 2 in three successive seasons: 40 goals in 1957–58, 42 in 1958–59 and 39 in 1959–60.

John Hickton (Middlesbrough) was top Div 2 scorer three times in four seasons: 24 goals in 1967–68, 24 in 1969–70 and 25 in 1970–71.

MOST HAT-TRICKS

Nine by **George Camsell** (Middlesbrough) in Div 2, 1926–27, is the record for one season. Most League hat-tricks in career: 37 by **Dixie Dean** for Tranmere and Everton (1924–38).

Most **top division** hat-tricks in a season since last War: six by **Jimmy Greaves** for Chelsea (1960–61). **Alan Shearer** scored five hat-tricks for Blackburn in the Premier League, season 1995–96.

Frank Osborne (Tottenham) scored three consecutive hat-tricks in Div 1 in Oct–Nov 1925, against Liverpool, Leicester (away) and West Ham

Tom Jennings (Leeds) scored hat-tricks in three successive Div 1 matches (Sep–Oct, 1926): 3 goals v Arsenal, 4 at Liverpool, 4 v Blackburn. Leeds were relegated that season.

Jack Balmer (Liverpool) scored his three hat-tricks in a 17-year career in successive Div 1 matches (Nov 1946): 3 v Portsmouth, 4 at Derby, 3 v Arsenal. No other Liverpool player scored during that 10-goal sequence by Balmer.

Gilbert Alsop scored hat-tricks in three successive matches for Walsall in Div 3 South in Apr 1939: 3 at Swindon, 3 v Bristol City and 4 v Swindon.

Alf Lythgoe scored hat-tricks in three successive games for Stockport (Div 3 North) in Mar 1934: 3 v Darlington, 3 at Southport and 4 v Wrexham.

TRIPLE HAT-TRICKS

There have been at least three instances of **3 hat-tricks** being scored for one team in a Football League match:

Apr 21, 1909: Enoch West, Billy Hooper and Alfred Spouncer for Nottm Forest (12-0 v Leicester Fosse, Div 1).

Mar 3, 1962: Ron Barnes, Wyn Davies and Roy Ambler in Wrexham's 10-1 win against Hartlepool (Div 4).

Nov 7, 1987: Tony Adcock, Paul Stewart and David White for Manchester City in 10-1 win at home to Huddersfield (Div 2).

For the first time in the Premiership, **three hat-tricks** were scored on one day (Sep 23, 1995): **Tony Yeboah** for Leeds at Wimbledon; **Alan Shearer** for Blackburn v Coventry; **Robbie Fowler** with 4 goals for Liverpool v Bolton

In the FA Cup, **Jack Carr**, **George Elliott** and **Walter Tinsley** each scored 3 in Middlesbrough's 9-3 first round win against Goole in Jan, 1915. **Les Allen** scored 5, **Bobby Smith** 4 and **Cliff Jones** 3 when Tottenham beat Crewe 13-2 in a fourth-round replay in Feb 1960.

HAT-TRICKS v THREE KEEPERS

When West Ham beat Newcastle 8-1 (Div 1) on Apr 21, 1986 **Alvin Martin** scored 3 goals against different goalkeepers: Martin Thomas injured a shoulder and was replaced, in turn, by outfield players Chris Hedworth and Peter Beardsley.

Jock Dodds of Lincoln had done the same against West Ham on Dec 18, 1948, scoring past Ernie Gregory, Tommy Moroney and George Dick in 4-3 win.

David Herd (Manchester Utd) scored against Sunderland's Jim Montgomery, Charlie Hurley and Johnny Parke in 5-0 First Division home win on Nov 26, 1966.

Brian Clark, of Bournemouth, scored against Rotherham's Jim McDonagh, Conal Gilbert and Michael Leng twice in 7-2 win (Div 3) on Oct 10, 1972.

On Oct 16, 1993 (Div 3) **Chris Pike** (Hereford) scored a hat-trick in 5-0 win over Colchester, who became the first team in league history to have two keepers sent off in the same game.

On Dec 18, 2004 (Lge 1), in 6-1 defeat at Hull, Tranmere used **John Achterberg** and **Russell Howarth**, both retired injured, and defender **Theo Whitmore**.

On Mar 9, 2008, Manchester Utd had three keepers in their 0-1 FA Cup quarter-final defeat by Portsmouth. **Tomasz Kuszczak** came on at half-time for **Edwin van der Sar** but was sent off when conceding a penalty. **Rio Ferdinand** went in goal and was beaten by Sulley Muntari's spot-kick

Derby used three keepers in a 4-1 defeat at Reading (Mar 10, 2010, Champ). **Saul Deeney**, who took over when **Stephen Bywater** was injured, was sent off for a foul and **Robbie Savage** replaced him.

EIGHT-DAY HAT-TRICK TREBLE

Joe Bradford, of Birmingham, scored three hat-tricks in eight days in Sep 1929–30 v Newcastle (won 5-1) on the 21st, 5 for the Football League v Irish League (7-2) on the 25th, and 3 in his club's 5-7 defeat away to Blackburn on the 28th.

PREMIERSHIP DOUBLE HAT-TRICK

Robert Pires and **Jermaine Pennant** each scored 3 goals in Arsenal's 6-1 win at home to Southampton (May 7, 2003).

TON UP – BOTH ENDS

Manchester City are the only club to score and concede a century of League goals in the same season. When finishing fifth in the 1957–58 season, they scored 104 and gave away 100.

TOURNAMENT TOP SHOTS

Most individual goals in a World Cup Final series: 13 by **Just Fontaine** for France, in Sweden 1958. Most in European Championship Finals: 9 by **Michel Platini** for France, in France 1984.

MOST GOALS ON CLUB DEBUT

Jim Dyet scored eight in King's Park's 12-2 win against Forfar (Scottish Div 2, Jan 2, 1930). **Len Shackleton** scored six times in Newcastle's 13-0 win v Newport (Div 2, Oct 5, 1946) in the week he joined them from Bradford Park Avenue

MOST GOALS ON LEAGUE DEBUT

Five by **George Hilsdon**, for Chelsea (9-2) v Glossop, Div 2, Sep 1, 1906. **Alan Shearer**, with three goals for Southampton (4-2) v Arsenal, Apr 9, 1988, became, at 17, the youngest player to score a First Division hat-trick on his full debut.

CLEAN-SHEET RECORDS

On the way to promotion from Div 3 in season 1995–96, Gillingham's ever-present goalkeeper **Jim Stannard** set a clean-sheet record. In 46 matches. He achieved 29 shut-outs (17 at home, 12 away), beating the 28 by **Ray Clemence** for Liverpool (42 matches in Div 1, 1978–79) and the previous best in a 46-match programme of 28 by Port Vale (Div 3 North, 1953–54). In conceding only 20 League goals in 1995–96, Gillingham created a defensive record for the lower divisions.

Chris Woods, Rangers' England goalkeeper, set a British record in season 1986–87 by going 1,196 minutes without conceding a goal. The sequence began in the UEFA Cup match against Borussia Moenchengladbach on Nov 26, 1986 and ended when Rangers were sensationally beaten 1-0 at home by Hamilton in the Scottish Cup 3rd round on Jan 31, 1987 with a 70th-minute goal by **Adrian Sprott**. The previous British record of 1,156 minutes without a goal conceded was held by Aberdeen goalkeeper **Bobby Clark** (season 1970–01).

Manchester Utd set a new Premier League clean-sheet record of 1,333 minutes (including 14 successive match shut-outs) in season 2008–9 (Nov 15-Feb 21). **Edwin van der Sar's** personal British league record of 1,311 minutes without conceding ended when United won 2-1 at Newcastle on Mar 4, 2009

Most clean sheets in season in top English division: **28** by **Liverpool** (42 matches) in 1978–79; **25** by **Chelsea** (38 matches) in 2004–05.

There have been three instances of clubs keeping 11 consecutive clean sheets in the Football League: **Millwall** (Div 3 South, 1925–26), **York** (Div 3, 1973–74) and **Reading** (Div 4, 1978–79). In his sequence, Reading goalkeeper **Steve Death** set the existing League shut-out record of 1,103 minutes.

Sasa Ilic remained unbeaten for over 14 hours with 9 successive shut-outs (7 in Div 1, 2 in play-offs) to equal a Charlton club record in Apr/May 1998. He had 12 clean sheets in 17 first team games after winning promotion from the reserves with 6 successive clean sheets.

Sebastiano Rossi kept a clean sheet in 8 successive away matches for AC Milan (Nov 1993–Apr 1994).

A world record of 1,275 minutes without conceding a goal was set in 1990–01 by **Abel Resino**, the Atletico Madrid goalkeeper. He was finally beaten by Sporting Gijon's Enrique in Atletico's 3-1 win on Mar 19, 1991.

In international football, the record is held by **Dino Zoff** with a shut-out for Italy (Sep 1972 to Jun 1974) lasting 1,142 minutes.

LOW SCORING

Fewest goals by any club in season in Football League: 18 by Loughborough (Div 2, 34 matches, 1899–1900); in 38 matches 20 by Derby (Prem Lge, 2007–08); in 42 matches, 24 by Watford (Div 2, 1971–72) and by **Stoke** (Div 1, 1984–85)); in 46-match programme, 27 by **Stockport** (Div 3, 1969–70).

Arsenal were the lowest Premier League scorers in its opening season (1992–93) with 40 goals in 42 matches, but won both domestic cup competitions. In subsequent seasons the lowest Premier League scorers were **Ipswich** (35) in 1993–94, **Crystal Palace** (34) in 1994–95, **Manchester City** (33) in 1995–96 and Leeds (28) in 1996–97 until **Sunderland** set the Premiership's new fewest-goals record with only 21 in 2002–03. Then, in 2007–08, **Derby** scored just 20.

LONG TIME NO SCORE

The world international non-scoring record was set by **Northern Ireland** when they played 13 matches and 1,298 minutes without a goal. The sequence began against Poland on Feb 13, 2002 and ended 2 years and 5 days later when David Healy scored against Norway (1-4) in Belfast on Feb 18, 2004.

Longest non-scoring sequences in Football League: 11 matches by Coventry City in 1919–20 (Div 2); 11 matches in 1992–93 (Div 2) by **Hartlepool**, who after beating Crystal Palace 1-0 in the FA Cup 3rd round on Jan 2, went 13 games and 2 months without scoring (11 League, 1 FA Cup, 1 Autoglass Trophy). The sequence ended after 1,227 blank minutes with a 1-1 draw at Blackpool (League) on Mar 6.

In the Premier League (Oct–Jan season 1994–95) **Crystal Palace** failed to score in nine consecutive matches.

The British non-scoring club record is held by **Stirling**: 14 consecutive matches (13 League, 1 Scottish Cup) and 1,292 minutes play, from Jan 31 1981 until Aug 8, 1981 (when they lost 4-1 to Falkirk in the League Cup).

In season 1971–72, **Mansfield** did not score in any of their first nine home games in Div 3. They were relegated on goal difference of minus two.

FA CUP CLEAN SHEETS

Most consecutive FA Cup matches without conceding a goal: 11 by **Bradford City**. The sequence spanned 8 rounds, from 3rd in 1910–11 to 4th. Round replay in 1911–12, and included winning the Cup in 1911.

GOALS THAT WERE WRONGLY GIVEN

Tottenham's last-minute winner at home to Huddersfield (Div 1) on Apr 2, 1952: Eddie Baily's corner-kick struck referee W.R Barnes in the back, and the ball rebounded to Baily, who crossed for Len Duquemin to head into the net. Baily had infringed the Laws by playing the ball twice, but the result (1-0) stood. Those two points helped Spurs to finish Championship runners-up; Huddersfield were relegated.

The second goal (66 mins) in **Chelsea**'s 2-1 home win v Ipswich (Div 1) on Sep 26, 1970: Alan Hudson's shot hit the stanchion on the outside of goal and the ball rebounded on to the pitch. But instead of the goal-kick, referee Roy Capey gave a goal, on a linesman's confirmation. TV pictures proved otherwise. The Football League quoted from the Laws of the Game: 'The referee's decision on all matters is final.'

When **Watford's** John Eustace and **Reading's** Noel Hunt challenged for a 13th minute corner at Vicarage Road on Sep 20, 2008, the ball was clearly diverted wide. But referee Stuart Attwell signalled for a goal on the instruction on his assistant and it went down officially as a Eustace own goal. The Championship match ended 2-2.

Sunderland's 1-0 Premier League win over **Liverpool** on Oct 17, 2009 was decided by one of the most bizarre goals in football history when Darren Bent's shot struck a red beach ball thrown from the crowd and wrong-footed goalkeeper Jose Reina. Referee Mike Jones wrongly allowed it to stand. The Laws of the Game state: 'An outside agent interfering with play should result in play being stopped and restarted with a drop ball.'

Blackburn's 59th minute equaliser (2-2) in 3-3 draw away to Wigan (Prem) on Nov 19, 2011 was illegal. Morten Gamst Pedersen played the ball to himself from a corner and crossed for Junior Hoilett to net.

The Republic of Ireland were deprived of the chance of a World Cup place in the second leg of their play-off with France on Nov 18, 2009. They were leading 1-0 in Paris when Thierry Henry blatantly handled before setting up William Gallas to equalise in extra-time time and give his side a 2-1 aggregate victory. The FA of Ireland's call for a replay was rejected by FIFA.

• The most notorious goal in World Cup history was fisted in by Diego Maradona in **Argentina's** 2-1 quarter-final win over England in Mexico City on Jun 22, 1986.

ATTENDANCES

GREATEST WORLD CROWDS

World Cup, Maracana Stadium, Rio de Janeiro, Jul 16, 1950. Final match (Brazil v Uruguay) attendance 199,850; receipts £125,000.

Total attendance in three matches (including play-off) between Santos (Brazil) and AC Milan for the Inter-Continental Cup (World Club Championship) 1963, exceeded 375,000.

BRITISH RECORD CROWDS

Most to pay: 149,547, Scotland v England, at Hampden Park, Glasgow, Apr 17, 1937. This was the first all-ticket match in Scotland (receipts £24,000).

At Scottish FA Cup Final: 146,433, Celtic v Aberdeen, at Hampden Park, Apr 24, 1937. Estimated another 20,000 shut out.

For British club match (apart from a Cup Final): 143,470, Rangers v Hibernian, at Hampden Park, Mar 27, 1948 (Scottish Cup semi-final).

FA Cup Final: 126,047, Bolton v West Ham, Apr 28, 1923. Estimated 150,000 in ground at opening of Wembley Stadium.

New Wembley: 89,874, FA Cup Final, Cardiff v Portsmouth, May 17, 2008.

World Cup Qualifying ties: 120,000, Cameroon v Morocco, Yaounde, Nov 29, 1981; 107,580, Scotland v Poland, Hampden Park, Oct 13, 1965.

European Cup: 135,826, Celtic v Leeds (semi-final, 2nd leg) at Hampden Park, Apr 15, 1970.

European Cup Final: 127,621, Real Madrid v Eintracht Frankfurt, at Hampden Park, May 18, 1960.

European Cup-Winners' Cup Final: 100,000, West Ham v TSV Munich, at Wembley, May 19, 1965.

Scottish League: 118,567, Rangers v Celtic, Jan 2, 1939.

Scottish League Cup Final: 107,609, Celtic v Rangers, at Hampden Park, Oct 23, 1965.

Football League old format: First Div: 83,260, Manchester Utd v Arsenal, Jan 17, 1948 (at Maine Road); **Div 2** 70,302 Tottenham v Southampton, Feb 25, 1950; **Div 3S:** 51,621, Cardiff v Bristol City, Apr 7, 1947; **Div 3N:** 49,655, Hull v Rotherham, Dec 25, 1948; **Div 3:** 49,309, Sheffield Wed v Sheffield Utd, Dec 26, 1979; **Div 4:** 37,774, Crystal Palace v Millwall, Mar 31, 1961.

Premier League: 76,098, Manchester Utd v Blackburn, Mar 31, 2007.

Football League – New Div 1: 41,214, Sunderland v Stoke, Apr 25, 1998; **New Div2:** 32,471, Manchester City v York, May 8, 1999; **New Div 3:** 22,319, Hull v Hartlepool Utd, Dec 26, 2002. **New Champs:** 52,181, Newcastle v Ipswich, Apr 24, 2010; **New Lge 1:** 38,256, Leeds v Gillingham, May 3, 2008; **New Lge 2:** 17,250, MK Dons v Morecambe, May 3, 2008.

In English Provinces: 84,569, Manchester City v Stoke (FA Cup 6), Mar 3, 1934.

Record for Under-21 International: 55,700, England v Italy, first match at New Wembley, Mar 24, 2007.

Record for friendly match: 104,679, Rangers v Eintracht Frankfurt, at Hampden Park, Glasgow, Oct 17, 1961.

FA Youth Cup: 38,187, Arsenal v Manchester Utd, at Emirates Stadium, Mar 14, 2007.

Record Football League aggregate (season): 41,271,414 (1948–49) – 88 clubs.

Record Football League aggregate (single day): 1,269,934, December 27, 1949, previous day, 1,226,098.

Record average home League attendance for season: 75,691 by Manchester Utd in 2007–08.

Long-ago League attendance aggregates: 10,929,000 in 1906–07 (40 clubs); 28,132,933 in 1937–38 (88 clubs).

Last 1m crowd aggregate, League (single day): 1,007,200, December 27, 1971.

Record Amateur match attendance: 100,000 for FA Amateur Cup Final, Pegasus v Harwich & Parkeston at Wembley, Apr 11, 1953.

Record Cup-tie aggregate: 265,199, at two matches between Rangers and Morton, in Scottish Cup Final, 1947–48.

Abandoned match attendance records: In England – 63,480 at Newcastle v Swansea City FA Cup 3rd round, Jan 10, 1953, abandoned 8 mins (0-0), fog.

In Scotland: 94,596 at Scotland v Austria (4-1), Hampden Park, May 8, 1963. Referee Jim Finney ended play (79 minutes) after Austria had two players sent off and one carried off.

Colchester's record crowd (19,072) was for the FA Cup 1st round tie v Reading on Nov 27, 1948, abandoned 35 minutes (0-0), fog.

SMALLEST CROWDS

Smallest League attendances: 450 Rochdale v Cambridge Utd (Div 3, Feb 5, 1974); 469, Thames v Luton (Div 3 South, December 6, 1930).

Only 13 people paid to watch Stockport v Leicester (Div 2, May 7, 1921) at Old Trafford, but up to 2,000 stayed behind after Manchester Utd v Derby earlier in the day. Stockport's ground was closed.

Lowest Premier League crowd: 3,039 for Wimbledon v Everton, Jan 26, 1993 (smallest top-division attendance since War).

Lowest Saturday post-war top-division crowd: 3,231 for Wimbledon v Luton, Sep 7, 1991 (Div 1).

Lowest Football League crowds, new format – Div 1: 849 for Wimbledon v Rotherham, (Div 1) Oct 29, 2002 (smallest attendance in top two divisions since War); 1,054 Wimbledon v Wigan (Div 1), Sep 13, 2003 in club's last home match when sharing Selhurst Park; **Div 2:** 1,077, Hartlepool Utd v Cardiff, Mar 22, 1994; **Div 3:** 739, Doncaster v Barnet, Mar 3, 1998.

Lowest top-division crowd at a major ground since the war: 4,554 for Arsenal v Leeds (May 5, 1966) – fixture clashed with live TV coverage of Cup-Winners' Cup Final (Liverpool v Borussia Dortmund).

Smallest League Cup attendances: 612, Halifax v Tranmere (1st round, 2nd leg) Sep 6, 2000; 664, Wimbledon v Rotherham (3rd round), Nov 5, 2002.

Smallest League Cup attendance at top-division ground: 1,987 for Wimbledon v Bolton (2nd Round, 2nd Leg) Oct 6, 1992.

Smallest Wembley crowds for England matches: 15,628 v Chile (Rous Cup, May 23, 1989 – affected by Tube strike); 20,038 v Colombia (Friendly, Sep 6, 1995); 21,432 v Czech.

(Friendly, Apr 25, 1990); 21,142 v Japan (Umbro Cup, Jun 3, 1995); 23,600 v Wales (British Championship, Feb 23, 1983); 23,659 v Greece (Friendly, May 17, 1994); 23,951 v East Germany (Friendly, Sep 12, 1984); 24,000 v N Ireland (British Championship, Apr 4, 1984); 25,756 v Colombia (Rous Cup, May 24, 1988); 25,837 v Denmark (Friendly, Sep 14, 1988).

Smallest international modern crowds: 221 for Poland v N Ireland (4-1, friendly) at Limassol, Cyprus, on Feb 13, 2002. Played at neutral venue at Poland's World Cup training base. 265 (all from N Ireland) at their Euro Champ qual against Serbia in Belgrade on Mar 25, 2011. Serbia ordered by UEFA to play behind closed doors because of previous crowd trouble.

Smallest international modern crowds at home: N Ireland: 2,500 v Chile (Belfast, May 26, 1989 – clashed with ITV live screening of Liverpool v Arsenal Championship decider); Scotland: 7,843 v N Ireland (Hampden Park, May 6, 1969); Wales: 2,315 v N Ireland (Wrexham, May 27, 1982).

Smallest attendance for post-war England match: 2,378 v San Marino (World Cup) at Bologna (Nov 17, 1993). Tie clashed with Italy v Portugal (World Cup) shown live on Italian TV.

Smallest paid attendance for British first-class match: 29 for Clydebank v East Stirling, CIS Scottish League Cup 1st round, Jul 31, 1999. Played at Morton's Cappielow Park ground, shared by Clydebank. Match clashed with the Tall Ships Race which attracted 200,000 to the area.

FA CUP CROWD RECORD (OUTSIDE FINAL)

The first FA Cup-tie shown on closed-circuit TV (5th round, Saturday, Mar 11, 1967, kick-off 7pm) drew a total of 105,000 spectators to Goodison Park and Anfield. At Goodison, 64,851 watched the match 'for real', while 40,149 saw the TV version on eight giant screens at Anfield. Everton beat Liverpool 1-0.

LOWEST SEMI-FINAL CROWD

The smallest FA Cup semi-final attendance since the War was 17,987 for the Manchester Utd–Crystal Palace replay at Villa Park on Apr 12, 1995. Palace supporters largely boycotted tie after a fan died in car-park clash outside pub in Walsall before first match.

Previous lowest: 25,963 for Wimbledon v Luton, at Tottenham on Apr 9, 1988.

Lowest quarter-final crowd since the war: 8,735 for Chesterfield v Wrexham on Mar 9, 1997.

Smallest FA Cup 3rd round attendances for matches between League clubs: 1,833 for Chester v Bournemouth (at Macclesfield) Jan 5, 1991; 1,966 for Aldershot v Oxford Utd, Jan 10, 1987.

PRE-WEMBLEY CUP FINAL CROWDS

AT CRYSTAL PALACE

1895 42,560	1902 48,036	1908 74,967
1896 48,036	Replay 33,050	1909 67,651
1897 65,891	1903 64,000	1910 76,980
1898 62,017	1904 61,734	1911 69,098
1899 73,833	1905 101,117	1912 54,434
1900 68,945	1906 75,609	1913 120,028
1901 110,802	1907 84,584	1914 72,778

AT OLD TRAFFORD

1915   50,000

AT STAMFORD BRIDGE

1920 50,018	1921 72,805	1922 53,000

INTERNATIONAL RECORDS

MOST APPEARANCES

Peter Shilton, England goalkeeper, then aged 40, retired from international football after the 1990 World Cup Finals with the European record number of caps – 125. Previous record (119) was set by **Pat Jennings**, Northern Ireland's goalkeeper from 1964–86, who retired on his 41st birthday during the 1986 World Cup Finals in Mexico. Shilton's England career spanned 20 seasons from his debut against East Germany at Wembley on Nov 25, 1970.

Six players have completed a century of appearances in full international matches for England. **Billy Wright** of Wolves, was the first, retiring in 1959 with a total of 105 caps. **Bobby Charlton**, of Manchester Utd, beat Wright's record in the World Cup match against West Germany in Leon, Mexico, in Jun 1970 and **Bobby Moore**, of West Ham, overtook Charlton's 106 caps against Italy in Turin, in Jun 1973. Moore played 108 times for England, a record that stood until **Shilton** reached 109 against Denmark in Copenhagen (Jun 7, 1989). In season 2008–09, **David Beckham** (LA Galaxy/AC Milan) overtook Moore as England's most-capped outfield player. In the vastly different selection processes of their eras, Moore played 108 full games for his country, whereas Beckham's total of 115 to the end of season 2009–10, included 58 part matches, 14 as substitute and 44 times substituted.

Kenny Dalglish became Scotland's first 100-cap international v Romania (Hampden Park, Mar 26, 1986).

World's most-capped player: Ahmed Hassan, 181 for Egypt (1995–2012).

Most-capped European player: Vitalijs Astafjevs, 167 for Latvia (1992–1010).

Most-capped European goalkeeper: Thomas Ravelli, 143 Internationals for Sweden (1981–97).

Gillian Coultard, (Doncaster Belles), England Women's captain, received a special presentation from Geoff Hurst to mark 100 caps when England beat Holland 1-0 at Upton Park on Oct 30, 1997. She made her international debut at 18 in May 1981, and retired at the end of season 1999–2000 with a record 119 caps (30 goals).

BRITAIN'S MOST-CAPPED PLAYERS

(As at start of season 2012–13)

England

Peter Shilton	125
David Beckham	115
Bobby Moore	108
Bobby Charlton	106
Billy Wright	105

Scotland

Kenny Dalglish	102
Jim Leighton	91
Alex McLeish	77
Paul McStay	76
Tommy Boyd	72

Wales

Neville Southall	92
Gary Speed	85

Dean Saunders	75
Peter Nicholas	73
Ian Rush	73

Northern Ireland

Pat Jennings	119
David Healy	92
Mal Donaghy	91
Sammy McIlroy	88
Maik Taylor	88

Republic of Ireland

Shay Given	125
Robbie Keane	119
Kevin Kilbane	110
Steve Staunton	102
Damien Duff	100

MOST ENGLAND CAPS IN ROW

Most consecutive international appearances: 70 by **Billy Wright**, for England from Oct 1951 to May 1959. He played 105 of England's first 108 post-war matches.

England captains most times: Billy Wright and **Bobby Moore**, 90 each.

England captains – 4 in match (v Serbia & Montenegro at Leicester Jun 3, 2003): **Michael Owen** was captain for the first half and after the interval the armband passed to **Emile Heskey** (for 15 minutes), **Philip Neville** (26 minutes) and substitute **Jamie Carragher** (9 minutes, including time added).

MOST SUCCESSIVE ENGLAND WINS

10 (Jun 1908–Jun 1909. Modern: 8 (Oct 2005–Jun 2006).

ENGLAND'S LONGEST UNBEATEN RUN

19 matches (16 wins, 3 draws), Nov 1965–Nov 1966.

ENGLAND'S TALLEST

At **6ft 7in**, **Peter Crouch** became England's tallest-ever international when he made his debut against Colombia in New Jersey, USA on May 31, 2005.

MOST PLAYERS FROM ONE CLUB IN ENGLAND SIDES

Arsenal supplied seven men (a record) to the England team v Italy at Highbury on Nov 14, 1934. They were: Frank Moss, George Male, Eddie Hapgood, Wilf Copping, Ray Bowden, Ted Drake and Cliff Bastin. In addition, Arsenal's Tom Whittaker was England's trainer.

Since then until 2001, the most players from one club in an England team was six from **Liverpool** against Switzerland at Wembley in Sep 1977. The side also included a Liverpool old boy, Kevin Keegan (Hamburg).

Seven **Arsenal** men took part in the England – France (0-2) match at Wembley on Feb 10, 1999. Goalkeeper David Seaman and defenders Lee Dixon, Tony Adams and Martin Keown lined up for England. Nicolas Anelka (2 goals) and Emmanuel Petit started the match for France and Patrick Vieira replaced Anelka.

Manchester Utd equalled Arsenal's 1934 record by providing England with seven players in the World Cup qualifier away to Albania on Mar 28, 2001. Five started the match – David Beckham (captain), Gary Neville, Paul Scholes, Nicky Butt and Andy Cole – and two went on as substitutes: Wes Brown and Teddy Sheringham.

INTERNATIONAL SUBS RECORDS

Malta substituted all 11 players in their 1-2 home defeat against England on Jun 3, 2000. Six substitutes by England took the total replacements in the match to 17, then an international record.

Most substitutions in match by **England**: 11 in second half by Sven-Goran Eriksson against Holland at Tottenham on Aug 15, 2001; 11 against Italy at Leeds on Mar 27, 2002; Italy sent on 8 players from the bench – the total of 19 substitutions was then a record for an England match; 11 against Australia at Upton Park on Feb 12, 2003 (entire England team changed at half-time); 11 against Iceland at City of Manchester Stadium on Jun 5, 2004.

Forty three players, a record for an England match, were used in the international against Serbia & Montenegro at Leicester on Jun 3, 2003. England sent on 10 substitutes in the second half and their opponents changed all 11 players.

The **Republic of Ireland** sent on 12 second-half substitutes, using 23 players in all, when they beat Russia 2-0 in a friendly international in Dublin on Feb 13, 2002.

First England substitute: Wolves winger **Jimmy Mullen** replaced injured Jackie Milburn (15 mins) away to Belgium on May 18, 1950. He scored in a 4-1 win.

ENGLAND'S WORLD CUP-WINNERS

At Wembley, Jul 30, 1966, 4-2 v West Germany (2-2 after 90 mins), scorers Hurst 3, Peters. Team: Banks; Cohen, Wilson, Stiles, J Charlton, Moore (capt), Ball, Hurst, R Charlton, Hunt, Peters. Manager **Alf Ramsey** fielded that same eleven in six successive matches (an England record): the World Cup quarter-final, semi-final and Final, and the first three games of the following season. England wore red shirts in the Final and The Queen presented the

Cup to Bobby Moore. The players each received a £1,000 bonus, plus £60 World Cup Final appearance money, all less tax, and Ramsey a £6,000 bonus from the FA The match was shown live on TV (in black and white).

England's non-playing reserves – there were no substitutes – also received the £1,000 bonus, but no medals. That remained the case until FIFA finally decided that non-playing members and staff of World Cup-winning squads should be given replica medals. England's 'forgotten heroes' received theirs at a reception in Downing Street on June 10, 2009 and were later guests of honour at the World Cup qualifier against Andorra at Wembley. The 11 reserves were: Springett, Bonetti, Armfield, Byrne, Flowers, Hunter, Paine, Connelly, Callaghan, Greaves, Eastham.

BRAZIL'S RECORD RUN

Brazil hold the record for the longest unbeaten sequence in international football: 45 matches from 1993–97. The previous record of 31 was held by Hungary between Jun 1950 and Jul 1954.

ENGLAND MATCHES ABANDONED

May 17, 1953 v **Argentina** (Friendly, Buenos Aires) after 23 mins (0-0) – rain.
Oct 29, 1975 v **Czechoslovakia** (Euro Champ qual, Bratislava) after 17 mins (0-0) – fog. Played next day.
Feb 15, 1995 v **Rep of Ireland** (Friendly, Dublin) after 27 mins (1-0) – crowd disturbance.

ENGLAND POSTPONEMENTS

Nov 21, 1979 v **Bulgaria** (Euro Champ qual, Wembley, postponed for 24 hours – fog; Aug 10, 2011 v Holland (friendly), Wembley, postponed after rioting in London

ENGLAND UNDER COVER

England played indoors for the first time when they beat Argentina 1-0 in the World Cup at the Sapporo Dome, Japan, on Jun 7, 2002.

ALL-SEATED INTERNATIONALS

The first **all-seated crowd** (30,000) for a full international in Britain saw **Wales** and **WestGermany** draw 0-0 at Cardiff Arms Park on May 31, 1989. The terraces were closed.
England's first all-seated international at Wembley was against Yugoslavia (2-1) on December 13, 1989 (attendance 34,796). The terracing behind the goals was closed for conversion to seating.
The first **full-house all-seated** international at Wembley was for England v Brazil (1-0) on Mar 28, 1990, when a capacity 80,000 crowd paid record British receipts of £1,200,000.

FIRST BLACK CAPS

First black player for **England** in a senior international was Nottm Forest full-back **Viv Anderson** against Czechoslovakia at Wembley on Nov 29, 1978.
Aston Villa's **Ugo Ehiogu** was **England's** first black captain (U-21 v Holland at Portsmouth, Apr 27, 1993).
Paul Ince (Manchester Utd) became the first black player to captain **England** in a **full international** (v USA, Boston, Jun 9, 1993).
First black British international was **Eddie Parris** (Bradford Park Avenue) for Wales against N Ireland in Belfast on December 5, 1931.

MOST NEW CAPS IN ENGLAND TEAM

6, by **Sir Alf Ramsey** (v Portugal, Apr 3, 1974) and **by Sven-Goran Eriksson** (v Australia, Feb 12, 2003; 5 at half-time when 11 changes made).

PLAYED FOR MORE THAN ONE COUNTRY

Multi-nationals in senior international football include: **Johnny Carey** (1938–53) – caps Rep of Ireland 29, N Ireland 7; **Ferenc Puskas** (1945–62) – caps Hungary 84, Spain 4; **Alfredo di Stefano** (1950–56) – caps Argentina 7, Spain 31; **Ladislav Kubala** (1948–58) – caps, Hungary 3, Czechoslovakia 11, Spain 19, only player to win full international honours with 3 countries. Kubala also played in a fourth international team, scoring twice for FIFA v England at Wembley in 1953. Eleven players, including **Carey**, appeared for both N Ireland and the Republic of Ireland in seasons directly after the last war.

Cecil Moore, capped by N Ireland in 1949 when with Glentoran, played for USA v England in 1953.

Hawley Edwards played for England v Scotland in 1874 and for Wales v Scotland in 1876.

Jack Reynolds (Distillery and WBA) played for both Ireland (5 times) and England (8) in the 1890s.

Bobby Evans (Sheffield Utd) had played 10 times for Wales when capped for England, in 1910–11. He was born in Chester of Welsh parents.

In recent years, several players have represented USSR and one or other of the breakaway republics. The same applies to Yugoslavia and its component states. **Josip Weber** played for Croatia in 1992 and made a 5-goal debut for Belgium in 1994.

THREE-GENERATION INTERNATIONAL FAMILY

When Bournemouth striker **Warren Feeney** was capped away to Liechtenstein on Mar 27, 2002, he became the third generation of his family to play for Northern Ireland. He followed in the footsteps of his grandfather James (capped twice in 1950) and father Warren Snr. (1 in 1976).

FATHERS & SONS CAPPED BY ENGLAND

George Eastham senior (pre-war) and **George Eastham** junior; **Brian Clough** and **Nigel Clough**; **Frank Lampard** snr and **Frank Lampard** jnr; **Mark Chamberlain** and **Alex Oxlade-Chamberlain**

FATHER & SON SAME-DAY CAPS

Iceland made father-and-son international history when they beat Estonia 3-0 in Tallin on Apr 24, 1996. **Arnor Gudjohnsen** (35) started the match and was replaced (62 mins) by his 17-year-old son Eidur.

LONGEST UNBEATEN START TO ENGLAND CAREER

Steven Gerrard, 21 matches (W16, D5) 2000–03.

SUCCESSIVE ENGLAND HAT-TRICKS

The last player to score a hat-trick in consecutive England matches was **Dixie Dean** on the summer tour in May 1927, against Belgium (9-1) and Luxembourg (5-2).

POST-WAR HAT-TRICKS v ENGLAND

Nov 25, 1953, **Nandor Hidegkuti** (England 3, Hungary 6, Wembley); May 11, 1958, **Aleksandar Petakovic** (Yugoslavia 5, England 0, Belgrade); May 17, 1959, **Juan Seminario** (Peru 4, England 1, Lima); Jun 15, 1988, **Marco van Basten** (Holland 3, England 1, European Championship, Dusseldorf).

NO-SAVE GOALKEEPERS

Chris Woods did not have one save to make when England beat San Marino 6-0 (World Cup) at Wembley on Feb 17, 1993. He touched the ball only six times.

Gordon Banks had a similar no-save experience when England beat Malta 5-0 (European Championship) at Wembley on May 12, 1971. Malta did not force a goal-kick or corner, and the four times Banks touched the ball were all from back passes.

Robert Green was also idle in the 6-0 World Cup qualifying win over Andorra at Wembley on Jun 10, 2009

WORLD/EURO MEMBERS

FIFA has 208 member countries, **UEFA** has 33

FIFA WORLD YOUTH CUP (UNDER-20)

Finals: 1977 (Tunis) Soviet Union 2 Mexico 2 (Soviet won 9-8 on pens.); **1979** (Tokyo) Argentina 3 Soviet Union 1; **1981** (Sydney) W Germany 4 Qatar 0; **1983** (Mexico City) Brazil 1 Argentina 0; **1985** (Moscow) Brazil 1 Spain 0; **1987** (Santiago) Yugoslavia 1 W Germany 1 (Yugoslavia won 5-4 on pens.); **1989** (Riyadh) Portugal 2 Nigeria 0; **1991** (Lisbon) Portugal 0 Brazil 0 (Portugal won 4-2 on pens.); **1993** (Sydney) Brazil 2 Ghana 1; **1995** (Qatar) Argentina 2 Brazil 0; **1997** (Kuala Lumpur) Argentina 2 Uruguay 1; **1999** (Lagos) Spain 4 Japan 0; **2001** (Buenos Aires) Argentina 3 Ghana 0; **2003** (Dubai) Brazil 1 Spain 0; **2005** (Utrecht) Argentina 2 Nigeria 1; **2007** (Toronto) Argentina 2 Czech Republic 1; **2009** (Cairo) Ghana 0 Brazil 0 (aet, Ghana won 4-3 on pens); **2011** (Bogota) Brazil 3 Portugal 2 (aet).

FAMOUS CLUB FEATS

Chelsea were Premiership winners in 2004–05, their centenary season with the highest points total (95) ever recorded by England Champions. They set these other records: Most Premiership wins in season (29); most clean sheets (25) and fewest goals conceded (15) in top-division history. They also won the League Cup in 2005.

Arsenal created an all-time English League record sequence of 49 unbeaten Premiership matches (W36, D13), spanning 3 seasons, from May 7, 2003 until losing 2-0 away to Manchester Utd on Oct 24, 2004. It included all 38 games in season 2003–04.

The Double: There have been 11 instances of a club winning the Football League/Premier League title and the FA Cup in the same season. **Manchester Utd** and **Arsenal** have each done so three times: **Preston** 1888–89; **Aston Villa** 1896–97; **Tottenham** 1960–61; **Arsenal** 1970–71, 1997–98, 2001–02; **Liverpool** 1985–86; **Manchester Utd** 1993–94, 1995–96, 1998–99; **Chelsea** 2009–10.

The Treble: Liverpool were the first English club to win three major competitions in one season when in 1983–84, Joe Fagan's first season as manager, they were League Champions, League Cup winners and European Cup winners.

Sir Alex Ferguson's **Manchester Utd** achieved an even more prestigious treble in 1998–99, completing the domestic double of Premiership and FA Cup and then winning the European Cup. In season 2008– 09, they completed another major triple success – Premier League, Carling Cup and World Club Cup.

Liverpool completed a unique treble by an English club with three cup successes under Gerard Houllier in season 2000–01: the League Cup, FA Cup and UEFA Cup.

Liverpool the first English club to win five major trophies in one calendar year (Feb– Aug 2001): League Cup, FA Cup, UEFA Cup, Charity Shield, UEFA Super Cup.

As Champions in season 2001–02, **Arsenal** set a Premiership record by winning the last 13 matches. They were the first top-division club since Preston in the League's inaugural season (1888–89) to maintain an unbeaten away record.

(See Scottish section for treble feats by Rangers and Celtic.)

Record Home Runs: Liverpool went 85 competitive first-team games unbeaten at home between losing 2-3 to Birmingham on Jan 21, 1978 and 1-2 to Leicester on Jan 31, 1981. They comprised 63 in the League, 9 League Cup, 7 in European competition and 6 FA Cup.

Chelsea hold the record unbeaten home League sequence of 86 matches (W62, D24) between losing 1-2 to Arsenal, Feb 21, 2004, and 0-1 to Liverpool, Oct 26, 2008.

Third to First: Charlton, in 1936, became the first club to advance from the Third to First Division in successive seasons. **Queens Park Rangers** were the second club to achieve the feat in 1968, and **Oxford Utd** did it in 1984 and 1985 as Champions of each division. Subsequently, **Derby** (1987), **Middlesbrough** (1988), **Sheffield Utd** (1990) and **Notts Co** (1991) climbed from Third Division to First in consecutive seasons.

Watford won successive promotions from the modern Second Division to the Premier League in 1997–98, 1998–99. **Manchester City** equalled the feat in 1998–99, 1999–2000. Norwich climbed from League 1 to the Premier League in seasons 2009–10, 2010–11. Southampton did the same in 2010–11 and 2011–12.

Fourth to First: Northampton , in 1965 became the first club to rise from the Fourth to the First Division. **Swansea** climbed from the Fourth Division to the First (three promotions in four seasons), 1977–78 to 1980–81. **Wimbledon** repeated the feat, 1982–83 to 1985–86 **Watford** did it in five seasons, 1977–8 to 1981–82. **Carlisle** climbed from Fourth Division to First, 1964–74.

Non-League to First: When **Wimbledon** finished third in the Second Division in 1986, they completed the phenomenal rise from non-League football (Southern League) to the First Division in nine years. Two years later they won the FA Cup.

Tottenham, in 1960–61, not only carried off the First Division Championship and the FA Cup for the first time that century but set up other records by opening with 11 successive wins, registering most First Division wins (31), most away wins in the League's history (16), and equalling Arsenal's First Division records of 66 points and 33 away points. They already held the Second Division record of 70 points (1919–20).

Arsenal, in 1993, became the first club to win both English domestic cup competitions (FA Cup and League Cup) in the same season. Liverpool repeated the feat in 2000–01.

Chelsea achieved the FA Cup/Champions League double in May 2012.

Preston, in season 1888–89, won the first League Championship without losing a match and the FA Cup without having a goal scored against them. Only other English clubs to remain unbeaten through a League season were **Liverpool** (Div 2 Champions in 1893–94) and **Arsenal** (Premiership Champions 2003–04).

Bury, in 1903, also won the FA Cup without conceding a goal.

Everton won Div 2, Div 1 and the FA Cup in successive seasons, 1930–31, 1931–32, 1932–33.

Wolves won the League Championship in 1958 and 1959 and the FA Cup in 1960.

Liverpool won the title in 1964, the FA Cup in 1965 and the title again in 1966. In 1978 they became the first British club to win the European Cup in successive seasons. Nottm Forest repeated the feat in 1979 and 1980.

Liverpool won the League Championship six times in eight seasons (1976–83) under **Bob Paisley's** management.

Sir Alex Ferguson's **Manchester Utd** have won the Premier League in 12 of its 20 seasons (1992–2012). They were runners-up five times and third three times.

Most Premiership wins in season: 29 by Chelsea in 2004–05, 2005–06.

Biggest points-winning margin by League Champions: 18 by Manchester Utd (1999– 2000).

COVENTRY UNIQUE

Coventry are the only club to have played in the Premier League, all four previous divisions of the Football League, in both sections (North and South) of the old Third Division and in the modern Championship. They will start the 2012–13 season in League 1.

FAMOUS UPS & DOWNS

Sunderland: Relegated in 1958 after maintaining First Division status since their election to the Football League in 1890. They dropped into Division 3 for the first time in 1987.

Aston Villa: Relegated with Preston to the Third Division in 1970.

Arsenal up: When the League was extended in 1919, Woolwich Arsenal (sixth in Division Two in 1914–15, last season before the war) were elected to Division One. Arsenal have been in the top division ever since.

Tottenham down: At that same meeting in 1919 Chelsea (due for relegation) retained their place in Division One but the bottom club (Tottenham) had to go down to Division Two.

Preston and **Burnley down**: Preston, the first League Champions in season 1888–89, dropped into the Fourth Division in 1985. So did Burnley, also among the League's original members in 1888. In 1986, Preston had to apply for re-election.

Wolves' fall: Wolves, another of the Football League's original members, completed the fall from First Division to Fourth in successive seasons (1984–5–6).

Lincoln out: Lincoln became the first club to suffer automatic demotion from the Football League when they finished bottom of Div 4, on goal difference, in season 1986–87. They were replaced by Scarborough, champions of the GM Vauxhall Conference. Lincoln regained their place a year later.

Swindon up and down: In the 1990 play-offs, Swindon won promotion to the First Division for the first time, but remained in the Second Division because of financial irregularities.

MOST CHAMPIONSHIP WINS

Manchester Utd became champions of England for a record 19th time (7 Football League, 12 Premier League) by winning the title in season 2010–11. They overtook Liverpool (18), with Arsenal third on 13 wins.

LONGEST CURRENT MEMBERS OF TOP DIVISION

Arsenal (since 1919), **Everton** (1954), **Liverpool** (1962), **Manchester Utd** (1975).

CHAMPIONS: FEWEST PLAYERS

Liverpool used only **14** players (five ever-present) when they won the League Championship in season 1965–66. **Aston Villa** also called on no more than 14 players to win the title in 1980–81, with seven ever-present.

UNBEATEN CHAMPIONS

Only two clubs have become Champions of England with an unbeaten record: **Preston** as the Football League's first winners in 1888–89 (22 matches) and **Arsenal**, Premiership winners in 2003–04 (38 matches).

LEAGUE HAT-TRICKS

Huddersfield created a record in 1924–5–6 by winning the League Championship three years in succession.

Arsenal equalled this hat-trick in 1933–4–5, **Liverpool** in 1982–3–4 and **Manchester Utd** in 1999–2000–01. Sir Alex Ferguson's side became the first to complete two successive hat-tricks (2007– 8– 9).

'SUPER DOUBLE' WINNERS

Since the War, there have been three instances of players appearing in and then managing FA Cup and Championship-winning teams:

Joe Mercer: Player in Arsenal Championship teams 1948, 1953 and in their 1950 FA Cup side; manager of Manchester City when they won Championship 1968, FA Cup 1969.

Kenny Dalglish: Player in Liverpool Championship-winning teams 1979, 1980, 1982, 1983, 1984, player-manager 1986, 1988, 1990: player-manager when Liverpool won FA Cup (to complete Double) 1986; manager of Blackburn, Champions 1995.

George Graham: Played in Arsenal's Double-winning team in 1971, and as manager took them to Championship success in 1989 and 1991 and the FA Cup – League Cup double in 1993.

ORIGINAL TWELVE

The original 12 members of the Football League (formed in 1888) were: **Accrington, Aston Villa, Blackburn, Bolton, Burnley, Derby, Everton, Notts Co, Preston, Stoke, WBA and Wolves.**

Results on the opening day (Sep 8, 1888): Bolton 3, Derby 6; Everton 2, Accrington 1; Preston 5, Burnley 2; Stoke 0, WBA 2; Wolves 1, Aston Villa 1. Preston had the biggest first-day crowd: 6,000. Blackburn and Notts Co did not play that day. They kicked off a week later (Sep 15) – Blackburn 5, Accrington 5; Everton 2, Notts Co 1.

Accrington FC resigned from the league in 1893 and later folded. A new club, Accrington Stanley, were members of the league from 1921 until 1962 when financial problems forced their demise. The current Accrington Stanley were formed in 1968 and gained league status in 2007.

FASTEST CLIMBS
Three promotions in four seasons by two clubs – **Swansea City**: 1978 third in Div 4; 1979 third in Div 3; 1981 third in Div 2; **Wimbledon**: 1983 Champions of Div 4; 1984 second in Div 3; 1986 third in Div 2.

MERSEYSIDE RECORD
Liverpool is the only city to have staged top-division football – through Everton and/or Liverpool – in **every season** since League football began in 1888.

EARLIEST PROMOTIONS TO TOP DIVISION POST-WAR
Mar 23, 1974, Middlesbrough; Mar 25, 2006, Reading.

EARLIEST RELEGATIONS POST-WAR
From top division: **QPR** went down from the old First Division on Mar 29, 1969; **Derby** went down from the Premier League on Mar 29, 2008, with 6 matches still to play. From modern First Division: **Stockport** on Mar 16, 2002, with 7 matches still to play; **Wimbledon** on Apr 6, 2004, with 7 matches to play.

LEAGUE RECORDS

DOUBLE CHAMPIONS
Nine men have played in and managed League Championship-winning teams:
Ted Drake Player – Arsenal 1934, 1935, 1938. Manager – Chelsea 1955.
Bill Nicholson Player – Tottenham 1951. Manager – Tottenham 1961.
Alf Ramsey Player – Tottenham 1951. Manager – Ipswich 1962.
Joe Mercer Player – Everton 1939, Arsenal 1948, 1953. Manager – Manchester City 1968.
Dave Mackay Player – Tottenham 1961. Manager – Derby 1975.
Bob Paisley Player – Liverpool 1947. Manager – Liverpool 1976, 1977, 1979, 1980, 1982, 1983.
Howard Kendall Player – Everton 1970. Manager – Everton 1985, 1987.
Kenny Dalglish Player – Liverpool 1979, 1980, 1982, 1983, 1984. Player-manager – Liverpool 1986, 1988, 1990. Manager – Blackburn 1995.
George Graham Player – Arsenal 1971. Manager – Arsenal 1989, 1991.

GIGGS RECORD COLLECTION
Ryan Giggs (Manchester Utd) has collected the most individual honours in English football with a total of 32 prizes to the end of season 2011– 12. They comprise: 12 Premier League titles, 4 FA Cups, 3 League Cups, 2 European Cups, 1 UEFA Super Cup, 1 Inter-Continental Cup, 1 World Club Cup, 8 Charity Shields/Community Shields.

CANTONA'S FOUR-TIMER
Eric Cantona played in four successive Championship-winning teams: Marseille 1990–01, Leeds 1991–92, Manchester Utd 1992–93 and 1993–94.

ARRIVALS AND DEPARTURES
The following are the Football League arrivals and departures since 1923:

Year	In	Out
1923	Doncaster	Stalybridge Celtic
	New Brighton	

1927	Torquay	Aberdare Athletic
1928	Carlisle	Durham
1929	York	Ashington
1930	Thames	Merthyr Tydfil
1931	Mansfield	Newport Co
	Chester	Nelson
1932	Aldershot	Thames
	Newport Co	Wigan Borough
1938	Ipswich	Gillingham
1950	Colchester, Gillingham	
	Scunthorpe, Shrewsbury	
1951	Workington	New Brighton
1960	Peterborough	Gateshead
1962	Oxford Utd	Accrington (resigned)
1970	Cambridge Utd	Bradford PA
1972	Hereford	Barrow
1977	Wimbledon	Workington
1978	Wigan	Southport
1987	Scarborough	Lincoln
1988	Lincoln	Newport Co
1989	Maidstone	Darlington
1990	Darlington	Colchester
1991	Barnet	
1992	Colchester	Aldershot, Maidstone (resigned)
1993	Wycombe	Halifax
1997	Macclesfield	Hereford
1998	Halifax	Doncaster
1999	Cheltenham	Scarborough
2000	Kidderminster	Chester
2001	Rushden	Barnet
2002	Boston	Halifax
2003	Yeovil, Doncaster	Exeter, Shrewsbury
2004	Chester, Shrewsbury	Carlisle, York
2005	Barnet, Carlisle	Kidderminster, Cambridge Utd
2006	Accrington, Hereford	Oxford Utd, Rushden & Diamonds
2007	Dagenham, Morecambe	Torquay, Boston
2008	Aldershot, Exeter	Wrexham, Mansfield
2009	Burton, Torquay	Chester, Luton
2010	Stevenage, Oxford Utd	Grimsby, Darlington
2011	Crawley, AFC Wimbledon	Lincoln, Stockport
2012	Fleetwood, York	Hereford, Macclesfield

Leeds City were expelled from Div 2 in Oct, 1919; Port Vale took over their fixtures.

EXTENSIONS TO FOOTBALL LEAGUE

Clubs	Season	Clubs	Season
12 to 14	1891–92	44 to 66†	1920–21
14 to 28*	1892–93	66 to 86†	1921–22
28 to 31	1893–94	86 to 88	1923–24
31 to 32	1894–95	88 to 92	1950–51
32 to 36	1898–99	92 to 93	1991–92
36 to 40	1905–06	(Reverted to 92 when Aldershot closed, Mar 1992)

*Second Division formed. † Third Division (South) formed from Southern League clubs.
†Third Division (North) formed.
Football League reduced to 70 clubs and three divisions on the formation of the FA Premier

League in 1992; increased to 72 season 1994–95, when Premier League reduced to 20 clubs.

RECORD RUNS

Arsenal hold the record unbeaten sequence in the English League – 49 Premiership matches (36 wins, 13 draws) from May 7, 2003 until Oct 24, 2004 when beaten 2-0 away to Manchester Utd. The record previously belonged to **Nottm Forest** – 42 First Division matches (21 wins, 21 draws) from Nov 19, 1977 until beaten 2-0 at Liverpool on December 9, 1978.

Huddersfield set a new Football League record of 43 League 1 matches unbeaten from Jan 1, 2011 until Nov 28, 2011 when losing 2-0 at Charlton.

Best debuts: Ipswich won the First Division at their first attempt in 1961–62.

Peterborough in their first season in the Football League (1960–1) not only won the Fourth Division but set the all-time scoring record for the League of 134 goals. **Hereford** were promoted from the Fourth Division in their first League season, 1972–73.

Wycombe were promoted from the Third Division (via the play-offs) in their first League season, 1993–94. Stevenage were promoted from League 2 (via the play-offs) in their first League season, 2010–11. Crawley gained automatic promotion in their first season in 2011–12.

Record winning sequence in a season: 14 consecutive League victories (all in Second Division): **Manchester Utd** 1904–05, **Bristol City** 1905–06 and **Preston** 1950–51.

Best winning start to League season: 13 successive victories in Div 3 by **Reading**, season 1985–86.

Best starts in 'old' First Division: 11 consecutive victories by **Tottenham** in 1960–61; 10 by **Manchester Utd** in 1985–86. In 'new' First Division, 11 consecutive wins by **Newcastle** in 1992–93 and by **Fulham** in 2000–01.

Longest unbeaten sequence (all competitions): 40 by **Nottm Forest**, Mar–December 1978. It comprised 21 wins, 19 draws (in 29 League matches, 6 League Cup, 4 European Cup, 1 Charity Shield).

Longest unbeaten starts to League season: 38 matches (26 wins, 12 draws) in **Arsenal's** undefeated Premiership season, 2003–04; 29 matches – **Leeds**, Div 1 1973–74 (19 wins, 10 draws); **Liverpool**, Div 1 1987–88 (22 wins, 7 draws).

Most consecutive League matches unbeaten in a season: 38 **Arsenal** Premiership season 2003–04 (see above); 33 **Reading** (25 wins, 8 draws) 2005–06.

Longest winning sequence in Div 1: 13 matches by **Tottenham** – last two of season 1959–60, first 11 of 1960–61.

Longest winning one-season sequences in League Championship: 13 matches by **Preston**, 1891–92; **Sunderland**, also 1891–92; **Arsenal** 2001–02.

Longest unbeaten home League sequence in top division: 86 matches (62 wins, 24 draws) by **Chelsea** (Mar 2004– Oct 2008).

League's longest winning sequence with clean sheets: 9 matches by **Stockport** (Lge 2, 2006–07 season).

Premier League – best starts to season: **Arsenal**, 38 games, 2003–04; **Manchester City**, 14 games, 2011–12

Best winning start to Premiership season: 9 consecutive victories by **Chelsea** in 2005–06.

Premier League – most consecutive wins (two seasons): 14 by **Arsenal**, Feb-Aug, 2002. Single season: 13 by **Arsenal** (Feb-May, 2002).

Premier League – most consecutive home wins: 20 by **Manchester City** (last 5 season 2010–11, first 15 season 2011–12).

Most consecutive away League wins in top flight: 11 by **Chelsea** (3 at end 2007– 08 season, 8 in 2008– 9)

Premier League – longest unbeaten away run: 27 matches (W17, D10) by **Arsenal** (Apr 5, 2003–Sep 25, 2004).

Record home-win sequences: Bradford Park Avenue won 25 successive home games in Div 3 North – the last 18 in 1926–7 and the first 7 the following season. Longest run of home wins in the top division is 21 by **Liverpool** – the last 9 of 1971–72 and the first 12 of 1972–73.

British record for successive League wins: 25 by **Celtic** (Scottish Premier League), 2003–04.

WORST SEQUENCES

Derby experienced the longest run without a win in League history in season 2007–08 – 32 games from Sep 22 to the end of the campaign (25 lost, 7 drawn). They finished bottom by a 24-pt margin. The sequence increased to 36 matches (28 lost, 8 drawn) at the start of the following season.

Cambridge Utd had the previous worst of 31 in 1983–84 (21 lost, 10 drawn). They were bottom of Div 2.

Worst losing start to a League season : 12 consecutive defeats by **Manchester Utd** (Div 1), 1930–31.

Worst Premier League start: Swindon 15 matches without win (6 draws, 9 defeats), 1993–94.

Premier League – most consecutive defeats: 20 **Sunderland** last 15 matches, 2002–03, first five matches 2005–06.

Longest non-winning start to League season: 25 matches (4 draws, 21 defeats) by **Newport**, Div 4. Worst no-win League starts since then: 16 matches by **Burnley** (9 draws, 7 defeats in Div 2, 1979–80); 16 by **Hull** (10 draws, 6 defeats in Div 2, 1989–90); 16 by **Sheffield Utd** (4 draws, 12 defeats in Div 1, 1990–91).

Most League defeats in season: 34 by **Doncaster** (Div 3) 1997–98.

Fewest League wins in season: 1 by **Loughborough** (Div 2, season 1899–1900). They lost 27, drew 6, goals 18-100 and dropped out of the League. (See also Scottish section). 1 by **Derby** (Prem Lge, 2007–08). They lost 29, drew 8, goals 20-89.

Most consecutive League defeats in season: 18 by **Darwen** (Div 1, 1898–99); 17 by **Rochdale** (Div 3 North, 1931–32).

Fewest home League wins in season: 1 by **Loughborough** (Div 2, 1899–1900), **Notts Co** (Div 1, 1904–05), **Woolwich Arsenal** (Div 1, 1912–13), **Blackpool** (Div 1, 1966–67), **Rochdale** (Div 3, 1973–74), **Sunderland** (Prem Lge, 2005–06); **Derby** (Prem Lge, 2007–08).

Most home League defeats in season: 18 by **Cambridge Utd** (Div 3, 1984–85).

Away League defeats record: 24 in row by **Crewe** (Div 2) – all 15 in 1894–95 followed by 9 in 1895–96; by **Nelson** (Div 3 North) – 3 in Apr 1930 followed by all 21 in season 1930–31. They then dropped out of the League.

Biggest defeat in Champions' season: During **Newcastle's** title-winning season in 1908–09, they were beaten 9-1 at home by Sunderland on December 5.

WORST START BY EVENTUAL CHAMPIONS

Sunderland took only 2 points from their first 7 matches in season 1912–13 (2 draws, 5 defeats). They won 25 of the remaining 31 games to clinch their fifth League title.

DISMAL DERBY

Derby were relegated in season 2007–08 as the worst-ever team in the Premier League: fewest wins (1), fewest points (11); fewest goals (20), first club to go down in March (29th).

UNBEATEN LEAGUE SEASON

Only three clubs have completed an English League season unbeaten: **Preston** (22 matches in 1888–89, the League's first season), **Liverpool** (28 matches in Div 2, 1893–94) and **Arsenal** (38 matches in Premiership, 2003–04).

100 PER CENT HOME RECORDS

Six clubs have won every home League match in a season: Sunderland (13 matches)' in 1891–92 and four teams in the old Second Division: **Liverpool** (14) in 1893–94, **Bury** (15) in 1894–5, **Sheffield Wed** (17) in 1899–1900 and **Small Heath** (subsequently **Birmingham** (17) in 1902–03. The last club to do it, **Brentford**, won all 21 home games in Div 3 South in 1929–30. Rotherham just failed to equal that record in 1946–47. They won their first 20 home matches in Div 3 North, then drew the last 3-3 v Rochdale.

BEST HOME LEAGUE RECORDS IN TOP FLIGHT

Sunderland, 1891–92 (P13, W13); **Newcastle**, 1906–07 (P19, W18, D1); **Chelsea**, 2005–06 (P19, W18, D1); **Manchester Utd**, 2010–11 (P19, W18, D1); **Manchester City**, 2011–12 (P 19, W18, D1).

MOST CONSECUTIVE CLEAN SHEETS

Premier League – 14: **Manchester Utd** (2008– 09); **Football League** – 11: **Millwall** (Div 3 South 1925–26); **York** (Div 3 1973–74); **Reading** (Div 4, 1978–79).

WORST HOME RUNS

Most consecutive home League defeats: 14 **Rochdale** (Div 3 North) seasons 1931–32 and 1932–33; 10 **Birmingham** (Div 1) 1985–86; 9 **Darwen** (Div 2) 1897–98; 9 **Watford** (Div 2) 1971–72.

Between Nov 1958 and Oct 1959 **Portsmouth** drew 2 and lost 14 out of 16 consecutive home games.

West Ham did not win in the Premiership at Upton Park in season 2002–03 until the 13th home match on Jan 29.

MOST AWAY WINS IN SEASON

Doncaster won 18 of their 21 away League fixtures when winning Div 3 North in 1946–47.

AWAY WINS RECORD

Most consecutive away League wins: 11 **Chelsea** (Prem Lge) – 8 at start of 2008–09 after ending previous season with 3.

100 PER CENT HOME WINS ON ONE DAY

Div 1 – All 11 home teams won on Feb 13, 1926 and on Dec 10, 1955. **Div 2** – All 12 home teams won on Nov 26, 1988. **Div 3**, all 12 home teams won in the week-end programme of Oct 18–19, 1968.

NO HOME WINS IN DIV ON ONE DAY

Div 1 – 8 away wins, 3 draws in 11 matches on Sep 6, 1986. **Div 2** – 7 away wins, 4 draws in 11 matches on Dec 26, 1987. **Premier League** – 6 away wins, 5 draws in 11 matches on Dec 26, 1994.

The week-end **Premiership** programme on Dec 7–8–9, 1996 produced no home win in the ten games (4 aways, 6 draws). There was again no home victory (3 away wins, 7 draws) in the week-end **Premiership** fixtures on Sep 23–24, 2000.

MOST DRAWS IN A SEASON (FOOTBALL LEAGUE)

23 by **Norwich** (Div 1, 1978–79), **Exeter** (Div 4, 1986–87). **Cardiff** and **Hartlepool** (both Div 3, 1997–98). **Norwich** played 42 matches, the others 46.

MOST DRAWS IN PREMIER LEAGUE SEASON

18 (in 42 matches) by **Manchester City** (1993–94), **Sheffield Utd** (1993–94), **Southampton** (1994–95)

MOST DRAWS IN ONE DIV ON ONE DAY

On Sep 18, 1948 **nine** out of 11 First Division matches were drawn.

MOST DRAWS IN PREMIER DIV PROGRAMME

Over the week-ends of December 2–3–4, 1995, and Sep 23–24, 2000, **seven** out of the ten matches finished level.

FEWEST DRAWS IN SEASON

In 46 matches: 3 by **Reading** (Div 3 South, 1951–52); **Bradford PA** (Div 3 North, 1956–57); **Tranmere** (Div 4, 1984–85); **Southend** (Div 3, 2002–03); in 42 matches: 2 by **Reading** (Div 3 South, 1935–36); **Stockport** (Div 3 North, 1946–47); in 38 matches: 2 by **Sunderland** (Div 1, 1908–09).

HIGHEST-SCORING DRAWS IN LEAGUE

Leicester 6, **Arsenal** 6 (Div 1 Apr 21, 1930); **Charlton** 6, **Middlesbrough** 6 (Div 2. Oct 22, 1960)

Latest **6-6** draw in first-class football was between **Tranmere** and **Newcastle** in the Zenith Data Systems Cup 1st round on Oct 1, 1991. The score went from 3-3 at 90 minutes to 6-6 after extra time, and Tranmere won 3-2 on penalties. In Scotland: **Queen of the South** 6, **Falkirk** 6 (Div 1, Sep 20, 1947).

Most recent **5-5** draws in top division: **Southampton** v **Coventry** (Div 1, May 4, 1982); **QPR** v **Newcastle** (Div 1, Sep 22, 1984).

DRAWS RECORDS

Most consecutive drawn matches in Football League: 8 by Torquay (Div 3, 1969–70), **Middlesbrough** (Div 2, 1970–71), **Peterborough** (Div 4, 1971–72), **Birmingham** (Div 3 (1990–91), **Southampton** (Champ, 2005–06), **Chesterfield** (Lge 1, 2005–06), **Swansea** (Champ, 2008–09).

Longest sequence of draws by the same score: six 1-1 results by QPR in season 1957–58. Tranmere became the first club to play **five consecutive 0-0 League draws**, in season 1997–98.

IDENTICAL RECORDS

There is only **one instance** of two clubs in one division finishing a season with identical records. In 1907–08, **Blackburn** and **Woolwich Arsenal** were bracketed equal 14th in the First Division with these figures: P38, W12, D12, L14, Goals 51-63, Pts. 36.

The total of **1195 goals** scored in the Premier League in season 1993–94 was repeated in 1994–95.

DEAD LEVEL

Millwall's record in Division Two in season 1973–74 was P42, W14, D14, L14, F51, A51, Pts 42.

CHAMPIONS OF ALL DIVISIONS

Wolves, Burnley and **Preston** are the only clubs to have won titles in the old Divisions1, 2, 3 and 4. Wolves also won the Third Division North and the new Championship.

POINTS DEDUCTIONS

2000–01: Chesterfield 9 for breach of transfer regulations and falsifying gate receipts.

2002–03: Boston 4 for contractual irregularities.

2004–05: Wrexham, Cambridge Utd 10 for administration.

2005–06: Rotherham 10 for administration.

2006–07: Leeds, Boston 10 for administration; Bury 1 for unregistered player.

2007–08: Leeds 15 over insolvency rules; Bournemouth, Luton,Rotherham 10 for administration.

2008–09: Luton 20 for failing Insolvency rules, 10 over payments to agents; **Bournemouth, Rotherham** 17 for breaking administration rules; **Southampton,Stockport** 10 for administration – Southampton with effect from season 2009–10 **Crystal Palace** 1 for ineligible player.

2009–10: Portsmouth 9, **Crystal Palace** 10 for administration; Hartlepool 3 for ineligible player.

2010–11: Plymouth 10 for administration; Hereford 3, **Torquay** 1, each for ineligible player

2011–12: Portsmouth and Port Vale both 10 for administration.

Among previous points penalties imposed:

Nov 1990: **Arsenal** 2, **Manchester Utd** 1 following mass players' brawl at Old Trafford.

Dec 1996: **Brighton** 2 for pitch invasions by fans.

Jan 1997: **Middlesbrough** 3 for refusing to play Premiership match at Blackburn because of injuries and illness.

Jun 1994: **Tottenham** 12 (reduced to 6) and banned from following season's FA Cup for making illegal payments to players. On appeal, points deduction annulled and club re-instated in Cup.

NIGHTMARE STARTS

Most goals conceded by a goalkeeper on League debut: 13 by **Steve Milton** when Halifax lost 13-0 at Stockport (Div 3 North) on Jan 6, 1934.

Post-war: 11 by Crewe's new goalkeeper **Dennis Murray** (Div 3 North) on Sep 29, 1951, when Lincoln won 11-1.

RELEGATION ODD SPOTS

None of the Barclays Premiership relegation places in season 2004–05 were decided until the last day (Sunday, May 15). **WBA** (bottom at kick-off) survived with a 2-0 home win against Portsmouth, and the three relegated clubs were **Southampton** (1-2 v Manchester Utd), **Norwich** (0-6 at Fulham) and **Crystal Palace** (2-2 at Charlton).

In season 1937–38, **Manchester City** were the highest-scoring team in the First Division with 80 goals (3 more than Champions Arsenal), but they finished in 21st place and were relegated – a year after winning the title. They scored more goals than they conceded (77).

That season produced the **closest relegation battle** in top-division history, with only 4 points spanning the bottom 11 clubs in Div 1. **WBA** went down with **Manchester City**.

Twelve years earlier, in 1925–26, City went down to Division 2 despite totalling 89 goals – still the most scored in any division by a relegated team. Manchester City also scored 31 FA Cup goals that season, but lost the Final 1-0 to Bolton Wanderers.

Cardiff were relegated from Div 1 in season 1928–29, despite conceding fewest goals in the division (59). They also scored fewest (43).

On their way to relegation from the First Division in season 1984–85, **Stoke** twice lost ten matches in a row.

RELEGATION TREBLES

Two Football League clubs have been relegated three seasons in succession. **Bristol City** fell from First Division to Fourth in 1980–1–2 and **Wolves** did the same in 1984–5–6.

OLDEST CLUBS

Oldest Association Football Club is **Sheffield FC** (formed in 1857). The oldest Football League clubs are **Notts Co**, 1862; **Nottm Forest**, 1865; and **Sheffield Wed**, 1866.

FOUR DIVISIONS

In **May, 1957**, the Football League decided to re-group the two sections of the Third Division into Third and Fourth Divisions in **season 1958–59**.

The Football League was reduced to three divisions on the formation of the Premier League in **1992**.

In season 2004–05, under new sponsors Coca-Cola, the titles of First, Second and Third Divisions were changed to League Championship, League One and League Two.

THREE UP – THREE DOWN

The Football League annual general meeting of Jun 1973 agreed to adopt the promotion and relegation system of three up and three down.

The **new system** came into effect in **season 1973–74** and applied only to the first three divisions; four clubs were still relegated from the Third and four promoted from the Fourth.

It was the first change in the promotion and relegation system for the top two divisions in 81 years.

MOST LEAGUE APPEARANCES

Players with more than 700 English League apps (as at end of season 2011–12)
1005 Peter Shilton 1966–97 (286 Leicester, 110 Stoke, 202 Nottm Forest, 188

Southampton, 175 Derby, 34 Plymouth Argyle, 1 Bolton, 9 Leyton Orient).

931 Tony Ford 1975–2002 (423 Grimsby, 9 Sunderland, 112 Stoke, 114 WBA, 5 Bradford City, 76 Scunthorpe, 103 Mansfield, 89 Rochdale).

840 Graham Alexander 1991–2012 (159 Scunthorpe, 152 Luton, 372 Preston, 157 Burnley)

824 Terry Paine 1956–77 (713 Southampton, 111 Hereford).

795 Tommy Hutchison 1968–91 (165 Blackpool, 314 Coventry City, 46 Manchester City, 92 Burnley, 178 Swansea). In addition, 68 Scottish League apps for Alloa 1965–68, giving career League app total of 863.

790 Neil Redfearn 1982–2004 (35 Bolton, 100 Lincoln, 46 Doncaster, 57 Crystal Palace, 24 Watford, 62 Oldham, 292 Barnsley, 30 Charlton, 17 Bradford City, 22 Wigan, 42 Halifax, 54 Boston, 9 Rochdale).

782 Robbie James 1973–94 (484 Swansea, 48 Stoke, 87 QPR, 23 Leicester, 89 Bradford City, 51 Cardiff).

777 Alan Oakes 1959–84 (565 Manchester City, 211 Chester, 1 Port Vale).

773 Dave Beasant 1980–2003 (340 Wimbledon, 20 Newcastle, 6 Grimsby, 4 Wolves, 133 Chelsea, 88 Southampton, 139 Nottm F, 27 Portsmouth, 16 Brighton).

770 John Trollope 1960–80 (all for Swindon, record total for one club).

769 David James 1990–2012 (89 Watford, 214 Liverpool, 67 Aston Villa, 91 West Ham, 93 Manchester City, 134 Portsmouth, 81 Bristol City)

764 Jimmy Dickinson 1946–65 (all for Portsmouth).

761 Roy Sproson 1950–72 (all for Port Vale).

760 Mick Tait 1974–97 (64 Oxford Utd, 106 Carlisle, 33 Hull, 240 Portsmouth, 99 Reading, 79 Darlington, 139 Hartlepool Utd).

758 Billy Bonds 1964–88 (95 Charlton, 663 West Ham).

758 Ray Clemence 1966–88 (48 Scunthorpe, 470 Liverpool, 240 Tottenham).

757 Pat Jennings 1963–86 (48 Watford, 472 Tottenham, 237 Arsenal).

757 Frank Worthington 1966–88 (171 Huddersfield Town, 210 Leicester, 84 Bolton, 75 Birmingham, 32 Leeds, 19 Sunderland, 34 Southampton, 31 Brighton, 59 Tranmere, 23 Preston, 19 Stockport).

755 Wayne Allison 1986–2008 228 (84 Halifax, 7 Watford, 195 Bristol City, 103 Swindon, 76 Huddersfield, 102 Tranmere, 73 Sheffield Utd, 115 Chesterfield).

749 Ernie Moss 1968–88 (469 Chesterfield, 35 Peterborough, 57 Mansfield, 74 Port Vale, 11 Lincoln, 44 Doncaster, 26 Stockport, 23 Scarborough, 10 Rochdale).

746 Les Chapman 1966–88 (263 Oldham, 133 Huddersfield Town, 70 Stockport, 139 Bradford City, 88 Rochdale, 53 Preston).

744 Asa Hartford 1967–90 (214 WBA, 260 Manchester City, 3 Nottm Forest, 81 Everton, 28 Norwich, 81 Bolton, 45 Stockport, 7 Oldham, 25 Shrewsbury).

743 Alan Ball 1963–84 (146 Blackpool, 208 Everton, 177 Arsenal, 195 Southampton, 17 Bristol Rov.).

743 John Hollins 1963–84 (465 Chelsea, 151 QPR, 127 Arsenal).

743 Phil Parkes 1968–91 (52 Walsall, 344 QPR, 344 West Ham, 3 Ipswich).

737 Steve Bruce 1979–99 (205 Gillingham, 141 Norwich, 309 Manchester Utd 72 Birmingham, 10 Sheffield Utd).

734 Teddy Sheringham 1983–2007 (220 Millwall, 5 Aldershot, 42 Nottm Forest, 104 Manchester Utd, 236 Tottenham, 32 Portsmouth, 76 West Ham, 19 Colchester)

732 Mick Mills 1966–88 (591 Ipswich, 103 Southampton, 38 Stoke).

731 Ian Callaghan 1959–81 (640 Liverpool, 76 Swansea, 15 Crewe).

731 David Seaman 1982–2003 (91 Peterborough, 75 Birmingham, 141 QPR, 405 Arsenal, 19 Manchester City).

725 Steve Perryman 1969–90 (655 Tottenham, 17 Oxford Utd, 53 Brentford).

722 Martin Peters 1961–81 (302 West Ham, 189 Tottenham, 207 Norwich, 24 Sheffield Utd).

718 Mike Channon 1966–86 (511 Southampton, 72 Manchester City, 4 Newcastle, 9 Bristol Rov, 88 Norwich, 34 Portsmouth).

716	Ron Harris 1961–83 (655 Chelsea, 61 Brentford).
716	Mike Summerbee 1959–79 (218 Swindon, 357 Manchester City, 51 Burnley, 3 Blackpool, 87 Stockport).
714	Glenn Cockerill 1976–98 (186 Lincoln, 26 Swindon, 62 Sheffield Utd, 387 Southampton, 90 Leyton Orient, 40 Fulham, 23 Brentford).
705	Keith Curle 1981–2003 (32 Bristol Rov, 16 Torquay, 121 Bristol City, 40 Reading, 93 Wimbledon, 171 Manchester City, 150 Wolves, 57 Sheffield Utd, 11 Barnsley, 14 Mansfield.
705	Phil Neal 1968–89 (186 Northampton, 455 Liverpool, 64 Bolton).
705	John Wile 1968–86 (205 Peterborough, 500 WBA).
701	Neville Southall 1980–2000 (39 Bury, 578 Everton, 9 Port Vale, 9 Southend, 12 Stoke, 53 Torquay, 1 Bradford City).

- **Stanley Matthews** made 701 League apps 1932–65 (322 Stoke, 379 Blackpool), incl. 3 for Stoke at start of 1939–40 before season abandoned (war).
- Goalkeeper **John Burridge** made a total of 771 League appearances in a 28-season career in English and Scottish football (1968–96). He played 691 games for 15 English clubs (Workington, Blackpool, Aston Villa, Southend, Crystal Palace, QPR, Wolves, Derby, Sheffield Utd, Southampton, Newcastle, Scarborough, Lincoln, Manchester City and Darlington) and 80 for 5 Scottish clubs (Hibernian, Aberdeen, Dumbarton, Falkirk and Queen of the South).

LONGEST LEAGUE APPEARANCE SEQUENCE

Harold Bell, centre-half of Tranmere, was ever-present for the first nine post-war seasons (1946–55), achieving a League record of 401 consecutive matches. Counting FA Cup and other games, his run of successive appearances totalled 459.

The longest League appearance since Bell's was 394 appearances by goalkeeper **Dave Beasant** for Wimbledon, Newcastle and Chelsea. His nine-year run began on Aug 29, 1981 and was ended by a broken finger sustained in Chelsea's League Cup-tie against Portsmouth on Oct 31, 1990. Beasant's 394 consecutive League games comprised 304 for Wimbledon (1981–88), 20 for Newcastle (1988–89) and 70 for Chelsea (1989–90).

Phil Neal made 366 consecutive First Division appearances for Liverpool between December 1974 and Sep 1983, a remarkable sequence for an outfield player in top-division football.

MOST CONSECUTIVE PREMIER LEAGUE APPEARANCES

304 by goalkeeper **Brad Friedel** (152 Blackburn, 114 Aston Villa, 38 Tottenham) in 8 ever-present seaaons (2004–12).

EVER-PRESENT DEFENCE

The **entire defence** of Huddersfield played in all 42 Second Division matches in season 1952–53, namely, Bill Wheeler (goal), Ron Staniforth and Laurie Kelly (full-backs), Bill McGarry, Don McEvoy and Len Quested (half-backs). In addition, Vic Metcalfe played in all 42 League matches at outside-left.

FIRST SUBSTITUTE USED IN LEAGUE

Keith Peacock (Charlton), away to Bolton (Div 2) on Aug 21, 1965.

FROM PROMOTION TO CHAMPIONS

Clubs who have become Champions of England a year after winning promotion: **Liverpool** 1905, 1906; **Everton** 1931, 1932; **Tottenham** 1950, 1951; **Ipswich** 1961, 1962; **Nottm Forest** 1977, 1978. The first four were placed top in both seasons: Forest finished third and first.

PREMIERSHIP'S FIRST MULTI-NATIONAL LINE-UP

Chelsea made history on December 26, 1999 when starting their Premiership match at Southampton without a single British player in the side.

Fulham's Unique XI: In the Worthington Cup 3rd round at home to Bury on Nov 6, 2002, Fulham fielded 11 players of 11 different nationalities. Ten were full Internationals, with Lee Clark an England U–21 cap.

On Feb 14, 2005 **Arsenal** became the first English club to select an all-foreign match squad when Arsene Wenger named 16 non-British players at home to Crystal Palace (Premiership).

Fifteen nations were represented at Fratton Park on Dec 30, 2009 (Portsmouth 1 Arsenal 4) when, for the first time in Premier League history, not one Englishman started the match. The line-up comprised seven Frenchmen, two Algerians and one from each of 13 other countries.

Players from 22 nationalities (subs included) were involved in the Blackburn-WBA match at Ewood Park on Jan 23, 2011.

PREMIER LEAGUE'S FIRST ALL-ENGLAND LINE-UP

On Feb 27, 1999 Aston Villa (at home to Coventry) fielded the first all-English line up seen in the Premier League (starting 11 plus 3 subs).

THREE-NATION CHAMPIONS

Trevor Steven earned eight Championship medals in three countries: two with Everton (1985, 1987); five with Rangers (1990, 1991, 1993, 1994, 1995) and one with Marseille in 1992. **David Beckham** won a League title in three countries: with Manchester Utd six times (1996–97–99–2000–01–03), Real Madrid (2007) and LA Galaxy (2011).

LEEDS NO WIN AWAY

Leeds, in 1992–93, provided the first instance of a club failing to win an away League match as reigning Champions.

PIONEERS IN 1888 AND 1992

Three clubs among the twelve who formed the Football League in 1888 were also founder members of the Premier League: **Aston Villa, Blackburn** and **Everton**.

CHAMPIONS (MODERN) WITH TWO CLUBS – PLAYERS

Francis Lee (Manchester City 1968, Derby 1975); **Ray Kennedy** (Arsenal 1971, Liverpool 1979, 1980, 1982); **Archie Gemmill** (Derby 1972, 1975, Nottm Forest 1978); **John McGovern** (Derby 1972, Nottm Forest 1978) **Larry Lloyd** (Liverpool 1973, Nottm Forest 1978); **Peter Withe** (Nottm Forest 1978, Aston Villa 1981); **John Lukic** (Arsenal 1989, Leeds 1992); **Kevin Richardson** (Everton 1985, Arsenal 1989); **Eric Cantona** (Leeds 1992, Manchester Utd 1993, 1994, 1996, 1997); **David Batty** (Leeds 1992, Blackburn 1995); **Bobby Mimms** (Everton 1987, Blackburn 1995), **Henning Berg** (Blackburn 1995, Manchester Utd 1999, 2000); **Nicolas Anelka** (Arsenal 1998, Chelsea 2010); **Ashley Cole** (Arsenal 2002, 2004, Chelsea 2010); **Gael Clichy** (Arsenal 2004, Manchester City 2012); **Kolo Toure** (Arsenal 2004, Manchester City 2012); **Carlos Tevez** (Manchester Utd 2008, 2009, Manchester City 2012).

TITLE TURNABOUTS

In Jan 1996, **Newcastle** led the Premier League by 13 points. They finished runners-up to Manchester Utd

At Christmas 1997, **Arsenal** were 13 points behind leaders Manchester Utd and still 11 points behind at the beginning of Mar 1998. But a run of 10 wins took the title to Highbury.

On Mar 2, 2003, **Arsenal**, with 9 games left, went 8 points clear of Manchester Utd, who had a match in hand. United won the Championship by 5 points.

In Mar 2002, **Wolves** were in second (automatic promotion) place in Nationwide Div 1, 11 points ahead of WBA, who had 2 games in hand. They were overtaken by Albion on the run-in, finished third, then failed in the play-offs. A year later they won promotion to the Premiership via the play-offs.

CLUB CLOSURES

Four clubs have left the Football League in mid-season: **Leeds City** (expelled Oct 1919); **Wigan Borough** (Oct 1931, debts of £20,000); **Accrington Stanley** (Mar 1962, debts £62,000); **Aldershot** (Mar 1992, debts £1.2m). **Maidstone**, with debts of £650,000, closed Aug 1992, on the eve of the season.

FOUR-DIVISION MEN

In season 1986–87, goalkeeper **Eric Nixon**, became the first player to appear in **all four divisions** of the Football League **in one season**. He served two clubs in Div 1: Manchester City (5 League games) and Southampton (4); in Div 2 Bradford City (3); in Div 3 Carlisle (16); and in Div 4 Wolves (16). Total appearances: 44.

Harvey McCreadie, a teenage forward, played in four divisions over two seasons inside a calendar year – from Accrington (Div 3) to Luton (Div 1) in Jan 1960, to Div 2 with Luton later that season and to Wrexham (Div 4) in Nov.

Tony Cottee played in all four divisions in season 2000–01, for Leicester (Premiership), Norwich (Div 1), Barnet (Div 3, player-manager) and Millwall (Div 2).

FATHERS AND SONS

When player-manager **Ian** (39) and **Gary** (18) **Bowyer** appeared together in the **Hereford** side at Scunthorpe (Div 4, Apr 21, 1990), they provided the first instance of father and son playing in the same team in a Football League match for 39 years. Ian played as substitute, and Gary scored Hereford's injury-time equaliser in a 3-3 draw.

Alec (39) and **David** (17) **Herd** were the previous father-and-son duo in League football – for Stockport, 2-0 winners at Hartlepool (Div 3 North) on May 5, 1951.

When Preston won 2-1 at Bury in Div 3 on Jan 13, 1990, the opposing goalkeepers were brothers: **AlanKelly** (21) for Preston and **Gary** (23) for Bury. Their father, **Alan** (who kept goal for Preston in the 1964 FA Cup Final and won 47 Rep of Ireland caps) flew from America to watch the sons he taught to keep goal line up on opposite sides.

George Eastham Snr (manager) and son **George Eastham Jnr** were inside-forward partners for Ards in the Irish League in season 1954–55.

FATHER AND SON REFEREE PLAY-OFF FINALS

Father and son refereed two of the 2009 Play-off Finals. **Clive Oliver**, 46, took charge of Shrewsbury v Gillingham (Lge 2) and **Michael Oliver**, 26, refereed Millwall v Scunthorpe (Lge 1) the following day.

FATHER & SON BOTH CHAMPIONS

John Aston snr won a Championship medal with Manchester Utd in 1952 and **John Aston snr** did so with the club in 1967. **Ian Wright** won the Premier League title with Arsenal in 1998 and **Shaun Wright-Phillips** won with Chelsea in 2006.

FATHER & SON RIVAL MANAGERS

When **Bill Dodgin Snr** took Bristol Rov to Fulham for an FA Cup 1st Round tie in Nov 1970, the opposing manager was his son, **Bill Jnr.**

FATHER & SON ON OPPOSITE SIDES

It happened for the first time in FA Cup history (1st Qual Round on Sep 14, 1996) when 21-year-old **Nick Scaife** (Bishop Auckland) faced his father **Bobby** (41), who played for Pickering. Both were in midfield. Home side Bishops won 3-1.

THREE BROTHERS IN SAME SIDE

Southampton provided the first instance for 65 years of three brothers appearing together in a Div 1 side when **Danny Wallace** (24) and his 19-year-old twin brothers **Rodney** and **Ray** played against Sheffield Wed on Oct 22, 1988. In all, they made 25 appearances together for Southampton until Sep 1989.

A previous instance in Div 1 was provided by the Middlesbrough trio **William, John** and **George Carr** with 24 League appearances together from Jan 1920 to Oct 1923.

The **Tonner** brothers, **Sam, James** and **Jack**, played together in 13 Second Division matches for Clapton Orient in season 1919–20.

Brothers **David, Donald** and **Robert Jack** played together in Plymouth's League side in 1920.

TWIN TEAM-MATES (see also Wallace twins above)

Twin brothers **David** and **Peter Jackson** played together for three League clubs (Wrexham, Bradford City and Tranmere) from 1954–62. The **Morgan** twins, **Ian** and **Roger**, played regularly in the QPR forward line from 1964–68. WBA's **Adam** and **James Chambers**, 18, were the first twins to represent England (v Cameroon in World Youth Championship, Apr 1999). They first played together in Albion's senior team, aged 19, in the League Cup 2nd. Round against Derby in Sep 2000. Brazilian identical twins **Rafael** and **Fabio Da Silva** (18) made first team debuts at full-back for Manchester Utd in season 2008– 09. Swedish twins **Martin** and **Marcus Olsson** played together for Blackburn in season 2011–12

SIR TOM DOES THE HONOURS

Sir Tom Finney, England and Preston legend, opened the Football League's new headquarters on their return to Preston on Feb 23, 1999. Preston had been the League's original base for 70 years before the move to Lytham St Annes in 1959.

SHORTENED MATCHES

The 0-0 score in the **Bradford City v Lincoln** Third Division fixture on May 11, 1985, abandoned through fire after 40 minutes, was subsequently confirmed as a result. It is the shortest officially- completed League match on record, and was the fourth of only five instances in Football League history of the score of an unfinished match being allowed to stand.

The other occasions: **Middlesbrough 4, Oldham 1** (Div 1, Apr 3, 1915), abandoned after 55 minutes when Oldham defender Billy Cook refused to leave the field after being sent off; **Barrow 7, Gillingham 0** (Div 4, Oct 9, 1961), abandoned after 75 minutes because of bad light, the match having started late because of Gillingham's delayed arrival.

A crucial **Manchester** derby (Div 1) was abandoned after 85 minutes, and the result stood, on Apr 27, 1974, when a pitch invasion at Old Trafford followed the only goal, scored for City by Denis Law, which relegated United, Law's former club.

The only instance of a first-class match in England being abandoned **'through shortage of players'** occurred in the First Division at Bramall Lane on Mar 16, 2002. Referee Eddie Wolstenholme halted play after 82 minutes because **Sheffield Utd** were reduced to 6 players against **WBA**. They had had 3 men sent off (goalkeeper and 2 substitutes), and with all 3 substitutes used and 2 players injured, were left with fewer than the required minimum of 7 on the field. Promotion contenders WBA were leading 3-0, and the League ordered the result to stand.

The last 60 seconds of **Birmingham v Stoke** (Div 3, 1-1, on Feb 29, 1992) were played behind locked doors. The ground had been cleared after a pitch invasion.

A First Division fixture, **Sheffield Wed v Aston Villa** (Nov 26, 1898), was abandoned through bad light after 79 mins with Wednesday leading 3-1. The Football League ruled that the match should be completed, and the remaining 10.5 minutes were played four months later (Mar 13, 1899), when Wednesday added another goal to make the result 4-1.

FA CUP RECORDS

(See also Goalscoring section)

CHIEF WINNERS

11 Manchester Utd; **10** Arsenal; **8** Tottenham; **7** Aston Villa, Chelsea, Liverpool; **6** Blackburn, Newcastle

Three times in succession: The Wanderers (1876–7–8) and Blackburn (1884–5–6).

Trophy handed back: The FA Cup became the Wanderers' absolute property in 1878, but they handed it back to the Association on condition that it was not to be won outright by any club.

In successive years by professional clubs: Blackburn (1890 and 1891); Newcastle (1951 and 1952); Tottenham (1961 and 1962); Tottenham (1981 and 1982); Arsenal (2002 and 2003); Chelsea (2009–10).

Record Final-tie score: Bury 6, Derby 0 (1903).

Most FA Cup Final wins at Wembley: Manchester Utd 9, Arsenal 7, Chelsea 6, Tottenham 6, Liverpool 5, Newcastle 5.

SECOND DIVISION WINNERS

Notts Co (1894), **Wolves** (1908), **Barnsley** (1912), **WBA** (1931), **Sunderland** (1973), **Southampton** (1976), **West Ham** (1980). When **Tottenham** won the Cup in 1901 they were a Southern League club.

'OUTSIDE' SEMI-FINALISTS

Wycombe, in 2001, became the eighth team from outside the top two divisions to reach the semi-finals, following **Millwall** (1937), **Port Vale** (1954), **York** (1955), **Norwich** (1959), **Crystal Palace** (1976), **Plymouth** (1984) and **Chesterfield** (1997). None reached the Final.

FOURTH DIVISION QUARTER-FINALISTS

Oxford Utd (1964), **Colchester** (1971), **Bradford City** (1976), **Cambridge Utd** (1990).

FOURTH ROUND – NO REPLAYS

No replays were necessary in the 16 fourth round ties in January 2008 (7 home wins, 9 away). This had not happened for 51 years, since 8 home and 8 away wins in season 1956–57.

FOUR TROPHIES

The latest FA Cup, first presented at Wembley in 1992, is a replica of the one it replaced, which had been in existence since 1911. 'It was falling apart and was not going to last much longer,' said the FA.

The new trophy is the fourth FA Cup. These were its predecessors:

1895: First stolen from shop in Birmingham while held by Aston Villa. Never seen again.

1910: Second presented to Lord Kinnaird on completing 21 years as FA president. This trophy was bought by Birmingham chairman David Gold at Christie's (London) for £420,000 in May 2005 and presented to the National Football Museum at Preston.

1992: Third 'gracefully retired' after 80 years' service (1911–91).

There are three FA Cups currently in existence. The retired model is still used for promotional work. The present trophy stays with the winners until the following March. A third, identical Cup is secreted in the FA vaults as cover against loss of the existing trophy.

FINALISTS RELEGATED

Five clubs have reached the FA Cup Final in a season of relegation and all lost at Wembley: **Manchester City** 1926, **Leicester** 1969, **Brighton** 1983, **Middlesbrough** 1997; **Portsmouth** 2010.

FA CUP SHOCKS DOWN THE YEARS

(2011 = season 2010–11; rounds shown in brackets; R=replay)

1922 (1)	Everton	0	Crystal Palace	6	**1988 (F)**	Wimbledon	1	Liverpool	0
1933 (3)	Walsall	2	Arsenal	0	**1989 (3)**	Sutton	2	Coventry	1
1939 (F)	Portsmouth	4	Wolves	1	**1990 (2)**	Whitley Bay	2	Preston	0
1948 (3)	Arsenal	0	Bradford PA	1	**1991 (3)**	WBA	2	Woking	4
1948 (3)	Colchester	1	Huddersfield	0	**1992 (1)**	Fulham	0	Hayes	2
1949 (4)	Yeovil	2	Sunderland	1	**1992 (1)**	Telford	2	Stoke	1R

1954 (4)	Arsenal	1	Norwich	2	1992 (3)	Wrexham	2	Arsenal	1
1955 (5)	York	2	Tottenham	1	1993 (1)	Cardiff	2	Bath	3
1956 (2)	Derby	1	Boston	6	1993 (3)	Liverpool	0	Bolton	2R
1957 (4)	Wolves	0	Bournemouth	1	1994 (3)	Birmingham	1	Kidderminster	2
1957 (5)	Bournemouth	3	Tottenham	1	1994 (3)	Liverpool	0	Bristol City	1R
1958 (4)	Newcastle	1	Scunthorpe	3	1994 (4)	Arsenal	1	Bolton	3R
1959 (3)	Norwich	3	Man Utd	0	2001 (1)	Port Vale	1	Canvey Is	2R
1959 (3)	Worcester	2	Liverpool	1	2001 (1)	Nuneaton	1	Stoke	0R
1961 (3)	Chelsea	1	Crewe	2	2001 (4)	Wycombe	2	Wolves	1
1964 (3)	Aldershot	2	Aston Villa	1R	2001 (4)	Everton	0	Tranmere	3
1964 (3)	Newcastle	1	Bedford	2	2002 (1)	Wigan	0	Canvey Island	1
1965 (4)	Peterborough	2	Arsenal	1	2002 (2)	Canvey Is	1	Northampton	0
1967 (3)	Swindon	3	West Ham	0R	2002 (3)	Cardiff	2	Leeds	1
1967 (4)	Man Utd	1	Norwich	2	2003 (1)	QPR	1	Vauxhall Mot	1R
1971 (5)	Colchester	3	Leeds	2	*(Vauxhall won 4-3 on pens)*				
1972 (3)	Hereford	2	Newcastle	1R	2003 (3)	Shrewsbury	2	Everton	1
1973 (F)	Sunderland	1	Leeds	0	2005 (3)	Oldham	1	Man City	0
1975 (3)	Burnley	0	Wimbledon	1	2006 (3)	Fulham	1	Leyton Orient	2
1978 (4)	Wrexham	4	Newcastle	1R	2008 (2)	Chasetown	1	Port Vale	0R
1978 (4)	Stoke	2	Blyth	3	2008 (2)	Notts Co	0	Havant	1
1980 (3)	Chelsea	0	Wigan	1	2008 (3)	Havant	4	Swansea	2R
1980 (3)	Harlow	1	Leicester	0R	2008 (5)	Liverpool	1	Barnsley	2
1980 (3)	Halifax	1	Man City	0	2008 (6)	Barnsley	1	Chelsea	0
1981 (4)	Exeter	3	Leicester	1R	2009 (1)	Histon	1	Swindon	0
1981 (5)	Exeter	4	Newcastle	0R	2009 (2)	Histon	1	Leeds	0
1984 (3)	Bournemouth	2	Man Utd	0	2010 (3)	Man Utd	0	Leeds	1
1985 (3)	Orient	2	WBA	1	2010 (4)	Liverpool	1	Reading	2R
1985 (4)	York	1	Arsenal	0	2010 (4)	Wigan	0	Notts Co	2R
1985 (4)	Wimbledon	3	Nottm Forest	0R	2011 (1)	Rochdale	2	FC United	3
1986 (3)	Peterborough	1	Leeds	0	2011 (3)	Stevenage	3	Newcastle	1
1986 (3)	Birmingham	1	Altrincham	2	2011 (3)	Sunderland	1	Notts Co	2
1987 (1)	Chorley	3	Wolves0 (at Bolton)		2011 (3)	Sunderland	1	Notts Co	2

YEOVIL TOP GIANT-KILLERS

Yeovil's victories over Colchester and Blackpool in season 2000–01 gave them a total of 20 FA Cup wins against League opponents. They set another non-League record by reaching the third round 13 times.

This was Yeovil's triumphant (non-League) Cup record against League clubs: 1924–25 Bournemouth 3-2; 1934–35 Crystal Palace 3-0, Exeter 4-1; 1938–39 Brighton 2-1; 1948–49 Bury 3-1, Sunderland 2-1; 1958–59 Southend 1-0; 1960–61 Walsall 1-0; 1963–64 Southend 1-0, Crystal Palace 3-1; 1970–71 Bournemouth 1-0; 1972–73 Brentford 2-1; 1987–88 Cambridge Utd 1-0; 1991–92 Walsall 1-0; 1992–93 Torquay 5-2, Hereford 2-1; 1993–94 Fulham 1-0; 1998–9 Northampton 2-0; 2000–01 Colchester 5-1, Blackpool 1-0.

NON-LEAGUE BEST

Since League football began in 1888, three non-League clubs have reached the FA Cup Final. **Sheffield Wed** (Football Alliance) were runners-up in 1890, as were **Southampton** (Southern League) in 1900 and 1902. **Tottenham** won the Cup as a Southern League team in 1901.

Otherwise, the furthest progress by non-League clubs has been to the 5th round on 6 occasions: **Colchester** 1948, **Yeovil** 1949, **Blyth Spartans** 1978, **Telford** 1985, **Kidderminster** 1994, Crawley 2011.

Greatest number of non-League sides to reach the **3rd round** is **8** in 2009: **Barrow, Blyth, Eastwood, Forest Green, Histon, Kettering, Kidderminster and Torquay.**

Most to reach **Round 4: 3** in 1957 (**Rhyl, New Brighton, Peterborough**) and 1975 (**Leatherhead, Stafford** and **Wimbledon**).

Five non-League clubs reaching **round 3** in 2001 was a Conference record. They were **Chester, Yeovil, Dagenham, Morecambe** and **Kingstonian**.

In season 2002–3, Team Bath became the first University-based side to reach the FA Cup 1st Round since **Oxford University** (Finalists in 1880).

NON-LEAGUE 'LAST TIMES'

Last time no non-League club reached round 3: 1951. Last time only one did so: 1969 (**Kettering**).

TOP-DIVISION SCALPS

Victories in FA Cup by non-League clubs over top-division teams since 1900 include: 1900–1 (Final, replay), **Tottenham** 3, Sheffield Utd 1 (Tottenham then in Southern League); 1919–20 **Cardiff** 2, Oldham 0, and Sheffield Wed 0, **Darlington** 2; 1923–24 **Corinthians** 1, Blackburn 0; 1947–48 **Colchester** 1, Huddersfield 0; 1948–9 **Yeovil** 2, Sunderland 1; 1971–2 **Hereford** 2, Newcastle 1; 1974–75 Burnley 0, **Wimbledon** 1; 1985–86 Birmingham 1, **Altrincham** 2; 1988–89 **Sutton** 2, Coventry 1.

MOST WINNING MEDALS

Ashley Cole has won the trophy seven times, with (Arsenal 2002–3–5) and Chelsea (2007–9–10–12). **The Hon Arthur Kinnaird** (The Wanderers and Old Etonians), **Charles Wollaston** (The Wanderers) and **Jimmy Forrest** (Blackburn) each earned five winners' medals. Kinnaird, later president of the FA, played in nine of the first 12 FA Cup Finals, and was on the winning side three times for The Wanderers, in 1873 (captain), 1877, 1878 (captain), and twice as captain of Old Etonians (1879, 1882).

MANAGERS' MEDALS BACKDATED

In 2010, the FA agreed to award Cup Final medals to all living managers who took their teams to the Final before 1996 (when medals were first given to Wembley team bosses). Lawrie McMenemy had campaigned for the award since Southampton's victory in 1976.

MOST WINNERS' MEDALS AT WEMBLEY

4 – **Mark Hughes** (3 for Manchester Utd, 1 for Chelsea), **Ashley Cole** (all Chelsea).

3 – **Dick Pym** (3 clean sheets in Finals), **Bob Haworth, Jimmy Seddon, Harry Nuttall, Billy Butler** (all Bolton); **David Jack** (2 Bolton, 1 Arsenal); **Bob Cowell, Jack Milburn, Bobby Mitchell** (all Newcastle); **Dave Mackay** (Tottenham); **Frank Stapleton** (1 Arsenal, 2 Manchester Utd); **Bryan Robson** (3 times winning captain), **Arthur Albiston, Gary Pallister** (all Manchester Utd); **Bruce Grobbelaar, Steve Nicol, Ian Rush** (all Liverpool); **Roy Keane, Peter Schmeichel, Ryan Giggs** (all Manchester Utd); **Dennis Wise** (1 Wimbledon, 2 Chelsea).

Arsenal's **David Seaman** and **Ray Parlour** have each earned 4 winners' medals (2 at Wembley, 2 at Cardiff) as have Manchester Utd's **Roy Keane** and **Ryan Giggs** (3 at Wembley, 1 at Cardiff).

MOST WEMBLEY FINALS

Nine players appeared in five FA Cup Finals at Wembley, replays excluded:

● Joe Hulme (Arsenal: 1927 lost, 1930 won, 1932 lost, 1936 won; Huddersfield: 1938 lost).

● Johnny Giles (Manchester Utd: 1963 won; Leeds: 1965 lost, 1970 drew at Wembley, lost replay at Old Trafford, 1972 won, 1973 lost).

● Pat Rice (all for Arsenal: 1971 won, 1972 lost, 1978 lost, 1979 won, 1980 lost).

● Frank Stapleton (Arsenal: 1978 lost, 1979 won, 1980 lost; Manchester Utd; 1983 won, 1985 won).

● Ray Clemence (Liverpool: 1971 lost, 1974 won, 1977 lost; Tottenham: 1982 won, 1987 lost).

- Mark Hughes (Manchester Utd: 1985 won, 1990 won, 1994 won, 1995 lost; Chelsea: 1997 won).
- John Barnes (Watford: 1984 lost; Liverpool: 1988 lost, 1989 won, 1996 lost; Newcastle: 1998 sub, lost): – first player to lose Wembley FA Cup Finals with three different clubs.
- Roy Keane (Nottm Forest: 1991 lost; Manchester Utd: 1994 won, 1995 lost, 1996 won, 1999 won).
- Ryan Giggs (Manchester Utd: 1994 won, 1995 lost, 1996 won, 1999 won, 2007 lost).
- Clemence, Hughes and Stapleton also played in a replay, making six actual FA Cup Final appearances for each of them.
- Glenn Hoddle also made six appearances at Wembley: 5 for Tottenham (incl. 2 replays), in 1981 won, 1982 won and 1987 lost, and 1 for Chelsea as sub in 1994 lost.
- Paul Bracewell played in four FA Cup Finals without being on the winning side – for Everton 1985, 1986, 1989, Sunderland 1992.

MOST WEMBLEY/CARDIFF FINAL APPEARANCES

8 by **Ashley Cole** (Arsenal: 2001 lost; 2002 won; 2003 won; 2005 won; Chelsea: 2007 won; 2009 won; 2010 won, 2012 won).

7 by **Roy Keane** (Nottm Forest: 1991 lost; Manchester Utd: 1994 won; 1995 lost; 1996 won; 1999 won; 2004 won; 2005 lost).

7 by **Ryan Giggs** (Manchester Utd): 1994 won; 1995 lost; 1996 won; 1999 won; 2004 won; 2005 lost; 2007 lost.

6 by **Paul Scholes** (Manchester Utd): 1995 lost; 1996 won; 1999 won; 2004 won; 2005 lost; 2007 lost.

5 by **David Seaman** and **Ray Parlour** (Arsenal): 1993 won; 1998 won; 2001 lost; 2002 won; 2003 won; **Dennis Wise** (Wimbledon 1988 won; Chelsea 1994 lost; 1997 won; 2000 won; Millwall 2004 lost); Patrick Vieira (Arsenal): 1998 won; 2001 lost; 2002 won; 2005 won; (Manchester City) 2011 won

BIGGEST FA CUP SCORE AT WEMBLEY

5-0 by Stoke v Bolton (semi-final, Apr 17, 2011.

WINNING GOALKEEPER-CAPTAINS

1988 **Dave Beasant** (Wimbledon); 2003 **David Seaman** (Arsenal).

MOST-WINNING MANAGER

Sir Alex Ferguson (Manchester Utd) 5 times (1990, 1994, 1996, 1999, 2004).

PLAYER-MANAGERS IN FINAL

Kenny Dalglish (Liverpool, 1986); **Glenn Hoddle** (Chelsea, 1994); **Dennis Wise** (Millwall, 2004).

DEBUTS IN FINAL

Alan Davies (Manchester Utd v Brighton, 1983); **Chris Baird** (Southampton v Arsenal, 2003); **Curtis Weston** (Millwall sub v Manchester Utd, 2004).

SEMI-FINALS AT WEMBLEY

1991 Tottenham 3 Arsenal 1; **1993** Sheffield Wed 2 Sheffield Utd 1, Arsenal 1 Tottenham 0; **1994** Chelsea 2 Luton 0, Manchester Utd 1 Oldham 1; **2000** Aston Villa beat Bolton 4-1 on pens (after 0-0), Chelsea 2 Newcastle 1; **2008** Portsmouth 1 WBA 0, Cardiff 1 Barnsley 0; **2009** Chelsea 2 Arsenal 1, Everton beat Manchester Utd 4-2 on pens (after 0-0); **2010** Chelsea 3 Aston Villa 0, Portsmouth 2 Tottenham 0; **2011** Manchester City 1 Manchester Utd 0, Stoke 5 Bolton 0; **2012** Liverpool 2 Everton 1, Chelsea 5 Tottenham 1.

CHELSEA'S FA CUP MILESTONES

Their victory over Liverpool in the 2012 Final set the following records:

Captain John Terry first player to lift the trophy four times for one club; Didier Drogba first to sacore in four Finals; Ashley Cole first to earn seven winner's medals (Arsenal 3, Chelsea 4); Roberto Di Matteo first to score for and manage the same winning club (player for Chelsea 1997, 2000, interim manager 2012).

Chelsea's four triumphs in six seasons (2007–12) the best winning sequence since Wanderers won five of the first seven competitions (1872–78) and Blackburn won five out of eight (1884–91).

FIRST ENTRANTS (1871–72)

Barnes, Civil Service, Crystal Palace, Clapham Rov, Donnington School (Spalding), Hampstead Heathens, Harrow Chequers, Hitchin, Maidenhead, Marlow, Queen's Park (Glasgow), Reigate Priory, Royal Engineers, Upton Park and Wanderers. Total 15.

FA CUP FIRSTS

Out of country: Cardiff, by defeating Arsenal 1-0 in the 1927 Final at Wembley, became the first and only club to take the FA Cup out of England.
All-English Winning XI: First club to win the FA Cup with all-English XI: Blackburn Olympic in 1883. Others since: WBA in 1888 and 1931, Bolton (1958), Manchester City (1969), West Ham (1964 and 1975).
Non-English Winning XI: Liverpool in 1986 (Mark Lawrenson, born Preston, was a Rep of Ireland player).
Won both Cups: Old Carthusians won the FA Cup in 1881 and the FA Amateur Cup in 1894 and 1897. **Wimbledon** won Amateur Cup in 1963, FA Cup in 1988.

MOST GAMES NEEDED TO WIN

Barnsley played a record 12 matches (20 hours' football) to win the FA Cup in season 1911–12. All six replays (one in round 1, three in round 4 and one in each of semi-final and Final) were brought about by goalless draws.
Arsenal played 11 FA Cup games when winning the trophy in 1979. Five of them were in the 3rd round against Sheffield Wed.

LONGEST TIES

6 matches: (11 hours): Alvechurch v Oxford City (4th qual round, 1971–72). Alvechurch won 1-0.
5 matches: (9 hours, 22 mins – record for competition proper): Stoke v Bury (3rd round, 1954–55). Stoke won 3-2.
5 matches: Chelsea v Burnley (4th round, 1955–56). Chelsea won 2-0.
5 matches: Hull v Darlington (2nd round, 1960–61). Hull won 3-0.
5 matches: Arsenal v Sheffield Wed (3rd round, 1978–79). Arsenal won 2-0.
Other marathons (qualifying comp, all 5 matches, 9 hours): Barrow v Gillingham (last qual round, 1924–25) – winners Barrow; Leyton v Ilford (3rd qual round, 1924–25) – winners Leyton; Falmouth v Bideford (3rd qual round, 1973–74) – winners Bideford.
End of Cup Final replays: The FA decided that, with effect from 1999, there would be no Cup Final replays. In the event of a draw after extra-time, the match would be decided on penalties. This happened for the first time in 2005, when Arsenal beat Manchester Utd 5-4 on penalties after a 0-0 draw. A year later, Liverpool beat West Ham 3-1 on penalties after a 3-3 draw.
FA Cup marathons ended in season 1991–92, when the penalty shoot-out was introduced to decide ties still level after one replay and extra-time.
In 1932–33 **Brighton** (Div 3 South) played 11 FA Cup games, including replays, and scored 43 goals, without getting past round 5. They forgot to claim exemption and had to play from 1st qual round.

LONGEST ROUND

The longest round in FA Cup history was the **3rd round** in **1962–63**. It took 66 days to complete, lasting from Jan 5 to Mar 11, and included 261 postponements because of bad weather.

LONGEST UNBEATEN RUN

23 matches by **Blackburn** In winning the Cup in three consecutive years (1884–5–6), they won 21 ties (one in a replay), and their first Cup defeat in four seasons was in a first round replay of the next competition.

RE-STAGED TIES

Sixth round, Mar 9, 1974: Newcastle 4, Nottm Forest 3. Match declared void by FA and ordered to be replayed following a pitch invasion after Newcastle had a player sent off. Forest claimed the hold-up caused the game to change its pattern. The tie went to two further matches at Goodison Park (0–0, then 1–0 to Newcastle).

Third round, Jan 5, 1985: Burton 1, Leicester 6 (at Derby). Burton goalkeeper Paul Evans was hit on the head by a missile thrown from the crowd and continued in a daze. The FA ordered the tie to be played again, behind closed doors at Coventry (Leicester won 1–0).

First round replay, Nov 25, 1992: Peterborough 9 (Tony Phillliskirk 5), Kingstonian 1. Match expunged from records because, at 3–0 after 57 mins, Kingstonian were reduced to ten men when goalkeeper Adrian Blake was concussed by a 50 pence coin thrown from the crowd. The tie was re-staged on the same ground behind closed doors (Peterborough won 1–0).

Fifth round: Within an hour of holders Arsenal beating Sheffield Utd 2-1 at Highbury on Feb 13, 1999, the FA took the unprecedented step of declaring the match void because an unwritten rule of sportsmanship had been broken. With United's Lee Morris lying injured, their goalkeeper Alan Kelly kicked the ball into touch. Play resumed with Arsenal's Ray Parlour throwing it in the direction of Kelly, but Nwankwo Kanu took possession and centred for Marc Overmars to score the 'winning' goal. After four minutes of protests by manager Steve Bruce and his players, referee Peter Jones confirmed the goal. Both managers absolved Kanu of cheating but Arsenal's Arsene Wenger offered to replay the match. With the FA immediately approving, it was re-staged at Highbury ten days later (ticket prices halved) and Arsenal again won 2-1.

PRIZE FUND

The makeover of the FA Cup competition took off in 2001–02 with the introduction of round-by-round prize-money.

FA CUP FOLLIES

1999–2000 The FA broke with tradition by deciding the 3rd round be moved from its regular Jan date and staged before Christmas. Criticism was strong, gates poor and the 3rd round in 2000–01 reverted to the New Year. By allowing the holders Manchester Utd to withdraw from the 1999–2000 competition in order to play in FIFA's inaugural World Club Championship in Brazil in Jan, the FA were left with an odd number of clubs in the 3rd round. Their solution was a 'lucky losers' draw among clubs knocked out in round 2. Darlington, beaten at Gillingham, won it to re-enter the competition, then lost 2-1 away to Aston Villa.

HAT-TRICKS IN FINAL

There have been three in the history of the competition: **Billy Townley** (Blackburn, 1890), **Jimmy Logan** (Notts Co, 1894) and **Stan Mortensen** (Blackpool, 1953).

MOST APPEARANCES

88 by **Ian Callaghan** (79 for Liverpool, 7 for Swansea City, 2 for Crewe); **87** by **John Barnes** (31 for Watford, 51 for Liverpool, 5 for Newcastle); **86** by **Stanley Matthews** (37 for Stoke, 49 for Blackpool); **84** by **Bobby Charlton** (80 for Manchester Utd, 4 for Preston); **84** by **Pat Jennings** (3 for Watford, 43 for Tottenham, 38 for Arsenal); **84** by **Peter Shilton** for seven clubs (30 for Leicester, 7 for Stoke, 18 for Nottm Forest, 17 for Southampton, 10 for Derby, 1 for Plymouth Argyle, 1 for Leyton Orient); **82** by **David Seaman** (5 for Peterborough, 5 for Birmingham, 17 for QPR, 54 for Arsenal, 1 for Manchester City).

THREE-CLUB FINALISTS

Five players have appeared in the FA Cup Final for three clubs: **Harold Halse** for Manchester Utd (1909), Aston Villa (1913) and Chelsea (1915); **Ernie Taylor** for Newcastle (1951), Blackpool (1953) and Manchester Utd (1958); **John Barnes** for Watford (1984), Liverpool (1988, 1989, 1996) and Newcastle (1998); **Dennis Wise** for Wimbledon (1988), Chelsea (1994, 1997, 2000), Millwall (2004); **David James** for Liverpool (1996), Aston Villa (2000) and Portsmouth (2008, 2010).

CUP MAN WITH TWO CLUBS IN SAME SEASON

Stan Crowther, who played for Aston Villa against Manchester Utd in the 1957 FA Cup Final, appeared for both Villa and United in the 1957–58 competition. United signed him directly after the Munich air crash and, in the circumstances, he was given dispensation to play for them in the Cup, including the Final.

CAPTAIN'S CUP DOUBLE

Martin Buchan is the only player to have captained Scottish and English FA Cup-winning teams – Aberdeen in 1970 and Manchester Utd in 1977.

MEDALS BEFORE AND AFTER

Two players appeared in FA Cup Final teams before and after the War: **Raich Carter** was twice a winner (Sunderland 1937, Derby 1946) and **Willie Fagan** twice on the losing side (Preston 1937, Liverpool 1950).

DELANEY'S COLLECTION

Scotland winger **Jimmy Delaney** uniquely earned Scottish, English, Northern Ireland and Republic of Ireland Cup medals. He was a winner with Celtic (1937), Manchester Utd (1948) and Derry City (1954) and a runner-up with Cork City (1956).

STARS WHO MISSED OUT

Internationals who never won an FA Cup winner's medal include: Tommy Lawton, Tom Finney, Johnny Haynes, Gordon Banks, George Best, Terry Butcher, Peter Shilton, Martin Peters, Nobby Stiles, Alan Ball, Malcolm Macdonald, Alan Shearer, Matthew Le Tissier, Stuart Pearce, Des Walker, Phil Neal, Ledley King.

CUP WINNERS AT NO COST

Not one member of **Bolton's** 1958 FA Cup-winning team cost the club a transfer fee. Each joined the club for a £10 signing-on fee.

11-NATIONS LINE-UP

Liverpool fielded a team of 11 different nationalities in the FA Cup 3rd round at Yeovil on Jan 4, 2004.

HIGH-SCORING SEMI-FINALS

The **record team score** in FA Cup semi-finals is **6**: 1891–92 WBA 6, Nottm Forest 2; 1907–08 Newcastle 6, Fulham 0; 1933–34 Manchester City 6, Aston Villa 1.

Most goals in semi-finals (aggregate): 17 in 1892 (4 matches) and 1899 (5 matches). In modern times: 15 in 1958 (3 matches, including Manchester Utd 5, Fulham 3 – highest-scoring semi-final since last war); 16 in 1989–90 (Crystal Palace 4, Liverpool 3; Manchester Utd v Oldham 3-3, 2-1. **All 16 goals** in those three matches were scored by **different players**.

Stoke's win against Bolton at Wembley in 2011 was the first 5-0 semi-final result since Wolves beat Grimsby at Old Trafford in 1939.

Last hat-trick in an FA Cup semi-final was scored by **Alex Dawson** for Manchester Utd in 5-3 replay win against Fulham at Highbury in 1958.

SEMI-FINAL VENUES

Villa Park has staged more such matches (55 including replays) than any other ground. Next is Hillsborough (33).

ONE IN A HUNDRED

The 2008 semi-finals included only one top-division club, Portsmouth, for the first time in 100 years – since Newcastle in 1908.

FOUR SPECIAL AWAYS

For the only time in FA Cup history, **all four quarter-finals** in season 1986–87 were won by the away team.

DRAWS RECORD

In season 1985–86, **seven** of the eight 5th round ties went to replays – a record for that stage of the competition.

LUCK OF THE DRAW

In the FA Cup on Jan 11, 1947, eight of **London's** ten Football League clubs involved in the 3rd round were drawn at home (including Chelsea v Arsenal). Only Crystal Palace played outside the capital (at Newcastle).

In the 3rd round in Jan 1992, Charlton were the only London club drawn at home (against Barnet), but the venue of the Farnborough v West Ham tie was reversed on police instruction. So Upton Park staged Cup ties on successive days, with West Ham at home on the Saturday and Charlton (who shared the ground) on Sunday.

Arsenal were drawn away in every round on the way to reaching the Finals of 1971 and 1972.
Manchester Utd won the Cup in 1990 without playing once at home.

The 1999 finalists, **Manchester Utd** and **Newcastle**, were both drawn at home every time in Rounds 3–6.

On their way to the semi-finals of both domestic Cup competitions in season 2002–03, **Sheffield Utd** were drawn at home ten times out of ten and won all ten matches – six in the League's Worthington Cup and four in the FA Cup.

ALL TOP-DIVISION VICTIMS

The only instance of an FA Cup-winning club meeting top-division opponents in every round was provided by Manchester Utd in 1947–48. They beat Aston Villa, Liverpool, Charlton, Preston, then Derby in the semi-final and Blackpool in the Final.

In contrast, these clubs have reached the Final without playing top-division opponents on the way: West Ham (1923), Bolton (1926), Blackpool (1948), Bolton (1953), Millwall (2004).

WON CUP WITHOUT CONCEDING GOAL

1873 **The Wanderers** (1 match; as holders, exempt until Final); 1889 **Preston** (5 matches); 1903 **Bury** (5 matches). In 1966 **Everton** reached Final without conceding a goal (7 matches), then beat Sheffield Wed 3-2 at Wembley.

HOME ADVANTAGE

For the first time in FA Cup history, all eight ties in the 1992–93 5th round were won (no replays) by the **clubs drawn at home**. Only other instance of eight home wins at the last 16 stage was in 1889–90, in what was then the 2nd round.

NORTH-EAST WIPE-OUT

For the first time in 54 years, since the 4th round in Jan, 1957, the North-East's 'big three' were knocked out on the same date, Jan 8, 2011 (3rd round). All lost to lower-division opponents – Newcastle 3-1 at Stevenage, Sunderland 2-1 at home to Notts County and Middlesbrough 2-1 at Burton.

FEWEST TOP-DIVISION CLUBS IN LAST 16 (5th ROUND)

5 in 1958; **6** in 1927, 1970, 1982; **7** in 1994, 2003; **8** in 2002, 2004.

SIXTH-ROUND ELITE

For the first time in FA Cup 6th round history, dating from 1926 when the format of the competition changed, all **eight quarter-finalists** in 1995–96 were from the top division.

SEMI-FINAL – DOUBLE DERBIES

There have been three instances of both FA Cup semi-finals in the same year being local derbies: **1950** Liverpool beat Everton 2-0 (Maine Road), Arsenal beat Chelsea 1-0 after 2-2 draw (both at Tottenham); **1993** Arsenal beat Tottenham 1-0 (Wembley), Sheffield Wed beat Sheffield Utd 2-1 (Wembley); **2012** Liverpool beat Everton 2-1 (Wembley), Chelsea beat Tottenham 5-1 (Wembley).

TOP CLUB DISTINCTION

Since the Football League began in 1888, there has never been an FA Cup Final in which **neither club** represented the top division.

CLUBS THROWN OUT

Bury expelled (Dec 2006) for fielding an ineligible player in 3-1 2nd rd replay win at Chester. **Droylsden** expelled for fielding a suspended player in 2-1 2nd rd replay win at home to Chesterfield (Dec 2008).

SPURS OUT – AND IN

Tottenham were banned, pre-season, from the 1994–95 competition because of financial irregularities, but were re-admitted on appeal and reached the semi-finals.

FATHER & SON FA CUP WINNERS

Peter Boyle (Sheffield Utd 1899, 1902) and **Tommy Boyle** (Sheffield Utd 1925); **Harry Johnson Snr** (Sheffield Utd 1899, 1902) and **Harry Johnson Jnr** (Sheffield Utd 1925); **Jimmy Dunn Snr** (Everton 1933) and **Jimmy Dunn Jnr** (Wolves 1949); **Alec Herd** (Manchester City 1934) and **David Herd** (Manchester Utd 1963); **Frank Lampard Snr** (West Ham 1975, 1980) and **Frank Lampard Jnr** (Chelsea 2007, 2009, 2010, 2012).

BROTHERS IN FA CUP FINAL TEAMS (Modern Times)

1950 **Denis** and **Leslie Compton** (Arsenal); 1952 **George** and **Ted Robledo** (Newcastle); 1967 **Ron** and **Allan Harris** (Chelsea); 1977 **Jimmy** and **Brian Greenhoff** (Manchester Utd); 1996 and 1999 **Gary** and **Phil Neville** (Manchester Utd).

FA CUP SPONSORS

Littlewoods Pools became the first sponsors of the FA Cup in season 1994–95 in a £14m, 4-year deal. French insurance giants **AXA** took over (season 1998–99) in a sponsorship worth £25m over 4 years. German energy company **E.ON** agreed a 4-year deal worth £32m from season 2006–07 and extended it for a year to 2011. American beer company **Budweiser** began a three-year sponsorship worth £24m in season 2011–12.

FIRST GOALKEEPER-SUBSTITUTE IN FINAL

Paul Jones (Southampton), who replaced injured Antti Niemi against Arsenal in 2003.

LEAGUE CUP RECORDS
(See also Goalscoring section)

Highest scores: West Ham 10-0 v Bury (2nd round, 2nd leg 1983-84; agg 12-1); Liverpool 10-0 v Fulham (2nd round, 1st leg 1986-87; agg 13-2).

Most League Cup goals (career): 49 Geoff Hurst (43 West Ham, 6 Stoke, 1960-75); 49 Ian Rush (48 Liverpool, 1 Newcastle, 1981-98).

Highest scorer (season): 12 Clive Allen (Tottenham 1986-87 in 9 apps).

Most goals in match: 6 Frank Bunn (Oldham v Scarborough, 3rd round, 1989-90).

Most winners' medals: 5 Ian Rush (Liverpool).

Most appearances in Final: 6 Kenny Dalglish (Liverpool 1978-87), Ian Rush (Liverpool 1981-95).

League Cup sponsors: Milk Cup 1981-86, Littlewoods Cup 1987-90, Rumbelows Cup 1991-92, Coca-Cola Cup 1993-98. Worthington Cup 1999-2003, Carling Cup 2003-12; Capital One Cup from season 2012-13.

Up for the cup, then down: In 2011, Birmingham became only the second club to win a major trophy (the Carling Cup) and be relegated from the top division. It previously happened to Norwich in 1985 when they went down from the old First Division after winning the Milk Cup.

Liverpool's League Cup records: Winners a record 8 times. **Ian Rush** only player to win 5 times. Rush also first to play in 8 winning teams in Cup Finals **at Wembley**, all with Liverpool (FA Cup 1986-89-92; League Cup 1981-82-83-84-95).

Britain's first under-cover Cup Final: Worthington Cup Final between Blackburn and Tottenham at Cardiff's Millennium Stadium on Sunday, Feb 24, 2002. With rain forecast, the retractable roof was closed on the morning of the match.

DISCIPLINE

SENDINGS-OFF

Season 2003-4 set an **all-time record** of 504 players sent off in English domestic football competitions. There were 58 in the Premiership, 390 Nationwide League, 28 FA Cup (excluding non-League dismissals), 22 League Cup, 2 in Nationwide play-offs, 4 in LDV Vans Trophy.

Most sendings-off in Premier League programme (10 matches): 9 (8 Sat, 1 Sun, Oct 31-Nov 1, 2009)

The 58 Premiership red cards was 13 fewer than the record English **top-division** total of 71 in 2002-03. **Bolton** were the only club in the English divisions without a player sent off in any first-team competition that season.

Worst day for dismissals in English football was Boxing Day, 2007, with **20 red cards** (5 Premier League and 15 Coca-Cola League). Three players, Chelsea's Ashley Cole and Ricardo Carvalho and Aston Villa's Zat Knight were sent off in a 4-4 draw at Stamford Bridge. Luton had three men dismissed in their game at Bristol Rov, but still managed a 1-1 draw.

Previous worst day was Dec 13, 2003, with **19 red cards** (2 Premiership and the 17 Nationwide League).

In the entire first season of post-war League football (1946-47) only 12 players were sent off, followed by 14 in 1949-50, and the total League dismissals for the first nine seasons after the War was 104.

The worst pre-War total was 28 in each of seasons 1921-22 and 1922-23.

ENGLAND SENDINGS-OFF

In a total of 13 England dismissals, David Beckham and Wayne Rooney have been red-carded twice. Beckham is the only England captain to be sent off and Robert Green the only goalkeeper.

| Jun 5, 1968 | Alan Mullery | v Yugoslavia (Florence, Euro Champ) |
| Jun 6, 1973 | Alan Ball | v Poland (Chorzow, World Cup qual) |

Jun 12, 1977	**Trevor Cherry**	v Argentina (Buenos Aires, friendly)
Jun 6, 1986	**Ray Wilkins**	v Morocco (Monterrey, World Cup Finals)
Jun 30, 1998	**David Beckham**	v Argentina (St. Etienne, World Cup Finals)
Sep 5, 1998	**Paul Ince**	v Sweden (Stockholm, Euro Champ qual)
Jun 5, 1999	**Paul Scholes**	v Sweden (Wembley, Euro Champ qual)
Sep 8, 1999	**David Batty**	v Poland (Warsaw, Euro Champ qual)
Oct 16, 2002	**Alan Smith**	v Macedonia (Southampton, Euro Champ qual)
Oct 8, 2005	**David Beckham**	v Austria (Old Trafford, World Cup qual)
Jul 1, 2006	**Wayne Rooney**	v Portugal (Gelsenkirchen, World Cup Finals)
Oct 10, 2009	**Robert Green**	v Ukraine (Dnipropetrovsk, World Cup qual)
Oct 7, 2011	**Wayne Rooney**	v Montenegro (Podgorica, Euro Champ qual)

Other countries: Most recent sendings-off of players representing other Home Countries:
N Ireland – Adam Thompson (Carling Cup v Rep of Ireland, Dublin, May 24, 2011).
Scotland – Steven Whittaker (European Champ qual v Spain, Hampden Park, Oct 12, 2010).
Wales – Chris Gunter (European Champ qual v Bulgaria, Cardiff, Oct 8, 2010).
Rep of Ireland– Keith Andrews (European Champ v Italy, Poznan, Jun 18, 2012).
England dismissals at other levels:
U-23: Stan Anderson (v Bulgaria, Sofia, May 19, 1957); **Alan Ball** (v Austria, Vienna, Jun 2, 1965); **Kevin Keegan** (v E Germany, Magdeburg, Jun 1, 1972); **Steve Perryman** (v Portugal, Lisbon, Nov 19, 1974).
U-21: Sammy Lee (v Hungary, Keszthely, Jun 5, 1981); **Mark Hateley** (v Scotland, Hampden Park, Apr 19, 1982); **Paul Elliott** (v Denmark, Maine Road, Manchester, Mar 26, 1986); **Tony Cottee** (v W Germany, Ludenscheid, Sep 8, 1987); **Julian Dicks** (v Mexico, Toulon, France, Jun. 12, 1988); **Jason Dodd** (v Mexico, Toulon, May 29, 1991; 3 Mexico players also sent off in that match); **Matthew Jackson** (v France, Toulon, May 28, 1992); **Robbie Fowler** (v Austria, Kafkenberg, Oct 11, 1994); **Alan Thompson** (v Portugal, Oporto, Sep 2, 1995); **Terry Cooke** (v Portugal, Toulon, May 30, 1996); **Ben Thatcher** (v Italy, Rieti, Oct 10, 1997); **John Curtis** (v Greece, Heraklion, Nov 13, 1997); **Jody Morris** (v Luxembourg, Grevenmacher, Oct 13, 1998); **Stephen Wright** (v Germany, Derby, Oct 6, 2000); **Alan Smith** (v Finland, Valkeakoski, Oct 10, 2000); **Luke Young** and **John Terry** (v Greece, Athens, Jun. 5, 2001); **Shola Ameobi** (v Portugal, Rio Maior, Mar 28, 2003); **Jermaine Pennant** (v Croatia, Upton Park, Aug 19, 2003); **Glen Johnson** (v Turkey, Istanbul, Oct 10, 2003); **Nigel Reo-Coker** (v Azerbaijan, Baku, Oct 12, 2004); **Glen Johnson** (v Spain, Henares, Nov 16, 2004); **Steven Taylor** (v Germany, Leverkusen, Oct 10, 2006); **Tom Huddlestone** (v Serbia & Montenegro, Nijmegen, Jun 17, 2007); **Tom Huddlestone** (v Wales, Villa Park, Oct 14, 2008); **Michael Mancienne** (v Finland, Halmstad, Jun 15, 2009); **Fraizer Campbell** (v Sweden, Gothenburg, Jun 26, 2009); Ben Mee (v Italy, Empoli, Feb 8, 2011).
England 'B' (1): **Neil Webb** (v Algeria, Algiers, Dec 11, 1990).

MOST DISMISSALS IN INTERNATIONAL MATCHES

19 (10 Chile, 9 Uruguay), Jun 25, 1975; **6** (2 Mexico, 4 Argentina), 1956; **6** (5 Ecuador, 1 Uruguay), Jan 4, 1977 (4 Ecuadorians sent off in 78th min, match abandoned, 1-1); **5** (Holland 3, Brazil 2), Jun 6, 1999 in Goianio, Brazil.

INTERNATIONAL STOPPED THROUGH DEPLETED SIDE

Portugal v Angola (5-1), friendly international in Lisbon on Nov 14, 2001, abandoned (68 mins) because Angola were down to 6 players (4 sent off, 1 carried off, no substitutes left).

MOST 'CARDS' IN WORLD CUP FINALS MATCH

20 in Portugal v Holland quarter-final, Nuremberg, Jun 25, 2006 (9 yellow, 2 red, Portugal; 7 yellow, 2 red, Holland).

FIVE OFF IN ONE MATCH

For the first time since League football began in 1888, five players were sent off in one match (two

Chesterfield, three Plymouth) in Div 2 at Saltergate on **Feb 22, 1997.** Four were dismissed (two from each side) in a goalmouth brawl in the last minute. Five were sent off on Dec 2, 1997 (4 Bristol Rov, 1 Wigan) in Div 2 match at Wigan, four in the 45th minute. The third instance occurred at Exeter on **Nov 23, 2002** in Div 3 (three Exeter, two Cambridge United) all in the last minute. On Mar 27, 2012 (Lge 2) three Bradford players and two from Crawley were shown red cards in the dressing rooms after a brawl at the final whistle at Valley Parade.

Matches with **four** Football League club players being sent off in one match:

Jan 8, 1955: Crewe v Bradford City (Div 3 North), two players from each side.

Dec 13, 1986: Sheffield Utd (1 player) v Portsmouth (3) in Div 2.

Aug 18, 1987: Port Vale v Northampton (Littlewoods Cup 1st Round, 1st Leg), two players from each side.

Dec 12, 1987: Brentford v Mansfield (Div 3), two players from each side.

Sep 6, 1992: First instance in British first-class football of four players from one side being sent off in one match. Hereford's seven survivors, away to Northampton (Div 3), held out for a 1-1 draw.

Mar 1, 1977: Norwich v Huddersfield (Div 1), two from each side.

Oct 4, 1977: Shrewsbury (1 player), Rotherham (3) in Div 3.

Aug 22, 1998: Gillingham v Bristol Rov (Div 2), two from each side, all after injury-time brawl.

Mar 16, 2001: Bristol City v Millwall (Div 2), two from each side.

Aug 17, 2002: Lincoln (1 player), Carlisle (3) in Div 3.

Aug 26, 2002: Wycombe v QPR (Div 2), two from each side.

Nov 1, 2005: Burnley (1 player) v Millwall (3) in Championship.

Nov 24, 2007: Swindon v Bristol Rov (Lge 1), two from each side.

Mar 4, 2008: Hull v Burnley (Champ) two from each side.

Four Stranraer players were sent off away to Airdrie (Scottish Div 1) on Dec 3, 1994, and that Scottish record was equalled when four Hearts men were ordered off away to Rangers (Prem Div) on Sep 14, 1996. Albion had four players sent off (3 in last 8 mins) away to Queen's Park (Scottish Div 3) on Aug 23, 1997.

In the **Island Games** in Guernsey (Jul 2003), five players (all from Rhodes) were sent off against Guernsey for violent conduct and the match was abandoned by referee Wendy Toms.

Most dismissals one team, one match: Five players of America Tres Rios in first ten minutes after disputed goal by opponents Itaperuna in Brazilian cup match in Rio de Janeiro on Nov 23, 1991. Tie then abandoned and awarded to Itaperuna.

Eight dismissals in one match: Four on each side in South American Super Cup quarter-final (Gremio, Brazil v Penarol, Uruguay) in Oct 1993.

Five dismissals in one season – Dave Caldwell (2 with Chesterfield, 3 with Torquay) in 1987–88.

First instance of four dismissals in Scottish match: three Rangers players (all English – Terry Hurlock, Mark Walters, Mark Hateley) and Celtic's Peter Grant in Scottish Cup quarter-final at Parkhead on Mar 17, 1991 (Celtic won 2-0).

Four players (3 Hamilton, 1 Airdrie) were sent off in Scottish Div 1 match on Oct 30, 1993.

Four players (3 Ayr, 1 Stranraer) were sent off in Scottish Div 1 match on Aug 27, 1994.

In Scottish Cup first round replays on Dec 16, 1996, there were two instances of three players of one side sent off: Albion Rov (away to Forfar) and Huntly (away to Clyde).

FASTEST SENDINGS-OFF

World record – 10 sec: Giuseppe Lorenzo (Bologna) for striking opponent in Italian League match v Parma, Dec 9, 1990. Goalkeeper **Preston Edwards** (Ebbsfleet) for bringing down opponent and conceding penalty in Blue Square Premier League South match v Farnborough, Feb 5, 2011.

World record (non-professional) – 3 sec: David Pratt (Chippenham) at Bashley (British Gas Southern Premier League, Dec 27, 2008).

Domestic – 13 sec: Kevin Pressman (Sheffield Wed goalkeeper at Wolves, Div 1, Sunday, Aug 14, 2000); **15 sec: Simon Rea** (Peterborough at Cardiff, Div 2, Nov 2, 2002). **19 secs: Mark Smith** (Crewe goalkeeper at Darlington, Div 3, Mar 12, 1994). **Premier League – 72 sec: Tim Flowers** (Blackburn goalkeeper v Leeds Utd, Feb 1, 1995).

In **World Cup – 55 sec: Jose Batista** (Uruguay v Scotland at Neza, Mexico, Jun 13, 1986).
In **European competition – 90 sec: Sergei Dirkach** (Dynamo Moscow v Ghent UEFA Cup 3rd round, 2nd leg, Dec 11, 1991).
Fastest FA Cup dismissal – 52 sec: Ian Culverhouse (Swindon defender, deliberate hand-ball on goal-line, away to Everton, 3rd Round, Sunday Jan 5, 1997).
Fastest League Cup dismissal – 33 sec: Jason Crowe (Arsenal substitute v Birmingham, 3rd Round, Oct 14, 1997). Also fastest sending off on debut.
Fastest Sending-off of substitute – 0 sec: Walter Boyd (Swansea City) for striking opponent before ball in play after he went on (83 mins) at home to Darlington, Div 3, Nov 23, 1999.
15 secs: Keith Gillespie (Sheffield Utd) for striking an opponent at Reading (Premiership), Jan 20, 2007. **90 sec: Andreas Johansson** (Wigan), without kicking a ball, for shirt-pulling (penalty) away to Arsenal (Premiership), May 7, 2006.

MOST SENDINGS-OFF IN CAREER

21 **Willie Johnston** , 1964–82 (Rangers 7, WBA 6, Vancouver Whitecaps 4, Hearts 3, Scotland 1)
21 **Roy McDonough**, 1980–95 (13 in Football League – Birmingham, Walsall, Chelsea, Colchester, Southend, Exeter, Cambridge Utd plus 8 non-league)
13 **Steve Walsh** (Wigan, Leicester, Norwich, Coventry)
13 **Martin Keown** (Arsenal, Aston Villa, Everton)
13 **Alan Smith** (Leeds, Manchester Utd, Newcastle, England U–21, England)
12 **Dennis Wise** (Wimbledon, Chelsea, Leicester, Millwall)
12 **Vinnie Jones** (Wimbledon, Leeds, Sheffield Utd, Chelsea, QPR)
12 **Mark Dennis** (Birmingham, Southampton, QPR)
12 **Roy Keane** (Manchester Utd, Rep of Ireland)
10 **Patrick Vieira** (Arsenal)
10 **Paul Scholes** (Manchester Utd, England)
Most Premier League sendings-off: Patrick Vieira 9, Duncan Ferguson 8, Richard Dunne 8, Vinnie Jones 7, Roy Keane 7
● **Carlton Palmer** holds the unique record of having been sent off with each of his five Premiership clubs: Sheffield Wed, Leeds, Southampton, Nottm Forest and Coventry.

FA CUP FINAL SENDINGS-OFF

Kevin Moran (Manchester Utd) v Everton, Wembley, 1985; **Jose Antonio Reyes** (Arsenal) v Manchester Utd, Cardiff, 2005

WEMBLEY SENDINGS-OFF

Aug 1948	**Branko Stankovic** (Yugoslavia) v Sweden, Olympic Games
Jul 1966	**Antonio Rattin** (Argentina captain) v England, World cup quarter-final
Aug 1974	**Billy Bremner** (Leeds) and **Kevin Keegan** (Liverpool), Charity Shield
Mar 1977	**Gilbert Dresch** (Luxembourg) v England, World Cup
May 1985	**Kevin Moran** (Manchester Utd) v Everton, FA Cup Final
Apr 1993	**Lee Dixon** (Arsenal) v Tottenham, FA Cup semi-final
May 1993	**Peter Swan** (Port Vale) v WBA, Div 2 Play-off Final
Mar 1994	**Andrei Kanchelskis** (Manchester Utd) v Aston Villa, League Cup Final
May 1994	**Mike Wallace, Chris Beaumont** (Stockport) v Burnley, Div 2 Play-off Final
Jun 1995	**Tetsuji Hashiratani** (Japan) v England, Umbro Cup
May 1997	**Brian Statham** (Brentford) v Crewe, Div 2 Play-off Final
Apr 1998	**Capucho** (Portugal) v England, friendly
Nov 1998	**Ray Parlour** (Arsenal) and **Tony Vareilles** (Lens), Champions League
Mar 1999	**Justin Edinburgh** (Tottenham) v Leicester, League Cup Final
Jun 1999	**Paul Scholes** (England) v Sweden, European Championship qual
Feb 2000	**Clint Hill** (Tranmere) v Leicester, League Cup Final
Apr 2000	**Mark Delaney** (Aston Villa) v Bolton, FA Cup semi-final
May 2000	**Kevin Sharp** (Wigan) v Gillingham, Div 2 Play-off Final

Aug 2000	**Roy Keane** (Manchester Utd captain) v Chelsea, Charity Shield
May 2007	**Marc Tierney** (Shrewsbury) v Bristol Rov, Lge 2 Play-off Final
May 2007	**Malt Gill** (Exeter) v Morecambe, Conf Play-off Final
May 2009	**Jamie Ward** (Sheffield Utd) and **Lee Hendrie** (Sheffield Utd) v Burnley, Champ Play-off Final (Hendrie after final whistle)
May 2009	**Phil Bolland** (Cambridge Utd) v Torquay, Blue Square Prem Lge Play-off Final
May 2010	**Robin Hulbert** (Barrow) and **David Bridges** (Stevenage), FA Trophy Final
Apr 2011	**Paul Scholes** (Manchester Utd) v Manchester City, FA Cup semi-final
Apr 2011	**Toumani Diagouraga** (Brentford) v Carlisle, Johnstone's Paint Trophy Final

WEMBLEY'S SUSPENDED CAPTAINS

Suspension prevented four **club captains** playing at Wembley in modern finals, in successive years.

Three were in FA Cup Finals – **Glenn Roeder** (QPR, 1982), **Steve Foster** (Brighton, 1983), **Wilf Rostron** (Watford, 1984). Sunderland's **Shaun Elliott** was banned from the 1985 Milk Cup Final. Roeder was banned from QPR's 1982 Cup Final replay against Tottenham, and Foster was ruled out of the first match in Brighton's 1983 Final against Manchester Utd.

BOOKINGS RECORDS

Most players of one Football League club booked in one match is **TEN** – members of the Mansfield team away to Crystal Palace in FA Cup third round, Jan 1963.

Fastest bookings – 3 seconds after kick-off, **Vinnie Jones** (Chelsea, home to Sheffield Utd, FA Cup fifth round, Feb 15, 1992); 5 seconds after kick-off: **Vinnie Jones** (Sheffield Utd, away to Manchester City, Div 1, Jan 19, 1991). He was sent-off (54 mins) for second bookable offence.

FIGHTING TEAM-MATES

Charlton's **Mike Flanagan** and **Derek Hales** were sent off for fighting each other five minutes from end of FA Cup 3rd round tie at home to Southern League Maidstone on Jan 9, 1979.

Bradford City's **Andy Myers** and **Stuart McCall** had a fight during the 1-6 Premiership defeat at Leeds on Sunday, May 13, 2001.

On Sep 28, 1994 the Scottish FA suspended Hearts players **Graeme Hogg** and **Craig Levein** for ten matches for fighting each other in a pre-season 'friendly' v Raith.

Blackburn's England players **Graeme Le Saux** and **David Batty** clashed away to Spartak Moscow (Champions League) on Nov 22, 1995. Neither was sent off.

Newcastle United's England Internationals **Lee Bowyer** and **Kieron Dyer** were sent off for fighting each other at home to Aston Villa (Premiership on Apr 2, 2005).

Arsenal's **Emmanuel Adebayor** and **Nicklas Bendtner** clashed during the 5-1 Carling Cup semi-final 2nd leg defeat at Tottenham on Jan 22, 2008. Neither was sent off; each fined by their club.

Stoke's **Richardo Fuller** was sent off for slapping his captain, Andy Griffin, at West Ham in the Premier League on Dec 28, 2008

FOOTBALL'S FIRST BETTING SCANDAL

A Football League investigation into the First Division match which ended Manchester Utd 2, Liverpool 0 at Old Trafford on Good Friday, Apr 2, 1915 proved that the result had been 'squared' by certain players betting on the outcome. Four members of each team were suspended for life, but some of the bans were lifted when League football resumed in 1919 in recognition of the players' war service.

PLAYERS JAILED

Ten professional footballers found guilty of conspiracy to fraud by 'fixing' matches for betting purposes were given prison sentences at Nottingham Assizes on Jan 26, 1965.

Jimmy Gauld (Mansfield), described as the central figure, was given four years. Among the others sentenced, **Tony Kay** (Sheffield Wed, Everton & England), **Peter Swan** (Sheffield

Wed & England) and **David 'Bronco' Layne** (Sheffield Wed) were suspended from football for life by the FA.

DRUGS BANS

Abel Xavier (Middlesbrough) was the first Premiership player found to have taken a performance-enchancing drug. He was banned by UEFA for 18 months in Nov 2005 after testing positive for an anabolic steroid. The ban was reduced to a year in Jul 2006 by the Court of Arbitration for Sport. **Paddy Kenny** (Sheffield Utd goalkeeper) was suspended by an FA commission for 9 months from July, 2009 for failing a drugs test the previous May. Kolo Toure (Manchester City) received a 6-month ban in May 2011 for a doping offence. It was backdated to Mar 2.

LONG SUSPENSIONS

The longest suspension (8 months) in modern times for a player in British football was imposed on two Manchester Utd players. First was **Eric Cantona** following his attack on a spectator as he left the pitch after being sent off at Crystal Palace (Prem League) on Jan 25, 1995. The club immediately suspended him to the end of the season and fined him 2 weeks' wages (est £20,000). Then, on a disrepute charge, the FA fined him £10,000 (Feb 1995) and extended the ban to Sep 30 (which FIFA confirmed as world-wide). A subsequent 2-weeks' jail sentence on Cantona for assault was altered, on appeal, to 120 hours' community service, which took the form of coaching schoolboys in the Manchester area.

On **Dec 19, 2003** an FA Commission, held at Bolton, suspended **Rio Ferdinand** from football for 8 months (plus £50,000 fine) for failing to take a random drug test at the club's training ground on Sep 23. The ban operated from Jan 12, 2004.

Aug 1974: Kevin Keegan (Liverpool) and **Billy Bremner** (Leeds) both suspended for 10 matches and fined £500 after being sent off in FA Charity Shield at Wembley.

Jan 1988: Mark Dennis (QPR) given 8-match ban after 11th sending-off of his career.

Oct 1988: Paul Davis (Arsenal) banned for 9 matches for breaking the jaw of Southampton's Glenn Cockerill.

Oct 1998: Paolo Di Canio (Sheff Wed) banned for 11 matches and fined £10,000 for pushing referee Paul Alcock after being sent off at home to Arsenal (Prem), Sep 26.

Mar 2005: David Prutton (Southampton) banned for 10 matches (plus 1 red card) and fined £6,000 by FA for shoving referee Alan Wiley when sent off at home to Arsenal (Prem), Feb 26.

Sep 2008: Joey Barton (Newcastle) banned for 12 matches (6 suspended) and fined £25,000 by FA for training ground assault on former Manchester City team-mate **Ousmane Dabo**.

May 2012: Joey Barton (QPR) suspended for 12 matches and fined £75,000 for violent conduct when sent off against Manchester City on final day of Premier League season.

Seven-match ban: Frank Barson, 37-year-old Watford centre-half, sent off at home to Fulham (Div 3 South) on Sep 29, 1928, was suspended by the FA for the remainder of the season.

Twelve-month ban: Oldham full-back **Billy Cook** was given a 12-month suspension for refusing to leave the field when sent off at Middlesbrough (Div 1), on Apr 3, 1915. The referee abandoned the match with 35 minutes still to play, and the score (4-1 to Middlesbrough) was ordered to stand.

Long Scottish bans: Sep 1954: Willie Woodburn, Rangers and Scotland centre-half, suspended for rest of career after fifth sending-off in 6 years.

Billy McLafferty, Stenhousemuir striker, was banned (Apr 14) for 8 and a half months, to Jan 1, 1993, and fined £250 for failing to appear at a disciplinary hearing after being sent off against Arbroath on Feb 1.

Twelve-match ban: On May 12, 1994 Scottish FA suspended Rangers forward **Duncan Ferguson** for 12 matches for violent conduct v Raith on Apr 16. On Oct 11, 1995, Ferguson (then with Everton) sent to jail for 3 months for the assault (served 44 days); Feb 1, 1996 Scottish judge quashed 7 matches that remained of SFA ban on Ferguson.

On Sep 29, 2001 the SFA imposed a **17-match suspension** on Forfar's former Scottish international **Dave Bowman** for persistent foul and abusive language when sent off against Stranraer on Sep 22. As his misconduct continued, he was shown **5 red cards** by the referee.

On Apr 3, 2009, captain **Barry Ferguson** and goalkeeper **Allan McGregor** were banned for life from playing for Scotland for gestures towards photographers while on the bench for a World Cup qualifier against Iceland.

On Dec 20, 2011 Liverpool and Uruguay striker **Luis Suarez** was given an 8-match ban and fined £40,000 by the FA for making 'racially offensive comments' to Patrice Evra of Manchester Utd (Prem Lge, Oct 15)

TOP FINES

Clubs: £5,500,000 West Ham: Apr 2007, for breaches of regulations involving 'dishonesty and deceit' over Argentine signings Carlos Tevez and Javier Mascherano; **£1,500,000** (increased from original £600,000) Tottenham: Dec 1994, financial irregularities; **£875,000** QPR: May 2011 for breaching rules when signing Argentine Alejandro Faurlin; **£300,000** (reduced to £75,000 on appeal) Chelsea: Jun 2005, illegal approach to Arsenal's Ashley Cole; **£175,000** Arsenal: Oct 2003, players' brawl v Manchester Utd; **£150,000** Leeds: Mar 2000, players' brawl v Tottenham; **£150,000** Tottenham: Mar 2000, players brawl v Leeds; **£115,000** West Ham: Aug 25, 2009, crowd misconduct at Carling Cup; v Millwall; **£105,000** Chelsea: Jan 1991, irregular payments; **£100,000** Boston Utd: Jul 2002, contract irregularities; **£100,000** Arsenal and Chelsea: Mar 2007 for mass brawl after Carling Cup Final; **£100,000** (including suspended fine)Blackburn: Aug 2007, poor disciplinary record; **£62,000** Macclesfield: Dec 2005, funding of a stand at club's ground.

Players: £150,000 Roy Keane (Manchester Utd): Oct 2002, disrepute offence over autobiography; **£100,000** (reduced to £75,000 on appeal) Ashley Cole (Arsenal): Jun 2005, illegal approach by Chelsea; **£75,000** (plus 12-match ban) Joey Barton (QPR): May 2012, violent conduct v Manchester City; **£45,000** Patrick Vieira (Arsenal): Oct 1999, tunnel incidents v West Ham; **£40,000** Lauren (Arsenal): Oct 2003, players' fracas v Manchester Utd; **£32,000** Robbie Fowler (Liverpool): Apr 1999, simulating drug-taking and incident with Graeme Le Saux v Chelsea; **£30,000** Lee Bowyer (Newcastle): Apr 2005, fighting with team-mate Kieron Dyer v Aston Villa.

*In eight seasons with Arsenal (1996–2004) **Patrick Vieira** was fined a total of £122,000 by the FA for disciplinary offences.

Managers: £200,000 (reduced to £75,000 on appeal) Jose Mourinho (Chelsea): Jun 2005, illegal approach to Arsenal's Ashley Cole; **£33,000** and 3-match Euro touchline ban Arsene Wenger (Arsenal) for criticism of referee after Champions League defeat by AC Milan; **£30,000** Sir Alex Ferguson (Manchester Utd): Mar 2011 criticising referee Martin Atkinson v Chelsea; **£20,000** Graeme Souness (Newcastle): Jun 2005, criticising referee v Everton; **£20,000** Sir Alex Ferguson (Manchester Utd): Oct 2009, questioning referee's fitness; **£15,000** Graeme Souness (Blackburn): Oct 2002, sent off v Liverpool; **£15,000** Arsene Wenger (Arsenal): Dec 2004, comments about Manchester Utd's Ruud van Nistelrooy.

• Jonathan Barnett, Ashley Cole's agent was fined **£100,000** in Sep 2006 for his role in the 'tapping up' affair involving the player and Chelsea.

*£68,000 FA: May 2003, pitch invasions and racist chanting by fans during England v Turkey, Sunderland.

MANAGERS

INTERNATIONAL RECORDS

(As at start of season 2012–13)

	P	W	D	L	F	A
Roy Hodgson (England – appointed May 2012)	6	4	2	0	7	3
Craig Levein (Scotland – appointed Dec 2009)	19	9	3	7	25	25
Chris Coleman (Wales – appointed Jan 2012)	1	0	0	1	0	2

Michael O'Neil (Northern Ireland – appointed Oct 2011)	2	0	0	2	0	9I
Giovanni Trapattoni (Republic of Ireland – appointed May 2008)	48	20	17	11	62	46

FINAL RECORDS

Fabio Capello (England: Dec 2007–Feb 2012)	42	28	8	6	89	35
Gary Speed (Wales: Dec 2010–Nov 2011)	10	5	0	5	13	13
Nigel Worthington (Northern Ireland: May 2007–October 2011)	41	9	10	22	35	55

previous ENGLAND'S MANAGERS

		P	W	D	L
1946–62.	**Walter Winterbottom**	139	78	33	28
1963–74	**Sir Alf Ramsey**	113	69	27	17
1974	**Joe Mercer**, caretaker	7	3	3	1
1974–77	**Don Revie**	29	14	8	7
1977–82	**Ron Greenwood**	55	33	12	10
1982–90	**Bobby Robson**	95	47	30	18
1990–93	**Graham Taylor**	38	18	13	7
1994–96	**Terry Venables**	23	11	11	1
1996–99	**Glenn Hoddle**	28	17	6	5
1999	**Howard Wilkinson**, caretaker	1	0	0	1
1999–2000	**Kevin Keegan**	18	7	7	4
2000	**Howard Wilkinson**, caretaker	1	0	1	0
2000	**Peter Taylor**, caretaker	1	0	0	1
2001–6	**Sven–Goran Eriksson**	67	40	17	10
2006–7	**Steve McClaren**	18	9	4	5
2007–12	**Fabio Capello**	42	28	8	6

INTERNATIONAL MANAGER CHANGES

England: Walter Winterbottom 1946–62 (initially coach); **Alf Ramsey** (Feb 1963–May 1974); Joe Mercer (caretaker May 1974); **Don Revie** (Jul 1974–Jul 1977); **Ron Greenwood** (Aug 1977–Jul 1982); **Bobby Robson** (Jul 1982–Jul 1990); **Graham Taylor** (Jul 1990–Nov 1993); **Terry Venables**, coach (Jan 1994–Jun 1996); **Glenn Hoddle**, coach (Jun 1996–Feb 1999); **Howard Wilkinson** (caretaker Feb 1999); **Kevin Keegan coach** (Feb 1999–Oct 2000); **Howard Wilkinson** (caretaker Oct 2000); **Peter Taylor** (caretaker Nov 2000); **Sven–Goran Eriksson** (Jan 2001–Aug 2006); **Steve McClaren** (Aug 2006–Nov 2007); **Fabio Capello** (Dec 2007–Feb 2012); **Roy Hodgson** (since May 2012).

Scotland (modern): Bobby Brown (Feb 1967–Jul 1971); Tommy Docherty (Sep 1971–Dec 1972); **Willie Ormond** (Jan 1973–May 1977); **Ally MacLeod** (May 1977–Sep 1978); Jock Stein (Oct 1978–Sep 1985); Alex Ferguson (caretaker Oct 1985–Jun 1986); Andy Roxburgh, coach (Jul 1986–Sep 1993); Craig Brown (Sep 1993–Oct 2001); Berti Vogts (Feb 2002–Oct 2004); **Walter Smith** (Dec 2004–Jan 2007); **Alex McLeish** (Jan 2007–Nov 2007); **George Burley** (Jan 2008–Nov 2009); **Craig Levein** (since Dec 2009).

Northern Ireland (modern): Peter Doherty (1951–62); Bertie Peacock (1962–67); Billy Bingham (1967–Aug 1971); Terry Neill (Aug 1971–Mar 1975); Dave Clements (player-manager Mar 1975–1976); Danny Blanchflower (Jun 1976–Nov 1979); Billy Bingham (Feb 1980–Nov 1993); Bryan Hamilton Feb 1994–Feb 1998); Lawrie McMenemy (Feb 1998–Nov 1999); Sammy McIlroy (Jan 2000–Oct 2003); Lawrie Sanchez (Jan 2004–May 2007); Nigel Worthington (May 2007–Oct 2011); Michael O'Neill (since Oct 2011).

Wales (modern): Mike Smith (Jul 1974–Dec 1979); Mike England (Mar 1980–Feb 1988);

David Williams (caretaker Mar 1988); **Terry Yorath** (Apr 1988–Nov 1993); **John Toshack** (Mar 1994, one match); **Mike Smith** (Mar 1994–Jun 1995); **Bobby Gould** (Aug 1995–Jun 1999); **Mark Hughes** (Aug 1999 – Oct 2004); **John Toshack** (Nov 2004–Sep 2010); Brian Flynn (caretaker Sep–Dec 2010); **Gary Speed** (Dec 2010–Nov 2011); **Chris Coleman** (since Jan 2012).

Republic of Ireland (modern): Liam Tuohy (Sep 1971–Nov 1972); **Johnny Giles** (Oct 1973–Apr 1980, initially player–manager); **Eoin Hand** (Jun 1980–Nov 1985); **Jack Charlton** (Feb 1986–Dec 1995); **Mick McCarthy** (Feb 1996–Oct 2002); **Brian Kerr** (Jan 2003–Oct 2005); **Steve Staunton** (Jan 2006–Oct 2007); **Giovanni Trapattoni** (since May 2008).

WORLD CUP-WINNING MANAGERS

1930 Uruguay (Alberto Suppici); 1934 and 1938 Italy (Vittorio Pozzo); 1950 Uruguay (Juan Lopez Fontana); 1954 West Germany (Sepp Herberger); 1958 Brazil (Vicente Feola); 1962 Brazil (Aymore Moreira); 1966 England (Sir Alf Ramsey); 1970 Brazil (Mario Zagallo); 1974 West Germany (Helmut Schon); 1978 Argentina (Cesar Luis Menotti); 1982 Italy (Enzo Bearzot); 1986 Argentina (Carlos Bilardo); 1990 West Germany (Franz Beckenbauer); 1994 Brazil (Carlos Alberto Parreira); 1998 France (Aimee Etienne Jacquet); 2002 Brazil (Luiz Felipe Scolari); 2006 Italy (Marcello Lippi); 2010 Spain (Vicente Del Bosque).
Each of the 19 winning teams had a manager/coach of that country's nationality

FIRST BLACK ENGLAND MANAGER

Chris Ramsey, 36, in charge of England's U-20 squad for World Youth Championship in Nigeria, Apr 1999. He was Brighton's right-back in the 1983 FA Cup Final v Manchester Utd.

FIRST BLACK MANAGER IN FOOTBALL LEAGUE

Tony Collins (Rochdale 1960–68).

YOUNGEST LEAGUE MANAGERS

Ivor Broadis, 23, appointed player-manager of Carlisle, Aug 1946; **Chris Brass**, 27, appointed player-manager of York, Jun 2003; **Terry Neill**, 28, appointed player manager of Hull, Jun 1970; **Graham Taylor**, 28, appointed manager of Lincoln, Dec 1972.

LONGEST-SERVING LEAGUE MANAGERS – ONE CLUB

Fred Everiss, secretary–manager of WBA for 46 years (1902–48); **George Ramsay**, secretary–manager of Aston Villa for 42 years (1884–1926); **John Addenbrooke**, Wolves, for 37 years (1885–1922). Since last war, **Sir Matt Busby**, in charge of Manchester Utd for 25 seasons (1945–69, 1970–71); **Dario Gradi** at Crewe for 26 years (1983–2007, 2009–11); **Jimmy Seed** at Charlton for 23 years (1933–56); **Sir Alex Ferguson** at Manchester Utd for 26 seasons (1986–2012); **Brian Clough** at Nottm Forest for 18 years (1975–93).

WARNOCK'S SEVEN PROMOTIONS

In his managerial career, **Neil Warnock** has won promotion seven times: 1987 Scarborough (won Conference); 1990 Notts Co (won Div 3 play-offs); 1991 Notts Co (won Div 2 play-offs); 1995 Huddersfield (won Div 2 play-offs); 1996 Plymouth (won Div 3 play-offs); 2006 Sheffield Utd (Champ runners-up); 2011 QPR (won Champ).

LAST ENGLISH MANAGER TO WIN CHAMPIONSHIP

Howard Wilkinson (Leeds), season 1991–92.

1,000-TIME MANAGERS

Only five have managed in more than **1,000 English League games**: Alec Stock, Brian Clough, Jim Smith, Graham Taylor and Dario Gradi.
Sir Matt Busby, Dave Bassett, Lennie Lawrence, Alan Buckley, Denis Smith, Joe Royle, Sir Alex Ferguson, Ron Atkinson, Brian Horton, Neil Warnock, Harry Redknapp and Steve Coppell have each managed more than **1,000 matches in all first class competitions**.

SHORT-TERM MANAGERS

Departed

3 days	Bill Lambton (Scunthorpe)	Apr 1959
7 days	Tim Ward (Exeter)	Mar 1953
7 days	Kevin Cullis (Swansea City)	Feb 1996
10 days	Dave Cowling (Doncaster)	Oct 1997
10 days	Peter Cormack (Cowdenbeath)	Dec 2000
13 days	Johnny Cochrane (Reading)	Apr 1939
13 days	Micky Adams (Swansea City)	Oct 1997
16 days	Jimmy McIlroy (Bolton)	Nov 1970
19 days	Martin Allen (Barnet)	Apr 2011
20 days	Paul Went (Leyton Orient)	Oct 1981
27 days	Malcolm Crosby (Oxford Utd)	Jan 1998
28 days	Tommy Docherty (QPR)	Dec 1968
28 days	Paul Hart (QPR)	Jan 2010
32 days	Steve Coppell (Manchester City)	Nov 1996
34 days	Niall Quinn (Sunderland)	Aug 2006
36 days	Steve Claridge (Millwall)	Jul 2005
39 days	Paul Gascoigne (Kettering)	Dec 2005
41 days	Steve Wicks (Lincoln)	Oct 1995
41 days	Les Reed (Charlton)	Dec 2006
44 days	Brian Clough (Leeds)	Sep 1974
44 days	Jock Stein (Leeds)	Oct 1978
48 days	John Toshack (Wales)	Mar 1994
48 days	David Platt (Sampdoria coach)	Feb 1999
49 days	Brian Little (Wolves)	Oct 1986
49 days	Terry Fenwick (Northampton)	Feb 2003
61 days	Bill McGarry (Wolves)	Nov 1985

- In May 1984, Crystal Palace named **Dave Bassett** as manager, but he changed his mind four days later, without signing the contract, and returned to Wimbledon.
- In May 2007, **Leroy Rosenior** was reportedly appointed manager of Torquay after relegation and sacked ten minutes later when the club came under new ownership.
- **Brian Laws** lost his job at Scunthorpe on Mar 25, 2004 and was reinstated three weeks later.
- In an angry outburst after a play-off defeat in May 1992, Barnet chairman Stan Flashman sacked manager **Barry Fry** and re-instated him a day later.

EARLY-SEASON MANAGER SACKINGS

2011: Jim Jefferies (Hearts) 9 days; **2010** Kevin Blackwell (Sheffield Utd) 8 days; **2009** Bryan Gunn (Norwich) 6 days; **2007:** Neil McDonald (Carlisle) 2 days; Martin Allen (Leicester) 18 days; **2004:** Paul Sturrock (Southampton) 9 days; **2004:** Sir Bobby Robson (Newcastle) 16 days; **2003:** Glenn Roeder (West Ham) 15 days; **2000:** Alan Buckley (Grimsby) 10 days; **1997:** Kerry Dixon (Doncaster) 12 days; **1996:** Sammy Chung (Doncaster) on morning of season's opening League match; **1996:** Alan Ball (Manchester City) 12 days; **1994:** Kenny Hibbitt (Walsall) and Kenny Swain (Wigan) 20 days; **1993:** Peter Reid (Manchester City) 12 days; **1991:** Don Mackay (Blackburn) 14 days; **1989:** Mick Jones (Peterborough) 12 days; **1980:** Bill McGarry (Newcastle) 13 days; **1979:** Dennis Butler (Port Vale) 12 days; **1977:** George Petchey (Leyton O.) 13 days; **1977:** Willie Bell (Birmingham) 16 days; **1971:** Len Richley (Darlington) 12 days.

RECORD START FOR MANAGER

Arsenal were unbeaten in 17 League matches from the start of season 1947–48 under new manager Tom Whittaker.

MANAGER CHOSEN BY POLL

A month after being sacked by Third Division promotion winners Hartlepool, **Mike Newell** became manager of Luton in Jun 2003. He was appointed via a telephone poll which the club, under a new board, conducted among fans, players, shareholders and season-ticket holders.

CARETAKER SUPREME

As Chelsea's seaaon collapsed, Andre Villas-Boas was sacked in March 2012 after eight months as manager, 2012. Roberto Di Matteo was appointed caretaker and by the season's end his team had won the FA Cup and the Champions League.

MANAGER DOUBLES

Four managers have won the League Championship with different clubs: **Tom Watson**, secretary–manager with Sunderland (1892–3–5) and Liverpool (1901); **Herbert Chapman** with Huddersfield (1923–24, 1924–25) and Arsenal (1930–31, 1932–33); **Brian Clough** with Derby (1971–72) and Nottm Forest (1977–78); **Kenny Dalglish** with Liverpool (1985–86, 1987–88, 1989–90) and Blackburn (1994–95).

Managers to win the FA Cup with different clubs: **Billy Walker** (Sheffield Wed 1935, Nottm Forest 1959); **Herbert Chapman** (Huddersfield 1922, Arsenal 1930).

Kenny Dalglish (Liverpool) and **George Graham** (Arsenal) completed the Championship/FA Cup double as both player and manager with a single club. **Joe Mercer** won the title as a player with Everton, the title twice and FA Cup as a player with Arsenal and both competitions as manager of Manchester City.

CHAIRMAN–MANAGER

On Dec 20, 1988, after two years on the board, Dundee Utd manager **Jim McLean** was elected chairman, too. McLean, Scotland's longest-serving manager (appointed on Nov 24, 1971), resigned at end of season 1992–93 (remained chairman).

Ron Noades was chairman-manager of Brentford from Jul 1998–Mar 2001. **John Reames** did both jobs at Lincoln from Nov 1998–Apr 2000)

Niall Quinn did both jobs for five weeks in 2006 before appointing Roy Keane as manager of Sunderland.

TOP DIVISION PLAYER–MANAGERS

Les Allen (QPR 1968–69); **Johnny Giles** (WBA 1976–77); **Howard Kendall** (Everton 1981–82); **Kenny Dalglish** (Liverpool, 1985–90); **Trevor Francis** (QPR, 1988–89); **Terry Butcher** (Coventry, 1990–91), **Peter Reid** (Manchester City, 1990–93), **Trevor Francis** (Sheffield Wed, 1991–94), **Glenn Hoddle**, (Chelsea, 1993–95), **Bryan Robson** (Middlesbrough, 1994–97), **Ray Wilkins** (QPR, 1994–96), **Ruud Gullit** (Chelsea, 1996–98), **Gianluca Vialli** (Chelsea, 1998–2000).

FIRST FOREIGN MANAGER IN ENGLISH LEAGUE

Uruguayan **Danny Bergara** (Rochdale 1988–89).

COACHING KINGS OF EUROPE

When **Jose Mourinho** lifted the Champions League trophy with Inter Milan in 2010, he became only the third coach in European Cup history to win the world's greatest club prize with two different clubs. He had previously done it with Porto in 2004. The others to achieve this double were **Ernst Happel** with Feyenoord (1970) and Hamburg (1983) and **Ottmar Hitzfeld** with Borussia Dortmund (1997) and Bayern Munich (2001).

FOREIGN TRIUMPH

Former Dutch star **Ruud Gullit** became the first foreign manager to win a major English competition when Chelsea took the FA Cup in 1997.

Arsene Wenger and Gerard Houllier became the first foreign managers to receive recognition when they were awarded honorary OBEs in the Queen's Birthday Honours in Jun 2003 'for their contribution to English football and Franco–British relations'.

MANAGERS OF POST-WAR CHAMPIONS (*Double winners)

1947 George Kay (Liverpool); **1948** Tom Whittaker (Arsenal); **1949** Bob Jackson (Portsmouth). **1950** Bob Jackson (Portsmouth); **1951** Arthur Rowe (Tottenham); **1952** Matt Busby (Manchester Utd); **1953** Tom Whittaker (Arsenal); **1954** Stan Cullis (Wolves); **1955** Ted Drake (Chelsea); **1956** Matt Busby (Manchester Utd); **1957** Matt Busby (Manchester Utd); **1958** Stan Cullis (Wolves); **1959** Stan Cullis (Wolves).

1960 Harry Potts (Burnley); **1961** *Bill Nicholson (Tottenham); **1962** Alf Ramsey (Ipswich); **1963** Harry Catterick (Everton); **1964** Bill Shankly (Liverpool); **1965** Matt Busby (Manchester Utd); **1966** Bill Shankly (Liverpool); **1967** Matt Busby (Manchester Utd); **1968** Joe Mercer (Manchester City); **1969** Don Revie (Leeds).

1970 Harry Catterick (Everton); **1971** *Bertie Mee (Arsenal); **1972** Brian Clough (Derby); **1973** Bill Shankly (Liverpool); **1974** Don Revie (Leeds); **1975** Dave Mackay (Derby); **1976** Bob Paisley (Liverpool); **1977** Bob Paisley (Liverpool); **1978** Brian Clough (Nottm Forest); **1979** Bob Paisley (Liverpool).

1980 Bob Paisley (Liverpool); **1981** Ron Saunders (Aston Villa); **1982** Bob Paisley (Liverpool); **1983** Bob Paisley (Liverpool); **1984** Joe Fagan (Liverpool); **1985** Howard Kendall (Everton); **1986** *Kenny Dalglish (Liverpool – player/manager); **1987** Howard Kendall (Everton); **1988** Kenny Dalglish (Liverpool – player/manager); **1989** George Graham (Arsenal).

1990 Kenny Dalglish (Liverpool); **1991** George Graham (Arsenal); **1992** Howard Wilkinson (Leeds); **1993** Alex Ferguson (Manchester Utd); **1994** *Alex Ferguson (Manchester Utd); **1995** Kenny Dalglish (Blackburn); **1996** *Alex Ferguson (Manchester Utd); **1997** Alex Ferguson (Manchester Utd); **1998** *Arsene Wenger (Arsenal); **1999** *Alex Ferguson (Manchester Utd).

2000 Sir Alex Ferguson (Manchester Utd); **2001** Sir Alex Ferguson (Manchester Utd); **2002** *Arsene Wenger (Arsenal); **2003** Sir Alex Ferguson (Manchester Utd); **2004** Arsene Wenger (Arsenal); **2005** Jose Mourinho (Chelsea); **2006** Jose Mourinho (Chelsea); **2007** Sir Alex Ferguson (Manchester Utd); **2008** Sir Alex Ferguson (Manchester Utd); **2009** Sir Alex Ferguson (Manchester Utd); **2010** *Carlo Ancelotti (Chelsea); **2011** Sir Alex Ferguson (Manchester Utd); **2012** Roberto Mancini (Manchester City).

SIR ALEX IS TOPS

With 47 major prizes, **Sir Alexander Chapman Ferguson** is the most successful manager in the history of British football. At **Aberdeen** (1978–86) he won 3 Scottish Championships, 4 Scottish Cups, 1 Scottish League Cup, 1 Cup-Winners' Cup, 1 European Super Cup. His triumphs for **Manchester Utd** since taking over in November, 1986 total 37. They comprise: 12 Premier League titles, 5 FA Cups, 4 League Cups, 2 European Cups, 1 Cup-Winners' Cup, 1 UEFA Super Cup, 1 Inter-Continental Cup, 1 FIFA Club World Cup, 10 Charity/ Community Shields. Under him, United have set a record of 19 League titles. In Jan 2012, he received the FIFA President's Award for services to football.

BOB PAISLEY'S HONOURS

Bob Paisley won 13 major competitions for Liverpool (1974–83): 6 League Championships, 3 European Cups, 3 League Cups, 1 UEFA Cup.

MOURINHO'S RECORD

Jose Mourinho, who left Chelsea on September 19, 2007, was the most successful manager in the club's history. Appointed in June 2004 after taking Porto to successive Portuguese League titles, he won six trophies in three seasons at Stamford Bridge: Premiership in 2005 and 2006, League Cup in 2005 and 2007, FA Cup in 2007 and Community Shield in 2005. Under Mourinho, Chelsea were unbeaten at home in the Premier League with his record:

P60 W46 D14 F123 A28. He won the Italian title with Inter Milan in 2009 and completed the treble of League, Cup and Champions League the following season before taking over at Real Madrid. There, in 2012, he achieved his seventh League title in ten years in four countries, Portugal, England, Italy and Spain.

RECORD MANAGER FEE

Chelsea paid Porto a record £13.25m compensation when they appointed **Andre Villas-Boas** as manager in June 2011. He lasted less than nine months at Stamford Bridge. He was appointed Tottenham manager in July 2012.

FATHER AND SON MANAGERS WITH SAME CLUB

Fulham: Bill Dodgin Snr 1949–53; Bill Dodgin Jnr 1968–72. **Brentford:** Bill Dodgin Snr 1953–57; Bill Dodgin Jnr 1976–80. **Bournemouth:** John Bond 1970–73; Kevin Bond 2006–08. **Derby:** Brian Clough 1967–73; Nigel Clough 2009.

SIR BOBBY'S HAT-TRICK

Sir Bobby Robson, born and brought up in County Durham, achieved a unique hat-trick when he received the Freedom of Durham in Dec 2008. He had already been awarded the Freedom of Ipswich and Newcastle. He died in July 2009 and had an express loco named after him on the East Coast to London line.

MANAGERS WITH MOST FA CUP SUCCESSES

5 Sir Alex Ferguson (Manchester Utd); 4 Arsene Wenger (Arsenal); 3 Charles Foweraker (Bolton), John Nicholson (Sheffield Utd), Bill Nicholson (Tottenham).

HOLE-IN-ONE MANAGER

Three days after appointing **Bobby Williamson** manager, from Hibernian, Plymouth Argyle clinched promotion and the Second Division Championship by beating QPR 2-1 on Apr 24, 2004.

RELEGATION 'DOUBLES'

Managers associated with two clubs relegated in same season: **John Bond** in 1985–86 (Swansea City and Birmingham); **Ron Saunders** in 1985–86 (WBA – and their reserve team – and Birmingham); **Bob Stokoe** in 1986–87 (Carlisle and Sunderland); **Billy McNeill** in 1986–87 (Manchester City and Aston Villa); **Dave Bassett** in 1987–88 (Watford and Sheffield Utd); **Mick Mills** in 1989–90 (Stoke and Colchester).

WEMBLEY STADIUM

NEW WEMBLEY

A new era for English football began in March 2007 with the completion of the new national stadium. The 90,000-seater arena was hailed as one of the finest in the world – but came at a price. Costs soared, the project fell well behind schedule and disputes involving the FA, builders Multiplex and the Government were rife. The old stadium, opened in 1923, was built for £750,000. The new one, originally priced at £326m in 2000, ended up costing around £800m. The first international after completion was an Under-21 match between England and Italy. The FA Cup Final returned to its spiritual home after being staged at the Millennium Stadium in Cardiff for six seasons. Then, England's senior team were back for a friendly against Brazil.

DROGBA'S WEMBLEY RECORD

Didier Drogba's FA Cup goal for Chelsea against Liverpool in May 2012 meant that he had scored in all his 8 competitive appearances for the club at Wembley. (7 wins, 1 defeat). They came in: 2007 FA Cup Final (1-0 v Manchester Utd); 2008 League Cup Final (1-2 v Tottenham); 2009 FA Cup semi-final (2-1 v Arsenal); 2009 FA Cup Final (2-1 v Everton); 2010 FA Cup semi-final (3-0 v Aston Villa); 2010 FA Cup Final (1-0 v Portsmouth); 2012 FA Cup semi-final (5-1 v Tottenham); 2012 FA Cup Final (2-1 v Liverpool).

INVASION DAY

Memorable scenes were witnessed at the first **FA Cup Final at Wembley**, Apr 28, 1923, between **Bolton** and **West Ham**. An accurate return of the attendance could not be made owing to thousands breaking in, but there were probably more than 200,000 spectators present. The match was delayed for 40 minutes by the crowd invading the pitch. Official attendance was 126,047.

Gate receipts totalled £27,776. The two clubs and the FA each received £6,365 and the FA refunded £2,797 to ticket-holders who were unable to get to their seats. Cup Final admission has since been by ticket only.

REDUCED CAPACITY

Capacity of the all-seated Wembley Stadium was 78,000. The last 100,000 attendance was for the 1985 FA Cup Final between Manchester Utd and Everton. Crowd record for New Wembley: 89,874 for 2008 FA Cup Final (Portsmouth v Cardiff).

WEMBLEY'S FIRST UNDER LIGHTS

Nov 30, 1955 (England 4, Spain 1), when the floodlights were switched on after 73 minutes (afternoon match played in damp, foggy conditions).

First Wembley international played throughout under lights: England 8, N Ireland 3 on evening of Nov 20, 1963 (att: 55,000).

MOST WEMBLEY APPEARANCES BY PLAYER

59 by **Tony Adams** (24 Arsenal, 35 England).

WEMBLEY HAT-TRICKS

Three players have scored hat-tricks in major finals at Wembley: **Stan Mortensen** for Blackpool v Bolton (FA Cup Final, 1953), **Geoff Hurst** for England v West Germany (World Cup Final, 1966) and **David Speedie** for Chelsea v Manchester City (Full Members Cup, 1985).

ENGLAND'S WEMBLEY DEFEATS

England have lost 22 matches to foreign opponents at Wembley:

Nov 1953	3-6 v Hungary	**May 1990**	1-2 v Uruguay
Oct 1959	2-3 v Sweden	**Sep 1991**	0-1 v Germany
Oct 1965	2-3 v Austria	**Jun 1995**	1-3 v Brazil
Apr 1972	1-3 v W Germany	**Feb 1997**	0-1 v Italy
Nov 1973	0-1 v Italy	**Feb 1998**	0-2 v Chile
Feb 1977	0-2 v Holland	**Feb 1999**	0-2 v France
Mar 1981	1-2 v Spain	**Oct 2000**	0-1 v Germany
May 1981	0-1 v Brazil	**Aug 2007**	1-2 v Germany
Oct 1982	1-2 v W Germany	**Nov 2007**	2-3 v Croatia
Sep 1983	0-1 v Denmark	**Nov 2010**	1-2 v France
Jun 1984	0-2 v Russia	**Feb 2012**	2-3 v Holland

A further defeat came in **Euro 96**. After drawing the semi-final with Germany 1-1, England went out 6-5 on penalties.

FASTEST GOALS AT WEMBLEY

In first-class matches: **25 sec** by **Louis Saha** for Everton in 2009 FA Cup Final against Chelsea; **38 sec** by **Bryan Robson** for England's against Yugoslavia in 1989; **42 sec** by

Roberto Di Matteo for Chelsea in 1997 FA Cup Final v Middlesbrough; **44 sec** by **Bryan Robson** for England v Northern Ireland in 1982;

Fastest goal in **any** match at Wembley: **20 sec** by **Maurice Cox** for Cambridge University against Oxford in 1979.

FOUR WEMBLEY HEADERS

When **Wimbledon** beat Sutton 4-2 in the FA Amateur Cup Final at Wembley on May 4, 1963, Irish centre-forward **Eddie Reynolds** headed all four goals.

WEMBLEY ONE-SEASON DOUBLES

In 1989, **Nottm Forest** became the first club to win two Wembley Finals in the same season (Littlewoods Cup and Simod Cup).

In 1993, **Arsenal** made history there as the first club to win the League (Coca-Cola) Cup and the FA Cup in the same season. They beat Sheffield Wed 2-1 in both finals.

In 2012, **York** won twice at Wembley in nine days at the end of the season, beating Newport 2-0 in the FA Trophy Final and Luton 2-1 in the Conference Play-off Final to return to the Football League.

SUDDEN-DEATH DECIDERS

First Wembley Final decided on sudden death (first goal scored in overtime): Apr 23, 1995 – **Birmingham** beat Carlisle (1-0, Paul Tait 103 mins) to win Auto Windscreens Shield.

First instance of a golden goal deciding a major international tournament was at Wembley on Jun 30, 1996, when **Germany** beat the Czech Republic 2-1 in the European Championship Final with Oliver Bierhoff's goal in the 95th minute.

FOOTBALL TRAGEDIES

DAYS OF TRAGEDY – CLUBS

Season 1988–89 brought the worst disaster in the history of British sport, with the death of 96 Liverpool supporters (200 injured) at the **FA Cup semi-final** against Nottm Forest at **Hillsborough, Sheffield**, on Saturday, Apr 15. The tragedy built up in the minutes preceding kick-off, when thousands surged into the ground at the Leppings Lane end. Many were crushed in the tunnel between entrance and terracing, but most of the victims were trapped inside the perimeter fencing behind the goal. The match was abandoned without score after six minutes' play. The dead included seven women and girls, two teenage sisters and two teenage brothers. The youngest victim was a boy of ten, the oldest 67-year-old Gerard Baron, whose brother Kevin played for Liverpool in the 1950 Cup Final. (*Total became 96 in Mar 1993, when Tony Bland died after being in a coma for nearly four years).

The two worst disasters in one season in British soccer history occurred at the end of 1984–85. On May 11, the last Saturday of the League season, 56 people (two of them visiting supporters) were burned to death – and more than 200 taken to hospital – when fire destroyed the main stand at the **Bradford City–Lincoln** match at Valley Parade.

The wooden, 77-year-old stand was full for City's last fixture before which, amid scenes of celebration, the club had been presented with the Third Division Championship trophy. The fire broke out just before half-time and, within five minutes, the entire stand was engulfed.

Heysel Tragedy

Eighteen days later, on May 29, at the European Cup Final between **Liverpool** and **Juventus** at the Heysel Stadium, Brussels, 39 spectators (31 of them Italian) were crushed or trampled to death and 437 injured. The disaster occurred an hour before the scheduled kick-off when Liverpool supporters charged a Juventus section of the crowd at one end of the stadium, and a retaining wall collapsed. The sequel was a 5-year ban by UEFA on English clubs generally in European competition, with a 6-year ban on Liverpool.

On May 26 1985 ten people were trampled to death and 29 seriously injured in a crowd panic on the way into the **Olympic Stadium, Mexico City** for the Mexican Cup Final between local clubs National University and America.

More than 100 people died and 300 were injured in a football disaster at **Nepal's national stadium** in Katmandu in Mar 1988. There was a stampede when a violent hailstorm broke over the capital. Spectators rushed for cover, but the stadium exits were locked, and hundreds were trampled in the crush.

In South Africa, on Jan 13 1991 40 black fans were trampled to death (50 injured) as they tried to escape from fighting that broke out at a match in the gold-mining town of Orkney, 80 miles from Johannesburg. The friendly, between top teams **Kaiser Chiefs** and **Orlando Pirates**, attracted a packed crowd of 20,000. Violence erupted after the referee allowed Kaiser Chiefs a disputed second-half goal to lead 1-0.

Disaster struck at the French Cup semi-final (May 5, 1992), with the death of 15 spectators and 1,300 injured when a temporary metal stand collapsed in the Corsican town of Bastia. The tie between Second Division **Bastia** and French Champions **Marseille** was cancelled. Monaco, who won the other semi-final, were allowed to compete in the next season's Cup-Winners' Cup.

A total of 318 died and 500 were seriously injured when the crowd rioted over a disallowed goal at the National Stadium in Lima, Peru, on May 24, 1964. **Peru** and **Argentina** were competing to play in the Olympic Games in Tokyo.

That remained **sport's heaviest death** toll until Oct 20, 1982, when (it was revealed only in Jul 1989) 340 Soviet fans were killed in Moscow's Lenin Stadium at the UEFA Cup second round first leg match between **Moscow Spartak** and **Haarlem** (Holland). They were crushed on an open stairway when a last-minute Spartak goal sent departing spectators surging back into the ground.

Among other crowd disasters abroad: Jun, 1968 – 74 died in Argentina. Panic broke out at the end of a goalless match between River Plate and Boca Juniors at Nunez, Buenos Aires, when Boca supporters threw lighted newspaper torches on to fans in the tiers below.

Feb 1974 – 49 killed in **Egypt** in crush of fans clamouring to see Zamalek play Dukla Prague.

Sep 1971 – 44 died in **Turkey**, when fighting among spectators over a disallowed goal (Kayseri v Siwas) led to a platform collapsing.

The then worst disaster in the history of British football, in terms of loss of life, occurred at Glasgow Rangers' ground at **Ibrox Park**, Jan 2 1971. Sixty-six people were trampled to death (100 injured) as they tumbled down Stairway 13 just before the end of the **Rangers v Celtic** New Year's match. That disaster led to the 1975 Safety of Sports Grounds legislation.

The Ibrox tragedy eclipsed even the Bolton disaster in which 33 were killed and about 500 injured when a wall and crowd barriers collapsed near a corner-flag at the **Bolton v Stoke** FA Cup sixth round tie on Mar 9 1946. The match was completed after half an hour's stoppage.

In a previous crowd disaster at **Ibrox** on Apr 5, 1902, part of the terracing collapsed during the Scotland v England international and 25 people were killed. The match, held up for 20 minutes, ended 1-1, but was never counted as an official international.

Eight leading players and three officials of **Manchester Utd** and eight newspaper representatives were among the 23 who perished in the air crash at **Munich** on Feb 6, 1958, during take-off following a European Cup-tie in Belgrade. The players were Roger Byrne, Geoffrey Bent, Eddie Colman, Duncan Edwards, Mark Jones, David Pegg, Tommy Taylor and Liam Whelan, and the officials were Walter Crickmer (secretary), Tom Curry (trainer) and Herbert Whalley (coach). The newspaper representatives were Alf Clarke, Don Davies, George Follows, Tom Jackson, Archie Ledbrooke, Henry Rose, Eric Thompson and Frank Swift (former England goalkeeper of Manchester City).

On May 14, 1949, the entire team of Italian Champions **Torino**, 8 of them Internationals, were killed when the aircraft taking them home from a match against Benfica in Lisbon crashed at Superga, near Turin. The total death toll of 28 included all the club's reserve players, the manager, trainer and coach.

On Feb 8, 1981, 24 spectators died and more than 100 were injured at a match in **Greece**. They were trampled as thousands of the 40,000 crowd tried to rush out of the stadium at Piraeus after Olympiacos beat AEK Athens 6-0.

On Nov 17, 1982, 24 people (12 of them children) were killed and 250 injured when fans stampeded at the end of a match at the Pascual Guerrero stadium in **Cali, Colombia**. Drunken spectators hurled fire crackers and broken bottles from the higher stands on to people below and started a rush to the exits.

On Dec 9, 1987, the 18-strong team squad of **Alianza Lima**, one of Peru's top clubs, were wiped out, together with 8 officials and several youth players, when a military aircraft taking them home from Puccalpa crashed into the sea off Ventillana, ten miles from Lima. The only survivor among 43 on board was a member of the crew.

On Apr 28, 1993, 18 members of **Zambia's international squad** and 5 ZFA officials died when the aircraft carrying them to a World Cup qualifying tie against Senegal crashed into the Atlantic soon after take-off from Libreville, Gabon.

On Oct 16 1996, 81 fans were crushed to death and 147 seriously injured in the '**Guatemala Disaster**' at the World Cup qualifier against Costa Rica in Mateo Flores stadium. The tragedy happened an hour before kick-off, allegedly caused by ticket forgery and overcrowding – 60,000 were reported in the 45,000-capacity ground – and safety problems related to perimeter fencing.

On Jul 9, 1996, 8 people died, 39 injured in riot after derby match between **Libya's two top clubs** in Tripoli. Al-Ahli had beaten Al-Ittihad 1-0 by a controversial goal.

On Apr 6, 1997, 5 spectators were crushed to death at **Nigeria's national stadium** in Lagos after the 2-1 World Cup qualifying victory over Guinea. Only two of five gates were reported open as the 40,000 crowd tried to leave the ground.

It was reported from the **Congo** (Oct 29, 1998) that a bolt of lightning struck a village match, killing all 11 members of the home team Benatshadi, but leaving the opposing players from Basangana unscathed. It was believed the surviving team wore better-insulated boots.

On Jan 10, 1999, eight fans died and 13 were injured in a stampede at **Egypt's Alexandria Stadium**. Some 25,000 spectators had pushed into the ground. Despite the tragedy, the cup-tie between Al-Ittihad and Al-Koroum was completed.

Three people suffocated and several were seriously injured when thousands of fans forced their way into **Liberia's national stadium** in Monrovia at a goalless World Cup qualifying match against Chad on Apr 23, 2000. The stadium (capacity 33,000) was reported 'heavily overcrowded'.

On Jul 9, 2000, 12 spectators died from crush injuries when police fired tear gas into the 50,000 crowd after South Africa scored their second goal in a World Cup group qualifier against Zimbabwe in **Harare**. A stampede broke out as fans scrambled to leave the national stadium. Players of both teams lay face down on the pitch as fumes swept over them. FIFA launched an investigation and decided that the result would stand, with South Africa leading 2-0 at the time of the 84th-minute abandonment.

On Apr 11, 2001, at one of the biggest matches of the South African season, 43 died and 155 were injured in a crush at **Ellis Park, Johannesburg**. After tearing down a fence, thousands of fans surged into a stadium already packed to its 60,000 capacity for the Premiership derby between top Soweto teams Kaizer Chiefs and Orlando Pirates.

The match was abandoned at 1-1 after 33 minutes. In Jan 1991, 40 died in a crowd crush at a friendly between the same clubs at Orkney, 80 miles from Johannesburg.

On Apr 29, 2001, seven people were trampled to death and 51 injured when a riot broke out at a match between two of Congo's biggest clubs, Lupopo and Mazembe at **Lubumbashi**, southern Congo.

On May 6, 2001, two spectators were killed in Iran and hundreds were injured when a glass fibre roof collapsed at the over-crowded Mottaqi Stadium at Sari for the match between Pirouzi and Shemshak Noshahr.

On May 9, 2001, in Africa's worst football disaster, 123 died and 93 were injured in a stampede at the national stadium in **Accra, Ghana**. Home team Hearts of Oak were leading 2-1 against Asante Kotoko five minutes from time, when Asanti fans started hurling bottles on to the pitch. Police fired tear gas into the stands, and the crowd panicked in a rush for the exits, which were locked. It took the death toll at three big matches in Africa in Apr/May to 173.

On Aug 12, 2001, two players were killed by lightning and ten severely burned at a **Guatemala** Third Division match between Deportivo Culquimulilla and Pueblo Nuevo Vinas.

On Nov 1, 2002, two players died from injuries after lightning struck Deportivo Cali's training ground in **Colombia**.

On Mar 12 2004, five people were killed and more than 100 injured when spectators stampeded shortly before the Syrian Championship fixture between Al-Jihad and Al-Fatwa in **Qameshli**, Northern Syria. The match was cancelled.

On Oct 10, 2004, three spectators died in a crush at the African Zone World Cup qualifier between **Guinea** and **Morocco** (1-1) at Conakry, Guinea.

On Mar 25, 2005, five were killed as 100,000 left the Azadi Stadium, **Tehran**, after Iran's World Cup qualifying win (2-1) against Japan.

On Jun 2, 2007, 12 spectators were killed and 46 injured in a crush at the Chillabombwe Stadium, **Zambia**, after an African Nations Cup qualifier against Congo.

On Mar 29, 2009, 19 people died and 139 were injured after a wall collapsed at the Ivory Coast stadium in **Abidjan** before a World Cup qualifier against Malawi. The match went ahead, Ivory Coast winning 5-0 with two goals from Chelsea's Didier Drogba. The tragedy meant that, in 13 years, crowd disasters at club and internationals at ten different grounds across Africa had claimed the lives of 283 people.

On Jan 8, 2010, terrorists at **Cabinda**, Angola machine-gunned the Togo team buses travelling to the Africa Cup of Nations. They killed a driver, an assistant coach and a media officer and injured several players. The team were ordered by their Government to withdraw from the tournament.

On Oct 23, 2010, seven fans were trampled to death when thousands tried to force their way into the Nyayo National Stadium in **Nairobi** at a Kenya Premier League match between the Gor Mahia and AFC Leopards clubs.

On Feb 1, 2012, 74 died and nearly 250 were injured in a crowd riot at the end of the Al-Masry v Al-Ahly match in **Port Said** – the worst disaster in Egyptian sport.

DAYS OF TRAGEDY – PERSONAL

Sam Wynne, Bury right-back, collapsed five minutes before half-time in the First Division match away to Sheffield Utd on Apr 30, 1927, and died in the dressing-room.

John Thomson, Celtic and Scotland goalkeeper, sustained a fractured skull when diving at an opponent's feet in the Rangers v Celtic League match on Sep 5, 1931, and died the same evening.

Sim Raleigh (Gillingham), injured in a clash of heads at home to Brighton (Div 3 South) on Dec 1, 1934, continued to play but collapsed in second half and died in hospital the same night.

James Thorpe, Sunderland goalkeeper, was injured during the First Division match at home to Chelsea on Feb 1, 1936 and died in a diabetic coma three days later.

Derek Dooley, Sheffield Wed centre-forward and top scorer in 1951–52 in the Football League with 46 goals in 30 matches, broke a leg in the League match at Preston on Feb 14, 1953, and, after complications set in, had to lose the limb by amputation.

John White, Tottenham's Scottish international forward, was killed by lightning on a golf course at Enfield, North London in Jul, 1964.

Tony Allden, Highgate centre-half, was struck by lightning during an Amateur Cup quarter-final with Enfield on Feb 25, 1967. He died the following day. Four other players were also struck but recovered.

Roy Harper died while refereeing the York–Halifax (Div 4) match on May 5, 1969.

Jim Finn collapsed and died from a heart attack while refereeing Exeter v Stockport (Div 4) on Sep 16, 1972.

Scotland manager **Jock Stein**, 62, collapsed and died at the end of the Wales-Scotland World Cup qualifying match (1-1) at Ninian Park, Cardiff on Sep 10, 1985.

David Longhurst, York forward, died after being carried off two minutes before half-time in the Fourth Division fixture at home to Lincoln on Sep 8, 1990. The match was abandoned (0-0).

The inquest revealed that Longhurst suffered from a rare heart condition.

Mike North collapsed while refereeing Southend v Mansfield (Div 3) on Apr 16, 2001 and died shortly afterwards. The match was abandoned and re-staged on May 8, with the receipts donated to his family.

Marc-Vivien Foe, on his 63rd appearance in Cameroon's midfield, collapsed unchallenged in the centre circle after 72 minutes of the FIFA Confederations Cup semi-final against Colombia in Lyon, France, on Jun 26, 2003, and despite the efforts of the stadium medical staff he could not be revived. He had been on loan to Manchester City from Olympique Lyonnais in season 2002–03, and poignantly scored the club's last goal at Maine Road.

Paul Sykes, Folkestone Invicta (Ryman League) striker, died on the pitch during the Kent Senior Cup semi-final against Margate on Apr 12, 2005. He collapsed after an innocuous off-the-ball incident.

Craig Gowans, Falkirk apprentice, was killed at the club's training ground on Jul 8, 2005 when he came into contact with power lines.

Peter Wilson, Mansfield goalkeeping coach, died of a heart attack after collapsing during the warm-up of the League Two game away to Shrewsbury on Nov 19, 2005.

Matt Gadsby, Hinckley defender, collapsed and died while playing in a Conference North match at Harrogate on Sep 9, 2006.

Phil O'Donnell, 35-year-old Motherwell captain and Scotland midfield player, collapsed when about to be substituted near the end of the SPL home game against Dundee Utd on Dec 29, 2007 and died shortly afterwards in hospital.

GREAT SERVICE

'For services to Association Football', **Stanley Matthews** (Stoke, Blackpool and England), already a CBE, became the first professional footballer to receive a knighthood. This was bestowed in 1965, his last season. Before he retired and five days after his 50th birthday, he played for Stoke to set a record as the oldest First Division footballer (v Fulham, Feb 6, 1965).

Over a brilliant span of 33 years, he played in 886 first-class matches, including 54 full Internationals (plus 31 in war time), 701 League games (including 3 at start of season 1939–40, which was abandoned on the outbreak of war) and 86 FA Cup-ties, and scored 95 goals. He was never booked in his career.

Sir Stanley died on Feb 23, 2000, three weeks after his 85th birthday. His ashes were buried under the centre circle of Stoke's Britannia Stadium. After spending a number of years in Toronto, he made his home back in the Potteries in 1989, having previously returned to his home town, Hanley in 1987 to unveil a life-size bronze statue of himself. The inscription reads: 'Sir Stanley Matthews, CBE. Born Hanley, 1 Feb 1915.

His name is symbolic of the beauty of the game, his fame timeless and international, his sportsmanship and modesty universally acclaimed. A magical player, of the people, for the people.' On his home-coming in 1989, Sir Stanley was made President of Stoke, the club he joined as a boy of 15 and served as a player for 20 years between 1931 and 1965, on either side of his spell with Blackpool.

In Jul 1992 FIFA honoured him with their 'Gold merit award' for outstanding services to the game.

Former England goalkeeper **Peter Shilton** has made more first-class appearances (1,387) than any other footballer in British history. He played his 1,000th League game in Leyton Orient's 2-0 home win against Brighton on Dec 22, 1996 and made 9 appearances for Orient in his final season. He retired from international football after the 1990 World Cup in Italy with 125 caps, then a world record. Shilton kept a record 60 clean sheets for England.

Shilton's career spanned 32 seasons, 20 of them on the international stage. He made his League debut for Leicester in May 1966, two months before England won the World Cup.

His 1,387 first-class appearances comprise a record 1,005 in the Football League, 125

Internationals, 102 League Cup, 86 FA Cup, 13 for England U-23s, 4 for the Football League and 52 other matches (European Cup, UEFA Cup, World Club Championship, Charity Shield, European Super Cup, Full Members' Cup, Play-offs, Screen Sports Super Cup, Anglo-Italian Cup, Texaco Cup, Simod Cup, Zenith Data Systems Cup and Autoglass Trophy).

Shilton appeared more times at Wembley (57) than any other player: 52 for England, 2 League Cup Finals, 1 FA Cup Final, 1 Charity Shield match, and 1 for the Football League. He passed a century of League appearances with each of his first five clubs: Leicester (286), Stoke (110), Nottm Forest (202), Southampton (188) and Derby (175) and subsequently played for Plymouth, Bolton and Leyton Orient.

His club honours, all gained with Nottm Forest: League Championship 1978, League Cup 1979, European Cup 1979 and 1980, PFA Player of Year 1978.

Six other British footballers have made more than 1,000 first-class appearances:

Ray Clemence , formerly with Tottenham, Liverpool and England, retired through injury in season 1987–88 after a goalkeeping career of 1,119 matches starting in 1965–66.

Clemence played 50 times for his first club, Scunthorpe; 665 for Liverpool; 337 for Tottenham; his 67 representative games included 61 England caps.

A third great British goalkeeper, **Pat Jennings**, ended his career (1963–86) with a total of 1,098 first-class matches for Watford, Tottenham, Arsenal and N Ireland. They were made up of 757 in the Football League, 119 full Internationals, 84 FA Cup appearances, 72 League/Milk Cup, 55 European club matches, 2 Charity Shield, 3 Other Internationals, 1 Under-23 cap, 2 Texaco Cup, 2 Anglo-Italian Cup and 1 Super Cup. Jennings played his 119th and final international on his 41st birthday, Jun 12, 1986, against Brazil in Guadalajara in the Mexico World Cup.

Yet another outstanding 'keeper, **David Seaman**, passed the 1,000 appearances milestone for clubs and country in season 2002–03, reaching 1,004 when aged 39, he captained Arsenal to FA Cup triumph against Southampton.

With Arsenal, Seaman won 3 Championship medals, the FA Cup 4 times, the Double twice, the League Cup and Cup-Winners' Cup once each. After 13 seasons at Highbury, he joined Manchester City (Jun 2003) on a free transfer. He played 26 matches for City before a shoulder injury forced his retirement in Jan 2004, aged 40.

Seaman's 22-season career composed 1,046 first-class matches: 955 club apps (Peterborough 106, Birmingham 84, QPR 175, Arsenal 564, Manchester City 26); 75 senior caps for England, 6 'B' caps and 10 at U-21 level.

Defender **Graeme Armstrong**, 42-year-old commercial manager for an Edinburgh whisky company and part-time assistant-manager and captain of Scottish Third Division club Stenhousemuir, made the 1000th first team appearance of his career in the Scottish Cup 3rd Round against Rangers at Ibrox on Jan 23, 1999. He was presented with the Man of the Match award before kick-off.

Against East Stirling on Boxing Day, he had played his 864th League game, breaking the British record for an outfield player set by another Scot, Tommy Hutchison, with Alloa, Blackpool, Coventry, Manchester City, Burnley and Swansea City.

Armstrong's 24-year career, spent in the lower divisions of the Scottish League, began as a 1-match trialist with Meadowbank Thistle in 1975 and continued via Stirling Albion, Berwick Rangers, Meadowbank and, from 1992, Stenhousemuir.

Tony Ford became the first English outfield player to reach 1000 senior appearances in Rochdale's 1-0 win at Carlisle (Auto Windscreens Shield) on Mar 7, 2000. Grimsby-born, he began his 26-season midfield career with Grimsby and played for 7 other League clubs: Sunderland (loan), Stoke, WBA, Bradford City (loan), Scunthorpe, Mansfield and Rochdale. He retired, aged 42, in 2001 with a career record of 1072 appearances (121 goals) and his total of 931 League games is exceeded only by Peter Shilton's 1005.

On Apr 16, 2011, **Graham Alexander** reached 1,000 appearances when he came on as a sub for Burnley at home to Swansea. Alexander, 40, ended a 22-year career with the equaliser for Preston against Charlton (2-2, Lge 1) on Apr 28, 2012 – his 1,023rd appearance. He also played for Luton and Scunthorpe and was capped 40 times by Scotland.

KNIGHTS OF SOCCER

Players, managers and administrators who have been honoured for their services to football: **Charles Clegg** (1927), **Stanley Rous** (1949), **Stanley Matthews** (1965), **Alf Ramsey** (1967), **Matt Busby** (1968), **Walter Winterbottom** (1978) **Bert Millichip** (1991), **Bobby Charlton** (1994), **Tom Finney** (1998), **Geoff Hurst** (1998), **Alex Ferguson** (1999), **Bobby Robson** (2002), **Trevor Brooking** (2004), **Dave Richards** (2006), **Doug Ellis** (2011).

FOOTBALL IN STATUE

In recognition of **Brian Clough's** outstanding achievements as manager, a 9ft bronze statue was unveiled by his widow Barbara in Market Square, Nottingham on Nov 6, 2008. The bulk of the £60,000 cost was met by supporters of Forest, the club he led to back-to-back European Cup triumphs. There is also a statue of Clough in his home town, Middlesbrough, and at Derby's Pride Park stands a combined statue of the famous management team of Clough and Peter Taylor. Other leading managers and players have been honoured over the years. They include **Sir Matt Busby** (Manchester Utd), **Bill Shankly** (Liverpool), **Sir Alf Ramsey** and **Sir Bobby Robson** (Ipswich), **Stan Cullis** (Wolves), **Jackie Milburn** (Newcastle), **Bob Stokoe** (Sunderland), **Ted Bates** (Southampton), **Nat Lofthouse** (Bolton) and **Billy Bremner** (Leeds). **Bobby Moore**, England's World Cup-winning captain, is immortalised by a statue at the new Wembley, where there is a bust of Sir Alf in the tunnel corridor. There are statues of **Sir Stanley Matthews** and **Sir Tom Finney** recognising their playing achievements with Stoke and Preston, and one honouring Manchester Utd's **Sir Bobby Charlton, George Best** and **Denis Law** outside Old Trafford. At Upton Park, there is a combined statue of West Ham's World Cup-winning trio, **Bobby Moore, Sir Geoff Hurst** and **Martin Peters**. Similarly, Fulham legend **Johnny Haynes** and Charlton's greatest goalkeeper **Sam Bartram** are honoured. So, too, is Everton great **William Ralph 'Dixie' Dean** at Goodison Park. The original bust of **Herbert Chapman** remains on its plinth at Arsenal's former home at Highbury (now converted into apartments). A replica is in place at the Emirates Stadium, which also has a bust of the club's most successful manager, **Arsene Wenger**. A bust of **Derby's** record scorer, **Steve Bloomer**, is at Pride Park and there is one of Blackburn's former owner, **Jack Walker**, at Ewood Park. Chelsea honourerd **Peter Osgood** in 2010 and Blackpool did the same for **Jimmy Armfield** the following year. 2011 also saw statues unveiled of **Herbert Chapman, Thierry Henry** and **Tony Adams** as part of Arsenal's 125th anniversary and **Jimmy Hill** at Coventry. In 2012, **Sir Bobby Robson** was honoured at Newcastle.

PENALTIES

The **penalty-kick** was introduced to the game, following a proposal to the Irish FA in 1890 by William McCrum, son of the High Sheriff for Co Omagh, and approved by the International Football Board on Jun 2, 1891.

First penalty scored in a first-class match in England was by John Heath, for Wolves v Accrington Stanley (5-0 in Div 1, Sep 14, 1891).

The greatest influence of the penalty has come since the 1970s, with the introduction of the shoot-out to settle deadlocked ties in various competitions.

Manchester Utd were the first club to win a competitive match in British football via a shoot-out (4-3 away to Hull, Watney Cup semi-final, Aug 5, 1970); in that penalty contest, George Best was the first player to score, Denis Law the first to miss.

The shoot-out was adopted by FIFA and UEFA the same year (1970).

In season 1991–92, penalty shoot-outs were introduced to decide FA Cup ties still level after one replay and extra time.

Wembley saw its first penalty contest in the 1974 Charity Shield. Since then many major matches across the world have been settled in this way, including:

1974	**FA Charity Shield (Wembley):**	Liverpool beat Leeds 6-5 (after 1-1).
1976	**Euro Champ Final (Belgrade):**	Czech beat West Germany 5-3 (after 2-2).

1980	**Cup-Winners' Cup Final (Brussels):** Valencia beat Arsenal 5-4 (after 0-0).
1980	**Euro Champ 3rd/4th place play-off (Naples):** Czech beat Italy 9-8 (after 1-1).
1982	**World Cup semi-final (Seville):** West Germany beat France 5-4 (after 3-3).
1984	**European Cup Final (Rome):** Liverpool beat Roma 4-2 (after 1-1).
1984	**UEFA Cup Final:** Tottenham (home) beat Anderlecht 4-3 (2-2 agg).
1984	**Euro Champ semi-final (Lyon):** Spain beat Denmark 5-4 (after 1-1).
1986	**European Cup Final (Seville):** Steaua Bucharest beat Barcelona 2-0 (after 0-0). Barcelona's four penalties were all saved.
1987	**Freight Rover Trophy Final (Wembley):** Mansfield beat Bristol City 5-4 (after 1-1).
1987	**Scottish League (Skol) Cup Final (Hampden Park):** Rangers beat Aberdeen 5-3 (after 3-3).
1988	**European Cup Final (Stuttgart):** PSV Eindhoven beat Benfica 6-5 (after 0-0).
1988	**UEFA Cup Final:** Bayer Leverkusen (home) beat Espanyol 3-2 after 3-3 (0-3a, 3-0h).
1990	**Scottish FA Cup Final (Hampden Park):** Aberdeen beat Celtic 9-8 (after 0-0).
1990	**World Cup 2nd Round (Genoa):** Rep of Ireland beat Romania 5-4 (after 0-0); **quarter-final (Florence):** Argentina beat Yugoslavia 3-2 (after 0-0); **semi-final (Naples):** Argentina beat Italy 4-3 (after 1-1); **semi-final (Turin):** West Germany beat England 4-3 (1-1).
1991	**European Cup Final (Bari):** Red Star Belgrade beat Marseille 5-3 (after 0-0).
1991	**Div 4 Play-off Final (Wembley):** Torquay beat Blackpool 5-4 (after 2-2).
1992	**FA Cup semi-final replay (Villa Park):** Liverpool beat Portsmouth 3-1 (after 0-0).
1992	**Div 4 Play-off Final (Wembley):** Blackpool beat Scunthorpe 4-3 (after 1-1).
1992	**Euro Champ semi-final (Gothenburg):** Denmark beat Holland 5-4 (after 2-2).
1993	**Div 3 Play-off Final (Wembley):** York beat Crewe 5-3 (after 1-1).
1993	**FA Charity Shield (Wembley):** Manchester Utd beat Arsenal 5-4 (after 1-1).
1994	**Autoglass Trophy Final (Wembley):** Swansea City beat Huddersfield 3-1 (after 1-1).
1994	**World Cup Final (Los Angeles):** Brazil beat Italy 3-2 (after 0-0).
1994	**Scottish League (Coca-Cola) Cup Final (Ibrox Park):** Raith beat Celtic 6-5 (after 2-2).
1995	**Cup-Winners' Cup semi-final:** Arsenal beat Sampdoria away 3-2 (5-5 agg)
1995	**Copa America Final (Montevideo):** Uruguay beat Brazil 5-3 (after 1-1).
1996	**European Cup Final (Rome):** Juventus beat Ajax 4-2 (after 1-1).
1996	**European U-21 Champ Final (Barcelona):** Italy beat Spain 4-2 (after 1-1).
1996	**Euro Champ quarter-final (Wembley):** England beat Spain 4-2 after 0-0; **semi-final (Wembley):** Germany beat England 6-5 (after 1-1); **semi-final (Old Trafford):** Czech Republic beat France 6-5 (after 0-0).
1997	**Auto Windscreens Shield Final (Wembley):** Carlisle beat Colchester 4-3 (after 0-0)
1997	**UEFA Cup Final:** FC Schalke beat Inter Milan 4-1 (after 1-1 agg).
1998	**Div 1 Play-off Final (Wembley):** Charlton beat Sunderland 7-6 (after 4-4).
1998	**World Cup 2nd round (St Etienne):** Argentina beat England 4-3 (after 2-2).
1999	**Div 2 Play-off Final (Wembley):** Manchester City beat Gillingham 3-1 (after 2-2).
1999	**Women's World Cup Final (Pasedena):** USA beat China 5-4 (after 0-0).
2000	**African Nations Cup Final (Lagos):** Cameroon beat Nigeria 4-3 (after 0-0).
2000	**FA Cup semi-final (Wembley):** Aston Villa beat Bolton 4-1 (after 0-0).
2000	**UEFA Cup Final (Copenhagen):** Galatasaray beat Arsenal 4-1 (after 0-0).
2000	**Euro Champ semi-final (Amsterdam):** Italy beat Holland 3-1 (after 0-0). Holland missed 5 penalties in match – 2 in normal play, 3 in shoot-out.
2000	**Olympic Final (Sydney):** Cameroon beat Spain 5-3 (after 2-2).
2001	**League (Worthington) Cup Final (Millennium Stadium):** Liverpool beat Birmingham 5-4 (after 1-1).
2001	**Champions League Final (Milan):** Bayern Munich beat Valencia 5-4 (after 1-1).
2002	**Euro U-21 Champ Final (Basle):** Czech Republic beat France 3-1 (after 0-0).
2002	**Div 1 Play-off Millennium Stadium):** Birmingham beat Norwich 4-2 (after 1-1).
2002	**World Cup 2nd round: (Suwon):** Spain beat Rep of Ireland 3-2 (after 1-1).

2003	**Champions League Final (Old Trafford):** AC Milan beat Juventus 3–2 (after 0–0).
2003	**FA Community Shield (Millennium Stadium):** Manchester Utd beat Arsenal 4-3 (after 1-1).
2004	**Div 3 Play-off Final (Millennium Stadium):** Huddersfield beat Mansfield 4-1 (after 0-0).
2004	**Euro Champ quarter-final (Lisbon):** Portugal beat England 6-5 (after 2-2).
2004	**Copa America Final (Lima):** Brazil beat Argentina 4-2 (after 2-2).
2005	**FA Cup Final (Millennium Stadium):** Arsenal beat Manchester Utd 5-4 (after 0-0).
2005	**Champions League Final (Istanbul):** Liverpool beat AC Milan 3-2 (after 3-3).
2006	**African Cup of Nations Final (Cairo):** Egypt beat Ivory Coast 4-2 (after 0-0).
2006	**FA Cup Final (Millennium Stadium):** Liverpool beat West Ham 3-1 (after 3-3).
2006	**Scottish Cup Final (Hampden Park):** Hearts beat Gretna 4-2 (after 1-1).
2006	**Lge 1 Play-off Final (Millennium Stadium):** Barnsley beat Swansea City 4-3 (after 2-2).
2006	**World Cup 2nd round (Cologne):** Ukraine beat Switzerland 3-0 (after 0-0); **quarter-final (Berlin):** Germany beat Argentina 4-2 (after 1-1); **quarter-final (Gelsenkirchen):** Portugal beat England 3-1 (after 0-0); **Final (Berlin):** Italy beat France 5-3 (after 1-1).
2007	**UEFA Cup Final (Hampden Park):** Sevilla beat Espanyol 3-1 (after 2-2).
2007	**Euro U-21Champ semi-final (Heerenveen):** Holland beat England 13-12. (after 1-1).
2007	**FA Community Shield (Wembley):** Manchester Utd beat Chelsea 3-0 (after 1-1).
2008	**Champions League Final (Moscow):** Manchester Utd beat Chelsea 6-5 (after 1-1).
2008	**Euro Champ quarter-final (Vienna):** Turkey beat Croatia 3-1 (after 1-1).
	Euro Champ quarter-final (Vienna): Spain beat Italy 4-2 (after 0-0).
2008	**Scottish League Cup Final (Hampden Park):** Rangers beat Dundee Utd 3-2 (after 2-2).
2008	**FA Community Shield (Wembley):** Manchester Utd beat Portsmouth 3-1 (after 0-0).
2009	**League (Carling) Cup Final (Wembley):** Manchester Utd beat Tottenham 4-1 (after 0-0).
2009	**Community Shield (Wembley):** Chelsea beat Manchester Utd 4-1 (after 2-2).
2010	**World Cup round of 16 (Pretoria):** Paraguay beat Japan 5-3 (after 0-0); **quarter-finals (Johannesburg, Soccer City):** Uruguay beat Ghana 4-2 (after 1-1).
2011	**Women's World Cup Final:** Japan beat USA 3-1 (after 2-2).
2012	**League Cup Final (Wembley):** Liverpool beat Cardiff 3-2 (after 2-2)
2012	**Champions League Final (Munich):** Chelsea beat Bayern Munich 4-3 (after 1-1).
2012	**Lge 1 Play-off Final:** Huddersfield beat Sheffield Utd 8-7 (after 0-0).
2012	**Africa Cup of Nations Final (Gabon):** Zambia beat Ivory Coast 8-7 (after 0-0).
2012	**Euro Champ quarter-final (Kiev):** Italy beat England 4-2 (after 0-0).
2012	**Euro Champ semi-final (Donetsk):** Spain beat Portugal 4-2 (after 0-0)

In South America in 1992, in a 26-shot competition, **Newell's Old Boys** beat America 11-10 in the Copa Libertadores.

Longest-recorded penalty contest in first-class matches was in Argentina in 1988 – from 44 shots, **Argentinos Juniors** beat Racing Club 20-19. Genclerbirligi beat Galatasaray 17-16 in a Turkish Cup-tie in 1996. Only one penalty was missed.

Highest-scoring shoot-outs in international football: **North Korea** beat Hong Kong 11-10 (after 3-3 draw) in an Asian Cup match in 1975; and **Ivory Coast** beat Ghana 11-10 (after 0-0 draw) in African Nations Cup Final, 1992.

Most penalties needed to settle an adult game in Britain: **44** in Norfolk Primary Cup 4th round replay, Dec 2000. Aston Village side **Freethorpe** beat Foulsham 20-19 (5 kicks missed). All 22 players took 2 penalties each, watched by a crowd of 20. The sides had drawn 2-2, 4-4 in a tie of 51 goals.

Penalty that took 24 days: That was how long elapsed between the award and the taking of a penalty in an Argentine Second Division match between **Atalanta** and Defensores in 2003. A riot ended the original match with 5 minutes left. The game resumed behind closed doors with the penalty that caused the abandonment. Lucas Ferreiro scored it to give Atalanta a 1–0 win.

INTERNATIONAL PENALTIES, MISSED

Four penalties out of five were missed when **Colombia** beat Argentina 3-0 in a Copa America group tie in Paraguay in Jul 1999. Martin Palmeiro missed three for Argentina and Colombia's Hamilton Ricard had one spot-kick saved.

In the European Championship semi-final against Italy in Amsterdam on Jun 29, 2000, **Holland** missed five penalties – two in normal time, three in the penalty contest which Italy won 3-1 (after 0-0). Dutch captain Frank de Boer missed twice from the spot.

ENGLAND'S SHOOT-OUT RECORD

England have been beaten in seven out of nine penalty shoot-outs in major tournaments:

1990 (World Cup semi-final, Turin) 3-4 v West Germany after 1-1.
1996 (Euro Champ quarter-final, Wembley) 4-2 v Spain after 0-0.
1996 (Euro Champ semi-final, Wembley) 5-6 v Germany after 1-1.
1998 (World Cup 2nd round., St Etienne) 3-4 v Argentina after 2-2.
2004 (Euro Champ quarter-final, Lisbon) 5-6 v Portugal after 2-2.
2006 (World Cup quarter-final, Gelsenkirchen) 1-3 v Portugal after 0-0.
2007 (Euro U-21 Champ semi-final, Heerenveen) 12-13 v Holland after 1-1.
2009 (Euro U-21 Champ semi-final, Gothenbury) 5-4 v Sweden after 3-3.
2012 (Euro Champ quarter-final, Kiev) 2-4 v Italy after 0-0.

FA CUP SHOOT-OUTS

First penalty contest in the FA Cup took place in 1972. In the days of the play-off for third place, the match was delayed until the eve of the following season when losing semi-finalists Birmingham and Stoke met at St Andrew's on Aug 5. The score was 0-0 and Birmingham won 4-3 on penalties.

Highest-scoring: Preliminary round replay (Aug 30, 2005): Tunbridge Wells beat Littlehampton 16-15 after 40 spot-kicks (9 missed).

Competition proper: Macclesfield beat Forest Green 11-10 in 1st round replay (Nov 28, 2001) – 24 kicks.

Shoot-out abandoned: The FA Cup 1st round replay between Oxford City and Wycombe at Wycombe on Nov 9, 1999 was abandoned (1-1) after extra-time. As the penalty shoot-out was about to begin, a fire broke out under a stand. Wycombe won the second replay 1-0 at Oxford Utd's ground.

First FA Cup Final to be decided by shoot-out was in 2005 (May 21), when Arsenal beat Manchester Utd 5-4 on penalties at Cardiff's Millennium Stadium (0-0 after extra time). A year later (May 13) Liverpool beat West Ham 3-1 (3-3 after extra-time).

MARATHON SHOOT-OUT BETWEEN LEAGUE CLUBS

Highest recorded score in shoot-out between league clubs: Dagenham & Redbridge 14-13 against Leyton Orient (after 1-1) in Johnstone's Paint Trophy southern section on Sep 7, 2011

MISSED CUP FINAL PENALTIES

John Aldridge (Liverpool) became the first player to miss a penalty in an FA Cup Final at Wembley when Dave Beasant saved his shot in 1988 to help Wimbledon to a shock 1-0 win. Seven penalties before had been scored in the Final at Wembley.
Previously, **Charlie Wallace**, of Aston Villa, had failed from the spot in the 1913 Final against Sunderland at Crystal Palace, which his team won 1-0

Gary Lineker (Tottenham) had his penalty saved by Nottm Forest's Mark Crossley in the 1991 FA Cup Final.

For the first time, two spot-kicks were missed in an FA Cup Final. In 2010, Petr Cech saved from Portsmouth's **Kevin-Prince Boateng** while Chelsea's **Frank Lampard** put his kick wide.

Another miss at Wembley was by Arsenal's **Nigel Winterburn**, Luton's Andy Dibble saving his spot-kick in the 1988 Littlewoods Cup Final, when a goal would have put Arsenal 3-1 ahead. Instead, they lost 3-2.

Winterburn was the third player to fail with a League Cup Final penalty at Wembley, following **Ray Graydon** (Aston Villa) against Norwich in 1975 and **Clive Walker** (Sunderland), who shot wide in the 1985 Milk Cup Final, also against Norwich who won 1-0. Graydon had his penalty saved by Kevin Keelan, but scored from the rebound and won the cup for Aston Villa (1-0).

Derby's Martin Taylor saved a penalty from **Eligio Nicolini** in the Anglo-Italian Cup Final at Wembley on Mar 27, 1993, but Cremonese won 3-1.

LEAGUE PENALTIES RECORD

Most penalties in Football League match: Five – 4 to Crystal Palace (3 missed), 1 to Brighton (scored) in Div 2 match at Selhurst Park on Mar 27 (Easter Monday), 1989. Crystal Palace won 2-1. Three of the penalties were awarded in a 5-minute spell. The match also produced 5 bookings and a sending-off. Other teams missing 3 penalties in a match: Burnley v Grimsby (Div 2), Feb 13, 1909; Manchester City v Newcastle (Div 1), Jan 17, 1912.

HOTTEST MODERN SPOT-SHOTS

Matthew Le Tissier ended his career in season 2001–02 with the distinction of having netted 48 out of 49 first-team penalties for Southampton. He scored the last 27 after his only miss when Nottm Forest keeper Mark Crossley saved in a Premier League match at The Dell on Mar 24, 1993.

Graham Alexander scored 78 out of 84 penalties in a 22-year career (Scunthorpe, Luton, Preston twice and Burnley) which ended in 2112.

SPOT-KICK HAT-TRICKS

Right–back **Joe Willetts** scored three penalties when Hartlepool beat Darlington 6-1 (Div 3N) on Good Friday 1951.

Danish international **Jan Molby**'s only hat-trick in English football, for Liverpool in a 3-1 win at home to Coventry (Littlewoods Cup, 4th round replay, Nov 26, 1986) comprised three goals from the penalty spot.

It was the first such hat-trick in a major match for two years – since **Andy Blair** scored three penalties for Sheffield Wed against Luton (Milk Cup 4th round, Nov 20 1984).

Portsmouth's **Kevin Dillon** scored a penalty hat-trick in the Full Members Cup (2nd round) at home to Millwall (3-2) on Nov 4, 1986.

Alan Slough scored a hat-trick of penalties in an away game, but was on the losing side, when Peterborough were beaten 4-3 at Chester (Div 3, Apr 29, 1978).

Penalty hat-tricks in **international football**: Dimitris Saravakos (in 9 mins) for Greece v Egypt in 1990. He scored 5 goals in match. **Henrik Larsson**, among his 4 goals in Sweden's 6-0 home win v Moldova in World Cup qualifying match, Jun 6, 2001.

MOST PENALTY GOALS (LEAGUE) IN SEASON

13 out of 13 by **Francis Lee** for Manchester City (Div 1) in 1971–72. His goal total for the season was 33. In season 1988–89, **Graham Roberts** scored 12 League penalties for Second Division Champions Chelsea. In season 2004–05, **Andrew Johnson** scored 11 Premiership penalties for Crystal Palace, who were relegated.

PENALTY–SAVE SEQUENCES

Ipswich goalkeeper **Paul Cooper** saved eight of the ten penalties he faced in 1979–80. **Roy Brown** (Notts Co) saved six in a row in season 1972–73.

Andy Lomas, goalkeeper for Chesham (Diadora League) claimed a record eighth **consecutive** penalty saves – three at the end of season 1991–92 and five in 1992–93.

Mark Bosnich (Aston Villa) saved five in two consecutive matches in 1993–94: three in Coca-Cola Cup semi-final penalty shoot–out v Tranmere (Feb 26), then two in Premiership at Tottenham (Mar 2).

MISSED PENALTIES SEQUENCE

Against Wolves in Div 2 on Sep 28, 1991, **Southend** missed their seventh successive penalty (five of them the previous season).

SCOTTISH RECORDS
(See also under 'Goals' & 'Discipline')

RANGERS' MANY RECORDS

Rangers' record-breaking feats include:

League Champions: 54 times (once joint holders) – world record.

Winning every match in Scottish League (18 games, 1898–99 season).

Major hat-tricks: Rangers have completed the domestic treble (League Championship, League Cup and Scottish FA Cup) a record seven times (1948–49, 1963–64, 1975–76, 1977–78, 1992–93, 1998–99, 2002–03).

League & Cup double: 17 times.

Nine successive Championships (1989–97). Four men played in all nine sides: Richard Gough, Ally McCoist, Ian Ferguson and Ian Durrant.

115 major trophies: Championships 54, Scottish Cup 33, League Cup 27, Cup-Winners' Cup 1.

CELTIC'S GRAND SLAM

Celtic's record in 1966–67 was the most successful by a British club in one season. They won the **Scottish League,** the **Scottish Cup,** the **Scottish League Cup** and became the first British club to win the **European Cup.** They also won the **Glasgow Cup.**

Celtic have 3 times achieved the Scottish treble (League Championship, League Cup and FA Cup), in 1966–67, 1968–69 and 2000–01 (in Martin O'Neill's first season as their manager). They became Scottish Champions for 2000–01 with a 1-0 home win against St. Mirren on Apr 7 – the earliest the title had been clinched for 26 years, since Rangers' triumph on Mar 29, 1975.

They have won the Scottish Cup 35 times, and have completed the League and Cup double 14 times.

Celtic won nine consecutive Scottish League titles (1966–74) under Jock Stein.

They set a **British record** of 25 consecutive League wins in season 2003–04 (Aug 15 to Mar 14). They were unbeaten for 77 matches (all competitions) at Celtic Park from Aug 22, 2001, to Apr 21, 2004. They have won the Scottish Championship 43 times.

UNBEATEN SCOTTISH CHAMPIONS

Celtic and **Rangers** have each won the Scottish Championship with an unbeaten record: Celtic in 1897–98 (P18, W15, D3), Rangers in 1898–99 (P18, W18).

LARSSON SUPREME

After missing most of the previous campaign with a broken leg, Swedish international **Henrik Larsson,** with 53 goals in season 2000–01, set a post-war record for Celtic and equalled the Scottish Premier League record of 35 by **Brian McClair** (Celtic) in 1986–87. Larsson's 35 earned him Europe's **Golden Shoe** award.

His 7 seasons as a Celtic player ended, when his contract expired in May 2004, with a personal total of 242 goals in 315 apps (third-highest scorer in the club's history). He helped Celtic win 4 League titles, and at 32 he moved to Barcelona (free) on a 2-year contract.

SCOTTISH CUP HAT-TRICKS

Aberdeen's feat of winning the Scottish FA Cup in 1982–3–4 made them only the third club to achieve that particular hat-trick. **Queen's Park** did it twice (1874–5–6 and 1880–1–2), and **Rangers** have won the Scottish Cup three years in succession on three occasions: 1934–5–6, 1948–9–50 and 1962–3–4.

SCOTTISH CUP FINAL DISMISSALS

Five players have been sent off in the Scottish FA Cup Final: **Jock Buchanan** (Rangers v Kilmarnock, 1929); **Roy Aitken** (Celtic v Aberdeen, 1984); **Walter Kidd** (Hearts captain v Aberdeen, 1986); **Paul Hartley** (Hearts v Gretna, 2006); **Pa Kujabi** (Hibernian v Hearts, 2012).

RECORD SEQUENCES

Celtic hold Britain's League record of 62 matches undefeated, from Nov 13, 1915 to Apr 21, 1917, when Kilmarnock won 2-0 at Parkhead. They won 49, drew 13 (111 points) and scored 126 goals to 26.

Greenock Morton in 1963–64 accumulated 67 points out of 72 and scored 135 goals.

Queen's Park did not have a goal scored against them during the first seven seasons of their existence (1867–74, before the Scottish League was formed).

EARLIEST PROMOTIONS IN SCOTLAND

Dundee promoted from Div 2, Feb 1, 1947; **Greenock Morton** promoted from Div 2, Mar 2, 1964; **Gretna** promoted from Div 3, Mar 5, 2005.

WORST HOME SEQUENCE

After gaining promotion to Div 1 in 1992, **Cowdenbeath** went a record 38 consecutive home League matches without a win. They ended the sequence (drew 8, lost 30) when beating Arbroath 1-0 on Apr 2, 1994, watched by a crowd of 225.

ALLY'S RECORDS

Ally McCoist became the first player to complete 200 goals in the Premier Division when he scored Rangers' winner (2-1) at Falkirk on Dec 12, 1992. His first was against Celtic in Sep 1983, and he reached 100 against Dundee on Boxing Day 1987.

When McCoist scored twice at home to Hibernian (4-3) on Dec 7, 1996, he became Scotland's record post-war League marksman, beating Gordon Wallace's 264.

Originally with St Johnstone (1978–81), he spent two seasons with Sunderland (1981–83), then joined Rangers for £200,000 in Jun 1983.

In 15 seasons at Ibrox, he scored 355 goals for Rangers (250 League), and helped them win 10 Championships (9 in succession), 3 Scottish Cups and earned a record 9 League Cup winner's medals. He won the European Golden Boot in consecutive seasons (1991–92, 1992–93).

His 9 Premier League goals in three seasons for Kilmarnock gave him a career total of 281 Scottish League goals when he retired at the end of 2000–01. McCoist succeeded Walter Smith as manager of Rangers in May 2011.

SCOTLAND'S MOST SUCCESSFUL MANAGER

Bill Struth, 30 trophies for Rangers, 1920–54 (18 Championships, 10 Scottish Cups, 2 League Cups).

SMITH'S IBROX HONOURS

Walter Smith, who retired in May, 2011, won a total of 21 trophies in two spells as Rangers manager (10 League titles, 5 Scottish Cups, 6 League Cups).

RANGERS PUNISHED

In April 2012, Rangers (in administration) were fined £160,000 by the Scottish FA and given a 12-month transfer ban on charges relating to their finances. The ban was later overturned in court. The club had debts estimated at around £135m and on June 12, 2012 were forced into liquidation. A new company emerged, but Rangers were voted out of the Scottish Premier League and demoted to Division Three for the start of the 2012-13 season. Dundee, runners-up in Division One, replaced them in the top flight.

FIVE IN A MATCH

Paul Sturrock set an individual scoring record for the Scottish Premier Division with 5 goals in Dundee Utd's 7-0 win at home to Morton on Nov 17, 1984. **Marco Negri** equalled the feat with all 5 when Rangers beat Dundee Utd 5-1 at Ibrox (Premier Division) on Aug 23, 1997, and **Kenny Miller** scored 5 in Rangers' 7-1 win at home to St. Mirren on Nov 4, 2000. **Kris**

Boyd scored all Kilmarnock's goals in a 5-2 SPL win at home to Dundee Utd on Sep 25, 2004. **Boyd** scored another 5 when Rangers beat Dundee Utd 7-1 on Dec 30, 2009. That took his total of SPL goals to a record 160. **Gary Hooper** netted all Celtic's goals in 5-0 SPL win against Hearts on May 13, 2012

NEGRI'S TEN-TIMER

Marco Negri scored in Rangers' first ten League matches (23 goals) in season 1997-98, a Premier Division record. The previous best sequence was 8 by **Ally MacLeod** for Hibernian in 1978.

DOUBLE SCOTTISH FINAL

Rangers v Celtic drew **129,643** and **120,073** people to the Scottish Cup Final and replay at Hampden Park, Glasgow, in 1963. Receipts for the two matches totalled £50,500.

MOST SCOTTISH CHAMPIONSHIP MEDALS

13 by **Sandy Archibald** (Rangers, 1918-34). Post-war record: 10 by **Bobby Lennox** (Celtic, 1966-79).

Alan Morton won **nine** Scottish Championship medals with Rangers in 1921-23-24-25-27-28-29-30-31. **Ally McCoist** played in the Rangers side that won nine successive League titles (1989-97).

Between 1927 and 1939 **Bob McPhail** helped Rangers win nine Championships, finish second twice and third once. He scored 236 League goals but was never top scorer in a single season.

TOP SCOTTISH LEAGUE SCORERS IN SEASON

Raith Rovers (Div 2) 142 goals in 1937-38; **Morton** (Div 2) 135 goals in 1963-64; **Hearts** (Div 1) 132 goals in 1957-58; **Falkirk** (Div 2) 132 goals in 1935-36; **Gretna** (Div 3) 130 goals in 2004-05.

SCOTTISH CUP – NO DECISION

The **Scottish FA** withheld their Cup and medals in 1908-09 after Rangers and Celtic played two drawn games in the Final. Spectators rioted.

FEWEST LEAGUE WINS IN SEASON

In modern times: 1 win by **Ayr** (34 matches, Div 1, 1966-67); **Forfar** (38 matches, Div 2, 1973-74); **Clydebank** (36 matches, Div 1, 1999-2000).

Vale of Leven provided the only instance of a British team failing to win a single match in a league season (Div 1, 18 games,1891-92).

HAMPDEN'S £63M REDEVELOPMENT

On completion of redevelopment costing £63m **Hampden Park**, home of Scottish football and the oldest first-class stadium in the world, was re-opened full scale for the Rangers-Celtic Cup Final on May 29, 1999.

Work on the 'new Hampden' (capacity 52,000) began in 1992. The North and East stands were restructured (£12m); a new South stand and improved West stand cost £51m. The Millennium Commission contributed £23m and the Lottery Sports Fund provided a grant of £3.75m.

GRETNA'S RISE AND FALL

Gretna, who joined the Scottish League in 2002, won the Bell's Third, Second and First Division titles in successive seasons (2005-6-7). They also become the first team from the third tier to reach the Scottish Cup Final, taking Hearts to penalties (2006). But then it all turned sour. Businessman Brooks Mileson, who had financed this rise to the Premier League, withdrew his backing, causing the club to collapse. They went into administration, finished bottom of the SPL, were demoted to Division Three, then resigned from the League.

DEMISE OF AIRDRIE AND CLYDEBANK

In May 2002, First Division **Airdrieonians**, formed in 1878, went out of business. They had debts of £3m. Their place in the Scottish League was taken by **Gretna**, from the English Unibond League, who were voted into Div 3. Second Division **Clydebank** folded in Jul 2002 and were taken over by the new **Airdrie United** club.

FASTEST GOAL IN SPL

12.4 sec by **Anthony Stokes** for Hibernian in 4-1 home defeat by Rangers, Dec 27, 2009.

YOUNGEST SCORER IN SPL

Fraser Fyvie, aged 16 years and 306 days, for Aberdeen v Hearts (3-0) on Jan 27, 2010.

12 GOALS SHARED

There was a record aggregate score for the SPL on May 5, 2010, when **Motherwell** came from 6-2 down to draw 6-6 with **Hibernian**.

25-POINT DEDUCTION

Dundee were deducted 25 points by the Scottish Football League in November 2010 for going into administration for the second time. It left the club on minus 11 points, but they still managed to finish in mid-table in Division One.

GREAT SCOTS

In Feb 1988, the Scottish FA launched a national **Hall of Fame**, initially comprising the first 11 Scots to make 50 international appearances, to be joined by all future players to reach that number of caps. Each member receives a gold medal, invitation for life at all Scotland's home matches, and has his portrait hung at Scottish FA headquarters in Glasgow.

MORE CLUBS IN 2000

The **Scottish Premier League** increased from 10 to 12 clubs in season 2000–01. The **Scottish Football League** admitted two new clubs – Peterhead and Elgin City from the Highland League – to provide three divisions of 10 in 2000–01.

NOTABLE SCOTTISH 'FIRSTS'

- The father of League football was a Scot, **William McGregor**, a draper in Birmingham. The 12–club Football League kicked off in Sep 1888, and McGregor was its first president.
- **Hibernian** were the first British club to play in the European Cup, by invitation. They reached the semi–final when it began in 1955–56.
- **Celtic** were Britain's first winners of the European Cup, in 1967.
- Scotland's First Division became the **Premier Division** in season 1975–76.
- Football's **first international** was staged at the West of Scotland cricket ground, Partick, on Nov 30, 1872: Scotland 0, England 0.
- Scotland introduced its **League Cup** in 1945–46, the first season after the war. It was another 15 years before the Football League Cup was launched.
- Scotland pioneered the use in British football of **two subs** per team in League and Cup matches.
- The world's **record football score** belongs to Scotland: Arbroath 36, Bon Accord 0 (Scottish Cup 1st rd) on Sep 12, 1885.
- The Scottish FA introduced the penalty **shoot-out** to their Cup Final in 1990.
- On Jan 22, 1994 all six matches in the **Scottish Premier Division** ended as draws.
- Scotland's new Premier League introduced a **3-week shut-down** in Jan 1999 – first instance of British football adopting the winter break system that operates in a number of European countries. The SPL ended its New Year closure after 2003.
- **Rangers** made history at home to St. Johnstone (Premier League, 0-0, Mar 4, 2000) when

fielding a team entirely without Scottish players.

John Fleck, aged 16 years, 274 days, became the youngest player in a Scottish FA Cup Final when he came on as a substitute for Rangers in their 3-2 win over Queen of the South at Hampden Park on May 24, 2008

SCOTTISH CUP SHOCK RESULTS

1885–86	(1)	Arbroath 36 Bon Accord 0
1921–22	(F)	Morton 1 Rangers 0
1937–38	(F)	East Fife 4 Kilmarnock 2 (replay, after 1-1)
1960–61	(F)	Dunfermline 2 Celtic 0 (replay, after 0-0)
1966–67	(1)	Berwick 1 Rangers 0
1979–80	(3)	Hamilton 2 Keith 3
1984–85	(1)	Stirling 20 Selkirk 0
1984–85	(3)	Inverness 3 Kilmarnock 0
1986–87	(3)	Rangers 0 Hamilton 1
1994–95	(4)	Stenhousemuir 2 Aberdeen 0
1998–99	(3)	Aberdeen 0 Livingston 1
1999–2000	(3)	Celtic 1 Inverness 3
2003–04	(5)	Inverness 1 Celtic 0
2005–06	(3)	Clyde 2 Celtic 1
2008–09	(6)	St Mirren 1 Celtic 0
2009–10	(SF)	Ross Co 2 Celtic 0
Scottish League (Coca-Cola) Cup Final		
1994–95		Raith 2, Celtic 2 (Raith won 6-5 on pens)

MISCELLANEOUS

NATIONAL ASSOCIATIONS FORMED

FA	**1863**
FA of Wales	**1876**
Scottish FA	**1873**
Irish FA	**1904**
Federation of International Football Associations (FIFA)	**1904**

NATIONAL & INTERNATIONAL COMPETITIONS LAUNCHED

FA Cup	**1871**
Welsh Cup	**1877**
Scottish Cup	**1873**
Irish Cup	**1880**
Football League	**1888**
Premier League	**1992**
Scottish League	**1890**
Scottish Premier League	**1998**
Scottish League Cup	**1945**
Football League Cup	**1960**
Home International Championship	**1883–4**
World Cup	**1930**
European Championship	**1958**
European Cup	**1955**
Fairs/UEFA Cup	**1955**
Cup-Winners' Cup	**1960**
European Champions League	**1992**
Olympic Games Tournament, at Shepherd's Bush	**1908**

INNOVATIONS

Size of Ball: Fixed in **1872**.

Shinguards: Introduced and registered by Sam Weller Widdowson (Nottm Forest & England) in **1874**.

Referee's whistle: First used on Nottm Forest's ground in **1878**.

Professionalism: Legalised in England in the summer of **1885** as a result of agitation by Lancashire clubs.

Goal-nets: Invented and patented in **1890** by Mr JA Brodie of Liverpool. They were first used in the North v South match in Jan, **1891**.

Referees and linesmen: Replaced umpires and referees in Jan, **1891**.

Penalty-kick: Introduced at Irish FA's request in the season **1891–92**. The penalty law ordering the goalkeeper to remain on the goal-line came into force in Sep, **1905**, and the order to stand on his goal-line until the ball is kicked arrived in **1929–30**.

White ball: First came into official use in **1951**.

Floodlighting: First FA Cup-tie (replay), Kidderminster Harriers v Brierley Hill Alliance, **1955**. First Football League match: Portsmouth v Newcastle (Div 1), **1956**.

Heated pitch to beat frost tried by Everton at Goodison Park in **1958**.

First soccer closed-circuit TV: At Coventry ground in Oct **1965** (10,000 fans saw their team win at Cardiff, 120 miles away).

Substitutes (one per team) were first allowed in Football League matches at the start of season **1965–66**. Three substitutes (one a goalkeeper) allowed, two of which could be used, in Premier League matches, **1992–93**. The Football League introduced three substitutes for **1993–94**.

Three points for a win: Introduced by the Football League in **1981–82**, by FIFA in World Cup games in **1994**, and by the Scottish League in the same year.

Offside law amended, player 'level' no longer offside, and 'professional foul' made sending-off offence, **1990**.

Penalty shoot-outs introduced to decide FA Cup ties level after one replay and extra time, **1991–92**.

New back-pass rule: goalkeeper must not handle ball kicked to him by team-mate, **1992**.

Linesmen became 'referees' assistants', **1998**.

Goalkeepers not to hold ball longer than 6 seconds, **2000**.

Free-kicks advanced by ten yards against opponents failing to retreat, **2000**. This experimental rule in England was scrapped in 2005).

YOUNGEST AND OLDEST

Youngest Caps

	Age
Gareth Bale (Wales v Trinidad & Tobago, May 27, 2006)	**16 years 315 days**
Norman Whiteside (N Ireland v Yugoslavia, Jun 17, 1982)	**17 years 41 days**
Theo Walcott (England v Hungary, May 30, 2006)	**17 years 75 days**
Johnny Lambie (Scotland v Ireland, Mar 20, 1886)	**17 years 92 days**
Jimmy Holmes (Rep of Ireland v Austria, May 30, 1971)	**17 years 200 days**

Youngest England scorer: Wayne Rooney (17 years, 317 days) v Macedonia, Skopje, Sep 6, 2003.

Youngest England hat-trick scorer: Theo Walcott (19 years, 178 days) v Croatia, Zagreb, Sep 10, 2008.

Youngest England captains: Bobby Moore (v Czech., Bratislava, May 29, 1963), 22 years, 47 days; Michael Owen (v Paraguay, Anfield, Apr 17, 2002), 22 years, 117 days.

Youngest England players to reach 50 caps: Michael Owen (23 years, 6 months) v Slovakia at Middlesbrough, Jun 11, 2003; Bobby Moore (25 years, 7 months) v Wales at Wembley, Nov 16, 1966.

Youngest player in World Cup Final: Pele (Brazil) aged 17 years, 237 days v Sweden in Stockholm, Jun 12, 1958.

Youngest player to appear in World Cup Finals: Norman Whiteside (N Ireland v Yugoslavia in Spain – Jun 17, 1982, age 17 years and 42 days.

Youngest First Division player: Derek Forster (Sunderland goalkeeper v Leicester, Aug 22, 1964) aged 15 years, 185 days.

Youngest First Division scorer: At 16 years and 57 days, schoolboy Jason Dozzell (substitute after 30 minutes for Ipswich at home to Coventry on Feb 4, 1984). Ipswich won 3-1 and Dozzell scored their third goal.

Youngest Premier League player: Matthew Briggs (Fulham sub at Middlesbrough, May 13, 2007) aged 16 years and 65 days.

Youngest Premier League scorer: James Vaughan (Everton, home to Crystal Palace, Apr 10, 2005), 16 years, 271 days.

Youngest Premier League captain: Lee Cattermole (Middlesbrough away to Fulham, May 7, 2006) aged 18 years, 47 days.

Youngest player sent off in Premier League: Wayne Rooney (Everton, away to Birmingham, Dec 26, 2002) aged 17 years, 59 days.

Youngest First Division hat-trick scorer: Alan Shearer, aged 17 years, 240 days, in Southampton's 4-2 home win v Arsenal (Apr 9, 1988) on his full debut. Previously, Jimmy Greaves (17 years, 309 days) with 4 goals for Chelsea at home to Portsmouth (7-4), Christmas Day, 1957.

Youngest to complete 100 Football League goals: Jimmy Greaves (20 years, 261 days) when he did so for Chelsea v Manchester City, Nov 19, 1960.

Youngest players in Football League: Reuben Noble-Lazarus (Barnsley 84th minute sub at Ipswich, Sep 30, 2008, Champ) aged 15 years, 45 days; Mason Bennett (Derby at Middlesbrough, Champ, Oct 22, 2011) aged 15 years, 99 days; Albert Geldard (Bradford PA v Millwall, Div 2, Sep 16, 1929) aged 15 years, 158 days; Ken Roberts (Wrexham v Bradford Park Avenue, Div 3 North, Sep 1, 1951) also 15 years, 158 days.

Youngest Football League scorer: Ronnie Dix (for Bristol Rov v Norwich, Div 3 South, Mar 3, 1928) aged 15 years, 180 days.

Youngest player in Scottish League: Goalkeeper Ronnie Simpson (Queens Park) aged 15 in 1946.

Youngest player in FA Cup: Andy Awford, Worcester City's England Schoolboy defender, aged 15 years, 88 days when he substituted in second half away to Boreham Wood (3rd qual round) on Oct 10, 1987.

Youngest player in FA Cup proper: Luke Freeman, Gillingham substitute striker (15 years, 233 days) away to Barnet in 1st round, Nov 10, 2007.

Youngest FA Cup scorer: Sean Cato (16 years, 25 days), second half sub in Barrow Town's 7-2 win away to Rothwell Town (prelim rd), Sep 3, 2011.

Youngest Wembley Cup Final captain: Barry Venison (Sunderland v Norwich, Milk Cup Final, Mar 24, 1985 – replacing suspended captain Shaun Elliott) – aged 20 years, 220 days.

Youngest FA Cup-winning captain: Bobby Moore (West Ham, 1964, v Preston), aged 23 years, 20 days.

Youngest FA Cup Final captain: David Nish aged 21 years and 212 days old when he captained Leicester against Manchester City at Wembley on Apr 26, 1969.

Youngest FA Cup Final player: Curtis Weston (Millwall sub last 3 mins v Manchester Utd, 2004) aged 17 years, 119 days.

Youngest FA Cup Final scorer: Norman Whiteside (Manchester Utd v Brighton, 1983 replay, Wembley), aged 18 years, 19 days.

Youngest FA Cup Final managers: Stan Cullis, Wolves (33) v Leicester, 1949; Steve Coppell, Crystal Palace (34) v Manchester Utd, 1990; Ruud Gullit, Chelsea (34) v Middlesbrough, 1997.

Youngest player in Football League Cup: Chris Coward (Stockport) sub v Sheffield Wed, 2nd Round, Aug 23, 2005, aged 16 years and 31 days.

Youngest Wembley scorer: Norman Whiteside (Manchester Utd v Liverpool, Milk Cup Final, Mar 26, 1983) aged 17 years, 324 days.

Youngest Wembley Cup Final goalkeeper: Chris Woods (18 years, 125 days) for Nottm Forest v Liverpool, League Cup Final on Mar 18, 1978.

Youngest Wembley FA Cup Final goalkeeper: Peter Shilton (19 years, 219 days) for Leicester v Manchester City, Apr 26, 1969.

Youngest senior international at Wembley: Salomon Olembe (sub for Cameroon v England, Nov 15, 1997), aged 16 years, 342 days.

Youngest winning manager at Wembley: Roy McDonough, aged 33 years. 6 months, 24 days as player-manager of Colchester, FA Trophy winners on May 10, 1992.

Youngest scorer in full international: Mohamed Kallon (Sierra Leone v Congo, African Nations Cup, Apr 22, 1995), reported as aged 15 years, 192 days.

Youngest English scorer in Champions League: Alex Oxlade-Chamberlain (Arsenal v Olympiacos, Sep 28, 2011) aged 18 years 1 month, 13 days

Youngest player sent off in World Cup Final series: Rigobert ong (Cameroon v Brazil, in USA, Jun 1994) aged 17 years, 358 days.

Youngest FA Cup Final referee: Kevin Howley, of Middlesbrough, aged 35 when in charge of Wolves v Blackburn, 1960.

Youngest player in England U-23 team: Duncan Edwards (v Italy, Bologna, Jan 20, 1954), aged 17 years, 112 days.

Youngest player in England U-21 team: Theo Walcott (v Moldova, Ipswich, Aug 15, 2006), aged 17 years, 152 days.

Youngest player in Scotland U-21 team: Christian Dailly (v Romania, Hampden Park, Sep 11, 1990), aged 16 years, 330 days.

Youngest player in senior football: Cameron Campbell Buchanan, Scottish-born outside right, aged 14 years, 57 days when he played for Wolves v WBA in War-time League match, Sep 26, 1942.

Youngest player in peace-time senior match: Eamon Collins (Blackpool v Kilmarnock, Anglo-Scottish Cup quarter-final 1st leg, Sep 9, 1980) aged 14 years, 323 days.

World's youngest player in top division match: Centre-forward Fernando Rafael Garcia, aged 13, played for 23 minutes for Peruvian club Juan Aurich in 3-1 win against Estudiantes on May 19, 2001.

Oldest player to appear in Football League: New Brighton manager Neil McBain (51 years, 120 days) as emergency goalkeeper away to Hartlepool (Div 3 North, Mar 15, 1947).

Other oldest post-war players: Sir Stanley Matthews (Stoke, 1965, 50 years, 5 days); Peter Shilton (Leyton Orient 1997, 47 years, 126 days); Kevin Poole (Burton, 2010, 46 years, 291 days); Dave Beasant (Brighton 2003, 44 years, 46 days); Alf Wood (Coventry, 1958, 43 years, 199 days); Tommy Hutchison (Swansea City, 1991, 43 years, 172 days).

Oldest Football League debutant: Andy Cunningham, for Newcastle at Leicester (Div 1) on Feb 2, 1929, aged 38 years, 2 days.

Oldest post-war debut in English League: Defender David Donaldson (35 years, 7 months, 23 days) for Wimbledon on entry to Football League (Div 4) away to Halifax, Aug 20, 1977.

Oldest player to appear in First Division: Sir Stanley Matthews (Stoke v Fulham, Feb 6, 1965), aged 50 years, 5 days – on that his last League appearance, the only 50-year-old ever to play in the top division.

Oldest players in Premier League: Goalkeepers John Burridge (Manchester City v QPR, May 14, 1995), aged 43 years, 5 months, 11 days; Alec Chamberlain (Watford v Newcastle, May 13, 2007) aged 42 years, 11 months, 23 days; Steve Ogrizovic (Coventry v Sheffield Wed, May 6, 2000), aged 42 years, 7 months, 24 days; Neville Southall (Bradford City v Leeds, Mar 12, 2000), aged 41 years, 5 months, 26 days. Outfield: Teddy Sheringham (West Ham v Manchester City, Dec 30, 2006), aged 40 years, 8 months, 28 days. Gordon Strachan (Coventry City v Derby, May 3, 1997), aged 40 years, 2 months, 24 days.

Oldest player for British professional club: John Ryan (owner-chairman of Conference club Doncaster, played as substitute for last minute in 4-2 win at Hereford on Apr 26, 2003), aged 52 years, 11 months, 3 weeks.

Oldest FA Cup Final player: Walter (Billy) Hampson (Newcastle v Aston Villa on Apr 26, 1924), aged 41 years, 257 days.

Oldest captain and goalkeeper in FA Cup Final: David James (Portsmouth v Chelsea, May 15, 2010) aged 39 years, 287 days.

Oldest FA Cup Final scorers: Bert Turner (Charlton v Derby, Apr 27, 1946) aged 36 years, 312 days. Scored for both sides. Teddy Sheringham (West Ham v Liverpool, May 13, 2006) aged 40 years, 41 days. Scored in penalty shoot-out.

Oldest FA Cup-winning team: Arsenal 1950 (average age 31 years, 2 months). Eight of the players were over 30, with the three oldest centre-half Leslie Compton 37, and skipper Joe Mercer and goalkeeper George Swindin, both 35.

Oldest World Cup-winning captain: Dino Zoff, Italy's goalkeeper v W Germany in 1982 Final, aged 40 years, 92 days.

Oldest player capped by England: Stanley Matthews (v Denmark, Copenhagen, May 15, 1957), aged 42 years, 103 days.

Oldest England scorer: Stanley Matthews (v N Ireland, Belfast, Oct 6, 1956), aged 41 years, 248 days.

Oldest British international player: Billy Meredith (Wales v England at Highbury, Mar 15, 1920), aged 45 years, 229 days.

Oldest 'new caps': Goalkeeper Alexander Morten, aged 41 years, 113 days when earning his only England Cap against Scotland on Mar 8, 1873; Arsenal centre-half Leslie Compton, at 38 years, 64 days when he made his England debut in 4-2 win against Wales at Sunderland on Nov 15, 1950. **For Scotland:** Goalkeeper Ronnie Simpson (Celtic) at 36 years, 186 days v England at Wembley, Apr 15, 1967.

Longest Football League career: This spanned 32 years and 10 months, by Stanley Matthews (Stoke, Blackpool, Stoke) from Mar 19, 1932 until Feb 6, 1965.

Shortest FA Cup-winning captain: 5ft 4in – Bobby Kerr (Sunderland v Leeds, 1973).

SHIRT NUMBERING

Numbering players in Football League matches was made compulsory in 1939. Players wore numbered shirts (1-22) in the FA Cup Final as an experiment in 1933 (Everton 1-11 v Manchester City 12-22).

Squad numbers for players were introduced by the Premier League at the start of season 1993–94. They were optional in the Football League until made compulsory in 1999–2000.

Names on shirts: For first time, players wore names as well as numbers on shirts in League Cup and FA Cup Finals, 1993.

SUBSTITUTES

In **1965**, the Football League, by 39 votes to 10, agreed that **one substitute** be allowed for an injured player at any time during a League match. First substitute used in Football League: Keith Peacock (Charlton), away to Bolton in Div 2, Aug 21, 1965.

Two substitutes per team were approved for the League (Littlewoods) Cup and FA Cup in season 1986–87 and two were permitted in the Football League for the first time in 1987–88.

Three substitutes (one a goalkeeper), two of which could be used, introduced by the Premier League for 1992–93. The Football League followed suit for 1993–94.

Three substitutes (one a goalkeeper) were allowed at the World Cup Finals for the first time at US '94.

Three substitutes (any position) introduced by Premier League and Football League in 1995–96.

Five named substitutes (three of which could be used) introduced in Premier League in 1996–97, in FA Cup in 1997–98, League Cup in 1998–99 and Football League in 1999–2000.

Seven named substitutes for Premier League, FA Cup and League Cup in 2008–09. Still only three to be used. Football League adopted this rule for 2009–10, reverted to five in 2011–12 and went back to seven for the 2012–13 season.

First substitute to score in FA Cup Final: Eddie Kelly (Arsenal v Liverpool, 1971). The **first recorded use** of a substitute was in 1889 (Wales v Scotland at Wrexham on Apr 15) when Sam Gillam arrived late – although he was a Wrexham player – and Allen Pugh (Rhostellyn) was allowed to keep goal until he turned up. The match ended 0-0.

When **Dickie Roose**, the Welsh goalkeeper, was injured against England at Wrexham, Mar 16, 1908, **Dai Davies** (Bolton) was allowed to take his place as substitute. Thus Wales used 12 players. England won 7-1.

END OF WAGE LIMIT

Freedom from the maximum wage system – in force since the formation of the Football League in 1888 – was secured by the Professional Footballers' Association in 1961. About this time Italian clubs renewed overtures for the transfer of British stars and Fulham's **Johnny Haynes** became the first British player to earn £100 a week.

THE BOSMAN RULING

On Dec 15, 1995 the **European Court of Justice** ruled that clubs had no right to transfer fees for out-of-contract players, and the outcome of the 'Bosman case' irrevocably changed football's player-club relationship. It began in 1990, when the contract of 26-year-old **Jean-Marc Bosman**, a midfield player with FC Liege, Belgium, expired. French club Dunkirk wanted him but were unwilling to pay the £500,000 transfer fee, so Bosman was compelled to remain with Liege. He responded with a lawsuit against his club and UEFA on the grounds of 'restriction of trade', and after five years at various court levels the European Court of Justice ruled not only in favour of Bosman but of all professional footballers.

The end of restrictive labour practices revolutionised the system. It led to a proliferation of transfers, rocketed the salaries of elite players who, backed by an increasing army of agents, found themselves in a vastly improved bargaining position as they moved from team to team, league to league, nation to nation. Removing the limit on the number of foreigners clubs could field brought an increasing ratio of such signings, not least in England and Scotland.

Bosman's one-man stand opened the way for footballers to become millionaires, but ended his own career. All he received for his legal conflict was 16 million Belgian francs (£312,000) in compensation, a testimonial of poor reward and martyrdom as the man who did most to change the face of football.

By 2011, he was living on Belgian state benefits, saying: 'I have made the world of football rich and shifted the power from clubs to players. Now I find myself with nothing.'

INTERNATIONAL SHOCK RESULTS

1950	USA 1 England 0 (World Cup).
1953	England 3 Hungary 6 (friendly).
1954	Hungary 7 England 1 (friendly)
1966	North Korea 1 Italy 0 (World Cup).
1982	Spain 0, Northern Ireland 1; Algeria 2, West Germany 1 (World Cup).
1990	Cameroon 1 Argentina 0; Scotland 0 Costa Rica 1; Sweden 1 Costa Rica 2 (World Cup).
1990	Faroe Islands 1 Austria 0 (European Champ qual).
1992	Denmark 2 Germany 0 (European Champ Final).
1993	USA 2 England 0 (US Cup tournament).
1993	Argentina 0 Colombia 5 (World Cup qual).
1993	France 2 Israel 3 (World Cup qual).
1994	Bulgaria 2 Germany 1 (World Cup).
1994	Moldova 3 Wales 2; Georgia 5 Wales 0 (European Champ qual).
1995	Belarus 1 Holland 0 (European Champ qual).
1996	Nigeria 4 Brazil 3 (Olympics).
1998	USA 1 Brazil 0 (Concacaf Gold Cup).
1998	Croatia 3 Germany 0 (World Cup).
2000	Scotland 0 Australia 2 (friendly).
2001	Australia 1 France 0; Australia 1, Brazil 0 (Confederations Cup).
2001	Honduras 2 Brazil 0 (Copa America).
2001	Germany 1 England 5 (World Cup qual).

2002	France 0 Senegal 1; South Korea 2 Italy 1 (World Cup).
2003:	England 1 Australia 3 (friendly)
2004:	Portugal 0 Greece 1 (European Champ Final).
2005:	Northern Ireland 1 England 0 (World Cup qual).

GREAT RECOVERIES – DOMESTIC FOOTBALL

On Dec 21, 1957, **Charlton** were losing 5-1 against Huddersfield (Div 2) at The Valley with only 28 minutes left, and from the 15th minute, had been reduced to ten men by injury, but they won 7-6, with left-winger Johnny Summers scoring five goals. **Huddersfield** (managed by Bill Shankly) remain the only team to score six times in a League match and lose.

Among other notable comebacks: on Nov 12, 1904 (Div 1), **Sheffield Wed** were losing 0-5 at home to Everton, but drew 5-5. At Anfield on Dec 4, 1909 (Div 1), **Liverpool** trailed 2-5 to Newcastle at half-time, then won 6-5. On Boxing Day, 1927, in Div 3 South, **Northampton** won 6-5 at home to Luton after being 1-5 down at half-time. On Apr 12, 1993 (Div 1) **Swindon** were 1-4 down at Birmingham with 30 minutes left, but won 6-4.

Other turnabouts in Div 1 include: **Grimsby** (3-5 down) won 6-5 at WBA on Apr 30, 1932; and Derby beat Manchester Utd 5-4 (from 1-4) on Sep 5, 1936. With 5 minutes to play, **Ipswich** were losing 3-0 at Barnsley (Div 1, Mar 9, 1996), but drew 3-3. On Sunday, Jan 19, 1997 (Div 1), **QPR** were 0-4 down away to Port Vale at half-time and still trailing 1-4 with 5 minutes left. They drew 4-4. On Nov 19, 2005, **Leeds** retrieved a 3-0 deficit against Southampton in the final 20 minutes to win their **Championship** game 4-3. **Cardiff** were four goals down at the break in their Championship match at Peterborough (Dec 28, 2009) and recovered to gain a point.

Tranmere retrieved a 3-0 half-time deficit to beat Southampton 4-3 in an FA Cup fifth round replay at home on Feb 20, 2001.

Premier League comebacks: Jan 4, 1994 – Liverpool were 3 down after 24 mins at home to Manchester Utd, drew 3-3; Nov 8, 1997 – Derby led 3-0 after 33 mins at Elland Road, but Leeds won 4-3 with last-minute goal; Sep 29, 2001 – Manchester Utd won 5-3 at Tottenham after trailing 3-0 at half-time; Apr 18, 2010 – Wigan beat Arsenal 3-2 after trailing 2-0 with 80 minutes played.

Season 2003–04 produced some astonishing turn-rounds. **Premiership** (Oct 25): In bottom-two clash at Molineux, **Wolves** were 3 down at half-time v Leicester, but won 4-3. Feb 22: **Leicester**, down to 10 men, rallied from 3-1 down at Tottenham to lead 4-3. Result 4-4.

First Division (Nov 8): **West Ham** led 3-0 after 18 mins at home to WBA, but lost 4-3.

FA Cup 4th Round replay (Feb 4): At half-time, Tottenham led 3-0 at home to **Manchester City**, but City, reduced to 10 men, won 4-3.

Season 2010–11 produced a Premier League record for **Newcastle**, who came from 4-0 down at home to Arsenal to draw 4-4. Previous instance of a team retrieving a four-goal deficit in the top division to draw was in 1984 when Newcastle trailed at QPR in a game which ended 5-5. Preston came back from trailing 4-1 at Leeds to win 6-4 in the Championship in 2010.

MATCHES OFF

Worst day for postponements: Feb 9, 1963, when 57 League fixtures in England and Scotland were frozen off. Only 7 Football League matches took place, and the entire Scottish programme was wiped out.

Other weather-hit days:
Jan 12, 1963 and Feb 2, 1963 – on both those Saturdays, only 4 out of 44 Football League matches were played.
Jan 1, 1979 – 43 out of 46 Football League fixtures postponed.
Jan 17, 1987 – 37 of 45 scheduled Football League fixtures postponed; only 2 Scottish matches survived.
Feb 8–9, 1991 – only 4 of the week-end's 44 Barclays League matches survived the freeze-up (4 of the postponements were on Friday night). In addition, 11 Scottish League matches were off.

Jan 27, 1996 – 44 Cup and League matches in England and Scotland were frozen off. On the weekend of Jan 9, 10, 11, 2010, 46 League and Cup matches in England and Scotland were victims of the weather. On the weekend of Dec 18-21, 2010, 49 matches were frozen off in England and Scotland.

Fewest matches left on one day by postponements was during the Second World War – Feb 3, 1940 when, because of snow, ice and fog only one out of 56 regional league fixtures took place. It resulted Plymouth Argyle 10, Bristol City 3.

The Scottish Cup second round tie between Inverness Thistle and Falkirk in season 1978–79 was **postponed 29 times** because of snow and ice. First put off on Jan 6, it was eventually played on Feb 22. Falkirk won 4-0.

Pools Panel's busiest days: Jan 17, 1987 and Feb 9, 1991 – on both dates they gave their verdict on 48 postponed coupon matches.

FEWEST 'GAMES OFF'

Season 1947–48 was the best since the war for English League fixtures being played to schedule. Only six were postponed.

LONGEST SEASON

The latest that League football has been played in a season was **Jun 7, 1947** (six weeks after the FA Cup Final). The season was extended because of mass postponements caused by bad weather in mid-winter.

The latest the FA Cup competition has ever been completed was in season 1981–82, when Tottenham beat QPR 1-0 in a Final replay at Wembley on May 27.

Worst winter hold-up was in season 1962–63. The Big Freeze began on Boxing Day and lasted until Mar, with nearly 500 first-class matches postponed. The FA Cup 3rd round was the longest on record – it began with only three out of 32 ties playable on Jan 5 and ended 66 days and 261 postponements later on Mar 11. The Lincoln–Coventry tie was put off 15 times. The Pools Panel was launched that winter, on Jan 26, 1963.

HOTTEST DAYS

The Nationwide League kicked off season 2003–04 on Aug 9 with pitch temperatures of 102 degrees recorded at Luton v Rushden and Bradford v Norwich. On the following day, there was a pitch temperature of 100 degrees for the Community Shield match between Manchester Utd and Arsenal at Cardiff's Millennium Stadium. Wembley's pitch-side thermometer registered 107 degrees for the 2009 Chelsea–Everton FA Cup Final.

FOOTBALL ASSOCIATION SECRETARIES/CHIEF EXECUTIVES

1863– 66 Ebenezer Morley; 1866– 68 **Robert Willis**; 1868– 70 **RG Graham**; 1870– 95 **Charles Alcock** (paid from 1887); 1895–1934 **Sir Frederick Wall**; 1934–62 **Sir Stanley Rous**; 1962–73 **Denis Follows**; 1973–89 **Ted Croker** (latterly chief executive); 1989–99 **Graham Kelly** (chief executive); 2000–02 **Adam Crozier** (chief executive); 2003–04 **Mark Palios** (chief executive); 2005– 08: **Brian Barwick** (chief executive); 2009–10 **Ian Watmore** (chief executive); 2010 **Alex Horne** (general secretary).

FOOTBALL'S SPONSORS

Football League: Canon 1983–86; Today Newspaper 1986–87; Barclays 1987–93; Endsleigh Insurance 1993–96; Nationwide Building Society 1996–2004; Coca-Cola 2004–10; Npower from 2010.

League Cup: Milk Cup 1982–86; Littlewoods 1987–90; Rumbelows 1991–92; Coca-Cola 1993–98; Worthington 1998–2003; Carling 2003–12; Capital One from 2012.

Premier League: Carling 1993–2001; Barclaycard 2001–04; Barclays from 2004.

FA Cup: Littlewoods 1994–98; AXA 1998–2002; E.ON 2006–2011; Budwesier from 2011.

SOCCER HEADQUARTERS

Football Association: Wembley Stadium, Wembley, Middx.
Premier League: 30 Gloucester Place, London W1U 8PL.
Football League: Edward VII Quay, Navigation Way, Preston PR2 2YF. London Office: 30 Gloucester Place, London W1U 8FL.
Professional Footballers' Association: 2 Oxford Court, Bishopsgate, Manchester M2 3WQ.
Scottish Football Association: Hampden Park, Glasgow G42 9AY.
Scottish Premier League: Hampden Park, Glasgow G42 9DE.
Scottish Football League: Hampden Park, Glasgow G42 9EB.
Irish Football Association: 20 Windsor Avenue, Belfast BT9 6EG.
Irish Football League: Benmore House, 343-353 Lisburn Road, Belfast BT9 7EN.
League of Ireland: Sports Campus, Abbotstown, Dublin 15.
Football Association of Ireland: Sports Campus, Abbotstown, Dublin 15
Welsh Football Association: 11/12 Neptune Court, Vanguard Way, Cardiff CF24 5PJ.
FIFA: P.O. Box 85, 8030 Zurich, Switzerland.
UEFA: Route de Geneve, CH-1260, Nyon, Geneva, Switzerland.

NEW HOMES OF SOCCER

Newly-constructed League grounds in England since the war: 1946 Hull (Boothferry Park); 1950 Port Vale (Vale Park); 1955 Southend (Roots Hall); 1988 Scunthorpe (Glanford Park); 1990 Walsall (Bescot Stadium); 1990 Wycombe (Adams Park); 1992 Chester (Deva Stadium); 1993 Millwall (New Den); 1994 Huddersfield (McAlpine Stadium); 1994 Northampton (Sixfields Stadium); 1995 Middlesbrough (Riverside Stadium); 1997 Bolton (Reebok Stadium); 1997 Derby (Pride Park); 1997 Stoke (Britannia Stadium); 1997 Sunderland (Stadium of Light); 1998 Reading (Madejski Stadium); 1999 Wigan (JJB Stadium); 2001 Southampton (St. Mary's Stadium); 2001 Oxford Utd (Kassam Stadium); 2002 Leicester (Walkers Stadium); 2002 Hull (Kingston Communications Stadium); 2003 Manchester City (City of Manchester Stadium); 2003 Darlington (New Stadium); 2005 Coventry (Ricoh Arena); Swansea (Stadium of Swansea, Morfa); 2006 Arsenal (Emirates Stadium); 2007 Milton Keynes Dons (Stadium: MK); Shrewsbury (New Meadow); 2008 Colchester (Community Stadium); 2009 Cardiff City Stadium; 2010 Chesterfield (b2net Stadium), Morecambe (Globe Arena); 2011 Brighton (American Express Stadium); 2012 Rotherham (New York Stadium).

Huddersfield now Galpharm Stadium; Leicester now King Power Stadium; Manchester City now Etihad Stadium; Shrewsbury now Greenhous Meadow Stadium; Swansea now Liberty Stadium; Walsall now Banks's Stadium; Wigan now DW Stadium

NATIONAL FOOTBALL CENTRE

The FA's new £100m centre at St George's Park, Burton upon Trent is set in 330 acres of countryside and will be the base for England teams of all ages. It comprises 12 football pitches, five gyms, a 90-seat lecture theatre, conference rooms, two hotels and, for the treatment of injuries, a hydrotherapy unit with swimming pool.

GROUND-SHARING

Crystal Palace and **Charlton** (Selhurst Park, 1985–91); **Bristol Rov** and **Bath City** (Twerton Park, Bath, 1986–96); **Partick Thistle** and **Clyde** (Firhill Park, Glasgow, 1986–91; in seasons 1990–01, 1991–92) **Chester** shared **Macclesfield's** ground (Moss Rose).
Crystal Palace and **Wimbledon** shared Selhurst Park, from season 1991–92, when **Charlton** (tenants) moved to rent Upton Park from **West Ham**, until 2003 when Wimbledon relocated to Milton Keynes. **Clyde** moved to Douglas Park, **Hamilton Academical's** home, in 1991–92. **Stirling Albion** shared **Stenhousemuir's** ground, Ochilview Park, in 1992–93. In 1993–94, **Clyde** shared **Partick's** home until moving to Cumbernauld. In 1994–95, **Celtic** shared Hampden Park with **Queen's Park** (while Celtic Park was redeveloped); **Hamilton** shared **Partick's** ground. **Airdrie** shared **Clyde's** Broadwood Stadium. **Bristol Rov** left **Bath City's**

ground at the start of season 1996–97, sharing Bristol Rugby Club's Memorial Ground. **Clydebank** shared **Dumbarton's** Boghead Park from 1996–97 until renting **Greenock Morton's** Cappielow Park in season 1999–2000. **Brighton** shared **Gillingham's** ground in seasons 1997–98, 1998–99. **Fulham** shared **QPR's** home at Loftus Road in seasons 2002–03, 2003–04, returning to Craven Cottage in Aug 2004.
Inverness Caledonian Thistle moved to share **Aberdeen's** Pittodrie Stadium in 2004–05 after being promoted to the SPL; **Gretna's** home matches on arrival in the SPL in 2007–08 were held at Motherwell and Livingston.

ARTIFICIAL TURF

QPR were the first British club to install an artificial pitch, in 1981. They were followed by **Luton** in 1985, and **Oldham** and **Preston** in **1986**. QPR reverted to grass in 1988, as did Luton and promoted Oldham in season 1991–92 (when artificial pitches were banned in Div 1). **Preston** were the last Football League club playing 'on plastic' in 1993–94, and their Deepdale ground was restored to grass for the start of 1994–95.
Stirling were the **first Scottish club** to play on plastic, in season 1987–88.

DOUBLE RUNNERS-UP

There have been nine instances of clubs finishing runner-up in **both the League Championship and FA Cup** in the same season: 1928 Huddersfield; 1932 Arsenal; 1939 Wolves; 1962 Burnley; 1965 and 1970 Leeds; 1986 Everton; 1995 Manchester Utd; 2001 Arsenal.

CORNER-KICK RECORDS

Not a single corner-kick was recorded when **Newcastle** drew 0-0 at home to **Portsmouth** (Div 1) on Dec 5, 1931.
The record for **most corners** in a match for one side is believed to be **Sheffield Utd's 28** to **West Ham's 1** in Div 2 at Bramall Lane on Oct 14, 1989. For all their pressure, Sheffield Utd lost 2-0.
Nottm Forest led **Southampton** 22-2 on corners (Premier League, Nov 28, 1992) but lost the match 1-2.
Tommy Higginson (Brentford, 1960s) once passed back to his own goalkeeper from a corner kick.
When **Wigan** won 4-0 at home to Cardiff (Div 2) on Feb 16, 2002, all four goals were headed in from corners taken by N Ireland international **Peter Kennedy**.
Steve Staunton (Rep of Ireland) is believed to be the only player to score direct from a corner in **two** Internationals.
In the 2012 Champions League Final, **Bayern Munich** forced 20 corners without scoring, while **Chelsea** scored from their only one.

SACKED AT HALF-TIME

Leyton Orient sacked **Terry Howard** on his 397th appearance for the club – at half-time in a Second Division home defeat against Blackpool (Feb 7, 1995) for 'an unacceptable performance'. He was fined two weeks' wages, given a free transfer and moved to Wycombe.
Bobby Gould resigned as **Peterborough's** head coach at half-time in their 1-0 defeat in the LDV Vans Trophy 1st round at Bristol City on Sep 29, 2004.
Harald Schumacher, former Germany goalkeeper, was sacked as Fortuna Koln coach when they were two down at half-time against Waldhof Mannheim (Dec 15, 1999). They lost 5-1.

MOST GAMES BY 'KEEPER FOR ONE CLUB

Alan Knight made 683 League appearances for Portsmouth, over 23 seasons (1978–2000), a record for a goalkeeper at one club. The previous holder was Peter Bonetti with 600 League games for Chelsea (20 seasons, 1960–79).

PLAYED TWO GAMES ON SAME DAY

Jack Kelsey played full-length matches for both club and country on Wednesday Nov 26, 1958. In the afternoon he kept goal for Wales in a 2-2 draw against England at Villa Park, and he then drove to Highbury to help Arsenal win 3-1 in a prestigious floodlit friendly against Juventus.

On the same day, winger **Danny Clapton** played for England (against Wales and Kelsey) and then in part of Arsenal's match against Juventus.

On Nov 11, 1987, **Mark Hughes** played for Wales against Czechoslovakia (European Championship) in Prague, then flew to Munich and went on as substitute that night in a winning Bayern Munich team, to whom he was on loan from Barcelona.

On Feb 16, 1993 goalkeeper **Scott Howie** played in Scotland's 3-0 U-21 win v Malta at Tannadice Park, Dundee (ko 1.30pm) and the same evening played in Clyde's 2-1 home win v Queen of South (Div 2).

Ryman League **Hornchurch**, faced by end-of-season fixture congestion, played **two matches** on the same night (May 1, 2001). They lost 2-1 at home to Ware and drew 2-2 at Clapton.

RECORD LOSS

Manchester City made a record loss of £194.9m in the 2010–11 financial year.

FIRST 'MATCH OF THE DAY'

BBC TV (recorded highlights): Liverpool 3, Arsenal 2 on Aug 22, 1964. **First complete match to be televised:** Arsenal 3, Everton 2 on Aug 29, 1936. **First League match televised in colour:** Liverpool 2, West Ham 0 on Nov 15, 1969.

'MATCH OF THE DAY' – BIGGEST SCORES

Football League: Tottenham 9, Bristol Rov 0 (Div 2, 1977–78). **Premier League:** Nottm Forest 1, Manchester Utd 8 (1998–99); Portsmouth 7 Reading 4 (2007–08).

FIRST COMMENTARY ON RADIO

Arsenal 1 Sheffield Utd 1 (Div 1) broadcast on BBC, Jan 22, 1927.

OLYMPIC FOOTBALL WINNERS

1908 Great Britain (in London); **1912** Great Britain (Stockholm); **1920** Belgium (Antwerp); **1924** Uruguay (Paris); **1928** Uruguay (Amsterdam); **1932** No soccer in Los Angeles Olympics; **1936** Italy (Berlin); **1948** Sweden (London); **1952** Hungary (Helsinki); **1956** USSR (Melbourne); **1960** Yugoslavia (Rome); **1964** Hungary (Tokyo); **1968** Hungary (Mexico City); **1972** Poland (Munich); **1976** E Germany (Montreal); **1980** Czechoslovakia (Moscow); **1984** France (Los Angeles); **1988** USSR (Seoul); **1992** Spain (Barcelona); **1996** Nigeria (Atlanta); **2000** Cameroon (Sydney); **2004** Argentina (Athens); **2008** Argentina (Beijing).

Highest scorer in Final tournament: Ferenc Bene (Hungary) 12 goals, 1964.

Record crowd for Olympic Soccer Final: 108,800 (France v Brazil, Los Angeles 1984).

MOST AMATEUR CUP WINS

Bishop Auckland set the FA Amateur Cup record with 10 wins, and in 1957 became the only club to carry off the trophy in three successive seasons. The competition was discontinued after the Final on Apr 20, 1974. (Bishop's Stortford 4, Ilford 1, at Wembley).

FOOTBALL FOUNDATION

This was formed (May 2000) to replace the **Football Trust**, which had been in existence since 1975 as an initiative of the Pools companies to provide financial support at all levels, from schools football to safety and ground improvement work throughout the game.

SEVEN-FIGURE TESTIMONIALS

The first was **Sir Alex Ferguson**'s at Old Trafford on Oct 11, 1999, when a full-house of 54,842 saw a Rest of the World team beat Manchester Utd 4-2. United's manager pledged that a large percentage of the estimated £1m receipts would go to charity.

Estimated receipts of £1m and over came from testimonials for **Denis Irwin** (Manchester Utd) against Manchester City at Old Trafford on Aug 16, 2000 (45,158); **Tom Boyd** (Celtic) against Manchester Utd at Celtic Park on May 15, 2001 (57,000) and **Ryan Giggs** (Manchester Utd) against Celtic on Aug 1, 2001 (66,967).

Tony Adams' second testimonial (1-1 v Celtic on May 13, 2002) two nights after Arsenal completed the Double, was watched by 38,021 spectators at Highbury. Of £1m receipts, he donated £500,000 to Sporting Chance, the charity that helps sportsmen/women with drink, drug, gambling problems.

Sunderland and a Republic of Ireland XI drew 0-0 in front of 35,702 at the Stadium of Light on May 14, 2002. The beneficiary, **Niall Quinn**, donated his testimonial proceeds, estimated at £1m, to children's hospitals in Sunderland and Dublin, and to homeless children in Africa and Asia.

A record testimonial crowd of 69,591 for **Roy Keane** at Old Trafford on May 9, 2006 netted more than £2m for charities in Dublin, Cork and Manchester. Manchester Utd beat Celtic 1-0, with Keane playing for both teams.

Alan Shearer's testimonial on May 11, 2006, watched by a crowd of 52,275 at St James's Park, raised more than £1m. The club's record scorer, in his farewell match, came off the bench in stoppage time to score the penalty that gave Newcastle a 3-2 win over Celtic. Total proceeds from his testimonial events, £1.64m, were donated to 14 charities in the north-east.

Ole Gunnar Solskjaer, who retired after 12 years as a Manchester Utd player, had a crowd of 68,868, for his testimonial on Aug 2, 2008 (United 1 Espanyol 0). He donated the estimated receipts of £2m to charity, including the opening of a dozen schools In Africa.

Liverpool's **Jamie Carragher** had his testimonial against Everton (4-1) on Sep 4, 2010. It was watched by a crowd of 35,631 and raised an estimated £1m for his foundation, which supports community projects on Merseyside.

Gary Neville donated around £1m from his testimonial against Juventus (2-1) in front of 42,000 on May 24, 2011, to charities and building a Supporters' Centre near Old Trafford.

Paul Scholes had a crowd of 75,000 for his testimonial, Manchester United against New York Cosmos, on Aug 5, 2011. Receipts were £1.5m.

WHAT IT USED TO COST

Minimum admission to League football was one shilling in 1939 After the war, it was increased to 1s 3d in 1946; 1s 6d in 1951; 1s 9d in 1952; 2s in 1955; 2s 6d.

in 1960; 4s in 1965; 5s in 1968; 6s in 1970; and 8s (40p) in 1972 After that, the fixed minimum charge was dropped.

Wembley's first Cup Final programme in 1923 cost three pence ($1^1/4$p in today's money). The programme for the 'farewell' FA Cup Final in May, 2000 was priced £10.

FA Cup Final ticket prices in 2011 reached record levels – £115, £85, £65 and £45.

WHAT THEY USED TO EARN

In the 1930s, First Division players were on £8 a week (£6 in close season) plus bonuses of £2 win, £1 draw. The maximum wage went up to £12 when football resumed post-war in 1946 and had reached £20 by the time the limit was abolished in 1961.

EUROPEAN TROPHY WINNERS

European Cup/Champions League: 9 Real Madrid; **7** AC Milan; **5** Liverpool; **4** Ajax, Barcelona, Bayern Munich; **3** Inter Milan, Manchester Utd; **2** Benfica, Juventus, Nottm Forest, Porto; **1** Aston Villa, Borussia Dortmund, Celtic, Chelsea, Feyenoord, Hamburg, Marseille, PSV Eindhoven, Red Star Belgrade, Steaua Buchares

Cup-Winners' Cup: 4 Barcelona; **2** Anderlecht, Chelsea, Dynamo Kiev, AC Milan; **1** Aberdeen, Ajax, Arsenal, Atletico Madrid, Bayern Munich, Borussia Dortmund, Dynamo Tbilisi, Everton, Fiorentina, Hamburg, Juventus, Lazio, Magdeburg, Manchester City, Manchester

Utd, Mechelen, Paris St. Germain, Parma, Rangers, Real Zaragoza, Sampdoria, Slovan Bratislava, Sporting Lisbon, Tottenham, Valencia, Werder Bremen, West Ham.

UEFA Cup: 3 Barcelona, Inter Milan, Juventus, Liverpool, Valencia; **2** Borussia Moenchengladbach, Feyenoord, Gothenburg, Leeds, Parma, Real Madrid, Sevilla, Tottenham; **1** Anderlecht, Ajax, Arsenal, Bayer Leverkusen, Bayern Munich, CSKA Moscow, Dynamo Zagreb, Eintracht Frankfurt, Ferencvaros, Galatasaray, Ipswich, Napoli, Newcastle, Porto, PSV Eindhoven, Real Zaragoza, Roma, Schalke, Shakhtar Donetsk, Zenit St Petersburg.

Europa League: 2 Atletico Madrid, 1 Porto
- The Champions League was introduced into the European Cup in 1992–93 to counter the threat of a European Super League. The UEFA Cup became the Europa League, with a new format, in season 2009–10.

BRITAIN'S 33 TROPHIES IN EUROPE

European Cup/Champions League (13)	Cup-Winners' Cup (10)	Fairs/UEFA Cup (10)
1967 Celtic	1963 Tottenham	1968 Leeds
1968 Manchester Utd	1965 West Ham	1969 Newcastle
1977 Liverpool	1970 Manchester City	1970 Arsenal
1978 Liverpool	1971 Chelsea	1971 Leeds
1979 Nottm Forest	1972 Rangers	1972 Tottenham
1980 Nottm Forest	1983 Aberdeen	1973 Liverpool
1981 Liverpool	1985 Everton	1976 Liverpool
1982 Aston Villa	1991 Manchester Utd	1981 Ipswich
1984 Liverpool	1994 Arsenal	1984 Tottenham
1999 Manchester Utd	1998 Chelsea	2001 Liverpool
2005 Liverpool		
2008 Manchester Utd		
2012 Chelsea		

ENGLAND'S EUROPEAN RECORD

Manchester Utd, Chelsea, Arsenal and Liverpool all reached the Champions League quarter-finals in season 2007–08 – the first time one country had provided four of the last eight. For the first time, England supplied both finalists in 2008 (Manchester Utd and Chelsea) and have provided three semi-finalists in 2007–08–09).

END OF CUP-WINNERS' CUP

The **European Cup-Winners' Cup**, inaugurated in 1960–61, terminated with the 1999 Final. The competition merged into a revamped **UEFA Cup**.

From its inception in 1955, the **European Cup** comprised only championship-winning clubs until 1998–99, when selected runners-up were introduced. Further expansion came in 1999–2000 with the inclusion of clubs finishing third in certain leagues and fourth in 2002.

EUROPEAN CLUB COMPETITIONS – SCORING RECORDS

European Cup – record aggregate: 18-0 by Benfica v Dudelange (Lux) (8-0a, 10-0h), prelim rd, 1965–66.

Record single-match score: 11-0 by Dinamo Bucharest v Crusaders (rd 1, 2nd leg, 1973-74 (agg 12-0).

Champions League – record single-match score: Liverpool 8-0 v Besiktas, Group A qual (Nov 6, 2007).

Highest match aggregate: 13 – Bayern Munich 12 Sporting Lisbon 1 (5-0 away, 7-1 at home, 1st ko rd, 2008–09)

Cup-Winners' Cup – *record aggregate: 21-0 by Chelsea v Jeunesse Hautcharage (Lux) (8-0a, 13-0h), 1st rd, 1971–72.

Record single-match score: 16-1 by Sporting Lisbon v Apoel Nicosia, 2nd round, 1st leg, 1963–64 (aggregate was 18-1).

UEFA Cup (prev Fairs Cup) – *Record aggregate: 21-0 by Feyenoord v US Rumelange (Lux) (9-0h, 12-0a), 1st round, 1972–73.

Record single-match score: 14-0 by Ajax Amsterdam v Red Boys (Lux) 1st rd, 2nd leg, 1984–85 (aggregate also 14-0).

Record British score in Europe: 13-0 by **Chelsea** at home to Jeunesse Hautcharage (Lux) in Cup-Winners' Cup 1st round, 2nd leg, 1971–72. Chelsea's overall 21-0 win in that tie is highest aggregate by British club in Europe.

Individual scoring record for European tie (over two legs): 10 goals (6 home, 4 away) by Kiril Milanov for Levski Spartak in 19-3 agg win Cup-Winners' Cup 1st round v Lahden Reipas, 1976–77. Next highest: **8** goals by Jose Altafini for AC Milan v US Luxembourg (European Cup, prelim round, 1962–63, agg 14-0) and by **Peter Osgood** for Chelsea v Jeunesse Hautcharage (Cup-Winners' Cup, 1st round 1971–72, agg 21-0). Altafini and Osgood each scored 5 goals at home, 3 away.

Individual single-match scoring record in European competition: **6** by Mascarenhas for Sporting Lisbon in 16-1 Cup-Winner's Cup 2nd round, 1st leg win v Apoel, 1963–64; and by **Lothar Emmerich** for Borussia Dortmund in 8-0 CWC 1st round, 2nd leg win v Floriana 1965–66; and by **Kiril Milanov** for Levski Spartak in 12-2 CWC 1st round, 1st leg win v Lahden Reipas, 1976–77.

Most goals in single European campaign: 15 by **Jurgen Klinsmann** for Bayern Munich (UEFA Cup 1995–96).

Most goals by British player in European competition: 30 by **Peter Lorimer** (Leeds, in 9 campaigns).

Most individual goals in Champions League match: 5 by **Lionel Messi** (Barcelona) in 7-1 win at home to Bayer Leverkusen in round of 16 second leg, 2011–12.

Most European Cup goals by individual player: 49 by **Alfredo di Stefano** in 58 apps for Real Madrid (1955–64).

(*Joint record European aggregate)

First European treble: Clarence Seedorf became the first player to win the European Cup with three clubs: Ajax in 1995, Real Madrid in 1998 and AC Milan in 2003.

EUROPEAN FOOTBALL – BIG RECOVERIES

In the most astonishing Final in the history of the European Cup/Champions League, **Liverpool** became the first club to win it from a 3-0 deficit when they beat AC Milan 3-2 on penalties after a 3-3 draw in Istanbul on May 25, 2005. Liverpool's fifth triumph in the competition meant that they would keep the trophy.

The following season, **Middlesbrough** twice recovered from three-goal aggregate deficits in the **UEFA Cup**, beating Basle 4-3 in the quarter finals and Steaua Bucharest by the same scoreline in the semi-finals.

In 2010, **Fulham** beat Juventus 5-4 after trailing 1-4 on aggregate in the second leg of their Europa League, Round of 16 match at Craven Cottage.

Only four clubs have survived a **4-goal** deficit in any of the European club competitions after the first leg had been completed:

1961–62 (Cup-Winners' Cup 1st round): Leixoes (Portugal) beat Chaux de Fonds (Luxembourg) 7-6 on agg (lost 2-6a, won 5-0h).

1962–63 (Fairs Cup 2nd round): Valencia (Spain) beat Dunfermline 1-0 in play-off in Lisbon after 6-6 agg (Valencia won 4-0h, lost 2-6a).

1984–85 (UEFA Cup 2nd round): Partizan Belgrade beat QPR on away goals (lost 2-6 away, at Highbury, won 4-0 home).

1985–86 (UEFA Cup 3rd round): Real Madrid beat Borussia Moenchengladbach on away goals (lost 1-5a, won 4-0h) and went on to win competition.

Two Scottish clubs have won a European tie from a 3-goal, first leg deficit: **Kilmarnock** 0-3, 5-1 v Eintracht Frankfurt (Fairs Cup 1st round, 1964–65); **Hibernian** 1-4, 5-0 v Napoli (Fairs

Cup 2nd Round, 1967–68).
English clubs have three times gone out of the **UEFA Cup** after leading 3-0 from the first leg: 1975–76 (2nd Rd) **Ipswich** lost 3-4 on agg to Bruges; 1976–77 (quarter-final) **QPR** lost on penalties to AEK Athens after 3-3 agg; 1977–78 (3rd round) **Ipswich** lost on penalties to Barcelona after 3-3 agg.
• In the **1966 World Cup quarter-final** (Jul 23) at Goodison Park, North Korea led Portugal 3-0, but Eusebio scored 4 times to give **Portugal** a 5-3 win.

HEAVIEST ENGLISH-CLUB DEFEATS IN EUROPE

(Single-leg scores)
European Cup: Artmedia Bratislava 5, **Celtic** 0 (2nd qual round), Jul 2005 (agg 5-4); Ajax 5, **Liverpool** 1 (2nd round), Dec 1966 (agg 7-3); Real Madrid 5, **Derby** 1 (2nd round), Nov 1975 (agg 6-5).
Cup-Winners' Cup: Sporting Lisbon 5, **Manchester Utd** 0 (quarter-final), Mar 1964 (agg 6-4).
Fairs/UEFA Cup: Bayern Munich 6, **Coventry** 1 (2nd round), Oct 1970 (agg 7-3). **Combined London** team lost 6-0 (agg 8-2) in first Fairs Cup Final in 1958. Barcelona 5, **Chelsea** 0 in Fairs Cup semi-final play-off, 1966, in Barcelona (after 2-2 agg).

SHOCK ENGLISH CLUB DEFEATS

1968–69 (Eur Cup, 1st round): **Manchester City** beaten by Fenerbahce, 1-2 agg.
1971–72 (CWC, 2nd round): **Chelsea** beaten by Atvidaberg on away goals.
1993–94 (Eur Cup, 2nd round): **Manchester Utd** beaten by Galatasaray on away goals.
1994–95 (UEFA Cup, 1st round): **Blackburn** beaten by Trelleborgs, 2-3 agg.
2000–01 (UEFA Cup, 1st round): **Chelsea** beaten by St. Gallen, Switz 1-2 agg.

PFA FAIR PLAY AWARD (Bobby Moore Trophy from 1993)

1988	Liverpool	2001	Hull
1989	Liverpool	2002	Crewe
1990	Liverpool	2003	Crewe
1991	Nottm Forest	2004	Crewe
1992	Portsmouth	2005	Crewe
1993	Norwich	2006	Crewe
1994	Crewe	2007	Crewe
1995	Crewe	2008	Crewe
1996	Crewe	2009	Stockport
1997	Crewe	2010	Rochdale
1998	Cambridge Utd	2011	Rochdale
1999	Grimsby	2012	Chesterfield
2000	Crewe		

RECORD MEDAL SALES

West Ham bought (Jun 2000) the late **Bobby Moore's** collection of medals and trophies for £1.8m at Christie's auction. It was put up for sale by his first wife Tina and included his World Cup-winner's medal.
A No. 6 duplicate red shirt made for England captain **Bobby Moore** for the 1966 World Cup Final fetched £44,000 at an auction at Wolves' ground in Sep, 1999. Moore kept the shirt he wore in that Final and gave the replica to England physio Harold Shepherdson.
Sir Geoff Hurst's 1966 World Cup-winning shirt made a record £91,750 at Christie's in Sep, 2000. His World Cup Final cap fetched £37,600 and his Man of the Match trophy £18,800. Proceeds totalling £274,410 from the 129 lots went to Hurst's three daughters and charities of his choice, including the Bobby Moore Imperial Cancer Research Fund.
In Aug, 2001, Sir Geoff sold his World Cup-winner's medal to his former club West Ham Utd (for their museum) at a reported £150,000.
'The **Billy Wright** Collection' – caps, medals and other memorabilia from his illustrious career – fetched over £100,000 at Christie's in Nov, 1996.

At the sale in Oct 1993, trophies, caps and medals earned by **Ray Kennedy**, former England, Arsenal and Liverpool player, fetched a then record total of £88,407. Kennedy, suffering from Parkinson's Disease, received £73,000 after commission. The PFA paid £31,080 for a total of 60 lots – including a record £16,000 for his 1977 European Cup winner's medal – to be exhibited at their Manchester museum. An anonymous English collector paid £17,000 for the medal and plaque commemorating Kennedy's part in the Arsenal Double in 1971.

Previous record for one player's medals, shirts etc collection: £30,000 (**Bill Foulkes**, Manchester Utd in 1992). The sale of **Dixie Dean**'s medals etc in 1991 realised £28,000.

In Mar, 2001, **Gordon Banks'** 1966 World Cup-winner's medal fetched a new record £124,750. TV's Nick Hancock, a Stoke fan, paid £23,500 for **Sir Stanley Matthews's** 1953 FA Cup-winner's medal. He also bought one of Matthews's England caps for £3,525 and paid £2,350 for a Stoke Div 2 Championship medal (1963).

Dave Mackay's 1961 League Championship and FA Cup winner's medals sold for £18,000 at Sotherby's. Tottenham bought them for their museum.

A selection of England World Cup-winning manager **Sir Alf Ramsey**'s memorabilia – England caps, championship medals with Ipswich etc. – fetched more than £80,000 at Christie's. They were offered for sale by his family, and his former clubs Tottenham and Ipswich were among the buyers.

Ray Wilson's 1966 England World Cup-winning shirt fetched £80,750. Also in Mar, 2002, the No. 10 shirt worn by **Pele** in Brazil's World Cup triumph in 1970 was sold for a record £157,750 at Christies. It went to an anonymous telephone bidder.

In Oct, 2003, **George Best**'s European Footballer of the Year (1968) trophy was sold to an anonymous British bidder for £167,250 at Bonham's. It was the then most expensive item of sporting memorabilia ever auctioned in Britain.

England captain **Bobby Moore**'s 1970 World Cup shirt, which he swapped with Pele after Brazil's 1-0 win in Mexico, was sold for £60,000 at Christie's in Mar, 2004.

Sep, 2004: England shirt worn by tearful **Paul Gascoigne** in 1990 World Cup semi-final v Germany sold at Christie's for £28,680. At same auction, shirt worn by Brazil's **Pele** in 1958 World Cup Final in Sweden sold for £70,505.

May, 2005: The **second FA Cup** (which was presented to winning teams from 1896 to 1909) was bought for £420,000 at Christie's by Birmingham chairman David Gold, a world record for an item of football memorabilia. It was presented to the National Football Museum, Preston. At the same auction, the World Cup-winner's medal earned by England's **Alan Ball** in 1966 was sold for £164,800.

Oct, 2005: At auction at Bonham's, the medals and other memorabilia of Hungary and Real Madrid legend **Ferenc Puskas** were sold for £85,000 to help pay for hospital treatment.

Nov, 2006: A ball used in the 2006 World Cup Final and signed by the winning **Italy** team was sold for £1.2m (a world record for football memorabilia) at a charity auction in Qatar. It was bought by the Qatar Sports Academy.

Feb, 2010: A pair of boots worn by **Sir Stanley Matthews** in the 1953 FA Cup Final was sold at Bonham's for £38,400.

Oct, 2010: Trophies and memorabilia belonging to **George Best** were sold at Bonham's for £193,440. His 1968 European Cup winner's medal fetched £156,000.

Oct–Nov 2010: **Nobby Stiles** sold his 1966 World Cup winner's medal at an Edinburgh auction for a record £188,200. His old club, Manchester Utd, also paid £48,300 for his 1968 European Cup medal to go to the club's museum at Old Trafford. In London, the shirt worn by Stiles in the 1966 World Cup Final went for £75,000. A total of 45 items netted £424,438. **George Cohen** and **Martin Peters** had previously sold their medals from 1966.

Oct 2011: **Terry Paine** (who did not play in the Final) sold his 1966 World Cup medal for £27,500 at auction.

LONGEST UNBEATEN CUP RUN

Liverpool established the longest unbeaten Cup sequence by a Football League club: 25 successive rounds in the League/Milk Cup between semi-final defeat by Nottm Forest (1-2 agg) in 1980 and defeat at Tottenham (0-1) in the third round on Oct 31, 1984. During this period Liverpool won the tournament in four successive seasons, a feat no other Football League club has achieved in any competition.

NEAR £1M RECORD DAMAGES

A High Court judge in Newcastle (May 7, 1999) awarded Bradford City's 28-year-old striker **Gordon Watson** record damages for a football injury: £909,143. He had had his right leg fractured in two places by Huddersfield's Kevin Gray on Feb 1, 1997. Huddersfield were 'proven negligent for allowing their player to make a rushed tackle'. The award was calculated at £202,643 for loss of earnings, £730,500 for 'potential career earnings' if he had joined a Premiership club, plus £26,000 to cover medical treatment and care. Watson, awarded £50,000 in an earlier legal action, had a 6-inch plate inserted in the leg. He resumed playing for City in season 1998–99.

BIG HALF-TIME SCORES

Tottenham 10, Crewe 1 (FA Cup 4th round replay, Feb 3, 1960; result 13-2); Tranmere 8, Oldham 1 (Div 3N., Dec 26, 1935; result 13-4); **Chester City 8, York 0** (Div 3N., Feb 1, 1936; result 12-0; believed to be record half-time scores in League football).

Nine goals were scored in the first half – **Burnley 4, Watford 5** in Div 1 on Apr 5, 2003. Result: 4-7.

Stirling Albion led Selkirk 15-0 at half-time (result 20-0) in the Scottish Cup 1st round, Dec 8, 1984.

World record half-time score: **16-0** when **Australia** beat **American Samoa** 31-0 (another world record) in the World Cup Oceania qualifying group at Coff's Harbour, New South Wales, on Apr 11 2001.

• On Mar 4 1933 **Coventry** beat QPR (Div 3 South) 7-0, having led by that score at half-time. This repeated the half-time situation in Bristol City's 7-0 win over Grimsby on Dec 26, 1914.

TOP SECOND-HALF TEAM

Most goals scored by a team in one half of a League match is **11. Stockport** led Halifax 2-0 at half-time in Div 3 North on Jan 6 1934 and won 13-0.

FIVE NOT ENOUGH

Last team to score **5** in League match and lose: **Burton**, beaten 6-5 by Cheltenham (Lge 2, Mar 13, 2010).

LONG SERVICE WITH ONE CLUB

Bill Nicholson, OBE, was associated with Tottenham for 67 years – as a wing-half (1938–55), then the club's most successful manager (1958–74) with 8 major prizes, subsequently chief advisor and scout. He became club president, and an honorary freeman of the borough, had an executive suite named after him at the club, and the stretch of roadway from Tottenham High Road to the main gates has the nameplate Bill Nicholson Way. He died, aged 85, in Oct 2004.

Ted Bates, the Grand Old Man of Southampton with 66 years of unbroken service to the club, was awarded the Freedom of the City in Apr, 2001. He joined Saints as an inside-forward from Norwich in 1937, made 260 peace-time appearances for the club, became reserve-team trainer in 1953 and manager at The Dell for 18 years (1955–73), taking Southampton into the top division in 1966. He was subsequently chief executive, director and club president. He died in Oct 2003, aged 85.

Dario Gradi, MBE, stepped down after completing 24 seasons and more than 1,000 matches as manager of Crewe (appointed Jun 1983). Never a League player, he previously managed Wimbledon and Crystal Palace. At Crewe, his policy of finding and grooming young talent has earned the club more than £20m in transfer fees. He stayed with Crewe as technical director, and twice took charge of team affairs again following the departure of the managers who succeeded him, Steve Holland and Gudjon Thordarson.

Bob Paisley was associated with Liverpool for 57 years from 1939, when he joined them from Bishop Auckland, until he died in Feb 1996. He served as player, trainer, coach, assistant-manager, manager, director and vice-president. He was Liverpool's most successful manager, winning 13 major trophies for the club (1974–83).

Ronnie Moran, who joined Liverpool in as a player 1952, retired from the Anfield coaching staff in season 1998–99.

Ernie Gregory served West Ham for 52 years as goalkeeper and coach. He joined them as boy of 14 from school in 1935, retired in May 1987.

Ted Sagar, Everton goalkeeper, 23 years at Goodison Park (1929–52, but only 16 League seasons because of War).

Alan Knight, goalkeeper, played 23 seasons (1977–2000) for his only club, Portsmouth.

Roy Sproson, defender, played 21 League seasons for his only club, Port Vale (1950–71).

Allan Ball, goalkeeper, 20 seasons with Queen of the South (1963–83).

Pat Bonner, goalkeeper, 19 seasons with Celtic (1978–97).

Danny McGrain, defender, 17 years with Celtic (1970–87).

TIGHT AT HOME

Fewest home goals conceded in League season (modern times): 4 by **Liverpool** (Div 1, 1978–9); 4 by **Manchester Utd** (Premier League, 1994–95) – both in 21 matches.

FOOTBALL POOLS

Littlewoods launched them in 1923 with a capital of £100. Coupons were first issued (4,000 of them) outside Manchester Utd's ground, the original 35 investors staking a total of £4 7s 6d (pay-out £2 12s).

Vernons joined Littlewoods as the leading promoters. The Treble Chance, leading to bonanza dividends, was introduced in 1946 and the Pools Panel began in Jan 1963, to counter mass fixture postponements caused by the Big Freeze winter.

But business was hard hit by the launch of the National Lottery in 1994. Dividends slumped, the work-force was drastically cut and in Jun 2000 the Liverpool-based Moores family sold Littlewoods Pools in a £161m deal. After 85 years, the name Littlewoods disappeared from Pools betting in Aug 2008. The New Football Pools was formed. Vernons and

Zetters continued to operate under their own name in the ownership of Sportech.

The record prize remains the £2,924,622 paid to a Worsley, Manchester, syndicate in Nov 1994.

Fixed odds football – record pay-out: £654,375 by Ladbrokes (May 1993) to Jim Wright, of Teignmouth, Devon. He placed a £1,000 each-way pre-season bet on the champions of the three Football League divisions – Newcastle (8–1), Stoke (6–1) and Cardiff (9–1).

Record match accumulators: £164,776 to £4 stake on 18 correct results, Oct 5, 6, 7, 2002. The bet, with Ladbrokes in Colchester, was made by Army chef Mark Simmons; £272,629 for £2.50 stake on 9 correct scores (6 English Prem Lge, 3 Spanish Cup) on Jan 5, 2011, by an anonymous punter at Ladbrokes in Berkshire.

TRANSFER WINDOW

This was introduced to Britain in Sep 2002 via FIFA regulations to bring uniformity across Europe (the rule previously applied in a number of other countries).

The transfer of contracted players is restricted to two periods: Jun 1–Aug 31 and Jan 1–31).

On appeal, Football League clubs continued to sign/sell players (excluding deals with Premiership clubs).

PROGRAMME PIONEERS

Chelsea pioneered football's magazine-style programme when they introduced a 16-page issue for their First Division match against Portsmouth on Christmas Day 1948. It cost sixpence (2.5p). A penny programme from the 1909 FA Cup Final fetched £23,500 at a London auction in May, 2012.

TRIBUNAL-FEE RECORDS

Top tribunal fee: £2.5m for **Chris Bart-Williams** (Sheffield Wed to Nottm Forest, Jun 1995).
Biggest discrepancy: Andy Walker, striker, Bolton to Celtic, Jun 1994: Bolton asked £2.2m, Celtic offered £250,000. Tribunal decided £550,000.

LONG THROW EXPERTS

Andy Legg's throws for Notts Co were measured at 41m in season 1994–95) and claimed as the longest by any footballer in the world. Then, in 1997–98,
Dave Challinor (Tranmere) reached 46.3 metres. A range of throws not previously encountered by Premier League defences was provided by Stoke's **Rory Delap** in season 2008–09. Reaching an estimated 37mph, they averaged 38m and were delivered in a combination of high, looping throws and those with a flatter trajectory. Stoke scored nine goals from them.
In 2010, Denmark's Thomas Gronnemark was reported to have thrown 51.3m.

BALL JUGGLING: WORLD RECORD CLAIMS

Sam Ik (South Korea) juggled a ball non-stop for 18 hours, 11 minutes, 4 seconds in Mar 1995. Thai footballer **Sam-Ang Sowanski** juggled a ball for 15 hours without letting it touch the ground in Bangkok in Apr 2000.
Milene Domingues, wife of Brazilian star Ronaldo and a player for Italian women's team Fiammamonza, Milan, became the 'Queen of Keepy Uppy' when for 9 hours, 6 minutes she juggled a ball 55,187 times.

SUBS' SCORING RECORD

Barnet's 5-4 home win v Torquay (Div 3, Dec 28, 1993) provided the first instance of all **four substitutes** scoring in a major League match in England.

WORLD'S OLDEST FOOTBALL ANNUAL

Now in its 126th edition, this publication began as the 16-page Athletic News Football Supplement & Club Directory in 1887. From the long-established Athletic News, it became the Sunday Chronicle Annual in 1946, the Empire News in 1956, the News of the World & Empire News in 1961 and the News of the World Annual from 1965 until becoming the Nationwide Annual in 2008.

BARCLAYS PREMIER LEAGUE CLUB DETAILS AND SQUADS 2012–13

(At time of going to press)

ARSENAL

Ground: Emirates Stadium, Highbury, London, N5 1BU
Telephone: 0207 704 4000. **Club nickname:** Gunners
Colours: Red and white shirts; white shorts; white socks
Record transfer fee: £17.4m to Seville for Jose Antonio Reyes, Jan 2004
Record fee received: £35m from Barcelona for Cesc Fabregas, Aug 2011
Record attendance: Highbury: 73,295 v Sunderland (Div 1) 9 Mar, 1935. Wembley: 73,707 v Lens (Champ Lge) Nov 1998. Emirates Stadium: 60,161 v Manchester Utd (Prem Lge) 3 Nov, 2007
Capacity: 60,361. **Main sponsor:** Emirates
League Championship: Winners 1930–31, 1932–33, 1933–34, 1934–35, 1937–38, 1947–48, 1952–53, 1970–71, 1988–89, 1990–91, 1997–98, 2001–02, 2003–04
FA Cup: Winners 1930, 1936, 1950, 1971, 1979, 1993, 1998, 2002, 2003, 2005
League Cup: Winners 1987, 1993
European competitions: Winners Fairs Cup 1969–70, Cup-Winners' Cup 1993–94
Finishing positions in Premier League: 1992–93 10th, 1993–94 4th, 1994–95 12th, 1995–96 5th, 1996–97 3rd, 1997–98 1st, 1998–99 2nd, 1999–2000 2nd, 2000–01 2nd, 2001–02 1st, 2002–03 2nd, 2003–04 1st, 2004–05 2nd, 2005–06 4th, 2006–07 4th, 2007–08 3rd, 2008–09 4th, 2009–10 3rd, 2010–11 4th, 2011–12 3rd
Biggest win: 12-0 v Loughborough (Div 2) 12 Mar, 1900
Biggest defeat: 0-8 v Loughborough (Div 2) 12 Dec, 1896
Highest League scorer in a season: Ted Drake 42 (1934–35)
Most League goals in aggregate: Thierry Henry 175 (1999–2007) and (2012)
Longest unbeaten League sequence: 49 matches (2003–04)
Longest sequence without a League win: 23 matches (1912–13)
Most capped player: Thierry Henry (France) 81

Name	Height ft in	Previous club	Birthplace	Birthdate
Goalkeepers				
Fabianski, Lukasz	6.3	Legia Warsaw	Kostrzyn, Pol	18.04.85
Mannone, Vito	6.3	Atalanta	Desio, It	02.03.88
Szczesny, Wojciech	6.5	–	Warsaw, Pol	18.04.90
Defenders				
Bartley, Kyle	6.3	Bolton	Manchester	22.05.91
Djourou, Johan	6.3	Etoile Carouge	Abidjan, Iv C	18.01.87
Gibbs, Kieran	5.10	–	Lambeth	26.09.89
Koscielny, Laurent	6.1	Lorient	Tulle, Fr	10.09.85
Mertesacker, Per	6.6	Werder Bremen	Hannover, Ger	29.09.84
Sagny, Bacari	5.9	Auxerre	Sens, Fr	14.02.83
Santos, Andre	5.11	Fenerbahce	Sao Paulo, Br	08.03.83
Squillaci, Sebastien	6.1	Sevilla	Toulon, Fr	11.08.80
Vermaelen, Thomas	6.0	Ajax	Kapellen, Bel	14.11.85
Midfielders				
Arshavin, Andrey	5.8	Zenit St Petersburg	St Petersburg, Rus	29.05.81
Arteta, Mikel	5.9	Everton	San Sebastian, Sp	28.03.82
Coquelin, Francis	5.10	Lavallois	Laval, Fr	13.05.91
Diaby, Abou	6.2	Auxerre	Paris, Fr	11.05.86

Frimpong, Emmanuel	6.0	–		Accra, Gh	10.01.92
Lansbury, Henri	6.0	–		Enfield	12.10.90
Oxlade-Chamberlain, Alex	5.11	Southampton		Portsmouth	15.08.93
Rosicky, Tomas	5.10	Borussia Dortmund		Prague, Cz	04.10.80
Ramsey, Aaron	5.11	Cardiff		Caerphilly	26.12.90
Song, Alex	6.1	Bastia		Douala, Cam	09.09.87
Walcott, Theo	5.8	Southampton		Newbury	16.03.89
Wilshere, Jack	5.8	–		Stevenage	01.01.92

Forwards

Bendtner, Nicklas	6.3	–		Copenhagen, Den	16.01.88
Chamakh, Marouane	6.2	Bordeaux		Tonneins, Fr	10.01.84
Gervinho	5.11	Lille		Anyama, Iv C	27.05.87
Giroud, Olivier	6.4	Montpellier		Chambery, Fr	30.09.86
Ju-Young Park	6.0	Monaco		Daegu, SKor	10.07.85
Miyaichi, Ryo	6.0	–		Aichi, Jap	14.12.92
Podolski, Lukas	6.0	Cologne		Gliwice, Pol	04.06.85
Van Persie, Robin	6.0	Feyenoord		Rotterdam, Hol	06.08.83
Vela, Carlos	5.7	Guadalajara		Cancun, Mex	01.03.89

ASTON VILLA

Ground: Villa Park, Trinity Road, Birmingham, B6 6HE
Telephone: 0871 423 8101. **Club nickname:** Villans
Colours: Claret and blue shirts; white shorts; blue socks
Record transfer fee: £24m to Sunderland for Darren Bent, Jan 2011
Record fee received: £24m for James Milner from Manchester City, Aug 2010
Record attendance: 76,588 v Derby Co (FA Cup 6) 2 Mar, 1946
Capacity: 42,785. **Main sponsor:** Genting
League Championship: Winners 1893–94, 1895–96, 1896–97, 1898–99, 1899–1900, 1909–10, 1980–81
FA Cup: Winners 1887, 1895, 1897, 1905, 1913, 1920, 1957
League Cup: Winners 1961, 1975, 1977, 1994, 1996
European competitions: Winners European Cup 1981–82, European Super Cup 1982–83
Finishing positions in Premier League: 1992–93 2nd, 1993–94 10th, 1994–95 18th, 1995–96 4th, 1996–97 5th, 1997–98 7th, 1998–99 6th, 1999–2000 6th, 2000–01 8th, 2001–02 8th, 2002–03 16th, 2003–04 6th, 2004–05 10th, 2005–06 16th, 2006–07 11th, 2007–08 6th, 2008–09 6th, 2009–10 6th, 2010–11 9th, 2011–12 16th
Biggest win: 12-2 v Accrington (Div 1) 12 Mar, 1892; 11-1 v Charlton (Div 2) 24 Nov, 1959; 10-0 v Sheffield Wed (Div 1) 5 Oct, 1912, v Burnley (Div 1) 29 Aug, 1925. Also: 13-0 v Wednesbury (FA Cup 1) 30 Oct, 1886
Biggest defeat: 0-7 in five League matches from Blackburn (Div 1) 19 Oct, 1889 to Manchester Utd (Div 1) 24 Oct, 1964
Highest League scorer in a season: 'Pongo' Waring 49 (1930–31)
Most League goals in aggregate: Harry Hampton 215 (1904–1915)
Longest unbeaten League sequence: 15 matches (1897, 1909–10 and 1949)
Longest sequence without a League win: 12 matches (1973–74 and 1986–87)
Most capped player: Steve Staunton (Republic of Ireland) 64

Goalkeepers

Given, Shay	6.1	Manchester City	Lifford, Ire	20.04.76
Guzan, Bradley	6.4	Chivas	Evergreen Park, US	09.09.84
Marshall, Andy	6.2	Coventry	Bury St Edmunds	14.04.75

Defenders

Baker, Nathan	6.3	–	Worcester	23.04.91

Clark, Ciaran	6.2	–	Harrow	26.09.89
Collins, James	6.2	West Ham	Newport	23.08.83
Dunne, Richard	6.2	Manchester City	Dublin, Ire	21.09.79
Hutton, Alan	6.1	Tottenham	Glasgow	30.11.84
Lichaj, Eric	5.10	Chicago	Illinois, US	17.11.88
Lowton, Matthew	5.11	Sheffield Utd	Chesterfield	09.06.89
Stevens, Enda	6.0	Shamrock	Dublin, Ire	09.07.90
Warnock, Stephen	5.10	Blackburn	Ormskirk	12.12.81
Midfielders				
Albrighton, Mark	6.1	–	Tamworth	18.11.89
Bannan, Barry	5.11	Derby	Airdrie	01.12.89
Carruthers, Samir	5.8	Arsenal	Islington	04.04.93
Delph, Fabian	5.9	Leeds	Bradford	05.05.91
El Ahmadi, Karim	5.10	Feyenoord	Enschede, Hol	27.01.85
Gardner, Gary	6.2	–	Solihull	29.06.92
Herd, Chris	5.8	–	Perth, Aus	04.04.89
Ireland, Stephen	5.8	Manchester City	Cork, Ire	22.08.86
N'Zogbia, Charles	5.8	Wigan	Harfleur, Fr	28.05.86
Petrov, Stiliyan	5.10	Celtic	Montana, Bul	05.07.79
Forwards				
Agbonlahor, Gabriel	5.11	–	Birmingham	13.10.86
Bent, Darren	5.11	Sunderland	Wandsworth	06.02.84
Delfouneso, Nathan	6.1	–	Birmingham	02.02.91
Holman, Brett	5.10	AZ Alkmaar	Bankstown, Aus	27.03.84
Weimann, Andreas	6.2	–	Vienna, Aut	05.08.91

CHELSEA

Ground: Stamford Bridge Stadium, London SW6 1HS
Telephone: 0871 984 1955. **Club nickname:** Blues
Colours: Blue shirts; blue shorts; white socks
Record transfer fee: £50m to Liverpool for Fernando Torres, Jan 2011
Record fee received: £24.5m from Real Madrid for Arjen Robben, Aug 2007
Record attendance: 82,905 v Arsenal (Div 1) 12 Oct, 1935
Capacity: 42,449. **Main sponsor:** Samsung
League Championship: Winners 1954–55, 2004–05, 2005–06, 2009–10
FA Cup: Winners 1970, 1997, 2000, 2007, 2009, 2010, 2012
League Cup: Winners 1965, 1998, 2005, 2007
European competitions: Winners Champions League 2011–12; Winners Cup-Winners' Cup 1970–71, 1997–98
Finishing positions in Premier League: 1992–93 11th, 1993–94 14th, 1994–95 11th, 1995–96 11th, 1996–97 6th, 1997–98 4th, 1998–99 3rd, 1999–2000 5th, 2000–01 6th, 2001–02 6th, 2002–03 4th, 2003–04 2nd, 2004–05 1st, 2005–06 1st, 2006–07 2nd, 2007–08 2nd, 2008–09 3rd, 2009–10 1st, 2010–11 2nd, 2011–12 6th
Biggest win: 9-2 v Glossop (Div 2) 1 Sep, 1906 and 7-0 in four League matches. Also: 13-0 v Jeunesse Hautcharage, (Cup-Winners' Cup 1) 29 Sep, 1971
Biggest defeat: 1-8 v Wolves (Div 1) 26 Sep, 1923; 0-7 v Leeds (Div 1) 7 Oct, 1967, v Nottm Forest (Div 1) 20 Apr, 1991
Highest League scorer in a season: Jimmy Greaves 41 (1960–61)
Most League goals in aggregate: Bobby Tambling 164 (1958–70)
Longest unbeaten League sequence: 40 matches (2004–05)
Longest sequence without a League win: 21 matches (1987–88)
Most capped player: Frank Lampard (England) 88

Goalkeepers

Cech, Petr	6.5	Rennes	Plzen, Cz	20.05.82
Hilario, Henrique	6.3	Nacional	Sao Pedro, Por	21.10.75
Turnbull, Ross	6.1	–	Bishop Auckland	04.01.85

Defenders

Bertrand, Ryan	5.10	–	Southwark	05.08.89
Cahill, Gary	6.2	Bolton	Sheffield	19.12.85
Cole, Ashley	5.8	Arsenal	Stepney	20.12.80
Ferreira, Paulo	6.0	Porto	Lisbon, Por	18.01.79
Hutchinson, Sam	6.0	–	Slough	03.08.89
Ivanovic, Branislav	6.2	Lok Moscow	Mitrovica, Serb	22.02.84
Luiz, David	6.2	Benfica	Didema, Br	22.04.87
Terry, John	6.1	–	Barking	07.12.80

Midfielders

Benayoun, Yossi	5.10	Liverpool	Dimona, Isr	05.05.80
De Bruyne, Kevin	5.11	Genk	Drongen, Bel	28.06.91
Essien, Michael	6.0	Lyon	Accra, Gh	03.12.82
Hazard, Eden	5.8	Lille	La Louviere, Bel	07.01.91
Lampard, Frank	6.0	West Ham	Romford	20.06.78
Malouda, Florent	5.11	Lyon	Cayenne, Gui	13.06.80
Marin, Marko	5.7	Werder Bremen	Gradiska, Bos	13.03.89
Mata, Juan	5.7	Valencia	Burgos, Sp	28.04.88
McEachran, Josh	5.10	–	Oxford	01.03.93
Meireles, Raul	5.11	Liverpool	Porto, Por	17.03.83
Mikel, John Obi	6.2	Lyn Oslo	Plato State, Nig	22.04.87
Oscar	5.10	Internacional	Americana, Br	09.09.91
Ramires	5.11	Benfica	Rio de Janeiro, Br	24.03.87
Romeu, Oriol	6.0	Barcelona	Ulldecona, Sp	24.09.91

Forwards

Kakuta, Gael	5.8	Lens	Lille, Fr	21.06.91
Lukaku, Romelu	6.3	Anderlecht	Antwerp, Bel	13.05.93
Sturridge, Daniel	6.2	Manchester City	Birmingham	01.09.89
Torres, Fernando	6.1	Liverpool	Madrid, Sp	20.03.84

EVERTON

Ground: Goodison Park, Liverpool L4 4EL
Telephone: 0870 442 1878. **Club nickname**: Toffees
Colours: Blue shirts; white shorts; white socks
Record transfer fee: £15m to Standard Liege for Marouane Fellaini, Aug 2008
Record fee received: £27m from Manchester Utd for Wayne Rooney, Aug 2004
Record attendance: 78,299 v Liverpool (Div 1) 18 Sep, 1948
Capacity: 40,157. **Main sponsor**: Chang
League Championship: Winners 1890–91, 1914–15, 1927–28, 1931–31, 1938–39, 1962–63, 1969–70, 1984–85, 1986–87
FA Cup: Winners 1906, 1933, 1966, 1984, 1995
League Cup: Runners up 1977, 1984
European competitions: Winners Cup-Winners' Cup 1984–85
Finishing positions in Premier League: 1992–93 13th, 1993–94 17th, 1994–95 15th, 1995–96 6th 1996–97 15th 1997–98 14th 1998–99 14th, 1999–2000 13th, 2000–01 16th, 2001–02 15th, 2002–03 7th, 2003–04 17th, 2004–05 4th, 2005–06 11th, 2006–07 6th, 2007–08 5th, 2008–09 5th, 2009–10 8th, 20010–11 7th, 2011–12 7th
Biggest win: 9-1 v Manchester City (Div 1) 3 Sep, 1906, v Plymouth (Div 2) 27 Dec, 1930. Also: 11-2 v Derby (FA Cup 1) 18 Jan, 1890

Biggest defeat: 0-7 v Portsmouth (Div 1) 10 Sep, 1949 and v Arsenal (Prem Lge) 11 May, 2005
Highest League scorer in a season: Ralph 'Dixie' Dean 60 (1927–28)
Most League goals in aggregate: Ralph 'Dixie' Dean 349 (1925–37)
Longest unbeaten League sequence: 20 matches (1978)
Longest sequence without a League win: 14 matches (1937)
Most capped player: Neville Southall (Wales) 92

Goalkeepers

Howard, Tim	6.3	Manchester Utd	North Brunswick, US	03.06.79
Mucha, Jan	6.3	Legia Warsaw	Cirochou, Cz	05.12.82

Defenders

Baines, Leighton	5.7	Wigan	Liverpool	11.12.84
Coleman, Seamus	5.10	Sligo	Donegal, Ire	11.10.88
Distin, Sylvain	6.4	Portsmouth	Paris, Fr	16.12.77
Duffy, Shane	6.4	–	Derry	01.01.92
Heitinga, Johnny	5.11	Atletico Madrid	Alphen, Hol	15.11.83
Hibbert, Tony	5.10	–	Liverpool	20.02.81
Jagielka, Phil	5.11	Sheffield Utd	Manchester	17.08.82
Neville, Phil	5.11	Manchester Utd	Bury	21.01.77

Midfielders

Barkley, Ross	6.2	–	Liverpool	05.12.93
Fellaini, Marouane	6.4	Standard Liege	Etterbeek, Bel	22.11.87
Francisco Junior	5.5	Benfica	Guinea-Bissau	18.01.92
Gibson, Darron	5.9	Manchester Utd	Derry	25.10.87
Osman, Leon	5.8	–	Billinge	17.05.81
Rodwell, Jack	6.1	–	Birkdale	17.09.89

Forwards

Anichebe, Victor	6.1	–	Lagos, Nig	23.04.88
Baxter, Jose	5.10	–	Bootle	07.02.92
Gueye, Magaye	5.10	Strasbourg	Nogent, Fr	06.07.90
Jelevic, Nikica	6.2	Rangers	Capljina, Cro	27.08.85
McAleny, Conor	5.10	–	Liverpool	12.08.92
Naismith, Steven	5.10	Rangers	Irvine	14.09.86
Silva, Joao	6.2	Desportivo	Vila das Aves, Por	21.05.90
Vellios, Apostolos	6.3	Iraklis	Thessalonika, Gre	08.01.92

FULHAM

Ground: Craven Cottage, Stevenage Road, London SW6 6HH
Telephone: 0870 442 1222. **Club nickname**: Cottagers
Colours: White and black shirts; black shorts; white socks
Record transfer fee: £11.5m to Lyon for Steve Marlet, Aug 2001
Record fee received: £12.8m from Manchester Utd for Louis Saha, Jan 2004
Record attendance: 49,335 v Millwall (Div 2) 8 Oct, 1938
Capacity: 25,700. **Main sponsor**: FxPro
League Championship: 7th 2008–09
FA Cup: Runners-up 1975
League Cup: 5th rd 1968, 1971, 2000
European positions: Europa League Final 2009–10
Finishing positions in Premier League: 2001–02 13th, 2002–03 14th, 2003–04 9th, 2004–05 13th, 2005–06 12th, 2006–07 16th 2007–08 17th, 2008–09 7th; 2009–10 12th, 2010–11 8th, 2011–12 9th
Biggest win: 10-1 v Ipswich (Div 1) 26 Dec, 1963
Biggest defeat: 0-10 v Liverpool (League Cup 2) 23 Sep, 1986

Highest League scorer in a season: Frank Newton 43 (1931–32)
Most League goals in aggregate: Gordon Davies 159 (1978–84 and 1986–91)
Longest unbeaten League sequence: 15 matches (1999)
Longest sequence without a League win: 15 matches (1950)
Most capped player: Johnny Haynes (England) 56

Goalkeepers

Etheridge, Neil	6.2	Chelsea	Enfield	07.02.90
Schwarzer, Mark	6.4	Middlesbrough	Sydney, Aus	06.10.72
Somogyi, Csaba	6.3	Rakospalotai	Dunaujvaros, Hun	07.04.85
Stockdale, David	6.3	Darlington	Leeds	28.09.85

Defenders

Baird, Chris	5.10	Southampton	Ballymoney	25.02.82
Briggs, Matthew	6.2	–	Wandsworth	09.03.91
Halliche, Rafik	6.2	Benfica	Algiers, Alg	02.09.86
Hangeland, Brede	6.5	Copenhagen	Houston, US	20.06.81
Hughes, Aaron	6.1	Aston Villa	Cookstown	08.11.79
Kelly, Stephen	5.11	Birmingham	Dublin, Ire	06.09.83
Riise John Arne	6.2	Roma	Molde, Nor	24.09.80
Senderos, Philippe	6.3	Arsenal	Geneva, Swi	14.02.85

Midfielders

Davies, Simon	5.11	Everton	Haverfordwest	23.10.79
Dempsey, Clint	6.1	New England	Nacogdoches, US	09.03.83
Diarra, Mahamadou	6.0	Monaco	Bamako, Mali	18.05.81
Duff, Damien	5.10	Newcastle	Dublin, Ire	02.03.79
Etuhu, Dickson	6.2	Sunderland	Kano, Nig	08.06.82
Frei, Kerim	5.7	–	Feldkirch, Aut	19.11.93
Gecov, Marcel	5.11	Slovan Liberec	Prague, Cz	01.01.88
Kacaniklic, Alex	5.11	Liverpool	Helsingborg, Swe	13.08.91
Kasami, Pajtim	6.2	Palermo	Struga, Mac	02.06.92
Riether, Sascha	5.9	Cologne (loan)	Lahr, Ger	23.03.83
Sidwell, Steve	5.10	Aston Villa	Wandsworth	14.12.82

Forwards

Dembele, Moussa	6.1	AZ Alkmaar	Wilrijk, Bel	16.07.87
Petric, Mladen	6.1	Hamburg	Dubrave Brcko, Bos	01.01.81
Rodallega, Hugo	6.0	Wigan	El Carmelo, Col	25.07.85
Ruiz, Bryan	6.2	Twente	Aljuela, C Rica	18.08.85

LIVERPOOL

Ground: Anfield, Liverpool L4 OTH
Telephone: 0151 263 2361. **Club nickname**: Reds or Pool
Colours: All red
Record transfer fee: £35m to Newcastle for Andy Carroll, Jan 2011
Record fee received: £50m from Chelsea for Fernando Torres, Jan 2011
Record attendance: 61,905 v Wolves, (FA Cup 4), 2 Feb, 1952
Capacity: 45,276. **Main sponsor**: Standard Chartered
League Championship: Winners 1900–01, 1905–06, 1921–22, 1922–23, 1946–47, 1963–64, 1965–66, 1972–73, 1975–76, 1976–77, 1978–79, 1979–80, 1981–82, 1982–83, 1983–84, 1985–86, 1987–88, 1989–90
FA Cup: Winners 1965, 1974, 1986, 1989, 1992, 2001, 2006
League Cup: Winners 1981, 1982, 1983, 1984, 1995, 2001, 2003, 2012
European competitions: Winners European Cup/Champions League 1976–77, 1977–78, 1980–81, 1983–84, 2004–05; UEFA Cup 1972–73, 1975–76, 2000–01; European Super Cup 1977, 2005

Finishing positions in Premier League: 1992–93 6th, 1993–94 8th, 1994–95 4th, 1995–96 3rd, 1996–97 4th, 1997–98 3rd, 1998–99 7th, 1999–2000 4th, 2000–01 3rd, 2001–02 2nd, 2002–03 5th, 2003–04 4th, 2004–05 5th, 2005–06 3rd, 2006–07 3rd, 2007–08 4th, 2008–09 2nd, 2009–10 7th, 2010–11 6th, 2011–12 8th
Biggest win: 10-1 v Rotherham (Div 2) 18 Feb, 1896. Also: 11-0 v Stromsgodset (Cup-Winners' Cup 1) 17 Sep, 1974
Biggest defeat: 1-9 v Birmingham (Div 2) 11 Dec, 1954
Highest League scorer in a season: Roger Hunt 41 (1961–62)
Most League goals in aggregate: Roger Hunt 245 (1959–69)
Longest unbeaten League sequence: 31 matches (1987–88))
Longest sequence without a League win: 14 matches (1953–54))
Most capped player: Steven Gerrard (England) 96

Goalkeepers

Doni, Alexander	6.5	Roma	Sao Paulo, Br	22.10.79
Gulacsi, Peter	6.3	MTK Hungaria	Budapest, Hun	06.05.90
Jones, Brad	6.3	Middlesbrough	Armadale, Aus	19.03.82
Reina, Jose	6.2	Villarreal	Madrid, Sp	31.08.82
Defenders				
Agger, Daniel	6.3	Brondby	Hvidovre, Den	12.12.84
Carragher, Jamie	6.1	–	Liverpool	28.01.78
Coates, Sebastian	6.6	Nacional	Montevideo, Uru	07.10.90
Flanagan, John	5.11	–	Liverpool	01.01.93
Johnson, Glen	5.11	Portsmouth	Greenwich	23.08.84
Jose Enrique	6.0	Newcastle	Valencia, Sp	23.01.86
Kelly, Martin	6.3	–	Whiston	27.04.90
Robinson, Jack	5.7	–	Warrington	01.09.93
Skrtel, Martin	6.3	Zenit St Petersburg	Trencin, Slovak	15.12.84
Wilson, Danny	6.2	Rangers	Livingston	27.12.91
Midfielders				
Adam, Charlie	6.1	Blackpool	Dundee	10.12.85
Aquilani, Alberto	6.1	Roma	Rome, It	07.07.84
Cole, Joe	5.9	Chelsea	Islington	08.11.81
Downing, Stewart	6.0	Aston Villa	Middlesbrough	02.07.84
Gerrard, Steven	6.1	–	Whiston	30.05.80
Henderson, Jordan	5.10	Sunderland	Sunderland	17.06.90
Lucas Leiva	5.10	Gremio	Dourados, Br	09.01.87
Pacheco, Daniel	5.6	Barcelona	Malaga, Sp	05.01.91
Shelvey, Jonjo	6.0	Charlton	Romford	27.02.92
Spearing, Jay	5.6	–	Wirral	25.11.88
Forwards				
Bellamy, Craig	5.9	Manchester City	Cardiff	13.07.79
Borini, Fabio	5.11	Roma	Bentivoglio, It	29.03.91
Carroll, Andy	6.3	Newcastle	Gateshead	06.01.89
Eccleston, Nathan	5.10	–	Manchester	30.12.90
Suarez, Luis	5.11	Ajax	Salto, Uru	24.01.87

MANCHESTER CITY

Ground: Etihad Stadium, Etihad Campus, Manchester M11 3FF
Telephone: 0870 062 1894. **Club nickname**: City
Colours: Sky blue shirts; white shorts; sky blue socks
Record transfer fee: £38.5m to Atletico Madrid for Sergio Aguero, Jul 2011
Record fee received: £21m from Chelsea for Shaun Wright-Phillips, Jul 2005

Record attendance: Maine Road: 84,569 v Stoke (FA Cup 6) 3 Mar, 1934 (British record for any game outside London or Glasgow). Etihad Stadium: 48,000 v QPR (Prem Lge) 13 May, 2012
Capacity: 48,000. **Main sponsor**: Etihad
League Championship: Winners 1936–37, 1967–68, 2011–12
FA Cup: Winners 1904, 1934, 1956, 1969, 2011
League Cup: Winners 1970, 1976
European competitions: Winners Cup-Winners' Cup 1969–70
Finishing positions in Premier League: 1992–93 9th, 1993–94 16th, 1994–95 17th, 1995–96 18th, 2000–01: 18th, 2002–03 9th, 2003–04 16th, 2004–05 8th, 2005–06 15th, 2006–07 14th, 2007–08 9th, 2008–09 10th, 2009–10 5th, 2010–11 3rd, 2011–12 1st
Biggest win: 10-1 Huddersfield (Div 2) 7 Nov, 1987. Also: 10-1 v Swindon (FA Cup 4) 29 Jan, 1930
Biggest defeat: 1-9 v Everton (Div 1) 3 Sep, 1906
Highest League scorer in a season: Tommy Johnson 38 (1928–29)
Most League goals in aggregate: Tommy Johnson, 158 (1919–30)
Longest unbeaten League sequence: 22 matches (1946–47)
Longest sequence without a League win: 17 matches (1979–80)
Most capped player: Colin Bell (England) 48

Goalkeepers				
Hart, Joe	6.3	Shrewsbury	Shrewsbury	19.04.87
Nielsen, Gunnar	6.3	Blackburn	Torshavin, Faroes	07.10.83
Pantilimon, Costel	6.8	Timisoara	Bacau, Rom	01.02.87
Defenders				
Boyata, Dedryck	6.2	Brussels	Uccle, Bel	28.11.90
Clichy, Gael	5.11	Arsenal	Paris, Fr	26.07.85
Kompany, Vincent	6.4	Hamburg	Uccle, Bel	10.04.86
Kolarov, Aleksandar	6.2	Lazio	Belgrade, Serb	10.11.85
Lescott, Joleon	6.2	Everton	Birmingham	16.08.82
Richards, Micah	5.11	–	Birmingham	24.06.88
Savic, Stefan	6.1	Partizan	Mojkovac, Mont	08.01.91
Toure, Kolo	6.0	Arsenal	Bouake, Iv C	19.03.81
Zabaleta, Pablo	5.10	Espanyol	Buenos Aires, Arg	16.01.85
Midfielders				
Barry, Gareth	6.0	Aston Villa	Hastings	23.02.81
De Jong, Nigel	5.8	Hamburg	Amsterdam, Hol	30.11.84
Ibrahim, Abdisalam	6.2	Fjellhamar	Mogadishu, Som	01.05.91
Johnson, Adam	5.9	Middlesbrough	Sunderland	14.07.87
Johnson, Michael	6.0	–	Urmston	03.03.88
Milner, James	5.11	Aston Villa	Leeds	04.01.86
Nasri, Samir	5.10	Arsenal	Marseille, Fr	26.06.87
Razak, Abdul	5.11	QPR	Abidjan, Iv C	11.11.92
Silva, David	5.7	Valencia	Arguineguin, Sp	08.01.86
Toure, Yaya	6.3	Barcelona	Bouake, Iv C	13.05.83
Weiss, Vladimir	5.8	Inter Bratislava	Bratislava, Slovak	30.11.89
Forwards				
Aguero, Sergio	5.8	Atletico Madrid	Quilmes, Arg	02.06.88
Adebayor, Emmanuel	6.3	Arsenal	Lome, Tog	24.12.84
Balotelli, Mario	6.3	Inter Milan	Palermo, It	12.08.90
Dzeko, Edin	6.4	Wolfsburg	Sarajevo, Bos	17.03.86
Guidetti, John	6.0	Brommapojkarna	Stockholm, Swe	15.04.92
Santa Cruz, Roque	6.2	Blackburn	Asuncion, Par	16.08.81
Tchuimeni–Nimely, Alex	5.11	Cotonsport	Monrovia, Lib	11.05.91
Tevez, Carlos	5.8	Manchester Utd	Ciudadela, Arg	05.02.84

MANCHESTER UNITED

Ground: Old Trafford Stadium, Sir Matt Busby Way, Manchester, M16 ORA
Telephone: 0161 868 8000. **Club nickname**: Red Devils
Colours: Red shirts; white shorts; black socks
Record transfer fee: £30.7m to Tottenham for Dimitar Berbatov, Sep 2008
Record fee received: £80,000,000 from Real Madrid for Cristiano Ronaldo, Jun 2009
Record attendance: 75,811 v Blackburn (Prem Lge), 31 Mar, 2007. Also: 76,962 Wolves v Grimsby (FA Cup semi-final) 25 Mar, 1939. Crowd of 83,260 saw Manchester Utd v Arsenal (Div 1) 17 Jan, 1948 at Maine Road – Old Trafford out of action through bomb damage
Capacity: 75,797. **Main sponsor**: AON
League Championship: Winners 1907–08, 1910–11, 1951–52, 1955–56, 1956–7, 1964–65, 1966–67, 1992–93, 1993–94, 1995–96, 1996–97, 1998–99, 1999–2000, 2000–01, 2002–03, 2006–07, 2007–08, 2008–09, 2010–11
FA Cup: Winners 1909, 1948, 1963, 1977, 1983, 1985, 1990, 1994, 1996, 1999, 2004
League Cup: Winners 1992, 2006, 2009
European competitions: Winners European Cup/Champions League 1967–68, 1998–99, 2007–08; Cup-Winners' Cup 1990–91; European Super Cup 1991
World Club Cup: Winners 2008
Finishing positions in Premier League : 1992–93 1st, 1993–94 1st, 1994–95 2nd, 1995–96 1st, 1996–97 1st, 1997–98 2nd, 1998–99 1st, 1999–2000 1st, 2000–01 1st, 2001–02 3rd, 2002–03 1st, 2003–04 3rd, 2004–05 3rd, 2005–06 2nd, 2006–07 1st, 2007–08 1st, 2000–09 1st, 2009–10 2nd, 2010–11 1st,
2011–12 2nd
Biggest win: As Newton Heath: 10-1 v Wolves (Div 1) 15 Oct, 1892. As Manchester Utd: 9-0 v Ipswich (Prem Lge), 4 Mar, 1995. Also: 10-0 v Anderlecht (European Cup prelim rd) 26 Sep, 1956
Biggest defeat: 0-7v Blackburn (Div 1) 10 Apr, 1926, v Aston Villa (Div 1) 27 Dec 1930, v Wolves (Div 2) 26 Dec, 1931
Highest League scorer in a season: Dennis Viollet 32 (1959–60)
Most League goals in aggregate: Bobby Charlton 199 (1956–73)
Longest unbeaten League sequence: 29 matches (1998–99)
Longest sequence without a League win: 16 matches (1930)
Most capped player: Bobby Charlton (England) 106

Goalkeepers

Amos, Ben	6.1	–	Macclesfield	10.04.90
De Gea, David	6.4	Atletico Madrid	Madrid, Sp	07.11.90
Lindegaard, Anders	6.4	Aalesund	Odense, Den	13.04.84

Defenders

Da Silva Rafael	5.6	Fluminense	Petropolis, Br	09.07.90
Evans, Jonny	6.2	–	Belfast	03.01.88
Evra, Patrice	5.8	Monaco	Dakar, Sen	15.05.81
Ferdinand, Rio	6.2	Leeds	Peckham	08.11.78
Jones, Phil	5.11	Blackburn	Blackburn	21.02.92
Smalling, Chris	6.1	Fulham	Greenwich	22.11.89
Vidic, Nemanja	6.3	Spartak Moscow	Uzice, Serb	21.10.81

Midfielders

Anderson	5.0	Porto	Alegre, Br	13.04.88
Carrick, Michael	6.0	Tottenham	Wallsend	28.07.81
Cleverley, Tom	5.10	–	Basingstoke	12.08.89
Fletcher, Darren	6.0	–	Edinburgh	01.02.84
Giggs, Ryan	5.11	–	Cardiff	29.11.73
Kagawa, Shinji	5.8	Borussia Dortmund	Kobe, Jap	17.03.89
Nani	5.10	Sporting Lisbon	Amadora, Por	17.11.86

Scholes, Paul	5.7	–	Salford	16.11.74
Valencia, Antonio	5.10	Wigan	Lago Agrio, Ec	04.08.85
Young, Ashley	5.10	Aston Villa	Stevenage	09.07.85
Forwards				
Bebe	6.2	Vitoria Guimaraes	Agualva, Por	12.07.90
Berbatov, Dimitar	6.2	Tottenhaam	Blagoevgrad, Bul	30.01.81
Hernandez, Javier	5.8	Chivas	Guadalajara, Mex	01.06.88
Macheda, Federico	6.0	Lazio	Rome, It	22.08.91
Powell, Nick	6.0	Crewe	Crewe	23.03.94
Rooney, Wayne	5.10	Everton	Liverpool	24.10.85
Welbeck, Danny	5.10	–	Manchester	26.11.90

NEWCASTLE UNITED

Ground: Sports Direct Arena. Newcastle-upon-Tyne, NE1 4ST
Telephone: 0844 372 1892. **Club nickname**: Magpies
Colours: Black and white shirts; black shorts; black socks
Record transfer fee: £16m to Real Madrid for Michael Owen, Aug 2005
Record fee received: £35m from Liverpool for Andy Carroll, Jan 2011
Record attendance: 68,386 v Chelsea (Div 1) 3 September, 1930
Capacity: 52,409. **Main sponsor**: Virgin Money
League Championship: Winners 1904–05, 1906–07, 1908–09, 1926–27
FA Cup: Winners 1910, 1924, 1932, 1951, 1952, 1955
League Cup: Runners-up 1976
European competitions: Winners Fairs Cup 1968–69, Anglo-Italian Cup 1972–73
Finishing positions in Premier League: 1993–94 3rd 1994–95 6th 1995–96 2nd 1996–97
2nd 1997–98 13th 1998–99 13th, 1999–2000 11th, 2000–01 11th, 2001–02 4th,
2002–03 3rd, 2003–04 5th, 2004–05 14th, 2005–06 7th, 2006–07 13th, 2007–08 12th;
2008–09 18th, 2010–11 12th, 2011–12 5th
Biggest win: 13-0 v Newport (Div 2) 5 Oct, 1946
Biggest defeat: 0-9 v Burton (Div. 2) 15 Apr, 1895
Highest League scorer in a season: Hughie Gallacher 36 (1926–27)
Most League goals in aggregate: Jackie Milburn 177 (1946–57)
Longest unbeaten League sequence: 14 matches (1950)
Longest sequence without a League win: 21 matches (1978)
Most capped player: Shay Given (Republic of Ireland) 83

Goalkeepers				
Elliot, Rob	6.3	Charlton	Chatham	30.04.86
Harper, Steve	6.2	–	Easington	14.03.75
Krul, Tim	6.3	Den Haag	Den Haag, Hol	03.04.88
Defenders				
Coloccini, Fabricio	6.0	Dep La Coruna	Cordoba, Arg	22.01.82
Ferguson, Shane	5.11	–	Derry	12.07.91
Simpson, Danny	6.0	Manchester Utd	Salford	04.01.87
Perch, James	6.0	Nottm Forest	Mansfield	28.09.85
Santon, Davide	6.2	Inter Milan	Portomaggiore, It	02.01.91
Tavernier, James	5.9	–	Bradford	31.10.91
Taylor, Ryan	5.8	Wigan	Liverpool	19.08.84
Taylor, Steven	6.2	–	Greenwich	23.01.86
Williamson, Mike	6.4	Portsmouth	Stoke	08.11.83
Midfielders				
Abeid, Mehdi	5.10	Lens	Montreuil, Fr	06.08.92
Amalfitano, Romain	5.9	Reims	Nice, Fr	27.08.89
Ben Arfa, Hatem	5.10	Marseille	Clamart, Fr	07.03.87

Bigirimana, Gael	5.10	Coventry	Bujumbura, Bur	22.10.93
Cabaye, Yohan	5.9	Lille	Tourcoing, Fr	14.01.86
Gosling, Dan	5.10	Everton	Brixham	02.02.90
Gutierrez, Jonas	6.0	Real Mallorca	Saenz Pena, Arg	05.07.82
Marveaux, Sylvain	5.8	Rennes	Vannes, Fr	15.04.86
Obertan, Gabriel	6.2	Manchester Utd	Pantin, Fr	26.02.89
Tiote, Cheik	5.11	Twente	Yamoussoukro, Iv C	21.06.86
Vuckic, Haris	6.2	Domzale	Ljubljana, Sloven	21.08.92
Forwards				
Ameobi, Sammy	6.4	–	Newcastle	01.05.92
Ameobi, Shola	6.3	–	Zaria, Nig	12.10.81
Cisse, Papiss	6.0	Freiburg	Dakar, Sen	03.06.85
Demba Ba	6.3	Hoffenheim	Sevres, Fr	25.05.85
Ranger, Nile	6.2	–	Highgate	11.04.91

NORWICH CITY

Ground: Carrow Road, Norwich NR1 1JE
Telephone: 01603 760760. **Club nickname**: Canaries
Colours: Yellow shirts; green and yellow shorts; yellow socks
Record transfer fee: £3.5m to WBA for Robert Earnshaw, Jan 2006
Record fee received: £7.2m from West Ham for Dean Ashton, Jan 2006
Record attendance: 43,984 v Leicester City (FA Cup 6), 30 Mar, 1963
Capacity: 27,010. **Main sponsor**: Aviva
League Championship: 3rd 1993
FA Cup: semi-finals 1959, 1989, 1992
League Cup: Winners 1962, 1985
European competitions: UEFA Cup rd 3 1993–94
Finishing positions in Premier League: 1992–93: 3rd, 1993–94 12th, 1994–95 20th, 2004–05 19th, 2011–12 12th
Biggest win: 10-2 v Coventry (Div 3S) 15 Mar, 1930. Also: 8-0 v Sutton (FA Cup 4) 28 Jan, 1989
Biggest defeat: 2-10 v Swindon (Southern Lge) Sep 5, 1908
Highest League scorer in a season: Ralph Hunt 31 (1955–56)
Most League goals in aggregate: Johnny Gavin 122 (1945–54, 55–58)
Longest unbeaten League sequence: 20 matches (1950)
Longest sequence without a League win: 25 matches (1956–7)
Most capped player: Mark Bowen (Wales) 35

Goalkeepers				
Rudd, Declan	6.1	–	Diss	16.01.91
Ruddy, John	6.4	Everton	St Ives, Cam	24.10.86
Steer, Jed	6.3	–	Norwich	23.09.92
Defenders				
Ayala, Daniel	6.3	Liverpool	El Saucejo, Sp	07.11.90
Barnett, Leon	6.1	WBA	Stevenage	30.11.85
Bennett, Ryan	6.2	Peterborough	Orsett	06.03.90
Francomb, George	6.0	–	Hackney	08.09.91
Martin, Russell	6.0	Peterborough	Brighton	04.01.86
Tierney, Marc	6.0	Colchester	Prestwich	23.08.85
Ward, Elliott	6.1	Coventry	Harrow	19.01.85
Whittaker, Steven	6.1	Rangers	Edinburgh	16.06.84
Midfielders				
Adeyemi, Tom	6.0	–	Norwich	24.10.91
Bennett, Elliott	5.9	Brighton	Telford	18.12.88

Butterfield, Jacob	5.11	Barnsley	Bradford	10.06.90
Crofts, Andrew	5.11	Brighton	Chatham	29.05.84
Fox, David	5.9	Norwich	Leek	13.12.83
Hoolahan, Wes	5.7	Blackpool	Dublin, Ire	10.08.83
Howson, Jonathan	5.11	Norwich	Leeds	21.05.88
Johnson, Bradley	6.0	Leeds	Hackney	28.04.87
Lappin, Simon	5.11	St Mirren	Glasgow	25.01.83
Pilkington, Anthony	6.0	Huddersfield	Blackburn	06.06.88
Surman, Andrew	5.11	Wolves	Johannesburg SA	20.08.86
Smith, Korey	6.0	–	Hatfield	31.01.91
Forwards				
Holt, Grant	6.0	Shrewsbury	Carlisle	12.04.81
Jackson, Simeon	5.8	Gillingham	Kingston	28.03.87
Martin, Chris	5.10	–	Beccles	04.11.88
Morison, Steve	6.2	Millwall	Enfield	29.08.83
Vaughan, James	5.11	Everton	Birmingham	14.07.88

QUEENS PARK RANGERS

Ground: Loftus Road Stadium, South Africa Road, London W12 7PA
Telephone: 0208 743 0262. **Club nickname:** Hoops
Colours: Blue and white shirts; blue shorts; blue and white socks
Record transfer fee: £5m to Fulham for Bobby Zamora, Jun 2012
Record fee received: £6m from Newcastle for Les Ferdinand, Jun 1995
Record attendance: 35,353 v Leeds (Div 1) 27 Apr, 1974
Capacity: 18,439. **Main sponsor:** Air Asia
League Championship: Runners-up 1975–76
FA Cup: Runners-up 1982
League Cup: Winners 1967
European competitions: UEFA Cup quarter-finals 1976–77
Finishing positions in Premier League: 1992–93 5th, 1993–94 9th, 1994–95 8th, 1995–96 19th, 2011–12 17th
Biggest win: 9-2 v Tranmere (Div 3) 3 Dec, 1960. Also: 8-1 v Bristol Rov (FA Cup 1) 27 Nov, 1937; 8-1 v Crewe (Lge Cup 1) 3 October 1983
Biggest defeat: 1-8 v Mansfield (Div 3) 15 Mar 1965; 1-8 v Manchester Utd (Div 1) 19 Mar 1969
Highest League scorer in a season: George Goddard 37 (1929–30)
Most League goals in aggregate: George Goddard 172 (1926–34)
Longest unbeaten League sequence: 20 matches (1972)
Longest sequence without a League win: 20 matches (1968–69)
Most capped player: Alan McDonald (Northern Ireland) 52

Goalkeepers				
Cerny, Radek	6.4	Slavia Prague	Prague, Cz	18.02.74
Green, Robert	6.2	West Ham	Chertsey	18.01.80
Murphy Brian	6.0	Ipswich	Waterford, Ire	07.05.83
Defenders				
Connolly, Matthew	6.1	Arsenal	Barnet	24.09.87
Da Silva, Fabio	5.6	Manchester Utd (loan)	Petropolis, Br	09.07.90
Ferdinand, Anton	6.0	Sunderland	Peckham	18.02.85
Hill, Clint	6.0	Crystal Palace	Liverpool	22.02.80
Nelsen, Ryan	6.0	Tottenham	Christchurch, NZ	18.10.77
Onuoha, Nedum	6.2	Manchester City	Warri, Nig	12.11.86
Traore, Armand	6.1	Arsenal	Paris, Fr	08.10.89

| Young, Luke | 6.0 | Aston Villa | Harlow | 19.07.79 |

Midfielders

Barton, Joey	5.9	Newcastle	Huyton	02.09.82
Derry, Shaun	5.10	Crystal Palace	Nottingham	06.12.77
Diakite, Samba	6.1	Nancy	Montfermeil, Fr	24.01.89
Ehmer, Max	6.2	–	Frankfurt, Ger	03.02.92
Ephrain, Hogan	5.9	West Ham	Islington	31.03.88
Faurlin, Alejandro	6.1	Instituto	Rosario, Arg	09.08.86
Ji–Sung Park	5.9	Manchester Utd	Seoul, S Kor	25.02.81
Taarabt, Adel	5.11	Tottenham	Taza, Mor	24.05.89
Wright–Phillips, Shaun	5.6	Manchester City	Greenwich	25.10.81

Forwards

Bothroyd, Jay	6.3	Cardiff	Islington	05.05.82
Campbell, Dudley	5.11	Blackpool	Hammersmith	12.11.81
Cisse, Djibril	6.0	Lazio	Arles, Fr	12.08.81
Helguson, Heidar	5.10	Bolton	Akureyri, Ice	22.08.77
Hulse, Rob	6.1	Derby	Crewe	25.10.79
Johnson, Andrew	5.9	Fulham	Bedford	10.02.81
Mackie, Jamie	5.8	Plymouth	Dorking	22.09.85
Smith, Tommy	5.10	Portsmouth	Hemel Hempstead	22.05.80
Zamora, Bobby	6.0	Fulham	Barking	16.01.81

READING

Ground: Madejski Stadium, Junction 11 M4, Reading RG2 0FL
Telephone: 0118 968 1100. **Club nickname:** Royals
Colours: Blue and white shirts; blue shorts; blue socks
Record transfer fee: £2.5m to Nantes for Emerse Fae, Aug 2007
Record fee received: £7m from Hoffenheim for Gylfi Sigurdsson, Aug 2010
Record attendance: Elm Park: 33,042 v Brentford (FA Cup 5) 19 Feb, 1927. Madejski Stadium: 24,135 v Manchester Utd (Prem Lge) 19 Jan, 2008
Capacity: 24,169. **Main sponsor:** Waitrose
League Championship: 8th 2007
FA Cup: semi-finals 1927
League Cup: 5th rd 1996, 1998
Finishing positions in Premier League: 2006–07 8th, 2007–08 18th
Biggest win: 10-2 v Crystal Palace (Div 3S) 4 Sep, 1946
Biggest defeat: 0-18 v Preston (FA Cup 1) 27 Jan, 1894
Highest League scorer in a season: Ronnie Blackman 39 (1951–52)
Most League goals in aggregate: Ronnie Blackman 158 (1947–54)
Longest unbeaten League sequence: 19 matches (1973)
Longest sequence without a League win: 14 matches (1927)
Most capped player: Kevin Doyle (Republic of Ireland) 26

Goalkeepers

Andersen, Mikkel	6.5	Copenhagen	Herlev, Den	17.12.88
Federici, Adam	6.2	Sardenga	Nowra, Aus	31.01.85
McCarthy, Alex	6.4	–	Guildford	03.12.89

Defenders

Cummings, Shaun	6.0	Chelsea	Hammersmith	28.02.89
Gorkss, Kaspars	6.3	QPR	Riga, Lat	06.11.81
Gunter, Chris	5.11	Nottm Forest	Newport	21.07.89
Harte, Ian	5.10	Carlisle	Drogheda, Ire	31.08.77
Mariappa, Adrian	5.11	Watford	Harrow	03.10.86

Morrison, Sean	6.1	Swindon	Plymouth	08.01.91
Pearce, Alex	6.0	–	Oxford	09.11.88
Shorey, Nicky	5.9	WBA	Romford	19.02.81
Midfielders				
Antonio, Michail	5.11	Tooting	Wandsworth	28.03.90
D'Ath, Lawson	5.9	–	Oxford	24.12.92
Gunnarsson, Brynjar	6.1	Watford	Reykjavik, Ice	16.10.75
Guthrie, Danny	5.9	Newcastle	Shrewsbury	18.04.87
Karacan, Jem	5.10	–	Catford	21.02.89
Kebe, Jimmy	5.9	Lens	Vitry, Fr	19.01.84
Leigertwood, Mikele	6.1	QPR	Enfield	12.11.82
McAnuff, Jobi	5.11	Watford	Edmonton	09.11.81
Obita, Jordan	5.11	–	Oxford	08.12.93
Robson-Kanu, Hal	6.0	–	Acton	21.05.89
Tabb, Jay	5.7	Coventry	Tooting	21.02.84
Taylor, Jake	5.10	–	Ascot	01.12.91
Forwards				
Bignall, Nicholas	5.10	–	Reading	11.07.90
Church, Simon	6.0	–	High Wycombe	10.12.88
Hunt, Noel	5.8	Dundee Utd	Waterford	26.12.82
Le Fondre, Adam	5.9	Rotherham	Stockport	02.12.86
McCleary, Garath	5.11	Nottm Forest	Bromley	15.05.87
Pogrebnyak, Pavel	6.2	Fulham	Moscow, Rus	08.11.83
Roberts, Jason	5.11	Blackburn	Park Royal	25.01.78
Sheppard, Karl	5.11	Shamrock	Dublin, Ire	14.02.91

SOUTHAMPTON

Ground: St Mary's Stadium, Britannia Road, Southampton, SO14 5FP
Telephone: 0845 688 9448. **Club nickname**: Saints
Colours- White and red shirts; red shorts; black socks
Record transfer fee: £6m to Burnley for Jay Rodriguez, Jun 2012
Record fee received: £12m from Arsenal for Alex Oxlade-Chamberlain, Aug 2011
Record attendance: The Dell: 31,044 v Manchester Utd (Div 1) 8 Oct, 1969;
St Mary's: 32,363 v Coventry (Champ) 28 April, 2012
Capacity: 32,689. **Main sponsor**: aap
League Championship: 2nd 1983–84
FA Cup: Winners 1976
League Cup: Runners-up 1979
European competitions: Fairs Cup rd 3 1969–70; Cup-Winners' Cup rd 3 (qf) 1976–77
Finishing positions in Premier League: 1992–93 18th, 1993–94 18th, 1994–5 10th,
1995–96 17th, 1996–97 16th, 1997–98 12th, 1998–99 17th, 1999–200 15th, 2000–01
10th, 2001–02 11th, 2002–03 8th, 2003–04 12th, 2004–05 20th
Biggest win: 8-0 v Northampton (Div 3S) 24 Dec, 1921
Biggest defeat: 0-8 v Tottenham (Div 2) 28 Mar, 1936 and v Everton (Div 1) 20 Nov, 1971
Highest League scorer in a season: Derek Reeves 39 (1959–60)
Most League goals in aggregate: Mick Channon 185 (1966–82)
Longest unbeaten League sequence: 19 matches (1921)
Longest unbeaten League sequence: 20 matches (1969)
Most capped player: Peter Shilton (England) 49

Goalkeepers

Davis, Kelvin	6.1	Sunderland	Bedford	29.09.76
Gazzaniga, Paulo	6.5	Gillingham	Murphy, Arg	02.01.92

Defenders

Butterfield, Danny	5.9	Crystal Palace	Boston	21.11.79
Clyne, Nathaniel	5.9	Crystal Palace	Stockwell	05.04.91
Dickson, Ryan	5.10	Brentford	Saltash	14.12.86
Fonte, Jose	6.2	Crystal Palace	Penafiel, Por	22.12.83
Fox, Danny	6.0	Burnley	Winsford	29.05.86
Harding, Dan	6.0	Ipswich	Gloucester	23.12.83
Hooiveld, Jos	6.4	Celtic	Zeijen, Hol	22.04.83
Martin, Aaron	6.1	Eastleigh	Newport, IOW	29.09.89
Richardson, Frazer	5.11	Charlton	Rotherham	29.10.82
Seaborne, Daniel	6.0	Exeter	Barnstaple	15.03.87

Midfielders

Chaplow, Richard	5.9	Preston	Accrington	02.02.85
Cork, Jack	6.1	Chelsea	Carshalton	25.06.89
Davis, Steven	5.8	Rangers	Ballymena	01.01.85
De Ridder, Steve	5.10	De Graafschap	Ghent, Bel	25.02.87
Do Prado, Guly	6.2	Cesena	Campinas, Br	31.12.81
Hammond, Dean	6.0	Colchester	Hastings	07.03.83
Lallana, Adam	5.10	St Albans	Bournemouth	10.05.88
Puncheon, Jason	5.8	Plymouth	Croydon	26.06.86
Schneiderlin, Morgan	5.11	Strasbourg	Zellwiller, Fr	08.11.89

Forwards

Barnard, Lee	5.10	Southend	Romford	18.07.84
Forte, Jonathan	6.0	Scunthorpe	Sheffield	25.07.86
Lambert, Rickie	5.10	Bristol Rov	Liverpool	16.02.82
Lee, Tadanari	6.0	Hiroshima	Nishitokyo, Jap	19.12.85
Rodriguez, Jay	6.1	Burnley	Burnley	29.07.89
Sharp, Billy	5.8	Doncaster	Sheffield	05.02.86

STOKE CITY

Ground: Britannia Stadium, Stanley Matthews Way, Stoke-on-Trent ST4 7EG
Telephone: 0871 663 2008. **Club nickname**: Potters
Colours: Red and white shirts; white shorts; white socks
Record transfer fee:£10m to Tottenham for Peter Crouch, Aug 2012
Record fee received: £4,500,000 from Wolfsburg for Tuncay, Jan 2011
Record attendance: Victoria Ground: 51,380 v Arsenal (Div 1) 29 Mar, 1937
Britannia Stadium: 28,218 v Everton (FA Cup 3) 5 Jan, 2002
Capacity: 27,740. **Main sponsor**: Britannia
League Championship: 4th 1935–36, 1946–47
FA Cup: Final 2011
League Cup: Winners 1972
Finishing positions in Premier League: 2008–09 12th, 2009–10 11th, 2010–11 13th, 2011–12 14th
European competitions: Europa League rd of 32 2011–12
Biggest win: 10-3 v WBA (Div 1) 4 Feb, 1937
Biggest defeat: 0-10 v Preston (Div 1) 14 Sep, 1889
Highest League scorer in a season: Freddie Steele 33 (1936–37)
Most League goals in aggregate: Freddie Steele 142 (1934–49)
Longest unbeaten League sequence: 25 matches (1992–93)
Longest sequence without a League win: 17 matches (1989)
Most capped player: Glenn Whelan (Republic of Ireland) 42

Goalkeepers

Begovic, Asmir	6.5	Portsmouth	Trebinje, Bos	20.06.87

Nash, Carlo	6.5	Everton	Bolton	13.09.73
Sorensen, Thomas	6.5	Aston Villa	Federica, Den	12.06.76
Defenders				
Collins, Danny	6.0	Sunderland	Chester	06.08.80
Higginbotham, Danny	6.1	Sunderland	Manchester	29.12.78
Huth, Robert	6.2	Middlesbrough	Berlin, Ger	18.08.84
Shawcross, Ryan	6.3	Manchester Utd	Chester	04.10.87
Shotton, Ryan	6.3	–	Stoke	30.09.88
Upson, Matthew	6.1	West Ham	Eye	18.04.79
Wilkinson, Andy	5.11	–	Stone	06.08.84
Midfielders				
Arismendi, Diego	6.2	Nacional	Montevideo, Uru	25.01.88
Delap, Rory	6.0	Sunderland	Sutton Coldfield	06.07.76
Etherington, Matthew	5.10	West Ham	Truro	14.08.81
Ness, Jamie	5.10	Rangers	Irvine	02.03.91
Palacios, Wilson	6.0	Tottenham	La Ceiba, Hond	29.07.84
Pennant, Jermaine	5.8	Real Zaragoza	Nottingham	15.01.83
Tonge, Michael	5.11	Sheffield Utd	Manchester	07.04.83
Whitehead, Dean	5.11	Sunderland	Abingdon	12.01.82
Whelan, Glenn	5.10	Sheffield Wed	Dublin, Ire	13.01.84
Wilson, Marc	6.2	Portsmouth	Belfast	17.08.87
Forwards				
Crouch, Peter	6.7	Tottenham	Macclesfield	30.01.81
Jerome, Cameron	6.1	Birmingham	Huddersfield	14.08.86
Jones, Kenwyne	6.2	Sunderland	Point Fortin, Trin	05.01.84
Moult, Lewis	6.0	–	Stoke	14.05.92
Sidibe, Mamady	6.4	Gillingham	Bamako, Mali	18.12.79
Walters, Jon	6.0	Ipswich	Birkenhead	20.09.83

SUNDERLAND

Ground: Stadium of Light, Sunderland SR5 1SU
Telephone: 0191 551 5000. **Club nickname**: Black Cats
Colours: Red and white shirts; black shorts; red and white socks
Record transfer fee: £13m to Rennes for Asamoah Gyan, Aug 2010
Record fee received: £24m from Aston Villa for Darren Bent, Jan 2011
Record attendance: At Roker Park: 75,118 v Derby (FA Cup 6 replay) 8 Mar, 1933. At Stadium of Light: 48,707 v Liverpool (Prem Lge) 13 Apr, 2002
Capacity: 49,000. **Main sponsor**: Invest In Africa
League Championship: Winners 1891–92, 1892–93, 1894–95, 1901–02, 1912–13, 1935–36
FA Cup: Winners 1937, 1973
League Cup: Runners-up 1985
European competitions: Cup-Winners' Cup rd 2 1973–74
Finishing positions in Premier League: 1996–97 18th, 1999–2000 7th, 2000–01 7th, 2001–02 17th, 2002–03 20th, 2005–06 20th, 2007–08 15th, 2008–09 16th, 2009–10 13th, 2010–11 10th, 2011–12 13th
Biggest win: 9-1 v Newcastle (Div 1) 5 Dec, 1908. Also: 11-1 v Fairfield (FA Cup 1) 2 Feb, 1895
Biggest defeat: 0-8 v Sheffield Wed (Div 1) 26 Dec, 1911, v West Ham (Div 1) 19 Oct 1968, v Watford (Div 1) 25 Sep, 1982
Highest League scorer in a season: Dave Halliday 43 (1928–29)
Most League goals in aggregate: Charlie Buchan 209 (1911–25)
Longest unbeaten League sequence: 19 matches (1998–99)
Longest sequence without a League win: 22 matches (2003–04)
Most capped player: Charlie Hurley (Republic of Ireland) 38

Goalkeepers

Mignolet, Simon	6.4	Sint-Truidense	Sint-Truiden, Bel	06.08.88
Westwood, Keiren	6.1	Coventry	Manchester	23.10.84

Defenders

Bardsley, Phil	5.11	Manchester Utd	Salford	28.06.85
Bramble, Titus	6.1	Wigan	Ipswich	21.07.81
Brown, Wes	6.1	Manchester Utd	Manchester	13.10.79
Cuellar, Carlos	6.3	Aston Villa	Madrid, Sp	23.08.81
Kilgallon, Matthew	6.1	Sheffield Utd	York	08.01.84
O'Shea, John	6.3	Manchester Utd	Waterford, Ire	30.04.81
Richardson, Kieran	5.10	Manchester Utd	Greenwich	21.10.84
Turner, Michael	6.4	Hull	Lewisham	09.11.83

Midfielders

Elmohamady, Ahmed	5.11	ENPPI	Basyoun, Egy	09.09.87
Cattermole, Lee	5.10	Wigan	Stockton	21.03.88
Colback, Jack	5.10	–	Killingworth	24.10.89
Gardner, Craig	5.10	Birmingham	Solihull	25.11.86
Larsson, Sebastian	5.10	Birmingham	Eskiltuna, Swe	06.06.85
McClean, James	5.11	Derry	Derry	22.04.89
Meyler, David	6.2	Cork	Cork, Ire	29.05.89
Sessegnon, Stephane	5.8	Paris SG	Allahe, Benin	01.06.84
Vaughan, David	5.7	Blackpool	Rhuddlan	18.02.83

Forwards

Campbell, Fraizer	5.11	Manchester Utd	Huddersfield	13.09.87
Ji Dong-won	6.1	Chunnam	Jeju-do, S Kor	28.05.91
Noble, Ryan	6.0	–	Sunderland	06.11.91
Wickham, Connor	6.3	Ipswich	Colchester	31.03.93

SWANSEA CITY

Ground: Liberty Stadium, Morfa, Swansea SA1 2FA
Telephone: 01792 616600. **Club nickname**: Swans
Colours: All white
Record transfer fee: £3.5m to Watford for Danny Graham, Jun 2011
Record fee received: £2m from Wigan for Jason Scotland, Jun 2009
Record attendance: Vetch Field: 32,796 v Arsenal (FA Cup 4) 17 Feb, 1968; Liberty Stadium: 20,605 v Liverpool (Prem Lge) 13 May, 2012
Capacity: 20,700. **Main sponsor**: 32Red
League Championship: 6th 1981–82
FA Cup: Semi-finals 1926, 1964
League Cup: 4th rd 1965, 1977, 2009
Finishing position in Premier League: 2011–12 11th
European competitions: Cup-winners' Cup rd 2 1982–83
Biggest win: 8-0 v Hartlepool (Div 4) 1 Apr, 1978. Also: 12-0 v Sliema (Cup-winners' Cup 1st rd 1st leg), 15 Sep, 1982
Biggest defeat: 0-8 v Liverpool (FA Cup 3) 9 Jan, 1990; 0-8 v Monaco (Cup-winners' Cup 1st rd 2nd leg) 1 October, 1991
Highest League scorer in a season: Cyril Pearce 35 (1931–32)
Most League goals in aggregate: Ivor Allchuch 166 (1949–58, 1965–68)
Longest unbeaten League sequence: 19 matches (1970–71)
Longest sequence without a League win: 15 matches (1989)
Most capped player: Ivor Allchuch (Wales) 42

Goalkeepers

Cornell, David	6.0	–	Swansea	28.03.91

Tremmel, Gerhard	6.3	Salzburg	Munich, Ger	16.11.78
Vorm, Michel	6.0	Utrecht	Nieuwegein, Hol	20.10.83
Defenders				
Alfei, Daniel	5.11	–	Swansea	23.02.92
Bessone, Federico	5.11	Leeds	Cordoba, Arg	23.01.84
Flores, Jose Manuel	6.2	Genoa	Cadiz, Sp	06.03.87
Monk, Garry	6.0	Barnsley	Bedford	06.03.79
Obeng, Curtis	5.8	Wrexham	Manchester	14.02.89
Rangel, Angel	5.11	Terrassa	Tortosa, Sp	28.10.82
Situ, Darnel	6.2	Lens	Rouen, Fr	18.03.92
Tate, Alan	6.1	Manchester Utd	Easington	02.09.82
Taylor, Neil	5.9	Wrexham	St Asaph	07.02.89
Williams, Ashley	6.0	Stockport	Wolverhampton	23.08.84
Midfielders				
Agustien, Kenny	5.10	AZ Alkmaar	Willemstad, Hol	20.08.86
Allen, Joe	5.7	–	Carmarthen	14.03.90
Britton, Leon	5.5	Sheffield Utd	Merton	16.09.82
Edwards, Gwion	5.7	–	Carmarthen	01.03.93
Davies, Ben	5.6	–	Neath	24.04.93
De Guzman, Jonathan	5.9	Villarreal (loan)	Scarborough, Can	13.09.87
Dyer, Nathan	5.10	Southampton	Trowbridge	29.11.87
Gower, Mark	5.11	Southend	Edmonton	05.10.78
Lucas, Lee	5.9	–	Aberdare	10.06.92
March, Kurtis	5.9	–	Swansea	30.03.93
Michu	6.1	Rayo Vallecano	Oviedo, Sp	21.03.86
Orlandi, Andrea	6.0	Alaves	Barcelona, Sp	03.08.84
Richards, Ashley	6.1	–	Swansea	12.04.91
Routledge, Wayne	5.7	Newcastle	Sidcup	07.01.85
Sinclair, Scott	5.10	Chelsea	Bath	25.03.89
Forwards				
Dobbie, Stephen	5.10	Queen of South	Glasgow	05.12.82
Donnelly, Rory	6.2	Cliftonville	Belfast	18.02.92
Graham, Danny	6.1	Watford	Gateshead	12.08.85
Lita, Leroy	5.9	Middlesbrough	Kinshasa, DR Con	28.12.84
Moore, Luke	5.10	WBA	Birmingham	13.02.86

TOTTENHAM HOTSPUR

Ground: White Hart Lane, Tottenham, London N17 OAP
Telephone: 0844 499 5000. **Club nickname**: Spurs
Colours: All white
Record transfer fee: £16.6m to Dinamo Zagreb for Luka Modric, Jun 2008
Record fee received: £30.7m from Manchester United for Dimitar Berbatov, Aug 2008
Record attendance: 75,038 v Sunderland (FA Cup 6) 5 Mar, 1938
Capacity: 36,230. **Main sponsor**: Autonomy
League Championship: Winners 1950–51, 1960–61
FA Cup: Winners 1901, 1921, 1961, 1962, 1967, 1981, 1982, 1991
League Cup: Winners 1971, 1973, 1999, 2008
European competitions: Winners Cup-Winners' Cup 1962–63, UEFA Cup 1971–72, 1983–84
Finishing positions in Premier League: 1992–93 8th, 1993–94 15th, 1994–95 7th, 1995–96 8th, 1996–97 10th, 1997–98 14th, 1998–99 11th, 1999–2000 10th, 2000–01 12th, 2001–02 9th, 2002–03 10th, 2003–04 14th, 2004–05 9th, 2005–06 5th, 2006–07 5th, 2007–08 11th, 2008–09 8th, 2009–10 4th, 2010–11 5th, 2011–12 4th
Biggest win: 9-0 v Bristol Rov (Div 2) 22 Oct, 1977. Also: 13-2 v Crewe (FA Cup 4 replay) 3 Feb, 1960

Biggest defeat: 0–7 v Liverpool (Div 1) 2 Sep, 1979. Also: 0–8 v Cologne (Inter Toto Cup) 22 Jul, 1995
Highest League scorer in a season: Jimmy Greaves 37 (1962–63)
Most League goals in aggregate: Jimmy Greaves 220 (1961–70)
Longest unbeaten League sequence: 22 matches (1949)
Longest sequence without a League win: 16 matches (1934–35)
Most capped player: Pat Jennings (Northern Ireland) 74

Goalkeepers

Cudicini, Carlo	6.1	Chelsea	Milan, It	06.09.73
Friedel, Brad	6.3	Aston Villa	Lakewood, US	18.05.71
Gomes, Heurelho	6.2	PSV Eindhoven	Joao Pinheiro, Br	15.12.81

Defenders

Assou–Ekotto, Benoit	5.10	Lens	Arras, Fr	24.03.84
Dawson, Michael	6.2	Nottm Forest	Northallerton	18.11.83
Gallas, William	6.1	Arsenal	Asnieres, Fr	17.08.77
Kaboul, Younes	6.3	Portsmouth	St Julien, Fr	04.01.86
Khumalo, Bongani	6.2	Supersport	Manzini, Swaz	06.01.87
Naughton, Kyle	5.10	Sheffield Utd	Sheffield	11.11.88
Vertonghen, Jan	6.2	Ajax	Sint-Niklaas,Bel	24.04.87
Walker, Kyle	5.10	Sheffield Utd	Sheffield	28.05.90

Midfielders

Bale, Gareth	6.0	Southampton	Cardiff	16.07.89
Bentley, David	5.10	Arsenal	Peterborough	27.08.84
Huddlestone, Tom	6.1	Derby	Nottingham	28.12.86
Jenas, Jermaine	6.0	Newcastle	Nottingham	18.02.83
Lennon, Aaron	5.5	Leeds	Leeds	16.04.87
Livermore, Jake	6.2	–	Enfield	14.11.89
Modric, Luka	5.7	Dinamo Zagreb	Zadar, Cro	09.09.85
Parker, Scott	5.7	West Ham	Lambeth	13.10.80
Pienaar, Steven	5.9	Tottenham	Johannesburg, SA	17.03.82
Rose, Danny	5.8	Leeds	Doncaster	02.07.90
Sandro	6.2	Internacional	Riachinho, Br	15.03.89
Sigurdsson, Gylfi	6.1	Hoffenheim	Hafnarfjordur, Ice	08.09.89
Townsend, Andros	6.0	–	Leytonstone	16.07.91
Van der Vaart, Rafael	5.10	Real Madrid	Heemskerk, Hol	11.02.83

Forwards

Defoe, Jermain	5.7	Portsmouth	Beckton	07.10.82
Dos Santos, Giovanni	5.9	Barcelona	Monterrey, Mex	11.05.89

WEST BROMWICH ALBION

Ground: The Hawthorns, Halfords Lane, West Bromwich B71 4LF
Telephone: 0871 271 1100. **Club nickname**: Baggies
Colours: Blue and white shirts; white shorts; blue socks
Record transfer fee: £4.7m to Real Mallora for Borja Valero, Aug 2008
Record fee received: £8.5m from Aston Villa for Curtis Davies, July 2008
Record attendance: 64,815 v Arsenal (FA Cup 6) 6 Mar, 1937.
Capacity: 26,360. **Main sponsor**: Bodog
League Championship: Winners 1919–20
FA Cup: Winners 1888, 1892, 1931, 1954, 1968
League Cup: Winners 1966
European competitions: Cup-Winners' Cup quarter-finals 1968–69. UEFA Cup quarter-finals 1978–79
Finishing positions in Premier League: 2002–03 19th, 2004–5 17th, 2005–6 19th; 2008–09

20th, 2010–11 11th, 2011–12 10th
Biggest win: 12-0 v Darwen (Div 1) 4 Apr, 1892
Biggest defeat: 3-10 v Stoke (Div 1) 4 Feb, 1937
Highest League scorer in a season: William Richardson 39 (1935–36)
Most League goals in aggregate: Tony Brown 218 (1963–79)
Longest unbeaten League sequence: 17 matches (1957)
Longest sequence without a League win: 14 matches (1995)
Most capped player: Stuart Williams (Wales) 33

Goalkeepers

Daniels, Luke	6.4	Manchester Utd	Bolton	05.01.88
Foster, Ben	6.2	Birmingham	Leamington	03.04.83
Myhill, Boaz	6.3	Hull	Modesto, US	09.11.82

Defenders

Dawson, Craig	6.2	Rochdale	Rochdale	06.05.90
Gayle, Cameron	5.11	Crewe	Birmingham	22.11.92
Hurst, James	5.8	Portsmouth	Sutton Coldfield	31.01.92
Jones, Billy	5.11	Preston	Shrewsbury	24.03.87
McAuley, Gareth	6.3	Ipswich	Larne	05.12.79
Olsson, Jonas	6.4	Nijmegen	Landskrona, Swe	10.03.83
O'Neil, Liam	5.11	Histon	Cambridge	31.07.93
Reid, Steven	6.1	Blackburn	Kingston	10.03.81
Ridgewell, Liam	5.10	Birmingham	Bexley	21.07.84
Tamas, Gabriel	6.2	Auxerre	Brasov, Rom	09.11.83

Midfielders

Allan, Scott	5.9	Dundee Utd	Glasgow	28.11.91
Brown, Kayleden	6.2	–	Birmingham	15.04.92
Brunt, Chris	6.1	Sheffield Wed	Belfast	14.12.84
Dorrans, Graham	5.9	Livingston	Glasgow	05.05.87
El Ghanassy, Yassine	5.8	Gent (loan)	La Louviere, Bel	12.07.90
Jara, Gonzalo	5.10	Colo Colo	Santiago, Chil	29.08.85
Mantom, Sam	5.9	–	Stourbridge	20.02.92
Morrison, James	5.10	Middlesbrough	Darlington	25.05.86
Mulumbu, Youssouf	5.10	Paris SG	Kinshasa, DR Con	25.01.87
Roofe, Kemar	5.10	–	Walsall	06.01.93
Sawyers, Romaine	5.9	–	Birmingham	02.11.91
Thomas, Jerome	6.1	Portsmouth	Wembley	23.03.83
Thorne, George	6.2	–	Chatham	04.01.93
Yacob, Claudio	5.11	Racing Club	Carcarana, Arg	18.07.87

Forwards

Berahino, Saido	5.10	–	Burundi	04.08.93
Cox, Simon	5.10	Swindon	Reading	28.04.87
Fortune, Marc-Antoine	6.0	Celtic	Cayenne, Fr Gui	02.07.81
Gera, Zoltan	6.0	Fulham	Pecs, Hun	22.04.79
Long, Shane	5.10	Reading	Gortnahoe, Ire	22.01.87
Nabi, Adil	5.8	–	Birmingham	28.02.94
Odemwingie, Peter	6.0	Lok Moscow	Tashkent, Uzbek	15.07.81
Wood, Chris	6.3	–	Auckland, NZ	07.12.91

WEST HAM UNITED

Ground: Boleyn Ground, Upton Park, London E13 9AZ
Telephone: 0208 548 2748. **Club nickname:** Hammers
Colours: Claret and blue shirts; white shorts; white socks

Record transfer fee: £7.5m to Liverpool for Craig Bellamy, Jul 2007
Record fee received: £18m from Leeds for Rio Ferdinand, Nov 2000
Record attendance: 43,322 v Tottenham (Div 1) 17 Oct, 1970
Capacity: 35,303. **Main sponsor:** SBOBET
League Championship: 3rd 1985–86
FA Cup: Winners 1964, 1975, 1980
League Cup: Runners-up 1966, 1981
European competitions: Winners Cup-Winners' Cup 1964–65
Finishing positions in Premier League: 1993–94 13th, 1994–95 14th, 1995–96 10th, 1996–97 14th, 1997–98 8th, 1998–99 5th, 1999–2000 9th, 2000–01 15th, 2001–02 7th, 2002–03 18th, 2005–06 9th, 2006–07 15th, 2007–08 10th, 2008–09: 9th, 2009 10 17th, 2010–11 20th
Biggest win: 8-0 v Rotherham (Div 2) 8 Mar, 1958, v Sunderland (Div 1) 19 Oct, 1968. Also: 10-0 v Bury (League Cup 2) 25 Oct, 1983
Biggest defeat: 0-7 v Barnsley (Div 2) 1 Sep, 1919, v Everton (Div 1) 22 Oct, 1927, v Sheffield Wed (Div 1) 28 Nov, 1959,
Highest League scorer in a season: Vic Watson 42 (1929–30)
Most League goals in aggregate: Vic Watson 298 (1920–35)
Longest unbeaten League sequence: 27 matches (1980–81)
Longest sequence without a League win: 17 matches (1976)
Most capped player: Bobby Moore (England) 108

Goalkeepers

Henderson, Stephen	6.3	Portsmouth	Dublin, Ire	02.05.88
Jaaskelainen, Jussi	6.4	Bolton	Mikkeli, Fin	17.04.75
Defenders				
Demel, Guy	6.3	Hamburg	Orsay, Fr	13.06.81
Driver, Callum	5.7	–	Bexley	23.10.92
McCartney, George	6.0	Sunderland	Belfast	29.04.81
O'Brien, Joey	6.2	Bolton	Dublin, Ire	17.02.86
Potts, Daniel	5.8	–	Romford	13.04.94
Reid, Winston	6.3	Midtjlland	Auckland, NZ	03.07.88
Spence, Jordan	6.0	–	Woodford	24.05.90
Tomkins, James	6.3	–	Basildon	29.03.89
Midfielders				
Collison, Jack	6.0	–	Watford	02.10.88
Diame, Mohamed	6.1	Wigan	Creteil, Fr	14.06.87
Morrison, Ravel	5.10	Manchester Utd	Wythenshawe	02.02.93
Noble, Mark	5.11	–	West Ham	08.05.87
Nolan, Kevin	6.1	Newcastle	Liverpool	24.06.82
O'Neil, Gary	5.10	Middlesbrough	Beckenham	18.05.83
Taylor, Matt	5.10	Bolton	Oxford	27.11.81
Forwards				
Baldock, Sam	5.8	MK Dons	Bedford	15.03.89
Cole, Carlton	6.3	Chelsea	Croydon	12.10.83
Maiga, Modibo	6.1	Sochaux	Bamako, Mali	03.09.87
Maynard, Nicky	5.11	Bristol City	Winsford	11.12.86
Vaz Te, Ricardo	6.2	Barnsley	Lisbon, Por	01.10.86

WIGAN ATHLETIC

Ground: DW Stadium, Robin Park, Wigan WN5 0UZ
Telephone: 01942 774000. **Club nickname:** Latics
Colours: Blue and white shirts; blue shorts; white socks

Record transfer fee: £7m to Newcastle for Charles N'Zogbia, Feb 2009
Record fee received: £15.2m from Manchester Utd for Antonio Valencia, Jun 2009
Record attendance: Springfield Park: 27,526 v Hereford (FA Cup 2)
12 Dec, 1953. DW Stadium: 25,133 v Manchester Utd (Prem Lge) 11 May, 2008
Capacity: 25,133. **Main sponsor**: 188Bet
League Championship: 10th 2005–06
FA Cup: 6th rd 1987
League Cup: Final 2006
Finishing positions in Premier League: 2005–06 10th, 2006–07 17th, 2007–08 14th,
2008–09 11th, 2009–10 16th, 2010–11 16th, 2011–12 15th
Biggest win: 7-1 v Scarborough (Div 3) 11 Mar, 1997). Also: 6-0 v Carlisle (FA Cup 1) 24
Nov, 1934
Biggest defeat: 1-9 v Tottenham (Prem Lge) 22 Nov, 2009
Highest League scorer in a season: Graeme Jones 31 (1996–97)
Most League goals in aggregate: Andy Liddell 70 (1998–2004)
Longest unbeaten League sequence: 25 matches (1999–2000)
Longest sequence without a League win: 14 (1989)
Most capped player: Maynor Figueroa (Honduras)

Goalkeepers

Al Habsi, Ali	6.5	Bolton	Muscat, Oman	30.12.81
Pollitt, Mike	6.4	Rotherham	Farnworth	29.02.72

Defenders

Alcaraz, Antolin	6.2	Bruges	San Roque, Par	30.07.82
Boyce, Emmerson	5.11	Crystal Palace	Aylesbury	24.09.79
Caldwell, Gary	5.11	Celtic	Stirling	12.04.82
Figueroa, Maynor	5.11	Olimpia	Juticalpa, Hond	02.05.83
Golobart, Roman	6.4	Espanyol	Barcelona, Sp	21.03.92
Lopez, Adrian	6.0	Dep La Coruna	As Pontes, Sp	25.02.87
Mustoe, Jordan	5.11	–	Wirral	28.01.91
Stam, Ronnie	5.9	Twente	Breda, Hol	18.06.84

Midfielders

Beausejour, Jean	5.11	Birmingham	Santiago, Chi	01.06.84
Crusat, Albert	5.5	Almeria	Barcelona, Sp	13.05.82
Dicko, Nouha	5.8	Strasbourg	Paris, Fr	14.05.92
Fyvie, Fraser	5.8	Aberdeen	Aberdeen	27.03.93
Gomez, Jordi	5.10	Espanyol	Barcelona, Sp	24.05.85
Jones, David	5.10	Wolves	Southport	04.11.84
Maloney, Shaun	5.7	Celtic	Miri, Malay	24.01.83
McArthur, James	5.7	Hamilton	Glasgow	07.10.87
McCarthy, James	5.11	Hamilton	Glasgow	12.11.90
Moses, Victor	5.10	Crystal Palace	Kaduna, Nig	12.12.90
Watson, Ben	5.10	Crystal Palace	Camberwell	09.07.85

Forwards

Boselli, Mauro	6.0	Estudiantes	Buenos Aires, Arg	22.05.85
Di Santo, Franco	6.4	Chelsea	Mendoza, Arg	07.04.89
McManaman, Callum	5.11	Everton	Knowsley	25.04.91
Sammon, Conor	6.1	Kilmarnock	Dublin, Ire	06.11.86

NPOWER LEAGUE PLAYING STAFFS 2012–13

(at time of going to press)

CHAMPIONSHIP

BARNSLEY

Ground: Oakwell Stadium, Barnsley S71 1ET
Telephone: 01226 211211. **Club nickname:** Tykes
Colours: Red shirts; white shorts; red socks. **Capacity:** 23,287
Record attendance: 40,255 v Stoke (FA Cup 5) 15 Feb, 1936

Name	Height ft in	Previous club	Birthplace	Birthdate
Goalkeepers				
Alnwick, Ben	6.0	Tottenham	Prudhoe	01.01.87
Steele, Luke	6.2	WBA	Peterborough	24.09.84
Defenders				
Collins, Lee	5.11	Port Vale	Telford	28.09.88
Edwards, Rob	6.1	Blackpool	Madeley	25.12.82
Foster, Stephen	5.11	Burnley	Warrington	10.09.80
Golbourne, Scott	5.9	Exeter	Bristol	29.02.88
Hassell, Bobby	5.9	Mansfield	Derby	04.06.80
McNulty, Jim	6.0	Brighton	Liverpool	13.02.85
Silva, Toni	6.0	Liverpool	Bissau, Guin-Biss	15.09.93
Stones, John	5.10	–	Barnsley	28.05.94
Wiseman, Scott	6.0	Rochdale	Hull	13.12.85
Midfielders				
Clark, Jordan	5.10	–	Hoyland	22.09.93
Dawson, Stephen	5.6	Leyton Orient	Dublin, Ire	04.12.85
Digby, Paul	6.3	–	Sheffield	02.02.95
Done, Matt	5.10	Rochdale	Oswestry	22.07.88
Etuhu, Kelvin	6.1	Portsmouth	Kano, Nig	30.05.88
Mellis, Jacob	5.11	Chelsea	Nottingham	08.01.91
O'Brien, Jim	6.0	Motherwell	Vale of Leven	28.09.87
Perkins, David	5.6	Colchester	Heysham	21.06.82
Forwards				
Dagnall, Chris	5.8	Scunthorpe	Liverpool	15.04.86
Davies, Craig	6.2	Chesterfield	Burton	09.01.86
Mido	6.2	Zamalek	Cairo, Egy	23.02.83
Noble-Lazarus, Reuben	5.11	–	Huddersfield	16.08.93
Rose, Danny	5.10	–	Barnsley	10.12.93

BIRMINGHAM CITY

Ground: St Andrew's, Birmingham B9 4NH
Telephone: 0844 557 1875. **Club nickname:** Blues
Colours: All blue. **Capacity:** 29,409
Record attendance: 66,844 v Everton (FA Cup 5) 11 Feb, 1939

Name	Height ft in	Previous club	Birthplace	Birthdate
Goalkeepers				
Butland, Jack	6.4	–	Bristol	10.03.93
Doyle, Colin	6.5	–	Cork, Ire	12.08.85
Lucas, David	6.1	Rochdale	Preston	23.11.77

Defenders

Caldwell, Steven	5.11	Wigan	Stirling	12.09.80
Carr, Stephen	5.9	Newcastle	Dublin, Ire	29.08.76
Davies, Curtis	6.2	Aston Villa	Waltham Forest	15.03.85
Ibanez, Pablo	6.4	WBA	Madrigueras, Sp	03.08.81
Murphy, David	6.1	Hibernian	Hartlepool	01.06.84
Spector, Jonathan	6.1	West Ham	Arlington Heights, US	03.01.86

Midfielders

Ambrose, Darren	5.11	Crystal Palace	Harlow	29.02.84
Burke, Chris	5.9	Cardiff	Glasgow	02.12.83
Elliott, Wade	5.10	Burnley	Eastleigh	14.12.78
Fahey, Keith	5.10	St Patrick's	Dublin, Ire	15.01.83
Gomis, Morgaro	5.7	Dundee Utd	Paris, Fr	14.07.85
Mullins, Hayden	6.0	Portsmouth	Reading	27.03.79
Redmond, Nathan	5.8	–	Birmingham	06.03.94

Forwards

Jervis, Jake	6.3	Shrewsbury	Birmingham	17.09.91
King, Marlon	6.1	Coventry	Dulwich	26.04.80
Lovenkrands, Peter	6.0	Newcastle	Horsholm, Den	29.01.80
Rooney, Adam	6.2	Inverness	Dublin, Ire	21.04.88
Zigic, Nikola	6.8	Valencia	Backa Topola, Serb	25.09.80

BLACKBURN ROVERS

Ground: Ewood Park, Blackburn BB2 4JF
Telephone: 0871 702 1875. **Club nickname:** Rovers
Colours: Blue and white shirts; white shorts; white socks. **Capacity:** 31,154
Record attendance: 62,522 v Bolton (FA Cup 6) 2 Mar, 1929

Goalkeepers

Bunn, Mark	6.0	Northampton	Southgate	16.11.84
Kean, Jake	6.4	Derby	Derby	04.02.91
Robinson, Paul	6.2	Tottenham	Beverley	15.10.79

Defenders

Anderson, Myles	6.0	Aberdeen	Westminster	09.01.90
Dann, Scott	6.2	Birmingham	Liverpool	14.02.87
Givet, Gael	6.0	Marseille	Arles, Fr	09.10.81
Hanley, Grant	6.2	–	Dumfries	20.11.91
Henley, Adam	5.10	–	Knoxville, US	14.06.94
Morris, Josh	5.10	–	Preston	30.09.91
O'Connor, Anthony	6.2	–	Cork, Ire	25.10.92
Olsson, Martin	5.7	Hogaborgs	Gavle, Swe	17.05.88
Orr, Bradley	6.0	QPR	Liverpool	01.11.82
Ribeiro, Bruno	5.8	Gremio	Tupa, Br	01.04.83

Midfielders

Dunn, David	5.10	Birmingham	Blackburn	27.12.79
Formica, Mauro	5.10	Newell's OB	Rosario, Arg	04.04.88
Linganz, Amine	6.1	St Etienne	Algiers	16.11.89
Lowe, Jason	6.0	–	Wigan	02.09.91
Murphy, Danny	5.9	Fulham	Chester	18.03.77
Fabio Nunes	5.11	Portimonese	Porto Alegre, Br	15.01.80
N'Zonzi, Steven	6.3	Amiens	La Garenne, Fr	15.12.88
Olsson, Marcus	5.11	Halmstad	Gavle, Swe	17.05.88
Petrovic, Radosav	6.4	Partizan	Ub, Serb	08.03.89
Pedersen, Morten Gamst	5.11	–	Vadso, Nor	08.09.81

Vukcevic, Simon	5.11	Sporting	Titograd, Mont	29.01.86
Forwards				
Best, Leon	6.1	Newcastle	Nottingham	19.09.86
Blackman, Nick	5.10	Macclesfield	Whitefield	11.11.89
Nuno Gomes	6.0	Braga	Amarante, Por	05.07.76
Goodwillie, David	5.9	Dundee Utd	Stirling	28.03.89
Rochina, Ruben	5.11	Barcelona	Sagunto, Sp	23.03.91
Slew, Jordan	6.3	Sheffield Utd	Sheffield	07.09.92

BLACKPOOL

Ground: Bloomfield Road, Blackpool FY1 6JJ
Telephone: 0871 622 1953. **Club nickname**: Seasiders
Colours: Tangerine shirts; white shorts; tangerine socks. **Capacity**: 16,007
Record attendance: 38,098 v Wolves (Div 1) 17 Sep, 1955

Goalkeepers				
Gilks, Matthew	6.1	Norwich	Rochdale	04.06.82
Halstead, Mark	6.3	–	Blackpool	01.01.90
Defenders				
Baptiste, Alex	5.11	Mansfield	Sutton–in–Ashfield	31.01.86
Bignot, Paul	6.1	Newport	Birmingham	14.02.86
Cathcart, Craig	6.2	Manchester Utd	Belfast	06.02.89
Crainey, Stephen	5.9	Leeds	Glasgow	22.06.81
Eardley, Neal	5.11	Oldham	Llandudno	06.11.88
Eastham. Ashley	6.3	–	Preston	22.03.91
Evatt, Ian	6.3	QPR	Coventry	19.11.81
Harris, Robert	5.8	Queen of South	Glasgow	28.08.87
Midfielders				
Basham, Chris	5.11	Bolton	Hebburn	18.02.88
Bruna, Gerardo	5.9	Liverpool	Mendoza, Arg	29.01.91
Caprice, Jake	5.10	Crystal Palace	London	11.11.92
Ferguson, Barry	5.10	Birmingham	Glasgow	02.02.78
Ince, Thomas	5.10	Liverpool	Stockport	30.01.92
Martinez, Angel	5.9	Girona	Girona, Sp	31.01.86
Osbourne, Isaiah	6.2	Hibernian	Birmingham	15.11.87
Phillips, Matt	6.0	Wycombe	Aylesbury	13.03.91
Southern, Keith	5.10	Everton	Gateshead	21.04.84
Sylvestre, Ludovic	6.0	Mlada Boleslav	Paris, Fr	05.02.84
Tiago Gomes	5.8	Hercules	Vila Franca, Por	18.08.85
Forwards				
Amond, Louis	5.11	–	Blackburn	05.01.92
Phillips, Kevin	5.7	Birmingham	Hitchin	25.07.73
Sutherland, Craig	6.0	North Carolina	Edinburgh	17.12.88
Taylor–Fletcher, Gary	6.0	Huddersfield	Liverpool	04.06.81

BOLTON WANDERERS

Ground: Reebok Stadium, Burnden Way, Lostock, Bolton BL6 6JW
Telephone: 0844 871 2932. **Club nickname**: Trotters
Colours: All white. **Capacity**: 28,101
Record attendance: Burnden Park: 69,912 v Manchester City (FA Cup 5) 18 Feb, 1933;
Reebok Stadium: 28,353 v Leicester (Prem Lge) 28 Dec, 2003

Goalkeepers				
Bogdan, Adam	6.4	Vasas	Budapest, Hun	27.09.87

Lainton, Rob	6.1	–	Ashton-under-Lyne	12.10.89
Lonergan, Andy	6.4	Leeds	Preston	19.10.83
Defenders				
Alonso, Marcos	6.2	Real Madrid	Madrid, Sp	28.12.90
Knight, Zat	6.6	Aston Villa	Solihull	02.05.80
Mears, Tyrone	5.11	Burnley	Stockport	18.02.83
Mills, Matt	6.3	Leicester	Swindon	14.07.86
Ream, Tim	6.1	NY Red Bulls	St Louis, US	05.10.87
Ricketts, Sam	6.1	Hull	Aylesbury	11.10.81
Wheater, David	6.4	Middlesbrough	Redcar	14.02.87
Midfielders				
Andrews, Keith	6.0	WBA	Dublin, Ire	13.09.80
Chung–Yong Lee	5.11	Seoul	Seoul, S Kor	02.07.88
Davies, Mark	5.11	Wolves	Wolverhampton	18.02.88
Eagles, Chris	6.0	Burnley	Hemel Hempstead	19.11.85
Holden, Stuart	5.10	Houston	Aberdeen	01.08.85
McKee, Joe	5.11	Livingston	Glasgow	31.10.92
Muamba, Fabrice	5.11	Birmingham	Kinshasa, DR Con	06.04.88
Pratley, Darren	6.0	Swansea	Barking	22.04.85
Petrov, Martin	5.11	Manchester City	Vzatza, Bul	15.01.79
Wylde, Greg	5.10	Rangers	Kirkintilloch	23.03.91
Forwards				
Davies, Kevin	6.0	Southampton	Sheffield	26.03.77
Eaves, Tom	6.4	Oldham	Liverpool	14.01.92
Ngog, David	6.3	Liverpool	Gennevilliers, Fr	01.04.89
O'Halloran, Michael	6.2	–	Glasgow	06.01.91
Sordell, Marvin	5.10	Watford	Brent	17.02.91

BRIGHTON AND HOVE ALBION

Ground: American Express Stadium, Village Way, Brighton BN1 9BL
Telephone: 01273 878288. **Club nickname:** Seagulls
Colours: Blue and white shirts; blue shorts; white socks. **Capacity:** 22,500
Record attendance: Goldstone Ground: 36,747 v Fulham (Div 2) 27 Dec, 1958; Withdean Stadium: 8,729 v Manchester City (Carling Cup2) 23 Sep, 2008; American Express Stadium: 21,897 v Liverpool (Lge Cup 3) 21 Sep, 2011

Goalkeepers				
Ankergren, Casper	6.3	Leeds	Koge, Den	09.11.79
Brezonan, Peter	6.6	Swindon	Bratislava, Slovak	09.12.79
Kuszczak, Thomasz	6.3	Manchester Utd	Krosno, Pol	20.03.82
Defenders				
Bridge, Wayne	5.10	Manchester City (loan)	Southampton	05.08.80
Calderon, Inigo	5.11	Alaves	Vitoria, Sp	04.01.82
Dunk, Lewis	6.4	–	Brighton	21.11.91
El-Abd, Adam	6.0	–	Brighton	11.09.84
Elphick, Tommy	5.11	–	Brighton	07.09.87
Greer, Gordon	6.2	Swindon	Glasgow	14.12.80
Painter, Marcos	6.0	Swansea	Birmingham	17.08.86
Saltor, Bruno	5.11	Valencia	El Masnou, Sp	01.10.80
Vincelot, Romain	5.10	Dagenham	Poitiers, Fr	29.10.85
Midfielders				
Bridcutt, Liam	5.9	Chelsea	Reading	08.05.89
Dicker, Gary	6.0	Stockport	Dublin, Ire	31.07.86
Harley, Ryan	5.9	Swansea	Bristol	22.01.85

LuaLua, Kazenga	5.11	Newcastle	Kinshasa, DR Con	10.12.90
Noone, Craig	6.3	Plymouth	Fazackerley	17.11.87
Sparrow, Matt	5.10	Scunthorpe	Wembley	03.10.81
Vicente	5.10	Valencia	Valencia, Sp	16.07.81
Forwards				
Agdestien, Torbjorn	6.1	Stord	Stord, Nor	18.09.91
Barnes, Ashley	6.0	Plymouth	Bath	31.10.89
Bergkamp, Roland	6.3	Excelsior	Amstelveen, Hol	03.04.91
Buckley, Will	6.0	Watford	Oldham	12.08.88
Hoskins, Will	5.10	Bristol Rov	Nottingham	06.05.86
Mackail-Smith, Craig	6.3	Peterborough	• Watford	25.02.84

BRISTOL CITY

Ground: Ashton Gate, Bristol BS3 2EJ
Telephone: 0871 222 6666. **Club nickname**: Robins
Colours: Red shirts; white shorts; red socks. **Capacity**: 21,804
Record attendance: 43,335 v Preston (FA Cup 5) 16 Feb, 1935

Goalkeepers				
Gerken, Dean	6.2	Colchester	Southend	04.08.85
Carey, Lewis	6.0	Gloucester	–	02.06.93
Defenders				
Carey, Louis	5.10	Coventry	Bristol	22.01.77
Cunningham, Greg	6.0	Manchester City	Carnmore, Ire	31.01.91
Edwards, Joe	5.8	–	Gloucester	31.10.90
Fontaine, Liam	6.3	Fulham	Beckenham	07.01.83
Foster, Richard	5.9	Aberdeen	Aberdeen	31.07.85
Nyatanga, Lewin	6.2	Derby	Burton	18.08.88
Stewart, Damion	6.3	Bradford	Kingston, Jam	08.08.80
Wilson, James	6.2	–	Chepstow	26.02.89
Midfielders				
Bolasie, Yannick	6.2	Plymouth	Kinshasa, DR Con	24.05.89
Bryan, Joe	5.7	–	Bristol	17.09.93
Cisse, Kalifa	6.1	Reading	Dreux, Fr	09.01.84
Elliott, Marvin	6.0	Millwall	Wandsworth	15.09.84
Kilkenny, Neil	5.8	Leeds	Enfield	19.12.85
Morris, Jody	5.5	St Johnstone	Hammersmith	22.12.78
Pearson, Stephen	6.0	Derby	Lanark	02.10.82
Reid, Bobby	5.7	–	Bristol	02.02.93
Skuse, Cole	5.9	–	Bristol	29.03.86
Woolford, Martyn	6.0	Scunthorpe	Pontefract	13.10.85
Forwards				
Adomah, Albert	6.1	Barnet	Lambeth	13.12.87
Pitman, Brett	6.0	Bournemouth	St Helier, Jer	03.01.88
Stead, Jon	6.3	Ipswich	Huddersfield	07.04.83
Taylor, Ryan	6.2	Rotherham	Rotherham	04.05.88

BURNLEY

Ground: Turf Moor, Harry Potts Way, Burnley BB10 4BX
Telephone: 0871 221 1882. **Club nickname**: Clarets
Colours: Claret and blue shirts; white shorts; white socks. **Capacity**: 21,940.
Record attendance: 54,775 v Huddersfield (FA Cup 3) 23 Feb, 1924

Goalkeepers

Grant, Lee	6.2	Sheffield Wed	Hemel Hempstead	27.01.83
Jensen, Brian	6.1	WBA	Copenhagen, Den	08.06.75
Stewart, Jon	6.3	Bournemouth	Brent	13.03.89

Defenders

Bartley, Marvin	5.11	Bournemouth	Reading	01.07.89
Duff, Mike	6.1	Cheltenham	Belfast	11.01.78
Edgar, David	6.2	Newcastle	Kitchener, Can	19.05.87
Lafferty, Daniel	6.1	Derry	Derry	01.04.89
Long, Kevin	6.2	Cork	Cork, Ire	18.08.90
Mee, Ben	5.11	Manchester City	Sale	23.09.89
Mills, Joseph	5.9	Reading (loan)	Swindon	30.10.89
O'Neill, Luke	6.0	Mansfield	Slough	20.08.91
Shackell, Jason	6.4	Derby	Stevenage	27.09.83
Trippier, Kieran	5.10	Manchester City	Bury	19.09.90

Midfielders

Hewitt, Steven	5.7	–	Manchester	05.12.93
Howieson, Cameron	5.10	Mosgiel	Blenheim, NZ	22.12.94
MacDonald, Alex	5.7	–	Chester	14.04.90
McCann, Chris	6.1	–	Dublin, Ire	21.07.87
Marney, Dean	5.11	Hull	Barking	31.01.84
Porter, George	5.10	Leyton Orient	Sidcup	27.06.92
Treacy, Keith	6.0	Preston	Dublin, Ire	13.09.88
Wallace, Ross	5.6	Preston	Dundee	23.05.85

Forwards

Austin, Charlie	6.2	Swindon	Hungerford	05.07.89
Ings, Danny	5.10	Bournemouth	Winchester	16.03.92
Fletcher, Wes	5.10	–	Ormskirk	28.02.90
Jackson, Joe	5.10	–	Barrow	03.02.93
McCartan, Shay	5.10	Glenavon	Newry	18.05.94
Paterson, Martin	5.9	Scunthorpe	Tunstall	13.05.87
Stanislas, Junior	6.0	West Ham	Eltham	26.11.89

CARDIFF CITY

Ground: Cardiff City Stadium, Leckwith Road, Cardiff CF11 8AZ
Telephone: 0845 365 1115. **Club nickname**: Bluebirds
Colours: Red shirts; black shorts; red socks. **Capacity**: 26,828
Record attendance: Ninian Park: 61,566 Wales v England, 14 Oct, 1961; Club: 57,893 v Arsenal (Div 1) 22 Apr, 1953; Cardiff City Stadium: 26,058 v QPR (Champ) 23 Apr, 2011

Goalkeepers

Lewis, Joe	6.5	Peterborough	Broome	06.10.87
Marshall, David	6.3	Norwich	Glasgow	05.03.85
Parish, Elliot	6.2	Aston Villa	Northampton	20.05.90

Defenders

Gerrard, Anthony	6.2	Walsall	Liverpool	06.02.86
Hudson, Mark	6.3	Charlton	Guildford	30.03.82
McNaughton, Kevin	5.10	Aberdeen	Dundee	28.08.82
Taylor, Andrew	5.10	Middlesbrough	Hartlepool	01.08.86
Turner, Ben	6.4	Coventry	Birmingham	21.08.88

Midfielders

Blake, Darcy	5.10	–	Caerphilly	13.12.88
Conway, Craig	5.8	Dundee Utd	Irvine	02.05.85
Cowie, Don	5.11	Watford	Inverness	15.02.83

Gunnarsson, Aron	5.11	Coventry	Akureyri, Ice	22.04.89
Harris, Kadeem	5.9	Wycombe	Westminster	08.06.93
Kiss, Filip	6.1	Slovan Bratislava	Dunajska, Slovak	13.10.90
McPhail, Stephen	5.10	Barnsley	Westminster	09.12.79
Mutch, Jordon	5.9	Birmingham	Birmingham	02.12.91
Ralls, Joe	6.0	–	Aldershot	13.10.93
Whittingham, Peter	5.10	Aston Villa	Nuneaton	08.09.84
Forwards				
Gestede, Rudy	6.4	Metz	Nancy, Fr	10.10.88
Mason, Joe	5.10	Plymouth	Plymouth	13.05.91
Miller, Kenny	5.10	Bursaspor	Edinburgh	23.12.79
Velikonja, Etien	5.10	Maribor	Sempeter, Sloven	26.12.88

CHARLTON ATHLETIC
Ground: The Valley, Floyd Road, London SE7 8BL
Telephone: 0208 333 4000. **Club nickname**: Addicks
Colours: Red shirts; white shorts; red socks. **Capacity**: 27,111
Record attendance: 75,031 v Aston Villa (FA Cup 5) 12 Feb, 1938

Goalkeepers				
Hamer, Ben	6.4	Reading	Taunton	20.11.87
Pope, Nick	6.3	Bury Town	–	19.04.92
Sullivan, John	6.2	Millwall	Brighton	08.03.88
Defenders				
Cort, Leon	6.3	Burnley	Southwark	11.09.79
Cousins, Jordan	5.10	–	Greenwich	06.03.94
Evina, Cedric	5.9	Oldham	Cameroon	16.11.91
Hughes, Andy	5.11	Scunthorpe	Manchester	02.01.78
Mambo, Yado	6.3	–	Kilburn	22.10.91
Morrison, Michael	6.1	Sheffield Wed	Bury St Edmunds	03.03.88
Solly, Chris	5.8	–	Rochester	20.01.90
Taylor, Matt	5.10	Exeter	Ormskirk	30.01.82
Wiggins, Rhoys	5.9	Bournemouth	Hillingdon	04.11.87
Wilson, Lawrie	5.10	Stevenage	Collier Row	11.09.87
Midfielders				
Green, Danny	6.0	Dagenham	Harlow	09.07.88
Harriott, Callum	5.5	–	Norbury	04.03.94
Haynes, Danny	5.11	Barnsley	Peckham	19.01.88
Hollands, Danny	5.11	Bournemouth	Ashford, Surrey	06.11.85
Izquierdo, Ruben	5.7	Halesowen	Majorca	24.06.92
Jackson, Johnnie	6.1	Notts Co	Camden	15.08.82
Pritchard, Bradley	6.1	Hayes	Harare, Zim	19.12.85
Stephens, Dale	5.7	Oldham	Bolton	12.06.89
Wagstaff, Scott	5.11	–	Maidstone	31.03.90
Forwards				
Clarke, Leon	6.2	Swindon	Wolverhampton	10.02.85
Cook, Jordan	5.9	Sunderland	Sunderland	20.03.90
Hayes, Paul	6.0	Preston	Dagenham	20.09.83
Kermorgant, Yann	6.1	Leicester	Vannes, Fr	08.11.81
Smith, Michael	6.4	Darlington	Wallsend	17.10.91
Wright-Phillips, Bradley	5.8	Plymouth	Lewisham	12.03.85

CRYSTAL PALACE

Ground: Selhurst Park, Whitehorse Lane, London SE25, 6PU
Telephone: 0208 768 6000. **Club nickname:** Eagles
Colours: Red and blue shirts; blue shorts; blue socks. **Capacity:** 26,225
Record attendance: 51,482 v Burnley (Div 2), 11 May, 1979

Goalkeepers

Fitzsimons, Ross	6.1	–	Hammersmith	28.05.94
Price, Lewis	6.3	Derby	Bournemouth	19.07.84
Speroni, Julian	6.1	Dundee	Federal, Arg	18.05.79

Defenders

McCarthy, Patrick	6.1	Charlton	Dublin, Ire	31.05.83
Moxey, Dean	5.11	Derby	Exeter	14.01.86
Parr, Jonathan	6.0	Aalesund	Oslo, Nor	21.10.88
Parsons, Matthew	5.10	–	London	25.12.91
Ward, Joel	6.2	Portsmouth	Portsmouth	29.10.89
Wright, David	5.11	Ipswich	Warrington	01.05.80
Wynter, Alex	6.0	–	Beckenham	15.09.93

Midfielders

Cadogan, Kieron	6.4	–	Wandsworth	16.08.90
Dikgacoi, Kagisho	5.11	Fulham	Brandford SA	24.11.84
De Silva, Kyle	5.7	–	Croydon	29.11.93
Dorman, Andy	6.1	St Mirren	Chester	01.05.82
Garvan, Owen	6.0	Ipswich	Dublin, Ire	29.01.88
Holland, Jack	6.3	–	Bromley	01.03.92
Jedinak, Mile	6.3	Genclerbirligi	Sydney, Aus	03.08.84
O'Keefe, Stuart	5.8	Southend	Norwich	04.03.91
Williams, Jonathan	5.7	–	Pembury	09.10.93

Forwards

Appiah, Kwesi	5.8	Margate	Hendon	12.08.90
Easter, Jermaine	5.10	MK Dons	Cardiff	15.01.82
Murray, Glenn	6.2	Brighton	Maryport	25.09.83
Pedroza, Antonio	5.7	Jaguares	Chester	20.02.91
Sekajja, Ibra	5.11	–	Croydon	31.10.92
Wilbraham, Aaron	6.3	Norwich	Knutsford	21.10.79
Zaha, Wilf	5.10	–	Abidjan, Iv C	10.11.92

DERBY COUNTY

Ground: Pride Park Stadium, Pride Park, Derby DE24 8XL
Telephone: 0871 472 1884. **Club nickname:** Rams
Colours: White shirts; black shorts; white socks. **Capacity:** 33,502
Record attendance: Baseball Ground: 41,826 v Tottenham (Div 1) 20 Sep, 1969.
Pride Park: 33,597 (England v Mexico) 25 May, 2011; Club: 33,475 v Rangers (Ted McMinn testimonial) 1 May, 2006

Goalkeepers

Deeney, Saul	6.1	Burton	Derry	23.03.83
Fielding, Frank	6.0	Blackburn	Blackburn	04.04.88
Legzdins, Adam	6.0	Burton	Stafford	23.11.86

Defenders

Barker, Shaun	6.2	Blackpool	Nottingham	19.09.82
Brayford, John	5.8	Crewe	Stoke	29.12.87
Buxton, Jake	5.11	Burton	Sutton-in-Ashfield	04.03.85
Keogh, Richard	6.2	Coventry	Harlow	11.08.86

Naylor, Tom	6.2	Mansfield	Sutton-in-Ashfield	28.06.91
O'Brien, Mark	5.11	Cherry Orchard	Dublin, Ire	20.11.92
Roberts, Gareth	5.8	Doncaster	Wrexham	06.02.78
Midfielders				
Bailey, James	6.0	Crewe	Macclesfield	18.09.88
Bryson, Craig	5.8	Kilmarnock	Rutherglen	06.11.86
Coutts, Paul	6.1	Preston	Aberdeen	22.07.88
Davies, Ben	5.6	Notts Co	Birmingham	27.05.81
Hendrick, Jeff	6.1	–	Dublin, Ire	31.01.92
Hughes, Will	6.1	–	Surrey	07.04.95
Jacobs, Michael	5.9	Northampton	Rothwell	04.11.91
Forwards				
Bennett, Mason	5.10	–	Langwith	15.07.96
Davies, Steve	6.1	Tranmere	Liverpool	29.12.87
Doyle, Conor	6.2	Creighton	McKinney, US	13.10.91
Robinson, Theo	5.9	Millwall	Birmingham	22.01.89
Tyson, Nathan	6.0	Nottm Forest	Reading	04.05.82
Ward, Jamie	5.5	Sheffield Utd	Birmingham	12.05.86

HUDDERSFIELD TOWN

Ground: Galpharm Stadium, Huddersfield HD1 6PX
Telephone: 0870 444 4677. **Club nickname**: Terriers
Colours: Blue and white shirts; white shorts; white socks. **Capacity**: 24,554
Record attendance: Leeds Road: 67,037 v Arsenal (FA Cup 6) 27 Feb, 1932;
Galpharm Stadium: 23,678 v Liverpool (FA Cup 3) 12 Dec, 1999

Goalkeepers				
Allinson, Lloyd	6.2	–	Rothwell	07.09.93
Bennett, Ian	6.0	Sheffield Utd	Worksop	10.10.71
Colgan, Nick	6.2	Grimsby	Drogheda, Ire	19.09.73
Smithies, Alex	6.1	–	Huddersfield	25.03.90
Defenders				
Clarke, Peter	6.0	Southend	Southport	03.01.82
Clarke, Tom	5.11	–	Halifax	21.12.87
Dixon, Paul	5.10	Dundee Utd	Aberdeen	22.11.86
Hunt, Jack	5.9	–	Leeds	06.12.90
Lynch, Joel	6.1	Nottm Forest	Eastbourne	03.10.87
McCombe, Jamie	6.5	Bristol City	Pontefract	01.01.83
Ridehalgh, Liam	5.10	–	Halifax	20.04.91
Wallace, Murray	6.2	Falkirk	Glasgow	10.01.93
Woods, Callum	5.11	Dunfermline	Liverpool	05.02.87
Midfielders				
Arfield, Scott	5.10	Falkirk	Livingston	01.11.88
Atkinson, Chris	6.1	–	Halifax	13.02.92
Clayton, Adam	5.9	Leeds	Manchester	14.01.89
Crooks, Matty	6.0	–	Huddersfield	20.01.94
Gobern, Oscar	6.3	Southampton	Birmingham	26.01.91
Kay, Antony	5.11	Tranmere	Barnsley	21.10.82
Norwood, Oliver	5.11	Manchester Utd	Burnley	12.04.91
Robinson, Anton	6.0	Bournemouth	Brent	17.02.86
Forwards				
Higginbotham, Kallum	5.11	Falkirk	Salford	15.06.89
Lee, Alan	6.2	Crystal Palace	Galway, Ire	21.08.78
Novak, Lee	6.0	Gateshead	Newcastle	28.09.88

Rhodes, Jordan	6.1	Ipswich	Oldham	05.02.90
Scannell, Sean	5.9	Crystal Palace	Croydon	21.03.89
Spencer, James	6.1	–	Leeds	13.12.91
Ward, Danny	6.0	Bolton	Bradford	11.12.91

HULL CITY

Ground: Kingston Communications Stadium, Anlaby Road, Hull, HU3 6HU
Telephone: 0870 837 0003. **Club nickname:** Tigers
Colours: Amber shirts; black shorts; black socks. **Capacity:** 25,404
Record attendance: Boothferry Park: 55,019 v Manchester Utd. (FA Cup 6) 26 Feb, 1949;
Kingston Communications Stadium: 25,030 v Liverpool (Prem Lge) 9 May, 2010; Also:
25,280 for England U21 v Holland, 17 Feb, 2004

Goalkeepers
| Jakupovic, Eldin | 6.4 | Aris Salonika | Kozarac, Bos | 02.10.84 |
| Oxley, Mark | 6.3 | Rotherham | Sheffield | 02.06.90 |

Defenders
Bradley, Sonny	6.4	–	Hull	13.09.91
Chester, James	5.10	Manchester Utd	Warrington	23.01.89
Cooper, Liam	6.0	–	Hull	30.08.91
Dawson, Andy	5.9	Scunthorpe	Northallerton	20.10.78
Dudgeon, Joe	5.9	Manchester Utd	Leeds	26.11.90
Faye, Abdoulaye	6.2	West Ham	Dakar, Sen	26.02.78
Hobbs, Jack	6.3	Leicester	Portsmouth	18.08.88
McShane, Paul	6.0	Sunderland	Kilpeddar, Ire	06.01.86
Rosenior, Liam	5.10	Reading	Wandsworth	15.12.84

Midfielders
Aluko, Sone	5.8	Rangers	Hounslow	19.02.89
Cairney, Tom	6.0	–	Nottingham	20.01.91
Devitt, James	5.10	–	Dublin, Ire	06.07.90
Evans, Corry	5.11	Manchester Utd	Belfast	30.07.90
Koren, Robert	5.10	WBA	Radlje, Sloven	20.09.80
McKenna, Paul	5.8	Nottm Forest	Chorley	20.10.77
Olofinjana, Seyi	6.4	Stoke	Lagos, Nig	30.06.80
Stewart, Cameron	5.8	Manchester Utd	Manchester	08.04.91

Forwards
Cullen, Mark	5.10	–	Ashington	21.04.92
Fryatt, Matty	5.10	Leicester	Nuneaton	05.03.86
Mclean, Aaron	5.6	Peterborough	Hammersmith	25.05.83
Proschwitz, Nick	6.3	Paderborn	Weibenfels, Ger	28.11.86
Simpson, Jay	5.11	Arsenal	Enfield	01.12.88

IPSWICH TOWN

Ground: Portman Road, Ipswich IP1 2DA
Telephone: 01473 400500. **Club nickname:** Blues/Town
Colours: Blue shirts; white shorts; blue socks. **Capacity:** 30,311
Record attendance: 38,010 v Leeds (FA Cup 6) 8 Mar, 1975

Goalkeepers
Cropper, Cody	6.3	–	Atlanta, US	16.02.93
Lee-Barrett, Arran	6.2	Hartlepool	Ipswich	28.02.84
Loach, Scott	6.2	Watford	Nottingham	14.10.79

Defenders
| Ainsley, Jack | 5.11 | – | Ipswich | 17.09.91 |

Chambers, Luke	5.11	Nottm Forest	Kettering	29.08.85
Cresswell, Aaron	5.7	Tranmere	Liverpool	15.12.89
Hewitt, Elliott	5.11	Macclesfield	Bodelwyddan	30.05.94
Delaney, Damien	6.2	Hull	Cork, Ire	29.07.81
Peters, Jaime	5.7	–	Ottawa, Can	04.05.87
Smith, Tommy	6.1	–	Macclesfield	31.03.90
Whight, Joe	5.10	–	Ipswich	06.01.94
Midfielders				
Bullard, Jimmy	5.10	Hull	Newham	23.10.78
Carson, Josh	5.9	–	Ballymena	03.06.93
Drury, Andy	5.11	Luton	Chatham	28.11.83
Edwards, Carlos	5.11	Sunderland	Port of Spain, Trin	24.10.78
Emmanuel-Thomas, Jay	6.3	Arsenal	Forest Gate	27.12.90
Hyam, Luke	5.10	–	Ipswich	24.10.91
Lawrence, Byron	5.10	–	Cambridge	12.03.96
Luongo, Massimo	5.9	Tottenham (Loan)	Sydney	25.09.92
Martin, Lee	5.10	Manchester Utd	Taunton	09.02.87
Stevenson, Ryan	5.11	Hearts	Irvine	24.08.84
Forwards				
Chopra, Michael	5.9	Cardifff	Gosforth	23.12.83
Murray, Ronan	5.8	–	Mayo, Ire	12.09.91
Scotland, Jason	5.9	Wigan	Morvant, Trin	18.02.79

LEEDS UNITED

Ground: Elland Road, Leeds LS11 OES
Telephone: 0871 334 1919. **Club nickname**: Whites
Colours: White shirts; white shorts; blue, white and yellow socks. **Capacity**: 37,697
Record attendance: 57,892 v Sunderland (FA Cup 5 replay) 15 Mar, 1967

Goalkeepers				
Ashdown, Jamie	6.3	Portsmouth	Reading	30.11.80
Cairns, Alex	6.0	–	Doncaster	04.01.93
Kenny, Paddy	6.1	QPR	Halifax	17.05.78
Defenders				
Bromby, Leigh	5.11	Sheffield Utd	Dewsbury	02.06.80
Connolly, Paul	6.0	Derby	Liverpool	29.09.83
Drury, Adam	5.10	Norwich	Cambridge	29.08.78
Kisnorbo, Patrick	6.2	Leicester	Melbourne, Aus	24.03.81
Lees, Tom	6.1	–	Warwick	18.11.90
Pearce, Jason	5.11	Portsmouth	Hillingdon	06.12.87
White, Aidan	5.7	–	Leeds	10.10.91
Midfielders				
Brown, Michael	5.10	Portsmouth	Hartlepool	25.01.77
Green, Paul	5.10	Derby	Sheffield	10.04.83
Nunez, Ramon	5.7	Olimpia	Tegucigalpa, Hond	14.11.85
Pugh, Danny	6.0	Stoke	Manchester	19.10.82
Forwards				
Becchio, Luciano	6.2	Merida	Cordoba, Arg	28.12.83
Gray, Andy	6.1	Barnsley	Harrogate	15.11.77
McCormack, Ross	5.10	Cardiff	Glasgow	18.08.86
Paynter, Billy	6.0	Swindon	Liverpool	13.07.84
Rogers, Robbie	5.10	Columbus	Palos Verdes, US	12.05.87
Snodgrass, Robert	6.0	Livingston	Glasgow	07.09.87
Somma, Davide	6.1	San Jose	Johannesburg, SA	26.03.85
Varney, Luke	5.11	Portsmouth	Leicester	28.09.82

LEICESTER CITY

Ground: King Power Stadium, Filbert Way, Leicester, LE2 7FL
Telephone: 0844 815 6000. **Club nickname**: Foxes
Colours: Blue shirts; white shorts; blue socks. **Capacity**: 32,312
Record attendance: Filbert Street: 47,298 v. Tottenham (FA Cup 5) 18 Feb, 1928;
King Power Stadium: 32,188 v Real Madrid (friendly) 30 July, 2011

Goalkeepers

Schmeichel, Kasper	6.0	Leeds	Copenhagen, Den	05.11.86
Smith, Adam	6.0	Middlesbrough	Sunderland	23.01.92

Defenders

De Laet, Ritchie	6.1	Manchester Utd	Antwerp, Bel	28.11.88
Kennedy, Tom	5.11	Rochdale	Bury	24.06.85
Konchesky, Paul	5.10	Liverpool	Barking	15.05.81
Morgan, Wes	5.11	Nottm Forest	Nottingham	21.01.84
Moore, Liam	6.1	–	Leicester	31.01.93
Parkes, Tom	6.3	–	Mansfield	15.01.92
Peltier, Lee	5.10	Huddersfield	Liverpool	11.12.86
St Ledger, Sean	6.0	Preston	Birmingham	28.12.84
Taft, George	6.3	–	Leicester	29.07.93
Whitbread, Zak	6.2	Norwich	Houston, US	04.03.84

Midfielders

Danns, Neil	5.9	Crystal Palace	Liverpool	23.11.82
Drinkwater, Danny	5.10	Manchester Utd	Manchester	05.03.90
Dyer, Lloyd	5.9	MK Dons	Birmingham	13.09.82
James, Matty	5.10	Manchester Utd	Bacup	22.07.91
King, Andy	6.0	–	Maidenhead	29.10.88
Schlupp, Jeffrey	5.8	–	Hamburg, Ger	23.12.92
Wellens, Richie	5.9	Doncaster	Manchester	26.03.80

Forwards

Beckford, Jermaine	6.2	Everton	Ealing	09.12.83
Futacs, Marko	6.5	Portsmouth	Budapest, Hun	22.02.90
Gallagher, Paul	6.0	Blackburn	Glasgow	09.08.84
Marshall, Ben	6.0	Stoke	Salford	29.09.91
Nugent, David	5.11	Portsmouth	Liverpool	02.05.85
Vardy, Jamie	5.10	Fleetwood	Sheffield	11.01.87
Waghorn, Martyn	5.10	Sunderland	South Shields	23.01.90

MIDDLESBROUGH

Ground: Riverside Stadium, Middlesbrough, TS3 6RS
Telephone: 0844 499 6789. **Club nickname**: Boro
Colours: Red shirts; white shorts; red socks. **Capacity**: 34,998
Record attendance: Ayresome Park:53,536 v Newcastle (Div 1) 27 Dec, 1949; Riverside
Stadium: 34,836 v Norwich (Prem Lge) 28 Dec, 2004; Also: 35,000 England v Slovakia 11
Jun, 2003

Goalkeepers

Steele, Jason	6.2	–	Bishop Auckland	18.08.90
Ripley, Connor	6.1	Blackburn	Middlesbrough	13.02.93

Defenders

Bates, Matthew	5.8	–	Stockton	10.12.86
Bennett, Joe	5.8	–	Rochdale	28.03.90
Hines, Seb	6.2	–	Wetherby	29.05.88
McManus, Stephen	6.2	Celtic	Lanark	10.09.82

Parnaby, Stuart	5.10	Birmingham	Durham	19.07.82
Williams, Rhys	6.1	Joondalup	Perth, Aus	07.07.88
Woodgate, Jonathan	6.2	Stoke	Middlesbrough	22.01.80

Midfielders

Arca, Julio	5.9	Sunderland	Quilmes, Arg	30.01.81
Bailey, Nicky	5.10	Charlton	Hammersmith	10.06.84
Halliday, Andrew	5.11	Livingston	Glasgow	18.10.91
Haroun, Faris	6.2	Germinal	Brussels, Bel	22.09.85
Leadbitter, Grant	5.9	Ipswich	Chester-le-Street	07.01.86
Ledesma, Emmanuel	5.11	Walsall	Quilmes, Arg	24.05.88
Thomson, Kevin	5.11	Rangers	Edinburgh	14.10.84
Zemmama, Merouane	5.7	Hibernian	Sale, Mor	07.10.83

Forwards

Emnes, Marvin	5.11	Sparta Rotterdam	Rotterdam, Hol	27.05.88
Jutkiewicz, Lukas	6.1	Coventry	Southampton	20.03.89
Main, Curtis	5.10	Darlington	South Shields	20.06.92
McDonald, Scott	5.8	Celtic	Melbourne, Aus	21.08.83
Williams, Luke	6.1		Middlesbrough	11.06.93

MILLWALL

Ground: The Den, Zampa Road, London SE16 3LN
Telephone: 0207 232 1222. **Club nickname**: Lions
Colours: All blue. **Capacity**: 19,734
Record attendance: The Den: 48,672 v Derby (FA Cup 5) 20 Feb, 1937;
New Den: 20,093 v Arsenal (FA Cup 3) 10 January, 1994

Goalkeepers

Forde, David	6.2	Cardiff	Galway, Ire	20.12.79
Mildenhall, Steve	6.4	Southend	Swindon	13.05.78
Taylor, Maik	6.4	Leeds	Hildesheim, Ger	04.09.71

Defenders

Dunne, Alan	5.10	–	Dublin, Ire	23.08.82
Lowry, Shane	6.1	Aston Villa	Perth, Aus	12.06.89
Mkandawire, Tamika	6.1	Leyton Orient	Mzunu, Malaw	28.05.83
Osborne, Karleigh	6.2	Brentford	Southall	19.03.83
Robinson, Paul	6.1	–	Barnet	07.01.82
Smith, Jack	5.11	Swindon	Hemel Hempstead	14.11.83
Ward, Darren	6.3	Wolves	Kenton	13.09.78

Midfielders

Abdou, Nadjim	5.10	Plymouth	Martigues, Fr	13.07.84
Barron, Scott	5.10	Ipswich	Preston	02.09.85
Feeney, Liam	6.0	Bournemouth	Hammersmith	28.04.86
Henry, James	6.1	Reading	Reading	10.06.89
Racon, Therry	5.10	Charlton	Villeneuve, Fr	01.05.84
Malone, Scott	6.2	Bournemouth	Rowley Regis	25.03.91
Taylor, Chris	5.11	Oldham	Oldham	20.12.86
Trotter, Liam	6.2	Ipswich	Ipswich	24.08.88
Wright, Josh	6.1	Scunthorpe	Tower Hamlets	06.11.89

Forwards

Batt, Shaun	6.2	Peterborough	Luton	22.02.87
Henderson, Darius	6.2	Sheffield Utd	Sutton	07.09.81
Keogh, Andy	6.0	Wolves	Dublin, Ire	16.05.86
Marquis, John	6.1	–	Lewisham	16.05.92
N'Guessan, Dany	6.1	Leicester	Ivry, Fr	11.08.87

NOTTINGHAM FOREST

Ground: City Ground, Pavilion Road, Nottingham NG2 5FJ
Telephone: 0115 982 4444. **Club nickname**: Forest
Colours: Red shirts; white shorts; red socks. **Capacity**: 30,576
Record attendance: 49,946 v Manchester Utd (Div 1) 28 Oct, 1967

Goalkeepers

Camp, Lee	6.0	QPR	Derby	22.08.84
Darlow, Karl	61	Aston Villa	Northampton	08.10.90

Defenders

Cohen, Chris	5.11	Yeovil	Norwich	05.03.87
Freeman, Kieron		–	Bestwood	21.03.92
Guedioura, Adlene	6.0	Wolves	La Roche, Fr	12.11.85
Lascelles, Jamaal	6.2	–	Derby	11.11.93
Moloney, Brendan	5.10	–	Beaufort	18.01.89

Midfielders

Greening, Jonathan	5.11	Fulham	Scarborough	02.01.79
McGugan, Lewis	5.10	–	Long Eaton	25.10.88
Majewski, Radoslav	5.7	Polonia Warsaw	Pruszkow, Pol	
Moussi, Guy	6.2	Angers	Bondy, Fr	23.01.85
Reid, Andy	5.7	Blackpool	Dublin	29.07.82

Forwards

Blackstock, Dexter	6.2	Nottm Forest	Oxford	20.05.86
Derbyshire, Matt	6.1	Olympiacos	Blackburn	14.04.86
Findley, Robbie	5.9	Real Salt Lake	Phoenix, US	04.08.85
McGoldrick, David	6.1	Southampton	Nottingham	29.11.87
Miller, Ishmael	6.3	WBA	Manchester	05.03.87
Tudgay, Marcus	5.10	Sheffield Wed	Shoreham	03.02.83

PETERBOROUGH UNITED

Ground: London Road Stadium, Peterborough PE2 8AL
Telephone: 01733 563947. **Club nickname**: Posh
Colours: Blue shirts; white shorts; white socks. **Capacity**: 14,793
Record attendance: 30,096 v Swansea (FA Cup 5) 20 Feb, 1965

Goalkeepers

Day, Joe	6.1	Rushden	Brighton	13.08.90
Olejnik, Bobby	6.0	Torquay	Vienna, Aut	26.11.86

Defenders

Alcock, Craig	5.8	Yeovil	Truro	08.12.87
Brisley, Shaun	6.2	Macclesfield	Macclesfield	06.05.90
Knight-Percival, Nat	6.0	Wrexham	Cambridge	31.03.87
Little, Mark	6.1	Wolves	Worcester	20.08.88
Ntlhe, Kgosi	5.9	–	Pretoria, SA	21.02.94
Zakuani, Gabriel	6.1	Fulham	Kinshasa, DR Con	31.05.86

Midfielders

Bostwick, Michael	6.1	Stevenage	Greenwich	17.05.88
Frecklington, Lee	5.8	Lincoln	Lincoln	08.09.85
Kearns, Daniel	5.10	Dundalk	Belfast	26.08.91
McCann, Grant	5.10	Scunthorpe	Belfast	14.04.80
Mendez-Laing, Nathaniel	5.10	Wolves	Birmingham	15.04.92
Newell, Joe	5.11	–	Tamworth	15.03.93
Rowe, Tommy	5.11	Stockport	Manchester	01.05.89
Swanson, Danny	5.7	Dundee Utd	Leith	28.12.86

Tomlin, Lee	5.11	Rushden	Leicester	12.01.89

Forwards

Ajose, Nicky	5.8	Manchester Utd	Bury	07.10.91
Barnett, Tyrone	6.3	Crawley	Birmingham	28.10.85
Boyd, George	5.10	Stevenage	Chatham	02.10.85
Clarke-Harris, Jonson	5.10	Coventry	Leicester	20.07.94
Hibbert, Dave	6.2	Shrewsbury	Stafford	28.01.86
Sinclair, Emile	6.0	Macclesfield	Leeds	29.12.87
Taylor, Paul	5.11	Anderlecht	Liverpool	04.10.87

SHEFFIELD WEDNESDAY

Ground: Hillsborough, Sheffield, S6 1SW
Telephone: 0871 995 1867. **Club nickname**: Owls
Colours: Blue and white shirts; blue shorts; blue socks. **Capacity**: 39,812
Record attendance: 72,841 v Manchester City (FA Cup 5) 17 Feb, 1934

Goalkeepers

Bywater, Stephen	6.2	Derby	Manchester	07.06.81
Jameson, Arron	6.3	–	Sheffield	07.11.89
Kirkland, Chris	6.3	Wigan	Leicester	02.05.81
Weaver, Nicky	6.3	Burnley	Sheffield	02.03.79

Defenders

Beevers, Mark	6.4	–	Barnsley	21.11.89
Bennett, Julian	6.1	Nottm Forest	Nottingham	17.12.84
Buxton, Lewis	6.1	Stoke	Newport, IOW	10.12.83
Gardner, Anthony	6.5	Crystal Palace	Stafford	18.08.81
Johnson, Reda	6.3	Plymouth	Marseille, Fr	21.03.88
Jones, Daniel	6.2	Wolves	Wordsley	23.12.86
Jones, Rob	6.7	Scunthorpe	Stockton	03.11.79
Llera, Miguel	6.4	Blackpool	Castilleja, Sp	07.08.79
Mattock, Joe	6.0	WBA	Leicester	15.05.90
Reynolds, Mark	6.1	Motherwell	Motherwell	07.05.87
Semedo, Jose	6.0	Charlton	Setubal, Por	11.01.85

Midfielders

Amado, Diogo	5.10	Uniao Leiria	Lagos Por	21.01.90
Coke, Giles	6.0	Motherwell	Westminster	03.06.86
Johnson, Jermaine	5.9	Bradford	Kingston, Jam	25.06.80
Jones, Mike	6.0	Bury	Birkenhead	15.08.87
Lee, Kieran	6.1	Oldham	Tameside	22.06.88
Lines, Chris	6.2	Bristol Rov	Bristol	30.11.85
Pecnik, Nejc	6.2	CD National	Dravograd, Sloven	03.01.86
Prutton, David	6.1	Swindon	Hull	12.09.81

Forwards

Lowe, Ryan	5.11	Bury	Liverpool	18.09.78
Madine, Gary	6.4	Carlisle	Gateshead	24.08.90
Maguire, Chris	5.8	Derby	Bellshill	16.01.89
O'Grady, Chris	6.1	Rochdale	Nottingham	25.01.86

WATFORD

Ground: Vicarage Road Stadium, Vicarage Road, Watford WD18 0ER
Telephone: 0844 856 1881. **Club nickname**: Hornets
Colours: Yellow shirts, black shorts, yellow socks. **Capacity**: 17,477
Record attendance: 34,099 v Manchester Utd (FA Cup 4 replay) 3 Feb, 1969

Goalkeepers

Bond, Jonathan	6.3	–	Hemel Hempstead	19.05.93
Bonham, Jack	6.0	–	–	14.09.93

Defenders

Bennett, Dale	5.11	–	Enfield	06.01.90
Dickinson, Carl	6.1	Stoke	Swadlincote	31.03.87
Doyley, Lloyd	5.10	–	Whitechapel	01.12.82
Hoban, Thomas	6.2	–	Waltham Forest	24.01.94
Hodson, Lee	5.11	–	Borehamwood	02.10.91
Mirfin, David	6.1	Scunthorpe	Sheffield	18.04.85
Nosworthy, Nyron	6.0	Sunderland	Brixton	11.10.80
Pudil, Daniel	6.0	Granada (loan)	Prague, Cz	27.09.85
Taylor, Martin	6.4	Birmingham	Ashington	09.11.79
Thompson, Adrian	6.2	–	Harlow	28.09.92

Midfielders

Assombalonga, Britt	5.10	–	Kinshasa, DR Con	06.12.92
Bauben, Prince	5.10	Dundee Utd	Akosombo, Gh	23.04.88
Eustace, John	5.11	Stoke	Solihull	03.11.79
Forsyth, Craig	6.0	Dundee	Carnoustie	24.02.89
Hogg, Jonathan	5.7	Aston Villa	Middlesbrough	06.12.88
Jenkins, Ross	5.11	–	Watford	09.11.90
McGinn, Stephen	5.10	St Mirren	Glasgow	02.12.88
Mingoia, Piero	5.7	–	Enfield	20.10.91
Murray, Sean	5.9	–	Abbots Langley	11.10.93
Smith, Connor	5.11	–	Ireland	18.02.93
Whichelow, Matt	6.4	–	Islington	28.09.91
Yeates, Mark	5.9	Sheffield Utd	Dublin, Ire	11.01.85

Forwards

Garner, Joe	5.10	Nottm Forest	Blackburn	12.04.88
Iwelumo, Chris	6.3	Burnley	Coatbridge	01.08.78
Massey, Gavin	5.10	–	Watford	14.10.92
Vydra, Matej	5.11	Udinese (loan)	Chotebor, Cz	01.05.92

WOLVERHAMPTON WANDERERS

Ground: Molineux Stadium, Waterloo Road, Wolverhampton WV1 4QR
Telephone: 0871 222 2220. **Club nickname**: Wolves
Colours: Gold shirts; black shorts; black socks. **Capacity**: 29,303
Record attendance: 61,315 v Liverpool (FA Cup 5) 11 Feb, 1939

Goalkeepers

De Vries, Dorus	5.11	Swansea	Beverwijk, Hol	29.12.80
Hennessey, Wayne	6.0	–	Bangor, Wal	24.01.87
Ikeme Carl	6.2	–	Sutton Coldfield	08.06.86

Defenders

Batth, Danny	6.3	–	Brierley Hill	21.09.90
Berra, Christophe	6.1	Hearts	Edinburgh	31.01.85
Doherty, Matt	5.11	–	Dublin	16.01.92
Elokobi, George	6.0	Colchester	Mamfe, Cam	31.01.86
Foley, Kevin	5.9	Luton	Luton	01.11.84
Jonsson, Eggert	6.2	Hearts	Reykjavik, Ice	18.08.88
Johnson, Roger	6.3	Birmingham	Ashford, Surr	28.04.83
Mouyokolo, Steven	6.3	Hull	Melun, Fr	24.01.87
Rekord, Jamie	5.10	–	Wolverhampton	09.03.92
Stearman, Richard	6.2	Leicester	Wolverhampton	19.08.87

Name	Height ft in	Previous club	Birthplace	Birthdate
Ward, Stephen	5.11	Bohemians	Dublin, Ire	20.08.85
Zubar, Ronald	6.1	Marseille	Les Abymes, Guad	20.09.85
Midfielders				
Davis, David	5.8	–	Smethwick	20.02.91
Edwards, David	5.11	Luton	Pontesbury	03.02.85
Forde, Anthony	5.9	–	Ballingarry, Ire	16.11.93
Gorman, Johnny	5.10	–	Sheffield	26.10.92
Hammill, Adam	5.10	Barnsley	Liverpool	25.01.88
Henry, Karl	6.1	Stoke	Wolverhampton	26.11.82
Hunt, Stephen	5.8	Hull	Port Laoise, Ire	01.08.80
Jarvis, Matt	5.8	Gillingham	Middlesbrough	22.05.86
Kightly, Michael	5.11	Grays	Basildon	24.01.86
Milijas, Nenad	6.2	Red Star Belgrade	Belgrade, Serb	30.04.83
O'Hara, Jamie	5.11	Tottenham	Dartford	25.09.86
Forwards				
Doyle, Kevin	5.11	Reading	Wexford, Ire	18.09.83
Ebanks–Blake, Sylvan	5.10	Plymouth	Cambridge	29.03.86
Fletcher, Steven	6.1	Burnley	Shrewsbury	26.03.87
Nouble, Frank	6.3	West Ham	Lewisham	24.09.91
Sigurdarson, Bjorn	6.1	Lillestrom	Akranes, Ice	26.02.91
Vokes, Sam	5.11	Bournemouth	Lymington	21.10.89
Winnall, Sam	5.11	–	Wolverhampton	19.01.91

LEAGUE ONE

BOURNEMOUTH

Ground: Dean Court, Bournemouth BH7 7AF
Telephone: 01202 726300. **Club nickname**: Cherries
Colours: Red and black shirts; black shorts; red and black socks. **Capacity**: 9,776
Record attendance: 28,799 v Manchester Utd (FA Cup 6) 2 Mar, 1957

Name	Height ft in	Previous club	Birthplace	Birthdate
Goalkeepers				
Flahavan, Darryl	5.11	Portsmouth	Southampton	28.11.78
Jalal, Shwan	6.2	Peterborough	Baghdad, Iraq	14.08.83
Thomas, Dan	6.2	–	Poole	01.09.91
Defenders				
Addison, Miles	6.3	Derby	Newham	07.01.89
Barrett, Adam	5.10	Crystal Palace	Dagenham	29.11.79
Cook, Steve	6.1	Brighton	Hastings	19.04.91
Francis, Simon	6.0	Charlton	Nottingham	16.02.85
Purches, Stephen	5.11	Leyton Orient	Ilford	14.01.80
Strugnell, Dan	5.11	–	Christchurch	30.06.92
Zubar, Stephane	6.2	Plymouth	Pointe, Guad	09.10.86
Midfielders				
Arter, Harry	5.9	Woking	Eltham	28.12.89
Daniels, Charlie	5.10	Leyton Orient	Harlow	07.09.86
Fogden, Wes	5.9	Brighton	Havant	12.04.88
Gregory, Steven	6.1	Wimbledon	Aylesbury	19.03.87
MacDonald, Shaun	6.1	Swansea	Swansea	17.06.88
McDermott, Donal	5.9	Huddersfield	Ashbourne, Ire	19.10.89
Partington, Joe	5.11	–	Portsmouth	01.04.90

Pugh, Marc	5.11	Hereford	Bacup	02.04.87

Forwards

Demouge, Frank	5.11	Utrecht	Nijmegen, Hol	25.06.82
Fletcher, Steve	6.3	Crawley	Hartlepool	26.07.72
Grabban, Lewis	6.0	Rotherham	Croydon	12.01.88
McQuoid, Josh	5.10	Millwall	Southampton	15.12.89
Sheringham, Charlie	6.0	Dartford	Chingford	14.04.88
Stockley, Jayden	6.2	–	Poole	15.09.93
Thomas, Wes	5.11	Crawley	Barking	23.01.87
Tubbs, Matt	5.9	Crawley	Salisbury	15.07.84

BRENTFORD

Ground: Griffin Park, Braemar Road, Brentford TW8 0NT
Telephone: 0845 345 6442. **Club nickname**: Bees
Colours: Red and white shirts; black shorts; black socks. **Capacity**: 12,763
Record attendance: 39,626 v Preston (FA Cup 6) 5 Mar, 1938

Goalkeepers

Gounet, Antoine	6,1	Tours	–	16.10.88
Lee, Richard	5.11	Watford	Oxford	05.10.82
Moore, Simon	6.3	Farnborough	IOW	19.05.90

Defenders

Craig, Tony	6.0	Millwall	Greenwich	20.04.85
Legge, Leon	6.1	Tonbridge	Hastings	28.04.85
Logan, Shaleum	6.1	Manchester City	Manchester	06.11.88

Midfielders

Dallas, Stuart	6.0	Crusaders	Cookstown	19.04.91
Dean, Harlee	5.10	Southampton	Basingstoke	26.07.91
Diagouraga, Toumani	6.3	Peterborough	Paris, Fr	09.06.87
Douglas, Jonathan	5.11	Swindon	Monaghan, Ire	22.11.81
Forshaw, Adam	6.1	Everton	Liverpool	08.10.91
O'Connor, Kevin	5.11	–	Blackburn	24.02.82
Reeves, Jake	5.7	–	Greenwich	30.05.93
Saunders, Sam	5.11	Dagenham	Greenwich	29.08.83
Weston, Myles	5.11	Notts Co	Lewisham	12.03.88

Forwards

Donaldson, Clayton	6.1	Crewe	Bradford	07.02.84
El Alagui, Farid	5.11	Falkirk	Bordeaux, Fr	10.02.85
Forrester, Harry	5.10	Aston Villa	Milton Keynes	02.01.91
German, Antonio	6.1	Stockport	Harlesden	26.12.91
Norris, Luke	6.1	Hitchin	Stevenage	03.06.93

BURY

Ground: Gigg Lane, Bury BL9 9HR
Telephone: 08445 790009. **Club nickname**: Shakers
Colours: White shirts; blue shorts; blue socks. **Capacity**: 11,313
Record attendance: 35,000 v Bolton (FA Cup 3) 9 Jan, 1960

Goalkeepers

Belford, Cameron	5.11	Coventry	Nuneaton	16.10.88
Carson, Trevor	6.0	Sunderland	Killyleagh	05.03.88
Dibble, Christian	6.3	–	Wilmslow	11.05.94

Defenders

Futcher, Ben	6.6	Sheffield Utd	Bradford	04.06.81

Hughes, Mark	6.2	North Queensland	Liverpool	09.12.86
Lockwood, Adam	6.0	Doncaster	Wakefield	26.10.81
McLaughlin, Dalton	5.8	–	Salford	13.05.94
Melia, Jordan	5.10	–	Bolton	09.03.94
Picken, Phil	5.9	Chesterfield	Droylsden	12.11.85
Skarz, Joe	6.0	Huddersfield	Huddersfield	13.07.89
Sodje, Efe	6.1	Gillingham	Greenwich	05.10.72
Midfielders				
Carrington, Mark	6.2	Hamilton	Warrington	04.05.87
Harrop, Max	5.8	–	Oldham	30.06.93
Jones, Andrai	5.11	Everton	Liverpool	01.01.92
Marshall, Marcus	5.10	Rotherham	Hammersmith	07.10.89
Schumacher, Steven	6.0	Crewe	Liverpool	30.04.84
Sweeney, Peter	6.0	Grimsby	Glasgow	25.09.84
Worrall, David	6.0	WBA	Manchester	12.06.90
Forwards				
Bishop, Andy	6.0	York	Stone	19.10.82
Boswell, Liam	5.7	–	Bury	25.01.95
Elford-Alliyu, Lateef	5.8	WBA	Ibadan, Nig	01.06.92
Harrad, Shaun	5.10	Northampton	Nottingham	11.12.84
John-Lewis, Lenell	5.11	Lincoln	Hammersmith	17.05.89
McCarthy, Luke	5.10	–	Bolton	07.07.93

CARLISLE UNITED

Ground: Brunton Park, Warwick Road, Carlisle CA1 1LL
Telephone: 01228 526237. **Club nickname**: Cumbrians
Colours: Blue shirts; white shorts; white socks. **Capacity**: 17,902
Record attendance: 27,500 v Birmingham City (FA Cup 3) 5 Jan, 1957, v Middlesbrough (FA Cup 5) 7 Jan, 1970

Goalkeepers				
Caig, Tony	6.0	Workington	Whitehaven	11.04.74
Collin, Adam	6.1	Workington	Carlisle	09.12.84
Gillespie, Mark	6.0	–	Newcastle	27.03.92
Defenders				
Edwards, Mike	6.1	Notts Co	Hessle	25.04.80
Livesey, Danny	6.3	Bolton	Salford	31.12.84
Michalik, Lubomir	6.4	Leeds	Cadca, Slovak	13.08.83
Murphy, Peter	5.11	Blackburn	Dublin, Ire	27.10.80
Simek, Frankie	6.0	Sheffield Wed	St Louis, US	13.10.84
Midfielders				
Berrett, James	5.10	Huddersfield	Halifax	13.01.89
Chantler, Chris	5.10	Manchester City	Manchester	16.12.90
Kavanagh, Graham	5.10	Sunderland	Dublin, Ire	02.12.73
McGovern, Jon-Paul	5.10	Swindon	Glasgow	03.10.80
Noble, Liam	5.8	Sunderland	Cramlington	08.05.91
Potts, Brad	6.2	–	Hexham	03.07.94
Robson, Matty	5.10	Hartlepool	Durham	23.01.85
Thirlwell, Paul	5.11	Derby	Springwell	13.02.79
Welsh, Andy	5.8	Yeovil	Manchester	24.11.83
Forwards				
Beck, Mark	6.5	–	Sunderland	02.04.94
Cadamarteri, Danny	5.9	Huddersfield	Cleckheaton	12.10.79
Loy, Rory	5.10	Rangers	Dumfries	19.03.88

Madden, Patrick	5.11	Bohemians	Dublin, Ire	04.03.90
Miller, Lee	6.2	Middlesbrough	Lanark	18.05.83
Zoko, Francois	6.0	Oostende	Daloa, Iv C	13.09.83

COLCHESTER UNITED

Ground: Weston Homes Community Stadium, United Way, Colchester CO4 5HE
Telephone: 01206 755100. **Club nickname**: U's
Colours: Blue and white shirts; blue shorts; blue socks. **Capacity**: 10,105
Record attendance: Layer Road:19,072 v Reading (FA Cup 1) 27 Nov, 1948;
Community Stadium: 10,064 v Norwich (Lge 1) 16 Jan, 2010

Goalkeepers
| Cousins, Mark | 6.1 | – | Chelmsford | 09.01.87 |
| Pentney, Carl | 6.0 | Leicester | Colchester | 29.10.89 |

Defenders
Aldred, Tom	6.2	Watford	Bolton	11.09.90
Bean, Marcus	5.11	Brentford	Hammersmith	02.11.84
Bender, Thomas	6.3	–	Harlow	19.01.93
Eastman, Tom	6.3	Ipswich	Colchester	21.10.91
Hamilton, Bradley	6.0	–	Newham	30.08.92
Heath, Matt	6.4	Leeds	Leicester	01.11.81
Okuonghae, Magnus	6.4	Dagenham	Croydon	16.02.86
Rose, Michael	5.11	Swindon	Salford	28.07.82
White, John	6.0	–	Colchester	25.07.86
Wilson, Brian	5.10	Bristol City	Manchester	09.05.83

Midfielders
Bond, Andy	5.11	Barrow	Wigan	16.03.86
Coker, Ben	5.11	Bury Town	Cambridge	01.07.90
Duguid, Karl	5.8	Plymouth	Hitchin	21.03.78
Izzet, Kemal	5.8	Charlton	Whitechapel	29.09.80
O'Toole, John-Joe	6.2	Watford	Harrow	30.09.88
Sanderson, Jordan	6.0	–	Waltham Forest	07.08.93
Wordsworth, Anthony	6.1	–	Camden	03.01.89

Forwards
Henderson, Ian	5.9	Ankaraguco	Thetford	24.01.85
Ladapo, Freddie	5.11	–	Romford	01.02.93
Morrison, Clinton	6.0	Sheffield Wed	Tooting	14.05.79
Sears, Freddie	5.10	West Ham	Hornchurch	27.11.89

COVENTRY CITY

Ground: Ricoh Arena, Foleshill, Coventry CV6 6GE
Telephone: 0844 873 1883. **Club nickname**: Sky Blues
Colours: All sky blue. **Capacity**: 32,604
Record attendance: Highfield Road: 51,455 v Wolves (Div 2) 29 Apr, 1967; Ricoh Arena:
31,407 v Chelsea (FA Cup 6), 7 Mar 2009

Goalkeepers
| Dunn, Chris | 6.4 | Northampton | Brentwood | 23.10.87 |
| Murphy, Joe | 6.2 | Scunthorpe | Dublin, Ire | 21.08.81 |

Defenders
Brown, Reece	6.1	Manchester Utd (loan)	Manchester	01.11.91
Cameron, Nathan	6.2	–	Birmingham	21.11.91
Clarke, Jordan	6.0	–	Coventry	19.11.91
Edjenguele, William	6.2	Panetolikos	Paris, Fr	07.05.87
Hussey, Chris	5.10	Wimbledon	Hammersmith	02.01.89

Kilbane, Kevin	6.0	Hull	Preston	01.02.77
Malaga, Kevin	6.2	Nice	Toulon, Fr	24.06.87
Wood, Richard	6.3	Sheffield Wed	Ossett	05.07.85
Midfielders				
Baker, Carl	6.2	Stockport	Whiston	26.12.82
Bell, David	5.10	Norwich	Kettering	21.01.84
Deegan, Gary	5.9	Bohemians	Dublin, Ire	28.09.87
Fleck, John	5.7	Rangers	Glasgow	24.08.91
Jennings, Steven	5.7	Motherwell	Liverpool	28.10.84
McSheffrey, Gary	5.8	Birmingham	Coventry	13.08.72
Forwards				
Ball, Callum	6.2	Derby (loan)	Leicester	08.10.92
Elliott, Stephen	5.9	Hearts	Dublin, Ire	06.01.84
Jeffers, Sean	6.1	–	Bedford	14.04.92
McDonald, Cody	6.0	Norwich	Witham	30.05.86
O'Donovan, Roy	5.7	Sunderland	Cork, Ire	10.08.85
Wilson, Callum	5.11	–	Coventry	27.02.92

CRAWLEY TOWN

Ground: Broadfield Stadium, Winfield Way, Crawley RH11 9RX
Telephone: 01293 410000. **Club nickname**: Reds
Colours: All red. **Capacity**: 5,500
Record attendance: 4,723 v Crewe (Lge 2) 6 Apr, 2012

Goalkeepers				
Jones, Paul	6.3	Peterborough	Maidstone	28.06.86
Kuipers, Michael	6.2	Brighton	Amsterdam, Hol	26.06.72
Defenders				
Connolly, Mark	6.1	Bolton	Monaghan, Ire	16.12.91
Cooper, Shaun	5.10	Bournemouth	Newport, IOW	05.10.83
Davis, Claude	6.3	Crystal Palace	Kingston	06.03.79
McFadzean, Kyle	6.1	Alfreton	Sheffield	28.02.87
Sadler, Mat	5.11	Walsall	Birmingham	26.02.85
Midfielders				
Adams, Nicky	5.10	Rochdale	Bolton	16.10.86
Akpan, Hope	6.0	Everton	Liverpool	14.08.91
Bulman, Dannie	5.8	Oxford	Ashford, Surrey	24.01.79
Clarke, Billy	5.8	Blackpool	Cork, Ire	13.12.87
Davies, Scott	6.0	Reading	Aylesbury	10.03.88
Hunt, David	5.11	Brentford	Dulwich	10.09.82
Neilson, Scott	5.10	Bradford	Enfield	15.05.87
Simpson, Josh	5.9	Peterborough	Cambridge	06.03.87
Torres, Sergio	5.11	Peterborough	Mar del Plata, Arg	08.11.83
Forwards				
Akinde, John	6.2	Bristol City	Gravesend	08.07.89
Alexander, Gary	5.11	Brentford	Lambeth	15.08.79

CREWE ALEXANDRA

Ground: Alexandra Stadium, Gresty Road, Crewe CW2 6EB
Telephone: 01270 213014. **Club nickname**: Railwaymen
Colours: Red shirts; white shorts; red socks. **Capacity**: 10,109
Record attendance: 20,000 v Tottenham (FA Cup 4) 30 Jan, 1960

Goalkeepers				
Garratt, Ben	6.1	–	Shrewsbury	25.04.93

Martin, Alan	6.1	Ayr	Glasgow	01.01.89
Phillips, Steve	6.1	Crewe	Bath	06.05.78
Defenders				
Davis, Harry	6.2	–	Burnley	24.09.91
Dugdale, Adam	6.3	Telford	Liverpool	13.09.87
Ellis, Mark	6.2	Torquay	Plymouth	30.09.88
Ray, George	6.0	–	Warrington	13.10.93
Robertson, Gregor	6.0	Chesterfield	Edinburgh	19.01.84
Tootle, Matt	5.8	–	Knowsley	11.10.90
Turton, Oliver	5.11	–	Manchester	06.12.92
Westwood, Ashley	5.8	–	Nantwich	01.04.90
White, Andy	5.11	–	Chester	08.10.92
Midfielders				
Mellor, Kelvin	6.2	Nantwich	Crewe	25.01.91
Murphy, Luke	6.2	–	Alsager	21.10.89
Forwards				
Clayton, Max	5.9	–	Crewe	09.08.94
Connerton, Jordan	5.10	Lancaster	Lancaster	02.10.89
Daniels, Brendan	5.11	–	Stoke	24.09.93
Leitch-Smith, Ajay	5.11	–	Crewe	06.03.90
Miller, Shaun	5.10	–	Alsager	25.09.87
Moore, Byron	6.0	–	Stoke	24.08.88
Pogba, Mathias	6.3	Wrexham	Paris, Fr	19.08.90

DONCASTER ROVERS

Ground: Keepmoat Stadium, Stadium Way, Doncaster DN4 5JW
Telephone: 01302 764664. **Club nickname**: Rovers
Colours: Red and white shirts; black shorts; black socks. **Capacity**: 15,231
Record attendance: Belle Vue: 37,149 v Hull (Div 3 N) 2 Oct, 1948; Keepmoat Stadium: 15,001 v Leeds (Lge 1) 1 Apr, 2008

Goalkeepers				
Sullivan, Neil	6.0	Leeds	Sutton	24.02.70
Woods, Gary	6.0	Manchester Utd	Kettering	01.10.90
Defenders				
Beye, Habib	6.0	Aston Villa	Suresnes, Fr	19.10.77
Friend, George	6.0	Wolves	Barnstaple	19.10.87
Husband, James	5.11	–	Leeds	03.01.94
Martis, Shelton	6.2	WBA	Willemstad, Cur	29.11.82
O'Connor, James	5.10	Bournemouth	Birmingham	20.11.84
Spurr, Tommy	6.1	Sheffield Wed	Leeds	30.09.87
Midfielders				
Bennett, Kyle	5.5	Bury	Telford	09.09.90
Cotterill, David	5.9	Barnsley	Cardiff	04.12.87
Gillett, Simon	5.6	Southampton	Oxford	06.11.85
Stock, Brian	5.10	Preston	Winchester	24.12.81
Syers, David	5.10	Bradford	Leeds	30.11.87
Woods, Martin	5.11	Rotherham	Airdrie	01.01.86
Forwards				
Blake, Robbie	5.9	Bolton	Middlesbrough	04.03.76
Brown, Chris	6.3	Preston	Doncaster	11.12.84
Coppinger, James	5.7	Exeter	Middlesbrough	10.01.81

HARTLEPOOL UNITED

Ground: Victoria Park, Clarence Road, Hartlepool TS24 8BZ
Telephone: 01429 272584. **Club nickname:** Pool
Colours: Blue and white shirts; blue shorts; white socks. **Capacity:** 7,749
Record attendance: 17,426 v Manchester Utd (FA Cup 3) 5 Jan, 1957

Goalkeepers

Flinders, Scott	6.4	Crystal Palace	Rotherham	12.06.86
Rafferty, Andy	5.11	Guisborough	Guisborough	27.05.88

Defenders

Austin, Neil	5.10	Darlington	Barnsley	26.04.83
Baldwin, Jack	6.1	Faversham	Redbridge	30.06.93
Collins, Sam	6.2	Hull	Pontefract	05.06.77
Hartley, Peter	6.1	Sunderland	Hartlepool	03.04.88
Holden, Darren	5.11	–	Krugersdorp, SA	27.08.93
Horwood, Evan	6.0	Carlisle	Hartlepool	10.03.86
Johnson, Paul	5.11	–	Sunderland	05.04.92
Rowbotham, Josh	5.11	–	Stockton	07.01.93

Midfielders

Hawkins, Lewis	5.10	–	Hartlepool	15.06.93
Humphreys, Richie	5.11	Cambridge Utd	Sheffield	30.11.77
Luscombe, Nathan	5.8	Sunderland	Gateshead	06.11.89
Monkhouse, Andy	6.1	Swindon	Leeds	23.10.80
Murray, Paul	5.7	Shrewsbury	Carlisle	31.08.76
Richards, Jordan	5.9	–	Sunderland	25.04.93
Sweeney, Anthony	6.0	–	Stockton	05.09.83
Walton, Simon	6.1	Plymouth	Leeds	13.09.87

Forwards

Franks, Jonathan	5.7	Middlesbrough	Stockton	08.04.90
Howard, Steve	6.3	Leicester	Durham	10.05.76
James, Luke	5.11	–	Amble	04.11.94
Nish, Colin	6.3	Hibernian	Edinburgh	07.03.81
Poole, James	5.11	Manchester City	Stockport	20.03.90

LEYTON ORIENT

Ground: Matchroom Stadium, Brisbane Road, London E10 5NE
Telephone: 0871 310 1881. **Club nickname:** O's
Colours: All red. **Capacity:** 9,311
Record attendance: 34,345 v West Ham (FA Cup 4) 25 Jan, 1964

Goalkeepers

Allsop, Ryan	6.1	Millwall	Birmingham	17.06.92
Butcher, Lee	6.0	Tottenham	Waltham Forest	11.10.88
Jones, Jamie	6.0	Everton	Kirkby	18.02.89

Defenders

Baudry, Mathieu	6.2	Bournemouth	Le Havre, Fr	24.02.88
Chorley, Ben	6.3	Tranmere	Sidcup	30.09.82
Clarke, Nathan	6.2	Huddersfield	Halifax	30.11.83
Cuthbert, Scott	6.2	Swindon	Alexandria, Sco	15.06.87
Sawyer, Gary	6.0	Bristol Rov	Bideford	05.07.85

Midfielders

Brunt, Ryan	6.1	Stoke (loan)	Birmingham	26.05.93
Cox, Dean	5.5	–	Brighton	12.08.87
Griffith, Anthony	6.0	Port Vale	Huddersfield	28.10.86
James, Lloyd	5.11	Colchester	Bristol	16.02.88

Laird, Marc	6.1	Millwall	Edinburgh	23.01.86
McSweeney, Leon	6.1	Hartlepool	Cork, Ire	19.02.83
Odubajo, Moses	5.10	–	Greenwich	28.07.93
Smith, Jimmy	6.1	Chelsea	Newham	07.01.87
Forwards				
Lisbie, Kevin	5.10	Ipswich	Hackney	17.10.78
Lobjoit, Billy	5.10	–	Edgware	03.09.93
Mooney, David	6.2	Reading	Dublin, Ire	30.10.84
Symes, Michael	6.3	Bournemouth	Great Yarmouth	31.10.83

MILTON KEYNES DONS

Ground: stadiummk, Stadium Way West, Milton Keynes MK1 1ST
Telephone: 01908 622922. **Club nickname**: Dons
Colours: All white. **Capacity**: 21,189
Record attendance: 19,506 v QPR (FA Cup 3) 7 Jan, 2012. Also: 20,222 England v Bulgaria
(U-21 int) 16 Nov, 2007

Goalkeepers				
Martin, David	6.2	Liverpool	Romford	22.01.86
McLoughlin, Ian	6.3	Ipswich	Dublin, Ire	09.08.91
Defenders				
Chicksen, Adam	5.8	–	Milton Keynes	01.11.90
Doumbe, Mathias	6.1	Plymouth	Drancy, Fr	28.10.79
Flanagan, Tom	6.2	–	Hammersmith	30.12.91
Lewington, Dean	5.11	Wimbledon	Kingston	18.05.84
MacKenzie, Gary	6.3	Dundee	Lanark	15.10.85
Otsemobor, Jon	5.10	Sheffield Wed	Liverpool	23.03.83
Midfielders				
Baldock, George	5.9	–	Buckingham	26.01.93
Chadwick, Luke	5.11	Norwich	Cambridge	18.11.80
Gleeson, Stephen	6.2	Wolves	Dublin, Ire	03.08.88
O'Shea, Jay	6.0	Birmingham	Dublin, Ire	10.08.88
Potter, Darren	5.10	Sheffield Wed	Liverpool	21.12.84
Powell, Daniel	6.2	–	Luton	12.03.91
Smith, Alan	5.10	Newcastle	Rothwell	28.10.80
Williams, Shaun	6.0	Sporting Fingal	Dublin, Ire	19.09.86
Forwards				
Bowditch, Dean	5.11	Yeovil	Bishop's Stortford	15.06.86
Collins, Charlie	6.0	–	Wandsworth	22.11.91
Ibehre, Jabo	6.2	Walsall	Islington	28.01.83
MacDonald, Charlie	5.10	Brentford	Southwark	13.02.81

NOTTS COUNTY

Ground: Meadow Lane, Nottingham NG2 3HJ
Telephone: 0115 952 9000. **Club nickname**: Magpies
Colours: White and black shirts; black shorts; black socks. **Capacity**: 20,280
Record attendance: 47,310 v York (FA Cup 6) 12 Mar, 1955

Goalkeepers				
Bialkowski, Bartosz	6.0	Southampton	Braniewo, Pol	06.07.87
Mitchell, Liam	6.3	Lewes	–	18.09.92
Defenders				
Hughes, Jeff	6.1	Bristol Rov	Larne	29.05.85
Kelly, Julian	5.9	Reading	Enfield	06.09.89

Leacock, Dean	6.3	Leyton Orient	Thornton Heath	10.06.84
Pearce, Krystian	6.1	Huddersfield	Birmingham	05.01.90
Sheehan, Alan	5.11	Swindon	Athlone, Ire	14.09.86
Smith, Manny	6.2	Walsall	Birmingham	08.11.88
Thompson, John	6.0	Oldham	Dublin, Ire	12.10.81

Midfielders

Campbell-Ryce, Jamal	5.7	Bristol City	Lambeth	06.04.83
Bencherif, Hamza	6.0	Macclesfield	Paris, Fr	09.02.88
Bishop, Neal	6.0	Barnet	Stockton	07.08.81
Judge, Alan	6.0	Blackburn	Dublin, Ire	11.11.88
Labadie, Joss	6.3	Tranmere	Croydon	30.09.90
Liddle, Gary	6.1	Hartlepool	Middlesbrough	15.06.86
Mahon, Gavin	6.1	QPR	Birmingham	02.01.77

Forwards

Arquin, Yoann	6.2	Hereford	Le Havre, Fr	15.04.88
Hughes, Lee	5.10	Oldham	Smethwick	22.05.76
Showunmi, Enoch	6.4	Tranmere	Kilburn	21.04.82

OLDHAM ATHLETIC

Ground: Boundary Park, Oldham OL1 2PA
Telephone: 0161 624 4972. **Club nickname**: Latics
Colours: Blue shirts; white shorts; white socks. **Capacity**: 10,850
Record attendance: 47,761 v Sheffield Wed (FA Cup 4) 25 Jan, 1930

Goalkeepers

Bouzanis, Dean	6.1	Liverpool	Sydney, Aus	02.10.90
Cisak, Alex	6.4	Accrington	Krakow, Pol	19.05.89
Jacob, Liam	6.3	Manchester Utd	Sydney, Aus	18.08.94

Defenders

Belezika, Glenn	5.11	Stalybridge	Camden	24.12.94
Brown, Connor	5.9	Sheffield Utd	Sheffield	22.08.92
Grounds, Jonathan	6.1	Middlesbrough	Thornaby	02.02.88
Mvoto, Jean Yves	6.4	Sunderland	Paris, Fr	06.09.88

Midfielders

Croft, Lee	5.11	Derby (loan)	Billinge	21.06.85
Furman, Dean	5.11	Rangers	Cape Town, SA	22.06.88
Hughes, Connor	5.10	–	Bolton	06.05.93
M'Changama, Youssouf	5.8	Troyes	Marseille, Fr	29.08.90
Mellor, David	5.10	Manchester Utd	Oldham	10.07.93
Wesolowski, James	5.9	Peterborough	Sydney, Aus	25.08.87
Winchester, Carl	6.0	Linfield	Belfast	12.04.93

Forwards

Millar, Kirk	5.9	Linfield	Belfast	07.07.92
Simpson, Robbie	6.0	Huddersfield	Cambridge	15.03.85
Smith, Matt	6.6	Solihull Mot	Birmingham	07.06.89
Taylor, Daniel	5.11	Newcastle	Newcastle	17.03.93

PORTSMOUTH

Ground: Fratton Park, Frogmore Road, Portsmouth, PO4 8RA
Telephone: 0239 273 1204. **Club nickname**: Pompey
Colours: Blue shirts; white shorts; red socks. **Capacity**: 21,178
Record attendance: 51,385 v Derby (FA Cup 6) 26 Feb, 1949

Goalkeepers
Defenders

Halford, Greg	6.4	Wolves	Chelmsford	08.12.84
Webster, Adam	6.3	–	Chichester	04.01.95
Midfielders				
Ben Haim, Tal	6.0	Manchester City	Rishon, Isr	31.03.82
Lawrence, Liam	5.9	Stoke	Retford	14.12.81
Norris, David	5.8	Ipswich	Peterborough	22.02.81
Forwards				
Harris, Ashley	5.8	–	Poole	09.12.93
Huseklepp, Erik	6.2	Bari	Baerum, Nor	05.09.84
Kanu, Nwankwo	6.4	WBA	Owerri, Nig	01.08.76
Kitson, Dave	6.3	Stoke	Hitchin	21.01.80

PRESTON NORTH END

Ground: Deepdale, Sir Tom Finney Way, Preston PR1 6RU
Telephone: 0844 856 1964. **Club nickname:** Lilywhites
Colours: White shirts; navy shorts; white socks. **Capacity:** 23,404
Record attendance: 42,684 v Arsenal (Div 1) 23 Apr, 1938

Goalkeepers				
Stuckmann, Thorsten	6.6	Aachen	Gutersloh, Ger	17.03.81
Defenders				
Buchanan, David	5.9	Tranmere	Rochdale	06.05.86
Cansdell-Sheriff, Shane	6.0	Shrewsbury	Sydney, Aus	10.11.82
Huntington, Paul	6.2	Yeovil	Carlisle	17.09.87
Laird, Scott	5.9	Stevenage	Taunton	15.05.88
Morgan, Craig	6.0	Peterborough	St Asaph	18.06.85
Robertson, Chris	6.3	Torquay	Dundee	11.10.86
Wright, Bailey	5.10	VIS	Melbourne, Aus	28.07.92
Midfielders				
Barton, Adam	5.10	Blackburn	Blackburn	07.01.91
Hayhurst, Will	5.10	–	Blackburn	24.02.94
Holmes, Lee	5.8	Southampton	Mansfield	02.04.87
Keane, Keith	5.9	Luton	Luton	20.11.86
Mayor, Danny	6.0	–	Leyland	18.10.90
Monakana, Jeffrey	5.11	Arsenal	Edmonton	05.11.93
Mousinho, John	6.1	Stevenage	Isleworth	30.04.86
Procter, Andy	5.11	Accrington	Blackburn	13.03.83
Welsh, John	6.0	Tranmere	Liverpool	10.01.84
Wroe, Nicky	5.11	Shrewsbury	Sheffield	28.09.85
Forwards				
Amoo, David	5.10	Liverpool	Southwark	13.04.91
Cummins, Graham	5.10	Cork	Cork, Ire	29.12.87
Holroyd, Chris	5.11	Rotherham	Nantwich	24.10.86
Hume, Iain	5.7	Barnsley	Brampton, Can	31.10.83
Procter, Jamie	6.2	–	Preston	25.03.92
Trundle, Lee	6.0	Neath	Liverpool	10.10.76

SCUNTHORPE UNITED

Ground: Glanford Park, Doncaster Road, Scunthorpe DN15 8TD
Telephone: 0871 221 1899. **Club nickname:** Iron
Colours: Claret and blue shirts, blue shorts; blue socks. **Capacity:** 9,144
Record attendance: Old Show Ground: 23,935 v Portsmouth (FA Cup 4) 30 Jan, 1954; Glanford Park: 8,921 v Newcastle (Champ) 20 Oct, 2009

Goalkeepers

Severn, James	6.3	Derby	Nottingham	10.10.91
Slocombe, Sam	6.0	Bottesford	Scunthorpe	05.06.88

Defenders

Canavan, Niall	6.3	–	Leeds	11.04.91
Kennedy, Callum	6.1	Swindon	Chertsey	09.11.89
Reid, Paul	6.2	Colchester	Carlisle	18.02.82
Ribeiro, Christian	6.0	Bristol City	Neath	14.12.89

Midfielders

Barcham, Andy	5.9	Gillingham	Basildon	16.12.86
Collins, Michael	6.0	Huddersfield	Halifax	30.04.86
Duffy, Mark	5.9	Morecambe	Liverpool	07.10.85
Gibbons, Robbie	5.11	Larnaca	Knocklyon, Ire	08.10.91
Mozika, Damien	6.1	Bury	Corbeil-Essonnes, Fr	15.04.87
Ryan, Jimmy	5.10	Accrington	Maghull	06.09.88
Walker, Josh	5.11	Watford	Newcastle	21.02.89

Forwards

Godden, Matt	5.10	–	Canterbury	29.07.91
Grant, Bobby	5.11	Accrington	Blackpool	01.07.90
Grella, Mike	5.11	Bury	Glen Cove, US	23.01.87
Jennings, Connor	6.0	Stalybridge	Manchester	29.01.91

SHEFFIELD UNITED

Ground: Bramall Lane, Sheffield S2 4SU
Telephone: 0871 995 1899. **Club nickname:** Blades
Colours: Red and white shirts; black shorts; black socks. **Capacity:** 32,609
Record attendance: 68,287 v Leeds (FA Cup 5) 15 Feb, 1936

Goalkeepers

Howard, Mark	6.1	Blackpool	Southwark	21.09.86
Long, George	6.4	–	Sheffield	05.11.93

Defenders

Collins, Neil	6.3	Leeds	Troon	02.09.83
Lescinel, Jean-Francois	6.2	Swindon	Cayenne, F Gui	02.10.86
Maguire, Harry	6.2	–	Sheffield	05.03.93
Morgan, Chris	6.1	Barnsley	Barnsley	09.11.77
Westlake, Darryl	5.9	Walsall	Sutton Coldfield	01.03.91
Williams, Marcus	5.8	Reading	Doncaster	08.04.86

Midfielders

Doyle, Michael	5.10	Coventry	Dublin, Ire	08.07.81
Flynn, Ryan	5.7	Falkirk	Edinburgh	04.09.88
Harriott, Matty	6.0	–	Luton	23.09.92
McAllister, David	5.11	St Patrick's	Dublin, Ire	29.12.88
McDonald, Kevin	6.2	Burnley	Carnoustie	04.11.88
Montgomery, Nick	5.9	–	Leeds	28.10.81
Philliskirk, Danny	5.10	Chelsea	Oldham	10.04.91
Quinn, Stephen	5.6	–	Dublin, Ire	04.04.86
Tonne, Erik	6.0	Strindheim	Trondheim, Nor	03.07.91
Williamson, Lee	5.10	Watford	Derby	07.06.82

Forwards

Cresswell, Richard	6.1	Stoke	Bridlington	20.09.77
Philliskirk, Danny	5.10	Chelsea	Oldham	10.04.91
Porter, Chris	6.1	Derby	Wigan	12.12.83

SHREWSBURY TOWN

Ground: Greenhous Meadow Stadium, Oteley Road, Shrewsbury SY2 6ST
Telephone: 01743 289177. **Club nickname**: Shrews
Colours: Blue and yellow shirts; blue shorts; blue socks. **Capacity**: 9,875
Record attendance: Gay Meadonw: 18,917 v Walsall (Div 3) 26 Apr, 1961; Greenhous
Meadow: 9,441 v Dagenham (Lge 2) 28 Apr, 2012

Goalkeepers				
Anyon, Joe	6.2	Lincoln	Lytham	29.12.86
Weale, Chris	6.2	Leicester	Yeovil	09.02.82
Defenders				
Goldson, Connor	6.3	–	Wolverhampton	18.12.92
Grandison, Jermaine	6.4	Coventry	Birmingham	15.12.90
Jacobson, Joe	5.11	Accrington	Cardiff	17.11.86
Jones, Darren	6.1	Aldershot	Newport	26.08.83
Midfielders				
Hall, Asa	6.2	Oxford	Sandwell	29.11.86
Parry, Paul	5.11	Preston	Chepstow	19.08.80
Purdie, Rob	5.9	Hereford	Leicester	28.09.82
Richards, Matt	5.9	Walsall	Harlow	26.12.84
Summerfield, Luke	6.0	Cheltenham	Shrewsbury	06.12.87
Taylor, Jon	5.11	–	Liverpool	20.07.92
Wildig, Aaron	5.9	Cardiff	Hereford	15.04.92
Wright, Mark	5.11	Bristol Rov	Wolverhampton	24.02.82
Forwards				
Bradshaw, Tom	5.6	Aberystwyth	Shrewsbury	27.07.92
Doble, Ryan	5.10	Southampton	Abergavenny	01.02.91
Gornell, Terry	5.11	Accrington	Liverpool	16.12.89
Morgan, Marvin	6.4	Aldershot	Manchester	13.04.83

STEVENAGE

Ground: Lamex Stadium, Broadhall Way, Stevenage SG2 8RH
Telephone: 01438 223223. **Club nickname**: Boro
Colours: White shirts; red shorts; red socks. **Capacity**: 6,722
Record attendance: 8,040 v Newcastle (FA Cup 4) 25 January, 1998

Goalkeepers				
Arnold, Steve	6.4	Wycombe	Welham Green	22.08.89
Day, Chris	6.2	Millwall	Walthamstow	28.07.75
Defenders				
Ashton, Jon	6.2	Grays	Nuneaton	04.10.82
Charles, Darius	6.1	Ebbsfleet	Ealing	10.12.87
Hills, Lee	5.10	Crystal Palace	Croydon	13.04.90
N'Gala, Bondz	6.2	Yeovil	Forest Gate	13.09.89
Gray, David	5.11	Preston	Edinburgh	04.05.88
Roberts, Mark	6.1	Northwich	Northwich	16.10.83
Midfielders				
Dunne, James	5.11	Exeter	Farnborough	18.09.89
Grant, Anthony	5.10	Southend	Lambeth	04.06.87
Morais, Filipe	5.9	Oldham	Benavente, Por	21.11.85
Shroot, Robin	5.11	Birmingham	Hammersmith	26.03.88
Sinclair, Rob	5.10	Salisbury	Bedford	29.08.89
Tansey, Greg	6.1	Inverness	Huyton	21.11.88
Thalassitis, Michael	6.1	–	Edmonton	19.01.93

Forwards

Cowan, Don		Longford	New York, US	16.11.89
Freeman, Luke	5.9	Arsenal	Dartford	22.03.92
Haber, Marcus	6.3	St Johnstone	Vancouver, Can	11.01.89

SWINDON TOWN

Ground: County Ground, County Road, Swindon SN1 2ED
Telephone: 0871 423 6433. **Club nickname**: Robins
Colours: Red shirts; white shorts; red socks. **Capacity**: 14,983
Record attendance: 32,000 v Arsenal (FA Cup 3) 15 Jan, 1972

Goalkeepers

Bedwell, Leigh	6.2	–	Wantage	08.01.94
Foderingham, Wes	6.1	Crystal Palace	Shepherd's Bush	14.01.91

Defenders

Archibald-Henville, Troy	6.2	Exeter	Newham	04.11.88
Caddis, Paul	5.7	Celtic	Irvine	19.04.88
Cibocchi, Alessandro	6.0	Porto Summaga	Terni, It	18.09.82
Devera, Joe	6.2	Barnet	Southgate	06.02.87
Flint, Aden	6.2	Alfreton	Nottingham	11.07.89
McEveley, Jay	6.1	Barnsley	Liverpool	11.02.85
Smith, Chris	5.11	Stone	Stoke	12.10.90
Thompson, Nathan	5.10	–	Chester	22.04.91

Midfielders

Ferry, Simon	5.8	Celtic	Dundee	11.01.88
McCormack, Alan	5.8	Charlton	Dublin, Ire	10.01.84
Miller, Tommy	6.1	Huddersfield	Shotton	08.01.79
Navarro, Alan	5.10	Brighton	Liverpool	31.05.81
Risser, Oliver	6.2	KuPS	Windhoek, Nam	17.09.80
Ritchie, Matt	5.8	Portsmouth	Gosport	10.09.89
Roberts, Gary	5.10	Huddersfield	Chester	18.03.84
Rooney, Luke	5.11	Gillingham	Bermondsey	28.12.90
Thompson, Louis	5.11	–	Bristol	19.12.94

Forwards

Benson, Paul	6.2	Charlton	Rochford	12.10.79
Collins, James	6.1	Shrewsbury	Coventry	01.12.90
De Vita, Raffaela	5.11	Livingston	Rome, It	23.09.87
Storey, Miles	5.11	–	Sandwell	04.01.94
Williams, Andy	5.11	Yeovil	Hereford	14.08.86

TRANMERE ROVERS

Ground: Prenton Park, Prenton Road West, Birkenhead CH42 9PY
Telephone: 0871 221 2001. **Club nickname**: Rovers
Colours: All white. **Capacity**: 16,151
Record attendance: 24,424 v Stoke (FA Cup 4) 5 Feb, 1972

Goalkeepers

Fon Williams, Owain	6.4	Rochdale	Caernarfon	17.03.87

Defenders

Bakayogo, Zoumana	6.0	Alfortville	Paris, Fr	17.08.86
Black, Paul	6.0	Oldham	Middleton	18.05.90
Goodison, Ian	6.3	Hull	Kingston, Jam	21.11.72
Holmes, Danny	6.0	New Saints	Wirral	06.01.89
Kay, Michael	6.1	Sunderland	Shotley Bridge	12.09.89

McChrystal, Mark	6.1	Derry	Derry	26.06.84
Taylor, Ash	6.0	–	Bromborough	02.09.90
Midfielders				
Harrison, Danny	5.11	Rotherham	Liverpool	04.11.82
Palmer, Liam	5.11	Sheffield Wed (loan)	Worksop	19.09.91
Power, Max	5.11	–	Birkenhead	27.07.93
Robinson, Andy	5.9	Leeds	Birkenhead	03.11.79
Wallace, James	6.0	Everton	Fazackerley	19.12.91
Forwards				
Akins, Lucas	6.0	Hamilton	Huddersfield	25.02.89
Akpa Akpro, Jean-Louis	6.0	Rochdale	Toulouse, Fr	04.01.85
Burgess, Ben	6.3	Notts Co	Buxton	09.11.81
McGurk, Adam	5.10	Hednesford	Larne	24.01.89

WALSALL

Ground: Banks's Stadium, Bescot Crescent, Walsall WS1 4SA
Telephone: 01922 622791. **Club nickname**: Saddlers
Colours: Red shirts; white shorts; red socks. **Capacity**: 10,989
Record attendance: Fellows Park: 25,453 v Newcastle (Div 2) 29 Aug, 1961; Bescot Stadium: 11,049 v Rotherham (Div 1) 10 May, 2004

Goalkeepers				
Grof, David	6.3	Notts Co	Budapest, Hun	17.04.89
Walker, Jimmy	5.11	Tottenham	Sutton-in-Ashfield	09.07.73
Defenders				
Benning, Malvind	5.10	–	Sandwell	02.11.93
Butler, Andy	6.0	Huddersfield	Doncaster	04.11.83
Chambers, Adam	5.10	Leyton Orient	Sandwell	20.11.80
Holden, Dean	6.1	Rochdale	Salford	15.09.79
Taundry, Richard	6.0	–	Walsall	15.02.89
Midfielders				
Beevers, Lee	6.2	Colchester	Doncaster	04.12.83
Cuvelier, Florent	6.0	Stoke (loan)	Anderlecht, Bel	12.09.92
Hemmings, Ashley	5.7	Wolves	Lewisham	03.03.91
Jones, Jake	5.10	–	Birmingham	06.04.93
Forwards				
Bowerman, George	5.10	–	Wordsley	06.11.91
Butlin, Joey	5.10	–	Birmingham	17.03.93
Grigg, Will	5.11	Stratford	Solihull	03.07.91
Paterson, Jamie	5.9	–	Coventry	20.12.91

YEOVIL TOWN

Ground: Huish Park, Lufton Way, Yeovil BA22 8YF
Telephone: 01935 423662. **Club nickname**: Glovers
Colours: Green and white shirts; white shorts; white socks. **Capacity**: 9,565
Record attendance: 9,527 v Leeds (Lge 1) 25 Apr, 2008

Goalkeepers				
Stech, Marek	6.3	West Ham	Prague, Cz	28.01.90
Stewart, Gareth	6.0	Welling	Preston	03.02.80
Defenders				
Ayling, Luke	6.1	Arsenal	Lambeth	25.08.91
Haynes-Brown, Curtis	6.2	Lowestoft	Ipswich	15.04.89
Hinds, Richard	6.2	Lincoln	Sheffield	22.08.80

Name	Height ft in	Previous club	Birthplace	Birthdate
McAllister, Jamie	5.11	Bristol City	Glasgow	26.04.78
Webster, Byron	6.4	Northampton	Leeds	31.03.87
Midfielders				
Blizzard, Dominic	6.2	Bristol Rov	High Wycombe	02.09.83
Ince, Rohan	6.4	Chelsea (loan)	Whitechapel	08.11.92
Marsh-Brown, Keanu	5.9	Oldham	Hammersmith	10.08.92
Ralph, Nathan	5.9	Peterborough	Essex	14.02.93
Upson, Ed	5.10	Ipswich	Bury St Edmunds	21.11.89
Williams, Gavin	5.11	Bristol Rov	Merthyr	20.07.80
Young, Lewis	5.9	Northampton	Stevenage	27.09.89
Forwards				
Foley, Sam	6.0	Newport	Upton-on-Severn	17.10.86
Hayter, James	5.9	Doncaster	Newport, IOW	09.04.79
Reid, Reuben	6.0	Oldham	Bristol	26.07.88
Ugwu, Gozie	5.10	Reading (loan)	Oxford	22.04.93

LEAGUE TWO

ACCRINGTON STANLEY

Ground: Crown Ground, Livingstone Road, Accrington BB5 5BX
Telephone: 0871 434 1968. **Club nickname**: Stanley
Colours: Red shirts; white shorts; red and white socks. **Capacity**: 5,070
Record attendance: 4,368 v Colchester (FA Cup 3) 3 Jan, 2004

Name	Height ft in	Previous club	Birthplace	Birthdate
Goalkeepers				
Dunbavin, Ian	6.1	Halifax	Knowsley	27.05.80
Defenders				
Clark, Luke	5.10	Preston	Liverpool	24.05.94
Liddle, Michael	5.8	Sunderland	Hounslow	25.12.89
Murphy, Peter	6.0	–	Liverpool	13.02.90
Nsiala, Aristote	6.4	Everton	Kinshasa, DR Con	25.03.92
Richardson, Leam	5.7	Blackpool	Leeds	19.11.79
Winnard, Dean	5.9	Blackburn	Wigan	20.08.89
Midfielders				
Barnett, Charlie	5.8	Tranmere	Liverpool	19.09.88
Dixon, Bohan	6.4	–	Liverpool	17.10.89
Hatch, Lewis	5.9	Liverpool	Liverpool	04.09.94
Hatfield, Will	5.8	Leeds	Dewsbury	10.10.91
Hopper, Ryan	5.11	–	Manchester	13.11.93
Hughes, Bryan	5.9	Vestmannaeyjar	Liverpool	19.06.76
Joyce, Luke	5.11	Carlisle	Bolton	09.07.87
Miller, George	5.9	Preston	Eccleston	25.11.91
Forwards				
Carver, Marcus	5.11	–	Blackburn	22.10.93
Lindfield, Craig	6.0	Macclesfield	Wirral	07.09.88

AFC WIMBLEDON

Ground: Kingsmeadow, Kingston Road, Kingston upon Thames KT1 3PB
Telephone: 0208 547 3528. **Club nickname**: Dons
Colours: All blue. **Capacity**: 5,194
Record attendance: 4,722 v St Albans (Blue Sq South Lge) 25 April, 2009

Goalkeepers

Brown, Seb	6.0	Brentford	Sutton	24.11.89

Defenders

Balkestein, Pim	6.3	Brentford	Gouda, Hol	29.04.87
Cummings, Warren	5.9	Bournemouth	Aberdeen	15.10.80
McNaughton, Callum	6.2	West Ham	Harlow	25.10.91
Mitchel-King, Mat	6.4	Crewe	Cambridge	12.09.83
Osano, Curtis	5.11	Luton	Nakuru, Ken	08.03.87

Midfielders

Harris, Louis	5.11	Wolves	Sutton Coldfield	07.12.92
Kiernan, Brendan	5.9	Crystal Palace	Lambeth	10.11.92
Long, Stacy	5.8	Stevenage	Bromley	11.01.85
Moore, Sammy	5.8	Dover	Deal	07.09.87
Yussuf, Rashid	6.1	Gillingham	Poplar	23.09.89

Forwards

Harrison, Byron	6.2	Stevenage	Wandsworth	15.06.87
Jolley, Christian	5.11	Kingstonian	Aldershot	12.05.88
Midson, Jack	6.2	Oxford	Stevenage	21.09.83
Moore, Luke	5.11	Ebbsfleet	Gravesend	27.04.88
Prior, Jason	6.1	Bognor	Portsmouth	20.12.88

ALDERSHOT TOWN

Ground: EBB Stadium, High Street, Aldershot GU11 1TW
Telephone: 01252 320221. **Club nickname**: Shots
Colours: Red shirts; blue shorts; blue socks. **Capacity**: 6,835
Record attendance: 19,138 v Carlisle (FA Cup 4 replay) 28 Jan, 1970

Goalkeepers

Worner, Ross	6.1	Charlton	Hindhead	03.10.89
Young, Jamie	5.11	Wycombe	Brisbane, Aus	25.08.85

Defenders

Bergqvist, Doug	5.11	QPR	Stockholm, Swe	29.03.93
Branston, Guy	6.2	Bradford	Leicester	09.01.79
Brown, Troy	5.10	Rotherham	Croydon	17.09.90
Herd, Ben	5.10	Shrewsbury	Welwyn Garden City	21.06.85
Lancashire, Olly	6.1	Walsall	Basingstoke	13.12.88
Morris, Aaron	6.0	Cardiff	Rumney	30.12.89
Tonkin, Anthony	5.11	Oxford	Newlyn	17.01.80

Midfielders

Breimyr, Henrik	5.11	Reading	Stavanger, Nor	20.07.93
Mekki, Adam	5.9	Reading	Chester	24.12.91
Payne, Josh	6.0	Oxford	Basingstoke	25.11.90
Roberts, Jordan	5.11	Peterborough	Watford	05.01.94
Stanley, Craig	5.8	Bristol Rov	Bedworth	03.03.83
Vincenti, Peter	6.2	Stevenage	St Peter, Jer	07.07.86

Forwards

Connolly, Reece	6.0	–	Frimley	22.01.92
Hylton, Danny	6.0	–	Camden	25.02.89
Madjo, Guy	6.0	Stevenage	Douala, Cam	01.06.84
Rankine, Michael	6.2	York	Doncaster	15.01.85
Reid, Craig	5.10	Stevenage	Coventry	17.12.85
Risser, Wilko	6.3	Floriana	Windhoek, Nam	11.08.82
Rodman, Alex	6.2	Tamworth	Sutton Coldfield	15.12.87

BARNET

Ground: Underhill Stadium, Barnet EN5 2DN
Telephone: 0208 441 6932. **Club nickname**: Bees
Colours: Black and yellow shirts; black shorts; black socks. **Capacity**: 6,023
Record attendance: 11,026 v Wycombe (FA Amateur Cup 4), Feb 23, 1952

Goalkeepers				
Cowler, Sam	6.0	West Ham	–	26.10.92
O'Brien, Liam	6.4	Portsmouth	Harrow	03.11.91
Defenders				
Brown, Jordan	5.5	Crewe	Benfleet	11.10.91
Kamdjo, Clovis	5.11	Reading	Cameroon	15.12.90
Saville, Jack	6.3	Southampton	Camberley	02.04.91
Senda, Danny	5.11	Bristol Rov	Harrow	17.04.81
Midfielders				
Abdulla, Ahmed	5.9	Dagenham	Saudi Arabia	12.11.91
Byrne, Mark	5.9	Nottm Forest	Kilnamanagh, Ire	09.11.88
Edgar, Anthony	5.7	Yeovil	Newham	30.09.90
Lee, Olly	5.11	West Ham	Havering	11.07.91
Vilhete, Mauro	5.9	–	Lisbon, Por	10.05.93
Warren, Freddie	5.10	Charlton	Barking	02.11.92
Yiadom, Andy	6.0	Braintree	Camden	02.12.91
Forwards				
Holmes, Ricky	6.2	Chelmsford	Uxbridge	19.06.87
Kabba, Steve	5.10	Brentford	Lambeth	07.03.81
Nurse, Jon	5.9	Dagenham	Bridgetown, Barb	01.03.81

BRADFORD CITY

Ground: Coral Windows Stadium, Valley Parade, Bradford BD8 7DY
Telephone: 01274 773355. **Club nickname**: Bantams
Colours: Yellow and claret shirts; claret shorts; claret socks. **Capacity**: 25,136
Record attendance: 39,146 v Burnley (FA Cup 4) 11 Mar, 1911

Goalkeepers				
Duke, Matt	6.5	Hull	Sheffield	16.06.77
McLaughlin, Jon	6.2	Harrogate	Edinburgh	09.09.87
Defenders				
Darby, Stephen	5.9	Liverpool	Liverpool	06.10.88
Davies, Andrew	6.2	Stoke	Stockton	17.12.84
McArdle, Rory	6.1	Aberdeen	Sheffield	01.05.87
Meredith, James	6.1	York	Albury, Aus	04.04.88
Oliver, Luke	6.4	Wycombe	Hammersmith	04.09.82
Midfielders				
Atkinson, Will	5.10	Hull	Beverley	14.10.88
Jones, Gary	5.10	Rochdale	Birkenhead	03.06.77
Jones, Ritchie	6.1	Oldham	Manchester	26.09.86
Ravenhill, Ricky	5.10	Notts Co	Doncaster	16.01.81
Reid, Kyel	5.11	Charlton	Deptford	26.11.87
Thompson, Garry	5.11	Scunthorpe	Kendal	24.11.80
Forwards				
Connell, Alan	5.11	Swindon	Enfield	05.02.83
Hannah, Ross	5.11	Matlock	Sheffield	14.05.8
Hanson, James	6.4	Guiseley	Bradford	09.11.87
Wells, Nahki	5.9	Carlisle	Bermuda	01.06.90

BRISTOL ROVERS

Ground: Memorial Stadium, Filton Avenue, Horfield, Bristol BS7 0BF
Telephone: 0117 909 6648. **Club nickname**: Pirates
Colours: Blue and white shirts; blue shorts; blue socks. **Capacity**: 11,626
Record attendance: Eastville: 38,472 v Preston (FA Cup 4) 30 Jan, 1960; Memorial Stadium: 12,011 v WBA (FA Cup 6) 9 Mar, 2008

Goalkeepers				
Bevan, Scott	6.6	Torquay	Southampton	19.09.79
Gough, Conor	6.5	Charlton	Ilford	09.08.93
Defenders				
Brown, Lee	6.0	QPR	Farnborough	10.08.90
Brown, Wayne	5.9	Fulham	Kingston	06.08.88
Clucas. Seanan	5.10	Preston	Dungannon	08.11.92
Lund, Matthew	6.0	Stoke (loan)	Manchester	21.11.90
Smith, Michael	5.11	Ballymena	Ballyclare	04.09.88
Virgo, Adam	6.2	Yeovil	Brighton	25.01.83
Woodards, Danny	5.11	MK Dons	Forest Gate	08.10.83
Midfielders				
Anyinsah, Joe	5.8	Charlton	Bristol	08.10.84
Clarke, Ollie	5.11	–	Bristol	29.06.92
Gill, Matt	5.11	Norwich	Cambridge	08.11.80
Norburn, Oliver	5.10	Leicester	Bolton	26.10.92
Paterson, Jim	5.10	Shamrock	Bellshill	25.09.79
Forwards				
Carayol, Mustapha	5.10	Lincoln	Banjul, Gam	10.06.89
Harrold, Matt	6.1	Shrewsbury	Leyton	25.07.84
Richards, Elliot	5.10	–	New Tredegar	10.09.91
Zebroski, Chris	6.1	Torquay	Swindon	29.10.86

BURTON ALBION

Ground: Pirelli Stadium, Princess Way, Burton upon Trent DE13 AR
Telephone: 01283 565938. **Club nickname**: Brewers
Colours: Yellow and black shirts; black shorts; black socks. **Capacity**: 6,912
Record attendance: 6,192 v Oxford Utd (Blue Square Prem Lge) 17 Apr, 2009

Goalkeepers				
Atkins, Ross	6.0	Derby (loan)	Derby	03.11.89
Lyness, Dean	6.3	Kidderminster	Halesowen	20.07.91
Defenders				
Corbett, Andy	6.0	Nuneaton	Worcester	20.02.80
Diamond, Zander	6.2	Oldham	Alexandria, Sco	12.03.85
Holness, Marcus	6.0	Rochdale	Salford	08.12.88
McCrory, Damien	6.2	Dagenham	Croom, Ire	23.02.90
Palmer, Chris	5.8	Gillingham	Derby	16.10.83
Stanton, Nathan	5.9	Rochdale	Nottingham	06.05.81
Webster, Aaron	6.2	–	Burton	19.12.80
Midfielders				
Dyer, Jack	5.10	Aston Villa	Sutton Coldfield	11.12.91
Maghoma, Jacques	5.11	Tottenham	Lubumbashi, DR Con	23.10.87
McGrath, John	5.10	Tamworth	Limerick, Ire	27.03.80
Phillips, Jimmy	5.7	Stoke	Stoke	20.09.89
Taylor, Cleveland	5.9	St Johnstone	Leicester	09.09.83
Weir, Robbie	5.9	Tranmere	Belfast	09.12.88

Forwards

Kee, Billy	5.9	Torquay	Leicester	01.12.90
Richards, Justin	6.0	Port Vale	Sandwell	16.10.80
Yussuf, Adi	6.1	–	Zanzibar, Tanz	03.10.92

CHELTENHAM TOWN

Ground: Abbey Business Stadium, Whaddon Road, Cheltenham GL52 5NA
Telephone: 01242 573558. **Club nickname:** Town
Colours: Red shirts ; red shorts; black socks. **Capacity:** 7,133
Record attendance: 8,326 v Reading (FA Cup 1) 17 Nov, 1956

Goalkeepers

Brown, Scott	6.0	Bristol City	Wolverhampton	26.04.85

Defenders

Andrew, Danny	5.11	Peterborough	Boston	23.12.90
Bennett, Alan	6.2	Wycombe	Cork, Ire	04.10.81
Elliott, Steve	6.2	Bristol Rov	Derby	29.10.78
Jombati, Sido	6.1	Bath	Lisbon, Por	20.08.87
Hooman, Harry	6.1	Shrewsbury	Worcester	27.04.91
Jones, Billy	6.1	Exeter	Gillingham	26.06.83
Lowe, Keith	6.2	Hereford	Wolverhampton	13.09.85

Midfielders

Deering, Sam	5.6	Barnet	Tower Hamlets	26.02.91
Graham, Bagasan	5.11	QPR	Plaistow	06.10.92
McGlashan, Jermaine	5.7	Aldershot	Croydon	14.04.88
Pack, Marlon	6.2	Portsmouth	Portsmouth	25.03.91
Penn, Russ	6.0	Burton	Wordsley	08.11.85
Summerfield, Luke	6.0	Plymouth	Plymouth	06.12.87

Forwards

Duffy, Darryl	5.11	Bristol Rov	Glasgow	16.04.84
Goulding, Jeff	6.2	Bournemouth	Reading	13.05.84
Mohamed, Kaid	5.11	AFC Wimbledon	Cardiff	23.07.84

CHESTERFIELD

Ground: b2net Stadium, Whittington Moor, Chesterfield S41 8NZ
Telephone: 01246 209765. **Club nickname:** Spireites
Colours: Blue shirts; white shorts; blue socks. **Capacity:** 10,300
Record attendance: Saltergate: 30,561 v Tottenham (FA Cup 5) 12 Feb, 1938; b2net Stadium: 10,089 v Rotherham (Lge 2) 18 Mar, 2011

Goalkeepers

Lee, Tommy	6.2	Macclesfield	Keighley	03.01.86
O'Donnell, Richard	6.2	Sheffield Wed	Sheffield	12.09.88

Defenders

Forbes, Terrell	6.0	Leyton Orient	Southwark	17.08.81
Hird, Sam	5.8	Doncaster	Doncaster	07.09.87
Smith, Nathan	6.0	Yeovil	Enfield	11.01.87
Trotman, Neal	6.2	Rochdale	Manchester	11.03.87

Midfielders

Allott, Mark	5.11	Tranmere	Manchester	03.10.77
Clay, Craig	5.11	–	Nottingham	05.05.92
Darikwa, Tendayi	6.2	–	Nottingham	13.12.91
Randall, Mark	6.0	Arsenal	Milton Keynes	28.09.89
Togwell, Sam	5.11	Scunthorpe	Maidenhead	14.10.84

Whittaker, Danny	5.10	Oldham	Manchester	14.11.80
Forwards				
Boden, Scott	5.11	Sheffield Utd	Sheffield	19.12.89
Bowery, Jordan	6.1	–	Nottingham	02.07.91
Lester, Jack	5.10	Nottm Forest	Sheffield	08.10.75
Richards, Marc	5.11	Port Vale	Wolverhampton	08.07.82
Talbot, Drew	5.10	Luton	Barnsley	19.07.86
Westcarr, Craig	5.11	Notts Co	Nottingham	29.01.85

DAGENHAM AND REDBRIDGE

Ground: Dagenham Stadium, Victoria Road, Dagenham RM10 7XL
Telephone: 0208 592 1549. **Club nickname**: Daggers
Colours: Red and blue shirts; blue shorts; red socks. **Capacity**: 6,070
Record attendance: 5,949 v Ipswich (FA Cup 3), 5 Jan, 2002

Goalkeepers				
Hogan, David	6.0	–	Harlow	31.05.89
Lewington, Chris	6.2	Fisher	Sidcup	23.08.88
Defenders				
Bingham, Billy	5.10	Crystal Palace	Greenwich	15.07.90
Doe, Scott	6.1	Weymouth	Reading	06.11.88
Hoyte, Gavin	5.11	Arsenal	Waltham Forest	06.06.90
Ilesanmi, Femi	6.1	Ashford	Southwark	18.04.91
Reynolds, Duran	6.0	Southend	Boston	27.09.91
Rose, Richard	5.10	Hereford	Tunbridge Wells	08.09.82
Spillane, Michael	6.1	Brentford	Cambridge	23.03.89
Midfielders				
Elito, Medy	5.11	Colchester	Kinshasa, DR Con	20.03.90
Green, Danny	6.0	Billericay	Harlow	04.08.90
Green, Dominic	5.6	Peterborough	West Ham	05.07.89
Howell, Luke	5.11	Lincoln	Cuckfield	05.01.87
Maher, Kevin	6.0	Gillingham	Ilford	17.10.76
Ogogo, Abu	5.10	Arsenal	Epsom	03.11.89
Saunders, Matthew	5.11	Fulham	Chertsey	12.09.89
Wilkinson, Luke	6.2	Portsmouth	Wells	02.12.91
Forwards				
Edmans, Rob	6.6	Chelmsford	Greenwich	25.01.87
Osborn, Alex	5.11	Grays	Walthamstow	25.07.93
Gayle, Dwight	5.8	Stansted	–	20.10.90
Reed, Jake	5.10	Gt Yarmouth	Gt Yarmouth	13.05.91
Scott, Josh	6.2	Hayes	London	10.05.85
Williams, Sam	6.1	Yeovil	Greenwich	09.06.87
Woodall, Brian	5.10	Gresley	–	28.12.87

EXETER CITY

Ground: St James Park, Stadium Way, Exeter EX4 6PX
Telephone: 01392 411243. **Club nickname**: Grecians
Colours: Red and white shirts, black shorts, red and black socks. **Capacity**: 8,830
Record attendance: 20,984 v Sunderland (FA Cup 6 replay) 4 Mar, 1931

Goalkeepers				
Evans, Rhys	6.1	Staines	Swindon	27.01.82
Krysiak, Artur	6.4	Birmingham	Lodz, Pol	11.08.89
Defenders				
Amankwaah, Kevin	6.1	Rochdale	Kenton	19.05.82

Baldwin, Pat	6.0	Southend	London	12.11.82
Bennett, Scott	5.10	–	Truro	30.11.90
Coles, Danny	6.1	Bristol Rov	Bristol	31.10.81
Tully, Steve	5.9	Weymouth	Paignton	10.02.80
Woodman, Craig	5.9	Brentford	Tiverton	22.12.82
Midfielders				
Davies, Arron	5.9	Northampton	Cardiff	22.06.84
Dawson, Aaron	5.11	–	Exeter	24.03.92
Doherty, Tommy	5.8	Bath	Bristol	17.03.79
Freear, Elliott	5.8	–	Exeter	11.09.90
Keohane, Jimmy	5.11	Bristol City	Aylesbury	22.01.91
Sercombe, Liam	5.10	–	Exeter	25.04.90
Forwards				
Bauza, Guillem	6.0	Northampton	Palma, Maj	25.10.84
Gow, Alan	6.0	East Bengal	Clydebank	09.10.82
Nichols, Tom	5.10	–	Taunton	28.08.93
O'Flynn, John	5.11	Barnet	Cobh, Ire	11.07.82

FLEETWOOD TOWN

Ground: Highbury Stadium, Park Avenue, Fleetwod FY7 6TX
Telephone: 01253 775080. **Club nickname**: Fishermen
Colours: Red shirts, white shorts; red socks. **Capacity**: 5,094
Record attendance: 5,092 v Blackpool (FA Cup 3) 7 Jan, 2012

Goalkeepers				
Davies, Scott	6.0	Morecambe	Thornton Cleveleys	27.02.87
Maxwell, Chris	6.1	Wrexham	St Asaph	30.07.90
Defenders				
Atkinson, Rob	6.1	Grimsby	Beverley	29.04.87
Beeley, Shaun	5.10	Southport	Stockport	21.11.88
Brown, Junior	5.9	Northwich	Crewe	07.05.89
Charnock, Kieran	5.11	Morecambe	Preston	03.08.84
Goodall, Alan	5.9	Stockport	Birkenhead	02.12.81
Howell, Dean	6.1	Crawley	Burton upon Trent	29.11.80
McLaughlin, Conor	6.0	Preston	Belfast	26.07.91
McNulty, Steve	6.1	Barrow	Liverpool	26.09.83
Midfielders				
Barry, Anthony	5.7	Chester	Liverpool	29.05.86
Crowther, Ryan	5.11	Hyde	Stockport	17.09.88
Fowler, Lee	5.7	Wrexham	Cardiff	10.06.83
Johnson, Damien	5.10	Plymouth	Lisburn	18.11.78
Milligan, Jamie	5.7	Fylde	Blackpool	03.01.80
McGuire, Jamie	5.5	Droylsden	Birkenhead	13.11.83
Nicholson, Barry	5.8	Preston	Dumfries	24.08.78
Rose, Danny	5.7	Newport	Bristol	21.02.88
Forwards				
Ball, David	6.0	Peterborough	Whitefield	14.12.89
Gillespie, Steven	5.9	Colchester	Liverpool	04.06.85
Mangan, Andy	5.9	Wrexham	Liverpool	30.08.86
Parkin, Jon	6.4	Cardiff	Barnsley	30.12.81
Rowe, Danny	–	Kendal	–	29.01.90
Titchiner, Alex	5.7	Witton	St Asaph	13.06.91

GILLINGHAM

Ground: Priestfield Stadium, Redfern Avenue, Gillingham ME7 4DD
Telephone: 01634 300000. **Club nickname**: Gills
Colours: Blue shirts; blue shorts; white socks. **Capacity**: 11,440
Record attendance: 23,002 v QPR. (FA Cup 3) 10 Jan, 1948

Goalkeepers

Flitney, Ross	6.3	Dover	Hitchin	01.06.84
Forecast, Tommy	6.6	Southampton	Newham	15.10.86
Nelson, Stuart	6.1	Notts Co	Stroud	17.09.81

Defenders

Allen, Charlie	6.0	Notts Co	Barking	24.03.92
Davies, Callum	6.1	–	Chatham	08.02.93
Essam, Connor	6.0	–	Chatham	09.07.92
Fish, Matt	–	Dover	Croydon	05.01.89
Frampton, Andy	5.11	Millwall	Wimbledon	03.09.79
Fuller, Barry	5.10	Stevenage	Ashford, Kent	25.08.84
Jackman, Danny	5.5	Northampton	Worcester	03.01.83

Midfielders

Lee, Charlie	5.11	Peterborough	Whitechapel	05.01.87
Martin, Joe	6.0	Blackpool	Dagenham	29.11.89
Montrose, Lewis	6.2	Wycombe	Manchester	17.11.88
Payne, Jack	5.9	–	Gravesend	05.12.91
Whelpdale, Chris	6.0	Peterborough	Harold Wood	27.01.87

Forwards

Birchall, Adam	5.7	Dover	Maidstone	02.12.84
Kedwell, Danny	5.11	Wimbledon	Gillingham	03.08.83
Miller, Ashley	5.7	–	Dover	08.06.94
Strevens, Ben	6.1	Wycombe	Islington	24.05.80

MORECAMBE

Ground: Globe Arena, Christie Way, Westgate, Morecambe LA4 4TB
Telephone: 01524 411797. **Club nickname**: Shrimps
Colours: Red shirts; white shorts; red socks. **Capacity**: 6,400
Record attendance: Christie Park: 9,234 v Weymouth (FA Cup 3) 6 Jan 1962; Globe Arena: 5,003 v Burnley (League Cup 2) 24 Aug, 2010

Goalkeepers

Roche, Barry	6.4	Chesterfield	Dublin, Ire	06.04.82

Defenders

Fenton, Nick	6.1	Rotherham	Preston	23.11.79
Haining, Will	6.0	St Mirren	Glasgow	02.10.82
McCready, Chris	6.1	Northampton	Chester	05.09.81
Parkinson, Dan	5.11	–	Preston	02.11.92
Parrish, Andy	6.0	Bury	Bolton	22.06.88
Threlfall, Robbie	6.0	Bradford	Liverpool	28.11.88

Midfielders

Drummond, Stewart	6.2	Shrewsbury	Preston	11.12.75
Ellison, Kevin	6.0	Rotherham	Liverpool	23.02.79
Fleming, Andy	5.11	Wrexham	Liverpool	05.10.87
McDonald, Gary	6.1	Hamilton	Irvine	10.04.82
McGee, Joe	5.11	–	Liverpool	06.03.93
Mwasile, Joe	5.9	–	-	06.07.93
Reid, Izak	5.5	Macclesfield	Sheffield	13.09.89

Wright, Andrew	6.1	Scunthorpe	Liverpool	15.01.85
Forwards				
Alessandra, Lewis	5.10	Oldham	Oldham	08.02.89
Brodie, Richard	6.2	Crawley (loan)	Gateshead	08.07.87
Carlton, Danny	6.0	Bury	Leeds	22.12.83
Redshaw, Jack	5.6	Altrincham	Salford	20.11.90

NORTHAMPTON TOWN

Ground: Sixfields Stadium, Upton Way, Northampton NN5 5QA
Telephone: 01604 683700. **Club nickname**: Cobblers
Colours: Claret and white shirts; white shorts; white socks. **Capacity**: 7,300
Record attendance: County Ground: 24,523 v Fulham (Div 1) 23 Apr, 1966; Sixfields Stadium: 7,557 v Manchester City (Div 2) 26 Sep, 1998

Goalkeepers				
Higgs, Shane	6.3	Leeds	Oxford	13.05.77
Kitson, Neal	6.0	Rochester	New York, US	04.01.86
Defenders				
Charles, Anthony	6.1	Aldershot	Isleworth	11.03.81
Johnson, John	6.0	Middlesbrough	Middlesbrough	16.09.88
Nana-Ofori, Seth	5.8	Peterborough	Accra, Gh	15.05.90
Tozer, Ben	6.1	Newcastle	Plymouth	01.03.90
Widdowson, Joe	6.0	Rochdale	Forest Gate	29.03.89
Midfielders				
Demontagnac, Ishmel	5.10	Notts Co	Newham	15.06.88
Guttridge, Luke	5.8	Aldershot	Barnstaple	27.03.82
Hackett, Chris	6.0	Millwall	Oxford	01.03.83
Harding, Ben	6.1	Wycombe	Carshalton	06.09.84
Forwards				
Akinfenwa, Adebayo	6.1	Gillingham	West Ham	10.05.82
Langmead, Kelvin	6.1	Peterborough	Coventry	23.03.85
Nicholls, Alex	5.10	Walsall	Stourbridge	09.12.87
Platt, Clive	6.4	Coventry	Wolverhampton	27.10.77
Robinson, Jake	5.8	Shrewsbury	Brighton	23.10.86
Wilson, Lewis	5.10	Newport Pagnall	Milton Keynes	19.02.93

OXFORD UNITED

Ground: Kassam Stadium, Grenoble Road, Oxford OX4 4XP
Telephone: 01865 337500. **Club nickname**: U's
Colours: All yellow. **Capacity**: 12,500.
Record attendance: Manor Ground: 22,750 v Preston (FA Cup 6) 29 February, 1964; Kassam Stadium: 12,243 v Leyton Orient (Lge 2) 6 May, 2006

Goalkeepers				
Brown, Wayne	6.1	Supersport	Southampton	14.01.77
Clarke, Ryan	6.3	Salisbury	Bristol	30.04.82
Defenders				
Batt, Damien	5.10	Grays	Hoddesdon	16.09.84
Capaldi, Tony	6.0	Morecambe	Porsgrunn, Nor	12.08.81
Duberry, Michael	6.1	St Johnstone	Enfield	14.10.75
McGinty, Sean	6.1	Manchester Utd (loan)	Maidstone	11.08.93
Raynes, Michael	6.3	Rotherham	Manchester	15.10.87
Whing, Andy	6.0	Leyton Orient	Birmingham	20.09.84
Worley, Harry	6.4	Leicester	Warrington	25.11.88
Wright, Jake	5.11	Brighton	Keighley	11.03.86

Midfielders

Chapman, Adam	5.10	Sheffield Utd	Doncaster	29.11.89
Cox, Lee	6.0	Swindon (loan)	Leicester	26.06.90
Davis, Liam	6.1	Northampton	Wandsworth	23.11.86
Forster-Caskey, Jake	5.10	Brighton(loan)	Southend	25.04.94
Heslop, Simon	5.11	Barnsley	York	01.05.87
Leven, Peter	5.11	MK Dons	Glasgow	27.09.83
Potter, Alfie	5.7	Peterborough	Islington	09.01.89
Rigg, Sean	5.9	Port Vale	Bristol	01.10.88

Forwards

Constable, James	6.2	Shrewsbury	Malmesbury	04.10.84
Craddock, Tom	5.11	Luton	Darlington	14.10.86
Pittman, Jon-Paul	5.9	Wycombe	Oklahoma City, US	24.10.86
Smalley, Deane	5.10	Oldham	Chadderton	05.09.88

PLYMOUTH ARGYLE

Ground: Home Park, Plymouth PL2 3DQ
Telephone: 01752 562561. **Club nickname**: Pilgrims
Colours: Green shirts; white shorts; white socks. **Capacity**: 16,388
Record attendance: 43,596 v Aston Villa (Div 2) 10 Oct, 1936

Goalkeepers

Chenoweth, Ollie	6.1	Bideford	Liskeard	17.02.92
Cole, Jake	6.3	Barnet	Hammersmith	11.09.85
Gilmartin, Rene	6.5	Watford	Dublin, Ire	31.05.87

Defenders

Berry, Durrell	5.11	Aston Villa	Derby	27.05.92
Bhasera, Onismo	5.8	Kaizer Chiefs	Mutare, Zim	07.01.86
Blanchard, Maxime	6.0	Tranmere	Alencon, Fr	27.09.86
Nelson, Curtis	6.0	Stoke	Newcastle-under-Lyme	21.05.93
Purse, Darren	6.2	Millwall	Stepney	14.02.77
Richards, Jamie	5.10	–	Newton Abbot	24.06.94
Soukouna, Ladjie	6.4	Creteil	Paris, Fr	15.12.90

Midfielders

Copp, Jordan	5.9	–	Saltash	28.09.93
Harper-Penman, Jed	5.7	–	Bideford	02.02.94
Hourihane, Conor	6.0	Ipswich	Cork, Ire	02.02.91
Lennox, Joe	5.7	Bristol City	Bristol	22.11.91
Lowry, Jamie	6.0	Chesterfield	Newquay	18.03.87
Williams, Robbie	5.10	Rochdale	Pontfract	02.10.84
Wotton, Paul	5.11	Yeovil	Plymouth	17.08.77
Young, Luke	5.10	–	Plymouth	22.02.93

Forwards

Chadwick, Nick	6.0	Stockport	Stoke	26.10.82
Cowan-Hall, Paris	5.8	Woking	Hillingdon	05.10.90
Feeney, Warren	5.10	Oldham	Belfast	17.01.81
Lecointe, Matt	5.10	–	Plymouth	28.10.94
Sims, Jared	5.9	–	Truro	26.10.93
Vassell, Isaac	5.7	–	Newquay	09.09.93

PORT VALE

Ground: Vale Park, Hamil Road, Burslem, Stoke-on-Trent ST6 1AW
Telephone: 01782 655800. **Club nickname**: Valiants
Colours: Black and white shirts, black shorts, black socks. **Capacity**: 19,148
Record attendance 49,768 v Aston Villa (FA Cup 5) 20 Feb, 1960

Goalkeepers

Johnson, Sam	6.6	Stoke	Newcastle-u-Lyme	01.12.92
Neal, Chris	6.2	Shrewsbury	St Albans	23.10.85

Defenders

Artell, David	6.2	Crewe	Rotherham	22.11.80
Davis, Joe	5.10	–	Burnley	10.11.93
Duffy, Richard	5.11	Exeter	Swansea	30.08.85
James, Kingsley	6.1	Sheffield Utd	Rotherham	17.02.92
McCombe, John	6.2	Hereford	Pontefract	07.05.85
McDonald, Clayton	6.6	Walsall	Liverpool	06.12.88
Owen, Gareth	6.1	Stockport	Stoke	21.09.82
Yates, Adam	5.10	Morecambe	Stoke	28.05.83

Midfielders

Burge, Ryan	5.10	Hyde	Cheltenham	12.10.88
Dodds, Louis	5.10	Leicester	Sheffield	08.10.86
Haldane, Lewis	6.0	Bristol Rov	Trowbridge	13.03.85
Loft, Doug	6.0	Brighton	Maidstone	25.12.86
Lloyd, Ryan	5.10	–	Newcastle-u-Lyme	01.02.94
Morsy, Sam	5.9	–	Wolverhampton	10.09.91
Murphy, Darren	6.1	Stevenage	Cork, Ire	28.07.85
Myrie-Williams, Jennison	6.0	Stevenage	Lambeth	17.05.88
Shuker, Chris	5.5	Morecambe	Huyton	09.05.82
Taylor, Rob	6.0	Nuneaton	Shrewsbury	16.01.85

Forwards

Pope, Tom	6.3	Rotherham	Stoke	27.08.85
Vincent, Ashley	6.0	Colchester	Birmingham	26.05.85
Williamson, Ben	5.11	Hyde	Lambeth	25.12.88

ROCHDALE

Ground: Spotland, Wilbutts Lane, Rochdale OL11 5DS
Telephone: 01706 644648. **Club nickname:** Dale
Colours: Blue and black shirts; white shorts; blue and black socks. **Capacity:** 10,149
Record attendance: 24,231 v Notts Co (FA Cup 2) 10 Dec, 1949

Goalkeepers

Edwards, Matthew	6.3	Leeds	Liverpool	01.08.91
Lillis, Josh	6.0	Scunthorpe	Derby	24.06.87

Defenders

Bennett, Rhys	6.3	Bolton	Manchester	01.09.91
Byrne, Neill	–	Nottm Forest	Portmarnock, Ire	02.02.93
Cavanagh, Peter	5.11	Fleetwood	Liverpool	14.10.81
Jordan, Stephen	6.0	Sheffield Utd	Warrington	06.03.82
Minihan, Sam	5.11	–	Rochdale	16.02.94

Midfielders

Barry-Murphy, Brian	6.0	Bury	Cork, Ire	27.07.78
Grimes, Ashley	6.0	Millwall	Swinton	09.12.86
Kennedy, Jason	6.1	Darlington	Stockton	11.09.86
McIntyre, Kevin	5.10	Accrington	Liverpool	23.12.77
Thompson, Joe	6.0	–	Rochdale	05.03.89
Tutte, Andrew	5.9	Manchester City	Liverpool	21.09.90

Forwards

Abadaki, Godwin	5.10	–	Manchester	04.03.94
Donnelly, George	5.9	Macclesfield	Kirkby	28.05.88
Gray, Reece	5.7	–	Oldham	01.09.92

ROTHERHAM UNITED

Ground: New York Stadium
Telephone: TBC. **Club nickname**: Millers
Colours: Red and white shirts; red shorts; red socks. **Capacity**: 12,000
Record attendance: Millmoor: 25,170 v Sheffield Wed (Div 2) 26 Jan, 1952 and v Sheffield Wed (Div 2) 13 Dec, 1952; Don Valley Stadium: 7,082 v Aldershot (Lge 2 play-off semi-final, 2nd leg) 19 May 2010

Goalkeepers

Shearer, Scott	6.2	Crawley	Glasgow	15.02.81
Warrington, Andy	6.3	Bury	Sheffield	10.06.76

Defenders

Arnason, Kari	6.3	Aberdeen	Gothenburg, Swe	13.10.82
Hunt, Nicky	6.1	Preston	Westhoughton	03.09.83
Mullins, John	5.11	Stockport	Hampstead	06.11.85
Sharps, Ian	6.4	Shrewsbury	Warrington	23.10.80
Tonge, Dale	5.10	Barnsley	Doncaster	07.05.85
Wilson, Laurence	5.10	Morecambe	Liverpool	10.10.86

Midfielders

Ainsworth, Lionel	5.9	Shrewsbury	Nottingham	01.10.87
Bradley, Mark	6.0	Walsall	Wordsley	14.01.88
Evans, Gareth	6.0	Bradford	Macclesfield	26.04.88
Noble, David	6.0	Exeter	Hitchin	02.02.82
O'Connor, Michael	6.1	Scunthorpe	Belfast	06.10.87
Pringle, Ben	6.1	Derby	Newcastle	27.05.89
Schofield, Danny	5.10	Millwall	Doncaster	10.04.80
Taylor, Jason	6.2	Stockport	Ashton-under-Lyne	28.01.87

Forwards

Nardiello, Daniel	5.11	Exeter	Coventry	22.10.82
Odejayi, Kayode	6.2	Colchester	Ibadon, Nig	21.02.82
Revell, Alex	6.3	Leyton Orient	Cambridge	07.07.83

SOUTHEND UNITED

Ground: Roots Hall, Victoria Avenue, Southend SS2 6NQ
Telephone: 01702 304050. **Club nickname**: Shrimpers
Colours: Blue shirts; white shorts; white socks. **Capacity**: 12,163
Record attendance: 31,090 v Liverpool (FA Cup 3) 10 Jan, 1979

Goalkeepers

Bentley, Daniel	6.2	–	Basildon	13.07.93

Defenders

Barker, Chris	6.0	Plymouth	Sheffield	02.03.80
Bilel, Mohsni	6.3	St Genevieve	Paris, Fr	21.07.87
Clohessy, Sean	5.10	Bath	Croydon	12.12.86
Coughlan, Graham	6.2	Shrewsbury	Dublin, Ire	18.11.74
Cresswell, Ryan	6.2	Rotherham	Rotherham	22.12.87
Leonard, Ryan	6.1	Plymouth	Plymouth	24.05.92
Phillips, Mark	6.2	Brentford	Lambeth	27.01.82
Prosser, Luke	6.3	Port Vale	Enfield	28.05.88
Straker, Anthony	5.9	Aldershot	Ealing	23.09.88

Midfielders

Ferdinand, Kane	6.1	–	Newham	07.10.92
Hall, Ryan	5.10	Bromley	Dulwich	04.01.88
Hurst, Kevan	6.0	Walsall	Chesterfieldf	27.08.85

Martin, David	5.9	Derby	Erith	03.06.85
Timlin, Michael	5.8	Swindon	Lambeth	19.03.85
Forwards				
Benyon, Elliot	5.9	Swindon	High Wycombe	29.08.87
Corr, Barry	6.3	Exeter	Newcastle, NI	02.04.85
Eastwood, Freddy	5.11	Coventry	Epsom	29.10.83
Harris, Neil	5.11	Millwall	Orsett	12.07.77
Tomlin, Gavin	5.10	Dagenham	Lewisham	21.08.83

TORQUAY UNITED

Ground: Plainmoor, Torquay TQ1 3PS
Telephone: 01803 328666. **Club nickname**: Gulls
Colours: Yellow and blue shirts; yellow shorts; yellow socks. **Capacity**: 6,000
Record attendance: 21,908 v Huddersfield (FA Cup 4) 29 Jan, 1955

Goalkeepers				
Poke, Michael	6.2	Brighton	Ashford, Surrey	21.11.85
Rice, Martin	5.11	Truro	Exeter	07.03.86
Defenders				
Cruise, Tom	6.0	Arsenal	Islington	09.03.91
Downes, Aaron	6.1	Chesterfield	Mudgee, Aus	15.05.85
Nicholson, Kevin	5.8	Forest Green	Derby	02.10.80
Leadbitter, Daniel	6.3	–	Newcastle	07.10.90
Oastler, Joe	6.1	QPR	Portsmouth	03.07.90
Saah, Brian	6.1	Cambridge Utd	Rush Green	16.12.86
Midfielders				
Bodin, Billy	5.11	Swindon	Swindon	24.03.92
Craig, Nathan	5.11	Caernarfon	Caernarfon	25.10.91
Easton, Craig	5.10	Dunfermline	Bellshill	26.02.79
Halpin, Sean	6.1	–	Truro	31.05.91
Mansell, Lee	5.9	Oxford	Gloucester	23.09.82
Morris, Ian	6.0	Scunthorpe	Dublin, Ire	27.02.87
O'Kane, Eunan	5.8	Coleraine	Derry	10.07.90
Stevens, Danny	5.10	Luton	Enfield	26.11.86
Lathrope, Damon	5.10	Norwich	Stevenage	28.10.89
Forwards				
Howe, Renee	6.0	Peterborough	Bedford	22.10.86
Jarvis, Ryan	6.1	Walsall	Fakenham	11.07.86
Macklin, Lloyd	5.9	Swindon	Camberley	02.08.91
Yeoman, Ashley	5.10	–	Kingsbridge	25.02.92

WYCOMBE WANDERERS

Ground: Adams Park, Hillbottom Road, High Wycombe HP12 4HJ
Telephone: 01494 472100. **Club nickname**: Chairboys
Colours: Light and dark blue shirts; dark blue shorts; dark and light blue socks. **Capacity**: 10,000
Record attendance: 10,000 v Chelsea (friendly) 13 July, 2005

Goalkeepers				
Bull, Nikki	6.2	Brentford	Hastings	02.10.81
Ingham, Matt	6.2	–	–	18.12.93
Defenders				
Basey, Grant	6.1	Peterborough	Bromley	30.11.88
Doherty, Gary	6.1	Charlton	Donegal, Ire	31.01.80

Dunne, Charles	5.10	–	Lambeth	13.02.93
Foster, Danny	6.1	Brentford	Enfield	23.09.84
Johnson, Leon	6.0	Gillingham	London	10.05.81
McCoy, Marvin	6.0	Wealdstone	Waltham Forest	02.10.88
Stewart, Anthony	6.0	–	Lambeth	18.09.92
Winfield, Dave	6.3	Aldershot	Aldershot	24.03.88

Midfielders

Ainsworth, Gareth	5.9	QPR	Blackburn	10.05.73
Angol, Lee	5.10	Tottenham	Carshalton	04.08.94
Bloomfield, Matt	5.8	Ipswich	Felixstowe	08.02.84
Grant, Joel	6.0	Crewe	Hammersmith	27.08.87
Kewley-Graham, Jesse	6.0	–	Hounslow	30.11.93
Lewis, Stuart	5.11	Dagenham	Welwyn Garden City	15.10.87
Scowen, Josh	5.10	–	Enfield	28.03.93
Spring, Matthew	6.0	Leyton Orient	Harlow	17.11.79
Wood, Sam	6.0	Brentford	Bexley	09.08.86

Forwards

Beavon, Stuart	5.10	Weymouth	Reading	05.05.84
Henderson, Liam	5.11	Watford	Gateshead	28.12.89
Logan, Richard	6.1	Exeter	Bury St Edmunds	04.01.82
McClure, Matt	5.10	Crystal Palace	Slough	17.11.91
Oli, Dennis	6.0	Gillingham	Newham	28.01.84

YORK CITY

Ground: Bootham Crescent, York, YO30 7AQ
Telephone: 01904 624447. **Club nickname**: Minstermen
Colours: Red shirts; blue shorts; white socks. **Capacity**: 7,872
Record attendance: 28,123 v Huddersfield (FA Cup 6) 5 Mar, 1938

Goalkeepers

Ingham, Michael	6.4	Hereford	Preston	07.09.80
Musselwhite, Paul	6.2	Lincoln	Portsmouth	22.12.68

Defenders

Blanchett, Danny	5.11	Burton	Wembley	06.05.87
Doig, Chris	6.2	Aldershot	Dumfries	13.02.81
Fyfield, Jamal	5.9	Maidenhead	–	17.03.89
McGurk, David	6.0	Darlington	Middlesbrough	30.09.82
Oyebanjo, Lanre	6.1	Histon	London	27.04.90
Parslow, Daniel	6.1	Cardiff	Rhymney	09.11.85
Smith, Chris	5.10	Mansfield	Derby	30.06.81

Midfielders

Blair, Matty	5.9	Kidderminster	Warwick	30.11.87
Bullock, Lee	6.0	Bradford	Thornaby	22.05.81
Challinor, Jon	5.11	Kettering	Northampton	02.12.80
Chambers, Ashley	5.10	Leicester	Leicester	01.08.90
Kerr, Scott	5.8	Lincoln	Leeds	11.12.81
McLaughlin, Patrick	6.2	Newcastle	Larne	14.01.91
McReady, John	5.10	Darlington	South Shields	24.07.92
Potts, Michael	5.10	Blackburn	–	26.11.91
Smith, Jonathan	5.8	Swindon	Preston	17.10.86

Forwards

Coulson, Michael	5.10	Grimsby	Scarborough	04.04.88
Johnson, Oli	5.11	Oxford	Wakefield	06.11.87
Reed, Jamie	6.0	Bangor	Connah's Quay	13.08.87
Walker, Jason	5.9	Luton	Barrow	21.02.84

CLYDESDALE SCOTTISH PREMIER LEAGUE SQUADS 2012–13

(at time of going to press)

ABERDEEN
Ground: Pittodrie Stadium, Pittodrie Street, Aberdeen AB24 5QH. **Capacity:** 21,421
Telephone: 01224 650400. **Manager:** Craig Brown. **Colours:** Red and white. **Nickname:** Dons
Goalkeepers: Jason Brown, Jamie Langfield, Danny Rogers
Defenders: Russell Anderson, Andrew Considine, Clark Robertson
Midfielders: Chris Clark, Ryan Fraser, Jonny Hayes , Stephen Hughes, Ryan Jack, Jamie Masson, Niall McGinn Robert Milsom, Isaac Osbourne, Peter Pawlett, Gavin Rae
Forwards: Rory Fallon, Josh Magennis, Declan McManus, Mitchel Megginson, Michael Paton, Cameron Smith, Scott Vernon

CELTIC
Ground: Celtic Park, Glasgow G40 3RE. **Capacity:** 60, 355. **Telephone:** 0871 226 1888.
Manager: Neil Lennon. **Colours:** Green and white. **Nickname:** Bhoys
Goalkeepers: Fraser Forster, Lukasz Zaluska
Defenders: Andre Blackman, Emilio Izaguirre, Mikael Lustig, Adam Matthews, Charlie Mulgrew, Thomas Rogne, Josh Thompson, Lewis Toshney, Kevin Wilson
Midfielders: Scott Brown, Kris Commons, James Forrest, Rabiu Ibrahim, Beram Kayal, Ki Sung-Yueng, Joe Ledley, Pat McCourt, Dylan McGeouch, Paul Slane, Filip Twardzik, Patrik Twardzik, Victor Wanyama
Forwards: Mohamed Bangura, Gary Hooper, James Keatings, Daryl Murphy, Morten Rasmussen, Georgios Samaras, Anthony Stokes, Tony Watt

DUNDEE
Ground: Dens Park, Sandeman Street, Dundee DD3 7JY. **Capacity:** 12,085. **Telephone:** 01382 889966. **Manager:** Barry Smith. **Colours:** Blue and white. **Nickname:** The Dee
Goalkeepers: Rab Douglas, John Gibson
Defenders: Kyle Benedictus, Declan Gallagher, Gary Irvine, Matthew Lockwood, Neil McGregor
Midfielders: Ryan Conroy, Iain Davidson, Kevin McBride, Jamie McCluskey, Stephen O'Donnell, Nicky Riley, Graham Webster
Forwards: John Baird, Carl Finnigan, Leighton McIntosh, Steven Milne

DUNDEE UNITED
Ground: Tannadice Park, Tannadice Street, Dundee DD3 7JW. **Capacity:** 14,223. **Telephone:** 01382 833166. **Manager:** Peter Houston. **Colours:** Tangerine and white. **Nickname:** Terrors
Goalkeepers: Radoslaw Cierzniak, Marc McCallum, Filip Mentel
Defenders: Patrick Barrett, Sean Dillon, Barry Douglas, Gavin Gunning, Brian McLean, Ross Smith, Keith Watson
Midfielders: Stuart Armstrong, Willo Flood, Gary Mackay-Steven, Mark Millar, John Rankin, Willie Robertson, Richie Ryan
Forwards: Jon Daly, Ryan Dow, Michael Gardyne, Dale Hilson, Milos Lacny, Johnny Russell, Robert Thomson

HEART OF MIDLOTHIAN
Ground: Tynecastle Stadium, McLeod Street Edinburgh EH11 2NL. **Capacity:** 17,590.
Telephone: 0871 663 1874. **Manager:** John McGlynn. **Colours:** Maroon and white. **Nickname:** Jam Tarts
Goalkeepers: Marian Kello, Jamie MacDonald, Mark Ridgers

Defenders: Darren Barr, Ismael Bouzid, Danny Grainger, Ryan McGowan, Kevin McHattie, Brad McKay, Fraser Mullen, Jason Thomson, Andy Webster, Marius Zaliukas
Midfielders: Andrew Driver, Jamie Hamill, Colin Hamilton, Jason Holt, Chris Kane, Dylan McGowan, Denis Prychynenko, Mehdi Taouil
Forwards: Aryvdas Novikovas, Scott Robinson, David Smith, Gordon Smith, John Sutton, David Templeton

HIBERNIAN

Ground: Easter Road Stadium, Albion Place, Edinburgh EH7 5QG. **Capacity:** 20,250.
Telephone: 031 661 2159. **Manager:** Pat Fenlon. **Colours:** Green and white. **Nickname:** Hibees
Goalkeepers: Calum Antell, Paul Grant, Ben Williams
Defenders: Callum Booth, Tim Clancy, Paul Hanlon, James McPake, Sean O'Hanlon, Pa Saikou Kujabi, Scott Smith, David Stephens
Midfielders: Paul Cairney, Jorge Claros, Danny Galbraith, Sam Stanton, Lewis Stevenson, David Wotherspoon
Forwards: Ross Caldwell, Eoin Doyle, Leigh Griffiths

INVERNESS CALEDONIAN THISTLE

Ground: Caledonian Stadium, Stadium Road, Inverness IV1 1FF. **Capacity:** 7,750. **Telephone:** 01463 222880. **Manager:** Terry Butcher. **Colours:** Blue and red. **Nickname:** Caley Thistle
Goalkeepers: Ryan Esson, Antonio Reguero
Defenders: Chris Hogg, Josh Meekings, David Raven, Graeme Shinnie, Gary Warren
Midfielders: Aaron Doran, Ross Draper, Martin Laing, Gavin Morrison, Conor Pepper, Liam Polworth, Nick Ross, Andrew Shinnie, Owain Tudur Jones
Forwards: Richie Foran, Billy McKay, Jason Oswell, Shane Sutherland

KILMARNOCK

Ground: Rugby Park, Kilmarnock KA 1 2DP. **Capacity:** 18,128. **Telephone:** 01563 545300.
Manager: Kenny Shiels. **Colours:** White and blue. **Nickname:** Killie
Goalkeepers: Cameron Bell, Anssi Jaakkola, Kyle Letheren
Defenders: Lee Ashcroft, Ross Barbour, Billy Berntsson, Ross Fisher, James Fowler, Garry Hay, Rory McKeown, Michael Nelson, Ryan O'Leary, Alex Pursehouse, Mohamadou Sissoko, Jeroen Tesselaar
Midfielders: Ross Davidson, James Dayton, Gary Harkins, Lee Johnson, Liam Kelly, Matthew Kennedy, Leon Panikar, Danny Racchi, Manuel Pascali, Dean Shiels, Jude Winchester
Forwards: Rory Boulding, Jorge Galan, William Gros, Paul, Heffernan, Chris Johnston

MOTHERWELL

Ground: Fir Park, Firpark Street, Motherwell ML1 2QN. **Capacity:** 13,677. **Telephone:** 01698 333333. **Manager:** Stuart McCall. **Colours:** Clarent and amber. **Nickname:** Well
Goalkeepers: Lee Hollis, Darren Randolph
Defenders: Steven Hammell, Tom Hateley, Shaun Hutchinson, Jonathan Page, Simon Ramsden, Steven Saunders
Midfielders: Stuart Carswell, Omar Daley, Chris Humphrey, Keith Lasley, Nicky Law
Forwards: Michael Higdon, Robert McHugh, Jamie Murphy, Henrik Ojamaa

ROSS COUNTY

Ground: Victoria Park Stadium, Jubilee Road, Dingwall IV15 9QZ. **Capacity:** 6,000
Telephone: 01349 860860. **Manager:** Derek Adams. **Colours:** Blue and white. **Nickname:** Staggies
Goalkeepers: Michael Fraser, Joe Malin
Defenders: Jon Bateson, Scott Boyd, Marc Fitzpatrick, Mihael Kovacevic, Grant Munro, Ross Tokely

Midfielders: Richard Brittain, Alex Cooper, Mark Corcoran, Russell Duncan, Marc Fitzpatrick, Stuart Kettlewell, Paul Lawson, Rocco Quinn, Martin Scott, Iain Vigurs
Forwards: Steven Craig, Kurtis Byrne, Gary Glen, Colin McMenamin, Sam Morrow

ST JOHNSTONE

Ground: McDiarmid Park, Crieff Road, Perth PH1 2SJ. **Capacity**: 10,673. **Telephone**: 01738 459090. **Manager**: Steve Lomas. **Colours**: Blue and white. **Nickname**: Saints
Goalkeepers: Zander Clark, Alan Mannus, Jonathan Tuffey
Defenders: Steven Anderson, Callum Davidson, David Mackay, David McCracken, Gary Miller, Tam Scobbie, Frazer Wright
Midfielders: Jamie Adams, Liam Caddis, Liam Craig, Patrick Cregg, Murray Davidson, Chris Millar, Kevin Moon, David Robertson
Forwards: Nigel Hasselbaink, Sean Higgins, Stevie May, Gregory Tade

ST MIRREN

Ground: St Mirren Park, Greenhill Road, Paisley PA3, 1RU. **Capacity**: 8,029. **Telephone**: 0141 889 2558. **Manager**: Danny Lennon. **Colours**: Black and white. **Nickname**: Buddies
Goalkeepers: Craig Samson
Defenders: David Barron, Sean Kelly, Lee Mair, Mark McAusland, Darren McGregor, Jason Naismith, David van Zanten
Midfielders: Graham Carey, Jim Goodwin, Mark Lamont, Paul McGowan, Jamie McKernon, Kenny McLean, Jon Robertson, Gary Teale
Forwards: Lewis Guy, Dougie Imre, Sam Parkin, Thomas Reilly, Jon Scullion, Steven Thompson

ENGLISH FIXTURES 2012–2013

Friday, 17 August
npower Championship
Cardiff v Huddersfield

Saturday, 18 August
Barclays Premier League
Arsenal v Sunderland
Fulham v Norwich
Newcastle v Tottenham
QPR v Swansea
Reading v Stoke
WBA v Liverpool
West Ham v Aston Villa

npower Championship
Barnsley v Middlesbrough
Birmingham v Charlton
Burnley v Bolton
Crystal Palace v Watford
Derby v Sheffield Wed
Hull v Brighton
Ipswich v Blackburn
Leeds v Wolves
Leicester v Peterborough
Millwall v Blackpool
Nottm Forest v Bristol City

npower League 1
Bury v Brentford
Crawley v Scunthorpe
Crewe v Notts Co
Hartlepool v Swindon
MK Dons v Oldham
Portsmouth v Bournemouth
Preston v Colchester
Sheffield Utd v Shrewsbury
Stevenage v Carlisle
Tranmere v Leyton Orient
Walsall v Doncaster
Yeovil v Coventry

npower League 2
AFC Wimbledon v Chesterfield
Bristol Rov v Oxford
Cheltenham v Dag & Red
Exeter v Morecambe
Fleetwood v Torquay
Gillingham v Bradford
Plymouth v Aldershot
Port Vale v Barnet
Rochdale v Northampton
Rotherham v Burton
Southend v Accrington
York v Wycombe

Sunday, 19 August
Barclays Premier League
Manchester City v Southampton
Wigan v Chelsea

Monday, 20 August
Barclays Premier League
Everton v Manchester Utd

Tuesday, 21 August
npower Championship
Blackpool v Leeds
Bolton v Derby
Brighton v Cardiff
Bristol City v Crystal Palace
Charlton v Leicester
Huddersfield v Nottm Forest
Middlesbrough v Burnley
Peterborough v Millwall
Sheffield Wed v Birmingham
Watford v Ipswich
Wolves v Barnsley

npower League 1
Bournemouth v MK Dons
Brentford v Yeovil
Carlisle v Tranmere
Colchester v Portsmouth
Coventry v Sheffield Utd
Doncaster v Bury
Leyton Orient v Stevenage
Notts Co v Hartlepool
Oldham v Walsall
Scunthorpe v Crewe
Shrewsbury v Preston
Swindon v Crawley

npower League 2
Accrington v Port Vale
Aldershot v Exeter
Barnet v Bristol Rov
Bradford v Fleetwood
Burton v AFC Wimbledon
Chesterfield v Rochdale
Dag & Red v Plymouth
Morecambe v York
Northampton v Rotherham
Oxford v Southend
Torquay v Cheltenham
Wycombe v Gillingham

Wednesday, 22 August
npower Championship
Blackburn v Hull

Friday, 24 August
npower Championship
Bolton v Nottm Forest

Saturday, 25 August
Barclays Premier League
Aston Villa v Everton
Chelsea v Newcastle
Man Utd v Fulham
Norwich v QPR
Southampton v Wigan
Sunderland v Reading
Swansea v West Ham
Tottenham v WBA

npower Championship
Blackburn v Leicester
Blackpool v Ipswich
Brighton v Barnsley
Bristol City v Cardiff
Charlton v Hull
Huddersfield v Burnley
Middlesbrough v Crystal Palace
Peterborough v Leeds
Sheffield Wed v Millwall
Watford v Birmingham
Wolves v Derby

npower League 1
Bournemouth v Preston
Brentford v Crewe
Carlisle v Portsmouth
Colchester v Sheffield Utd
Coventry v Bury
Doncaster v Crawley
Leyton Orient v Hartlepool
Notts Co v Walsall
Oldham v Stevenage
Scunthorpe v Yeovil
Shrewsbury v Tranmere
Swindon v MK Dons

npower League 2
Accrington v Exeter
Aldershot v Cheltenham
Barnet v York
Bradford v AFC Wimbledon
Burton v Fleetwood
Chesterfield v Rotherham
Dag & Red v Gillingham
Morecambe v Port Vale
Northampton v Southend
Oxford v Plymouth
Torquay v Rochdale
Wycombe v Bristol Rov

Sunday, 26 August
Barclays Premier League
Liverpool v Manchester City
Stoke v Arsenal

Saturday, 1 September
Barclays Premier League
Chelsea v Reading
Man City v QPR
Swansea v Sunderland
Tottenham v Norwich
WBA v Everton
West Ham v Fulham
Wigan v Stoke

npower Championship
Barnsley v Bristol City
Birmingham v Peterborough
Burnley v Brighton
Crystal Palace v Sheffield Wed
Derby v Watford
Hull v Bolton
Ipswich v Huddersfield
Leeds v Blackburn
Leicester v Blackpool
Millwall v Middlesbrough
Nottm Forest v Charlton

npower League 1
Bury v Notts Co
Crawley v Leyton Orient
Crewe v Coventry
Hartlepool v Scunthorpe
MK Dons v Carlisle
Portsmouth v Oldham
Sheffield Utd v Bournemouth
Stevenage v Shrewsbury
Tranmere v Colchester
Walsall v Brentford
Yeovil v Doncaster

npower League 2
AFC Wimbledon v Dag & Red
Bristol Rov v Morecambe
Cheltenham v Accrington
Exeter v Burton
Fleetwood v Aldershot
Gillingham v Chesterfield
Plymouth v Northampton
Port Vale v Torquay
Rochdale v Barnet
Rotherham v Bradford
Southend v Wycombe
York v Oxford

Sunday, 2 September
Barclays Premier League
Liverpool v Arsenal;
Newcastle v Aston Villa
Southampton v Manchester Utd

npower Championship
Cardiff v Wolves

npower League 1
Preston v Swindon

Saturday, 8 September
npower League 1
Brentford v Colchester
Bury v Preston
Crewe v Tranmere
Doncaster v Oldham
Hartlepool v Carlisle
Notts Co v Shrewsbury
Scunthorpe v Sheffield Utd
Swindon v Leyton Orient
Walsall v MK Dons
Yeovil v Bournemouth

npower League 2
Accrington v Bradford
Barnet v Gillingham
Bristol Rov v Aldershot
Morecambe v Fleetwood
Northampton v AFC Wimbledon
Oxford v Exeter
Port Vale v Rotherham
Rochdale v Burton
Southend v Dag & Red
Torquay v Plymouth
Wycombe v Cheltenham
York v Chesterfield

Sunday, 9 September
npower League 1
Coventry v Stevenage
Crawley v Portsmouth

Thursday, 13 September
npower League 1
Leyton Orient v Brentford

Friday, 14 September
npower Championship
Brighton v Sheffield Wed
Charlton v Crystal Palace

Saturday, 15 September
Barclays Premier League
Arsenal v Southampton
Aston Villa v Swansea
Fulham v WBA
Man Utd v Wigan
Norwich v West Ham
QPR v Chelsea
Stoke v Man City
Sunderland v Liverpool

npower Championship
Barnsley v Blackpool
Bolton v Watford
Bristol City v Blackburn

Burnley v Peterborough
Cardiff v Leeds
Huddersfield v Derby
Hull v Millwall
Middlesbrough v Ipswich
Nottm Forest v Birmingham
Wolves v Leicester

npower League 1
Bournemouth v Hartlepool
Carlisle v Swindon
Colchester v Doncaster
MK Dons v Yeovil
Oldham v Notts Co
Portsmouth v Walsall
Preston v Crawley
Sheffield Utd v Bury
Shrewsbury v Scunthorpe
Stevenage v Crewe
Tranmere v Coventry

npower League 2
AFC Wimbledon v Rochdale
Aldershot v Morecambe
Bradford v Barnet
Burton v Oxford
Cheltenham v Southend
Chesterfield v Wycombe
Dag & Red v Accrington
Exeter v York
Fleetwood v Northampton
Gillingham v Bristol Rov
Plymouth v Port Vale
Rotherham v Torquay

Sunday, 16 September
Barclays Premier League
Reading v Tottenham

Monday, 17 September
Barclays Premier League
Everton v Newcastle

Tuesday, 18 September
npower Championship
Birmingham v Bolton
Blackpool v Middlesbrough
Crystal Palace v Nottm Forest
Derby v Charlton
Ipswich v Wolves
Leeds v Hull
Leicester v Burnley
Millwall v Cardiff
Peterborough v Bristol City
Watford v Brighton

npower League 1
Bournemouth v Brentford
Carlisle v Crewe

Colchester v Crawley
Leyton Orient v Yeovil
MK Dons v Notts Co
Oldham v Scunthorpe
Portsmouth v Swindon
Preston v Hartlepool
Sheffield Utd v Doncaster
Shrewsbury v Coventry
Stevenage v Walsall
Tranmere v Bury

npower League 2
AFC Wimbledon v Torquay
Aldershot v Barnet
Bradford v Morecambe
Cheltenham v Oxford
Chesterfield v Accrington
Dag & Red v Northampton
Exeter v Wycombe
Fleetwood v Port Vale
Gillingham v Southend
Plymouth v Bristol Rov
Rotherham v Rochdale

Wednesday, 19 September
npower Championship
Blackburn v Barnsley
Sheffield Wed v Huddersfield

npower League 2
Burton v York

Friday, 21 September
npower Championship
Blackburn v Middlesbrough

Saturday, 22 September
Barclays Premier League
Chelsea v Stoke
Newcastle v Norwich
Southampton v Aston Villa
Swansea v Everton
WBA v Reading
West Ham v Sunderland
Wigan v Fulham

npower Championship
Birmingham v Barnsley
Blackpool v Huddersfield
Crystal Palace v Cardiff
Derby v Burnley
Ipswich v Charlton
Leeds v Nottm Forest
Leicester v Hull
Millwall v Brighton
Peterborough v Wolves
Sheffield Wed v Bolton
Watford v Bristol City

npower League 1
Brentford v Oldham
Bury v MK Dons
Coventry v Carlisle
Crawley v Tranmere
Crewe v Leyton Orient
Doncaster v Stevenage
Hartlepool v Shrewsbury
Notts Co v Portsmouth
Scunthorpe v Colchester
Swindon v Bournemouth
Walsall v Preston
Yeovil v Sheffield Utd

npower League 2
Accrington v Aldershot
Barnet v Rotherham
Bristol Rov v Fleetwood
Morecambe v Plymouth
Northampton v Chesterfield
Oxford v Bradford
Port Vale v Gillingham
Rochdale v Dag & Red
Southend v Exeter
Torquay v Burton
Wycombe v AFC Wimbledon
York v Cheltenham

Sunday, 23 September
Barclays Premier League
Liverpool v Manchester Utd
Manchester City v Arsenal
Tottenham v QPR

Friday, 28 September
npower League 2
Cheltenham v Morecambe

Saturday, 29 September
Barclays Premier League
Arsenal v Chelsea
Everton v Southampton
Fulham v Man City
Man Utd v Tottenham
Norwich v Liverpool
Reading v Newcastle
Stoke v Swansea
Sunderland v Wigan

npower Championship
Barnsley v Ipswich
Bolton v Crystal Palace
Brighton v Birmingham
Bristol City v Leeds
Burnley v Millwall
Cardiff v Blackpool
Charlton v Blackburn
Huddersfield v Watford
Hull v Peterborough

Middlesbrough v Leicester
Wolves v Sheffield Wed

npower League 1
Bournemouth v Walsall
Carlisle v Crawley
Colchester v Hartlepool
Leyton Orient v Doncaster
MK Dons v Crewe
Oldham v Coventry
Portsmouth v Scunthorpe
Preston v Yeovil
Sheffield Utd v Notts Co
Shrewsbury v Swindon
Stevenage v Bury
Tranmere v Brentford

npower League 2
AFC Wimbledon v Accrington
Aldershot v York
Bradford v Port Vale
Burton v Northampton
Chesterfield v Torquay
Dag & Red v Wycombe
Exeter v Bristol Rov
Fleetwood v Barnet
Gillingham v Rochdale
Plymouth v Southend
Rotherham v Oxford

Sunday, 30 September
Barclays Premier League
Aston Villa v WBA

npower Championship
Nottm Forest v Derby

Monday, 1 October
Barclays Premier League
QPR v West Ham

Tuesday, 2 October
npower Championship
Barnsley v Peterborough
Bolton v Leeds
Brighton v Ipswich
Bristol City v Millwall
Burnley v Sheffield Wed
Cardiff v Birmingham
Charlton v Watford
Huddersfield v Leicester
Hull v Blackpool
Wolves v Crystal Palace

npower League 1
Brentford v Shrewsbury
Bury v Carlisle
Coventry v MK Dons
Crawley v Bournemouth

Crewe v Oldham
Doncaster v Preston
Hartlepool v Sheffield Utd
Notts Co v Stevenage
Scunthorpe v Tranmere
Swindon v Colchester
Walsall v Leyton Orient
Yeovil v Portsmouth

npower League 2
Accrington v Rotherham
Barnet v Exeter
Morecambe v Chesterfield
Northampton v Gillingham
Oxford v AFC Wimbledon
Port Vale v Dag & Red
Rochdale v Bradford
Southend v Burton
Torquay v Aldershot
Wycombe v Plymouth
York v Fleetwood

Wednesday, 3 October
npower Championship
Middlesbrough v Derby
Nottm Forest v Blackburn

npower League 2
Bristol Rov v Cheltenham

Saturday, 6 October
Barclays Premier League
Chelsea v Norwich
Liverpool v Stoke
Man City v Sunderland
Swansea v Reading
WBA v QPR
West Ham v Arsenal
Wigan v Everton

npower Championship
Birmingham v Huddersfield
Blackburn v Wolves
Blackpool v Charlton
Crystal Palace v Burnley
Derby v Brighton
Ipswich v Cardiff
Leeds v Barnsley
Leicester v Bristol City
Millwall v Bolton
Peterborough v Nottm Forest
Sheffield Wed v Hull
Watford v Middlesbrough

npower League 1
Brentford v Crawley
Bury v Swindon
Coventry v Bournemouth
Crewe v Hartlepool
Doncaster v Shrewsbury

Leyton Orient v Sheffield Utd
MK Dons v Portsmouth
Notts Co v Tranmere
Oldham v Preston
Stevenage v Scunthorpe
Walsall v Carlisle
Yeovil v Colchester

npower League 2
Accrington v Rochdale
Aldershot v Chesterfield
Bristol Rov v Northampton
Cheltenham v Fleetwood
Dag & Red v Bradford
Exeter v Port Vale
Morecambe v Burton
Oxford v Gillingham
Plymouth v AFC Wimbledon
Southend v Barnet
Wycombe v Torquay
York v Rotherham

Sunday, 7 October
Barclays Premier League
Newcastle v Manchester Utd
Southampton v Fulham
Tottenham v Aston Villa

Saturday, 13 October
npower League 1
Bournemouth v Leyton Orient
Carlisle v Notts Co
Colchester v Stevenage
Crawley v Bury
Hartlepool v Doncaster
Portsmouth v Crewe
Scunthorpe v Brentford
Sheffield Utd v Oldham
Swindon v Coventry
Tranmere v Yeovil

npower League 2
AFC Wimbledon v Cheltenham
Barnet v Plymouth
Bradford v York
Burton v Bristol Rov
Chesterfield v Dag & Red
Fleetwood v Wycombe
Gillingham v Aldershot
Northampton v Exeter
Rochdale v Morecambe
Rotherham v Southend
Torquay v Accrington

Sunday, 14 October
npower League 1
Preston v MK Dons
Shrewsbury v Walsall

Monday, 15 October
npower League 2
Port Vale v Oxford

Friday, 19 October
npower Championship
Sheffield Wed v Leeds

npower League 2
Barnet v Northampton

Saturday, 20 October
Barclays Premier League
Fulham v Aston Villa
Liverpool v Reading
Man Utd v Stoke
Norwich v Arsenal
Swansea v Wigan
Tottenham v Chelsea
WBA v Man City
West Ham v Southampton

npower Championship
Birmingham v Leicester
Bolton v Bristol City
Brighton v Middlesbrough
Burnley v Blackpool
Charlton v Barnsley
Crystal Palace v Millwall
Derby v Blackburn
Huddersfield v Wolves
Hull v Ipswich
Nottm Forest v Cardiff
Watford v Peterborough

npower League 1
Bournemouth v Tranmere
Colchester v Carlisle
Coventry v Notts Co
Doncaster v Brentford
Hartlepool v Crawley
MK Dons v Stevenage
Oldham v Leyton Orient
Portsmouth v Shrewsbury
Preston v Sheffield Utd
Swindon v Scunthorpe
Walsall v Crewe
Yeovil v Bury

npower League 2
Aldershot v Rotherham
Bradford v Cheltenham
Bristol Rov v Torquay
Exeter v Chesterfield
Fleetwood v AFC Wimbledon
Gillingham v Burton
Morecambe v Southend
Oxford v Accrington
Plymouth v Rochdale

Port Vale v Wycombe
York v Dag & Red

Sunday, 21 October
Barclays Premier League
QPR v Everton
Sunderland v Newcastle

Tuesday, 23 October
npower Championship
Barnsley v Crystal Palace
Blackpool v Nottm Forest
Bristol City v Burnley
Cardiff v Watford
Ipswich v Derby
Leeds v Charlton
Leicester v Brighton
Middlesbrough v Hull
Millwall v Birmingham
Peterborough v Huddersfield
Wolves v Bolton

npower League 1
Brentford v Coventry
Bury v Hartlepool
Carlisle v Oldham
Crawley v MK Dons
Crewe v Swindon
Leyton Orient v Colchester
Notts Co v Bournemouth
Scunthorpe v Preston
Sheffield Utd v Walsall
Shrewsbury v Yeovil
Stevenage v Portsmouth
Tranmere v Doncaster

npower League 2
AFC Wimbledon v Bristol Rov
Accrington v York
Burton v Port Vale
Cheltenham v Plymouth
Chesterfield v Fleetwood
Dag & Red v Exeter
Northampton v Bradford
Rochdale v Oxford
Rotherham v Morecambe
Southend v Aldershot
Torquay v Gillingham
Wycombe v Barnet

Wednesday, 24 October
npower Championship
Blackburn v Sheffield Wed

Saturday, 27 October
Barclays Premier League
Arsenal v QPR
Everton v Liverpool
Man City v Swansea

Newcastle v WBA
Reading v Fulham
Stoke v Sunderland
Wigan v West Ham

npower Championship
Barnsley v Nottm Forest
Blackburn v Watford
Blackpool v Brighton
Bristol City v Hull
Cardiff v Burnley
Ipswich v Sheffield Wed
Leeds v Birmingham
Leicester v Crystal Palace
Middlesbrough v Bolton
Millwall v Huddersfield
Peterborough v Derby
Wolves v Charlton

npower League 1
Brentford v Hartlepool
Bury v Walsall
Carlisle v Bournemouth
Crawley v Oldham
Crewe v Yeovil
Leyton Orient v Coventry
Notts Co v Doncaster
Scunthorpe v MK Dons
Sheffield Utd v Portsmouth
Shrewsbury v Colchester
Stevenage v Swindon
Tranmere v Preston

npower League 2
AFC Wimbledon v Gillingham
Accrington v Bristol Rov
Burton v Bradford
Cheltenham v Exeter
Chesterfield v Barnet
Dag & Red v Aldershot
Northampton v Port Vale
Rochdale v Fleetwood
Rotherham v Plymouth
Southend v York
Torquay v Morecambe
Wycombe v Oxford

Sunday, 28 October
Barclays Premier League
Aston Villa v Norwich
Chelsea v Manchester Utd
Southampton v Tottenham

Saturday, 3 November
Barclays Premier League
Fulham v Everton
Man Utd v Arsenal
Norwich v Stoke
Sunderland v Aston Villa
Swansea v Chelsea

Tottenham v Wigan
West Ham v Man City

npower Championship
Birmingham v Ipswich
Bolton v Cardiff
Brighton v Leeds
Burnley v Wolves
Charlton v Middlesbrough
Crystal Palace v Blackburn
Derby v Blackpool
Huddersfield v Bristol City
Hull v Barnsley
Nottm Forest v Millwall
Sheffield Wed v Peterborough
Watford v Leicester

Sunday, 4 November
Barclays Premier League
Liverpool v Newcastle
QPR v Reading

Monday, 5 November
Barclays Premier League
WBA v Southampton

Tuesday, 6 November
npower Championship
Birmingham v Bristol City
Bolton v Leicester
Brighton v Peterborough
Burnley v Leeds
Charlton v Cardiff
Crystal Palace v Ipswich
Derby v Barnsley
Huddersfield v Blackburn
Hull v Wolves
Nottm Forest v Middlesbrough
Sheffield Wed v Blackpool
Watford v Millwall

npower League 1
Bournemouth v Shrewsbury
Colchester v Notts Co
Coventry v Crawley
Doncaster v Crewe
Hartlepool v Tranmere
MK Dons v Leyton Orient
Oldham v Bury
Portsmouth v Brentford
Preston v Carlisle
Swindon v Sheffield Utd
Walsall v Scunthorpe
Yeovil v Stevenage

npower League 2
Aldershot v Wycombe
Barnet v Torquay

Bradford v Chesterfield
Bristol Rov v Southend
Exeter v AFC Wimbledon
Fleetwood v Rotherham
Gillingham v Cheltenham
Morecambe v Accrington
Oxford v Dag & Red
Plymouth v Burton
Port Vale v Rochdale
York v Northampton

Saturday, 10 November
Barclays Premier League
Arsenal v Fulham
Aston Villa v Man Utd
Everton v Sunderland
Newcastle v West Ham
Reading v Norwich
Southampton v Swansea
Stoke v QPR
Wigan v WBA

npower Championship
Barnsley v Huddersfield
Blackburn v Birmingham
Blackpool v Bolton
Cardiff v Hull
Ipswich v Burnley
Leeds v Watford
Leicester v Nottm Forest
Middlesbrough v Sheffield Wed
Millwall v Derby
Peterborough v Crystal Palace
Wolves v Brighton

npower League 1
Brentford v Carlisle
Bury v Portsmouth
Coventry v Scunthorpe
Crewe v Colchester
Doncaster v Bournemouth
Leyton Orient v Shrewsbury
MK Dons v Sheffield Utd
Notts Co v Crawley
Oldham v Tranmere
Stevenage v Preston
Walsall v Swindon
Yeovil v Hartlepool

npower League 2
Accrington v Northampton
Aldershot v Bradford
Bristol Rov v Chesterfield
Cheltenham v Burton
Dag & Red v Rotherham
Exeter v Fleetwood
Morecambe v Barnet
Oxford v Torquay
Plymouth v Gillingham
Southend v Port Vale

Wycombe v Rochdale
York v AFC Wimbledon

Sunday, 11 November
Barclays Premier League
Chelsea v Liverpool
Manchester City v Tottenham

npower Championship
Bristol City v Charlton

Friday, 16 November
npower League 2
Barnet v Accrington

Saturday, 17 November
Barclays Premier League
Arsenal v Tottenham
Liverpool v Wigan
Man City v Aston Villa
Newcastle v Swansea
Norwich v Man Utd
QPR v Southampton
Reading v Everton
WBA v Chelsea

npower Championship
Birmingham v Hull
Bolton v Barnsley
Bristol City v Blackpool
Burnley v Charlton
Cardiff v Middlesbrough
Crystal Palace v Derby
Huddersfield v Brighton
Leicester v Ipswich
Nottm Forest v Sheffield Wed
Peterborough v Blackburn
Watford v Wolves

npower League 1
Bournemouth v Oldham
Carlisle v Leyton Orient
Colchester v Bury
Crawley v Walsall
Hartlepool v Coventry
Portsmouth v Doncaster
Preston v Brentford
Scunthorpe v Notts Co
Sheffield Utd v Stevenage
Shrewsbury v Crewe
Swindon v Yeovil
Tranmere v MK Dons

npower League 2
AFC Wimbledon v Aldershot
Bradford v Exeter
Burton v Dag & Red
Chesterfield v Oxford

Fleetwood v Plymouth
Gillingham v Morecambe
Northampton v Wycombe
Port Vale v York
Rochdale v Bristol Rov
Rotherham v Cheltenham
Torquay v Southend

Sunday, 18 November
Barclays Premier League
Fulham v Sunderland

npower Championship
Millwall v Leeds

Monday, 19 November
Barclays Premier League
West Ham v Stoke

Tuesday, 20 November
npower League 1
Bournemouth v Stevenage
Carlisle v Doncaster
Colchester v Coventry
Crawley v Yeovil
Hartlepool v Oldham
Portsmouth v Leyton Orient
Preston v Notts Co
Scunthorpe v Bury
Sheffield Utd v Crewe
Shrewsbury v MK Dons
Swindon v Brentford
Tranmere v Walsall

npower League 2
AFC Wimbledon v Southend
Barnet v Oxford
Bradford v Plymouth
Burton v Aldershot
Chesterfield v Cheltenham
Fleetwood v Accrington
Gillingham v Exeter
Northampton v Morecambe
Port Vale v Bristol Rov
Rochdale v York
Rotherham v Wycombe
Torquay v Dag & Red

Saturday, 24 November
Barclays Premier League
Aston Villa v Arsenal
Everton v Norwich
Man Utd v QPR
Southampton v Newcastle
Stoke v Fulham
Swansea v Liverpool
Wigan v Reading

npower Championship

Barnsley v Cardiff
Blackburn v Millwall
Blackpool v Watford
Brighton v Bolton
Charlton v Huddersfield
Derby v Birmingham
Hull v Burnley
Ipswich v Peterborough
Leeds v Crystal Palace
Middlesbrough v Bristol City
Sheffield Wed v Leicester
Wolves v Nottm Forest

npower League 1

Brentford v Sheffield Utd
Bury v Bournemouth
Coventry v Portsmouth
Crewe v Crawley
Doncaster v Scunthorpe
Leyton Orient v Preston
MK Dons v Colchester
Notts Co v Swindon
Oldham v Shrewsbury
Stevenage v Tranmere
Walsall v Hartlepool
Yeovil v Carlisle

npower League 2

Accrington v Gillingham
Aldershot v Port Vale
Bristol Rov v Bradford
Cheltenham v Barnet
Dag & Red v Fleetwood
Exeter v Rotherham
Morecambe v AFC Wimbledon
Oxford v Northampton
Plymouth v Chesterfield
Southend v Rochdale
Wycombe v Burton
York v Torquay

Sunday, 25 November
Barclays Premier League
Chelsea v Manchester City
Sunderland v WBA
Tottenham v West Ham

Tuesday, 27 November
Barclays Premier League
Aston Villa v Reading
Southampton v Norwich
Stoke v Newcastle
Sunderland v QPR
Swansea v WBA

npower Championship
Barnsley v Burnley
Blackpool v Birmingham
Brighton v Bristol City

Charlton v Peterborough
Derby v Cardiff
Hull v Crystal Palace
Ipswich v Nottm Forest
Leeds v Leicester
Middlesbrough v Huddersfield
Sheffield Wed v Watford
Wolves v Millwall

Wednesday, 28 November
Barclays Premier League
Chelsea v Fulham
Everton v Arsenal
Manchester Utd v West Ham
Tottenham v Liverpool
Wigan v Manchester City

npower Championship
Blackburn v Bolton

Saturday, 1 December
Barclays Premier League
Arsenal v Swansea
Fulham v Tottenham
Liverpool v Southampton
Man City v Everton
Newcastle v Wigan
Norwich v Sunderland
QPR v Aston Villa
Reading v Man Utd
WBA v Stoke
West Ham v Chelsea

npower Championship
Birmingham v Middlesbrough
Bolton v Ipswich
Bristol City v Wolves
Burnley v Blackburn
Crystal Palace v Brighton
Huddersfield v Leeds
Leicester v Derby
Millwall v Charlton
Nottm Forest v Hull
Peterborough v Blackpool
Watford v Barnsley

Sunday, 2 December
npower Championship
Cardiff v Sheffield Wed

Saturday, 8 December
Barclays Premier League
Arsenal v WBA
Aston Villa v Stoke
Fulham v Newcastle
Man City v Man Utd
Southampton v Reading
Sunderland v Chelsea

Swansea v Norwich
West Ham v Liverpool
Wigan v QPR

npower Championship
Blackburn v Cardiff
Charlton v Brighton
Crystal Palace v Blackpool
Derby v Leeds
Huddersfield v Bolton
Ipswich v Millwall
Leicester v Barnsley
Nottm Forest v Burnley
Peterborough v Middlesbrough
Sheffield Wed v Bristol City
Watford v Hull
Wolves v Birmingham

npower League 1
Brentford v MK Dons
Bury v Leyton Orient
Carlisle v Sheffield Utd
Colchester v Oldham
Coventry v Walsall
Crawley v Shrewsbury
Hartlepool v Stevenage
Preston v Crewe
Scunthorpe v Bournemouth
Swindon v Doncaster
Tranmere v Portsmouth
Yeovil v Notts Co

npower League 2
Barnet v AFC Wimbledon
Bradford v Torquay
Bristol Rov v Dag & Red
Fleetwood v Southend
Northampton v Cheltenham
Oxford v Aldershot
Plymouth v York
Port Vale v Chesterfield
Rochdale v Exeter
Rotherham v Gillingham
Wycombe v Morecambe

Sunday, 9 December
Barclays Premier League
Everton v Tottenham

npower League 2
Burton v Accrington

Saturday, 15 December
Barclays Premier League
Chelsea v Southampton
Liverpool v Aston Villa
Man Utd v Sunderland
Newcastle v Man City
Norwich v Wigan
QPR v Fulham

Reading v Arsenal
Stoke v Everton
Tottenham v Swansea
WBA v West Ham

npower Championship
Barnsley v Sheffield Wed
Birmingham v Crystal Palace
Blackpool v Blackburn
Bolton v Charlton
Brighton v Nottm Forest
Bristol City v Derby
Burnley v Watford
Cardiff v Peterborough
Hull v Huddersfield
Leeds v Ipswich
Middlesbrough v Wolves
Millwall v Leicester

npower League 1
Bournemouth v Colchester
Crewe v Bury
Doncaster v Coventry
Leyton Orient v Scunthorpe
MK Dons v Hartlepool
Notts Co v Brentford
Oldham v Swindon
Portsmouth v Preston
Sheffield Utd v Tranmere
Shrewsbury v Carlisle
Stevenage v Crawley
Walsall v Yeovil

npower League 2
AFC Wimbledon v Rotherham
Accrington v Wycombe
Aldershot v Rochdale
Cheltenham v Port Vale
Chesterfield v Burton
Dag & Red v Barnet
Exeter v Plymouth
Gillingham v Fleetwood
Morecambe v Oxford
Southend v Bradford
Torquay v Northampton
York v Bristol Rov

Friday, 21 December
npower Championship
Derby v Hull

npower League 1
Bury v Shrewsbury

npower League 2
Barnet v Burton
Rochdale v Cheltenham
Southend v Chesterfield

Saturday, 22 December
Barclays Premier League
Chelsea v Aston Villa
Liverpool v Fulham
Man City v Reading
Newcastle v QPR
Southampton v Sunderland
Swansea v Man Utd
Tottenham v Stoke
WBA v Norwich
West Ham v Everton
Wigan v Arsenal

npower Championship
Birmingham v Burnley
Blackburn v Brighton
Blackpool v Wolves
Crystal Palace v Huddersfield
Ipswich v Bristol City
Leeds v Middlesbrough
Leicester v Cardiff
Millwall v Barnsley
Peterborough v Bolton
Sheffield Wed v Charlton
Watford v Nottm Forest

npower League 1
Brentford v Stevenage
Coventry v Preston
Crawley v Sheffield Utd
Crewe v Bournemouth
Doncaster v MK Dons
Hartlepool v Portsmouth
Notts Co v Leyton Orient
Scunthorpe v Carlisle
Swindon v Tranmere
Walsall v Colchester
Yeovil v Oldham

npower League 2
Accrington v Plymouth
Bristol Rov v Rotherham
Morecambe v Dag & Red
Northampton v Aldershot
Oxford v Fleetwood
Port Vale v AFC Wimbledon
Torquay v Exeter
Wycombe v Bradford
York v Gillingham

Wednesday, 26 December
Barclays Premier League
Arsenal v West Ham
Aston Villa v Tottenham
Everton v Wigan
Fulham v Southampton
Man Utd v Newcastle
Norwich v Chelsea
QPR v WBA
Reading v Swansea

Stoke v Liverpool
Sunderland v Man City

npower Championship
Barnsley v Birmingham
Bolton v Sheffield Wed
Brighton v Millwall
Bristol City v Watford
Burnley v Derby
Cardiff v Crystal Palace
Charlton v Ipswich
Huddersfield v Blackpool
Hull v Leicester
Middlesbrough v Blackburn
Nottm Forest v Leeds
Wolves v Peterborough

npower League 1
Bournemouth v Yeovil
Carlisle v Hartlepool
Colchester v Brentford
Leyton Orient v Swindon
MK Dons v Walsall
Oldham v Doncaster
Portsmouth v Crawley
Preston v Bury
Sheffield Utd v Scunthorpe
Shrewsbury v Notts Co
Stevenage v Coventry
Tranmere v Crewe

npower League 2
AFC Wimbledon v Northampton
Aldershot v Bristol Rov
Bradford v Accrington
Burton v Rochdale
Cheltenham v Wycombe
Chesterfield v York
Dag & Red v Southend
Exeter v Oxford
Fleetwood v Morecambe
Gillingham v Barnet
Plymouth v Torquay
Rotherham v Port Vale

Saturday, 29 December
Barclays Premier League
Arsenal v Newcastle
Aston Villa v Wigan
Everton v Chelsea
Fulham v Swansea
Man Utd v WBA
Norwich v Man City
QPR v Liverpool
Reading v West Ham
Stoke v Southampton
Sunderland v Tottenham

npower Championship
Barnsley v Blackburn
Bolton v Birmingham

Brighton v Watford
Bristol City v Peterborough
Burnley v Leicester
Cardiff v Millwall
Charlton v Derby
Huddersfield v Sheffield Wed
Hull v Leeds
Middlesbrough v Blackpool
Nottm Forest v Crystal Palace
Wolves v Ipswich

npower League 1
Bournemouth v Crawley
Carlisle v Bury
Colchester v Swindon
Leyton Orient v Walsall
MK Dons v Coventry
Oldham v Crewe
Portsmouth v Yeovil
Preston v Doncaster
Sheffield Utd v Hartlepool
Shrewsbury v Brentford
Stevenage v Notts Co
Tranmere v Scunthorpe

npower League 2
AFC Wimbledon v Oxford
Aldershot v Torquay
Bradford v Rochdale
Burton v Southend
Cheltenham v Bristol Rov
Chesterfield v Morecambe
Dag & Red v Port Vale
Exeter v Barnet
Fleetwood v York
Gillingham v Northampton
Plymouth v Wycombe
Rotherham v Accrington

Tuesday, 1 January
Barclays Premier League
Chelsea v QPR
Liverpool v Sunderland
Man City v Stoke
Newcastle v Everton
Southampton v Arsenal
Swansea v Aston Villa
Tottenham v Reading
WBA v Fulham
West Ham v Norwich
Wigan v Man Utd

npower Championship
Birmingham v Cardiff
Blackburn v Nottm Forest
Blackpool v Hull
Crystal Palace v Wolves
Derby v Middlesbrough
Ipswich v Brighton
Leeds v Bolton

Leicester v Huddersfield
Millwall v Bristol City
Peterborough v Barnsley
Sheffield Wed v Burnley
Watford v Charlton

npower League 1
Brentford v Bournemouth
Bury v Tranmere
Coventry v Shrewsbury
Crawley v Colchester
Crewe v Carlisle
Doncaster v Sheffield Utd
Hartlepool v Preston
Notts Co v MK Dons
Scunthorpe v Oldham
Swindon v Portsmouth
Walsall v Stevenage
Yeovil v Leyton Orient

npower League 2
Accrington v Chesterfield
Barnet v Aldershot
Bristol Rov v Plymouth
Morecambe v Bradford
Northampton v Dag & Red
Oxford v Cheltenham
Port Vale v Fleetwood
Rochdale v Rotherham
Southend v Gillingham
Torquay v AFC Wimbledon
Wycombe v Exeter
York v Burton

Saturday, 5 January
npower League 1
Brentford v Leyton Orient
Bury v Sheffield Utd
Coventry v Tranmere
Crawley v Preston
Crewe v Stevenage
Doncaster v Colchester
Hartlepool v Bournemouth
Notts Co v Oldham
Scunthorpe v Shrewsbury
Swindon v Carlisle
Walsall v Portsmouth
Yeovil v MK Dons

npower League 2
Accrington v Dag & Red
Barnet v Bradford
Bristol Rov v Gillingham
Morecambe v Aldershot
Northampton v Fleetwood
Oxford v Burton
Port Vale v Plymouth
Rochdale v AFC Wimbledon
Southend v Cheltenham
Torquay v Rotherham

Wycombe v Chesterfield
York v Exeter

Saturday, 12 January
Barclays Premier League
Arsenal v Man City
Aston Villa v Southampton
Everton v Swansea
Fulham v Wigan
Man Utd v Liverpool
Norwich v Newcastle
QPR v Tottenham
Reading v WBA
Stoke v Chelsea
Sunderland v West Ham

npower Championship
Barnsley v Leeds
Bolton v Millwall
Brighton v Derby
Bristol City v Leicester
Burnley v Crystal Palace
Cardiff v Ipswich
Charlton v Blackpool
Huddersfield v Birmingham
Hull v Sheffield Wed
Middlesbrough v Watford
Nottm Forest v Peterborough
Wolves v Blackburn

npower League 1
Bournemouth v Swindon
Carlisle v Coventry
Colchester v Scunthorpe
Leyton Orient v Crewe
MK Dons v Bury
Oldham v Brentford
Portsmouth v Notts Co
Preston v Walsall
Sheffield Utd v Yeovil
Shrewsbury v Hartlepool
Stevenage v Doncaster
Tranmere v Crawley

npower League 2
AFC Wimbledon v Wycombe
Aldershot v Accrington
Bradford v Oxford
Burton v Torquay
Cheltenham v York
Chesterfield v Northampton
Dag & Red v Rochdale
Exeter v Southend
Fleetwood v Bristol Rov
Gillingham v Port Vale
Plymouth v Morecambe
Rotherham v Barnet

Friday, 18 January
npower League 2
Morecambe v Cheltenham

Saturday, 19 January
Barclays Premier League
Chelsea v Arsenal
Liverpool v Norwich
Man City v Fulham
Newcastle v Reading
Southampton v Everton
Swansea v Stoke
Tottenham v Man Utd
WBA v Aston Villa
West Ham v QPR
Wigan v Sunderland

npower Championship
Birmingham v Brighton
Blackburn v Charlton
Blackpool v Cardiff
Crystal Palace v Bolton
Derby v Nottm Forest
Ipswich v Barnsley
Leeds v Bristol City
Leicester v Middlesbrough
Millwall v Burnley
Peterborough v Hull
Sheffield Wed v Wolves
Watford v Huddersfield

npower League 1
Brentford v Tranmere
Bury v Stevenage
Coventry v Oldham
Crawley v Carlisle
Crewe v MK Dons
Doncaster v Leyton Orient
Hartlepool v Colchester
Notts Co v Sheffield Utd
Scunthorpe v Portsmouth
Swindon v Shrewsbury
Walsall v Bournemouth
Yeovil v Preston

npower League 2
Accrington v AFC Wimbledon
Barnet v Fleetwood
Bristol Rov v Exeter
Northampton v Burton
Oxford v Rotherham
Port Vale v Bradford
Rochdale v Gillingham
Southend v Plymouth
Torquay v Chesterfield
Wycombe v Dag & Red
York v Aldershot

Friday, 25 January
npower League 2
Cheltenham v Rochdale

Saturday, 26 January
npower Championship
Barnsley v Millwall
Bolton v Peterborough
Brighton v Blackburn
Bristol City v Ipswich
Burnley v Birmingham
Cardiff v Leicester
Charlton v Sheffield Wed
Huddersfield v Crystal Palace
Hull v Derby
Middlesbrough v Leeds
Nottm Forest v Watford
Wolves v Blackpool

npower League 1
Bournemouth v Crewe
Carlisle v Scunthorpe
Colchester v Walsall
Leyton Orient v Notts Co
MK Dons v Doncaster
Oldham v Yeovil
Portsmouth v Hartlepool
Preston v Coventry
Sheffield Utd v Crawley
Shrewsbury v Bury
Stevenage v Brentford
Tranmere v Swindon

npower League 2
AFC Wimbledon v Port Vale
Aldershot v Northampton
Bradford v Wycombe
Burton v Barnet
Chesterfield v Southend
Dag & Red v Morecambe
Exeter v Torquay
Fleetwood v Oxford
Gillingham v York
Plymouth v Accrington
Rotherham v Bristol Rov

Tuesday, 29 January
Barclays Premier League
Aston Villa v Newcastle
Norwich v Tottenham
QPR v Man City
Reading v Chelsea
Stoke v Wigan
Sunderland v Swansea

Wednesday, 30 January
Barclays Premier League
Arsenal v Liverpool
Everton v WBA

Fulham v West Ham
Manchester Utd v Southampton

Friday, 1 February
npower League 1
Sheffield Utd v Coventry

npower League 2
Bristol Rov v Barnet

Saturday, 2 February
Barclays Premier League
Arsenal v Stoke
Everton v Aston Villa
Fulham v Man Utd
Man City v Liverpool
Newcastle v Chelsea
QPR v Norwich
Reading v Sunderland
WBA v Tottenham
West Ham v Swansea
Wigan v Southampton

npower Championship
Birmingham v Nottm Forest
Blackburn v Bristol City
Blackpool v Barnsley
Crystal Palace v Charlton
Derby v Huddersfield
Ipswich v Middlesbrough
Leeds v Cardiff
Leicester v Wolves
Millwall v Hull
Peterborough v Burnley
Sheffield Wed v Brighton
Watford v Bolton

npower League 1
Bury v Doncaster
Crawley v Swindon
Crewe v Scunthorpe
Hartlepool v Notts Co
MK Dons v Bournemouth
Portsmouth v Colchester
Preston v Shrewsbury
Stevenage v Leyton Orient
Tranmere v Carlisle
Walsall v Oldham
Yeovil v Brentford

npower League 2
AFC Wimbledon v Burton
Cheltenham v Torquay
Exeter v Aldershot
Fleetwood v Bradford
Gillingham v Wycombe
Plymouth v Dag & Red
Port Vale v Accrington
Rochdale v Chesterfield
Rotherham v Northampton
Southend v Oxford
York v Morecambe

Saturday, 9 February
Barclays Premier League
Aston Villa v West Ham
Chelsea v Wigan
Liverpool v WBA
Man Utd v Everton
Norwich v Fulham
Southampton v Man City
Stoke v Reading
Sunderland v Arsenal
Swansea v QPR
Tottenham v Newcastle

npower Championship
Blackburn v Ipswich
Blackpool v Millwall
Bolton v Burnley
Brighton v Hull
Bristol City v Nottm Forest
Charlton v Birmingham
Huddersfield v Cardiff
Middlesbrough v Barnsley
Peterborough v Leicester
Sheffield Wed v Derby
Watford v Crystal Palace
Wolves v Leeds

npower League 1
Bournemouth v Portsmouth
Brentford v Bury
Carlisle v Stevenage
Colchester v Preston
Coventry v Yeovil
Doncaster v Walsall
Leyton Orient v Tranmere
Notts Co v Crewe
Oldham v MK Dons
Scunthorpe v Crawley
Shrewsbury v Sheffield Utd
Swindon v Hartlepool

npower League 2
Accrington v Southend
Aldershot v Plymouth
Barnet v Port Vale
Bradford v Gillingham
Burton v Rotherham
Chesterfield v AFC Wimbledon
Dag & Red v Cheltenham
Morecambe v Exeter
Northampton v Rochdale
Oxford v Bristol Rov
Torquay v Fleetwood
Wycombe v York

Friday, 15 February
npower League 2
Exeter v Accrington

Saturday, 16 February
npower Championship
Barnsley v Brighton
Birmingham v Watford
Burnley v Huddersfield
Cardiff v Bristol City
Crystal Palace v Middlesbrough
Derby v Wolves
Hull v Charlton
Ipswich v Blackpool
Leeds v Peterborough
Leicester v Blackburn
Millwall v Sheffield Wed
Nottm Forest v Bolton

npower League 1
Bury v Coventry
Crawley v Doncaster
Crewe v Brentford
Hartlepool v Leyton Orient
MK Dons v Swindon
Portsmouth v Carlisle
Preston v Bournemouth
Sheffield Utd v Colchester
Stevenage v Oldham
Tranmere v Shrewsbury
Walsall v Notts Co
Yeovil v Scunthorpe

npower League 2
AFC Wimbledon v Bradford
Bristol Rov v Wycombe
Cheltenham v Aldershot
Fleetwood v Burton
Gillingham v Dag & Red
Plymouth v Oxford
Port Vale v Morecambe
Rochdale v Torquay
Rotherham v Chesterfield
Southend v Northampton
York v Barnet

Tuesday, 19 February
npower Championship
Barnsley v Wolves
Birmingham v Sheffield Wed
Burnley v Middlesbrough
Cardiff v Brighton
Crystal Palace v Bristol City
Derby v Bolton
Hull v Blackburn
Ipswich v Watford
Leeds v Blackpool
Leicester v Charlton
Millwall v Peterborough
Nottm Forest v Huddersfield

Saturday, 23 February
Barclays Premier League
Arsenal v Aston Villa

Fulham v Stoke
Liverpool v Swansea
Man City v Chelsea
Newcastle v Southampton
Norwich v Everton
QPR v Man Utd
Reading v Wigan
WBA v Sunderland
West Ham v Tottenham

npower Championship
Blackburn v Leeds
Blackpool v Leicester
Bolton v Hull
Brighton v Burnley
Bristol City v Barnsley
Charlton v Nottm Forest
Huddersfield v Ipswich
Middlesbrough v Millwall
Peterborough v Birmingham
Sheff Wed v Crystal Palace
Watford v Derby

npower League 1
Bournemouth v Sheffield Utd
Brentford v Walsall
Carlisle v MK Dons
Colchester v Tranmere
Coventry v Crewe
Doncaster v Yeovil
Leyton Orient v Crawley
Notts Co v Bury
Oldham v Portsmouth
Scunthorpe v Hartlepool
Shrewsbury v Stevenage
Swindon v Preston

npower League 2
Accrington v Cheltenham
Aldershot v Fleetwood
Barnet v Rochdale
Bradford v Rotherham
Burton v Exeter
Chesterfield v Gillingham
Dag & Red v AFC Wimbledon
Morecambe v Bristol Rov
Northampton v Plymouth
Oxford v York
Torquay v Port Vale
Wycombe v Southend

Sunday, 24 February
npower Championship
Wolves v Cardiff

Tuesday, 26 February
npower League 1
Bournemouth v Coventry
Carlisle v Walsall
Colchester v Yeovil
Crawley v Brentford

Hartlepool v Crewe
Portsmouth v MK Dons
Preston v Oldham
Scunthorpe v Stevenage
Sheffield Utd v Leyton Orient
Shrewsbury v Doncaster
Swindon v Bury
Tranmere v Notts Co

npower League 2
AFC Wimbledon v Plymouth
Barnet v Southend
Bradford v Dag & Red
Burton v Morecambe
Chesterfield v Aldershot
Fleetwood v Cheltenham
Gillingham v Oxford
Northampton v Bristol Rov
Port Vale v Exeter
Rochdale v Accrington
Rotherham v York
Torquay v Wycombe

Friday, 1 March
npower Championship
Derby v Crystal Palace

Saturday, 2 March
Barclays Premier League
Aston Villa v Man City
Chelsea v WBA
Everton v Reading
Man Utd v Norwich
Southampton v QPR
Stoke v West Ham
Sunderland v Fulham
Swansea v Newcastle
Tottenham v Arsenal
Wigan v Liverpool

npower Championship
Barnsley v Bolton
Blackburn v Peterborough
Blackpool v Bristol City
Brighton v Huddersfield
Charlton v Burnley
Hull v Birmingham
Ipswich v Leicester
Leeds v Millwall
Middlesbrough v Cardiff
Sheffield Wed v Nottm Forest
Wolves v Watford

npower League 1
Brentford v Scunthorpe
Bury v Crawley
Coventry v Swindon
Crewe v Portsmouth
Doncaster v Hartlepool
Leyton Orient v Bournemouth
MK Dons v Preston
Notts Co v Carlisle

Oldham v Sheffield Utd
Stevenage v Colchester
Walsall v Shrewsbury
Yeovil v Tranmere

npower League 2
Accrington v Torquay
Aldershot v Gillingham
Bristol Rov v Burton
Cheltenham v AFC Wimbledon
Dag & Red v Chesterfield
Exeter v Northampton
Morecambe v Rochdale
Oxford v Port Vale
Plymouth v Barnet
Southend v Rotherham
Wycombe v Fleetwood
York v Bradford

Tuesday, 5 March
npower Championship
Birmingham v Blackpool
Bolton v Blackburn
Bristol City v Brighton
Burnley v Barnsley
Cardiff v Derby
Crystal Palace v Hull
Huddersfield v Middlesbrough
Leicester v Leeds
Millwall v Wolverhampton
Nottm Forest v Ipswich
Peterborough v Charlton
Watford v Sheff Wed

npower League 2
Cheltenham v Chesterfield

Saturday, 9 March
Barclays Premier League
Arsenal v Everton
Fulham v Chelsea
Liverpool v Tottenham
Man City v Wigan
Newcastle v Stoke
Norwich v Southampton
QPR v Sunderland
Reading v Aston Villa
WBA v Swansea
West Ham v Man Utd

npower Championship
Birmingham v Derby
Bolton v Brighton
Bristol City v Middlesbrough
Burnley v Hull
Cardiff v Barnsley
Crystal Palace v Leeds
Huddersfield v Charlton
Leicester v Sheffield Wed
Millwall v Blackburn
Nottm Forest v Wolves

Peterborough v Ipswich
Watford v Blackpool

npower League 1
Bournemouth v Doncaster
Carlisle v Brentford
Colchester v Crewe
Crawley v Notts Co
Hartlepool v Yeovil
Portsmouth v Bury
Preston v Stevenage
Scunthorpe v Coventry
Sheffield Utd v MK Dons
Shrewsbury v Leyton Orient
Swindon v Walsall
Tranmere v Oldham

npower League 2
AFC Wimbledon v York
Barnet v Morecambe
Bradford v Aldershot
Burton v Cheltenham
Chesterfield v Bristol Rov
Fleetwood v Exeter
Gillingham v Plymouth
Northampton v Accrington
Port Vale v Southend
Rochdale v Wycombe
Rotherham v Dag & Red
Torquay v Oxford

Tuesday, 12 March
npower League 1
Brentford v Swindon
Bury v Scunthorpe
Coventry v Colchester
Crewe v Sheffield Utd
Doncaster v Carlisle
Leyton Orient v Portsmouth
MK Dons v Shrewsbury
Notts Co v Preston
Oldham v Hartlepool
Stevenage v Bournemouth
Walsall v Tranmere
Yeovil v Crawley

npower League 2
Accrington v Fleetwood
Aldershot v Burton
Bristol Rov v Port Vale
Dag & Red v Torquay
Exeter v Gillingham
Morecambe v Northampton
Oxford v Barnet
Plymouth v Bradford
Southend v AFC Wimbledon
Wycombe v Rotherham
York v Rochdale

Saturday, 16 March
Barclays Premier League
Aston Villa v QPR

Chelsea v West Ham
Everton v Man City
Man Utd v Reading
Southampton v Liverpool
Stoke v WBA
Sunderland v Norwich
Swansea v Arsenal
Tottenham v Fulham
Wigan v Newcastle

npower Championship
Barnsley v Watford
Blackburn v Burnley
Blackpool v Peterborough
Brighton v Crystal Palace
Charlton v Millwall
Derby v Leicester
Hull v Nottm Forest
Ipswich v Bolton
Leeds v Huddersfield
Middlesbrough v Birmingham
Sheffield Wed v Cardiff
Wolves v Bristol City

npower League 1
Brentford v Preston
Bury v Colchester
Coventry v Hartlepool
Crewe v Shrewsbury
Doncaster v Portsmouth
Leyton Orient v Carlisle
MK Dons v Tranmere
Notts Co v Scunthorpe
Oldham v Bournemouth
Stevenage v Sheffield Utd
Walsall v Crawley
Yeovil v Swindon

npower League 2
Accrington v Barnet
Aldershot v AFC Wimbledon
Bristol Rov v Rochdale
Cheltenham v Rotherham
Dag & Red v Burton
Exeter v Bradford
Morecambe v Gillingham
Oxford v Chesterfield
Plymouth v Fleetwood
Southend v Torquay
Wycombe v Northampton
York v Port Vale

Saturday, 23 March
npower League 1
Bournemouth v Bury
Carlisle v Yeovil
Colchester v MK Dons
Crawley v Crewe
Hartlepool v Walsall
Portsmouth v Coventry

Preston v Leyton Orient
Scunthorpe v Doncaster
Sheffield Utd v Brentford
Shrewsbury v Oldham
Swindon v Notts Co
Tranmere v Stevenage

npower League 2
AFC Wimbledon v Morecambe
Barnet v Cheltenham
Bradford v Bristol Rov
Burton v Wycombe
Chesterfield v Plymouth
Fleetwood v Dag & Red
Gillingham v Accrington
Northampton v Oxford
Port Vale v Aldershot
Rochdale v Southend
Rotherham v Exeter
Torquay v York

Friday, 29 March
npower Championship
Blackburn v Blackpool
Derby v Bristol City
Watford v Burnley

npower League 1
Brentford v Notts Co
Bury v Crewe
Carlisle v Shrewsbury
Colchester v Bournemouth
Crawley v Stevenage
Hartlepool v MK Dons
Preston v Portsmouth
Scunthorpe v Leyton Orient
Tranmere v Sheffield Utd
Yeovil v Walsall

npower League 2
Barnet v Dag & Red
Bradford v Southend
Northampton v Torquay
Oxford v Morecambe
Port Vale v Cheltenham
Rotherham v AFC Wimbledon
Rochdale v Aldershot
Wycombe v Accrington

Saturday, 30 March
Barclays Premier League
Arsenal v Reading
Aston Villa v Liverpool
Everton v Stoke
Fulham v QPR
Man City v Newcastle
Southampton v Chelsea
Sunderland v Man Utd
Swansea v Tottenham
West Ham v WBA
Wigan v Norwich

npower Championship
Charlton v Bolton
Crystal Palace v Birmingham
Huddersfield v Hull
Ipswich v Leeds
Leicester v Millwall
Nottm Forest v Brighton
Peterborough v Cardiff
Sheffield Wed v Barnsley
Wolves v Middlesbrough

npower League 1
Coventry v Doncaster
Swindon v Oldham

npower League 2
Bristol Rov v York
Burton v Chesterfield
Fleetwood v Gillingham
Plymouth v Exeter

Monday, 1 April
npower Championship
Barnsley v Leicester
Birmingham v Wolves
Blackpool v Crystal Palace
Bolton v Huddersfield
Bristol City v Sheffield Wed
Burnley v Nottm Forest
Cardiff v Blackburn
Hull v Watford
Leeds v Derby
Millwall v Ipswich

npower League 1
Bournemouth v Scunthorpe
Crewe v Preston
Doncaster v Swindon
Leyton Orient v Bury
MK Dons v Brentford
Notts Co v Yeovil
Oldham v Colchester
Portsmouth v Tranmere
Sheffield Utd v Carlisle
Shrewsbury v Crawley
Stevenage v Hartlepool
Walsall v Coventry

npower League 2
AFC Wimbledon v Barnet
Accrington v Burton
Aldershot v Oxford
Cheltenham v Northampton
Chesterfield v Port Vale
Dag & Red v Bristol Rov
Exeter v Rochdale
Gillingham v Rotherham
Morecambe v Wycombe
Southend v Fleetwood
Torquay v Bradford

York v Plymouth

Tuesday, 2 April
npower Championship
Brighton v Charlton
Middlesbrough v Peterborough

Friday, 5 April
npower League 2
Port Vale v Burton

Saturday, 6 April
Barclays Premier League
Chelsea v Sunderland
Liverpool v West Ham
Man Utd v Man City
Newcastle v Fulham
Norwich v Swansea
QPR v Wigan
Reading v Southampton
Stoke v Aston Villa
Tottenham v Everton
WBA v Arsenal

npower Championship
Birmingham v Millwall
Bolton v Wolves
Brighton v Leicester
Burnley v Bristol City
Charlton v Leeds
Crystal Palace v Barnsley
Derby v Ipswich
Huddersfield v Peterborough
Hull v Middlesbrough
Nottm Forest v Blackpool
Sheffield Wed v Blackburn
Watford v Cardiff

npower League 1
Bournemouth v Notts Co
Colchester v Leyton Orient
Coventry v Brentford.
Doncaster v Tranmere
Hartlepool v Bury
MK Dons v Crawley
Oldham v Carlisle
Portsmouth v Stevenage
Preston v Scunthorpe
Swindon v Crewe
Walsall v Sheffield Utd
Yeovil v Shrewsbury

npower League 2
Aldershot v Southend
Barnet v Chesterfield
Bradford v Northampton
Bristol Rov v AFC Wimbledon
Exeter v Dag & Red
Fleetwood v Rochdale

Gillingham v Torquay
Morecambe v Rotherham
Oxford v Wycombe
Plymouth v Cheltenham
York v Accrington

Friday, 12 April
npower League 2
Southend v Bristol Rov

Saturday, 13 April
Barclays Premier League
Arsenal v Norwich
Aston Villa v Fulham
Chelsea v Tottenham
Everton v QPR
Man City v WBA
Newcastle v Sunderland
Reading v Liverpool
Southampton v West Ham
Stoke v Man Utd
Wigan v Swansea

npower Championship
Barnsley v Charlton
Blackburn v Derby
Blackpool v Burnley
Bristol City v Bolton
Cardiff v Nottm Forest
Ipswich v Hull
Leeds v Sheffield Wed
Leicester v Birmingham
Middlesbrough v Brighton
Millwall v Crystal Palace
Peterborough v Watford
Wolves v Huddersfield

npower League 1
Brentford v Portsmouth
Bury v Oldham
Carlisle v Preston
Crawley v Coventry
Crewe v Doncaster
Leyton Orient v MK Dons
Notts Co v Colchester
Scunthorpe v Walsall
Sheffield Utd v Swindon
Shrewsbury v Bournemouth
Stevenage v Yeovil
Tranmere v Hartlepool

npower League 2
AFC Wimbledon v Exeter
Accrington v Morecambe
Burton v Plymouth
Cheltenham v Gillingham
Chesterfield v Bradford
Dag & Red v Oxford
Northampton v York
Rochdale v Port Vale
Rotherham v Fleetwood

Torquay v Barnet
Wycombe v Aldershot

Tuesday, 16 April
npower Championship
Barnsley v Derby
Blackpool v Sheffield Wed
Bristol City v Birmingham
Cardiff v Charlton
Ipswich v Crystal Palace
Leeds v Burnley
Leicester v Bolton
Middlesbrough v Nottm Forest
Millwall v Watford
Peterborough v Brighton
Wolves v Hull

Wednesday, 17 April
npower Championship
Blackburn v Huddersfield

Saturday, 20 April
Barclays Premier League
Fulham v Arsenal
Liverpool v Chelsea
Man Utd v Aston Villa
Norwich v Reading
QPR v Stoke
Sunderland v Everton
Swansea v Southampton
Tottenham v Man City
WBA v Newcastle
West Ham v Wigan

npower Championship
Birmingham v Leeds
Bolton v Middlesbrough
Brighton v Blackpool
Burnley v Cardiff
Charlton v Wolves
Crystal Palace v Leicester
Derby v Peterborough
Huddersfield v Millwall
Hull v Bristol City
Nottm Forest v Barnsley
Sheffield Wed v Ipswich
Watford v Blackburn

npower League 1
Bournemouth v Carlisle
Colchester v Shrewsbury
Coventry v Leyton Orient
Doncaster v Notts Co
Hartlepool v Brentford
MK Dons v Scunthorpe
Oldham v Crawley
Portsmouth v Sheffield Utd
Preston v Tranmere
Swindon v Stevenage
Walsall v Bury
Yeovil v Crewe

npower League 2

Aldershot v Dag & Red
Barnet v Wycombe
Bradford v Burton
Bristol Rov v Accrington
Exeter v Cheltenham
Fleetwood v Chesterfield
Gillingham v AFC Wimbledon
Morecambe v Torquay
Oxford v Rochdale
Plymouth v Rotherham
Port Vale v Northampton
York v Southend

Saturday, 27 April
Barclays Premier League

Arsenal v Man Utd
Aston Villa v Sunderland
Chelsea v Swansea
Everton v Fulham
Man City v West Ham
Newcastle v Liverpool
Reading v QPR
Southampton v WBA
Stoke v Norwich
Wigan v Tottenham

npower Championship

Barnsley v Hull
Blackburn v Crystal Palace
Blackpool v Derby
Bristol City v Huddersfield
Cardiff v Bolton
Ipswich v Birmingham
Leeds v Brighton
Leicester v Watford
Middlesbrough v Charlton
Millwall v Nottm Forest
Peterborough v Sheffield Wed
Wolves v Burnley

npower League 1

Brentford v Doncaster
Bury v Yeovil
Carlisle v Colchester
Crawley v Hartlepool
Crewe v Walsall
Leyton Orient v Oldham
Notts Co v Coventry
Scunthorpe v Swindon
Sheffield Utd v Preston
Shrewsbury v Portsmouth
Stevenage v MK Dons
Tranmere v Bournemouth

npower League 2

AFC Wimbledon v Fleetwood
Accrington v Oxford
Burton v Gillingham
Cheltenham v Bradford
Chesterfield v Exeter

Dag & Red v York
Northampton v Barnet
Rochdale v Plymouth
Rotherham v Aldershot
Southend v Morecambe
Torquay v Bristol Rov
Wycombe v Port Vale

Saturday, 4 May
Barclays Premier League

Fulham v Reading
Liverpool v Everton
Man Utd v Chelsea
Norwich v Aston Villa
QPR v Arsenal
Sunderland v Stoke
Swansea v Man City
Tottenham v Southampton
WBA v Wigan
West Ham v Newcastle

npower Championship

Birmingham v Blackburn
Bolton v Blackpool
Brighton v Wolves
Burnley v Ipswich
Charlton v Bristol City
Crystal Palace v Peterborough
Derby v Millwall
Huddersfield v Barnsley
Hull v Cardiff
Nottm Forest v Leicester
Sheffield Wed v Middlesbrough
Watford v Leeds

Sunday, 12 May
Barclays Premier League

Arsenal v Wigan
Aston Villa v Chelsea
Everton v West Ham
Fulham v Liverpool
Man Utd v Swansea
Norwich v WBA
QPR v Newcastle
Reading v Man City
Stoke v Tottenham
Sunderland v Southampton

Sunday, 19 May
Barclays Premier League

Chelsea v Everton
Liverpool v QPR
Man City v Norwich
Newcastle v Arsenal
Southampton v Stoke
Swansea v Fulham
Tottenham v Sunderland
WBA v Man Utd
West Ham v Reading
Wigan v Aston Villa

SCOTTISH FIXTURES 2012–2013

The Scottish Premier League fixtures are subject to change where they have Dundee, who replaced Rangers, at home on the same day as Dundee Utd.

Saturday, 4 August
Clydesdale Bank Premier League
Celtic v Aberdeen
Hearts v St Johnstone
Kilmarnock v Dundee
Ross Co v Motherwell
St Mirren v Inverness

Sunday, 5 August
Clydesdale Bank Premier League
Dundee Utd v Hibernian

Saturday, 11 August
Clydesdale Bank Premier League
Aberdeen v Ross Co
Celtic v Dundee Utd
Dundee v St Mirren
Hibernian v Hearts
Inverness v Kilmarnock
Motherwell v St Johnstone

Irn-Bru First Division
Airdrie v Dumbarton
Cowdenbeath v Dunfermline
Morton v Livingston
Partick v Falkirk
Raith v Hamilton

Irn-Bru Second Division
Alloa v East Fife
Ayr v Stenhousemuir
Brechin v Albion
Queen of South v Forfar
Stranraer v Arbroath
Irn-Bru Third Division
Berwick v Elgin
East Stirling v Queens Park
Montrose v Clyde
Peterhead v Rangers
Stirling v Annan

Saturday, 18 August
Clydesdale Bank Premier League
Dundee Utd v Dundee
Hearts v Inverness
Kilmarnock v Motherwell
Ross Co v Celtic
St Johnstone v Aberdeen
St Mirren v Hibernian

Irn-Bru First Division
Dumbarton v Cowdenbeath
Dunfermline v Partick
Falkirk v Raith
Hamilton v Morton
Livingston v Airdrie

Irn-Bru Second Division
Albion v Alloa
Arbroath v Ayr
East Fife v Queen of South
Forfar v Stranraer
Stenhousemuir v Brechin

Irn-Bru Third Division
Annan v Berwick
Clyde v Peterhead
Elgin v Stirling
Queens Park v Montrose
Rangers v East Stirling

Saturday, 25 August
Clydesdale Bank Premier League
Dundee v Ross Co
Hibernian v St Johnstone
Inverness v Celtic
Kilmarnock v Dundee Utd
Motherwell v St Mirren

Irn-Bru First Division
Airdrie v Dunfermline
Cowdenbeath v Hamilton
Morton v Falkirk
Partick v Dumbarton
Raith v Livingston

Irn-Bru Second Division
Alloa v Arbroath
Ayr v Forfar
Brechin v East Fife
Queen of South v Albion
Stranraer v Stenhousemuir

Irn-Bru Third Division
Berwick v Rangers
East Stirling v Elgin
Montrose v Annan
Peterhead v Queens Park
Stirling v Clyde

Sunday, 26 August
Clydesdale Bank Premier League
Aberdeen v Hearts

Saturday, 1 September
Clydesdale Bank Premier League
Aberdeen v St Mirren
Celtic v Hibernian
Motherwell v Inverness
Ross Co v Kilmarnock
St Johnstone v Dundee Utd

Irn-Bru First Division
Airdrie v Cowdenbeath
Dunfermline v Raith
Falkirk v Livingston
Morton v Dumbarton
Partick v Hamilton

Irn-Bru Second Division
Brechin v Alloa
East Fife v Albion
Queen of South v Arbroath
Stenhousemuir v Forfar
Stranraer v Ayr

Irn-Bru Third Division
Berwick v East Stirling
Clyde v Annan
Peterhead v Montrose
Rangers v Elgin
Stirling v Queens Park

Sunday, 2 September
Clydesdale Bank Premier League
Hearts v Dundee

Saturday, 15 September
Clydesdale Bank Premier League
Dundee v Motherwell
Dundee Utd v Ross Co
Hibernian v Kilmarnock
Inverness v Aberdeen
St Johnstone v Celtic
St Mirren v Hearts

Irn-Bru First Division
Cowdenbeath v Morton
Dumbarton v Dunfermline
Hamilton v Falkirk
Livingston v Partick
Raith v Airdrie

Irn-Bru Second Division
Albion v Stranraer
Alloa v Stenhousemuir
Arbroath v East Fife
Ayr v Queen of South
Forfar v Brechin

Irn-Bru Third Division
Annan v Rangers
East Stirling v Stirling
Elgin v Peterhead
Montrose v Berwick
Queens Park v Clyde

Saturday, 22 September
Clydesdale Bank Premier League
Aberdeen v Motherwell
Celtic v Dundee

Dundee Utd v Hearts
Hibernian v Inverness
Kilmarnock v St Mirren
Ross Co v St Johnstone

Irn-Bru First Division
Dumbarton v Hamilton
Dunfermline v Livingston
Falkirk v Airdrie
Morton v Raith
Partick v Cowdenbeath

Irn-Bru Second Division
Albion v Stenhousemuir
Alloa v Stranraer
Arbroath v Forfar
Brechin v Queen of South
East Fife v Ayr

Irn-Bru Third Division
Annan v Peterhead
Berwick v Stirling
East Stirling v Clyde
Elgin v Queens Park
Rangers v Montrose

Saturday, 29 September
Clydesdale Bank Premier League
Aberdeen v Hibernian
Dundee v St Johnstone
Hearts v Kilmarnock
Inverness v Dundee Utd
Motherwell v Celtic
St Mirren v Ross Co

Irn-Bru First Division
Airdrie v Morton
Cowdenbeath v Falkirk
Hamilton v Dunfermline
Livingston v Dumbarton
Raith v Partick

Irn-Bru Second Division
Ayr v Brechin
Forfar v Albion
Queen of South v Alloa
Stenhousemuir v Arbroath
Stranraer v East Fife

Saturday, 6 October
Clydesdale Bank Premier League
Celtic v Hearts
Hibernian v Dundee
Inverness v Ross Co
Kilmarnock v Aberdeen
Motherwell v Dundee Utd
St Johnstone v St Mirren

Irn-Bru First Division
Airdrie v Hamilton

Falkirk v Dunfermline
Livingston v Cowdenbeath
Morton v Partick
Raith v Dumbarton

Irn-Bru Second Division
Arbroath v Brechin
Ayr v Albion
Forfar v Alloa
Stenhousemuir v East Fife
Stranraer v Queen of South

Irn-Bru Third Division
Clyde v Elgin
Montrose v East Stirling
Peterhead v Berwick
Queens Park v Annan
Stirling v Rangers

Saturday, 20 October
Clydesdale Bank Premier League
Dundee v Inverness
Dundee Utd v Aberdeen
Hearts v Motherwell
Ross Co v Hibernian
St Johnstone v Kilmarnock
St Mirren v Celtic

Irn-Bru First Division
Cowdenbeath v Raith
Dumbarton v Falkirk
Dunfermline v Morton
Hamilton v Livingston
Partick v Airdrie

Irn-Bru Second Division
Albion v Arbroath
Alloa v Ayr
Brechin v Stranraer
East Fife v Forfar
Queen of South v Stenhousemuir

Irn-Bru Third Division
Berwick v Clyde
East Stirling v Peterhead
Elgin v Annan
Rangers v Queens Park
Stirling v Montrose

Saturday, 27 October
Clydesdale Bank Premier League
Aberdeen v Dundee
Celtic v Kilmarnock
Hearts v Ross Co
Inverness v St Johnstone
Motherwell v Hibernian
St Mirren v Dundee Utd

Irn-Bru First Division
Dumbarton v Airdrie
Dunfermline v Cowdenbeath
Falkirk v Partick
Hamilton v Raith
Livingston v Morton

Irn-Bru Second Division
Alloa v Albion
Ayr v Arbroath
Brechin v Stenhousemuir
Queen of South v East Fife
Stranraer v Forfar

Irn-Bru Third Division
Annan v East Stirling
Clyde v Rangers
Montrose v Elgin
Peterhead v Stirling
Queens Park v Berwick

Saturday, 3 November
Clydesdale Bank Premier League
Dundee v Hearts
Dundee Utd v Celtic
Hibernian v St Mirren
Kilmarnock v Inverness
Ross Co v Aberdeen
St Johnstone v Motherwell

Saturday, 10 November
Clydesdale Bank Premier League
Celtic v St Johnstone
Hibernian v Dundee Utd
Inverness v Hearts
Kilmarnock v Ross Co
Motherwell v Dundee
St Mirren v Aberdeen

Irn-Bru First Division
Airdrie v Livingston
Cowdenbeath v Dumbarton
Morton v Hamilton
Partick v Dunfermline
Raith v Falkirk

Irn-Bru Second Division
Albion v Brechin
Arbroath v Stranraer
East Fife v Alloa
Forfar v Queen of South
Stenhousemuir v Ayr

Irn-Bru Third Division
Annan v Stirling
Clyde v Montrose
Elgin v Berwick
Queens Park v East Stirling
Rangers v Peterhead

Saturday, 17 November
Clydesdale Bank Premier League
Aberdeen v Celtic
Dundee v Hibernian
Dundee Utd v Kilmarnock
Hearts v St Mirren
Inverness v Motherwell
St Johnstone v Ross Co

Irn-Bru First Division
Cowdenbeath v Airdrie
Dumbarton v Morton
Hamilton v Partick
Livingston v Falkirk
Raith v Dunfermline

Irn-Bru Second Division
Albion v East Fife
Alloa v Brechin
Arbroath v Queen of South
Ayr v Stranraer
Forfar v Stenhousemuir
Irn-Bru Third Division
Berwick v Annan
East Stirling v Rangers
Montrose v Queens Park
Peterhead v Clyde
Stirling v Elgin

Saturday, 24 November
Clydesdale Bank Premier League
Celtic v Inverness
Hibernian v Aberdeen
Kilmarnock v St Johnstone
Motherwell v Hearts
Ross Co v Dundee Utd
St Mirren v Dundee

Irn-Bru First Division
Airdrie v Raith
Dunfermline v Dumbarton
Falkirk v Hamilton
Morton v Cowdenbeath
Partick v Livingston

Irn-Bru Second Division
Brechin v Forfar
East Fife v Arbroath
Queen of South v Ayr
Stenhousemuir v Alloa
Stranraer v Albion

Irn-Bru Third Division
Annan v Clyde
Elgin v Rangers
Montrose v Peterhead
Queens Park v Stirling

Sunday, 25 November
Irn-Bru Third Division
East Stirling v Berwick

Wednesday, 28 November
Clydesdale Bank Premier League
Aberdeen v Inverness
Dundee v Kilmarnock
Dundee Utd v Motherwell
Hearts v Celtic
Ross Co v St Mirren
St Johnstone v Hibernian

Saturday, 1 December
Irn-Bru Third Division
Berwick v Montrose
Clyde v Queens Park
Peterhead v Elgin
Rangers v Annan
Stirling v East Stirling

Saturday, 8 December
Clydesdale Bank Premier League
Dundee v Dundee Utd
Hearts v Aberdeen
Inverness v Hibernian
Kilmarnock v Celtic
Motherwell v Ross Co
St Mirren v St Johnstone

Irn-Bru First Division
Airdrie v Falkirk
Cowdenbeath v Partick
Hamilton v Dumbarton
Livingston v Dunfermline
Raith v Morton

Irn-Bru Second Division
Albion v Forfar
Alloa v Queen of South
Arbroath v Stenhousemuir
Brechin v Ayr
East Fife v Stranraer

Irn-Bru Third Division
Annan v Queens Park
Berwick v Peterhead
East Stirling v Montrose
Elgin v Clyde
Rangers v Stirling

Saturday, 15 December
Clydesdale Bank Premier League
Aberdeen v Kilmarnock
Celtic v St Mirren
Dundee Utd v Inverness
Hibernian v Motherwell
Ross Co v Dundee
St Johnstone v Hearts

Irn-Bru First Division
Dumbarton v Livingston
Dunfermline v Hamilton
Falkirk v Cowdenbeath
Morton v Airdrie
Partick v Raith

Irn-Bru Second Division
Ayr v East Fife
Forfar v Arbroath
Queen of South v Brechin
Stenhousemuir v Albion
Stranraer v Alloa

Irn-Bru Third Division
Clyde v East Stirling
Montrose v Rangers
Peterhead v Annan
Queens Park v Elgin
Stirling v Berwick

Saturday, 22 December
Clydesdale Bank Premier League
Aberdeen v St Johnstone
Celtic v Ross Co
Hearts v Dundee Utd
Inverness v Dundee
Kilmarnock v Hibernian
St Mirren v Motherwell

Wednesday, 26 December
Clydesdale Bank Premier League
Dundee v Celtic
Dundee Utd v St Johnstone
Hibernian v Ross Co
Inverness v St Mirren
Kilmarnock v Hearts
Motherwell v Aberdeen

Irn-Bru First Division
Cowdenbeath v Livingston
Dumbarton v Raith
Dunfermline v Falkirk
Hamilton v Airdrie
Partick v Morton

Irn-Bru Second Division
Albion v Ayr
Alloa v Forfar
Brechin v Arbroath
East Fife v Stenhousemuir
Queen of South v Stranraer

Irn-Bru Third Division
Berwick v Queens Park
East Stirling v Annan
Elgin v Montrose
Rangers v Clyde
Stirling v Peterhead

Saturday, 29 December
Clydesdale Bank Premier League
Dundee v Aberdeen
Dundee Utd v St Mirren
Hibernian v Celtic
Motherwell v Kilmarnock
Ross Co v Hearts
St Johnstone v Inverness

Irn-Bru First Division
Airdrie v Partick
Falkirk v Dumbarton
Livingston v Hamilton
Morton v Dunfermline
Raith v Cowdenbeath

Irn-Bru Second Division
Arbroath v Albion
Ayr v Alloa
Forfar v East Fife
Stenhousemuir v Queen of South
Stranraer v Brechin

Irn-Bru Third Division
Annan v Elgin
Clyde v Berwick
Montrose v Stirling
Peterhead v East Stirling
Queens Park v Rangers

Wednesday, 2 January
Clydesdale Bank Premier League
Aberdeen v Dundee Utd
Celtic v Motherwell
Hearts v Hibernian
Ross Co v Inverness
St Johnstone v Dundee
St Mirren v Kilmarnock

Irn-Bru First Division
Airdrie v Cowdenbeath
Dunfermline v Raith
Falkirk v Livingston
Morton v Dumbarton
Partick v Hamilton

Irn-Bru Second Division
Albion v Stranraer
Alloa v Stenhousemuir
Arbroath v East Fife
Ayr v Queen of South
Forfar v Brechin

Irn-Bru Third Division
Annan v Rangers
East Stirling v Stirling
Elgin v Peterhead
Montrose v Berwick
Queens Park v Clyde

Saturday, 5 January
Irn-Bru First Division
Cowdenbeath v Morton
Dumbarton v Dunfermline
Hamilton v Falkirk
Livingston v Partick
Raith v Airdrie

Irn-Bru Second Division
Brechin v Alloa
East Fife v Albion
Queen of South v Arbroath
Stenhousemuir v Forfar
Stranraer v Ayr

Irn-Bru Third Division
Berwick v East Stirling
Clyde v Annan
Peterhead v Montrose
Rangers v Elgin
Stirling v Queens Park

Saturday, 12 January
Irn-Bru First Division
Dumbarton v Partick
Dunfermline v Airdrie
Falkirk v Morton
Hamilton v Cowdenbeath
Livingston v Raith

Irn-Bru Second Division
Albion v Queen of South
Arbroath v Alloa
East Fife v Brechin
Forfar v Ayr
Stenhousemuir v Stranraer

Irn-Bru Third Division
Annan v Montrose
Clyde v Stirling
Elgin v East Stirling
Queens Park v Peterhead
Rangers v Berwick

Saturday, 19 January
Clydesdale Bank Premier League
Celtic v Hearts
Hibernian v Dundee
Inverness v Aberdeen
Kilmarnock v Dundee Utd
Motherwell v St Johnstone
St Mirren v Ross Co

Irn-Bru First Division
Airdrie v Dumbarton
Cowdenbeath v Dunfermline
Morton v Livingston
Partick v Falkirk
Raith v Hamilton

Irn-Bru Second Division
Alloa v East Fife
Ayr v Stenhousemuir
Brechin v Albion
Queen of South v Forfar
Stranraer v Arbroath

Irn-Bru Third Division
Berwick v Elgin
East Stirling v Queens Park
Montrose v Clyde
Peterhead v Rangers
Stirling v Annan

Saturday, 26 January
Clydesdale Bank Premier League
Aberdeen v Hibernian
Dundee v St Mirren
Dundee Utd v Ross Co
Hearts v Motherwell
Inverness v Kilmarnock
St Johnstone v Celtic

Irn-Bru First Division
Dumbarton v Hamilton
Dunfermline v Livingston
Falkirk v Airdrie
Morton v Raith
Partick v Cowdenbeath
Irn-Bru Second Division
Albion v Stenhousemuir
Alloa v Stranraer
Arbroath v Forfar
Brechin v Queen of South
East Fife v Ayr

Irn-Bru Third Division
Annan v Peterhead
Berwick v Stirling
East Stirling v Clyde
Elgin v Queens Park
Rangers v Montrose

Wednesday, 30 January
Clydesdale Bank Premier League
Celtic v Kilmarnock
Hearts v Dundee
Motherwell v Dundee Utd
Ross Co v Hibernian
St Johnstone v Aberdeen
St Mirren v Inverness

Saturday, 2 February
Irn-Bru Second Division
Ayr v Brechin
Forfar v Albion
Queen of South v Alloa
Stenhousemuir v Arbroath
Stranraer v East Fife

Irn-Bru Third Division

Clyde v Elgin
Montrose v East Stirling
Peterhead v Berwick
Queens Park v Annan
Stirling v Rangers

Saturday, 9 February
Clydesdale Bank Premier League

Aberdeen v St Mirren
Dundee v Ross Co
Dundee Utd v Hearts
Hibernian v St Johnstone
Inverness v Celtic
Kilmarnock v Motherwell

Irn-Bru First Division

Airdrie v Morton
Cowdenbeath v Falkirk
Hamilton v Dunfermline
Livingston v Dumbarton
Raith v Partick

Irn-Bru Second Division

Albion v Arbroath
Alloa v Ayr
Brechin v Stranraer
East Fife v Forfar
Queen of South v Stenhousemuir

Irn-Bru Third Division

Berwick v Clyde
East Stirling v Peterhead
Elgin v Annan
Rangers v Queens Park
Stirling v Montrose

Saturday, 16 February
Clydesdale Bank Premier League

Aberdeen v Dundee
Celtic v Dundee Utd
Hearts v Kilmarnock
Motherwell v Inverness
Ross Co v St Johnstone
St Mirren v Hibernian

Irn-Bru First Division

Airdrie v Hamilton
Falkirk v Dunfermline
Livingston v Cowdenbeath
Morton v Partick
Raith v Dumbarton

Irn-Bru Second Division

Arbroath v Brechin
Ayr v Albion
Forfar v Alloa
Stenhousemuir v East Fife
Stranraer v Queen of South

Irn-Bru Third Division

Annan v East Stirling
Clyde v Rangers
Montrose v Elgin
Peterhead v Stirling
Queens Park v Berwick

Saturday, 23 February
Clydesdale Bank Premier League

Celtic v Dundee
Dundee Utd v Hibernian
Hearts v Inverness
Kilmarnock v Aberdeen
Ross Co v Motherwell
St Johnstone v St Mirren

Irn-Bru First Division

Cowdenbeath v Raith
Dumbarton v Falkirk
Dunfermline v Morton
Hamilton v Livingston
Partick v Airdrie

Irn-Bru Second Division

Alloa v Arbroath
Ayr v Forfar
Brechin v East Fife
Queen of South v Albion
Stranraer v Stenhousemuir

Irn-Bru Third Division

Berwick v Rangers
East Stirling v Elgin
Montrose v Annan
Peterhead v Queens Park
Stirling v Clyde

Wednesday, 27 February
Clydesdale Bank Premier League

Aberdeen v Ross Co
Dundee v St Johnstone
Hibernian v Kilmarnock
Inverness v Dundee Utd
Motherwell v Celtic
St Mirren v Hearts

Saturday, 2 March
Irn-Bru First Division

Dumbarton v Cowdenbeath
Dunfermline v Partick
Falkirk v Raith
Hamilton v Morton
Livingston v Airdrie

Irn-Bru Second Division

Albion v Alloa
Arbroath v Ayr
East Fife v Queen of South
Forfar v Stranraer
Stenhousemuir v Brechin

536

Saturday, 2 March
Irn-Bru Third Division
Annan v Berwick
Clyde v Peterhead
Elgin v Stirling
Queens Park v Montrose
Rangers v East Stirling

Saturday, 9 March
Clydesdale Bank Premier League
Aberdeen v Motherwell
Dundee v Inverness
Hibernian v Hearts
Ross Co v Celtic
St Johnstone v Kilmarnock
St Mirren v Dundee Utd

Irn-Bru First Division
Airdrie v Dunfermline
Cowdenbeath v Hamilton
Morton v Falkirk
Partick v Dumbarton
Raith v Livingston

Irn-Bru Second Division
Brechin v Forfar
East Fife v Arbroath
Queen of South v Ayr
Stenhousemuir v Alloa
Stranraer v Albion

Irn-Bru Third Division
Berwick v Montrose
Clyde v Queens Park
Peterhead v Elgin
Rangers v Annan
Stirling v East Stirling

Saturday, 16 March
Clydesdale Bank Premier League
Celtic v Aberdeen
Dundee Utd v Dundee
Hearts v St Johnstone
Inverness v Ross Co
Kilmarnock v St Mirren
Motherwell v Hibernian

Irn-Bru First Division
Cowdenbeath v Airdrie
Dumbarton v Morton
Hamilton v Partick
Livingston v Falkirk
Raith v Dunfermline

Irn-Bru Second Division
Albion v East Fife
Alloa v Brechin
Arbroath v Queen of South
Ayr v Stranraer
Forfar v Stenhousemuir

Irn-Bru Third Division
Annan v Clyde

East Stirling v Berwick
Elgin v Rangers
Montrose v Peterhead

Saturday, 23 March
Irn-Bru First Division
Airdrie v Raith
Dunfermline v Dumbarton
Falkirk v Hamilton
Morton v Cowdenbeath
Partick v Livingston

Irn-Bru Second Division
Albion v Forfar
Alloa v Queen of South
Arbroath v Stenhousemuir
Brechin v Ayr
East Fife v Stranraer

Irn-Bru Third Division
Annan v Queens Park
Berwick v Peterhead
East Stirling v Montrose
Elgin v Clyde
Rangers v Stirling

Saturday, 30 March
Clydesdale Bank Premier League
Aberdeen v Hearts
Dundee v Motherwell
Hibernian v Inverness
Ross Co v Kilmarnock
St Johnstone v Dundee Utd
St Mirren v Celtic

Irn-Bru First Division
Airdrie v Falkirk
Cowdenbeath v Partick
Hamilton v Dumbarton
Livingston v Dunfermline
Raith v Morton

Irn-Bru Second Division
Ayr v East Fife
Forfar v Arbroath
Queen of South v Brechin
Stenhousemuir v Albion
Stranraer v Alloa

Irn-Bru Third Division
Clyde v East Stirling
Montrose v Rangers
Peterhead v Annan
Queens Park v Elgin
Stirling v Berwick

Saturday, 6 April
Clydesdale Bank Premier League
Celtic v Hibernian

537

Dundee Utd v Aberdeen
Hearts v Ross Co
Inverness v St Johnstone
Kilmarnock v Dundee
Motherwell v St Mirren

Irn-Bru First Division
Dumbarton v Livingston
Dunfermline v Hamilton
Falkirk v Cowdenbeath
Morton v Airdrie
Partick v Raith

Irn-Bru Second Division
Arbroath v Albion
Ayr v Alloa
Forfar v East Fife
Stenhousemuir v Queen of South
Stranraer v Brechin

Irn-Bru Third Division
Annan v Elgin
Clyde v Berwick
Montrose v Stirling
Peterhead v East Stirling
Queens Park v Rangers

Tuesday, 9 April
Irn-Bru First Division
Cowdenbeath v Livingston
Dumbarton v Raith
Dunfermline v Falkirk
Hamilton v Airdrie
Partick v Morton

Saturday, 13 April
Irn-Bru First Division
Airdrie v Partick
Falkirk v Dumbarton
Livingston v Hamilton
Morton v Dunfermline
Raith v Cowdenbeath

Irn-Bru Second Division
Albion v Ayr
Alloa v Forfar
Brechin v Arbroath
East Fife v Stenhousemuir
Queen of South v Stranraer

Irn-Bru Third Division
Berwick v Queens Park
East Stirling v Annan
Elgin v Montrose
Rangers v Clyde
Stirling v Peterhead

Saturday, 20 April
Irn-Bru First Division
Dumbarton v Airdrie
Dunfermline v Cowdenbeath
Falkirk v Partick

Hamilton v Raith
Livingston v Morton

Irn-Bru Second Division
Albion v Brechin
Arbroath v Stranraer
East Fife v Alloa
Forfar v Queen of South
Stenhousemuir v Ayr

Irn-Bru Third Division
Annan v Stirling
Clyde v Montrose
Elgin v Berwick
Queens Park v East Stirling
Rangers v Peterhead

Saturday, 27 April
Irn-Bru First Division
Airdrie v Livingston
Cowdenbeath v Dumbarton
Morton v Hamilton
Partick v Dunfermline
Raith v Falkirk

Irn-Bru Second Division
Alloa v Albion
Ayr v Arbroath
Brechin v Stenhousemuir
Queen of South v East Fife
Stranraer v Forfar

Irn-Bru Third Division
Berwick v Annan
East Stirling v Rangers
Montrose v Queens Park
Peterhead v Clyde
Stirling v Elgin

Saturday, 4 May
Irn-Bru First Division
Dumbarton v Partick
Dunfermline v Airdrie
Falkirk v Morton
Hamilton v Cowdenbeath
Livingston v Raith

Irn-Bru Second Division
Albion v Queen of South
Arbroath v Alloa
East Fife v Brechin
Forfar v Ayr
Stenhousemuir v Stranraer

Irn-Bru Third Division
Annan v Montrose
Clyde v Stirling
Elgin v East Stirling
Queens Park v Peterhead
Rangers v Berwick

BLUE SQUARE PREMIER LEAGUE
FIXTURES 2012–2013

Friday, 10 August
Hereford v Macclesfield

Saturday, 11 August
Barrow v AFC Telford
Braintree v Hyde
Dartford v Tamworth
Forest Green v Cambridge Utd
Lincoln v Kidderminster
Luton v Gateshead
Mansfield v Newport
Nuneaton v Ebbsfleet
Southport v Grimsby
Stockport v Alfreton
Wrexham v Woking

Tuesday, 14 August
AFC Telford v Forest Green
Alfreton v Southport
Cambridge Utd v Lincoln
Ebbsfleet v Braintree
Gateshead v Mansfield
Grimsby v Stockport
Hyde v Barrow
Kidderminster v Luton
Macclesfield v Wrexham
Newport v Nuneaton
Tamworth v Hereford
Woking v Dartford

Saturday, 18 August
AFC Telford v Braintree
Alfreton v Hereford
Cambridge Utd v Southport
Ebbsfleet v Wrexham
Gateshead v Forest Green
Grimsby v Nuneaton
Hyde v Luton
Kidderminster v Mansfield
Macclesfield v Dartford
Newport v Lincoln
Tamworth v Stockport
Woking v Barrow

Saturday, 25 August
Barrow v Alfreton
Braintree v Newport
Dartford v Kidderminster
Forest Green v Woking
Hereford v Ebbsfleet
Lincoln v Macclesfield
Luton v AFC Telford
Mansfield v Hyde
Nuneaton v Cambridge Utd
Southport v Tamworth

Stockport v Gateshead
Wrexham v Grimsby

Monday, 27 August
AFC Telford v Stockport
Alfreton v Nuneaton
Cambridge Utd v Dartford
Ebbsfleet v Luton
Gateshead v Lincoln
Grimsby v Mansfield
Hyde v Southport
Kidderminster v Forest Green
Macclesfield v Barrow
Newport v Hereford
Tamworth v Wrexham

Tuesday, 28 August
Woking v Braintree

Saturday, 1 September
Barrow v Kidderminster
Braintree v Tamworth
Dartford v Alfreton
Forest Green v Hyde
Hereford v Grimsby
Lincoln v Ebbsfleet
Luton v Macclesfield
Mansfield v Woking
Nuneaton v Gateshead
Southport v AFC Telford
Stockport v Cambridge Utd
Wrexham v Newport

Tuesday, 4 September
Barrow v Grimsby
Braintree v Kidderminster
Dartford v Newport
Forest Green v Ebbsfleet
Hereford v Woking
Lincoln v Alfreton
Luton v Cambridge Utd
Mansfield v Tamworth
Nuneaton v AFC Telford
Southport v Gateshead
Stockport v Macclesfield
Wrexham v Hyde

Saturday, 8 September
AFC Telford v Lincoln
Alfreton v Luton
Cambridge Utd v Wrexham
Ebbsfleet v Mansfield
Gateshead v Dartford
Grimsby v Forest Green
Hyde v Hereford

Kidderminster v Southport
Macclesfield v Braintree
Newport v Stockport
Tamworth v Barrow
Woking v Nuneaton

Saturday, 15 September
Barrow v Newport
Cambridge Utd v AFC Telford
Dartford v Hereford
Forest Green v Alfreton
Gateshead v Tamworth
Kidderminster v Grimsby
Lincoln v Hyde
Luton v Wrexham
Mansfield v Braintree
Nuneaton v Macclesfield
Southport v Ebbsfleet
Stockport v Woking

Saturday, 22 September
AFC Telford v Mansfield
Alfreton v Kidderminster
Braintree v Stockport
Ebbsfleet v Barrow
Grimsby v Luton
Hereford v Cambridge Utd
Hyde v Nuneaton
Macclesfield v Forest Green
Newport v Southport
Tamworth v Lincoln
Woking v Gateshead
Wrexham v Dartford

Tuesday, 25 September
AFC Telford v Newport
Braintree v Dartford
Cambridge Utd v Kidderminster
Ebbsfleet v Woking
Grimsby v Gateshead
Hereford v Forest Green
Hyde v Alfreton
Lincoln v Nuneaton
Macclesfield v Mansfield
Southport v Stockport
Tamworth v Luton
Wrexham v Barrow

Saturday, 29 September
Alfreton v Braintree
Barrow v Cambridge Utd
Dartford v Hyde
Forest Green v Lincoln
Gateshead v AFC Telford
Kidderminster v Macclesfield
Luton v Southport
Mansfield v Hereford
Newport v Grimsby
Nuneaton v Wrexham
Stockport v Ebbsfleet
Woking v Tamworth

Saturday, 6 October
AFC Telford v Woking
Braintree v Barrow
Cambridge Utd v Mansfield
Ebbsfleet v Kidderminster
Grimsby v Dartford
Hereford v Stockport
Hyde v Gateshead
Lincoln v Luton
Macclesfield v Alfreton
Southport v Nuneaton
Tamworth v Newport
Wrexham v Forest Green

Tuesday, 9 October
Alfreton v Grimsby
Barrow v Southport
Dartford v AFC Telford
Forest Green v Tamworth
Gateshead v Macclesfield
Kidderminster v Hyde
Luton v Braintree
Mansfield v Lincoln
Newport v Ebbsfleet
Nuneaton v Hereford
Stockport v Wrexham
Woking v Cambridge Utd

Saturday, 13 October
AFC Telford v Grimsby
Barrow v Dartford
Ebbsfleet v Alfreton
Gateshead v Cambridge Utd
Hereford v Braintree
Hyde v Tamworth
Luton v Nuneaton
Macclesfield v Newport
Mansfield v Forest Green
Stockport v Kidderminster
Woking v Southport
Wrexham v Lincoln

Saturday, 27 October
Alfreton v AFC Telford
Braintree v Wrexham
Cambridge Utd v Hyde
Dartford v Mansfield
Forest Green v Luton
Grimsby v Macclesfield
Kidderminster v Gateshead
Lincoln v Stockport
Newport v Woking
Nuneaton v Barrow
Southport v Hereford
Tamworth v Ebbsfleet

Tuesday, 6 November
AFC Telford v Ebbsfleet
Dartford v Forest Green
Gateshead v Alfreton

Hereford v Luton
Hyde v Grimsby
Lincoln v Braintree
Macclesfield v Tamworth
Newport v Cambridge Utd
Nuneaton v Mansfield
Southport v Wrexham
Stockport v Barrow
Woking v Kidderminster

Saturday, 10 November
Alfreton v Newport
Barrow v Lincoln
Braintree v Gateshead
Cambridge Utd v Macclesfield
Ebbsfleet v Hyde
Forest Green v Stockport
Grimsby v Woking
Kidderminster v Nuneaton
Luton v Dartford
Mansfield v Southport
Tamworth v AFC Telford
Wrexham v Hereford

Saturday, 17 November
AFC Telford v Kidderminster
Barrow v Forest Green
Cambridge Utd v Tamworth
Dartford v Southport
Grimsby v Braintree
Lincoln v Hereford
Macclesfield v Ebbsfleet
Mansfield v Luton
Newport v Hyde
Nuneaton v Stockport
Woking v Alfreton
Wrexham v Gateshead

Saturday, 1 December
Alfreton v Cambridge Utd
Braintree v Macclesfield
Ebbsfleet v Grimsby
Forest Green v Nuneaton
Gateshead v Newport
Hereford v AFC Telford
Hyde v Woking
Kidderminster v Wrexham
Luton v Barrow
Southport v Lincoln
Stockport v Mansfield
Tamworth v Dartford

Tuesday, 4 December
AFC Telford v Barrow
Alfreton v Wrexham
Braintree v Forest Green
Ebbsfleet v Cambridge Utd
Gateshead v Grimsby
Hereford v Mansfield
Lincoln v Woking

Macclesfield v Hyde
Newport v Luton
Nuneaton v Dartford
Stockport v Southport
Tamworth v Kidderminster

Saturday, 8 December
Barrow v Hereford
Cambridge Utd v Gateshead
Dartford v Lincoln
Forest Green v Macclesfield
Grimsby v Tamworth
Hyde v AFC Telford
Kidderminster v Newport
Luton v Alfreton
Mansfield v Ebbsfleet
Southport v Braintree
Woking v Stockport
Wrexham v Nuneaton

Saturday, 22 December
AFC Telford v Luton
Alfreton v Barrow
Cambridge Utd v Nuneaton
Ebbsfleet v Hereford
Gateshead v Stockport
Grimsby v Wrexham
Hyde v Mansfield
Kidderminster v Dartford
Macclesfield v Lincoln
Newport v Braintree
Tamworth v Southport
Woking v Forest Green

Wednesday, 26 December
Barrow v Gateshead
Braintree v Cambridge Utd
Dartford v Ebbsfleet
Forest Green v Newport
Hereford v Kidderminster
Lincoln v Grimsby
Luton v Woking
Mansfield v Alfreton
Nuneaton v Tamworth
Southport v Macclesfield
Stockport v Hyde
Wrexham v AFC Telford

Saturday, 29 December
Barrow v Macclesfield
Braintree v Woking
Dartford v Cambridge Utd
Forest Green v Kidderminster
Hereford v Newport
Lincoln v Gateshead
Luton v Ebbsfleet
Mansfield v Grimsby
Nuneaton v Alfreton
Southport v Hyde
Stockport v AFC Telford
Wrexham v Tamworth

Tuesday, 1 January
AFC Telford v Wrexham
Alfreton v Mansfield
Cambridge Utd v Braintree
Ebbsfleet v Dartford
Gateshead v Barrow
Grimsby v Lincoln
Hyde v Stockport
Kidderminster v Hereford
Macclesfield v Southport
Newport v Forest Green
Woking v Luton

Wednesday, 2 January
Tamworth v Nuneaton

Saturday, 5 January
AFC Telford v Southport
Alfreton v Dartford
Cambridge Utd v Stockport
Ebbsfleet v Lincoln
Gateshead v Nuneaton
Grimsby v Hereford
Hyde v Forest Green
Kidderminster v Barrow
Macclesfield v Luton
Newport v Wrexham
Tamworth v Braintree
Woking v Mansfield

Saturday, 12 January
Barrow v Woking
Braintree v AFC Telford
Dartford v Macclesfield
Forest Green v Gateshead
Hereford v Alfreton
Lincoln v Newport
Luton v Hyde
Mansfield v Kidderminster
Nuneaton v Grimsby
Southport v Cambridge Utd
Stockport v Tamworth
Wrexham v Ebbsfleet

Saturday, 19 January
AFC Telford v Alfreton
Braintree v Grimsby
Ebbsfleet v Tamworth
Gateshead v Woking
Hereford v Dartford
Hyde v Cambridge Utd
Lincoln v Wrexham
Macclesfield v Kidderminster
Newport v Barrow
Nuneaton v Luton
Southport v Mansfield
Stockport v Forest Green

Tuesday, 22 January
AFC Telford v Gateshead

Barrow v Stockport
Cambridge Utd v Ebbsfleet
Dartford v Braintree
Forest Green v Hereford
Grimsby v Hyde
Luton v Lincoln
Mansfield v Nuneaton
Tamworth v Macclesfield
Woking v Newport
Wrexham v Southport

Saturday, 26 January
Alfreton v Tamworth
Cambridge Utd v Grimsby
Dartford v Barrow
Gateshead v Hereford
Hyde v Ebbsfleet
Kidderminster v Woking
Lincoln v Forest Green
Luton v Stockport
Macclesfield v AFC Telford
Nuneaton v Braintree
Southport v Newport
Wrexham v Mansfield

Tuesday, 29 January
Kidderminster v AFC Telford

Saturday, 2 February
AFC Telford v Cambridge Utd
Barrow v Luton
Braintree v Lincoln
Ebbsfleet v Macclesfield
Forest Green v Wrexham
Grimsby v Alfreton
Hereford v Southport
Mansfield v Dartford
Newport v Kidderminster
Stockport v Nuneaton
Tamworth v Gateshead
Woking v Hyde

Saturday, 9 February
Alfreton v Woking
Braintree v Hereford
Ebbsfleet v Gateshead
Grimsby v AFC Telford
Hyde v Macclesfield
Kidderminster v Cambridge Utd
Lincoln v Dartford
Luton v Forest Green
Mansfield v Barrow
Newport v Tamworth
Nuneaton v Southport
Wrexham v Stockport

Tuesday, 12 February
AFC Telford v Hyde
Cambridge Utd v Alfreton
Dartford v Luton

Forest Green v Braintree
Gateshead v Kidderminster
Hereford v Wrexham
Macclesfield v Nuneaton
Newport v Mansfield
Southport v Barrow
Stockport v Lincoln
Tamworth v Grimsby
Woking v Ebbsfleet

Saturday, 16 February
AFC Telford v Tamworth
Alfreton v Macclesfield
Barrow v Nuneaton
Braintree v Southport
Ebbsfleet v Stockport
Forest Green v Dartford
Gateshead v Wrexham
Hereford v Lincoln
Hyde v Kidderminster
Luton v Newport
Mansfield v Cambridge Utd
Woking v Grimsby

Saturday, 23 February
Cambridge Utd v Hereford
Dartford v Stockport
Grimsby v Ebbsfleet
Kidderminster v Alfreton
Lincoln v Barrow
Luton v Mansfield
Macclesfield v Gateshead
Newport v AFC Telford
Nuneaton v Forest Green
Southport v Woking
Tamworth v Hyde
Wrexham v Braintree

Tuesday, 26 February
Alfreton v Hyde
Barrow v Wrexham
Braintree v Luton
Dartford v Grimsby
Lincoln v Mansfield
Newport v Gateshead
Nuneaton v Kidderminster
Stockport v Hereford
Tamworth v Cambridge Utd

Saturday, 2 March
Barrow v Tamworth
Cambridge Utd v Forest Green
Gateshead v Braintree
Hereford v Nuneaton
Hyde v Newport
Kidderminster v Ebbsfleet
Macclesfield v Grimsby
Mansfield v AFC Telford
Southport v Dartford
Stockport v Luton

Woking v Lincoln
Wrexham v Alfreton

Saturday, 9 March
AFC Telford v Macclesfield
Braintree v Nuneaton
Cambridge Utd v Woking
Dartford v Wrexham
Ebbsfleet v Newport
Forest Green v Barrow
Gateshead v Hyde
Grimsby v Kidderminster
Lincoln v Southport
Luton v Hereford
Mansfield v Stockport
Tamworth v Alfreton

Tuesday, 12 March
Alfreton v Ebbsfleet
Macclesfield v Woking
Southport v Forest Green

Saturday, 16 March
Alfreton v Gateshead
Ebbsfleet v Southport
Forest Green v Mansfield
Grimsby v Cambridge Utd
Hereford v Barrow
Hyde v Dartford
Kidderminster v Tamworth
Newport v Macclesfield
Nuneaton v Lincoln
Stockport v Braintree
Woking v AFC Telford
Wrexham v Luton

Saturday, 23 March
Barrow v Ebbsfleet
Braintree v Alfreton
Dartford v Gateshead
Forest Green v Grimsby
Hereford v Hyde
Lincoln v AFC Telford
Luton v Tamworth
Mansfield v Macclesfield
Nuneaton v Woking
Southport v Kidderminster
Stockport v Newport
Wrexham v Cambridge Utd

Saturday, 30 March
AFC Telford v Nuneaton
Alfreton v Lincoln
Cambridge Utd v Luton
Ebbsfleet v Forest Green
Gateshead v Southport
Grimsby v Barrow
Hyde v Wrexham
Kidderminster v Braintree
Macclesfield v Stockport

Newport v Dartford
Tamworth v Mansfield
Woking v Hereford
Monday, 1 April
Barrow v Hyde
Braintree v Ebbsfleet
Dartford v Woking
Forest Green v AFC Telford
Hereford v Tamworth
Lincoln v Cambridge Utd
Luton v Kidderminster
Mansfield v Gateshead
Nuneaton v Newport
Southport v Alfreton
Stockport v Grimsby
Wrexham v Macclesfield

Saturday, 6 April
AFC Telford v Dartford
Alfreton v Stockport
Barrow v Mansfield
Cambridge Utd v Newport
Ebbsfleet v Nuneaton
Gateshead v Luton
Grimsby v Southport
Hyde v Braintree
Kidderminster v Lincoln
Macclesfield v Hereford
Tamworth v Forest Green

Woking v Wrexham

Saturday, 13 April
Braintree v Mansfield
Cambridge Utd v Barrow
Ebbsfleet v AFC Telford
Forest Green v Southport
Hereford v Gateshead
Lincoln v Tamworth
Luton v Grimsby
Newport v Alfreton
Nuneaton v Hyde
Stockport v Dartford
Woking v Macclesfield
Wrexham v Kidderminster

Saturday, 20 April
AFC Telford v Hereford
Alfreton v Forest Green
Barrow v Braintree
Dartford v Nuneaton
Gateshead v Ebbsfleet
Grimsby v Newport
Hyde v Lincoln
Kidderminster v Stockport
Macclesfield v Cambridge Utd
Mansfield v Wrexham
Southport v Luton
Tamworth v Woking